The Blackwell Encyclopaedia of
Political Science

The Blackwell Encyclopaedia of Political Science

Edited by
Vernon Bogdanor

BLACKWELL
Reference

Copyright © Basil Blackwell 1987, 1991
© Editorial organization Vernon Bogdanor 1987, 1991

First published in hardback (as *The Blackwell
Encyclopaedia of Political Institutions*) 1987
First published (with corrections) in paperback 1991

Blackwell Publishers
108 Cowley Road, Oxford OX4 1JF, UK

3 Cambridge Center
Cambridge, Massachusetts 02142, USA

ISBN 0 631 18304 3

CIP catalogue records for this book are available from the British Library
and the Library of Congress.

Typeset in 9½ on 11 pt Linotron Ehrhardt
by Columns of Reading
Printed and bound in Great Britain by
Butler & Tanner Ltd, Frome and London

Contents

Editor's Introduction

The purpose of this encyclopaedia is to provide a succinct guide to the central concepts used in the study of the political institutions of advanced industrial societies, the principal political organizations and movements in these societies and the main types of political community. It includes entries on leading political scientists of the past, but excludes political scientists still living as well as politicians (Woodrow Wilson, for instance, is included as a political scientist, not as the twenty-eighth President of the United States) and items relating to particular events or places on which information is easily available elsewhere. Also excluded are entries relating either to international relations or to purely local matters. There are, however, entries for some culture–specific terms that have either passed into general use, or whose use is confined to Britain, the United States and Western Europe. The *Encyclopaedia* is designed to be a source of reference for students and teachers of politics, history and allied subjects, and, more generally, for the large number of general readers looking for elucidation of the concepts and ideas used in the discussion of government and politics. It is hoped that this volume will prove complementary to *The Blackwell Encyclopaedia of Political Thought*.

Each entry is intended to be complete in itself, but where it might be helpful to consult other entries, cross-references are printed in capitals in the text. There is a general index at the end of the volume through which the reader can trace all references to a specific individual or subject. Almost every entry is followed by suggestions for further reading, and all works referred to are listed with full publication details.

I am deeply indebted to Dr David Butler and Professor S.E. Finer who offered advice, encouragement and stimulation during every stage of the preparation of this *Encyclopaedia*. Their influence extends considerably beyond the entries which they have themselves contributed. I should also like to thank Michael Steed for the care with which he read an earlier draft of the *Encyclopaedia* and for his critical comments.

The following have also given valuable advice on various aspects of the *Encyclopaedia*: Dr Marco Brusati; Professor Leon Epstein; Dr R.J.W. Evans; Professor Barry Nicholas; Professor Philip Norton; Miss Gillian Peele; Professor Gerald Pomper; Professor Austin Ranney; Dr John Rowett; Dr Vincent Wright.

I should also like to thank the 247 contributors from thirteen countries for putting their skill and expertise at the disposal of the *Encyclopaedia*. I am, however, entirely responsible for the selection of entries, which I have in some cases cut substantially, and the choice of contributors.

Jo Hadley, Carol Le Duc and Ann McCall of Blackwells worked heroically to transform pages of untidy copy into readable prose; while Janet Godden has supervised the *Encyclopaedia* from inception to completion with a rare mixture of imperturbable cheerfulness and unfailing efficiency.

It was with great sadness that the Editor and Publishers learnt as the *Encyclopaedia* was going to press of the deaths of three valued contributors: Sir Norman Chester, Dr J.D. Lees and Professor W.H. Walsh.

Vernon Bogdanor
Brasenose College, Oxford
1 February 1987

Introduction to Paperback Edition

I have taken the opportunity of this paperback edition to correct some infelicities and ambiguities in the hardback edition. I am grateful to those correspondents who have pointed these out. But no attempt has been made to bring the text up to date. It remains broadly as it was in 1987.

The Editor and Publishers were sad to learn of the death of Professor Peter G. Richards, a valued contributor to the *Encyclopaedia*.

Vernon Bogdanor
Brasenose College, Oxford
June 1991

Contributors

Frank Aarebrot **FA**
University of Bergen

Charles R. Adrian **CRA**
University of California, Riverside

Martin Albrow **MCA**
University College, Cardiff

Erik Allardt **EA**
University of Helsinki

H.J.B. Allen **HJBA**

Graham T. Allison **GTA**
Harvard University

Gabriel A. Almond **GAA**
Stanford University

Christopher Andrew **CMA**
Corpus Christi College, Cambridge

Douglas E. Ashford **DEA**
University of Pittsburgh

Shlomo Avineri **SA**
Hebrew University of Jerusalem

Michael Banton **MPB**
University of Bristol

Rodney Barker **RB**
London School of Economics & Political Science

Frank Bealey **FWB**
University of Aberdeen

David Beetham **DB**
University of Leeds

John Bell **JSB**
Wadham College, Oxford

Lord Beloff **B**
All Souls College, Oxford

Robert Benewick **RJB**
University of Sussex

Elias Berg **EB**
University of Stockholm

R.N. Berki **RNB**
University of Hull

Hugh Berrington **HBB**
University of Newcastle upon Tyne

Jean Blondel **JFPB**
European University Institute, Florence

Jay G. Blumler **JGB**
University of Leeds

Noel T. Boaden **NTB**
University of Liverpool

Vernon Bogdanor **VBB**
Brasenose College, Oxford

Tom Bottomore **TBB**
University of Sussex

Karl Dietrich Bracher **KDB**
University of Bonn

CONTRIBUTORS

A.W. Bradley **AWB**
University of Edinburgh

Sir Kenneth Bradshaw **KB**
House of Commons, Westminster

Steven J. Brams **SJB**
New York University

Jack Brand **JAB**
University of Strathclyde

Michael Brock **MGB**
St George's House, Windsor

Hugh Brogan **HB**
University of Essex

Eric C. Browne **ECB**
University of Wisconsin, Milwaukee

P.A. Brunt **PAB**
Brasenose College, Oxford

Ian Budge **IB**
University of Essex

J. Bulpitt **JB**
University of Warwick

John H. Bunzel **JHB**
Hoover Institution, Stanford University

David Butler **DEB**
Nuffield College, Oxford

Mario Caciagli **MC**
University of Padua

Naomi Caiden **NJC**
California State University, San Bernardino

Bruce E. Cain **BEC**
California Institute of Technology

Peter Calvert **PARC**
University of Southampton

Sir Raymond Carr **RC**
St Antony's College, Oxford

Alan Cawson **AC**
University of Sussex

Richard A. Chapman **RAC**
University of Durham

Jean Charlot **JC**
Fondation Nationale des Sciences Politiques, Paris

Monica Charlot **MCh**
Maison Française, Oxford

Sir Norman Chester **DNC**
Late of *Nuffield College, Oxford*

K. Alec Chrystal **KAC**
University of Sheffield

Irene Collins **IC**
University of Liverpool

Paul Compton **PAC**
The Queen's University of Belfast

Rt. Hon. Sir Zelman Cowen **ZC**
Oriel College, Oxford

Paul Craig **PPC**
Worcester College, Oxford

Maurice Cranston **MWC**
London School of Economics & Political Science

Bernard Crick **BRC**
Birkbeck College, London

John Curtice **JKC**
University of Strathclyde

Lloyd N. Cutler **LNC**
Washington DC

Hans Daalder **HD**
University of Leiden, Netherlands

Ivo H. Daalder **IHD**
Massachusetts Institute of Technology

Robert A. Dahl **RAD**
Yale University

John Darwin **JGD**
Nuffield College, Oxford

Alan Doig **ADo**
University of Liverpool

Robert E. Dowse **RED**
University of Western Australia

Ivo D. Duchacek **IDD**
City University of New York

P.J. Dunleavy **PJD**
London School of Economics &
Political Science

Andrew Dunsire **AD**
University of York

Kenneth Dyson **KD**
University of Bradford

Jeremy Eades **JSE**
University of Kent at Canterbury

David Easton **DE**
University of California, Irvine

D.A.O. Edward **DAOE**
University of Edinburgh

Sir George Engle QC **GE**
Formerly *First Parliamentary Counsel,*
Whitehall

Leon D. Epstein **LDE**
University of Madison-Wisconsin

R.J.W. Evans **RJWE**
Brasenose College, Oxford

Sir James Fawcett QC **JESF**
Former *Member and President of European*
Commission of Human Rights

James W. Fesler **JWF**
Yale University

S.E. Finer **SEF**
All Souls College, Oxford

Peter C. Fishburn **PCF**
AT & T Bell Laboratories

Peter Frank **PF**
University of Essex

Mark N. Franklin **MNF**
University of Strathclyde

Michael Freeden **MSF**
Mansfield College, Oxford

Mark Freedland **MRF**
St John's College, Oxford

Michael Freeman **MDAF**
University College, London

Andrew Gamble **AMG**
University of Sheffield

Ernest Gellner **EG**
University of Cambridge

Jean Gottmann **JG**
Hertford College, Oxford

S.J. Gould **SJG**
University of Nottingham

W.P. Grant **WPG**
University of Warwick

Christine Gray **CDG**
St Hilda's College, Oxford

Ted Robert Gurr **TRG**
University of Colorado, Boulder

Emanuel Gutmann **EGu**
Hebrew University of Jerusalem

A.H. Halsey **AHH**
Nuffield College, Oxford

J.E.S. Hayward **JESH**
University of Hull

A. Heath **AFH**
Nuffield College, Oxford

Guy Hermet **GH**
Fondation Nationale des Sciences Politiques,
Paris

R.H. Hilton **RHH**
University of Birmingham

David Hine **DJH**
Christ Church, Oxford

Christopher Hood **CCH**
London School of Economics & Political Science

Christopher Hughes **CJH**
University of Leicester

CONTRIBUTORS

Christopher T. Husbands **CTH**
London School of Economics & Political Science

Richard Hyman **RH**
University of Warwick

Ronald Inglehart **RI**
University of Michigan, Ann Arbor

Ghiţa Ionescu **GI**
University of Manchester

Edmund Ions **ESAI**
University of Oxford

Ronald Irving **REMI**
University of Edinburgh

William I. Jenkins **WIJ**
University of Kent at Canterbury

R.J. Johnston **RJJ**
University of Sheffield

Charles O. Jones **COJ**
University of Virginia, Charlottesville

A. Grant Jordan **AGJ**
University of Aberdeen

Jeffrey Jowell **JLJ**
University College, London

Tony R. Judt **TRJ**
New York University

Max Kaase **MK**
University of Mannheim

Dennis Kavanagh **DK**
University of Nottingham

B. Keith-Lucas **BK-L**
University of Kent at Canterbury

Ellen Kennedy **ELK**
University of York

Benedict Kingsbury **BK**
Exeter College, Oxford

K. Kirkwood **KK**
St Antony's College, Oxford

Eva Kolinsky **EK**
Aston University

Stein Kuhnle **SK**
University of Bergen

Jan-Erik Lane **J-EL**
University of Umeå

J.A. Laponce **JAL**
University of British Columbia

Philip Laundy **PACL**
House of Commons, Ottawa

Michael Laver **MJL**
University College, Galway

Sir Frank Layfield QC **FL**
Temple, London

John D. Lees **JDL**
Late of *University of Keele*

David Levene **DSL**
Brasenose College, Oxford

Karl Leyser **KL**
All Souls College, Oxford

Arend Lijphart **AL**
University of California, San Diego

J. Linz **JLi**
Yale University

Gerhard Loewenberg **GL**
University of Iowa

Colin Lucas **CL**
Balliol College, Oxford

John Lukacs **JL**
Chestnut Hill College, Philadelphia

A. Maass **AM**
Harvard University

N. MacCormick **NMacC**
University of Edinburgh

H. Machin **HM**
London School of Economics & Political Science

Tom Mackie   **TTM**
University of Strathclyde

Donald Gunn MacRae   **DGM**
London School of Economics & Political Science

A.F. Madden   **AFM**
Nuffield College, Oxford

J.T.S. Madeley   **JTSM**
London School of Economics & Political Science

Peter Mair   **PMM**
University of Manchester

B.S. Markesinis   **BSM**
Queen Mary College, London

Geoffrey Marshall   **GM**
The Queen's College, Oxford

David Marsland   **DM**
Brunel University

Richard Mayne   **RJM**
Encounter, *London*

Alan McBriar   **AMMcB**
Monash University

Martin McCauley   **MMcC**
School of Slavonic & East European Studies,
London

F.E. McDermott   **FEMcD**
University of Sheffield

Iain McLean   **IMcL**
University College, Oxford

T.P. McNeill   **TPMcN**
University of Hull

Kenneth D. McRae   **KDMcR**
Carleton University, Ottawa

Edward McWhinney   **EMcW**
Simon Fraser University, British Columbia

Yves Mény   **YM**
University of Paris II

James Michael   **JRM**
Polytechnic of Central London

Ralph Miliband   **RM**
London

David Millar   **DMcWM**
Formerly European Parliament, Strasbourg

Fergus Millar   **FGBM**
Brasenose College, Oxford

David Miller   **DLM**
Nuffield College, Oxford

William Miller   **WLM**
University of Glasgow

Kenneth Minogue   **KRM**
London School of Economics & Political Science

Kenneth O. Morgan   **KOM**
The Queen's College, Oxford

Richard Mulgan   **RGM**
University of Auckland

William D. Muller   **WDM**
State University of New York, Fredonia

Colin Munro   **CRM**
University of Manchester

R.E. Neustadt   **REN**
Harvard University

Kenneth Newton   **KN**
University of Essex

Barry Nicholas   **JKBN**
Brasenose College, Oxford

Jeremy Noakes   **JDN**
University of Exeter

Philip Norton   **PN**
University of Hull

Geoffrey Ostergaard   **GNO**
University of Birmingham

Øyvind Østerud   **ØØ**
University of Oslo

E.C. Page   **ECP**
University of Hull

CONTRIBUTORS

Khayyam Z. Paltiel **KZP**
Carleton University, Ottawa

G. Parker **GP**
University of Birmingham

Geraint Parry **GBP**
University of Manchester

W.E. Paterson **WEP**
University of Warwick

Gillian Peele **GRP**
Lady Margaret Hall, Oxford

Anton Pelinka **AP**
Innsbruck University

B. Guy Peters **BGP**
University of Pittsburgh

John Pinder **JP**
London

William Plowden **WP**
*Royal Institute of Public
Administration, London*

J.R. Pole **JRP**
St Catherine's College, Oxford

Gerald M. Pomper **GMP**
Rutgers University

Peter Pulzer **PGJP**
All Souls College, Oxford

R.M. Punnett **RMP**
University of Strathclyde

L. Pye **LWP**
Massachusetts Institute of Technology

T.H. Qualter **THQ**
University of Waterloo, Ontario

Nicol C. Rae **NCR**
Florida International University

Austin Ranney **AR**
University of California, Berkeley

D.E. Regan **DER**
University of Nottingham

Peter G. Richards **PGR**
Late of the University of Southampton

Marvin Rintala **MR**
Boston College, Massachusetts

Bert A. Rockman **BAR**
University of Pittsburgh

David Rohde **DWR**
Michigan State University, East Lansing

Richard Rose **RR**
University of Strathclyde

F. Rosen **FR**
University College, London

Jeffrey Ian Ross **JIR**
University of Colorado, Boulder

John Rowett **JSR**
Brasenose College, Oxford

Michael Ryle **MTR**
House of Commons, Westminster

Larry Sabato **LJS**
University of Virginia

David Sanders **DJS**
University of Essex

Alberta Sbragia **AMS**
University of Pittsburgh

John R. Schmidhauser **JRS**
University of Southern California

George Schöpflin **GSch**
*London School of Economics &
Political Science*

S.R. Schram **SRS**
School of Oriental and African Studies, London

Raymond Seidelman **RMS**
Sarah Lawrence College, New York

Patrick Seyd **PS**
University of Sheffield

Byron E. Shafer **BES**
Nuffield College, Oxford

Hyun Shin **HS**
Magdalen College, Oxford

Barbara L. Sinclair **BLS**
University of California, Riverside

Anthony D. Smith **ADS**
*London School of Economics &
Political Science*

Gordon Smith **GSm**
*London School of Economics &
Political Science*

Albert Somit **AS**
Southern Illinois University at Carbondale

Donald Southgate **DGS**
Bridford, Devon

John L. Stanley **JLS**
University of California, Riverside

Michael Steed **MS**
University of Manchester

D.L. Stockton **DLS**
Brasenose College, Oxford

J.A.A. Stockwin **JAAS**
Nissan Institute of Japanese Studies, Oxford

Kaare Strom **KS**
University of Minnesota

Gerald Studdert-Kennedy **GS-K**
University of Birmingham

Michael Taylor **MJT**
University of Essex

Michael Taylor **MWT**
Lincoln College, Oxford

Niels Aage Thorsen **NT**
University of Copenhagen

Henry Tudor **HT**
University of Durham

Derek W. Urwin **DWU**
University of Warwick

Henry Valen **HV**
University of Oslo

Elizabeth Vallance **EMV**
Queen Mary College, London

Douglas Verney **DVV**
York University, Ontario

Maurice Vile **MJCV**
University of Kent at Canterbury

K. von Beyme **KvB**
University of Heidelberg

Helen Wallace **HW**
*The Royal Institute of International Affairs,
London*

W.H. Walsh **WHW**
Late of *University of Edinburgh*

Ronald L. Watts **RLWa**
Queen's University, Ontario

Stephen Welch **SW**
St Antony's College, Oxford

Patrick Weller **PMW**
Griffith University, Queensland

Roger L. Wettenhall **RLW**
Canberra College of Advanced Education

Michael Wheeler-Booth **MAJW-B**
House of Lords, Westminster

Stephen White **SLW**
University of Glasgow

Paul Wilkinson **PW**
University of Aberdeen

G.L. Williams **GLW**
University of Sheffield

Roger Williams **RW**
University of Manchester

Raymond E. Wolfinger **REW**
University of California, Berkeley

CONTRIBUTORS

David Worswick **GDNW**
Magdalen College, Oxford

Anthony Wright **AWW**
University of Birmingham

Deil Wright **DSW**
University of North Carolina at Chapel Hill

V. Wright **VW**
Nuffield College, Oxford

David Yardley **DCMY**
Commission for Local Administration in England

Zvi Yavetz **ZY**
Tel-Aviv University

John Zvesper **JZ**
University of East Anglia

A

absentee voting Many democracies provide facilities for absentee voting for those who might have difficulty through infirmity or absence in recording their vote at the polling booth. There are five types of absentee voting: *advance voting* in Canada, Finland, Israel, Japan, Norway and New Zealand by which the polling booth is open before the date of the election either for all those unable to vote on the appointed day or, as in Israel, Japan and Norway, for special categories; *postal voting* in fifteen countries; *proxy voting* in eight countries; *special polling booths* in hospitals, prisons, old people's homes etc. in eight countries and *constituency transfer* in seven countries.

The various arrangements make little difference to rates of TURNOUT. Postal voting, the most important of the provisions, is only taken advantage of in Britain by approximately 2 per cent of the electorate.   DEB

Reading

Crewe, I.: Electoral participation. In *Democracy at the Polls*, ed. D. Butler, H.R. Penniman and A. Ranney. Washington, DC: American Enterprise Institute, 1981.

absolute government/absolutism is government with plenary powers, freed from legal constraints (*legibus absolutus*, hence the word) and constitutional controls; normally monarchical. The term enjoys common use in European history, but there is much disagreement about the period to which it may properly be applied, as also about the relation between its status in political practice and in the writings of theorists. Despite antecedents in Plato and the medieval canonists, and

notwithstanding the arguments for strong monarchy deployed from the Renaissance onwards, the main impetus towards absolute government seems to have come from an extension of the activities of rulers and consolidation of their courts which proceeded swiftly after the early sixteenth century. The first stage was heavily confessional in character, as the state gained dominance over the church – especially in Protestant countries, where the process is often described as Erastianism – and used religion as a legitimating channel ('divine right of kings'). The most important manifestations were in Habsburg Spain and in the France of Louis XIV. Yet the executive authority of such rulers remained comparatively weak. Only the eighteenth century saw a more thoroughgoing development of absolutism, as monarchs – controlling large bureaucracies and standing armies – mounted major reform programmes in the economic, social, and legal spheres, which were justified in largely secular terms as serving the public good. The most celebrated 'enlightened absolutists' were Frederick II of Prussia (1740–86), Catherine II of Russia (1762–96) and Joseph II of Austria (1780–90). Most parts of Europe experienced such regimes, the main exceptions being Britain, the Netherlands, and Poland. Obstacles to efficient government, however, remained great, and in France the inability of absolutism to promote change led directly to the Revolution. Absolutist forms were widely reinstated in the period of restoration after the French Revolution; Napoleon I has frequently been claimed as a ruler in this tradition. Yet Bonapartism, with its plebiscitary style and extensive social mobility, introduced

1

different accents, and by the time of its final fling during the 1850s and 1860s absolute government in Europe was losing its distinctive features.

As a construction in political philosophy, absolutism was fed by the experience of anarchy and the fear of barbarism. Its greatest expositors were Niccolo MACHIAVELLI, who drew on the Roman imperial example and exalted the strong prince over his own indecisive Florentine republic; Jean BODIN, who stressed the need for undivided sovereignty against a background of religious strife in France; and Thomas HOBBES, whose *Leviathan* written at the time of the English civil war, proposed a free and total subjugation of individual wills (*pactum subjectionis*) to the will of a single governor in return for protection. Not least because of its associations with reason of state, and above all in Britain and America, absolutism has often carried negative connotations, being identified with arbitrary rule, alien and bureaucratic government, social and economic regimentation, and sometimes with militarism. But its advocates, especially in central Europe, have pointed to the achievements of absolute monarchs in promoting equality before the law, rational administration, state education, economic development, public order and welfare. In fact absolutism embodied a complex blend of old assumptions and new initiatives; while frequently able to rally the support of rising middle-class commercial, professional, and intellectual interests, its proponents usually remained conservative in their view of society, maintaining the status of nobles while undermining their political privileges. Properly speaking, absolutism should be distinguished from DESPOTISM, which describes perverted or oriental forms of government, though enlightened absolutists have often been mischievously described as 'enlightened despots', and Russian AUTOCRACY (*samoderzhavie*) which represents an intermediate stage. It should also be distinguished from twentieth-century TOTALITARIANISM, since absolute monarchs were restrained, not only by a much less efficient repressive apparatus which usually confined its attention to the public sphere, but also by the claims of custom, Christian morality, and natural law.   RJWE

Reading

Anderson, P.: *Lineages of the Absolutist State*. London: New Left Books, 1974.

Behrens, C.B.A.: *The Ancien Régime*. London: Thames & Hudson, 1967.

Bluche, F.: *Le Despotisme éclairé*. Paris: Fayard, 1968.

Meinecke, F.: *Machiavellism: the doctrine of raison d'état and its place in modern history*, ed. W. Stark, and trans. D. Scott. London: Routledge & Kegan Paul, 1957.

Raeff, M.: *The Well-Ordered Police State: social and institutional change through law in the Germanies and Russia 1600–1800*. New Haven, Conn.: Yale University Press, 1983.

Shennan, J.H.: *The Origins of the Modern European State 1450–1725*. London: Hutchinson, 1974.

————: *Liberty and Order in Early Modern Europe: the subject and the state 1650–1800*. London: Longman, 1986.

Skinner, Q.: *The Foundations of Modern Political Thought*. 2 vols. Cambridge: Cambridge University Press, 1978.

acephalous political systems   See PRE-STATE POLITICAL SYSTEMS.

accountability   See RESPONSIBILITY.

Act   A BILL that has been sanctioned by a LEGISLATURE and that has also passed through any other procedure required by the constitution of a state before it is accepted as a law. Once a bill has become an act it will be enforced by the courts of law. An act or sections of it may not come into effect immediately if the act itself requires that these sections shall not come into force until a further STATUTORY INSTRUMENT has been issued. Lawyers commonly refer to acts as statutes.   PGR

Adams, John (1735–1826)   Born in Braintree, Massachusetts, educated at Harvard College, and practised law. He was highly-strung and intensely ambitious, emotions which he transferred to his country in the form of resentment of British sovereignty. Adams's first publication, *Dissertation on the Canon and Feudal Law* (1765), was a violent attack on feudal and ecclesiastical influences in government. A signer of the Declaration of Independence, diplomatic emissary in Europe and first US minister at the Court of St James, Adams was first Vice-President and Washington's successor as President of the USA (1797–1801). He wanted republican government genuinely deriving from the people, but he also wanted it securely based on the rule of law. The Massachusetts Declaration of Rights accompanying the Constitution of 1780, which he helped to draft, contains a full articulation of the principle of the SEPARATION OF POWERS 'to the end that it be a government of laws and not of men'. Similar views expressed in a pamphlet, *Thoughts on Government* (1776), influenced the constitution-makers of Virginia. During the War of Independence Adams became sceptical of the virtue of his fellow countrymen, but defended their political arrangements at great length in his learned but rambling *Defence of the Constitutions of the United States* (1787) evoked by French criticisms of the state constitutions. Here Adams defended separation of powers and balanced government against democratic unicameralism. He believed emulation to be the cardinal human motive – an insight into his own character – and also held that the haughtiness of the aristocracy would always render them difficult to govern. For this reason he advocated an upper chamber as 'a kind of ostracism'. He missed the Philadelphia Convention of 1787 (being in London) but soon came to support the stronger form of government as necessary to continental unity. Though still dedicated to separation of powers, he came to believe in a stronger executive, and signed the highly oppressive and questionably constitutional Alien and Sedition Acts. JRP

Reading

Adams, C.F. ed.: *The Works of John Adams*. 10 vols. Boston, Mass.: Little, Brown, 1850–6.

Bowen, C.D.: *John Adams and the American Revolution*. Boston, Mass.: Little, Brown, 1950.

Chinard, G.: *Honest John Adams*. Boston, Mass.: Little, Brown, 1933.

Howe, J.R. Jr: *The Changing Political Thought of John Adams*. Princeton, NJ: Princeton University Press, 1966.

Shaw, P.: *The Character of John Adams*. Chapel Hill: University of North Carolina Press, 1976.

Smith, P.: *John Adams*. 2 vols. New York: Doubleday, 1962.

additional member system Term used for an ELECTORAL SYSTEM such as that in the Federal Republic of Germany in which a single-member constituency element is combined with proportional representation, the 'additional members' being derived either from a party list – whether national or regional – or, as in the electoral system of Baden-Württemberg, from losing candidates in the constituencies with the highest percentages of votes. VBB

adjudication The application by courts or tribunals of legal rules to particular cases or controversies. Historically the theory of the SEPARATION OF POWERS treated adjudication as one of three governmental functions along with the making and execution of laws. In modern constitutions in which powers are constitutionally allocated to the legislative, executive and judicial branches there has been much difficulty in defining the idea of adjudication or judicial action. A similar difficulty arises in administrative law as to the precise meaning of acting 'judicially'. Most definitions emphasize the idea that an adjudicative act is one that decides upon the allocation in a binding manner in a suit between parties of rights that are presumed to be already determined in principle by existing law. The British Committee on Ministers' Powers in 1932 concluded:

A true judicial decision presupposes an existing dispute between two or more parties, and then invokes four requisites:
(1) the presentation (not necessarily orally) of their case by the parties to the dispute;
(2) if the dispute between them is a question of fact, the ascertainment of the fact by means of evidence adduced by the parties to the dispute;
(3) if the dispute between them is a question of law the submission of legal argument by the parties;
(4) a decision which disposes of the whole matter by a finding upon the facts in dispute and an application of the law of the land to the facts so found, including, where required, a ruling upon any disputed question of law.

The clarity of the distinction between the three functions of government is threatened by the fact that executive as well as judicial officers may be authorized to apply rules to individual cases, and judges or adjudicators may create new law or in effect legislate in the course of carrying out their adjudicative function.

In the United States the role of adjudication in constitutional cases has been a constant subject of debate among legal and political commentators, especially where federal and state legislation is reviewed by the federal courts. Major disagreements have arisen, for example, as to whether in applying the broad guarantees of the constitution, judges should attempt to discover and give weight to the historical intentions of those who draft it, or whether they should interpret the constitution in the light of present-day political morality. In all jurisdictions judges may also be divided between a concept of their function that emphasizes an active policy-making role and one that sees non-elected judicial officers as owing a duty in a democratic political system to exercise restraint and deference to the elective branch of government and to limit their own policy-making role.

To some extent this dilemma arises in all legal systems in the ordinary business of interpreting statutory enactments and developing judicial doctrine from case to case. In addition, in the interpretation of any instrument, adjudicators may be torn between efforts to infer the intentions of those who originated the document and treating the task of interpretation as one of drawing out the meaning of the terms in question with the aid of linguistic rules or conventions. In the United Kingdom recourse to the proceedings of the legislature as an aid to statutory interpretation is severely restricted. In the United States and many other countries recourse to such legislative material is permitted.

Among legal theorists, as well as administrative and constitutional lawyers, adjudication has been a major topic of debate. Legal realists in the United States and Scandinavia have always emphasized the factual and psychological elements in the judicial role as against the so-called formal character of the legal rules. In recent years debate about the character of legal rules themselves as elements in a legal system has involved British and American legal theorists in extended arguments about the nature of the judicial process. A main feature of the controversy has been the theory of adjudication advanced in the writings of Ronald Dworkin and in particular the analysis of the judicial role in so-called 'hard cases' in which existing law presents no clear answers to a legal controversy and courts are involved in balancing apparently conflicting rights and weighing issues of public policy. These controversies reflect more general disagreements about the nature of legal rules, legal systems, and legal rights.   GM

Reading

Abraham, H.J.: *The Judicial Process*. 4th edn. New York and Oxford: Oxford University Press, 1980.

Bell, J.: *Policy Arguments in Judicial Decisions*. Oxford: Oxford University Press, 1983.

Cross, R.: *Statutory Interpretation*. London: Butterworths, 1976.

————: *Precedent in English Law*. Oxford: Clarendon Press, 1961.

Dworkin, R.M.: *Taking Rights Seriously*. 2nd edn, chs 2–6. London: Duckworth, 1978.

Fuller, L.L: The forms and limits of adjudication. *Harvard Law Review* 92 (1978) 358.

MacCormick, N.: *Legal Theory and Legal Reasoning*. Oxford: Clarendon Press, 1978.

Marshall, G.: *Constitutional Theory*, ch. 4. Oxford: Oxford University Press, 1971.

Report of the Committee on Ministers' Powers. London: HMSO Cmd 4060, 1932.

Twining, W. and Miers, D.: *How to do things with Rules*. 2nd edn. London: Weidenfeld & Nicolson, 1982.

administration   In general terms, the tidying-up side of life. In an army camp, or a coal mine, or a hospital, the administration block is where paper is pushed around, in contrast with the 'proper' work of the place: soldiering, or digging coal, or treating patients. Professional men similarly tend to distinguish part of their work (which they often call administration) from what they are 'really there for'. Administration as 'the paperwork' is a widespread experience, whatever it is called, and whether or not there actually is paper involved.

If we were to analyse this paperwork more formally, in a medium-sized or large organization, so that the various kinds of work show up, there are several ways in which we could do it. For instance, by *format*: letters or correspondence; memoranda, minutes, notes or other messages; printed forms or vouchers; entries in ledgers and the like – or nowadays by the electronic equivalents of these things. By *subject-matter*: paper concerned with the production of the organization's goods or services; or with financial matters; with purchasing and supplies, sales or public relations, research and development, or staffing – recruitment, promotion, training and so on; or with the maintenance of the plant and fabric. By *function*: paper dealing with what the organization should be doing, its objectives and standards, targets and rules of procedure ('directing information'); paper dealing with what is actually happening, in the organization and outside it, reports and accounts and 'feedback' of all sorts ('detecting information'); or paper dealing with internal instructions, flow of work, quotas, and the co-ordination and dovetailing of 'production' ('effecting information').

The labels given to these three functions indicate that administration is being seen as, first, a matter of dealing with information, and second, a matter of maintaining control. Control here does not signify being in command: rather that the controller knows what should be happening, knows what is happening, and has means of bringing the second into line with the first where there is a discrepancy. No one can be in control of anything without these three requirements. The paperwork, from this point of view, is the way in which the leaders of an organization are kept informed of what should be done if their ends are to be attained, what is being done, and what adjustments need to be made to current operations.

This distinction between being in command and being in control is quite important in this context. Of course the person who is in command of something is often also in control of it; but it is equally common for the leader to rely on others to keep control, once he or she

has determined the objectives, set the standards, given the targets and laid down the rules to be followed. The controllers, strictly speaking, are exceeding their function if they invent their own norms.

The root meaning of administration is the same as that of 'to minister unto': the act of assisting, or serving, or being someone's steward. But just as a minister may be the king's servant and yet by that very fact be a most important person, so administration can exercise great powers. The word's connotations in Britain have changed somewhat, from being the collective noun for the highest servants of the state (the Gladstone administration – cf. the Reagan administration), to being not what ministers do but what they have done for them by others (Dunsire 1973, chs 1–3). In that latter sense we have a difficulty. Either administration means what any public servant does when he or she is 'pushing paper around'; or else we have to make the earlier distinction between directional and control information paperwork and other kinds.

In some corners of public administration there is little difficulty: the army, coal mines and hospitals are, after all, parts of public administration in the United Kingdom (though not in all countries). If we look closely into the more typical ministries (say the Department of Health and Social Security or the Inland Revenue), we find that they do have a product or service, or several such, which is 'what they are there for', even if it takes the form of pieces of paper. They need the directional and control information paperwork alongside their 'line production' paperwork just as much as do the army, coal mines and hospitals. For yet other departments, such as the Treasury and the Foreign Office, on the other hand, we might decide that their work consists almost entirely of directional and control information paperwork. This was the standard British usage of the term administration as in the Administrative Class of the Civil Service. It was the label used for the highest ranks between 1920 and 1969, with duties concentrating on assisting ministers in the formulation of policy and in the running of the department. Now the Administration Group includes all ranks up to that level who are not in a specialist occupational group; the operational meaning of administration in the Civil Service has clearly changed. Top civil servants are now encouraged to think of themselves less as policy advisers to ministers and more as managers (which we might interpret as concentrating on the control side within the system, rather than on the extra-system norm-setting).

The British Civil Service's operating definition of administration as the work of the top directing staff (institutionally contrasted with both executive work, done by middle ranks, and specialist advice, which should be filtered by the administrative mind before going to ministers) led it away from any emphasis on a distinction between administration and politics or policy making. In what Schaffer (1973, p. 252) called the 'public service bargain' in the late nineteenth century (not a real negotiation, but everyone behaved as though there had been such a bargain), officials had offered loyalty, proficient performance, anonymity, and sacrifice of some political rights, in return for permanency, adequate remuneration and pension, and honourable social status. The mandarins felt themselves able to advise ministers on all aspects of a proposal; not only on its administrative feasibility, their stock-in-trade, but also on its political feasibility – and to advise ministers of a succeeding government of a different colour just as expertly and as loyally. Administrative work included policy work, however policy was defined, but ministers were entitled to take advice or reject it, to substitute their own decisions, and to enjoy total access to departmental activities (because they bore total responsibility).

It had been somewhat different in the United States, where reformers wished to limit the SPOILS SYSTEM by which a large proportion of the public service might lose office if the presidency went to a different party, and gain more assurance in regard to the recruitment and development of necessary skills and expertise, of experience and continuity, in the public service. In this context, a professor of political science, Woodrow WILSON wrote a very influential paper, 'The study of administration', in which he characterized administration as a technical matter, almost a professional sphere such as engineering, with which politics should not interfere:

The field of administration is a field of business. . . . It is a part of political life only as the methods of the counting-house are a part of the life of society; only as machinery is part of the manufactured product. Administrative questions are not political questions. Although politics sets the tasks for administration, it should not be suffered to manipulate its offices. (Wilson 1887, p. 211)

Moreover, administrative techniques can be transferred across regimes:

If I see a murderous fellow sharpening a knife cleverly, I can borrow his way of sharpening the knife without borrowing his probable intention to commit murder with it; and so, if I see a monarchist dyed in the wool managing a public bureau well, I can learn his business methods without changing one of my republican spots. (ibid, p. 220)

The politics/administration dichotomy was invented. It was not only the theoretical basis for the limitation of the spoils system in American federal government, but also the spur to the development of the academic subject of public administration (borrowing from the parallel scientific management movement in manufacturing industry), with its highwater mark in the publication of *Papers on the Science of Administration* (Gulick and Urwick 1937). Administration here meant almost the same as management in business, including the new subjects of organization and human relations, but particularly in the state sphere. So far as academic scholars are concerned the death-blow to the politics/administration dichotomy was given by Paul Appleby in *Policy and Administration* (1949), and the scientific pretensions of public administration never really recovered from an attack by Herbert Simon in an article entitled 'The proverbs of administration' (1946). Yet both were orthodoxy for a generation, and survive in the popularly-understood difference of role generally understood between elected politicians and career officials: politicians make policy, and officials administer it.

The politics/administration dichotomy was intended to keep the politicians out of the officials' territory. Today in Britain, although it is not conducted in terms of the meaning of the word administration, there is a similar anxiety about whether too much political commitment is not being expected of top civil servants, so that a successor government might find their loyalty not credible (Fry 1985). Indeed, Britain is almost alone now in having no class of officials (save for a few political advisers) who are not elected but who expect to come in and go out of office along with ministers (see CIVIL SERVICE). But the more pressing worry in many countries today is that public administration is itself out of control, that the mandarins and not ministers are the real rulers of the country; that in the modern state there are so many decisions to be taken, and many of them so technical, that elected representatives have neither the time nor the expertise even to keep up with BUREAUCRACY, let alone oversee and check it. It is perhaps not helpful to suggest that not only democratic theory but also the etymology and the control-theory understanding of administration make it wrong for administrators to set their own norms: we know it is wrong; we are just unsure how to avoid it.

This is part of the governmental OVERLOAD thesis, and many avenues are being explored to cope with it (see DEVOLUTION, IMPLEMENTATION, PUBLIC CHOICE THEORY). After a certain size and complexity of organization, administration, even in its narrow sense of directional and control information, comes up against its limits (Hood 1976). Yet within these limitations there is much development of purely administrative expertise to come – in the choice of instruments required to achieve some policy end (Hood 1983), and in administrative analysis generally. We have spent so much effort in fruitlessly trying to delineate the frontier regions of administration (as against politics, management, judicial process, and so on) that we have neglected the study of its heartland.   AD

Reading

Appleby, P.H.: *Policy and Administration*. Montgomery: University of Alabama Press, 1949.

Dunsire, A.: *Administration: the Word and the Science*. London: Martin Robertson; New York: Wiley, 1973.

Fry, G.K.: *The Changing Civil Service*. London: Allen & Unwin, 1985.

Gulick, L. and Urwick, L.F. eds: *Papers on the Science of Administration*. New York: Institute of Public Administration, 1937.

Hood, C.C.: *The Limits of Administration*. Chichester and New York: Wiley, 1976.

———: *The Tools of Government*. London: Macmillan, 1983.

Schaffer, B.B.: *The Administrative Factor*. London: Cass, 1973.

Simon, H.A.: The proverbs of administration. *Public Administration Review* 4 (1946) 53–67.

———: *Administrative Behaviour*. New York: Macmillan, 1947.

Wilson, W.: The study of administration. *Political Science Quarterly* 2 (1887) 197–222; repr. *American Political Science Review* 56 (1941) 481–506.

administrative board In general terms the administration of a public function by a corporate body, for example PUBLIC CORPORATION and QUANGO; more particularly, the use of such a body to take joint responsibility for the operation of a government department. Until well into the nineteenth century it was quite usual for a department to be headed by a Board, for example, the Treasury Board, the Board of Trade and the Local Government Board. This device was thought to avoid the concentration of power which might occur if all authority were vested in one person. It could also enlarge the patronage of the crown.

The increasing power of the UK HOUSE OF COMMONS following the waning influence of the crown meant an increasing stress on individual responsibility. Parliament could not secure accountability when the DECISION MAKING was, in theory at least, distributed between half a dozen or so individuals: they demanded that one person should be accountable to them in the case of each department. And so even when the Board form continued it was in name only, it being well understood that only one member of it – the minister – could be called to account. In the words of John Stuart Mill's *Representative Government*, Boards 'are not a fit instrument for executive business'.

In Scotland the Board form of central

administration was very popular and had a greater measure of independence. Boards were seen as manifestations of Scottish national distinctiveness in the absence of a Secretary of State for Scotland.

In the United States, however, administrative boards have been more widely used, especially since 1913, at the federal, state and local levels. They offered the advantage of freedom from political interference in cases of policy making where it was held that political considerations should carry no weight; but they have been criticized on the grounds of diffusion, in some cases of evasion, of responsibility; and also on occasion of corruption. It has also been argued that they make the co-ordination of administration more difficult.

See also COMMISSION; PUBLIC ADMINISTRATION.   DNC

Reading

Chester, N.: *The English Administrative System.* Oxford: Clarendon Press, 1981.

Willson, F.M.G.: Ministries and boards: some aspects of administrative development since 1832. *Public Administration* (1955) 43–58.

administrative court A judicial body specializing in litigation over questions of ADMINISTRATIVE LAW. 'Judicial' means here settling questions concerning rights and powers in a definitive and non-hierarchical way by the application of legal rules and principles. In this sense, many ADMINISTRATIVE TRIBUNALS may properly be considered administrative courts.

The establishment of a specialized administrative court arises from a number of considerations, notably the particularity of the legal and factual questions involved, the expertise of judges, and the need for specialized procedures. Whether or not a particular legal system creates a specialist administrative court or courts depends on the importance attached to these considerations and upon the extent to which they can be accommodated within the ordinary judicial system.

The particularity of administrative law issues goes beyond the nature of the facts and legal rules in dispute. Firstly, the litigation very often involves a conflict between the public interest for which the administration acts and the private interests of the individuals specially affected by a decision, and this differs in character from litigation between private individuals. Secondly, the administration includes bodies which are politically responsible and whose control poses issues different from the control of private organizations.

The specialist character of the issues involved may require the selection of expert judges. In some cases this expertise may lie in a technical knowledge either of the factual problems involved or of the law in the area. In others the expertise may lie in knowledge of the social milieu in which the rules operate – either knowledge of the administration, as in the case of French administrative judges, or of the citizens affected, as in the case of some tribunals.

The public interest may require that the legality of administrative action be settled more rapidly than in ordinary civil procedure. The responsibilities of the administration towards citizens and their relatively weak position in litigation may justify a greater scrupulousness on the part of the court to ensure that justice is done to litigants. Both arguments favour a special procedure for administrative law cases.

A specialist administrative court is usually institutionally separate from courts concerned with private law litigation, with a distinct manpower and competence. Some legal systems, for example those in Britain and the United States, have no separate institution, but have a special procedure within the ordinary court system for handling administrative law matters. Institutional or procedural distinctions of this kind can create significant problems for the litigant in choosing the appropriate jurisdiction or procedure. Given the difficulties most legal systems have in determining the scope of administrative law such problems are not easily resolved. This reason weighs heavily against the advantages of a separate administrative court system.

See also CONSEIL D'ÉTAT.   JSB

Reading

Brown, L.N. and Garner, J.A.: *French Administrative*

Law. 2nd edn, chs 3 and 6. London: Butterworth, 1983.

Davis, K.C.: *Administrative Law Treatise*. 2nd edn, chs 11–17. San Diego, Calif.: Davis, 1980.

Racz, A.: *Courts and Tribunals: a comparative study*, chs 1 and 2. Budapest: Akademia: Kiado, 1980.

Schwartz, B. and Wade, H.W.R.: *Legal Control of Government*, ch. 9. Oxford: Oxford University Press, 1972.

Whitmore, H.: *Principles of Australian Administrative Law*. 5th edn, chs 9 and 10. Sydney: Law Book Co., 1980.

administrative law   The branch of public law governing the powers and functions of the administration. Its primary concern is the use of power by the executive organs of the state. In some legal systems, administrative law also controls other forms of corporatist power. Whereas CONSTITUTIONAL LAW is concerned with the allocation of power by the constitution and with the protection of fundamental liberties, administrative law is concerned with the exercise of power, derived from any source, by the executive branch of government. Its development in the twentieth century is a product of the growth of the modern STATE, and the need for its manifold activities to be regulated by law. Its significance for the student of political institutions is as a limitation upon the power of the executive.

There are broadly three models of administrative law. The first is the legal integrationist model which recognizes no radical distinction between public and private law, and which treats rules of law governing the administration as an integral element of the rules governing all subjects of the law. Such an approach is traditional in common law systems which originated in England, but now are found in the United States and in many Commonwealth countries. In this century, the approach has been weakened by the creation of specialist institutions to adjudicate on disputes with the administration the ADMINISTRATIVE TRIBUNALS, and by the development of specialized administrative law procedures in the ordinary courts.

Many continental European legal systems adopt a legal separationist model which requires the creation of separate bodies of public and private law, typically administered by separate courts. A clear separation of both the corpus of legal rules applicable to the administration and of the courts which adjudicate upon them is to be found in France, where the CONSEIL D' ÉTAT presides over a system of administrative courts which are distinct from the civil courts and apply distinct legal rules. This model has been followed in many countries, though others have wished to avoid damaging conflicts between distinct systems of rules and courts.

The third model is that of administrative supervision, which is prevalent in the communist countries of Eastern Europe. Founded in 1722 by Peter the Great, the Procuracy was revived in 1922 in the Soviet Union. The Procurator is a state official whose task is to supervise the legality of administrative action. He frequently has the power to suspend administrative decisions which appear illegal and to pursue the matter before the appropriate administrative or judicial authority for a penal or disciplinary sanction.

Particular systems may adopt elements from more than one model in seeking ways to control the administration.

Scope of administrative law

In a wide sense, administrative law includes all legal rules and principles governing the powers and functions of the administration. But this is unnecessarily encyclopaedic. If its primary concern is the use of state power, it is not obviously necessary to treat a contract to buy stationery for the mayor or an accident caused by his official car under a different legal category from similar actions for or by ordinary individuals. The term is therefore properly reserved for those rules and principles peculiar to the functioning of the administration which may be identified by a number of criteria.

The administration: Whereas continental legal systems have been able to develop a coherent concept of the administration, common law systems have no such concept. In essence, this is connected with the abilities of these legal systems to define the state, whose powers the administration exercises. However, even within continental legal systems, the notion of the

9

administration is under strain. Although it clearly covers national and local government departments, problems are caused by the proliferation of QUANGOS, and the public ownership of some service and commercial enterprises, such as transport or banking. Legal systems differ widely on how far such bodies should be governed by administrative law.

Administrative activity: Not all actions of the administration are governed by administrative law. Administrative law regulates those activities which are integrally related to its exercise of state power in the public interest. These may be unilateral acts by which the administration gives orders or grants benefits, e.g. in controlling immigration or granting welfare benefits, or consensual acts, e.g. the placing of defence contracts. Most legal systems find it necessary to divide these categories of administrative acts into those that are integral to the exercise of state power and those that are merely incidental thereto, but the criteria for such a division are rarely satisfactory.

Jurisdictional competence: In those countries with separate ADMINISTRATIVE COURTS, administrative law is often defined in practice as the rules of law applied by those courts. However, since the jurisdiction of those courts is often defined by reference to such concepts as 'an administrative body' or 'an administrative law matter', the definition risks circularity.

Pedagogical definition: In the end writers on administrative law in most countries adopt a pragmatic definition. While recognizing the importance of the criteria just mentioned, they tend to reserve the term 'administrative law' for the general rules and principles applicable to the exercise of power by an administrative body. Rules and principles applicable exclusively to specific administrative bodies or activities, especially where these are submitted to specialized administrative courts or tribunals, tend to be treated in separate works. There are special works on immigration law, military law, planning law, taxation, and so on.

Content of administrative law

Administrative law establishes both primary rules governing the competence and procedures of the functioning of the administration, and secondary rules governing the remedies available for the failure to observe the primary rules.

Primary rules: Administrative law establishes the rules of competence and of procedure in relation to the three principal aspects of an administration's functioning: its *relations with the citizen*, its *internal organization*, and its *relations with other administrations*.

Actions of the administration frequently have direct effects on citizens. Primarily, administrative law defines the conditions under which the administration's duties and powers arise, the principles which must govern their exercise, and the procedures to be adopted. However, such rules are defined so as to respect, as much as possible, the rights of citizens affected by administrative action, whether they be fundamental rights or those conferred by particular legislation or case-law. This is particularly the case where the citizen is the specific object of administrative action, e.g. the grant of planning permission, or where he is particularly affected by the decision, e.g. where a new road affects the enjoyment of his property. In this indirect way, administrative law is part of the fundamental guarantees of a citizen's rights and may give him a special status as regards administrative action.

Although most of the internal operation of the administration is not the subject-matter of legal regulation, administrative law is particularly concerned with two areas. Firstly, the institutional competence of the various persons within a specific branch of the administration is frequently defined by law. Thus, it may require some decisions to be taken or signed by a minister or mayor personally, rather than by a subordinate official. Secondly, public employment raises many questions of a legal character concerning the entry, deployment, promotion, salaries, and dismissal of the officials and employees of the administration. In continental legal systems, such questions are typically governed by special legal principles and are litigated before administrative courts. In common law systems, the fundamental rules are those of ordinary labour law and do not form an important branch of administrative law, which is limited to noting any special rules applicable to public service.

While the practical interaction between different administrations cannot successfully be the subject-matter of legal rules, the law normally determines the basic framework of the relations between them. Typically, such rules will determine the extent to which one organ can intervene in or control the operation of another. This is especially the case with supervisory powers, such as those of a minister or government representative over local authorities or organizations independent from a government department. At times of divergence of opinion or policy between different administrations, such rules provide a guarantee of institutional autonomy and may protect pluralism in a democracy. At other times, they may simply ensure the efficient co-ordination and co-operation of administrations by the transfer of information or by provisions for consultation before decisions are taken.

Secondary rules: Where the primary rules of administrative law are breached, a person aggrieved may seek redress through administrative, judicial, or other channels. The secondary rules of administrative law govern the *procedure* for bringing complaints before courts or tribunals, the admissible *grounds of complaint*, and the remedies which may be granted.

Legal systems differ widely on the procedures for legal redress against the administration. Some require the exhaustion of administrative redress before a legal action can be brought, while others allow legal proceedings even before the administration has made a decision on an individual's case. There are three important aspects to procedure: the competence of the jurisdiction, the standing of the complainant, and the methods of proof. For those legal systems where administrative courts are separate from civil courts, it is important to know which court is competent to hear a complaint. Even in other systems, courts may refuse to entertain litigation which properly belongs to the competence of an administrative tribunal. Such rules may be rigid, as in France, where most administrative law questions must be submitted

to the administrative courts, even if they arise incidentally in a private law suit. Other systems are more flexible so as to avoid dividing a single dispute between several courts. Most legal systems do not permit a popular action by a citizen simply to enforce the law. A complainant must have a personal interest in the litigation. Although most systems initially recognized only the interest of a person against whom an administrative decision was taken, today the indirect interests of associations, pressure groups and unions suffice in the United States, France, West Germany, and, to a lesser extent, in Britain, where the decision affects an interest which they were set up to protect. The spectrum of procedures ranges from the investigatory model of the French administrative courts or of the Soviet Procurator to the formal adversary proceedings before common law courts. In the former, the court takes charge of compiling the dossier and obtaining the necessary information from the parties. In the latter, it is up to the complainant to furnish the relevant evidence and to obtain discovery of documents held by the administration, so the judicial role is more that of an umpire. All the same, even in the investigatory system, the burden of proof may still be on the complainant to show that the documents in the dossier justify the complaint. The rules for obtaining evidence and for the burden of proof differ according to jurisdictions and types of complaint.

Depending on the competence of the court or tribunal before which litigation is brought, a complainant may be able to challenge all the grounds of law and fact on which a decision was made, or may be restricted to questions of law, which is frequently the case before appellate jurisdictions. Three kinds of ground may be distinguished. *Questions of legality* concern the competence of the administration to make the decision, the legal validity of the reasons given, and the regularity of the procedure adopted in reaching the decision. These can nearly always be challenged before a court or tribunal. *Questions of merits* concern the substantive grounds on which the decision was reached, either reasons of fact, or of mixed questions of law and fact. Since this amounts to challenging the judgment of the administration, such a ground of challenge is not always available and may be restricted to certain types of decisions, e.g. those affecting individual liberty. While ADMINISTRATIVE TRIBUNALS often can consider such questions, courts may operate only a limited control, ensuring merely that the decision is not manifestly unreasonable. *Questions of liability* concern the consequences of a decision or act and not its validity. Particularly in some European continental systems, such as in France and West Germany, the administration may be liable without proof of fault for actions which place an undue burden on particular citizens. In other cases, the liability of the administration will require proof of fault, or a breach of contract, or the violation of the rules on restitution. Unlike the French, most legal systems give competence on these latter questions to the ordinary civil courts.

Where a complaint is successful, a number of *remedies* are available, over which the court or tribunal enjoys varying degrees of discretion. Whereas the quashing of a decision permits the administration to re-examine the facts in the light of a judicial ruling, the substitution by the court or tribunal of what it considers to be the correct decision raises delicate questions about the respective roles of the administration and its judges. In general, a decision will only be substituted where the administration enjoys little discretion in dealing with the case. The award of compensation is an independent remedy and indemnifies the complainant for losses suffered as a result of an administrative act or decision.

See also CIVIL RIGHTS; CIVIL SERVICE; OMBUDSMAN. JSB

Reading

Brown, L.N. and Garner, J.A.: *French Administrative Law.* 2nd edn. London: Butterworth, 1983.

Chapman, B.: *The Profession of Government.* London: Allen & Unwin, 1959.

Craig, P.: *Administrative Law.* London: Sweet & Maxwell, 1983.

Davis, K.C.: *Administrative Law Treatise.* 2nd edn. chs 11–17. San Diego, Calif.: Davis, 1980.

Harlow, C. and Rawlings, R.: *Law and Administration.* London: Weidenfeld & Nicolson, 1984.

Morstein-Marx, F.: *The Administrative State.* Chicago, Ill.: University of Chicago Press, 1957.

Schwartz, B. and Wade, H.W.R.: *Legal Control of Government*, chs 1 and 9. Oxford: Oxford University Press, 1972.

administrative tribunal An independent body set up to resolve disputes between the administration and citizens. There are two broad types of tribunal: those that are substitutes for courts and those that are policy-oriented bodies.

Court-substitute tribunals resolve disputes by applying the law in an authoritative decision on questions of law and fact, acting like a court. Compared with ordinary courts a tribunal may have a number of advantages. Its procedure may be more informal, more investigatory, and more accessible to the citizen than the formal, adversary system run by lawyers before the ordinary courts. The citizen may be better able to participate in the decision and bring out his or her case. Especially where legal representation is not permitted, such a procedure may be cheaper both for citizens and for the administration. A tribunal is typically composed of persons with expertise in the social or technical problems involved, but who are not all lawyers. This permits a greater manpower and expertise than could be found among the professional judiciary. Finally, the greater number and procedural simplicity of many tribunals permits a speedier resolution of disputes than would be possible if all administrative law disputes were submitted to the courts.

The various tribunals have these characteristics to a greater or lesser extent, but their existence is explained by the desire to remove specialized questions from the courts for speedier, cheaper and more satisfactory resolution elsewhere. It is before tribunals, rather than before courts, that the vast bulk of administrative law litigation is resolved in Britain. Countries with a specialized court system have less resort to tribunals. This is not surprising as, in essence, administrative tribunals are a way of creating specialist administrative courts. The division of tasks between courts and tribunals depends, *inter alia*, on the competence, procedures and costs of the ordinary courts for administrative law matters.

Policy-oriented tribunals make policy decisions in relation to specific disputes, such as whether particular bus routes should be continued or not. In performing such tasks, the tribunal is essentially a regulatory body which is institutionally independent of the government. Its decision is the concrete application of a policy, and the tribunal may enjoy greater or less freedom to develop a policy of its own in the area subject to its control.

It is hard to distinguish such policy-oriented tribunals from the category of QUANGOS, since both are independent bodies created to implement policies free from ordinary political pressures. The only substantial distinction is that tribunals are properly limited to settling disputes between citizens and the administration, while quangos have a wider role in the creation and the administration of policies in their area of control. However, since the primary issue for both is the appropriate application of a general policy, the distinction is not very clear.

Since some courts, such as the Restrictive Practices Court or magistrates dealing with licensing applications, may also arbitrate on the implementation of policies, a wide difference between the two categories of tribunal is hard to substantiate.

See also ADMINISTRATIVE COURT; ADMINISTRATIVE LAW.   JSB

Reading

Farmer, J.A.: *Tribunals and Government*. London: Weidenfeld & Nicolson, 1974.

Racz, A.: *Courts and Tribunals: a comparative study*, chs 1 and 2. Budapest: Akademia: Kiado, 1980.

Report of the Committee on Administrative Tribunals and Enquiries London: HMSO Cmnd 218, 1957.

Schwartz, B. and Wade, H.W.R.: *Legal Control of Government*, chs 5 and 6. Oxford: Oxford University Press, 1972.

Wraith, R.E. and Hutchesson, P.G.: *Administrative Tribunals*. London: Hutchinson, 1973.

administrator plan   The twentieth century has seen a trend towards professional administration in LOCAL GOVERNMENT under a chief administrative officer (CAO) who is chosen on the basis of formal training and management experience. The CAO generally tries to avoid becoming openly involved in political issues but otherwise serves as a leader in policy development and usually appoints the department heads. The CAO may be an appointee of the council, as in the COUNCIL-MANAGER PLAN and COUNTY-MANAGER PLAN, or of the mayor in the MAYOR-ADMINISTRATOR PLAN. The CAO typically serves at pleasure, with no job protection. Variations on this plan are common in the Irish Republic, the Federal Republic of Germany, and the United States.
                                                                    CRA

adversary politics   A situation in which electoral competition in a basically two-party system produces over-polarized ('adversary') party manifestos and styles of government (see PARTY SYSTEMS). The term was coined during the 1970s by S. E. Finer and used extensively by liberal political scientists in Britain to explain why the proportion of people voting for the previously dominant Conservative and Labour parties had declined. Critics have frequently dismissed the concept as vague and biased, useful only to Liberal (and latterly Social Democratic) politicians in Britain for attacking the older parties. The term adversary politics has now been more formally defined, however, to describe an important class of situations which meet four requirements.

(1) The voting mechanism protects established parties from the threat of new competitors, as plurality and majority systems do in Britain, the USA and Australia.

(2) Both the major parties are controlled by ideologists who give little priority to electoral popularity. Exceptionally these might be the party leaders, financial backers or parliamentarians, but these groups are usually concerned to win elections. Parties controlled by activists, however, are often less prepared to compromise ideological principles in order to win votes, hence those systems with democratically-run MASS MEMBERSHIP PARTIES are more likely to show adversary characteristics than those with only CADRE PARTIES.

(3) Both parties adopt very distinctive policy positions, which are more polarized to the left

and right than are the views of the large majority of voters. Voters must consequently choose between the lesser of two evils at election time, and are denied the opportunity to vote for the consensual policies which they would prefer. This situation may continue for a long period where casting a ballot for a third party is ineffective, and hence the major parties do not have to worry about new parties eroding their vote base or parliamentary representation.

(4) Both political parties when in government reverse a great deal of previous legislation, creating a climate of political uncertainty. Political/business cycle models predict that all governments (left and right) introduce necessary but unpopular economic measures early in their term of office, and reflate in time for the next election. But the adversary politics model predicts that left parties will begin by reflating the economy and right-wing parties by being excessively fiscally conservative. In mid term however both types of government make a U-turn, departing from polarizing positions, and adopting more pragmatic policies to try to restore economic prosperity in time for the next election.

In such situations, the adversary politics model is held to show why the Downsian model of the working of two-party systems, according to which they converge towards the centre, does not hold.

See also ELECTORAL SYSTEMS; SPATIAL MODELS. PJD

Reading

Cox, A.: *Adversary Politics and Land: the conflict over land and public policy in post-war Britain.* Cambridge: Cambridge University Press, 1984.

Dunleavy, P.J. and Husbands, C.: *British Democracy at the Crossroads: voting and party competition in the 1980s,* chs 2–4. London: Allen & Unwin, 1985.

Finer, S.E. ed.: *Adversary Politics and Electoral Reform.* London: Anthony Wigram, 1975.

———: *The Changing British Party System 1945–79.* Washington, DC: American Enterprise Institute, 1980.

Gamble, A.M. and Walkland, S.A.: *The British Political System and Economic Policy 1945–83: studies in adversary politics.* Oxford: Oxford University Press, 1984.

Robertson, D.: Adversary politics, public opinion and electoral change. In *Comparative Government and Politics,* ed. D. Kavanagh and G. Peele. London: Heinemann, 1984.

advertising, political Forms of communication and messages which parties and candidates purchase and use to persuade voters to vote for them. It is usually at its peak during election campaigns, particularly in the press and broadcasting media and the use of posters. In the United States most broadcasting channels are privately owned, and parties and candidates buy time like other advertisers. In most other western states television is state-controlled, provides some free time for party and candidate broadcasts, and does not allow further purchase. In contrast to Australia and the United States, most states in Western Europe forbid political advertising on radio and television. This helps to equalize opportunities between parties and candidates which vary greatly in economic resources. Precluded from television, campaigns concentrate on the national and regional press. Most states have regulatory agencies which rule on the 'fairness' of campaign advertisements. Does advertising switch votes? Early research, which emphasized the selective interpretation of information by most voters, suggested not. Later studies of political communications have shown the voters to be more open-minded and therefore more likely to be open to persuasion. Nevertheless for all the attention paid to television spot advertising in the United States, research suggests that it has little effect in moving voters.

See also MASS COMMUNICATION; POLITICAL COMMUNICATION. DK

advice and consent Under the United States Constitution (Article II, section 2) the advice and consent of the Senate is needed in two circumstances. Treaties with foreign nations require the approval of two-thirds of the Senate, while a majority vote is required to confirm the appointment of ambassadors, Supreme Court justices, and such major officers as heads of Cabinet departments. Legislation has enlarged this requirement to include lower court judges, members of regulatory commissions, military officers and prominent executives such as the directors of the Central Intelligence Agency and the Federal Bureau of Investigation. While the Senate's 'advice' is usually informal, consent is by formal roll call. The procedure has both direct and indirect effects. On some occasions the Senate has exercised this power to reject treaties (most notably the Versailles treaty after the first world war) or appointees (such as two of President Nixon's nominees for the Supreme Court). An indirect effect is that the power restricts the power of the president, and induces him to consult important senators in advance of any action. For example, President Truman brought Republican leaders into the development of NATO, while President Carter did not submit the SALT II arms control agreement, because he contemplated its rejection by the Senate. GMP

Reading

Harris, J.: *The Advice and Consent of the Senate.* Berkeley: University of California Press, 1953.
Harris, R.: *Decision.* New York: Dutton, 1971.

affirmative action Public and private sector policies designed to incorporate racial and ethnic minority group citizens (as well as women) into a variety of political, social and economic institutions. These policies have been adopted in a large number of democracies, but the term is usually applied to the United States where the policy has been the subject of considerable debate.

The first use of the term was in the 1961 Executive Order (No. 10925), issued by President John F. Kennedy. This Order instructed contractors to the United States government to act 'affirmatively', to recruit workers on a non-discriminatory basis. In 1965 President Lyndon B. Johnson expanded the order (No. 11246), requiring the contractor to take 'affirmative action' to ensure non-discrimination in all employment practices. This affirmative action to promote 'equal employment opportunity' enjoyed wide support in the United States. By the early 1970s the promulgation of court orders, government regulations and voluntary measures had transformed many affirmative action policies from

merely encouraging equal opportunity for all individuals to mandating equality of results among selected minority groups. This 'race-conscious' affirmative action is itself varied – ranging from the consideration of minority group membership as a positive factor in hiring and other decisions, to quotas requiring statistical parity among certain minority groups. Arguments supporting such measures include the state interest in promoting minority progress, the justice of compensating minority groups which have suffered discrimination, and the failure of neutral criteria to achieve minority representation in various institutions. Arguments opposing such measures include the injustice of punishing individuals who have not discriminated against minorities, the divisiveness of dispensing public goods on the basis of race, and the awarding of public goods to persons who may not require special assistance.

Because the legal standards governing affirmative action are rather vague, the definition of permissible affirmative action remains ambiguous. JHB

Reading

Affirmative Action Symposium. *Wayne Law Review* (July, 1980).
Consultations on the Affirmative Action Statement of the US Commission on Civil Rights, Vols I and II, 10 February and 10–11 March, 1981.
Glazer, N.: *Affirmative Discrimination: ethnic inequality and public policy.* New York: Basic Books, 1975.
Goldman, A.H.: *Justice and Reverse Discrimination.* Princeton, NJ: Princeton University Press, 1979.

agenda setting The political agenda is that necessarily rather short list of issues which are generally regarded as the most important; agenda setting or agenda building is the process by which political issues are continually sifted and sorted according to the importance attached to them.

The term agenda setting is invariably used to describe the role of the mass media which, it is said, cannot tell people what to think, but can and do exercise a strong influence over what people think about. In other words the term rests upon a distinction between how people evaluate any given set of issues, what they know about the issues, and how they rank them in importance. Research has consistently failed to find any clear evidence that the mass media have a strong and direct effect on the evaluation and interpretation of political issues, but investigation carried out since the 1970s has found solid evidence of an indirect, agenda-setting influence in which the media emphasize some things but not others.

This is not to claim that the media alone create the political agenda, simply that all the political organizations and interests which struggle over the agenda have to go through the media which therefore enjoy a strategic position. Nor does recent research claim that the general public blindly accepts the media's agenda; on the contrary it shows that agenda setting involves constant interaction between the media and audience. The media sort out news items for presentation; the public sort out these items according to their own values and priorities. The public, however, cannot be aware of, and therefore cannot care about what is not reported.

The most important and controversial aspect of the media's agenda-setting powers concerns the ability to keep matters out of sight and out of mind. Some argue that the diversity of media sources ensures that most issues will be given an airing. Others claim that the media are big business, and that their own commercial interests cause them to maintain an agenda which both supports the status quo and is alarmingly narrow. Others point out that 'news' consists, almost by definition, of dramatic events and personalities which may be superficial, rather than an analysis of underlying trends, causes, and consequences. Research seems to have found an important agenda-setting role for the media; exactly how powerful this is, and exactly how it works, is still to be established.

See also MASS COMMUNICATION.   KN

Reading

Qualter, T.H.: *Opinion Control in the Democracies*. London: Macmillan, 1985.

Roberts, D.F. and Bachen, C.M.: Mass communication effects. In *Annual Review of Psychology*, pp. 332–6, ed. M.R. Rosenzweig and L.W. Porter. Palo Alto, Calif.: Annual Reviews Inc., 1981.

aggregation (of interests)   See INTEREST ARTICULATION AND AGGREGATION.

agrarian parties   Political organizations that claim to represent and present policies on behalf of agricultural producers or, more generally, the rural sector of society. Under the stimulus of the expansion of the suffrage, agrarian parties first appeared in Western Europe and North America in the opening decades of the twentieth century. They also enjoyed an ephemeral flowering in Eastern Europe between the world wars, and have sporadically appeared in Latin America. As a durable political phenomenon, however, agrarian parties have been significant only in Scandinavia.

Until fairly recently most people everywhere lived on or from the land. Agricultural questions have therefore always been politically important. Agrarian politics have arisen from two related factors. The first is the nature of the urban rural relationship, especially in economic matters. Economic defence of agrarian interests has formed the core of an urban rural cleavage in the commodity market: the food producers want the highest possible profit from their products and labour, while consumers want to eat as cheaply as possible. The second factor is agrarian structure. There are two constraints of agrarian structure which have shaped the character of political activity: the nature of land ownership, and the impact of the market on the individual farm enterprise. Before the emergence of agrarian organizations such as farmers' associations and co-operative institutions in the late nineteenth century, agricultural political activity – sometimes cathartic, sometimes millenarian – tended to be sporadic and violent. The agrarian uprising or rebellion has been a regular feature of history in most parts of the world.

Market conditions stimulated the formation of the first agrarian parties in the West. The initiative to form a party, to press demands within rather than against the political institutions of the state, was usually taken by a farmers' association dissatisfied with its ability to work within established liberal or conservative parties which, under predominantly urban leaderships, tended to lack an appreciation of the technical and economic problems of farming. In Scandinavia the agrarian parties were originally designed as the political adjuncts of the farming associations and agricultural co-operative societies. They were essentially political pressure groups concerned with the economic position of the farmer. Like the other western agrarian parties they have lacked any kind of distinctive ideology. While committed to the notion of private property, their desire for economic security has meant that they have not been averse to demanding government assistance for, intervention in, and controls over agriculture. Because of this entrepreneurial radicalism, they cannot be easily categorized politically as left or right. They are perhaps best described as 'centrist', usually being prepared to look in either direction for political allies in return for economic promises. Red-Green alliances became a common feature of politics in Scandinavia after the 1930s, although more recently the agrarian parties, except in Finland, have looked more to the right for political co-operation and alliances.

The agrarian parties that emerged elsewhere did so in less developed societies where national independence was an issue or had only recently been achieved, where the question of land ownership had just been resolved or still had to be settled, and where the urban rural dimension of politics and society had the ideological overtones of a moral struggle between good and evil. This was the context in Eastern Europe where the agrarian parties can more appropriately be described as peasantist. Building upon the ideas of Russian populism, they sought to develop an ideology which elevated the peasantry to the status of the chosen people and the only class worthy of political power. Agrarian dictatorships were attempted in Bulgaria, Estonia and Latvia. Peasantist parties were concerned more with the social and political status of the cultivator than with economic improvement. They were defending the idea of small farm units owned by people possessing some vaguely conceived

moral virtues. The peasantist mystique saw the problems and situation of individual and society as being intimately related, but it failed to develop strong roots or any cohesive ideology. It remained little more than a collection of vague notions which at the extreme spurned working relationships with other groups and sought to prevent the contamination of the peasantry by the market economy. Quite often the leadership was urban in origin; it tended not to understand agricultural economics and to use what organization it possessed, including co-operatives, for its own and other political purposes. The agrarian parties which have appeared outside Europe have also displayed many of these peasantist characteristics. Although the peasantist parties of Eastern Europe were violently anti-Marxist, elsewhere they have to a greater or lesser extent taken on board Marxist ideas and analyses of society.

By contrast, in more complex industrial societies, the commercialization of agriculture did not spawn an ideologically motivated politics of agrarian defence. There developed a more pragmatic style of interest politics which treated each issue on its own merit and sought to capitalize upon differences between other political parties to gain economic benefits for farmers. Nowhere, however, have agrarian parties succeeded in mobilizing all cultivators behind their political banner. In most countries the size of the agricultural and rural population was such that in terms of electoral support all parties were agrarian. Other cleavages, especially religious, ethnic and linguistic, divided the rural community and provided for a variegated pattern of party mobilization.

Where agriculture became more heavily market-oriented it also became more specialized, determined by climate and soil conditions. In turn this meant that weather and market conditions did not affect all farmers in the same way. In large countries such as the United States, France and West Germany, this explains why agrarian parties tended to be regional in nature and crop-specific. In the more uniform climatic conditions of Scandinavia, agrarian parties could more easily attempt to be national parties.

As agriculture came to employ fewer people,

and as societies became more urbanized, agrarian parties were faced with a serious challenge to their *raison d'etre*. If they wished to avoid declining in importance, they would have to broaden their electoral appeal and modify their policies. Both of these possibilities have been observed in recent decades. In countries such as France and West Germany the urban rural cleavage has diminished rapidly in importance leading to the elimination of their small regional-based agrarian parties. These tendencies are even more noticeable in Scandinavia. Around 1960 the agrarian parties of Finland, Norway and Sweden changed their names to Centre, symbolizing not just their perceived position on the political spectrum, but also a new deliberate strategy of recruiting non-agrarian support. This strategy was successful only in Sweden, and even there only partially: the Scandinavian Centre parties are still essentially agrarian parties in policy, membership and support. Even so, in recent elections they have declined still further, not just because of the continued shrinkage of the agricultural population, but also because of a loss of support within their traditional clientele to other parties. Their long-term future seems far from secure. DWU

Reading

Landsberger, H.A. ed.: *Latin American Peasant Movements*. Ithaca, NY: Cornell University Press, 1969.

Linz, J.J.: Patterns of land tenure, division of labor, and voting behavior in Europe. *Comparative Politics* 8 (1976) 365–430.

Mitrany, D.: *Marx against the Peasant*. Chapel Hill: University of North Carolina Press, 1951.

Paige, J.M.: *Agrarian Revolution: social movements and export agriculture in the underdeveloped world*. New York: Free Press, 1975.

Stavenhagen, R. ed.: *Agrarian Problems and Peasant Movements in Latin America*. New York: Doubleday, 1970.

Stincombe, A.L.: Agricultural enterprise and rural class relations. *American Journal of Sociology* 67 (1961) 165–76.

Urwin, D.W.: *From Ploughshare to Ballotbox: the politics of agrarian defence in Europe*. Oslo: Universitetsforlaget, 1980.

aldermen In Anglo-Saxon England the *ealdormen* were the leading officials of a county, presiding over the county court and leading the county's armed forces; they were superseded by earls and sheriffs. In the medieval boroughs the aldermen, together with the mayor, formed the governing body of the corporation. The Municipal Corporations Act (1835) provided that in all boroughs aldermen should be chosen by the council for a period of six years, and have the same powers as the elected councillors – the purpose being to introduce elements of continuity and stability into the new councils. In 1888 the system was extended to the counties. The Local Government Act (1972) abolished aldermen (except in the City of London) on the grounds that their method of election was undemocratic. The English system of aldermen was introduced into several Commonwealth countries when municipal corporations were established. In Canada the word alderman is now used only as an alternative to 'councillor'. Several European countries, for example Sweden and Holland, have patterns of local administration which include small executive bodies (*magistrat*) which may be seen as the equivalent of the pre-1835 aldermen in England. BK-L

Reading

Jewell, H.: *English Local Administration in the Middle Ages*. Newton Abbot: David & Charles, 1972.

Report of the Royal Commission on the Municipal Corporations 116 XXIII–XXVI, 1835; repr. Irish University Press, 1969.

Webb, S. and Webb, B.: *English Local Government: the manor and the borough* (1908). repr. London: Cass, 1963.

alternative vote An ELECTORAL SYSTEM based upon preferential voting in single-member constituencies. The voter is required to mark his ballot paper not with an X as in Britain, but with the figure '1' by his most favoured candidate, '2' by the next most favoured and so on. In Australia where voting is compulsory, a vote is only valid if a preference is placed against every candidate whose name appears on the ballot paper; but this is not an essential feature of the system.

Like the second ballot system, the alternative vote allows more than one candidate from the same party or bloc to stand in an election without splitting the vote as occurs under the plurality system. This system, which has been used for elections to the Australian lower house since 1919, ensures that no candidate is elected on a minority vote of his or her constituents. It does not, however, ensure proportional representation, since, under the alternative vote, as under the plurality system, the number of seats that a party wins will depend not only upon the number of votes that it receives, but also upon their geographical distribution. Indeed, it can, under certain circumstances, yield more disproportionate results than the plurality system. The political consequences of the alternative vote are similar to, though not identical with, those of the second ballot.

Australia is the only country that has used the alternative vote in general elections over an extended period. The Irish Republic, however, uses this system for by-elections and presidential elections. The alternative vote has been on the margins of the electoral reform debate in Britain for many years. It was recommended by a Royal Commission in 1910, by the 1917 Speaker's Conference for most constituencies and in a bill in 1930. On each of these latter two occasions it was defeated by the House of Lords.   VBB

Reading

Bogdanor, V.: *What is Proportional Representation? A Guide to the Issues*, ch. 3. Oxford: Martin Robertson, 1984.

American Revolution The successful revolt of the American colonies against British rule which resulted in the establishment of American independence. It was also an episodic and ill-defined transformation in American politics as a result of the forces let loose by the need to invoke popular support to fight a War of Independence. The war began in April 1775 at Lexington and Concord though only in July did the Continental Congress officially vote to take up arms and appoint Washington as commander-in-chief. While Washington kept the army together, only

winning occasional successes, the Congress maintained a form of continental government and negotiated for the aid of foreign powers. From 1781 Robert Morris as Finance Secretary contributed as much on the economic front as Washington did on the military. French intervention in 1778 gave the United States the prospect of victory, and the French fleet freed Washington's army to take Yorktown in 1781. Peace was concluded at Paris in 1783. Social forces of a democratic nature took a large part in domestic politics, particularly at the state level, during these and subsequent years. These forces continued to operate largely regardless of official politics. The Constitution of 1787–8 both contained and reformulated them, giving the United States a 'republican' rather than a 'democratic' government. The social revolution was an amorphous process whose dates are a matter of emphasis rather than definition.   JRP

Reading

Bailyn, B.: *The Ideological Origins of the American Revolution*. Cambridge, Mass.: Harvard University Press, 1964.

Christie, I.R.: *Crisis of Empire*. London: Arnold, 1966.

Jameson, J.F.: *The American Revolution Considered as a Social Movement*. Princeton, NJ: Princeton University Press, 1926.

Jensen, M.: *The American Revolution within America*. New York: New York University Press, 1974.

Pole, J.R.: *The Decision for American Independence*. London: Arnold, 1977.

Wood, G.S.: *The Creation of the American Republic*. Chapel Hill: University of North Carolina Press, 1969.

anarchism (from the Greek, *anarkhia* = absence of rule). An umbrella term for those political outlooks that unequivocally reject the state along with other coercive forms of authority, and look forward to a social order based entirely on voluntary co-operation between individuals and groups. In popular belief anarchists are terrorists, and it is true that certain groups of anarchists have advocated the assassination of heads of state and politicians to further their ends. Between 1892 and 1901 a number of prominent political leaders were assassinated by anarchists, but the vast majority of anarchists repudiate terrorism. The popular usage of 'anarchy' is the equivalent of 'chaos' or total disorder, but this is wholly removed from the self-regulated but orderly society which anarchists assume would emerge if the state were abolished.

Anarchists differ sharply among themselves over the shape of this new society: at one extreme there are those who see its main organizing principle as market exchange between self-interested individuals, at the other those who anticipate a communal form of association in which altruistically-motivated people provide without material reward for one another's welfare. All agree, however, that the state is an unnecessary encumbrance on social relations, and exists primarily to allow a small ruling class to exploit and coerce the remainder of society.

The bearing of anarchism on political institutions is therefore essentially negative and critical. On a theoretical plane anarchist criticism of the state aims to show that, beneath the constitutional facades of different regimes, the same power relations always obtain. In particular, anarchists have dismissed parliamentary democracy as little more than a legitimating device, a means whereby a ruling class is able to co-opt the most vociferous of its opponents. On those grounds they have normally advocated a policy of abstention, refusing not only to stand for election, but in many cases even to vote.

They have also been among the most outspoken critics of state socialism; even those in sympathy with the ultimate ends of socialism have argued that these cannot be realized through centralized authority, which inevitably brings into existence a new political class.

In practice anarchists have demonstrated their opposition to the state in a variety of ways, ranging from acts of civil disobedience such as tax-refusal, through direct action against government policies and personnel (including, on occasion, acts of violence), to full-scale participation in revolutionary movements. They have been most effective when acting in collaboration with other political forces, when the strength of their commitment has often compensated for their lack of numbers. In the second half of the nineteenth century anarchists played a significant role in the European socialist movement, forming a far left wing alongside revolutionary Marxists and parliamentary socialists. Their greatest influence came with the formation of syndicalist trade unions in France and Italy (and after 1900 in Spain) inside which anarchists were able to wield influence far in excess of their numerical strength (see SYNDICALISM). Spain in 1936 provided the one occasion on which the anarchists were able to play a leading role in a revolutionary uprising, revealing both the strengths and the weaknesses of their decentralized forms of organization.

There have been no large-scale anarchist organizations since the defeat of the Spanish revolution, but individuals and small groups have continued to act on the margins of politics, often now in association with liberals. There has, for instance, been a significant anarchist presence in the European peace movement. In the USA individualist anarchists have joined forces with classical liberals to form the Libertarian Party, which polled nearly one million votes in the 1980 presidential election. Anarchist ideas have also flowed into the cultural critique of advanced technological society, influencing the commune movement of the 1960s and early 1970s, and more recently the radical wing of the ecology movement – these movements tending to by-pass mainstream political institutions rather than engaging with them directly. In addition, anarchist ideas, especially in their modified Nozickian form, have influenced the libertarian ideas of the NEW RIGHT.   DLM

Reading

Apter, D.E. and Joll, J. eds: *Anarchism Today*. London: Macmillan, 1971.

Bookchin, M.: *The Spanish Anarchists: the heroic years 1868–1936*. New York: Free Life Editions, 1977.

Joll, J.: *The Anarchists*. 2nd edn. London: Methuen, 1979.

Maitron, J.: *Le Mouvement anarchiste en France*. Paris: Maspero, 1975.

Miller, D.: *Anarchism*. London: Dent, 1984.

Nozick, R.: *Anarchy, State and Utopia*. Oxford: Blackwell, 1974.

Rothbard, M.: *For a New Liberty: the libertarian manifesto*. New York: Collier, 1978.

Woodcock, G.: *Anarchism*. Harmondsworth: Penguin, 1963.

anthropology, political The branch of social or cultural anthropology which deals with relationships of power and authority and with competition and conflict in social life. It is concerned with political processes in all types of society, from small PRE-STATE POLITICAL SYSTEMS to large NATION-STATES, with the entire range of political institutions which this entails. Political anthropology also adopts an holistic approach to politics, assuming that all areas of social life may be in some way related to political processes. Thus, even in very complex societies, certain processes may be explicable only with reference to kinship organization and the network of family ties as in ancient Rome, or current world views and religious ideology as in post-revolutionary Iran.

The origins of political anthropology lie in the evolutionary ideas of the nineteenth-century social theorists such as Henry Maine, Karl MARX and Friedrich Engels (especially *The Origin of the Family*), and the evolution of the state is still a major issue (Service 1975). But in the twentieth century the emphasis shifted to first-hand observation of non-western societies, many of them under colonial control. Some of these were 'centralized', with recognizable chiefship institutions. Other societies lacked them, and here political integration was achieved through lineages (groups descended from a common ancestor), cult organizations, or divisions on the basis of age and sex.

By the 1960s the emphasis was less on plain institutional description and more on problems of change and conflict. The collection and use of historical data in anthropological analysis had become increasingly sophisticated, and a major issue was now the place of the local-level political structures in the nation-state (Swartz 1969). Studies of ETHNICITY, class formation and political conflict proliferated, as a new generation of radical students turned to Marxist theory.

There was also a steady growth of research in the complex societies of Europe and North America themselves. At first anthropologists concentrated on rural areas, discovering, as Blok did in Sicily, rich material on peasant politics, violence, patrons and clients. Some anthropologists, like Bailey, began to apply anthropological concepts to exotic subcultures like those of politicians and academics. But increasingly political anthropology has become concerned with more central political issues affecting the LEGITIMACY and stability of the state itself – unemployment, urban decay, racial and ethnic conflict, NATIONALISM and separatist political movements (see Gellner 1983) – as well as with the informal structures of politics and with the symbols, rhetoric and IDEOLOGY through which leaders attempt to sustain their authority.   JSE

Reading

Aronoff, M.J. ed.: *Political Anthropology Yearbook*, vols 1– . New Brunswick, NJ: Transaction Books, 1980– .

Bailey, F.G.: *Stratagems and Spoils*. Oxford: Blackwell, 1969.

Blok, A.: *The Mafia of a Sicilian Village, 1860–1960*. Oxford: Blackwell, 1974.

Cohen, R. and Middleton, J. eds: *Comparative Political Systems*. Garden City, NY: The Natural History Press, 1967.

Engels, F.: *The Origin of the Family, Private Property and the State* (1884). London: Lawrence & Wishart, 1972; New York: Pathfinder, 1973.

Gellner, E.: *Nations and Nationalism*. Oxford: Blackwell, 1983.

Lewellen, T.: *Political Anthropology*. South Hadley, Mass.: Bergin & Garvey, 1983.

Service, E.R.: *Origins of the State and Civilization*. New York: Norton, 1975.

Swartz, M.J. ed.: *Local-level Politics*. London: University of London Press, 1969.

anticlericalism Political attitude of hostility to the influence of the ministers of organized religion ('clerics') in political and social affairs. Christianity, unlike many other world religions (for example Buddhism, Islam, Hinduism) has on the whole embodied itself in highly organized and hierarchical structures, i.e. in 'churches'. From the very origins of the Christian church, and until 150 years ago, these churches and notably the Roman Catholic church were highly involved in the determination of major social policies, particularly those relating to public morals, marriage and divorce, and education. The creeds of such churches often brought them into collision with the civil authorities. This is particularly true of the Roman Catholic church which has consistently maintained that its origin was independent of the establishment of the state, and its authority in certain areas (for example as above) was superior, since it derived from divine ordinance. During the middle ages, the popes and the emperors of the HOLY ROMAN EMPIRE engaged in three centuries of struggle for supremacy, and anti-clerical resentment among the people and the governments of the individual states of Europe can also be discerned, at various times during the Middle Ages. Modern anti-clericalism has taken three main forms.

(1) Eighteenth-century opposition, the opposition of the *Enlightenment*, especially in France, to the material privileges and alleged corruption of the higher priesthood as established in feudal days and to what were regarded as the unenlightened beliefs of the Roman Catholic church, the latter being enforced through censorship and the church's control of education. This anticlericalism culminated in the acts of the French Revolution (1789) which abolished priestly privileges, confiscated church properties and ended by persecuting the church.

(2) Nineteenth-century opposition, the opposition of *Liberalism*, which accused the church of buttressing despotic governments and enforcing unscientific thought. In most European states and notably France, Italy, Spain and Germany, where the influence of the Roman Catholic church was strong, anti-clerical movements and/or political parties arose which advocated the suppression of the religious orders, the separation of the church from the state (i.e. making the church a purely voluntary body financed by its own adherents), civil marriage and divorce, and lay education.

This led to struggles between the pro-church and the anticlerical parties. In the Third French Republic (established in 1870) the conflict was exacerbated by the hostility of the church to Alfred Dreyfus, and culminated in the Act separating church and state in 1905.

When Rome became the capital of united Italy in 1870 this bitterly offended the Roman Catholic church, since the pope had governed not only the city of Rome but the province around it as a civil as well as religious ruler. From 1874 to 1919 successive popes forbade Catholics to participate in Italian politics; for their part the anticlerical parties were unable to enact civil divorce (which had to wait until 1974) or to ban religious instruction in schools. A similar conflict in Germany, known as the *Kulturkampf* (struggle between cultures) occurred from 1871 to 1878, ending in compromise; similar struggles occurred in Belgium, Spain, and the Austro-Hungarian Empire, and, to a marked and often bloody degree, in the newly independent states of Latin America.

(3) Opposition from COMMUNISM and to a lesser extent from NATIONAL SOCIALISM in the twentieth century. The doctrine of Marxist–Leninist communism always regarded religion as the 'opiate of the people', diverting it from the class struggle and appreciation of the laws of social development. Everywhere in communist countries the church has been separated from the state and has become a purely voluntary body, education is secular, and marriage and divorce are civil functions. In addition, in some of these states, notably the USSR, the government has encouraged antireligious organizations. The anticlerical movement has been most successful in those countries where the prevailing form of Christianity is the Greek Orthodox kind, but in Poland and Hungary, for instance, where the Roman Catholic church is strong, governments have been forced to reach an uneasy compromise. In Western Europe anticlericalism has waned as a major political issue since 1945, although it can resurface when issues such as abortion, divorce and primary education come to the fore. It persists in certain groups (such as primary school teachers or Masonic circles in France), as well as some political

parties of the left. This has coincided with the rise of CHRISTIAN DEMOCRACY and can be of significance in domestic politics. Socialists and communists on the continent of Europe are almost always anticlerical; in addition there survive from the nineteenth century a number of parties which, although conservative, on economic questions are also anticlerical. The Liberal parties in Belgium, Holland, and Italy, and the Radicals in France are all of this type, and conflicts on issues concerning civil liberties and the role of women in society prevent co-operation between otherwise similar parties of the centre-right.

It is also worth noting the distinctive political form which anticlericalism has assumed in Britain. In the nineteenth and twentieth centuries, independent sects, and the nonconformist churches, have opposed the Church of England not so much on doctrinal questions, but because of its alleged political and economic privilege as the established church. At the beginning of the century, this was an important factor distinguishing the vote for the Liberal and Labour parties from the vote for the Conservatives, the party of the Church of England. Such differences are of little importance in contemporary Britain, however, and there is no British counterpart to the secular radical movements of France and other countries of continental Europe. In the modern world, anticlericalism is now strongest in countries such as Israel and in developing countries with powerful religious fundamentalist movements.   SEF

Reading

Chadwick, O.: *The Secularisation of the European Mind in the Nineteenth Century*. Cambridge: Cambridge University Press, 1976.

Devlin, J.J.: *Spanish Anticlericalism: a study in modern alienation*. New York: Las Americas Publishing Co., 1966.

Mellor, A.: *Histoire de l'Anticléricalisme Français*. Paris: Mame, 1966.

Rémond, R.: *L'Anticléricalisme en France de 1815 à nos jours*. Paris: Fayard, 1976.

Sanchez, J.M.: *Anticlericalism: a brief history*. Notre Dame: Indiana University Press, 1972.

Schapiro, J.S.: *Anticlericalism: conflict between church and state in France, Italy and Spain*. Princeton, NJ: Princeton University Press, 1967.

Anti-Federalism   A misnomer which has passed into historical usage. The Anti-Federalists took their name from their opposition to the Federal Constitution drafted at Philadelphia in 1787. They claimed however that it was they who believed in truly federal government while their opponents, who had appropriated the name of Federalists, were really nationalists believing in central government. The Anti-Federalists' weakness was the lack of any central principle, since they wanted the states to retain a large measure of sovereignty and the Congress to have power to act for the states only where the states could not act for themselves – notably foreign policy, western settlement and issues arising between states. Some Anti-Federalists objected on republican grounds to the concentration of powers, particularly the Senate, which they feared would become an OLIGARCHY. Others, to be found mainly in the mercantile states and cities, expressed fears that the rich and educated merchants and lawyers would operate the new machinery of government in their own interests, at the expense of the poor. These fears were allied to those expressed by Patrick Henry of Virginia that the north-east would dominate the new government at the expense of the south and west. Anti-Federalists came very close to rejecting the Constitution in Virginia, and constituted large minorities in Pennsylvania, New York and Massachusetts, but some were won over by implied promises of a BILL OF RIGHTS to protect the citizen against centralized power – redeemed by the first ten amendments to the Constitution, passed by the first Congress. In general the Anti-Federalists lacked control of the press and were poor in organization and in qualities of leadership.

See also   FEDERALISM;   FEDERALIST PAPERS.   JRP

Reading

Jensen, M.: *The New Nation 1781–1789*. Chapel Hill: University of North Carolina Press, 1950.

Kenyon, M. ed.: *The Anti-Federalists*. Indianapolis,

New York and Kansas City: Bobbs-Merrill, 1966.

Main, J.T.: *The Anti-Federalists: critics of the constitution 1781–1788*. Chapel Hill: University of North Carolina Press, 1969.

Wood, G.S.: *The Creation of the American Republic 1776–1787*. Chapel Hill: University of North Carolina Press, 1969.

anti-party group The name given by Khrushchev and his supporters to a temporary coalition in the Soviet Presidium (see POLITBURO) which, objecting to the pace of de-Stalinization and to other policies such as the rapprochement with Yugoslavia and administrative decentralization, called for his resignation in June 1957. Khrushchev successfully demanded that the CENTRAL COMMITTEE of the CPSU, which formally elects the First Secretary (see GENERAL SECRETARY), be convened in plenary session. After eight days of debate the plenum issued a resolution condemning the opposition. Since Khrushchev did not wish it to be obvious that he had been in a minority in the Presidium the names of the group's members – Bulganin, Kaganovich, Malenkov, Molotov, Peruvkhin, Saburov, Voroshilov and candidate member Shepilov – were released gradually. These men lost their Presidium and Central Committee membership but significantly were transferred to minor administrative posts, retaining their pension rights, rather than executed. The subsequent reconstruction of the Presidium confirmed Khrushchev's dominance.   SW

Reading

Hough, J.F. and Fainsod, M.: *How the Soviet Union is Governed*. Cambridge, Mass. and London: Harvard University Press, 1979.

Linden, C.A.: *Khrushchev and the Soviet Leadership 1957–1964*. Baltimore, Md.: The Johns Hopkins University Press, 1966.

Pethybridge, R.: *A Key to Soviet Politics: the crisis of the anti-party group*. London: Allen & Unwin, 1962.

Schapiro, L.: *The Communist Party of the Soviet Union*. 2nd edn. London: Methuen, 1970.

Tatu, M.: *Power in the Kremlin: from Khrushchev to collective leadership*. London: Collins, 1969.

anti-Semitism The term was coined in 1879 by the German journalist Wilhelm Marr to emphasize the antagonism between Jews and 'Aryans', based not on religion, occupation or interest but on the unalterable, apparently scientific, basis of biological descent. The introduction of this racial argument marked an intensification of a prejudice as old as the dispersion of Jews as a minority in the civilized world, following the sack of Jerusalem by the Romans in AD 70. Systematic discrimination followed with the spread of Christianity throughout Europe. Exclusion from more and more occupations and the ownership of land increasingly restricted Jews to trade and money-lending. Discrimination led only slowly to persecution; it was not until the thirteenth century that Jews were obliged to wear distinctive dress, including the yellow patch, and the early sixteenth century that they were residentially confined to *ghettoes*. It is from this period of incipient segregation that the most common superstitions about Jews date – their alleged involvement in sorcery, the poisoning of wells, the desecration of the host and above all of 'ritual murder', that is the use of Christian blood in the making of Passover bread.

However, the political movement that Marr named anti-Semitism differed in kind from these earlier episodic persecutions, for those had not threatened the Jews' existence as a people. So long as the Jew was a second-class citizen he or she did not threaten the status of others. Anti-Semitism as a political phenomenon is the product of two features of the modern world: the emancipation of the Jews and the emancipation of the masses. The ending of religious discrimination, which began with the French Revolution and spread gradually through Europe in the nineteenth century, turned the Jew from pariah to citizen and opened all callings to him, at least in theory. In an age of rapid economic and constitutional change Jews were able to take advantage of new opportunities in commerce, industry, politics and intellectual life. Anyone who feared or resented the new order was tempted to suppose that because Jews benefited from it they must have instigated it.

Hence two new features were added to traditional Jew-hatred. The first was the belief that the Jew was not only inferior but dangerous: the alleged power and wealth of Jews, often exaggerated, could be explained only by conspiracy. Evidence for this belief was produced in the *Protocols of the Elders of Zion*, published in Russia in 1905 and in western translations, including English, since 1920. Though shown to be a forgery, this document continues to be reprinted, most recently in Britain in 1972. The second was the assertion that what differentiated Jews from their neighbours was race: hence any civic equality, assimilation or inter-marriage was to be resisted. Economic and political crises have given rise to periodic outbursts of this newer type of anti-Semitism. The stereotype of the Jew as traitor surfaced in the Dreyfus Affair in France in the 1890s, over a Jewish officer falsely accused of espionage. Both the Russian Revolution of 1917 and Germany's military defeat in 1918 fed beliefs in Jewish-inspired conspiracies.

Increasingly, politicians and governments saw fit to exploit popular anti-Semitic beliefs as safety valves for political discontent. The *pogroms* that swept Russia after the assassination of Tsar Alexander II in 1881 exemplify this device. With the extension of the suffrage and the growth of a popular press anti-Semitic political parties developed. The first, the Christian-Social Workers' Party, was founded in Berlin in 1878 by the court preacher Adolf Stoecker. Karl Lueger, leader of the Austrian Christian-Social Party, was elected Mayor of Vienna in 1895, and the *Ligue antisémitique* flourished in France at the time of the Dreyfus Affair. International anti-Semitic conventions, the first in Dresden in 1882, took place.

Anti-Semitism in general intensified in the social disorganization after the first world war and the economic despair brought about by the Great Depression. These enabled Adolf Hitler's National Socialist German Workers' Party (Nazis) to gain power in Germany in 1933. Under them anti-Semitism as public policy, combining the belief in conspiracy and in race, culminated in the deportation and murder of around six million Jews, mostly in specially constructed EXTERMINATION CAMPS, such as Auschwitz and Treblinka.

Though Hitler's defeat in 1945 discredited anti-Semitism, it survives as a motif in parties such as the National Front in Britain, the *Front national* in France, the West German National Democratic Party and various white supremacist groups in the USA. It has also surfaced from time to time in the Soviet Union and other parts of the Soviet bloc and occasionally appears in controversies about Israel and ZIONISM.

See also NAZISM; RACE IN POLITICS.

PGJP

Reading

Cohn, N.: *Warrant for Genocide. The Myth of the Jewish World conspiracy and the protocols of the Elders of Zion*. London: Eyre & Spottiswoode, 1967.

Katz, J.: *From Prejudice to Destruction: Anti-Semitism 1700–1933*. Cambridge, Mass.: Harvard University Press, 1980.

Parkes, J.: *The Conflict of the Church and the Synagogue*. New York: Meridian, 1961.

Poliakov, L.: *The History of Anti-Semitism*. 3 vols. London: Routledge, 1974–5; Vol IV. Oxford: Oxford University press, 1985.

Pulzer, P.: *The Rise of Political Anti-Semitism in Germany and Austria*. 2nd edn. London: Peter Halban, 1989.

Reichmann, E.: *Hostages of Civilisation*. London: Gollancz, 1950.

anti-system party A term normally applied to parties in a political system which refuse to accept the normal rules of democratic party competition. The concept of anti-system parties has been applied frequently to extremist parties of the left and of the right, which may threaten the democratic order. The classic case is that of Weimar Germany, which has profoundly influenced later political analysts. Ferdinand Hermens ascribed the fall of the Weimar republic to the nefarious effect of proportional representation (PR) which in his view fragments political will and ideologizes politics; Maurice Duverger has argued that PR systems are particularly liable to a sudden entry of anti-system parties, while Giovanni Sartori has used the Weimar experience to illustrate his model of POLARIZED PLURALISM.

As a result of Weimar, safeguards have been suggested or adopted to defend the democratic order against parties which might try to overthrow it; the Basic Law of the

Federal German Republic requires that parties must respect the principles of a democratic order and entrusts the Federal Constitutional Court with the authority to ban parties which do not. A high electoral threshold and the constructive motion of no-confidence are also regarded as possible defences against a repetition of the events of 1933. The concept has also been applied to *Poujadist* or TAX REVOLT PARTIES (such as the Danish Progress Party since 1973.

Historically interesting and relevant examples are parties that have rejected the legitimacy of a particular state or constitutional order, for example the Roman Catholics in Italy after the fall of the Papal States in 1870, Fianna Fail in the Republic of Ireland between 1921 and 1932, or certain sections of the Gaullist movement between 1946 and 1958. In the same vein, nationalist and regionalist parties which demand independence, or at least greater autonomy in a given state, can develop into anti-system parties when they refuse to adhere to the existing constitutional arrangements for party competition.

See also COMMUNIST PARTIES; FASCISM; GAULLISM; NAZISM; POUJADISM.   HD

Reading

Kirchheimer, O.: Germany: the vanishing opposition. In *Political Oppositions in Western Democracies*, ed. R.A. Dahl. New Haven, Conn.: Yale University Press, 1966.

Sartori, G.: *Parties and Party Systems: a framework for analysis*. New York and Cambridge: Cambridge University Press, 1976.

apartheid Afrikaans word for 'apartness', a policy aimed at segregating whites and non-whites in the Republic of South Africa. It was the official policy of South Africa since its chief exponents, the Nationalist Party, took power in 1948, although it has been considerably modified in the 1980s. Its basis is classification by race. A person's rights are determined by his or her race as defined by the state. In practice it has installed baaskap (white supremacy). Blacks may neither vote nor sit in the central parliament. Instead, four tribal quasi-

independent homelands and six self-governing areas have been set up, exclusively for Blacks, with their own elected governments. These enjoy a limited authority under the overriding authority of the South African Parliament. Apartheid involved forbidding marriage between white and non-white persons, dividing rural and city areas into white and non-white zones; segregating schools, universities, transport facilities, libraries, cinemas and theatres, and economic discrimination, for example, reserving certain occupations which were non-accessible to Blacks, and discrimination in property rights. The movement of Blacks was controlled by an internal passport system. In 1983 a new constitution was approved giving some participation to Indians and Coloureds, but not to the majority Black population: and there have been some reforms, most notably in liberalizing the laws forbidding marriage and sexual relations between whites and non-whites. Apartheid has been vigorously denounced by many countries as a violation of human rights.   SEF

Reading

Omond, P.: *The Apartheid Handbook*. 2nd edn. Harmondsworth: Penguin, 1986.

apparatchik A member of the full-time staff of party, state, or other organizations in communist-ruled countries. The term is used more particularly to refer to the full-time party bureaucracy at both local and national levels. Nominally subordinate to elected party committees and holders of elected posts, the full-time party bureaucracy has in fact played a dominant role in most communist regimes since their inception. Party statutes generally make little reference to the full-time apparatus, though the revised rules of the Communist Party of the Soviet Union adopted in 1986 for the first time made formal provision for the existence of an 'apparatus' attached to all levels of the party organization whose responsibilities included 'organizing and checking up on the fulfilment of party decisions' and 'rendering assistance to the lower organizations in their activities' (rule 23). The apparatus plays a similar role in most other communist or Marxist–Leninist parties.

SLW

Reading

Hill, R.J. and Frank, P.: *The Soviet Communist Party*. 3rd edn. London: Allen & Unwin, 1987.

Simons, W.B. and White, S. eds: *The Party Statutes of the Communist World*. The Hague: Nijhoff, 1984.

apparentement A provision in a list system of proportional representation by which separate parties can declare themselves linked for the purposes of vote counting and seat allocation. The votes of these separate parties are counted together as though cast for a single list. The political aim of *apparentement* is to encourage co-operative parties and penalize the intransigent.

See ELECTORAL SYSTEMS. VBB

Reading

Williams, P.M.: *Crisis and Compromise: Politics in the Fourth Republic*, ch. 22. London: Longman, 1964.

apportionment See REDISTRIBUTION.

appropriations See BUDGET/BUDGETING.

approval voting A voting system whereby people can vote for as many candidates as they wish in an election with more than two candidates. For example, if there are five candidates voters can vote for two or more if they have no clear favourite, but only one vote can be cast for each approved candidate. The candidate with the most approval votes wins.

Potential advantages of approval voting are as follows:

(1) The system gives voters more flexible options: they can vote for a single favourite if they wish – but should they have no such favourite they can express this by voting for all the candidates they find acceptable. Furthermore, if their favourite candidate has little chance of winning they can also vote for a more viable second or third choice. This increased flexibility of options encourages a larger turnout.

(2) The system elects the strongest candidate without depriving weaker candidates of their proper due. The candidate with the greatest overall support will win, but lesser candidates do not suffer from the wasted-vote phenomenon whereby votes are taken away from them to be given to stronger contenders – this has proved very disruptive in plurality elections. Approval voting is relatively insensitive both to the number of candidates running and to assessments of their standing.

(3) The system is simple for voters to understand, it does not appear to violate any constitutions, and it can be implemented on existing voting machines. This makes it more practical to operate than more complex preferential voting systems, useful though these may be in achieving proportional representation in multiple-winner elections.

Approval voting minimises strategic calculations but does not eliminate them, because approval of a less-preferred candidate could hurt a more-preferred approved candidate. Presumably, the voter will vote for a less-preferred candidate if that candidate, though less acceptable, has a better chance of winning.

Approval voting is now widely used in private organizations, professional societies, and universities; bills to implement approval voting have been introduced in some state legislatures in the United States. It is particularly recommended in party primaries, which often attract large fields of candidates and wherein strong minority candidates on the left and right have often defeated centrists, who would probably be helped by approval voting.

See also ELECTORAL SYSTEMS. SJB/PCF

Reading

Brams, S.J. and Fishburn, P.C.: *Approval Voting*. Cambridge, Mass.: Birkhäuser Boston, 1983.

areal division of power The term was first used in 1956 to identify a model devised by a group of American political scientists for comparing alternative institutional arrangements that divide governmental power among areas (Maass et al. 1959). It was intended, in part, to be a conceptual framework to guide research in LOCAL GOVERNMENT and inter-governmental relations.

The model devised by Maass et al. is based on four initial arguments.

(1) Quoting Friedrich (1950, p. 5), 'division of power is the basis of civilized government; it is what is meant by constitutionalism.'

(2) Division of power, like governmental institutions generally, is a function of community values.

(3) The extent to which governmental power is divided and the methods by which the divisions are affected are also functions of the community power structure – of the 'non-governmental division of power'.

(4) Although the areal division of power (*adp*) is as important as the SEPARATION OF POWERS or capital division of power (*cdp*) in serving community values, political scientists had not developed systematic analytical models for studying it.

Community values used as examples are liberty, equality, and welfare. In order to promote liberty, governmental power can be so divided as to protect the individual and groups against arbitrary governmental action and against great concentrations of political and economic power – a restraining, 'constitutional' effect. In order to promote equality, governmental power can be so divided as to provide broad opportunities for citizen participation in public policy – a 'democratic' effect. In order to promote welfare, governmental power can be so divided as to ensure that governmental action will be effective in meeting the needs of society – a service or facilitating effect. From these macro-values various instrumental values are derived.

The model has two basic building blocks.

(1) Governmental power can be divided among institutions at the capital (*cdp*) and among component areas (*adp*) according to the *processes* used in government, for example, legislation, administration, the *functions* or activities of government, and the *constituencies* represented by institutions and areas. Process,

function, and constituency are interrelated as methods for dividing power. For example, functions can be divided among units of government which also represent unique constituencies.

(2) The assignment of processes, functions, and constituencies to governmental units at the capital and to component areas can be either exclusive or shared. The function of coining money could be given exclusively to the central government, whereas the function of public welfare could be shared by both central and provincial governments. There are many possible elaborations of this two-part distinction. The assignment of power to the units or areas sharing a function, process or constituency can either be spelled out exactly, so as to allow a minimum of overlap or discord, or it can be designed to allow or promote competition and conflict. Furthermore, the assignment of exclusive or shared powers can either be by delegation which proceeds from a single source (other than a constitution) and which can be withdrawn by that source, or it can be by constitutional provision which can be changed formally only by constitutional amendment. The *adp* technique of analysis can be applied equally to federal and to unitary states, and it is dynamic in form and intent.

Using this framework and the basic community values of liberty, equality and welfare, the next step was to develop criteria for dividing governmental power on an areal basis. More specifically, Ylvisaker postulated the conditions under which *adp* would tend to maximize realization of the community values. These conditions were called maxims for a 'proper' areal division of power. The first maxim, for example, is that the assignment of powers to component areas should always be general, covering the whole range of governmental functions, rather than partial and related only to particular functions.

The model, as elaborated by Maass and Ylvisaker, was applied to US metropolitan areas by Wood, to US states by Willbern, and to Canadian federalism by Dupré. For example, Wood considered Ylvisaker's maxim in the light of data from a number of metropolitan areas and concluded:

Ylvisaker's requirement that the power to govern be a general one does not mean necessarily and at once a power to govern generally (i.e. with respect to all matters) for the entire metropolitan region, although it certainly can and probably does mean this for the long run. But in the less than mature system, a transitional device may be to select one or a group of powers, institutionalize them, and nurse them along in such a way that they lead to greater cohesion for the region, and as a consequence, to a more general power to govern. The essential point is that the powers granted should be stated in terms of the community and constituency affected and the political process involved, and that they should be powers – not functions.

The model was also used to reinterpret some of the classic political science literature on division of power. Huntington, reviewing the writings of the founding fathers of the US Constitution – ADAMS, JEFFERSON and MADISON – found a significant correlation between their proposed configurations of *adp* and *cdp* on the one hand, and their preferences for one or other of the community values of liberty, equality and welfare on the other. Hoffmann, however, found that for the French thinkers BODIN, MONTESQUIEU, ROUSSEAU, TOCQUEVILLE, Taine, and Proudhon any concern for *adp* was part of a more general concern for creating a healthy balance of forces in society. In the French context there was a more serious concern than there was in the American about relations between governmental and non-governmental divisions of power.

The principal criticism of the *adp* model has been that the criteria or maxims need to be developed into more precise hypotheses before they can be used as a framework for further empirical research and tested. Though this has not been done in any systematic way the analytical framework of *adp* has proved to be suggestive for a number of important scholarly studies of regional and local governments, for example, Robert Putnam on REGIONALISM in Italy and Steven Reed on local government in Japan.

See also FEDERALISM.   AM

Reading

Friedrich, C.J.: *Constitutional Government and Democracy*, chs 10 and 11. Boston, Mass.: Ginn, 1950.

Maass, A. ed. with Dupré, J.S., Huntington, S.P., Hoffmann, S., Willbern, Y., Wood R.C. and Ylvisaker, P.: *Area and Power: a theory of local government*. Glencoe, Ill.: Free Press of Glencoe, 1959.

Putnam, R., Leonard, R. and Nanetti, R. eds: *La Pianta e le radici: il radicamento dell'istituto regionale nel sistema politico italiano*. Bologna: Societa editrice il Mulino, 1985.

Arendt, Hannah (1906–1975)   German-American philosopher. The first book of Hannah Arendt's to become widely known was the magisterial *Origins of Totalitarianism* (1951). This made a great impact on American political theory, but less on the insular British scene. She was the first to argue on a large scale that there were common elements in NAZISM and STALINISM. However different the content of their ideologies, both believed that ideology furnished 'the key to history', and they were each creating a new system of government with world-changing aspirations. Even the worst of the old autocracies had had only limited ambitions. Hannah Arendt saw the origins of the idea of total power in the by-ways of European intellectual history, ideas of cranks and fanatics which became plausible when in the first quarter of this century, 'two demons', total war and mass unemployment, destroyed the widespread belief in liberal rationality. Above all she was obsessed with trying to explain why the CONCENTRATION CAMPS became EXTERMINATION CAMPS.

Her later books can be seen as attempts to elaborate, and to ground philosphically, positions taken up in her great first book. *The Human Condition* (1958) blended ARISTOTLE, KANT and Heidegger in a view of politics as the essential example of free human action, divorced from considerations of utility, success or failure. This underlay her study of *Eichmann in Jerusalem* (1963) which aroused anger because, although she extended pity to her people, she argued both that the Jews lacked a political tradition, and that an important element of a political tradition was hopeless resistance. Her political essays are a curious mixture of conservative scepticism about mass action, and socialist affection for small groups. Her *On Violence* (1970) contains masterful and terse definitions.   BRC

Reading

Arendt, H. : *The Origins of Totalitarianism* (1951), repr. Cleveland, Ohio: Meridian, 1966.

———: *The Human Condition*. Oxford: Oxford University Press, 1958.

———: *Between Past and Future*. London: Faber; Cleveland, Ohio and New York: Viking, 1961.

———: *Eichmann in Jerusalem*. London: Faber, 1963.

———: *On Violence*. London: Allen Lane; Penguin, 1970.

———: *Men in Dark Times*. London: Penguin, 1973.

Beiner, R. ed.: *Hannah Arendt: Lectures on Kant's Political Philosophy*. Chicago, Ill.: University of Chicago Press, 1982.

Canovan, M.: *The Political Thought of Hannah Arendt*. London: Methuen, 1977.

Hill, M.R. ed.: *Hannah Arendt: the Recovery of the Public World*. New York: St Martin's, 1979.

Young-Bruehl, E.: *Hannah Arendt*. New Haven, Conn: Yale University Press, 1982.

aristocracy   The term has various historical connotations.

(1) In its original sense in classical Greece it meant 'government by the best'(*aristos* = best + *kratia* = rule); what is meant by best and how the best are selected, educated or trained for government are perennial problems in political philosophy. PLATO and ARISTOTLE sought answers to these problems in their discussions of the ideal form of government. The aristocracy required special sets of qualities to make them fit for government, and Plato in particular devoted much of his thinking to the problem of selecting, and educating, those who would become the guardians or rulers of the state. Their rule would be in the interests of the people and for the common good, and not for their own self-interest. However both Plato and Aristotle were very conscious that aristocracy can easily degenerate to OLIGARCHY which in turn could become plutocracy, where the pursuit of private wealth becomes the chief aim of the oligarchs.

(2) Aristocracy, as a plural concept, is always to be distinguished from monarchy where a single ruler governs by divine right or by the hereditary principle. The aristocracy is not necessarily loyal or subservient to the monarch, and there are many historical examples where an aristocracy has been engaged in a struggle for power against a reigning monarch.

(3) In the modern era, aristocracy is almost invariably discussed in its connotation of a special class or caste of persons having special privileges but also, as they would normally assert, special responsibilities. The essential characteristics of an aristocracy are kinship, birth, and breeding within a determined group. Wealth, the possession of property, or special forms of education are not defining characteristics although some of them are usually deemed important by the members of an aristocracy themselves. The European aristocracies have been historically associated with hereditary titles, both before and after the revolutions of the nineteenth and twentieth centuries.

(4) In modern socialist thought, aristocracy is viewed as part of the detritus handed down from feudalism, to be swept away by revolutionary means along with other aspects of privilege and inequality seen to be preserved and sustained by capitalism.   ESAI

Reading

Barker, E.: *Greek Political Theory: Plato and his predecessors*. London: Methuen, 1960.

Bottomore, T.B.: *Classes in Modern Society*. London: Allen & Unwin, 1965.

Giddens, A.: *The Class Structure of the Advanced Societies*. London: Hutchinson, 1973.

Parkin, F.: *Marxism and Class Theory: a bourgeois critique*. London: Tavistock, 1979.

Ponsonby, A.W.H.: *The Decline of Aristocracy*. London: Unwin, 1912.

Aristotle   (384–322 BC)   Greek philosopher, the most famous pupil of the Greek philosopher PLATO, Aristotle wrote treatises on a wide range of philosophical and scientific subjects, including ethics and politics. His *Politics* is a posthumously edited collection of essays which together form the most comprehensive pre-modern account of POLITICAL SCIENCE. Like other Aristotelian sciences, political science is generalized knowledge based on first principles and providing causal explanations. As a science dealing with human action, it is necessarily imprecise and its generalizations hold true only 'for the most part' and not absolutely. It is also a practical science, providing guidance for the statesman and aiming at appropriate action rather than simply knowledge for its own sake.

The overall purpose of the political community is that its citizens should achieve the good life or happiness, which is discussed in Aristotle's two ethical treatises, the *Eudemian* and the *Nicomachean Ethics*, which are closely linked to the *Politics*. In the *Politics*, Aristotle concentrates almost exclusively on the institutions of the Greek city-state (*polis*) which he considers the most developed and civilized form of political organization. He and his pupils recorded the political structure and history of 158 cities, the first instance of systematic empirical research in the history of political studies. (Only one of these accounts, the *Constitution of Athens*, survives.)

Aristotle's approach to political analysis is not narrowly legalistic or institutional but places considerable weight on what would now be called socio-economic and ideological factors. The central concept is 'constitution' (*politeia*) which provides the identity of each *polis* and includes not only the main institutions of government but also the values and goals of those holding power.

As usual, Aristotle gives particular attention to problems of classification. In classifying constitutions, he adopts the traditional Greek classification according to the size of the ruling body (one, few or many) and the ethical nature (goodness or badness) of the regime. This provides six general types: good and bad forms of monarchy, i.e. kingship and tyranny; good and bad forms of rule by the few, i.e. aristocracy and oligarchy; good and bad forms of rule by the many, i.e. 'polity' (the generic term for 'constitution', *politeia*, used in a

specific sense) and democracy. The traditional criteria are considerably developed and refined, particularly in relation to OLIGARCHY and DEMOCRACY, the two commonest types of constitution: the number of those in power is less important than their economic condition, whether rich (oligarchy) or poor (democracy); each type of constitution also has a dominant principle or conception of justice, e.g. wealth for oligarchy and freedom for democracy, which is the overriding value of those in power and determines the distribution of power and other goods.

Constitutions can also be distinguished by their methods of organizing the three elements of government. These elements are: the deliberative, which makes the most important decisions in domestic and foreign policy, and is responsible for legislation and the appointment of officials; the official, which includes all appointed officials and magistrates; and the judicial. The deliberative and judicial functions are normally exercised by those who control the regime, for example, the wealthy in an oligarchy, free males in a democracy. This group also constitutes the citizen body, citizenship being defined as participation in deliberative or judicial office. Officials may be chosen by birth, by election or by lot. Election, with its assumption of selecting the most able candidates, is seen as characteristic of aristocracy, the type of constitution most concerned with virtue and merit; the method of selection appropriate to democracy is lot because it assumes equality of merit and desert.

Constitutions are further divided into those where the rulers govern in accordance with law ('the rule of law') or absolutely, by decree. Each of the general types is divided into generalized sub-types ranging from the more extreme, in which the characteristics of the type are realized in a pure or extreme form, to the more moderate which share some of the characteristics of other, cognate types. In analysing actual individual constitutions, Aristotle uses his categories in the manner of ideal types, showing how a particular constitution may share features of different general types or sub-types.

The best type of constitution for any city will depend on the nature and composition of its population. The ideally best constitution is rule by a man or men of complete virtue, a form of kingship or aristocracy. Absolute rule where a person or persons of exceptional ability rule above the law would be justifiable if sufficiently superior people could be found; more likely is a larger citizen body of virtuous land-owners which would share in ruling and being ruled in a form of ideal aristocracy (the subject of the last two books of the *Politics*). But this too is utopian. A more realistic aim is some form of 'polity'. In the central, so-called 'realistic' books of the *Politics* (IV, V and VI), polity emerges not so much as a good form of democracy but more as a mixture of, or compromise between, the extremes of oligarchy and democracy, giving power to those of moderate wealth rather than to the rich or the poor. Such a regime is both more just and more likely to provide political stability which, for Aristotle, is the major aim and value in everyday non-ideal politics.

Not every city will have a middle class large enough to sustain a polity but all regimes are capable of improvements which will lessen the risk of instability. Aristotle therefore analyses in considerable detail the various causes of constitutional change and political disorder (*stasis*), drawing heavily on his school's researches into the history of individual Greek cities. This section (Books V and VI) best illustrates Aristotle's political science, as it works towards general explanations, based on firm empirical evidence and directed towards an issue of practical relevance. The analysis is always open-ended, giving weight both to ideological factors, such as differing conceptions of justice, and to socio-economic factors, such as demographic changes or economic conflict. He also includes personal or accidental factors which may act as triggers to revolution even if they do not provide the underlying causes. In the light of these findings he recommends various measures to reduce the risk of disorder and revolution. In general, they involve making the constitution more moderate by sharing power more widely and by reducing the grievances of potential opponents.

Among other sections of the *Politics* is an analysis of the household (Book I) which contains historically influential accounts of slavery, defended as natural, and of the acquisition of wealth, in which usury is condemned as unnatural.   RGM

Reading

Aristotle: *Politics*.
————: *The Ethics*.
————: *Constitution of Athens*.
Barnes, J.: *Aristotle*. Oxford: Oxford University Press, 1982.
Mulgan, R.G.: *Aristotle's Political Theory*. Oxford: Clarendon Press, 1977.

Aron, Raymond (1905–1983)   Aron's career and his work are both tripartite. Professionally, he was equally celebrated as a journalist, as a writer and as a teacher. And his work, although harmonized in a global perspective, is divided into social science, philosophy, and history. As a philosopher Aron stands out as one of the most French and French-rooted contemporary political philosophers, in an age in which French philosophy and political theory was under strong German influence. This trend was started by Sartre (his antagonistic twin). Oddly enough, Aron, whose doctoral thesis and first book, *Introduction to the Philosophy of History* (1938) was an examination of German historical sociology (Dilthey, Rickert, Simmel and Weber) – conserved his French authenticity; while Sartre fell irretrievably under Heidegger's spell, Aron's sole masters were MONTESQUIEU and TOCQUEVILLE – and beyond both of them, Montaigne and his specifically French quality of understanding, in the double sense of the word. As a journalist, Edward Shils rightly said that at the end of his life 'Raymond Aron was the most prominent and most esteemed expert in modern societies and in international relations'. *Les Guerres en chaîne* and *Clausewitz* form a classic trilogy on the history of modern war and international relations.

Although he was professionally described as a sociologist, Aron himself believed, in an Aristotelian way, that political philosophy links together and comprehends sociology, economics and political science – thus emulating both Montesquieu and Tocqueville. His distinctive approach to political institutions lay in his attempt to understand the internal logic of different political systems, a notion deriving from Max WEBER's theory of ideal types. 'The political regime', he believed 'conditions the style of the collectivity. In the age of industrial society, it is the political regime which provides the specific difference between collectivities belonging to the same type'. Aron distinguishes between regimes in terms of party competition. He divided industrial societies into *monopolistic*, such as the USSR, where the one-party state exerts a monopoly on society, and *constitutional–pluralistic*, where the Constitution or the laws of the state guarantee and protect the social, national, economic, cultural and political pluralism. Monolithic political types were in his view abnormal and precarious. Although monopolistic and constitutional–pluralistic societies are both submitted to such 'iron laws' of the industrial societies as rationalization, hierarchical relations of production, social stratification and scientific–technological priorities, there would be no 'convergence' as long as the political structures of the two regimes remain diametrically opposed to each other. Only a basic alteration in the monopolistic political regime could, according to Aron, lead to some convergence of industrial societies.

Aron stressed that there are four interrelated rules of modern political analysis: the political system must be considered in the light of its representative institutions; at the same time, the exercise of decision-making power depends on social groups, on their interests and their conflicts; the analysis must also examine the phenomenon of bureaucracy by itself; the historical environment of the political system must form the necessary background to the analysis. 'Every political system is influenced, if not determined, by the accumulation of traditions, values, mentalities and behaviour peculiar to each country.' This last rule especially distinguished Aron's method of modern political analysis from that of sociological and political science behavioural 'systems'. But he stressed that all four rules should be observed together.

GI

Reading

Aron, R.: *Introduction to the Philosophy of History* (1938). Boston, Mass.: Beacon, 1951.

———: *Les Guerres en châine*. Paris: Gallimard, 1951. Trans. as *The Century of Total War*. New York: Doubleday, 1954.

———: *On War: atomic weapons and global diplomacy* (1957). London: Secker & Warburg, 1958; New York: Doubleday, 1959.

———: *Paix et guerre entre les nations*. Paris: Calmann-Lévy, 1952. Trans. as *Peace and War: a theory of international relations*. London: Weidenfeld & Nicolson; New York: Doubleday, 1966.

———: *Industrial Society*. London: Weidenfeld & Nicolson, 1967.

———: *Democracy and Totalitarianism* (1958). London: Weidenfeld & Nicolson, 1968.

———: *Essai sur les libertés*. Paris: Calmann-Lévy, 1965.

———: *The Imperial Republic: the United States and the world 1945–73*. Englewood Cliffs, NJ.: Prentice-Hall, 1974.

———: *Penser la guerre: Clausewitz*. 2 vols. Paris: Gallimard, 1976.

Colquhoun, R.: *Raymond Aron*. 2 vols. London: Gage, 1986.

———: *Commentaire: Raymond Aron, histoire et politique*. Paris: Juillard, 1985 (a commemorative volume).

Pierce, R.: *Contemporary French Political Thought*, ch. 8. London: Oxford University Press, 1966.

Articles of Confederation

The first formal Constitution of the United States. It is a remarkable fact that the articles were not ratified until 1781 and that the Continental Congress acted as an effective war-time government – raising an army, managing supply and finance and conducting foreign policy – from the summer of 1775 without a grant of formal authority. The articles were substantially agreed by 1777 after strenuous debates about the distribution of power between the Congress and the states. The latter largely prevailed and the Congress, which operated through executive boards or committees of its own members, had no direct powers of taxation. Requisitions had to be raised on and by the states. Ratification was delayed largely because Maryland, a state with a fixed western boundary, wanted a share of the proceeds of the lands claimed by Virginia and New York. Maryland acceded in 1781 under French pressure; Virginia and New York ceded their claims to the Congress. But although the War of Independence was won and the Peace of Paris concluded by a Congressional delegation, the Congress was unable to raise sufficient requisitions to finance itself. No major alteration to the Articles could be made without unanimous agreement of the states, and two schemes for strengthening the financial system, in 1781 and 1783, failed for want of one state's consent. Notwithstanding these failings, the Congress under the Articles issued the land ordinances of 1785 and 1787, the latter establishing a permanent system later incorporated under the Constitution, for the orderly settlement and government of western territories and the admission of new states. The Articles were superseded by the Constitution in 1789.   JRP

Reading

Jensen, M.: *The Articles of Confederation*. Wisconsin: University of Wisconsin Press, 1940.

Onuf, P.S.: *The Origins of the Federal Republic 1775–1787*. Philadelphia: University of Pennsylvania Press, 1983.

Rakove, J.N.: *The Beginnings of National Politics: an interpretive history of the continental congress*. New York: Knopf, 1979.

Wood, G.S.: *The Creation of the American Republic 1776–1787*. Chapel Hill: University of North Carolina Press, 1969.

articulation (of interests) See INTEREST ARTICULATION AND AGGREGATION.

authoritarianism A form of government, or the philosophy that advocates such a form, where the rulers impose their values on society irrespective of its members' wishes. A family may be run in an authoritarian way: equally a state. The term denotes a wide class of governmental systems of which DESPOTISM, TYRANNY, FASCISM, NAZISM and TOTALITARIANISM are special sub-classes. Fascist, Communist and most single-party regimes outside these, as well as military dictatorships

are all examples of authoritarian rule. The three major characteristics are: the techniques of decision by public discussion and voting are largely or wholly supplanted by the decision of those in authority; these dispose of sufficient power to dispense with any constitutional limitations; and the authority that they claim does not necessarily nor usually derive from the consent of the governed but from some special quality which they alone possess. This quality may be *divine*: Joseph de Maistre, the French moralist (1773–1821) asserted that the authority of the Christian religion was the source and justification of all government; *institutional*: the German philosopher Hegel (1770–1831), for instance, considered that the state was itself 'the march of God on earth'; ruling Communist parties claim authority to govern from their superior knowledge of the 'scientific laws of social development' derived from Marxism–Leninism; or *personal*: such leaders as Mussolini and Hitler have claimed (and many of their subjects have agreed) that they personally possessed extraordinary qualities by virtue of which they alone were qualified to rule.

The term is sometimes used today in a more specific sense to distinguish regimes that rule without public discussion or constitutional limitation and expect compliance with their orders but exercise power only in a limited sphere, as opposed to *totalitarian* regimes that attempt to control all aspects of life and mobilize their populations into active support of their policies.

See also AUTOCRACY.   SEF

authority In every society there are some people, and some rules, which ought to be obeyed in appropriate circumstances; such people have authority, and such rules are laws. Rules in turn become law because they have been authorized by some recognized process.

The word authority derives from the Latin *auctoritas* and registers the enormous impact of the Romans upon subsequent European politics. An *auctor* was an originator of something: poem, statute, law and so on, but especially of a family and of a city. Each Roman father embodied *auctoritas* in the family, but the supreme *auctor* was Romulus, the notional founder of Rome itself. This quality was passed on to the Senate, originally composed of elders of the patrician class, and later of experienced office-holders including plebeians. They guided the Roman state by virtue not of the *potestas* or power of the offices (such as the consulship) which they held, but by virtue of their special claim to *auctoritas*. The advice they gave was less than a command but more than advice. This understanding of the nature and limits of government was passed on to medieval and modern Europe.

In the modern European state authority came to be recognized as supremely possessed by whoever was sovereign, and it depended upon current political beliefs. In the early modern period kings were often thought to have authority by divine right; in Calvinist states, the elders and magistrates of a community were often recognized as authoritative. In recent centuries the prevalent belief has been that authority can only be conferred by the people through the electoral process. Democracy must be understood as a theory of authority, not (as is sometimes confusedly suggested) its antithesis. This confusion has generated the pejorative term 'authoritarian' which seems to refer not to a right to obedience but to a manner of claiming it, and especially to an officious propensity to try to regulate the affairs of subjects.

Authority is quite distinct from power: the authority of the governments which went into exile as a result of Nazi conquest in 1940–1 was not affected by defeat, but their power certainly was. The modern theory of authority was classically laid out in HOBBES' *Leviathan* (1651). Sovereignty, Hobbes argued, arises from the authorization of those over whom it is exercised, and consists in the power to make laws conducive to the peace and defence of a community. Authority correlated with the obligation of the subject to conform his behaviour to law. It appears as a device for generating binding decisions about any matters on which widespread dispute threatens the peace of the community. The vital point about authority thus conceived is that it makes no claim to rationality and so leaves men free to retain their own judgments about any matter, so long as their conduct accords with the

decision. Although commonly regarded as absolutist in later times, Hobbes was in his own day often thought subversive because he derived authority not from God but from the people themselves. Later writers such as LOCKE and ROUSSEAU thought that the somewhat coerced authorization he conceived was inadequate to generate real authority; the process of authorization in later times came to be conceived in an increasingly democratic way so that it is not only the holder of the sovereign office but the actual policies he adopts which must in some measure be authorized by the subjects. Thus have the idea of authority, and hence the imperatives of an orderly society, been aligned with the central European value of self-determination.

Modern political scientists have tried to analyse especially the relationship between different styles of authority and social attitudes and practices. They have been particularly concerned with the relationship between patterns of authority and forms of government. Co-operative, cross-national studies, such as those of Almond and Verba, have used probability sampling methods to show how different styles of POLITICAL CULTURE affect attitudes to authority. In addition, political scientists have tried to show how attitudes towards authority are derived from early experiences. The concept of authority is thus of crucial importance in contemporary political science.

See also LEGITIMACY; POLITICAL SOCIALIZATION. KRM

Reading

Almond, G.A. and Verba, S.: *The Civic Culture: political attitudes and democracy in five nations*. Princeton, NJ: Princeton University Press, 1963.

————: *The Civic Culture Revisited: an analytic study*. Boston, Mass.: Little, Brown, 1980.

Arendt, H.: What is authority? In *Between Past and Future*. London: Faber; Cleveland, Ohio and New York: Viking, 1961.

Eckstein, H. and Gurr, T.R.: *Patterns of Authority: a structural basis for political inquiry*. London: Wiley, 1975.

Friedrich, C.J.: *Tradition and Authority*. London: Pall Mall, 1972.

Green, L.: Authority and convention. *Philosophical Quarterly* 35 (1985) 329–46.

Hart, H.L.A.: *The Concept of Law*. Oxford: Oxford University Press, 1961.

Hobbes, T.: *Leviathan* (1651).

Watt, E.D. *Authority*. London: Croom Helm, 1982.

Weber, M. *Economy and Society: an outline of interpretative sociology*. 3 vols. ed. G. Roth and C. Wittich. New York: Bedminster, 1968.

autochthony The notion of autochthony was popularized by the late Sir Kenneth Wheare in his post-war writings on the constitutional structure of the Commonwealth. It is clearly explained by Marshall (*Constitutional Conventions*, p. 206) in the following terms. 'Some members of the Commonwealth wished to establish not merely that their systems of government were no longer subordinate to that of the United Kingdom, but that their constitutions had the force of law within their territory through their own native authority and not because they were enacted or authorized in the United Kingdom. They wished to be something more than autonomous. They wanted to be constitutionally rooted in their own soil.'

In the inter-war years it was the view of the Irish Free State (which was then a member of the Commonwealth and formally remained a member until 1949) that the Constitution of 1922 derived its legal base from an Irish and not from a United Kingdom source, though this view was not accepted as valid by the United Kingdom. The later Irish Constitution of 1937 clearly asserted a base in 'native authority', which in this case was the approval of the constitution by popular referendum. In the early post-war period it was the clear intendment of the Indian constitution makers that the source of authority for the constitution of 1950 was the will of the Indian people and did not rest on an ultimate United Kingdom grant of legislative authority. So it was that the constitution was adopted by the constituent assembly but not submitted to the GOVERNOR-GENERAL for assent.

It may be, as Wheare says, that in the modern Commonwealth a constitution with an historic United Kingdom source may now be seen in a different light. So he writes, in the context of Australia: 'If by some means the Constitution could be deprived of its quality of a British act, Australians would still regard it as having force of law. If the Constitution obtained its life in the seed bed at Westminster and was transplanted to Australia, it has struck root in the Australian soil, and owes its life now to Australia and not to Britain.' (*Constitutional Structure of the Commonwealth*, p. 108.)

Recent events leading to the enactment of the Canada Act 1982, which involved the issue of 'patriation' of that constitution, raise questions which may bear on autochthony. That act of the United Kingdom parliament gave Canada for the first time a domestic constitutional amendment power, and the Act expressly renounced any further power in the United Kingdom Parliament to legislate for Canada. A similar renunciation was made in respect of Australia early in 1986. In the context of autochthony, there is a question whether this termination of United Kingdom authority is reversible. In Australian and Canadian courts, there can be little doubt that it would be seen as 'complete, effective and irreversible'. Whether United Kingdom courts would view the matter in this light is not so clear. The judgment that 'it is better to suppose that the United Kingdom Parliament is capable of making a legally effective abdication of its authority to legislate for particular territories and that it has done so' (Marshall 1984, p. 208) is persuasive, not least because it brings constitutional doctrine into line with contemporary realities.   ZC

Reading

Hogg, P.W.: Patriation of the Canadian Constitution: has it been achieved? *Queen's University Law Journal* 8 (1983) 123.

Marshall, G.: *Constitutional Conventions*. Oxford: Oxford University Press, 1984.

Wheare, K.C.: *The Constitutional Structure of the Commonwealth*, ch. 4. Oxford: Oxford University Press, 1960.

autocracy Literally, rule by one person not responsible to any followers or subordinates; in effect AUTHORITARIANISM with a single ruler. The complete absence of restraints – constitutional or legal – is the defining characteristic of the autocrat whose rule cannot be challenged and who embodies sovereignty and state power. There are no recognized limits to the autocrat's rule, which is arbitrary and unconfined. It is difficult to distinguish the term conceptually from DESPOTISM, but it is distinguished from TOTALITARIANISM in that the autocrat does not exercise total control over the lives of his subjects.

As a type of government or rule, autocracy can only persist through time under certain kinds of social and economic conditions. These include an uneducated, backward people with little or no conception of natural rights, and lacking any concerted political aspirations to improve their condition. The autocrat has a personal, vested interest in maintaining these conditions. Russia under the rule of the tsars was an example of autocratic rule.

In modern times the terms autocrat and autocratic powers have been applied somewhat more broadly and loosely to those who wield their powers within organizations and institutions in an arbitrary manner without reference to followers or subordinates. In this modern rendering of the term, the autocrat may in principle be constrained by a constitution, by legal norms, or by rules and conventions, but the term 'autocratic' is invoked as a pejorative characterization of the manner and methods by which power is exercised. It continues to be one of the strongest words in the political lexicon, and lies at the opposite pole to the term democracy or rule by the people.

See also ABSOLUTE GOVERNMENT.

ESAI

Reading

Arendt, H.: *The Origins of Totalitarianism* (1951), repr. Cleveland, Ohio: Meridian, 1966.

Friedrich, C.J. and Brzezinski, Z. eds: *Totalitarian Dictatorship and Autocracy*, 2nd edn. Cambridge, Mass.: Harvard University Press, 1966.

Popper, K.: *The Open Society and its Enemies*. 2 vols. London: Routledge & Kegan Paul, 1945.

Wittfogel, K.: *Oriental Despotism: a comparative study of total power*. New Haven, Conn.: Yale University Press, 1957.

B

Bagehot, Walter (1826–1877) Best known for *The English Constitution* (1865–7) in which he attempted to penetrate beyond the formal analysis of the Constitution, and relate it to social attitudes, or as it would now be called, POLITICAL CULTURE. He regarded national character as 'by far and out of all question the most important' factor in the analysis of political institutions, and believed that the English character, because it found so large a role for DEFERENCE, was peculiarly suited to parliamentary government which he regarded as the best form of government.

Bagehot sought to go beyond a paper description of the Constitution so as to understand its 'living reality'. He distinguished between the 'dignified' parts of the constitution, such as the monarchy and the House of Lords, which enjoyed little effective power but played a vital role in fostering reverence for authority; and the 'efficient' parts, such as the cabinet and the House of Commons, which played an important part in the government of the country. Bagehot undermined earlier ideas that the English Constitution was a balanced constitution characterized by the separation of powers. He showed that, on the contrary, the 'efficient secret' of the constitution was 'the close union, the nearly complete fusion of the executive and legislative powers' through the cabinet, 'a combining committee – a *hyphen* which joins, a *buckle* which fastens, the legislative part of the state to the executive part of the state'.

Bagehot's work has enjoyed enduring influence. He was one of the earliest writers to analyse political institutions comparatively, in his discussion of the relative merits of parliamentary and PRESIDENTIAL government. His account of constitutional MONARCHY, in which he laid down that a constitutional monarch enjoyed three rights: 'the right to be consulted, the right to encourage, the right to warn' – adding that 'a king of great sense and sagacity would want no others', has come to be accepted as authoritative. Bagehot's approach to political analysis has influenced writers such as Woodrow WILSON whose book *Congressional Government* (1885) sought, in Wilson's words 'to treat the American Constitution as Mr Bagehot . . . has treated the English Constitution'; Sidney Low in *The Governance of England* (1904); and Richard Rose whose influential *Politics in England* (1965) explicitly acknowledges a debt to Bagehot; while R. H. S. Crossman argued in 1963 that the cabinet itself was now part of the 'dignified' machinery of government, since the 'efficient' ruler was the prime minister. This argument, however, is not accepted by many political scientists.

Bagehot was editor of *The Economist* for the last seventeen years of his life, and was a prolific writer of political journalism. His other main work of political analysis was *Physics and Politics*, an attempt to follow Sir Henry Maine in applying evolutionary ideas in political analysis. Bagehot attempted, by this method, to prove the superiority of government by discussion as a method of organizing society.

MCh

Reading

Bagehot, W.: *The English Constitution*, vol. 5; *Physics and Politics*; vol. 7. In *Collected Works*. 15 vols, ed. N. St John-Stevas. London: The Economist, 1965–86.

Buchan, A.: *The Spare Chancellor: the life of Walter Bagehot*. London: Chatto & Windus, 1959.

Crossman, R.H.S.: Introduction to *Bagehot: the English Constitution*. London: Fontana, 1963.

ballot   In early examples of secret voting, a ballot or little ball was dropped into an urn as an indicator of preference and the term was extended to refer to the papers issued to electors as mass democracy and secret voting spread in the nineteenth century.

Voting in elections can be open or secret. The open declaration of preference makes voters responsible for their choice but renders them liable to bribery and intimidation. Although various forms of secret voting such as the use of boxes with concealed compartments can be traced back to ancient times, the first state to introduce the secret ballot as a general principle was South Australia in 1856; consequently the system became known as the Australian ballot during the world-wide arguments over its introduction in the decades that followed. In Britain the Ballot Act of 1872 superseded the centuries old practice of open voting at the hustings; while the secret ballot was first introduced to the United States in Kentucky in 1888.

There are many variants of secret voting. In most countries under the Westminster model, ballot papers are printed by the state and issued at the polling station to electors whose names are checked off against a prepared electoral register. They are then required to mark their preference with a cross or a number in a concealed booth and to place the ballot, folded, in a sealed box. In the United States, the ballot paper takes a variety of different forms, and in many states, the ballot also contains REFERENDUM propositions on which voters are asked to express their view. This can render ballot papers very long and complicated.

In other countries, ballot papers are prepared by the contesting parties and distributed outside the polling station. Inside, the voter is issued with an official envelope into which he or she can place the individually chosen paper. Strict procedures are needed to prevent forged or duplicate papers being inserted into the ballot box at any point. In the United States, voting machines are widely used as a defence against fraud.

In many regimes which profess to have free and secret voting, the safeguards of secrecy are nullified by, for example, only requiring negative votes to be marked.   DEB

Reading

Ranney, A. and Kendall, W.: *The American Party System*, ch. 14. New York: Harcourt Brace, 1956.

bargaining theory   Applies non-zero-sum GAME THEORY to politics. A non-zero-sum game is any game in which some outcomes yield a higher aggregate payoff than others. In all non-zero-sum games there is therefore some scope for cooperation, coordination and bargaining among the players, but no guarantee that any of these will occur. Every game has at least one 'non-cooperative' or 'Nash' equilibrium. An equilibrium is any point from which it pays no player to depart; a Nash equilibrium is one which the players can reach with no cooperation or coordination among themselves. In many games the Nash equilibrium is 'defective': that is, there is at least one other equilibrium which is better for all players. Two well known examples are Prisoners' Dilemma (PD) and Chicken. These are most easily understood in two-person form. In the diagram (p. 40) each player has the options Cooperate and Defect. In each cell, the number before the comma is the row player's ranking of the outcome (4 = that player's best, 1 = that player's worst), and the number after the comma is the column player's. Nash equilibria are circled.

In PD, the outcome where both players cooperate is always superior to the Nash equilibrium, and in repeated plays of Chicken it may be. Bargaining may get the players from the non-cooperative equilibrium to a cooperative one. This has been extensively explored for the repeated PD, notably by Axelrod (1984) who argues that tit-for-tat (cooperate in the first game; thereafter do what your opponent did in the previous game) is a winning strategy if discount rates are low enough. Wage bargaining and some international bargaining games – most famously the Cuban missile crisis of 1962 – are Chicken

Prisoners' Dilemma

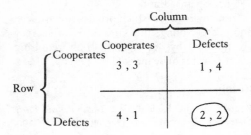

Reading

Axelrod, R.: *The Evolution of Cooperation*. New York: Basic Books, 1984.

Rapoport, A.: *Fights, Games and Debates*. Ann Arbor: University of Michigan Press, 1960.

Schelling, T.C.: *Micromotives and Macrobehavior*. New York: Norton, 1978.

Shubik, M.: *Game Theory in the Social Sciences: concepts and solutions*. Cambridge, Mass.: MIT Press, 1982.

Chicken

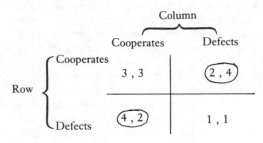

games. In Chicken each player tries to get his or her best outcome by committing himself or herself not to cooperate, but if both do that the outcome is the worst for both. Wage bargaining which ends in a strike is an example, and a Cuban missile crisis which ended in nuclear war would have been another. There are many other political and social bargaining games. For discussions in ascending order of difficulty, see Rapoport (1960), Schelling (1978) or Shubik (1982).

There is also scope for bargaining in many-person zero-sum games because any subset of the players may gang up against the others by forming a coalition. COALITION THEORY deals in particular with government-formation games and 'log-rolling' games. Log-rolling means offering another player a favour now in return for another favour later. It is frequently alleged to be characteristic of Congressional behaviour in the USA. Bargaining theory – more strictly, coalition theory – predicts that logs will be rolled, but it cannot predict which.

IMcL

behaviouralism   A reaction of the 1950s and 1960s against the then dominant methods of POLITICAL SCIENCE and international studies; it involved a rejection of the legal orientation, the moral biases and the narrow focus of 'comparative' analysis on the main European countries that characterized much of political science after the second world war (Ranney 1962; Lijphart 1974). In the 1970s the movement faded away as what was basically sound in the new methodology had become generally accepted, and what was extreme and exaggerated had met with fierce opposition (Dahl 1961).

The negative aim of behavouralism, explicitly formulated in the search for a new political science in contradistinction to the old, was complemented by a positive aim spelling out what the new political science amounted to: behaviouralism is fundamentally a more or less coherent political science methodology and includes a rather extreme version of the scientific method.

Formalism versus behaviour: 'Behaviour' is a key element in behaviouralism. It denotes what is essential in social systems and what should be the basic unit of analysis in political science. To study behaviour is to look at what really happens within legal frameworks and political ideologies. Behaviour can include attitudes as well as action; it is considered more fundamental than rules or norms stating what should take place, because it refers to living politics. This does not mean that norms or ideologies are unimportant in political life, only that their relevance derives from their role in human behaviour; to understand the political system it is not enough to focus on the normative framework surrounding political activities: the core is political behaviour itself.

Relevance of data: In order to substantiate the claim that behaviour is the essence of politics, behaviouralists needed to collect a variety of data about actual modes of behaviour. Given the distinction between legal framework and patterns of behaviour other types of information had to be searched for in place of the focus on legal documents. This implied a fundamental reorientation of political science towards the employment of more sophisticated techniques for the collection and mastering of empirical information in the form of surveys and ecological data. It also meant an emphasis on quantitative approaches to empirical information involving the use of various kinds of multivariate tools. The reorientation of political science towards data and tools for analysing empirical information was expressed in the undertaking of a number of large scale projects in the fields of voter behaviour, public policy and evaluation.

Facts versus theory: To behaviouralists the statement of what actually takes place was not an end in itself; the analysis of single events or processes was in order to establish scientific laws or statistical regularities: behaviouralism entails a commitment to the belief in scientific methodology, its possibility and usefulness for the scientific enterprise (Kaplan 1964). Political phenomena like any other kind of phenomena may be explained in terms of models covering a range of diverse events. The ultimate aim of political science is to identify such generalizations, whether these are law-like or statistical in nature. The commitment to such a philosophy of science involves the employment of a theoretical approach to the data as well as the employment of techniques for testing model implications in relation to some set of data. The ideal in behaviouralism was a hypothetical-deductive mode of scientific analysis (Popper 1968), but the actual practice was more in line with the inductive tradition of research. It is symptomatic of the broad spectrum of behaviouralism that it included efforts towards a positive theory (Riker and Ordeshook 1973) as well as the detailed study of attitudes at some particular

point of time (Campbell, Converse, Miller and Stokes 1960).

Moral inquiry versus scientific argument: Behaviouralists distinguish between moral or ethical inquiry and scientific argument. How this distinction is made was a matter of dispute. Some behaviouralists assume that there is a sharp gulf between statements of fact and value judgements, and that science only encompasses the former; moral directives or normative prescriptions would therefore fall outside of the domain of science and its claim to truth which, however, does imply that empirical inquiries into moral attitudes or actually existing norms is unscientific. For others the demarcation line between values and science is drawn in a broader way: not disregarding the relevance of moral questions or problems of social justice, they would only insist that it is made clear when the validity of a moral proposition and when it is the truth-claim of a scientific proposition that is in question. Both may be valid enterprises but they are separate types of enquiry.

Problems of behaviouralism: It cannot be doubted that the behaviouralist movement was successful in reorienting the focus and methodology of political science. In a sense it was so successful that the movement could dissolve itself. There were however a few basic problems in behaviouralist theory which did provoke a strong reaction (Storing 1962; Wolin 1969). First there was the danger of empiricism. Behaviouralists could degenerate into the collection of huge data banks without having an explicit theoretical focus. Second it might encourage overemphasis on methods, in particular quantitative techniques, thereby assuming that all kinds of empirical information about politics should be handled by statistical techniques requiring the fulfilment of strong assumptions about the nature of the data. Third, it could fall into *scientism* or the belief that political life was governed by a set of natural laws to be found by the conduct of massive empirical inquiry. Finally, the neglect of moral issues could lead to the relegation of crucial questions concerning justice as belonging merely to some unscientific domain of reasoning (Easton 1969). These negative expressions of behaviouralism provoked a reaction in the 1970s which looked for new ways to understand political problems while emphasizing the validity of normative analysis as well as the central place of theory (Connolly 1967).

The core of behaviouralism: The conduct of scientific investigations into political phenomena has to be based on a methodological balance between theory and data. Without data theoretical propositions are empty because they have no basis in or relevance for the real world. One and the same phenomenon may be accounted for by means of alternative theoretical frameworks, but how could we choose between competing explanations except by reference to empirical tests or data? Without the employment of data how could there be any claim to truth in the sense of correspondence to facts? On the other hand, data without theory would be just as inadequate, because empirical information has to be interpreted; it would be blind, because there is no limit to the amount of empirical information to be reported. Theories or theoretical approaches direct the search for data and imply the kinds of data that would confirm or falsify the hypotheses at stake. This balance between theory and data, between test implications and actual tests, is struck by emphasizing both elements to the same extent.

Behaviouralism claims that the theory–data distinction may be substantiated by distinguishing between concepts and indicators or indices. Concepts may be measured by tying indicators to them. These indicators may be employed to identify various dimensions in theoretical concepts at the same time as the concepts are used to find the indicators most suitable for observations. The conduct of a scientific inquiry has to be based on an interaction between theory and data, concepts and indicators. Concepts are not identical to their indicators as they have an openness of meaning that derives from the theoretical contexts in which they operate. Indicators could be assigned to concepts by various methods: by conventional fiat, by analytical reasoning, or by the observation of casual

relationships such as in the analysis of latent variables by means of a bundle of manifest variables. Behaviouralism emphasizes that the concepts of science must somehow be measurable in terms of empirical information (Hempel 1952), although very few behaviouralists would adhere to the dogmas of operationalism or extreme logical positivist notions of meaning.

For behaviouralists, concepts should be clarified as far as possible in order to reduce ambiguity (Sartori 1984). Behaviouralists argue for concept clarification and explication because the ambiguity of words in ordinary language is regarded as an obstacle to scientific clarity. Although the various meanings of words may be of interest in themselves, behaviouralists would argue that it is vital to be alert to the semantic problems in their use in scientific contexts. Different senses should therefore be kept separate and distinct; it may be necessary to stipulate meanings in order to make clear how key words are being used.

Behaviouralists favour the search for generalizations more than the statement of individual facts. These generalizations could be of various kinds, from model principles to inductive regularities. Generalizations of some type are necessary for the explanatory goal of science. A scientific theory is a bundle of hypotheses which explains the facts. Scientific theories may be more or less well structured. Formalized or axiomatized theories are not abundant in the social sciences, but a particular mode of presentation of theories is not necessary for the conduct of inquiry. Often a scientific theory is a pattern of hypotheses adduced to take account of interesting facts and to be tried by means of severe tests. These generalizations may form some more or less coherent whole, though their interrelationship may be far from clear or explicit. Scientific knowledge grows by the process of rational elimination of conjectures. Theories come and go as a result of the fierce competition between them.

Behaviouralism has a basic comparative orientation as a result of its emphasis on the search for general relationships between the variables, preferably of some causal character.

Explanations of single cases or events are always tentative as long as there is no test of their implications on other relevant and comparable cases of events. The fundamental logic of reasoning in behaviouralism is the test of generalizations where variables are isolated from each example and the interaction between two or more are compared in order to look for partial effects. Behaviouralism favours the construction of typologies and conceptual schemes that make comparisons possible, stating similarities and differences between cases (Lijphart 1971): model building is at the heart of the scientific project of behaviouralism as it provides a clearly defined structure allowing basic hypotheses to be stated explicitly and their implications to be more easily derived and tested in relation to a clearly defined set of data.

What behaviouralism is not: It seems necessary to point out that behaviouralism is not a substantive doctrine or theory about politics. Its association with the pluralist approach to understanding politics or the SYSTEMS ANALYSIS framework was purely contingent. The criticism of these two substantive theories (Bachrach and Baratz 1962, 1963), behaviouralism and PLURALISM, carried over into the accusation that pluralism, functionalism and behaviouralism were indistinguishable. It is possible to outline a sound version of behaviouralism and at the same time adhere to different substantive approaches. Behaviouralism deals with the necessity to strike a balance between theory and data or models and empirical information in scientific work. Without a balanced interaction between the two basic elements of scientific inquiry political science will either have a narrow empiricist focus or run into the danger of theoreticism, that is the proliferation of theoretical arguments without any empirical test to sort out those that are true from those that are false.   See also QUANTITATIVE METHODS IN POLITICS.   J-EL

Reading

Bachrach, P. and Baratz, M.S.: Two faces of power. *American Political Science Review* 56 (1962) 947–52.
———: Decisions and nondecisions: an analytical

framework. *American Political Science Review* 57 (1963) 632–42.

Campbell, A., Converse, P.E., Miller, W.E. and Stokes, D.E.: *The American Voter.* New York and London: Wiley, 1960.

Connolly, W.E.: *Political Science and Ideology.* New York: Atherton, 1967.

Dahl, R.A.: The behavioural approach in political science: epitaph for a monument to a successful protest. *American Political Science Review* 55 (1961) 763–72.

Easton, D.: The new revolution in political science. *American Political Science Review* 63 (1969) 1051–61.

Hempel, C.G.: *Fundamentals of Concept Formation in Empirical Science.* Chicago, Ill.: University of Chicago Press, 1952.

Kaplan, A.: *The Conduct of Inquiry.* San Francisco: Chandler, 1969.

Lijphart, A.: Comparative politics and comparative method. *American Political Science Review* 65 (1971) 682–93.

———: The structure of theoretical revolution in international relations. *International Studies Quarterly* 18 (1974) 41–74.

Popper, K.R.: *Conjectures and Refutations.* New York: Harper Torchbook, 1968.

Ranney, A. ed.: *Essays on the Behavioural Study of Politics.* Urbana: University of Illinois Press, 1962.

Riker, W.H. and Ordeshook, P.C.: *An Introduction to Positive Political Theory.* Englewood Cliffs, NJ: Prentice-Hall, 1973.

Sartori, G.: *Social Science Concepts.* Beverly Hills, Calif.: Sage, 1984.

Storing, H.T. ed.: *Essays on the Scientific Study of Politics.* New York: Holt, Rinehart & Winston, 1962.

Wolin, S.: Political theory as a vocation. *American Political Science Review* 63 (1969) 1062–82.

Bentham, Jeremy (1748–1832) Utilitarian philosopher, jurist, economist, and reformer, Bentham did not come to the systematic study of political institutions until after the age of sixty, when in 1809–10 he began his career as an advocate of radical reform. Nevertheless, in his earlier writings many of his later ideas had already been developed. In his first major work, *A Fragment on Government* (1776), he presented a critique of Blackstone's conception of the English constitution, establishing his reputation and preparing him for the task of moving the political thought of his period out of the Lockeian mould into which it had been shaped by numerous writers including MONTESQUIEU, De Lolme and Blackstone. Bentham put together, in several earlier works, a formidable critique of such notions as natural rights ('simple nonsense'), natural and imprescriptible rights ('nonsense upon stilts'), the state of nature, the social contract, consent, SOVEREIGNTY, and MIXED GOVERNMENT. Although he drew on HUME's earlier criticism of Lockeian political ideas (as he also drew on Helvetius and others), he brought to his analyses a critical dimension and an attention to method and detail which were not present in Hume or in any other earlier modern political theorist.

Bentham's analytical skills first emerge fully in his writings on jurisprudence which were originally part of a larger study of penal law and offences. In *An Introduction to the Principles of Morals and Legislation* (printed in 1780 and published in 1789) he presented an account of utilitarian philosophy that, whatever its faults and limitations, has formed the basis of one major strand of contemporary political philosophy, which was distinctive in its claims to deal critically (and philosophically) with the practical details of ethics, law and politics. It was this capacity to join philosophy and practice which later, especially after the launch of the *Westminster Review* in 1824, led to Bentham and his radical followers being called the 'Philosophic Radicals'. These and other ideas were brought together in the massive, unfinished work on government, the *Constitutional Code*, which was begun in April 1822 in response to an invitation from the Portuguese Cortes to draft civil, penal and constitutional codes.

From his earlier writings on Panopticon, the model prison, Bentham drew on the ideas of inspection, publicity and accountability in administration. From his writings on parliamentary reform he incorporated the doctrines of equal sovereignty, secret ballot, annual parliaments and 'virtual' universal suffrage, as well as the lengthy and often bitter criticisms of the institutions and practices of all aspects of British government. From his earlier writings on public economy and also on parliamentary reform, he developed at length an emphasis on efficient and inexpensive government, perhaps best summarized in the phrase, 'Official Aptitude Maximized, Expense Minimized', which became a motto of his theory of government – emphasizing the enlistment of the best talent available for public office, the reduction of the expense of government and, hence, the burden of taxation on the people. From numerous works on judicial organization and legal reform, he set forth a telling attack on the corruption and inefficiency of the English legal system – 'Judge and Co' – which led in the *Constitutional Code* to a simplified judicial system with access equally available to rich and poor.

Unlike earlier writers in the Lockeian tradition, Bentham was more concerned with justifying the specific institutions of government than with exploring in abstract terms the grounds of political obligation. He saw the science of government as both normative and empirical. He was a close student of the political systems of many countries and especially an admirer (though not an uncritical one) of what he called the Anglo-American United States, where political democracy had been established successfully without any danger of the confiscation of property. He conceived of government as a system of power, with power limited by the careful delineation of the functions of every office from the prime minister to the lowest porter and watchman. To limit the abuse of power in the exercise of these functions he devised what he called 'securities for appropriate aptitude', various means by which the apt performance of duties could be secured by those who were subject to the exercise of political power. These securities were both legal and non-legal and ranged from the impeachment and trial of various officials to inspection and publicity by the press, the main organ of what he called the 'Public Opinion Tribunal'.

In the *Constitutional Code* Bentham put forward in a comprehensive and detailed manner a system of representative democracy far in advance of any system yet adopted by contemporary governments or even proposed by other thinkers. He offered it to 'all Nations and all Governments professing Liberal

Opinions'. The *Code* provided for a representative system having annual elections to the legislature; a prime minister elected for a four-year term by the legislature; a justice minister (as head of the judiciary); thirteen ministers covering such fields as health, education, defence, transport, finance, police, trade, poverty and public works; and a military service and a judiciary fully accountable not only to the legislature but also to the electorate. Bentham's desire to combine good government with democratic accountability led him to develop some novel and interesting practices. Although all administrative and judicial officers, including ministers, were to be appointed for life through a thoroughly meritocratic system of education and competitive examination, they were easily dismissible not only by their superiors but also by petition and vote by the electorate. Even members of the legislature must have passed through the system of education and examination to be eligible for office, though they would not be eligible for a second term until there was a pool of former experienced members from which to choose new legislators. This was designed to prevent one experienced deputy from obtaining a grip on his constituency whence it was virtually impossible to unseat him, whatever his conduct.

Bentham's ideas almost certainly influenced the great reforms of the Victorian period. By conceiving the ends of legislation to include security, subsistence, abundance and equality, and by conceiving security as encompassing far more than security of property, he foresaw the needs and aspirations of the modern democratic state and laid some of the theoretical foundations for the development of the WELFARE STATE. His work also forms an important bridge between the political theory of the eighteenth century and the more empirically-based science of politics of the present day.

See also LOCKE; MIXED GOVERNMENT; REPRESENTATION; REPRESENTATIVE GOVERNMENT   FR

Reading

Bentham, J.: *The Collected Works of Jeremy Bentham*, ed. J.H. Burns, J.R. Dinwiddy and F. Rosen. London: Athlone; Oxford: Clarendon Press, 1968–.

————:*The Works of Jeremy Bentham*, ed. J. Bowring. Edinburgh: Tate, 1838–43.

————: *An Introduction to the Principles of Morals and Legislation*, ed. J.H. Burns and H.L.A. Hart. London: Athlone, 1970.

————: *A Comment on the Commentaries* and *A Fragment on Government*, ed. J.H. Burns and H.L.A. Hart. London: Athlone, 1977.

————: *Of Laws in General*, ed. H.L.A. Hart. London: Athlone, 1970.

————: *Constitutional Code*, Vol. I, ed. F. Rosen and J.H. Burns. Oxford: Clarendon Press, 1983.

Dinwiddy, J.R.: Bentham's transition to political radicalism 1809–10. *Journal of the History of Ideas* 26 (1975) 683–700.

Halévy, E.: *La Formation du radicalisme philosophique*. 3 vols. Paris: Alcan, 1901–4; trans. M. Morris, *The Growth of Philosophic Radicalism*. London: Faber & Faber, 1952.

Harrison, R.: *Bentham*. London: Routledge & Kegan Paul, 1983.

Hart, H.L.A.: *Essays on Bentham: Jurisprudence and Political Theory*. Oxford: Clarendon Press, 1982.

Hume, L.J.: *Bentham and Bureaucracy*. Cambridge: Cambridge University Press, 1981.

Rosen, F.: *Jeremy Bentham and Representative Democracy: a study of the constitutional code*. Oxford: Clarendon Press, 1983.

Bentley, Arthur F. (1870–1957) Bentley is now widely regarded as one of the major intellectual influences on the methodology of American political and social science. His career contrasts sharply with other social scientists of the early twentieth century. After receiving a doctorate from The Johns Hopkins University in 1895, he taught at the University of Chicago for only a year, abandoning an academic career first for journalism and later to manage a farm in Paoli, Indiana. Writing outside the academic mainstream, Bentley penned his most famous work, *The Process of Government*, in 1908. Between the 1920s and 1940s he continued his writing with rather more obscure work in sociological method, linguistic analysis, psychology and, with John Dewey, philosophy.

Bentley was a proponent of the scientistic strain in American social science. Bentley's central aim in *The Process of Government* was to

45

show that what he called 'soul stuff' – feeling, motivation, ideas and institutions – were not the basic causes of political or social behaviour. He sought 'to fashion a tool' (*Process of Government* p. vii) for the investigation of such behaviour, suggesting that it was best studied by describing the interactions of groups. He also emphasized the importance of quantitative measurement in political science. Bentley believed that if political life could be understood in terms of overt activity, the foundation for a science based on precise measurement would have been laid.

Although Bentley modified many of his ideas in later works, it is *The Process of Government* which has remained the basic source of his influence. It is a classical text of BEHAVIOURALISM, and modern PLURALISM. Bentley's work has found resonance in such areas as the study of voting behaviour, ROLL-CALL ANALYSIS, and INTEREST GROUPS, although political scientists have tended to analyse interest groups less in terms of their activities than in terms of their organization, purposes and functions. Moreover, Bentley did not share the conservative political orientation of many of those who claimed his legacy.

Bentley's conception of the political process has been attacked as ignoring 'non-decisions', the ability of powerful groups to confine decision making to relatively non-controversial areas, excluding more contentious matters from the scope of legitimate political activity. Perhaps the most fundamental weakness of Bentley's thought, however, lies in his mechanistic conception of scientific activity, and his failure to give proper weight to ideologies and to human intentions.

See also POLITICAL SCIENCE. RMS

Reading

Bachrach, P. and Baratz, M.: Two faces of power. *American Political Science Review* 56 (1962) 947–52.

––––––: Decisions and non-decisions: an analytical framework. *American Political Science Review* 57 (1963) 632–42.

Bentley, A.F.: *The Process of Government* (1948). Evanston, Ill.: Principia, 1949. [The introduction to this edition contains a statement of Bentley's basic position.]

––––––: *Makers, Users and Masters*. Syracuse, NY: Syracuse University Press, 1969.

Dewey, J. and Bentley, A.F.: *Knowing and the Known*. Boston, Mass.: Beacon, 1949.

Golembiewski, R.T.: The group basis of politics: notes on analysis and development. *American Political Science Review* 54 (1960) 962–71.

Hale, M.Q.: The cosmology of Arthur F. Bentley. *American Political Science Review* 54 (1960) 955–61.

Kress, P.: *Social Science and the Idea of Process: the ambiguous legacy of Arthur F. Bentley*. Urbana: University of Illinois Press, 1969.

Seidelman, R.: *Disenchanted Realists: political science and the American crisis* 1884–1904, ch. 3. Albany, NY: State University of New York Press, 1985.

Taylor, R.W.: Arthur F. Bentley's political science. *Western Political Quarterly* 5 (1952) 214–30.

–––––– ed.: *Life, Language, Law: essays in honour of Arthur F. Bentley*. Yellow Springs, Ohio: Antioch, 1957.

––––––: Bentley, Arthur F. In *International Encyclopedia of the Social Sciences*, Vol II, pp. 58–62. ed. P.L. Sills. New York: Macmillan and The Free Press, 1968.

Truman, D.: *The Governmental Process*. New York: Knopf, 1971.

bicameralism See SECOND CHAMBERS.

bill The draft of a proposed new law being considered by a LEGISLATURE. In the United Kingdom Parliament the sub-divisions of a bill are known as clauses. Further detailed provisions added as appendices to a bill are known as schedules.

The procedure under which a legislature considers a bill, and potentially approves it, varies from state to state. The process will depend on whether a legislature has one chamber or two, on whether the country is a MONARCHY or a REPUBLIC, and on the nature of the relationship between the legislature and the EXECUTIVE. In the United Kingdom a bill has to be passed by the HOUSE OF COMMONS and the HOUSE OF LORDS and be assented to by the monarch.

Exceptionally, under the terms of the Parliament Acts 1911 and 1949, a bill passed by the Commons may receive the Royal Assent without the agreement of the Lords. Such a bill must have been passed by the

Commons in two successive sessions, providing that a year has elapsed between the bill's first second reading in the Commons and its second third reading. The second reading provides an opportunity to consider the principles of a bill; the third reading is the final chance to accept or reject it after details have been considered at the committee stage.

In the United States a bill has to be passed by both Houses of Congress and be accepted by the President. The form seems similar to that of the United Kingdom. However, no British monarch has failed to assent to a bill since the early days of the eighteenth century. The United States president quite often fails to concur. His power of VETO can be overridden if both Houses of Congress vote to support a vetoed bill by a margin of two-thirds of those voting.   PGR

Reading

Bradshaw, K. and Pring, D.: *Parliament and Congress*. London: Quartet, 1981.

Englefield, D.: *Whitehall and Westminster*. London and New York: Longman, 1985.

May, T.E.: *Parliamentary Practice*. 20th edn. London: Butterworths, 1983.

Preparation of Legislation. Report of Committee 1974–5. Cmnd 6053. British Parliamentary Papers xii.

bill of rights Constitutional charters today commonly include a formal listing of citizens' rights which are specially protected against state (governmental) control and which are changeable only by some extraordinary constitutional process different from, and more difficult than, the amendment of ordinary legislation. It is in this sense that we speak of an 'entrenched' bill of rights. The principal archetypes or models are the American Bill of Rights, of which the first twelve articles were adopted almost contemporaneously with the Constitution of the United States of 1787, and the French DECLARATON OF THE RIGHTS OF MAN AND THE CITIZEN of 1789, which was placed at the head of the Revolutionary era Constitution of 1791 and which was incorporated into the post-war French Constitutions of 1946 and of 1958 (the Fifth Republic, still in force).

Constitutional charters are increasingly accompanied today by institutionally-based enforcement procedures, of which the best-known and most popular is the special CONSTITUTIONAL COURT, having jurisdiction over the observance and application of the charter's guarantees and to which, in most cases, the private citizen and private interest groups may bring their legal complaints. Once again United States constitutionalism provides the principal model, in the historical practice of the SUPREME COURT in its exercise of a wide-ranging civil rights jurisdiction. But American experience has been reinforced and refined today in continental European institutions such as the West German Federal Constitutional Court (which has served as a model for socialist Yugoslavia and for post-Franco Spain) and also the somewhat hybrid French CONSEIL CONSTITUTIONNEL. The basic alternative to the modern, US-derived, conception of constitutional rights of the citizen guaranteed by a written constitutional charter that is itself enforced by the courts, is the historical English conception of a RULE OF LAW that does not rest on any notional distinction between constitutional rights and other legal rights but finds its realization in the self-restraint of executive and legislative power and its practical expression in the ordinary decisions of the ordinary courts of the land in cases arising before them. DICEY's conception of the rule of law was hostile to the American, charter-and-court approach to civil liberties, and had obvious links to similar continental European *Rechtsstaat* notions which prevailed until the new wave of constitution-making after the second world war. In the constitutional 'patriation' debate in Canada, during the period 1980–2, over constitutional renewal and modernization, original English constitutional influences were engaged in a last-ditch, and ultimately unsuccessful, battle against the newer US constitutional doctrines which preached the case for an entrenched Charter of Rights and Freedoms and for a prime role for the courts in their enforcement.

The American and the French constitutional charters, understandably for documents conceived and framed at the end of the eighteenth century, reflect liberal-democratic values and show a preoccupation with what we would today identify as 'open society' values: liberties of the person and guarantees of fair criminal processes, liberties of speech, expression and association. The post-Civil War 13th, 14th, and 15th Amendments, added to the United States charter in the late 1860s in the historical design of integrating the newly freed slaves into American society, embodied equality and equal protection values. They were soon used, however, during a period of judicial interpretation by the Supreme Court lasting until the late 1930s, to achieve and protect *laissez-faire* economic values and immunize property interests of large corporations and entrepreneurs from the incipient social welfare legislation being introduced, first, by various state legislatures and, ultimately, by the federal legislature (Congress) in fulfilment of President Franklin Roosevelt's 'New Deal' programme. The 'Court Revolution' of 1937 meant the end of this *laissez-faire*, 'liberty-of-contract', court-imposed jurisprudence; the main legal recourse to the US Bill of Rights, aided by recent additions such as the 24th (Civil Rights) Amendment, adopted in 1964, is now to secure the elimination of all forms of disability based on racial origin, colour, religion or sex. The new constitutional charters of the post-1945 period – with those of post-decolonization India, socialist Yugoslavia, the Soviet Union (constitution of 1977), and the People's Republic of China (constitution of 1978), as prime examples – actively incorporate socialist values into their bills of rights, with a panoply of new, social democratic rights (in contradistinction to the old, liberal democratic rights) that have the social and economic welfare of the citizens as their stated principal goal. The Indian constitution of 1950 straddles the old and the new: its Fundamental Rights reflect the older liberal, *laissez-faire* values, but are accompanied by new Directive Principles of State Policy which are unashamedly social democratic and reformist in content and objectives. This has created some interpretive problems for the Indian Supreme Court in trying to resolve the contradiction thereby created, especially in regard to AFFIRMATIVE ACTION (reverse discrimination) programmes where governments positively intervene on behalf of socially and economically disadvantaged groups within society by introducing quota systems legally favouring their entry into particular professions, occupations or educational institutions. The Indian experience in this has been more systematic, and rather more successful, than in the United States. The notion of affirmative action, when it was decided upon in the United States, had to be grafted on to already existing, liberal-democratic constitutional guarantees which, as a matter of constitutional history, had not really comprehended or encouraged other than a formal, notional juridical equality for all citizens, irrespective of their origins. The intellectual barrier involved not merely displacement of such notional individual equality in favour of quota systems, but also acceptance of the idea of collective or group, as opposed to individual, rights. While collective rights are at the core of socialist (communist) constitutionalism and have also begun to recur in continental European constitutional thinking in relation to ethno-culturally-based language and other rights inhering in national minorities within the state today, they are not part of historical US constitutionalism. The history of bills of rights demonstrates, however, a continuing expansion of their range and impact in response to changing societal needs and expectations, and a correlative capacity of the courts, as main institutional safeguards for the enforcement of the charter guarantees, creatively to adapt old law to new society.

EMcW

Reading

Corwin, E.S.: *The 'Higher Law' Background of American Constitutional Law*. Ithaca, NY: Cornell University Press, 1928.

Friedrich, C.J.: *The Impact of American Constitutionalism Abroad*. Boston, Mass.: Boston University Press, 1967.

Griswold, E.N.: *The 5th Amendment Today*. Cambridge, Mass.: Harvard University Press, 1955.

Hand, L.: *The Bill of Rights*. Cambridge, Mass.: Harvard University Press, 1958.

McWhinney, E.: *Constitution-Making: principles, process, practice*. Toronto: University of Toronto Press, 1981.

Rémond, R.: *L'Anticléricalisme en France de 1815 à nos jours*. Paris: Fayard, 1976.

biopolitics An approach to political science whose proponents use biological concepts and research techniques in studying POLITICAL BEHAVIOUR. Originating in the latter half of the 1960s, biopolitics received formal disciplinary recognition in 1973 with the establishment of the International Political Science Association's Research Committee on Biology and Politics. This was followed by the organization of the Association for Politics and the Life Sciences in 1982 and the launching two years later of its journal, *Politics and the Life Sciences*. The Association now has approximately 300 members and, although still predominantly American, includes political scientists from some fifteen countries.

Practitioners of biopolitics generally agree on three propositions:

(1) Human political behaviour (and especially such manifestations of it as aggression, altruism, xenophobia, dominance, and territoriality) is to a significant degree influenced by biological make-up and genetic legacy.
(2) Human political and social behaviour can be modified by changes in physiological functioning induced by illness, stress, drugs, pain, fatigue, malnutrition, and so forth.
(3) Physiological measures, such as galvanic skin response, heart-beat rate, body posture, eye blink, blood pressure, can be used, directly or indirectly, to assess emotional states and/or behavioural potential.

The biological sources from which biopolitics has most heavily drawn are ethology, sociobiology, physiology, and neurology. The literature falls into four broad categories: that in which ethological/socio-biological concepts and techniques are used to study and explain political behaviour; that in which some aspect of physiological functioning serves as the independent, and political behaviour as the dependent, variable; that in which one (or more) of the above-mentioned physiological measures is employed to ascertain emotional states or behavioural propensities; that which deals with such biologically-based public policy issues as genetic engineering, treatment of the terminally ill, environmental pollution, radiation levels, and birth control.

Understandably, much early biopolitical writing tried to persuade other political scientists that genetic and biological factors did play an important part in human political behaviour. In recent years there has been a marked tendency simply to take this relationship for granted and to focus instead on demonstrating that biologically derived concepts and research tools can be fruitfully employed by political scientists. This demonstration, though still in its early phases, has been increasingly successful.   AS

Reading

Corning, P.: *The Synergism Hypothesis*. New York: McGraw-Hill, 1983.

Somit, A.: *Biology and Politics: recent exploration*. Paris: Maison des Sciences de l'Homme, 1976.

———— et al.: *The Literature of Biopolitics*. Rev edn. DeKalb: Northern Illinois University Center for Biopolitical Research, 1980.

Wiegele, T.C.: *Biopolitics: search for a more human political science*. Boulder, Col.: Westview, 1979.

block grant A payment by the central government in support of local government activity but carrying no specific direction as to how it should be spent or on which area of public service. Block grant was introduced in Britain in 1958 in order to reduce the degree of control which the central government could exercise through grants which were earmarked for specific purposes. In theory the local authority can decide how it will spend its block grant, though in practice local governments are restricted by statutory requirements imposed by central legislation relating to each service.   NTB

block vote
(1) A variant of the plurality system of voting, whereby each selector has one vote for each vacancy to be filled in a multi-member constituency: for example three votes in a constituency returning three members. This system is used in a number of British local authority elections.

49

(2) The method by which the trade unions vote at British Labour Party annual conferences, and at annual Trades Union Congress conferences. Affiliated unions vote as a block without registering minority opinion, so increasing the influence of the larger unions and reducing that of constituency parties in the Labour Party.

See ELECTORAL SYSTEMS.   VBB

Bodin, Jean (1529/30–1596) French jurist and polymath born in Anjou and trained in law, Bodin's mature years coincided with the crisis of monarchical authority in France during the Wars of Religion. His political ideas are developed mainly in *Les Six livres de la république* (1576, Latin edition 1586) and in his *Methodus ad facilem historiarum cognitionem* (1566).

Bodin's theory of SOVEREIGNTY represented a major advance in the systematic analysis of political AUTHORITY. Sovereignty, he argued, was a necessary characteristic of all stable political regimes. Although under most conditions he preferred the monarchical form, the concept was also applicable to aristocracies or democracies. While best exercised when the sovereign observed the higher norms of divine and natural law, it was also applied with clinical neutrality to despotic and tyrannical regimes that by definition did not observe these norms. Not fully emancipated from medieval constitutional traditions, Bodin's theory still allows for a few rules governing the transmission of sovereignty (such as the Salic law) or the manner of its exercise (special majorities, methods of voting) which he designates as *leges imperii* and tends to consider as beyond the authority of the sovereign to change.

The *République* is a massive political treatise, containing much descriptive empirical material on the locus of sovereignty in European and non-European societies, both classical and contemporary, but also on a wide range of political and social institutional questions. Bodin's theory of environmental influences embraces both celestial and geographic factors; with respect to the latter, he is an important precursor of MONTESQUIEU.

Bodin's major contribution was to free political authority from medieval particularist constraints and to place it under more universalist and abstract norms of natural and divine law. In doing so he became an unwitting contributor to theories of rational ABSOLUTISM in the seventeenth and eighteenth centuries. But the theory of sovereignty also promoted significant advances in political integration and state-building, and it provided foundations for the modern state system of sovereign entities linked through international law.   KDMcR

Reading

Bodin, J.: *Method for the Easy Comprehension of History*, trans. and ed. B. Reynolds. New York: Columbia University Press, 1945.

——: *The Six Books of a Commonweale*, trans. R. Knolles, ed. K.D. McRae. Cambridge, Mass.: Harvard University Press, 1962; repr. New York: Arno, 1979.

Franklin, J.H.: *Jean Bodin and the Rise of Absolutist Theory*. Cambridge: Cambridge University Press, 1973.

Moreau-Reibel, J.: *Jean Bodin et le droit public comparé dans ses rapports avec la philosophie de l'histoire*. Paris: Vrin, 1933.

Bolshevism   The political philosophy of the party which won power in the October Revolution of 1917 in Russia, and hence more generally of Marxist revolution on the Soviet pattern; it comprises both Marxist ideals and historical analysis (see MARX) and the organizational principles established by the Bolsheviks before and after the revolution. Its chief theoretician and tactician was LENIN, and it is only in connection with his belief in the short-term feasibility of a proletarian revolution in Russian and in the decisive role to be played therein by a vanguard party of professional revolutionaries that the history of Bolshevism can be understood.

Bolshevism should be distinguished, firstly, from Marxism–Leninism, the official ideology of the Soviet Union. While there is a good deal of overlap between these concepts it is useful to restrict the reference of the term Bolshevism to the political philosophy of the formative years of the Soviet revolution, from 1903 to about 1930, using Marxism–Leninism to refer to the body of thought developed in the post-revolutionary phase by official Soviet interpreters of Marx and, much more prominently, Lenin. This distinction rests partly on the different function of each: Bolshevism was a set of doctrines designed to provide guidance for a revolutionary party in the context of a collapsing autocratic state amid multiple challenges for future hegemony, whereas Marxism–Leninism is the ideology of established state power of the Soviet type, having at most evolutionary rather than revolutionary content. Another ground for the distinction is the vaguer one of the revolutionary-heroic connotation of the term Bolshevism, a connotation which fixes it in time much more clearly than the more abstract notion of Marxism–Leninism.

The term Bolshevik derives from the Russian word *bol'shinstvo*, or majority, implying a second distinction, between Bolshevism and the views of the Mensheviks, or minoritarians. These labels were coined (by the winning side) at the Second Congress of the Russian Social Democratic and Labour Party (RSDLP) in 1903. The split was initiated by a dispute over the criteria for party membership, Lenin, opposed by Yu. Martov, advocating more restricted criteria requiring 'personal participation in one of the party organizations'. While losing the vote on this particular issue Lenin was able to exploit the resulting division and succeeded in establishing himself and his supporters as sole occupants of the top leadership positions. Although this victory was soon reversed the split proved irreversible.

At the time of the schism it was the Mensheviks' opposition to Lenin's conspiratorial methods which chiefly united them; their views varied widely, and many were in sympathy with the political aims of the Bolsheviks. However, the Bolsheviks' (and especially Lenin's) accusations that the Mensheviks wanted to liquidate the underground party and instead create a mass party, thereby deferring the revolution until the eventual development of proletarian class consciousness, serve to highlight by contrast the distinctive features of Bolshevism itself. Lenin had been attacking similar views since the 1890s, when they had been represented by

the group he labelled the Economists, and they clearly had no place within his own faction. Moreover, the accusations were not entirely misplaced, since theoretical and tactical issues were of course related, and the views of some Mensheviks came increasingly to resemble Lenin's caricature. Lenin's theoretical inventiveness, typified by his 'law of unequal development', which was an attempt to reconcile revolutionary aspirations with Marxist doctrine, contrasted with the more rigid thinking of the Mensheviks, and complemented the political opportunism displayed by the Bolsheviks in their seizure of power in October 1917.

The Bolsheviks (who became a separate party in April 1917, having decisively broken with the Mensheviks in 1912) were in government faced with numerous external threats, among them severe economic dislocation and armed intervention by foreign powers. Within the party, existing tensions came to the surface, and the new circumstances brought new disagreements. The substantial differences between War Communism (1918–21) and the New Economic Policy (1921–8) demonstrate to how small an extent Bolshevism comprised a detailed post-revolutionary political programme. In terms of organizational rather than substantive principles, however, continuity can be detected. The centralist tendency represented by Lenin was challenged both by the Workers' Opposition, advocating greater autonomy for the trade unions, and by the Democratic Centralists, who advocated democratic procedures within the party, but true centralism was victorious at the Tenth Party Congress of 1921, which coincided with the Kronstadt rebellion: in an atmosphere of threat, the congress enacted a resolution on party unity which prohibited factions on pain of expulsion. Thus was DEMOCRATIC CENTRALISM, which had been established as an organizational norm of the RSDLP since 1906, given its final form as the definitive principle of Bolshevik political organization.

The word Bolshevik was not dropped from the title of the party until 1952; however it is debatable whether the term Bolshevism is appropriate to describe the political practices and ideology of the STALIN period. While continuity was apparent in the extension of centralist principles from the party to the whole of society, and in the unchallenged hegemony of the party (and while Stalin's political opportunism was in no sense in conflict with Bolshevik traditions), features of Stalinism such as its economic policies, physical repression of opponents within the party and the use of mass terror mark it as a distinctive political system and philosophy.

See also COMMUNIST PARTIES.   SW

Reading

Harding, N.: *Lenin's Political Thought*. 2 vols. London: Macmillan, 1977, 1981.

————: *Marxism in Russia: key documents 1879–1906*. Cambridge: Cambridge University Press, 1983.

Hosking, G.: *A History of the Soviet Union*. London: Fontana, 1985.

Hough, J.F. and Fainsod, M.: *How the Soviet Union is Governed*. Cambridge, Mass. and London: Harvard University Press, 1979.

Lenin, V.I.: What is to be Done? In *Collected Works*, Vol I. London: Lawrence & Wishart, 1965.

Schapiro, L.: *The Communist Party of the Soviet Union*. 2nd edn. London: Methuen, 1970.

Bonapartism Having three distinct, yet interrelated, strands, Bonapartism relates to a specific political movement, a set of governmental practices, and a number of political principles (often referred to as a programme). Bonapartism as a political movement was shaped by the need to provide support for the dynasty founded by Napoleon Bonaparte and that provided France with two Empires during the nineteenth century. As an effective movement it dates from the Second Republic and more specifically from the December 1848 election of Louis Napoleon (nephew of Napoleon I) to the presidency by universal manhood suffrage. During and after the campaign there emerged a doctrine, a programme and an electorate which were quite distinct from those of the traditional conservative parties. This dynastically-inspired political movement survived the collapse of the Second Empire in September 1870 but slowly disintegrated after the death of the Prince Imperial in 1879.

As a governmental system, Bonapartism embodied certain practices: strong, even authoritarian, and hierarchically organized leadership based on a powerful executive headed by one man; a weak legislature; a centralized system of territorial government (a legacy from the Jacobins) with centrally-appointed PREFECTS enjoying wide-ranging powers at local level; a depoliticized decision-making process in which appointed officials were given wide powers and in which ministers were often chosen for their technical rather than their political skills.

The third dimension of Bonapartism is doctrinal or programmatic – a set of ideas which, however, were never systematically expressed. A pervasive NATIONALISM underpins the doctrine: Bonapartism inherited from Jacobinism an exalted idea of France's place in the world; as a conveyor of certain universalistic and civilized values France had a duty to the rest of mankind. A strong and impartial state is essential to ensure the successful implementation of this universal vocation. It is also required to hold together a divided society and to impose order and stability in a nation shaken by the political and social turbulence of the First and Second Republics. In that sense Bonapartism must be seen as a reaction against the Revolutions of 1789 and of 1848. In other senses, however, Bonapartism represented a defence of the revolutionary settlements. There was no attempt, for instance, during the First Empire to restore the power and privileges enjoyed by the Church during the *ancien régime*. Nor was any attempt made to upset the centralized system of government established by the Jacobins. The Second Empire fully integrated universal manhood suffrage into its political practices and proclaimed that authority emanated directly from the popular will. Bonapartism may be seen as the heir of Jacobinism in another essential way: a deep-seated mistrust of traditional elites and of intermediary bodies such as political parties, provinces, Church or trade associations, which reflect the divisions of the nation. Guizot summed up the complexity of Bonapartism when he claimed that it was a symbol of national glory, a principle of authority and a guarantor of the Revolution.

Yet the complexity lies not only in its various dimensions but also in the gulf between the principles and practice of Bonapartism (dislike yet dependency upon traditional elites; adherence to popular sovereignty yet political oppression; a centralized system based on prefects but tolerance of the power of local notables). Moreover, Bonapartism as a political movement always embraced a disparate collection of elements, ranging from opportunistic conservatives to democratic and populist radicals.

The influence of Bonapartism in France has been unquestionable, and has been felt in two directions. In the first place, and by way of reaction, it created in Republican circles a fear of the strong leader (who was always viewed as a potential dictator) and an attachment to parliamentary institutions. The principles and practices of the Third and Fourth Republics were shaped by the persistent fear of a Bonapartist revival. The influence of Bonapartism may also be seen in the nationalism which pervades most French political discourse, in the nostalgia for strong leadership, for order and for discipline. Finally, there were, unquestionably, many Bonapartist elements in GAULLISM.   VW

Reading

Rémond, R.: *La Droite en France*. Paris: Aubier, 1982.

Rothney, J.: *Bonapartism after Sedan*. Ithaca, NY: Cornell University Press, 1969.

boss   A somewhat pejorative term for the leader of a political party organization in an American city, county, or state. The label is widely applied in political rhetoric to impute excessive or improperly derived power exercised in an unrestrained manner. It is not a precise term. A boss is best thought of as the clearly dominant leader of an organization that controls a bloc of votes for the nomination of candidates at some level of government; and that is sustained primarily by PATRONAGE (see MACHINE).

A boss may be an elected or, less commonly, appointed official, usually in municipal government. The base of the boss's power is his ability to deliver votes in whatever procedure is used to nominate candidates (see CAUCUS; PRIMARY). In turn, this ability depends on his influence over the distribution of the 'spoils' of state and/or local government (see SPOILS SYSTEM): jobs, contracts, and favouritism. Other than the distribution of patronage, the boss need have no responsibility for governing. Hence many bosses hold no governmental position and are largely indifferent to substantive policy questions, which they consider divisive and irrelevant to the 'real business of politics'.

Although the number and power of bosses have declined, they are by no means an extinct species, particularly in the Northeast and some industrial Great Lakes states. Their power is greatest when public interest is low and the great national and world issues that animate idealistic 'amateurs' are less germane. They are most influential in filling local offices and less important in nominating presidents and members of Congress.   REW

Reading

Key, V.O. Jr: *Politics, Parties and Pressure Groups*. New York: Crowell, 1964.

Riordan, W.L.: *Plunkitt of Tammany Hall*. New York: McClure, Phillips, 1948.

Whyte, W.F.: *Street Corner Society*. Enlarged edn. Chicago, Ill.: University of Chicago Press, 1955.

Wolfinger, R.E.: *The Politics of Progress*. Englewood Cliffs, NJ: Prentice-Hall, 1974.

breakdown and regime change   Polities change, states disintegrate, regimes undergo processes of installation, consolidation, crisis, re-equilibration, decay, breakdown, overthrow and sometimes restoration. There are changes within a regime and changes of regime, which are not always easy to distinguish (for example in the Soviet Union from Lenin to Stalin, or from him to his successors). Those processes can be due to causes external (Germany, 1945–9) or endogenous to the society, or often a combination of both (Italy in 1943, Eastern Europe and Turkey after the first world war), and it is not easy to assign the proper weight to internal and external factors. Regime changes can be peaceful or violent; they can lead to deep social changes or just political change. Some can be dated, while others take place slowly and without the full awareness of participants, although symbolic events later date the rise of a new regime (the March on Rome of 1922, the first Mussolini cabinet). Historians provide us with a chronological account of events (Bracher 1957; De Felice 1966); social scientists attempt to conceptualize and classify types of change and explain why some regimes have attained a persistence and stability, although experiencing change within the institutional framework and values legitimizing them (the changes in DEMOCRACIES resulting from ELECTIONS and government change), while other regimes have led from autocracy to democracy, from democracy to AUTHORITARIANISM or TOTALITARIANISM, or from non-democratic to democratic government (Morlino 1980; Linz and Stepan 1978; Rouquié 1985; O'Donnell, Schmitter and Whitehead, 1987).

Regime changes defined as changes in the basic political institutions and principles of legitimation of AUTHORITY, not just of governments, are not necessarily violent and more often involve a transfer of power, *Machtubergabe* rather than *Machtergreifung* (Lepsius 1971). Some bring with them radical social and economic changes while others bring only changes in political institutions. The shift in Spain in 1975–7 from an authoritarian regime without political freedoms to a parliamentary democracy took place by a process of *reforma pactada–ruptura pactada*, negotiated reform and negotiated break without discontinuity, and with the paradox that the last prime minister before democracy became the first parliamentary prime minister after a free election. This model has had considerable impact on the transitions from authoritarianism to democracy in Latin America. Regime change is only exceptionally revolutionary and more often the result of slow continuous and complex processes leading from the loss of power of one regime to the transfer of power to another; the result of decay and disintegration rather than overthrow, assaults on 'winter palaces' or civil wars. In many parts of the world, military coups lead to changes of regime and more often of rulers within the same type of authoritarian regime.

Theories of regime breakdown and change emphasize a wide range of factors from very general ones to those specific to particular types of regimes, societies, and historical periods. They place the emphasis on sociological and economic structural factors, or more specifically, political processes. Those differences reflect intellectual orientations: Marxism, cultural determinism, the recognition or denial of autonomy to politics, great man theories of history, and emphasis on the *Zeitgeist* and ideology. The complexity of reality is not exhausted by any of them, although in each case or type of cases some seem more adequate than others.

The stability of a regime ultimately depends on the LEGITIMACY of its institutions as it is perceived by significant proportions of the population and, in particular, with respect to specific resources and influence: armed forces, religious leaders, the business community, intellectuals, political activists and even foreign powers and foreign public opinion. They divide on which type of regime they consider most desirable for a society in a particular crisis, in some cases producing the situation of dual sovereignty (Tilly 1975) that can lead to civil war. In ordinary circumstances, most people whether or not they support the regime comply with the orders of those in power (Rose 1970), but in crisis situations where there is a loss of legitimacy, and with the appeal of alternative legitimacy principles, the regime is contested. A regime which is considered illegitimate might obtain the compliance of its citizens by the absence of an alternative, or by coercion, assuring its persistence but not its ultimate stability. Legitimacy, the belief in the right to demand obedience and in the duty to obey in crisis situations, has been based on different principles. In modern times it has shifted from its basis in tradition to legal–rational authority: the enactment of decisions following procedures established in a constitution or other system of rules, and increasingly on democratic authority derived from free and competitive elections within a constitutional order. An alternative principle has been the commitment to a political party with an ideology representing the prospect of a better society, national independence, religious values, and to its sometimes charismatic leader or leaders.

A separate but interrelated dimension is the efficacy or performance of a regime (Lipset 1960; Linz 1980; Eckstein 1971, Gurr et al. 1971; Zimmermann 1986): the capacity to satisfy the requirements of the population in terms of security, legal order, the territorial integrity of the state, and its basic social and economic needs. The levels of efficacy demanded of governments vary as a result of expectations, generated in part by the regimes and in part by comparisons between societies; they are therefore relative rather than absolute. There is a complex relation between legitimacy and efficacy which suggests that legitimate regimes can afford losses of efficacy better than less legitimate ones and that efficacy, economic prosperity, social progress, international prestige, and cultural achievements, contribute to legitimate regimes. Successful performance however does not appear to lead to the legitimation of regimes whose principles and values are considered illegitimate; this appears to be the case with authoritarian rule: military regimes, personal autocratic rule by small oligarchies whose values differ from those of the population, and rule imposed by foreign powers. In those cases, efficacy can neutralize opposition but does not assure ultimate regime stability. Defeat in war, the continuation of war without the capacity or means to achieve its goals, have led to the loss of legitimacy and the breakdown of regimes (for example, the provisional government of Kerensky; Italian Fascism in 1943; the Fourth French Republic; Caetano in Portugal, 1974). There are problems that become unsolvable, leading to the prolonged crisis of a regime and its eventual breakdown, or permanent regime instability (for example Northern Ireland, Cyprus, Lebanon). Ethnic, national, religious and racial conflicts are probably the most serious causes of the instability and breakdown of not just regimes but polities.

The theories and analyses of the crises and breakdowns in European democracies between the two world wars have been particularly rich. Some have argued that the democracies born around 1918 were structurally weak and were never really consolidated. Others (for example Linz, 1978) have placed greater emphasis on the crises confronting them, arguing for example that the rise of fascism as an anti-democratic popular movement was a result of the dislocations in the social structure caused by the first world war. Others still, mainly on the basis of the German case, have argued the incompatibility of CAPITALISM and democracy and noted the impact of the world depression in the 1930s. These analyses do not consider those democracies that experienced crises without the rise of strong fascist movements, and which did not break down. Some, such as the United States and the social democracies of Scandinavia, experienced political and social change in response to the crisis without breakdown while others such as the Netherlands, Belgium and the United Kingdom remained stable. This comparison suggests the need to take into account political, cultural and social factors in addition to the economic crisis. The crises and breakdowns of democracies in the inter-war years in Europe, both in the structural economic interpretations and the historical analyses, have been linked with the problem of the rise of fascism and other rightist anti-democratic movements: their origin, strengths, social basis, indirect supports, and tactics of gaining power (Allen 1965; Bracher 1957; De Felice 1966; Gregor 1974; Laqueur 1976; Linz 1980; Payne 1980; Wippermann 1976). From another perspective, Bracher and Linz concentrated their attention on the sequence of events leading to the breakdown, focusing on the democratic parties and leaders and the overall process rather than on the challengers of democracy, on the important role not only of disloyal anti-system oppositions but of semi-loyal political forces, and on phases in the crises of regimes; that is, not only on the why but also the how of the breakdown, developing a descriptive model of the process of loss of power, power vacuum and transfer of power through an attempted co-optation of the anti-democrats leading to totalitarian and authoritarian regimes.

The breakdown is a result of the process initiated by the incapacity of governments, specifically the democratic parties and their leaders, to solve problems for which the disloyal opposition offers itself as a solution. Problems are either objectively unsolvable or made unsolvable within the institutional framework due to the ideological commitments of political parties and/or the identification with interest groups that do not allow them to negotiate solutions assuring political stability. This leads to: frequent cabinet crises; anticipated dissolutions and elections; fragmentation of parties; a general abdication of the responsibility to govern and refusal of the top leaders to do so; reliance on cabinets of experts rather than party leaders; incorporation of the military in the decision making process; transfer of decisions to the courts; a growing in strength of the neutral powers (kings and presidents); narrowing of the political arena with the exclusion of parliament and the participation of small non-responsible groups and individuals; attempts to neutralize the anti-system opposition by concessions; negotiations to incorporate it in the government in order to 'domesticate' it; in the end, a giving way to the opposition's demand for power and with the transfer of power the establishment of a new regime. These processes within the political elite are accompanied by: growing ELECTORAL VOLATILITY; rigidities in the confrontation of parties and outbidding; defamation of the political class as a whole; growing POLITICAL VIOLENCE and loss of the monopoly of legitimate force due to the ambiguity of the courts, the police and the army toward political extremists, whose goals are shared although their means are illegal, resulting in a climate of incertitude and pressures to reach a decision to end the crisis, if necessary, by a regime change. In this context, the anti-system critique gains strength, negative majorities make the democratic political process unviable, and key institutions take their distance from the democratic regime parties; at the same time intellectuals express their dissatisfaction with the political leadership, contributing to the loss of power and the power vacuum surrounding the institutions of the regime. The result is an acceleration of the political process in a narrow arena that prevents the supporters of the regime from uniting in its

defence, and opens the door to anti-system leaders, combining legal action with the threat of violence or its actual use, to demand power which, once transferred, is used to destroy the regime and create a new authoritarian or totalitarian political system. Exceptionally the leadership can at the last minute refuse the transfer of power, or call on a leader of the opposition who, while changing the regime, does not put into question the democratic principles. This leads to what might be called a process of re-equilibration (an example is De Gaulle in the transition from the Fourth to the Fifth Republic). The timing of decisions becomes critical and the outcome will differ depending on the social, institutional and political context in which the new regime undertakes its consolidation.

See also MILITARY GOVERNMENT; REVOLUTION AND COUNTER-REVOLUTION.   JLi

Reading

Allen, W.S.: *The Nazi Seizure of Power: the experience of a single German town, 1930–1935*. Chicago, Ill.: Quadrangle, 1965.

Bracher, K.D.: *Die Auflosung der Weimarer Republik*. Stuttgart: Ring-Verlag, 1957.

Collier, D. ed.: *The New Authoritarianism in Latin America*. Princeton, NJ: Princeton University Press, 1979.

De Felice, R.: *Mussolini il fascista: la conquista del potere, 1921–1925*. Torino: Einaudi, 1966.

Eckstein, H.: The evaluation of political performance: problems and dimensions. *Comparative Politics* 01–017 (1971).

Gregor, A.J.: *Interpretations of Fascism*. Morristown, NJ: General Learning Press, 1974.

Gurr, T.R. and McClelland, M.: *Political Performance: a twelve-nation study*. Beverly Hills, Calif.: Sage, 1971.

Laqueur, W. ed.: *Fascism: a reader's guide*. London: Wildwood House, 1976.

Lepsius, M.R.: Machtübernahme und Machtübergabe: zur Strategie des Regimewechsels. In *Sozialtheorie und Soziale Praxis: Homage to Eduard Baumgarten*. Mannheimer Sozialwissenschaftliche Studien Vol III, ed. H. Albert et al. Meisenheim: Hain, 1971.

Linz, J.J.: Political space and fascism as a latecomer: conditions conducive to the success or failure of fascism as a mass movement in inter-war

Europe. In *Who were the fascists?*, ed. S.U. Larsen, B. Hagtvet and J.P. Myklebust. Bergen: Universitetsforlaget, 1980.

—— and Stepan, A. eds: *The Breakdown of Democratic Regimes*. Baltimore, Md.: The Johns Hopkins University Press, 1978.

Lipset, S.M.: *Political Man: the social bases of politics*, ch. 3. London: Heinemann, 1959; New York: Doubleday, 1960.

Morlino, L.: *Come Cambiano i regimi politici*. Milan: Angeli, 1980.

O'Donnell, G.A.: *Modernization and Bureaucratic-Authoritarianism: studies in South American politics*. Berkeley: Institute of International Studies, University of California, 1973.

—— , Schmitter, P. and Whitehead, L. eds: *Transitions from Authoritarian Rule: prospects for democracy*. Baltimore, Md.: The Johns Hopkins University Press, 1987.

Payne, S.G.: *Fascism: comparison and definition*. Madison: University of Wisconsin Press, 1980.

Rose, R.: The dynamics of a divided regime. In *Government and Opposition* 5.2 (1970).

Rouquié, A.: Changement politique et transformation des régimes. In *Traité de science politique*, vol. II, ed. M. Grawitz and J. Leca. Paris: Presses Universitaires de France, 1985.

Tilly, C.: Revolution and collective violence. In *Handbook of Political Science: macropolitical Theory*, ed. F.I. Greenstein and N.W. Polsby, vol. III. Reading, Mass.: Addison-Wesley, 1975.

Wippermann, W.: *Faschismustheorien zum stand der gegenwärtigen Diskussion*. Darmstadt: Wissenschaftliche Buchgesellschaft, 1976.

Zimmermann, E.: *Political Violence, Crises and Revolutions*. Cambridge, Mass.: Schenkman, 1983.

——: The 1930s world economic crisis in six European countries: a first report on causes of political instability and reactions to crisis. In *Rhythms in Politics and Economics*, ed. P.M. Johnson and W.R. Thompson. New York: Praeger, 1985.

——: Government stability in six European countries during the world economic crisis of the 1930s: some preliminary considerations. *European Journal of Political Research* 14 (1986).

Bryce, James, Lord (1838–1922) Political scientist and historian. James Bryce was educated at Glasgow and Oxford universities where he showed outstanding distinction in classics, history and law. He was appointed to the chair of civil law at Oxford in 1870 at the age of thirty-two. In that same year he travelled to the United States with his friend A. V. DICEY, chiefly to New England but also to Chicago and the Midwest. These and subsequent visits made profound impressions on Bryce. In 1888 he published his magnum opus *The American Commonwealth* which analysed American political institutions at three levels – federal, state, and local or municipal government – and also contained a detailed treatment of party and party organization at all levels. Bryce used his immense knowledge of other systems of government from ancient to recent history to illuminate his analysis throughout. He blazed a trail which others, such as OSTROGORSKI, MICHELS, R. T. MCKENZIE, adapted in their own works especially in the detailed study of political parties. His book *Modern Democracies* (1921) is one of the earliest works on comparative government and Bryce is one of the founding fathers of the discipline.

In his collection of essays, *Studies in History and Jurisprudence* (1901), Bryce drew a distinction between two types of constitution in past and present experience. These were 'flexible' and 'rigid' constitutions. The flexible type were unwritten, not contained in any special or sacred document, and alterable by legislative authority. The rigid type, found mostly since the seventeenth century, had a document or instrument superior to the legislature and any laws it passed. Notable examples were the American and Australian constitutions. Modern scholars may find the distinction unhelpful and by no means clear-cut, since written constitutions invariably have some provision for amendment, and the process often involves the legislature at crucial stages. A criticism of Bryce would be that he carried Aristotle's penchant for classification to extremes. His chief legacy remains the detailed study of party organization and the study of government by the comparative method.

ESAI

Reading

Bryce, J.: *The American Commonwealth* (1888). 2 vols. London and New York: Macmillan, 1914.

————: *Studies in History and Jurisprudence*. 2 vols. Oxford: Clarendon Press, 1901.

————: *Modern Democracies*. 2 vols. London and New York: Macmillan, 1921.

Ions, E.S.: *James Bryce and American Democracy 1870–1922*. London: Macmillan, 1968.

budget/budgeting A means of systematically relating financial resources to planned objectives. At its simplest a budget is a document setting out expected revenues and expenditures for a specified future period. Since their origins in early nineteenth-century Europe, however, public budgets have taken on multiple functions and have developed as key elements in governmental policy making and management. The meaning of public budgeting has expanded accordingly, and it has been defined in different ways according to three major perspectives – economics, management and political science – each of which has conceptualized the subject within the boundaries of its own assumptions. But recent changes in budgets and their environments have overtaken these older views and are forcing reconceptualizations of budget processes.

Modern governmental budgeting began as an innovative way of handling state finances on the restoration of the French monarchy following the Napoleonic wars. Until then governmental revenues and expenditures all over Europe had typically been handled through decentralized funds or accounts, often in private hands, and on a cash-flow basis without benefit of planning or systematic control. The system was highly vulnerable to abuse and breakdown, entailed high administrative and borrowing costs, and above all, left authorities responsible for financial management without information or control. Some piecemeal reforms, such as the establishment of the Treasury and enactment of the Consolidated Fund in England, and the elimination of the tax farmers in France, ameliorated the position. But it was not until 1815 in what has been claimed as 'the first budget in Europe' (Bruguière 1969, p. 1) that an attempt was made to present to a legislature an exact evaluation of departmental needs and the ways and means of meeting them. Within a few years the mechanics of budgeting became routine: annual estimate and prediction of expenditures, consolidation of revenues, controls over payments, and preparation of audited accounts at the end of the financial year.

The idea of the budget quickly became the idealized and ubiquitous norm for civilized public financial management. A classical theory of budgeting was enunciated, setting up principles which served as standards for correct financial management and the achievement of accountability. According to the criterion of *annuality*, estimates, decisions and accounts should be for a single year; the principle of *unity* required that all financial transactions should be included in a single document; all expenditures were to be sanctioned by legal *appropriation* and subject to *audit*.

Changes in the role of the state during the twentieth century brought unprecedented growth in government budgets and corresponding elaboration of their functions. Although the general framework and routines of budgeting continued to follow classical principles, their purposes were transformed. The exigencies of modern warfare, which permeated virtually every aspect of national life, involved handling a far greater volume of revenues than previously experienced, while governmental expenditures extended into new areas. The WELFARE STATE required DECISION MAKING on the level, kind and delivery of services to large populations, as well as raising issues of the extent and nature of redistribution of income. Perhaps most important, worldwide economic depression and cyclical volatility resulted in national governmental commitment to Keynesian fiscal policy. Governments gained responsibility for economic stability, including the prevention of depression and inflation, the maintenance of full employment, and the ensuring of economic growth through manipulation of key economic indicators by deliberate decisions on budgetary deficits and surpluses. Budgets were transformed from mechanisms providing funding for minimal governmental functions in an accountable manner, to multi-purpose instruments for the attainment of programme information, efficiency and effectiveness; determination of revenue and expenditure policies over a wide range of governmental activities; control and direction of the economy.

Budgeting, thus defined as a process for resource allocation, may be viewed in a number of ways. In practice, until recently, its study was dominated by a triple paradigm in which economists, management experts and political scientists each pursued their own directions, separating rather than uniting different aspects and emphasizing professional jurisdictions rather than common ground. On a macro-level economists defined budgets as instruments of fiscal policy, hypothesizing the impacts of revenue and expenditure decisions upon aggregates such as savings, consumption, employment and prices. Their concern was with budget totals, forecasting effects of economic trends, and determining appropriate macro-policies to influence or counteract them. At a micro-level, economists extended their traditional interest in the efficiency of tax measures into the propriety and efficiency of governmental expenditures. Applying marginal economic analysis they saw budgets as a means of societal welfare maximization, equalizing satisfaction for the last dollar of expenditure between public and private sectors and for different categories of public expenditure. According to this conception, public budgeting should be concerned with distinguishing the special economic attributes of public activity, the criteria to be applied in judging the economic efficiency of various budget policies, and their effects upon market choices and behaviour.

From these issues it was but a short step to asking how collective social choices, as compared with market choices, were made. In the United States the famous question of the political scientist V. O. Key 'On what basis shall it be decided to allocate X dollars to activity A instead of activity B?' (Key 1940, p. 1137) gave an analytical thrust to practical debates about how budget processes should be organized. A budget reform movement, which may be traced back to the efforts of good government reformers and so-called scientific management enthusiasts in the early years of the twentieth century, emphasized efficiency and effectiveness in the use of public resources. During the 1960s, in accordance with the goals of the War on Poverty, budgeting came to be seen as the maximization of societal return from public expenditures. A normative managerial approach tried to transform routine budget processes so as to rationalize budget choices through such measures as performance and productivity techniques, cost-benefit applications, and SYSTEMS ANALYSIS (see PPBS). These reforms, despite poor results in their home setting, were widely advocated in other countries and form an accepted international standard for budgeting practice.

The difficulties of implementing managerial reforms brought to the fore the nature of budgeting as a political process, a means of resolving conflicts. Budgets are political statements, demonstrating the real choices and values of those who have participated in formulating them. Budgeting is the focus of a political struggle, the outcome of which determines who gets what, when and how. But because the annual time frame of the budget cycle rules out prolonged conflict and forces decision making according to set deadlines, this struggle has to take place within a framework of accepted rules. These rules, which are both formal and informal, reflect the nature of the political process; however in budget systems where decision making takes place primarily behind closed doors in the executive branch of government, they are difficult to discern.

In the United States where the legislative branch and its committees play a leading role in budgetary decision making, political analysis of the budget process was more feasible. In the mid 1960s the concept of incrementalism, the regular addition of amounts to the base of the previous budget, emerged as a dominant description of budgetary behaviour at the time, and as a possible universal norm.

Budgeting might be viewed in a number of ways – a means of accountability for the handling of revenues and expenditures, a macro-economic tool for economic stabilization, an instrument for efficient allocation of societal resources, a managerial and analytical mechanism for the rationalization of programme choices, or a political process for the resolution of conflicts. Each of these definitions had practical recognition in accepted concepts of budgetary conceptualization and organization: the macro-economic approach in Keynesian fiscal policy, the micro-economic approach in a theory of public goods and economic analysis, the managerial approach in budget process reforms, and the political approach in theories of budgetary behaviour and incrementalism.

But by the last quarter of the twentieth century these accepted formulations began to appear increasingly isolated from reality. In the industrialized countries of western Europe and North America, stagflation, declining rates of economic growth, and volatile business cycles posed a challenge to Keynesian economic policies.

Budgets too had changed. Instead of cohesive instruments deciding allocations of resources for a future fixed period, they became indeterminate, fragmented and disputed reflections of strained political processes. An increasing proportion of national budgets had become 'uncontrollable', that is, composed of contracts and entitlement payments not subject to alteration by normal budget processes in a single year. In this sense budgets were 'rigid', merely recording expenditures made automatically beyond the annual resource allocation process. Because many of these expenditures were related to economic performance (for example, payments indexed to the rate of inflation) budget forecasts were also sensitive to cyclical fluctuations. This sensitivity was heightened by corresponding uncertainties on the revenue side of the budget which was also dependent on the level of economic activity. As revenues persistently lagged behind expenditures the budgetary position was worsened by fragmentation: enactment of expenditures outside the regular budget, such as 'off-budget' categories, government loans or special amendments to the tax code (tax expenditures). In this situation the classic principles of unity, annuality and appropriation appeared inapplicable. Managerial budget reform and

concepts of economic efficiency seemed irrelevant. Incrementalism was an inappropriate means of resolving conflicts where the majority of expenditures were made automatically and no increment was available. Governments cast about for innovative ways to prevent budgetary breakdown under heavy pressures and with constrained resources.

The difficulties of the industrialized countries, however, were but a pale echo of those under which governments of poor or developing countries had laboured for decades. In these countries poverty and uncertainty had made annual budgeting itself virtually impossible. Despite repeated attempts to introduce advanced budget reforms such as PPBS, public financial management in most poor countries continued as an entrenched process of repetitive budgeting. Because resources were inadequate for needs and budgetary authorities could not forecast for an uncertain future, initial allocations were subject to constant recalculation and renegotiation during the fiscal year. The budget in fact was typically a fiction and resource allocation was a repetitive process of pre-audit throughout the year. Not surprisingly, programme agencies subjected to this system responded with their own strategies such as padding estimates and seeking autonomous funds beyond the reach of the budget authorities. In this way, participants passed on uncertainties to one another in a vicious circle. The practice of repetitive budgeting violated every principle of budgetary theory, but its participants none the less were responding rationally to their environment. Its persistence demonstrated the dependence of the accepted budget model on appropriate conditions, particularly adequate resources and stable expectations.

In contemporary public budgeting, fiscal stress, economic fluctuations and the need to accommodate seemingly irreconcilable demands have narrowed options and heightened conflict. Even more significantly they have altered the formal and informal rules according to which budgeting is carried out. As budget processes and institutions have reacted to fluctuating and conflicting demands upon them, the situation appears fluid, unstable and ambiguous. A bewildering variety of developments makes it difficult to define adaptations currently taking place, but it is possible to discern their outlines. First, the primacy of annual allocations has given way to a stress on formulas and assumptions relating to the future behaviour of entitlements. From regarding this area as 'uncontrollable' governments have moved to the adoption of measures to control it. Budgeting by formula has become an acknowledged practice, though its pitfalls remain. The intertwining of budget and economy has not only reduced the predictability of the budget but changed its very nature from a purposeful plan of action to a projection which may or may not be fulfilled. Second, budgets are increasingly made up of 'packages', units for decision making. These packages are the framework for setting agendas, resolving conflicts, and determining limits and possibilities. They may take a number of forms, dividing the budget into manageable areas, taking account of diverse forms of expenditure, and grouping politically feasible measures together. Third, budgeting has become continuous, reflecting the flow of financial transactions, prevailing uncertainties and the multi-year implications of most budgetary decisions. Finally, incrementalism has been replaced by norms of budget cutting which heighten conflict and destabilize budget processes, placing strain on institutions, and even immobilizing them entirely.

Budgets and budgeting are open to a number of definitions and interpretations. Their meaning has expanded from the original conception of annual estimation of government financial needs and control of funds to societal allocation of resources and control of the economy, a management device to gain efficiency and effectiveness in government expenditures, and a political means for resolving conflicts. But with changes in the nature of governmental finances and their environment, it seems that budget processes are once again in a state of flux, and their future shape is open to speculation.   NJC

Reading

Bruguière, M.: *La Première restauration et son budget*. Geneva: Droz, 1969.

Burkehead, J.: *Government Budgeting*. New York: Wiley, 1956.

Caiden, N.: The new rules of the federal budget game. *Public Administration Review* Mar/Apr (1984) 109–18.

———— and Wildavsky, A.: *Planning and Budgeting in Poor Countries*. New York: Wiley; 1974; repr. New Brunswick, NJ: Transaction Books, 1980.

Key, V.O.: The lack of a budgetary theory. *American Political Science Review* 34 (1940) 1137–144.

Schick, A.: *Congress and Money*. Washington, DC: The Urban Institute, 1980.

Tarschys, D.: The scissors crisis in public finance. *Policy Science* 15 (1983) 205–24.

Wildavsky, A.: *Budgeting: a comparative theory of budgetary processes*. 2nd edn. New Brunswick, NJ: Transaction Books, 1986.

————: *The Politics of the Budgetary Process*. 4th edn. Boston: Little, Brown, 1984.

bureaucracy The idea of bureaucracy (rule by the bureau) crystallized in the early nineteenth century to become the most important addition so far to the ancient Greek classification of types of rule, monarchy, aristocracy and democracy. In its early usage the term meant simply rule by officials but from the beginning different slants could be attached to it depending on whether the collective body of officials (*the bureaucracy*) or the machinery of such rule was the centre of attention. Over the last 150 years the term has acquired numerous extensions to its meaning and there is no sign of a decline in its everyday and academic use. Towards the end of the nineteenth century its use was extended to cover the ADMINISTRATION by trained professionals not just of the state but of all large organizations and by the middle of the twentieth century it could be used as a synonym for 'large organization'. It is now commonplace to speak of the bureaucratic nature of modern society as a whole.

The clue to understanding the popularity of the term was contained in its first recorded use in 1764. The French philosopher Baron de Grimm attributed its invention to the physiocrat, de Gournay, who complained that the real spirit of the laws in France was the subordination of the public interest to offices and officials and that it was in effect a new form of government. The term very neatly captures the feeling that means have become ends, that systems have acquired independence from the people they are supposed to serve. It then easily becomes a term of abuse, but it emerges out of a real dilemma of modern social life, namely that the increasing application of rational procedures so often results in a feeling of loss of control.

'Bureaucracy' therefore contains both the eighteenth century's promise of the fruits of rationality and the unease with which both conservative and radical critics of rationalism view modern government. In the nineteenth century bureaucracy became associated above all with the centralized European STATE, being brought to a fine art in Prussia with its specialized CIVIL SERVICE trained in ADMINISTRATIVE LAW and its comprehensive regulation of the life of its citizens. It was regularly contrasted with what was seen as the British system of self-government. The eighteenth century's hopes for rationality in the machinery of government reached its culminating expression in HEGEL's *Philosophy of Right* (1821). Hegel linked the ethical rationalism of KANT and German idealism to the realities of the social structure of the Prussia of his day. He saw the state as the embodiment of rationality and universal principles of human action but also as the vehicle for personal and collective fulfilment for individual citizens. In this elaborate synthesis of philosophical concepts and social commentary Hegel accorded civil servants a position more exalted than they have occupied in any account, before or since. The civil servant was entrusted with the maintenance of the state's universal interest and of legality in general. The class of civil servants was one of the three great classes of society, the others being the agricultural and industrial. Unlike the others it worked only for the universal interest and its private interest was satisfied in that work. Both the realization of state projects and the confidence of the public in government depended on their conduct and culture. Hence their education had to be appropriate to the task and their demeanour had to match the great tasks with which they were entrusted. They formed the 'greater part of the middle class, the class in which the consciousness of right and the developed intelligence of the mass of the people is found' (*Philosophy of Right* 1942 edn, p. 193).

At the same time as Hegel was writing, reforms of the administrative systems of European states, impelled by pressures brought about by the centralized Napoleonic state, led to the idea of bureaucracy being elaborated into a doctrine of administrative efficiency. In Austria and Prussia particularly administrative reforms were instituted which replaced the old committees or *collegia* with a hierarchy of offices under the control of individual officials; all this was introduced with the help of a developing theory of administration. Hegel's treatise, which can equally be translated *Philosophy of Law*, linked these real developments in the modern state with an account of the nature of rationality and interpreted them as inevitably connected. In this way he provided a set of potential legitimations for bureaucracy which have been rehearsed by officials and governments since.

It is helpful also to refer to MARX's critique of Hegel, for this too presages a tradition of opposition to bureaucracy and enables us to see why the Hegelian sentiments anticipate some of the deepest ideological cleavages of the modern world. Marx wrote his *Critique of Hegel's Philosophy of Law* at the beginning of his career in 1843 and it was not published until 1927, but in it we can find both key elements in later Marxist doctrine and the exploration of feelings which have so often been expressed in popular protest against modern government before and after. He inveighed against Hegel's identification of the state with rationality insisting that it was simply the work of people of flesh and blood and only properly constituted in a democracy. Where a constitution was not democratic the state became something abstract opposed to the people, and bureaucracy confronted them as a closed society.

Marx followed this with an array of criticisms of bureaucracy that contradict the justification Hegel cited and that have been employed in arguments against bureaucracy ever since. Bureaucracy exists in collusion with the great corporations of society, by working in the same spirit of formalism and invoking an imaginary general interest. It turns formalism into an end in itself, creates a hierarchy of knowledge, converts knowledge into mystery and secrets, binds officials to a career of chasing promotion, and guarantees them greater security than anyone else. The only checks against these defects are themselves unwarranted privileges for corporations and an education unduly restricted to the middle estate.

Marx shifted his interest to capital and labour and so did not follow up this account of bureaucracy with more substantial analysis; it was left to Max WEBER (1865–1920) to provide what became the starting point for modern scientific accounts of bureaucracy. The rationality of bureaucracy became its central characteristic in the sense of binding administration to rules and requiring knowledge to be the basis of DECISION MAKING. Weber's account was quite devoid of Hegelian philosophizing but, like his predecessor, he was prepared to draw on the administrative theory of his day to provide the guidelines for his description of the workings of a key modern institutional structure. This fitted very happily with his own theory of social scientific methodology which gave a privileged place to rationality. Rational bureaucracy operated as a pure notion in theory, or 'ideal type', which, if implemented in practice, guaranteed reliability, predictability, and maximized efficiency. Hence the practices of Prussian bureaucracy of his time – the hierarchy of office, strict separation of office and person, selection by examination, career structures, salaries, pensions, disciplinary provision – all within a framework comprehensively regulated by law – became the hallmarks of the 'ideal type' of bureaucracy.

Weber was equally aware of the general criticism of bureaucracy as formalistic and capable of producing accumulations of power in the hands of officials. It was indeed a friend of his, Roberto MICHELS, who in *Political Parties* (1911) gave such prominence to the IRON LAW OF OLIGARCHY and the tendency of power to accumulate in the hands of officials. But Weber was not inclined to radical solutions to this problem and after reviewing a variety of

possible alternatives to bureaucracy, such as the collegial principle, amateur administration, SEPARATION OF POWERS and DIRECT DEMOCRACY, he concluded that free parliaments and responsible elected leadership were about the best checks which could be expected under modern conditions.

The general nature of Weber's account was such that not only did he extend the idea of bureaucracy, in a way already implicit in Hegel's and Marx's accounts to all large organizations so that it applied equally to state, church, political party and business corporation, but he also asserted that the rationalization of the modern world was such that bureaucracy would flourish in both capitalist and socialist types of society. In this way he provided the basis for and anticipated a great deal of both internal and external criticisms of socialist theory and practice in the twentieth century.

Bureaucracy has indeed been a recurrent problem for socialist societies in that, time and again, significant opposition to the state and party control has focused on complaints against bureaucracy as departing a long way from the democratic inspirations of Marx. LENIN found it necessary to praise bureaucratic principles in his attempts to organize a revolutionary party, and then to disavow them in order to gain control of the Soviet state. He was outdone by TROTSKY who made criticism of bureaucracy a main plank of his campaign against STALIN. When Tito led Yugoslavia out of Soviet control in the early 1950s he attacked Soviet bureaucracy only to be attacked in turn by Milovan Djilas who in *The New Class* (1957) broke fundamentally with Marxist doctrine by identifying the party and state machine with a bureaucracy and arguing that it formed a class. In China MAO ZEDONG used attacks on bureaucracy as a justification for initiating the cultural revolution which involved the systematic removal of office holders in all walks of life.

In the West the growth of state activity and state employment has led to repeated attempts by right-wing parties to focus popular feelings of resentment against the ills of bureaucracy and to call for the dismantling of welfare and the reduction of taxes. Bureaucracy has become regarded as the core of the modern state. Weber himself regarded the development of bureaucracy as inevitable, and gloomily foresaw a world of highly specialized roles with human qualities constrained by the machine-like structures of modern organization, whether in the state or in the large corporation. But the weight of empirical social scientific research since his time has tended to emphasize the fact that the ideal type of bureaucracy is neither so rational nor, in its operation, so machine-like as he saw it. Much more emphasis has been placed on the scope for discretion by holders of offices of all kinds and the range of human qualities, which the modern world calls for in addition to detachment, self-control and integrity.

As yet, however, there has been no major statement to compare with Hegel's and Weber's which would revise the idea of bureaucracy in the light of contemporary social and theoretical developments. Key social changes which have taken place over the last sixty years include the growth of the professionalization of occupations, the ever-increasing inter-penetration of state and private business, the extension of ownership and rights in property and the rationalization of the media of communication and exchange. In the world of theory the idea of rationality has been elaborated in different directions by Karl Popper with his emphasis on the necessity for criticism, by Jürgen Habermas with his stress on communicability and by Niklas Luhmann emphasizing systems rationality. Developments in theoretical ideas may well be seen as part expressions of changes in social structure. They express both the extension of rationality into every sphere of life and at the same time an increase in refinement and sophistication in its use. If the dominant image of bureaucracy in Weber's time was the black-coated official behind his desk facing the citizen applying for a licence, in the late 1980s the equivalent is perhaps the couple filling in their tax return in the living-room with the aid of a microcomputer. But the intellectual synthesis of these changes, ideas and images is not yet available.

MCA

Reading

Albrow, M.: *Bureaucracy*. London: Macmillan, 1970.

Blau, P.M. and Meyer, M.W.: *Bureaucracy in Modern Society*. New York: Random House, 1971.

Habermas, J.: Reason and the rationalization of society. In *The Theory of Communicative Action*, Vol. I, trans. T. McCarthy. London: Heinemann, 1984.

Hegel, G.W.F.: *Philosophy of Right* (1821). trans. T.M. Knox. Oxford: Oxford University Press, 1942.

Hummel, R.: *The Bureaucratic Experience*. New York: St Martin's, 1977.

Kamenka, E. and Krygier, M.: *Bureaucracy*. London: Arnold, 1979.

Luhmann, N.: *The Differentiation of Society*. New York: Columbia University Press, 1982.

Marx, K.: Contribution to the Critique of Hegel's Philosophy of Law. In Karl Marx and Friedrich Engels *Collected Works*, pp. 175–87. London: Lawrence & Wishart, 1975.

Page, E.C.: *Political Authority and Bureaucratic Power*. Brighton, Sussex: Wheatsheaf, 1985.

Popper, K.R.: *The Logic of Scientific Discovery*. London: Hutchinson, 1959.

Rizzi, B.: *The Bureaucratization of the World*. London: Tavistock, 1985.

Weber, M.: Bureaucracy. In *From Max Weber*, pp. 196–244, ed. H.H. Gerth and C. Wright Mills. London: Routledge & Kegan Paul, 1948.

Burke, Edmund (1729–1797)

British parliamentarian and prolific political pamphleteer. During his career as a propagandist for the Rockinghamite Whigs Burke published his *Thoughts on the Cause of the Present Discontents* (1770) which contains an important analysis of party. Burke held that George III's attempts to extend the royal prerogative and to rule by cabal undermined the historic relationship between the executive and parliament, and he advocated the combination of men of virtue to restore the constitution. Hence he was at pains to show that party was not necessarily factious or a vicious aberration from normal political life, as both Chatham and the king's supporters believed, but was essential to the preservation of liberty. A party, Burke wrote, 'is a body of men united for promoting by their joint endeavours the national interest upon some particular principle in which they are all agreed'. The *Present Discontents* has been often interpreted as a defence of party government and even as an anticipation of the dual party system. Such a view is challenged by revisionist scholarship (Brewer 1971; O'Gorman 1973) which attributes to Burke a more limited ambition. He did not envisage the existence of permanent disciplined parties or the institutionalization of party conflict, and sought only to demonstrate the legitimacy of certain specific types of political association, especially the Rockingham connexion and a united opposition to the king. Party was merely an expedient for ending the partisanship of George III's reign. Of Burke's other writings, the *Speech to the Electors of Bristol* (1774) gives a powerful defence of a member of parliament's right to independent judgement and the *Reflections on the Revolution in France* (1790) is credited with being the first theoretical statement of conservatism.   MWT

Reading

Brewer, J.: Party and the double cabinet: two facets of Burke's *Thoughts. Historical Journal* 14 (1971).

Burke, E.: *Writings and Speeches of Edmund Burke*, ed. P. Langford. Oxford: Oxford University Press 1981– .

Cone, C.B.: *Burke and the Nature of Politics: the Age of the American Revolution*. Lexington: University of Kentucky Press, 1957.

Courtenay, C.P.: *Montesquieu and Burke*. Oxford: Oxford University Press, 1963.

Mansfield, H.C.: *Statesmanship and Party Government*. Chicago: University of Chicago Press, 1965.

O'Gorman, F.: *Edmund Burke: his political philosophy*. London: Allen & Unwin, 1973.

C

cabinet/cabinet government A form of government in which a group of ministers, usually drawn from the majority party or parties of a parliament, combine to make collective decisions about the country's policies. Originally developed in Britain it was later exported to most Commonwealth countries and established in several European nations, such as Sweden, Norway, West Germany and Italy. Two points are central to the concept. First, the decisions of a cabinet are meant to be collective, not those of a single person; ministers are bound by the doctrine of collective responsibility publicly to support all the decisions taken by cabinet. Second, the cabinet acts as a political link between the executive and the parliament because ministers are answerable to the parliament. Cabinet government needs to be differentiated from the cabinet in a PRESIDENTIAL SYSTEM where the cabinet, again a meeting of leading executives, only offers advice to a president who is responsible for the final decisions.

The cabinet first appeared in the reign of Charles II and was initially a meeting of those advisers whom the monarch chose to consult. By the nineteenth century the monarch did not attend meetings or decide what would be discussed. The survival of the cabinet depended on its capacity to retain the support of the HOUSE OF COMMONS. The cabinet has no formal constitutional status and when the older colonial constitutions were created the role of the cabinet in a system of RESPONSIBLE GOVERNMENT was taken for granted. It is therefore never mentioned in their constitutions and it continues to work behind the fiction that decisions of government are taken by the monarch in consultation with the Executive Council. The precise role of the cabinet is therefore open to interpretation and manipulation.

Initially the procedures of the cabinet depended on the style of the PRIME MINISTER; there were few records and little formal need for submissions. But the pressures of business, in Britain during the first world war and in Canada and Australia during the second, required the creation of a cabinet secretariat and a system of formalized submissions, minutes and decisions that laid the foundation for the highly organized cabinet structures of the modern day.

Members of the cabinet are generally chosen by the prime minister. This power gives the prime minister scope for patronage, but it is always circumscribed by the need to take account of the personal weight of leading colleagues, factional alignments, bi-cameral demands and, particularly in federations, state or provincial representation. In coalition governments the demands of coalition partners have to be negotiated. Cabinets are therefore likely to include many of the prime minister's rivals and other powerful individuals (particularly state or provincial representatives in federations) because they cannot all be excluded. It is not likely to consist only of sycophants and friends. Prime ministers normally have the power to sack ministers for poor performance, for mistakes or simply because they want to change the image of the government; it is a power used readily in Britain but more sparingly in Canada and Australia where there is a preference for not allowing enemies to act as a focus of discontent on the backbenches.

In the case of Labour governments in Australia and New Zealand, ministers are not chosen by the prime minister but elected by the parliamentary parties (the CAUCUS) and prime ministers retain the right only to distribute and redistribute portfolios. They can sack ministers only on the grounds of some significant error and even then will effectively need to obtain caucus endorsement.

Some systems distinguish between senior cabinet ministers and their less important colleagues outside the cabinet. In Britain the cabinet usually contains around twenty-three out of a total of nearly a hundred ministers; in Australia fifteen out of twenty-seven are in the cabinet. The largest cabinet is in Canada where numbers rose gradually to forty by 1985; since the cabinet plays an important representational function, it is regarded as invidious to divide ministers into inner and outer groups. One result is that the important decisions are taken by committees of cabinet.

The agenda of cabinet is decided by the prime minister on the advice of the Cabinet Office or equivalent body. In Britain there are two standing items – parliamentary business and foreign affairs (and for a time Northern Ireland). Most business in all cabinet systems is presented in a ministerial submission that includes details of a problem or proposition. It will normally be circulated in advance to obtain the views of interested departments. Unless intended simply to inform cabinet, it will include a set of recommendations. The prime minister retains the right to refuse to list an item for discussion, but as the management of cabinet business has become more routinized so it seems that this power is exercised less often. Nevertheless if the prime minister and the minister responsible for a policy combine to keep an item off the agenda there is nothing that other ministers can do to force a discussion. Items not listed on the agenda, such as approval of appointments or reports on emerging crises, can usually be raised only with the prior agreement of the prime minister. The size of the agenda may vary from around six or eight items in Britain to twenty or more in smaller systems where ministers may feel less secure and want to gain

the imprimatur of cabinet before making decisions. Large agendas also provide a means for prime ministers to keep a close check on what is happening.

Prime ministers chair cabinet meetings, determining the order in which items are taken, the terms in which they will be discussed, and the time available for debate. At the end of the discussion the prime minister summarizes the feeling of the meeting. He or she will occasionally go round the table and count heads, but as some ministers' opinions are given greater weight than others the summary need not precisely reflect the numbers. Formal votes are rare, although they have been taken in Australian Labor cabinets (even then some ministers thought that the prime minister didn't count accurately!). Ministers may challenge the prime minister's conclusion, but seldom do. Cabinet decisions are written in the cabinet offices, drawing on the recommendations included in the submissions and on the debate in cabinet as reflected in the prime minister's summary. Draft decisions may be cleared with the prime minister, but usually they are immediately circulated to the relevant ministers and agencies. That circulation may be restricted so that not all cabinet ministers know all the decisions taken in their name. Cabinet decisions then become the authoritative weapons in bureaucratic battles.

The cabinet system refers not only to meetings of the full cabinet but also to the activities of its committees. Every cabinet system includes committees, even though in Britain their existence was long regarded as secret and their membership and terms of reference are rarely announced. Elsewhere all these details are available. Committees carry much of the workload of cabinet. Sometimes they pre-digest complicated issues so that they can bring proposals to full cabinet. They are often delegated responsibility for the final decisions. In Canada and Australia the main discussion on most items occurs in committee and decisions are listed in bulk for formal cabinet endorsement, in Canada as an addendum to the agenda. These decisions will rarely be challenged.

At times the existence of key committees of

leading ministers has led to charges that they are de facto inner cabinets. Since prime ministers are responsible for deciding the membership and terms of reference of committees, they can arrange for sensitive items to be considered in arenas where their support is highest. Economic committees may sometimes be the only arena where a full debate on fiscal strategy takes place. The war cabinet and economic committees in Britain, the co-ordination committee in Australia, the priorities and planning committee in Canada, have indeed been the central powerhouses where prime ministers have consulted with a small number of select senior ministers and made crucial policy choices; once those senior bodies have made decisions it will be rare for them to be overturned. All other ministers are still bound to support them by the principle of collective responsibility. However these committees are part of the formal cabinet structure; they should therefore be distinguished from kitchen cabinets which are groups that have no official status or authority.

The importance of the cabinet in a political system depends in part on the degree of independence given to individual ministers. Where great weight is given to the idea of co-ordination, as in Westminster systems, cabinet is regarded as central. Where, as in European countries such as Denmark and West Germany, ministers have greater freedom to exercise their independent judgement and cabinet has little authority to direct them, its position is less pivotal.

Several criticisms have been made of the way in which the cabinet works. In general terms Richard Crossman and John Mackintosh argued that the prime minister now so dominates the cabinet that cabinet government has been replaced by PRIME MINISTERIAL GOVERNMENT and that the cabinet is now, like the monarch, a dignified but ineffectual part of the constitution. More specifically they and others have claimed that cabinet is little more than a forum for rampant departmentalism, with ministers as adversaries arguing their portfolio's interest, and unable to question the often technical advice provided by civil servants. They argue that cabinet is unable to develop any coherent strategy or to act as an effective political forum – both of which they regard as desirable. Government is too *ad hoc*, dominated by sequential DECISION MAKING from narrow departmental viewpoints.

By contrast, Edmund Dell has suggested that the cabinet is managerially inefficient. He argued that the doctrine of collective responsibility often means that all members want to be involved in all items, regardless of their expertise, and that the cabinet is therefore a poor forum for making sensible decisions. He also pointed to the futility of weekend meetings during which the cabinet collectively discusses general directions and strategy; he saw that process as getting in the way of real work on specific problems. Canadian commentators have shown that although the cabinet developed a sophisticated decision-making system, attempts to set general strategy, as in the 1975–6 priorities exercise, failed and that all the large initiatives were in fact taken outside the official structure. The system, however well-designed, could not deliver efficient strategic results.

Each critic of cabinet can provide evidence for his case, but each assumes that cabinet ought to fill particular functions: either as strategic planner (Crossman) or as managerial and technical decision-maker (Dell). In fact the cabinet must try to fulfil both of these functions, and also others. Its functions cannot be neatly described; cabinets pay attention to problems not on account of their inherent importance but because of their political sensitivity and intractability. Cabinet is the forum for determining what cannot be settled elsewhere – in departments, by ministers, or by cabinet committees. It must arbitrate between ministers, make difficult policy decisions and allocate resources. It must act as a forum in which technical advice is put under the political microscope. It may try to set general directions, at least implicitly, in its budget parameters. It can also act as a rubber stamp and as an information exchange. But it cannot do any of these exclusively, and may not do any one particularly well.

Cabinet is a forum that must be judged by political, not managerial criteria. It is after all a committee of the powerful, faced by difficult problems with extensive ramifications.

Although its procedures have become more routine they are still open to manipulation, usually, but not always, by the prime minister. But so long as government remains collective, prime ministers need to maintain the support and consent of cabinet however it is obtained. Cabinet government remains a real and living, if changing, concept.

See also EXECUTIVES; MONARCHY.

PMW

Reading

Bogdanor, V.: The Crossman diaries. *Political Studies* 25 (1977) 110–22.

Crossman, R.H.S.: *The Diaries of a Cabinet Minister.* 3 vols. London: Hamish Hamilton, 1975, 1976, 1977.

————: *Introduction to Walter Bagehot: the English Constitution.* London: Fontana, 1963.

Dell, E.: Collective responsibility: fact, fiction or facade? In *Policy and Practice: the experience of government.* London: RIPA, 1980.

French, R.: *How Ottawa Decides.* Toronto: Lorimer, 1980.

Hennessy, P.: *Cabinet.* Oxford: Blackwell, 1986.

Jennings, I.: *Cabinet Government.* Rev. edn. Cambridge: Cambridge University Press, 1959.

Keith, A.: *The British Cabinet System.* London: Stevens, 1952.

Mackie, T.T. and Hogwood, B.W. eds: *Unlocking the Cabinet: cabinet structures in comparative perspective.* London: Sage, 1985.

Mackintosh, J.P.: *The British Cabinet.* 3rd edn. London: Stevens, 1977.

Weller, P.: *First Among Equals: prime ministers in Westminster systems.* Sydney and Boston, Mass.: Allen & Unwin, 1985.

cabinet ministériel The minister's personal team of advisers. *Cabinets* exist in many West European countries, for example Austria and Italy, but have been longest established in France. The *cabinet* offers one solution to the problem of establishing political control over the BUREAUCRACY. The majority of *cabinet* members in France have been civil servants personally chosen by the minister.

VBB

cadre party One of the oldest party types originating at a time when the franchise was restricted. In its loose organization and the absence of any emphasis on securing party members the cadre party is best contrasted with the MASS MEMBERSHIP PARTY. The limited number of voters meant that little advantage was gained in building up a mass organization, and cadre parties performed mainly a vote-getting function. For organizational purposes it was sufficient to rely on an informal group of leaders who, through their social and political connections, were able to supply co-ordination necessary to contest elections as well as to use their powers of patronage to achieve results. Until the extension of the franchise and the rise of mass membership parties there was no incentive for 'parties of notables' to change their character. Later, when they were forced to compete, the 'mass democratic' aspect was to some extent made to co-exist with the old-style elitism of the cadre party.

The term cadre is used in a different sense to apply to a party relying on a core of disciplined party activists, strictly organized and centrally directed. It accords with LENIN's ideas of a revolutionary COMMUNIST party, organized on quasi-military lines and firmly authoritarian. Its elitist character may be disguised by encouraging a fairly wide general membership, but the role of the membership will be largely supportive to the leadership and serve as a source of recruitment to the leading party cadres.

See also APPARATCHIK; BOLSHEVISM.

GSm

Reading

Blondel, J.: Types of parties and types of society. In *Comparative Government*, ed. J. Blondel. London: Macmillan, 1969.

Duverger, M.: *Political Parties: their organisation and activity in the modern state.* London: Methuen, 1964.

Epstein, L.D.: *Political Parties in Western Democracies.* New Brunswick, NJ: Transaction Books, 1980.

Caesarism A typically nineteenth-century concept which was necessary to help explain the emotional and demagogic factors in the government of the two Napoleons. Historians and political scientists in the nineteenth century made more frequent use of the term Caesarism than their twentieth-century counterparts. François Auguste Romieu, an enthusiastic Bonapartist used it for the first time in his *Ere des Césars* in 1850. Theodor Mommsen did not take exception to this usage and it can be found in his *History of Rome* (1956), despite the fact that in contrast to Romieu, Mommsen loathed BONAPARTISM and especially Napoleon III.

In his *Umrisse zur Naturlehre des Caesarisumus* (1888) W. Roscher emphasized the fact that under Caesarism everything is promised to everyone, and only the leader's genius can preserve a certain unity. No rational acts can bridge the contradictions of this problem. It depends simply and solely on blind belief in the super-human capabilities of the ruler. Napoleon I promised the Jacobins that he would destroy the ancient nobility; and to the old aristocracy he promised the opposite. Napoleon III promised peace ('l'empire c'est la paix') only to entangle France a few months later in the hopeless Crimean war. He promised his support to the Italian Nationalists and the Pope alike, only to ultimately disappoint both. Hence, A. J. P. Taylor's devastating judgement: 'The more we strip off the disguises the more the disguises appear. Such was Louis Napoleon the man of mystery, conspirator and statesman, dreamer and realist, despot and democrat, maker of wars and peace, creator and muddler.'

In 1895 Robert von Poehlman published his *Enstehung des Caesarismus*, asserting that Roman Caesarism had its origin in the later Greek tyrannies. Dionysius of Syracuse, Agathocles and Nabis of Sparta must have been the models for Caesarism. All of them were indifferent to the concepts of morality, justice and law. It was therefore not difficult for them to be two-faced by appearing to be absolute monarchs to some, and extreme democrats to others. Most nineteenth-century scholars were agreed that Caesarism was the outcome of the degenerate democracy and that the rise of the dictator was usually facilitated by the unavoidable conflict between the love of freedom – characteristic of the wealthy and educated classes – and the desire for equality among the masses.

These objectives, being mutually exclusive and incompatible in the long run, must bring about a crisis. In these circumstances the most able withdraw from politics and while the gulf between the social classes deepens, the field is left wide open for demagogues to intensify their efforts. Unrest breaks out and eventually people begin to yearn for the benefactor as sole ruler. In the last resort the masses prefer to permit person and property to be consumed by a single lion rather than by a hundred jackals or even a thousand rats.

Karl Marx rejected the term Caesarism in his *18 Brumaire of Louis Bonaparte*, characterized it as a schoolboy expression (*Schulphrase*) and criticized its use as a superficial analogizing of history. Lenin, on the other hand, continued to use Caesarism in his writings and therefore the term can still be found in Soviet historiography. Nor did political thinkers in the west in the twentieth century give it up altogether. Antonio Gramsci made use of the terms 'progressive' and 'regressive' Caesarism, maintaining that Caesar and Napoleon were examples of progressive Caesarism because under their regimes the revolutionary element put the conservative in the shade. The German historian Oswald Spengler (1918) believed that democracy was doomed and predicted the approach of a new Caesarism, since this was the end of all life cycles of all cultures. Ortega Y Gasset, in *Revolt of the Masses* (1930), shocked and disappointed by the brutal empire of the masses, looked for a new Caesar, some new charismatic figure to point the way to the unification of Europe; only a new Caesar could counteract the decadence of Europe, since Julius Caesar, one of the only two clear heads in the ancient world (the other was Themistocles), had the imagination to look beyond the limits of the classical city state to a new international empire.

In 1937 Albert Camus was hoping for a new Mediterranean culture based on Greek ideals of tragic freedom, human dignity, rational lucidity and beauty. In contrast to Ortega he does not blame the disasters of the century on falsely aspiring masses, but on intellectual Nihilism and the totalitarian Caesarism of both the right and left alike (Nazism and Stalinism).

For Amaury de Riencourt in *The Coming Caesars* (1958) Caesarism is neither dictatorship nor brutal seizure of power through revolution, nor one man's overriding ambition, but rather a slow unconscious development that ends in the voluntary surrender of a free people to one autocratic master. This process had already begun in the United States where Roosevelt is seen as Julius Caesar and Eisenhower as Caesar Augustus.

Professional historians could not agree with such generalizations, so it is not surprising that Momigliano pointed out that Caesarism was utterly unintelligible to the man of antiquity and too inexact for the modern man. In books and scholarly articles written by ancient historians and professional classicists, the term Caesarism seems to be more and more avoided.

See also DICTATORSHIP.   ZY

Reading

Momigliano, A.: Per un riesame della storia dell'idea di Cesarismo. *Rivista Storica Italiana* 68 (1956) 220–29.

————: Burckhardt e la parola Cesarismo. *Rivista Storica Italiana* 74 (1962) 369–71.

Yavetz, Z.: *Julius Caesar and his Public Image.* London: Thames & Hudson, 1983.

Calhoun, John C. (1782–1850) An American politician and constitutional theorist.
In a political career of almost forty years' duration John C. Calhoun of South Carolina, while never attaining the coveted office of president of the United States, filled almost every other post open to ambition: congressman, senator (twice), secretary of war, vice-president, secretary of state. But he is better known for his role in the growing sectional divergences that culminated in the secession of the South and the American Civil War, and for his contribution to the doctrines about the nature and origins of the American federal constitution upon which advocates of the Southern cause relied both before and after the war.

While originally a partisan of a strong national economic policy, Calhoun became convinced that the industrial protectionism that was a necessary part of it would be harmful to the planting interests of South Carolina. He took a leading part in the state's opposition to federal policy which culminated in the 'nullification ordinance' of 1833. Calhoun's argument, worked out in a series of speeches and writings over the preceding five years, had been that the federal constitution was a compact between originally sovereign states delegating certain powers to common institutions but giving these no direct rights over individual citizens. The states were therefore entitled to interpose their authority when they disputed whether a given power had been so delegated, and prevent such legislation taking effect until the constitution had been amended to confer the disputed power. In the last resort the state could secede from the Union and resume full independence. Calhoun was, therefore, one of the originators of the doctrine of STATES RIGHTS. The failure of South Carolina to get its way and his dissatisfaction with the eventual compromise shifted Calhoun's interests towards developing a common front among the Southern states based upon their most compelling common interest, the preservation of negro slavery, now increasingly under attack from elements in the North.

Since most of the concrete issues in the contest did not involve legislation affecting Southern states themselves, nullification no longer suited Calhoun's purpose; indeed he was bound to denounce its use by the Northern states when they asserted their right to impede the enforcement of the fugitive slave law – nor could it help to make the case for legitimizing slavery in new territories. Calhoun shared MADISON's view (*Federalist Papers* No. 10), that a republican government was in danger of being ruled by an exclusive party or FACTION, but he found the measures which Madison proposed to counteract this danger inadequate.

As a safeguard for limited government against party domination and for the protection, as he saw it, of property of all kinds, Calhoun developed the doctrine of what he sometimes called the 'concurring majority', but latterly more usually the CONCURRENT MAJORITY – that is to say that a valid exercise of federal power in a country divided into distinct sections or interests should only be valid if a majority for it could be found in every section. The South should have an inbuilt veto perhaps through the device of a dual presidency. During the last years of his life Calhoun worked on two books designed to expound his particular version of limited government: *A Disquisition on Government* and *A Discourse on the Constitutional Government of the United States*, published posthumously in 1851 as the first volume of his collected works. His work has exerted considerable influence on the theory of CONSOCIATIONAL DEMOCRACY, and more generally upon attempts to secure democracy in plural societies.   B

Reading

Calhoun, J.C.: *A Disquisition on Government*, with selections from the *Discourse*, ed. C.G. Post. Indianapolis, Minn.: Bobbs-Merrill, 1953.

Cralle, R.K. ed.: *The Works of John C. Calhoun* (1851), Vol. I. New York: Russell & Russell, 1968.

Current, N.: *John C. Calhoun*. New York: Twayne, 1963.

Meriwether, R.L. et al. eds: *The Papers of John C. Calhoun*, Vols I–XVI. Columbia: University of South Carolina Press, 1959–

Wiltse, C.M.: *John C. Calhoun*. 3 vols. Indianapolis, Minn.: Bobbs-Merrill, 1944, 1949 and 1951.

candidate selection The mainly extralegal processes by which political parties decide who will be designated on ballots and election communications as their recommended candidates. The term is sometimes confused with *nomination*, which is the mainly legal procedure by which election authorities certify persons as qualified candidates for office and print their names on the official ballots.

In most democratic countries the law is silent on candidate selection, and each party establishes and administers its own rules without government regulation. There are a few exceptions. In West Germany the national election law requires parties to select their candidates for the *Bundestag* in each district either by secret votes of the district's dues-paying party members or by district nominating conventions elected by the members. In

Turkey a national law stipulates that all but 5 per cent of each party's candidates for the National Assembly must be selected by the direct vote of the dues-paying party members in the legislative districts. The United States has the most elaborate regulations: the laws of most states stipulate in detail how all candidates are to be chosen by direct primary elections administered by public authorities.

Democratic political parties vary widely in the relative power of national, regional, and local organizations over candidate selection. Power is most centralized in Israel and Venezuela, where national party committees select all candidates for the national legislature after hearing (often perfunctorily) suggestions from local party committees and interest groups. In India, Japan, Sri Lanka, and the Netherlands national party committees also make the final selections but often accept names strongly urged by their regional and local affiliates. At the other extreme, in Norway, Turkey, and the United States, all candidates for the national legislature are selected by regional and district organizations with no national supervision of any kind so that control of the party's label is entirely in local hands.

The most common arrangement is one in which the party's district or regional organizations choose the candidates subject to supervision by a national agency. In Britain, for example, the national extra-parliamentary organizations of both the Conservative and Labour parties maintain lists of persons recommended for candidature. On several occasions national leaders have tried to persuade the organizations in winnable constituencies to select senior members who had lost their seats in previous general elections, but more often than not the constituency organizations have rejected such suggestions as unwarranted invasions of their prerogatives. Similar local rebellions have sometimes occurred in leading parties in Scandinavia, Belgium, and France. Even in the more centralized parties the national organizations' 'placement' powers often look more powerful than they are.

National supervision usually involves some kind of veto power as well: party rules provide that no candidate selected locally or regionally for the national legislature can be designated as the official party candidate until the national party organization has given its approval. Many parties have such a national veto power, for example the leading parties of Scandinavia, Belgium, and Britain. It is seldom used, but its existence generally causes the local organizations to pass over aspirants who might not be acceptable to their national organizations.

In several federal democracies, notably Australia, West Germany, and Switzerland, regional organizations (in the states, *länder*, and cantons respectively) rather than the national party organizations prescribe the rules for and supervise the administration of candidate selection by the district organizations.

Democratic parties also vary widely in the number of people who participate in candidate selection. At one extreme stand the leading parties in Israel, in each of which a national nominating committee composed of a handful of party leaders not only chooses the candidates on the national party list (Israel has no subnational districts for electing members of the Knesset) but also determines their rank order on the list and therefore their chances of being elected. At the other extreme stand the parties of the United States, where state laws require that any registered voter who wishes to vote in the primary elections of any party must be allowed to do so, and in the states with 'open' and 'blanket' primaries the voter does not even have to state his choice publicly let alone pay dues or assume any other obligation to the party. As a result, far more people participate in candidate selection in the USA than in other nations. For example, in 1984 over 25 million people voted in the primaries and caucuses that selected the Democratic and Republican presidential candidates. In most democratic countries, on the other hand, the candidates are chosen by small assemblies of local party members or officials, and the total size of the 'selectorate' is less than 1 per cent of the voters.

However it is organized, candidate selection plays a critical role in all large-scale modern democracies. For one thing it determines who wins the most important stake of power in any political party. The core of a party is the beliefs and actions of the people it elects to public office, not the platforms and manifestos written by party activists outside government. Consequently, by selecting from among its many members who would like to represent the party in government the few who have a serious chance of doing so, the party decides what (that is, who) it is.

Even more important, candidate selection makes democratic elections possible in large-scale modern democracies. In every such polity millions of people are legally eligible for public office, and no voter can possibly make an informed choice among all of them. By selecting and publicizing their candidates the parties effectively reduce the alternatives to very small numbers among which voters can rationally choose. They also provide many voters with their best cue for distinguishing the good candidates from the bad – their party labels. Thus candidate selection is as essential to realizing the ideal of free elections as free elections are to realizing the ideal of government by the consent of the governed.

See also PARTY ORGANIZATION; PRIMARY, DIRECT.

AR

Reading

Epstein, L.D.: *Political Parties in Western Democracies*, ch. 8. New Brunswick, NJ: Transaction Books, 1980.

Obler, J.: The role of national party leaders in the selection of parliamentary candidates: the Belgian case. *Comparative Politics* 5 (1973) 157–84.

Ranney, A.: *Pathways to Parliament*. London: Macmillan, 1965.

————: Candidate selection. In *Democracy at the Polls: a comparative study of competitive national elections*, pp. 75–106. ed. D. Butler, H.R. Penniman and A. Ranney. Washington, DC: American Enterprise Institute, 1981.

Rush, M.: *The Selection of Parliamentary Candidates*. London: Nelson, 1969.

Scarrow, H.A.: Nomination and local party organization in Canada: a case study. *Western Political Quarterly* 17 (1964) 55–64.

Valen, H.: The recruitment of parliamentary nominees in Norway. *Scandinavian Political Studies*. New York: Columbia University Press, 1966.

capitalism A term that came into general use to describe the new form of economic organization that became dominant in industrial societies during the nineteenth century. MARX spoke of the capitalist mode of production and bourgeois society rather than of capitalism, but it is from his writings that the modern concept of capitalism has emerged. He conceived capitalism as a specific stage in economic development, and attempted to grasp its essential features in order to analyse its laws of motion and to identify what differentiated capitalism from other modes of production.

This approach was in marked contrast to the classical economists, who tended to treat capitalism not as a new form of economic organization but as the expression of a universal aspect of economic behaviour. This conflict in approach has remained in later writing on capitalism, and in part explains why the term has been used more by the left than by the right since its use is sometimes taken to imply acceptance of the socialist argument that there is an alternative and superior way of organizing a modern industrial society. Despite this, the term is still widely used to denote the economic institutions of the advanced industrial countries outside the Soviet bloc: private ownership of the means of production, wage labour, and economic co-ordination through free markets.

Marx argued that the main characteristic which differentiated societies from one another historically was the way in which their labour process was organized. The modes of production dominant since the advent of agriculture had tended to be class modes in which the exclusive ownership by one class of the technical and natural resources available for production created a dependent class of non-owners, forced to work not only to secure their own means of subsistence but to create a surplus for the ruling class.

Capitalism was founded not on relationships of coercion, however, but on voluntary exchange between free and sovereign individuals. Marx argued that it was still a class mode of production despite appearances because it rested on private ownership of the means of production which created a dependent class of wage labourers. The only property that the proletariat could sell to secure their means of subsistence was their labour power. By buying labour power at its market value in a free and voluntary exchange the capitalist bought the one commodity which could create new value, and properly used could yield a surplus value.

Capitalism was a unique mode of production according to Marx because it combined formal freedom and legal equality of all economic agents in the market place with subordination and coercion at work. The two key institutions of capitalism were therefore private ownership of the means of production and free labour. Labour had to be free in a double sense: workers had to be free to exchange their labour power for wages with any potential employer, and they could own nothing except their labour power.

The conflict between bourgeoisie and proletariat over the production and appropriation of surplus value, and competition between different capitals, are the source of the dynamism of the capitalist mode of production. In the last two hundred years capitalism has been associated with an enormous increase in production and a great enlargement of the world market. Marx predicted that the relentless drive to accumulate capital would produce increasingly severe crises. Overcoming these crises would involve constant revolutionizing of the techniques of production, the concentration and centralization of capital, and the creation of a large industrial reserve army or surplus population. As full automation of production was approached capitalism would encounter barriers which could not be overcome. The existence of such barriers indicated that capitalism was a transient mode of production which in due course would be replaced by SOCIALISM.

This conclusion was sharply contested by critics of MARXISM, such as Max WEBER, who argued that capitalism is a universal aspect of all social and economic systems. What justifies modern societies being called capitalist on this view is that they give special prominence and encouragement to rational economic conduct. Economizing behaviour, technical rationality, the choice of the best available means at the lowest cost, become institutionalized through private ownership of the means of production, techniques of calculation, and the development of markets for all goods and services including money. This leads to increased competition and specialization, and a widening and deepening division of labour. In Weber's view the increased wealth which flowed from capitalism was inseparable from the institutions that promoted technical rationality, including the division of labour and private ownership of the means of production. He therefore regarded the possibility of a socialist economy preserving the wealth created by capitalism while abolishing the institutions which created that wealth as a fantasy.

Much contemporary discussion has focused on whether capitalism has evolved into something else, and whether the essential characteristic of capitalism is its class relations of production or its unity as a world market which has been developing since the sixteenth century. Many social scientists have treated capitalism as an early variant of industrial society. Such terms as post-capitalism and welfare capitalism now abound. The changes that are most often cited in arguing that contemporary industrial societies are no longer capitalist are first the divorce of ownership from control with the rise of modern corporate capital; second the greatly expanded role of the state; third the political influence exercised by the working class through trade unions and a democratic political system.

Capitalism has undergone considerable modification as a result of these factors. In the nineteenth century the role of government in some capitalist societies tended to *laissez-faire*, but the twentieth century has seen increasing government intervention and regulation designed to achieve high levels of employment, rapid rates of growth and stable prices, to improve social welfare, and to regulate monopoly. Landmarks in this process have included in the United States the NEW DEAL, and in Britain the reforms of the 1945–51 Labour government aimed at strengthening the WELFARE STATE. Some claimed that a new form of industrial society was emerging which transcended both capitalism and socialism. More recently many, especially on the NEW RIGHT, have restated the case for capitalism arguing that capitalist countries suffer from an excessive degree of government intervention, and that their economies would be more efficient if government control were to be lessened and democracy curbed. Such warnings about the dangers of political interference in the market order of capitalist societies are often taken to imply that it is political rather than economic or technological factors, which have proved to be the fundamental determinants of developments in capitalism. There has been a long debate about the dependence of capitalism on democracy and democracy on capitalism. Some have claimed that capitalist states are generally characterized 'by a high degree and wide extent of pluralism' and by a 'separation of economic and political powers' (Hoover, pp. 294–302), while others, following Lenin, have regarded democracy as the 'best possible shell for capitalism'.

Many of the strongest supporters of capitalism such as Max Weber and Joseph SCHUMPETER have been pessimistic about the chances of survival of capitalism because it tends to undermine the institutions which give it legitimacy. But capitalism is not only the most productive but also the most flexible and adaptable economic system in history, and shows few signs of withering away.

See also KEYNES.

AMG

Reading

Giddens, A.: *Capitalism and Modern Social Theory*. Cambridge: Cambridge University Press, 1971.

Hoover, C.B.: Capitalism. In *International Encyclopedia of the Social Sciences*, Vol. II. New York: Macmillan and The Free Press, 1968.

O'Connor, J.: *Accumulation Crisis*. Oxford: Blackwell, 1984.

Schumpeter, J.A.: *Capitalism, Socialism and Democracy*. 5th edn. London: Allen & Unwin, 1976.

Shonfield, A.: *Modern Capitalism*. London and Oxford: Oxford University Press, 1965.

Wallerstein, I.: *The Modern World System*. New York: Academic Press, 1974.

caretaker government An interim government; a term first used in Britain by Joseph Chamberlain to refer to the Conservative minority government in 1885; used later to refer to Winston Churchill's brief Conservative administration of May–July 1945, formed after the dissolution of the wartime coalition until the results of the general election were known. The term is also used in other democracies. By convention, a caretaker government abstains from controversial legislation. In the words of the 1953 Danish Constitution (§ 15 (2)), a caretaker government may 'do only what is necessary for the purpose of the uninterrupted conduct of official business'.

In some of the multi-party systems of the European continent, such as Finland and the Netherlands, caretaker governments play a wider role as part of the GOVERNMENT FORMATION PROCESS. They may be appointed either to take a decision for which the politicians do not wish to take responsibility, or to allow time for one or more of the coalition partners to distance themselves from coalition policy positions as the election approaches.   VBB

catch-all party Term coined by the German-American political scientist Otto Kirchheimer (1905–1965) to characterize the increasing tendency of bourgeois parties of individual respresentation (see also CADRE PARTIES) and mass parties of integration (see MASS MEMBERSHIP PARTIES) to become parties which try to appeal to as many different groups of voters as possible. The major characteristics of the catch-all party were in his view:

(a) drastic reduction of the party's ideological baggage . . . ; (b) . . . strengthening of the top leadership groups; (c) downgrading of the role of the individual party member . . . ; (d) de-emphasis of the . . . specific social-class or denominational clientele, in favor of recruiting voters among the population at large; (e) securing access to a variety of interest groups.

Kirchheimer who had earlier analysed what he termed the tendency towards 'a waning of oppositions' gave as major examples of catch-all parties those in the United States, the German CDU (Christlich Demokratische Union) and SPD (Sozialdemokratische Partei Deutschlands) (at the period of the adoption of its new Bad Godesberg programme in 1959), the Austrian SPOe (Sozialistische Partei Österreichs) and the French UNR (Union pour la Nouvelle République). The notion of the catch-all party forms part of the end of ideology literature, as developed by Raymond ARON, Daniel Bell, Edward Shils and S. M. Lipset, although as a left-socialist Kirchheimer regretted the trends he analysed. In its emphasis on a market-orientation in party strategies the concept is also influenced by the so-called economic theories of democracy, as developed in his time in the writings of J. A. SCHUMPETER, and Anthony Downs' 'spatial analysis' of party systems.

See SPATIAL MODELS.   HD

Reading

Dittrich, K.: Testing the catch-all thesis: some difficulties and possibilities. In *Western European Party Systems: continuity and change*, pp. 257–66, ed. H. Daalder and P. Mair. Beverly Hills, Calif. and London: Sage, 1983.

Kirchheimer, O.: The transformation of the Western European party systems. In *Political Parties and Political Development*, pp. 177–200, ed. J. La Palombara and M. Weiner. Princeton, NJ: Princeton University Press, 1966; repr. in *Politics, Law and Social Change: selected essays of Otto Kirchheimer*, pp. 346–71, ed. F.S. Burin and K.L. Shell. New York and London: Columbia University Press, 1969.

Wolinetz, S.B.: The transformation of the European party system revisited. *West European Politics* 2 (1979) 4–28.

caucus Historically, a private meeting of a political party or factional group.

In England in 1868 the Liberal Party committee in Birmingham organized the party membership so as to win the greatest number of seats; and this committee was referred to as the Liberal 'caucus'. The term is not much used in Britain today except sometimes in an unfavourable sense to refer to party organizations in local government.

In the United States the word was originally coined in 1763. The caucus was a meeting limited to persons with a common characteristic, usually members of a political party from a locality, for the purpose of nominating the party's candidates in the general election. This method has been largely replaced by primary elections (see PRIMARY, DIRECT). The major exception is nominating presidential and vice-presidential candidates, which is still done by the major parties at national conventions. About 30 per cent of the delegates to these conventions represent states in which delegates are chosen by a complex process that begins with caucuses in precincts (neighbourhoods). These meetings, held on the same evening everywhere in a state, are open to all party members in the precinct. They choose delegates to a convention at the next level, usually the county. The county convention may pick delegates to a state convention, or there may be another level of meetings before the final state-wide gathering, where delegates to the national convention are chosen.

The precinct caucus is the crucial one, where the basic political alignment of the delegates is set. Attending such meetings is relatively demanding, hence they tend to be limited to people who are either committed to a candidate or mobilized by a strong local party organization, if there is one. The caucus-convention method therefore favours candidates with good organizations or intense activist supporters. Because few people other than party activists know when and where the precinct caucus is held, small numbers of party workers can, and do, pack the caucuses. Local caucuses thus favour the continued power of 'old-fashioned' political machines (see MACHINE).

There is another sort of caucus: not a meeting but a group in a legislature (or other political assembly) based on a characteristic shared by the group's members. The most important historical examples are the Democratic and Republican caucuses in the US Senate and House of Representatives. Composed of all the party's members in their respective chamber, the caucuses are the ultimate authorities of their parties in Congress. They assign members to committees and make decisions about various procedural and organizational matters. In contrast to the early days of this century, no party caucus now tries to instruct party members how to vote on pending legislation.

In the 1970s legislators began to form caucuses to express a variety of purposes. Some were based on legislators' characteristics (the Congressional Black Caucus); others on constituency characteristics (the New England Caucus); a third type gave expression to a point of view on an issue (the Military Reform Caucus). In 1986 there were 32 such groups in the House of Representatives and 17 in the Senate. Some of these caucuses were fairly informal; others charged dues, had paid staffs, held their own hearings, provided detailed information, mobilized support for particular legislative measures; in short, they performed some of the functions of formally established committees. The growth of these caucuses was one of the causes of the fragmentation of power in Congress.　　REW

Readings

Jones, C.O.: *The United States Congress*, ch. 9. Homewood, Ill.: Dorsey, 1982.

Ranney, A.: Candidate selection. In *Democracy at the Polls: a comparative study of competitive national elections*, ed. D. Butler, H.R. Penniman and A. Ranney. Washington, DC: American Enterprise Institute, 1981.

caudillo, caudillismo　　This term owes its origins to the chiefs of armed bands of the medieval period struggling against Muslim domination in the Iberian peninsula. During the nineteenth century, in Latin America, it came to designate leaders who held power by force during the period immediately following colonial domination. During the Spanish Civil War General Franco applied the term to himself, using it in a new sense which combined the medieval origins of the term with the German idea of the Führer. In fact, the term caudillo came to be almost synonymous with Führer or Duce, the titles of the leaders of the national socialist and fascist regimes, but it also had a catholic connotation in virtue of its association with the reconquest of Iberia from the Arabs.   GH

cell   See PRIMARY PARTY ORGANIZATION.

censorship   The practice of imposing restrictions on or suppressing the expression of information, opinions, ideas or the arts. The term is used particularly of, and sometimes reserved for, official systems of supervision where authorization is required before publication. Among the pretexts advanced for the practice have been the security of the state, the prevention of revolutionary or dangerous ideas, the protection of morals or religion, and the imposition of a conformity of views.

Censorship has been practised in many societies. Forms of it existed in ancient China and India, Israel and Greece, where the corrupting effects of Socrates' opinions on the young was one of the charges against him, which led to his execution. The term is derived from the Roman office of censor, a magistrate whose functions included the regulation of morals. After the fall of the Roman empire, the church of Rome, which controlled what education and culture survived in Europe, punished infractions when they occurred. The threat posed by the invention of printing engendered a more systematic response. The Inquisition under Pope Paul IV issued the first Index of Prohibited Books in 1559. That became the basis of an extensive system of restriction, in force until 1966.

In countries where the Reformation took hold, the controlling function was taken over by rulers and reformed churches. In England various methods were employed during the sixteenth and seventeenth centuries, including the granting of a printing monopoly to the Stationers' Company, the use of prerogative powers by the Star Chamber, and licensing systems provided for under legislation. Since 1695 books and journals have been free from legal restrictions before publication, although taxation and other methods were sometimes used as inhibitions. Legal consequences after publication remained possible in the form of prosecutions for seditious, obscene, blasphe-

mous or defamatory libels. The licensing of drama lasted from 1549 to 1968, and in the twentieth century legislation has provided for cinema licensing and the regulation of broadcasting.

Censorship was eloquently opposed by Spinoza, Milton and Locke, and movements for toleration and freedom developed in the seventeenth century and gained ground subsequently. Censorship is a denial of FREEDOM OF SPEECH, which came to be regarded as a fundamental civil liberty in democracies, though guarantees of freedom of speech have generally not been expressed or interpreted in absolute terms. Freedom of expression under the EUROPEAN CONVENTION ON HUMAN RIGHTS may be limited on such grounds as security and morality, and does not prevent the licensing of broadcasting or cinema enterprises. In the United States the FIRST AMENDMENT to the Constitution has been interpreted as generally prohibiting prior restraints on political or religious expression, but prior restraints on account of obscenity have been upheld. In democracies generally censorship designed to prevent corruption or offence has become the most prominent, although wider censorship is common in war time. Censorship is more prevalent in dictatorships, and was especially pervasive in the Soviet Union and other countries aspiring to communism, where disconformity was regarded as delaying that goal.   CRM

Reading

Craig, A.: *The Banned Books of England and other Countries*. London: Allen & Unwin, 1962.

Ernst, M.L. and Schwartz, A.U.: *Censorship: the search for the obscene*. New York: Macmillan, 1964.

O'Higgins, P.: *Censorship in Britain*. London: Nelson, 1972.

Wiggins, J.R.: *Freedom or Secrecy*. New York: Oxford University Press, 1964.

Central Committee (of the CPSU)
According to Soviet party rules, the Central Committee of the Communist Party of the Soviet Union is the highest authority in the party between congresses: party decisions are usually issued in its name. But by 1919 de

facto power had already switched to the newly-formed POLITBURO owing to the unwieldy size of the Central Committee, which has continued to grow to its current level – after the Twenty-Seventh Congress of 1986 – of 307 full and 170 candidate (nonvoting) members.

Membership of the Central Committee in general attaches to the most important positions in Soviet society, and indeed is to some extent a measure of the importance of an office in the eyes of the leadership. Members drawn from the cultural and scientific fields, and from the proletariat, form a small proportion of the total. The connection between offices and membership implies a certain rigidity in the selection process, but some scope for patronage remains. The party congress elects the Central Committee, invariably approving a slate presented by the Politburo. But analysis of the changing composition of the Central Committee suggests that within the Politburo the General Secretary has a disproportionately large share of the patronage involved.

The Central Committee convenes at least twice a year, but seldom much more than this, and its sessions are usually short (one or two days). Little is known of the substance of its meetings, stenographic reports having been available only during the later Khrushchev years. The influence of the Central Committee has sometimes been direct and decisive, as in the leadership crises of 1957 and 1964 (see ANTI-PARTY GROUP; GENERAL SECRETARY). Khrushchev's ouster is a reminder of the dangers to the General Secretary of ignoring Central Committee opinion, and to this extent a diffuse background influence is maintained. Moreover, external circumstances such as an international crisis may prompt increased use of the Central Committee plenum as a forum in which to canvass opinion about possibly competing policies.

The Secretariat of the Central Committee is a body of, currently, eleven members formally elected by the Central Committee but nominated by the Politburo. It is second in importance only to the Politburo itself, and secretaries who are also in the Politburo

('senior secretaries', as some western scholars call them) are the most influential men in Soviet politics. The Secretariat directs the work of the Central Committee apparatus, which is the permanent staff of the Central Committee, comprising over twenty departments of which most supervise a group of government ministries, the departments being further divided into sections. Some heads of department are Central Committee secretaries, but more commonly a secretary oversees several departments, whose heads are then subordinate officials.

The size of the apparatus is most convincingly estimated (by Hough) at about 1500 responsible officials, placing obvious limitations on the control which the departments can exercise over the much larger ministries, whatever the Constitution specifies about the supremacy of the party. Aside from supervision of ministries, the departments have two further responsibilities: selection of personnel for top administrative posts (the highest level of the NOMENKLATURA system by which the party controls public career advancement) and the gathering of information as part of the decision-making process within the top leadership organs.   SW

Reading

Avtorkhanov, A.: *The Communist Party Apparatus.* Chicago, Ill.: Regnery, 1966.

Hill, R.J. and Frank, P.: *The Soviet Communist Party.* 3rd edn. London: Allen & Unwin, 1986.

Hough, J.F. and Fainsod, M.: *How the Soviet Union is Governed.* Cambridge, Mass. and London: Harvard University Press, 1979.

Schapiro, L.: The General Department of the CC of the CPSU. *Survey* 21 (1975) 53–65.

central/local relations Structural and dynamic relationships between centre and periphery, between the whole and its parts, exist in any and every organization. Some manifestations of central/local relations have been on the grand scale (for example the Great Wall of China or Caesar crossing the Rubicon) but this discussion restricts itself primarily to relations between unitary states and the province-states of federal polities on the one hand and their political and administrative subdivisions on the other. Even this relatively limited field is affected by many multi-dimensional factors: geography, history, demography, economics, and even mythology are among the disciplines that bear on the subject as much as political or administrative science. Several key variables can be identified.

(1) The scope and variety of functions administered respectively by the centre, by the localities, and by specialized agencies;
(2) The number and size of different local units and their relationships with one another horizontally and vertically;
(3) Their personnel: whether locally or centrally recruited or controlled; whether hereditary, appointed, or elected directly or indirectly by proportional or plurality systems;
(4) Their relative shares of public revenues: whether large or small and more or less elastic, and their powers to increase or decrease these, or their expenditures, recurrent or capital;
(5) The constitutional status and popular image of the various actors, and the extent and nature of the pressures that any one of them can bring to bear on another;
(6) The political, economic, administrative and other controls over local units available to the centre or its agents;
(7) Macro-economics and micro-economics, both ephemeral and long-term.

Yet another variable is the nature of the central/local interface itself – an interface that in every polity is likely to change with the point at issue, whether legal, financial, administrative, or political. In some systems of governance there is a fulcrum in the form of a person or body relating directly both to centre and to locality: the French *maire*, for instance, popularly elected as municipal chief executive but thereby becoming the local representative of the state; or the combination of locally elected councillors and centrally appointed field officials forming district committees in socialist countries of eastern Europe and in many former colonial territories. Some central ministries or departments are of particular significance in relations with local bodies – those responsible for law and order, for finance, and for general local co-ordination:

but these functions may be combined or dispersed at central level, or administered through local field agents. The local authorities, too, may articulate their approach to the centre in many ways: as individual units, through political power brokers or through one or more representative, and sometimes competitive, associations. All these actors can have greater or less degrees of autonomy in DECISION MAKING.

Furthermore, very few of these factors are ever static, so that it is highly misleading to think of central/local relations as a simple confrontational dichotomy: on the contrary, the central and the local polities in all countries interpenetrate and are mutually supportive on a continuum comprising many strands. To isolate and examine any one strand of that continuum in one country at any particular time, and on that basis to make comparisons with any other country – or even with that same country at a different time – is perilous, even if satisfactory common criteria for measurement can be identified. Despite this, in country after country policies for central/local relations are determined by studies of this sort which ignore fundamental issues – such as, notoriously, finance. A few illustrations may serve to demonstrate the futility of drawing conclusions from isolated factors. First, local authorities in the Netherlands raise a far smaller proportion of their revenue for themselves or in their localities than any of their neighbours, yet they enjoy conspicuously more 'autonomy' and directly administer many more services than local authorities in Belgium, England, or France. Second, it is at least doubtful whether local authorities are freer to act in countries like Czechoslovakia or Portugal or states like South Carolina or Queensland which grant constitutionally based discretionary authority to their local governments, than are their equivalents in the United Kingdom or North Carolina or New South Wales which do not. Third, it has been argued that 'local self-government' is impossible in any state in which the localities are subject to the doctrine of *ultra vires* (or 'Dillon's rule'); nevertheless, 'local home rule', through the devolution of discretionary powers, can give far more real autonomy than exists where local bodies enjoy 'general competence' yet are denied adequate finance, or are subject under the Napoleonic system of *tutelle* (see TUTELAGE) to intrusive central review of the minutiae of local decision making.

Advantages and disadvantages of CENTRALIZATION AND DECENTRALIZATION are discussed elsewhere. Broadly speaking there are two fundamentally contrasting attitudes to dispersed authority within the state, and these colour all central/local relations. They can be termed the partnership and the agency models and they predominate in countries with contrasting historical origins.

The partnership model
In those countries that were formed initially by the coming together of autonomous small communities for mutual help and support (for example Switzerland, the Netherlands, Yugoslavia, the New England states) LOCAL GOVERNMENT continues to be understood as essentially the organic self-expression of the community – that is to say, machinery allowing the local citizens of each settlement in the nation to provide necessary services for themselves. Only when an essential service is proved incontrovertibly to exceed the total capacities of the local community is power to provide that service grudgingly conceded to a more remote level of government.

Such a philosophy requires each local authority to be small enough for every citizen to be able to identify with it. In a populous country this means a very large number of local units – over 3000 municipalities in Switzerland, for example, and over 80,000 local bodies elected for general or special purposes in the USA. For central/local relations to be manageable in such circumstances mechanisms must be devised for access and co-ordination: either more or less voluntary joint bodies for groups of small authorities, or one or more intermediate tiers of government – directly elected like Belgium's provinces or Italy's regions, indirectly elected like Yugoslavia's urban and regional communities, or else field units of central government, like the *Bezirksregierungen* of several West German states.

In these 'community-based' countries public revenues, whether centrally or locally raised, are always seen to be the property of the citizenry as a whole. The allocation of these resources between the partners at centre and periphery and among the different local units generates heated controversy, but there is no supposition that either central or local governments have any exclusive rights over income directly raised by them, nor that transfers by one level to another are in the nature of charitable donations or 'grants'. In these countries the distribution of public resources is normally determined statutorily by the legislature, leaving the central executive little scope for discriminatory treatment of local authorities. In Holland, for example, parliament decides what proportion of the national tax revenues shall be assigned directly to local government, and a committee dominated by local government representatives approves the principles whereby this 'municipal fund' shall be distributed among the different municipalities. If individual central departments then wish to use local authorities as agents to implement specific policies they must provide further funds as specific grants from their own quotas of the national budget, but these allocations do not affect the local bodies' entitlement to their share of the general revenue. In the German Federal Republic these principles are re-emphasized by the fact that the local authorities, too, transfer a proportion of their own local tax income to their partners at state level.

Protagonists claim that in such countries the local/central partnership is least adversarial, the local councillors and staff enjoy high prestige in the community, and voluntary participation in public affairs is most assiduous, with the consequence that among these polities may be found most of the strongest economies and highest standards of living in the world.

The agency model
The majority of countries, however, were not formed historically by a voluntary drawing together of autonomous local communities; rather, they were dominated directly or in-

directly by powerful monarchies such as England, France, Russia, Spain, or Turkey. Practically all third world countries fall into this group, since they were subjected to domination by one or other colonial power, or had monarchies of their own sufficiently strong to resist such domination (for example Thailand, Ethiopia). In all these countries local government is looked upon primarily as a subordinate agent – no more than one of several convenient mechanisms whereby the paternalist central state can ensure the provision of decentralized services for its citizens. Local government here has little more than a residual function: most nationally important services are provided by the centre, either directly through FIELD SERVICE ADMINISTRATION, or through specialist agencies, or perhaps using local government bodies for such services as education or trunk roads, but simply as agents under strict central control.

These attitudes are sustained by the bureaucracy of the central public service; even where the civil servants are professedly apolitical they tend to be at one in adhering to the prerogative of central government, whatever its political colouring, to rule without undue concern for local democracy.

Advocates of this school argue that local government cannot be local self-government by the community: it is simply the administration of governmental functions at the local level, and its objective is service provision rather than local representation. The state, it is claimed, is the guardian of efficiency and effectiveness, and it alone can ensure high and equitable standards of social and economic services, while preserving citizens from the wastefulness of myopic local maladministration. Degrees of central intervention can vary greatly: even within the same ministry, as Griffith points out, the administration may approach the local authorities in a continuum ranging from *laissez-faire* through regulatory to promotional policies. However, the underlying preconceptions effectively emasculate political decentralization, whether it be France's *déparisination* or Tanzania's *ujamaa*.

In all these countries the centre's tech-nocratic pursuit of economies of scale is reinforced by bureaucratic desire for manageable spans of control. In consequence reforms in many countries from the United Kingdom to Bulgaria have drastically reduced the number of local authorities, while formerly monolithic countries such as France and Spain have been cautious to ensure that real power be devolved to only a limited number of large units. Some of these 'local' authorities are as large as NATION-STATES, so that on the one hand they can pose formidable political challenges to the centre while on the other they tend to be remote from the local citizenry they purport to serve.

It is a lamentable fact that almost everywhere both central and local levels of government are wont to use the other as a political scapegoat. Nevertheless, 'it is not local government *versus* central government but the two working together, recognizing their interdependence, which will produce the greatest results' (Maddick, p. 197). Several countries have established a standing advisory council on inter-governmental relations, such as exist in Australia, India, and in the USA and many of its constituent states. An optimal balance between the partnership and the agency approach tends to be seldom and fleetingly achieved: perhaps the Swiss and the Nordic countries can boast that in recent times they have held closest to that ideal.

See also FEDERALISM; LOCAL GOVERNMENT FINANCE; LOCAL GOVERNMENT REORGANIZATION; LOCAL POLITICS; PREFECT.   HJBA

Reading

Davey, K.J.: *Financing Regional Government: International practices and their relevance to the third world.* Chichester: Wiley, 1983.

Griffith, J.A.G.: *Central Departments and Local Authorities.* London: Allen & Unwin, 1966.

Hill, D.M.: *Democratic Theory and Local Government.* London and Boston, Mass.: Allen & Unwin, 1974.

Jones, G.W. ed.: *New Approaches to the Study of Central-Local Government Relations.* Farnborough: Gower/SSRC, 1980.

Jones, M.A.: *Local Government and the People.* West Melbourne: Hargreen, 1981.

Leemans, A.F.: *Changing Patterns of Local Government*. The Hague: IULA, 1970.

Maddick, H.: *Democracy, Decentralization and Development*. New York: Asia Publishing House, 1963.

Rhodes, R.A.W.: *Control and Power in Central-Local Government Relations*. Farnborough: Gower/SSRC, 1981.

Smith, B.C.: *Decentralization: the territorial dimension of the state*. London: Allen & Unwin, 1985.

Zimmermann, J.F.: *State–Local Relations: a partnership approach*. New York: Praeger, 1983.

centralization and decentralization

Alternative characterizations of a process, condition, or trend in the distribution of power between government and the private sector, between the governments of large and of component geographic areas, or among a single government's administrative levels.

Decentralization in relation to the private sector exists when the governmental sector performs a minimal role in society. Centralization exists when that sector extensively regulates and financially supports individuals and private enterprises, operates major business-type enterprises, and spends a large share of the gross domestic product (GDP). By this last criterion, selected western democracies ranged as follows, in 1984: Sweden (64 per cent), Denmark (61 per cent), Italy (57 per cent), Belgium (55 per cent), France (53 per cent), Norway (49 per cent), Germany, the United Kingdom, and Canada (48 per cent), and the United States (38 per cent) – (figures from OECD 1986).

Within the governmental sector as a whole centralization and decentralization refer to the vertical distribution of power among governments, which is to say among large governmental areas and those of smaller compass. Such distribution is constitutionally inherent in FEDERALISM and is a practical feature of INTERGOVERNMENTAL RELATIONS. In the United States constitutional interpretations by the Supreme Court vest the national government with broad discretion in matters of centralization and decentralization, a discretion scarcely distinguishable from that of the British Parliament in relation to LOCAL GOVERNMENTS. In practice, American state governments retain a large range of functions, though many are partly financed by a conditional federal GRANT IN AID. National centralization reflects increased nationalization of a society and greater valuation of the national governments' power to remedy geographically based social and economic inequalities. Costly externalities of local and intermediate governments' autonomy, if not corrected by expansion of boundaries, invite transfer of authority to higher governmental levels having broader geographical jurisdictions. Countering such centralizing tendencies is an ideology that identifies decentralization with individual liberty, a pluralistic society, grass-roots democracy, and local self-government. Such an ideology is reinforced in nations with geographically concentrated ethnic minorities that seek DEVOLUTION. In contrast, centralization lacks a supportive ideology, though national integration requires some degree of centralization, and decentralization enhances the role of subnational governments that may themselves centralize power.

Within any single government the terms refer to two overlapping patterns. One is the vertical distribution of authority within the executive branch's central hierarchy at the capital (or city hall). The other is the distribution of authority between the executive branch's headquarters and its field-administration outposts.

At the capital, decentralization is most feasible in an organizational structure that groups together such programmes as are interrelated, such sets of programmes being distinct from those of parallel organizations. Centralization trends in the twentieth century have reflected the erosion of this condition as governmental activities multiplied, their web of interrelations became complex, and their grouping in self-contained organizations proved unachievable. Power has moved upward to presidents' and prime ministers' offices as problems no longer fit within individual departments and ministries. However, bureaux that have a network of supportive clienteles, professions, and legislators often preserve substantial autonomy.

CENTRALIZATION AND DECENTRALIZATION

Decentralization to a government's FIELD SERVICE ADMINISTRATION operates through variants of two pure-form models. In the *prefectoral* model the government prescribes a single set of geographical districts and delegates authority in each to a generalist field agent (for example, a PREFECT) to whom all district field agents of the government's departments are subordinated. In the *functional* model each bureau establishes its own field-administration districts, each district director reports directly to his or her bureau's headquarters, and the bureau determines the degree of decentralization appropriate to the function. Between these pure types is a set of departmental field services in which each department mimics the prefectoral model by prescribing uniform geographical districts, each headed by a district director to whom field agents of the department's bureaux are subordinated. In practice both the prefectoral model and its departmental variation are vulnerable to fragmentation by functionally specialized units. These units resist decentralization if power lodges in generalist district directors rather than in the units' professional counterparts in the field.

In most countries the distribution of power varies in different sectors of the society, polity, or government. Formal governmental decentralization may be countered by centralization within political parties or, as in the United States, vice versa. Formal administrative centralization may be tempered by clientele referenda and local advisory committees whose judgements are ignored at peril. Formal administrative decentralization may disguise staff members' conformity to agency-favoured values, which are instilled by professional training, recruitment policies, in-service training, and socialization to the agency's culture.

No term exists for the continuum between the poles of centralization and decentralization or for the middle range where the tendencies are roughly in balance. No overall measure exists for specifying the degrees of centralization and decentralization at different times in one country or for comparing several countries at one time. France and England have traditionally been regarded as centralized and decentralized respectively. Recent scholars have reversed this characterization. Measurement of the shift of power to national governments commonly neglects the simultaneous, and sometimes greater, expansion of the scope and intensity of subnational governments' activities.

The absence of comprehensive measurement, however, does not preclude reasonable judgement of the tendency of specific actions and proposals. Denationalization or deregulation of an industry decentralizes power within the society unless the private industry is monopolistic. The abandoning of welfare programmes by higher-level governments decentralizes responsibility to other governments, to charitable organizations, or to the poor.

See also CENTRAL/LOCAL RELATIONS; LOCAL POLITICS.   JWF

Reading

Ashford, D.E.: *British Dogmatism and French Pragmatism: central–local policymaking in the welfare state*. London, Boston, Mass. and Sydney: Allen & Unwin, 1982.

Fesler, J.W.: *Area and Administration*. Alabama: University of Alabama Press, 1949, 1964.

Fried, R.C.: *The Italian Prefects: a study in administrative politics*. New Haven, Conn. and London: Yale University Press, 1963.

Jacob, H.: *German Administration since Bismarck: central authority versus local autonomy*. New Haven, Conn. and London: Yale University Press, 1963.

Kaufman, H.: *The Forest Ranger: a study in administrative behavior*. Baltimore, Md.: The Johns Hopkins University Press, 1960.

Mudd, J.: *Neighborhood Services: making big cities work*. New Haven, Conn. and London: Yale University Press, 1984.

Organization for Economic Cooperation and Development.: *Economic Outlook* 39 (May 1986), Table R. 8 at p. 81.

Sharpe, L.J. ed.: *Decentralist Trends in Western Democracies*. London and Beverly Hills, Calif.: Sage, 1979.

Smith, B.C.: *Decentralization: the territorial dimension of the state*. London, Boston, Mass. and Sydney: Allen & Unwin, 1985.

Tarrow, S., Katzenstein P.J., and Graziano, L. eds: *Territorial Politics in Industrial Nations*. New York and London: Praeger, 1978.

United States Advisory Commission on Inter-governmental Relations: *Reports*. Washington, DC: US Advisory Commission on Intergovernmental Relations.

centre party Term widely used in the description of multi-party systems to indicate a party located in a party space with other parties on either side. The label was adopted by German Roman Catholics who formed the *Zentrum* in the nineteenth century, and is frequently identified with Christian demo-cratic parties generally. But the label centre party has also been consciously adopted by other parties attempting to expand their electoral following (for example, former AGRARIAN PARTIES in Scandinavia, some new parties in the re-emerging democracies of Southern Europe, and as a euphemism by clearly rightist parties in other political systems).

In political science, the major authors who have occupied themselves with the notion of a centre and centre parties in multi-party systems are Maurice Duverger, Anthony Downs and Giovanni Sartori. Duverger regarded centre parties in the French Fourth Republic as part of the *marais éternel* which caused unstable cabinets and prevented clear choices in politics and policy. Downs and Sartori tend to share Duverger's view that two-party systems (or systems of moderate pluralism which operate in a two-bloc fashion) are likely to encourage a movement of parties to a moderate centre. If the centre is occupied by one or more parties, according to Sartori, as in systems of POLARIZED PLURALISM, centrifugal competition is likely to result in a strengthening of extremist parties and a growing ideological polarization.

On closer inspection the terms centre, and centre parties, mean rather different things, depending on assumptions of uni-dimensionality or multi-dimensionality of cleavage systems. The term is also used in rather different metaphors (for example, average or median positions of a group of persons arranged on some scale pro or contra a given decision, or some policy preference; centripetal versus centrifugal movements; a

balancing of scales; equilibrium of different social groups; a person or party which may give a majority to one side or another, etc.). Although the term is usually associated with forces of moderation, it can also stand for avoidance of choices and decisions. Given the lack of clarity in both normative and empirical assumptions, the analytical use of the term centre party is inevitably limited.

See also POLITICAL CLEAVAGES.   HD

Reading

Daalder, H.: In search of the center in European party systems. *American Political Science Review* 78 (1984) 92–109.

Sartori, G.: *Parties and Party Systems: a framework for analysis*. New York and Cambridge: Cambridge University Press, 1976.

centre/periphery analysis Twin con-cepts that denote the geographical element of social differentiation and POLITICAL CLEAVAGES. They refer to the territorial sources of political groupings whose concerns may also be economic and/or cultural. They therefore relate to the degree of both geo-graphical and social remoteness from the mainstream of society, and can refer to both territory and social groups. The concepts are difficult to apply in empirical analysis because centres and peripheries may vary considerably in their nature from country to country. The dichotomy refers to the total relationship of all areas within a country. These relationships could take at least nine alternative forms, as a country could have nil, one, or more than one centre, and nil, one, or more than one periphery. Most usefully the concepts have been applied within the context of state and NATION BUILDING, where they are taken to be two elements in a spatial archetype in which the periphery is subordinate to the authority of the centre. Within the archetype the centre represents the seat of authority, the periphery those geographical locations at the furthest distance from the centre, but still within the territory controlled by the latter.

Centres are a form of temporal imperialism. They are privileged locations within a territory where the holders of key political, economic and cultural resources tend to congregate in institutions for decision making. A high concentration of the three kinds of resources in one small area indicates a monocephalic territorial structure. By contrast, a marked geographical dispersion of the different types of decision-making institutions across several locations indicates a polycephalic structure: a pattern of spatial segmentation of different types of resource-holders and a chain of distinctive centres, each with its own profile of elite groups. Centres can also be identified by seeing what people do: how they make their living, and the networks of · co-operative activity in which they participate. In terms of human activity, a centre as part of a spatial system of authority and subordination is that location within a territorial system which possesses the largest concentration of people with the ability to tell others what to do. The centre possesses a decisive voice in the processing and communication of information and instructions over long distances. The key concepts for centre structures are the endowment of resources, distances, and channels of communication: a centre holds the bulk of the transactions among the holders of resources across a territory; it tends to be close to the resource-rich areas within the territory; it dominates the communication flow, typically through the territorial diffusion of a standard language and through its control of a set of institutions for consultation and direction.

Peripheries control at best only their own resources, tend to be isolated from other regions, and contribute little to the total communication flow within their territory. A periphery is dependent upon one or more centres, with little control over its own fate. It tends to be culturally distinctive with at least some minimal sense of a separate identity, usually expressed in terms of a different language and/or religion, but with minimal resources for the defence of its distinctiveness. It is often a conquered or annexed territory, administered by officials whose loyalty is to the centre, and who are responsive less to the desires of the periphery than to instructions from a remote centre. A periphery is located at some distance from the dominant centre, and its transactions with the latter are fraught with

costs and disadvantages. Typically it will have a poorly developed economy, or one that is dependent upon a single commodity that makes it an easy victim of fluctuations in demand and prices over which it has little or no control. Peripherality can exist in three distinctive domains of public life: in politics, economics and culture. Whatever the domain, the periphery depends upon one or more centres, and its situation cannot be understood apart from the latter. Distance is crucial for dependence. Distance structures territorial economies. It affects and can set limits to state-building: the longer the distance between centre and periphery, the greater the costs of controlling the latter. Similarly, the greater the cultural (for example language) distance, the greater the likelihood of distortion in and barriers against the communication flow.

In the three territorial dimensions – politics, economics, culture – of state and nation building the centre/periphery relationship is reciprocal. Peripheral boundaries are easily penetrated by at least some agencies of the central authorities. The kind and degree of penetration affects the structure of both the periphery and the state. Analyses of the centre periphery relationship should therefore look at three types of transactions across boundaries: economic (import/export of goods, services, labour, investments, credits, subsidies); cultural (messages, norms, life styles, ideologies, myths, rituals); political (wars, invasions, elite alliances). While these types of transaction constitute the major dimension of centre/periphery relationships, the three subsets do not necessarily form a single cluster. An annexed periphery may escape economic dependence on the political (for example Catalonia, the Basque lands). Cultural standardization may not be an inevitable consequence of political penetration (for example Wales). Processes of centralization and boundary penetration are however continuous and interactive: for example, peripheries that are becoming more economically dependent may find it more difficult to maintain their previous level of cultural distinctiveness.

Analysis of centre/periphery relationships

also forms an important part of the theory of the generation of European PARTY SYSTEMS, put forward by S. M. Lipset and Stein ROKKAN. They regarded the relationships of conflict or compromise formed during the period of nation-building between centre and periphery as one of the three factors explaining differences between European party systems. In addition, they used the centre/periphery dichotomy to explain the existence of parties of territorial defence in certain European countries.

However, components of the centre/periphery relationships enter into a variety of configurations, and should be analysed developmentally. For each case we must ask questions about the strength and distinctiveness of the boundaries between periphery and centre: how dependent upon the centre is each aspect of periphery life; which sectors and groups offer the most persistent resistance to the removal of boundaries and further territorial integration? Furthermore, a state cannot be studied in isolation. Each centre/periphery relationship must also be considered in a broader geopolitical, geoeconomic and geocultural perspective. Only in that way can the comparative distinctiveness of any periphery be assessed. Peripherality has to be measured in terms of distances from alternative territorial centres outside the state, the proximity to and degree of dependence upon major international trade networks, and the degree of cultural distinctiveness within the overall cross-national map of cultural groupings. While there are many examples of single country case studies of centre/periphery relationships, broader comparative exercises have been restricted to Europe where processes of state and nation building have been extremely complex.

See also TERRITORIAL POLITICS.   DWU

Reading

Gottmann, J.: The evolution of the concept of territory. *Social Science Information* 14 (1975) 29–47.

Innis, H.: *The Bias of Communication*. Toronto: University of Toronto Press, 1951.

Lipset, S.M. and Rokkan, S.: The Introduction of *Party Systems and Voter Alignments: cross-national perspectives*. London: Collier-Macmillan; New York: Free Press, 1967.

Mény, Y. and Wright, V. eds: *Centre/Periphery Relations in Western Europe*. London: Allen & Unwin, 1986.

Rokkan, S. and Urwin, D.W.: *Economy, Territory, Identity: politics of West European peripheries*. London: Sage, 1983.

——: *The Politics of Territorial Identity: studies in European regionalism*. London: Sage, 1982.

Rose, R. and Urwin, D.W.: *Territorial Differentiation and Political Unity in Western Nations*. Beverly Hills, Calif. and London: Sage, 1975.

Tarrow, S.: *Between Center and Periphery: grassroots politicians in Italy and France*. New Haven, Conn.: Yale University Press, 1977.

charisma This New Testament term (literally 'gift of grace') was popularized as a political concept by Max WEBER who defined charismatic authority as a form of authority which derived from the extraordinary qualities of an individual rather than from the occupation of an established office or post. It was an exceptional form of authority claimed by leaders of revolutionary and other social movements and acknowledged by their followers, which was often associated with periods of social distress or upheaval. By its nature anti-institutional, this authority would always experience acute problems of consolidation and perpetuation, unless the leader's charisma could be 'routinized' through the establishment of an elective office or hereditary line of succession. Since Weber's time the term 'charismatic' has come to be used of any figure enjoying exceptional popular authority, even where the basis of this authority is the occupation of a recognized office such as a premiership or presidency. Since such popular authority can be acquired by the exercise of fairly mundane political skills and by the manipulation of a leader's image, the use of the term 'charisma' to indicate extraordinary personal qualities has become largely arbitrary and subjective. For this reason it belongs more to the realm of personal adulation than to the academic study of politics.   DB

Reading

Weber, M.: Charismatic authority. In *Economy and Society: an outline of interpretive sociology*, pp. 241–70, 1111–57. 3 vols. ed. G. Roth and C. Wittich. New York: Bedminster, 1968.

charter A written instrument through which the state or other supreme authority grants certain privileges. In Britain, a formal document issued under royal prerogative power used for the creation and regulation of privileged bodies corporate such as, for example, municipal boroughs until 1835, universities, medieval guilds (including the great London livery companies), 'regulated companies' such as the Merchant Adventurers, 'chartered companies' such as the Russia Company 1555, Levant Company 1581, the Bank of England 1694, and the British Broadcasting Corporation 1927: a PUBLIC CORPORATION acting as Trustee for the national interest.

These charters constituted delegations of power and grants of a degree of autonomy to the recipients as for instance to the founders of the thirteen American colonies in the seventeenth century, whether companies or proprietors. Often they conferred monopoly privileges for the purpose of promoting British commerce, accompanied in the case of the East India Company (1600) and the Hudson's Bay Company (1670), both chartered joint-stock companies, by the power to acquire territory and to govern it. His Majesty's Government deprived the East India Company of its commercial powers in 1833 but did not annex its territories until 1858. The Royal Niger Company (1886) and the British East Africa Company (1888) had to be relieved of their unprofitable governmental responsibilities as early as 1900 and 1895 respectively, and the British South Africa Company (1888) was allowed similarly to bail out of Rhodesia in 1923.

When the editor of Stubbs's *Charters* claimed that 'the whole of the constitutional history of England is a commentary on the Charter', he was of course referring to Magna Carta, dated 15 June 1215, a charter of liberties 'which the barons seek and the lord king grants'. Taken out of its feudal context it was glorified in the seventeenth century by the opponents of 'royal tyranny'. When aggrieved radical working men sought political democracy, they petitioned parliament three times between 1839 and 1848 to enact their six-point 'People's Charter' and were proud to be dubbed Chartists. A paper signed by Churchill and Roosevelt in August 1941 became known as the Atlantic Charter. The Moscow Declaration of 1 January 1942 made adherence to its 'purposes and principles' the test for membership of the UNITED NATIONS whose written constitution, signed at San Francisco on 26 June 1945, is now called 'the Charter'.   DGS

checks and balances Two major theories of limited government have been influential in the development of western constitutional thought: MIXED GOVERNMENT and the SEPARATION OF POWERS. Both of these ideas are however rather abstract, without much empirical basis in the actual working of political institutions. The theory of mixed government relies upon balancing the power of different sections or classes in society: monarchy, aristocracy and democracy. The doctrine of the separation of powers relies upon a functional distribution of authority between three branches of government: the legislature, the executive and the judiciary. The idea of checks and balances within a political system is a much more practical concept, and one which grew out of the eighteenth-century constitution in Britain to become the mechanism by which the Constitution of the United States prevented the excessive exercise of power by those who controlled one or other of its branches.

PLATO and ARISTOTLE developed the view that the most effective way of controlling the power of one class of society was to check it by setting up a 'mixed' CONSTITUTION in which the differing sections of the community each had control over one of its parts, and this idea was taken up in medieval Europe and in the seventeenth and eighteenth centuries became the basis of the British 'balanced constitution'. In Britain however the equilibrium between the parts of the system of government was maintained, not simply by juxtaposing them, but by giving to each branch a means of influencing or controlling the others. This theory of checks and balances was set forth very clearly by Charles I in 1642 in his *Answer to the Nineteen Propositions*. The three ESTATES of the realm, King, Lords and Commons, shared the exercise of the legislative power, but each also had independent powers with which to check the others. The king made treaties, chose the officers of state and the judges, created peers, raised armies and granted pardons. The House of Lords exercised the final judicial power, and the Commons raised taxes and had the power of impeachment. In this way each estate could ensure that neither of the others could destroy the balance of the constitution. After 1689 this became the established theory of the constitution and was elaborated by Bolingbroke, MONTESQUIEU and Blackstone.

It was also received enthusiastically in the British colonies in America until in the 1760s and 1770s their desire to rid themselves of the irritating constraints of imperial rule made the 'matchless constitution' seem unbearable. As a result, in the revolutionary fervour leading up to 1776 all those aspects of the balanced constitution associated with monarchy and aristocracy were rejected, and the early constitutions of the newly established States reflected this reliance upon the almost unrestrained exercise of power by representative legislatures. The state legislatures and their committees soon showed that they were capable of tyrannies as great as those of George III, and in the words of James MADISON, 'The legislative department is everywhere extending the sphere of its activity, and drawing all power into its impetuous vortex'. By the time the constitutional convention met in Philadelphia in 1787 the need to place limits upon the power of legislatures as well as upon kings and governors was well recognized. Simply to erect 'parchment barriers' to the exercise of power was not enough, Madison wrote. Experience had taught 'that it is necessary to introduce such a balance of powers and interests, as will guarantee the provisions on paper'. In addition to balancing the powers of the federal government by those of the states, the Constitution gave to the president a power to veto legislation, subject to the overriding power of two-thirds of both Houses of Congress, and the power to nominate justices of the Supreme Court and other high officials; the Senate was given the power to ratify treaties and to confirm appointments to the Supreme Court and to senior offices in the administration; the House of Representatives was given the power to impeach the president and other officials for trial by the Senate, and the exclusive right to initiate financial bills; the Supreme Court was given the power, by implication and according to the clear intention of a number of the Founding Fathers, to invalidate acts of the legislature, as well as of the president and his or her administration, which were in conflict with the Constitution. In this way many of the elements of the pre-revolutionary checks and balances of the British constitution were reimported into the newly established Constitution of the United States.   MJCV

Reading

Bailyn, B.: *The Origins of American Politics*. New York: Vintage Books, 1970.

Hamilton, A., Madison, J. and Jay, J.: *The Federalist Papers*, ed. C. Rossiter. New York: Mentor, 1964.

Robbins, C.A.: *The Eighteenth-Century Commonwealth Man*. Cambridge, Mass.: Harvard University Press, 1959.

Vile, M.J.C.: *Constitutionalism and the Separation of Powers*. Oxford: Oxford University Press, 1967.

Christian Democracy   A major political force in most west European, and a few Latin American countries since 1945. Christian Democracy arose in the nineteenth century as a counter to individualism and sought to combat *laissez-faire* as well as ANTI-CLERICALISM. It encouraged the growth of Christian trade union organizations and these remain important in Belgium, Italy and the Netherlands. It combines Catholic views on social and economic justice (although not all Christian Democratic parties draw their membership exclusively from Catholics) with liberal views on political democracy. It cannot be categorized simply as 'of the right' or 'of the left'. Christian Democracy is 'conservative' in so far as it defends traditional values – notably those of the Church and family. It is 'progressive' in so far as it supports economic interventionism and significant social welfare programmes. It is distinctive in the strength of its commitment to class reconciliation and transnational co-operation. Just as the movement is difficult to categorize, so the typology of the Christian Democratic parties varies considerably. Those Christian Democratic parties which absorbed conservative parties – as has been the case in West Germany, Austria and Chile – are now themselves essentially conservative. In contrast, those parties which still compete with conservative parties, e.g. those of Italy, the Netherlands, France and Venezuela – are essentially centrist in orientation.

Latin American Christian Democracy may be dealt with fairly summarily. Like the European movement, it is essentially a post-war phenomenon. Unlike traditional South American parties, the Christian Democratic parties are inter-class organizations committed to political democracy and social and economic justice. Despite high hopes in the immediate post-war period and the setting up of the Organization of Christian Democrats of America, only the Chilean Partida Democrata Christiano (PDC) and the Venezuelan Comitado Organizado pro Elecciones Independientes (COPEI) have been politically important.

In Western Europe Christian Democracy may be said to have gone through three phases since 1945 – emergence in strength during the decade after the war; decline during the 1960s and early 1970s; and revival during the late 1970s and early 1980s.

The rapid and powerful emergence of Christian Democracy after 1945 was not surprising. The extreme right was discredited by FASCISM and the extreme left by STALINISM. The traditional bourgeois parties were also unpopular, partly on account of their *attentiste* attitude to fascism, but principally because of their association with *laissez-faire* capitalism. The Christian Democrats, in contrast, could not be blamed for the political, social and economic bankruptcy of the inter-war years. They had a respectable record of resistance to fascism. They promised a new style of politics, based on participation, co-operation (at home and abroad), and traditional moral values. This vague but comforting platform was ideally suited to filling the post-war political vacuum, and the Christian Democratic parties received a further boost as the Cold War developed, for they were seen as the main bulwark against communism. By the early 1950s, the Christian Democratic parties of Italy, Germany, Belgium, the Netherlands, and Austria, were all polling over 40 per cent and constituted the sole or major element in their respective national governments. In France the Christian Democratic party constituted the fulcrum of a series of centrist governments in the Fourth Republic (1946–58). Meanwhile, as the nations of western Europe began to co-operate more closely, the chief advocates of European integration were all Christian Democrats: Konrad Adenauer, chancellor of Germany; Alcide de Gasperi, prime minister of Italy; and Robert Schuman, foreign minister of France.

The second phase in the history of post-war Christian Democracy – the period of relative decline – occurred during the late 1960s and early 1970s. As communism became less threatening and detente became a key theme in East–West relations, many conservatives, who had taken shelter under the Christian Democratic umbrella at the height of the Cold War, returned to their own parties (especially true of France, and to a lesser extent of Italy, Belgium and the Netherlands). At the same time Socialist parties tended to become more centrist, less doctrinaire and less anticlerical; as they began to appeal directly to liberally minded Catholics in the 1960s and 1970s there was clear evidence that the progressive and trade union wings of the Christian Democratic parties were being undermined by the Socialists (especially true of Germany and the Netherlands). In addition, growing secularization and 'deconfessionalization', unwittingly assisted by the Second Vatican Council, undermined the Christian Democratic parties and their support organizations further. Finally, many young voters in the late 1960s and early 1970s expressed a desire for more clear-cut 'ideological' politics, i.e. they wanted parties to state their objectives clearly and implement them when in power. They considered the Christian Democratic parties to be far too pragmatic.

There was in consequence a strong electoral reaction against Christian Democracy: the German Christian Democrats were ousted from power by the Socialist–Liberal coalition in 1969, and in 1972 the Social Democrats outpolled the Christian Democrats for the first time (the latter still received over 40 per cent of the votes cast); the Belgian Christian Democrats lost a third of their electorate between 1958 and 1971 (dropping from 45 per cent to 30 per cent); the Dutch Christian Democrats fell back from 50 per cent to 30 per cent between 1963 and 1972; meanwhile, in Italy the gap between the Christian Democrats and Communists was narrowing, although between a third and two-fifths of the electorate still voted for the Christian Democrats.

However, the decline of the Christian Democrats levelled out in the mid-1970s. By the mid 1980s, the Christian Democrats were the leading party of government in Germany (nearly 50 per cent of the poll in 1983), Italy (33 per cent in 1983), Belgium (30 per cent in 1985), the Netherlands (30 per cent in 1982) and Luxemburg (35 per cent in 1984), while in Austria with 43 per cent in 1983 they were the leading party of opposition. At the European Parliament elections of 1984 the Christian Democrats polled more votes than any other group (31 million to the Socialists' 30 million). Their average poll throughout the Community (excluding the United Kingdom which has no Christian Democratic party) was about 32 per cent. In Scandinavia, Christian Democratic parties play a different role. They are small parties of recent provenance whose aim is to combat the evils of the permissive society which they believe the secular parties to have encouraged. (See PROTESTANT PARTIES.)

Altogether, then, Christian Democracy continues to be a major political force in Western Europe. Why has it revived? Christian Democracy does still have a distinctive political philosophy based on religiosity, social concern and a strong commitment to liberal democracy.

Its very pragmatism has appealed to many in the post-oil-crisis world, in which both neo-Keynesian and neo-Marxist remedies have been found wanting. The Christian Democrats have no simple solutions to the problems of unemployment, drug abuse and disarmament (to name but three), but they have a solid sociological and electoral base, and are judged by a significant number of voters to be at least as capable of governing equitably and competently as any of their rivals. REMI

Reading

Bakvis, H.: *Catholic Power in the Netherlands.* McGill: Queen's University Press, 1981.

Fogarty, M.P.: *Christian Democracy in Western Europe, 1820–1953.* London: Routledge & Kegan Paul, 1957.

Irving, R.E.M.: *Christian Democracy in France.* London: Allen & Unwin, 1973.

——: *The Christian Democratic Parties of Western Europe.* London: RIIA/Allen & Unwin, 1979.

Pridham, G.: *Christian Democracy in Western Germany.* London: Croom Helm, 1977.

Sigmund, P.E.: *The Overthrow of Allende and the Politics of Chile, 1964–76.* Pittsburgh: Pittsburgh University Press, 1979.

Vaussard, M.: *Storia della Democrazia Christiana.* Bologna: Cappelli, 1969.

Veen, H-J. ed.: *Christlich-demokratische und konservative Parteien in Westeuropa.* Paderborn: Schoningh, 1983.

Williams, E.J.: *Latin American Christian Democratic Parties.* Knoxville: University of Tennessee Press, 1967.

church and state Relations between church and state have provided a central focus of political argument and conflict in Christendom from the earliest to the most recent times. As one of the areas where the interaction of religion and politics achieves particular significance the complexities of church–state relations as such can only be observed in those contexts where particular religious traditions have given rise to church-type institutions. While the idea of a church can be traced back to Old Testament times when the Jews lost their state but continued to maintain their religious identity, its full development occurred only with the spread of Christianity. Although the other world religions have given rise to more or less independent institutions which can be counterposed to the state, only Christianity developed the form of the church as a religious community served by a priesthood claiming to exercise spiritual authority by divine right and independently of any secular authority.

The evolution of the Christian cult from one of a number of obscure sects to become finally the established religion of the Roman Empire was accompanied by a major change in its orientation to the institutions of civil authority. While the sectarian tradition of distrust for state institutions and disapproval for the principles of the wider social order never quite disappeared, the church's leadership eventually came to see the holders of political power as valuable protectors and allies in the task of diffusing Christian beliefs, values and practices. Relations were rarely easy however and during the medieval period a whole series of contests occurred between the holders of political and religious authority from the popes and emperors down – over the right to appoint bishops and clergy, the control of the church's wealth, the scope of rival jurisdictions, and so on. In the western church, maximalist claims were advanced by Pope Boniface VIII among others to the effect that the supremacy of the church extended to temporal affairs and that lay rulers only enjoyed such authority as the church delegated to them. Such claims were rarely given practical effect however. In the eastern church where the secular institutions of empire survived much longer than in the west a quite different and much more stable pattern of church–state relations became established. There the emperors maintained their influence over the church by summoning councils, investing patriarchs, :uing ecclesiastical decrees and so on. Tɪɪs eastern tradition of civil supremacy within the church, sometimes rather inaccurately called caesaropapism, has continued to affect the management of church–state relations in areas where the Orthodox church has been dominant, even where, as in the Soviet Union and parts of eastern Europe, communist regimes have in recent times exercised civil authority.

In western Europe the era of the Reformation and wars of religion saw on the one hand the development of the modern NATION-STATE with its claim for sovereign authority and on the other the emergence of a much more variegated pattern of church–state relations. The broad geographical pattern was more or less permanently fixed by the Peace of Westphalia in 1648 when the principle was finally adopted that the established religion of a particular territory should be that of its prince. Since then Europe has been divided between, broadly, a Roman Catholic south, a Protestant north (with variously Anglican, Lutheran and Calvinist established churches) and an intervening area of mixed confession. In all parts of Europe at least until the time of the FRENCH REVOLUTION state and church authorities were generally closely linked, with the secular arm invariably in the ascendant. In the south and in the overseas colonies of the Iberian states this took the form of mutually beneficial throne-and-altar alliances between the Roman Catholic church and the *ancien régime* authorities; in the north it varied between the Erastian pattern of almost complete dominance of the church by the secular authorities in the Lutheran territories, to the relative but still qualified independence of the church in certain areas where the Calvinist tradition was dominant. Almost everywhere however religious conformity was the rule and failure to conform usually attracted such civil penalties as disqualification from civil office.

The eighteenth century saw some advances in the direction of religious toleration particularly in the United Kingdom and some of its American territories but later also in those European states where the ideas of the Enlightenment were adopted by particular rulers. In almost all cases the old pattern of church establishment continued to obtain however and it was only under the impact of the French Revolution at the turn of the century that this arrangement was seriously challenged. In southern or Roman Catholic Europe in particular the new revolutionary ideas were regarded as deeply subversive of true religion and morality as well as of the state, and church–state relations tended to become a focus for bitter conflict between anticlerical forces and the partisans of the church under clericalist leadership (see CLERICALISM; ANTICLERICALISM) as they vied for political influence and power. In Italy the contest between modernizing elites and the church was complicated by the severe threat posed by Italian nationalism to the temporal power of the papacy, a matter which was only finally resolved sixty years after the unification of the country in 1929. In Ireland and Poland by contrast, where Roman Catholicism tended to lend extra strength to nationalist movements, church–state relations became close and mutually supportive after the successful achievement of national independence. In Protestant Europe and the territories of mixed confession where the Protestants were in the ascendant, issues affecting church–state relations tended to centre on the rights of those who were not members of the established churches, whether Roman Catholic, non-conforming Protestant, or of no religion. The existence in the north of alternative religious traditions which could be relied on to fight for what they considered to be their rights meant that the left or reform-oriented forces only rarely took on the character of anticlerical movements and often acquiesced in the maintenance of the church establishment as long as it did not affect their enjoyment of full religious freedom.

The introduction of universal systems of public education gave rise to some of the hardest fought struggles in the field of church–state relations in almost all parts of Europe in the nineteenth and early twentieth centuries. The defenders of established or majority religious traditions fought for the inclusion in the public school curriculum of orthodox religious instruction or for the public funding of confessional schools. The supporters of minority religious traditions on the other hand opposed any arrangement which gave a privileged status in education to the dominant church and occasionally joined anticlericals and other secularists who opposed the use of public funding for the support of religious instruction. This issue more than any other led to the formation of CONFESSIONAL PARTIES in Europe. Although church–state

conflicts in the field of education do occasionally recur in the West, for example in France in 1984, the main areas of controversy in recent decades have concerned what might be called the politics of morality: divorce and contraception in Roman Catholic countries and abortion, pornography and homosexuality more widely. In eastern Europe and the Third World by contrast church–state tensions and conflicts have centred on basic questions of political order and social justice as the various church traditions and institutions have tended to become vehicles of protest and political mobilization.

See also CHRISTIAN DEMOCRACY.

JTSM

Reading

Berger, S. ed.: *Religion in West European Politics.* London: Cass, 1983.

Mecham, J.L.: *Church and State in Latin America.* Chapel Hill: University of North Carolina Press, 1966.

Merkl, P. and Smart, N. eds: *Religion and Politics in the Modern World.* New York: University of New York Press, 1983.

Nicholls, D.: *Church and State in Britain since 1820.* London: Routledge, 1967.

Pfeffer, L.: *Church, State and Freedom.* Boston, Mass.: Beacon, 1967.

Silvert, K.H. ed.: *Churches and States.* New York: American Universities Field Staff, 1967.

Smith, D.E.: *Religion and Political Development.* Boston, Mass.: Little, Brown, 1970.

Whyte, J.H.: *Catholics in Western Democracies.* Dublin: Gill & Macmillan, 1981.

Cicero, Marcus Tullius (106 – 43 BC)

Political theorist. The idea that there are fundamentally only three distinct types of constitution – MONARCHY, ARISTOCRACY, DEMOCRACY – is at least as old as Herodotus (*History III*. 82), and the notion that the best polity is a 'mixed' one which combines the strengths and eschews the weaknesses of each of them was already long established when Cicero composed his two essays on political theory, *De republica* and *De legibus* in imitation of PLATO's *Republic* and *Laws*. Although Cicero was not an original political theorist, these works reflect the contributions made to thought on the subject by historians and philosophers since ARISTOTLE. The rise of Rome to world dominion during the second century BC had been rapid and remarkable; and the Greek historian POLYBIUS was not the only contemporary observer who looked for an explanation of Rome's success in the excellence of her 'balanced' constitution. For him, as for Cicero, Rome had achieved this over long centuries of empirical adaptation. What Cicero provides is a nostalgic and hence considerably idealized and largely uncritical model of the Roman state as it had come to be before the disruptive tribunates of the Gracchi (133, 123–122 BC; see Stockton 1979): the consuls represented the 'monarchic' element, the senate the 'aristocratic', the citizen assemblies the 'democratic'. Although they add little or nothing new to ancient political theory, Cicero's essays were widely read and very influential in later times; they give a valuable insight into the sort of practical arrangements which for conservative thinkers such as Cicero exemplified a successful 'mixed' or 'balanced' constitution, *viz.* collegiality and strict limitation of tenure for the (elected) executive officers of state, a powerful permanent advisory council of state, and a limited but essential degree of popular participation in elections and decision taking.

See also MIXED GOVERNMENT.   DLS

Reading

Cicero: *De republica* and *De legibus*.

Fritz, K. von: *The Theory of the Mixed Constitution in Antiquity: a critical analysis of Polybius' political ideas.* New York: Columbia University Press, 1954.

Rawson, E.: *Cicero: a portrait*, ch. 9. London: Allen Lane, 1974.

Stockton, D.L.: *Cicero: a political biography*, ch. 2 and appendix 4C. Oxford: Oxford University Press, 1971.

————: *The Gracchi*. Oxford: Oxford University Press, 1979.

citizen initiative   A term used during the last two decades by political analysts to describe movements outside traditional political parties and pressure groups aimed at influencing decision makers. Citizen initiatives are com-

paratively spontaneous; plebiscitarian because they are a coalition of individuals without an established organizational framework; autonomous because they have to abstain from being integrated into political parties or permanently existing pressure groups; limited because they concentrate on specific issues; radically democratic because they are claiming democratic values as justification for their pressures. Citizen initiative is a contemporary version of a single issue pressure group, based on democratic grass root ideology.

As a phenomenon within advanced western industrialized societies, the citizen initiative is the modern heir of an old theoretical claim: government by the people. It is a consequence of the rise of new issues, especially ecological issues such as the anti-nuclear power movements. In certain countries, the United States and the Federal Republic of Germany for instance, different data show a clear preference for citizen initiatives at the local level. Data also demonstrate that citizen initiatives are usually an instrument of better educated white collar voters, who are able to use such action to influence public opinion without the backing of an established organization.   AP

Reading

Birnbaum, P. et al. eds: *Democracy, Consensus and Social Contract.* London and Beverly Hills, Calif.: Sage, 1978.

Duncan, G. ed.: *Democratic Theory and Practice.* Cambridge: Cambridge University Press, 1983.

Guggenberger, B. and Kempf, U. eds: *Bürgerinitiativen und repräsentatives System.* 2nd edn. Opladen: Westdeutscher Verlag, 1984.

citizenship   The term denotes the full and responsible membership of an individual in a state. In the social sciences it has been used primarily to denote the status of individuals in the development of modern nation-states. Citizenship refers to rights which a state confers upon certain or all individuals in a territory over which it has control. According to Bendix, a core element in nation-building is the codification of the rights and duties of all adults who are classified as citizens. Conditions of citizenship are determined within each state in accordance with its own legal provisions.

Most societies have developed from a condition in which the vast majority of the people were considered objects of rule to a condition in which rights have become as important as duties and in which the rights of citizenship have gradually become universal.

In *Citizenship and Social Class*, T. H. Marshall offered what has become a classic example of analysis of the concept of citizenship within an evolutionary perspective. He created a simple threefold typology of citizenship rights and applied it to the historical development of rights and duties in England since the eighteenth century. In Marshall's perspective, the eighteenth century brought civil rights (or *civil citizenship*): equality before the law, liberty of the person, freedom of speech, thought, and faith, the right to own property and conclude contracts. The nineteenth century saw the development of political rights (or *political citizenship*): the right to take part in elections, the right to serve in bodies invested with political authority, whether legislatures or cabinets. Finally, the exercise of political rights in the twentieth century brought social rights (or *social citizenship*): the right to a certain standard of economic and social welfare, the right to share to the full in the social heritage. Four sets of public institutions correspond to these three types of rights: the courts, representative political bodies, the social services and the schools.

Citizenship denotes individual membership in a nation-state. International law does not recognize any distinction between nationality and citizenship: nationality determines citizenship. Modern life patterns in the western world, however, have given rise to a development towards a kind of multiple citizenship. A Turkish guest-worker in Sweden may in a short period of time acquire most of the citizenship rights and duties of Swedish nationals, while simultaneously upholding the citizenship rights (and duties) of a Turkish citizen. This is not merely a question of definition; it is also a practical problem since citizenship denotes a relationship between an individual and the state by which the individual owes allegiance and the state owes protection. The citizen who has a right to be consulted in the conduct of the political system is also supposed to be bound by the results of the consultation. A serious difficulty would arise if the two (or more) states in which an individual maintained important citizenship rights were to go to war with one another. The trend towards a greater number of 'multinational individuals' seems to require the development of rules to determine the instances in which one type of citizenship has priority over others. The development of an international citizenship for such individuals is one possibility.

See also WELFARE STATE.   SK

Reading

Bendix, R: *Nation-Building and Citizenship.* Berkeley: University of California Press, 1977.

Kuhnle, S. and Rokkan, S.: T.H. Marshall. In *International Encyclopedia of the Social Sciences*, Vol. XVIII. New York: Free Press, 1969.

Marshall, T.H.: *Citizenship, Social Class, and other Essays.* Cambridge: Cambridge University Press, 1950.

Svarlien, O.: Citizenship. In *A Dictionary of the Social Sciences*, ed. J. Gould and W. Kolb. London: Tavistock, 1964.

city government Involves the formal arrangements for controlling local affairs and exercising some or all state powers within a city. City government must be distinguished from urban or metropolitan government and some agreed definition is required which is not restricted to capital cities or to the great cities of the world which are not capitals. There is little international agreement as to what constitutes a city, and in practice different countries adopt different definitions. In some countries the formal title is given to settlements with more than a few thousand inhabitants, but that is not a workable or sensible measure. Historically in Britain cities were towns which had cathedrals and royal CHARTERS, but those characteristics became redundant as criteria during the nineteenth century when population growth and industrialization produced large numbers of urban settlements with neither cathedral nor charter. Common sense suggests that any definition of practical use involves an element of population size and density and a geographical independence of other similar settlements. This avoids confusion by ruling out the small and very large urban areas and means that most developed countries have substantial numbers of cities whose government has to be secured. Such cities are not easily governed by the central government nor even by regional governments and all developed countries have established some form of LOCAL GOVERNMENT.

There are two elements which distinguish a city with a government from a city with simply a local administration. One is its power to raise revenue from some or all of its population and to have some discretion over how that revenue is spent. The other is some form of REPRESEN-TATION and consequent accountability which gives the population ultimate formal control over the membership of the city government. Together these characteristics distinguish government from ADMINISTRATION and most developed countries have such city government. This does not remove the need for city administration, but simply makes it accountable to a locally elected body rather than a remote central government. Inevitably city government and administration have to operate within a framework of national laws but within them they enjoy some autonomy.

Even with these limitations cities vary widely in size and character and city governments vary equally widely. Several forms of city governments are to be found in the United States and even the highly centralized British system allows for diverse local practice though the form is standardized. Variations relate to the functions undertaken by city government and to the form and character which that government takes. In terms of function the city government may provide all of the basic public services in its area, as in Britain, or it may share those tasks with other agencies established for particular purposes, as in the United States. The latter makes for problems of effective co-ordination between agencies while the former creates easier possibilities of corporate development though these are often not realized.

In terms of form and character, city governments vary according to the degree of emphasis given to democratic accountability as against efficient and effective decision making. At one extreme lies the British city council with its large membership made up usually of three representatives from each quite small electoral division, the ward. This can produce as many as a hundred elected councillors, many of whom see their roles as representing their ward electorate. A few see themselves as directing the affairs of the city and determining policy and practice in public services. These few tend to be removed from public pressure by their colleagues and the whole structure depends on party politics to cement organization and organize support. At the other extreme lies the case of the elected mayor or his or her equivalent, sometimes supported by a small elected council. Such systems simplify control and ease the process of DECISION MAKING but at the same time democratic control may become more difficult. Ward voting may apply, even to small councils, but the tendency is to have direct election by the city electorate as a whole. This invariably leads to a broadening of the platform on which candidates stand for election and can lead to non-partisan politics. This may generate a sense of solidarity and shared interest though the diverse character of city populations can make it hard to sustain, especially where government is heavily involved in economic and social provision. Inequalities inevitably occur and local political processes often reflect them.

It is worth noting that these formal political arrangements are supported by elaborate organizational structures to implement policy decisions, coinciding with the range of functions performed by city government (but the pattern is not uniform). At one extreme lie highly professionalized, often quite small departments, running the treasury or the planning service. Equally professional but much larger in scale are departments such as education or the public welfare service. By contrast, the departments which deal with highways or public transport or cleansing are led by professionals but staffed by large numbers of manual workers. Combining these varied elements, and their widely varied costs, into coherent public programmes is one of the main tasks of city government. Departments are not always mutually aware of what others are doing, and are seldom ready to accept the implications of budgetary limitations. Competition is as common among them as cooperation.

Having distinguished local government from administration, the presence of such elaborate structures raises questions about the relative influence of appointed staff in relation to elected councillors; the picture is by no means clear. Theoretically the councillors determine policy and officials carry it out; in practice IMPLEMENTATION often determines what is really policy and in any case officials play an advisory role in determination of policy. Precise roles are unclear, but if councillors wield power in its formal sense, officials are nevertheless highly influential. Their more elaborate role is greatly enhanced by the fact that they enjoy extensive contact with the public, especially between elections.

All these aspects of city government are constantly changing and adapting to changes in social and economic conditions both in cities and around them. There are however certain general pressures which pose a threat to the basic idea of city government. One of these is the rigidity of city boundaries in relation to those who live in suburbs outside the city yet commute for work and leisure. This produces demands on public services from non-local tax payers and may involve loss of revenue as the more affluent move out. It can also involve considerable pressure on services from remaining residents who may be more deprived and needy.

These population pressures have been accompanied by economic changes which are equally damaging. Inevitably the economic base of many cities is founded on historical circumstances, of location or raw material availability. When these change the impact of economic decline hits city government in terms of its resources and the needs to be met as well as the challenging task of assisting economic change. This has not been helped by the shift in industry from locally based to multinational forms of organization. Economic decision making has been removed from local control, and local considerations loom much smaller in the minds of decision makers. Again, the implications for city government are negative.

Such strains have produced reforms in and pressures on city government. Suburban spread can convert the city into a metropolis and this generates a search for metropolitan government. This may leave some functions with a 'city' government within the metropolitan area but it leaves major question marks about the status of such cities in relation to the definitions arrived at above. More important, the fiscal and service strain has produced centralizing tendencies which undermine the character of city government. On the fiscal side central (or regional) governments have had to provide more and more resources with doubts being raised about the tax autonomy of city government. In Britain this has led to central government directly limiting local tax powers, though not only for city governments. At the same time the pressure from the disadvantaged cities has produced specific central government initiatives to deal with deprivation and relative inequality. These policies in their turn pose a challenge to the concept of city government.

See also LOCAL GOVERNMENT FINANCE; LOCAL GOVERNMENT REORGANIZATION; LOCAL POLITICS.   NTB

Reading

Banfield, E.C. and Wilson, J.Q.: *City Politics*. New York: Vintage Books, 1963.
Dunleavy, P.J.: *Urban Political Analysis: the politics of collective consumption*. London: Macmillan, 1980.
Elliot, B. and McCrone, D.: *The City: patterns of domination and conflict*. London: Macmillan, 1982.
Goldsmith, M.: *Politics, Planning and the City*. London: Hutchinson, 1980.
Hicks, U.K.: *The Large City*. London: Macmillan, 1974.
McKay, D.H. and Cox, A.W.: *The Politics of Urban Change*. London: Croom Helm, 1979.
Newton, K.: *Second City Politics: democratic processes and decision-making in Birmingham*. Oxford: Oxford University Press, 1976.
Robson, W.A. and Regan, D.E. eds: *Great Cities of the World: their government, politics and planning*. 3rd edn. London: Allen & Unwin, 1972.
Sharpe, L.J. ed.: *The Local Fiscal Crisis in Western Europe: myths and realities*. London: Sage, 1981.

city state Denotes the *polis* of classical

Greece and by analogy other similar political communities, e.g. Carthage, Republican Rome, and some medieval cities, especially in Flanders and Italy. Unlike the latter which owed allegiance, sometimes nominal, to a monarch or lord, the *polis* acknowledged no external sovereign. It was not usually a city in the modern sense but had an urban centre, generally fortified, for political and religious purposes; most citizens might live in the country. The *polis* (see STATE) was the citizens; 'the Athenians' officially constitute the state, while Athens is the urban centre. The citizens, sometimes a minority of all adult male inhabitants, alone possessed any political rights. In a DEMOCRACY such as Athens a primary assembly, in which each member had one vote, met often and took all important decisions, e.g. on finance, foreign policy and military operations; the magistrates and council were its servants. But in many Greek city states power was almost entirely vested in the council and annual magistrates qualified by birth or wealth. In some, monarchic control was usurped by a 'tyrant'; the term originally indicated only his lack of legal authority. According to PLATO each *polis* was divided into one of the rich and one of the poor; democracy favoured the poor. The frequency of social conflicts and political revolutions generated political theory, designed to determine the form of institutions under which the citizens could lead the best life, or which would preserve stability. Many thinkers held that a 'mixed' or balanced CONSTITUTION, with monarchic, aristocratic and democratic features, could best achieve a consensus and be most enduring. Rome was taken to be an example of this type. In fact with hundreds of thousands of citizens spread throughout Italy Rome outstripped the appropriate dimensions of a city state; the primary assemblies, which retained important powers, were not truly representative of the people. Idealized accounts of the Greek city state have, since ROUSSEAU formed the basis of many accounts of democracy in which the virtue of participation is stressed. ARISTOTLE'S *Politics* remains the best analysis of its real character.

See also MIXED GOVERNMENT.

PAB

Reading

Aristotle: *Politics*, rev edn. ed. T.J. Saunders and trans. T.A. Sinclair. Harmondsworth: Penguin, 1981.

———: *Constitution of Athens*, trans. K. von Gritz and E. Kapp. New York: Haffner, 1950.

Burke, P.: City-states. In *States in History*, pp. 137–53, ed. J.A. Hale. Oxford and New York: Blackwell, 1986.

Forrest, W.G.: *The Emergence of Greek Democracy 800–400 BC*. London: Weidenfeld & Nicolson, 1966.

Hignett, C.: *A History of the Athenian Constitution*. Oxford: Oxford University Press, 1952.

Jones, A.H.M.: *Athenian Democracy*. Oxford: Blackwell, 1977.

Plato: *Republic*.

Waley, D.P.: *The Italian City-Republics*. London: Longman, 1978.

civic culture A psychological theory of democratic stability. Though it was formulated in the early 1960s in the context of a comparative survey of attitudes towards DEMOCRACY in Britain, Germany, Italy, the United States, and Mexico, it is part of a long tradition of efforts to explain political stability, going back to Aristotle, including Polybius and Cicero, Tocqueville, John Stuart Mill, Bagehot, Schumpeter and many others. What all these theorists had in common was a recognition of the problematics of democracy based on historical experience – for Aristotle and Polybius the excesses of Athenian democracy, for Cicero the disorders in Rome, for Tocqueville the French Revolution, for Mill and Bagehot English and French historical experience, for Schumpeter and a whole generation of political theorists from the 1930s, 1940s and 1950s, the collapse of Weimar democracy.

In elaborating the psychological requirements of democratic stability Aristotle spoke of 'political friendliness', a sense of 'partnership' and 'political restraint'; Tocqueville wrote of 'self interest rightly understood', 'temperance, moderation, and self command'; Bagehot wrote of 'animated moderation'; and Eckstein stressed the importance of 'balanced disparities'. The Civic Culture study sought to demonstrate the connection of attitudes of this

kind with the historical experience of democratic stability – contrasting attitudes in Britain
and the United States with attitudes in
Germany and Italy.

The logic of the theory held that effective
performance of a democracy required the
reconciliation of the power of leaders to
initiate and to act – for the government to
govern – on the one hand, with participation of
citizens in the political process on the other.
With no political division of labour it is
difficult to see how political choices could be
made, and how an informed electorate could
evaluate the performance of political leaders.
What kind of citizenry would be congruent
with a proper balance of power and responsiveness, and democratic stability? The
Civic Culture study suggested that a political
culture congruent with stable democracy
would be a mixed political culture, one in
which activity and passivity, obligation and
performance, consensus and cleavage, would
be balanced and combined.

Citizens would not always be participating
to the full; they would have a 'civic reserve' –
skills and commitments available for issues
important to them. They would balance activity
and passivity, and so enable leaders both to
exercise power and to respond to citizen
demands. There would be a tension between
civic obligation and actual civic performance.
Most citizens would acknowledge the obligation to participate, and believe in the
accessibility of government to their participation; but their performance would be
selective, and would fall short of their sense of
obligation. Finally there would be a tension
between consensus and cleavage. Conflict is
the essence of politics; hence political
antagonism is unavoidable, particularly in
open democratic systems. But in a stable
democracy antagonism between parties and
groups is contained within an overarching
national loyalty, and support of the political
system.

This theory of the psychological components of stable democracy has not been
disproven by attitude changes which have
occurred in Europe and the United States in
recent decades. Political polarization and
declining national pride and confidence in

Britain and the United States, have been
associated with the declining effectiveness and
performance of the British and American
governments and economies, just as the rise of
civic propensities in Germany has been
associated with effective political and
economic performance. These fluctuations in
cultural patterns demonstrate the dependence
of the civic culture on democratic performance. Nevertheless, as a theory of
democratic stability it is too dependent on the
British and American cases. The Low
Countries and Austria – Lijphart's CON-
SOCIATIONAL DEMOCRACIES – have found
their way to stability through the development
of an elite accommodative culture, and a set of
arrangements protecting the interests of
ethnic, religious, and social groups. Schmitter's
and Katzenstein's CORPORATISM may be
another route to democratic stability in small
countries particularly vulnerable to the
fluctuations of international trade. Here
interest groups, otherwise involved in conflictual, destabilizing activities, engage in
coordinated bargaining activities, with parliamentary leaders and bureaucrats, around the
issues of wages and conditions of work,
welfare benefits, prices, and investment policy.
The adoption of arrangements like these
implies growing consensus and system
support.   GAA

Reading

Aristotle: *Politics*.

Almond, G.A. and Verba, S.: *The Civic Culture:
political attitudes and democracy in five nations*.
Princeton, NJ: Princeton University Press, 1963.

——— and Verba, S.: *The Civic Culture Revisited: an
analytical study*. Boston, Mass.: Little, Brown, 1980.

Bagehot, W.: *The English Constitution*. In *Collected
Works*, Vol. V, ed. N. St John-Stevas. London: The
Economist, 1965–86.

Eckstein, H.: *Division and Cohesion in Democracy*.
Princeton, NJ: Princeton University Press, 1966.

Katzenstein, P.: *Small States and World Markets*.
Ithaca, NY: Cornell University Press, 1985.

Lijphart, A.: *The Politics of Accommodation*. Berkeley,
Calif.: University of California Press, 1968.

Polybius: *The Histories*.

Schmitter, P. and Lehmbruch, G. eds: *Trends*

Toward Corporatist Intermediation. London and Beverly Hills, Calif.: Sage, 1979.

Schumpeter, J. *Capitalism, Socialism and Democracy.* New York: Harper & Row, 1942; London: Allen & Unwin, 1976.

Thompson, D.: *John Stuart Mill and Representative Government.* Princeton, NJ: Princeton University Press, 1977.

Tocqueville, A. de: *Democracy in America* (2 vols. 1835, 1840), trans. G. Lawrence, ed. J.P. Mayer and M. Lerner. New York: Harper, 1966; London: Fontana, 1968.

civil liberties   Those liberties to which the individual citizen is entitled by virtue of his or her humanity. The modern idea of civil liberties is based on a notion of common humanity, rather than upon contingent factors such as status or performance.

The evolution in the nature and character of western-based constitutionalism and CONSTITUTIONAL GOVERNMENT from its earlier 'patrician' era in the seventeenth, eighteenth and nineteenth centuries, when the franchise was deliberately restricted, by law and practice, to propertied (land-owning or salaried) classes, to twentieth-century participatory democracy based on universal adult suffrage, is nowhere better illustrated than in the emergence of the modern concept of civil liberties. Some might argue today that it has become the prime principle of democratic constitutionalism. Where earlier constitutional charters tended to limit themselves to detailing the machinery of government – law-making institutions and processes – the more contemporary constitutional charter also inscribes fundamental community values, the limits of governmental decision making in relation to the individual citizen and, sometimes the rights of private interest groups and associations. In its most affirmative form, the conception of constitutional liberties of the citizen availing against the state and state authority, is embodied in an entrenched BILL OF RIGHTS, of which the US and French models have been the historically strongest influence upon constitution makers operating in the western, liberal democratic tradition. But the conception is present, also, in the constitutionalism of other western societies that do not have an enacted constitution. The English constitutional idea of the RULE OF LAW, celebrated by the jurist A. V. DICEY, identifies absence of arbitrary power and equality before the law as basic premises of the constitutional system, to be applied by the government as limitations on the otherwise legally unqualified, sovereign powers of Parliament and as controls on executive–administrative discretion in the application of laws. The links to the continental Western European, classical notion of the *Rechtsstaat*, and also to the contemporary Soviet and Eastern European Principle of Socialist Legality are clear enough.

The term civil liberties, in its historical development, implies a prime concern with procedure and process – on access to, and participation in, community decision making, and the removal of political–legal clogs or obstructions to its free operation. This is what Justice (later Chief Justice) Stone of the US Supreme Court meant with his political process concept; the encouragement of the 'Open Society' values of freedom of speech and association and access to information, as necessary pre-conditions of informed involvement in community decisions, are a logical application and extension. Civil liberties, as a constitutional idea belongs, more properly to the liberal democratic era of constitutionalism, and falls short of the more modern notion of CIVIL RIGHTS with its more substantive (rather than procedural) emphasis, and its commitment to political and legal activism.   EMcW

Reading

Commager, H.S.: *Majority Rule and Minority Rights.* New York: Smith, 1950.

Corwin, E.S.: *Liberty Against Government: the rise, flowering and decline of a famous judicial concept.* Baton Rouge: Louisiana State University Press, 1948.

Dicey, A.V.: *Introduction to the Study of the Law of the Constitution.* 10th edn (1959), ed. E.C.S. Wade. Basingstoke: Macmillan, 1985.

Friedrich, C.J.: *Limited Government: a comparison.* Englewood Cliffs, NJ: Prentice-Hall, 1974.

Gastil, R.D. ed.: *Freedom in the World: Political Rights and Civil Liberties.* Boston, Mass.: Hall, 1978– , annually.

McWhinney, E.: *Constitution-Making: principles,*

process, practice. Toronto: Toronto University Press, 1981.

O'Higgins, P.: *Cases and Materials on Civil Liberties.* London: Sweet & Maxwell, 1980.

Street, H.: *Freedom, the Individual and the Law.* 6th edn. Harmondsworth: Penguin, 1989.

civil–military relations In its broadest sense the term relates to attitudes and behaviour which the general public and the members of the armed forces of society exhibit towards each other (see Girardet 1953; Luckham 1971), but the narrower and specifically political sense pursued here connotes the relationships of superordination or subordination existing between the armed forces and the lawfully constituted public authorities of the state. The conceptual distinction between the two terms *civil* and *military* has not always been applicable in practice. Societies have existed such as the Mongol nomads, *circa* tenth to twelfth centuries AD, where the ruler and the tribesmen were also the war-leader and the armed horde. (Something analogous might be said of, say, MAO ZEDONG's 8th Route Army in the late 1930s, or Fidel Castro's 'July 26th Movement' before the conquest of the state in 1959.) Similarly in the feudal monarchies of Europe the barons were both the warriors and the political leaders. Even where the armed forces were fully differentiated from the general public as a standing professional army, as in eighteenth-century European monarchies, the armies were officered by aristocratic families who doubled as the courtiers and ministers of the ruler who was both their political leader and the ex-officio commander-in-chief of the armed forces.

After the French Revolution of 1789 loyalty to the nation eclipsed the previous loyalty of the officer corps to their dynastic sovereign, or even to elected authorities. Secondly, the officer corps became a career-oriented long-term professionalized corporation whose life styles, training, social status and (often) material interests could significantly diverge from those of the general public. The twin development made possible a divergence of outlook between the armed forces and the government of the day, and since that time such collisions, manifested in military COUPS D'ÉTAT, have become commonplace.

Today there are three broad categories of civil–military relations.

(1) States where the military have overthrown the lawful government and have installed their own members as rulers (see MILITARY GOVERNMENT).

(2) The *permeation* or *subjective control* relationship of which the paradigm (and best researched case) is the USSR, but the pattern is found in all Marxist states and a number of others where an ideological single or hegemonic party holds rule (Burma, Iraq). The aspiration is to make the military's outlook conform to and therefore uphold that of the ruling party and this is attempted by: permeating the forces by cells of the ruling party so as to carry out propaganda and maintain surveillance; closing officer positions to all who are not members of the ruling party; assigning to all units party-controlled political officers whose words override those of the equivalent field officers; and penetration by the security services and secret police. In the socialist states this mode of relationship has been effective in preventing what they call 'Bonapartism', the attempted armed overthrow by the military. The method is effective only to the extent that the party is centralized, solidary, and with a clear-cut ideology. Hence it is not very effective in Syria or Iraq, for instance, where the ruling Ba'ath party state is less numerous, less tightly organized, and has a less defined ideology than the communist parties in socialist states. The method is ineffective in quasi-Marxist states such as Benin or the Congolese Republic, where the official parties are largely nominal. This pattern cannot be applied in liberal–democratic states where there is no official ideology and the parties compete and alternate in office. Hence in these states the pattern is some variant of the third type of relationship.

(3) The *liberal* or *objective control* relationship is one where the aspiration is that the armed forces can be depoliticized and so become entirely subservient instruments of the political incumbents of the day, irrespective of who they are or what their views are. This form of

relationship however need not preclude the military high command from exercising very considerable political influence, providing only that the civil authorities have the final word.

Huntington (1957) argued that this condition could be met when the army was made fully 'professional'. This is, however, a necessary and not a sufficient condition, and it does not follow that armies, like the Japanese which certainly intervened in politics during the 1930s, were by definition not fully professional. In practice moreover even the most professonal armies have interests and outlooks that encroach on 'civilian' spheres - for example foreign policy, manpower policy, economic policy (home-based industries etc.). The guarantee of de-politicization needs two requirements over and above professionalization. It requires the military to internalize the principle of civil supremacy as indeed has happened in the USA, the UK *et al*. It also requires that the civil authorities treat the military in a way accordant with their self respect (status) and material interests (promotion, career patterns and so forth). The two conditions can be summarized as: first, a state of affairs where a civilian government is self-standing (i.e. has sufficient legitimacy and popular support to stand without reliance on the military), and, second, where the military for its part, being treated according to what it sees as its deserts, does not require any particular incumbent or regime to satisfy it.

These conditions have been met in the older liberal democracies since 1945 (Greece and Portugal are, significantly, less industrialized states with a long history of political instability) but have often been lacking in the newer third world states. Here the military have frequently found their views and interests colliding with those of the government of the day either because they perceive the national interest differently or because they feel their own class/communal/ethnic/corporate (status, pay, promotion etc.) interests threatened, or even because of the personal ambitions of some of their leaders. Though such cleavages between the military's perceptions and those of the civil authorities do not in themselves

provoke a clash and possibly a coup, they are, alone or in combination, a necessary condition.   SEF

Reading

Best, G.: *War and Society in Revolutionary Europe, 1770–1870*. London: Fontana, 1983.

Bond, B.: *War and Society in Europe, 1870–1970*. London: Fontana, 1984.

Finer, S.E.: *The Man on Horseback*. 2nd edn. Harmondsworth: Penguin, 1976.

———: State and nation-building in Europe: the role of the military. In *The Formation of National States in Western Europe*, ed. C. Tilly. Princeton, NJ: Princeton University Press, 1975.

Girardet, R.: *La Société militaire dans la France contemporaine*. Paris: Plon 1953.

Hale, J.R.: *War and Society in Renaissance Europe. 1450–1620*. London: Fontana, 1985.

Herspring, D.R. and Volgyes, I.: *Civil-Military Relations in Communist Systems*. Boulder, Col.: Westview, 1978.

Huntington, S.P.: *The Soldier and the State*. Cambridge, Mass.: Harvard University Press, 1957.

———: *Political Order in Changing Societies*. New Haven, Conn.: Yale University Press, 1968.

Janowitz, M.: *The Military in the Political Development of New Nations*. Chicago, Ill.: University of Chicago Press, 1964.

Keegan, J.: *World Armies*, 2nd edn. London: Macmillan, 1983.

Kolkowicz, R. and Korbonski, A.: *Soldiers, Peasants and Bureaucrats*. London: Allen & Unwin, 1982.

Luckham, A.R.A.: A comparative typology of civil-military relations. *Government and Opposition* 6.1 (1971).

Nordlinger, E.A.: *Soldiers in Politics*. Englewood Cliffs, NJ: Prentice-Hall, 1977.

Perlmutter, A.: *The Military and Politics in Modern Times*. New Haven, Conn.: Yale University Press, 1977.

Rouquier, A.: *La Politique de Mars*. Paris, 1981.

civil rights The rights guaranteed to citizens by the state. In general, civil rights are distinguished from CIVIL LIBERTIES in two ways. First, in that they apply to the rights of groups, whether ethnic, racial or religious, as opposed to individual rights. The term is often used as a synonym for minority rights. In 1877, Lord Acton declared that 'the most certain test by which we judge whether a country is really free is the amount of security enjoyed by minorities'. In the twentieth century the struggle for civil rights has been an important feature of politics in many democratic countries, and international organizations such as the UNITED NATIONS and the Council of Europe have sought to protect minorities. The issue of civil rights has become a matter of universal concern.

Secondly, however, the idea of civil rights denotes the historical evolution from the classical, more limited conception of constitutional liberties as finding their expression and outlet in the constitutional self-restraint of the political–governmental elite in regard to the ordinary citizen (the continental European *Rechtsstaat*, the English and American 'Rule of Law'), to the far more contemporary idea that constitutional freedoms can only become concrete and meaningful through a form of vigilant, combative democracy. This implies direct political action through social and other pressure groups, especially organized for the purpose and operating upon the constitutional–governmental processes as a whole. While specifically American in its historical origins, the Civil Rights movement emerged through the coalition of various political action-oriented groups in the western, and western-influenced, world in the 1960s and 1970s, in the wake of the Vietnam war and more general student and citizen protest movements of the era.

This entry concentrates on the United States, for civil rights is historically most closely associated with the political–legal action movements, from the 1940s onwards, which were directed to ensure the full and concrete implementation of the constitutional guarantees of racial equality contained in the US Constitution's post-Civil War 13th, 14th, and 15th Amendments. Private organizations such as the American Civil Liberties Union and the National Association for the Advancement of Coloured Peoples prepared, directed and funded test cases before the Supreme Court and other federal courts in an attempt to compel state governments and their administrators, and also agencies receiving state funds, to observe the Bill of Rights'

guarantees in their full spirit as well as the letter. The most spectacular achievement of the Civil Rights movement before the law courts was in public education, culminating in the US SUPREME COURT's decision in 1954, in *Brown* v. *Board of Education*, rejecting the constitutionally long-sanctioned principle of 'separate but equal' and proclaiming an end to segregation, by race or colour, in the grade schools of the United States. But significant progress towards ending racial discrimination was also made, before the courts, in other areas such as voting rights. The initial emphasis upon court-based action reflected the political impasse at the time in Congress and also within the executive arm of government (the presidency). The cumulative effect of action in the courts and the political arenas led on, however, to the adoption in 1964 of the 24th Amendment to the Constitution (banning the Poll Tax as a device for restricting negro voting), and to the enactment of President Lyndon Johnson's federal Civil Rights Act in the same year.

The Civil Rights movement in the United States was broadened in its political base by the emergence of the protests against the Vietnam War, civil disobedience, and citizen activist groups in the late 1960s and early 1970s, resulting in a certain dilution of the earlier concentration on negro rights, as the ensuing litigation emphasized new and different constitutional law issues such as the limitations on the executive's power to conduct military operations abroad without prior Congressional authorization. At the same time, by the mid-1970s, a new and expanded substantive content was being sought for the constitutional prohibitions on racial discrimination by the political pressures for positive governmental intervention to help historically disadvantaged racial and other minorities in their pursuit of economic and social betterment. This was the constitutional concept of AFFIRMATIVE ACTION ('reverse discrimination'), to be achieved by the establishment of racial quotas reserved for such minorities in their access to employment, entry into educational institutions, and even electoral processes. In the result, this raised some still not completely resolved doctrinal–

legal conflicts (with the 14th Amendment 'equal protection' guarantee) in the courts, which occasionally saw traditional minority groups (negro rights organizations, Jewish rights groups) on opposing sides in the litigation.

See also EUROPEAN CONVENTION ON HUMAN RIGHTS; FUNDAMENTAL RIGHTS; MINORITIES, PROTECTION OF.   EMcW

Reading

Abraham, H.J.: *Freedom and the Court: civil rights and liberties in the United States*. 4th edn. Oxford: Oxford University Press, 1982.

Emerson, T.I. and Haber, D.: *Political and Civil Rights in the United States*. Buffalo, NY: Dennis, 1952.

Gastil, R.D. ed.: *Freedom in the World: political rights and civil liberties*. Boston, Mass.: Hall, 1978– , annually.

Hand, L.: *The Bill of Rights*. Cambridge, Mass.: Harvard University Press, 1958.

Konvitz, M.R.: *A Century of Civil Rights*. New York: Columbia University Press, 1961.

STREET, H.: *Freedom, the Individual and the Law*. 6th edn. Harmondsworth: Penguin, 1989.

civil service   The remunerated personnel, other than those serving in the armed forces, whose functions are to administer policies formulated by or approved by national governments. The term originates from the British administration in India where it referred to the officials employed by the government other than the armed forces and judiciary, but since the mid-nineteenth century it has been used in Britain to refer only to civilian officials working in departments of central government. In some countries today the term encompasses not only the civilian staff who work in government departments but also civilian personnel working with the armed forces, and armed forces personnel serving government in a civilian capacity, the judiciary, employees of local governments and public corporations, school and university teachers, police and other agencies. In Britain and many other countries today the term public service is generally used for this large number of different categories of employees, and civil service retains its specific and restricted

meaning. Much of the debate about its exact meaning has been transferred to the definition of other terms such as 'department of central government'. The term therefore only has a precise meaning when used in relation to particular national political systems.

The origins of the civil service in many developed countries can be traced from the time when its officials were the servants of the monarch or ruler, through a period when they were servants of ministers, to modern times when they are servants of the CROWN or STATE. In countries where the contemporary civil service can be more precisely defined it dates from the introduction of a new constitution.

Most civil servants in most countries are permanent officials who do not change when a government changes. This is the case for nearly all civil servants in the United Kingdom, though in recent years a small number of temporary appointments have been made for political reasons. In some countries, such as France, Belgium and Italy, the civil service includes a number of temporary 'political' positions through the CABINET MINISTÉRIEL system. But even in countries such as the United States or West Germany, where more positions change hands when a different party assumes power, most officials are permanent and regard their employment as a career. They are generally appointed to positions for which qualifications are stated and by procedures that are publicly known and approved. Their conditions of service are laid down in written documents, usually in statutes. Within their ministries or departments their duties are distributed in a fixed way and they are organized in a hierarchical structure (often in a horizontal class system, usually explicitly related to levels and types of educational qualifications upon entry) in grades to which known pay scales apply. Their methods of work are bureaucratic according to the generally accepted meaning of the term which involves a dependence on files containing records of decisions, enabling citizens to be treated in a uniform manner and ensuring that DECISION MAKING and ADMINISTRATION are accountable through the official hierachy and/or involving responsible ministers. These general remarks on the selection, conditions of service and duties of the civil service, can be illustrated from the experience of the United Kingdom.

The United Kingdom, which does not have an enacted CONSTITUTION has no statute which can be compared to the civil service statutes of most other countries. Conditions of service are laid down in a number of Orders in Council and official codes, and the maintenance of these rules together with the promulgation of new ones are the responsibility at present of the Management and Personnel Office (within the Cabinet Office), with the prime minister having the additional title of Minister of the Civil Service – though matters of a day to day nature are generally dealt with by a junior minister. The position of Head of the Home Civil Service is currently held by the Secretary of the Cabinet, though this has not invariably been the case. Since the Civil Service Department was disbanded in 1981 the responsibility for controlling civil service manpower, pay, superannuation and responsibility for the Central Computer and Telecommunications Agency was transferred to the Treasury and responsibility for management, organization, training and overall efficiency, including training and personnel policy, was transferred to the Management and Personnel Office. Civil servants may normally belong to unions, which look after the interests of individuals and groups of staff, make representations and negotiate on their behalf.

Civil servants in the United Kingdom are either recruited by the Civil Service Commission (which is part of the Management and Personnel Office, though the Commissioners have independent authority for selection decisions), or by departments using procedures that have been laid down or approved by the Civil Service Commission. Once recruited, they work in government departments or ministries, each of which has a minister who is answerable for it in parliament. The majority of British civil servants work away from London in regional or local offices, but most of those who are involved in formulating policy and advising ministers, or who are associated directly with parliamentary

duties, work in or near Whitehall. For purposes of good personnel management, civil servants (who in 1986 numbered nearly 600,000) are appointed to grades which are organized into categories and groups. They are trained within their departments or by attending courses at the Civil Service College or in courses at other educational or training institutions which have been officially approved or awarded training contracts. Civil servants do not contribute to an occupational pension fund but this is reflected in setting pay levels, and permanent officials are entitled to pensions on retirement and their entitlements relate to the number of years of service.

Criticisms of the civil service in any country tend to have certain characteristics in common. In general they arise either from the defects of BUREAUCRACY or from the political and administrative cultures within which civil servants perform their duties. These criticisms include delays in dealing with the public and over-devotion to precedent, elitism and remoteness from the rest of the community, lack of initiative and imagination, and unwillingness to take responsibility or make decisions. Other criticisms include: in France, the alleged political power of technocratic civil servants who initiate and implement policies; in Italy, the widespread practice of political patronage affecting appointment and promotion and having consequences in terms of inefficiencies and corruption.

Conscious efforts are made in most civil services to eliminate or reduce these deficiencies. In the United Kingdom for example, the Conservative government first elected in 1979 has placed considerable emphasis on achieving greater efficiency in the use of resources. It has employed various means to this end including a series of scrutinies overseen by the Efficiency Unit reporting to the prime minister and the introduction of the Financial Management Initiative (FMI) designed to ensure that all managers have a clear view of their objectives and the means to assess how far they are achieving them as well as a clear responsibility and accountability for making the best use of their resources and the information, training and expert advice they need.

Civil services are the means by which modern societies are held together. Their influence on the quality of life for the general population through the services they design and run is considerable. Civil servants have responsibilities for formulating policies, designing management systems for large scale complex tasks, and serving LEGISLATURES in executive capacities. Consequently many people find it difficult to distinguish between the responsibilities of civil service personnel and the policies of governments which they carry out but for which they are not politically accountable.   RAC

Reading

Barker, E.: *The Development of Public Services in Western Europe 1660–1930*. Oxford: Oxford University Press, 1944.

Cabinet Office: *Civil Service Yearbook*. London: HMSO, annually.

Campbell, C.: *Governments Under Stress: Political Executives and Key Bureaucrats in Washington, London and Ottawa*. Toronto: University of Toronto Press, 1983.

Chapman, B.: *The Profession of Government: the public service of Europe*. London: Allen & Unwin, 1959.

Chapman, R.A.: *Leadership in the British Civil Service: a study of Sir Percival Waterfield and the creation of the Civil Service Selection Board*. London: Croom Helm, 1984.

Dogan, M. ed.: *The Mandarins of Western Europe: the political role of top civil servants*. London: Halstead, 1975.

Garrett, J.: *Managing the Civil Service*. London: Heinemann, 1980.

Heclo, H. and Wildavsky, A.: *The Private Government of Public Money*. 2nd edn. London: Macmillan, 1981.

Sisson, C.H.: *The Spirit of British Administration and Some European Comparisons*. 2nd edn. London: Faber, 1966.

civil war Problems of definition occur because of the imprecision of both the word civil and the word war. 'Civil' implies that the war is between citizens of the same states but sometimes whether or not the combatants are members of one state is precisely what the war is about. 'War' implies both a large number of combatants and a substantial duration; if such a restrictive meaning is not applied all manner of events such as strikes, demonstrations, terrorist actions, insurrections, military coups could be considered to be wars. Not all civil wars are either revolutions or rebellions, for a civil war can take place between two antagonists with equally plausible claims to rulership, e.g. the war between King Stephen and Matilda in twelfth-century England. Not all rebellions are civil wars or lead to one: witness the almost bloodless and very rapid overthrow of President Marcos of the Philippine Republic in February 1986. Perhaps the best definition is the rough and ready one of civil war as a large-scale and sustained bout of hostilities between rival factions in a state for the possession of supreme political power, or between the government of a state and insurgents. It should be noted especially that in international law a state of civil war exists only if the two sides are recognized by other states as belligerents.

Though hundreds of studies have been devoted to individual civil wars such as the war between Caesar and Pompey, the English Civil War and the American Civil War, no comparative study has been made. The numerous monographs, essays, or hints as to how such a study might usefully be undertaken address questions which suggest four approaches. The first is a matter of quantification: how many such wars there have been in a given period, when, and with what set patterns (Sorokin 1937; Richardson 1960). A second might be the classification of the objectives of civil wars: Johnson (1964) has identified these, which he calls 'limited objectives', as political, economic, religious, nationalist and separatist, with a residual class in which they may be combined. A third approach could concentrate on identifying causes: Eckstein has shown that the factors stressed by scholars are sometimes intellectual, sometimes economic; sometimes they lie in the social structure, sometimes in the political arrangements. He shows that these explanations are both self-contradictory and too many in number. Finally, a fourth approach might be concerned with the way in which a civil war develops, through four stages: initial

violence, expansion, consolidation and victory.
See also GUERRILLA WARFARE.   SEF

Reading

Eckstein, H. ed.: *Internal War: problems and approaches*. New York: Collier-Macmillan, 1964.

————: On the etiology of internal wars. *History and Theory* (1965) 133–62.

Ellis, J.: *Armies in Revolution*. London: Croom Helm, 1973.

Feierabend, I.K., Feierabend, R.L. and Gurr, T.T. eds: *Anger, Violence, and Politics*. Englewood Cliffs, NJ: Prentice-Hall, 1972.

Gurr, T.R.: *Why Men Rebel*. Princeton, NJ: Princeton University Press, 1970.

Johnson, C.A.: *Revolution and the Social System*. Stanford, Calif.: The Hoover Institute; Stanford University Press, 1964.

Richardson, L.F.: *Statistics of Deadly Quarrels*. London: Stevens, 1960.

Sorokin, P.: *Fluctuations of Social Relationships, War, and Revolution*, Vol. III of *Social and Cultural Dynamics*. New York: American Book Co., 1937.

clericalism   A term used to describe the influence of religious hierarchies in political systems, particularly in the modern era. While it is occasionally applied to almost any context where religious functionaries take on a political role, its prime reference historically has been to the role of certain Roman Catholic hierarchies in countries or among populations where Catholicism has traditionally been dominant. As it is used in political debate the term has a pejorative connotation and almost always refers to the improper exercise of the influence of the clergy, in particular by 'exploiting' the loyalty of lay believers; occasionally it is used by loyal Roman Catholics themselves. Its most frequent usage however is found among secularists and anticlericals (see ANTICLERICALISM) to designate the thing they distinctively oppose and denounce; for example, Gambetta in 1877: 'le cléricalisme – voilà l'ennemi'.

In pre-modern times in particular, conflicts between CHURCH AND STATE were generally fought out without the church resorting to mobilization of lay support. It was only with the FRENCH REVOLUTION and the intense politicization of anti-church and anticlerical sentiments that clericalism, properly so-called, came to prominence. In the first half of the nineteenth century some liberal Roman Catholics argued that the church should come to terms with the modern world as represented by the principles of the French Revolution but, under the pontificate of Pius IX the church decisively resisted and committed itself to the defence and promotion of its interests and values through, *inter alia*, clericalist means. Because of this historical background the term has tended to be restricted to those occasions when clerical influence has been exercised either in the interests of the church itself or in the furthering of reactionary causes. In France where the right was very divided, Roman Catholic anti-revolutionary sentiment, which was energetically promoted by the clergy, was one of the few unifying factors. In many parts of Roman Catholic Europe the representative figure of clericalism was the clerical deputy, often elected as the member for a CONFESSIONAL PARTY, and in the 1920s the leaders or guiding spirits of such parties in Germany, Italy, Austria and the Netherlands were all priests. The emergence of CHRISTIAN DEMOCRACY as the principal vehicle for the influence of religion in the politics of the liberal democracies after the second world war brought the career of clericalism in Europe to a virtual end. In Latin America, where the opposition between clericalists and modernizing secularists had also been a central feature of political debate and conflict in the nineteenth and early twentieth centuries, clericalism also declined as a political factor, particularly after Vatican II, as other more open and progressive streams of Roman Catholic opinion came into prominence.

                                                    JTSM

Reading

Berger, S. ed.: *Religion in West European Politics*. London: Cass, 1983.

Merkl, P. and Smart, N. eds: *Religion and Politics in the Modern World*. New York: University of New York Press, 1983.

Smith, D.E.: *Religion and Political Development*. Boston, Mass.: Little, Brown, 1970.

Whyte, J.H.: *Catholics in Western Democracies*. Dublin: Gill & Macmillan, 1981.

clientelism The term used to describe informal power relations between individuals or groups in unequal positions, based on the exchange of benefits. The simplest bilateral relation is found in small communities and primitive societies. A person with higher status (the patron) takes advantage of his or her authority and resources to protect and benefit somebody with an inferior status (the client) who reciprocates with support and services.

In more complex societies clientelism networks allow for more complex multilateral relationships. Patrons are the gatekeepers and brokers who establish the connection between the central power which distributes resources and the masses who reciprocate. Political scientists distinguish between a traditional clientelism involving notables (vertical) and a new clientelism involving organizations (horizontal). The old clientelism is of a personal and affective nature. The patron relies upon his or her prestige and the client shows devotion and gratitude. The new clientelism involves only tangible benefits. Patrons control political organizations and use public resources (employment, pensions, social benefits), while clients, who can be organizations such as ethnic minorities or professional associations, reciprocate with the vote.

The main instrument of the new clientelism is the political MACHINE, led by a BOSS who plays the role of a broker and political manager. But in addition mass clientelistic parties were formed, parties which relied on strong organization rather than mass participation.

In each type of clientelism, relationships are both voluntary and coercive, based not upon collective solidarity, but upon particular interests. Clientelism, then, is a method of ruling through consensus. As such, it is found in different forms in political systems at different levels of development. In rural societies in some subcontinents (the Muslim Mediterranean and south-east Asia) clientelism has ancient roots and has shaped mentality and behaviour for centuries. Colonialism in Latin America and Africa favoured the survival of clientelism because it strengthened the relationships of dependence both within and between states.

Clientelism has been particularly noticeable in transitional societies, undergoing rapid and violent modernization. Decolonization and problems of national integration in developing countries increase the need for patronage of both the old and new types. Clientelism results also from urbanization and immigration in industrial countries, leading to the destruction of traditional institutions, ethnic, linguistic and religious fragmentation and arbitrariness in the distribution of resources.

Traditional clientelism including notables still exists in the third world. The patrons have names such as *caciques* in Mexico, *coroneles* in Brazil, *agas* in Turkey, *zaims* in the Middle East. There is machine politics in such new states as Ivory Coast, Senegal, Nigeria, but the prototype was first studied in the American metropolis with severe problems of immigration and unemployment. Mass clientelistic parties also exist in more modern societies (Christian Democrats in the Italian south, and the Gaullist party in the west of France). Finally, clientelism can also be found in specific subsystems such as local government and the bureaucracy.

See also FACTION; PATRONAGE.   MC

Reading

Clapham, C. ed.: *Private Patronage and Public Power: political clientelism in the modern state*. London: Pinter, 1982.

Eisenstadt, S.N. and Lemarchand, R. eds: *Political Clientelism, Patronage and Development*. Beverly Hills, Calif.: Sage, 1981.

Schmidt, S.W., Scott, J.C., Landé, C.H. and Guasti, L. eds: *Friends, Followers and Factions: a reader on political clientelism*. Berkeley, Calif., Los Angeles and London: University of California Press, 1977.

closure See PARLIAMENTARY OBSTRUCTION.

coalition/coalition government An interparty coalition is a set of several parties pursuing a common goal; a coalition government is a specific form of coalition. Coalition governments are commonly contrasted with single-party governments, in which only one party holds office. They should also be distinguished from non-partisan governments, within which cabinet members do not act as representatives of political parties. Coalition governments are party governments. The membership of a coalition government is conventionally defined as those parties that are represented in the cabinet. Some parliamentary governments however consistently co-operate with parties which do not hold cabinet portfolios. Government coalitions are only one form of coalition between political parties; other forms are *legislative* coalitions and *electoral* coalitions. Legislative coalitions are commonly formed by MINORITY GOVERNMENTS which need to broaden their parliamentary support; electoral coalitions are typically designed to avoid the penalties many ELECTORAL SYSTEMS impose on smaller parties.

In pure or modified two-party systems, such as New Zealand, the United Kingdom and Canada, coalition governments are very rare in peacetime. In many multiparty systems, such as Belgium and the Netherlands, virtually all governments are coalitions. Other multiparty countries, such as Denmark and Sweden, alternate between coalition and single-party (often minority) governments. Coalition governments normally consist of two to five parties. Governments with even more parties occasionally form in countries with very fragmented party systems or in situations of national emergency. Coalition governments may be majority or minority governments: whereas most majority governments in multiparty countries tend to be coalitions, most minority governments consist of only one party. A *grand coalition* is a government composed of all parliamentary parties. Grand coalitions are very rare, except in situations of war or other national emergencies – though Swiss governments regularly include all major parties. Coalition governments which include just enough parties to secure a parliamentary majority are called *minimal winning*. Most coalition theories of government formation predict that minimal winning coalitions will necessarily form, and in fact such govern-

ments are common; the Swiss experience however runs counter to this prediction, as does that of several other smaller democracies, such as Belgium.

Within coalition governments the distribution of cabinet portfolios among the participating parties is generally roughly proportional to their parliamentary strength. Small but pivotal parties are often able to secure greater representation than their size would warrant. Coalition governments have traditionally been viewed as less stable than those consisting of a single party. Recent studies have shown considerable variation in durability between different kinds of coalition governments. Minimal winning coalitions exhibit substantially greater stability than minority coalitions and oversized governments, and can prove as stable as single-party governments.   KS

Reading

Axelrod, R.: *Conflict of Interest.* Chicago, Ill.: Markham, 1970.

Blondel, J.: Party systems and patterns of government in western democracies. *Canadian Journal of Political Science* 1 (1968) 180–203.

Bogdanor, V. ed.: *Coalition Government in Western Europe.* London: Heinemann, 1983.

Browne, E.C. and Dreijmanis, J. eds: *Government Coalitions in Western Democracies.* New York: Longman, 1982.

Dodd, L.C.: *Coalitions in Parliamentary Government.* Princeton, NJ: Princeton University Press, 1976.

Lijphart, A.: *Democracies: patterns of majoritarian and consensus government in twenty-one countries.* New Haven, Conn. and London: Yale University Press, 1984.

Luebbert, G.M.: *Comparative Democracy: policy-making and governing coalitions in Europe and Israel.* New York: Columbia University Press, 1986.

Swaan, A. de: *Coalition Theories and Cabinet Formations.* Amsterdam: Elsevier, 1973.

Taylor, M. and Laver, M.: Coalition governments in Western Europe. *European Journal of Political Research* 1 (1973) 205–48.

Warwick, P.: The durability of coalition governments in parliamentary democracies. *Comparative Political Studies* 11 (1979) 465–98.

coalition theory   A sub-area of positive

political theory, a branch of political theory distinguished by its commitment to the development of axiomatically based, deduced theories of important political processes (cf. PUBLIC CHOICE THEORY; RATIONAL CHOICE; SOCIAL CHOICE THEORY). Introduced by William H. Riker, coalition theory is concerned with decision making in groups of three or more members, where the joining together of some of them will be necessary and sufficient to control a decisional outcome. To quote Riker: 'the process of making a decision in a group is the process of forming a subgroup which, by the rules accepted by all members, can decide for the whole. This subgroup is a coalition.' (*Theory of Political Coalitions*, ch. xii).

Coalition formation is assumed to be the outcome of strategic decision making by rational actors in some decisional context. Here, rationality connotes purposive behaviour, calculated to be efficient in the maximization of individual preferences (utility). This behaviour is typically analysed by the application of mathematical models drawn from the theory of n-person games. GAME THEORY models investigate allocations of game pay-offs (values associated with the game) under an assumption of individually rational behaviour. Subject to certain constraints that define a particular game, the object of analysis is to identify, from all possible pay-off divisions, that allocation (or allocations) which is pay-off maximizing for all game players. This particular division (or divisions) constitutes a 'solution' for the game being played.

Whereas game theory models are concerned with the identification of the pay-off division that is dominant over all others possible, coalition theories try to identify from the set of all actors the subset (or subsets) that may be expected to form a winning coalition. Again, based on the assumption of individually rational behaviour, that coalition (or coalitions) is expected to form which maximizes the pay-off shares of all its members, relative to the share they all could expect to receive from participation in alternative coalitions with other, similarly motivated, players.

In the construction of coalition theories, certain features of the decision making context are specified in advance so that analyses become tractable. These include a minimum number of relevant actors (three) and some effective standard of decisiveness (usually a majority decision rule). Also, some assumptions about the properties of available pay-offs are made, most commonly: the value of the pay-off to all winners is equal to the loss in value to all losers (the constant-sum condition); the value of the pay-off is constant over all coalitions that form (the simple game condition); and value may be allocated to individual coalition members from the coalition pay-off (the condition of transferable utility). Given conditions such as these and the general assumption of rational behaviour, hypotheses regarding the expected composition of winning coalitions are deduced. The most enduring hypothesis to have emerged is the expectation that the minimal winning coalition will form (that coalition with sufficient members to satisfy the decision rule, but no more) (see Riker 1962; Gamson 1961; Leiserson 1968).

Empirical testing of the implications of these minimal size theories, conducted mostly in the context of cabinet coalition formation in western European democracies, produced disappointing results. In consequence a family of new theories were developed based on a motivational assumption that actors seek to join coalitions which minimize the extent of preference disagreement among them. This conception assumes that actors create coalition pay-offs over a set of available alternatives by a bargained agreement (e.g. a set of policies). If the disparity (distance) between the most preferred alternatives of some decisive set of actors is minimized, then any agreement on alternatives they can reach will be closer to the ideal points of the actors involved than will be the case for all of them in alternative coalitions they each might join. Hypotheses are derived from this group of theories which predict the formation of those winning coalitions that minimize conflict of interest, or that minimize the policy distance separating actors (see Axelrod 1970; De Swaan 1973).

Since the appearance of these two kinds of

theories work has progressed along somewhat divergent paths, as a result of dissatisfaction with the mathematical, theoretical, and empirical adequacy of the early theories. First, the game theoretic basis of coalition theories (particularly constant-sum theories) was called into question by McKelvey, Ordeshook, and Winer (1978) with a new mathematical formulation, known as the 'competitive solution'. This model identifies stability conditions for the formation of coalitions and the allocation of pay-offs, applied to co-operative games with non-transferable utility. A special case of this model is able to handle MAJORITY RULE, spatial games, and is consistent with the view of the formation process advanced by the policy distance minimization theories.

A second issue concerns the static character of the early coalition theories that treated each formation as a separate episode, unrelated to consideration of former or future coalition formations in the same setting. This problem has been addressed by Bueno de Mesquita (1975) in the formulation of a coalition theory which incorporates a redistributive perspective on the process. This theory posits that actors in parliamentary situations attempt to attain majority actor status by using the acquisition of particular ministerial portfolios to enhance their parliamentary resources over time. Hence, this theory proposed that coalition formation be modelled as a supergame of successive formations, ending when some actor dominates the process alone.

Since all these theoretical treatments deal with coalition experiences at a relatively high level of formal abstraction, many scholars have expressed concern about their ability adequately to capture the empirical richness of the contexts to which they must inevitably be applied.

To meet this demand for more contextual specificity Dodd (1976) has offered an inductively based theory of coalition formation in multiparty parliaments. He identifies coalition formation as the result of variable conditions describing structural features of the political setting (e.g. degrees of multipartism) and particular characteristics of actors (e.g. their a priori willingness to bargain).

As may be seen, coalition theories have been preoccupied with the problem of identifying the processes which determine the composition of winning coalitions. These are seen as largely dependent on the way in which rational actors deal with the allocation of coalition pay-offs. Scholars have generally been unable to relate the process of pay-off distribution to the axiomatic structure of coalition theories in an entirely successful way. Browne and Franklin (1973) have produced strong evidence for the proposition that actors in winning (formed) cabinet coalitions allocate government ministries proportionally to their seat contributions to the coalition, but this distribution rule has not yet been derived in a formal coalition theory. Recent work by Schofield and Laver (1985), however, has demonstrated that predictions of ministerial allocations from bargaining set theory are successful when certain conditions are present in the context.

If there is a trend here it is away from the creation of coalition theories applied generally in favour of concentration on coalition phenomena in specific contexts. The most intensively studied area is that of cabinet coalitions. Interest has most recently focused on the issue of cabinet stability (durability) over time. A major hypothesis, being developed by Browne, Frendreis and Gleiber (1984), is that coalition formation is dependent on actor decision-making which is not only concerned with the maximization of benefits realized at the time of formation but also contingent on anticipated (or unanticipated) disruptions in an expected benefit stream over time. Here, formation becomes problematic (probabilistic) to the extent that actors attempt to build in considerations of future increments of benefit and loss.

Coalition theory has undergone considerable development since its inception in the early 1960s. The current preoccupation with stability demonstrates a commitment to bring these theories closer to the reality they try to inform. As this development becomes more refined we may expect increasing empirical relevance to displace the earlier scepticism which many voiced about its prospects.   ECB

Reading

Axelrod, R.: *Conflict of Interest*. Chicago, Ill.: Markham, 1970.

Browne, E. and Franklin, M.: Aspects of coalition payoffs in European parliamentary democracies. *American Political Science Review* 67 (1973) 453–69.

——— , Frendreis, J. and Gleiber, D.: An 'events' approach to the problem of cabinet stability. *Comparative Political Studies* 17 (1984) 167–97.

———: The process of cabinet dissolution: an exponential model of duration and stability in western democracies. *American Journal of Political Science* 30 (1986) 628–50.

Bueno de Mesquita, B.: *Strategy, Risk and Personality in Coalition Politics: the case of India*. Cambridge: Cambridge University Press, 1975.

Dodd, L.C.: *Coalitions in Parliamentary Government*. Princeton, NJ: Princeton University Press, 1976.

Gamson, W.: A theory of coalition formation. *American Sociological Review* 26 (1961) 373–82.

Leiserson, M.: Factions and coalitions in one-party Japan: an interpretation based on the theory of games. *American Political Science Review* 57 (1968) 770–87.

McKelvey, R., Ordeshook, P. and Winer, M.: The competitive solution for n-person games without transferable utility, with an application to committee games. *American Political Science Review* 72 (1978) 599–615.

Riker, W.H.: *The Theory of Political Coalitions*. New Haven, Conn.: Yale University Press, 1962.

Schofield, N. and Laver, M.: Bargaining theory and portfolio payoffs in European coalition governments 1945–83. *British Journal of Political Science* 15 (1985) 143–64.

Swaan, A. de: *Coalition Theories and Cabinet Formations*. Amsterdam: Elsevier, 1973.

cohabitation A colloquial term used to describe a situation in a SEMI-PRESIDENTIAL SYSTEM in which a directly elected president must live together with a parliamentary majority of an opposite colour. The term is particularly applied to the experience of France following the legislative elections of 1986 when, for the first time in the history of the Fifth Republic, a president of the Left faced a parliamentary majority of the Right; but the same situation has arisen in other semi-presidential regimes. The experience of *cohabitation* shows that a constitution does not delineate a unique governmental structure, and that different regimes can flourish within the same juridical framework according to the constellation of political forces at any particular time.   VBB

Cole, George Douglas Howard (1889–1959) British socialist, intellectual and polymath. His published output was prodigious across a range of disciplines, reflected in the fact that he was appointed, consecutively, to the Readership in economics at Oxford and then to the Chichele chair of social and political theory.

Cole is best remembered for his lifelong commitment to a form of decentralized, participatory socialism as the most desirable system of social organization. This was the central tenet of GUILD SOCIALISM, which flourished briefly as both doctrine and movement during the second decade of the century, and of which Cole was the leading theorist. Cole argued, on the basis of a political theory that rejected prevailing orthodoxies about the nature of the state and of REPRESENTATION, that an active DEMOCRACY required SELF-GOVERNMENT by the workers in industry and a political structure that represented people in a multiform way in relation to their functional and territorial loyalties. Hence both CAPITALISM and a collectivist SOCIALISM were defective as systems of industrial organization, just as parliament was an inadequate and restricted form of political representation. Cole attempted to describe a model of a (guild socialist) society which met the requirements of an active, pluralistic democracy. This attempt produced ever more elaborate schemes of co-ordinated functional and territorial representation, most notably in *Guild Socialism Re-stated* (1920).

Although guild socialism disappeared as a movement, and Cole later disavowed some of his more Byzantine system building, he always remained essentially a guild socialist. After many years of neglect Cole's ideas have been rediscovered by a generation dissatisfied with both the capitalist and socialist versions of democracy dominant in the twentieth century and concerned with extending ideas of democracy in new ways.   AWW

Reading

Cole, G.D.H.: *Self-Government in Industry*. London: Bell, 1917.

————: *Social Theory*. London: Methuen, 1920.

————: *Guild Socialism Restated*. London: Parsons, 1920.

Glass, S.T.: *The Responsible Society: the ideas of the English guild socialists*. London: Longman, 1966.

Wright, A.W.: *G.D.H. Cole and Socialist Democracy*. Oxford: Clarendon Press, 1979.

collective action   Since the publication of Mancur Olson's *Logic of Collective Action* (1965), the term has generally been understood to refer to the action taken by members of a group to further their common interest, especially (though not exclusively) where the common interest is in the provision of a public good. Collective action, or the potential for it, is ubiquitous. Examples include: attempts by farmers to persuade a government to maintain or increase price supports, or by the firms in some industry to secure protection against foreign competition, and similar lobbying efforts generally; the formation and maintenance of voluntary associations; collusive actions by producers designed to maintain the price of their product by restricting output (as, for example, the members of OPEC (Organization of Petroleum-Exporting Countries) sometimes endeavour to do); actions by neighbouring peasants to install or maintain communal irrigation facilities; demonstrations, strikes, rebellions and the like; efforts by any group of people to maintain order among themselves or to defend themselves against external aggression; mutual restraint in the exploitation of a scarce resource.

All these examples share a common feature: they each involve a good which a member of the group in question can consume (or in some way benefit from) whether or not he or she contributes to its provision. For example, a worker benefits from the wage rise which his fellow workers have brought about even if he has not contributed to their efforts, by paying dues to the relevant trade union, by participating in a strike, or whatever. A member of OPEC may similarly benefit from the higher price of oil which the actions of other members have brought about without cutting its own production of oil.

The ability of an individual to be a free rider on the efforts of others is possible because the good (or service) is a *public good*. A public good is not necessarily one provided by a government, nor one provided by a number of individuals acting jointly. It is one which is to some extent indivisible and also non-excludable. A good is indivisible if it can be consumed or used by one individual without reducing the amount available to other members of the public in question, and it is non-excludable if it is impossible or at least economically unfeasible to prevent any member of the public from consuming it.

If some or all of the members of a group take advantage of such opportunities to become free riders, there may be little or no collective action and the public good may be provided in sub-optimal amounts or not at all. The existence of a common interest among the members of some group is therefore no guarantee that they will act to further it. Such failure of collective action is widespread. For example, only a small minority of the substantial numbers of Americans who (as surveys repeatedly reveal) claim to care a great deal about the state of the environment are prepared to do anything about it.

Collective action is fundamental to politics, for most if not all political activity would not be necessary if individuals generally acted voluntarily to further the interests they share with others. The forms which political activity takes, the roles and institutions through and in which it takes place, are in part explicable in terms of the underlying collective action problems which it solves.

The ubiquity and importance of the collective action or free rider problem has come to be much more widely recognized since the publication of Olson's book. Olson's main contribution was to show that the problem was more acute in large groups than in small ones (thereby undermining the view that a group's effectiveness in influencing government policy is proportional to the number of individuals sharing the common interest it tries to promote). There are essentially three reasons for this size effect: first, the larger the group the smaller the benefit accruing to the individual from the additional amount of the public good resulting from his contribution – and the more likely, therefore that this benefit will be outweighed by the cost of making the contribution; second, the larger the number of people the greater the costs of organizing them; and third, the larger the group the less likely it is to contain one or more individuals who are prepared to shoulder the costs of providing the public good unilaterally and the less likely too that the group will be able to overcome the free rider problem through some form of conditional co-operation (in which each person contributes if and only if enough others do). In smaller groups, too, especially those with a slowly changing membership, informal social sanctions based on approval and disapproval can be used more effectively to induce co-operation. These size effects are no doubt among the reasons why many large political organizations and voluntary associations have a federal structure and mobilize support through local cells or branches.

Collective action may be organized or facilitated in larger groups by the efforts of 'political entrepreneurs' or leaders, who characteristically operate by providing selective incentives (goods or services available to the individual only if he contributes), by facilitating conditional co-operation, by persuading individuals that others too will co-operate only if they do, and in other ways persuading people that their contributions matter.

The failure of people to provide themselves with public goods voluntarily has been used to provide a justification for intervention by the STATE and more generally to argue, as Thomas HOBBES did, that people would want to institute government in order to ensure that at least the fundamental public goods of social order and national defence were provided.

MJT

Reading

Barry, B. and Hardin, R. eds: *Rational Man and Irrational Society?* Beverly Hills, Calif.: Sage, 1982.

Hardin, R.: *Collective Action.* Baltimore, Md. and London: The Johns Hopkins University Press, 1982.

Olson, M.: *The Logic of Collective Action: public goods and the theory of groups.* 2nd edn. Cambridge, Mass.: Harvard University Press, 1971.

Taylor, M.: *The Possibility of Co-operation.* Cambridge and New York: Cambridge University Press, 1987; rev. edn. of *Anarchy and Co-operation.* London: Wiley, 1976.

collective leadership The principle of shared authority in accordance with which the leaderships of COMMUNIST and Marxist–LENINIST parties are supposed to conduct their affairs. Collective leadership is described in the current rules of the Communist Party of the Soviet Union (CPSU) as the 'supreme principle of party leadership', which in turn is a prerequisite for the 'normal functioning of party organizations, the proper education of cadres, [and] the promotion of the activity and initiative of Communists' (rule 27). The principle of collective leadership is regarded as having been crudely violated during the STALIN era, together with other 'Leninist norms of party life' such as criticism and self-criticism. The twentieth Party Congress of 1956, which heard Khrushchev's 'secret speech' on the Stalin period, adopted a resolution calling for the elimination of the 'cult of personality' which had characterized those years, and for the full restoration of collective leadership and other norms of party life. In 1964 the CENTRAL COMMITTEE took matters further by resolving that, in order to guard against excessive concentration of power in the hands of a single person, the posts of prime minister and party leader should in future be held by different people. Other ruling communist parties operate upon similar principles and, like the CPSU, generally separate the party leadership from the prime ministership, although the party leader, for largely ceremonial reasons, may also hold the post of state president.

SLW

Reading

Schapiro, L.: *The Communist Party of the Soviet Union.* 2nd edn. London: Methuen, 1970.

Simons, W.B. and White, S. eds: *The Party Statutes of the Communist World.* The Hague: Nijhoff, 1984.

collectivism The term was first applied to

the anarchist socialism of Bakunin and his followers. A collective meant an autonomous self-governing association of individuals, founded on the principles of equality and co-operation. Such collectivism was intended as an alternative both to the competitive individualism of CAPITALISM and the centralized authority of state SOCIALISM. This meaning has been overshadowed in the last hundred years by the use of the word collectivism for the ideological orientation that is antagonistic to individualism. This has often made it a synonym for socialism and socialist economic theory, but its meaning goes wider still, embracing all those doctrines which have justified state interference in society and the economy. In this sense socialism becomes only one of many collectivist doctrines.

This wider meaning of collectivism was emphasized by DICEY who contrasted the principles of Benthamism or individualism with collectivism. Since the middle of the nineteenth century the tide of opinion had been flowing strongly towards collectivism. Dicey defined the fundamental principle of collectivism as 'faith in the benefit to be derived by the mass of the people from the action or intervention of the State' (Law and Public Opinion, 2nd edn, p. 259). Collectivists rejected *laissez-faire* as a principle of sound legislation; they supported governmental interference even when it greatly limited the sphere of individual choice and liberty. Dicey thought collectivism had begun to influence legislation in England in four main areas: the extension of protection, the restriction of freedom of contract, a preference for collective as opposed to individual action, and the equalization of advantages among individuals.

During the nineteenth century in England the rise of collectivism was a slow process that involved piecemeal acceptance of the need to extend the sphere of public responsibility and public action. The main areas of collectivist advance were state regulation to enforce minimum standards in such areas as the employment of women and children, the adulteration of food, subsidies for private interests, public provision of services such as health and education, and new forms of public enterprise at both national and local level. In many other countries, such as Germany and Japan, the rise of collectivism was a matter of deliberate state policy. The virtues of organization and efficiency were placed ahead of liberal ideals of the dispersal of power and individual autonomy.

Collectivism came to mean all those doctrines which asserted that the complexity of modern industrial societies required an expanding role for administrative DECISION MAKING by central bodies, overriding where necessary the preferences and outcomes established by individual exchanges through markets. Some critics of collectivism such as F. A. Hayek have argued that all collectivist measures, whatever their intent, lead irresistibly towards socialism, which he defines as the centralization of decision making in the hands of the state and the belief that social goals are best achieved by central direction.

Collectivism does not have to entail that the means of production, distribution and exchange should be owned collectively, and the proposition that collectivist measures start liberal societies on a slippery slope to serfdom and TOTALITARIANISM has not been convincingly demonstrated. What has persisted is a continuing debate about where the frontiers should be drawn between public and private provision, where administrative planning should be relied on in preference to markets, and how much the collective and interdependent basis of modern societies makes some form of collectivism in public policy unavoidable.

This debate does not run on party lines but takes place within political parties and within political IDEOLOGIES. W. H. Greenleaf presents the contrast between libertarianism and collectivism as the most fundamental contrast in attitudes and values underlying modern political debate and action in all modern societies. On this view, what is distinctive about collectivism is first its stress on notions of the public good and social justice, which justify the interests of the community being given priority over the interests of individuals; second, an emphasis on centralization of power and administration to ensure uniformity and consistency in the pursuit of social objectives; and third, a preference for extending the role and responsibilities of public authorities to deal with social and economic problems. Since collectivists do not believe that social harmony arises spontaneously through the activities of individuals, they favour an organization of society which rests on a permanent intervention by the state to secure the interests of the community and maintain social order. The task of the state is to ensure that all its citizens are treated equally and provided with equal opportunities so that all enjoy an adequate level of security and welfare. This usually means a preference for administrative rather than market solutions.

Collectivism in this broad sense covers much more than socialism. The rise of collectivism in the twentieth century in all industrial societies has been sponsored by parties from all parts of the political spectrum. Much of the collectivist legislation in Britain to which Dicey was so opposed was passed by Liberal and Conservative governments. The attack on *laissez-faire* came from New Liberals and Social Imperialists as well as Fabian socialists. Twentieth-century politics have often been labelled the politics of the collectivist age. There has been general acceptance of collective representation of interests through political parties and producer groups, as well as the acceptance of continuous intervention by government in both society and the economy.

The expectation however that the trend towards ever greater centralization of power and decision making would prove irresistible and irreversible has not been realized. All advanced industrial societies are now collectivist in the sense that they have large and growing public sectors and major areas of policy where political and administrative criteria prevail over market principles. But there is no uniform pattern, and a wide range of variation exists in the degree of reliance placed on market as opposed to collective criteria in the pursuit of social objectives.

AMG

Reading

Beer, S.H.: *Modern British Politics*. 3rd edn. London: Faber, 1982.

Dicey, A.V.: *Law and Public Opinion in England during the Nineteenth Century*. 2nd edn. London: Macmillan, 1962.

Greenleaf, W.H.: *The British Political Tradition*, Vol. I. (2 vols.) London: Methuen, 1983.

colonial government The essential characteristic concerns distance: where central control is impossible on a remote frontier, whether of a settled, ceded or protected DEPENDENCY, the problem is how much local autonomy can be tolerated and balanced by metropolitan supervision in the interest of continuing imperial unity. The issue was no different for Rome in the outlying provinces of Gaul or Britain, for the English crown in the palatinate of Durham or the 'pale' of Dublin, or for the *Real y Supremo Consejo de las Indias* over the Spanish empire from Lousiana to La Plata: and the government which emerged was always a compromise. By contrast with Phoenician or Greek colonies which owed no obedience to Carthage or Athens, Romans and subsequent EMPIRE builders sought for some control of sprawling empires: Spaniards and Portuguese; French, Dutch and Britons, Russians, Germans and Japanese. But always central authority or royal purpose was blunted by distance. Even an autocrat's powers were reduced: 'the Turk' wrote Burke, 'cannot govern Egypt and Arabia and Kurdistan as he governs Thrace'.

In government the options are always limited. Naturally colonial forms were influenced, if not dictated, by usage and precedent at home, but in the several empires, institutions were, if not identical, not wholly different. There was need for a representative of the sovereign, a governor or viceroy; for a central superintending council; and for a local advisory, even legislative body. Whether possessions of despotic or limited monarchies, the governments in colonies were projections of the mother country: a Spanish empire of overseas sister kingdoms under the crown as in Old Spain; a French centralizing impulse to impose on New France the dualism of governor and intendant of the French provinces; or a Dutch expedient of converting a commercial system into an administrative sub-department. But in practice what emerged was for the most part what the settlers sought to create locally, as their own variations or substitutes, on the basis of the laws and institutions naturally inherited from the metropolis. This was easier in predominantly 'settled' empires such as the British where, in contrast with that of Spain, for example, with its large indigenous populations, the American 'thirteen colonies' consisted largely of emigrants from the British Isles, who imported with them assumptions not only about English law, but also of their rights to representative government and self taxation.

Indeed the British entered into the imperial competition somewhat late and reluctantly. Devices from the medieval experience of governing distant dependencies, which were derived from feudal tenures and joint stock companies, were employed to delegate to individuals or to corporations an authority which might be revoked but which was soon virtually beyond all metropolitan restraint save persistent exhortation. Any continuing loyalty to the crown sprang shrewdly from the realization that too overt a disobedience or declaration of independence would mean no more than the exchange of one metropolitan government for another, and at least the British crown was the devil that was known and could often be disobeyed. Britain had not granted a WESTMINSTER MODEL to her settled colonies: what happened was that settlers tried in many respects (but not all, for example the unparliamentary executive committees in American assemblies) to create parliamentary forms on the foundation of the feudal or company charters they had received. When after the secession of the American colonies British governments were faced with new imperial responsibilities in colonies of non-British, even non-European, race where a British representative system was strongly rejected (as in Quebec) or seemed wholly inappropriate (as in India or Ceylon), new forms of paternal autocracy emerged – of governor and council without an elected assembly.

In 'crown colony government' the legislative council was at first purely nominated – a few officials and perhaps several influential colonists; but in time elected members were introduced. A separate executive council, first set up in the Canadas in 1791, became a normal feature too. When the number of elected members became a majority, it was customary to divide the legislative into two houses – an upper council and an elected assembly. At the next stage, following the example of Canada and other settled colonies in the middle of the nineteenth century after the Durham Report (1839), the executive became responsible in all internal matters to the assembly, and thereafter by securing control over finance, the tariff, commercial treaties, defence and foreign affairs, colonies were able to assert an identity on the international stage and to become acknowledged as having full 'DOMINION status': a category first recognized as a convenient shorthand borrowed from the title Canada had chosen in 1867 (but then without any implication of status) to distinguish self-governing colonies from the rest. Later, in flight from emotive words (for example, empire) and any implication of 'domination', it was replaced in 1949 by the more neutral 'Member of the COMMONWEALTH'. But realization of the burdens in diplomacy and defence placed on mini-states caused in the late 1960s a separate category of 'associate members' to emerge, whereby for a transitional period the United Kingdom at request undertook these external responsibilities.

The practices of colonial government were shaped by what was appropriate in local politics: they were of course transformed when, as in Canada, they had to be adapted to the needs of federal government. In all colonies metropolitan precedents would be claimed when convenient, but emphatically denied when not. Whereas some imperial powers (for example, France) were concerned to see colonial forms imitate the metropolitan model, British government (save in the briefest period after the second world war) had been regularly at pains to warn colonists (and Indians) that the British model was hardly an appropriate export. But on liberation from colonial status new states as often adopted constitutions with some similarity to the metropolitan model as they chose those quite different.   AFM

Reading

Keith, A.B.: *The First British Empire*. Oxford: Clarendon Press, 1930.

Perham, M.: *Native Administration in Nigeria*. Oxford: Oxford University Press, 1962.

Madden, A.F. with Fieldhouse, D.: *Select Documentation of the Constitutional History of the British Empire and Commonwealth, 1175–1914*. 4 vols. Westport and London: Greenwood Press, 1985.

Wight, M.: *The Development of the Legislative Council 1606–1945*. London: Faber, 1947.

commission A body of persons charged with some specific public function; from the word commit, meaning to give in trust. Commissions usually have a regulatory function, for example the Boundary Commissions for England, Northern Ireland, Scotland and Wales, and the Monopolies and Mergers Commission. But they may occasionally denote a form of public enterprise, for example the Forestry Commission. In the late seventeenth century it was fashionable to put one of the great offices of State, such as the Lord High Treasurer, into commission – in other words to spread responsibility from a single person to several.

See also ROYAL COMMISSION.   DNC

Commission (European Community)

This consists of seventeen members appointed by common accord of the twelve European Community member governments. At present there are two Britons, two French, two Germans, two Italians, and two Spaniards, and one member from each of the other countries. They are pledged by treaty (and under oath) not to act as national representatives, nor to seek or accept national instructions. Their collective task is to identify, represent, and promote the common interest of the Community as a whole, rather than the member states' national interests or the sum of these.

Formally, the Commission has four roles: it may act as the executant of decisions taken by the COUNCIL OF MINISTERS; it is intended, primarily, to be the source of the policy proposals on which the Council decides; it mediates within the Council, defending and if necessary modifying its proposals; and it is the guardian of the Treaties, bringing governments, firms, or individuals to book, and if necessary to the EUROPEAN COURT OF JUSTICE if they breach Community law.

The Commission, born of the merger in 1965 of the institutions of the European Coal and Steel Community, the European Atomic Energy Community, and the European Economic Community, has inherited the respective powers of the Commissions of the latter two communities and the High Authority of the European Coal and Steel Community. The High Authority was originally envisaged (see MONNET) as the potential embryo of a future SUPRANATIONAL GOVERNMENT; the Commission, as its more modest name implies, embodies a less ambitious concept. In practice the difference is less marked. The High Authority's powers were chiefly those of executing decisions already reached in the pre-Treaty negotiations; outside those limits, where new policies were required, its role was similar to that of the Commission. In recent years the Commission's central role has been gradually eroded. This has been due in part to the general resurgence of NATIONALISM (not exclusively but powerfully embodied by General de Gaulle); in part to a series of Commission presidents less adroit than the first of them, Walter Hallstein; and in part to the increasing intractability of the problems faced by the Community once it had abolished the more obvious barriers to internal trade and begun to tackle more politicized issues. This, together with the Community's expansion from six to twelve members, has led some observers to question the viability of the original institutional framework. In 1984 the EUROPEAN PARLIAMENT proposed a new Treaty of Union, while the EUROPEAN COUNCIL has adopted a Single European Act to streamline the process of DECISION MAKING.

Neither of these moves, however, seems likely to resolve the central paradox of the Commission's status – independent of governments which appoint its members, acting in some respects like a government of Europe with its own diplomatic representation but so far excluded, save as an observer and adviser, from the regular machinery of foreign policy co-operation among the member states.

These anomalies are reminders that the Community is not a finished product but a process of change which is subject to political pressure and conflict as it evolves.   RJM

Reading

Hallstein, W.: *Die Europäische Gemeinschaft*. Düsseldorf and Vienna: Econ Verlag, 1974.

————: *United Europe: challenge and opportunity*. Cambridge, Mass.: Harvard University Press, 1962.

————: *Der Unvollendete Bundestaat*. Düsseldorf and Vienna: Econ Verlag, 1969.

Wallace, H., Wallace, W. and Webb, C. eds: *Policy Making in the European Communities*. 2nd edn. Chichester: Wiley, 1983.

commission plan A now uncommon form of local administration plan restricted to North America in which the commissioners serve collectively as the governing body of the city and individually as department heads. The commission consists of three to seven members, nearly always elected at large. The commissioners usually select one of their own number as MAYOR to preside over meetings and to perform ceremonial functions, but sometimes all members are elected to specific positions. The plan originated as an emergency measure after the destructive Galveston, TX hurricane of 1901, was advanced by reformers and spread to hundreds of cities in Canada and the United States, but proved to have serious faults. After about 1917 it lost favour to the COUNCIL-MANAGER PLAN. It is no longer used in Canada and is employed in only about 200 cities in the United States.   CRA

Reading

Rice, B.R.: *Progressive Cities: the commission government movement in America*. Austin: University of Texas Press, 1977.

Committee of the Whole House A

working body, first known in the UK HOUSE OF COMMONS, which comprises all the members of the House presided over by a Chairman instead of by the SPEAKER. In modern times the concept of a committee consisting of all but one of the members of its parent body seems strange. Originally, how-

ever, the word committee meant no more than the person or persons to whom a task was given. The emphasis was not on the size of body to which the delegation was made but on the delegation itself; as Redlich put it, 'the formation of the word is the same as that of many other English words which denote the recipient in a bilateral relation of obligation, such as trustee, lessee, nominee, appointee' (1969, p. 204).

In the mid-nineteenth century when other legislatures, such as the United States Congress, already devolved much detailed work to small committees, the British House of Commons had for over two centuries regularly used committees of the whole to consider not only the details of legislation but also financial matters – both the raising of revenue and the authorization of expenditure. Committees of the whole House retained their prominence until well into the twentieth century by which time the use of *ad hoc* STANDING COMMITTEES became the normal mechanism for consideration of legislative details. The distinction remains between some legislatures in the Westminster tradition which retain an element of Committee of the Whole House procedure and others of different traditions which have never employed it.

Commonwealth countries such as Australia and Canada continue to know the committee of the whole procedure, although in the Australian House of Representatives its manifestations as committees of Supply and Ways and Means were brought to an end in 1963, three years before the British House of Commons abolished similar committees. In the Canadian Commons the use of committee of the whole for supply bills persists, while at Westminster the Commons considers the principal clauses of the annual Finance Bill and the details of BILLS of major constitutional import in committee of the whole rather than in standing committees. The device is also occasionally used for other bills which are urgently needed or are of minor importance.

In theory the British House of Commons could still consider matters other than bills in the committee of the whole, but it has not done so since the committees of Supply and Ways and Means were abolished. In the

Australian House of Representatives certain other matters may still be referred to committee of the whole. In the Indian Lok Sabha, however, there is no provision for a committee of the whole, although most legislation is considered by the assembly as a whole.

The main difference between proceedings in committee of the whole and those in the House is the greater informality of the former: members may speak more than once to the same question so that the details of the bill may have the most thorough consideration. Speakers in standing committees in the British House of Commons are similarly un-constrained with the result that debate there also may sometimes be inordinately pro-longed.   KB

Reading

Herman, V.: *Inter-Parliamentary Union: parliaments of the world*. 2nd edn. Aldershot: Gower, 1986.

Redlich, J.: *The Procedure of the House of Commons*, Vol. II. (3 vols.) London: Constable, 1908; repr. New York: AMS Press, 1969.

common law An expression used in a number of different but complementary ways. First, the systems of law in operation in much of the English-speaking world (England, most of the USA, Australia, New Zealand) are common law systems, as contrasted with civil law systems in much of the rest of the world. Common law systems are essentially non-codified, uninfluenced by Roman law and judge-made. STATUTE LAW is frequently seen as a 'stitch in time' rather than the fabric itself. Common law systems tend to be adversary or accusatorial in process, rather than in-quisitorial. In common law systems there tends to be a heavy reliance on precedent or *stare decisis*. Second, common law refers also to those branches of law within common law systems which are essentially the product of case law development, in particular the law of contract, tort and the principles of criminal law. Third, common law also means case law and refers to principles of law developed incrementally over a long period of time; for example it is a common law principle that contracts require consideration, but it is difficult to trace this 'rule' to a single datable

act. Fourth, common law also refers to the law developed in common law courts, as opposed to the law of equity which developed in the Courts of Chancery. Principles emanating from both streams have since 1875 been administered in all courts.   MDAF

Reading

Abraham, H.J.: *The Judicial Process*. 4th edn. New York and Oxford: Oxford University Press, 1980.

Lloyd, Lord and Freeman, M.D.A.: *Introduction to Jurisprudence*, ch. 12. London: Stevens, 1985.

Stein, P.: *Legal Institutions*. London: Butterworth, 1984.

Twining, W. and Miers, D.: *How To Do Things With Rules*. 2nd edn. London: Weidenfeld & Nicolson, 1982.

commonwealth An international organ-ization of independent states. The term was given currency, particularly by Rosebery, Shaw and Smuts, to distinguish the 'free association' of those self-governing colonies (first categorized as Dominions in 1907) which, within the British Empire, had acquired equality of status (if not of function, for the UK was still a great power) with one another and were united, first by allegiance to the CROWN in the Balfour formulation of 1926 and, later, by recognition of the monarch as Head of the Commonwealth in 1949. It was a compromise in 1926 between the 'freedom' claimed by Ireland, South Africa and Canada, and the 'association' then cherished by Australia, New Zealand and Newfoundland. But freedom gradually came to include the right to secede, to establish a republic, to have a military dictatorship or one-party rule, to be unaligned etc.; and the association, growing from six Dominions in 1926 to forty-nine Members comprising one-quarter of the world's population, in the next half century, became both more representative of world opinions and less coherent. While it is easy to underrate the importance of an organic association which had evolved from common experience under British rule, used English as a *lingua franca* and has been most notably shaped by the devotion of Elizabeth II, critics argue that the Commonwealth, enjoying no decision-making power, lacks standing, is suspect as a 'millstone', 'an empty durbar', 'a tattered old boys' club', and is questioned as having outlived its usefulness. Nevertheless, the very differences can be enriching. If members do no longer feel more secure or prosperous simply by belonging, all certainly believe that they are better informed and, if only by retaining membership, demonstrate some faith in its values.   AFM

Reading

Ball, M.M.: *The 'Open' Commonwealth*. Chapel Hill, NC: Duke University Commonwealth Studies Center, 1971.

Dawson, R.M.: *The Development of Dominion Status 1900–1936* (1936). London: Cass, 1965.

Ingram, P.: *The Imperfect Commonwealth*. London: Collins, 1977.

Mansergh, N.: *The Commonwealth Experience*. London: Weidenfeld & Nicolson, 1968.

Miller, J.D.B.: *The Commonwealth in the World*. London: Duckworth, 1965.

Walker, A.: *The Commonwealth: a new look*. Oxford: Pergamon, 1978.

Wheare, K.C.: *The Constitutional Structure of the Commonwealth*. Oxford: Oxford University Press, 1960.

Yearbook of the Commonwealth. London: Foreign and Commonwealth Office, 1969, annually.

communal representation Countries in which religious, linguistic, ethnic, or racial differences are of great political importance may use these differences as criteria by which to define communal categories of voters whose names appear on separate rolls and who elect their own representatives. Recent and contemporary examples of communal REPRESENTATION are the separate Greek and Turkish voter rolls in the 1960 election in Cyprus, the separate black and white rolls in the 1980 and 1985 elections in Zimbabwe, and the special Maori districts in New Zealand.

The advantage of communal representation is that it can guarantee adequate representation, or even over-representation, to a communal minority without abandoning the use of plurality or majority electoral methods; there are, though, two serious drawbacks. The first is the potentially invidious determination of which groups are entitled to guaranteed

representation and which are not. The second is that it may be difficult to assign individual voters to the communal categories and that the very principle of registering individuals according to such criteria as ethnicity and race may be controversial or unacceptable to many citizens. The first problem cannot be solved, but New Zealand exemplifies a partial solution of the second: the formerly rigid Maori districts were made optional in 1975 allowing Maori voters to register on either the Maori or the general roll. The only guarantee of minority representation that avoids both problems is proportional representation.

See also ELECTORAL SYSTEMS; ETHNICITY.

AL

Reading

Lijphart, A.: Proportionality by non-PR methods: ethnic representation in Belgium, Cyprus, Lebanon, New Zealand, West Germany, and Zimbabwe. In *Electoral Laws and their Political Consequences*, ch. 7, ed. B. Grofman and A. Lijphart. New York: Agathon, 1986.

Mackenzie, W.J.M.: *Free Elections: an elementary textbook*, ch. 4. London: Allen & Unwin, 1958.

McRobie, A.D.: Ethnic representation: the New Zealand experience. In *Politics in New Zealand: a reader*, ed. S. Levine. Sydney: Allen & Unwin, 1978.

Nohlen, D.: *Wahlsysteme der Welt-Daten und Analysen: ein handbuch*. Munich: Piper, 1978.

Sternberger, D. and Vogel, B. eds: *Die Wahl der Parlamente und anderer Staatsorgane: ein handbuch*. Berlin: De Gruyter, 1969.

communist parties Communist and Social Democratic parties have a common origin in the SOCIALIST PARTIES of nineteenth-century Europe, but were split as a result of the Russian Revolution and the triumph of BOLSHEVISM in 1917. The name was first applied to what was formerly the Russian Social Democratic Labour Party (Bolshevik). At the eighth Congress of that party, 6–8 March 1919, Lenin proposed that the party should change its name to Russian Communist Party (Bolshevik), completely breaking its past association with, and filiation to, the socialist parties and the Second International (Socialist). But the name already contained a contradiction.

For, while communist was the name proposed by Karl MARX for his theory in general and for the political organization animated by that theory, 'party' was not the definition Marx had chosen to give to that organization, which he called the *League* of Communists, stressing a voluntary, spontaneous and decentralized kind of organization. (Indeed, after the break with the Communist Party of the Soviet Union (CPSU) then still under STALIN's leadership, the Communist Party of Yugoslavia in 1952 ostentatiously changed its name to the *League of Communists* of Yugoslavia. They claimed that the name of 'party' had been so desecrated by the Stalinist dictatorship that it could not possibly continue to be used for the organization of a genuine and popular communism.) While communist was a Marxist concept, party was a Leninist one. LENIN had described the party as far back as 1902 in his *What is to Be Done?* as an organization in which he believed that a dozen experienced revolutionaries, no less professionally trained than the police, would centralize all the secret side of the work and appoint bodies of leaders for each urban district, for each factory district and for each educational institution.

Coming to power in 1917, the Communist Party transformed its illegal organization into a formal one. Its basic principle was described as DEMOCRATIC CENTRALISM, meaning that the 'monolithic' unity of the organization demanded the total subordination of the minority to the majority and the prohibition of 'factions' and 'fractions'. The Congress of the party is formally its supreme organ. It elects a CENTRAL COMMITTEE which elects a Presidium. At the eighth Congress in 1919 the Central Committee created three new organs: a political bureau (Politburo), an organizational bureau (Orgburo), and a Secretariat, with one First Secretary and five technical secretaries. The monolithic power of this eminently centralistic organization is therefore concentrated in the hands, first of the POLITBURO, but ultimately of the First Secretary: Lenin, Stalin, Khrushchev, Brezhnev, Gorbachev . . .

Although in *What is to be Done?* Lenin had claimed that he was writing only about the conditions of Tsarist Russia, not only did he continue to keep, after the Revolution, the same 'monolithic' organization of the party, and abolish all forms of opposition to it in the USSR, but when he created the *Third International* (Comintern) comprising new communist parties internationally, he constrained them to adopt the same clandestine and monolithic organization as that of the CPSU. Through the Comintern the USSR controlled all these parties. Under Stalin the control became even more stringent – both over the CPSU and over the foreign parties. The moment of truth for the European parties came during the Stalin–Hitler pact (1939–41) when they were ordered by the Comintern not to join in resistance against the Nazi armies. Once Hitler attacked the USSR they were ordered to do an about turn and to join the resistance. After the war when the USSR was able, through the military occupation of half of Europe, to install communist parties in power in Eastern and Central Europe, those parties had the same organization and used the same methods of government as the Stalinist CPSU. The communist parties in power became (like the CPSU since the tenth Congress in 1921) the political, administrative and ideological *apparat* of the Stalinist dictatorship. Under Stalin the SECRET POLICE apparat took the lead, putting the party-apparat under its control. In China, after the Cultural Revolution, the army displaced the Party for a while; the same has happened in Poland since 1982.

In Europe communist parties are distinguished by three characteristics – their recognition of the USSR as the leading Socialist country, their continued allegiance to democratic centralism, and their urge to transcend capitalist economic organization.

The communist parties in power and/or in opposition in industrial countries are faced now with the same fundamental problem: how to get rid of their Marxist–Leninist ideology and organization, which might have been suitable for the period of forcible industrialization of their countries, but which has become totally counter-productive in the conditions of modern transnational industrial–technological society. As most of the socialist parties, since the second world war, had rejected the obsolete Marxist creeds, so the communist parties tried to shake-up the formula of the

DICTATORSHIP OF THE PROLETARIAT, a Marxist–Leninist prescription which by itself, but especially under Stalin's leadership, was only a façade for a TOTALITARIAN system of dictatorship. But, because of its arch-centralistic character, that system was unsuited, from all points of view, to the running of the essentially decentralized industrial–technological society. Yugoslavia in 1952 and China in 1982 were the two countries where the communist parties in power directly disavowed their original Stalinist ideologies. The Hungarian and Czechoslovak parties in power, which attempted to do the same thing, were forced, by Soviet military intervention in their countries, to revert to the Soviet model.

To the communist parties in opposition, the crisis of the Marxist–Leninist–Stalinist ideology manifested itself increasingly in the form of a growing estrangement from the working class which these parties were supposed to represent in their respective countries. *Polycentrism*, an expression coined by the Italian Communist Party leader Togliatti, replaced the previous compulsory leadership of the communist world-movement by the CPSU. The Italian Communist Party itself went very far in its rejection of both the Marxist–Leninist ideology and the subordination to the CPSU. It publicly opposed most of the USSR's acts of aggression abroad and intolerance at home, thereby maintaining some popularity with the Italian electorate, and broke its links with the USSR in 1980. But the popularity of parties like the French one, which still tried to maintain some of the old Marxist–Leninist–Stalinist ideological tenets and organizational discipline, has shown a steady but continuous decline. The same situation prevails in most European countries. An attempt to build up a new and more modern programme for the *Eurocommunist* parties (as distinct from the CPSU and third world parties) soon faded away, in part because of the negative stand taken by the USSR, but above all because of the low credibility which any variation on Marxist–Leninist themes enjoys now in the eyes of the modern population of the industrial–technological countries, based on the market economy.   GI

Reading

Carr, E.H.: *The Bolshevik Revolution 1917–1973*. 2 vols. Harmondsworth: Penguin, 1966.

Duverger, M.: *Political Parties: their organisation and activity in the modern state*. London: Methuen, 1954.

Fischer-Galati, S. ed.: *The Communist Parties of Eastern Europe*. New York: Columbia University Press, 1979.

Guillermaz, J.: *The Chinese Communist Party in Power*. Folkestone, Kent: Dawson, 1976.

Harrison, J.P.: *The Long March to Power: a history of the Chinese Communist Party 1921–1972*. New York: Praeger, 1972.

Ionescu, G.: *The Politics of the European Communist State*. London: Weidenfeld & Nicolson, 1967.

———: *Comparative Communist Politics*. London: Macmillan, 1972.

Lange, P. and Vannicelli, M. eds: *The Communist Parties of Italy, France and Spain, Postwar Change and Continuity: a casebook*. London: Allen & Unwin, 1981.

Lenin, V.I.: *What is to be done?* In *Collected Works*, Vol. V. London: Lawrence & Wishart, 1961.

McInnes, N.: *The Communist Parties of Western Europe*. Oxford: Oxford University Press, 1975.

Middlemas, K.: *Power and the Party: changing faces of communism in western Europe*. London: Deutsch, 1980.

Rakovska-Harmstone, T. ed.: *Communism in Eastern Europe*. Manchester: Manchester University Press, 1984.

Ranney, A. and Sartori, G. eds: *Eurocommunism: the Italian case*. Washington, 1978.

Rigby, T.H.: *Communist Party Membership in the USSR*. Princeton, NJ: Princeton University Press, 1968.

Schapiro, L.: *The Origin of the Communist Autocracy*. London: London School of Economics, 1955.

———: *The Communist Party of the Soviet Union*. 2nd edn. London: Methuen, 1970.

———: *The Government and Politics of the Soviet Union*. 2nd edn. London: Eyre and Spottiswoode, 1970.

Tannahill, R.N.: *The Communist Parties of Western Europe*. Westport, Conn.: Greenwood, 1978.

competitive party systems

In a democratic system parties are not conceivable in isolation; even in pre-democratic systems the rise of one party usually entailed the rise of a counter-movement (for instance guelph-ghibelline). Most multi-party systems are competitive, with the exception of communist countries such as Bulgaria, China, Czechoslovakia, East Germany and Poland, where there are a number of different parties, but elections are not competitive. A fixed number of seats is allotted to each party, and the communist party makes sure that it retains its dominant position.

The leading modern theory of democratic party systems is that of Sartori (1976). This article, however, offers a modification of his typology in the light of changes that have occured since the publication of Vol. I of *Parties and Party Systems*.

It is not possible to make a fully schematic count of parties which have passed the hurdle of winning 2 per cent of votes and can therefore be regarded as 'relevant' (Table 1). Some parties have been included for qualitative reasons, although they have sometimes fallen below 2 per cent: the Republicans in Italy, for instance, dropped below the 2 per cent mark for a time (1953–63), but they did not cease to act as an important mediator between the power blocs.

Table 1: *Number of relevant parties with over 2 per cent of the votes*

	1946/47	1960	1970	1980	1983
Austria	3	4	3	3	3
Belgium	4	5	6	6	8
Denmark	5	7	5	11	9
FRG	8	3	4	3	4
Finland	7	8	7	8	7
France	5	7	6	8	5
Great Britain	3	3	3	4	5
Ireland	6	5	3	3	3
Iceland	4	4	5	5	5
Italy	6	7	7	8	8
Luxemburg	4	4	5	5	5
Netherlands	6	6	10	8*	5
Norway	6	7	6	7	7
New Zealand	2	3	3	3	3
Spain				6	6
Switzerland	7	7	9	8	10
Sweden	5	5	5	5	5

* (1981)

A few years after Sartori's work appeared (1976) many of his classifications needed revising, and those of Table 1 will presumably also soon be obsolete on some points. Counts

of parties which have played a 'relevant' part in parliament have shown that the number of parties dropped in European countries between 1949 (4.2) and 1953 (3.7), rising again after 1966 in most countries to reach a post-war peak in 1973 at 4.5.

If Sartori's typology is modified, we can identify four types of party systems with sub-groups (Table 2).

Two-party systems
These are more of an abstraction than a reality: even Britain, Canada, and New Zealand have only been two-party systems in some phases of their history because they were clinging to the idea of alternating governments to avoid coalitions.

Moderate pluralism
This is found in three sub-types: where parties alternate in government without coalitions (Britain, Canada, and Austria until 1983); where two major centre parties form a grand coalition, often tolerating a minority government (the Benelux states, Scandinavia – except Finland, and Switzerland). In Sartori's view there are three features of a moderate pluralist party system: relatively slight ideological distance between major parties; an inclination to coalition formation between parties of different views; predominantly centripetal competition.

But this too needs modifying. Some countries have never had polar coalition formation (Switzerland), while new conflicts have arisen to drive parties further apart and the ideological gap has widened. Ethnic parties have sometimes called into question centripetal competition (Belgium, Britain, Spain) and neo-populist protest parties have performed a similar function (Denmark, Norway, the Netherlands). As a whole, however, Sartori's view still holds and major areas of party systems have not changed.

Polarized pluralism
This cannot easily be distinguished from moderate pluralism, although Sartori once tried to do so. At one time the border between the two could be said to lie at between five and six parties in the system. But as the number of

Table 2: *Party systems in western democracies*

Two parties alternating in government	Moderate pluralism	Polarized pluralism	One hegemonial party in polarized pluralism
USA New Zealand	1 Alternating wing parties, preferably without coalitions: 　　Austria (up to 1983)(3) 　　Canada (4) 　　Great Britain (5)	1 With fundamental opposition eroding the Centre: 　　Weimar Republic 　　Second Spanish 　　Republic	Ireland (3) Israel (up to 1977) India Japan (6)
	2 Alternating wing parties with permanent coalition partners: 　　Australia (3, until 1983) 　　FRG (3, 1957–66, 　　1969–83)	2 Weakening centrifugal effects of fundamental opposition: 　　France (4 plus n) 　　Israel (6) 　　Spain (6) 　　Finland (7) 　　Italy (8)	
	3 Moderate pluralism with Centre coalitions or grand coalitions: 　　Belgium (8) 　　Iceland (5) 　　Netherlands (5) 　　Sweden (5) 　　Greece (6) 　　Norway (7) 　　Switzerland (10)		

parties and their fragmentation has been increasing since about 1974 (Denmark, the Netherlands, Norway, and Switzerland) the figures in some cases are now out of date. It is only in the case of Switzerland that this hardly seems to matter; because of the unique executive structure, the increase in the number of parties has not automatically brought an increase in the number of those which have a proportionate share in government.

Some of the coalition patterns which have been regarded as typical of POLARIZED PLURALISM are now only to be found in a weaker form, and it is no longer so easy to distinguish anti-system parties of this type. The Italian MSI (Movimento Sociale Italiano), however, is one. But the fundamental opposition is no longer so symmetrical as in Sartori's model. Even in 1976 Sartori's dis-

trust of the Italian Communist Party strongly affected his definitions. In fact the Italian Communist Party is much more strongly integrated into the system than Sartori's term 'negative integration' would suggest. It has for a long time been the most credible supporter of Euro-Communism in Europe, and however much mistrust may remain, it cannot be simply lumped together with the fascist and communist parties in fundamental opposition to the Weimar Republic and the Second Spanish Republic. Paolo Farneti has rightly called Italy the exemplary type of 'centripetal competition', with the MSI more expressly excluded the more the communists are drawn in. But the MSI alone is not enough over the longer term to justify the identification of Italy as a centrifugal system. After all, groups which are not so far to the right, such as the FPÖ (Freie

Partei Österreich) in Austria, were for a long time (until 1983) excluded from the coalition consensus, but no one would think of calling Austria an example of a centrifugal polity.

Developments in Finland and Iceland could also cast doubt on whether polarized pluralism stands as a class in itself. Both countries have experimented with coalitions containing the Communists. In both countries the Communists opted out of government on several occasions, and Sartori held that these were marginal cases and cannot be taken as proof that the Communists will generally fit into the western scheme of democratic government. Nowhere in Europe was polarized pluralism so embittered as it was in Chile, and this has been of major importance for the European communist parties. It is no longer justifiable to equate the Communist Party in Chile (which was not one of the most radical) with the Italian. Nor can parallels be drawn between Socialists and Communists. The Socialists began to integrate into the system at an earlier stage, having more in common with bourgeois democracy – at least in its radical interpretation – than did the Communists. The International they could draw on was, moreover, often overestimated and tended to crumble easily; it was not, like the Soviet Union, a world power from which even the Euro-Communists are unwilling to draw too far away.

For these reasons therefore it would appear advisable to subdivide polarized pluralist systems into two sub-groups: first, where right and left are in fundamental opposition (Weimar Republic, Second Spanish Republic) with a centre no longer capable of governing; second, those with centre parties which are capable of governing (France, Israel, Finland, Spain).

Systems with one dominant party

Here the DOMINANT PARTY generally forms the government and can only be displaced by a coalition of all or most of the opposition parties. Competition is most strongly restricted in such constellations, and this situation is typical of many developing countries. Mexico has been like this under the hegemony of the PRI (Partido Revolucionario Institucional) for decades. The Kemal movement in Turkey abandoned its claim to sole government, but not even Atatürk has been able to implement his conviction that a western multi-party system – or a least a two-party system – is possible in a developing country. He twice banned an opposition which he himself called into being, and it was not until 1945 that Turkey moved away from a system with one ruling party. At the end of the 1970s there was barely a system at all, and the parties – with the exception of the National Salvation Party – were virtually waging civil war with each other although they derived from the same founder. There are very few developing countries with full competition between political parties (Venezuela is a possible exception), and in many cases competition is artificially kept down through proportional arrangements for seats (Uruguay before the military dictatorship, and Colombia). Where competition did emerge it often collapsed again (Chile).

But some regimes which adopted western democratic methods of conflict settlement have also had one dominant party which regarded itself as 'the natural party of government'. All these systems have strong remnants of a traditionalist political culture with an orientation to clienteles. Even dominant party systems, however, have a functional equivalent of competitiveness: what they lack in competition between the parties they frequently develop in intra-party competition via factionalism (especially in India, Japan, and Italy).

Competitiveness has recently been growing in spite of the second wave of 'deideologization' because of the rise of new SOCIAL MOVEMENTS, the decline of traditional party identification, and increasing volatility of the voters.

See also ELECTORAL VOLATILITY; PARTY IDENTIFICATION; PARTY ORGANIZATION; PARTIES, POLITICAL: FUNCTIONS OF; PARTY SYSTEMS, TYPES OF.　　　　KvB

Reading

Beyme, K. von: *Political Parties in Western Democracies*. New York: St Martin's; Aldershot: Gower, 1985.

Epstein, L.D.: *Political Parties in Western Democracies*. New Brunswick, NJ: Transaction Books, 1980.

Farneti, P.: *The Italian Party System*. London: Pinter, 1985.

Kirchheimer, O.: The vanishing opposition. In *Political Oppositions in Western Democracies*, pp. 237–59, ed. R.A. Dahl. New Haven, Conn.: Yale University Press, 1966.

Merkl, P.H. ed.: *Western European Party Systems: trends and prospects*. New York: Free Press; London: Collier-Macmillan, 1980.

Sartori, G.: *Parties and Party Systems: a framework for analysis*. New York and Cambridge: Cambridge University Press, 1976.

compulsory voting

In most democracies voting is seen as a civic duty – but a voluntary one. In Australia, Belgium, Greece, Luxemburg and Venezuela voting is compulsory for all or most of the electorate. Abstention from voting without due reason is punishable by a small fine. In Italy the identity cards of abstainers are liable to be stamped 'did not vote'. In all these countries, except Greece, turnouts of over 90 per cent are normal although convictions and sanctions against non-voters are generally negligible.   DEB

Reading

Crewe, I.: Electoral participation. In *Democracy at the Polls: a comparative study of competitive national elections*, ed. D. Butler, H.R. Penniman and A. Ranney. Washington, DC: American Enterprise Institute, 1981.

comrades' courts

In the USSR, a system of informal courts for minor offences staffed by elected citizens. Although characteristic of Soviet state socialism, a court system of this kind also reflects pre-revolutionary Russian traditions of community self-regulation. As presently constituted under legislation of 1977, comrades' courts are 'elective social agencies' rather than state bodies and are supposed to play a persuasive rather than primarily coercive role within the communities in which they are located. Comrades' courts consider a variety of offences from violations of labour discipline to hooliganism and petty theft, and may impose 'measures of social pressure' such as public apologies or fines.
                SLW

Reading

Butler, W.E.: *Soviet Law*. London: Butterworths, 1983.

——— ed.: *Basic Documents on the Soviet Legal System*. New York: Oceana, 1983.

concentration camp

A concentration camp is an internment centre for those such as political opponents or minority groups who are considered a threat to state security. It is distinguished from a prison by the fact that its internees have not been convicted of a civil offence by due process of law and have normally been arrested under an executive decree or military order without indictment and often simply on the basis of their membership of a particular group.

Use of the term 'concentration camp' rather than the less pejorative 'internment camp' usually implies harsher and more punitive conditions because the term 'concentration camp' has become particularly associated with the *Konzentrationslager* in Nazi Germany (see NAZISM). In fact, the Nazis borrowed the term from the British, who during the Boer War (1899–1902) confined non-combatants in the Transvaal and Cape Colony in 'concentration camps' in order to prevent them from providing aid to the enemy and as a means of terrorizing the Boer population into surrender.

The first Nazi concentration camps were established early in 1933 for the confinement of their political opponents, at this stage mainly Communists and Social Democrats. From July 1934 onwards, the concentration camps came under the control of the SS (*Schutzstaffel* = defence echelons, the elite Nazi formation of blackshirts). The SS introduced a systematic form of terror in place of the arbitrary brutality of the SA (*Sturmabteilung* = storm detachments or brownshirts). Conditions were extremely harsh, with brutal physical punishments, backbreaking labour, and inadequate food and housing. The main categories of prisoner were: political prisoners, habitual criminals, anti-social elements, Jehovah's Witnesses, homosexuals, and Jews.

From 1938 onwards, and particularly during the war, the camps came to be used more and more for the economic benefit of the SS, which exploited the labour of the prisoners either in its own industries, such as the stone quarries in the camps at Mauthausen near Linz in Austria and Buchenwald near Weimar, or by hiring out labour to German industry for cash. As a result of this economic motive and of the increase in Nazi terror during the war, both in the occupied territories and against the German population, the number of concentration camps expanded dramatically. According to a survey of 15 January 1945, there were at that time in the Reich 714,211 concentration camp inmates, mostly foreigners, compared with 25,000 at the outbreak of war, mostly Germans. The war also saw the introduction of EXTERMINATION CAMPS, while in Buchenwald and in Dachau near Munich medical experiments were forcibly carried out on prisoners often with lethal results.

Concentration camps have been used to crush political opposition under a number of regimes. In the Soviet Union by 1922 there were twenty-three concentration camps which were used for both political and criminal offenders and, during the collectivization of the peasantry between 1928 and 1932 and the purges of 1936–8, a number of camps were established in northern Russia and Siberia. Since the death of Stalin in 1953 both the number of inmates and the degrees of arbitrariness involved in their detention has been reduced.   JDN

Reading

Broszat, M.: The Concentration Camps 1933–45. In *Anatomy of the SS State*, ed. H. Krausnick et al. London: Collins, 1968.

Hoess, R.: *Commandant of Auschwitz*. London: Weidenfeld & Nicolson, 1959.

Kogon, E.: *The Theory and Practice of Hell*. London, 1950.

concurrent majority   Refers to a maxim first expounded by John C. CALHOUN, the leading spokesman of the slaveholding South between 1828 and his death in 1850, and published in his posthumous book *Disquisition on the Constitution and Government of the United States*. This maxim requires that all important sectional interests affected by a decision must concur with it. Calhoun was obsessed by the

decline of the South's relative strength within the American Union and by the threat that this posed to slavery, the planter class, and white supremacy. Because he feared that the Northern, free-labour states would be able to outvote the Southern slave-states, he proposed that federal power should be exercised, not freely, by the elected representatives of the numerical majority of the whole country, but under the constraint of sectional veto. He proposed a constitutional structure in which each of the great economic, functional, and regional interests should name its own organ of self-expression. He wanted to give 'to each division or interest, [i.e. the North and the South] through its appropriate organ, either a concurrent voice in making and executing the laws or a veto on their execution'. He proposed that there should be two presidents, one answerable to the North, the other to the Southern slaveholders, each having a veto on the other's actions, and on Congressional legislation. Like Calhoun's other pet notions, nullification and secession, this scheme, if adopted, would have destroyed the United States, in this case by a kind of general paralysis, for the sake of preserving slavery. It never stood a chance of adoption, but to propound it was to increase the inter-sectional hostility that culminated in the Civil War.

Despite Calhoun's lack of success, the concurrent majority principle is often applied today in practice, though hardly ever so styled in public, in a number of important organizations. For example, the decision-making arrangements of the United Nations Security Council or those of the EUROPEAN COMMUNITY are for practical purposes applications of the concurrent majority principle. In addition the CORPORATIST practices followed in many democracies show some resemblance to the concurrent majority arrangement; while the theory of CONSOCIATIONAL DEMOCRACY is an attempt to build on the idea of the concurrent majority so as to evolve a formula for governing divided societies in a democratic manner.   HB

Reading

Calhoun, J.C.: Discourse on the Constitution and Government of the United States. In *Works*, Vol. I (1853–5); repr. New York: Russell & Russell, 1968.

Current, R.N.: *John C. Calhoun*. New York: Twayne, 1963.

condominium Literally co-ownership or joint tenancy; joint rule or sovereignty. Examples are Andorra which, since the thirteenth century, has had dual allegiance to two co-princes, the bishop of Urgel in Spain and the president in France; and the New Hebrides (now the independent republic of Vanuatu) which was administered jointly by Britain and France between 1906 and 1980. The so-called Anglo-Egyptian Condominium over the Sudan (1899–1955) was not a genuine condominium since Britain remained the dominant partner in the government of the Sudan.

Condominium is often suggested as an appropriate form of rule for territories whose ownership is in dispute, such as the Falkland Islands or Northern Ireland. The Anglo-Irish Agreement of 1985, although not establishing a condominium since the Irish Republic was granted only consultative rather than statutory rights over the domestic affairs of Northern Ireland, nevertheless aims at resolving an intractable conflict through an informal sharing of power.   VBB

confederation A qualified union. States sometimes share certain institutions of government by what is intended to be a permanent agreement. For example, a group of republics may share a common citizenship, an army, an arbitration tribunal, a secretariat, a Council of Ministers, import duties levied at the common frontier, or even one House of a bicameral legislature. Thereby they acquire a secondary collective personality and a name: this is confederation. But when a point of no return is passed, when unanimity is no longer required for vital ultimate decisions, the related concept FEDERALISM is appropriate.

The distinction between these two words in technical parlance did not become usual in English until after 1870. The practical distinction is as old as the United States Constitution which, first drafted in 1787, came into force in 1789 and was familiar to the authors of the FEDERALIST PAPERS: it was explicitly made by Hamilton in The *Federalist* No. 15.

But the usefulness of Hamilton's distinction is confined to American-style dual federalism, and is vitiated by a clause excepting a range of cases. Moreover, Hamilton and his contemporaries employed the two words indiscriminately, and this practice only gradually ceased after the outbreak of the American War (1861–5) of SECESSION. The memory of the Articles of Confederation, the usage in Article 6 of the US Constitution, and the fact that the Southern States had called their own union (which can nevertheless be interpreted as federal) a 'confederacy', imposed the modern usage among scholars, especially in the USA. In Germany however the thing and the words were distinguished clearly (*Staatenbund, Bundesstaat*) by 1815. The English synonym for confederation, namely confederacy, has remained unambiguous.

The most accessible example of a confederal government is that of the American Continental Congress of 1776–88. This body had declared independence from Britain, raised an army and fought a war of liberation, made a treaty with the king of France, printed its own currency notes and finally, supporting the French troops at war with Britain, accepted the capitulation of the British land forces at Yorktown. The treaty recognizing independence was made with the emissaries of the Congress. This demonstrates the statehood and potentialities of a confederation. But the experience of the USA after 1780 also demonstrates that an ill-constructed confederacy can become so impotent as to border on intelligent anarchy. Until the Fourteenth Amendment in 1868, the American Constitution itself displayed aspects of confederal government.

Until 1789, or even perhaps 1868, all republican equal unions were confederal. Two ancient confederacies survive as federal states in Europe today. The Swiss Confederacy, destroyed in 1798, certainly went back to 1315, possibly even to 1291, and was revived in a new form in 1813, continuing to 1847. The Germanic Union of 1815–66 was continued until 1870 in a new form, and thence again until 1918. The German *Zollverein* also falls within our definition.

In very recent years, both single purpose and multi-purpose confederations have proliferated and dominate diplomacy, for example NATO (North Atlantic Treaty Organization), UNO (United Nations Organization), EUROPEAN COMMUNITY. In the past, confederations have waged wars and were formed for this purpose; it follows that confederations may possess diplomatic capacity, and even jurisdiction in high treason, and so on.

The word is also used, through analogy, by private-law associations. See also CALHOUN; LEAGUE; MAJORITY RULE.   CJH

Reading

Davis, S.R.: *The Federal Principle*. Berkeley: University of California Press, 1978.

Forsyth, M.: *Unions of States: the theory and practice of confederation*. New York: Holmes & Meier; Leicester: Leicester University Press, 1981.

Huber, E.R.: *Deutsche Verfassungsgeschichte seit 1789*. Stuttgart: Kohlhammer, 1957.

Jensen, M.: *The New Nation: a history of the United States during the Confederation 1781–87* New York: Knopf and Vintage Books, 1950.

confessional parties Parties whose prime objective is to defend the interests of the Catholic church, especially the rights and privileges of Catholic schools. In pre-war Europe there were several such parties, for example the German Centre Party, a major party winning up to a quarter of the electorate from 1870 to 1933; the Italian Popular Party, polling *c.*20 per cent between 1918 and the full establishment of fascism in 1926; the Belgian and Dutch Catholic parties with polls of up to 50 per cent and 30 per cent respectively; and the Austrian Christian Social Party (30 per cent plus).

In the post-war period Christian Democratic parties nominally replaced the old confessional parties (see CHRISTIAN DEMOCRACY). But, in practice, the new parties remained essentially confessional until the Second Vatican Council of 1960–4. In terms of 'preferences' (electoral programmes), 'governmental output' (especially defence of Catholic schools), and 'structure' (Catholic

Action, Catholic trade unions, etc.), the Christian Democratic parties could legitimately be labelled 'confessional parties' until the 1960s. In Italy the DC (Partito Democrazia Cristiana) was very much the political wing of the Catholic church; indeed, one of the major problems of the DC in the 1970s and 1980s has been how to maintain its strength in an increasingly secular society. In the Netherlands the Catholic Party remained the political 'pillar' of the church until the late 1960s – from 1917 to 67 Catholics (about 30 per cent of the electorate) voted with remarkable consistency and solidarity for their party. Then with great rapidity the old 'pillars' within Dutch society disintegrated, and a strong 'deconfessionalized' Christian Democratic party (bringing together Catholics, Protestants and non-believers) came into being. In Belgium the change was less dramatic, and the Flemish branch of the Social Christian party remains strongly committed to the defence of Catholic schools. But in Germany the CDU (Christliche Demokratische Union) and CSU (Christliche Soziale Union) (the Bavarian branch of the CDU), especially the former, can no longer be labelled 'confessional'. However, this was not the case until the 1960s, for in spite of Adenauer's attempts to create a non-confessional Catholic–Protestant CDU, the Catholic bishops and Catholic integralists played a dominant role in the CDU: they constituted a solid bloc committed to the defence of Catholic schools and Catholic moral and social values. In France, too, the Christian Democratic MRP (Mouvement Républicain Populaire) (1944–67) remained in many respects a confessional party to the end.

Since the Second Vatican Council – and under the general influence of increasing secularization – the Christian Democratic parties have become much less dependent on the Catholic church. They are of course to some extent still parties of 'religious defence' (for example the German CDU–CSU's opposition to the abortion law in 1972 and the Italian DC's opposition to the divorce law in 1974). They remain 'confessional' too in their dependence on the general support of the faithful at elections. But the phrase 'confessional party' is largely outdated. 'Christian Democratic' is now generally more appropriate.

REMI

Reading

Bakvis, H.: *Catholic Power in the Netherlands*. McGill: Queen's University Press, 1981.

Fogarty, M.: *Christian Democracy in Western Europe, 1920–1953*. London: Routledge & Kegan Paul, 1957.

Irving, R.E.M.: *Christian-Democracy in France*. London: Allen & Unwin, 1973.

————: *The Christian Democratic Parties of Western Europe*. London: Allen & Unwin, 1979.

Moloney, J.N.: *The Emergence of Political Catholicism in Italy*. London: Croom Helm, 1977.

Moodey, J.N. ed.: *Church and Society: Catholic political thought and movements, 1789–1950*. New York: Arts Inc., 1950.

Vaussard, M.: *Historie de la democratie Chrétienne: France, Belgique, Italie*. Paris: Seuil, 1956.

Whyte, J.H.: *Catholics in Western Democracies*. Dublin: Gill & Macmillan, 1981.

Congress The national legislature of the United States, consisting of two chambers. In the 100-member Senate, the fifty states are equally represented; representation in the 435-member House of Representatives is based upon population but each state has at least one representative. Members of the House are popularly elected from single member districts for a term of two years. Senators were originally chosen by the LEGISLATURES of their states but, since the adoption of the Seventeenth Amendment in 1913, senators have been popularly elected. The Senate term is six years and one-third of the Senate is elected every two years.

For a BILL to become law it must be passed in identical form by both chambers and be signed by the PRESIDENT. If the President vetoes the legislation, a two-thirds vote by both chambers is required to override the VETO. All revenue bills must originate in the House. Treaties must be ratified by a two-thirds vote of the Senate; the Senate also has the power to advise and consent (see ADVICE AND CONSENT), by majority vote, to the President's nomination of high executive branch officers and federal judges.

The US Constitution of 1787 established a national government in which power is formally divided among three independent branches: executive, legislative and judicial. This governmental structure combined with the relatively weak American party system has resulted in Congress maintaining for itself an important decision-making role in the policy process independent of the executive. The Constitution vests all legislative power in the Congress; by specifying that the government may spend no money 'but in consequence of appropriations made by law' (article I, section 9), the Constitution specifically vests the power of the purse in the Congress. Consequently the President is dependent upon Congress not only for the passage of his new legislative proposals but also for the budget to maintain ongoing programmes.

The relative influence of Congress and the Presidency has varied over time. The post-civil war period (1865–1900), for example, was characterized by Congressional ascendency. Most scholars would contend that the twentieth century has seen a considerable though by no means uninterrupted increase in presidential power *vis-à-vis* Congress, while the 1970s witnessed a resurgence of Congressional assertiveness. Certainly Congress maintains and often exercises its power to kill or alter the President's policy proposals. Furthermore, Congress can and does initiate policy as well. Thus, the US Congress is uniquely powerful and independent for a modern legislature.

Congress's independence of the executive is a result not only of the governmental structure but also of the character of the American party system. Always decentralized, the American party system has become progressively weaker during the twentieth century. Few members of Congress are dependent upon their party – local, state or national – for election or re-election. Party nominations are won in Primaries not bestowed by party leaders. Typically the congressional candidate makes his or her own decision to run, builds his own organization and raises his or her own campaign funds. Consequently the President, though party leader, has only limited influence over members of his or her party in the Congress.

Parties and committees provide the primary basis for the internal organization of Congress. Since very early in their history, both houses of Congress have worked by means of a division of labour through a committee system. Currently, the Senate has sixteen standing committees and the House has twenty-two. It is in the committees that most of the substantive work on legislation is done. Members are assigned to committees – usually two in the House, three in the Senate – through a party mechanism but, once on a committee, a member is entitled to remain. Members often remain on a committee for most of their congressional career and over time develop considerable expertise in the committee's subject matter. The committee system thus fosters specialization and the development of expertise.

Majority party leaders are responsible for the flow of legislation to and on the floor. The SPEAKER of the House is the leader of the majority party and the presiding officer of the chamber. Because of its large membership, the House has strict rules governing floor conduct, including severe limitations on the length of floor debate. The Speaker's position as enforcer of the rules gives him or her considerable leverage over floor activity.

The Senate rules place very little constraint on the individual senator; once a senator has the floor, he can speak for as long as he likes. The tactic of holding the floor for a lengthy period of time in order to prevent action on some piece of legislation is called a filibuster. A filibuster can be cut off only by the invoking of a procedure called cloture which requires an extraordinary majority – usually sixty. The majority party leader in the Senate is not the presiding officer and, given the Senate's loose rules, his ability to control floor procedure is weaker than the House Speaker's.

The strength of Congressional party leaders has varied over time, closely paralleling the strength of the party system. The party leadership was strongest between 1890 and 1910. The extremely powerful speakership of that period was based upon the Speaker's control over the assignment of members to committees and the designation of committee chairmen. By about 1920 in the House and earlier in the Senate, party leaders' discretion was replaced by SENIORITY as the determinant of committee chairmanships. That is, the majority party member with the longest tenure on the committee automatically became its chairman. The seniority system made committee chairmen autonomous of the party leadership and of party majorities; the 1920–70 period saw numerous instances of committee chairmen thwarting the wishes of party leaders and of majorities of their party colleagues. Since 1970 the congressional parties have changed their rules and procedures so as to decrease the power of committee chairmen. Although chairmen are still usually chosen on the basis of seniority, the party membership can bypass seniority and has done so in extraordinary cases. The result has been to make chairmen much more sensitive to the wishes of their fellow party members.

These changes have strengthened the hand of the party leadership *vis-à-vis* the committee chairmen. Leaders' influence over rank and file members, however, has probably decreased in recent years. Congressional party leaders have seldom been able to affect significantly their members' chances of winning re-election. Since 1920 or so, they have not possessed the internal resources – control over the distribution of desirable committee assignments, for example – necessary to command. In recent years, the resources available to rank-and-file members – staff in particular – have expanded greatly; this has increased such members' ability to pursue their own goals regardless of the wishes of the party leadership. Party leaders, when attempting to build winning coalitions for major legislation, must bargain and persuade; they cannot command. Consequently, strict party-line voting is extremely rare in the Congress.

The 1970s saw both chambers distribute influence more equally and afford the individual member still greater latitude. As committee chairmen lost power, the chairmen of the 100-plus subcommittees in each chamber became more influential and the opportunities for rank-and-file members to participate in the legislative process increased significantly. As a result, the legislative process in both chambers became more democratic and more open; sometimes, however, these desirable characteristics seemed to make the resolution of conflict more difficult.

Two interrelated characteristics, then, make the US Congress very different from the typical European legislature. As a legislature it exercises power independent of the executive. Internally, its members exercise a very high degree of autonomy. Developments during the 1970s and 1980s have accentuated the second characteristic and, it can be argued, the first as well.

See also PRIMARY.   BLS

Reading

Dodd, C. and Oppenheimer, B.I. eds: *Congress Reconsidered*. 3rd edn. Washington, DC: Congressional Quarterly Press, 1985.

Fenno, R.F.: *Home Style: house members in their districts*. Boston: Little, Brown, 1978.

Goehlert, R.U. and Sayre, J.R.: *The United States Congress*, [Bibliographical]. Glencoe, Ill.: Free Press of Glencoe, 1981.

Jones, C.O.: *The United States Congress*. Homewood, Ill.: Dorsey Press, 1982.

Maass, A.: *Congress and the Common Good*. New York: Basic Books, 1983.

Mann, T.E. and Ornstein, N.J.: *The New Congress*. Washington, DC: American Enterprise Institute, 1981.

Parker, G.R. ed.: *Studies of Congress*. Washington, DC: Congressional Quaterly Press, 1985.

Conseil Constitutionnel The Constitutional Council has proved to be one of the most important innovations of the constitution of the Fifth French Republic. Its functions can be placed in three categories, one exceptional and two regular.

(1) Before the president exercises emergency powers, he must consult the Council (Art. 16 of the Constitution); if the president is for any reason incapable of discharging his functions, the Council declares the presidency vacant (Art. 7).
(2) The Council oversees the regularity of elections to the presidency and of referenda and it decides contested cases arising out of parliamentary elections (Arts. 58–60).

(3) The Council acts as a constitutional referee. It is this last function which has given it its political importance.

The council may act as a constitutional referee in three ways. First, the Constitution (Arts. 34 and 37) delimits the area within which parliament may legislate, leaving all other matters to be governed by administrative enactments. The council will, at the instance of the government, rule on whether a parliamentary bill or statute (*loi*) goes outside the legislative area. (The function of keeping administrative enactments out of the legislative area belongs to the CONSEIL D'ÉTAT.) Second, before *lois* of a constitutional character (*lois organiques*) or parliamentary standing orders are enacted, the council must rule on their constitutionality (Art. 61.1). Third, much more widely, the constitution (Art. 61.2) provides that the question of the conformity to the constitution of any *loi* (but only in the period before its promulgation) may be referred to the council. At first this third provision attracted little attention, but since 1971 it has been used to create what had always been regarded as foreign to the French tradition: a power of JUDICIAL REVIEW of legislation (though the council is not formally a court). The importance of this power was greatly increased by a constitutional amendment in 1974 which allowed reference to the council to be made not only, as thitherto, by the president, the prime minister or the president of the Senate or the Assembly, but also by sixty members of either Senate or Assembly.

The council has taken an adventurous view of the extent of the constitution, which it has held to incorporate, by a reference in its Preamble, not only the Declaration of the Rights of Man and the Citizen of 1789, but also the Preamble of the 1946 constitution, which in turn incorporates 'the fundamental principles recognized by the *lois* of the Republic' and a catalogue of 'political, economic and social principles'. This adventurous interpretation has been balanced by a sound sense of political realities and the council has rapidly acquired a wide public acceptance. However, the period of COHABITATION which began in 1986 when a president of one political colour faced a prime minister of an opposite political colour poses a new challenge for the council, and there is some disagreement over its role. Some argued that the council ought to be the arbiter of constitutional disputes, while others believed that, under the constitution, it was the president whose function it was to act as arbiter.

The council has nine members, three each being appointed (for nine years) by the president of the Republic and the presidents of the Senate and the Assembly. Most of those chosen have had long experience of political life, but there have also been distinguished public servants and professors of law.

See also CONSTITUTIONAL COURT.   JKBN

Reading

Brown, L.N. and Garner, J.F.: *French Administrative Law*, pp. 9–14, 3rd edn. London: Butterworths, 1983.

Favoreu, L. and Philip, L.: *Les Grandes décisions du Conseil Constitutionnel*. 3rd edn. Paris: Sirey, 1984.

Luchaire, F.: *Le Conseil Constitutionnel*. Paris: Economica, 1980.

Nicholas, B.: Fundamental rights and judicial review in France. *Public Law* (1978) 82–101, 155–177.

Conseil d'État   The supreme French administrative body, which has both advisory and judicial functions. It advises ministers on the formulation of legislative and administrative enactments and, more widely, on any proposed administrative action. All bills introduced into parliament by the government and all proposed administrative enactments must be submitted to the *Conseil* for advice. In the case of bills the advice need not be followed, but the *Conseil* in its judicial capacity may annul administrative acts which ignore its advice.

In its judicial capacity the *Conseil* acts, except in some special cases, as a court of appeal from subordinate administrative courts. It has two principal jurisdictions. In the *pleine juridiction* it deals with cases in which the complainant alleges that an administrative body has infringed a right of his or hers and seeks compensation. If the defendant were not an administrative body, the case would go to the ordinary courts, but under the French

version of the SEPARATION OF POWERS those courts are forbidden to intervene in matters affecting the administration. In deciding such matters the *Conseil* applies its own case-law, which broadly follows the civil law, but has a number of special features. It is, however, more especially the *juridiction d'annulation* which has given the *Conseil* its very high reputation both in France and abroad. On pain of annulment at the suit of anyone with a sufficient interest, the *Conseil* requires all administrative acts to conform not only to the enacted law, but also to 'the general principles of law' which the *Conseil* itself has evolved through its case-law and which provide a very extensive protection for the individual against the abuse of administrative power. The *Conseil* also has a *juridiction en cassation* to quash decisions of special tribunals, such as professional disciplinary bodies.

The *Conseil* is regarded as the elite of the civil service. It combines administrative expertise with rigorous independence; the principles which it applies are rational and flexible; its procedure is simple and cheap. On the other hand, the existence of the *pleine juridiction* alongside the jurisdiction of the ordinary courts gives rise to conflicts; there is considerable delay in disposing of cases; the *Conseil* has no means of enforcing its decisions (though the administration seldom deliberately fails to comply), and it can only annul an abusive act *ex post facto* – a limitation which, when combined with delay, may cause hardship. Nevertheless, despite these limitations the Conseil d'État is often regarded as a model of an ADMINISTRATIVE COURT, and many reformers have sought to adapt it to the circumstances of other countries where different legal traditions prevail.

See also ADMINISTRATION; ADMINISTRATIVE LAW; ADMINISTRATIVE TRIBUNALS.

JKBN

Reading

Brown, L.N. and Garner, J.F.: *French Administrative Law*. 3rd edn. London: Butterworth, 1983.

Hamson, C.J.: *Executive Discretion and Judicial Control*. London: Stevens, 1954.

Rendel, M.: *The Administrative Functions of the*

French Conseil d'État. London: Weidenfeld & Nicolson, 1970.

consensus A set of beliefs, values and norms shared by individuals living in a given geographical unit at a given time. In its political sense it refers to beliefs that pertain to the POLITICAL SYSTEM. In principle the concept of consensus is applicable to the study of all social entities composed of more than one unit. In politics and in POLITICAL SCIENCE the term is mainly used in reference to the NATION-STATE, or to regional sub-units – the latter most noteworthy in federal states – and in reference to group-related stratifications such as those between ELITES and mass publics. It is often argued that consensus is inextricably intertwined with conflict. Since conflict is a core element of the human condition, consensus is of prime importance as a prerequisite for the peaceful and orderly conduct of socio-political affairs; without some generally accepted values and norms neither society nor polity is possible.

Classical political theory has evolved two essential elements of consensus: a shared sense of the purpose of the collectivity, and a shared agreement on the procedures by which decisions are reached. In democratic politics some argue that beyond those two factors consensus also refers to a shared acceptance of specific public policies. As such, however, the term has no precise meaning.

Conceptually, consensus refers to a system state at a given time. It is important to distinguish this state from its conative component, consent, which pertains to concrete acts of support such as voting for political symbols or policies. Although both consensus and consent have to be observed and measured on the individual level, for example through public opinion research, the former must be aggregated to the level of the particular collective unity for which a statement is intended.

Evaluative yardsticks are obviously needed for an assessment of how widespread a consensus on any given goal or procedure is deemed necessary. There is, though, disagreement with respect to the appropriate thresholds and whether consensus by some

groups is more important than that by others. Furthermore, in pluralist theory the crucial distinction between the consensual and the controversial political sector is theoretically underdeveloped; it therefore cannot tell us precisely which values and procedures belong to which of the two and when.

Though conceivable in authoritarian and totalitarian regimes consensus is particularly relevant for democratic polities, where it emerges from the free will of the citizens and thereby establishes itself as a unique source of legitimation for the goals, procedures and outcomes of the political process.   MK

Reading

Dahl, R.A.: *A Preface to Democratic Theory.* Chicago, Ill. and London: University of Chicago Press, 1956.

Graham, F.G. Jr: Consensus. In *Social Science Concepts: a systematic analysis,* pp. 89–124, ed. G. Sartori. Beverly Hills, Calif., London and New Delhi: Sage, 1984.

Key, V.O. Jr: *Public Opinion and American Democracy.* New York: Knopf, 1961.

McClosky, H.: Consensus and ideology in American politics. *American Political Science Review* 58 (1964) 361–82.

Shils, E. and Lipsitz, L.: Consensus. In *International Encyclopedia of the Social Sciences,* Vol. III, pp. 260–71, ed. D.S. Sills. New York: Macmillan and the Free Press, 1968.

Wright, J.D.: *The Dissent of the Governed.* New York, San Francisco and London: Academic Press, 1976.

conservative parties Usually the second parties to develop when traditional structures were challenged by the rising bourgeoisie and its liberal parties. Conservatives were so strongly represented in the centres of power that they showed enormous reluctance to organize as a party – and where they did they frequently believed, following Bolingbroke, that they had to rally as a party around the monarch to fight the 'factions'. The term 'conservative party' was rarely accepted outside Britain in the 1830s. In the meaning of a political party it was first used by Chateaubriand in his periodical *Le Conservateur* (1817), and was applied to a party in Britain in 1834 by Sir Robert Peel in the Tamworth Manifesto. Conservative parties have sometimes avoided the very notion of party and prefer such terms as union, people's party or *Volkspartei*, Independents (France), National Coalition Party (Finland), Moderates (Sweden); only rarely (Norway) do they call themselves right wing. Even in the twentieth century conservative writers have regarded a Conservative party as degenerate, because such a party can so easily succumb to an ideological style and become one interest ideology among all the rest.

As the Conservative movement became increasingly democratic and middle class, and as it abandoned the aristocratic claim to be something higher than a party, its members became even less inclined to accept the concept 'conservative'. So whereas up to 1945 many had followed the British pattern and did not object to the use of the terms conservative or right wing, after the second world war a growing number of parties changed their names: in Finland the old right-wing party became the National Coalition Party in 1969, and in 1970 the Swiss Conservative People's Party changed its name to Christian-Democratic People's Party.

It is more difficult in the case of Conservative parties than in that of the Liberal, Radical and Socialist movements to generalize on programmatic principles for more than one country. There are two reasons for this: Conservative thinkers and politicians tend to define themselves as pragmatic opponents of general theories; and Conservative programmes have undergone much more far-reaching change than have the doctrines of other political groups.

Any attempt to generalize about the programmes of Conservative parties will encounter difficulties in that Conservatives tend to reject abstract theories and distrust 'sophisters and calculators', as Burke put it. Conservatives have tended to abhor 'isms', preferring to state in concrete terms what they want to conserve – the MONARCHY, the monarchic principle (where the monarchy was already constitutional), or the legitimist principle. Hence the terms monarchist, royalist, and legitimist occurred more frequently in the early nineteenth century.

Individual attempts have been made to draw up a canon of Conservative ideas: these include belief in divine providence, a sense of divine mystery and the wealth of traditional life, support for order and the stratification of society, recognition of the identity of private property and freedom, faith in tradition and traditional rights, as well as awareness that change and reform are not identical and that slow change is the means of preservation.

Old Conservatism was generally opposed to the modern capitalist economy. In France especially it was regarded as *de bon ton* for the classical right to show ignorance of economic matters with occasional defence of individual interest so long as this did not amount to a general economic theory. Modern Conservatism has overcome this and in many cases overtaken Liberalism as the prevailing attitude on economic policy.

One of the main reasons for the strong change in Conservative ideology is the shift in its social base. After 1815 Conservatism was largely a matter for the nobility, the clergy, and other social groups with class ties. Around the turn of the century a large part of the middle and upper middle class became Conservative and in the twentieth century, when the old equation every worker = a member of the workers' party was visibly losing its validity, large sections of the working class also became a recruiting ground for the Conservatives. Without this the Conservative and Christian Democrat parties would not have attained their present strength. Between the two world wars demagogic variants in the crisis of Conservatism made large sections of the workers vulnerable to ideas of FASCISM. A new feature of the period after the second world war was that the 'productive and not the parasitic classes' (Marcuse) became more receptive to a Conservative approach.

The strength of Conservative parties depends largely on the competing parties within the party system. Conservative parties remained weak where they had to compete with Christian Democratic parties (Germany, the Netherlands, Switzerland, Austria); where they were isolated in the ghetto of a lost dynastic cause (Orangists in Belgium, DNVP in the Weimar Republic, Monarchists in Italy after 1946); where they competed with fascist populist movements (POUJADISM, Glistrup). Regionalist (Deutsche Partei in Germany) or ethnic (Volksunie in Belgium) groups also absorbed large parts of the Conservative vote. Questions of national identity frequently changed the nature of Conservatism after the two world wars. Gaullism and Fianna Fáil, two parties which sit as a single group in the European Parliament, played a revolutionary role in their own countries and were partly responsible for changes in the system. It is because of the emphasis placed on the national role in their countries that they are not prepared to designate themselves 'Conservative' although at home they are playing the role of a Conservative party *par excellence*.

In the new democracies in southern Europe Conservative movements, such as the CDS (Centro Democrático Social) in Portugal, the UCD (Union del Centro Democrático) in Spain and the New Democratic Party (ND) in Greece, at first seemed to be strong, but eroded after a few years and left the party system with a more reactionary but smaller Conservative party which seemed to have little hope for a comeback to power without the help of a heterogeneous coalition. In Spain, however, the Alianza Popular has now become stronger than the UCD and is the main opposition party to the Socialists. After joining with the British Conservatives in the European Parliament, it then joined the Christian Democrat group – the European Peoples Party (EPP). Otherwise, however, except for Britain and some Commonwealth countries, Conservative parties today are in a minority position within a fragmented camp of bourgeois parties.

KvB

Reading

Laponce, J.A.: *Left and Right: the topography of political perceptions*. Toronto: University of Toronto Press, 1981.

Layton-Henry, Z. ed.: *Conservative Politics in Western Europe*. London: Macmillan, 1982.

Morgan, R. and Silvestri, S. eds: *Moderates and Conservatives in Western Europe*. London: Heinemann, 1982.

Rogger, H. and Weber, E. eds: *The European Right*. London: Weidenfeld & Nicolson, 1965.

consociational democracy As the principal alternative to the more familiar majoritarian or Westminster-style type of democracy, consociational democracy is particularly suitable for the governance of plural societies, that is societies which are deeply divided by religious, ideological, linguistic, regional, cultural, racial or ethnic differences, which form clearly separate and easily identifiable segments. Consociational democracy can be defined in terms of four basic principles: the two most important are *executive power-sharing* or grand coalition, and a high degree of *autonomy* for the segments of the plural society; the two secondary principles are *proportionality* and the *minority veto*.

Executive power-sharing entails government by a grand coalition of the representatives of all significant segments. It may take a variety of institutional forms. The most straightforward form is that of a grand coalition cabinet in a parliamentary system. In presidential systems power-sharing may be accomplished by distributing the presidency and other high offices among the different segments. The grand coalition principle stands in sharp contrast to the principle of concentrating power in one-party, baremajority, non-coalition cabinets which is typical of the majoritarian Westminster model of democracy.

The second consociational principle prescribes the delegation of as much decision making as possible to the separate segments. It complements the grand coalition principle: on all issues of common concern the decisions should be made jointly by the representatives of the segments; on all other issues, decision making should be left to each segment. For plural societies with geographically concentrated segments, an especially suitable form of segmental autonomy is FEDERALISM. If the segments are geographically interspersed, segmental autonomy has to take a mainly non-territorial form. In either form segmental autonomy contrasts sharply with the unitary and centralized character of majoritarian democracy.

Proportionality is the basic consociational standard of political representation, civil service appointments, and allocation of public funds. As a principle of representation it is particularly important as a guarantee for the fair representation of minority segments. Two extensions of the proportionality rule entail even greater minority protection: the over-representation of small segments, and parity of representation when all segments are represented equally regardless of size. Proportionality, minority over-representation, and parity all contrast with the disproportional representation favouring the majority or the largest party that is typical of the plurality electoral method (first past the post) in the Westminster model.

The *minority veto* is the ultimate weapon that minority segments need to protect their vital interests. Even when a minority's representatives participate in an executive grand coalition, they may be overruled or outvoted by the majority. This may not present a problem when trifling issues are being decided, but when a minority's vital interests are at stake the veto provides essential protection. It goes without saying that the minority veto is again antithetical to the majoritarian model of democracy.

There are nine conditions that favour the establishment of consociational democracy in a plural society and its successful operation: the absence of a majority segment; segments of roughly the same size; a relatively small number of segments, ideally between three and five; a relatively small total population; foreign threats that are perceived as a common danger; overarching loyalties that counterbalance the centrifugal effects of segmental loyalties; the absence of large socio-economic inequalities; geographical concentration of the segments; and pre-existing traditions of political accommodation. These are helpful conditions, but they should not be regarded as either necessary or sufficient. The presence of all or most of them does not guarantee consociationalism, nor does their absence prevent it.

There are many examples of consociational democracy in various parts of the world. In Europe, examples are Austria during the period of Catholic–Socialist power-sharing cabinets from 1945 to 1966; Belgium since the first world war and, as far as its linguistic division is concerned, especially since 1970; the Netherlands from 1917 to 1967; Luxemburg during roughly the same fifty-year period; Switzerland from 1943 onwards. In the third world, consociational democracy can be found in Lebanon from 1943 to 1975, Malaysia from 1955 onwards, Cyprus during the few years from its independence in 1960 until 1963, Surinam from 1958 to 1973, and the Netherlands Antilles from 1950 until the secession of Aruba at the end of 1985. Furthermore, there are two cases of partially consociational democracy: Israel since its independence in 1948 and Canada – both the contemporary Canadian system and, even more clearly, the pre-democratic United Province of Canada from 1840 to 1867. At the regional and local level many additional examples of consociationalism can be found. For instance most of the cantons in Switzerland have power-sharing executives like the Swiss federal executive. Power-sharing has also been the rule in all but one of the Länder of federal Austria.   AL

Reading

Barry, B.: Political accommodation and consociational democracy. *British Journal of Political Science* 5 (1975) 477–505.

————: The consociational model and its dangers. *European Journal of Political Research* 3.4 (1975) 393–412.

Bluhm, W.T.: *Building an Austrian Nation: the political integration of a western state.* New Haven, Conn.: Yale University Press, 1973.

Boulle, L.J.: *South Africa and the Consociational Option: a constitutional analysis.* Cape Town: Juta, 1984.

Daalder, H.: The consociational democracy theme. *World Politics* 26.4 (July 1974) 604–21.

Dew, E.: *The Difficult Flowering of Surinam: ethnicity and politics in a plural society.* The Hague: Nijhoff, 1978.

Hanf, T., Weiland, H. and Vierdag, G.: *South Africa and the Prospects of Peaceful Change: an empirical enquiry into the possibility of democratic conflict regulation.* London: Collins, 1981.

Lewis, W.A.: *Politics in West Africa.* London: Allen & Unwin, 1965.

Lijphart, A.: *Democracy in Plural Societies: a comparative exploration.* New Haven, Conn.: Yale University Press, 1977.

————: Power-sharing in South Africa. *Policy Papers in International Affairs* 24. Berkeley: Institute of International Studies, University of California, 1985.

McRae, K.D. ed.: *Consociational Democracy: political accommodation in segmented societies.* Toronto: McClelland & Stewart, 1974.

Powell, G.B. Jr: *Social Fragmentation and Political Hostility: an Austrian case study.* Stanford, Calif.: Stanford University Press, 1970.

Schendelen, M.P.C.M. van, ed.: Consociationalism, pillarization and conflict-management in the Low Countries. *Acta Politica* 1 (January 1984).

Slabbert, F. van Zyl and Welsh, D.: *South Africa's Options: strategies for sharing power.* New York: St Martin's, 1979.

Steiner, J.: *Amicable Agreement versus Majority Rule: conflict regulation in Switzerland.* Chapel Hill: University of North Carolina Press, 1974.

Vorys, K. von: *Democracy without Consensus: communalism and political stability in Malaysia.* Princeton, NJ: Princeton University Press, 1975.

Constant, Benjamin (1767–1830) A member of France's Chamber of Deputies under the restored Bourbon monarchy, Benjamin Constant became the best known liberal politician and writer on the continent of Europe. His antics during the Napoleonic period had not been prepossessing and his electoral success in the department of La Sarthe in 1819 was largely the result of skilful management, but thereafter his courageous speeches in defence of individual freedom gave wide appeal to his somewhat difficult writings.

Popular government had been discredited by the experience of the FRENCH REVOLUTION, and Constant was therefore at pains to dissociate 'modern' liberty from the 'ancient' liberty which both ROUSSEAU and the Jacobins had extolled. In ancient CITY STATES, Constant argued, emphasis had been placed on political participation to the neglect of private independence. The ancients had understood liberty in terms of citizenship, but this left no room for private rights. The time had come, Constant urged, not so much to reverse the emphasis as to establish a balance. In a large modern state a mass electorate could too easily be manipulated by un-

scrupulous politicians. The remedy was to encourage genuine participation by thinking people who saw their political rights as a means of safeguarding their personal authenticity. Constant argued, as against Rousseau, that REPRESENTATION could help to preserve liberty. He favoured CONSTITUTIONAL GOVERNMENT, and believed that MONARCHY had an important role to play by maintaining a balance between executive and legislature, but aristocracy based on birth was unjustifiable and equality before the law was essential. Society was important in that it fulfilled a natural instinct and enabled individuals to carry out tasks they could never accomplish alone, but on no account must freedom of speech, religion and education be sacrificed or the right to oppose the government restricted.

By stressing the importance of an intelligent approach to politics, Constant seemed to place a premium on restriction of the franchise. He did indeed support the idea of a property qualification, but only because he regarded economic independence as necessary to free action. The idea of extending the franchise to greater numbers of people did not in itself terrify him as it did most nineteenth century liberals, nor did he regard leisure as a prerequisite of thought.

Constant's ideas, though they were to some extent tailored to suit the times, have not lost their importance, and Constant can properly be regarded as one of the founders of modern liberalism.

IC

Reading

Berlin, I.: Two concepts of liberty. In *Four Essays on Liberty.* Oxford: Oxford University Press, 1969.

Constant, B.: *Oeuvres*, ed. A. Roulin, Paris: Pléiade, 1964.

Dodge, G.: *Benjamin Constant's Philosophy of Liberalism.* Chapel Hill: University of North Carolina Press, 1980.

Hofmann, E.: Les 'Principes de politique' de Benjamin Constant. Geneva: Droz, 1980.

Holmes, S.: *Benjamin Constant and the Making of Modern Liberalism.* New Haven, Conn. and London: Yale University Press, 1984.

Siedentop, L.A.: Two liberal traditions. In *The Idea of Freedom*, ed. A.J. Ryan. Oxford: Oxford University Press, 1979.

constituency The most widely used term for the territorial divisions which form a key element in the election of almost all representative assemblies in liberal democracies. This is not always apparent in descriptions of PARLIAMENTARY SYSTEMS and ELECTORAL SYSTEMS partly because of some linguistic confusion over the word itself. Constituency (*circonscription* in French; *Wahlkreis* in German) is most commonly used where the territorial divisions have boundaries drawn specifically for electoral purposes. But other English terms are used for such divisions: the Canadian parliament is elected by ridings, and in English local government lower tier councils are elected by wards and upper tier councils by electoral divisions. Elsewhere, elections are held by the territorial divisions which exist for other purposes; for example the cantons, the components of the Swiss federation, elect both chambers of the Swiss parliament and there is no need for a special electoral term for them. Territorial divisions in some form, henceforward referred to as constituencies, are almost universally present; the notable exception is the Israeli Knesset, elected by one single national constituency.

Variations in the type and role of constituencies in the election of representative assemblies cut across the familiar types of electoral system. Most majority systems (whether first-past-the-post, alternative vote or two-ballot) use single-member constituencies, though double-member or treble-member constituencies were not uncommon in the past (e.g. the UK House of Commons until 1885); Britain still retains multi-member elections in London boroughs and in parishes, and in Turkey multi-member constituencies (with up to sixty members) were used for first-past-the-post elections in 1950–60. Most proportional representation systems are based on multi-member constituencies of varying size (although in several countries with such systems there are a few special case single-member constituencies, e.g. the Aaland islands in Finland). But in the German speaking world the combination of single-member constituencies with proportional representation has been advocated and is at present the basis of the electoral system in the Federal Republic of Germany. Thus the differences between majority voting systems and proportional systems overlap the difference between single-member and multi-member constituency systems; there are four possible combinations of which two are relatively unusual.

The second distinction between types of constituency is that between those constituencies whose boundaries are especially drawn for electoral purposes and those constituencies which exist for other purposes – as historic provinces, local government units or recognizable separate communities. Historically representative assemblies were based on summoning representatives from existing communities, for example the counties and boroughs in the House of Commons. The practice of dividing the country into districts, with boundaries especially drawn for electoral purposes, started in the United States: while the Senate was based on the traditional principle (each state automatically a constituency), the House of Representatives was elected on the new single-member constituency principle. This new principle spread across Europe in the middle of the nineteenth century, only to retreat as it was found that equality of size of constituencies did not produce the accurate reflection of the voters' wishes that its advocates had expected. The multi-member principle now predominates overwhelmingly in Europe, but the single-member principle is the norm in the English-speaking world.

Where it is necessary to draw special boundaries for constituencies, the process and the outcome have often become politically controversial because in both majority voting systems and in those proportional systems in which the allocation of seats takes place solely within the constituency, the size and boundaries of constituencies can affect the fortunes of political parties. Two distinct processes are involved: the allocation of seats to different parts of the country or types of constituency (sometimes known as apportionment), and the drawing of boundaries. These are most controversial in countries with rapidly growing populations (where taking the census becomes a highly political act) and ethnic divisions; the dangers to democracy of such controversies are best illustrated in Nigeria. Where there are single-member constituencies regular re-allocation to maintain equality of ratios between electors and representatives requires regular redrawing of boundaries; it can more easily be done in multi-member constituencies by altering the numbers of members. But regular redrawing of boundaries need not necessarily reflect a regular re-allocation of numbers of representatives; the allocation of seats between England, Scotland and Wales has failed to be adjusted to changes to the movement of population over the last sixty years and is now seriously out of line with the equal ratio principle.

Such failures either to redraw boundaries or to re-allocate regularly can be a form of malapportionment or gerrymander when the previous allocations or boundaries which suit a particular political party are maintained but they are not unique to single-member constituencies; a similar gerrymander by default occurs in Norway with proportional representation where the rural counties are now seriously over-represented, to the benefit of the parties with more support in rural Norway. Positive gerrymandering consists in drawing constituency boundaries to benefit the party in charge of the redrawing process, and is particularly prevalent in the United States of America. Other single-member constituency countries (e.g. Australia, New Zealand, the United Kingdom) attempt to avoid this problem by using impartial boundary commissions. But once again the problem is not unique to the single-member constituency or majority voting; in Ireland positive gerrymandering has taken the form of deciding whether multi-member constituencies should have three, four or five members as suits the party in power.

Because of the overlap between types of constituencies and types of voting system the effects of different sorts of constituencies have not been isolated and studied by political scientists until very recently. Furthermore, it is clear that the effects that they do have interact heavily not only with electoral systems but also with other constitutional provisions and with

political traditions. Thus generally multi-member constituencies tend to favour the practice of members of parliament coming from their own constituencies. This is because, with several seats at stake, ambitious candidates have a reasonable chance of getting one and are looked at suspiciously if they try their luck elsewhere; single-member constituencies, however, are often held safely by one party or an incumbent which blocks any other local politician's hopes. Consequently most multi-member constituency systems in Europe produce representatives who are more closely in touch with their constituencies than are members of the British House of Commons. However, a residency rule in the United States, together with the primary system (allowing easy challenges) and the looseness of party, produces a strong localism among US members of Congress despite single-member constituencies.

The reality of multi-member constituencies can vary considerably. Members of the Swiss parliament are strongly attached to their twenty-three cantons; the Dutch parliament is elected by eighteen constituencies but the Dutch political system functions in a manner much closer to a national list system. In Switzerland the canton as constituency is strongly reinforced by the federal framework of government, the linguistic variety of the country and the highly decentralized party system; in the Netherlands a centralized political culture (in which the subdivisions have traditionally been religious or cultural segments rather than the provinces) has effectively overridden the territorial constituency element.

There is one effect, though, of the multi-member versus single-member constituency dichotomy which appears across the board: multi-member constituencies, especially if they elect several rather than two or three members together, are more favourable to the election of women. This is most clear in countries (e.g. Britain, West Germany and Japan) where electoral systems have involved different types of constituency simultaneously. It is an interesting comment on the pre-occupations of political science that while there has been a substantial controversy over the effect of electoral systems on party systems, this effect of the constituency element in electoral systems has, until very recently, been unnoticed.

See also ELECTORAL GEOGRAPHY; REDISTRIBUTION.   MS

Reading

Steed, M.: The constituency. In *Representatives of the People?*, ed. V. Bogdanor. Aldershot: Gower, 1985.

constitution/constitutionalism A collection of written and unwritten principles and rules that identify the sources, purposes, uses, and restraints of public power. With a very few exceptions such as the United Kingdom, Israel, Saudi Arabia and some newly established micro-states, constitutional principles and rules are contained in one single written document. But no worthwhile study of a constitutional system can be limited to that central document. Constitutional practices, judicial interpretations, general laws, traditions and customs have also to be examined. Modern constitutions are generally much longer and more detailed than their older models such as the succinct United States Constitution which came into force in 1789: the Indian Constitution, for example, has nearly 400 articles, many of which extend over several pages. The length of post-colonial constitutions in the British Commonwealth and French Communauté often reflects a desire on the part of the drafters to codify and thus perpetuate the preliberation unity and consensus.

A *legal* view of national constitutions is that of a supreme law of the land, a fundamental normative fountain from which all the other secondary norms such as statutory laws, executive orders, and ordinances are derived. When these secondary norms fail to conform to the constitution, various judicial bodies (courts or special constitutional tribunals) are to declare the unconstitutional laws invalid. The term of judicial or constitutional review applies to this procedure.

A *political* and functional view of a constitution is that of a political manifesto and organizational chart or 'power map' (see Duchacek 1973). Every constitution combines a declaration of political or ideological commitment with a blueprint for action, expressed in legal terms, and limited by various restraints, normally contained in a BILL OF RIGHTS. Well over one-half of the constitutional text deals with specific ways in which legal rules and political decisions will be made, applied, and adjudicated. A student of POLITICAL SYSTEMS may view a national constitution as a shorthand description of major organs and processes by which conflicts of interest between various groups are to be arbitrated and various demands ('inputs' according to David Easton) converted into binding and enforceable rules and policies (Easton's 'outputs').

Editorially, most constitutions contain four to five core segments.

(1) A *preamble*, a declaratory, non-legal portion of the constitution. The preamble as well as several articles describing national symbols (flag, motto, emblem, capital, anthem) and the duty to defend the fatherland, are primarily addressed to the people's emotions, collective memories, and dreams rather than to the rational, organizational or legal sense of the citizens. Declamatory portions of a constitution mirror the founding elites' world-view, their sense of national history and future, and their commitment to such principles or creeds as DEMOCRACY, SOCIALISM, Islam, WELFARE STATE, planned economy, or federal division of power. Modern preambles record with pride – and at length – the cost and glory of great common deeds in the past and the resolve to do collectively more in the future. They are classical statements of NATIONALISM. One of the goals of the emotional solemnity incorporated into the constitutional texts, propagandized both before and after their promulgations, is socialization of various groups and individuals into a territorial polity: 'Co-ordinated people's activities, expectations, and habits rather than threats keep things moving' (Karl W. Deutsch). Constitutional drafters hope that the existence and wording of the national constitution may contribute to such co-ordination.

(2) An *organizational* chart contains a rather detailed description of the various structures,

agencies and specific procedures to be followed by individuals and groups in achieving their various goals in an orderly and legal fashion. Such a prescription of the hierarchical assignment of specialized roles and responsibilities to various agencies and agents may make for dull reading as is usually the case with all organizational charts issued by the management in charge of complex corporate bodies. Nearly all national constitutions (democratic, communist, or fascist) follow the traditional pattern of 'tripartism' and separate legislative, executive, and judicial institutions and processes into three distinct chapters, with separate chapters or sub-chapters dealing with regional and local governments.

This so-called constitutional tripartism dates back to the eighteenth century when MONTESQUIEU (1689–1755), basing himself on his somewhat inaccurate observations of the workings of the British system, tended to view tripartism (separation of legislative, executive, and judiciary authority) as a guarantee of non-tyrannical government. Most modern constitutions have adopted some variant of the Westminster CABINET system, wherein the executive branch of government issues from, is accountable to, and removable by, a popularly elected chamber of the national legislature. Symbolically, even authoritarian systems and constitutions copy this pattern. The American presidential system is favoured in the western hemisphere only but the SEMI-PRESIDENTIAL form, introduced by de Gaulle in France, has been adopted by a number of other states. Despite the contemporary voracious legislative appetite of the executive branch, the majority of national constitutions today still place the legislative chapter before the executive. The 'editorial' preference given to the legislature is a reflection of the democratic hopes of the past centuries that rules and policies would primarily originate with the elected legislators and not, as is increasingly the case today, with the executive branch and its bureaucrats and technocrats.

(3) BILL OF RIGHTS, today an integral part of every written constitution (including those proclaimed by dictators), lists various individual and collective rights, and guarantees of citizens' access to and legal restraints on the uses of power. The constitutional guarantees usually include the right to vote and be elected, the right to create and maintain political parties for the purpose of running and (in democracies) opposing the government, and the right to promote group interests, including the right to organize labour and strikes. These guarantees of political inputs and controls in turn depend on the constitutional protection of various CIVIL RIGHTS and liberties, ranging from the freedom of the press, speech, and assembly to linguistic rights, the right of privacy, DUE PROCESS of law, and the right to impartial justice. When the new Canadian constitution was patriated in 1982, an elaborate Charter of Rights and Freedoms was its central feature. Several constitutions, adopted by modern welfare states, have added a list of economic, social and cultural rights (either in a separate bill or as part of the bill of rights). These new rights aim at expanding the role of the government in contrast to the traditional civil rights and liberties whose aim was to limit and restrain government. Implementation or violation of participatory and civil rights and liberties is the fundamental yardstick by which one can determine whether a nation which has a constitution also enjoys constitutional government, that is, a limited, accountable, and responsive public authority (see CONSTITUTIONAL GOVERNMENT).

(4) *Amendatory articles* provide for procedures to be followed when a revision of the supreme law of the land is desired. No constitution claims to be the final word in the political development of the national life. Some constitutions, described as flexible, make the amending process as easy as enacting a statutory law. Other constitutions, described as rigid, often combine the vote in the legislative body with popular referendums, new general elections, or, as is necessary in federal systems, ratification by the component territorial units (Switzerland, the United States, Canada, and Australia). While logically each nation has only one national constitution, federal unions usually have as many 'sub-

national' constitutions as they have territorial components (the United States, for example, has fifty state constitutions in addition to the national one of 1789). (See ENTRENCHMENT.)

In response to social, political, and technological changes the amending of older constitutions and the making of new ones goes on constantly. Violent upheavals are often immediately followed by constitution-making to legitimate the new reality or new leaders. Comparing the avalanche of new constitutions with their antecedents, one rarely discovers any fresh formula. The selective copying of old and modern foreign constitutional models, concepts, terminology, and slogans is general, open, deliberate, and occasionally unwitting; the modern drafting fathers seem to be constitutional copycats, beginning their work armed with verbatim copies of selected foreign constitutions. The principal models for the content and style of bills of rights have been the English Bill of Rights of 1689, the French DECLARATION OF THE RIGHTS OF MAN AND THE CITIZEN of 1789, and the American Bill of Rights of 1791. Many newly independent nations in Africa proclaim their acceptance of the United Nations Universal Declaration of Human Rights of 1948 instead of preparing their own bill of rights. They 'domesticate' foreign models by weaving into them their own personal and collective aims and values which their people now support or, in the opinion of the drafting elite, should support. As Kenneth Wheare suggested, many a constitution is thus being drawn and promulgated, 'because people wish to make a fresh start . . . to begin again'. As the record indicates, a fresh start seems to be difficult in all human matters, constitutional or not. In past centuries the general public, constitutional lawyers, and even political scientists tended to view constitutions and their bills of rights as major guarantees against tyranny, if not 'tickets to Utopia'; this is no more so today when violation rather than observation of the constitutional bills of civil and participatory rights is a daily occurrence in the majority of nations. The fate of the democratic and seemingly well-designed Weimar constitution in Nazi Germany and the contemporary proclaiming and propagandizing of new constitutions by communist one-party systems, fascist dictators, and military juntas have led to a substantial decline in the former view of a constitution as a centre of gravity for political systems.

See also JUDICIAL REVIEW. IDD

Reading

Blaustein, A.P. and Flanz, G.H.: *Constitutions of the Countries of the World*. Dobbs Ferry, NY: Oceana, 1972.

———: *Constitutions of Dependencies and Special Sovereignties*. Dobbs Ferry, NY: Oceana, 1972.

Duchacek, I.D.: *Power Maps: comparative politics of constitutions*. Santa Barbara, Calif. and Oxford: ABC-Clio, 1973.

Duverger, M.: *Constitutions et documents politiques*. Paris: Presses Universitaires de France, 1957.

Easton, D.: *A Systems Analysis of Political Life*. New York: Wiley, 1965; 2nd edn. Chicago, Ill.: University of Chicago Press, 1979.

Friedrich, C.J.: *Constitutional Government and Democracy*. Boston, Mass.: Ginn, 1950.

Peaslee, A.L.: *Constitutions of the Nations*. 8 vols. New York: Justice House, 1956–68.

Triska, J.E. ed.: *Constitutions of the Communist Party States*. Stanford, Calif.: Stanford University Press, 1968.

Wheare, K.C.: *Modern Constitutions*. 2nd edn. Oxford: Oxford University Press, 1966.

constitutional court A governmental judicial tribunal exercising the highest appellate jurisdiction in the entire judicial system of a particular nation. Constitutional courts were developed after the historic decline of absolute monarchy; their model was the SUPREME COURT of the United States. This was established as a result of the deliberations and compromises of the delegates to the Philadelphia Convention of 1787 and the state ratifying conventions of 1788. The hallmark of these courts is a high degree of functional separation from and independence of national executive and legislative authority. This characteristic was viewed by the American Founding Fathers as the fulfilment of some of the goals of the AMERICAN REVOLUTION: the creation of judicial independence and the safeguarding of this independence against intrusive executive authority. A second goal was that of ensuring a degree of stability for property rights, occasionally threatened by state legislative uncertainty. Perhaps of most importance to the United States was the acknowledged role of the Supreme Court as the final arbiter in federal–state relations. For some of the nations subsequently adopting the concept of a constitutional court, FEDERALISM became both the major rationale for the development of the court and the most divisive source of constitutional litigation once such a court was created. Australia, Canada, and West Germany are good examples of the congruence of federalism and constitutional courts. Yet these courts have also become an integral part of non-federal nations such as the Republic of Ireland, Italy and Japan. In the Anglo-American jurisdictions constitutional courts belong to the same system as cases dealing with ordinary lawsuits, while in the civil law jurisdictions of the Continent they are distinct. Further, while the Supreme Court of the United States is part of the PRESIDENTIAL SYSTEM, most other constitutional courts function in PARLIAMENTARY SYSTEMS.

The logic of legislative supremacy in parliamentary systems would seem to preclude the exercise of JUDICIAL REVIEW, but in some countries, Canada for example, such judicial review has evolved. The assumption of greater judicial responsibilities for protecting individual rights and liberties, especially in the twentieth century, has contributed to greater judicial supervision. The assertion of such power of review of the constitutionality of executive or legislative actions since the second world war has not been significant in very many of the nations in which constitutional courts were recently established: India is perhaps, in contrast to France and Italy, a notable exception. In most nations which have such a court the exercise of its authority has been very cautious. Canada is an excellent example of this careful development. The post-war era has seen a significant growth in the number of national constitutional courts. Many of these new courts however have not been granted, and neither have they asserted, strong judicial authority, nor have they engaged in the kind of judicial policy making character-

istic of the Supreme Court of the United States.

All contemporary constitutional courts are collegial, composed of more than one justice or judge. The Supreme Court of the United States always meets as a single institution, but other constitutional courts generally meet in panels. Notable examples are the High Court of Australia and the Supreme Courts of Canada, the Republic of Ireland and Japan. The procedures for judicial decision making in the Supreme Courts of Japan and the United States provide important examples of the similarities and differences among contemporary national constitutional courts. The basic constitutional framework from which these two courts evolved were separated by a century: the American Constitution of 1789 and the Meiji Constitution of 1889. Furthermore, in Japan formal independence from executive supervision was not established until the creation of the constitution of 1947 (the so-called MacArthur Constitution). In the American system, Judicial Review was initially applied as a definitive doctrine in 1803 in *Marbury* v. *Madison*. In Japan it is explicitly embodied in the Constitution of 1947. Article 81 provides that the Supreme Court of Japan is 'the court of last resort with power to determine the constitutionality of any law, order, regulation, or official act'.

In regard to personnel, both justices and supporting officials, the Japanese Court still maintains its emphasis upon professional training thereby continuing the continental European influence which had been significant before 1947. Individuals eligible for a seat on the Japanese Supreme Court must, with a few exceptions, be selected for professional training for a judicial career as distinguished from training for the practice of law. In the United States political identification and, increasingly, ideological purity are considered, with legal competence, as prerequisites for a judge-justiceship. Similarly, Japanese justices place greater emphasis upon professional judicial training in selecting supporting personnel than do American justices. Japanese research officials (Chosaken) assist justices in preparation of opinions as do American law clerks. But the former are chosen from the ranks of full time judges, generally with over five years of experience, while the latter are selected from among top ranked students just graduating from elite law schools.

Since the nineteenth century the American Supreme Court has consisted of nine members meeting as a single collegial body. The fifteen-man Supreme Court of Japan generally meets in panels of five justices except for clearly defined major constitutional issues when it is united as 'the Grand Bench'. Seniority in service on each court is important but is of greater institutional consequence for the Japanese Court because all members are subject to compulsory retirement. In contrast, members of the Supreme Court of the United States are constitutionally guaranteed life tenure on good behaviour. Because Japanese justices are generally eligible for the Chief Justiceship through seniority of Supreme Court service, Chief Justices rarely serve for very long. In fact, with the exception of Chief Justice Tanaka (March 1950–October 1960), Japanese Chief Justices rarely have held the position long enough to develop or assert the kind of leadership that American Chief Justices, with twenty or thirty years' service are sometimes able to establish.

See also CONSEIL CONSTITUTIONNEL; EUROPEAN CONVENTION ON HUMAN RIGHTS. JRS

Reading

Abraham, H.J.: *The Judicial Process*. 4th edn. Oxford: Oxford University Press, 1980.

Hayakawa, T. and Schmidhauser, J.R.: A comparative analysis of the internal procedure and customs of the Supreme Courts of Japan and the United States. In *Comparative Judicial Systems*, ed. J.R. Schmidhauser. London: Butterworth Scientific and The International Political Science Association, 1987.

Kelly, A.H., Harbison, W. and Belz, H.: *The American Constitution: its origins and development*. New York: Norton, 1983.

McWhinney, E.: *Canada and the Constitution, 1979–1982: patriation and the Charter of Rights*. Toronto: University of Toronto Press, 1982.

Murphy, W.F. and Tanenhaus, J.: *Comparative Constitutional Law: cases and commentaries*. London: Macmillan, 1977.

Schmidhauser, J.R.: *The Supreme Court as Final Arbiter in Federal–State Relations, 1789–1957*. Chapel Hill: University of North Carolina Press, 1958.

Wood, G.S.: *The Creation of the American Republic, 1776–1787*. New York: Norton, 1972.

constitutional government Government limited by regular legal and political restraints and accountable to the citizens. Under constitutional government both public authorities and citizens are equally subject to the law and the constitution. The concept of institutionalized and continuously practised constitutional government is broadly synonymous with plural democracy or POLYARCHY (see Dahl 1970): in fact, they are twin concepts since both presuppose freedom of thought, speech, the press, and assembly, the right to impartial justice (from *habeas corpus* and trial by jury to the right of appeal) as well as citizens' free access to political processes by means of elections, political parties and interest groups.

Restraints on government and guarantees of citizens' access to political processes are usually spelled out in a written and formally proclaimed constitution or other fundamental texts and traditions. In a few countries (Britain and Israel) constitutional government is practised without a formal constitution. Statutory laws of a fundamental nature coupled with political tradition are their 'constitutions'; Rousseau might have labelled them as being 'not graven on tablets or brass, but on the hearts of the citizen'.

On the other hand the mere presence of a constitution is not the same as constitutional government. Today, practically all nations have formal constitutions that promise constitutional government but only a small fragment of the total enjoy constitutional government in the sense of limited, responsive, and responsible government.

Two benchmarks are useful in evaluating the gap between constitutional text and actual practice. The first distinguishes between *constant* and *occasional* violations. Constitutions usually authorize the government to suspend some basic individual and collective rights and guarantees for a limited period of emergency, with the understanding that they will be restored as soon as the crisis is over. If such a suspension of constitutional government is prolonged and tends to become a habit with the ruling elites (as was the case in India under Indira Gandhi and Pakistan under its successive military dictators), a serious doubt arises about the existence and the future of constitutional government, and therefore democracy. The second yardstick tries to differentiate between violations by the government of the *organizational* and the *essential* provisions of a national constitution. In the light of what has been said above, a nation does not enjoy constitutional government if the organizational chart aspect of the constitution is scrupulously observed while the constitutional guarantees of participatory and CIVIL RIGHTS are constantly violated.

A controversy touching upon the meaning of constitutional government has developed around the issue of modern social, economic, and cultural rights. In the period of welfare and service states whose leading elites are committed to national planning or ownership of economic, social and cultural resources, many modern constitutions contain various guarantees of economic, social and cultural rights. They often include the citizens' rights to work, health, education, and clean environment. They are either grouped into a separate Bill of Social Rights or incorporated into the general Bill of Rights and Liberties. There is, however, a substantial difference between the two. Traditional bills of civil rights and liberties (with their distinct eighteenth-century flavour) aim at limiting or restraining government. In contrast, modern social and economic rights aim at more government, not less. Modern social rights are not dependent on government's restraint but primarily on the economic and social resources that the government is asked to mobilize in order to free its citizens from unemployment, sickness, illiteracy, polluted air, land, or water and so forth. The Indian Constitution, for example, stipulates that the state shall make effective provisions securing the right to work 'within the limits of economic capacity and development'. For this reason these new rights or claims, unlike civil rights and liberties, are

hardly enforceable by courts. Can a vigorous pursuit of social progress and economic redistribution on the part of a government be construed by itself as evidence of 'constitutional government'? Not if such a welfare commitment is to be implemented at the cost of individual and group rights and liberties. On the other hand, constitutional government may be deemed actually to exist if civil rights and liberties are fully observed even though the government has abstained from assuming an active role in economic, social and cultural affairs. The appropriate mix between individual rights and liberties, on the one hand, and the governmental role in the social and economic fields, on the other, is a matter of political and ideological controversy which extends deeper and wider than the texts of modern constitutions.

As to federal systems which divide the territorial authority between one general (federal or national) government and a series of territorial component governments, each independent within its own sphere of jurisdiction, constitutional government is a *conditio sine qua non*. By means of a written constitution (based on a preceding consensus among the territorial components) a federal system institutionalizes the dividing as well as the connecting lines between the two orders of government. To be fully operative FEDERALISM requires democratic participatory processes both within and among the federal components. A one-party authoritarian system (aiming at a maximum concentration of power in the hands of a few) and democratic federalism (committed to PLURALISM) are mutually exclusive: authoritarianism is, as it were, genetically unable to grant a significant portion of its power to any other political formation, be it a territorial community as a federal component, a political party, or interest group (such as the Solidarity trade union in communist Poland). When fascist and communist systems, military juntas, and one-tribe-dominated regimes claim to be federal, they are, in fact, either confederal leagues of territorial DICTATORSHIPS (Yugoslavia or United Arab Emirates) or marginally decentralized dictatorships (Czechoslovakia, Nigeria, the Soviet Union, and Tanzania).

147

CONSTITUTIONAL LAW

Among constitutional lawyers and political scientists in general, and specialists in federalism in particular, the issues of DEMOCRACY as a prerequisite of federalism and the incompatibility of federalism with dictatorship remain controversial.

See also BILL OF RIGHTS; CIVIL LIBERTIES; RULE OF LAW.   IDD

Reading

Andrews, W.G.: *Constitutions and Constitutionalism.* Princeton, NJ: Van Nostrand, 1968.

Dahl, R.A.: *Modern Political Analysis.* Englewood Cliffs, NJ: Prentice-Hall, 1963.

————: *Polyarchy.* New Haven, Conn.: Yale University Press, 1970.

Duchacek, I.D.: *Rights and Liberties in the World Today.* Santa Barbara, Calif. and Oxford: ABC–Clio, 1973.

————: *The Territorial Dimension of Politics within, among, and across Nations.* Boulder, Col.: Westview, 1986.

Hamilton, A., Madison, J. and Jay, J.: *The Federalist Papers*, ed. C. Rossiter. New York: Mentor, 1964.

Sartori, G.: Constitutionalism: a preliminary discussion. *American Political Science Review* 56.4 (1962).

Wheare, K.C.: *Federal Government.* Oxford: Oxford University Press, 1961.

constitutional law   That body of knowledge dealing with the law of the constitution in the broadest sense, i.e. not just the law pertaining to the written document entitled the constitution, but also all those matters pertaining to the organization of government and its relationship to the citizen. In countries influenced by the Roman law tradition, law tends to be divided into a series of codes, and there is a clear demarcation between constitutional law and other branches of the law. In common law countries, such as Britain, however, the legal order has traditionally been conceived of as unified and indivisible and it becomes more difficult to draw a clear line of demarcation. The constitutional historian F. W. Maitland once declared that, in England, 'there is hardly any department of law which does not, at one time or another, become of constitutional importance'.

Constitutional law covers a very broad field – the institution of government – the legislature, executive and judiciary, and the allocation of powers between them; and the limitations upon the power of government necessary to secure the rights, both of individuals and of groups, whether racial, religious, linguistic or ethnic. Where the state is organized along FEDERAL lines, the territorial division of powers will generally be part of the constitution. Even so, the nature of a country's form of government can hardly be understood from a perusal of the constitution alone. For in almost every society the law of the constitution is buttressed by CONVENTIONS OF THE CONSTITUTION, non-legal rules which serve to supplement and give life to the legal framework. In Britain, for example, the system of CABINET GOVERNMENT has developed through conventional and not legal rules, although in a number of Commonwealth countries, the rules have been enacted as law. This illustrates the point that there is no hard and fast line of demarcation between what is enacted in legal form, and what remains a convention. The constitutional lawyer must study both if he or she is to obtain a systematic view of the subject. He or she must also attempt to explain the main theories and explanatory doctrines of the constitution if the basic conceptual structure of the constitution is to be understood.

The form and content of constitutional rules, whether legal or conventional, whether written or unwritten, differ widely, and a number of different methods of classifying constitutions have been adopted. An obvious demarcation is that between written and unwritten constitutions, but this is not of great value for students of constitutional law for a number of reasons. First, the number of democracies without formal constitutions is very small – comprising at the time of writing, only the United Kingdom, Israel and New Zealand; second, even these countries have a number of rules relating to the organization of government and the rights of the citizen which are in fact in written form, even though not codified. It was for reasons such as this that as early as 1884, James Bryce declared that the distinction between written and unwritten constitutions was 'old-fashioned'. He substituted a distinction of his own between 'flexible' constitutions where the amending process was by simple parliamentary majority, and 'rigid' constitutions where there was some special amending procedure known as ENTRENCHMENT. But this distinction is not of very great value either, since the vast majority of constitutions are rigid in Bryce's sense in that they require some special procedure.

Contemporary political scientists tend to divide constitutions not in terms of rigid distinctions of kind, but rather in terms of degree. There are important differences between constitutions in terms of their origins, their degree of codification and their extent of written detail, but these are differences of degree, not of kind. Perhaps the most important distinction between constitutions relates to the ease or difficulty of amendment, but this requires some consideration of the political system and indeed of social factors as well as strictly constitutional factors.

The vast majority of states then, possess a particular document or documents, which is known as the constitution, and which embodies some of the important rules concerning the government of that country. While the content of such documents will vary markedly they normally contain provisions concerning the powers of differing branches of government, the methods by which laws are enacted, and limitations, both procedural and substantive, on what governments can do. Individual and/or collective rights may well be protected, and legislation which interferes with these rights will either be constitutionally prohibited, or will be allowed only if passed according to some special procedure, such as a two-thirds majority in the legislature. In countries which possess an enacted constitution, books on constitutional law will normally be commentary upon the constitution, including the historical circumstances which led to its adoption, the meaning to be ascribed to particular provisions and the methods by which the constitution may be amended.

The role of the JUDICIARY will often be extremely important in the interpretation of enacted constitutions. The constitution may explicitly grant the judiciary the power to strike down legislation which is inconsistent with the provisions of the constitution itself; or the judiciary may interpret the written document so as to invest itself with this power of constitutional review. In legal systems in which the judiciary possess this power, their role can become of further significance if the constitution contains broad, open textured terms which the judges will then interpret. The meaning to be given to terms, such as DUE PROCESS or EQUAL PROTECTION may alter depending upon the perspective of the individual judge, his or her own political view and the relationship which is perceived to exist between the founding document and current circumstances. Fundamental questions of political theory and philosophy will be involved in the interpretative process, and thus texts on constitutional law may come to resemble works on applied jurisprudence and political theory. Precisely because of the political nature of such constitutional decision making, the legitimacy of this aspect of the judicial role can become a hotly contested issue. There will be a plethora of conflicting interpretations as to what the appropriate role of the judiciary should be. Those who believe in a strict and narrow construction of the constitution will be challenged by those who advocate a more activist role for the judiciary. The power of the executive may also be indirectly augmented in legal systems which possess this form of constitutional review. If, as in the United States, the President possesses significant power in the appointment of judges, it can enable him to choose those who are more likely to be sympathetic to the policies of his own party. While this does not mean that judges, once appointed, will become the handmaiden of the executive, the outlook of appointees may well affect their interpretation of the open textured provisions of the constitution.

The United Kingdom has no enacted constitution in the sense adumbrated above. UK constitutional law is to be found in practices, conventions, particular statutes, judicial decisions and political behaviour, although, as has been seen, there may be disagreements on what topics should be included within the subject. The standard works include the following topics: the foundations of the constitution, the composition and role of the executive, the functions of Parliament, civil rights and police powers and some treatment of the armed forces. What is to be regarded as appropriate for inclusion within the subject will, however, not only vary with the views of the particular commentator, but will also alter over time. Thus, to take but one example it might well be suggested that the complex issue of the way in which government uses its economic power has fundamental ramifications for the structure of authority in the country as a whole. It raises questions concerning the legitimacy of executive action and should therefore be included in the treatment of constitutional law. Another example may be found in the context of pressure groups. A voluminous literature exists within the political sciences as to the power, impact and significance of such groups. The implications of these developments have received little systematic treatment in the standard texts on constitutional law. This may well be mistaken. If the object, or one of the objects, of constitutional law is to consider the distribution of power at the governmental level, and to draw normative conclusions as to how it ought to be exercised or controlled, then to ignore the operation of pressure groups is to present a distorted picture of how political decision making operates within society. One of the continuing problems for constitutional law is to ensure that its coverage does not remain static, and that it is capable of responding to new developments within society. There can be a dangerous tendency for the lawyer's conception of judicial precedent to be transferred from the courts to the sphere of academic literature, the result being that the subject is strictly defined by what has gone before.

The mere fact that a country does not possess an enacted constitution does not inevitably mean that constitutional review is absent or impossible. The accepted doctrine within the United Kingdom is however, that Parliament is sovereign, in the sense that the courts cannot strike down legislation duly enacted by Parliament on the ground that it is beyond Parliament's power, or that it is violative of some previous statute. Thus, it is said that Parliament can do anything except bind or commit its successors in any way. The force of this statement must be treated with some reserve, despite the fact that it has often been repeated by eminent writers such as Blackstone and DICEY. The arguments in favour of the traditional position on sovereignty are eclectic and have been challenged. Part of the argument is *a priori* in the sense that sovereignty is said to connote unlimited power; in part the doctrine is empirical, in the sense that writers point to past constitutional practice, and decisions of the courts which are said to prove or establish the traditional position; a further aspect of the argument derives its force from the properties alleged to reside in or flow from the type of democracy in which we live. Constitutional review has been felt by some to be unnecessary because our representative democracy will ensure that Parliament does not pass laws which conflict with the desires and interests of the people. These arguments are, as stated, not beyond challenge. Writers past and present have questioned the alleged logic of the *a priori* contention; others have reassessed the case law and argued that it is not as clear as the protagonists of the traditional position claim; yet others have begun to question the implicit or explicit assumptions concerning democracy which underpin the sovereignty doctrine.

What has flowed from this questioning of classical doctrine has been a growing debate as to whether the United Kingdom should develop a written constitution and/or enshrine a BILL OF RIGHTS. The growth in the power of the executive and expansion in the functions of government and governmental agencies have been of significance in this debate. Whether such a step is or is not taken within the United Kingdom remains to be seen.

The distinction between a legal system which possesses FUNDAMENTAL RIGHTS and constitutional review and one which does not should, however, be kept within perspective. It is not as sharp as might appear at first sight. Where a legal system does allow constitutional review the judiciary may not necessarily be proscribing the substantive ends which the legislature is seeking to obtain, but may rather be mandating procedural standards which the legislature must follow, or condemning legislation which is too vague. Even decisions made on substantive grounds may still leave an alternative route open to the legislature to achieve the desired goals. The power of the courts in a system where there is no constitutional review should, by way of contrast, not be underestimated. The courts will still have powers of non-constitutional review, through which they control the exercise of executive discretionary powers. Although in theory the courts when performing this role are simply interpreting the legislative intent, their decisions may well entail creative interpretation balancing various interests and rights in reaching their conclusion. While technically this decision may be altered by the legislature, constraints may exist. It may be difficult to find parliamentary time for the legislative reversal of the judicial decision. There may be political pressures which render this problematic. Drafting problems can exist, for example, when a court has found that the interpretation of a statute by an agency was unreasonable; revising the statute so as to ensure that a subsequent similar interpretation by the agency does not suffer a similar fate may not be easy. Even if all these problems are overcome legislation which overturns a judgment may be constrained by other constitutional principles; if the only way to achieve the desired legislative goal is to pass retrospective legislation this can be the subject of political controversy in its own right.

The distinction between systems which do and do not possess constitutional review should also be kept in perspective for a rather different reason. It can be easy for constitutional lawyers to overrate the significance of this aspect of constitutional law in the overall political system of which law forms but one part. Another way of making the same point is by saying that constitutional lawyers are not and should not be exclusively concerned with control of governmental structures from the 'top' via the judicial process. CIVIL RIGHTS may ultimately be as well, or even better protected, by concentrating upon other techniques to ensure accountability. Training and supervision of personnel, internal checking mechanisms within departments, citizen

participation in decision making and OPEN GOVERNMENT, may all have an important role to play in helping to ensure that citizens' rights are not abused and that government goals are effectively achieved.

A distinction can also be drawn between federal and unitary constitutions. The problems concerning the scope of judicial power mentioned above may well also exist here. The precise division between federal and unitary constitutions and the implications of this dichotomy for constitutional law can be relatively clear but can also be confusing depending upon the context.

Countries such as the United States and Australia are clearly federal states (see FEDERALISM). A fully federal system will normally necessitate an enacted constitution in which the division between federal and state power is demarcated. The relationship between the two will often be dynamic rather than static, and the precise dividing line may well reside with the highest judicial authorities who exercise the power of constitutional adjudication. Thus, in the United States the boundary between legitimate federal action and areas which are reserved for state authority has been strongly influenced by the differing interpretation of successive Supreme Courts which have drawn the line at different places, although the overall tendency has been for the expansion of federal power.

A further distinction is that between diarchical and non-diarchical constitutions. In a diarchical constitution there is a division of governmental competence within the state, between two or more authorities, otherwise than on a regional basis. For example, in some constitutions, law making authority may be divided between the legislature and the executive whereby the latter has an autonomous power to pass laws within a sphere defined by the constitution.

Formal labels must, however, be treated with as much caution in this area as in any other. Whether a constitution is formally diarchical or not, may tell one little as to the realities of power within that constitutional structure. For example, a reading of the EEC Treaty might lead one to believe that the EEC COMMISSION was the most important political unit within the Community, even though legislation had to receive the assent of the COUNCIL OF MINISTERS. This would, however, be to miss the important political, social and economic developments since the inception of the Treaty which have tended to limit the powers of the Commission and to augment the authority of the Council.

A similar point may be made with respect to the UK. Whether one chooses to regard the UK as having a diarchical constitutional structure because of the ability of the executive to act through the Royal Prerogative may well be debated. The relevance of this appellation is, however, of little significance for the development of constitutional norms, as compared with the simpler realization of executive power over the legislature. This power may be exercised in Parliament itself or through the ability of the executive to bypass Parliament altogether when achieving its aims. Responding to these developments as they manifest themselves in the late twentieth century is perhaps the most important task facing UK constitutional law.

It will be readily apparent from the preceding discussion that the form of the constitution within a particular country will not necessarily be an accurate basis from which to predict the nature of constitutional law which subsists therein. While the presence of a written constitution with a Bill of Rights, or the existence of a federal system, may be indicative of the content which can be expected within the rubric of constitutional law, there is no substitute for careful substantive analysis of a particular system. Only then can an accurate assessment be made as to the efficacy of such devices, the extent to which they mould the exercise of public power and the way in which they relate to other aspects of that political system.   PPC

Reading

Capelletti, M. and Cohen, W.: *Comparative Constitutional Law*. New York: Bobbs-Merrill, 1979.

Ely, J.H.: *Democracy and Distrust*. Cambridge, Mass.: Harvard University Press, 1980.

Marshall, G.: *Constitutional Theory*. Oxford: Oxford University Press, 1971.

Perry, M.J.: *The Constitution, the Courts, and Human Rights: an inquiry into the legitimacy of constitutional policymaking by the judiciary*. New Haven, Conn.: Yale University Press, 1982.

Tribe, L.H.: *American Constitutional Law*. New York: Foundation Press, 1978.

Vile, M.J.C.: *Constitutionalism and the Separation of Powers*. Oxford: Oxford University Press, 1967.

Wheare, K.C.: *Modern Constitutions*. 2nd edn. Oxford: Oxford University Press, 1966.

Wolf-Phillips, L.: *Constitutions of Modern States: selected texts and commentary*. London: Pall Mall, 1968.

convention

(1) An agreement between the participants in any organized activity. In international relations there are conventions reached between states, relating for example to the settling of disputes, the conduct of war, the regulation of copyright, maritime affairs and the Protection of the World Cultural and Natural Heritage. Permanent international organizations often promulgate conventions as guidance for national legislation (the conventions relating to labour law and practice agreed by the International Labour Organization). European governments who were members of the Council of Europe in 1950 signed and promulgated the European Convention for the Declaration of Human Rights and Freedoms. Conventions of governmental behaviour may arise out of usage and practice as well as from specific agreement (see CONVENTION OF THE CONSTITUTION).

(2) A meeting of delegates or participants in a common activity. Historically the term has been used for certain popular assemblies, for example the English Convention Parliaments of 1660 and 1688 which assumed representative authority and met without the crown's summons.

In the United States the Constitution was drafted by a Federal Convention, which met at Philadelphia in 1787. Article V of the Constitution of the United States, which sets out procedures for constitutional amendment, provides for amendments to be initiated either by two-thirds of both Houses of Congress or by the calling of a convention at the request of the legislatures of two-thirds of the states. Such amendments become valid when ratified by the legislatures of three-quarters of the states or by conventions held in those states. It is unclear whether a convention summoned by two-thirds of the states under Article V would have unlimited authority to propose amendments to any part of the constitution; probably not. Conventions are also held in the United States for revising state constitutions and for nominating national candidates to participate in elections for the presidency.

In the Commonwealth, conventions have been used for debating and initiating the provisions of new constitutional instruments (as for example the Constitution of Australia or some of the post-war independence constitutions). An elected convention met in Northern Ireland 1975–6 to seek agreement on a structure of government for Northern Ireland, but it failed to reach agreement on proposals acceptable to both communities or to the United Kingdom government. It has even been suggested that a formal constitution for the United Kingdom should be drafted by a constituent convention, but the likelihood of such an exercise proving popular with Members of Parliament as now constituted seems remote.   GM

Reading

Corwin, E.S.: *The Constitution and what it Means Today*. 14th edn. Princeton, NJ: Princeton University Press, 1978.

Denenburg, R.V.: *Understanding American Politics*. 2nd edn. London: Fontana, 1984.

Orfield, L.B.O.: *The Amending of the Federal Constitution*. Chicago, Ill.: University of Michigan Press, 1942.

Wheare, K.C.: *Modern Constitutions*. 2nd edn, ch. 8 Oxford: Oxford University Press, 1966.

convention of the constitution   A rule of practice governing the behaviour of officers or organs of government, defining their rights, duties or relationships, derived not from law but from past precedents, custom or agreement or the general principles of the constitution. Conventions are found in varying degrees in all systems of goverment and in the external relationships between states.

There is no exact or agreed definition of such conventional rules that will distinguish them from the wider body of usages or practices that may be common or customary but not obligatory. In Britain textbook writers have tended to reserve the term for a relatively small body of rules that has acquired an acknowledged status as defining the obligations or entitlements of the major participants in the scheme of government. Examples of conventions in British government are the rules or principles that govern the behaviour of the cabinet in relation to the House of Commons, the relations of the sovereign to his or her ministers and prime minister and some of the relations between the two Houses of Parliament. The relations between the United Kingdom and the member countries of the Commonwealth have also in part been governed by conventions, though some of them have been enacted into law. (For example the Statute of Westminster in 1931 enacted the previously agreed convention that the United Kingdom Parliament would not legislate for the independent DOMINION countries without their request and consent, thus giving formal legal effect to the conventional equality of Britain and the countries then enjoying dominion status.)

An important feature of conventions is that they modify the effect of powers that exist in strict law. In the absence of a formal enacted constitution in Britain this feature of the constitutional conventions is fundamental to the political system. In law parliament could enact any provisions whatsoever, however tyrannical, but by convention this unlimited sovereign power is confined. In law the sovereign's prerogative powers are extensive, but the conventions of the constitution require that they are exercised on the advice of ministers. In law members of the government hold their offices at the will of the crown and not parliament, but the conventions require that when the House of Commons withdraws its confidence from them the government must offer its resignation or advise the holding of a general election. In law an act of parliament requires the assent of sovereign, Lords and Commons, but by convention the sovereign must in normal circumstances give assent to legislation that has passed both Houses. It can be seen that in Britain the major conventions relate to the behaviour of ministers (collective and individual responsibility) and to the different elements in the legislative process, but there are others that define the relationships of the CIVIL SERVICE to ministers and that protect the independence of particular officials (for example the security of tenure of the higher judiciary, and the immunity from political pressures or government instructions of the Law Officers and the police).

In many cases the exact implications of a convention that is acknowledged in general terms may be unclear since there may be room for argument about the precedents and their bearing on a novel situation. This signals a clear difference between law and convention since no appeal can be made to the British courts to settle directly the meaning of a disputed convention. Disputes about conventions have however been referred to the courts in Canada under special reference legislation and in Britain courts have in many cases taken the existence of political conventions into account in the course of interpreting Acts of Parliament or the common law.

See also DICEY. GM

Reading

Dicey, A.V.: *Introduction to the Study of the Law of the Constitution*. 10th edn (1959), chs 1 and 4. Basingstoke: Macmillan, 1985.

Jennings, I.: *The Law and the Constitution*. 5th edn. London: University of London Press, 1959.

————: *Cabinet Government*. 3rd edn, ch. 1. Cambridge: Cambridge University Press, 1959.

Marshall, G.: *Constitutional Conventions*. Oxford: Oxford University Press, 1984.

Munro, C.: Laws and conventions distinguished. *Law Quarterly Review* 91 (1975) 218.

Wheare, K.C.: *Modern Constitutions*. 2nd edn, ch. 8. Oxford: Oxford University Press, 1966.

COREPER The Committee of Permanent Representatives prepares the deliberations of the COUNCIL OF MINISTERS of the EUROPEAN COMMUNITY. Meeting weekly at Ambassador and Deputy Ambassador levels with the Commission, COREPER tries to resolve as far as possible differences of view among governments before legislation is formally adopted in the Council. Its members and their important offices – the Permanent Representations – are based in Brussels and provide crucial links between the member governments, the Commission and the Council. COREPER's work is prepared in detail by some 200 working groups of national and commission officials each handling a series of legislative proposals. HW

Reading

Noel, E. and Etienne, H.: The Permanent Representatives' Committee and the 'Deepening' of the Communities. *Government and Opposition* 6 (1971) 98–123.

corporatism Until recently corporatist institutions were invariably associated with FASCISM and authoritarian rule, and their corporatist character tends to be publicly denied in those countries, such as Austria and Sweden, where it is most deeply embedded. Current usage identifies a distinction between state corporatism, found in such systems as Salazar's Portugal or Franco's Spain, and liberal or societal corporatism which has emerged incrementally within capitalist democracies (Schmitter and Lehmbruch 1979).

Liberal corporatism is a useful description of processes and institutions that exist alongside parliamentary, party and electoral channels of representation. The basis of corporatism is FUNCTIONAL REPRESENTATION, whereby organizations representing socio-economic interests are permitted a privileged position by public authorities in a bargaining process over public policies which takes place in usually informal institutions outside the reach of formal democratic controls such as parliamentary scrutiny or ministerial responsibility. In exchange for this privileged position, interest organizations deliver the compliance of their members to the terms of agreed policies.

Authoritarian corporatism describes a number of political regimes in Latin America, including post-1964 Brazil, Mexico and Peru, and also the dictatorships of Mussolini and

Salazar. These systems are marked by the limited extent of liberal democracy and popular participation, the dominance of a ruling elite, and their relatively undeveloped industrial economies. Corporatist institutions permit the disciplining and control of labour, while allowing relatively inefficient and backward industrial interests a considerable degree of protection from international competition during the transitional phase to industrial capitalism. Licensed associations are created as intermediaries between the state and economic producers which have the effect of restricting the independent organizational activities of producer groups (Williamson 1985).

Liberal corporatism, by contrast, arises from the tendency for interest organizations in mature capitalist countries to develop representational monopolies. Its preconditions include centralized interest organizations representing both capital and labour, which have the capacity to apply coercive sanctions against members who break the terms of collective agreements. In countries with a highly developed system of public law, as opposed to the common law tradition of Anglo-Saxon countries, there is often compulsory membership in chambers of commerce and industry, and a formal role for labour organizations in the workplace. Where corporatism has developed most fully, it is often social democratic governments which have compensated for the structural weakness of labour compared to capital by ensuring some form of parity for labour organizations in corporatist institutions.

Most students of corporatism agree that the prototypical case of macro-corporatism is Austria, followed by the Scandinavian countries, and especially Sweden. Austria has a system of compulsory membership in Chambers of Commerce, Labour, Agriculture and the professions, and every working citizen is a member of at least one of these. Each is a highly centralized organization, in which the national leadership maintains effective control over sectoral and territorial subdivisions. The peak trade union organization monopolizes the representation of labour, and individual unions are sub-units which depend on the centre for their financial resources. Parity of representation is guaranteed by the state in bargaining over price control and economic planning, and collective socio-economic bargaining is focused on a highly informal non-bureaucratic agency, the Parity Commission. The Austrian example demonstrates the effective institutionalization of the preconditions of macro-corporatism: monopolistic and centralized interest organizations, parity in class representation, and informal adjustment processes. All of these preconditions have emerged over a considerable historical period, and while none are unique to Austria, the combination of them certainly is (Marin 1985).

Less stable and successful examples of corporatist institutions can be found in a number of other countries. For some two decades after the second world war the Dutch Social and Economic Council effectively produced an inter-class consensus on economic policy, but its influence waned from the 1960s as interest organizations became more fragmented and the formalized system of functional representation failed to adapt. In other cases, such as West Germany, corporatist institutions have come under pressure as a consequence of economic crisis, whereby employers and sometimes individual unions have sought to circumvent centralized bargaining procedures. In general the resurgence of neo-liberal economic strategies since the 1970s has tended to undermine the preconditions of corporatism at the macro level (Goldthorpe 1984).

It is useful to distinguish varieties of corporatism according to the level of the state system at which bargaining takes place (Cawson 1986). Looking at meso and micro levels, we can see that corporatist institutions can flourish even where the national context is hostile to corporatism. In specific economic and policy sectors there exist many examples of interest organizations enjoying a privileged status which protects their sphere from market forces or bureaucratic intervention. Almost everywhere agriculture is organized along corporatist lines, with the details of intervention negotiated between the state and farmers' organizations to the exclusion of consumer and other interests. In Britain the

National Farmers Union occupies such a privileged position, and until recent challenges to its monopoly arising from managerial reforms, the British Medical Association both bargained and implemented policy within the National Health Service. In both declining (steel, textiles) and emerging (micro-electronics) sectors there is considerable evidence of meso-corporatist arrangements in many advanced industrial countries where it has been recognized that market processes by themselves will not produce the policy outcomes desired by governments. Such examples differ from conventional PLURALIST accounts of INTEREST GROUP politics, in that organizations tend to be 'involuntary' in the sense that they are created or transformed by the devolution of public authority (Cawson 1985).

In public and academic debate most attention has been given to corporatist institutions at the macro level, where bargains are struck between 'peak' organizations representing the interests of the major social classes, capital and labour. In Britain institutions such as the former Prices and Incomes Board are 'quasi-corporatist' in that they were constituted on the basis of functional representation, but the inability of either employers or trade unions to deliver the compliance of their members over more than a short period demonstrates the absence in Britain of the institutional preconditions for corporatism at the macro-level.

Finally, in all capitalist democracies there are examples of quasi-autonomous bodies (QUANGOs) which are constituted on the basis of functional representation (but most frequently of individuals rather than organizations), and operate outside the formal control of parliaments. Such bodies are not truly corporatist, in the sense that they do not rely on formally private interest organizations in order to implement policies, but their importance in such areas as training policy and urban re-development indicates the difficulty of organizing state intervention through liberal–individualist forms of representation.

See also LABOUR MOVEMENT; TRADE UNIONS.   AC

Reading

Berger, S. ed.: *Organizing Interests in Western Europe: pluralism, corporatism and the transformation of politics*. New York: Cambridge University Press, 1981.

Cawson, A.: *Corporatism and Political Theory*. Oxford: Blackwell, 1986.

—— ed.: *Organized Interests and the State: studies in meso-corporatism*. London: Sage, 1985.

Goldthorpe, J. ed.: *Order and Conflict in Contemporary Capitalism: studies in the political economy of Western European nations*. Oxford: Oxford University Press, 1984.

Lehmbruch, G. and Schmitter, P.C.: *Patterns of Corporatist Policy-making*. London: Sage, 1982.

Marin, J.: Austria: the paradigm case of liberal corporatism. In *The Political Economy of Corporatism*, ed. W. Grant. London: Macmillan, 1985.

Schmitter, P.C. and Lehmbruch, G. eds: *Trends Toward Corporatist Intermediation*. London: Sage, 1979.

Williamson, P.J.: *Varieties of Corporatism: theory and practice*. Cambridge: Cambridge University Press, 1985.

council-manager plan An ADMINISTRATOR PLAN that emphasizes professional management of cities; the city manager has widespread powers and is expected to provide community leadership. A council, usually of five to nine citizens (rarely professional politicians) and commonly chosen at large in nonpartisan elections, adopts policy and hires the manager. Supported by most municipal reformers the plan is commonly said to have been devised by Richard S. Childs in about 1910 but the basic idea has been traced to the 1890s. The plan spread rapidly and became a favourite of middle-sized cities and middle-class suburbs. By 1985 about 2,300 council-manager cities existed in the United States and variations were to be found in the Irish Republic and the Federal Republic of Germany.   CRA

Reading

Stillman, R.J., II: *The Rise of the City Manager*. Albuquerque: University of New Mexico Press, 1974.

Stone, H.A., Price, D.K. and Stone, K.H.: *City Manager Government in the United States*. Chicago, Ill.: Public Administration Service, 1940.

Council of Ministers (European Community)

The body through which European Community (EC) policies are negotiated and turned into legislation. It consists of ministerial representatives from the member states, the specific composition varying according to the subjects on the agenda. The 'senior' foreign affairs council meets monthly to deal with external relations and various other specific subjects such as regional policy, and to some extent co-ordinates EC work as a whole. Many other policy areas actively discussed in the EC have their own regular specialist councils, such as agriculture, economics and finance or the budget. Issues which departmental ministers cannot resolve are referred to the EUROPEAN COUNCIL. Policy issues not formally within the legal competence of the EC are considered by less formal conferences of ministers. A small Secretariat General services the Council and in particular the presidency, which rotates among the member states every six months. The role and burdens of the presidency have steadily grown. The EC treaties, their amendments and internal rules of procedure govern the Council's powers and operations, its role being weaker under the European Coal and Steel Community. Legislation is initiated and drafted by the COMMISSION, but it changes considerably in the negotiations among national officials in COREPER and ministers in response to the domestic preoccupations and priorities of member governments. Non-binding opinions also emanate from the European Parliament and the Economic and Social Committee. Legislation through regulation is directly binding and through directive requires further national implementation. The treaties permit weighted majority voting for some decisions and require unanimity for others. Since the Luxemburg 'compromise' of 1966 (permitting vetos to defend 'vital national interests') consensus methods have predominated. In 1985 governments, in the Single European Act, agreed to extend the use of majority voting.   HW

Reading

Henig, S.: *Power and Decision in Europe*. London: Europotentials Press, 1980.

O'Nuallain, C.: *The Presidency of the European Council of Ministers*. London: Croom Helm/RIPA, 1985.

Sasse, C. et al.: *Decision-making in the European Communities*. New York: Praeger, 1977.

Wallace, H.: Negotiation and coalition formation in the European Community. *Government and Opposition* 20 (1985) 453–72.

Council of Ministers (USSR)

Defined by the Constitution of the USSR (Article 128) as 'the highest executive and administrative body of state authority of the USSR', the Council of Ministers is formally appointed by a joint sitting of both chambers of the USSR Supreme Soviet to which it is accountable. Membership consists of the chairman of the Council of Ministers (the prime minister), first vice-chairmen and vice-chairmen, ministers and chairmen of state committees, and heads of certain other state bodies such as the state bank. Chairmen of the councils of ministers of the supreme soviets of the fifteen constituent republics of the USSR are members *ex officio* of the all-Union Council of Ministers. At the first session of the eleventh convocation of the USSR Supreme Soviet on 12 April 1984 a Council of Ministers was formed consisting of 128 members. Appointed chairman was N. A. Tikhonov; he resigned in September 1985 and was replaced by N. I. Ryzhkov.

The Soviet political process maintains scrupulous separation of the policy making, decision taking, leadership role – which is the exclusive preserve of the Communist Party – and policy implementation, which is the responsibility of several social and political institutions, and pre-eminently that of the Council of Ministers. These functions merge at the very apex of the system within the Communist Party's POLITBURO, of which the chairman of the Council of Ministers is conventionally a member as is one of the first vice-chairmen and one or two ministers or chairmen of state committees.

Similar arrangements exist in other Soviet-type political systems.   PF

Reading

Hill, R.J.: *The Soviet Union: politics, economics and society*, ch. 3. London: Pinter, 1985.

McCauley, M. and Carter, S. eds: *Leadership and Succession in the Soviet Union, Eastern Europe and China*. London: Macmillan, 1986.

county-manager plan The COUNCIL-MANAGER PLAN as it is applied to the American county, which was traditionally an agent of the state, performing largely routine functions. From the 1920s counties in many states have been authorized to perform most urban functions. These new activities pointed up the need for executive leadership. By 1985 about 35 per cent of all counties had appointed professional administrative heads. In 183 cases they carried the title of 'county manager'; about 885 others, with fewer powers, had more modest designations, such as 'county administrator'. Perhaps the best known county managership is that of Dade county (Miami), Florida where the county is also a metropolitan government. CRA

Reading

Sofen, E.: *The Miami Metropolitan Experiment*, rev. edn. Garden City, NY: Anchor, 1966.

county-mayor plan Urbanized US counties sometimes opt for executive leadership in the form of elected mayors, generally using some version of the STRONG-MAYOR PLAN. About 180 such offices had been created in counties of all sizes by 1985. Members of county governing boards (and sometimes mayors of large cities within those counties) have resisted the idea of powerful, independently elected county mayors who could reduce the significance of their own jobs and dominate publicity in the mass media. This plan is in use in all the counties in Arkansas, several populous counties in New York, and Wayne county (Detroit), Michigan. CRA

coup d'état Literally a stroke of state; a seizure of power by a group using the permanent employees of the state – bureaucracy, armed forces or the police – to capture and paralyse the nerve ends of government. The coup d'état is distinguished from a REVOLUTION in that it does not aim to alter the social and political structure, but merely to substitute one ruling group for another. The coup operates essentially by detaching the employees of the state from their loyalty to the legitimate government.

The coup was common in Europe in the nineteenth century and the first half of the twentieth century (for example, the coup of Louis-Napoleon in France in December 1851, or that of Marshal Pilsudski in Poland in May 1926), tending to occur in countries in which political opinion was polarized between extreme and mutually hostile groupings. In the latter half of the twentieth century, by contrast, the coup has been far more frequent in those third world countries in which political participation is confined to a small section of the population. In the modern world the coup is at least as common a method of changing governments as is the election, and more common than a revolutionary upheaval.

See also MILITARY REGIMES. VBB

Reading

Luttwak, E.: *Coup d'État: a practical handbook*. London: Allen Lane, 1968.

Malaparte, C.: *Technique of the Coup d'État*. Paris: Grasset, 1948.

critical election See REALIGNMENT.

crown An important concept in the law of the United Kingdom and of other Commonwealth countries, such as Canada, Australia and New Zealand, whose law derives from the English common law. This meaning of the crown may best be described with reference to a simplified model of constitutional development in Britain by which the main organs of the state (such as parliament, the courts and the departments of central government) came into existence as an offshoot of royal power, originating in a period when kings and queens ruled and did not merely reign. By a convenient fiction the crown has come to be regarded as a legal entity representing the organs of central government, and as such it serves to meet the need for a legal definition of the STATE, for example in the terms crown property, ministers of the crown, and crown servants; criminal prosecutions are conducted in the name of the crown, and so on. Though executive power in the United Kingdom is still formally vested in the crown it is in fact exercised by the government of the day. Departments of central government have inherited many of the powers, privileges and immunities that were once exercised by or for the sovereign in person. But these rights and powers are not always appropriate in a democratic society and parliament has frequently had to make the law more acceptable by limiting these rights and powers.

What survives of the royal power in government in Tudor or Stuart times is often referred to as the royal PREROGATIVE. By far the greater part of prerogative power is now exercised directly by ministers and civil servants or, if action by the Queen is still required, on the advice and responsibility of her ministers (for example, the control of the armed forces and the conduct of foreign affairs). But exceptional prerogatives survive which must be exercised by the sovereign in person and may in case of necessity involve the exercise of a choice (for example, inviting the leader of a political party to be prime minister when the electoral system has failed to produce any party with a clear majority of seats in the House of Commons).

In the heyday of the British Empire, the crown was regarded as unitary and indivisible. In fact in countries with a federal system, such as Australia and Canada, the division of powers between two levels of government necessarily meant a split in the concept of the crown, in accordance with the allocation of powers contained in the federal constitution. It is generally accepted today that the crown is separate and divisible for each particular country within the Commonwealth that accepts the monarchical system. Thus treaties which were concluded in the nineteenth century between the crown and the Indian peoples in Canada no longer bind the crown in right of the United Kingdom but are capable of binding the crown in respect of Canada, that is the Canadian government.

See also MONARCHY. AWB

Reading

Marshall, G.: *Constitutional Theory*, ch. 2. Oxford: Oxford University Press, 1971.

cube law A mathematical formula attempting to show that there is a regular relationship between votes cast and parliamentary seats won in an election held under the plurality method or the ALTERNATIVE VOTE, both single-member constituency ELECTORAL SYSTEMS. First propounded by J. Parker Smith in evidence to the British Royal Commission on Electoral Systems in 1909, it was based upon statistical work by his friend Major Macmahon. It was rediscovered in 1949 by the British psephologist, David Butler, who applied it to the results of the 1950 general election in Britain, with statistical support by Kendall and Stuart.

The law states that if two parties divide the vote between them in the ratio A : B, the seats gained will divide in the proportion $A^3 : B^3$ thereby exaggerating the majority gained by the winning party. The law has been held to depend upon the following two assumptions: a fairly uniform swing over all constituencies; and the existence of only two major parties, with class being the dominant cleavage, so giving rise to an approximately normal distribution of the voters for these two parties across constituencies. Thus, the law was seen to apply in the 1950s to Britain (but not to Northern Ireland where the parties divide on sectarian rather than class lines), New Zealand, the United States Congress (excluding the South), and Australia.

But the 'law' of cubic proportion has been shown not to be a law. In Britain for example a change in the distribution of marginal seats had by the 1970s made a 'square law' a more accurate description of the relation between seats and votes, and in the 1980s the exaggerative effect of the system continued to decline.

In the United Sates (where the cube law was always less applicable) the widespread drawing of boundaries to produce safe seats and the growth in the electoral benefits of incumbency have similarly reduced the exaggerative effect.

Thus the cube law cannot be held to prove a regular and invariant relationship between votes and seats. The relationship is likely to vary, often considerably, from country to country and across time. It is unlikely that any all-embracing formula summarizing the relationship can be found.   VBB

Reading

Butler, D.: An examination of the results. In *The British General Election of 1950*, ed. H.G. Nicholas. London: Macmillan, 1951.

Curtice, J. and Steed, M.: Electoral choice and the production of government: the changing operation of the electoral system in the United Kingdom since 1955. *British Journal of Political Science* 12 (1982) 249–298.

————: Proportionality and exaggeration in the British electoral system. *Electoral Studies* 5.3 (1986) 209–28.

Kendall, M.G. and Stuart, A.: The law of cubic proportions in election results. *British Journal of Sociology* 1 (1950) 183–197.

Qualter, T.: Seats and votes: an application of the cube law to the Canadian electoral system. *Canadian Journal of Political Science* 1 (1968) 336–44.

cult of personality   A term applied in particular to the extravagant idolization of J. V. STALIN during the last two decades of his life when he exercised dictatorial power in the USSR. The expression was popularized as a result of Nikita Khrushchev's extensive use of it in his 'secret' speech to the twentieth Congress of the Communist Party of the Soviet Union in 1956. A more accurate and more apposite rendering of the Russian *kul't lichnosti* is 'cult of the individual', since it emphasizes the contradiction between the adulation of one person and his arbitrary exercise of power, and the collectivist ideology on which the power of the party theoretically rests.   PF

Reading

Antonov-Ovseyenko, A.: *The Time of Stalin: portrait of tyranny*. New York and London: Harper & Row, 1983.

Graeme, G.: The Soviet leader cult: reflections on the structure of leadership in the Soviet Union. *British Journal of Political Science* 10 (1980) 167–86.

Medvedev, Zh. and Medvedev, R.: *N.S. Khrushchev: the secret speech*. Nottingham: Spokesman Books, 1976.

cumulative vote   An ELECTORAL SYSTEM in which an elector voting in a multi-member constituency can cast more than one of his or her votes for a single candidate. It was used in Britain for the election of school boards between 1870 and 1902, and cumulation is employed to elect the lower house of the Illinois legislature and in the proportional representation systems of Luxemburg and Switzerland where an elector is permitted to cumulate two votes on the same candidate. The main political consequence of the cumulative vote is to improve the representation of minorities.   VBB

D

dealignment A concept brought to prominence by Crewe, Särlvik and Alt (1977) in order to describe recent changes in British electoral politics. The 'alignment' of a party system is the way in which party support is predicated upon fundamental POLITICAL CLEAVAGES in social structure. The British party system in the post-war era was said to be aligned with the class cleavage, so that working class voters generally supported the Labour Party and middle class voters generally supported the Conservative Party. Historians and other commentators have long employed the word REALIGNMENT to refer to a fundamental restructuring of the party system along new lines of cleavage; however, the concept is not appropriate to describe recent changes in British and American electoral politics. To refer to these changes as dealignment avoids the need to anticipate future developments.

As it is employed in the United States (first by Inglehart and Hochstein 1972; more recently by Dalton et al. 1984), the term has lacked any specific focus on the linkage between SOCIAL STRUCTURE AND PARTY ALIGNMENT. Instead it has been employed quite loosely to refer to the breakdown of the electoral hegemony of the Democratic Party since the mid-1960s. In Britain many commentators similarly think of the dealignment of British politics in terms of the challenge to the two-party hegemony presented by the Social Democratic Party and Liberal Alliance. Seen in these terms, the dealignment of the British party system began in February 1974, the first post-war election to see significant numbers of non-Labour and non-Conservative MPs returned to parliament.

Careful analysis of survey data from the elections of 1974 also showed that more Conservative voters were working class and more Labour voters were middle class than was the case ten years earlier. Dealignment can therefore be seen as consistent with a decline in the class basis of British voting choice. Heath, Jowell and Curtice (1985) have challenged the alleged decline in the class basis of British voting behaviour but Franklin (1985) has argued that this decline was already apparent in 1970, before minor party voting increased.

MNF

Reading

Crewe, I., Särlvik, B. and Alt, J.: Partisan dealignment in Britain 1964–1974. *British Journal of Political Science* 7 (1977).

Dalton, R.J., Flanagan, S.C. and Beck, P.A. eds: *Electoral Change in Advanced Industrial Democracies: realignment or dealignment.* Princeton, NJ: Princeton University Press, 1984.

Franklin, M.: *The Decline of Class Voting in Britain.* Oxford: Oxford University Press, 1985.

Heath, A., Jowell, R. and Curtice, J.: *How Britain Votes.* Oxford: Pergamon, 1985.

Inglehart, R. and Hochstein, A.: Alignment and dealignment of the electorate in France and the United States. *Comparative Political Studies* 5 (1972).

Nie, N., Verba, S. and Petrocik, J.: *The Changing American Voter.* Cambridge, Mass. and London: Harvard University Press, 1981.

decision making The process of selecting an option for implementation. Decisions are formed by a decision maker (the one who makes the final choice) and a decision unit (all those in a small group, organization, or government who are involved in the process). They react to an identified problem or set of problems by analysing information, determining objectives, formulating options, evaluating the options, and reaching a conclusion. Decisions are affected by the nature of the problem, the external setting, the internal dynamics of the decision unit, and the personality of the decision maker. In a crisis, stress and the speed of events will alter, and often degrade, the decision process. In government, decision making occurs in situations as diverse as the casting of votes, the crafting of laws, the determination of judicial opinions, and the handling of international crises.

Political theorists since Aristotle have considered how decision making affects the quality of governance. For example, Machiavelli observed that rulers who make decisions slowly and ambiguously produce ruinous policies. During the twentieth century political scientists have systematically studied decision making, drawing on the newly-emerging social sciences, as well as history, mathematics and computer science. Researchers first examined large organizations and the way their bureaucracies generate decisions. After the second world war DECISION THEORY and GAME THEORY began to map the structure of rational decisions, including assessments of the probability and utility of different outcomes. Meanwhile, studies of psychology and GROUP THEORY shed light on the actual behaviour of individuals and groups making choices.

Analyses of decisions frequently emphasize one of three principal conceptual perspectives, although sometimes the approach is eclectic. According to the oldest tradition, decisions are made by a rational actor responding purposively to an external challenge. This rational actor is assumed to hold clear objectives, to weigh thoroughly the costs and benefits of each option, to pick the best option, and to fully implement that choice. A variant of the rational actor model posits a decision maker who 'satisfices', selecting the first satisfactory option rather than searching until the optimal solution is found. A second perspective emphasizes the impact of routines on decisions by organizations. It shows how organizational structures and routines, for example standard operating procedures, shape choices by limiting the information available about an issue, the menu of options for responding, and the implementation of whatever is chosen. Both as a matter of habit and from the necessity of co-ordinating the behaviour of large numbers of people, pre-planned routines are necessary. Organizations and their routines in this way reinforce continuity and decision making by incremental adaptation. A third conceptual lens magnifies the internal dynamics of the decision unit and the extent to which decisions result from political struggles in a bureaucracy. This perspective shows how bargaining among individuals with different interests and power can lead to an eventual compromise that was preferred by none of them. Decisions are therefore influenced by the number of actors involved, by their prestige, responsibilities, values and expertise, and by the impact of public opinion, pressure groups and the media. In addition psychological research has revealed individual needs for cognitive consistency and group pressure for conformity; in a decision unit these can foster misperception and miscalculation. Finally, decision making on one issue is also influenced by the presence of competing problems that distract attention, increase uncertainty, and make the process both more complex and psychologically more demanding.

See also POLICY ANALYSIS.   GTA

Reading

Allison, G.T.: *The Essence of Decision: explaining the Cuban missile crisis.* Boston: Little, Brown, 1971.

American Behavioral Scientist 20.1 Sept/Oct (1976).

Cyert, R.M. and March, J.G.: *A Behavioral Theory of the Firm.* Englewood Cliffs, NJ: Prentice-Hall, 1963.

George, A.: *Presidential Decision Making in Foreign Policy.* Boulder, Col.: Westview, 1980.

Halperin, M.H.: *Bureaucratic Politics and Foreign Policy.* Washington, DC: Brookings Institution, 1974.

Janis, I.L.: *Groupthink: psychological studies of policy decisions and fiascoes.* Boston, Mass.: Houghton Mifflin, 1982.

Neustadt, R.E.: *Presidential Power: the politics of leadership from FDR to Carter.* New York: Wiley, 1980.

Quade, E.S.: *Analysis for Public Decisions.* New York: American Elsevier, 1975.

Schelling, T.C.: *The Strategy of Conflict.* New York: Oxford University Press, 1963.

Sullivan, M.P.: *International Relations: theories and evidence*, ch. 3. Englewood Cliffs, NJ: Prentice-Hall, 1976.

decision theory The theory of rational individual choice between options. Rationality is taken to be strictly instrumental in the sense that individual objectives are clearly defined before the choice is made, and the rationality of actions is judged according to their efficacy in furthering these objectives. Also, the chooser is assumed to be aware of all the available options. The basic theory may be classified under three categories.

Rational behaviour under certainty pertains to the environments in which the consequences of choice are fully and definitely known to the chooser in advance. The rational choice is therefore that which best promotes the chooser's objective. It may be characterized mathematically by the optimization of an objective function subject to constraints arising from the structure of the problem.

The second and third categories apply to environments in which the consequences of individual choice are not known with certainty because the consequences of individual actions are determined not only by these actions themselves but by the 'state of the world' of which the chooser does not know in advance.

Rational choice under risk pertains to environments in which there exists an objective probability distribution over the possible states of the world. Examples of such cases are found in gambling problems. A fair coin will come up heads or tails with 50 per cent probability and a sum of money may be staked on the coin coming up heads. The consequence (amount of winning, if any) is then determined jointly by the action (amount staked) and the state of the world (heads or tails). Mathematically it has been shown that rational choice under risk is characterized by expected utility maximization (see von Neumann and Morgenstern 1944).

Rational choice under uncertainty is similar to rational choice under risk but has no objective probability distribution over the possible states of the world. Instead, the theory assumes that individual decision makers have a subjective probability distribution over the states of the world. It can be shown that if individual choice satisfies certain axioms of rational choice, the chooser will act so as to maximize subjective expected utility (see Savage 1954). This leads to the theory of statistical decision theory and the Bayesian theory of statistical inference.

Although the mathematical theory of decisions has been well developed it has some well-known problems and limitations. First, decision theory has been advanced both as a normative theory of how people should behave, and as a positive theory of how they do behave – though experimental evidence has shown that individuals frequently violate the pre-scriptions of the theory. Second, there is yet no satisfactory account of the relationship between decision theory and GAME THEORY. Since most individual decisions are taken within an environment of interdependent choice, this may be regarded as a limitation on the applicability of decision theory to the social sciences. See also DECISION MAKING.   HS

Reading

Dixit, A.: *Optimization in Economic Theory.* Oxford: Oxford University Press, 1976.

Luce, R.D. and Raiffa, H.: *Games and Decisions: introduction and critical survey.* New York: Wiley, 1957.

Neumann, J. von and Morgenstern, O.: *Theory of Games and Economic Behaviour.* Princeton, NJ: Princeton University Press, 1944.

Savage, L.: *The Foundations of Statistics.* New York: Wiley, 1954.

Declaration of Independence The document that proclaimed the freedom of the thirteen American colonies from British rule and the creation of the United States of America. It was the first formal pronounce-ment by an organized political community of its right to choose its government. The Declaration was drafted by Thomas JEFFERSON, on account of his acknowledged 'felicity of style' (John Adams), as a member of a committee appointed by the Continental Congress. It was amended both by the committee and by Congress, notably in striking out Jefferson's passage denouncing the slave trade, which offended many southern delegates' susceptibilities. On 2 July 1776 it was agreed and adopted, and on 4 July it was proclaimed. The Declaration falls into two parts. The Preamble is a general statement of principles based on the proposition that the natural rights of man, including life, liberty and the pursuit of happiness, are 'self-evident', and that government is instituted 'to secure these rights'. The remainder is a specific list of grievances against King George III. It is significant that the king and not parliament is blamed, since the position claimed is that the colonies are directly under the crown. The appeal was directed in no small part to convincing American public opinion, but the rhetoric of liberty reverberated through later American history. The Declaration is displayed in the National Archives, Washington DC; 4 July (Independence Day) is celebrated in the United States as a national holiday.   JRP

Reading

Becker, C.L.: *The Declaration of Independence*. New York: Harcourt, Brace, 1949.

Boyd, J.P. ed.: *The Papers of Thomas Jefferson*, Vol. I. Princeton, NJ: Princeton University Press, 1950.

Hawke, D.: *A Transaction of Free Men: the birth and course of the Declaration of Independence*. New York: Scribner, 1964.

White, M.G.: *The Political Philosophy of the American Revolution*. New York: Oxford University Press, 1978.

Declaration of the Rights of Man and the Citizen

A basic CHARTER of human liberties, comprising the principles of the FRENCH REVOLUTION. It was adopted in its final form by the French National Assembly on 26 August 1789 as the preamble to the eventual 1791 Constitution. It was a compromise which emerged only after passionate and heated debate. The Declaration is brief, comprising 17 Articles and some 500 words. Article 1 contains one of the most celebrated lines in politics: 'Men are born and remain free and equal in their rights', and continues: 'social distinctions may be founded only on public utility'. Some of the remaining sixteen articles outline 'the natural and imprescribable rights of man' (such as the right to property, and the right to be presumed innocent unless proven guilty), while others explore the bases of those rights.

The Declaration has always been the subject of considerable controversy. This controversy rages over its source (some see it as springing from the writings of the French *philosophes* while for others it is rooted in the BILL OF RIGHTS of the newly liberated United States), over its merits (the battle engaged between BURKE and Paine has continued ever since), and over its impact. What is clear is that the Declaration is a model that has been constantly emulated, and that it has been the philosophical underpinning for a considerable body of law. It asserts the basic principles of Natural Rights, the SEPARATION OF POWERS and the independence of the judiciary.

See also CIVIL LIBERTIES; CIVIL RIGHTS.

VW

deference   The predisposition of people to assent to the rule and the opinions of those whom they deem best fitted to govern, whether by virtue of birth, education, wealth or the holding of a particular office. In Britain, students of electoral behaviour have used the notion of deference to account for the numerous working-class electors who, since the enfranchisement of the working-classes have, against their own apparent class interests, supported the Conservative Party. Social deference therefore extends into political deference. Students of political behaviour increasingly use the term in a more general sense in relation to the political system as a whole.

The term was used by Walter BAGEHOT in the mid nineteenth century in his classic *The English Constitution* to account for the continuing political influence of the aristocracy, despite the wider suffrage introduced in 1832. For him England was an example of the 'type of deferential countries' (p. 378). Following Bagehot, modern scholars employ the term to denote the passive or acquiescent features, as opposed to the participatory tendencies, of the mass public. Like Bagehot they emphasize the fact that voluntary acceptance, within broad limits, of the rule of the elite enhances political stability. Such latitude is regarded as essential if elites are to have any room for manoeuvre. Scholars today put more weight on the significance of deference for the political system and less on its implications for partisan support.   HBB

Reading

Almond, G.A. and Verba, S.: *The Civic Culture: political attitudes and democracy in five nations.* Princeton, NJ: Princeton University Press, 1963.

Bagehot, W.: The English Constitution. In *Collected Works*, Vol. V, ed. N. St John-Stevas. London: The Economist, 1965–86.

Jessop, R.: *Traditionalism, Conservatism and British Political Culture.* London: Allen & Unwin, 1974.

McKenzie, R. and Silver, A.: *Angels in Marble.* London: Heinemann, 1968.

Nordlinger, E.A.: *The Working-Class Tories.* London: MacGibbon & Kee, 1967.

delegate   Person authorized by an electorate to make laws or other decisions on their behalf. In a more restricted sense the term can refer to someone with a relatively circumscribed authority to act as the representative of others, in contrast to one who is granted a more discretionary representative authority and is often referred to as a trustee. In this restricted sense a delegate is closely identified with his or her principals, through a mandate (see MANDATE THEORY). More loosely, individuals detached from some parent group as representatives but without power to make decisions, bearers of fraternal greetings and the like, may be called delegates.   GS-K

Reading

Pitkin, H.F.: *The Concept of Representation.* Berkeley: University of California Press, 1967.

delegated legislation   Subordinate legislation issued under the authority of an Act. An act conferring such powers is commonly known as a 'parent' act. In the United Kingdom items of delegated legislation are entitled STATUTORY INSTRUMENTS.

Delegated legislation has both advantages and dangers. It saves parliamentary time. It is appropriate for technical questions which depend upon expert opinion. It can be essential for complex schemes of reform where all the consequences may not be foreseen when the basic enabling legislation is debated. Delegation also provides flexibility and the opportunity to experiment. It is also vital in emergencies. The report of the Committee on Ministers' Powers commented (p. 23): 'The truth is that if Parliament was not willing to delegate law-making power, Parliament would be unable to pass the kind and quantity of legislation which modern public opinion requires.'

Even in peacetime delegated legislation can be used on issues of great importance. Nor is it a recent invention. The Poor Law Amendment Act 1834 authorized the Poor Law Commissioners to issue Orders which controlled the conditions of life in the workhouses. In times of war extensive use is made of delegation. But the danger is that delegated power may be abused. Those given unfettered power may use it in unexpected or arbitrary ways, though various safeguards against possible abuse exist. An independent JUDICIARY may rule that the use made of delegated power goes beyond that permitted by the parent act and, therefore, will not be upheld by the court. A LEGISLATURE can be alert and ready to challenge the unreasonable application of subordinate legislation: the hindrance is that a legislature is always hampered by lack of time and that most of the problems that arise from delegation are likely to be too technical or limited in scope to arouse much public interest. The basic safeguard is for a legislature to be wary when debating proposals for delegated authority. However, a government is normally sustained by a majority in the legislature and will not welcome objections from its supporters about the content of bills. Civil servants drafting legislation may attempt to use delegation provisions as a means of evading future political and administrative difficulties.

PGR

165

Reading

Allen, C.K.: *Law and Orders*. London: Stevens, 1950.

Beith, A.: Prayers unanswered. *Parliamentary Affairs* 34 (1981) 165–73.

Eaves, J.: *Emergency Powers and the Parliamentary Watchdog*. London: Hansard Society, 1957.

Ministers' Powers. Report of Committee 1931–2 Cmd 4060. British Parliamentary Papers xii.

democracy   Its meaning derives from the Greek words *demos* (people) and *kratia* (rule or authority), hence 'rule by the people'. Although the root meaning is simple and even self-evident, both 'rule by' and 'the people' have been interpreted in markedly different ways.

The word *demokratia* was first used by the Greeks towards the middle of the fifth century BC to designate a new conception of political life and the practices it promoted in many of their city states. The two central elements in the meaning of the word are problematic, and were subject to interpretation even then. What sort of equality is signified by *demokratia*? Before the word *demokratia* gained currency Athenians had already referred to certain kinds of equality as desirable characteristics of their political system: equality of all citizens in the right to speak in the governing assembly *isegoria* and equality before the law *isonomia*. As the assembly in which the 'people', the *demos*, met to act on public affairs came to be seen as the sovereign authority, however, the word democracy seems to have gained ground as the name for the new system, and democracy came to mean that the *demos* was the sovereign ruler. Democracy was therefore commonly distinguished from rule by the few (ARISTOCRACY or OLIGARCHY) or by one (MONARCHY or TYRANNY).

Who should compose the *demos* is a question to which advocates of democracy have given sharply different answers. Both in classical Greece and in modern times the citizen body has invariably excluded some persons as unqualified. In the seventh and sixth centuries BC, before the advent of democratic regimes, the *demos* appears to have referred to a more restricted group than it did in the fifth century. Yet even at the height of Athenian democracy in the fifth century 'the people' or those able to participate comprised only a small minority of the adult population of Athens. It was not until the twentieth century that in both theory and practice democracy came to mean that the suffrage, as well as other rights of full citizenship, ought to be open to all, or almost all, permanent residents of a country.

Just as ideas about what properly constitutes the people have changed, so too have conceptions as to what it means for the people to rule. The political institutions that have developed in modern democracies to facilitate 'rule by the people', and the ideas about political life that lend legitimacy to these institutions in democratic countries, are in some important ways radically different from those of classical Greece, the Roman Republic, or the Italian republics of the middle ages and early Renaissance; so different in fact that a citizen of fifth-century Athens might be unable or unwilling to recognize any modern regime as a democracy.

One of the most far-reaching changes has been the shift of the locus of democracy from the small scale of the CITY STATE to the large scale of the modern nation state. By the end of the eighteenth century the city state, which for over two millennia had been looked on as the natural and even exclusive setting for a democratic order – a view maintained by Rousseau in the *Social Contract* (1762) – had become almost everywhere so subordinate to the nation state that democratic efforts, ideas, and ideology were shifted away from the city state to the problem of democratizing the government of the nation state. The consequences of this shift in scale and location, from democracy as appropriate to the small scale of the city state to democracy as appropriate to the large, even gigantic, scale of the nation state, were momentous. Although these consequences were not clearly foreseen at least seven have proved to be particularly important.

(1) REPRESENTATION, which was anathema to Rousseau in the *Social Contract*, has become unavoidable and generally accepted as a proper democratic institution. Because 'the people' are far too numerous (and scattered) to rule directly by assembling together, they must

now exercise their sovereignty through elected representatives.

(2) Once representation is accepted as a solution to the problem of how a large and extended body of people may rule, the barriers to the size of a democratic unit set by the requirement that citizens rule through their own assembly are eliminated. As a result, representative democracy can be extended virtually without limits as to population or area.

(3) As a direct consequence of increasing size some forms of POLITICAL PARTICIPATION are necessarily reduced, often drastically. For example, in all except very small countries, only a small percentage of citizens can possibly engage in discussions with their representatives. The limits on direct participation through discussion may easily be shown by multiplying the number of communications between citizens and representatives that participation is assumed to require by the average time required for each communication. As this simple exercise reveals, the time required rapidly becomes astronomical as the number of citizens increases.

(4) The relatively homogeneous population of citizens united by common attachments to city, language, race, myth, history, and religion that was a conspicuous part of the classical, city-state vision of democracy becomes for all practical purposes impossible because of the greater diversity that results in part from the larger size of nation states.

(5) As a consequence POLITICAL CLEAVAGES are multiplied, political conflict becomes an inevitable aspect of political life, and political thought and practice tends to accept conflict as a normal and not aberrant feature of politics.

(6) An entirely new constellation of political institutions and practices develops that, taken in its entirety, distinguishes modern democracy not only from contemporary non-democratic regimes but from all regimes earlier than the nineteenth century, including democracies and republics. These institutions include universal suffrage; a more or less coextensive right of any citizen to run for public office; the right of political leaders to compete publicly for support; free and fair (normally secret) elections; the right of all citizens to form autonomous political parties in order to contest elections; their right to form other political associations, such as LOBBYING organizations and pressure groups in order to influence the conduct of the government; the existence of alternative sources of information independent of the control both of the government and of one another; institutions that ensure the peaceful departure of government leaders who lose elections, and their peaceful replacement by the winners. This combination of institutions constitutes a type of regime that is sometimes called POLYARCHY. No city state ever possessed the full panoply of polyarchal institutions. Even the Roman Republic, which expanded in territory and citizenship far beyond the confines of Rome itself, failed to develop representative institutions and competing political parties (though factional disputes were commonplace).

(7) Modern democratic regimes are distinguished by the existence, legality and legitimacy of a variety of autonomous organizations and associations that are relatively independent in relation to the government and to one another. This characteristic is often referred to as PLURALISM or, more narrowly, as organizational pluralism. This characteristic of modern representative democracies, frequently said to be 'pluralistic democracies', distinguishes them not only from authoritarian regimes in which autonomous organizations are much more limited in their autonomy or forbidden outright, but also from the city-state democracies and republics of earlier times. For in those, too, autonomous political organizations typically did not exist or, if they did, were illegal and widely thought to be illegitimate; because of this, the older democratic tradition could be said to have been monistic rather than pluralistic in its orientation. Here again the contrast between the views of ROUSSEAU in the *Social Contract* and TOCQUEVILLE in *Democracy in America* is instructive: Rousseau, following the older republican tradition, was hostile to associations as inimical to the public good, while seventy years later Tocqueville, though not without some reservations, lauded them as essential to democracy.

DEMOCRACY

Although the theory and practice of democracy were profoundly altered by the shift in locus from city state to nation state, in both instances the idea of democracy was meant to be applied to the government of the state. The state, however, is only one kind of human association (see STATE). Even the older tradition of monistic democracy assumed, as did ARISTOTLE, that other human associations, such as the family or economic organizations of various kinds, would exist within the state, and were indeed necessary to a good life and to a good state. In the seventeenth and eighteenth centuries some religious groups, particularly dissenters in Britain and the American colonies, applied democratic ideas to the internal government of their churches, the Congregationalists in New England, for example. Not surprisingly, the spread of democratic ideas and beliefs has greatly strengthened the tendency to apply the idea of democracy not only to governing the state but to the internal government of associations and organizations of many kinds – TRADE UNIONS, political parties, consumer and producer co-operatives, and so on.

The vision of a society in which authority in organizations is typically democratic rather than hierarchical is sometimes referred to as the idea or ideology of 'participatory democracy'. Advocates of participatory democracy generally emphasize the importance of decentralizing decision making to smaller associations, strengthening opportunities to participate in the decisions of regional and LOCAL GOVERNMENTS, and providing opportunities for REFERENDUMS and other plebiscitary devices. Enthusiasm for participatory democracy appears to wax and wane; partly, perhaps, because enthusiasts generally underestimate the costs in time and effort of actively participating in a rich associational life and overestimate the satisfactions most people derive from doing so.

Extending democratic ideas to associations other than the state invites us to consider whether democratic authority ought to be understood as the only legitimate form of authority, or whether other forms of authority might not also be legitimate in certain kinds of associations or under certain conditions.

Although the question is much too broad to be considered here, one aspect of it is reflected in the term economic democracy, which implies extending the idea of democracy to the economic order. The expression economic democracy is unfortunately highly ambiguous and is often used with radically different meanings; two of these which are apparently contradictory, can be clearly distinguished. One interpretation refers to a social system in which wealth and incomes are distributed more or less equally. Conceivably, however, in order to bring about and maintain such a distribution the government of the state might have to be undemocratic; that is, lacking in the institutions of modern representative democracy described earlier. Another interpretation, (sometimes called INDUSTRIAL DEMOCRACY) refers to a system in which economic organizations – firms, enterprises, businesses, and so on – are internally democratic; that is, governed through democratic processes by the people who work in them. Conceivably economic democracy in this sense might also be brought about or maintained by an undemocratic state. The institutions of self-management in Yugoslavia provide workers with extensive opportunities to participate in governing their enterprises. But the system was inaugurated from above by a regime that was not itself a democracy and has not yet evolved fully democratic institutions for governing the state. Most advocates of economic democracy in the second sense support their argument by drawing on the theory and practice of democracy in governing the state, and they see self-government in economic organizations as a straightforward extension of, and as complementary to, self-government in the state. Yet up to the time this article was written (spring 1986), except for isolated cases or partial achievements in some countries, their aspirations for economic democracy have remained unfulfilled.

See also DIRECT DEMOCRACY.   RAD

Reading

Barber, B.: *Strong Democracy: participatory politics for a new age.* Berkeley: University of California Press, 1984.

168

Dahl, R.A.: *Dilemmas of Pluralist Democracy*. New Haven, Conn.: Yale University Press, 1982.

————: *A Preface to Democratic Theory*. Chicago, Ill.: University of Chicago Press, 1956.

Finley, M.I.: *Democracy, Ancient and Modern*. New Brunswick, NJ: Rutgers University Press, 1972.

Macpherson, C.B.: *Democratic Theory: essays in retrieval*. Oxford: Clarendon Press, 1973.

Pennock, J.R. and Chapman, J.W. eds: *Liberal Democracy, Nomos XXV*. New York: New York University Press, 1983.

Plamenatz, J.: *Democracy and Illusion*. London: Longman, 1973.

Sartori, G.: *The Theory of Democracy Revisited*. (2 vols.) Chatham, NJ: Chatham House, 1987.

democratic centralism   The organizing principle of the Communist Party of the Soviet Union and allied Marxist–Leninist parties. In principle it allows for the election of leaders and unfettered discussion of policy at all levels of the party until such time as a decision is democratically agreed, at which point discussion ceases and the policy becomes a matter for unquestioning acceptance by all members irrespective of their personal views.

Were COMMUNIST PARTIES to abide by democratic centralism as it is described, there would be little difference between their internal functioning and that of parties of the liberal–democratic type. The practice of democratic centralism, however, diverges widely from what it purports to be. Its real utility is to free communist leaders from accountability to party members. Communist parties of the Leninist type function on the basis of strict hierarchy, the subordination of lower bodies to higher ones and military-type discipline over rank and file members. Top leaders are chosen by means of co-optation rather than by election; lower cadres are appointed by superior organs, not by the bodies formally vested with this right; decision making is jealously guarded as the exclusive preserve of self-selected, unaccountable ruling groups. Given this arrangement, the Communist Party functions strictly on a top-down basis which leaves little room for initiative from below. In fact attempts to initiate uncovenanted policy discussion or to question the party 'line' are dubbed 'anti-party' activities and fall foul of the proscription on factionalism. This means that in practice centralism is the dominant feature of democratic centralism; the democratic aspect is cosmetic and ascriptive.

See also LENIN/LENINISM.   TPMcN

Reading

Lenin, V.I.: What is to be done? In *Collected Works*, Vol. I. London: Lawrence & Wishart, 1965.

Luxemburg, R.: *Leninism or Marxism?*. Ann Arbor: University of Michigan Press, 1961.

Schapiro, L.: *The Communist Party of the Soviet Union*. 2nd edn. London: Methuen, 1970.

Waller, M.: *The Language of Communism*. London: Bodley Head, 1972.

————: *Democratic Centralism: an historical commentary*. Manchester: Manchester University Press, 1981.

Democratic Party   One of the two major parties in contemporary American politics, and also arguably the oldest continuing, self-conscious political party in the world. Comprised originally of forces and elements which had opposed adoption of the United States Constitution, through the so-called ANTI-FEDERALISM of the 1780s, the Democratic Party was already the leading opposition to the successful Federalist Party by the end of the eighteenth century. With the election of Thomas JEFFERSON as President in 1800, the party confirmed its arrival as either the dominant political organization or the leading opposition force in American politics for all the years to follow.

This basic continuity did not imply a continued similarity of programme, constituency, or structure. The party conquered its opposition so thoroughly in the early 1800s that it verged on being the representative of 'everyone'. It was given a more westerly and anti-establishment flavour by Andrew Jackson after 1828. It broke apart over slavery and secession during the Civil War of 1861–5, as the new Republican Party became the dominant actor in American politics. The Democratic Party recoalesced after the war as a combination of southern and western populists and conservatives, gaining intermittent national successes in the late nineteenth century. It suffered another period of Republican hegemony from 1896 to 1932, at times being reduced to its base in the solidly Democratic south. But it moved back to consistent majority status after Franklin Roosevelt brought his 'New Deal' to American politics at the height of the Great Depression in 1932, adding the big cities, ethnic, racial, and religious minorities, and blue-collar workers generally to the southern party base.

The recognized party symbol has long been the domestic donkey, or jackass. Party heroes include Thomas Jefferson, its first president; Andrew Jackson, symbol of 'the common man'; Woodrow WILSON, champion of progressivism; and Franklin Roosevelt, architect of the NEW DEAL and of the Democratic voting majority which followed from it. In the period after 1968 – perhaps another watershed in Democratic, and hence American, party politics – the party remained the majority preference of individual Americans, and it retained overwhelming preponderance in the state legislatures and in the House of Representatives. But it occasionally lost control of the Senate, and it only occasionally managed to hold the American presidency. Throughout this period commentators argued, and politicians struggled, over the new shape of the American national party system, leaving the evolution of the Democratic (and Republican) national parties again apparently in flux.   BES

Reading

Chambers, W.N. and Burnham, W.D. eds: *The American Party Systems: stages of political development.* New York and London: Oxford University Press, 1967.

Ladd, E.C. Jr. with Hadley, D.: *Transformations of the American Party System.* 2nd edn. New York: Norton, 1978.

Sundquist, J.L.: *Dynamics of the Party System: alignment and realignment of political parties in the United States,* rev. edn. Washington, DC: The Brookings Institution, 1973.

department   As used in government, the word has several meanings. The most general conforms to the broadest dictionary definition: 'separate part of a complex whole'. In this sense a section of a LOCAL GOVERNMENT or PUBLIC CORPORATION is often described as a department in the same way that we speak of history departments in universities or toy departments in shops.

A more refined sense uses 'department' as the class-name for major units of government under the direct supervision of top-level political officers. The central part of the United States federal administration is composed of executive departments (thirteen in 1985) of State, Defence, Labor etc., each presided over by a member of the president's cabinet. The executive office of the president and several score of INDEPENDENT AGENCIES stand outside this departmental complex.

Even more specifically, department has often been used in Westminster systems in association with the adjective 'ministerial', to denote a major unit of government headed by an elected MINISTER and subject to the constitutional convention of ministerial RESPONSIBILITY. This convention (in the form of the individual responsibility of ministers) taught that ministers were responsible to parliament for the activities of their departments, and through parliament to the electorate, to the point of resignation for serious failure or maladministration. In this special sense the department comprised the minister at the top and a pyramid of hierarchically arranged civil servants below, with the apexing office of permanent secretary/permanent head furnishing principal advice to the minister, managing the department, and providing the formal channel of communication between minister and departmental officers generally. The juxtaposition of transitory, lay but superordinate ministers and permanent, expert but subordinate advisers came to excite generations of writers about the WESTMINSTER MODEL, and to a considerable extent the administrative structures of adhering countries were reformed accordingly.

It followed that departments could also be visualized as the principal units of civil/public service organization. They were the civil service's first-order sub-divisions, themselves usually broken down into 'divisions', 'branches' and 'sections' in that order. In some systems, the MINISTRY has developed as a related organizational form: boundary problems are discussed under that heading.

Widespread use of departments in government has spawned two auxiliary words. 'Departmentalization' usually refers to associated design processes, including identification of criteria by which work may be divided among departments and finding answers to 'span of control' questions relating to number and size of departments. The British experiment of the 1960s and 1970s with 'giant departments' is to be seen as a part of this process. 'Departmentalism' is usually taken to represent something more insidious: the tendency of the inhabitants of a particular department to see that department as an organizational end in itself and not as part of a larger system of government.

An assumption long existed that ministerial departments formed a homogeneous group of organizations, and many critics lamented the increasing use of non-departmental agencies to overcome alleged shortcomings in departmental/civil-service administration. However, developing public administration research, beginning in the 1960s, has cast doubt on this homogeneity. Moreover ministerial responsibility has become increasingly suspect as a determining criterion. The notion of the ministerial department remains part of the grand design of Westminsterdom, and is undoubtedly influential in shaping administrative organization; however, a range of contingency factors must now be taken into account to provide full understanding of the workings of this still dominant administrative form.   RLW

Reading

Hood, C. and Dunsire, A.: *Bureaumetrics: the quantitative comparison of British central government agencies*. Farnborough: Gower, 1981.

Pitt, D.C. and Smith, B.C.: *Government Departments: an organizational perspective*. London: Routledge & Kegan Paul, 1981.

Pollitt, C.: *Manipulating the Machine: changing the pattern of ministerial departments*. London: Allen & Unwin, 1984.

Schaffer, B.B.: *The Administrative Factor*, ch. 3. London: Cass, 1973.

Wallace, S.: *Federal Departmentalization: a critique of theories of organization*. New York: Columbia University Press, 1941.

Wettenhall, R.L.: *Organising Government: the uses of ministries and departments*. Sydney: Croom Helm, 1986.

dependency   A territory dependent upon an external metropolis for government. For the most part dependencies were colonies, either settled from the metropolis or conquered and ceded to that imperial power by another rival after war. There were also (for example, under the Foreign Jurisdiction Acts) spheres of influence where a metropolis provided law and order, even administration, in protectorates or (where local regimes retained considerable coherence in government) in protected states. Later, by consent of victorious allies, certain territories might be allowed as a mandate (after 1919) or a trusteeship (after 1945): on occasion, the responsibility was shared in a CONDOMINIUM.   AFM

despotism   A form of government in which the relationship of the ruler to the ruled is that of a master to his slaves. It does not follow that such a form is illegal (see TYRANNY), and in the eighteenth century in Europe some authors, for example Voltaire (1694–1778), applied the term, favourably, to the government of Louis XV in France, Frederick the Great of Prussia, and Catherine the Great of Russia. These authors held that such a form of government could be good, providing that the despot was 'enlightened', hence the expression 'enlightened despotism'. A despotism is conceptually almost indistinguishable from an AUTOCRACY.

The original term derives from the Greek philosophers, notably PLATO and ARISTOTLE, in whose age *despotes* meant simply 'the master of a household', and since these households comprised women and slaves the word was taken as the equivalent of 'master of slaves'. Aristotle used the term to describe the oriental monarchies such as the Persian Empire which were, so far as his native Greece was concerned, what he considered bad or corrupt forms of one-man rule. The Romans translated the word as *dominus* (master) with the same unfavourable connotations as the Greeks. After the third century AD the term despot survived in the eastern and Greek-speaking half of the Roman Empire as a title of honour to the emperor and, at a later stage, to his close relatives. This in turn gave rise to an office with the title Despot which was given to the governors of certain dependent states, such as Epirus, Trebizond and Cyprus. When the Turks finally overran the Byzantine Empire, taking Constantinople in 1453, they retained this title as in the instance of 'the Despot of Serbia'.

See also ABSOLUTE GOVERNMENT.   SEF

devolution Literally, the handing down from a superior authority to an inferior; the transfer to a subordinate elected body on a geographical basis of functions exercised by a country's legislature or ministers. Devolution is distinguished from FEDERALISM in that the powers of the subordinate legislature are conferred by the centre which retains residual constitutional authority, whereas under a federal system the powers of both the centre and the provinces are determined by the constitution. In practice the difference may not be very great in normal circumstances, but the importance of the legal distinction was shown in 1972 when the British government found itself in conflict with the government of Northern Ireland and was able first to prorogue the devolved parliament of Northern Ireland, and then to abolish it, something that would not have been possible under a federal system of government.

Devolution has the political purpose of providing some degree of self-government as an alternative to separation – in Britain it was known as Home Rule until the 1920s – and also of securing DECENTRALIZATION, the dispersal of power and reducing the level of governmental OVERLOAD. Subordinate legislatures have existed for many years in Italy, and have recently been introduced in France and Spain, but proposals for devolution in Britain in the 1970s proved abortive for lack of sufficient popular support.

See also REGIONALISM.   VBB

Reading

Birrell, D. and Murie, A.: *Policy and Government in Northern Ireland: lessons of devolution*. Dublin: Gill & Macmillan, 1980.

Bogdanor, V.: *Devolution*. Oxford: Oxford University Press, 1979.

Cornford, J. ed.: *The Failure of the State*. London: Croom Helm, 1975.

d'Hondt method Named after the nineteenth-century Belgian mathematician Victor d'Hondt. A formula used in party list systems of proportional representation to allocate seats to parties. After the votes cast for each party list have been ascertained, the totals are divided by the numbers 1, 2, 3 — so far as may be necessary. The example below is taken from the 1979 election to fill Luxemburg's six seats in the European parliament.

Three Christian Socialists were elected, two Democrats and one Socialist Worker.

This method is designed to ensure that the average number of votes needed to elect a candidate is as nearly as possible the same for all parties. It is used in, for example Belgium and West Germany, but tends to encourage large parties and discourage splinters, although its effects can be mitigated by APPARENTE-

European Parliament Election, Luxemburg 1979

	Christian Socialist	Democrat	Socialist Worker	Social Democrat	Communist	Liberal	Revolutionary Communist
votes	351,942	274,345	211,097	68,310	48,738	5,595	5,027
divided by 2	175,971	137,173	105,549				
divided by 3	117,314	91,448					

(adapted from Lakeman 1982, p. 35)

MENT. Other highest average methods of allocation more favourable to smaller parties include the Sainte-Laguë method where the divisor is 1, 3, 5, 7 etc, and the modified Sainte-Laguë method used in Denmark, Norway and Sweden where the divisor is 1.4, 3, 5, 7, etc. The Hagenbach-Bischoff method is a highest average method using the DROOP QUOTA in the first stage.

The other main method of allocating is a largest remainder method which consists of dividing the vote polled by each party by a quota, with unallocated seats awarded in order to the highest remainders.

The quota may be the Droop quota, the Hare quota (valid votes divided by the number of seats), or the Imperial (Imperiali) quota (valid votes divided by the number of seats to be allocated plus two).

Amongst these methods, d'Hondt is distinctly favourable to large parties, while the largest remainder method favours small parties. Sainte-Laguë and modified Sainte-Laguë methods attempt to be fair as between large and small parties.

See also ELECTORAL SYSTEMS.   VBB

Reading

Brew, D.A.: Examples of methods of counting used in different systems of proportional representation. In *The European Parliament: towards a uniform procedure for direct elections*, ed. C. Sasse et al. Florence: European University Institute, 1981.

Carstairs, A.M.: *A Short History of Electoral Systems in Western Europe*. London: Allen & Unwin, 1980.

Lakeman, E.: *Power to Elect*. London: Heinemann, 1982.

Nohlen, E.: *Wahlsysteme der Welt: ein Handbuch: Daten und Analysen*. Munich: Piper, 1978.

Dicey, A. V. (1835–1922)

British jurist and the most influential of those who have written systematically about the British Constitution. In his most important work, *Introduction to the Study of the Law of the Constitution* (1885), Dicey suggested three fundamental principles of the Constitution – the SOVEREIGNTY of parliament, the RULE OF LAW and the role of CONVENTIONS OF THE CONSTITUTION.

The notion of the sovereignty of parliament derives from Coke, Blackstone, BENTHAM and John Austin's *The Province of Jurisprudence Determined* (1832). In Dicey's formulation, Parliament has 'the right to make or unmake any law whatever; and . . . no person or body is recognised by the law . . . as having a right to override or set aside the legislation of Parliament.' Parliament can legislate on any matter whatever; there can be no legal limitations upon Parliament, and there can in Britain be no competing authority with power to legislate. If this doctrine is correct, it stands in the way of entrenched constitutional guarantees, such as a BILL OF RIGHTS, intended to preserve certain rights from the possibility of alteration by parliamentary majority. Dicey himself hoped that the REFERENDUM could be employed as a practical, though not a legal, limit on the power of Parliament; he was the first advocate of its use in Britain.

The doctrine of the rule of law was derived from W. E. Hearn's *Government of England* (1867). In Dicey's formulation it entails the supremacy of the regular law and the absence of arbitrary or wide discretionary power; equality before the law with all, including government officials, being equally subject to the law of the land and the ordinary courts; with the laws of the constitution being, in Britain, 'not the source but the consequence of the rights of individuals, as defined and enforced by the courts . . . ' Dicey was sceptical of the value of declarations of rights, and believed that civil liberties were best guaranteed by the courts and the COMMON LAW. He underestimated the importance of statutory reform in the protection of CIVIL LIBERTIES, and did not explain how the rule of law could be made compatible with parliamentary sovereignty. Dicey's views on the rule of law would not be defended by many jurists today, but, nevertheless, the rule of law remains important in the broader sense as part of the juridical foundation of a liberal society.

Dicey's account of conventions was influenced by Austin, J. S. MILL, BAGEHOT, and, above all, by E. A. Freeman's *Growth of the English Constitution* (1872). Dicey defined conventions as rules regulating the 'conduct of the several members of the sovereign power' which yet 'are not in reality laws at all since they are not enforced by the courts'. In the first edition of the *Law of the Constitution* he followed Freeman in asserting that conventions were peculiar to an uncodified constitution such as the British and that they existed only in modern times; but in later editions he accepted that conventions formed an important part of all constitutions at all times, whether codified or not. Contrary to what is often suggested Dicey insisted that the analysis of conventions was a legitimate and indeed essential part of the study of the constitution.

The basic principles laid down by Dicey have stood the test of time astonishingly well. There was, admittedly, a severe reaction to his work between the wars when writers such as Jennings, Laski and Robson condemned Dicey's supposedly universal principles as a reflection of his WHIG political views, with no application in a collectivist society, but this criticism is not accepted as well founded by the majority of contemporary jurists. A more recent criticism is that Dicey saw the constitution as a summation of past experience, a series of inductive generalizations resulting from judicial decisions determining the rights of private persons, rather than a search for conscious principles: and that this evolutionary method of thinking about the constitution has hindered the search for instruments capable of limiting the power of the state. Some critics suggest that Dicey's principles have, contrary to what he would have wished, legitimized the omnicompetence of government. Nevertheless, whether these criticisms are justified or not, the lucidity and precision of Dicey's analysis of the British Constitution, have made a permanent contribution to our understanding of it.

See also CONSTITUTIONAL LAW.   VBB

Reading

Cosgrove, R.A.: *The Rule of Law: Albert Venn Dicey, Victorian jurist.* London: Macmillan, 1980.

Dicey, A.V.: *Introduction to the Study of the Law of the Constitution.* 10th edn (1959), ed. E.C.S. Wade. Repr. Basingstoke: Macmillan, 1985.

————: *Law and Public Opinion in England during the Nineteenth Century.* 2nd edn. London: Macmillan, 1962.

Jennings, I.: *The Law and the Constitution.* 5th edn.

London: University of London Press, 1959.

Dicey and the Constitution. *Public Law* special issue (Winter 1985).

Johnson, N.: *In Search of the Constitution.* Oxford: Pergamon, 1977.

Lawson, F.H.: Dicey revisited. *Political Studies* 7 (1959) 109–126, 207–221.

Marshall, G.: *Constitutional Conventions.* Oxford: Oxford University Press, 1984.

dictatorship/dictator Strictly, a mode of government characterized by the existence of a single ruler i.e. an AUTOCRACY. This autocrat is called a dictator since he enjoys authority in virtue of a personal claim, rather than by the operation of the monarchical or dynastic principle. The term dictatorship derives its modern meaning from this primordial sense. It is often used more loosely to designate authoritarian governments ruled collectively by military leaders or by a single party, though for these forms of government, the generic term AUTHORITARIAN seems preferable; or they can be distinguished more specifically as military governments, ONE-PARTY STATES or totalitarian regimes (see MILITARY REGIMES; TOTALITARIANISM).

Dictatorship was not always synonymous with arbitrary government. In its origins, in the early Roman Republic, it was exactly the opposite of an illegitimate despotism. The dictator was a supreme magistrate nominated by the consuls on the recommendation of the Senate and confirmed by the Comitia Curiata (a popular assembly), under exceptional circumstances of external menace or internal disorder. His mandate was temporary and limited to six months, so although he exercised absolute power, he appeared not as a tyrant but as a saviour. He was required to account for his actions and was responsible to those he governed and to the law. He was a constitutional dictator. Some modern constitutions, for example the French, the Italian and that of the Federal German Republic, make provision for the assumption by the executive of EMERGENCY POWERS within the law, a form of constitutional dictatorship.

The kind of dictatorship with which we are familiar today was born with Sulla, and with Caesar and Augustus in the last decades of the

Republic. Dictatorship lost its constitutional character and its temporary nature, and came to embrace legislative as well as executive power so that the dictator's power was virtually unlimited. Modern dictatorship resembles its Roman homologue less than this latter form of imperial authoritarianism; it also resembles tyranny in Greece where the despot based his authority on force and on contempt for the law. However it was the dictatorship of Cromwell in England which marked the point of transition between the ancient and the contemporary worlds. Cromwell repudiated legality when he forcibly dissolved Parliament in 1653, but he also appeared as a providential saviour of a shattered country. After Cromwell the term dictatorship did not become pejorative until the rise in France of Napoleon Bonaparte, often accused of being a dictator by his enemies. The nineteenth-century model of dictatorship was determined by references to Napoleon III, and Bismarck, as well as the proliferation of despotisms, both military and civilian, in the new states of Latin America. This last phenomenon gave rise to a new word in the vocabulary of politics – CAUDILLO, which designated an exotic dictator invested with the confidence of the people in a situation of general insecurity in which normal parliamentary government was impossible.

The essence of modern dictatorship is that the dictator is above the law. His power may be limited by his subordinates but he will not be restrained by constitutional checks and, above all, he will not be responsible to those whom he governs. Sometimes he will be a charismatic leader and his power may well rest in part upon popular opinion, but it will probably depend upon fear as well. In the twentieth century, IDEOLOGY has played an important part in providing LEGITIMACY for dictators, especially for the FASCIST and NAZI dictatorships. Some have also argued that Bolshevik ideology formed the underpinning for STALIN's dictatorship though this is more disputable.

Nevertheless a dictatorship which is strictly personal is very rare in the contemporary world. The term dictatorship has come to signify some form of authoritarian power, rather than the despotism of a single dictator.

The most useful and all-inclusive definition is provided by Franz Neumann: 'By dictatorship we understand the rule of a person or a group of persons who arrogate to themselves and monopolise power in the state, exercising it without restraint.'

See also ABSOLUTE GOVERNMENT; DESPOTISM.

GH

Reading

Collier, D. ed.: *The New Authoritarianism in Latin America*. Princeton: Princeton University Press, 1979.

Duverger, M.: *De la dictature*. Paris: Julliard, 1961.

Eisenstadt, S.N.: *Traditional Patrimonialism and Modern Neo-patrimonialism*. London: Sage, 1973.

Friedrich, C.J. and Brzezinski, Z.K.: *Totalitarian Dictatorship and Autocracy*. New York: Praeger, 1967.

Germani, G.: *Authoritarianism, Fascism and National Populism*. New Brunswick, NJ: Transaction Books, 1978.

Ionescu, G. and Gellner, E. eds: *Populism*. London: Weidenfeld & Nicolson, 1969.

Laqueur, W. ed.: *Fascism: a reader's guide*. London: Wildwood, 1976.

Linz, J.J.: Totalitarianism and authoritarian regimes. In *Handbook of Political Science*, vol iii, pp. 175–411, ed. F.I. Greenstein and N. Polsby. Reading, Mass.: Addison-Wesley, 1975.

Moore, B. Jr: *Social Origins of Dictatorship and Democracy*. Boston, Mass.: Beacon, 1966; London: Allen Lane; Penguin, 1967.

Neumann, F.: *The Democratic and the Authoritarian State*. Glencoe, Ill.: Free Press of Glencoe, 1957.

Schmitt, C.: *Die Diktatur*. Munich: Duncker & Humblot, 1921.

dictatorship of the proletariat The term used within the Marxian tradition to describe the transition from CAPITALISM to SOCIALISM. Mainly used by MARX in private correspondence, the term was not specifically elaborated upon by him, but since Marx envisaged the proletariat becoming a majority in modern industrialized society, the implication was always that it constituted a dictatorship by the majority of the population. To Marx all political rule was class domination, so proletarian rule was as much a 'dictatorship of the proletariat' as capitalist rule was a 'dictatorship of the capitalists'. The one difference was that proletarian rule was for the first time rule by majority: hence Marx called it 'winning the battle of democracy'.

In the *Communist Manifesto* (1848) Marx spelt out the ingredients of this form of government as constituting 'despotic inroads into the rights of property and on the conditions of bourgeois production'. This would include nationalization of land, transport and banking, progressive taxation and the abolition of inheritance, together with the development of a public industrial sector. All this would 'by degrees, wrest all capital from the bourgeoisie'. While Marx did not rule out the possibility that in societies like those of England and the United States this could be achieved through the ballot box, in countries like France and Germany with a large peasant population and a bureaucratic–authoritarian tradition a violent overthrow would be necessary.

Within the Russian revolutionary movement the term 'dictatorship of the proletariat' underwent significant transformation. Because the proletariat in Russia was weak and under-developed it was argued by LENIN that there was no chance of achieving power through majority rule; the strong Jacobin tradition within the radical Russian intelligentsia also contributed towards investing the term with a clear meaning of an elitist, dictatorial rule imposed on a recalcitrant majority by a radical minority of 'professional revolutionaries'. After 1917, with the emergence of a centralized Communist Party in power, the term meant the monopoly of power exercised on behalf of the proletariat by the party apparatus.   SA

Reading

Kautsky, K.: *The Dictatorship of the Proletariat*. London: National Labour Press, 1924.

Lenin, V.I.: State and Revolution. In *Collected Works*, Vol. XXV. London: Lawrence & Wishart, 1965.

————: The proletarian revolution and the renegade Kautsky. In *Collected Works*, Vol. XXVIII. London: Lawrence & Wishart, 1965.

Marx, K.: The Communist Manifesto; and The civil war in France. In *The Portable Marx*. Harmondsworth: Penguin, 1983.

direct action Direct pressure upon government as distinct from action through constitutional processes. Examples are demonstrations, passive resistance, strikes and sabotage. Various forms of collective political behaviour are resorted to by those who perceive their access to and influence upon decision making to be ineffective or denied. It is associated with extra-parliamentary opposition methods in which confrontation takes priority over negotiation. The objectives of groups employing direct action range from specific claims that can be processed within the existing political system to alternatives to the system itself.

Machiavelli describes direct action, but its origins are more commonly traced to ANARCHISM and SYNDICALISM: it is subsequently seen in Gandhi's non-violent resistance which influenced the CIVIL RIGHTS Movement in the United States and the Campaign for Nuclear Disarmament in Britain. The women's peace camp at Greenham Common air base in Berkshire in protest against the stationing of US cruise missiles in Britain is a contemporary example of sustained direct action.

Direct action has been described as a form of the 'New Politics' not because it is new but because of the growth in the number of issues and groups now involved in it. What constitutes direct action, violent or non-violent, legal or non-legal, varies with the context. Its limits are open to debate but range from symbolic protest at one end of the spectrum to POLITICAL VIOLENCE at the other.

Its critics see direct action as irrational and as a threat to democratic and liberal values. Although identified with the left it is also used by the political right and even by the state. It may be counter-productive in so far as it permits the state to bestow legitimacy selectively. But direct action can play a part in achieving political and institutional reform, for ruling groups have seldom relinquished power voluntarily and change has seldom occurred in the absence of pressure.   RJB

Reading

Benewick, R. and Smith, T. eds: *Direct Action and Democratic Politics*. London: Allen & Unwin, 1972.

Carter, A.: *Direct Action and Liberal Democracy*. London: Routledge & Kegan Paul; New York: Harper & Row, 1973.

Cook, A. and Kirk, G.: *Greenham Women Everywhere*. London: Pluto, 1983.

Hain, P.: *Radical Regeneration*. London: Quartet, 1975.

Machiavelli, N.: *The Prince and The Discourses*. Modern Library edn, p. 120. New York: Random House, 1950.

direct democracy The form of government under which the right to make political decisions rests in the entire body of citizens, unmediated by political organizations such as parties. (By contrast, representative democracy vests the right to make the political decisions in REPRESENTATIVES or delegates who are elected by the citizens.) Many examples of direct democracy can be found in Greece of the fifth century BC. The political unit was the *polis*, or CITY STATE, whose inhabitants seldom numbered more than ten thousand, most of whom were women or slaves, and so not citizens. All citizens were entitled to attend and vote in the general assembly and were eligible for a wide variety of judicial and administrative posts, which were filled either by election or by throwing lots. A more recent example is provided by the town meetings in seventeenth- and eighteenth-century America. Direct democracy still survives where political units are small enough to permit it; in England and Wales, for instance, in parish-meetings of the parishioners of those PARISHES which have fewer than three hundred inhabitants; in town-meetings in the smaller towns in the New England States of the USA such as in Connecticut and Rhode Island; and in the *Landsgemeinde* of five small cantons and half-cantons in central and eastern Switzerland. A number of states combine representative democracy with a measure of direct democracy, in that they refer certain matters to the vote of the citizens as a whole by means of the REFERENDUM. These include Switzerland, Italy, France and a number of the states of the USA. In addition, Switzerland, Italy and a number of states of the USA use the initiative while the RECALL is still practised in some of the American states.

See also INITIATIVE; RECALL; TOWN MEETING.

SEF

discretion The room for manoeuvre possessed by any decision maker. The concept is especially relevant to an official decision, when a public officer implementing a law has freedom of choice among possible courses of action and inaction. The extent of discretion cannot be precisely defined, but it ranges along a continuum. When it is high it allows the official to decide in accordance with broad criteria such as 'reasonableness', 'the public interest', or 'as he thinks fit'. When it is low, discretion may be confined by a number of factors (such as resources, or political or professional constraints), but especially by rules that specify the action to be followed.

The amount of discretion officials should be allowed is a question that faces legislators attempting to allocate scarce resources, or to control behaviour. For example, should welfare benefits be allocated in accordance with precise rules, or by means of an overall assessment of each case, allowing a wide number of factors to be taken into account? Should land development be controlled by a strict system of zoning, which specifies, through a detailed plan, what can or cannot be done in any area, or should officers grant or refuse planning permission in accordance with a plan that acts only as guidance but also allows 'other material considerations' to be taken into account in each case (the latter procedure giving more discretion to the decision maker than the former)?

The English constitutional lawyer, A. V. DICEY, writing at the end of the nineteenth century, based his concept of the RULE OF LAW around the prevention of arbitrary decisions, which he felt would be encouraged by discretionary powers, and which he opposed as contrary to 'regular law'. Later Lord Hewart and F. A. Hayek added their voices to the opposition to wide discretionary powers, while W. A. Robson and W. Ivor Jennings saw the attacks on discretion as veiled attacks on the then new WELFARE STATE which required, in their view, wide discretion in order to accomplish complex governmental tasks. In the 1960s the debate about discretion shifted from the merits and defects of the welfare state to a discussion about techniques of IMPLEMENTATION of necessary public functions. Welfare recipients in Britain and the United States objected to the fact that government 'largesse' was disbursed in accordance with a secret code and asked instead for a set of welfare 'rights'. Others, such as Richard Titmuss, however, opposed these challenges to the unconstrained exercise of official discretion and warned of a 'pathology of legalism' developing in its place.

Uncontrolled discretion can lead to decisions that are irrational, discriminatory or otherwise unfair. There is clearly a benefit in having standards laid down in advance so that affected persons can plan their actions, officials be held accountable, and like cases be treated alike. The defects of discretion must however be balanced against its virtues, particularly its capacity for flexible response to the particular circumstances of an individual case. In pollution law, for example, the benefits of strict enforcement might be balanced against the risk of the pollutor's going out of business as a result of the additional abatement costs. There are however certain questions (such as individual need and aesthetic judgement) which, because of their complexity, or individuality, require a degree of discretion for their resolution and cannot be confined to rules. Where discretion can be controlled, and where it is thought desirable to control it, K. C. Davis proposes three principal techniques: the confining of discretion (usually through a rule – discretion to enforce safe driving for example may be confined by a rule specifying precise speed limits); the structuring of discretion (through openness and public participation in standard-setting); and the checking of discretion (through internal administrative arrangements or external appeals).

The control of administrative discretion by the courts raises special problems, as courts are not designed nor equipped to interfere in policy decisions. The extent to which courts themselves have discretion is a problem for jurisprudence. Dworkin would allow judges a 'weak' discretion (such as the discretion of a sergeant to pick 'the five most experienced men' for a patrol), which, because it is bound by a standard, does not permit judges to 'make' law. He would not however allow judges a 'strong' discretion (such as the discretion of the sergeant to pick 'any five men he chooses' for a patrol), because that would give the judiciary the power that should properly rest with the legislature.   JLJ

Reading

Bull, D.: The anti-discretion movement in Britain: fact or phantom? *Journal of Social Welfare Law* 65 (1980).

Davis, K.C.: *Discretionary Justice: a preliminary inquiry*. Baton Rouge: Louisiana State University Press, 1969.

Dicey, A.V.: *Introduction to the Study of the Law of the Constitution*. 10th edn (1959), ed. E.C.S. Wade. Basingstoke: Macmillan, 1985.

Dworkin, R.M.: *Taking Rights Seriously*. London: Duckworth, 1977.

Hayek, F.A.: *The Road to Serfdom*. London: Routledge & Kegan Paul, 1943.

Hewart, Lord: *The New Despotism*. London: Benn, 1929.

Jennings, W.E.: *The Law and the Constitution*. 5th edn. London: University of London Press, 1959.

Jowell, J.L.: The legal control of administrative discretion. *Public Law* (1979).

———: The rule of law today. In *The Changing Constitution*, p. 3, ed. J.L. Jowell and D. Oliver. Oxford: Oxford University Press, 1985.

Reich, C.: The new property. *Yale Law Journal* 73 (1964) 733.

Robson, W.A.: *Justice and Administrative Law*. London: Stevens, 1928.

Titmuss, R.: Welfare 'rights', law and discretion. *Political Quarterly* 42 (1971) 113.

dissolution of parliament A remarkable institution which has survived the many changes parliamentary government has undergone throughout the centuries. Originally little more than a device enabling monarchs to rid themselves of troublesome or over-zealous popular assemblies, it eventually became a key institution in the elaborate system of CHECKS AND BALANCES that characterized nineteenth-century classical parliamentarism. As the duc de Broglie put it when announcing the unfortunate dissolution of the Chambre des

Deputés in 1877 that followed the defeat of his minority government: 'Messieurs, nous n'avons pas votre confiance, vous n'avez pas la nôtre'. Dissolution was seen as the legal counter-balance to Parliament's right to censure governments.

The advent of universal suffrage and the consequent growth of party politics resulted – especially in the United Kingdom – in the gradual decline of Parliament's ability to force governments (and even individual ministers) to resign. With one side of the equation gone the other should also have disappeared. Yet dissolution survived only to become first a cabinet and later a prime-ministerial power to be used – with disputed efficacy – equally against recalcitrant friend and unprepared foe. Of European democracies only Norway and Switzerland have fixed term parliaments, but several other states such as Portugal and Sweden have only a very limited facility for early dissolution.

The political unpheavals that may follow an unwise exercise of the power of dissolution have led many constitutions to adopt a myriad of controlling devices. For example: Article 5 of the 1875 French Constitutional Act required the concurring opinion of the Senate; Article 12 of the 1958 French Constitution prohibits a second dissolution within the year following the last elections. Note, also, the complicated provisions of Articles 67 and 68 of the German Constitution of 1949. Article 67 allows the Bundestag to express its lack of confidence in the Federal Chancellor only through a 'constructive vote of no confidence' nominating a successor. Article 68 allows the Federal Chancellor, after failing to win a vote of confidence, to ask the Federal President for a dissolution of the Bundestag.

In the United Kingdom, in the absence of written norms, the position is more fluid. Nevertheless, a set of rules has developed seriously limiting the royal powers in this respect. The exact ambit of these rules and, indeed, whether they should be described as CONVENTIONS or mere usages – a distinction nebulous in itself – is in doubt. What is not in doubt is that a monarch would hardly ever be in a position to deny a request for a dissolution to a majority prime minister and would have to proceed with extreme caution even in the case of a request coming from a defeated prime minister. For the dangers here of having to grant to the succeeding prime minister what, only a short time before, was denied to his or her predecessor, must not be underestimated. It is submitted that this cautious approach should prevail even if an effective three-party system were to be established. For, at a time when certain royal prerogative powers are coming under increasing judicial control, and the democratic (as opposed to the hereditary) element in the constitution is in the ascendancy, the related issues of dissolution and appointment of prime minister should be left to the politicians to work out, with no appearance of participation by the Sovereign. Experience from many countries – Australia most recently – underlines the serious political dangers that any HEAD OF STATE may face as a result of a controversial dissolution and thus supports such a counsel of caution.

Though royal powers are on the wane, prime-ministerial ascendancy remains unchallenged. The current trend is for prime ministers to decide when parliament should be dissolved. (Cabinet papers suggest that trusted political friends, but not necessarily the cabinet, are usually consulted before such a decision is reached.) The political dangers associated with party-motivated dissolutions are obvious but represent merely one symptom of what some have called the move towards an 'elective dictatorship'. The future fate of dissolution appears to be inextricably linked to the contemporary crisis experienced by the parliamentary form of government.

See also HOUSE OF COMMONS; HOUSE OF LORDS; MONARCHY.   BSM

Reading

Forsey, E.A.: *The Royal Power of Dissolution of Parliament in the British Commonwealth.* 2nd edn. Toronto: Oxford University Press, 1968.

Lauvaux, P.: *La Dissolution des assemblées parlementaires.* Paris: Economica, 1983.

Markesinis, B.: *The Theory and Practice of Dissolution of Parliament.* Cambridge: Cambridge University Press, 1972.

Marshall, G.: *Constitutional Conventions.* Oxford: Oxford University Press, 1984.

Velu, J.: *La Dissolution du parlement*. Brussels: Bruylant, 1966.

Zines, L.: The double dissolutions and joint sitting. In *Labour and the Constitution 1972–1975*, ed. G. Evans. Melbourne: Heinemann, 1977.

dominant party A party which enjoys a preponderant influence in a given party system. It is generally used with little specification of the causes or extent of dominance. Giovanni Sartori has therefore emphasized the need to differentiate between *one-party regimes* in which only one party legally exists, *hegemonic party systems* in which one party controls the polity but permits the existence of other parties without these parties being really free to compete, and *predominant party systems* where one party has a preponderant position but other parties can compete freely in open elections. Even in predominant party systems different criteria may be used to define a dominant party, for example the proportion of the electorate which a party must win to qualify as a dominant party; the number of successive elections in which it must win that proportion; the gap separating the largest party from the second-largest party; the possible substitution of a large share of seats in a representative assembly for a large proportion of a national vote (which makes the definition dependent on the concentrating effect of the ELECTORAL SYSTEM in force); the threshold to executive office (which is lower in political systems with coalition cabinets or systems which permit minority government than in systems which require a majority of seats and have single party majority cabinets).

Dominant parties should not be identified with parties which are perennially in government. There are parties which have a location in a political spectrum so central that they play a key role in determining whether other, possibly larger, parties will enter into office or must remain in opposition (see CENTRE PARTY). Such has been the case with some Christian Democratic parties, the West German FDP, and the Finnish Centre Party. To call such long-running governing parties 'dominant', begs the question whether such parties can translate their strategic position into a decisive influence on policy.

See also COMPETITIVE PARTY SYSTEMS; PARTY SYSTEMS. HD

Reading

Sartori, G.: *Parties and Party Systems: a framework for analysis*. New York and Cambridge: Cambridge University Press, 1976.

dominion/dominion status The word 'dominion' was used from the first decade of the twentieth century to describe a small number of self-governing colonies of the United Kingdom 'beyond the seas'. The states covered by the description were Australia, Canada, Newfoundland (which lost dominion status in the 1930s), New Zealand and South Africa; the Irish Free State was added in 1921. Associated with 'dominion' was the notion of 'dominion status', and during and after the first world war there was pressure on the part of some, though not all, of the dominions to define that status. At the Imperial Conference of 1926, with the clear support of the United Kingdom government, dominion status was identified in the words of the Balfour report. That report described the relations of the United Kingdom and the overseas dominions in terms of autonomous communities within the British Empire equal in status, in no way subordinate one to another in any aspect of their domestic or external affairs, though united by a common allegiance to the CROWN and freely associated as members of the British Commonwealth of Nations (see COMMONWEALTH). The conference formulated some conventions to give practical substance to the principle of equality so stated; so it was that in 1926 and further in 1930 conventions relating to the office of GOVERNOR GENERAL were agreed. In the years between 1926 and 1930 other agreements were formulated, and in 1931 the STATUTE OF WESTMINSTER was enacted by the United Kingdom. In this way, by CONVENTION and legislation, the principle of equality between the dominions and the United Kingdom was reinforced. For some time however, while equality was asserted in principle, there was in practice dependence on the United Kingdom in some fields.

In the early post-war years India and Pakistan moved to independence by way of an intermediate stage of dominion status. India and later Pakistan (which in 1972 left the Commonwealth) subsequently became republics within the COMMONWEALTH of Nations.   ZC

Reading

Mansergh, N. et al.: *Commonwealth Perspectives*. London: Duke University Press; Cambridge University Press, 1958.

Wheare, K.C. *The Statute of Westminster and Dominion Status*, 5th edn. Oxford: Oxford University Press, 1953.

Droop quota The minimum number of votes which a candidate needs to be sure of election under the single transferable vote system of proportional representation. The quota is

$$\frac{V}{S+1} +1$$

where V is the total number of valid votes cast in the constituency, and S the total number of seats. (See ELECTORAL SYSTEMS.)   VBB

Reading

Droop, H.R.: *Methods of Electing Representatives*. London: Macmillan, 1868.

dual executive An executive in which the powers of the head of the government are held concurrently by two different persons. These powers refer to the ability of the holder or holders to exercise continuous supervision over all the affairs of the state, in contrast with those of ordinary ministers who may at most exercise spasmodic influence in the context of occasional meetings of cabinets.

Dual executive arrangements occur relatively frequently. They have occurred in the past – as in the Roman Republic – and have again become fairly common over the last decades of the twentieth century. They can be found among communist states, where power is normally shared between the general secretary of the Party and the chairman of the Council of Ministers; they occur in some authoritarian monarchies and presidencies, where a prime minister is appointed by the Head of State to share the burden of leadership; they also occur in a few liberal countries, the best examples being those of Finland and of France after 1958 (see SEMI-PRESIDENTIAL SYSTEMS). On the other hand the large majority of presidential systems are led by a single executive; PARLIAMENTARY SYSTEMS should not be regarded as being normally led by a dual executive, as the monarch or president has only symbolic or 'last-resort' powers (and does not even have much influence in the selection of the prime minister who tends to emerge from the majority party or from an arrangement among parties): at some point in the past, however, parliamentary systems have typically been characterized by a dual executive arrangement; this was the case in Britain in the eighteenth and early nineteenth centuries.

The fact that the system of dual executive has given way to a single executive in western European parliamentary systems has led to the view that the arrangement was essentially transitional; moreover, it has also been criticized as being ineffective as there have been cases of bitter struggle among the two leaders, for instance in a number of African states, such as Zaire, Uganda, or Burundi. There are indeed signs that a dual executive in which there is equality between the two leaders or one in which these leaders represent markedly antagonistic social elements (such as tribes or ethnic groups) does not constitute a stable system of government; however dual executives do appear to function where there is a hierarchy between the two leaders one of whom is in ultimate charge of the affairs of the nation while the other is more specifically concerned with the daily supervision of the government and with co-ordination among the ministers. In such cases, which correspond to the situation in communist states and many authoritarian monarchies and presidencies – and indeed, except between 1986 and 1988, characterized the division of powers in the Fifth Republic French government – the 'second' leader, normally the prime minister, is primarily concerned with the direction of the administration or of the 'state' functions, to take communist terminology.

Whether the dual executive system is ultimately transitional in the very long term is of course a difficult question: it is one which can be asked of any political arrangement. What is clear is that this division of functions within the leadership appears to correspond to a need, especially in a period in which the powers of the bureaucracy have increased and in which it is therefore difficult to expect the leader both to be a truly national leader and to direct effectively the administration of the country.   JFPB

Reading

Blondel, J.: *World Leaders*. London and Los Angeles: Sage, 1980.

————: Dual leadership in the contemporary world: a step towards executive and regime stability. In *Comparative Government and Politics*, ed. D. Kavanagh and G. Peele. London: Heinemann, 1984.

Hayward, J.E.S.: *Governing France*. London: Weidenfeld & Nicolson, 1983.

McAuley, M.: *Politics and the Soviet Union*. Harmondsworth: Penguin, 1977.

due process of law   The Fifth Amendment of the United States Constitution proclaims that no person shall be deprived of life, liberty or property without due process of law, and the Fourteenth Amendment extends the same principle to state action. Upon these declarations has been built a vast superstructure of constitutional law that serves to ensure that governmental power is not used against individuals except in accordance with the law and with due regard for their rights. In criminal law an accused is entitled to a fair trial which entails *inter alia* prior notice of any charges, opportunity to prepare a defence, the right to counsel, the right to submit evidence and cross-examine, the right to a JURY verdict and an impartial judge. In US law such values also extend to civil proceedings between individuals and to decision making by administrative agencies whose powers may affect an individual's rights or freedoms. In 1970 the

Supreme Court opened up the application of procedural due process to a wide variety of the individual's relations with government, holding in *Goldberg* v. *Kelly* that an evidentiary hearing must be given before a social welfare agency decides to terminate the payment of benefit. One controversial branch of the due process doctrine, known as substantive due process, empowers courts to protect individual rights against regulatory measures in executive or legislative form which in substance intrude further upon individual autonomy than the judges consider reasonable. First seen early in this century (in *Lochner* v. *New York* 1905), when legislation affecting economic and property rights was struck down, but subsequently discredited as political opinion changed, substantive due process has been given new life more recently in the protection of personal privacy against laws banning abortion and the use of contraception.

Direct equivalents of procedural due process are found in most legal systems, since the concept of a fair trial is fundamental to the idea of law itself. The historical origin of due process may be traced to chapter 39 of Magna Carta (1215), which declared that no free man should be taken or imprisoned or dispossessed of property or privileges except by the lawful judgment of his peers or by the law of the land. These words influenced developments in English criminal procedure: judgment by peers evolved into trial by jury, and 'the law of the land' was interpreted by parliament in the fourteenth century and by Sir Edward Coke in the seventeenth century as meaning due process of common law. The term 'due process' did not take root in the language of English law, but numerous aspects of civil and criminal justice serve to promote the aim of a fair trial. In ADMINISTRATIVE LAW the doctrine of natural justice closely resembles procedural due process: it emphasizes the right to a fair hearing by an unbiased court or tribunal. Since the decision of the House of Lords in *Ridge* v. *Baldwin* (1963), there has been a strong flow of judicial decisions based on natural justice and the related notion of fairness, and the circle of interests protected by those means continues to widen.

Internationally, due process is enshrined in

such documents as the United Nations Covenant on Civil and Political Rights, and the EUROPEAN CONVENTION ON HUMAN RIGHTS. Article 5 of the Convention regulates the circumstances in which a person may be deprived of liberty; Article 6 provides for the right to a fair and public hearing by an independent court or tribunal established by law whenever an individual's civil rights and obligations are determined or when criminal charges are brought. Under Article 6, the European Court of Human Rights in Strasbourg ruled that a convicted prisoner in England has the right of access to a lawyer over a claim for damages that he or she might wish to bring against the prison authorities (*Golder* v. *United Kingdom*, 1975). AWB

Reading

Gunther, G.: *Constitutional Law, Cases and Materials.* 10th edn. Mineola: Foundation Press, 1980.

Schwartz, J. and Wade, H.W.R.: *Legal Control of Government.* Oxford: Oxford University Press, 1972.

Smith, S.A. de: *Judicial Review of Administrative Action.* 4th edn, ed. J.M. Evans. London: Stevens, 1980.

dyarchy A system of divided political authority usually associated with the constitutional reforms introduced by the British in India in 1919. It was applied to provincial not central government and created a divided executive with some departments under the control of Indian ministers responsible to the legislature, while others, for example finance and internal security, remained under British officials answerable to the Governor. The system was intended to satisfy Indian demands for participation in government; in fact it proved a recipe for conflict between the two halves of the provincial executive and was replaced after 1935 with full ministerial RESPONSIBILITY at provincial level. JGD

Reading

Baker, C.J.: *Politics in South India 1920–1937.* Cambridge: Cambridge University Press, 1976.

Indian Statutory Commission: *Report Volume I: Survey.* London: HMSO, 1930.

E

ecology/environmental parties   These parties object to what they regard as the adverse effects of technological modernization and unrestricted economic growth. Environmentalism became a politically salient issue which established parties were slow to embrace when POSTMATERIALIST value orientations emerged in western democracies. In the early 1970s ecological/environmental parties were founded in countries where environmental concerns and action groups had been an intrinsic part of the political culture (France, Britain). New ecological/environmental parties to enter politics in the 1980s in countries such as Belgium and West Germany, could also draw on anti-nuclear protests and new SOCIAL MOVEMENTS.

Electoral support for such parties in western Europe has not yet reached ten per cent. Their supporters are voters with specific environmental grievances, and well-educated young voters with a low degree of social/occupational integration. The balance between these two types of supporter varies with the party, the electoral level and the country. Parliamentary representation has depended on some form of proportional representation, electoral DEALIGNMENT and a party constellation unable to articulate new cleavages. By 1986 ecological/environmental parties including Greens had won seats in the national parliaments of Belgium, Finland, Switzerland and West Germany, in the 1984 European Parliament (Belgium, Holland, Luxemburg, West Germany), in several regional and local parliaments, and they belonged to a government coalition and at regional level in West Germany (1985–7). In Sweden the Centre Party, an AGRARIAN PARTY, and part of a governmental coalition between 1976 and 1982, had adopted anti-nuclear policies and come to function in some respects like an ecology party.

The future of ecological/environmental parties in parliamentary politics depends on their effectiveness in opposition or government, the salience of new issues and the degree of electoral loyalty among their supporters.   EK

Reading

Dalton, R.J., Flanagan, S.C. and Beck, P.A. eds: *Electoral Change in Advanced Industrial Democracies: realignment or dealignment.* Princeton, NJ: Princeton University Press, 1984.

Müller-Rommel, F.: Ecology parties in Western Europe. *West European Politics* (1982) 68–74.

Rüdig, W.: Die grüne Welle: zur Entwicklung ökologischer Parteien. *Aus Politik und Zeitgeschichte* B 45/85 (Nov. 1985) 3–18.

economic planning   Planning involves an ambitious set of problem-solving procedures aimed at implementing an economic policy. National economic planning means going beyond the habitual process of incremental and fragmented DECISION MAKING by engaging in a rational calculation of what objectives can collectively be attained as indicated by projections and forecasts; by attempting to reconcile the possible alternatives with politically preferable outcomes through the strategic use of the available policy instruments at the disposal of the government, acting where necessary in concert with other organizations; by pursuing resolutely explicit quantitative and/or qualitative objectives in the medium term (approximately five years), although this activity is also usually associated with short-term (one-year) or long-term (ten or more years) objectives. As a non-traditional form of policy making it may be contrasted not so much with market decision making as with Lindblom's 'muddling through' process by which policy decisions are usually taken. Such unplanned decision making has no overriding, comprehensive and long-term objective; action more often takes the form of piecemeal intervention, step by step marginal adjustment of existing policies arrived at within government and between government and the other actors (notably business and trade unions) by procedures ranging from bargaining, through consultation, to outright coercion.

Outside the communist countries economic planning is a very exceptional activity, and even in those countries what occurs in practice diverges markedly from the planning model. Why is economic planning such a difficult activity to carry out? The uncertainty of the future is only partly counteracted by extrapolation from past trends. Change often comes about through the intrusion of unforeseen events. It is seldom possible to work out a clear and consistent set of preferences embodying the desirable future. Furthermore, the attempt to do so in a precise and realistic way brings out the latent conflicts and sharpens the overt conflicts over problematic economic policy issues: prices, wages, the rate of exchange, the rate of interest and so forth. To avoid exacerbating such conflicts, governments are more inclined to be content with patching up piecemeal, short-term compromises between incompatible interests than to attempt a comprehensive co-ordination of economic policies. Both in communist and non-communist countries the planner is a technocrat whose expertise is utilized for political purposes that are usually far removed from a concern with planning. Any pretension to separate political ends from planning means is as illusory as the technocrat's claim to reduce partisan passions to the serene, scientific dimensions of a series of equations. Conceived as an agent of change, the planner paradoxically usually reinforces rather than

reconstructs the status quo, this being the price of securing at least partial attainment of the plan's economic policy objectives.

Because centralized economic planning is regarded as an integral part of democratic centralist decision making, it has a legitimacy in Soviet-style countries which it can never hope to attain in liberal democratic systems. Soviet planning is largely an intra-governmental activity, whereas in mixed economies firms in the private sector are often able either to block or to dictate decisions, unless the planning can be done by powerful and corporatized extra-governmental forces as has occurred at times in countries such as Austria. The pragmatic case for planning in the Sovet Union derived from the need to cope with the decision-making overload which resulted from the elimination of the market mechanism at the end of the 1920s. Using the external yardstick of the market economies, the Communist Party leadership decided upon certain grandiose policy objectives and entrusted to the bureaucratized planning process the task of working out their resource allocation, investment and production consequences. The Soviet planning system, always adapted with difficulty to agriculture, has proved less and less effective outside the heavy industry and military sectors, and the temptations of Hungarian-style 'market socialism' have become increasingly powerful. In any case, Soviet planning consists largely of incremental and improvisatory changes whose occasional bold brutality should not be confused with planning.

Economic planning has been integrated into institutional arrangements at two levels. Those responsible for the technocratic aspects of planning are usually located in a body such as the Planning Commissariat in France, which may be attached to the prime minister or the finance minister or have its own minister. (All these solutions have existed at various times in France.) Those concerned with the consultative and functional representative aspects may be located in a body such as the Economic and Social Council in France, which supplements the traditional parliamentary process. Such institutions either predate and adapt to suit the needs of economic planning – in the case of the Economic and Social Council – or are created specifically, as was the case with the Planning Commissariat. In the British instance, both the National Economic Development Office and the National Economic Development Council were set up in conjunction with the planning ventures of the 1960s but have survived even after the abandonment of national planning, albeit in an enfeebled form.

After the second world war a number of European countries experimented with forms of medium-term economic planning. In Britain they proved short-lived, both when tried by the Labour Government in the late 1940s and by Conservative and Labour Governments in the early 1960s, this time under the inspiration of misinterpreted French experience. France offered the example of a hitherto backward economy in which, under the aegis of national economic planning, a long tradition of state intervention to protect social and economic stability from foreign competition was converted into the promotion of rapid economic modernization and adaptation to an international market economy, initially through the creation of the European (Economic) Community. Despite changes of government and even of republic, successive economic plans from the 1940s to the 1980s have provided one of the instruments for the techno-bureaucratic economic leadership that was credited with the attainment of a high rate of economic growth until the 1970s. Since then, French governments have been more concerned with 'managing the unforeseeable' than with medium-term planning. None of the targets of the first seven plans had been implemented without a major hitch, and by the 1980s the inability to master the effects of international recession, notably the rise in unemployment and a decline in industrial competitiveness, meant that national economic planning lost the virtue of association with increasing prosperity and full employment. So France has – even under socialist management – been forced into a 'muddling through' style of economic decision making, in a context in which the pretension to planning has been subordinated to makeshift crisis management.

See also KEYNES/KEYNESIANISM; TECHNOCRACY.   JESH

Reading

Bornstein, M. ed.: *Economic Planning, East and West*. Cambridge, Mass.: Ballinger, 1975.

Estrin, S. and Holmes, P.: *French Planning in Theory and Practice*. London: Allen & Unwin, 1983.

Faludi, A.: *A Reader in Planning Theory*. Oxford: Pergamon, 1973.

Gunsteren, H.R. van: *The Quest for Control: a critique of the rational-central-rule approach in public affairs*. London: Wiley, 1976.

Hayward, J. and Narkiewicz, O.A. eds: *Planning in Europe*. London: Croom Helm, 1978.

—— and Watson, M. eds: *Planning, Politics and Public Policy: the British, French and Italian experience*. Cambridge: Cambridge University Press, 1975.

Leruez, J.: *Economic Planning and Politics in Britain*. London: Martin Robertson, 1975.

Lindblom, C.: Still muddling, not yet through. *Public Administration Review* (Nov–Dec 1979) 517–26.

Shonfield, A.: *Modern Capitalism*. London and Oxford: Oxford University Press, 1965.

election campaign The efforts by candidates and parties to win votes in the few weeks before an election. Media coverage is at its greatest at this time and, in some countries, free television and radio time is provided and parties are required to account for their financial receipts and expenditures. In the United States the effective campaign period is often longer because parties hold PRIMARIES to decide who their candidates will be at the election. Most states have both a national campaign, which is fought by party leaders or presidential candidates, and a series of local contests to decide who fills the seats in the legislature. In Britain local candidates, limited by a strict spending ceiling, have to rely on old-fashioned methods of door-to-door canvassing and public meetings. Developments in public relations, OPINION POLLS and MASS MEDIA are exploited by the national leaders, but have largely bypassed the local campaigns. In the United States however, where there are no spending limits, candidates for state and even local elections are able to exploit these developments.

In Britain it used to be part of the conventional wisdom to claim that election campaigns did not decide elections. Voting loyalties were fairly stable and net changes in voting support in the period of the campaign virtually cancelled each other out. Since 1970, however, there has been great ELECTORAL VOLATILITY between and during election campaigns. The stabilizing factors have weakened. In particular, there is ample evidence that PARTY allegiance or IDENTIFICATION has declined as has the class basis of party voting. The old party-identification model of voting behaviour assumed that an individual's party identification hardened over time and was passed on to his or her offspring: partisanship was more or less self-perpetuating and made for the continuity of the party system. The weakening of party loyalties gives more scope for the influence of short-term factors, including events associated with the build-up to an election, such as the miners' strike in 1974, industrial disruption in early 1979, and the Falklands war in 1982.

In the United States also, a decline in the influence of party identification and the weakening of party loyalties have left more scope for particular issues and personality factors to play a role. The institution of the presidency and the opportunity for split-ticket voting (see TICKET-SPLITTING) have always enhanced the influence of personality in presidential elections. There have also been signs of increasing electoral volatility and a weakening of party loyalty in many West European states, so increasing the electoral importance of the campaign.

Prerequisites of free election campaigning are basic freedoms of speech, assembly and organization, and an effective right to campaign for office. East-European states, even when they were one-party regimes, also held election campaigns, though these were regarded by the rulers not as opportunities to signify choice or dissent but to promote identification with the regime and raise political consciousness.

There is no good evidence that effective local organization actually decides many electoral outcomes. Most seats are usually 'safe' for the holder and 'hopeless' for the opposition. In marginal seats, however, a popular candidate and good organization may be worth a few hundred votes and be enough to affect the result. Voting by post allows scope for an efficient organization to gain an advantage – the older the register the more voters there are likely to be eligible for a postal vote. In Britain, Conservatives are usually better than Labour at organizing postal votes and their middle-class supporters are more likely to qualify and apply for them. There is also evidence that an established MP, because of the media attention he may attract and the constituency services he may provide, is able to build up a personal vote – i.e. support for himself as an individual rather than as a representative of his party.

In recent years, and particularly in the United States, election campaigning has been transformed by new technology. Candidates make increased used of opinion polls, television advertising, and direct mail appeals to special groups of voters. This has been accompanied by the rise of public relations firms and consultants who specialize in election campaigns and who are more interested in 'marketing' candidates than in parties. The activities of these firms and public reliance on television and opinion polls have led to the bypassing of political parties in contacting voters, and prompted concern about their decline as electioneering bodies.   DK

Reading

Agranoff, R.: *The New Style in Election Campaigns.* 2nd edn. Boston, Mass.: Holbrook, 1976.

Butler, D., Penniman, H. and Ranney, A. eds: *Democracy at the Polls.* Washington, DC: American Enterprise Institute, 1981.

Crewe, I. and Harrop, M.: *Political Communications: the general election campaign of 1983.* Cambridge: Cambridge University Press, 1986.

Penniman, H. ed.: *At the Polls: a series of election studies.* Washington, DC: American Enterprise Institute, 1975– .

Sabato, L.J.: *The Rise of Political Consultants.* New York: Basic Books, 1981.

election programme The review of policy published by political parties one to two months before an election. In the case of

American, British and British-influenced parties this takes the form of a booklet of between thirty and eighty printed pages called in North America the PLATFORM and in Britain the 'manifesto' of the party. In continental Europe it is often termed the 'action programme'. Its presentation at a press conference marks the beginning of the actual ELECTION CAMPAIGN, which takes up themes and issues from the programme. It is not much read by the public but strongly influences media comment.

In Britain selected extracts are reproduced in candidates' electoral addresses and distributed directly to constituency residents. The British manifesto in fact originated in the election addresses of party leaders within their own parliamentary constituencies (compare the 'Tamworth Manifesto' of Sir Robert Peel in 1834). The coincidence of national manifesto and leader's electoral address survived in the Liberal and Conservative parties until 1950, but its preparation is now highly professionalized. In the Conservative Party it is based on previously prepared specialized policy documents produced by the research department, drafted by a party committee and approved by the leader. This is in fact the way in which electoral programmes are generally composed in western and westernized democracies by parties of similar structure and ideology to the Conservatives. In the United States party platforms will also be drafted in this way where there is an unchallengeable contender for the presidential candidacy. Party participation in the drafting of the programme will be more widespread where no dominant candidate exists. It is invariably greater in continental European socialist and communist parties and all parties of northwest Europe. The Labour Party manifesto in Britain is supposed to be jointly written by the National Executive Committee (NEC) and the parliamentary leadership. Growing disagreement, beginning in the 1970s, saw attempts by the NEC to establish control over manifesto contents. These were evaded by the party leader delaying composition to the last possible moment and putting in his own ideas. The Liberal Party, in recent years, and the Social Democratic Party (SDP), have opened the writing process to widespread participation through specialized committees of members, following the example of the continental European socialist and communist parties and of Dutch and Scandinavian parties. Attempts by the Conference to control the writing of the British Labour party manifesto illustrate one view of the manifesto's role: a means of establishing membership control over party leaders and so enforcing intra-party democracy.

Another popular view of the role of the manifesto is that it presents to the electorate a comprehensive programme which the party will pursue if elected to government, allowing electors to make an informed choice between competing programmes, and giving the party elected a 'mandate' to carry through its manifesto programme once in government. In fact it is not clear whether electors do choose between parties on the basis of their programmes even as these are indirectly reflected through the media; or how far parties put their full programme into the manifesto or carry it out. A comparison of post-war Britain and Canada showed that in both cases approximately 72 per cent of specific pledges in the election programme were fulfilled (Rallings, ch. 1 in Budge et al. 1987). Pledges were not made, however, in areas of central importance such as employment policy. It may be, in spite of increasing length and growing numbers of specific pledges, that policy is more truly reflected in the emphases of the programme – for example the amount of space Labour gives to social welfare, or Conservatives to law and order – than in actual promises. Given the unforeseen contingencies that may overtake a party in government, election programmes have normally been composed with more of an eye to election strategy than to long-term policy plans. They therefore try to give prominence to the party's more appealing policy concerns and play down those which are less popular, rather than giving a balanced presentation of their plans.

See also MANDATE THEORY; MASS MEDIA.

IB

Reading
Budge, I., Robertson, D.R. and Hearl, D.: *Ideology,*

Strategy and Party Movement: a spatial analysis of party election programmes in nineteen democracies. London: Cambridge University Press, 1987.

Craig, F.W.S.: *British General Election Manifestos, 1918–1966.* London: Parliamentary Reference Publications, 1975.

Kavanagh, D.: The politics of manifestos. *Parliamentary Affairs* 34 (1981) 7–27.

elections If we exclude special uses of the term in law and in theology elections are easy to define. The term comes from the Latin verb *eligere*, to pick out. It is a form of procedure with recognized rules where all or some of a population choose a few people or one person to hold office. It should be distinguished from alternative methods of selection by appointment or by lot. This choice of leaders, or delegates, or REPRESENTATIVES is found in some form in almost every society, although the system of voting, the extent of the FRANCHISE and the fairness of the process vary widely. In the twentieth century even totalitarian regimes have thought it expedient to seek legitimacy through some form of election, though they offer voters no real choice. Probably not more than around one-third of the approximately 160 nations in the contemporary world hold genuinely competitive elections.

Free elections are the major precondition of democratic government, but they are of relatively recent origin. It is true that in ancient Athens and Rome the election of officials was systematized but the franchise was very limited and voting was, for the most part, open. Conceptually, however, the notion of election is earlier than that of representation. In the middle ages forms of election were developed to select popes and Holy Roman Emperors, and substantial elements of popular choice were manifest in Scandinavian *Things* or conclaves and in the English Parliament.

Except for antiquarian purposes, the history of elections is effectively a couple of centuries old. Since the eighteenth century governments have increasingly sought the legitimacy of broad popular endorsement and citizens have sought a say in the choice of government.

An organized election requires a precise definition of who should be entitled to vote. Many of the early battles in the establishment of DEMOCRACY were over the extension of the franchise. In Britain until 1832 there were no consistent rules but voting was limited to men over 21 who were owners of a certain amount of property or land – though some of these could vote in more than one place. The Great Reform Act standardized the qualification but until 1867 only householders were able to vote. By 1885 almost all men were theoretically qualified but until 1918 only about 60 per cent appeared on the electoral register. In 1918 women over 30 were given the vote and in 1928 this was extended to women over 21 and the electoral register became almost coterminous with the adult population. In 1950 all plural voting was abolished and in 1969 the age of voting was lowered to 18.

In other countries the move to full male suffrage came sometimes by similar stages, sometimes more abruptly. Extension of the suffrage was in general associated with the development of individualism and the view that the vote was a right and not a privilege. In 1893 New Zealand became the first country to authorize female suffrage for national elections, and by 1920 most democracies had given women the vote although France waited until 1945 and Switzerland until 1971 for equal suffrage.

The granting of a universal right to vote does not guarantee its full exercise. In the US only 53 per cent of adult citizens voted in the 1984 Presidential election, and only 73 per cent of the registered electorate cast their ballots in the 1983 British election. Even in Australia, with compulsory voting and a very efficient REGISTRATION system, the TURNOUT in recent elections has been at most 96 per cent. People may be ill or away from home or they may deliberately or inadvertently choose not to vote; but also they may not be on the electoral register.

An accurate list of qualified voters is an almost necessary prerequisite of a fair election (although it is possible to have a system – as Britain did until 1832 – where voters prove their qualifications on arrival at the polling booth). In most democracies local or other authorities are responsible for compiling and maintaining a register of qualified electors and in most advanced democracies this is usually relatively full and accurate (although government studies in Britain showed the error rate rising from 3 per cent in 1951 to 7 per cent in 1981). The United States is the only major democracy in which, except in four states, the individual elector is not automatically registered, but must take the initiative himself. Thus registration depends on voluntary activity and party zeal.

Although many private organizations practise open voting the secret BALLOT (or the Australian ballot as it used often to be called) has become universally accepted in public elections. First used in South Australia in 1856 it spread to almost all democracies within half a century and it has been a major factor in the development of free elections since. If the vote really is secret there can be no guarantee that voters who are bought or intimidated will record the desired choice.

One element in secret voting is the need for a ballot paper (or a simulacrum of one if voting machines are used). This involves the advance nomination of candidates together with, in most countries, their party designations. It also requires reliable arrangements for competent presiding officials, as well as party observers, to guarantee against fraud or intimidation at the polling station and at the counting of the votes. Procedures for voting and for counting vary widely but, although there have been disputed cases in every country, the technical requirements of fair and secret voting are now achieved in most advanced democracies. Despite this, however, the provision of safeguards against corrupt and unfair practices in the conduct of elections has raised and continues to raise major problems.

In the majority of democracies there are no fixed dates for elections though parliaments often last for their full three-, four- or five-year term. In the USA elections always take place on the Tuesday after 1 November every second year; some other countries have an immutable timetable, especially for presidential contests. Norway and Switzerland are the only democracies in Europe to have fixed-term parliaments with no provision for early dissolution; but several other states such as Portugal and Sweden have very limited facility for early dissolution.

If the government of the day can choose the date, it starts with a distinct tactical bonus. It may exploit favourable economic trends (or even manufacture them) or take advantage of a favourable turn of events – an opposition embarrassment or a patriotic national occasion – to maximize its own support.

Flexible election dates tend to produce shorter campaigns. In the United States state-regulated PRIMARY elections start eight months before the November contest and informal preliminaries begin long before that. But in most countries formal campaigning seldom begins before the announcement of the actual date of the poll – and that, usually, is announced only a month or so in advance. Too long a campaign can exhaust participants and voters alike; too short a campaign can deny the opposition a fair chance to make its case. Malaysia with 13 days between dissolution and election has one of the shortest of elections. In most democracies the period lies between 14 and 35 days.

Basic to any election is the system by which votes are turned into seats; while in any electoral system, but particularly in ones with single member constituencies, the drawing of boundaries is of great importance (see CONSTITUENCY; ELECTORAL SYSTEMS; REDISTRIBUTION).

But healthy elections depend on far more than a just and efficient administrative framework. For truth to win in a fair market, the arguments must be deployed on reasonably equal terms. The state has often to intervene to ensure that money or other influences do not distort the outcome too seriously.

Most states now impose some restraints on the amount of money that a candidate or a party may spend and on the ways in which it may be spent. The British Corrupt Practices Act of 1883 was notably successful in three ways. It established a law of agency ('no person other than the duly authorised agent of the candidate may incur expenditure with a view to the promotion of the candidature'); it banned certain forms of election expenditure such as treating voters to drinks and hiring bands; and it set ceilings to the amount a candidate could spend. These restrictions purified British elections in a very few years and have enabled the real cost of a serious parliamentary contest to be notably reduced.

However, such a law of agency falls foul of the First Amendment to the United States Constitution with its guarantee of freedom of speech. It is not possible to prevent the friends of candidates, or a POLITICAL ACTION COMMITTEE that supports their views, from spending money to help them. Therefore attempts to limit American campaign expenditure have largely failed. With television as the prime means of electioneering, the costs of a contest have soared and, increasingly, American politics has become a battleground for very rich candidates – or for candidates with access to large financial support.

In many countries the rising cost of elections has led to a clamour for state funding, and since the 1970s, the United States and most West European countries (though not Britain where there are, however, substantial subsidies in kind to parties and candidates) have provided subsidies for political parties, for candidates or for both.

In most democracies, the broadcasting of paid political advertisements is not allowed. Party coverage in television and radio news bulletins, as well as access to the airwaves to deliver party messages or to take part in interviews or debates, is regulated with differing levels of equity as between government and opposition and as between major and minor parties. Broadcasting is certainly now more important than the press as a campaign influence. The partisanship of the press and the extent to which all parties can get their case across to a mass public through daily print varies greatly. Newspapers with monopoly areas in the United States usually give more balanced coverage than is available in the British popular press. In 1983 it was observed that the only mass circulation paper, the *Daily Mirror*, which advocated a Labour vote, was critical of most of the party's policies.

Elections may satisfy all the formal conditions of secrecy, real choices and fairness and yet be subject to criticism. The chances of mood on a particular day or even of the weather, can decide who shall govern a nation for five years. The popular judgement on a multitude of complex and unforeseeable issues is reduced to a simple choice between individuals or groups of individuals. The voters' knowledge of the problems and personalities at stake is necessarily very limited. Yet, for want of a better alternative, general elections are accepted as the keystone of democracy. The style of debate echoes a jury trial in which a supposedly openminded electorate is asked to give a verdict on which party it wishes to form a government. But in fact, as voting studies have shown, many electors are not open to argument; in the past at least, they tended to support their habitual party on the basis of class or religion or family loyalty. The minority of swinging voters who decide the destiny of a nation are not necessarily the most sophisticated or rational assessors of the rival programmes.

However in most countries there has been some tendency towards an increase in ELECTORAL VOLATILITY with more voters switching sides in response to arguments or events; and some analysts of elections have commented upon greater voter rationality. It is arguable that, in a rather mystic, collective way, a majority of the sharp voting changes manifest in western democracies in recent years have been in the interest of the country concerned. Fear of the next election constantly influences the policy of governments, sometimes frightening them away from desirable but unpopular action, but at least as often deterring them from corrupt or arbitrary courses. Elections force the contenders for power to go through the motions of defending their past record and future promises, presenting themselves as plausible guardians of the public interest. The election outcome may be distorted by old style demagoguery or by new and expensive hucksters, applying the skills of commercial advertising and public relations. But ultimately the issue must be settled in adversarial conflict between well-known public figures, who are restrained in their campaign stances by party tradition, by pressures to present a consistent long-term image, and by an awareness that gimmicks can be counterproductive.

Elections have only become the object of

extensive academic study in the last two generations and since 1951 the word PSEPH-OLOGY has come into fashion to describe this activity. Lazarsfeld's *The People's Choice*, a local study of voting behaviour in the 1940 presidential election, was a pioneer work; in later years the University of Michigan has become a central force, with *The American Voter* 1960, unquestionably the leading work in the field, being copied in many other countries. In Britain the Nuffield College series of studies of individual general elections as political events have since 1945 set a widely followed example. The arrival of the sample survey and the availability of public opinion poll data have transformed thinking about elections. They have also provided a tool widely used by party strategists and by the new profession of campaign consultant to determine the most effective approaches to the electorate.

The focus of academic study and popular interest has been on national elections, contests for control of the central levers of government. But in every democracy there are several levels of democracy. Parish councils, county councils, state or regional assemblies (and the European Parliament), are normally subject to regular election, usually under much the same procedures as are used nationally. But the efforts put into these contests and the public attention given to them are usually comparatively small – and the votes often reflect judgements on the conduct of the national parties and their leaders and not on the performance of the local candidates. It is for this reason that they have been called 'second-order elections' (Reif). However in the United States where parties are less ideological and distances are greater than in Europe, mayoral and other contests can easily turn on personalities and local issues.

But, whatever may decide elections, the question remains, what do elections decide? There are some grounds for scepticism about their actual impact. Democracy only works when there is a fairly broad consensus about most of the national goals. Therefore, when elections lead to a change in the composition of governments the change seems often to be of men rather than of measures. The effect is usually to bring in new faces and energies rather than new directions. Elections are treated as historical landmarks but remarkably few of the really key events in most national histories are associated with a switch at the ballot box. Elections decide less than most people suppose. Yet they give life and flexibility to the political system. There are grounds for anxiety about the electoral process but not for despair. We can give two cheers for democracy.

See also MASS MEDIA; POLITICAL CORRUPTION; POLITICAL FINANCE; POLITICAL RECRUITMENT; WOMEN'S SUFFRAGE.

DEB

Reading

Akzin, B.: Election and appointment. *American Political Science Review* 54 (1960) 705–713.

Butler, D.E.: *The Electoral System in Britain since 1918*. Oxford: Oxford University Press, 1963.

Butler, D.E., Penniman, H.R. and Ranney, A. eds: *Democracy at the Polls*. Washington, DC: American Enterprise Institute, 1981.

Campbell, A., Converse, P.E., Miller, W.E. and Stokes, D.E.: *The American Voter*. New York and London: Wiley, 1960.

Lazarsfeld, P.F., Berelson, B. and Gaudet, H.: *The People's Choice: how the voter makes up his mind in a presidential election*. New York: Duell, Sloan, Pearce, 1944.

Mackenzie, W.J.M.: *Free Elections: an elementary textbook*. London: Allen & Unwin, 1958.

Mackie, T. and Rose, R.: *The International Almanac of Election History*. 2nd edn. London: Macmillan, 1982.

Pomper, G.M. and Lederman, S.S.: *Elections in America*. 2nd edn. London: Longman, 1980.

Pulzer, P.G.J.: *Political Representation and Elections in Britain*. 3rd edn. London: Allen & Unwin, 1975.

Reif, K.: National electoral cycles and European elections 1979 and 1984. *Electoral Studies* 3 (1984) 244–255.

Rokkan, S. and Meyriat, J. eds: *National Elections of Western Europe*, Vol. I of *International Guide to Election Statistics*. Paris: Mouton, 1967.

Seymour, C. and Frary, D.P.: *How the World Votes: the story of democratic development in elections*. 2 vols. Springfield, Mass.: Nichols, 1918.

electoral college A body of persons

charged with electing a candidate to some office. The College of Cardinals, for instance, is the body that elects a new pope. Often the members of the electoral college have themselves been elected from a wider electorate. Between 1958 and 1962 the Constitution of the Fifth Republic of France provided that the president of the republic would be elected by a college of 81,764 persons, comprising all the (elected) deputies and senators of the French parliament, and all the (elected) mayors and councillors of the local authorities. In the USA the president is still elected by an electoral college, although the members do not meet together in person. In the presidential elections electors do not vote directly for a particular candidate for the presidency but for a list of 'presidential electors' pledged to their candidate – although in many states the ballot forms do not even specify the names of these electors. The number of electors in each state varies: it is the sum of the number of senators for each state (two for every state) plus the number of representatives for that state (this varies with population). Each elector has one vote in the electoral college of the USA which is the sum of all the electors in all the fifty states and the District of Columbia. The presidential candidate who wins a plurality of the votes in a state captures all the electors of that state as a block. Under a statute of 1934 these state presidential electors then meet together in their respective states to cast their vote for the presidential candidate. Then, on the 6 January following the election (which takes place every four years on the first Tuesday after the first Monday in November) the two Houses of Congress meet in Washington to count and tabulate the votes for and against the rival candidates, which are telephoned to them. The candidate winning an absolute majority of these votes is declared elected.   SEF

Reading

Best, J.: *The Case against Direct Election of the President: a defence of the electoral college*. Ithaca, NY: Cornell University Press, 1975.

Bickel, A.M.: *Reform and Continuity: the electoral college, the convention and the party system*. New York: Harper & Row, 1971.

Longley, L.D. and Braun, A.G.: *The Politics of Electoral College Reform*. New Haven, Conn.: Yale University Press, 1972.

Peirce, N.R.: *The People's President*. New York: Simon & Schuster, 1968.

Sayre, W. and Parris, J.H.: *Voting for President*. Washington, DC: Brookings Institution, 1970.

US Congress: House Committee on the Judiciary. *Electoral College Reform*. Hearings. 91st Congress 1st session. Washington, DC: Government Printing Office, 1969.

————: Senate Committee on the Judiciary. *Electing the President*. Hearings. 91st Congress 1st session. Washington, DC: Government Printing Office, 1969.

————: Senate. *The Electoral College and Direct Election*. Hearings. 95th Congress 1st session. Washington, DC: Government Printing Office, 1977.

Wilmerding, L.: *The Electoral College*. New Brunswick, NJ: Rutgers University Press, 1958.

electoral geography   The study of three linked spatial components of elections – the geography of voting, the geography of representation and the geography of outcomes.

Study of the inputs involves the *geography of voting*. At each election the voter's choice is influenced both by previous POLITICAL SOCIALIZATION and by the current ELECTION CAMPAIGN. Socialization involves political parties and other actors mobilizing segments of the electorate around either or both of identified divisions within society and particular issues. The goal is to produce POLITICAL CLEAVAGES, stable divisions of society that provide core support for parties. Lipset and Rokkan (1967) identified four such cleavages in Europe – subject versus dominant culture, church versus government, primary versus secondary economy, workers versus employers: the United States' experience indicates a fifth – section, or region (Archer and Taylor 1981).

If each party mobilizes its segment of the electorate to the same extent in all places, the geography of voting is no more than the geography of the relevant cleavage(s). However most studies have shown this to be untrue: in many situations each party is much stronger in some places than expected (usually those where the geography of the cleavage

193

already suggested relative strength), and weaker in others, often extensively so, as in England at the 1983 general election (see Johnston 1985). Suggested explanations for these 'deviations' include local processes of inter-personal influence (often termed the neighbourhood effect), local campaigning, local issues, and local candidates. Emphasis has recently been placed on the role of political parties as agents of socialization (see Taylor 1985a; Johnston 1986b, 1986c).

In most ELECTORAL SYSTEMS, election is by place, and the *geography of representation* involves study of the transformation of votes into seats. This almost invariably produces a result that deviates from proportional representation, either because CONSTITUENCY boundaries have been deliberately manipulated to that end (through gerrymandering and/or malapportionment) or because of the spatial configuration of the geography of voting (Gudgin and Taylor 1979); with the latter, the determination of constituency boundaries by neutral agents can have substantial political effects (Johnston and Rossiter 1982).

Governments enact policies, many of which have a differential spatial impact. These produce a *geography of outcomes* that may be related to the inputs and transformations. In the United States, for example, the practice of pork-barrel politics refers to the ways in which representatives and parties direct spending towards particular, spatially-defined, constituencies in the search for votes (Johnston 1980; Rundquist 1980; for British examples see Hoare 1983).

Most studies of electoral geography focus on the geography of liberal democracy, and are therefore restricted in their application (Johnston 1986b). Recent theoretical developments have placed this geography into the context of a holistic social science, and have linked socialization in place with the operations of a global world-economy (see Taylor 1985a).

See also SOCIAL STRUCTURE AND PARTY ALIGNMENTS.   RJJ

Reading

Archer, J.C. and Taylor, P.J.: *Section and Party: a political geography of American presidential elections from Andrew Jackson to Ronald Reagan*. Chichester: Wiley, 1981.

Gudgin, G. and Taylor, P.J.: *Seats, Votes and the Spatial Organization of Elections*. London: Pion, 1979.

Hoare, A.G.: Pork-barrelling in Britain: a review. *Environment and Planning C: Government and Policy* 1 (1983) 413–38.

Johnston, R.J.: *The Geography of Federal Spending in the United States*. Chichester: Wiley, 1980.

————: *The Geography of English Politics: the 1983 general election*. London: Croom Helm, 1985.

————: Individual freedom in the world-economy. In *A World in Crisis? Geographical Perspectives*, pp. 173–95, ed. R.J. Johnston and P.J. Taylor. Oxford: Blackwell, 1986a.

————: The neighbourhood effect revisited. *Environment and Planning D: Society and Space* 4 (1986b) 41–45.

————: A space for place (or a place for space) in British psephology. *Environment and Planning A* 18 (1986c) 599–618.

Johnston, R.J. and Rossiter, D.J.: Constituency building, political representation and electoral bias in urban England. In *Geography and the Urban Environment*, pp. 113–56. Vol. V, ed. D.T. Herbert and R.J. Johnston. Chichester: Wiley, 1982.

Lipset, S.M. and Rokkan, S.: Cleavage structures, party systems, and voter alignments: an introduction. In *Party Systems and Voter Alignments: cross-national perspectives*, pp. 3–64. London: Collier-Macmillan; New York: Free Press, 1967.

Rundquist, B.S.: *Political Benefits*. Lexington, KY: Heath, 1980.

Taylor, P.J.: *Political Geography: world-economy, nation-state and locality*. London: Longman, 1985.

————: The geography of elections. In *Progress in Political Geography*, pp. 243–72, ed. M. Pacione. London: Croom Helm, 1985b.

Taylor, P.J. and Johnston, R.J.: *Geography of Elections*. London: Penguin, 1979.

electoral system A method of allocating offices to candidates and political parties, of translating votes into seats. Political scientists have long been interested in the classification of different systems and the analysis of their political effects.

Electoral systems can be analysed in three dimensions. First, the method of calculating votes or 'electoral formula' (Rae 1971) – the three main methods are plurality, majority and proportional; second, the size of the CONSTITUENCY or 'district magnitude' (see Rae) – constituencies may be single-member, multi-member or national; and third, the extent to which the voter enjoys choice of candidate.

The plurality method is at present used only in Britain and in democracies that have been at one time under British rule. The majority method is currently used only in Australia (see ALTERNATIVE VOTE) and in France (see SECOND BALLOT). These two methods are almost always combined with single-member constituencies. The plurality method offers no choice of candidate unless combined with a DIRECT PRIMARY, while the majority method does provide for choice since it allows each party or bloc to present multiple candidatures without fear of splitting the vote.

The plurality method derives from the medieval idea of representation of communities, and it is profoundly linked to the notion of territorial representation. The single-member constituency originated in the American colonies; it was not introduced into Britain until 1707, and it did not become the predominant basis of representation in Britain until 1885. With the growth of party and the eclipse of the idea of community representation, the plurality method came to be defended as a means of securing stable and effective government since it exaggerated the representation of large parties while systematically under-representing small parties that were not territorially concentrated. The relationship used to be expressed in terms of the CUBE LAW, but political scientists have shown that the working of the plurality method is in fact dependent upon the spatial distribution of support for the various parties (see Gudgin and Taylor); this in turn is dependent upon the POLITICAL CLEAVAGES in society. When the main cleavage is based upon social class the fact that different social groups are residentially segregated and are not randomly distributed will ensure that there is a reasonably predictable and reliable relationship between votes and seats, with voters for the main parties being distributed in specific clusters of constituencies.

Where, however, the basic cleavage is ethnic, religious, territorial or tribal, the plurality method will emphasize concentrations of support, and it will tend to emphasize territorial cleavages at the expense of socio-economic ones. In general, plurality and majority methods will work less successfully in deeply divided or PLURAL SOCIETIES than in homogeneous ones. It was, indeed, in ethnically heterogenous societies that many of the earliest moves towards proportional representation occurred – for instance in Denmark in 1855, the first use of any proportional system for elections to a legislature – for elections to the indirectly elected upper house in an unavailing attempt to conciliate the German minority in Schleswig; and in Finland, with its Swedish minority, which introduced proportional representation in 1906. In general, therefore, it seems that a national culture unified both ideologically and ethnically may be a precondition for the successful working of the plurality and majority methods.

Plurality and majority electoral methods also work less well in multi-party systems, producing results in which there can be an erratic relationship between the votes cast for a particular party and the number of seats which it obtains. The number of seats which a party secures in the legislature will depend not only upon the number of votes it receives, but also upon their spatial distribution, upon where these votes are cast. There is in fact a deep-seated conflict between the notion of territorial representation and the representation of parties. It is this conflict that proportional representation electoral methods attempt to overcome.

The first country to adopt a proportional system of elections for the popular chamber of the legislature was Belgium in 1899, precisely because the development of a three-party system made the future relationship between votes and seats unpredictable. At the time of writing, the majority of the world's democracies (and every European democracy except for Britain and France), employ proportional systems; although since the world's two largest democracies – India and the United States – employ the plurality method, the majority of those living in democratic countries are ruled by governments elected under that method.

Proportional representation is not the name of a single method of election. It is a generic term for a wide variety of methods whose aim is to bring about the representation of voters in proportion with their numbers. The basic idea seems first to have been expressed by Mirabeau in 1789 when he argued that a representative body should be to the people as a map to the country it represents. Different methods of proportional representation aim to give concrete embodiment to this idea in different ways, and the political consequences of these different methods can also be quite dissimilar.

No system of proportional representation achieves perfect proportionality. All offer some bonus, however minimal, to larger parties and discriminate against smaller ones. This occurs through the formulas used for the allocation of seats, with the D'HONDT METHOD favouring larger parties; and through the threshold which a party must surmount if it is to secure representation. Thresholds can be explicit as, for example, in Denmark, the Federal Republic of Germany, Israel, the Netherlands and Sweden, where parties failing to secure a certain percentage of the national vote, varying from 0.67 per cent in the Netherlands to 5 per cent in Germany, cannot participate in the national allocation of seats; or the threshold can in a multi-member constituency system be implicit, the height of the threshold varying inversely with the size of the constituency.

One consequence of the fact that no electoral system achieves perfect proportionality is that parliamentary majorities in most democracies, and not only in those employing the plurality and majority methods, are manufactured majorities, i.e. the majority in the legislature does not reflect a majority among the electorate. This qualifies the extent to which the principle of MAJORITY RULE is exemplified in representative democracies.

Proportional methods can be divided into two main types: party list methods and the single transferable vote (STV). List methods can in turn be subdivided into a number of different types depending upon the degree of choice of candidate which they offer to the voter. The premiss behind party list methods of proportional representation is that representation of opinion is secured through parties so

that an effective method of election should secure the proportional representation of parties. In some countries, such as Germany and Israel, the corollary is held to be that it is for the party rather than the elector to decide which candidates should carry the party banner in the legislature, and the elector is offered no choice of candidate. Most proportional methods, however, do offer some degree of choice, although this can sometimes be of limited practical effect.

Denmark, Finland, Italy, Luxemburg and Switzerland are examples of countries where a wide choice of candidate is offered. In Luxemburg and Switzerland this is achieved through the device of *panachage* (that is allowing electors to vote for candidates from more than one party list) and cumulation (that is allowing a candidate to use two of his votes for the same candidate). These devices tend to benefit minority candidates and parties. Italy employs preferential voting, while in Finland the voter is not presented with an ordered list at all but votes for an individual candidate. Under any party list method, whatever the degree of choice of candidate, every vote cast is a vote for a party list as well as an individual candidate, and so it could, under certain circumstances, be used to help elect a candidate on the list whom the voter might not support, and, indeed, might not approve of.

STV was developed by Thomas HARE and by a Danish mathematician Carl Andrae. It was warmly endorsed by John Stuart MILL, and is, indeed, a product of mid-Victorian liberalism whose basic thesis is that representation is of individuals not of communities or political parties, and that consequently the voter should be given the widest choice possible, not only between political parties but between individual candidates.

STV is a preferential method of voting in multi-member constituencies without ordered lists. A voter's first preference is transferred if it cannot be used to help elect the candidate of his first choice either because this candidate has no chance of election, or because the candidate has more votes than are needed to secure election. The number of votes necessary to secure election is calculated by means of the DROOP QUOTA. Under STV, the vote may be seen as taking the form of an instruction to the returning officer, directing him to transfer his vote in accordance with the voter's preference so that it can be of maximum use in helping to elect a candidate. Unlike party list methods, STV is a 'party-free' method of proportional representation; a vote cast under STV cannot be used to help elect a candidate whom the voter does not endorse, since it cannot be transferred unless the voter so directs. Moreover, because it allows the voter full freedom to express his or her preferences, STV combines a direct primary with a general election. (For a description of the working of STV see Bogdanor 1984.)

Whereas party list methods have been used only very rarely in Commonwealth countries where the notion of territorial representation still exerts a powerful influence, STV, apart from a brief experiment in Denmark from 1855, has been used only in Britain and in countries that are or have been part of the Commonwealth. The only countries in which it has been used for national elections are the Irish Republic and Malta, but it is used to elect the Australian Senate, and since 1973 it has been used for all elections other than parliamentary in Northern Ireland.

STV has never been employed as the main electoral method in a large-scale industrial society, and this makes it difficult to generalize about its effects. The countries that have used it have generally done so within the framework of a localist and face-to-face civic culture, and political scientists tend to agree that in such societies STV encourages intra-party competition, factionalism and social relationships in which CLIENTELISM and PATRONAGE play an important role. Further, STV has been shown to be less proportional in terms of accuracy of party representation than party list methods, and it can yield anomalous results although it is more proportional than plurality or majority methods.

Electoral systems are capable in theory of affecting many areas of a country's political life, and there is still lively dispute among political scientists as to the precise consequences of different electoral systems. As regards the effects of electoral systems upon POLITICAL RECRUITMENT, however, there is agreement that proportional representation favours higher levels of female representation and representation of ethnic minorities. This is widely thought to be a consequence of the multi-member element present in almost all proportional systems; for this, it is suggested, has the effect of encouraging political parties to present a balanced ticket in which the absence of women or members of ethnic minorities will be noticed, while in a single-member constituency it will be the *presence* of a candidate who deviates from the norm which will be noticed.

In considering the political effects of different electoral systems, political scientists have concentrated upon the connection between a country's electoral system and its party system. Early theories tended to regard the electoral system as a fundamental causative factor in the development of party systems, but few political scientists would accept such a view today. Investigation of the history of electoral systems (see Carstairs; Rokkan) has shown that many democracies altered their electoral systems from the plurality or majority methods to proportional representation to accommodate changes in the party system which had already occurred. Proportional representation, far from necessarily causing a multiplication in the number of parties, was merely a recognition of the fact that there was already a multi-party system in existence. At the same time studies of the development of modern party systems have shown that proportional representation is not necessarily a brake preventing a reduction in the number of parties (see Bogdanor and Butler 1983.) In general political scientists are cautious in asserting causal laws charting the effects of electoral systems. Most would agree with Rokkan's conclusion (1968) that 'It turned out to be simply impossible to formulate any single-variable statements about the political consequences of plurality as opposed to those of PR'.

This does not mean that the electoral system is wholly an expression of social cleavages mediated through the party system. What can be claimed is that proportional representation will reflect social cleavages more faithfully than plurality or majority methods. Plurality and majority methods, by contrast, will tend to refract, stressing some cleavages while suppressing others. It is thus difficult to make any general statements about the contribution which a specific electoral system can make to the stability of the political system without knowing something about the nature and intensity of the cleavages in a given society. Electoral systems will probably exert most effect in periods of major social change when the party system is in process of formation or dissolution; or when the polity is being reconstructed as with Germany in 1949 and France in 1958. At other times, to the extent that the freezing hypothesis holds, electoral systems will be less important than patterns of electoral behaviour in determining the configuration of parties. In general, perhaps the most judicious summing up of the consequences of electoral systems is that offered by Rae who argues that, although these consequences may be marginal, the electoral system is not 'inconsequential to the electoral process . . . the systematic repetition of marginal effects is a potentially important political force'. The interactions between electoral systems, party systems and the process of social change are, therefore, reciprocal and highly complex, and not such as can be summed up in scientific laws of any degree of generality.

See also ADDITIONAL MEMBER SYSTEM; APPARENTEMENT; APPROVAL VOTING; BLOCK VOTE; COMMUNAL REPRESENTATION; CUMULATIVE VOTE; ELECTIONS; FACTION; FRANCHISE; LIMITED VOTE; PARTY SYSTEMS, TYPES OF; SOCIAL STRUCTURE AND PARTY ALIGNMENTS; SUCCESSIVE VOTING. VBB

Reading

Bogdanor, V.: *What is Proportional Representation?* Oxford: Robertson, 1984.

———— and Butler, D.E. eds: *Democracy and Elections: electoral systems and their political consequences.* Cambridge: Cambridge University Press, 1983.

Carstairs, A.M.: *A Short History of Electoral Systems in Western Europe.* London: Allen & Unwin, 1980.

Gudgin, G. and Taylor, P.J.: *Seats, Votes and the Spatial Organization of Elections.* London: Pion, 1979.

Nohlen, D.: *Wahlsysteme der Welt: ein Handbuch.* Munich: Piper, 1978.

Rae, D.W.: *The Political Consequences of Electoral Laws,* rev. edn. New Haven: Yale University Press, 1971.

Rokkan, S.: Electoral systems. In *International Encyclopedia of the Social Sciences,* Vol. V, pp. 6–21, ed. D. Sills. New York: Macmillan, 1968; revised as ch. 4 of *Citizens, Elections, Parties.* Oslo: Universitetsforlaget, 1970.

Steed, M.: The constituency. In *Representatives of the People? Parliamentarians and Constituents in Western Democracies,* ed. V. Bogdanor. Aldershot: Gower, 1985.

————: *Thoughts on Classifying, Defining and Measuring Electoral Systems.* Paper prepared for ECPR Joint Session, 1984.

electoral volatility This term is a borrowing from chemistry where it refers to the readiness of a substance to change from one state to another, for example liquid to gas. Applied to electoral behaviour it refers to the switching of votes between elections, either from one party to another or from voting to non-voting and vice versa. It has both an individual level and an aggregate level reference; that is, it can refer either to the vote-switching of an individual elector or to that of the electorate as a body. The two are related but not necessarily the same. For example, a large but equal number of voters changing between two parties would not show up as an overall change: even though much gross change would have occurred there would be no net effects, and in terms of election results the party's overall vote would have remained the same. The term volatility is employed more in the sense of the aggregate electorate rather than individual electors, where the term 'vote-switching' is preferred. It is therefore defined (always at the aggregate level) as 'the net change within the electoral party system resulting from individual vote transfers' (Pedersen 1979). Operationally this leads to a measure of volatility formed by calculating the percentage change in each party's vote-share compared with the preceding election, and dividing by two.

Although the mechanics are clear-cut there are certain ambiguities about this definition and measure: should it include only parties which are significant in some sense, or all parties, or some combination of 'fringe' and 'significant' parties? Are some percentage changes (for example an increase in votes of a small party) more significant than others (Crewe and Denver 1985, pp. 9–10). A further distinction neglected by this definition is that between the normal fluctuation in aggregate votes between election and election, and more enduring changes that occur in a party's long-term support. The latter have been measured through net changes in the PARTY IDENTIFICATION of the electorate or through changes in the level of the parties' *basic votes*, that is the votes they would get in the absence of favourable and unfavourable issues in an election (Budge and Farlie 1982, pp. 74–83, 121–8).

Whatever the detailed measurement of volatility there is general agreement that electoral volatility has increased substantially in Britain during the post-war period, and that it has been clearly manifested in Denmark, Belgium and the Netherlands; Australia, Canada, Norway and Sweden appear among the less volatile and more stable systems. Presidential elections in the United States produce sharp switches in party vote from one election to another but under the impact of short-term forces (candidates and issues) rather than as a result of long-term shifts in the strength of Democrats versus Republicans. It has been calculated that twenty-two out of forty-four major parties or tendencies in twenty-three democracies have undergone basic change at different points in the post-war period (Budge and Farlie 1982, p. 129).

Electoral volatility is closely associated, both as a cause and a consequence, with changes in the number of parties and the entry of new parties into electoral politics. Increasing volatility can also be traced back to the many social changes that have taken place since the second world war, and possibly to the shift from 'materialist' to 'post-materialist' values (Inglehart, 1977) and the rise of the 'New Politics', with its greater emphasis on individual liberty and protection of the environment, which cross-cuts the appeals of the older parties.

See also POSTMATERIALISM; SOCIAL STRUCTURE AND PARTY ALIGNMENTS; SWING.

IB

Reading

Budge, I. and Farlie, D.J.: *Explaining and Predicting Elections: issue effects and party strategies in twenty-three democracies*. London: Allen & Unwin, 1982.

Crewe, I. and Denver, D. eds: *Electoral Change in Western Democracies: patterns and sources of electoral volatility*. London: Croom Helm, 1985.

Inglehart, R.: *The Silent Revolution: changing values and political styles among western publics*. Princeton, NJ: Princeton University Press, 1977.

Pedersen, M.N.: The dynamics of European party systems: changing patterns of electoral volatility. *European Journal of Political Research* 7 (1979) 1–27.

elites, doctrine of   The concept of elites is sometimes thought to be weak merely because no single tight definition covers the relevant phenomena of political life in institutions, in the state, or in society. It may be, however, that this very lack of apparent rigour is an advantage. The word elite means 'the pick of the crop', referring to the best grapes for a vintage, in other words, the chosen. From Plato to the Abbé de Saint-Pierre two overlapping but ultimately conflicting concepts are at work. One is that of the ideal legislator – say Lycurgus – who establishes a correct order in and for polity. (The Founding Fathers of the American Constitution as interpreted by strict contructionists provide an instance of the fact that the legislator does not have to be a single individual.) Alternatively the polity may be deemed to need a firm, controlling hand on its day-to-day conduct. In a word the polity may require a constant effort of what was once termed cybernetic social maintenance and this can only be conducted by a team or elite gifted with one or more of the following: virtue, practical wisdom, brute courage, flexibility, and opportunism. The guardians of PLATO, the new Samurai of H. G. Wells or the skilled higher administration desired by Sidney and Beatrice WEBB are examples of this kind of thinking.

It was Vilfredo PARETO (1848–1923) who most clearly attempted to examine elites, in terms not of the rational perfection of conduct, but of what actually goes on in societies, (*Trattato de sociologica generale*, 1916). To Pareto every identifiable grouping within society produces an elite, though the fact may often be of little importance. There is an elite of chess players, for example, but its membership is basically of interest only to chess buffs. The serious elites, according to Pareto, are political and in the twentieth century are most likely to be, though are not uniquely, parliamentary. Pareto profoundly believed that in modern societies the political order, though part of the social structure, stands apart from it in that, at least in the short run, a political order is always agent not patient. The number of possible situations or offices within the political order has to be limited, otherwise the result will be ochlocracy or mere anarchy. Who says politics says not merely influence but also power. (This does not mean that Pareto was not well aware of the capacity of the economic order to generate influence and power, but that when power was generated it usually did, and, in principle always could, operate apart from its economic base.) At this point Pareto is either realistic or muddled: his elite is not the RULING CLASS, but it is the dominant group with the wheels of authority at its disposal. He extends the idea of the elite, however, beyond merely those who are members of it exercising power at any one moment. The elite, he says, consists of those who have, who have had, or who will have power; all those, that is, at any one moment from whom the powerful have been recruited. Clearly this includes families, financial connections, descent groups, and so on. Once this is said the elite cannot be distinguished from the ruling class in the sense in which this phrase was used by Pareto's younger contemporary Gaetano MOSCA (*Elementi de scienza politica*, 1896). But the ruling class in this thought world is not a socio-economic class in the Marxist sense, or even something to be equated with a feudal Estate: we are, as Roberto MICHELS argued in his *Sociologica del partito politico nella democrazia moderna*, very far from the world of Max WEBER. The difference is that while Weber and Michels agreed that if mass democratic parties are to function they must be bureaucratic, Michels also argued that they must be oligarchic (see OLIGARCHY).

Pareto distinguishes two kinds of elite. In one the predominating sentiment (or *residue*) is

essentially conservative – dedicated to the maintenance not only of its own power but also of existing institutional arrangements; on the other hand there are elites that emerge and use their power to make new social and political combinations in their society. This second kind of innovatory and sometimes revolutionary elite will of course in due time be caught up in the continuing administration of power and will therefore become conservative with regard to the very social formation which it has initiated. As a result reactionary establishments very often arise out of revolutionary innovations. These elites tend to be particularly brutal and bloody as they consolidate both themselves and their creations. Having become conservative, or even preservative, they might maintain themselves by the prestige of tradition, the exercise of police and bureaucratic power and, of course, by mere chicane. Eventually, Pareto believed, society being an endless flux within a basically tideless sea, a disjunction would arise between the authority and competence of such an elite and the actual pressures of changing structure and political culture. The opportunity would thereby be created for the cycle to continue and an innovatory elite would establish itself by osmosis, successful mass politics, violence, or some combination of these.

The idea of an elite is simple but not operationally easy to define. (Attempts to do so even statistically have been made since the work of Mme Kolabinska in 1912, but they have not been particularly successful.) These simple ideas are however extremely useful. The history of practically every country outside the narrow frontiers of the western democracies in the twentieth century has been a confirmation of the utility of these basic rules and principles of transformation. Nor can it be denied, though its assertion approaches mere truism, that the Paretian ebb and flow is to be found in democratic party states. Generations of students of political parties, from the time of OSTROGORSKI at the beginning of the century until today, have hoped to escape from this ebb and flow. Theorists of the elite would say that all such efforts are vain for they either belong to the hopes of Utopia or to the legitimation of brutal power – and brutal power brings its own, however delayed, nemesis.

See also ELITES/ELITISM.   DGM

Reading

Aron, R.: Classe sociale, classe politique, classe dirigeante. *European Journal of Sociology* 1 (1960) 1–2, 260–81.

Burnham, J.: *The Machiavellians*. London: Putnam, 1943.

Finer, S.E.: *The Man on Horseback*. 2nd edn. Harmondsworth: Penguin, 1976.

——— ed.: *Pareto: Sociological Writings*. London: Pall Mall, 1966.

Guttsman, W.: *The British Political Elite*. London: MacGibbon & Kee, 1963.

Kolabinska, Mme: *La Circulation des élites*. Paris, 1912.

MacRae, D.G.: Foundations for the sociology of politics. *Political Quarterly* 37 (1966) 324–32.

Mosca, G.: *The Ruling Class* (1896), trans. and ed. H.D. Kahn and A. Livingston. New York: McGraw-Hill, 1939.

Pareto, V.: *Trattato di sociologia generale* (1916). 2 vols. Trans. and ed. A. Livingston and A. Bongioro as *The Mind and Society*. 4 vols. London: Cape; New York: Harcourt Brace, 1935.

elites/elitism

(1) *Elites* The term was given its wide currency in the social sciences by PARETO (1848–1923), who began by formulating a very general conception according to which the elite was composed of all those having the highest ability in every branch of human activity, and then concentrated his attention on what he called the 'governing elite' as contrasted with the non-elite or lower stratum of society (see Pareto 1916). Somewhat earlier Pareto's compatriot MOSCA (1896) had made a similar distinction, arguing that in all societies 'two classes of people appear – a class that rules and a class that is ruled'. These original elite doctrines were clearly directed against SOCIALISM – especially Marxist socialism (see MARXISM), – and to some extent against ideas of DEMOCRACY (Bottomore 1964), and in this respect they had an important influence on the thought of Max WEBER and MICHELS (Beetham 1981; Mommsen 1981).

One of the major issues that they raised concerns the relation between elites and social classes, with particular reference to the Marxist concept of a ruling class, and there has been much controversy on this subject. Aron (1950) attempted a synthesis of 'class' sociology and 'elite' sociology through a careful analysis of 'the relation between social differentiation and political hierarchy in modern societies', and later suggested a more discriminating terminology in studying both classes and elites (Aron 1960). On the other hand, Mills (1956) proposed to substitute the concept of a 'power elite' (comprising the heads of business corporations, political leaders and military chiefs) for that of a ruling class, which he considered a 'badly loaded phrase' containing the assumption that an economic class rules politically. Marxists, for their part, have generally dismissed elite theories as being essentially ideological attempts to justify class domination.

The elite theories, with their emphasis upon leadership, also have implications for conceptions of democracy, as is particularly evident in the writings of Weber and Michels, who not only dismiss the idea of effective government by the people as utopian, but also implicitly discourage the idea that democratic participation can be gradually extended or improved at all. From a different standpoint however Mannheim (1956) has emphasized the 'democratization of culture' and the emergence of 'democratic elites' which result from selection by merit and a reduction of the distance between elites and masses.

Since the 1950s studies of elites by political scientists, sociologists and historians have multiplied. The elite groups which have received particular attention are political leaders, including 'revolutionary elites' (Lasswell and Lerner 1965), the heads of business enterprises, high-ranking bureaucrats, military chiefs, and intellectuals. Much research, including historical studies, has been undertaken on particular elites or elites in general in individual countries, but there have also been some regional and comparative studies: one important issue has been the prominent role of the military in many developing countries of the third world (Janowitz 1964). Other comparative studies have dealt with the political influence of intellectuals, the power of the bureaucracy (especially in socialist countries), and the recruitment of political leaders. One salient issue in almost all these studies is the relation between elites and classes, and in particular the class origins of elite members. The research has shown generally a high degree of elite self-recruitment – or in class terms, recruitment from the upper and upper-middle classes – though with variations between countries, and significant differences in some socialist countries, especially during the period of transition. An analysis of social mobility in Britain (Heath 1981) also suggests that the degree of self-recruitment of elite groups has changed little between 1949 and 1972, although there has been an important change in their overall composition as a result of the great expansion of their numbers: in 1972 three-quarters of the members of elite groups had come from lower social origins. To a limited extent, therefore, it may be permissible to speak of the development of more 'democratic' elites in Britain and in other industrial countries; 'democratization' in Mannheim's second sense however, as a reduced distance between elites and masses, seems doubtful (in some socialist as well as capitalist countries), though little research has been devoted to this aspect. Moreover it may still be argued, as do Marxists of various persuasions, that the character of the recruitment of elites makes relatively little difference to the situation of domination by a ruling group, so long as the ownership or effective possession of major economic resources is concentrated in the hands of a small minority, whether this is a capitalist class or a 'new class' of bureaucrats or intellectuals.

(2) *Elitism* As distinct from elites this term refers not so much to specific social groups as to social, political and cultural attitudes. The term came into vogue in the 1960s and was widely used in the radical movements of that time, especially the student movement, to contest diverse forms of authority and domination which were conceived largely in terms of elites rather than classes (Jacobs and Landau 1966). The student movement, in particular, opposed to elitism the idea of 'participatory democracy', emphasizing the fundamental equality of human beings; but in some spheres this anti-elitism verged upon a rejection of all distinctions of intellectual or cultural quality and achievement. The term elitism is now less frequently used and radical criticism has largely reverted to a concern with the differences between specific social groups, in studies of class, gender and ethnic inequalities and oppression.

See also ELITES, DOCTRINE OF. TBB

Reading

Aron, R.: Social structure and the ruling class. *British Journal of Sociology* 1 (1950) 1–16, 126–43.

———: Classe sociale, classe politique, classe dirigeante. *European Journal of Sociology* 1 (1960) 1–2, 260–81.

Beetham, D.: Michels and his critics. *European Journal of Sociology* 22 (1981) 81–99.

Bottomore, T.B.: *Elites and Society*. Harmondsworth: Penguin, 1966.

Heath, A.: *Social Mobility*. London: Fontana, 1981.

Jacobs, P. and Landau, S. eds: *The New Radicals: a report with documents*. New York: Random House, 1966.

Lasswell, H.D. and Lerner, D.: *World Revolutionary Elites*. Cambridge, Mass.: MIT Press, 1965.

Mannheim, K.: *Essays on the Sociology of Culture*. London: Routledge & Kegan Paul, 1956.

Mills, C.W.: *The Power Elite*. New York: Oxford University Press, 1956.

Mommsen, W.J.: Max Weber and Roberto Michels: an asymmetrical partnership. *European Journal of Sociology* 22 (1981) 100–116.

Mosca, G.: *The Ruling Class* (1896), trans. and ed. H.D. Kahn and A. Livingston. New York: McGraw-Hill, 1939.

Pareto, V.: *Trattato di sociologia generale* (1916). 2 vols. Trans. and ed. A. Livingston and A. Bongioro as *The Mind and Society*. 4 vols. London: Cape; New York: Harcourt Brace, 1935.

emergency powers Democratic systems of government may make provision for the executive to suspend normal legislative powers, and perhaps also certain rights of the citizen, to meet an emergency situation. This emergency power may be explicitly written into the constitution. The Fifth Republic Constitution in France grants the president through Article 16 very wide powers in an emergency but the attempt to regulate them was shown, on the one occasion on which they have been used, in 1961, to be of little value. In the Weimar Republic the misuse of Article 48 allowing the president to govern by decree and suspend certain civil liberties, is held by some to have contributed to the collapse of democracy in Germany.

In the United States, although the Constitution does not explicitly mention emergency powers, Article II, sections 2 and 3, grant the president very broad powers which can be exercised in time of war, rebellion, or in the case of strikes or natural disasters. These powers are, however, subject to review by the Supreme Court.

In Britain, the Crown enjoys some emergency powers under the prerogative, but these are held to be too uncertain to rely upon; and parliament has conferred upon the executive the right to proclaim a state of emergency for one month, with the possibility of renewal, and subject to parliamentary control. There have been eight states of emergency in Britain between 1945 and 1984, mainly to deal with dislocation caused by strikes in essential services. In Northern Ireland, emergency legislation has since 1973 provided, inter alia, for trial by a judge sitting alone without a jury for certain scheduled offences, and for additional arrest and detention powers for the police and army, together with certain exceptional powers of search and seizure.

Although situations may arise in which the executive must act quickly and decisively to protect the state, nevertheless the concept of emergency powers inevitably gives rise to some uneasiness in democratic states since it is so difficult to discover a politically neutral and unbiased criterion for what is to count as an emergency; and difficult also, as the experience of the Fifth Republic has shown, to impose a time limit for the duration of the emergency. Yet, despite the potential for abuse, espousal of emergency powers may well prove the lesser evil if the constitutional order is to be defended against attempts to subvert it.

See MARTIAL LAW. VBB

Reading

Friedrich, C.J.: *Constitutional Reason of State: the survival of the constitutional order*. Providence, Rhode Island: Brown University Press, 1957.

Harrison, M.: The French experience of exceptional powers 1961. *Journal of Politics* 25 (1963) 139–58.

Pickles, W.: Special powers in France: Article 16. *Public Law* (1963).

Rossiter, C.: *Constitutional Dictatorship: crisis government in the modern democracies*. Princeton, NJ: Princeton University Press, 1948.

Smith, S.A. de: *Constitutional and Administrative Law*. 5th edn, ch. 25. Harmondsworth: Penguin, 1985.

empire   A state which governs a number of territories beyond its borders and comprises a diversity of peoples. Empires have existed at every stage of human history since ancient times, and all have had to grapple with the near-insoluble problem of imperial government: how is political control to be maintained over territories whose inhabitants lie in a subordinate relationship to the centre and are, therefore, likely to prove unwilling to accept imperial authority. Modern colonial empires, which developed from the end of the eighteenth century and lasted until the period of rapid decolonization following the second world war, were in general composed of territorially scattered units rather than contiguous territories as with the empires of the ancient world. Despite the growth of industrialism, and improvements in communications and military technology, the problem of governing culturally diverse peoples remained as intractable as it had always been.

Different empires developed their own distinctive theories of imperial rule. The British Empire was by far the largest – in 1933, at its peak, it comprised almost a quarter of the world's population and covered nearly a quarter of the world's land surface. It was also the only empire containing important colonies of settlement. These colonies were given a large degree of self-government, developing their own representative institutions, and, after the Durham Report of 1839, they were ruled according to the principles of responsible government. By contrast, the colonies of the dependent and Indian empires were governed in one of two different ways. Either they were ruled directly from Whitehall, but with extensive devolution of power to a governor assisted by a legislative council – usually non-elected – composed of British officials and local notables; or alternatively, they were governed by methods of INDIRECT RULE whereby the imperial presence was mediated through a local, indigenous ruler loosely supervised by a British resident. This was the pattern, for example, in the Indian princely states, of which there were around 600 in the nineteenth century, and it provided for considerable autonomy in domestic matters while also allowing native peoples to preserve their own identity. This conception of indirect rule was also applied by the Netherlands in its Indonesian Empire. However neither method of government, whether direct rule or indirect, succeeded in laying a firm basis for the development of democratic institutions in dependent territories.

The other modern world-wide empire, the French, was based in theory upon very different principles – those of the French Revolution and the one and indivisible French republic. These principles dictated that overseas colonies were but a geographical extension of France: the French pattern of government was to be applied to them with the objective of fully assimilating colonial peoples to the French prototype. France was the only imperial power to allow representatives of the colonies to sit as members of the imperial legislature, but these representatives were too few in number to be able to exert much influence on policy. The French ideology of empire had no place for the subordination of colonial peoples nor for the autonomy of colonial government. In practice, however, this ideology was honoured more in the breach than in the observance, and the French colonies were governed autocratically by a centralized bureaucracy in Paris mediated through local governors or governors-general and advisory (though not legislative) councils. Portugal, Russia and the United States sought, like France, to incorporate colonial dependencies, but only Russia was at all successful in doing so.

In general, ideologies of imperial government had comparatively little influence upon methods of rule which all tended towards the centralized, the bureaucratic and the paternalist, free from effective control either by local representative institutions or by the imperial legislature. Although the theory of empire in some countries emphasized the preparation of colonial peoples for self-government, nowhere was this carried out sufficiently rapidly, and the speed of decolonization caught every imperial power by surprise. By 1945 Germany, Italy and Japan had lost their empires through defeat in war, and in the next thirty-five years the other European empires all came to an end, undermined by the growth of colonial nationalism and by the liberal and socialist critique of imperialism which condemned it as involving an exploitative relationship between peoples, and as contrary to the principles of national self-determination.

See also COLONIAL GOVERNMENT; COMMONWEALTH; DYARCHY; PROTECTORATE; TRUSTEE SYSTEM/TRUSTEESHIP.   VBB

Reading

Fieldhouse, D.K.: *The Colonial Empires: a comparative survey from the eighteenth century.* 2nd edn. London: Macmillan, 1982.

———: *Colonialism 1879–1945: an introduction.* London: Weidenfeld & Nicolson, 1981.

Koebner, R. and Schmidt, H.D.: *Imperialism, 1840–1960.* Cambridge: Cambridge University Press, 1964.

Mansergh, N.: *The Commonwealth Experience.* London: Weidenfeld & Nicolson, 1969.

employers' organizations The term refers to any organization combining employers to defend their collective interests against government, organizations of employees, or other organized interests such as customers and suppliers. Employers' associations take a variety of forms. The term employers' organization (but sometimes, confusingly, employers' association) refers to an organization which bargains with labour over pay and conditions of employment, and deals with germane industrial relations matters. Trade associations look after the commercial interests of a particular industry or product group. Sometimes both functions are performed by one association, but when there are separate organizations for a particular industry there may be areas of overlap, for example training policy. Chambers of commerce organize all businesses in a particular city or region and are especially important in continental Europe where membership is obligatory for enterprises in countries such as Austria and West Germany. The territorial organization of employer interests continues to be of considerable importance in Italy. There are some organizations which represent employers as individuals, for example the Institute of Directors in Britain, but most associations organize firms which send individuals as representatives to meetings.

At the national level business is represented by 'peak associations'. Sometimes, as with the Confederation of British Industry (CBI), these organize both industry associations and firms; in other cases, they are federations of federations, for example Confindustria in Italy. The Swedish Employers Confederation, SAF, is highly centralized, reflecting a system of centralized wage-bargaining, although that came under challenge in the early 1980s. In some countries there are separate peak associations for employers' organizations and trade associations. In West Germany, for example, trade associations are organized in the Bundesverband der Deutschen Industrie (BDI) and employers' organizations are organized in the Bundesvereinigung der Deutschen Arbeitgeberverbände (BDA). Peak associations are particularly poorly developed in North America. Both the United States and Canada have a number of national associations claiming to speak for business, but none could be described as a comprehensive representative body for employers. In the United States the Business Round Table has acquired prominence as an organization for the largest companies, but it is not a substitute for a peak association bringing together sectoral organizations. Large firms in the United States and Canada are particularly likely to have their own government relations divisions, a practice that has spread to the United Kingdom.

The internationalization of the global economy, and the growing importance of various kinds of supranational organizations, has led to an increasing emphasis on the international organization of employers. There are very few global organizations, but organizations covering the EEC are assuming more importance, particularly at the product or sector level. This trend is particularly marked in the case of industries which tend to operate in terms of a single European market, e.g. chemicals.

Centralized systems of wage-bargaining may decrease in importance, but employers are likely to make increasing use of their associations to defend themselves against regulatory pressures emanating from governments, and particularly the EEC, in such areas as the environment and health and safety.   WPG

Reading

Grant, W. and Marsh, D.: *The CBI*. London: Hodder & Stoughton, 1977.

ILO Labour-Management Relations Series No. 39: *Role of Employers' Organizations in Asian Countries*. Geneva: International Labour Organisation, 1971.

King, R. ed.: *Capital and Politics*. London: Routledge & Kegan Paul, 1983.

Useem, M.: *The Inner Circle: large corporations and the rise of business political activity in the US and UK*. Oxford: Oxford University Press, 1984.

Wilson, G.: *Business and Politics: a comparative introduction*. Basingstoke: Macmillan, 1985.

Windmuller, J.P. and Gladstone, A. eds: *Employers' Associations and Industrial Relations: a comparative study*. Oxford: Oxford University Press, 1984.

entrenchment   The practice often found in written CONSTITUTIONS of trying to protect particular rules or institutions from being amended or abolished by ordinary legislation. Every national constitution provides for a legislative body with power to make new laws, and constitutional logic suggests that the legislature's powers should be limited by the constitution. Techniques of entrenchment include the requirement of a special majority in the legislature, endorsement by popular vote in a REFERENDUM or at a general election, adoption by all or a stated proportion of the states in a federation, and approval by some special body with the sole function of approving constitutional amendments. The extent and manner of entrenchment may be one of the most difficult decisions to be made when a new constitution is being formed. It may be argued, though, that the legislature should have 'constituent' power, that is power to legislate on constitutional matters. Within a federation, or where there are important communal or minority interests, it is essential that the legislature should not have power by ordinary majority vote to override the federal system or rights guaranteed by the constitution.

Most constitutions accordingly include an amendment clause stating the procedure to be followed before the text may be amended. Article 5 of the US Constitution, for example, makes provision that amendments may be proposed by a two-thirds majority vote in both Houses of Congress and must be ratified by three-quarters of the states. Under the Basic Law of the Federal Republic of Germany, an affirmative vote of two-thirds of each house of the legislature is required for the Basic Law to be amended, but no amendment may be made affecting the basic principles on which the Federal Republic is founded.

In British tradition, typified by DICEY's celebrated exposition of the legislative supremacy of parliament, it is often considered that there is no possibility of entrenching any aspect of the constitution since there is no legal rule which cannot be changed by a later Act of Parliament. On this view the one thing that a SOVEREIGN parliament may not do is to bind its successors; it would be impossible for Westminster to entrench a new BILL OF RIGHTS. There seems no reason, however, why the United Kingdom should in perpetuity have to accept that its parliament is sovereign in Dicey's sense. Current developments such as guarantees given for the future status of Northern Ireland, the status of Community law, and proposals for incorporating the EURO-PEAN CONVENTION ON HUMAN RIGHTS into national law may give political impetus to changes in legal theory. Within Scotland it is already argued that certain national institutions (the church and the judicial system) are entrenched by virtue of the Acts of Union passed by the English and Scottish parliaments in 1706, although the precise legal significance of this is unclear.

Entrenchment formerly featured in the legal history of apartheid. During the 1950s a series of cases concerned the 'entrenched clauses' in the South Africa Act 1909 which guaranteed voting rights of non-Europeans in the Cape province. In *Harris* v. *Minister of the Interior* (1952) it was held that these rights could be revoked only by legislation which observed the special requirements contained in the South Africa Act. But a later attempt by the Nationalist government to circumvent the entrenchment was successful when the composition of the Senate was altered by Act of the South African Parliament, enabling the entrenched voting rights to be removed.

See also FEDERALISM. AWB

Reading

Bradley, A.W.: The sovereignty of parliament – in perpetuity? In *The Changing Constitution*, ed. J. Jowell and D. Oliver. Oxford: Clarendon Press, 1985.

Marshall, G.: *Parliamentary Sovereignty and the Commonwealth*. Oxford: Clarendon Press, 1957.

Roberts-Wray, K.: *Commonwealth and Colonial Law*. London: Stevens, 1966.

Wheare, K.C.: *Modern Constitutions*. 2nd edn. London: Oxford University Press, 1966.

equal protection   A concept found in the constitution of certain states although it is interpreted differently in different legal systems. Perhaps the best known example is the equal protection clause to be found in the American Constitution, whose scope has altered with the changing pattern of opinion on the Supreme Court. Since a great number of laws classify people to some extent, they cannot be declared unconstitutional upon that ground alone. An important factor will therefore be the standard of review which the Court brings to bear upon the legislation. It may, for example, simply ask whether the classification is of a type which bears a reasonable or rational relationship to an end of government which is not prohibited by the Constitution. By way of contrast, the Court may employ a strict scrutiny test, and independently determine the degree of relationship which the classification bears to a constitutionally compelling end.

Even where there is no constitutionally

enshrined concept of equal protection there may well be other legal devices which directly or indirectly work towards the same end. Specific legislation may prohibit certain differences of treatment accorded to people on grounds, for example, of race or sex. There may, in addition, be Court developed doctrines such as propriety of purpose which indirectly allow the judiciary to adjudicate upon differences of treatment accorded to those in similar situations.   PPC

Reading

Nowak, J.E., Rotunda, R.D. and Nelson Young, J.: *Constitutional Law.* 3rd edn. St Paul, Minn.: West Publishing, 1986.

Polyviou, P.G.: *The Equal Protection of the Laws.* London: Duckworth, 1980.

Tribe, L.H.: *American Constitutional Law.* New York: Foundation Press, 1978.

estates An early form of FUNCTIONAL REPRESENTATION: the organization of society into groups rigidly defined by law, admission to which was regulated by birth and by other carefully stated criteria. European societies in the Middle Ages and the early modern period were commonly divided into three or four estates (also known as orders): clergy, nobility (or upper and lower nobles – lords and knights – separately), and the burghers of specified towns. In a few areas, such as Sweden and the Tyrol, peasants formed an estate of their own; while in France and, more loosely, England, division was into upper orders, or lords spiritual and temporal, and a 'third estate' comprising (in theory) the whole commonalty. Estates were in essence privileged corporations, and their most important right was that of political representation, either individually or by delegates, at assemblies where they could debate the business of royal government, especially taxation, present their own demands or grievances, and frequently exercise a legislative function. Such continental assemblies, corresponding roughly to the English Parliament, are normally described as diets, and might meet at both regional and national levels. In France the national assembly, known as the ESTATES GENERAL, proved unworkable

and ceased to be summoned between 1614 and 1789, when the deputies of the third estate used it as a platform to initiate radical reforms which soon escalated into the FRENCH REVOLUTION.   RJWE

Reading

Bush, M.: *Noble Privilege.* Manchester: Manchester University Press, 1983.

Koenigsberger, H.G.: *Estates and Revolutions.* Ithaca and London: Cornell University Press, 1971.

Major, J.R.: *Representative Government in Early Modern France.* New Haven, Conn.: Yale University Press, 1980.

Myers, A.R.: *Parliaments and Estates in Europe to 1789.* London: Thames & Hudson, 1975.

estates general The organization of society into rigidly defined groups, defined primarily by law. In a number of countries of western Europe, such as England, France and Spain, society was divided into three orders – clergy, nobility and commoners. Admission to the estates was regulated by birth and by certain other carefully stated criteria. Moreover, estates had considerable political significance since representatives for assemblies in England and France were recruited according to rank.

Estates general in France (the term may be used only from the mid-fifteenth century) was the representative assembly of the three orders, and enjoyed the power, as recognized by custom, to be consulted on succession to the crown, to assist in government when the king was a minor, to advise the king, and to consent to taxes. From the sixteenth century it met only in times of crisis. Its central weakness was that the three orders could not agree amongst themselves. It did not meet after 1614 until 1789 at the beginning of the FRENCH REVOLUTION which was initiated by the deputies of the third estate.   VBB

Reading

Lousse, E.: *La Société d'Ancien Régime: organisation et représentation corporatives.* Louvain: Université de Louvain, 1943.

Major, J.R.: *Representative Government in Early Modern France.* New Haven, Conn.: Yale University Press, 1980.

Rebillon, A.: *Les États de Bretagne*. Paris: Picard, 1932.

ethnic nationalism Properly, an *ideological movement* on behalf of the autonomy, unity and identity of a human population conceived by some of its members as an actual or potential 'nation' – the 'nation' in turn being defined in terms of a myth of ancestry and historic culture. Unlike 'territorial' NATIONALISMS ethnic nationalisms define the unit of the aspirations less in terms of a territory or polity than by reference to the myths, memories and symbols that comprise an existing or putative 'ethnic' culture, i.e. a culture of ascribed origins and descent. More generally, ethnic nationalism refers to *sentiments* of belonging and aspirations for the well-being and autonomy of human populations conceived as nations in terms of common cultural traits and historical experiences.

The definition of the nation in terms of its ethnic heritage and the ensuing demand for ethno-national autonomy, unity and identity owes much to the Rousseauian cult of nature and the Herderian belief in popular or folk culture – and it is common to oppose, in the tradition of Hans Kohn, a Western territorial to an Eastern European ethnic nationalism, though this is problematic. Nevertheless, it is probably true to say that while in the West territorial and ethnic nationalisms were combined, as during the French Revolution, in eastern Europe and the Middle East and south Asia, ethnic nationalism has tended to overshadow a purely territorial nationalism operating on behalf of units based on historic or colonial territories. Even in these areas, however, a territorial nationalism has sometimes been espoused by sections of the intelligentsia and the bureaucracy, from Czechoslovakia and Yugoslavia to India and Malaysia. Inevitably, such state-based nationalisms have had to grapple with the ideological aspirations and movements of a host of ethnic communities (*ethnie*) within the new states, particularly in sub-Saharan Africa, but also in south-east Asia. In fact, few new states have been free of incipient or developed ethnic nationalisms, and even in the industrialized, democratic and long-established states of the West (and in the Soviet Union) ethnic nationalism has made itself felt in more muted tones. Indeed, the 1960s and 1970s witnessed a remarkable 'ethnic revival' both in the West and in the third world, in which movements and ethnic parties appeared ·and flourished, intent on securing greater power and opportunities for hitherto neglected or oppressed ethnic communities, and creating in other populations a sense of their historic community and solidarity, from Occitanie and Frisia to Eritrea and the Philippine Moros. In its incidence and political impact, the ethnic variety of nationalism is undoubtedly the most important, given the large number of polyethnic states and the appeal of ascriptive ties and historic cultures. It is possible to subdivide this large category of nationalisms in terms of the goals of the movement and the degree of 'development' of the nationalism among the population concerned. We can talk of primitive and developed ethnic nationalisms, and of secessionist, irredentist, pan and diaspora movements, though in reality certain ethnic nationalisms may move from one sub-category to another (Kurds in Iraq may desire secession but they would also like to link up with Kurds in Iran, Turkey and Syria and 'redeem' their ethnic kinsmen). This illustrates the propensity of ethnic communities and their nationalisms to assimilate or differentiate their sub-communities and sub-categories, and to reconstruct a new self-definition and culture to fit changing political and ideological situations, within the limits set by a particular historical experience.

Explanations of ethnic nationalism, as of nationalism generally, fall into two main groups. The so-called 'primordialists' tend to see ethnicity as a given of the human condition and hence the striving for ethno-national autonomy as universal, if not natural. The so-called 'instrumentalists' regard ethnic communities and nations as malleable constructs and ethnic perception and national sentiment as situational; the boundaries of belonging and opposition vary with the situation of the perceiver. For the primordialists, ethnic cultures are viewed as durable repositories of human experience and memory;

ethnie and nations are perennial. For the instrumentalist, ethnic culture is fluid and manipulable, an instrument for mobilizing group emotion on behalf of causes used by ELITES in their competition for wealth and power. Many instrumentalists see the nation and nationalism as products of a secular, industrial modernity or of bourgeois capitalism, or even of a political messianism born in the French Revolution but harking back to a tradition of millennialism.

There are difficulties with all these views. As an ideological movement nationalism clearly dates from the eighteenth century, but national differences were noted much earlier. *Ethnie* appear frequently in ancient sources, Egyptian and Assyrian inscriptions, Greek writings and the Bible, and if not perennial, are certainly durable. Few theories link the modern phenomenon of ethnic national*ism* with the much older phenomenon of the *ethnie*; however it may be suggested that modern conditions, notably the bureaucratic state and inter-state system, ignite ethnic nationalism where ethnic ties and memories have been retained or can be reconstructed by an intelligentsia desirous of communal roots, or where populations are thrown together by ethnic exclusion and bureaucratic discrimination, and are compelled to forge a fairly novel ethnic identity based on any myths and memories to hand. But in the latter case we may expect that such ethnic 're-inventions' will be subject to fissiparous tendencies once the immediate nationalist struggle has abated.

Politically, ethnic nationalism appears as a disruptive and explosive force at odds with every conception of a stable world order and, given the economic, political and cultural disparities between *ethnie* and between states on a global scale, one unlikely to abate in the foreseeable future. In the West, where ethnicity is one of several key political issues and where ethnic nationalisms tend to be autonomist rather than separatist in aspirations (except for minority parties such as Euzkadi Ta Askatsuna in Spain, or parties that fail to win ethnic majority support such as the Scottish National Party or *Plaid Cymru*), the framework and boundaries of the territorial NATION-STATE would not appear to be en-

dangered; the same may well be true of centralized but culturally federal states such as Yugoslavia, India and the Soviet Union, where many aspirations of *ethnie* are met within varying political limits. But even in these areas and states ethnic nationalism may reappear in force – while in many parts of Africa and Asia, from Sri Lanka and Burma to Ethiopia and Zimbabwe, the threat or reality of a secessionist ethnic nationalism is all too apparent. Perhaps because of unfavourable international conditions and the often ethnically mixed character of the would-be secessionist areas, very few ethnic nationalisms have been able to achieve their goal of separation, exceptions being Bangla Desh and Singapore. International failure to recognize ethnic, as opposed to territorial nationalism, and genuine fears of 'Balkanization', militate against separatist success; so does the resolve of threatened new states to counter ethnic nationalism. More generally, the opposition between a strong entrenched and bureaucratized state system and the scattered and intermittently chronic demands of movements of ethnic nationalism is likely to keep large areas of Africa and Asia in turmoil and to determine the politics of most new states and influence the character and direction of both old and new states, without undermining them completely.

See also ETHNIC PARTIES; ETHNICITY; LANGUAGE AND POLITICS.   ADS

Reading

Armstrong, J.: *Nations before Nationalism*. Chapel Hill: University of North Carolina Press, 1982.

Anderson, B.: *Imagined Communities*. London: Verso, 1983.

Brass, P. ed.: *Ethnic Groups and the State*. Beckenham: Croom Helm, 1985.

Esman, M.J. ed.: *Ethnic Conflict in the Western World*. Ithaca, NY: Cornell University Press, 1977.

Gellner, E.: *Nations and Nationalism*. Oxford: Blackwell, 1983.

Glazer, N. and Moynihan, D. eds: *Ethnicity, Theory and Experience*. Cambridge, Mass: Harvard University Press, 1976.

Horowitz, D.L.: *Ethnic Groups in Conflict*. Berkeley: University of California Press, 1985.

Kohn, H.: *The Idea of Nationalism*. 2nd edn. London: Macmillan, 1967.

Seton-Watson, H.: *Nations and States*. London: Methuen, 1977.

Smith, A.D.: *The Ethnic Revival*. Cambridge: Cambridge University Press, 1981.

————: *The Ethnic Origins of Nations*. Oxford: Blackwell, 1986.

ethnic parties Organizations which claim to represent the needs of an ethnic group and to oppose control of their group by governments drawn from more powerful ethnic groups. They generally plan to implement this aim by taking over the government of the territory occupied by their own group. In doing so, they may aim at complete independence from the existing state or at some degree of autonomy within the existing state. The Scottish National Party, for example, advocates complete independence for Scotland while the Basque National Party would be happy to retain the connection with Spain so long as the major decisions affecting the Basque Provinces were made by a regional Basque government. Since the 1960s there has been an increase in the activity of these parties in all parts of the world. In Europe and in Canada this development has been widely discussed since many politicians and scholars had expected that socio-economic issues would increasingly predominate in politics so that historic conflicts over integration would dissolve over time, thus reducing what were seen as residual ethnic differences. The ethnic parties have enjoyed mixed success. In Belgium and Spain they have been very influential and have achieved most of their aims. In Scotland and Wales, by contrast, the SNP and Plaid Cymru had a brief heyday in the 1970s, but have now slipped in popularity. The defence of the ethnic culture and the language is often prominent in the manifestos of ethnic parties, but it is not universal. Many areas no longer possess a distinctive language. In others it exists only in remote pockets. While cultural distinctiveness is always important, the economic health of the ethnic region is much more important. Virtually all ethnic parties base their case upon the perceived economic exploitation and decline of their area. One explanation for the recent rise of nationalism and ethnic parties has been that

they were a reaction to a process of INTERNAL COLONIALISM.

See also ETHNIC NATIONALISM; ETHNICITY; LANGUAGE AND POLITICS. JAB

Reading

Anderson, B.: *Imagined Communities*. London: Verso, 1983.

Brand, J.: *The National Movement in Scotland*. London: Routledge & Kegan Paul, 1978.

Gellner, E.: *Nations and Nationalism*. Oxford: Blackwell, 1983.

Hechter, M.: *Internal Colonialism*. London: Routledge & Kegan Paul, 1975.

Nairn, T.: *The Break-up of Britain*. London: New Left Books, 1977.

Reece, J.: *The Bretons against France*. Chapel Hill: University of North Carolina Press, 1977.

Saywell, J.: *The Rise of the Parti Quebecqois*. Toronto: University of Toronto Press, 1981.

Sugar, P. ed.: *Ethnic Diversity and Conflict in Eastern Europe*. Santa Barbara, Calif.: ABC-Clio, 1980.

ethnicity Sentiments of loyalty to one's own ethnic group, culture or place of origin, which may prove important in group mobilization when political divisions and ethnic divisions are thought to coincide. Ethnicity is closely related to 'tribalism', and ETHNIC NATIONALISM. The precise meaning depends on the meaning of 'ethnic group'.

Whereas 'tribe' historically referred to what colonial administrators believed to be clearcut and stable groups with their own distinct cultural traditions (Cohen and Middleton 1970; p. 2), the term 'ethnic group' has been used in situations where people from different cultural or regional backgrounds interact with each other. Numerous definitions exist: Abner Cohen defines it widely as 'a collectivity of people who (a) share some patterns of normative behaviour and (b) form part of a larger population (1974, p. ix). Schildkrout and Horowitz add the notions of kinship and common origin, even though these links may be very distant or even mythical. Ethnic affiliation thus has more to do with how people classify themselves and their origins than where they objectively come from. The link with kinship, though, is important in accounting for the intense emotions which ethnicity arouses. The fact that in many societies notions of morality are bound up with support of kin means that, when 'kin' is equated with 'fellow ethnics', morality implies ethnic solidarity as well.

As Fried argues for tribes, ethnic groups only become significant units by virtue of the relations of their members with outsiders, and as the nature of these relations changes so do people's perceptions of ethnic identity and its political importance. In his discussion of informal interest groups Abner Cohen explains why ethnic groups are so often important in politics. It is not always possible for groups of people with common interests to organize formally to defend them, so they organize informally. To be successful they need to communicate, to make decisions, to maintain discipline and a common ideology, and to keep away outsiders. Ethnic groups, with their existing kinship networks and community structure, and sometimes their separate language and culture, solve these problems easily.

Struggles between ethnic groups are likely to be particularly intense when for historical reasons different groups occupy different positions in the labour market or the political system. The uneven process of development in many countries means that certain areas lose out in the competition for jobs, education or development funds, and lack of educational opportunities may mean that they are under-represented in the state apparatus itself. Demands for, and struggles over, these resources may well be at least partly organized within and between particular ethnic groups, and they may well be defined as 'ethnic' or 'tribal' conflicts as a result, despite their ultimate origin in the regional political economy.   JSE

Reading

Cohen, A.: *Custom and Politics in Urban Africa*. London: Routledge & Kegan Paul, 1969.

————: *Two-dimensional Man*. London: Routledge & Kegan Paul, 1974.

————, ed.: *Urban Ethnicity*. London: Tavistock, 1974.

Cohen, R. and Middleton, J. eds: *From Tribe to Nation in Africa*. Scranton, Penn.: Chandler, 1970.

Fried, M.H.: *The Notion of Tribe*. Menlo Park, Calif.: Cummings, 1975.

Horowitz, D.L.: *Ethnic Groups in Conflict*. Berkeley: University of California Press, 1985.

Krejčí, J. and Velímský, V.: *Ethnic and Political Nations in Europe*. London: Croom Helm, 1981.

Schildkrout, E.: *People of the Zongo*. Cambridge: Cambridge University Press, 1978.

Smith, A.D.: *The Ethnic Origins of Nations*. Oxford: Blackwell, 1986.

European Community (EC) A community of states covering most of Western Europe and engaged in a process of economic and POLITICAL INTEGRATION. The Community was founded after the second world war by France, the German Federal Republic, Italy, Belgium, the Netherlands, and Luxemburg. Its aims were to effect an historic reconciliation between France and Germany; to create a political union in which there would be no fear of war among the member-states; to develop their economies in a large common market. With Franco-German reconciliation and peaceful relations among the members finally established, the EC continues to be a framework for economic development, for promoting common external interests, and for political integration. Six new members have since joined: Britain, Denmark and Ireland in 1973; Greece in 1981; and Portugal and Spain in 1986.

The European Coal and Steel Community (ECSC) was founded in 1952 on the initiative of Jean MONNET, who insisted that the coal and steel industries in the member countries should be regulated by common institutions endowed with the power to make and apply community law. Britain and other European countries were not ready to accept this merger of sovereignty. After failing to form a European Defence Community the six founder members went on to establish in 1958 both the European Economic Community providing for economic integration in a common market, and Euratom for collaboration in the civilian sector of nuclear power. The three Communities were merged in 1967, and became known collectively as the European Community.

The impact of the EC has been decisive where the member-states have endowed it with substantial common policy instruments. Its customs union had a double effect. The liberalized trade among the members quadrupled in a decade. The common external tariff made the EC a trading power on the scale of the United States, which then accommodated this change in power relationships by initiating the Kennedy round of tariff negotiations, resulting in a major liberalization of trade among industrial countries. The common agricultural policy (CAP) consolidated the Franco-German reconciliation by providing benefits to France to set against the industrial free trade in the Community, which was of greater interest to Germany; and the CAP has eased the process of reducing agricultural employment in several member countries by more than half.

The institutions to which the common policy instruments have been entrusted have certain federal characteristics as well as providing a framework for intergovernmental cooperation. There is a COMMISSION, EUROPEAN COURT OF JUSTICE, and EUROPEAN PARLIAMENT, each with a direct relationship with EC economic agents and citizens. As in the Bundesrat of the German Federal Republic, the governments of member-states are represented by their ministers in the Council of the EC. A critical difference from federal institutions is however that the European Parliament controls jointly with the Council of Ministers only a part of the EC budget, while its legislative role is mainly consultative. The Council, moreover, while it legislates on the basis of proposals from the Commission, has generally sought unanimity for its decisions, although the Treaties provide for voting by a two-thirds weighted majority on a number of important matters such as external trade policy, agricultural policy and the budget. A EUROPEAN COUNCIL bringing together the heads of state and governments has also been established, normally proceeding by unanimity.

The practice of unanimous voting became established in the mid-1960s after President de Gaulle (see GAULLISM) asserted that the French government would not accept being outvoted by the other members on any matter where it might consider that very important interests were at stake. This assertion was recorded at the EC Council meeting in Luxemburg in January 1966, following six months during which de Gaulle's challenge to the Community had been backed by the withdrawal of French ministers from the Council. With the subsequent de facto acceptance in the so-called 'Luxemburg Compromise' by the other members of unanimous voting as the general practice, the EC entered a period of consolidation rather than dynamic development of its institutions and competences.

The next two decades saw the entry of the six new member-states, which enhanced the EC's economic and political potential but made unanimous agreement on developing EC policies and institutions yet harder to achieve. The Community nevertheless made some headway in fields such as industrial, research, regional, social and transport policy and in its relations with industrialized and third world countries. After the failure in the early 1970s of an attempt to launch a full economic and monetary union, the member-states established in 1978 a European Monetary System, whose principal feature is a mechanism for stabilizing exchange rates in which, however, a minority of member-states have not so far participated. Procedures of European Political Co-operation facilitated consultation on foreign policy and efforts to reach common positions. The application of Community law developed steadily, with important decisions in matters such as competition policy and women's rights. The European Council was constituted, direct elections to the European Parliament were implemented and the Parliament acquired the power of co-decision with the Council over part of the budget.

The Council of Ministers failed, however, to expedite many new developments or to make adequate progress in completing the common market and reforming the increasingly burdensome agricultural policy. This led to demands for more effective and democratic institutions; and the European Parliament passed a Draft Treaty for European

Union in 1984 providing for full co-decision between the Parliament and Council, for the phasing out of an individual government's right of veto, and for the reformed institutions not only to exercise existing EC competences but also to establish economic and monetary union. But the member governments reacted only with the Single European Act (1986), which provided for majority decision-making on matters connected with the completion of the internal market and formalized foreign policy co-operation, as well as strengthening the European Parliament. European union was left as a possibility for the future.

See also FEDERALISM; SUPRANATIONAL GOVERNMENT.   JP

Reading

Bieber, R., Jacqué, J.-P. and Weiler, J.H.H. eds: *An Ever Closer Union: a critical analysis of the Draft Treaty establishing the European Union.* Brussels: Commission of the EC for the European University Institute, 1985.

Commission of the European Community: *General Reports,* annual.

Coombes, D.: *Politics and Bureaucracy in the European Community.* London: Allen & Unwin, 1970.

Henig, S.: *Political Integration, Power and Decision in Europe: the political institutions of the European Community.* London: Europotentials Press, 1980.

Marquand, D.A.: *Parliament for Europe.* London: Cape, 1979.

Wallace, H.S., Wallace, W. and Webb, C. eds: *Policy-Making in the European Communities.* 2nd edn. Chichester: Wiley, 1983.

European Convention on Human Rights The Convention was drafted in the Council of Europe in 1949–50, and completed on 4 November 1950. It came into force on 3 September 1953; additional provisions were embodied in Protocol No. 1 (18 May 1954), and Protocol No. 4 (2 May 1968), and amendments of a structural character were made in Protocol No. 3 (21 September 1970: Articles 29, 30 and 34), and in Protocol No. 5 (20 December 1971: Articles 29 and 40). The Convention has been extended by the United Kingdom and Netherlands to certain of their dependent territories. All the members of the Council of Europe are now parties to the Convention (Austria, Belgium, Cyprus, Denmark, France, Federal Republic of Germany, Greece, Iceland, Ireland, Malta, Italy, Liechtenstein, Luxemburg, the Netherlands, Norway, Portugal, Spain, Sweden, Switzerland, Turkey, United Kingdom). The text of the Convention is expressed in English and French, both texts being equally authentic.

Inspired by the Universal Declaration of Human Rights (1948), it was the first international convention designed to secure in practice the rights and freedoms set out in the Declaration. Those were chosen for inclusion in the Convention, which the majority of Council of Europe countries were prepared to accept and implement.

The substantive provisions can be seen as covering what may be called personal rights and social rights – personal rights being those that involve the individual as such and to some degree alone, while social rights are those that are exercised in principle with or in relation to other people, and are therefore subject to some regulation in the public interest. The exercise of some rights may of course fall into both categories, for example the right to life (Article 2) and the 'peaceful enjoyment of possessions' (Protocol No. 1, Article 1). Among the personal rights and freedoms are the prohibition of torture, inhuman and degrading treatment (Article 2); the prohibition of slavery and forced labour (Article 4); the right to liberty and security of the person (Article 5); the access to justice in both civil and criminal proceedings (Article 6); the prohibition of retroactive offences or penalties (Article 7). Social rights may be found in the respect for private and family life, home and correspondence (Article 8); the right to freedom of thought, conscience and religion (Article 9); freedom of expression and freedom to receive and impart information (Article 10); freedom of peaceful assembly and association, including the right to form and join trade unions (Article 11); the right to marry and found a family (Article 12); the peaceful enjoyment of possessions (Article 1 of Protocol No. 1). These social rights are qualified by extensive exceptions in the public interest: for example Article 8 has a second paragraph which reads:

213

There shall be no interference by a public authority with the exercise of this right [to respect for private and family life, home and correspondence] except such as is in accordance with the law and is necessary in a democratic society in the interests of national security, public safety, or the economic well-being of the country, for the prevention of disorder or crime, for the protection of health or morals or for the protection of the rights and freedoms of others.

Further:

In time of war or other public emergency threatening the life of the nation, any High Contracting Party may take measures derogating from its obligations under this Convention to the extent strictly required by the exigencies of the situation ... (Article 15)

Finally, the rights and freedoms set forth in the Convention are to be 'secured without discrimination on any ground such as sex, race, colour, language, religion, political or other opinion, national or social origin, association with a national minority, property, birth, or other status' (Article 14).

The implementation of the Convention is achieved in two ways. First, its provisions may be incorporated into the domestic law of a country, and can be then invoked and applied in its courts; thirteen countries have so far incorporated the Convention into their internal law. Second, the Convention has established an international system of complaints of infringement or denial of Convention rights and freedoms: 'Any person, non-governmental organization, or group of individuals claiming to be a victim of a violation by one of the High Contracting Parties of the rights set forth in this Convention' (Article 25) may make an application to the European Commission of Human Rights provided that that party has recognized the right of individual petition; all the Convention countries have done so except Malta, Greece, Cyprus and Turkey. The Commission, composed of one member from each Convention country, who sit as individuals and not as government representatives, may conduct a full examination of an application, obtaining information from both the applicant and the respondent government, and may hold an oral hearing. It will express its opinion on whether there has been a breach of the Convention and, if it does not secure a settlement between applicant and government, make a report of the facts, with its opinion, to the Committee of Ministers of the Council of Europe, which has then to decide whether there has been a breach. Within three months of the case being referred to the Committee of Ministers, it may be referred by the Commission or the respondent government to the European Court of Human Rights. The Convention requires a respondent government to give effect to a decision of the Committee of Ministers or a judgment of the Court.

In practice, the bulk of Convention work lies with the Commission: it has over 11,000 registered applications, and its opinions have been on a number of occasions implemented by governments, by changes in the law or by administrative practice.

The Convention has in fact exercised a significant influence in the past thirty years on the law and social policy of Convention countries, by its incorporation in the internal law of thirteen countries – in the United Kingdom, where it is not so incorporated, there is increasing judicial recognition of its provisions. Further, it played a part in the movement to independence of the colonial territories of the United Kingdom and the Netherlands. Legislation and changes in administrative practice have followed the findings by its organs of breaches of the Convention: for example, on abortion law in the Federal Republic of Germany, on detention on remand in Austria, on the status of illegitimacy in Belgium, and on surveillance, contempt of court, and correspondence of prisoners, in the United Kingdom.

See also CIVIL LIBERTIES; CIVIL RIGHTS.

JESF

Reading

Miller, D.: *Social Justice*. Oxford: Oxford University Press, 1976.

Robertson, A.H.: *Human Rights in the World*. Manchester: Manchester University Press, 1972.

Sieghart, P.: *The International Law of Human Rights*. Oxford: Oxford University Press, 1983.

European Council   Two or three times a year since 1974 the European Council has convened heads of state and government from the member states of the EUROPEAN COMMUNITY (EC) to discuss and negotiate the major issues and conflicts arising out of EC business. They also deliberate on foreign policy questions emerging from the procedures of European Political Co-operation. Originally intended by President Giscard d'Estaing as an informal forum for intimate debate, the European Council has increasingly become a decision-making body. However its agreements have to be translated into formal legislation by the COUNCIL OF MINISTERS. Broadly its procedures follow those of the Council in that it is chaired by the Council Presidency and prepared by working groups of officials as well as the Foreign Affairs Council with servicing from the Council Secretariat and papers from the Commission. Votes, though unusual, may be taken. But the European Council can and does operate more flexibly and its activities reveal more sharply than the Council of Ministers the influences of personality and the differential bargaining power of individual member states. Its functions include acting as a court of appeal for the Council of Ministers, handling the most politically-charged issues and broaching new policy questions. Views differ as to the effectiveness of the European Council and on whether its role should be extended. Some governments, notably from smaller member states, prefer a limited role. Others would like to see it become the predominant guiding force of the EC.   HW

Reading

Bulmer, S.: The European Council's first decade: between interdependence and domestic politics. *Journal of Common Market Studies* 24 (1985) 89–104.

Bulmer, S. and Wessels, W.: *The European Council: decision-making in European politics.* London: Macmillan, 1987.

Morgan, A.: *From Summit to Council: evolution in the EEC.* London: PEP/Chatham House, 1976.

European Court of Justice   Each of the founding treaties of the European Commun-

ities (the European Coal and Steel Community (ECSC), the European Economic Community (EEC), and the European Atomic Energy Community (Euratom)) established a Court of Justice with the function of 'ensuring that in the interpretation and application of this Treaty the law is observed'. A convention signed at the same time as the EEC and Euratom treaties established a single Court of Justice for all three Communities. The Court sits at Luxemburg. The Court of Justice of the European Communities should be clearly distinguished from the European Court of Human Rights which sits at Strasburg and was established within the framework of the Council of Europe by the EUROPEAN CONVENTION ON HUMAN RIGHTS.

The Court of Justice now consists of thirteen judges, one from each member state plus one additional judge nominated by the member states in rotation (to ensure an odd number). The Court elects its own president. It may, and in some cases must, sit in plenary session but it frequently sits in chambers of three or five judges. In either case the Court operates on the principle of collegiality, all judgments being the judgment of the Court with no dissenting judgments. The judgments tend to be terse, sometimes to the point of delphic utterance. This may make them unexciting to those who are familiar with the COMMON LAW system, but it contributes to their political acceptablity in a multinational community.

The Court is assisted by six advocates-general, whose function is to deliver an independent opinion on the case. The opinions of the advocates-general, unlike the judgments of the Court, discuss the issues of law and fact, and are therefore in that respect comparable to the judgment of the judge of first instance under the common law system. They are themselves a source of law and are frequently the best guide to the thinking of the Court.

The jurisdiction of the Court is laid down by the founding treaties and falls, broadly speaking, into five categories: actions by the Commission against a member state, or by one member state against another, claiming that the defendant state has failed to fulfil a treaty obligation; actions for JUDICIAL REVIEW of the acts (or failure to act) of the Community institutions; actions of damages against the Community itself; references from national courts and tribunals on questions of Community law; and actions by members of the staff of the institutions relating to their conditions of employment (for which a new court of first instance is expected to be established in the near future).

The Court has also been given jurisdiction to determine questions arising under supplementary conventions, for example the Brussels (Judgments) Convention, and international agreements, for example the Lomé Convention.

Because the nature and scope of its jurisdiction are defined in the treaties, the Court is not a 'supreme court' and has no general or overriding power. The Court has, if anything, been cautious in keeping within the strict limits of its jurisdiction and has incurred some criticism on that account. But that may be a measure of its success because, in spite of the weakness of the EUROPEAN PARLIAMENT, the inertia of the COUNCIL OF MINISTERS and the shackling of the COMMISSION, it is through the Court that the momentum of integration has been maintained. The Court has therefore had a profound (if largely unnoticed) political influence in post-war Europe.

Essentially, the Court has insisted that the member states should honour the obligations they undertook in the treaties: to co-operate in achieving the objectives of the treaties; to accept the consequences of having agreed to exercise their sovereignty in decisive areas of policy through autonomous Community institutions; above all, to remove the multifarious barriers to freedom of movement in the economic life of their citizens. The principal legal doctrines developed by the Court for this purpose are the doctrine of the primacy (or supremacy) of Community law and the doctrine of direct effect.

The doctrine of primacy is based on the principle that if all member states are to honour their obligations equally, the law deriving from the treaties must be applied uniformly throughout the Community. Con-

sequently member states cannot be allowed to derogate unilaterally from Community law and national courts must apply it in preference to national law (including subsequent parliamentary legislation) which is inconsistent with it. This might be seen as a direct challenge to the doctrine of the supremacy of parliament and analogous doctrines in other member states, but although the treaties provide no machinery by which the Court can enforce its judgments, there have been very few cases where a member state or its courts have refused to respect and apply Community law. This has been so in spite of the political sensitivity of many of the issues coming before the Court (for example, in the United Kingdom, tachographs in lorries, fisheries, and the relative weight of taxation of beer and wine). The Court has been particularly alive to the susceptibilities of national courts and has stressed that the relationship between them is one of co-operation in applying a new system of law which is common to them all.

The doctrine of direct effect is based on the wording of the treaties themselves, from which the Court concluded that the contracting member states intended to confer rights, not only upon the Community institutions and upon each other, but also upon individuals. If these rights are to be effective, they must be enforceable by the national courts in disputes between individuals or between individuals and national authorities. Broadly speaking, the doctrine applies wherever the terms of the treaties or secondary Community legislation are such as to impose clear and unconditional obligations giving rise to corresponding rights. So the Court has given immediate and binding effect to the key provisions of the EEC treaty on freedom of movement of goods, persons, services and, to a limited extent, capital. Left to themselves, even with the negotiating machinery provided by COREPER and the Council of Ministers, it is inconceivable that the member states would have agreed to dismantle the many protectionist barriers which have been removed at a stroke by a few judgments of the Court.

The Court has therefore played a vital political role, first in defusing issues which could otherwise, individually or at least cumulatively, have led to renewed tension in Western Europe; second in making a reality (albeit only partial) of the internal market.

An area in which the political consequences of the Court's judgments are only beginning to be apparent is in relation to the powers of the European Parliament. Although the powers of the Parliament are severely limited, the Court has insisted that they be effective, and that the rights of the Parliament be respected by the other Community institutions. The Council of Ministers can no longer ignore the Parliament, and the Commission now finds it a valuable ally.

In the field of administrative law the Court has drawn upon the laws of the member states to develop a body of general principles for the law of the Community. The principles of natural justice in United Kingdom law have influenced this development, but other member states (particularly Germany) have had more reason to develop a coherent theory of the relationship between the citizen and the state and to provide the citizen with adequate armour against the power and pretensions of the executive. It is significant that the House of Lords has now begun to draw upon Community law as a source of inspiration to fill gaps in the patchy system of ADMINISTRATIVE LAW in the United Kingdom.

See also JUDICIAL FUNCTION AND PROCESS; JUDICIARY.   DAOE

Reading

Brown, L.N. and Jacobs, F.G.: *The Court of Justice of the European Communities*. 2nd edn. London: Sweet & Maxwell, 1983.

Collins, L.: *European Community Law in the United Kingdom*. 3rd edn. London: Butterworths, 1984.

Mackenzie Stuart, Lord: *The European Communities and the Rule of Law*. London: Stevens, 1977.

Schermers, H.G.: *Judicial Protection in the European Communities*. 3rd edn. Deventer: Kluwer, 1983.

European Parliament The world's first directly elected supranational legislature; the representative institution of the EUROPEAN COMMUNITY. It has three types of powers: supervisory, budgetary and the right to participate in Community legislation. Its powers are primarily consultative; although its functions are defined by Article 137 of the Treaty of Rome 1957 as 'advisory and supervisory', the Treaty of 1975 amended certain financial provisions and the Parliament became, with the Council of Ministers, the budgetary authority of the European Community with the power to adopt or to reject the general budget. The budget was in fact rejected in 1980 and 1985. This Treaty also empowered Parliament to amend that part of the budget covering expenditure not necessarily resulting from the Treaty or from other Community legislation.

The European Parliament gives advisory opinions to the Council of Ministers on legislative proposals made by the European Commission under Article 149 of the Treaty of Rome. Such opinions usually include amendments to the proposal; but Parliament has no power to insist that the Council should adopt such amendments. Parliament thus has the right to participate in the legislative process of the Community, although it is not the Community's legislative authority.

The relations between Parliament, the Council and the Commission are further governed by the Joint Declaration of 1975 on the conciliation procedure, which provides for discussions on amendments proposed by the Parliament to legislative proposals by the Commission, if such amendments are unacceptable to the Council.

Parliament, however, cannot initiate new Community policies, and it is in theory possible for Community policies to be adopted against its wishes. Its powers, limited as they are, are directed primarily at the Commission, but it is the Council of Ministers and the European Council which have turned out to be the most powerful institutions of the Community. By decisions of the Foreign Ministers of the Member States meeting in European Political Co-operation, information is given to Parliament in various ways on decisions taken by the Ministers on foreign policy matters affecting the Community itself, and the Member States acting in co-operation.

The election and composition of the Parliament are governed chiefly by Article 138 of the Rome Treaty, by the Act of 20 September

1976 governing direct elections to Parliament and by the Acts of Accession of Greece, Spain and Portugal.

The membership of Parliament is 518, of whom 81 members are elected from France, the Federal Republic of Germany, Italy and the United Kingdom, respectively, 60 from Spain, 25 from the Netherlands, 24 each from Belgium, Greece and Portugal, 16 from Denmark, 15 from Ireland, and 6 from Luxemburg. Each member state uses a different electoral system for the election of its members to the European Parliament, but in the elections held in June 1979 and June 1984, the United Kingdom was the only Member State to use an electoral system not based on proportional representation. However, the most significant political fact about the Parliament is that its members sit as members of transnational political groups, rather than as national delegations. In 1985 there were the following seven groups – Socialists, Christian Democrats in the European People's party, Conservatives in the European Democratic Group, Liberals, European Democratic Alliance (Gaullists and Fianna Fail), the Rainbow Group (Green) and the radical right in the European Right.

The Single European Act of 1986 widens Parliament's consultative powers, but it still lacks the powers enjoyed by most LEGISLATURES; and neither the COUNCIL OF MINISTERS nor the EUROPEAN COUNCIL is responsible to it.   DMcWM

Reading

Coombes, D.: *The Future of the European Parliament.* London: Policy Studies Institute, 1979.

European Parliament: *Forging Ahead: thirty years of the European Parliament.* 2nd edn. Luxembourg: Office for Official Publications of the European Communities, 1983.

Hrbek, R., Jamar, J. and Wessels, W.: *The European Parliament on the Eve of the Second Direct Election: balance sheet and prospects.* Bruges: De Tempel, Tempelhof, 1984.

Marquand, D.A.: *Parliament for Europe.* London: Cape, 1979.

Palmer, M.: *The European Parliament.* Oxford: Pergamon, 1981.

exchange theory A theory of social interaction. It draws on the economic theory of exchange as a source of insights but also points up the differences between social and economic exchange. A great deal of social interaction can be conceptualized as 'an exchange of activity, tangible or intangible, and more or less rewarding or costly, between at least two persons' (Homans 1961, p. 13). This includes not only the ceremonial giftgiving of Christmas but also the mutual assistance of colleagues at work or the exchange of favours between neighbours. The defining feature of an exchange is that each action is contingent on a rewarding reaction and ceases when the expected reaction is not forthcoming. Pure altruism is excluded, as is moral action motivated by conscience or a sense of duty. But a person whose conformity with a norm is contingent on social approval or on sanctions can be thought of as engaging in an exchange.

Once interaction is conceptualized as an exchange, economic analysis and economic analogies become possible. Such analogies have been particularly productive in the study of power in social relationships where an analogy can be drawn between the price which a monopolist can charge and the compliance which the supplier of a service can extract from his exchange partner (see Blau 1964). The essence of the theory is that the supplier's power will be greater if the recipient has no alternative supplier to turn to for the service and if he has nothing to offer in exchange which is valued by the supplier. Power is therefore inverse to the dependence of the individual on his exchange partner. This has been termed 'the principle of least interest' (Waller and Hill 1951) and has been applied illuminatingly to the analysis of power in love relationships (see Blood and Wolfe 1960). As well as drawing analogies with economic principles, exchange theorists have also been concerned to emphasize the differences between social and economic exchanges. In social exchange it is argued (following the classic work of Mauss, 1925) that there is an absence of explicit bargaining and the nature of the return must be left to the recipient's discretion. The norm of reciprocity (Gouldner

1960) becomes a central mechanism ensuring that a return is actually made. The study of the norms of social exchange, and the notion of fair exchange, distinguishes the theory of exchange from economic theory.

Exchange theory has been most successfully applied in the analysis of face-to-face interaction within small groups such as the family or the work group. It has been particularly influential in anthropological studies of politics (see for example Barth 1966; Bailey 1969). Its use of economic analysis means that it overlaps with RATIONAL CHOICE theory, and it is the latter which has proved more popular in contemporary political science.   AFH

Reading

Bailey, F.G.: *Stratagems and Spoils: a social anthropology of politics*. Oxford: Blackwell, 1969.

Barth, F.: The analytical importance of transaction. *Models of Social Organisation*. Glasgow: Royal Anthropological Institute, 1966.

Blau, P.M.: *Exchange and Power in Social Life*. New York: Wiley, 1964.

Blood, R.O. and Wolfe, D.M.: *Husbands and Wives: the dynamics of married living*. New York: Free Press, 1960.

Gouldner, A.W.: The norm of reciprocity: a preliminary statement. *American Sociological Review* 25 (1960) 161–78.

Heath, A.F.: *Rational Choice and Social Exchange*. Cambridge: Cambridge University Press, 1976.

Homans, G.C.: *Social Behaviour: its elementary forms*. London: Routledge & Kegan Paul, 1961.

Mauss, M.: *The Gift: forms and functions of exchange in archaic societies* (1925), trans. I. Cunnison. London: Cohen & West, 1954.

Waller, W. and Hill, R.: *The Family: a dynamic interpretation*. New York: Dryden, 1951.

executives Every country has a national executive; indeed the executive is perhaps the only element of the political system which exists in every nation. Moreover the executive is manifestly the central piece of the decision-making machinery of the STATE. Whatever their juridical powers, national executives are typically able – and called upon – to initiate the major policies of the nation, while they are also naturally involved in the implementation of these policies.

It is because of this dominant position that liberals have attempted to reduce or circumscribe the power of executives. However these efforts have been successful only to a limited extent: juridical limitations have often proved ineffective, either because the institutional requirements have been blatantly set aside or because the evolution of societies has made it impractical to abide by the letter of these arrangements. Of course some executives are weak while others are not merely strong but overwhelmingly powerful; these differences are due more to the behavioural characteristics of the political system and to the configuration of social forces than to the presence or absence of legal impediments. To be realistic the study of executives must therefore go well beyond formal powers and examine the effective conditions which prevail in a country.

Three main questions need to be raised with respect to executives, relating to their composition, their structure, and their power (or powers). The first question is more complex than might at first sight seem since the word executive is somewhat ambiguous. In its widest connotation it refers to a whole 'branch' of the political system, that branch which was defined by eighteenth-century political theorists as being in charge of the 'execution' of the policies of the state, alongside (and to an extent under) the legislative branch which was viewed as being in charge of the determination of the general rules. This broad connotation, which is reflected in some constitutional documents and in particular in the US Constitution, has gradually given way to a more restricted meaning: this is partly because the increased involvement of the state in the social and economic life of nations and the consequential growth of bureaucracies made it necessary to distinguish between the bulk of public servants and the small number at the top who seemed to be the essential elements of the decision-making machine.

If what is now regarded as the executive is only a small part of the 'executive branch', there is still considerable room for disagreement about precise boundaries. To begin with, the basis of the distinction cannot follow the division between politicians and administrators: in many countries administrators are at the top of the executive and occupy positions of ministers, as was the case in continental European monarchies both before and after the French Revolution. Nor is it possible to state that the executive is constituted by the members of the cabinet, for there are many countries in which there is no cabinet in the real sense of a group meeting at regular intervals to take major decisions. Moreover many executives have second- and third-level ministers (parliamentary secretaries, under-secretaries, etc.): these can be viewed as belonging to the executive although they are typically not members of the cabinet *sensu stricto*. Finally, principally in communist states but also elsewhere, the executive is divided into two bodies or sets of bodies, one of which is primarily concerned with policy making while the other deals mainly with co-ordination. The Soviet executive is composed of the POLITBURO of the CPSU (Communist Party of the Soviet Union) and of the COUNCIL OF MINISTERS – or at least its Presidium. The executive is thus organized in many different ways across the world: any definition has therefore to be relatively loose and pragmatic.

Given such differences in composition, differences in structure are not surprising. There are profound variations in the philosophy on which the structure of the executive is based, though the formal arrangements which have resulted from these philosophies have been markedly modified or even set aside. Two interconnected problems lie at the root of the differences in structure. One stems from the status of the leaders, the other from the relationship among the members of the executive. Jointly, these two problems raise the question of the extent to which the executive is a collective body or has a hierarchical character, though this hierarchy is modified by the fact that the overall relationship may be tighter or looser, centralized or decentralized.

There is no neat typology of all existing forms of executives, but a general classification can be made. In one type of executive members form a closely integrated group, take at least the most important decisions jointly, and are relatively if not entirely equal. In such a situation the head of the government is at most the chairman of an active committee.

This model, which is more or less approximated by the Swiss federal council, is relatively rare, whatever may be stated in principle. The PRIME MINISTER in most western European CABINET SYSTEMS, for instance, although officially described as *primus inter pares* has an appreciably more elevated position – in part because of his or her powers of appointment and dismissal, in part because of the departmental duties which necessarily involve ministers most of the time in specialized activities and, above all, because of the political status of the prime minister in parliament and in the country. Although there are variations, prime ministers are usually 'above' the other members of the executive and these are only involved in a limited manner in collective decision making.

What is true in practice in western European parliamentary systems is true in theory in PRESIDENTIAL SYSTEMS, even in those which are liberal in character, such as those of the United States and of a number of Latin American countries. In these systems the structure of the executive is both formally and in practice pyramidal. The president is the only member of the executive in charge of all the affairs of the nation, ministers being solely responsible for their departments and indeed solely responsible to the president in this respect. For this reason the model of executive structure which characterizes liberal presidential systems is not vastly different from that which obtains in more authoritarian presidencies and even in military regimes which are established as de facto presidencies. There too, the head of the government regards the members of the executive as being in charge only of a specific sector and as being responsible to him or her for the policies which are adopted and implemented in these sectors.

Yet, by a curious reversal of the formal situation, this highly pyramidal structure of presidential executives has been altered in some cases as a result of the lack of strong control of the head of the executive. While the requirements of modern politics exalted the position of the prime minister in parliamentary systems, the growth of state functions and the consequential increase in the size of the bureaucracy have resulted in each department being somewhat autonomous in many systems which are formally hierarchical. In the United States, for instance, the federal executive has become highly decentralized; in communist states, paradoxically, the complicated decision-making and co-ordinating arrangements of politburos, party secretariats, councils of ministers and presidiums of councils of ministers do not prevent individual ministers from being often semi-autonomous in their own sphere: the relationships between the departments have more the character of negotiations among states than of an orchestra playing under one conductor. While differences resulting from the principle of collective government in parliamentary systems and from that of hierarchical leadership elsewhere are not without significance, a certain convergence can be noticed as a result of the natural tendencies of executives both to need leadership and to be involved in increasingly complex policies.

A similar trend can be observed with respect to the powers of the executive: the practice is often very different from what the constitution asserts, even in states which can be described as liberal and pluralistic. Attempts to reduce markedly the role of the executive by constitutional provisions have rarely been successful: the real limitations to executive influence are often the result of economic and administrative constraints or of the intervention of interest groups.

Admittedly, considerable efforts have been made since the eighteenth century to ensure the executive's dependence on the legislative branch, at any rate to the extent that laws would be decided upon by an elective assembly; and also to ensure that the executive should be confined to 'executing' these laws. In western European constitutions it was further added that the executive needed the confidence of parliament to remain in office. Thus, formally, the principles on which the power of executives is based are in sharp contrast with those which obtain in authoritarian states where the executive is truly dominant in all aspects of policy making and indeed often does not even have to bother with a legislature.

Yet the power of the executive has grown well beyond the constitutional blueprint to a point where, except to an extent in the United States, the executive has in effect become the main lawmaker. Bills are prepared in ministerial departments, with some degree of supervision by ministers; they are then presented to parliaments for approval: although LEGISLATURES, especially through their committees, are able to discuss and to some extent amend these bills it is relatively rare for major alterations to occur. Thus, even in liberal states the executive has recovered the power to draft legislation, the main difference with authoritarian states being that bills are openly debated and indeed discussed in detail; however the strength of party discipline and the complexity of modern legislation have contributed to increases in the initiating role of the executive. Even in the United States, where the role of CONGRESS with regard to legislation has remained large, a popular president exercises considerable influence.

The power of the executive has also increased as a result of the development of extra-legislative policy making. This has always been true in the field of foreign affairs, which classical political theorists recognized to be a special area; a similar development however has occurred in the economic field, in which much of the daily management takes the form of adjustments of interest rates, increases or decreases in the availability of credit, or manipulation in the value of the currency. This is even true to an extent in the social field, where regulations of various types issued by the executive alone may have at least as important an effect on the lives of citizens as does formal legislation.

The role of the executive is not merely to execute, that is to say to implement, it is to initiate policies as well as to co-ordinate the action of the various ministerial departments – an activity which has become increasingly complex as a result of the development of state intervention. Yet it would be wrong to conclude that the power of the executive is unrestrained, not only in liberal polities, but even in authoritarian states. Indeed, it is easy to overestimate the power of absolutist executives of the past; they had to contend not just with the prevailing socio-economic conditions, but also with cultural habits and political privileges: executives could not easily modify laws relating to personal status or even commercial and labour rules. Modern developments, in communication and information in particular, enable the executive to interfere more deeply in the fabric of society; however technical improvements also give citizens and groups some corresponding means of action. In liberal polities in particular the executive is restrained to a marked extent by a variety of pressures and by the need to obtain the agreement of at least some organizations when it puts forward policies. The real bargaining takes place not so much in parliament but in the many formal and informal meetings which occur before bills are published. Developments of this kind are not unknown even in authoritarian states as the executive cannot have a real impact on society if it is confronted with total passivity on the part of the population; even dictatorships lack the manpower to ensure the implementation of their decisions in all corners of the country.

Executives are truly central to the life of the modern state. They are usually, though of course not always, powerful, but then they are likely to be replaced relatively rapidly. Executives encounter limitations to their power however for technical and political reasons – if not necessarily for legal reasons only – in many, indeed in most, polities. The fear that an all-powerful Leviathan will inevitably dominate all societies is ill-founded: tyrannies will no doubt continue to prevail in many nations, but there are also signs that the requirements of modern government give opportunities for increased citizen influence and introduce curbs to the strength of executives.   JFPB

Reading

Blondel, J.: *An Introduction to Comparative Government*. London: Weidenfeld & Nicolson, 1969.

————: *The Organization of Governments*. London and Los Angeles: Sage, 1982.

Hague, R. and Harrop, M.: *Comparative Government*. London: Macmillan, 1982.

Heclo, H.: *A Government of Strangers*. Washington, DC: Brookings Institution, 1977.

Jackson, R.H. and Rosberg, C.G.: *Personal Rule in Black Africa*. Berkeley: University of California Press, 1981.

King, A.S.: Executives. In *A Handbook of Political Science*, Vol. V, ed. F. Greenstein and N. Polsby. Philadelphia: Addison-Wesley, 1975.

LaPalombara, J.: *Politics Within Nations*. Englewood Cliffs, NJ: Prentice-Hall, 1974.

McAuley, M.: *Politics and the Soviet Union*. Harmondsworth: Penguin, 1977.

Rose, R. and Suleiman, E.N. eds: *Presidents and Prime Ministers*. Washington, DC: American Enterprise Institute, 1980.

extermination camps Established by the Nazi regime in 1941–2 in Poland specifically for the extermination of the Jewish population of German-occupied Europe (see NAZISM). In the summer and autumn of 1941 nearly a million Russian Jews were shot by SS (*Schutzstaffel*: defence echelons, the elite Nazi formation of blackshirts) task forces operating behind the invading German armies. The decision to liquidate all European Jews, probably taken by Hitler in summer 1941 although no written order by him has been found, prompted the SS to seek a secret and effective method of mass extermination. During 1940–1, chambers filled with carbon monoxide gas had already been used to kill some 70,000 mentally handicapped in Germany in the so-called 'euthanasia programme', which was halted on 24 August 1941 by Hitler under public pressure articulated by the churches. Its personnel and methods were available to be used against the Jews.

The first mass gassing of Jews took place at Chelmno in a part of western Poland incorporated into Germany as the Warthegau. Here, from 8 December 1941 at intervals until July 1944, Jews were loaded into vans into which the exhaust gases were fed. Some 150,000 died. During 1942, special camps were opened in Poland, at Belzec in the South East, Sobibor in Lublin district, and Treblinka in Warsaw district. They were small installations specifically designed for the rapid extermination of large numbers of human beings. The Jews arrived by train and after undressing were taken along a fenced path straight to the gas chambers, of which each camp possessed several disguised as showers. They were killed by carbon monoxide produced by the fumes of diesel engines. Their bodies were then buried, and later burnt on open pyres. In Treblinka between 900,000 and 1.2 million were killed. In the so-called 'high season' 10,000 were arriving each day and within hours were dead. In Belzec 500–600,000 were murdered; in Sobibor around 200,000. Most of those killed in these camps came from Poland.

Another camp which, although not exclusively an extermination camp, is generally regarded as such was Majdanek in Lublin. Here Poles, Polish Jews, and Russian prisoners of war were held and forced to work as slave labour in SS enterprises. During September and October 1942 three gas chambers were installed, and of the roughly 200,000 who died in the camp approximately twenty-five per cent were gassed.

The gas used at Majdanek was Zyklon B, a pesticide made of a cyanide compound which had proved more effective than the rather primitive method of exhaust fumes used at the other camps. It had been tested in trials carried out on Russian prisoners of war in the autumn of 1941 in what was to become the largest of all the extermination camps, Auschwitz-Birkenau (Auschwitz II) in the Warthegau. Although mass gassing began here in 1942, it was not until 1943, with the installation of four large gas chambers and crematoria that Birkenau surpassed the capacity of Treblinka. In the summer of 1944, 20,000 Jews a day were being gassed. Unlike Belzec, Sobibor and Treblinka, Jews arriving by train at Auschwitz were separated into the able-bodied, who were either employed in the CONCENTRATION CAMP, Auschwitz I, or in the IG Farben plant making artificial rubber (attached to Auschwitz), and those unfit for work, who went straight to the gas chambers in Birkenau. Most of those selected for work did not survive the war. Around one million Jews died in Auschwitz-Birkenau, mostly from Hungary, Poland, and western and southern Europe. In addition at least 6,000 gypsies were gassed and thousands of non-Jews in effect worked to death.

See also ANTI-SEMITISM.   JDN

Reading

Davidowicz, L.: *The War against the Jews 1933–45*. London: Penguin, 1983.

Gilbert, M.J.: *The Holocaust*. London: Collins, 1986.

Hilberg, R.: *The Destruction of the European Jews*. 3 vols. New York: Holmes & Meier, 1985; Leicester: Holmes & Meier/Leicester University Press, 1986.

Hoess, R.: *Commandant of Auschwitz*. London: Weidenfeld & Nicolson, 1959.

Krausnick, H.: The persecution of the Jews. In *Anatomy of the SS State*, ed. H. Krausnick et al. London: Collins, 1968.

Sereny, G.: *Into that Darkness*. London: Picador, 1977.

F

Fabians Strictly the term means members of the Fabian Society, a socialist group founded in London on 4 January 1884 (it took its name from the Roman general, Fabius Cunctator, who fought Hannibal with circumspect tactics) and enjoying a continuous existence to the present day, or of one of the provincial and university Fabian societies (autonomous, and not 'branches' of the London society), which have flourished from time to time in many parts of the United Kingdom and as far away as New Zealand and Australia. Sometimes the term is extended in British politics to include persons not actually members of those societies but who nevertheless believe in the kind of reformist socialism, based on representative democracy and gradual, piecemeal, evolutionary social change, that was advanced by the London Fabian Society in its best-selling book *Fabian Essays in Socialism* (1889), edited by George Bernard Shaw.

Sidney WEBB, who joined the Fabian Society in May 1885, played a leading role in formulating Fabian doctrine and directing the society's activities. His extension of the radical 'theory of rent' was intended to demonstrate that an unregulated economy would lead inevitably, through the 'unearned increment' accruing to capitalists as well as landlords, to social inequality and injustice. This theory provided a rationale for empirical investigations, conducted by the Fabians and published in a long series of *Fabian Tracts*, into a great variety of social problems; they revealed the need for efficient government intervention to furnish a 'national minimum' of well-being for all citizens, financed to a considerable extent out of progressive taxation on 'unearned

incomes', to promote social equality. These measures, the Fabians believed, could be implemented by an enlightened public opinion and forced ahead by the demands of the recently enfranchised working class. In the long run they were conceived as promoting a gradual transition from a capitalist to a socialist society.

The Fabian Society remained a small, select group drawn mainly from the professional classes, but it included a number of well-known Labour leaders. It saw itself as a power-house of social research and informed propaganda. Its principal achievements were as follows. To draw into its group some of the prominent intellectuals and literary figures of several generations, and to persuade them to call themselves not merely advanced radical liberals, but socialists; to provide a style of SOCIALISM assimilable by persons well steeped in British constitutional and liberal values; to give programmatic shape to policies of the Liberal–Labour 'Progressive' alliance, which dominated London municipal politics from the early 1890s to 1907; to take an influential part in the educational reforms of the metropolis in the 1890s and early twentieth century; to play, in a time when the civil service was less bureaucratized and introverted than it is today, a role comparable with that played in the early nineteenth century by the utilitarians.

Larger-scale claims of Fabian influence, such as a determining influence on the Independent Labour Party and the Labour Party or in the development of the British WELFARE STATE, have not stood up to detailed analysis by historians. The London Fabian Society was always divided in its belief in the prospective

224

success of an independent Labour Party before the first world war, with its majority sceptical; but the Liberal Party proved to be more impermeable to Fabian ideas than the Fabians had hoped, taking its own way, under the leadership of Lloyd George and Winston Churchill, in welfare policy. After the first world war the Fabian Society continued its special role but submerged its political independence in the reconstituted Labour Party.   AMMcB

Reading

Cole, M.: *The Story of Fabian Socialism*. London: Heinemann, 1961.

McBriar, A.M.: *Fabian Socialism and English Politics 1884–1918*. Cambridge: Cambridge University Press, 1962.

Mackenzie, N. and J.: *The First Fabians*. London: Weidenfeld & Nicolson, 1977.

Pease, E.R.: *The History of the Fabian Society*. London: Fabian Society and Allen & Unwin, 1916.

Pugh, P.: *Educate, Agitate, Organize: 100 years of Fabian socialism*. London: Methuen, 1984.

Wolfe, W.: *From Radicalism to Socialism: men and ideas in the formation of Fabian socialist doctrines 1881–1889*. New Haven, Conn: Yale University Press, 1975.

faction These exist in most types of organizations, but political scientists have principally focused on those within political parties. In western political thought factions within parties have generally been regarded pejoratively. Whereas 'party' is seen as a legitimate form of political aggregation, faction is regarded as selfish, non-constructive and disruptive. For instance Lasswell in 1931 defined factions as parts of larger units working for the advancement of particular persons or policies, differing from each other only on the details of the application of agreed principles, and impermanent or ephemeral, so that a 'solidification' of factions turns them into parties in their own right.

The reality which this definition suggests is, however, relatively recent even in western political history. Parties and factions in eighteenth-century Britain, for instance, were hard to distinguish from each other. Where, as in Britain, parties have now been fully insti-

tutionalized and legitimized, the difference is readily apparent. Where parties remain weakly institutionalized, parties themselves may approximate to factions in much of their behaviour. In the Philippines before martial law was imposed in 1972 there was little to distinguish the two principal parties from each other in terms of policy or base of support, and a faction within one of them would readily defect to the other party if it foresaw political advantage in doing so. Here Lasswell's argument about 'details of application' is of little relevance, since what motivated both parties and factions were essentially patron–client relationships.

A different pattern again is to be found in Japan where parties are relatively well institutionalized, there is a high level of political stability and government policy-making processes are sophisticated. Nevertheless, most political parties contain a number of factions whose histories may stretch back over decades. These factions are themselves well institutionalized and may be regarded as an integral part of the POLITICAL SYSTEM. They are in large part patronage machines which function to channel electoral funding and provide political posts for their members. In left-wing parties they may be distinguished along ideological lines, but policy differences are slight between the powerful factions of the ruling Liberal Democratic Party. The multi-member constituency system of election (with single non-transferable votes) serves to promote factionalism within the larger parties since candidates of the same party compete with each other in the same constituencies; other ELECTORAL SYSTEMS allowing the voter to choose between candidates of the same party have a similar effect. This however is not the full (or even principal) cause of factionalism. Benjamin and Ori argue that the high level of organizational complexity in pre-industrial society means that older models of political organization, such as faction, have not been superseded by modern forms, such as party.

The versatility of factionalism is indicated by the fact that in the Soviet Union and other Eastern bloc political systems, where power is highly centralized and factionalism specifically proscribed, personal factions are nevertheless well documented as a means whereby an aspirant political leader competes for elevation to top positions by placing a 'faction' of his supporters in strategic positions so that they can back him in his claims for high office. Again in societies such as India, which are deeply divided along ethnic, religious and caste lines, factions may in certain circumstances serve to modify such divsons by recruiting on a cross-cultural basis, with political ambition as the motivator. In other cases, it is true, recruitment follows the cultural divisions themselves.

Faction is thus a form of political organization which, though regarded as anachronistic in both liberal democratic and Marxist–Leninist traditions, has demonstrated surprising resilience and usefulness in many different political systems. It can hardly be regarded as a transitional form.

See also CLIENTELISM; PATRONAGE.   JAAS

Reading

Benjamin, R. and Ori, K.: *Tradition and Change in Postindustrial Japan: the role of political parties*, pp. 80–1. New York: Praeger, 1981.

Brass, P.R.: *Factional Politics in an Indian State: the Congress Party in Uttar Pradesh*. Berkeley and Los Angeles: University of California Press, 1965.

Katz, R.: *A Theory of Parties and Electoral Systems*. Baltimore, MD: The Johns Hopkins University Press, 1980.

Lasswell, H.D.: Faction. *Encyclopaedia of the Social Sciences*, V (1931).

Lemarchand, R.: Political clientelism and ethnicity in tropical Africa: competing solidarities in nation building. *American Political Science Review* 66.1 (March 1982) 91–113.

Nicholas, R.W.: Factions: a comparative analysis. In *Political Systems and the Distribution of Power*, pp. 21–6, ed. M. Banton. London: Tavistock, 1965.

Schmidt, S.W., Scott, J.C., Landé, C.H. and Guasti, L. eds: *Friends, Followers and Factions: a reader in political clientelism*. Berkeley, Los Angeles and London: University of California Press, 1977.

Stockwin, J.A.A.: A comparison of political factionalism in Japan and India. *Australian Journal of Politics and History* 16.3 (December 1970) 361–74.

fascism   A term designating a wide variety of violently nationalistic and authoritarian movements that reached the peak of their strength between 1930 and 1945. The term fascist derives from the *fasces* which were bundles of elm or birch rods bound with red cord and carried by the lictors in ancient Rome in attendance upon magistrates: the rods symbolized unity and authority.

The original fascist movement was that of Mussolini in Italy, organized in March 1921, although its origins lie in the first world war and, more deeply, in the intellectual reaction against liberalism which began in the latter half of the nineteenth century. The movement acquired various ideas and slogans which were to have a popular appeal among those hit by post-war disillusion and depression, and somewhat resentful of Italy's second-class status as a European power. It was ultra-patriotic, ultra-nationalist and pro-militarist in policy and style. Italian fascism was to some extent revolutionary: for example in its desire to shake off the constraints of bourgeois liberal democratic values and practices, in its dedication to modernization and industrial growth, in its exaltation of the role of youth. In other respects it was counter-revolutionary and reactionary: for example Mussolini offered the capitalists and the church a bulwark against Bolshevism, the style and practice of fascism favoured the continuance of the privileges and status of the Italian monarchy and aristocracy, the structure of fascist rule was rigidly elitist; Mussolini followed a colonialist policy traditionally associated with the Right.

Mussolini's Black Shirts had many imitators throughout Europe and Latin America – indeed nearly every European country had a fascist party in the 1930s – though there were enormous variations in ideology and programme. It was not so much the rather nebulous ideology of Italian fascism that proved so appealing (though certainly ultra-nationalism and anti-Bolshevism became identifying characteristics of all fascisms), but rather its mass revolutionist techniques. Drawing on his experience as a socialist party organizer and propagandist, Mussolini proved able to use the techniques of the mass movement with enormous *élan* and propaganda success. He learnt to use the symbolism and ritual of para-military organizations, uniforms, mass parades, demonstrations and the whole paraphernalia of youth movement and media manipulation, to consolidate his personal charisma and political power as dictator. In the long process of this consolidation, between 1921 and 1928, the inherent ambiguities and internal contradictions of fascism became apparent.

There was a running conflict over political aims and methods between the fascist movement's grass-roots militants and members of Mussolini's para-military militia, and the more conservative traditionalist forces in Italy which Mussolini was not powerful enough to destroy or control and upon whose tacit support the Mussolini regime depended for its survival. These were the army, the church, the monarchy, large landowners and major capitalist interests. There was, furthermore, an internal conflict within the fascist movement between the impetuous revolutionary zeal of the mass movement and the needs of the movement-regime to establish a stable, disciplined and centrally controlled party bureaucracy. There is evidence that not only the fascist movement organizers, but also Mussolini himself, became confused, baffled and vacillating, in the search for a fascist political strategy in the mid 1920s, on the eve of the 'second wave' of fascist illegality and intimidation.

The other European fascisms did not necessarily follow the Italian historical pattern. This does not, however, mean that we should abandon the term fascism. All these movements combined, to some degree, mass revolutionist strategies with reactionary ideologies compounded of virulent ultra-nationalism, exaltation of irrationality, illegality, violence and fanatical anti-communism. In Spain, the Falange only became temporarily dominant in the right-wing coalition of the 'national movement' between 1936 and 1941–42. During this period, its ideological militancy and sympathy with its brother movements, NAZISM and Italian fascism, were of indispensable value in acquiring the resources for Franco's Civil War victory. By the 1950s the ideological fanaticism of the Falange was an embarrassment to the Spanish regime.

Spanish and Italian fascisms also lacked the *völkisch* racialist and anti-Semitic ideology of Hitler's Nazism. (Italian fascism was not explicitly anti-Semitic until 1938, and did not engage in anti-Semitic persecution on a major scale until the SS itself directly intervened under the German occupation.) Furthermore, Hitler was vastly more successful both in his use of mass revolutionist strategies, mass propaganda and party organization, and the control of mass communications media, nationalist symbolism and slogans. He appealed to German youth, to the German propensities for authoritative dictatorial government and military glory, and to the German desire for revenge against the humiliations imposed by the Versailles powers. Hitler used the full repertoire of mass revolutionism both to further his racialist aims of pathological ANTI-SEMITISM and to bolster his own charisma and power as leader of the new 'revolution'. Through the agency of the Nazi para-military terror organizations, the SA, the SS and later the Gestapo, the Hitler regime was able to indulge in violent and sadistic mass terrorism, mass liquidation, racial persecution and racial extermination, secure in the knowledge that all popular bases for organized mass political opposition had been eliminated within the first twelve months of the Nazi revolution in 1933. Despite the considerable evidence that Hitler continued to meet stiff resistance to his will among individual members of the top military and state bureaucracy, the overwhelming actual and potential power over German society which fell to the Nazi party passed the threshold of TOTALITARIANISM appallingly rapidly after 1933. In Spain, Italy, Rumania and Hungary, fascist movements, despite their considerable influence as mass movements, did not achieve the scale of the Nazi hegemony.

It is not difficult to summarize the crude tenets of fascist ideology: the belief in the supremacy of the chosen national group over all other races and minorities; the total subordination of the individual to an absolute state under an absolute leader or Führer figure; the suppression of all autonomous secondary institutions; the rejection of the values and institutions of parliamentary democracy and their replacement by fascist dictatorships; total opposition to peaceful internationalism; a foreign policy of expansionism and conquest as the natural 'destiny' of the nation. As George Orwell observed in *The Road to Wigan Pier*: 'It is usual to speak of the fascist objective as the "beehive state", which does a grave injustice to bees. A world of rabbits ruled by stoats would be nearer the mark.'

Historians and social scientists have been baffled by the stubborn survival of small pockets of fascist belief and activity over forty years after the defeat of Hitler. The phenomenon of small neo-fascist movements, scattered not only in western Europe and North America but as far away as Australia and South Africa, defies all the established theories of political participation and rational political choice elaborated by political scientists. We perhaps come closer to explaining their continued existence if we view them as ideological–religious cult movements, sustained by a crude set of irrational dogmas, and paradoxically strengthened in their fanaticism by their total alienation from the norms and values of democratic societies. Wilkinson (1983) surveys the growth of tiny groups of this type and the problems they can create in liberal democratic societies.

But it would be dangerous to assume that neo-fascism will inevitably be confined to the role of tiny conspiratorial groups. There have been a number of remarkably effective attempts in western Europe since 1945 to develop neo-fascist parties with mass support, under a veneer of respectability. These include the National Democratic Party (NPD) in West Germany, the Italian Social Movement (MSI) in Italy (which managed to get fifty-six Deputies elected to the Chamber of Deputies in the 1972 elections), the National Front (NF) in Britain and the *Front National* in France. These movements have not succeeded in capturing power but they have shown their capacity to exploit certain populist fears and prejudices such as hostility to immigrants, racial prejudice, fear of large communist movements (in Italy and France), and general frustration with economic conditions in a period of recession.

See also RACE IN POLITICS.   PW

Reading

Felice, R. de: *Interpretations of Fascism*. Cambridge, Mass.: Harvard University Press, 1977.

Gentile, G.: The origins and doctrine of fascism. In *Italian Fascisms*, ed. A. Lyttleton. London: Cape, 1973.

Gregor, A.J.: *The Ideology of Fascism: the rationale of totalitarianism*. New York: Free Press, 1969.

Hagtvet, B., Larsen, S.U. and Myklebust, J.P.: *Who were the Fascists? Social Roots of European Fascism*. Oslo: Universitetsforlaget, 1980.

Laqueur, W. ed.: *Fascism: a reader's guide*. London: Wildwood, 1976.

Lyttleton, A. ed.: *Italian Fascisms from Pareto to Gentile*. London: Cape, 1973.

Mussolini, B.: *The Political and Social Doctrines of Fascism*. London: Hogarth, 1935.

Nolte, E.: *Three Faces of Fascism*. London: Weidenfeld & Nicolson, 1965.

Payne, S.G.: *Fascism: comparison and definition*. Madison: University of Wisconsin Press, 1980.

Weber, E.: *Varieties of Fascism*. New York: Van Nostrand, 1964.

Wilkinson, P.: *The New Fascists*, rev. edn. London: Pan Books, 1983.

Woolf, S. ed.: *Fascism in Europe*. London: Methuen, 1981.

federalism   A form of territorial political organization in which unity and regional diversity are accommodated within a single political system by distributing power among general and regional governments in a manner constitutionally safeguarding the existence and authority of each. Distinctive features are the distribution of authority between at least two levels of government and the coexistence of unity and regional diversity.

There has been much scholarly debate over the precise definition of federalism, and whether its essence lies in concepts of covenant and constitutionalism, in legal and political structures involving distributed authority, in noncentralized political processes, in pluralist ideology, or in underlying social, economic and political phenomena giving pluralism a territorial dimension. There have also been differences between those who favour inclusive or restricted definitions of the term.

Some scholars (e.g. Riker, Duchacek) have

argued for a broad inclusive definition encompassing a great variety of self-styled federations past and present that possess some element of internal autonomy but range from such highly centralized examples as the Soviet Union and some Latin American countries to the peripheralized federations with barely any central institutions at all found in the ancient world. Currently nearly two dozen states, including most of the large ones and containing about half the world's territory and over a third of the world's population, would fall within this classification. Among those usually cited are the USA, Canada, Mexico, Venezuela, Brazil, Argentina, Austria, West Germany, Switzerland, the USSR, Czechoslovakia, Yugoslavia, India, Pakistan, Malaysia, Australia, Nigeria and Cameroun.

Since these examples have so little in common as federations except the name, other scholars (e.g. Wheare; Sawer) have advocated a more restricted definition of the term based on a set of quintessential federations typified by the United States, Switzerland, Canada and Australia. This approach identifies the concept that neither the central nor the regional order of government should be legally or politically subordinate to the other as the basic federal principle. In this respect federal systems are contrasted with unitary systems in which the sub-units of government are subordinate to central governments, and with confederacies in which the central institutions, composed of delegates from the constituent state governments, are subordinate. Federalism is viewed as a compromise between extreme concentrations of power and loose confederacies. It makes possible the combination of effective central powers for handling common problems with the preservation of regional autonomy and distinctiveness. Federal political systems so conceived are not hierarchical systems of DECENTRALIZATION but non-centralized systems in which authority is diffused among independent but interacting centres. Both independence and interdependence, and both rivalry and co-operation, characterize relations between general and regional governments within federations.

The characteristic features found in federations consistent with the restricted definition above include the following: *two orders of government*, a general government and regional governments (usually but not invariably called states) existing in their own right under the constitution, each directly elected and acting directly upon citizens by legislation, administration and taxation; *a formal distribution of legislative and executive authority and of sources of revenue* between the two orders of government; *a written constitution* defining this distribution which is not unilaterally amendable in its fundamental provisions by one order of government alone; *an umpire*, usually a supreme court, to rule upon disputes over the respective constitutional powers of the two orders of governments; *specific processes and institutions* to facilitate intergovernmental administrative and political interaction; *central institutions*, including a bicameral legislature, designed to ensure that the interests of regional minorities and groups are accommodated in the processes of central policy making.

Within each federation the particular form of these institutions and processes has varied according to the strength and character of the historical, economic, social and political forces for integration and regionalism which the federal institutions have attempted to express and accommodate. Consequently there are significant variations among such federations as the United States, Switzerland, Canada, Australia, the Federal Republic of Germany and India in terms of: the number and relative size and wealth of the constituent units; the specific fields of jurisdiction and the revenues assigned to the two orders of government; the degree to which administrative responsibility for significant areas of central legislation is constitutionally assigned to the regional governments (West Germany, Switzerland and India being notable examples); the patterns of fiscal adjustment employed to balance governmental resources with responsibilities and to reduce regional disparities; the use of a supreme court, specialized constitutional court or (as in Switzerland) referenda to determine constitutionality of legislation; the specific institutions and processes through which intergovernmental consultation and co-operation are facilitated; and the provision of regional representation in the institutions for central policy making, such as the executive, the second chamber, the bureaucracy and regulatory agencies.

A particularly significant variation among federations is whether the principle of the 'SEPARATION OF POWERS' between the executive and legislature or 'responsible parliamentary government' has been incorporated in the central and regional governments. These have produced different processes for the role of political parties in achieving inter-regional consensus within general governments and for the conduct of intergovernmental relations. The former is typified by the presidential system in the USA and the collegial system in Switzerland. In both, the diffusion of authority within each order of government has resulted in the development of multiple points of contact and interpenetration administratively and politically between levels of government evoking the 'marble cake' image. In parliamentary federations, most notably Canada and Australia, the dominance of cabinets at both levels has made these the focus for relations between levels of government, and this 'executive federalism' has given these federations a more 'layer cake' character.

See also CONFEDERATION. RLWa

Reading

Duchacek, I.D.: *Comparative Federalism: the territorial dimension of politics*. New York: Holt, Rinehart & Winston, 1970.

————: *The Territorial Dimension of Politics Within, Among and Across Nations*. Boulder, Col. and London: Westview Press, 1986.

Elazar, D.J.: The ends of federalism: notes towards a theory of federal political arrangements. In *Federalismus als Partnerschaft* (Partnership in Federalism), pp. 25–56, ed. M. Frenkel. Bern: Peter Lang, 1977.

————: *American Federalism: a view from the states*. 3rd edn. New York: Harper & Row, 1984.

Hamilton, A., Madison, J. and Jay, J.: *The Federalist Papers*, ed. C. Rossiter. New York: Mentor, 1964.

Riker, W.H.: Federalism. In *The Handbook of Political Science*. Vol. V *Governmental Institutions and Processes*, pp. 93–172, ed. F.I. Greenstein and N.W. Polsby. Reading, Mass.: Addison-Wesley, 1975.

Sawer, G.: *Modern Federalism*. 2nd edn. London: Watts, 1976.

Stein, M.: Federal political systems and federal societies. *World Politics* 20 (1968) 721–737.

Wheare, K.C.: *Federal Government*. 4th edn. London: Oxford University Press, 1963.

Wildavsky, A. ed.: *American Federalism in Perspective*. Boston, Mass: Little, Brown, 1967.

Federalist Papers Usually known collectively as *The Federalist* and unique among major works in political theory in having been written for a precise and limited practical purpose, namely, to influence the voters of New York in favour of the new Constitution of the United States recently drafted by the Federal Convention at Philadelphia. The eighty-five papers appeared in serial form in the New York press betwen October 1787 and August 1788 above the signature 'Publius'. The actual authors, much indebted to contemporary British thought, were James MADISON (1751–1836) of Virginia, Alexander HAMILTON (1755–1804) and John Jay (1745–1829) both of New York. Madison had been a leading member of the Convention and Hamilton had also been present, although as the advocate of a far more centralized system than eventually emerged.

Madison's leading role in the drafting of the Constitution has made the *Federalist Papers* the most authoritative source for subsequent interpretation of the Constitution by American statesmen and in the courts. The authors had to persuade their readers that it was possible to create a political system strong enough to present a united aspect to the outside world but one in which the individual states would preserve the degree of autonomy in their domestic affairs which their citizens claimed as of right. They had also to reassure men of property that the diffusion of power between the Federal Government and the states would prove an adequate safeguard against confiscatory legislation. Finally they had to demonstrate that the concentration of authority at the centre in the hands of a single-person executive, the proposed president of the United States, would not lead to tyranny because of the CHECKS AND BALANCES inherent in the SEPARATION OF POWERS.

Although some systems in the ancient world and in Switzerland and the Netherlands were called federal, and although many of the devices of the Constitution itself could be traced to practice in the British Empire before the American Revolution – JUDICIAL REVIEW for instance – the Constitution of the United States is the first example of FEDERALISM as we have come to know it in modern times, and the *Federalist Papers*, the classic exposition of the principles of federal government.

The importance of the *Federalist Papers* has been greater in the English-speaking world than in continental Europe and they were used by English publicists to urge the cause of IMPERIAL FEDERATION at the beginning of the twentieth century and of ideas of world federation during and after the second world war. The *Federalist Papers* were also influential in the discussions leading to the Constitution of the Union of South Africa in 1909.

Although three French editions appeared in the 1790s, European federalism drew on other sources. The first Italian translation, which appeared in 1955, was, however, related to the movement for European unity. Today the *Federalist Papers* are studied mostly for the light they throw on the general problem of limited government.   B

Reading

Adair, D.: *Fame and the Founding Fathers*, ed. T. Colbourn. New York: Norton, 1974.

Cooke, J.E. ed.: *The Federalist*. Middletown, Conn.: Wesleyan University Press, 1961.

Hamilton, A., Madison, J. and Jay, J.: *The Federalist*, rev. edn, ed. M. Beloff. Oxford: Blackwell, 1987; also *The Federalist Papers*, ed. C. Rossiter. New York: Mentor, 1964.

Main, J.T.: *The Anti-Federalists: critics of the Constitution, 1781–1788*. Chapel Hill: University of North Carolina Press, 1969.

Onuf, P.S.: *The Origins of the Federal Republic 1775–1787*. Philadelphia: University of Pennsylvania Press, 1983.

Wills, G.W.: *Explaining America: The Federalist*. London: Athlone, 1981.

feminist movements Feminist theories of the eighteenth and nineteenth centuries were largely liberal in inspiration and based on claims of justice and fairness. The arguments of Mary Wollstonecraft, William Thompson, John Stuart MILL, and Harriet Taylor Mill had in common the idea of women's equality with men because of their common nature as free human beings. These thinkers sometimes explored the social and political changes which would be required if the idea of equality were to become a reality, but a movement developed only when their adherents began to advocate practical political programmes for its achievement.

In Britain, the commitment of many utilitarians to feminism meant the direct translation of the intellectual argument about equality into the public policy arena. As a result the feminist movement in Britain was initially mainly a pressure group for female suffrage, on the assumption that women's equality would be assured once they were equal citizens. In Sweden too, the oldest-established women's organization, the Fredrika Bremer Association, pressed for the vote from 1889 on and in 1903 spawned the National Association for Women's Suffrage. In America the suffrage was only one of the number of equality demands of the infant feminist movement born at the Seneca Falls Convention in 1848. From the middle of the nineteenth century American feminists were inspired by and strongly associated with the cause of slavery, and the comparison of the positions of women and blacks is one which runs through to the contemporary movement. In pre-revolutionary Russia, although the movement itself emphasized the vote, the 'woman question' was always also taken to involve educational equality and access to professional life, divorce, and contraception. In 1905 middle-class women founded the Union for Women's Equality and a feminist political party to press for these reforms. This so-called 'first-wave feminism' revolved around claims for equality with men, demands for the same legal and political rights, and in particular the vote. With the progressive granting of female suffrage in many countries during the first half of the twentieth century (see WOMEN'S SUFFRAGE) it became apparent that the god had failed; the vote gave only formal parity and equality had still not been achieved.

The feminist movements of the 1970s and 1980s have therefore concentrated on 'women's liberation', analysing women's role in society, denying the superior value of male criteria, and challenging the time-honoured distinction between the public and the private spheres where politics is located in the former and women in the latter (see GENDER AND POLITICS). In this context the movement has encouraged 'consciousness-raising' by an emphasis on the non-aggressive, non-hierarchical, and co-operative style which is seen as particularly female, and has largely rejected the individualistic assertiveness which is presented as characteristically male. 'Radical feminists' have often believed that mainstream electoral politics is so overwhelmingly dominated by men that women should eschew it; 'Liberal feminists' on the other hand have tended to argue that women will only be adequately politically represented when they are present, in far greater numbers, in national parliaments. But Iceland is the only democracy in which an explicitly feminist party is at present represented in the legislature.   EMV

Reading

Bradshaw, J. ed.: The women's liberation movement: Europe and North America. *Women's Studies International Quarterly* special issue, 4.4 (1981).

Charvet, J.: *Feminism*. London: Dent, 1982.

Elshtain, J.: *Public Man, Private Woman*. Princeton, NJ: Princeton University Press, 1981.

Freeman, J.: *The Politics of Women's Liberation*. New York and London: Longman, 1975.

Rowbotham, S.: *Hidden from History*. London: Pluto, 1974.

feudalism The term most commonly used to describe a network of social obligations within the ARISTOCRACY of early medieval Europe, and also, more contentiously, the relations of the aristocracy with the agrarian producers under their lordship and control. The very essence of these relationships was taken by nineteenth-century scholars and publicists to entail the decay of effective public authority and the fragmentation of state power as wielded in the later Roman Empire. In Marxist historical analysis feudalism was the mode of economic and social exploitation appropriate to the want of liquid resources and the collapse of urban life in late Antiquity and the early Middle Ages.

The fief (from *feudum*, fee) became the means by which service, especially military service, was increasingly organized and rewarded, a grant of land which bound a powerful man to his prince and humbler warriors to the powerful, both ecclesiastical and lay nobles. The most characteristic act denoting this dependence at all levels was that of commendation and the ceremony of homage when the man, the 'vassal', placed his hands into those of his lord and also swore security and fidelity to him. Many men were so tied without receiving fiefs, but to maintain horses, arms and the heavy equipment for the style of warfare developing from the ninth century onwards, it proved expedient to enfeoff (grant fiefs to) vassals, with land or revenues. The land was then deemed to be held by homage and service. Feudal tenures were contractual and never wholly unprecarious, although often enough they hardened into hereditary possession and became the hallmark of honorific status setting apart privileged from humiliating forms of dependence. The vassal followed his lord in war and in peace, kept guard at his castles, attended his court, advised, aided and supported him. His marriage, and the marriages of his children might be subject to the lord's discretion and the heir might owe the lord a 'relief' to succeed to the paternal fief. If he was a minor the lord might have the wardship and the issues of his fief until he came of age. All these 'incidents', as they were called by lawyers, lay embedded in the primal homage and service obligation. Conversely the lord must protect and defend his man against outside challengers.

France from the ninth to the thirteenth century and Anglo-Norman England became the classical homes of feudalism in this mould, though there were infinite regional variations and divergencies, between the north and the south for example, not to mention the colonial feudalisms established by the Norman conquerors in southern Italy and Sicily, and the Latins in Antioch and the Kingdom of Jerusalem. The bonds and the ethos which great lords shared with their knightly homagers gradually became stronger and the social divide between them and the dependent peasantry – the once free men who had owed fidelity and public services to Charlemagne and Louis the Pious (768–840) – widened. This process of social crystallization, accompanied as it was by much feuding, in the castellanies of central France for example, has sometimes been labelled 'feudal anarchy' by historians. Rapid economic growth, the need for safe communications, and the interests of ecclesiastical establishments, however, all helped to re-establish the powers of royal and princely overlords. In Anglo-Norman England especially the problems of the conquerors' own security dictated a form of feudalism which favoured lordship and above all kingship. The rulers could use feudal ties, such as wardships, marriages and reliefs, to shape baronial society to their advantage. The combinations of greater and lesser vassals eventually imposed stricter legal limits on royal exploitation of feudal rights but it did not end them. On the continent of Europe too, the princely, royal and imperial courts, as social and judicial centres and seats of lay culture, reveal feudal institutions that were able to sustain varying degrees of state power while at the same time resisting its abuse. Rousseau's scathing denunciation of 'feudal government' in the *Contrat Social* (bk. 3, ch. 15) was hardly justified.

In western and central Europe the tenurial structures of feudalism, tenure by homage and service, shaped and determined land law and proved capable of living side by side with burgeoning urban, commercial and monetary expansion. The employment of mercenaries and even the rise of professional armies did not quite break the back of relationships which had become second nature to the hierarchies of aristocratic European societies. In England only the Restoration of Charles II and in France only the Revolution and its imitators (the reformers in the wake of defeat by Napoleon's armies) were able to do this. Moreover, feudalism exerted a profound influence on the development of early forms of constitutional and representative government.

There remains the question whether the phenomena described here, vassalage, fiefs and incidents, were wholly peculiar to Europe or whether they also and at the same time shaped the development of societies elsewhere. The medieval Islamic world and Japan both, for example, possessed institutions and social bonds which have been called feudal even though the cultural context in each case differed profoundly from that of the Latin west.

See also SERFDOM.   KL

Reading

Bloch, M.: *Feudal Society*. 2 vols, trans. L.A. Manyon. London: Routledge & Kegan Paul, 1962.

Brown, E.A.R.: The tyranny of a construct: feudalism and historians of medieval Europe. *American Historical Review* 79 (1974) 1063–88.

Fourquin, G.: *Lordship and Feudalism in the Middle Ages*, trans. I. and A. Lytton-Sells. New York: Pica Press, 1976.

Ganshof, F.L.: *Feudalism*, trans. P. Grierson. London: Longman, 1952.

field service administration   Governmental *deconcentration* – the bureaucratic delegation of defined authority for decision making to a central administration's own employees working outside headquarters – directly affects more people in the world than the more glamorous DEVOLUTION. Moreover, in centralized and in decentralized countries alike, the majority of the personnel employed by central and state governments work 'in the field'; autonomous local authorities and parastatal bodies themselves exercise most of their devolved powers through their own field service administrations.

Models of field service administration range from France's Napoleonic integrated prefectoral system – familiar in many former colonies – organized primarily on a territorial basis with a fused hierarchy of deconcentrated and devolved authorities; through eastern Europe's 'dual subordination', under which field administrators are accountable vertically to specialist functional agencies and horizontally to generalist representative councils; to the split hierarchy of the 'Anglo-Saxon' tradition, organized primarily on a functional basis, with deconcentrated field officials and devolved authorities severally responsible for quite separate services.

Field administration enables the delegating authority to preserve unchallenged political control over decision making while at the same time through employed subordinates: accomplishing its tasks in every part of its territory (and beyond); enhancing its own managerial efficiency by dispersing the decision-making function; retaining adequate flexibility and responsiveness to local economic and social circumstances; and exercising appropriate supervision and control over agencies to which it has devolved power. Moreover, it is usually easier for central field agents than for politically vulnerable local authorities to implement desirable, but locally unpopular, policies.

See also CENTRALIZATION AND DE-CENTRALIZATION; LOCAL GOVERNMENT; PREFECT.   HJBA

Reading

Leemans, A.F.: *Changing Patterns of Local Government*. The Hague: IULA, 1970.

Maddick, H.: *Democracy, Decentralization and Development*. New York: Asia Publishing House, 1963.

Smith, B.C.: *Decentralization: the territorial dimension of the state*. London: Allen & Unwin, 1985.

Verebélyi, I.: *Development Trends in the Council Administration Systems of the Socialist Countries*. Budapest: IMPA, 1985; also in *International Review of Administrative Sciences*. Brussels, 1986.

Yin, R.K.: Decentralization of government agencies: What does it accomplish? In *Making Bureaucracies Work*, ed. C.H. Weiss and A.H. Barton. London and Beverly Hills, Calif.: Sage, 1980.

filibuster   See PARLIAMENTARY OBSTRUCTION.

Finer, Herman (1898–1969)   The son of Romanian Jewish parents, Finer joined the staff of the London School of Economics in 1920, resigning in 1942 to become professor of political science at the University of Chicago from 1945–68. A passionate democrat, a Fabian (see his *Road to Reaction* (1945)) he was anti-marxist and anti-fascist (see his still classical study, *Mussolini's Italy* (1935)).

Finer's major work is the *Theory and Practice of Modern Government* (1932, revised 1949), a study based largely upon four democracies: Britain, the USA, France and Weimar Germany. This work is seminal. It is some 1500 pages long and, as the author somewhat immodestly states, was based on all the (then) available written sources. It still exerts a profound influence since it differs sharply from preceding and some succeeding comparative studies. It remains the most powerful example of the institution-by-institution approach unlike the country-by-country approach used by Lowell and BRYCE. Their analysis cannot be pushed further than a set of topical essays, cross-cutting the descriptions of one country after another. It also differs, and even more sharply, from the reductionism of Almond et al.'s 'functionalism' in which the political mechanisms and institutions are submerged in the detailed description of the 'inputs'. The *Theory and Practice*, after stating the nature and conditions of state activity, dis-assembles the constituent institutions and mechanisms and then for each item, such as constitutions, representation, electoral systems etc. provides its rationale, its internal logic and the permissible limits of its variations. Though the model is mechanistic, this is a purely heuristic device; few political scientists were more aware of, or paid as much attention to, the historical antecedents of the state and its institutions Many of the sections in *Theory and Practice* remain unsurpassed. The outdated elements of the book are, naturally, the descriptive ones: the analytical parts remain as valid now as when written.   SEF

Reading

Finer, H.: *Representative Government and a Parliament of Industry*. London: Fabian Society; Allen & Unwin, 1923.

————: *Theory and Practice of Modern Government* (1932), rev. and enlarged edn. London: Methuen, 1949.

————: *Mussolini's Italy* (1935). London: Cass, 1964.

————: *Road to Reaction* (1945), rev. edn. London: Greenwood, 1977.

————: *The Governments of Greater European Powers*. New York: Holt, 1956.

——: *The Major Governments of Modern Europe.* Evanston, Ill.: Row, Peterson, 1960.

First Amendment freedoms

First Amendment freedoms The opening Article of the US Constitution's BILL OF RIGHTS includes not merely freedom of speech and of the press, but also guarantees against any official establishment of religion or any prohibition on its free exercise, plus the right of peaceful assembly and the right to petition the government. Yet in a popular sense the First Amendment is usually identified with freedom of speech and of the press – the original, basic 'open society' rights which are the starting point of democratic CONSTITU-TIONALISM since they are the key to the whole political process. Justice (later Chief Justice) Harlan Stone recognized this and provided a landmark in his opinion in the *Carolene Products* case in 1938; and the idea, though bitterly criticized by Justice Frankfurter a decade later, was built up by liberal activist judges such as Black and Douglas into a constitutional dogma of the 'preferred position' of the First Amendment free speech guarantee, making it rank ahead of all other constitutional rights.

Though the First Amendment was addressed only to the federal government, there seems general agreement, now, with Justice Black's 'shorthand' theory of its incorporation, together with the rest of the original Bill of Rights (the first ten Amendments to the Constitution), into the Fourteenth Amendment so that it should also become applicable to the state governments of the US federal system.

Compatibly with its priority constitutional status, the First Amendment free speech guarantee is not a constitutional absolute, for it must still be weighed against other, counter-vailing interests in the concrete circumstances of individual cases. Justice Holmes, in the *Schenck* case in 1919, rightly remarked that the 'most stringent protection of free speech would not protect a man falsely shouting fire in a theatre and causing a panic', thereby underlining the pragmatism and common sense necessary in the application of this, as with other, Bill of Rights provisions.

See also FREEDOM OF SPEECH, EXPRESSION AND THE PRESS.   EMcW

Reading

Chafee, Z. Jr: *Free Speech in the United States.* Cambridge, Mass.: Harvard University Press, 1954.

Frankfurter, F.: *Mr Justice Holmes and the Supreme Court.* Cambridge, Mass.: Belknap, 1961.

Mason, A.T.: *Harlan Fiske Stone: pillar of the law.* New York: Viking, 1956.

Mendelson, W.: *Justices Black and Frankfurter: conflict in the court.* Chicago, Ill.: University of Chicago Press, 1961.

O'Brien, F.W.: *Justice Reed and the First Amendment.* Washington, DC: Georgetown University Press, 1958.

fiscal crisis of the state

fiscal crisis of the state In the early 1970s the MARXIST economist James O'Connor coined this phrase to describe a specific situation in an advanced industrial society where the demands on state spending radically outstrip available tax and borrowing resources, with major implications for the LEGITIMACY of government. O'Connor's analysis assumes that state intervention in a CAPITALIST society fulfils two key functions. First, public expenditure and taxation are used to regulate the economy, dramatically reducing the frequency and depth of profitability crises. Previous economic crises under capitalism took the form of over-capitalization, the piling up of unsold goods, or a loss of business confidence in the future development of the economy which resulted in bank failures, stock exchange collapses, sharp falls in prices and disinvestment by business. Now however many crisis tendencies are displaced into the public sector as government commits resources to sustain the continued accumulation of capital or to maintain economically necessary activities which business can no longer perform profitably. State expenditures which directly enhance business profitability O'Connor describes as 'social investment' spending.

Second, state intervention is crucial in legitimizing the existing social order, making its arrangements seem fair and acceptable, promoting social stability and public order. The constant threat of disruptive social unrest under previous industrial capitalism has been partially countered by WELFARE STATE policies which aim to co-opt crucial sections of the labour force into a 'class compromise' with capital, particularly the unionized, stably employed, predominantly white workforces of monopoly corporations. Social insurance provisions and the provision of collective consumption services by government both increase the 'social wage', adding an extra element to living standards which is financed by general taxation rather than falling directly on employers. These provisions increase demand for consumer goods, stabilize demand, and attach people to the social system. O'Connor describes state expenditures which indirectly enhance business profitability by maintaining workers' living standards as 'social consumption' spending. He also distinguished a third category of expenditures which are functionally necessary for any society (not just a capitalist one) but which do not increase business profitability, which he termed 'social expenses'.

The fiscal crisis of the state stems directly from the constant political pressures to inflate social investment and social consumption spending, which divert more and more resources out of the profit-making process. State fiscal resources depend on business profitability and wage incomes. An increasing tax-take slows the accumulation process while simultaneously boosting business pressure for government intervention. Worsening economic prospects impair social stability and increase the need for 'band aid' interventions to cool city riots or union militancy. Since the public sector is highly unionized, state workers can generally keep their wages in line with other unionized workers in the large-firm sector. If labour productivity in government employment increases more slowly than in monopoly corporations, then the real cost of a given level of public services will rise over time, implying a rising tax-take just to maintain existing service levels. The impact of this trend on individual tax-payers is increased by corporations' ability to evade more and more of their nominal tax commitments.

Accumulation and legitimation pressures for spending exceed state resources when the economy stops growing and downturns sharply (as in many western countries following the 1973 oil price increase), or when a majority of voters begin to sharply resist further tax increases. Governments' first response may be to borrow more money, but deficit financing only increases spending commitments to meet escalating interest payments. Hence the state apparatus is forced into a situation where major reductions of state spending have to be pushed through quickly, creating severe legitimacy problems. Business pressure will ensure that the social investment programmes closest to their interests are protected from cutbacks, magnifying the pressures on social consumption programmes. Overall a process of 'recommodifying capital' is set in train, in which welfare state expenditures are selectively cut back at the same time as direct business support is maintained.

O'Connor argued that a potential exists for two groups to unite to defeat demands for spending reductions, in the process becoming radicalized into an awareness of their common interests. The first is the group left most outside the welfare state compromise, namely the generally non-unionized workers of the market sector, who are most exposed to unemployment and are disproportionately made up of the young or elderly, women and ethnic minorities. The second are state workers whose living standards and working conditions will come under direct attack during the fiscal crisis. The alliance between these sectoral groups in O'Connor's schema offers a substitute for the lost proletariat of orthodox Marxist theory, many of whom are co-opted into the class compromise in the large firm sector and firmest in their resistance to further income or consumer tax increases. Resistance to re-commodification could generalize the system crisis, radicalizing more people until they appreciate the fundamentally oppressive character of capitalism.

O'Connor's work had an immediate success because of its apparent application to conditions in the late 1970s, especially such incidents as the virtual bankruptcy of New York city in 1977 and the 1976 currency crisis in Britain, when the International Monetary Fund imposed public spending cutbacks on a Labour government as a condition of bailing out sterling with an international loan. His claim to be developing a detailed Marxist 'fiscal sociology' was also an attractive exception to the general scarcity of Marxist empirical work. His book influenced subsequent work on urban politics and the welfare state, but the approach was never developed and it rapidly became apparent that the social investment/ social consumption distinction cannot be operationalized. Expectations of a closer alliance between state workers and the state dependent population have also not been generally confirmed, despite isolated moves in this direction.   PJD

Reading

Heald, D.: *Public Expenditure: its defence and reform*, pp. 263–70. Oxford: Martin Robertson, 1983.

Newton, K. and Karran, T.J.: *The Politics of Local Expenditure*, ch. 3. London: Macmillan, 1985.

O'Connor, J.: *The Fiscal Crisis of the State*. New York: St Martin's, 1973.

Rose, R. and Peters, B.G.: *Can Government go Bankrupt?* New York: Basic Books, 1978; London: Macmillan, 1979.

floating voter   Someone who stands outside political parties scrutinizing and evaluating alternative electoral programmes before voting. This small but informal vote determines the outcome of elections where major parties command the stable support of large blocks of the electorate. The extent to which this model corresponds to reality, though, is a long-standing controversy in the field of voting studies. Past research (summarized in Benewick et al.) on elections has indicated that floating voters are less interested and less well-informed than loyal party supporters. These findings have implications for liberal democratic theory suggesting an irrational electoral process in which the balance is held by a small number of relatively ignorant voters. But voting is a more complex activity than the model suggests, and other factors beside party programmes must be taken into account. These include perceptions of Party image, ideology and leadership; the force of habit, issues and events; and the voter's background, values and socio-economic interests. Furthermore floating voters comprise a more hetero-

geneous group than was at first recognized, including intermittent abstainers, temporary and permanent converts, and strategic and instrumental voters.

There is now evidence that floating voters comprise a larger portion of and are more representative of the electorate, than earlier surveys had indicated (see Heath et al.; Rose and McAllister). This is suggested by the increase in ELECTORAL VOLATILITY; for the floating-voter model and its critiques assume that voting behaviour is relatively static and party allegiance stable. In Britain a significantly growing proportion of the electorate has been adrift since the mid-1960s, with a decline in turnout and in PARTY IDENTIFICATION, and a growth in ISSUE VOTING.   RJB

Reading

Benewick, R. et al.: The floating voter and the liberal view of representation. *Political Studies* 17 (1969) 177–95.

Heath, A. et al.: *How Britain Votes*. Oxford: Pergamon, 1985.

Rose, R. and McAllister, I.: *Voters Begin to Choose*. London: Sage, 1986.

Särlvik, B. and Crewe, I.: *Decade of Dealignment*. London and Cambridge: Cambridge University Press, 1983.

franchise   The term franchise is used to designate a set of public rules specifying how citizenship rights, or more precisely voting rights, are acquired within a territory. Franchise is a key concept in the development of equalitarian democratic ELECTIONS. The pre-revolutionary period was characterized by great local and regional variations in franchise practices. Territorial representation did not exist except in England. REPRESENTATION was based upon membership in ESTATES (nobility, clergy, the city corporations of merchants and artisans) and in most countries each estate constituted a separate chamber (see Hintze; Lousse; Palmer). The French Revolution brought about a fundamental change in the conception of representation: the individual citizen became the basic unit, and representation was no longer channelled through separate functional bodies but through a unified national assembly. The new system of territorial representation was introduced in France in a law of 1792 which gave the franchise to all men of 21 years or more, except paupers, servants and vagabonds. In the constitution of 1793 even paupers were included in the electorate. During the Restoration franchise rules were restricted, but estate representation never returned in France (see Bendix).

In the wake of the French and the American Revolutions there was a period of standardization of franchise rules. Five sets of criteria were used in limiting the franchise during this transitional period: traditional *estate* criteria, restriction of franchise to heads of households within established status groups defined by law; *régime censitaire*, restrictions based on property or income; *régime capacitaire*, restrictions based on literacy, formal education, or appointments to public office; *household responsibility* criteria, restrictions to heads of households occupying own dwellings of a minimum volume or for a minimum rent; *residence* criteria, restrictions to citizens registered as residents within specified constituency boundaries or within the national territory for a given length of time (see Bendix; Meyer; Rokkan; Williamson).

The February Revolution of 1848 gave rise to movements for representative democracy throughout Europe, and during the subsequent years franchise was greatly expanded. Formal inequalities of influence persisted, however, under arrangements for multiple votes or for differential ratios of votes to representatives.

Under the slogan 'one man, one vote, one value', the struggle for equal voting rights was carried on into the next phase, during which manhood suffrage was introduced. All significant economic and social criteria of qualification for men above a given age were abolished. Although formal restrictions had been removed, however, marked differences in the weight of votes across constituencies still existed (see Zwager).

The current and final phase has been characterized by continued democratization. The most important events are the enfranchisement of women, of younger age groups (the lowering of voting age to 20 and even to 18 years) and to short-term residents. Further-more, there has been a continued equalization of voter-representation ratios throughout the national territory.

The described sequences of franchise development have varied greatly from nation to nation. Thus the smooth step by step development in countries such as Britain and Sweden contrasts sharply with the abrupt and revolutionary changes in France. In Britain the process took more than one hundred years from the Reform Act of 1832 to the abolition of multiple votes in 1948 (see Seymour). In Sweden the system of estate representation was abolished in 1866, but substantial inequalities of electoral influence existed until 1921 (see Verney). In France on the other hand, the change from estate representation to the stage of manhood suffrage occurred within a period of four years, from 1789 to 1793. But this sudden thrust toward mass democracy proved short-lived. It was followed by the Terror and for decades France was torn between traditionalist attempts to restrict franchise to a narrow stratum of owners and high officials and radical-plebiscitarian pressures for universal and equal elections.

The electoral histories of the rest of Europe fall between these two models. In the German territories, development followed competing patterns. Most spectacular was Prussia in which two widely different systems coexisted for about half a century. Manhood suffrage was introduced in Prussia by a royal decree in 1849, but the weight of the votes of the 'lower orders' was infinitesimal compared with the middle classes and the landowners. By contrast, the Reichstag was elected on the basis of equal franchise for all men. This principle had been adopted by the German national assembly in Frankfurt in 1848, but it was not enforced until 1867, when Bismarck realized the significance of general elections as a source of legitimacy for his new Reich. The Habsburg empire went through a longer and more tortuous process towards democratization: first, estate representation; from 1861 corporate-interest representation in a system of four curiae to which a fifth one was added in 1896; finally, in 1907, a unified system of national representation based on suffrage with equal rights for all men.

Belgium followed a step by step development like Sweden and England. The Dutch pattern was less regular, but resembled the same model. Denmark and Norway, however, came closer to the French model with rather abrupt changes. Denmark, the most absolutist of the Nordic polities, introduced estate representation in 1831 and then went into a system of extensive manhood suffrage in 1849. In Norway the Constitution of 1814 gave the franchise to nearly half of the male population, and in 1898 manhood suffrage was introduced. Finland, which was a Grand Duchy under the Russian Czar from 1809–1917, maintained the inherited Swedish estate representation until 1906, and then all of a sudden adopted a system with full suffrage not only for men, but also for women.

By the end of the first world war the great majority of European and European settled nations had introduced suffrage for men, several also for women. Franchise for women (see Kraditor) came first in settler nations (Wyoming in 1890; the rest of the United States in 1920; New Zealand 1893; South Australia 1895) and in Scandinavia (Finland 1906; Norway 1910–13; Denmark 1915; Sweden 1918–21). The tendency was for Roman Catholic nations to be slower than the Protestant ones in giving the franchise to women. Switzerland was surprisingly slow in introducing this reform: until 1971 Swiss women were not permitted to vote in federal elections.

With the dismantling of colonial empires after the second world war and the subsequent establishment of a great number of new nations the principle of 'one man, one vote' has gained ground throughout the world. Interestingly enough there has been no repetition in the new nations of the discussion in nineteenth century Europe about restrictions of franchise owing to illiteracy or poverty. The most serious struggles of the old cry of 'one man, one vote' have occurred in the ethnically most divided nations like South Africa and Rhodesia. In most nations the franchise has been an element in a strategy for national unification and the control of dissidence (see Rokkan).

See also WOMEN'S SUFFRAGE.   HV

Reading

Bendix, R.: *Nation-building and Citizenship*. Berkeley: University of California Press, 1977.

Hintze, O.: *Staat und Verfassung: Gesammelte Abhandlungen zur allgeimeinen Verfassungsgeschichte*. Göttingen: Vandenhoeck & Ruprecht, 1962.

Kraditor, A.: *The Ideas of the Woman Suffrage Movement*. New York: Columbia University Press, 1965.

Lousse, E.: *La Société d'Ancien Régime: organisation et representation corporatives*. Louvain: Université de Louvain, 1943.

Meyer, G.: *Das parlamentarische Wahlrecht*. Berlin: Haering, 1901.

Palmer, R.R.: *The Challenge*. Vol. I of *The Age of the Democratic Revolution: a political history of Europe and America, 1760–1800*. Princeton, NJ: Princeton University Press, 1959.

Rokkan, S.: Electoral systems. In *International Encyclopedia of the Social Sciences*, Vol. V, pp. 6–21. ed. E. Sills. New York: Crowell-Collier & Macmillan, 1968.

Seymour, C.: *Electoral Reform in England and Wales: the development and operation of the parliamentary franchise, 1832–1885*. New Haven, Conn.: Yale University Press, 1915.

Verney, D.V.: *Parliamentary Reform in Sweden, 1866–1921*. Oxford: Clarendon Press, 1957.

Williamson, C.: *American Suffrage: from property to democracy, 1760–1860*. Princeton, NJ: Princeton University Press, 1960.

Zwager, H.H.: *De motivering van het algemen kiesrecht en Europa*. Gronnigen: Wolfers, 1958.

freedom of information   A term sometimes used loosely in connection with international debates over the free flow of information between countries, or as a synonym for 'freedom of expression'. In a more limited sense it was used by the US Congress as the title of the Freedom of Information Act (1966), which established a general right of public access to federal government records. It is now often used generically to describe similar legislation in other countries such as France (1978), the Netherlands (1978), Canada (1983), Australia (1983), and New Zealand (1983). Sweden was the first country, by two centuries, to adopt such legislation. The general right of access to government documents was first established as part of the

Swedish constitution in 1766. Known in Swedish as *offentlighetsprincip* (the publicity principle), it provided a model for other Scandinavian countries which adopted similar legislation, such as Finland (1951), Norway (1970), and Denmark (1970).

Laws which are described as providing freedom of information all establish a general right of access to government records without any requirement that a reason for requesting access to records (a 'need to know') be demonstrated (although some statutes limit the right of access to citizens and residents). All of them have exemptions from the rule of disclosure on request, commonly for matters relating to national security, diplomacy, personal privacy, trade secrets, and internal policy making. All of them have some procedure for appeals to an impartial arbiter to decide whether a government claim for exemption from disclosure is justified, although the arbiter may be a judge, OMBUDSMAN, special commission, or a combination of these.

See also OPEN GOVERNMENT. JRM

Reading

Civil Service Department: *Disclosure of Information: a report on overseas practice*. London: HMSO, 1979.

Cross, H.: *The People's Right to Know*. New York: Columbia University Press, 1953.

McMillan, J.: Making government accountable: a comparative analysis of freedom of information statutes. *New Zealand Law Journal* (1977).

Mathews, A.: *The Darker Reaches of Government: access to information about public administration in the United States, Britain, and South Africa*. Berkeley: University of California Press, 1978.

Rowat, D. ed.: *Administrative Secrecy in Developed Countries*. London: Macmillan, 1979.

freedom of religion An important CIVIL LIBERTY denoting the freedom to hold and exercise any religious belief or none, including the freedom to express it in speech and forms of worship.

In medieval Europe conformity to the Catholic church was enforced by church and state authorities, and dissent was punishable as heresy. After the Reformation civil authorities in Protestant countries generally continued to impose conformity, although

toleration was practised in Holland from the sixteenth century. America became a haven for those in search of tolerance, but there too the persecuted, when they became dominant, often became persecutors themselves. During the eighteenth century, however, a spirit of toleration began to prevail. The United States Constitution prohibited religious tests for office and the Bill of Rights guaranteed free exercise of religion and a separation of church and state. In England, France, and other European countries, toleration was enjoined or practised, and the disabilities attaching to religious minorities, atheists and Jews were substantially removed.

Most constitutions nowadays provide for freedom of religion. Many states however maintain an established or official religion and a number, by legislation or in practice, impede or restrict public worship or the observance of religious practices. Freedom of religion was propounded in Article 18 of the United Nations Universal Declaration of Human Rights (1948), and receives protection in the EUROPEAN CONVENTION ON HUMAN RIGHTS and other international covenants. Questions may of course arise as to whether or not certain beliefs (such as devil-worship) constitute religions and conflicts may arise between religious practices and prevailing legislation, ethics or social customs. CRM

Reading

Bury, J.B.: *A History of Freedom of Thought*. London: Williams & Norgate, 1913.

Pfeffer, L.: *Church, State and Freedom*. Boston, Mass.: Beacon, 1967.

Ruffini, F.: *Religious Liberty*. London: Williams & Norgate, 1912.

freedom of speech, expression, and the press One of the most important CIVIL LIBERTIES or RIGHTS. It denotes the freedom to communicate orally, in writing or print, or other medium. It is linked to freedom of opinion, conscience and religion since the freedom to hold ideas is devalued without the opportunity to express them. It is also linked to freedom of assembly, which allows numbers of persons to exercise together their rights of association and free speech.

In the despotisms and oligarchies of ancient China, India and Israel, laws were based on religion, and orthodoxy of expression was imposed. By contrast, considerable liberty was afforded in the democracy of Athens in the fifth century BC. Free-born Athenians had the right to attend and speak in the Assembly and participate in government. Freedom was by no means absolute however, for Aeschylus, Euripides, Socrates and Aristotle were variously exiled, condemned to death or forced into flight, and besides, freedom had only a brief flowering. If the Hellenistic polities laid the foundation of western culture, their philosophers provided justifications for censorship as well as for freedom. The justifications of defeating paganism and countering infidelity served to allow the punishment of heretics in Jewish, Christian and Islamic countries up to medieval times, and in many instances longer.

The Renaissance encouraged freer political and religious thought as well as artistic expression. The rise of humanism promoted scepticism of authority. When religious struggles associated with the Reformation took place in various countries, arguments were advanced for toleration of diversity, on philosophical and pragmatic grounds. In western Europe greater degrees of freedom of expression were often achieved as a by-product of the gaining of FREEDOM OF RELIGION.

Sometimes however restrictions were imposed on political, rather than religious, grounds. The development of printing and the gradual growth of literacy led to the appearance of newspapers and journals in seventeenth-century Europe. Governments responded by imposing controls. In England the Star Chamber tried to suppress newspapers, and later the granting of a monopoly, and licensing powers, were used. In 1694 Parliament refused to renew the Licensing Act, with the indirect and accidental result that prior restraints on publication were abolished, never to be re-introduced. This was freedom of a sort, even if harassment, prosecutions for libel, and taxation continued to be used to restrict or inhibit the radical press for more than a century.

The seventeenth-century champions of freedom of speech had included John Milton,

John Locke, and the Dutch philosopher Spinoza. The most notable later exponents were Voltaire, Thomas Paine, and, in the nineteenth century, John Stuart MILL. The demand for freedom of speech became characteristic of the Enlightenment. In revolutionary France there was greater freedom than before, although forms of CENSORSHIP and licensing emerged again in the nineteenth century.

Thomas JEFFERSON, James MADISON, and the other Founding Fathers of the United States Constitution were children of the Enlightenment. In the FIRST AMENDMENT, it was provided that 'Congress shall make no law . . . abridging the freedom of speech, or of the press; or the right of the people peaceably to assemble, and to petition the Government for a redress of grievances'. The numerical position, as the first article of the Bill of Rights, was symbolic of its primacy among freedoms. In 1925 it was finally established that the First Amendment prohibitions against the abridgement of free speech by the federal government were applicable to state governments as well. Although the First Amendment has generally been held to prohibit prior restraints on publication, *ex post facto* punishments have been held to be more readily justifiable. So the guarantee has not been interpreted as absolute, and laws penalizing sedition, defamation, and obscenity, for example, have been upheld. A general test adopted by the Supreme Court in 1919 was whether a 'clear and present danger' to the community justified the restriction, but the test has fallen into disfavour.

During the twentieth century the degree to which freedom of expression has obtained has varied from state to state. It generally obtains to a higher degree in democracies, of which indeed it may be regarded as a prerequisite as well as an aim. In Nazi Germany there was book burning, and in dictatorships generally the press has been required to serve the ends of government. In the Soviet Union and eastern Europe, freedom of expression did not extend to impediments on the road to communism. Accordingly there were pervasive controls on literature, arts and the press, although these did not prevent some clandestine circulation of uncensored writings. In the

Soviet Union the press is owned and run by the state, but it is not conceived as standing between the people and the government, who are perceived as having no essential difference of goal. The press freedom of capitalist societies was seen as illusory by Lenin, as being merely freedom for the rich to deceive the masses. It is true that a 'negative' conception of freedom, as an absence of legal restrictions, takes no account of other matters which merit consideration, such as the economics of production and opportunities of access to the media.

Since the second world war international protection has been sought for freedom of expression. The United Nations in its Universal Declaration of Human Rights (1948) proclaimed that: 'Everyone has the right to freedom of opinion and expression', and this has been amplified in the covenants adopted in different regions of the world. Typically the right is expressed in qualified terms: Under Article 10 of the EUROPEAN CONVENTION ON HUMAN RIGHTS, for example, it does not prevent the licensing of cinema or broadcasting enterprises, and is subject to such legal restrictions as are necessary in a democratic society 'in the interests of national security, territorial integrity or public safety, for the prevention of disorder or crime, for the protection of health or morals, for the protection of the reputation or rights of others, for preventing the disclosure of information received in confidence, or for maintaining the authority and impartiality of the judiciary'.

CRM

Reading

Bury, J.B.: *A History of Freedom of Thought.* London: Williams & Norgate, 1913.

Castberg, F.: *Freedom of Speech in the West.* Oslo: Oslo University Press, 1960.

Haiman, F.S.: *Speech and Law in a Free Society.* Chicago, Ill.: University of Chicago Press, 1981.

Hohenberg, J.: *Free Press, Free People.* New York: Free Press, 1973.

Mill, J.S.: *On Liberty* (1859), ed. J. Rees. Oxford: Oxford University Press, 1985.

Street, H.: *Freedom, the Individual and the Law.* 6th edn. Harmondsworth: Penguin, 1989.

freezing of party alternatives The alternatives between which voters choose at an election logically and historically come before individual decisions about casting a vote. In a classic comparative analysis of the origins of parties in modern Europe, Lipset and ROKKAN (1967) observed: 'the party systems of the 1960s reflect, with few but significant exceptions, the cleavage structures of the 1920s' (p. 50). They therefore considered it appropriate to speak of the 'freezing' of party alternatives. The concept emphasizes the importance of past history for present electoral choice. Political conditions before the birth of most voters lead to the creation of political parties that mobilize support from the electorate. Through a process of organizational persistence, reinforced by the transmission of party loyalties between generations through POLITICAL SOCIALIZATION within the family, parties maintain support through the decades. The maintenance of support reduces or frustrates the opportunity for new parties to be created, since it is difficult to become established in a party system when the alternatives are frozen. In this model there is oligopolistic competition between a small number of parties that collectively produce the alternatives between which voters can choose. These alternatives are very limited, because the parties are themselves highly constrained by their own past. By contrast, a consumer-oriented model of voting behaviour starts by examining the preferences of groups of voters, and assumes that parties will exist, adapt or be transformed to suit the dominant preferences of the moment.

Studies of a party's share of the national vote have emphasized a variety of points, some stressing the absolute steadiness of total vote shares, while others have emphasized tendencies for greater fluctuations in a party's vote from election to election. Evidence of weaker popular attachment to parties or greater movement between established parties qualifies but does not reject the idea of freezing, for the party alternatives remain the same. It is best tested by reference to changes in the names and number of parties between which voters can move. A variety of examples of parties persisting from one historical period to another can be cited. The Democrats and the Republicans were formed in America before its industrial revolution, and so too were the British Conservatives. Since the German Social Democratic Party was founded in 1875, Germany has experienced three changes of regime; the party has persisted.

A comprehensive test of the freezing hypothesis with data from nineteen western nations by Rose and Mackie found only partial support for the freezing hypothesis. Of 337 parties winning at least 1 per cent of the national vote in one election, only 19 per cent have persisted unchanged since their origin, and so may be considered frozen. An additional 13 per cent have persisted with marginal modifications. More than two-thirds of all parties sooner or later are 'melted down' (that is, undergo structural change through merger or split) or 'melt away' (disappear without leaving any successor party). Even when parties fighting fewer than four elections are discounted on the grounds that they are flash parties that have failed to become institutionalized, nearly half of the remaining parties have failed to become frozen into a share of electoral support. Contrary to the theory of Lipset and Rokkan, parties originating in the early days of electoral competition are less likely to persist intact. The tendency of many parties to split, merge or disappear is explained by Rose and Mackie as the outcome of contrasting pressures from within the party organization, trying to maintain the position in which the party was frozen in an earlier era, and pressures from the electorate to adapt to new circumstances. Failure to adapt to electoral pressures can lead to a loss of votes and disappearance; too great a change can lead to a party split, as traditionalists within the organization can refuse to accept electorally necessary changes.

See also ELECTORAL VOLATILITY; POLITICAL CLEAVAGES; SOCIAL STRUCTURE AND PARTY ALIGNMENTS.   RR

Reading

Crewe, I. and Denver, D. eds: *Electoral Change in Western Democracies: patterns and sources of electoral volatility*. London: Croom Helm, 1985.

Dalton, R.J., Flanagan, S.C. and Beck, P.A. eds: *Electoral Change in Advanced Industrial Democracies: realignment or dealignment*. Princeton, NJ: Princeton University Press, 1984.

Lipset, S.M. and Rokkan, S.: Cleavage structures, party systems, and voter alignments. In *Party Systems and Voter Alignments: cross-national perspectives*, ed. S.M. Lipset and S. Rokkan. London: Collier-Macmillan; New York: Free Press, 1967.

Rose, R. and Urwin, D.W.: Persistence and change in western party systems since 1945. *Political Studies* 18 (1970) 287–319.

———— and Mackie, T.T.: Do parties persist or disappear? The big tradeoff facing organizations. In *When Parties Fail*, ed. K. Lawson and P. Merkl. Princeton, NJ: Princeton University Press, 1987.

French Revolution The Revolution created a structure of institutions in deliberate contrast to those of the *ancien régime*. The latter comprised a confused patchwork of local, provincial and royal institutions as much sanctioned by history, local custom and negotiated agreements as imposed by the monarchy, and as much designed to entrench a complex system of rights and privileges as to govern effectively. The Revolution established a structure of uniform institutions described in a written constitution whose purpose was to implement the sovereignty of the nation, all of whose members enjoyed the same natural rights stated in a Declaration of Rights placed at the head of the constitution.

The uniformity of law and institutions reflected the universality which the Revolution claimed for its principles; it also effectively destroyed the *ancien régime*. The central principle that sovereignty resided in the nation was expressed in the sovereign legislative power of the National Assembly of elected representatives. The electoral expression of the sovereignty of the people was also applied to public offices, all but a very few of which were rendered elective even including judges, law and police officers, and parish priests (for as long as there was an established religion).

These basic outlines remained remarkably constant throughout the revolutionary decade despite changes of regime, reflected in the succession of three constitutions and declarations of rights (1791, 1793 and 1795), each of which none the less retained the structure outlined above. The constitutions of 1791 and 1793 prescribed unicameral legislatures, while that of 1795 prescribed a bicameral system; both the 1791 and 1795 constitutions established limited franchise on a property qualification, whereas the 1793 constitution decreed universal manhood suffrage.

The 1793 constitution was suspended under the emergency government of the Terror during the composite crisis of war and radicalism and was ultimately never implemented. The same principles of sovereignty expressed through the National Assembly and elected representatives prevailed during the Terror. In practice, however, the Assembly deferred to select committees of government; politically reliable appointees replaced purged elected local officials; parallel emergency institutions were set up locally in a complex relationship with the subsisting regular institutions.

All the regimes of the decade insisted in principle upon the separation of the legislative, executive and judicial powers. In practice this was to prove the period's most arduous problem. The relationship between the king at the head of the executive and the sovereign nation in the legislature failed to settle down; despite explanations of the fall of the monarch in terms of the direct exercise of sovereignty by the people, in practice it was the legislature which deposed, tried and executed the king.

Under the Terror, ministers (who were not elected at any point during the Revolution) became insignificant as the legislative in practice invaded the executive through the select committees and the 'representatives-on-mission' in the provinces. The attempt at separation under the 1795 constitution's creation of an Executive Directory of five elected directors foundered when the directors purged the legislative assemblies several times in defence of their own definition of revolutionary principles.

As for the judiciary, the civic guarantee offered by its independence was sidetracked during the Terror by the appearance of emergency tribunals. Under the Directory, by contrast, judges in many cases used their independence to sabotage the 1795 consti-

tution's objective of a society policed by the impartial rule of law. This eventually provoked the Executive Directory to purge many courts.

This inability to stabilize the relationship between the three branches of government pointed towards the eventual emergence of the Napoleonic system. It is unwise however to see the pre-eminence of the state in that system as necessarily foreshadowed in the centralized government of the Terror under the dictatorship of the legislature's committees.

See also DECLARATION OF THE RIGHTS OF MAN.   CL

Reading

Aulard, A.: L'Exercice de la souveraineté nationale sous le Directoire. In *La Révolution Française* 40 (1901).

Church, C.H.: *Revolution and Red Tape: the French Ministerial Bureaucracy 1770–1850*. Oxford: Clarendon Press, 1981.

Deslandres, M.: *Histoire constitutionnelle de la France*, Vol. I. Paris: Colin/Du Recueil Sirey, 1932.

Godechot, J.: *Les Institutions de la France sous la Révolution et l'Empire*. Paris: Presses Universitaires de France, 1951.

Hintze, O.: *Staatseinheit und Federalismus in alten Frankreich und in der Revolution*. Stuttgart: 1927.

Seignobos, C.: *Études de politique et d'histoire: la séparation des pouvoirs*. Paris: Presses Universitaires de France, 1934.

functional representation A concept based on the idea that society is divided into various groups or strata, and that each of these ought to be represented in government. It can be distinguished from territorial representation in which the section of society which is represented is defined in purely geographical terms, although the distinction blurs when spatial community is held to be the basis of group representation. The distinction is at its sharpest when it derives from a contrast between liberal individualist and collectivist social theories. In the latter case, groups are said to perform specific social functions, and their unity derives from objective conditions rather than from voluntary association. In modern society, the division of labour is often taken as the starting point for the identification of functional groups or classes as the basis for representation.

Although blueprints for functional representation have frequently been advocated, from G. D. H. COLE's GUILD SOCIALISM to Harold Macmillan's Central Economic Council proposed in 1933, there is no indication that industrial parliaments will ever formally supplant existing governmental institutions in Britain or in other liberal democracies. But there is considerable functional representation in the policy-making process, where groups representing economic and professional interests have achieved permanent consultative status, and often in addition a role in policy implementation which can be understood as a form of CORPORATISM.   AC

Reading

Beer, S.H.: *Modern British Politics*. 3rd edn. London: Faber & Faber, 1982.

Birch, A.H.: *Representation*. London: Pall Mall, 1971.

functionalism In POLITICAL SCIENCE functionalism has a complicated ancestry, drawing its inspiration from a variety of sources. Major anthropological and sociological theorists such as Karl MARX, Emile Durkheim, Max WEBER, Bronislaw Malinowski, A. R. Radcliffe-Brown and others explained primitive and modern societies and processes of social change in terms of the interaction of social institutions and values. Thus, economic processes may be viewed as explaining political structure and religious institutions as in Marx, or religious values and attitudes may be viewed as explaining economic and political patterns as in Weber. This view of societies as consisting of interacting institutions and cultural patterns was the common explanatory strategy of social theory as it developed in the nineteenth and twentieth centuries. More abstract and formal functional analysis developed after the second world war in the work of Talcott Parsons, Marion Levy and others. Here there were efforts at formalization, distinguishing manifest from latent functions as in Merton, schematizing the functional requisites of any society as in Parsons, or in Marion Levy, assimilating functional theory

into the broader strategy of scientific explanation as in the work of Carl Hempel and Ernest Nagel.

Functionalism entered political science through the work of David Easton, Gabriel Almond, S. M. Lipset, Stein ROKKAN, Robert Holt and John Turner, William Mitchell, and others. David Easton's work was more immediately influenced by cybernetic or information theory, though it also drew on the sociological tradition. His concept of the POLITICAL SYSTEM has been influential as a schematization of politics in the form of a model which receives inputs from its environment, converts these inputs into outputs within the political system, the outputs then affecting the environment. The process is a circular one as the environment affects the political system in a feedback loop. This system conception of politics has been widely adopted in studies of POLITICAL SOCIALIZATION, political institutions, and public policy analysis.

As developed in the work of Almond, Coleman, Verba, Powell and others, functionalism drew more substantially from the history of political theory, particularly SEPARATION OF POWERS as developed in MONTESQUIEU, and elaborated by James MADISON and Alexander HAMILTON in the FEDERALIST PAPERS. The executive, legislative, and judicial powers though assigned in the main to separate agencies of government, were to be variously commingled among them in order to avoid attenuation of any one of them, and to maintain a constitutional equilibrium. American political science research as it developed in the course of the nineteenth century was dominated by this threefold division of political functions. Descriptive and normative political theory was based upon this theory of CONSTITUTIONALISM.

The emergence of political parties, organized interest groups, and the media of communication in the late nineteenth century presented serious analytical problems. How could these obviously important structures be accommodated in this threefold functional division? Early efforts treated these institutions with some awkwardness as additional legislative chambers, or as quasi-legislative chambers.

One writer called the owners of the mass newspapers of the turn of the century the 'lords of the press', implying that they constituted a kind of legislative chamber. Political science functionalism was in considerable part a response to these anomalies. But it was also a response to the need for separating structure from function in order to make comparisons possible between very different kinds of political systems such as those coming into existence in the Third World, where the relationship between structure and function was often quite problematic. Functionalism provided a better approach to locating different aspects and phases of the political process, than did a structural approach.

Almond, Powell and their collaborators have recently been employing a threefold functional scheme for descriptive-comparative purposes. A set of system functions – socialization, POLITICAL RECRUITMENT; POLITICAL COMMUNICATION – describes the ways a political system maintains itself and adapts to change. A set of process functions – INTEREST ARTICULATION AND AGGREGATION, policy-making, IMPLEMENTATION, and ADJUDICATION – describes how a political system makes decisions. A set of policy functions – extraction, regulation, distribution, and symbolic outputs – describes the impact of the political system on its society and its international environment. There are other approaches to the categorization of these functions, particularly the process ones. Lasswell, Wildavsky, and others break the decision process down in other ways, for example, adding an intelligence, initiation, and a termination phase to those listed above. This would simply seem to involve adapting the scheme to different research foci.

The critique of functionalism has proceeded along two lines. It has been attacked as concerned only with the maintenance of political equilibrium or order, and hence biased toward conservatism, and not suitable to the analysis of change. From the methodological side it is viewed by some as reductionist, as obscuring the importance of the STATE and political institutions. While polemic about the specifics of analytic schemes is inevitable, some functional scheme appears to be un-avoidable in the comparative study of political regimes and processes.   GAA

Reading

Almond, G.A. and Coleman, J.: *The Politics of the Developing Areas*. Princeton, NJ: Princeton University Press, 1960.

Almond, G.A. and Powell, B.G.: *Comparative Politics: system, process, policy*. Boston, Mass.: Little, Brown, 1978.

Durkheim, E.: *The Rules of Sociological Method*. 8th edn, ed. G.E.G. Catlin. Glencoe, Ill.: Free Press of Glencoe, 1958.

Easton, D.: *A Systems Analysis of Political Life*. New York: Wiley, 1965; 2nd edn. Chicago, Ill.: University of Chicago Press, 1979.

Lasswell, H.D.: *The Decision Process*. Baltimore, Md.: Bureau of Governmental Research, 1956.

Levy, M.: *The Structure of Society*. Princeton, NJ: Princeton University Press, 1952.

Lipset, S.M. and Rokkan, S. eds: *Party Systems and Voter Alignments: cross-national perspectives*. London: Collier-Macmillan; New York: Free Press, 1967.

Malinowski, B.: *A Scientific Theory of Culture*. Chapel Hill: University of North Carolina Press, 1944.

Montesquieu, C.-L. de Secondat: *The Spirit of the Laws* (1750). Ed. F. Neumann, trans. T. Nugent. New York: Hafner, 1949.

Parsons, T.: *The Social System*. London: Tavistock, 1952; New York: Free Press, 1961.

Pateman, C.: *Participation and Democratic Theory*. Cambridge: Cambridge University Press, 1970.

Radcliffe-Brown, A.R.: *Structure and Function in Primitive Societies*. London: Cohen & West, 1952.

Wildavsky, A. and May, J.: *The Policy Cycle*. Beverly Hills, Calif.: Sage, 1978.

fundamental rights   The more important private rights of an individual which, it is believed, should be protected against infringement or abridgement. No list can be exhaustive but included are the right to life, freedom from starvation, from torture and from arbitrary deprivation of liberty. None of these can be given any greater protection than the CONSTITUTION which embodies them. Fundamental rights came into prominence with the rise of Lockeian individualism. They were then designated as natural rights and have often since been called human rights. Fundamental (or human) rights are said to be required in three different but related ways (see Gewirth 1982). First, they are requirements in the sense that their objects fulfil objectively important needs. Second, they are requirements in the sense of entitlements. This suggests the idea of 'title' in the quasi-legal sense of a justifying basis which serves to allocate to a person some good as his 'due' or property. Third, they are requirements in the sense of justified demands in regard to other persons who have correlative duties to ensure that the subjects concerned have the goods in question. In many countries, for example the USA and the Federal Republic of Germany, certain rights are entrenched. Courts are given the power to strike down legislation or governmental action in breach of rights guaranteed in this way. There is nothing in the British constitution guaranteed against alteration. The rights of the individual in relation to the state are therefore in no way entrenched, except to the limited extent that the United Kingdom is bound by international conventions to respect certain human rights.

There are, however, statements to the effect that British citizens have certain fundamental rights. For example Lord Scarman numbered among their 'fundamental human rights' those of 'peaceful assembly and public protest' (Report on the Red Lion Square Disorders, Cmnd 5919, 1975, p. 1). Lord Denning has vindicated the right to demonstrate (see *Hubbard* v. *Pitt* [1976] QB 142, 178) and has declared that the COMMON LAW recognizes freedom of association and the right to join a union (*Cheall* v. *Association of Professional, Executive, Clerical and Computer Staffs* [1983] QB 126, 136). Lords Scarman and Simon have said that freedom of communication is a basic right at common law (*Home Office* v. *Harman* [1983] 1 AC 280, 311). The courts also apply certain presumptions in favour of fundamental rights when interpreting statutes (*R* v. *Bhagwan* [1972] AC 60 – the right of a British subject to enter the UK; *Central Control Board* v. *Cannon Brewery Co.* [1919] AC 744, 752 – rights of property). On the other hand, judicial decisions have sometimes drastically narrowed rights of individuals against the state (*Liversidge* v. *Anderson* [1942] AC 206; *Azam* v. *Secretary of State for Home Department* [1974] AC 18; *R* v. *Secretary of State for Home Department ex parte Hosenball* [1977] 1 WLR 766). There are calls in the United Kingdom for the incorporation of the EUROPEAN CONVENTION ON HUMAN RIGHTS into domestic law which would have the effect of giving the United Kingdom a BILL OF RIGHTS (Zander 1985).

See also CIVIL LIBERTIES; CIVIL RIGHTS; ENTRENCHMENT.   MDAF

Reading

Dworkin, R.M.: *Taking Rights Seriously.* 2nd edn. London: Duckworth, 1978.

Finnis, J.M.: *Natural Law and Natural Rights.* Oxford: Oxford University Press, 1980.

Gewirth, A.: *Human Rights.* Chicago, Ill.: University of Chicago Press, 1982.

Zander, M.: *A Bill of Rights.* London: Sweet & Maxwell, 1985.

G

game theory An approach to the analysis of DECISION MAKING. It is based on the 'rational choice' paradigm, which means that decisions and actions are interpreted as being means to achieve certain specified ends. Game theory can be applied in situations where the outcome depends upon the interaction between the choices of two or more 'players'. It operates by specifying the options open to each player and by specifying the anticipated outcome of each possible combination of options that might be selected by the players. It assumes that each player selects the option that he or she expects will maximize his or her personal utility, in the light of the anticipated choices of all other players.

Such analyses can obviously become very complex. Modern game theory has developed both as a branch of applied mathematics and as one of the main sub-fields in the area of 'formal' political, economic or social theory, as well as international relations. Game theory is related to, but distinct from, the notion of 'gaming', the simulation of social interactions in stylized, but tightly controlled, experimental environments. (For an elaboration of this distinction, see Colman 1982.) Aspects of game theory may be tested empirically, but it represents a quintessentially *deductive* approach that stands or falls on the quality of its logic rather than on the reality of its assumptions. Indeed, it is the facility with which the theorist can manipulate and replace assumptions in a systematic manner that gives game theory its important *heuristic* value. This enables theorists to explore the logic or range of possible scenarios, and gives rise to one of game theory's most controversial applications, which

is in the field of nuclear strategy and diplomacy (see Schelling 1963). A more unusual application of the heuristic potential of game theory is to theology (see Brams 1983).

Much of modern game theory is based on detailed analysis of a limited number of games, held to evoke particularly pervasive patterns of social interaction. These include the Chicken Game (used to model nuclear confrontations, strikes, and other examples of brinkmanship) and the Prisoners' Dilemma (PD) game (used to model pollution, resource depletion and other examples of COLLECTIVE ACTION problems). Games are typically divided into three categories.

(1) Games of pure conflict (zero sum, or constant-sum games) in which one player's gain is another's loss.

(2) Games of pure co-operation, in which all players win or lose together. These games are typically products of communications blockages. An example is the problem facing two prisoners attempting to give the same alibi under separate cross-examinations.

(3) Mixed motive games (variable-sum games), such as Chicken and the PD game, that blend conflict and co-operation. Game theory has made its greatest contribution to social science in the classification and analysis of mixed motive interactions.

More complex and realistic analyses can be modelled as supergames. These are sequences of games played by the same group of players, in which moves in one game can be conditional on moves and outcomes in earlier games. 'Anarchistic' solutions to the PD supergame, for example, have been used to challenge the

248

view that the PD game forms a major argument for state intervention in collective action problems (Taylor 1976). MJL

Reading

Brams, S.F.: *Game Theory and Politics*. New York: Free Press, 1975.

———: *Superior Beings: if they exist, how would we know?* New York: Springer, 1983.

Colman, A.: *Game Theory and Experimental Games*. London: Pergamon, 1982.

Schelling, T.C.: *The Strategy of Conflict*. New York: Oxford University Press, 1963.

Taylor, M.: *Anarchy and Co-operation*. London: Wiley, 1976.

gate keeping The term was introduced by the sociologist R. E. Pahl to describe the ability of bureaucratic officials to determine access to, and the allocation of, services and facilities. It is used with particular reference to urban managers such as social workers, planners, and housing managers and the term urban managerialism is a synonym. This approach to the understanding of resource and service distribution is rooted in WEBER's claim that as modern society grows increasingly bureaucratic, so state functionaries exercise increasing power.

Pahl's theoretical work resulted in a number of empirical studies of the activities and attitudes of urban managers in Britain, particularly those concerned with planning and housing. In the United States similar research was done on 'street-level bureaucrats' with responsibilities for housing, social services, highways maintenance, education, and law enforcement. Many of these studies found that urban managers do indeed have some gate-keeping discretion, but they also established that this was strictly limited by the organizations in which they worked, and by the operations of the private market. This led Pahl to reformulate his original approach. First, he argued that urban managers should be seen not so much as independent actors as mediators between the public and private sectors, and between local residents and national government. Second, he restricted the term to public officials. Third, he shifted attention from the 'middle dogs' to the 'top dogs' in the bureaucratic hierarchy. Fourth, he linked the notions of gate keeping and managing into the broader theory of the corporatist state. This did not resolve the basic problem of deciding to what extent a gate-keeping role is exercised by state functionaries, and the question remains open.

See also CORPORATISM. KN

Reading

Pahl, R.E.: *Whose city?* ch. 13. Harmondsworth: Penguin, 1975.

Pinch, S.: *Cities and Services: the geography of collective consumption*, ch. 4. London: Routledge & Kegan Paul, 1985.

Saunders, P.: *Social Theory and the Urban Question*, ch. 4. London: Hutchinson, 1982.

Gauleiter The chief of a NAZI PARTY district organization (*Gau*). After its refounding on 26 February 1925, the party was structured into Gaus which varied greatly in size and were subject to considerable reorganization between 1925 and 1945. The Gauleiters were appointed by Hitler and, following the party's leadership principle, were given autocratic powers over the party within their Gaus. Despite the development of a central party apparatus, they declined to be incorporated into a hierarchy, preferring to regard themselves as Hitler's direct representatives in the regions, a position he generally endorsed.

Between 1925 and the Nazi take-over in 1933 the Gauleiters were mainly responsible for recruiting members and voters for the party and played a key role in its rise to power. With the establishment of the Nazi regime some acquired state offices either as Reich Governor (*Reichsstatthalter*) of a state or as Provincial Governor (*Oberpräsident*) of a Prussian province. Before the war their power was restricted since the roles of Reich and Provincial governor were largely supervisory and representational rather than executive in scope and the party's right to intervene in matters of state was circumscribed. Moreover the abilities required to achieve power in a crisis were not the same as those needed to wield it under normal conditions, particularly in competition with a trained bureaucracy. In 1936 Reichsstatthalter/Gauleiter Fritz Sauckel of Thuringia described the position of the Reichsstatthalter with some exaggeration as similar 'to that of the English king': 'He is by no means without influence; he can get somewhere by diplomacy, by persuasion, by threats, or through the party – but he can give no orders ... he can make quite a lot of his position through his energy and skill but largely outside the legal limits.' This situation created growing frustration and while some Gauleiters fought a constant battle with the state authorities for political control of their Gaus, others opted out, contenting themselves with a largely representational role and indulging in private pleasures.

After the outbreak of war, the Gauleiters increased their influence. They were appointed to the official position of Reich Defence Commissioner in their Gaus and, particularly after 1942, played an increasingly important role in coping with the impact of the war in their respective areas. Through the effects of allied bombing and the growing shortages of trained personnel and materials, the apparatus of state and local government came under growing strain. In this emergency Hitler looked to the Gauleiters to use their political authority as senior party figures to cut through red tape and deal with the crisis. Some Gauleiters found that the characteristics which had benefited them in the struggle for power – drive, self-assertion, ruthlessness – once more came into their own.

The term Gauleiter is now sometimes used as a synonym for an autocratic representative of an autocratic ruler, a modern version of the ancient Persian satrap. Ironically, however, it was only in the last months of the regime that Gauleiters became the absolute masters of their Gaus.

See also AUTOCRACY.   JDN

Reading

Broszat, M.: *The Hitler State: the foundations and the development of the internal structure of the Third Reich.* London: Arnold, 1981.

Hüttenberger, P.: *Die Gauleiter: Studien zum Wandel des Machtgefüges in der NSDAP.* Stuttgart: Deutsche Verlags-Anstalt, 1969.

Orlow, D.: *A History of the Nazi Party 1919–1945.* 2 vols. Newton Abbot: David & Charles, 1969 and 1973.

Gaullism/Gaullist party Gaullism is the name of a French political movement as well as of a doctrine, both derived from the thought of Charles de Gaulle (1890–1970), leader of the French Resistance during the second world war, founder of the Fifth French Republic and its first President from 1958 to 1969. The Gaullist movement was known in the Fourth Republic as the Rassemblement du Peuple Français (RPF) 1947–54; in the Fifth Republic, the Gaullist party has undergone a number of changes of name, but at the time of writing it is known as the Rassemblement pour la République (RPR).

As a political doctrine Gaullism emphasizes the primacy of the nation state which it sees as the foundation of political life. This implies, in international relations, hostility to what is perceived as American hegemony in western Europe – de Gaulle withdrew French troops from NATO's integrated command structure in 1966 – and hostility towards the creation of a federal Europe – Gaullist policy succeeded in giving to each member state of the EUROPEAN COMMUNITY a veto when its vital national interests were affected. According to Gaullists, the strength of the French nation in international affairs is dependent upon the strength of its government. This in turn requires a constitutional structure in which the head of the government derives legitimacy not from the legislature, but from the electorate. Gaullism is sympathetic to a plebiscitary conception of democracy based upon the notion of popular sovereignty, according to which the leader of the state is invested with authority by the people rather than by parliament, and this authority can be reinforced by use of the REFERENDUM. Gaullism is suspicious of political parties and indeed of all intermediaries such as pressure groups which divide the people from the state. From this point of view, Gaullism has something in common with BONAPARTISM, and should be distinguished from conservatism although, since de Gaulle's departure from power in 1969, the Gaullist party has come to take on more of the characteristics of a conservative party and has ceased to emphasize the plebiscitary elements of the doctrine.   VBB

Reading

Charlot, J.: *The Gaullist Phenomenon*. London: Allen & Unwin, 1971.

Debré, J.-L.: *Les Idées constitutionnelles de Général de Gaulle*. Paris: Pichon et Durand-Aujies, 1974.

Gaulle, C. de: *Mémoires de guerre*. 3 vols. Paris: Plon, 1970.

————: *Discours et messages*. 5 vols. Paris: Plon, 1970.

————: *Mémoires d'espoir*. Paris: Plon, 1970.

Rémond, R.: *The Right Wing in France from 1815 to de Gaulle*. Philadelphia: University of Pennsylvania Press, 1969.

Touchard, J.: *Le Gaullisme 1940–1969*. Paris: Éditions du Seuil, 1978.

gender and politics   The emergence of gender as a significant factor in political analysis is a fairly recent phenomenon. Until the 1970s certain assumptions about women were common among political scientists; for example that they tended to vote to the right of men, and that they had a much lower interest in politics and were therefore less likely to vote at all. These factors were often said to be related to women's private, domestic role which, it was claimed, gave them neither time for nor interest in the public world of politics. This explanation became less plausible as the birth rate fell and more and more women became involved in work outside the home. Researchers looked at women's political role anew and began to examine the relationship of gender and politics, as they had looked in the past at the relationship between, for example, class and politics (see Randall).

What emerged from these investigations was, *inter alia* a realization of the under-representation of women at the elite level in politics and a challenge to the stereotype of the woman voter. Whereas women make up over 50 per cent of the electorate world-wide they are consistently only a small proportion of political respresentatives. The average in Western European assemblies is well under 10 per cent: in the UK the figure has never been even 5 per cent of the House of Commons (see Vallance 1979), and in the United States House of Representatives it is barely 5 per cent (see Githens and Prestage). Only in Scandinavia have women made a significant breakthrough in this area: in both Denmark and Sweden the figure is 26 per cent, and in Norway it is 34 per cent.

Outside Europe and America women are either totally unrepresented or represented in very small numbers. The reasons for this are complex. Woman's role as homemaker and carer of children and men is not only time-consuming but productive of a self-image as secondary and supportive which sits uneasily alongside the assertive and opinionated political persona. Along similar lines it is often claimed that girls are socialized to care more about personal relations than personal success, and that the kind of careers they are encouraged to pursue (for example, the 'caring' professions of teaching, health and social work) do not give the kind of experience which is transferable to politics. Social attitudes may also militate against women's political chances if it is believed that femininity is incompatible with the wielding of power. It appears too that women are suspect to those who select candidates, so that they are predominantly offered marginal or hopeless seats – again limiting their chances of electoral success. There is also evidence that proportional ELECTORAL SYSTEMS, as used for example, in Scandinavia, help women to be selected on a list of candidates in all constituencies not just marginal ones; the poor performance of women in Britain and America where single-member, non-proportional systems exist, supports this thesis. For many reasons then, in spite of a few well-publicized individual achievements, women's penetration of the political sphere has not kept step with their involvement in other areas of social and working life. In most representative assemblies there are few, if any, more women now than there were immediately after the last world war (see Epstein and Coser).

Investigation of gender and politics has also meant a serious challenge to what had been the received view of the woman voter as conservative and often apolitical (see Goot and

Reid). To begin with, the identification of age as a variable in political allegiance, coupled with women's greater longevity, has led to the questioning of the idea of women as habitually more conservative than men. Indeed, in Britain, in all but the highest age group women have over the past twenty years shown a greater propensity to support the left than men. In the case of non-voting, at least in Europe, America and Japan, the trend is for increasing proportions of the female electorate to turn out while the male vote has remained more or less static. Recent figures show that in some cases women are now voting at a higher rate than men (see Siltanen and Stanworth).

This does not mean, however, that there is no difference between the political participation of men and women. Recent research has produced some evidence, most notably in America but also to some extent in the UK and the rest of Europe, of a 'gender gap', that is a difference in the political views and priorities of the sexes. In the American experience, women of both political parties were found in the early 1980s to be significantly more critical of both the policies and styles of the administration than were their male equivalents (see Klein). In 1983, for example, Gallup found that 51 per cent of men but only 34 per cent of women approved of President Reagan's record. In Europe as well as in America, women are consistently more favourable to equality policy than men. The extent of such a 'gap' fluctuates with time and place but overall it suggests that women's life-styles and experience, which are not the same as men's, may be reflected in their political opinions (see Norris 1985, Vallance 1986).

See also FEMINIST MOVEMENTS; WOMEN'S SUFFRAGE. EMV

Reading

Epstein, C. and Coser, R. eds: *Access to Power: cross-national studies of women and elites*. London: Allen & Unwin, 1981.

Githens, M. and Prestage, J. eds: *A Portrait of Marginality: the political behaviour of the American woman*. New York: Longman, 1977.

Goot, M. and Reid, E.: *Women and Voting Studies: mindless matrons or sexist scientism?* Sage Professional Papers in Comparative Political Sociology, 1975.

Klein, E.: *Gender Politics*. Cambridge, Mass.: Harvard University Press, 1984.

Norris, P.: The Gender Gap in Britain and America. *Parliamentary Affairs* 38.2 (1985).

Randall, V.: *Women and Politics*. London: Macmillan, 1982.

Siltanen, J. and Stanworth, M. eds: *Women and the Public Sphere: a critique of sociology and politics*. London: Hutchinson, 1984.

Vallance, E.: *Women in the House: a study of women members of parliament*. London: Athlone, 1979.

—— and Davies, E.: *Women of Europe: women MEP's and equality policy* Cambridge: Cambridge University Press, 1986.

General Secretary of the CPSU The most powerful politician in the Soviet Union, leader of the POLITBURO and the Secretariat of the CENTRAL COMMITTEE of the CPSU. The post of General Secretary (or First Secretary from 1953 to 1966) was created in 1922, and its first occupant was Joseph STALIN. After Lenin's death in 1924 the General Secretaryship quickly became the centre of power in the political system, but this power was neither institutionalized nor limited since it rested on Stalin's control of the secret police and on his CULT OF PERSONALITY. The end of the terror under Nikita Khrushchev enabled the Politburo to form a collective challenge to the leader (see ANTI-PARTY GROUP), and such a challenge eventually led to his downfall. Semi-institutionalized constraints came only with the advent of COLLECTIVE LEADERSHIP in 1964, since which time the General Secretary has never been more powerful than the rest of the Politburo combined.

The General Secretary is elected by the Central Committee but selected by the Politburo, and so arrives in office with a background level of support but also with some political debts. The chief resource at his disposal is the power of patronage. How easily and quickly this can be wielded depends on circumstances and on the individuals involved. It took Leonid Brezhnev seven years to build up enough strength in the Central Committee to effect a decisive change in Politburo membership, after which his authority visibly increased; whereas a less conciliatory style and widespread frustration at the immobilism of the preceding years have enabled Mikhail Gorbachev to make rapid changes at Politburo level. The General Secretary is, however, no longer a dictator, and even when unchallenged within the party leadership he may face resistance to his policies from the state apparatus. SW

Reading

Breslauer, G.W.: *Khrushchev and Brezhnev as Party Leaders: building authority in Soviet politics.* London: Allen & Unwin, 1982.

Brown, A.: Gorbachev: new man in the Kremlin. *Problems of Communism* 34 (1985) 1–23.

————: The power of the General Secretary of the CPSU. In *Authority, Power and Policy in the Soviet Union*, ed. T.H. Rigby, A. Brown and P. Reddaway. London: Macmillan, 1980.

Hough, J.F. and Fainsod, M.: *How the Soviet Union is Governed.* Cambridge, Mass. and London: Harvard University Press, 1979.

Rush, M.: *Political Succession in the USSR.* 2nd edn. New York: Columbia University Press, 1968.

general strike A form of collective stoppage of work by wage earners designed to paralyse all economic life of a nation in pursuit of economic, political or revolutionary ends. The economic general strike is primarily concerned with particular issues of industrial relations and is designed in the first instance to change the actions of employers. A political general strike uses industrial action to compel a government to adopt a particular policy, such as the extension of the suffrage. More general political aims may also be sought, such as a 'strike against war', frequently discussed though never acted upon by the Second International before 1914. The revolutionary general strike is designed to bring about the overthrow of the existing social order and the creation of a socialist society. It was this revolutionary strike, more an eschatological response to organizational weakness than a considered strategy or theory of action, which was identified in the early twentieth century with SYNDICALISM and with the political theorist Georges SOREL though his actual relations with and influence upon the revolutionary syndicalist movement were minimal.

While the idea of using industrial power on a nation-wide basis to secure political objectives, either narrowly or broadly conceived, is to be found within all LABOUR MOVEMENTS, the ideology of the general strike developed as a response to the changing structure both of industrial capitalism and the labour movement in Europe and the United States in the early twentieth century.

See also DIRECT ACTION; SOCIALISM; TRADE UNIONS. JSR

Reading

Cole, G.D.H.: *The World of Labour.* London: Bell, 1913.

Mommsen, W.J. and Husung, H.-G.: *The Development of Trade Unionism in Great Britain and Germany 1880–1914.* London: Allen & Unwin, 1985.

Penner, N. ed.: *Winnipeg 1919: the strikers' own history of the Winnipeg general strike.* Toronto: James Lewis & Samuel, 1973.

Phillips, G.A.: *The General Strike: the politics of industrial conflict.* London: Weidenfeld & Nicolson, 1976.

Ridley, F.F.: *Revolutionary Syndicalism in France: the direct action of its time.* Cambridge: Cambridge University Press, 1970.

Stearns, P.N.: *Revolutionary Syndicalism and French Labor.* New Brunswick, NJ: Rutgers University Press, 1971.

generalist See BUREAUCRACY.

genocide The extermination of a population – a people, nation, race or ethnic group – defined according to biological and cultural criteria. Mass slaughter on other grounds, for example politico-economic in Cambodia recently, has also been described as genocide. Genocidal processes have operated throughout history. Extinction, mainly as a consequence of ecological disruption, has been the fate of Tasmanid (1877) and comparably situated peoples. Large-scale inter-ethnic killings described as genocidal have also attended frontier adjustments and power struggles, as in the Indian sub-continent, Rwanda, Burundi.

Organized massacres, pogroms, encouraged by state and state-related authorities, are also salient. Convictions of religious superiority, or perceptions of serious threat from other religions, have underlain lethal inter- and intra-faith conflicts. Virtually all religions and denominations have been involved. 'Science' based philosophies and ideologies, especially those incorporating 'eugenic' and 'Social Darwinist' elements have also been potent in justifying hierarchical categorizations and extreme discriminatory policies. Nazi 'racial science' and 'hygiene' sanctioned the systematic extermination of nearly six million Jews as well as Europe's gypsies in specially constructed extermination camps.

The historic enormity of Nazi genocidal beliefs and practices, and the ruthless mobilization of modern technology in the service of mass slaughter, underlie the definition of genocide as 'a special form of murder: state sanctioned liquidation against a collective group, without regard to whether an individual has committed any specific and punishable transgression' (Horowitz 1980, p. 1). The term ethnocide connotes cultural not physical obliteration.

See also ANTI-SEMITISM; NAZISM; RACE IN POLITICS.   KK

Reading

Horowitz, I.L.: *Taking Lives: genocide and state power*. New Brunswick, NJ: Transaction Books, 1980.

Kuper, L.: *The Pity of it all: polarisation of racial and ethnic relations*. London: Duckworth, 1977.

———: *Genocide*. Harmondsworth: Penguin, 1981.

Reynolds, V., Falger, V.S.E. and Vine, I. eds: *The Sociobiology of Ethnocentrism: evolutionary dimensions of xenophobia, discrimination, racism and nationalism*. London: Croom Helm, 1987.

Rothschild, J.: *Ethnopolitics: a conceptual framework*. New York: Columbia University Press, 1981.

Smith, A.D.: *Nationalism in the Twentieth Century*. Oxford: Martin Robertson, 1979.

Stepan, N.: *The Idea of Race in Science: Great Britain 1800–1960*. London: Macmillan/St Antony's College Oxford, 1982.

Stone, J.: *Racial Conflict in Contemporary Society*. London: Fontana, 1985.

Van den Berghe, P.L.: *The Ethnic Phenomenon*. New York and Oxford: Elsevier, 1981.

geopolitics The study of states as spatial phenomena with a view to understanding the geographical bases of their power. State behaviour is examined against the background of such characteristics as territory, climate, organic and inorganic resources and location as well as human features such as population distribution, cultural attributes, economic activity and political structures. Each state is seen as a component part of the world's political space as a whole, and the consequent pattern of international relationships forms an essential part of the study. Geopolitics is holistic in its approach, the object being to bring together diverse phenomena and to describe and interpret these as a totality.

The development of modern geopolitical concepts owes much to the work of Friedrich Ratzel (1844–1904). Ratzel subscribed to late nineteenth-century Social Darwinism and saw the state as a spatial organism obeying quasi-organic laws of behaviour. The term geopolitics (*Geopolitik*) is attributed to Rudolf Kjellén (1846–1922) who defined it as being the science which conceives of the state as a geographical organism and phenomenon in space. He saw states as being in competition with one another, only the fittest surviving and prospering.

The most famous world geopolitical view was that of Sir Halford Mackinder (1861–1947) who held that the opposition of land power and sea power was the underlying theme of world history. He saw the centre of Eurasia, which he termed 'The Heartland', as the pivot of world power, and was fearful that the maritime powers – and in particular Britain – were under increasing threat. Mackinder's world view, much modified and adapted, underlies many subsequent attempts to explain the patterns of power and in particular the relationship of the two superpowers after the second world war.

During the period between the two wars the German school of *Geopolitik*, deriving many of its ideas from earlier geographical thinking, helped plan the regeneration of Germany. Led by Karl Haushofer (1869–1946), its exponents advocated the creation of a strong *Mitteleuropa* (Central Europe) dominated by Germany, and the acquisition of *Lebensraum* (living space) in the east. Outside Germany this was widely interpreted as being a crude attempt to justify aggressive expansion, and its close association with the NAZI regime produced widespread condemnation. This episode had an adverse effect on the academic standing of the subject and it came to be seen as being too closely associated with the formulation of state policy.

In recent years there has been a renewed interest in geopolitics and an appreciation of its contribution to the understanding of the contemporary world and its problems. It is closely associated with POLITICAL GEOGRAPHY, the exact divide between the two having been a matter of some debate. Its practitioners see it as providing a unique methodology for the examination of world issues from a dynamic spatial perspective. Areas of particular interest in contemporary geopolitics have been the emergence of new centres of world power; the impact of the location of natural resources; the spatial background to international conflict; the dominance of the western world and the relationship of this to the problems of the 'South'. In its examination of such matters, geopolitics relates closely to international relations, economics and POLITICAL SCIENCE.

GP

Reading

Cohen, S.B.: *Geography and Politics in a World Divided.* 2nd edn. New York, London and Toronto: Oxford University Press, 1973.

Kjellén, R.: *Der Staat als Lebensform.* Leipzig: Hirzel, 1917.

Mackinder, H.: *Democratic Ideals and Reality: a study in the politics of reconstruction.* London: Constable, 1919.

Parker, G.: *Western Geopolitical Thought in the Twentieth Century.* London: Croom Helm, 1985.

Taylor, P.J.: *Political Geography, World-Economy, Nation-State and Locality.* London: Longman, 1985.

Gestapo The *Ge[heime] Sta[ats] Po[lizei]* (Secret State Police) was the political police force responsible for repressing political opponents and ideological enemies of the Nazi regime (see NAZISM). Under the democratic Weimar Republic (1918–33) the political police were subordinate to the police departments in the various federal states and their role was confined to gathering information. On 26 April 1933 Hermann Göring, the new Nazi Prussian Minister of the Interior, created a separate Secret State Police Office (*Gestapa*) and then, with the appointment of the leader of the SS (*Schutzstaffel*: defence echelons, the elite Nazi formation of blackshirts) Heinrich Himmler as Inspector of the Gestapo on 30 April 1934, the Prussian Gestapo apparatus was extended to the remainder of the Reich, thereby creating a national political police force with full executive powers.

Although officially remaining a state body subordinate to the Reich Ministry of the Interior, in practice from April 1934 onwards the Gestapo became increasingly linked to the SS organization. Its chief of operations was Heinrich Müller, formerly in charge of the communist desk in the Bavarian political police during the Weimar Republic. Müller and his colleagues, most of whom were professional policemen, now placed their technical skills at the disposal of the SS, of which they became members.

The Gestapo was responsible for gathering information about opposition to the regime and then arresting and interrogating opponents. Those arrested were either put on trial in the courts under Nazi legislation designed to outlaw opposition and then imprisoned in ordinary prisons, or else were taken into 'protective custody' under §1 of the Decree for the Protection of People and State of 28 February 1933, which had suspended civil rights, and then consigned to a CONCENTRATION CAMP. The main targets of Gestapo activity were those deemed ideological enemies of the regime: the left (communists and social democrats), 'reaction' (conservatives and churches), and increasingly the Jews, whose deportation to the EXTERMINATION CAMPS it supervised. Since Nazism was a TOTALITARIAN movement, even relatively innocuous forms of opposition to measures of the regime, or failure to conform to its norms, were liable to be deemed political offences warranting intervention by the Gestapo. Through its widespread use of informers and its brutal methods of interrogation the Gestapo developed a formidable efficiency in the suppression of opposition. There was no redress against its actions. The name Gestapo came to epitomize a ruthless political police.

See also SECRET POLICE.   JDN

Reading

Aronson, S.: *Reinhard Heydrich und die Frühgeschichte von Gestapo und SD*. Stuttgart: Deutsche Verlagsanstalt, 1971.

Buchheim, H.: The SS: instrument of domination. In *Anatomy of the SS State*, ed. H. Krausnick et al. London: Collins, 1968.

Crankshaw, E.: *The Gestapo: instrument of tyranny*. New York: Viking, 1956.

Höhne, H.: *The Order of the Death's Head: the story of Hitler's SS*, trans. R. Barry. London: Secker & Warburg, 1969.

Koehl, R.: *The Black Corps: the structure and power struggles of the Nazi SS*. Madison: University of Wisconsin Press, 1983.

governability   The words government and governability are derived from a Greek word for steering; governability refers to the ability of a country's political institutions to direct its economy and society. That ability is dependent upon characteristics of the government itself, as well as the characteristics of the society that it is attempting to 'steer'. Governability is a particular problem for democratic countries because of the difficulty of translating a mandate from voters in an election into workable policies.

The governability of democratic political systems became a particular concern during the 1970s. The combination of increasing costs of government, the beginnings of an ideological movement in several countries which questioned the ability of government to solve social problems, and loss of public trust in government created a fear of 'ungovernability' in many western countries. These fears were exaggerated, but have required some re-examination of the manner in which governments carried out their business and their relationship to society.

Sundquist cites four characteristics of governments which affect their capacity to govern. The first is the quality of the public BUREAUCRACY. A public bureaucracy which is amateurish in nature, either because of inadequate education and training or because many senior posts are rotated with changes in government as in the United States, will not be capable of providing sound advice and leadership in policy-making. The expertise of bureaucrats is highly important in policy-making, so if this expertise is inadequate the policies made are likely to be inadequate. In particular, government will be less capable of responding in other than a reactive fashion to conditions which arise.

A second factor is the commitment of the bureaucracy to the goals of the government of the day as opposed to their own organizational or personal goals. Fragmented administrative systems, as in the United States or some of the Scandinavian countries, may allow organizations to continue along established policy paths rather than follow new directions when there is alternation in office, or to use the policy-making process as a means of expanding their own budgets and influence.

Third, the institutional environment of policy-making in government may influence governability. Parliamentary governments, everything else being equal, should be more capable of providing governance than those with SEPARATION OF POWERS. Similarly, governing systems which have JUDICIAL REVIEW over the constitutionality of government policies may find it more difficult to act decisively than countries lacking powerful courts. FEDERAL systems, especially those which depend upon sub-national governments to implement central government policy, e.g. the Federal Republic of Germany, may find governance more difficult.

Finally, the party system may influence governability, especially the ability to generate and implement a clear mandate for action. Multi-party systems, and in particular the more extreme versions which always produce COALITION GOVERNMENTS, make it difficult for governments to have a clear mandate on policy issues. However, parties in two-party systems may be non-programmatic so that there is no policy guidance from their electoral campaigns. Also, the degree to which parties have a basic consensus about policy or at least the rules of the game will enhance the stability of government and the governability of the country. Governability may be enhanced when there is a limited number of parties which make, and maintain, clear policy stances and which attempt to implement those policies while in office.

The characteristics of the society within which a government must attempt to function will clearly affect the success of its efforts. One important factor is the degree of fragmentation in the society. Countries which have deep POLITICAL CLEAVAGES over language, religion, race or region will be more difficult to govern that those which are more homogeneous. Furthermore, fragmentation of INTEREST GROUPS (especially unions) may make policy-making (especially economic policy) and co-ordination more difficult. Though most industrialized countries have developed mechanisms for coping with societal fragmentation of both a social and an economic nature, their existence constitutes a strain on the governability of the country. A second societal factor influencing governability is the value structure of the population. Governability is closely related to the LEGITIMACY and authority of the government of the day. Certain cultures place a higher value on political authority than do others, while in others traditional allegiances to family and other social groups may make government a less important source of authority. In some instances government may even be a negative symbol of authority and its actions may be considered almost inherently illegitimate. Governments will obviously have more difficulties in exercising control when they do not evoke a symbolic loyalty.   BGP

Reading

Hall, P.A.: Policy innovation and the structure of the state. *Annals of the American Academy of Political and Social Sciences* 466 (1983) 43–60.

Kavanagh, D.: Whatever happened to consensus politics. *Political Studies* 33 (1985) 529–46.

Peters, B.G.: The problem of bureaucratic government. *Journal of Politics* 43 (1981) 56–82.

Rose, R.: *The Problem of Party Government*. London: Macmillan, 1974.

Sundquist, J.L.: A comparison of policy-making capacity in the United States and five European countries: the case of population distribution. In *Population Policy Analysis*, ed. M.E. Kraft and M. Schneider. Lexington, Mass.: Heath, 1978.

government   In the sense of a condition of ordered rule, government is the authoritative expression of the STATE. Its formal functions include law-making, the execution and implementation of laws, and the interpretation and application of law. These functions broadly correspond to legislative, administrative, and juridical functions. The extent to which the functions correspond to specific institutional jurisdictions depends to some degree on the organization of governance in a society. In modern governments, however, extensive advisory, policy planning and design processes, and programme review and analysis activities also take place. The development of these activities and functions has occurred mostly within the administrative apparatus of government which is the part of government whose activities have undergone the greatest expansion over the course of the past century. This expanded scope of governmental activity addressed by modern governments has been paralleled by the development of new ministries engaged in developmental, welfare, and regulatory functions. The development of governmental activity from the spare profile of the mid-nineteenth century to the numerous functions undertaken today also has been largely paralleled by the development of a professionalized BUREAUCRACY and a career CIVIL SERVICE. Towards the top of these ministries, therefore, are career officials whose roles consist of defining future policy alternatives and advising ministers about present courses of action.

By contrast with one or two centuries ago, the scope of governmental activity has increased greatly. With regard to the constituent components of governmental size, three key elements indicate the level of government activity in society – laws, people, and money. These elements have grown substantially since the middle of the nineteenth century. Over the course of the last few decades, however, the growth in the number of governmental employees has flattened and in relative terms mostly has declined. The principal growth component of government has been in its expenditure and taxation levels, though the impetus for expenditure growth lies in older laws establishing broad-based entitlement benefits such as pensions and health insurance.

But the term government may also denote the method by which a society is governed. Governments can be classified in several ways. One simple distinction made of contemporary governments is between liberal CONSTITUTIONAL GOVERNMENT and various forms of AUTHORITARIAN government. Liberal constitutional governments may be republican in nature (for example, the United States or France) or constitutional monarchies (for example Britain or the Netherlands). In the former case the head of state is an elected official; in the latter case the head of state is a hereditary monarch. The principal political features of either form of liberal constitutional government are competitive political parties, rule by a majority party or a coalition of parties able to obtain a governing majority (potential, if modest, exceptions to this characteristic will be noted in the case of the United States and France), and constitutional or normative limitations to the power of the state. No matter where formal sovereignty is said to derive, in reality it inheres in the legitimacy given to electoral results. In such governments, a further distinction often exists between the elected government of temporary rulers and a permanent government of career officials who populate and operate the administrative arm of the state. Each is dependent upon the other, but the impulse of the elected government is to lead in new directions while that of permanent government is to balance between the new directions and the often overtowering residue of past commitments made by former governments.

Authoritarian governments can range considerably in form. A common distinction made in political rhetoric is between TOTALITARIAN forms and traditional authoritarian forms. Totalitarian forms of government are regarded as phenomena unique to the twentieth century. They are chiefly characterized by a dominant ruling party that uses the power of the governmental apparatus to actively socialize and control the citizenry through techniques of mass mobilization, propaganda, and active coercion. NAZI or National Socialist Germany and the Soviet Union under STALIN are regarded as prime examples of totalitarian government. More broadly, the term has become associated with ruling Communist governments despite the great variability in patterns of rule under such governments. Aside from the institutional dominance of a ruling Communist party apparatus, it is often unclear how such governments differ from other forms of authoritarian government except to the extent that widespread control over the labour market provides unusual levers for such a government to control the life opportunities of citizens suspected of dissidence.

Other modes of authoritarian government usually have less central control over non-political activities. Such governments range from one person or family rule (as exemplified by the Duvalier family in Haiti) to military governments that have dominated sub-Saharan Africa, Latin America during various periods, and many Asian countries as well, to a loosely organized 'one party' patronage apparatus such as that earlier wielded by Juan Peron in Argentina, Kwame Nkrumah in Ghana, or Getulio Vargas in Brazil. Distinctions between forms of authoritarian government often fade on close inspection. Frequently in non-communist authoritarian governments the instruments of coercion, by virtue of being less pervasive, are more dependent on the exercise of violence than in many communist governments whose systems for controlling potential opposition are more institutionalized. On the other hand, many governments under official Communist party rule are really little more than family run dictatorships. The Ceausescu regime in Romania and the Kim Il-sung regime in North Korea are of this nature.

In general, only a relatively small number of countries among the world's governments can be genuinely classified as liberal constitutional ones. Most of these are in western Europe and North America. Overall there is a fairly close relationship between a society's state of economic development and relative affluence, and whether it has a democratic form of government. Democratic governments tend disproportionately to be from among the richest countries in the world, although there are important exceptions such as India.

The distinction between liberal constitutional and authoritarian governments, broadly speaking, focuses on the relationships between the governors and the governed. A different way of distinguishing between governments is in terms of the relationship between governing institutions. Within the genre of governments we can call liberal constitutional, two ways of classifying the relationships between governing institutions are particularly significant. One such distinction is based on the concentration or diffusion of power within a single level of government. The other distinction is based on the relationship between levels of government. In general, the first distinction is between governments based on a PRESIDENTIAL system and those based on a CABINET system. The second distinction is between federal and unitary governments. If the first distinction has to do with the relative concentration or diffusion of authority horizontally, the second distinction, that between unitary and federal governments, has to do with the relative concentration or diffusion of authority vertically. (See FEDERALISM.)

Of the liberal constitutional political systems in the world today, the vast majority are cabinet governments. In a cabinet government, a parliamentary majority forms a government. Such a government most frequently is formed by a combination of two or more political parties. Normally the combination consists of a large, but not a majority, political party and a combination of two or more smaller parties. Since 1969, for example, the Federal Republic of Germany (West Germany) has been governed by a dominant party with at least 40 per cent of the parliamentary seats and a pivotal small party. The constant factor in these governments has been the small party, the Free Democratic Party, while two large parties, the Christian Democratic Union (Christian Social Union in Bavaria) and the Social Democratic Party have at different times coalesced with the small party, providing it with considerable political advantages disproportionate to its small share of the vote.

Often a larger combination of political parties forms a coalition government, but one of these is usually the dominant party. A current example of this condition is the Italian government which has had the Christian Democratic Party at the core of all coalition governments. Numerous other parties whose seat allotment in the Italian Chamber of Deputies ranges from modest to minuscule have been in coalition with the Christian Democrats since the early 1960s.

Rather infrequently, the two dominant parties will form a grand coalition government when the costs of forming coalitions with smaller parties are too great for either of the larger ones. Since 1984 the government of Israel, for example, has been a grand coalition of the Labor and Likud party blocs. Similarly, in West Germany between 1966 and 1969 the Christian Democratic/Christian Social Union and the Social Democrats formed a grand coalition government. Grand coalition governments are typically the product of inconclusive elections and excessive demands by small pivotal parties for coalition entry.

Since the number of viable political parties is influenced by the system of election and the procedures by which parliamentary seats are allocated, majority party governments are likely to emerge only under conditions of plurality or majority election. The British system is a 'first past the post' (plurality) election system, and thus it normally produces majority party governments. (See ELECTORAL SYSTEMS.)

While there are particular variations from one system to another as to whether or not cabinet members are required also to be members of the parliamentary body, the key feature of cabinet systems is the notion of a fusion between the parliamentary majority and the government, the latter being a term that encompasses the prime minister and the cabinet. Thus, in a cabinet system of government it is legitimate to speak of the government as the present political rulers, and so it is also necessary to distinguish between the government of the temporary rulers and that of the permanent professional bureaucracy whose role is to serve the state, not merely a given government.

In a presidential system, however, there is genuine independence between a legislative majority and the political leadership of the executive. Indeed, with some frequency, the party holding a legislative majority may differ from the one holding executive power. In fact, that condition preponderantly characterizes the American Federal Government over the past three decades.

The United States is certainly the best known of the presidential systems. The American system is often referred to as a SEPARATION OF POWERS or 'checks and balances' system. Strictly speaking, there is no ruling government. The president and the legislature are each important, powerful, and institutionally independent of one another while politically interdependent. The French Fifth Republic has grafted elements of both the presidential and the cabinet systems on to its government. The French system of government consists of a prime minister and cabinet whose status is defined by political majorities in the Assembly. However a president with considerable powers is elected independently of the Assembly (as is the American president). In 1986 for the first time in the history of the Fifth Republic, the President and the government represent distinctly different political tendencies. The President and the government represented distinctly different political tendencies. This arrangement, which existed until 1988, was called COHABITATION and represented a form of power-sharing. (See SEMI-PRESIDENTIAL SYSTEM.)

One fundamental distinction between cabinet and presidential government lies in the degree of institutional independence between the executive and the legislative function. Whereas a president rarely can be assured of a legislative majority for his or her proposals, a cabinet government can be so assured if it introduces a bill on which either the majority party or parties in the governing coalition have come to prior agreement. When a president cannot command a legislative majority for one of his or her proposals, however, he or she does not fall. When a cabinet government, on the other hand, fails to gain a majority on a matter of confidence it does mean that the government will have to be reconstituted.

Overall, cabinet government tends to fuse authority; presidential government tends to fragment it. From a different perspective, unitary and federal government also have the effects of fusing or fragmenting sources of governmental decision-making. While there also are considerable variations within both unitary and federal governments, the fundamental difference between the two is that a unitary government controls from the centre; local or provincial administration legally is an arm of the central government. Whatever actual autonomy is enjoyed at these levels of government is at the discretion of the central government. A federal system of government, alternatively, is one where provincial governments enjoy a certain measure of constitutional legal and political autonomy, although constitutional law differs on the extent of such autonomy. Britain, France, Japan, and Italy are current examples of unitary governments while the United States, West Germany, Canada, and India are current examples of federal governments. Despite these general tendencies, a tremendous range of variation exists within each form of government as to how concentrated the actual exercise of authority really is.

In broadest form, government constitutes the institutions of governance. These institutions help to define the ways in which the governors relate to one another, to the political opposition, and to the career officials who populate the most operative arm of government – the administrative apparatus. They also help to define the way in which the governors and governed relate to one another. Governing institutions are vital to understanding how these relationships are structured, but the actual operations of government and governing also are influenced deeply by societal factors extraneous to formal institutions.　　　　　　　　　　　BAR

Reading

Beer, S. and Ulam, A.: *Patterns of Government*. 3rd edn. New York: Random House, 1974.

Blondel, J.: *An Introduction to Comparative Government*. London: Weidenfeld & Nicolson, 1969.

Crick, B.: *Basic Forms of Government: a sketch and a model*. London: Macmillan, 1973.

Finer, H.: *The Theory and Practice of Modern Government*. 2 vols. London: Methuen, 1949.

Finer, S.E.: *Comparative Government*. London: Penguin, 1970.

Friedrich, C.J.: *Man and his Government: an empirical theory of politics*. New York: McGraw-Hill, 1963.

Rose, R.: On the priorities of government: a developmental analysis of public policies. *European Journal of Political Research* 4 (1976) 247–89.

———: *Understanding Big Government: the programme approach*. London: Sage, 1984.

Schapiro, L.: *Totalitarianism*. London: Pall Mall, 1976.

government formation process

The institutional procedures adopted when the result of a general election fails to yield an unequivocal answer as to who should be asked to form a government. This problem arises mainly, though not exclusively, in those multi-party systems in which political alignments are ill-defined and the head of state is a constitutional monarch. The problem for the sovereign is to ensure that the process does not compromise his or her political neutrality. There are three methods of achieving this objective. The first, characteristic of Denmark and Norway, is to develop a series of CONSTITUTIONAL CONVENTIONS which politicians come to observe and respect. The second, characteristic of Belgium and the Netherlands, is to use an INFORMATEUR to assist in the process by negotiating with party leaders to discover what political combinations are possible. This enables the sovereign to be shielded from political involvement. The third method is that adopted in Sweden, as provided for by· the 1974 constitution known as the Instrument of Government, whereby the sovereign's prerogatives are transferred to the Speaker. However, whether the process works smoothly depends less upon institutional arrangements than upon the willingness to agree and the degree of consensus amongst party leaders.

See also MONARCHY.   VBB

Reading

Andeweg, R.B., van der Tak, T. and Dittrich, K.: Government formation in the Netherlands. In *The Economy and Politics of the Netherlands*, ed. R.T. Griffiths. The Hague: Nijhoff, 1980.

Bogdanor, V. ed.: *Coalition Government in Western Europe*. London: Heinemann, 1983.

———: The government formation process in the constitutional monarchies of north-west Europe. In *Comparative Government and Politics*, ed. D. Kavanagh and G. Peele. London: Heinemann, 1984.

Hermerén, H.: Government formation in multi-party systems. *Scandinavian Political Studies* (1976) 131–46.

governor

The elected chief executive of each American state. The governor is a popularly elected constitutional officer in all fifty states – the only state official so established and elected universally. Approximately 2000 individuals have served as a state governor since the founding of the American Republic, and each has fulfilled certain qualifications specified in the state constitutions. In modern times, most state governors are required to be at least thirty years of age, an American citizen, and a citizen of the state for at least five years. In forty-seven states the governor's term of office is four years (with a two-year term existing in New Hampshire, Rhode Island, and Vermont). Four states – Kentucky, Mississippi, New Mexico, and Virginia – restrict the governor to a single term, while all others permit the governor to serve at least two consecutive terms. Only in recent years has the corps of governors been diversified to include women and non-whites. Women were occasionally elected governor to succeed their deceased, impeached, or ineligible husbands before 1974, but in that year Democrat Ella Grasso of Connecticut became the first woman elected state chief executive without following her spouse to office. Similar independent women have since been elected in Washington, Vermont, and Kentucky. Hispanics have captured the governorship in New Mexico and Arizona, but no black has yet been elected governor of any American state. Despite this failure of blacks in gubernatorial politics, the modern governorship is more representative than ever before, and it is now attracting younger, better-educated, and more thoroughly trained politicians than in the first half of the twentieth century. As one of the four primary pathways to the presidency (the others being the Senate, the cabinet, and the vice presidency), the governorship has served as training ground for seventeen of the forty presidents, most recently Jimmy Carter of Georgia and Ronald Reagan of California. LJS

Reading

Beyle, T.L. and Muchmore, L.: *Being Governor: views from the Office*. Durham, NC: Duke University Press, 1983.

Kallenbach, J.E.: *The American Chief Executive: the presidency and the governorship*. New York: Harper & Row, 1966.

Lipson, L.: *The American Governor: from figurehead to leader*. Chicago, Ill: University of Chicago Press, 1949.

Ransone, C.B. Jr: *The Office of Governor in the United States*. Alabama: University of Alabama Press, 1956.

Sabato, L.J.: *Goodbye to Good-time Charlie: the American governship transformed*. 2nd edn. Washington, DC: Congressional Quarterly Press, 1983.

Governor-General The representative of the monarch in each of those member states of the British COMMONWEALTH of Nations (other than the United Kingdom) which acknowledge the monarch as HEAD OF STATE. In Canada and Australia the governor-general is the crown's representative at the central or national level; in the Canadian provinces there are also lieutenant-governors and in the Australian states, governors.

The office of governor-general has undergone change in keeping with the evolving constitutional status of Commonwealth countries. In Canada and Australia the governor-general originally served as the representative of both the monarch and the British government; at the Imperial Conference of 1926 it was agreed that henceforth he should perform the same role in the country in which he served as did the monarch in relation to the United Kingdom government, which meant that he no longer acted as a representative of United Kingdom governments and interests. The formula for the appointment of a governor-general also changed: whereas in earlier days he was appointed on the advice of United Kingdom ministers (possibly in consultation with local ministers), it was established by agreement at the Imperial Conference of 1930 that the governor-general should be appointed on the advice of ministers of the Commonwealth country in question after in-

formal consultation with the monarch. This convention was settled in the course of debate over the proposal to appoint Sir Isaac Isaacs as the first Australian-born governor-general of Australia in 1930.

In some modern Commonwealth constitutions, provision is made for the election of a governor-general, as for example in Papua New Guinea, where the electoral body is the LEGISLATURE; otherwise the source of advice is the prime minister. In the older Commonwealth countries the governor-general holds office 'during pleasure', for a term of years; in some constitutions a specific term of appointment is provided for. In earlier days the governor-general normally came from and returned to the United Kingdom; today, the practice is to appoint a 'local' man, a citizen of the country.

The modern governor-general is a viceroy; he performs his functions without prior reference to the monarch he represents. While there have been dramatic exercises of power, as when the governor-general of Australia, Sir John Kerr, dismissed a ministry led by Gough Whitlam in 1975, the governor-general usually performs his constitutional and ceremonial functions very much as does the monarch in the United Kingdom.

See also MONARCHY. ZC

Reading

Cowen, Z.: Governor-Generalship in the Commonwealth. *Journal of the Royal Society of Arts* (August 1985) 650–51.

Evatt, H.V.: *The King and his Dominion Governors*. London: Oxford University Press, 1936.

Hasluck, P.: *The Office of Governor-General*. Melbourne: Melbourne University Press, 1979.

Report of Inter-Imperial Relations Committee, Imperial Conference 1926. London: HMSO Cmd 2768, 1926.

grant in aid Payment by the national government or, in federal countries, the state in support of expenditure determined by a LOCAL GOVERNMENT. Such grants may be related to specific services or to a range of activities undertaken by the local government. They may be specific to a particular action, to a particular year, or they may be provided on a recurrent basis. The amount of grant may be fixed, or it may vary according to local circumstances – levels of local service, the resources of the locality or particular local conditions. Grant in aid provides a means whereby the centre can exercise control over the locality.

See also LOCAL GOVERNMENT FINANCE.

NTB

green parties See ECOLOGY/ENVIRON-MENTAL PARTIES.

group theory A term with two very different uses, each with its own literature. One describes theories about pressure groups: their emergence, membership, resources, maintenance. Until the publication in 1965 of *The Logic of Collective Action* by Olson such matters were not seen as controversial. Common sense seemed a sufficient guide and Truman (1951, pp. 56–61) described how groups emerged automatically through increasing specialization in society or as a response to disturbances in political balance which stimulated new countervailing groups. Olson however argued that, 'If the members of a large group rationally seek to maximize their personal welfare they will *not* act to advance their common or group objectives unless there is coercion to force them to do so, or unless some separate incentive, distinct from the achievement of the group interest is offered to the members of the group individually . . .' (1965, p. 2). Thus the core of the Olson argument was that groups did not emerge simply out of shared interests: it is more logical for the individual to 'free-ride' than to participate unless the group offers him or her selective benefits rather than political lobbying alone which will result in advantages for members and non-members alike.

This simple observation had profound impact as it undercut the assumption in pluralism that significant interests would probably be represented in the political process. Much writing on pressure groups in the past twenty years has been in reaction to, or a development of, Olson's point. (For example see Moe 1980; Kimber 1980.)

The second more controversial use of group theory was especially prominent in the 1950s and 1960s. It concerned the influence of groups in policy making. The most prominent source is A. F. Bentley (1967, p. 208) with his famous dictum, 'When the groups are adequately stated, everything is stated. When I say everything I mean everything. The complete description will mean the complete science, in the study of social phenomena . . .' The common misunderstanding here was that Bentley simply meant that membership based pressure groups such as the National Farmers Union, the British Medical Association, etc. determined policy. Such an interpretation neglects Bentley's very wide conception of 'group'. The group for Bentley might not be membership based – and indeed could lack formal organization – see for example, his discussion of the residents of New York City (which is included in New York State) as being in two conflicting groups (p. 206).

Bentley's insistence that the group was the unit of analysis of political science has not been widely followed and the leading group author Truman (1951) has disclaimed the label 'group theorist' and the pretence at a *general* theory of politics and has stated (1960) instead that his aim was to provide a *special* (restricted) theory of INTEREST GROUPS and their role. To study groups in policy-making is greatly removed from saying that only groups are worth studying.

The study of organized interest groups is therefore not synonomous with group theory in Bentley's sense, even if empirical study suggested that groups were important. Bentley has not been followed literally but his work has been resurrected periodically for two main reasons. First, his stress on empirical study rejected the prescriptive, constitutionally and institutionally orientated studies of the nineteenth century. Second, his conception of a political process in a state of constant flux is a very approximate progenitor of the systems approach of the mid-twentieth century.

Group theory was also important in a normative sense of finding a democratically respectable interpretation of the pressure group politics uncovered by empirical study (such as Odegard's *Pressure Politics*, 1928). This reformulation of democratic practice compensated for what were seen as defects in the working of the United States political system in terms of the criteria of classical (electoral) democracy. Voters were ill informed, turnout was low, and political outputs had little connection with electoral processes. To define democracy in terms of group activity leap-frogged such difficulties. Furthermore groups became 'respectable' as their presence distinguished western societies from the Cold War competitors.

See also POLITICAL SYSTEM.   AGJ

Reading

Bentley, A.F.: *The Process of Government* (1908). Evanston, Ill.: Principia, 1949; also ed. P. Odegard. Cambridge, Mass.: Belknap, 1967.

Garson, G.D.: *Group Theories of Politics*. Beverly Hills, Calif. and London: Sage, 1978.

Kimber, R.H.: Collective action and the fallacy of the liberal fallacy. *World Politics* 1 (1980) 178–196.

Moe, T.: *The Organisation of Interests: incentives and the internal dynamics of political interest groups.* Chicago, Ill.: University of Chicago Press, 1980.

Odegard, P.: *Pressure Politics*. New York: Columbia University Press, 1928.

Olson, M.: *The Logic of Collective Action*. Cambridge, Mass.: Harvard University Press, 1965.

Truman, D.B.: *The Governmental Process*. New York: Knopf, 1951.

————: On the invention of systems. *American Political Science Review* 54 (1960) 494–5.

guerrilla warfare   Meaning literally 'small war', the term was first used to describe the activities of the bands of Spanish soldiers and civilians who fought the French army of occupation during the Peninsular War of 1808–1814. The classic pattern of guerrilla warfare involves the strategically weaker side going over to the tactical offensive using methods, times and places of their own choice and constantly trying to benefit from their major tactical advantage, the element of surprise.

As a method of struggle, guerrilla warfare long predates the emergence of the modern term guerrilla. There are, for example, frequent references in the Bible to this form of warfare, practised by leaders such as David, Gideon, Judas Maccabeus, and Jonathan.

In the eighteenth century, when guerrilla wars were relatively rare in Europe, a more systematic doctrine begins to appear. A number of military writers, such as De Jeney in *Le Partisan ou l'art de faire la petite guerre* (1759) and Andreas Emmerich in *Der Parteigänger in Krieg* (1791), emphasize the special qualities required of the successful partisan: intelligence, resourcefulness and imagination, energy, physical resilience, and close knowledge of the terrain.

The most effective modern leaders and theorists of guerrilla warfare have stressed that it is not a self-sufficient method of achieving victory. Only when the anti-guerrilla side underestimates the guerrilla threat or simply fails to commit its full resources to the conflict does a guerrilla have a chance of achieving, unaided, long-term political aims. In most twentieth-century cases, guerrilla warfare on a major scale has been linked to revolutionary warfare, a struggle between a non-government group and a government for political and social control of a people in a given national territory. Most revolutionary wars have moved through a guerrilla phase and have finally developed into a decisive struggle between conventional armed forces. It should be noted, however, that the guerrilla warfare method has also frequently been used as an auxiliary weapon in other types of conflict (for example, partisan warfare against Nazi Germany in the second world war and guerrilla attacks during the periods of full-scale limited war in Korea and, later, in Vietnam).

Many theories of guerrilla warfare formulated by revolutionary leaders proclaim that counter-insurgency measures by incumbent regimes cannot be effective, and assume that such measures will tend only to enhance popular support for the guerrillas. Guerrilla movements often use urban guerrilla and terrorist tactics in a deliberate effort to provoke the authorities into a counter-insurgent over-reaction, thereby inducing an effect on domestic and international opinion favourable to the guerrillas. Thompson is one of many writers who have argued against an over-emphasis on military aspects of counter-insurgency.

Among the twentieth-century revolutionary

war theorists there have been changing emphases and doctrines of guerrilla warfare. The LENINIST model for gaining political power was basically designed for urban areas and was to culminate in a form of revolutionary coup d'etat. It was therefore found unsuitable for transmission to Asia. MAO ZEDONG tried the route of insurrection in the cities, but this was a complete failure. Chiang Kai-shek was able to defeat the Chinese Communist Party in 1927. Mao concluded that henceforth communist revolutions could only take the form of revolutionary wars.

Mao stressed the vital importance of gaining the mass support of the peasants as a basis for revolutionary struggle. He developed the strategy of protracted war passing through three stages: the enemy's strategic offensive and the revolutionaries' strategic defensive; the enemy's strategic consolidation and the revolutionaries' preparation of the counter-offensive; and the revolutionaries' strategic counter-offensive and the enemy's strategic retreat. This emphasis on a protracted struggle was based on Mao's assumption of lack of external assistance to the revolutionaries and the initial superiority of the enemy's military forces.

During their conflict against French colonial rule, the Viet Minh adapted the doctrine of protracted war to Vietnamese circumstances. In South Vietnam, guerrilla warfare was undertaken mainly to exploit contradictions in the American and Saigon governments, and to achieve political victory by undermining the opponent's will to fight. This aim was particularly clear after 1969 when the struggle became basically a confrontation between the conventional forces of North Vietnam and those of the United States and South Vietnam. Obviously the North Vietnamese could not have hoped to win a conventional military victory over the United States forces. What the guerrilla struggle helped to achieve was the American withdrawal, leaving the path clear for a conventional victory over the demoralized South Vietnamese army.

The successful guerrilla campaign of the Cuban revolutionaries led by Fidel Castro, 1956–9, saw the development of the theory of the 'foco', a small group of armed men who themselves create a revolutionary situation by their attacks on the government forces. The revolutionary leadership of the 'foco' combines political and military command. The guerrilla band is seen as the party in embryo. But although these ideas did have some influence in Latin America, the Cuban model suffered a great setback when the attempt at revolution in Bolivia ended in Guevara's death. A major weakness of the *foco* concept was its elitism and its almost inevitable isolation from the peasant and urban masses.

In the late 1960s and early 1970s revolutionary theorists in Latin America and elsewhere tended to shift their attention from the countryside to the cities, launching a number of spectacular but relatively short-lived campaigns of urban violence. These efforts also ended in failure due to determined and ruthless efforts to suppress them, and the failure of the revolutionaries to gain substantial and lasting mass support.

It would be premature to assume that guerrilla warfare has become obsolete as a result of developments in military technology and counter-insurgency capabilities. Guerrilla warfare continues to prove effective in tying down large numbers of security forces, disrupting government and the economy, and as an auxiliary weapon in a wider revolutionary war. Guerrillas continue to be used, often highly effectively, in many parts of the world, sometimes with substantial help from friendly foreign governments. A major trend in the late 1970s and early 1980s has been the growth of United States-supported guerrilla movements waging freedom struggles against incumbent Marxist regimes, for example in Afghanistan, Angola and Nicaragua. If well led and well armed, guerrillas can still present a formidable threat to weak and unstable governments in divided societies, especially where the guerrillas have ample wild and inaccessible terrain from which to operate, and a friendly state across the border.

See also CIVIL WAR; REVOLUTION AND COUNTER-REVOLUTION; TERRORISM.

PW

Reading

Asprey, R.B.: *War in the Shadow: the guerrilla in*

history. 2nd edn. Garden City, NY: Doubleday, 1975.

Callwell, C.E.: *Small Wars: their principles and practice*. London: HMSO, 1906.

Chorley, K.C.: *Armies and the Art of Revolution*. London: Faber, 1943.

Crozier, B.: *The Rebels: study of post-war insurrection*. London: Chatto & Windus, 1960.

De Jeney: *Le Partisan ou l'art de faire la petite guerre*. The Hague: 1759.

Emmerich, A.: *Der Parteigänger in Krieg*. Dresden: 1791.

Fairbairn, G.: *Revolutionary Guerrilla Warfare: the countryside version*. Harmondsworth: Penguin, 1974.

Guevara, C.: *Guerrilla Warfare*. Harmondsworth: Penguin, 1969.

Gwynn, C.: *Imperial Policing*. New York: St Martin's, 1934.

Heilbrunn, O.: *Partisan Warfare*. London: Allen & Unwin, 1962.

Laqueur, W.: *Guerrilla*. London: Weidenfeld & Nicolson, 1977.

Mao Zedong: *On Guerrilla Warfare*. Peking, 1961.

guild socialism Primarily a theory of community, industrial democracy and REPRESENTATION which casts TRADE UNIONS as the crucial agents in the transition to a socialist society in which power would be fragmented as FUNCTIONAL REPRESENTATION assumed equal importance to political representation. Developed in Britain in the first and second decades of the twentieth century it was a highly eclectic and utopian doctrine which included elements from the moral and aesthetic critiques of industrial society associated with Ruskin and the arts and crafts movement, Roman Catholic distributists such as Chesterton, FABIAN collectivism, SYNDICALISM, and PLURALISM with its critique of state sovereignty and insistence on the autonomy of self-governing associations. Two themes were constant: a discontent with the highly developed division of labour and bureaucratic structures of modern society and a consequent desire to return to a less complex, more morally integrated social order; a more immediately radical concern with the unequal distribution of power within society generally, but above all in the workplace. The former was most apparent in the writings of A. J. Penty; the latter in those of S. G. Hobson and G. D. H. COLE, for whom the greatest social evil was 'wage slavery' which impoverished the worker both materially and psychologically and was to be ended only by the abolition of profit and the vesting of control over production in the hands of self-governing guilds, each covering all the workers in a particular industry. For a brief period at the end of the first world war these ideas influenced both the programmes and the public language of labour politics in Britain.

See also SOCIALISM; SOCIALIST AND SOCIAL DEMOCRATIC PARTIES. JSR

Reading

Cole, G.D.H.: *Guild Socialism Restated*. London: Parsons, 1920.

Foote, G.: *The Labour Party's Political Thought: a history*. London: Croom Helm, 1985.

Glass, S.T.: *The Responsible Society: the ideas of the English guild socialists*. London: Longman, 1966.

Pierson, S.: *British Socialists*. Cambridge, Mass.: Harvard University Press, 1979.

Wright, A.W.: *G.D.H. Cole and Socialist Democracy*. Oxford: Clarendon Press, 1979.

gulag See LABOUR CAMP.

H

habeas corpus   A Latin term derived from the opening words of the writ by which in medieval times the common law courts in England could require a person to be brought before them. It refers to the legal remedy, as strengthened by legislation, by which a person deprived of liberty by arrest or detention (or someone else acting on his or her behalf) may apply to a court for a decision on the legality of the arrest or detention. If the arrest or detention is unlawful, release of the person detained will be ordered by the court. Habeas corpus refers essentially to a procedure for the protection of individual liberty in accordance with the rule of law (and see article 5.4, European Convention on Human Rights). In the tradition of British constitutional law, however, habeas corpus provides no fundamental guarantee of liberty since, for example, detention without trial may be authorized by parliament and a court may not order the release of anyone whose detention is shown to be in accordance with legislation. Habeas corpus is sometimes used in English law as a means of redressing grievances arising out of criminal justice (for example, the improper refusal of bail). It is often used in the context of extradition, immigration and detention of mental patients.

Habeas corpus is known in all legal systems which are derived from the English COMMON LAW. Under Article 1, section 9 of the US Constitution, the privilege of habeas corpus is not to be suspended except in extreme cases of rebellion or invasion. Habeas corpus has been widely used in the USA as a means of enabling review by the federal courts of criminal convictions recorded under state law.   AWB

Reading

Sharpe, R.J.: *The Law of Habeas Corpus*. Oxford: Clarendon Press, 1976.

Hagenbach-Bischoff method
See D'HONDT METHOD.

Hamilton/Hamiltonianism
(1) *Hamilton, Alexander* (1755–1804)   American statesman, co-author with James Madison and John Jay of the FEDERALIST PAPERS of which he composed over half the essays, and author of several influential policy papers during the presidency of George Washington, whom he served as Secretary of the Treasury (1789–1795). Hamilton's distrust of democracy and support for an active central government, for the public encouragement of manufactures, and for a realistic foreign policy made him the object of much of the popular opposition to the administrations of Washington and John ADAMS that, in the first great REALIGNMENT of American party politics, culminated in the electoral defeat of the Federalists by the Republicans under Thomas JEFFERSON. Hamilton's realism and Jefferson's idealism offered competing visions of America's future and still resonate in American politics today. Although Hamilton enthusiastically supported the cause of American independence in the American Revolution, he always kept his distance from the more utopian dreams and popular enthusiasm it inspired. He did not lose sight of the need for energetic government. Somewhat optimistically he judged that the experience of weak central government during and after the revolutionary war had

'wrought a deep and solemn conviction in the public mind that greater energy of government is essential to the welfare of the community' (*The Federalist*, No. 26). He saw the Constitution of 1787 as a step in the right direction, but it needed to be supplemented with forceful national fiscal and economic policies. He proposed an expansion of domestic capital and subsidies for non-agricultural sectors of the economy. He thought these policies conformed to the 'busy nature of man' (*Report on Manufactures*, 1791). Unlike many of his compatriots Hamilton did not believe that American domestic policies could or should radically depart from their European counterparts, as though human nature were different in America. He applied the same reasoning to foreign policy. For the sake of developing the American economy he advocated a special relationship with Britain. This policy was realistic, but it was also increasingly unpopular after the antagonism of Americans towards Britain that accompanied the Revolution was exacerbated by American sympathy with the French in their conflicts with Britain after the French Revolution.

(2) *Hamiltonianism* has never been so popular in America as it has been elsewhere; however, it appeals to hardheaded administrators everywhere, and it has usually enjoyed a friendly reception in the American business community. Hamilton's support for broad-based economic development supervised by strong central political and financial institutions found less favour in early American party politics than Jeffersonian support for agrarian interests and frugal government. Hamiltonianism however survived better in practice than in rhetoric. This was particularly true after a second American war against Britain (1812–1815) revealed some of the weaknesses of Jeffersonian policies, and many Jeffersonians came to embrace such Hamiltonian devices as the national bank and support for domestic manufactures. The Whig party of the 1830s and 1840s and the new Republican party of the 1850s (to which the modern Republican party traces its origins) incorporated Hamiltonian policies. They were, however, most successful when they also voiced Jeffersonian rhetoric. JZ

Reading

Miller, J.C.: *Alexander Hamilton: portrait in paradox*. New York: Harper, 1959.

Stourzh, G.: *Alexander Hamilton and the Idea of Republican Government*. Stanford, Calif.: Stanford University Press, 1970.

Syrett, H.C. and Cooke, J.E. eds: *The Papers of Alexander Hamilton*. 26 vols. New York: Columbia University Press, 1961–1979.

Hansard   The Official Report of debates in both houses of the United Kingdom parliament (and in some Commonwealth legislatures). The name derives from T. C. Hansard, the first publisher in 1803. Hansard covers debates on the floor and also in STANDING COMMITTEES of the HOUSE OF COMMONS. The report is substantially verbatim, with repetitions and redundancies omitted and obvious mistakes corrected. Hansard also includes the answers to questions for written answer. It is published in daily and weekly parts; these are later bound with indexes for each volume and for each session.   MTR

Reading

Law, W.: *Our Hansard*. London: Pitman, 1950.

May, T.E.: *Parliamentary Practice*, pp. 249, 262–4. 20th edn. London: Butterworth, 1983.

Hare, Thomas (1806–1891)   The first to elaborate the single transferable vote (STV) method of proportional representation. Hare was a Conservative free trader who followed Peel out of the Conservative party in 1846, and based his advocacy of STV upon the desire to free the individual from restrictions upon his choice. He believed that the single-member constituency characteristic of the plurality method of election imposed an unnecessary geographical restriction upon the choice of the elector. He believed in a liberal theory of REPRESENTATION, according to which the representative represented opinions rather than interests. Hare's writing deeply influenced John Stuart MILL, and his conception of the purpose of REPRESENTATION has provided the dynamic for electoral reform movements in Britain and in Commonwealth countries. On the Continent, however, STV has not proved acceptable as an electoral system, and proportional electoral systems are based upon one or other of the various list methods.

See ELECTORAL SYSTEMS. VBB

Reading

Bagehot, W.: *The English Constitution* (1865–7). (For a criticism of Hare.)

Bogdanor, V.: *The People and the Party System: the referendum and electoral reform in British politics*, part III. Cambridge: Cambridge University Press, 1981.

Hare, T.: *The Machinery of Representation*. London: Maxwell, 1857.

————: *The Election of Representatives, Parliamentary and Municipal: a treatise*. 4th edn. London: Longmans, 1873.

head of government In authoritarian states and traditional MONARCHIES the head of state, whether DICTATOR or monarch, also acts as head of government. In PARLIAMENTARY SYSTEMS the two offices are separated. PRESIDENTIAL SYSTEMS like that of the United States combine both roles in the office of the president. Socialist countries, for example the Soviet Union, separate the administration of government from the policy process and assign responsibility for administration to the COUNCIL OF MINISTERS.

In parliamentary systems the head of government is usually called prime minister (in West Germany, chancellor). Heads of government are selected from among the party leaders in parliament. According to the WESTMINSTER MODEL, the HEAD OF STATE appoints the party leader most capable of securing the confidence of parliament. Elsewhere the selection of the head of government may be the responsibility of the parliamentary parties or (as in Sweden) of the Speaker. In principle at least, heads of government serve at the pleasure of members of parliament. By convention they resign not only when rejected by the voters in an election but also if defeated on a vote of confidence in the legislature. It is therefore a convention that the head of government is responsible to parliament and the people – but not to the head of state. The last occasion

when a British monarch dismissed a prime minister was in 1783.

Heads of government appoint other members of the government and chair meetings of the ministry. Where, as in the United Kingdom, members of the government as a whole may number a hundred or more, a distinction is drawn between members of the cabinet and non-cabinet ministers. By convention, government policy is determined by the twenty to thirty members of the British cabinet, but all members of the government are expected to support cabinet decisions. The cabinet governs by consensus rather than through formal votes, with the prime minister as head of government summing up the sense of the meeting on each issue. It was once thought that the prime minister was best described as first among equals (*primus inter pares*) but it is now generally accepted that in normal circumstances the prime minister exercises much greater authority and that there is a hierarchy of ministers, some of whom the prime minister consults individually. Not all parliamentary governments operate according to the British model. One reason is that party systems vary. A head of government dependent on a coalition of parties is unlikely to be in as strong a position as the leader of a majority party. In some countries ministers are not required to be members of parliament.

Unlike the American president, a parliamentary head of government is not individually responsible for all acts of government. The other ministers share responsibility in cabinet: hence the doctrine of cabinet solidarity and collective responsibility. In addition, ministers are individually responsible for the conduct of their departments.

Where the head of state is also head of government it is often impossible to distinguish between the two roles. In the United States, however, most people are able to draw a distinction between the office of the president as head of state for all Americans and the role of the president as head of government (often called 'the Administration') and party leader. Under a presidential system like that of the United States, the president appoints members of the cabinet. They are responsible to the President as head of government but are not responsible to the legislature. Indeed, because of the American principle of the separation of the executive and legislative powers (or rather, institutions), neither the head of government nor the members of the cabinet are allowed to serve in either the Senate or the House of Representatives. This means that all legislation, including finance, has to be introduced in Congress by members of the legislative branch on behalf of the executive.

There has been a growing tendency for heads of government to meet in order to exchange views and resolve differences. When parliamentary heads of government meet the American president, who acts as both head of government and head of state, questions of protocol arise. France has attempted to overcome this difficulty by transforming its head of state into an office with real power. Since 1958 the French president has acted as both head of state and head of government (at least until the Assembly elections of 1986), leaving the prime minister as leader in parliament (see SEMI-PRESIDENTIAL SYSTEMS). The head of government in socialist countries is in a different category from those in authoritarian, parliamentary and presidential systems. In socialist states, such as the Soviet Union, administration is in the hands of a council of ministers chaired by the minister who is treated as first (or prime) minister. But government policy is in practice determined by the communist party, especially through its politburo of about a dozen members. The politburo, which includes the head of government, is guided by a leading official of the party secretariat who holds the title of first or general secretary. It is this person who, from Stalin onwards, in effect acts as head of government.

In sum, there are considerable differences in the roles played by heads of government. In authoritarian and traditional societies the head of state plays both roles. In the United States the president is both head of government and head of state. In socialist systems neither the head of government nor head of state enjoys the power customarily wielded by the leader of the communist party. The term head of government is perhaps most appropriately employed in parliamentary systems where the

separation of the two institutions, head of government and head of state, is a key principle of government.   DVV

Reading

Blake, Lord: *The Office of Prime Minister*. London: Oxford University Press, 1975.

Bogdanor, V. ed.: *Coalition Government in Western Europe*. London: Heinemann, 1983.

Crossman, R.: *Inside View*. London: Cape, 1972.

Gordon-Walker, P.: *The Cabinet*, rev. edn. London: Cape, 1972.

Jennings, W.I.: *Cabinet Government*, rev. edn. Cambridge: Cambridge University Press, 1959.

Koenig, L.W.: *The Chief Executive*. 4th edn. New York: Harcourt, Brace Jovanovich, 1981.

Lijphart, A.: *Democracies: patterns of majoritarian and consensus government in twenty-one countries*. New Haven, Conn. and London: Yale University Press, 1984.

Punnett, R.M.: *The Prime Minister in Canadian Government and Politics*. Toronto: Macmillan, 1977.

Rose, R. and Suleiman, E. eds: *Presidents and Prime Ministers*. Washington, DC: American Enterprise Institute, 1980.

Weller, P.: *First Among Equals: prime ministers in Westminster systems*. Sydney and Boston, Mass.: Allen & Unwin, 1985.

head of state   All political systems have an office of head of state which gives legitimacy to the system. The head of state, usually a MONARCH or president, is the person to whom foreign envoys present their credentials. Some heads of state also act as HEAD OF GOVERNMENT.

Heads of state attain their position through a variety of avenues. Monarchs, once their right to the succession has been established, are customarily crowned or anointed. British monarchs, for example, are crowned by the Archbishop of Canterbury. Commonwealth GOVERNORS-GENERAL are appointed by the monarch on the recommendation of the government of the day. Some parliamentary presidents (for example in India) are elected by one or more legislative bodies. In non-parliamentary systems the head of state may be elected by the people, either directly (as in France) or through an ELECTORAL COLLEGE (as in the United States). Nowadays there are fewer hereditary heads of state and more who are appointed or elected. In Malaysia the office is rotated among the hereditary heads of the various states. Between the world wars heads of state who seized power gave themselves a variety of titles, such as *shah* (Iran), *duce* (Italy), *führer* (Germany) and *caudillo* (Spain). The 'efficient powers' of the head of state, to use Bagehot's terminology, are generally less significant than the 'dignified powers', but the former can be important in an emergency situtation; in some circumstances the head of state may enjoy a genuine discretion.

Parliamentary systems require both a head of state (usually a monarch or president) and a head of government, usually a prime minister (in West Germany, chancellor). The powers of the parliamentary head of state are limited, but on occasion they may be important. For example, the head of state usually appoints the prime minister and, where no party obtains a majority, the head of state may exercise discretion. The head of state in some systems may decline to accept the prime minister's recommendation that parliament be dissolved, on the grounds that no alternative government is available. In Sweden, however, the powers of the head of state were devolved to the Speaker in the 1974 Instrument of Government, while in Switzerland, the head of state is the president of the Confederation, elected annually from the seven-member Federal Council.

In federal parliamentary systems there may be state governors (as in Australia and India) or provincial lieutenant-governors (as in Canada) who also act in normal times as formal heads of state. They may, however, be required by the federal government to override the head of government of their state or province in times of crisis. In socialist states such as the Soviet Union, the communist party leader wields more power than either the head of government (chairman of the council of ministers) or the head of state (chairman of the presidium of the supreme soviet of the USSR). The office of head of state is essential for the carrying out of the symbolic and formal functions of government and the initiation of the GOVERNMENT FORMATION PROCESS. In Sweden this last function has been transferred to the Speaker, but elsewhere the role varies from the largely ceremonial (in the UK and the USSR) to that of chief executive (in the USA).

DVV

Reading

Bagehot, W.: The English Constitution. In *Collected Works*, Vol. V, ed. N. St John-Stevas. London: The Economist, 1965–86.

Bogdanor, V.: *Multi-Party Politics and the Constitution*. Cambridge: Cambridge University Press, 1983.

Derfler, L.: *President and Parliament: a short history of the French presidency*. Boca Raton: University Presses of Florida, 1983.

Forsey, E.A.: *The Royal Power of the Dissolution of Parliament in the British Commonwealth*. 2nd edn. Toronto: Oxford University Press, 1968.

Hermerén, H.: Government formation in multi-party systems. *Scandinavian Political Studies* (1976).

Marshall, G.: *Constitutional Conventions: the rules and forms of political accountability*. Oxford: Oxford University Press, 1984.

Pious, R.: *The American Presidency*. New York: Basic Books, 1979.

Rossiter, C.: *Constitutional Dictatorship: crisis government in the modern democracies*. New York: Harcourt, Brace & Wold, 1963.

Hegel, Georg Wilhelm Friedrich

(1770–1831) German philosopher. Hegel had a strong interest in both theoretical and practical politics from early life. As a young man he was enthusiastic about the French Revolution; later his outlook was more conservative, but he never abandoned his support for ordered constitutional arrangements.

Hegel's principal work on politics was his *Philosophy of Right* (1821), which treats of 'natural law and political science in outline'. Hegel insists from the first that his object is not to recommend a political ideal but rather to articulate and clarify the concept of the modern STATE, the principle which underlies modern politics as opposed to those of former times. In his view political theory cannot prescribe, only describe; philosophy comes on the scene only when 'a shape of life has grown old'. 'To comprehend what is, this is the task of philosophy, because what is, is reason.'

According to Hegel the main difference between the state as it was in antiquity and the modern state is the presence in the latter of a whole sector devoted to the private pursuits of apparently self-sufficient individuals, the sector of 'civil society' (*die bürgerliche Gesellschaft*). This is the sphere of economic life, with the social structure (property law, 'police', trade associations) which goes with it, and it is often confused by theorists with the state proper. It constitutes however only an 'external' state, the state proper being much wider. Properly understood the latter term signifies a complex entity not just political or socio-economic, but cultural, religious, ethical, legal as well. Citizens gain fulfilment from membership of this wider whole and from conscious pursuit of the various satisfactions it affords. The state is needed, too, to rectify the recurrent crises to which civil society is subject, crises which Hegel identified as surely as MARX (see *Philosophy of Right*, ¶ 243–8).

Hegel proceeds to sketch the institutional form of the typical modern state. It turns out to be a constitutional monarchy, the monarch having substantial powers in foreign affairs but making only limited interventions at home. The legislature, partly elected, is separate from the executive, but little or nothing is said about the independence of the judiciary. Nevertheless, the rule of law is presupposed as the foundation on which other arrangements rest. An interesting feature is the part played by 'Corporations', initially introduced to mitigate the extreme individualism of civil society by making masters and men alike members of the same trade guild, later used to counter the anonymity of political elections by organizing them on occupational lines.

In international politics Hegel agreed with KANT that sovereign states largely stand to each other as do individuals in a state of nature, demanding recognition of their fellows but by no means always getting it. His conclusion from this was however that the Kantian project for 'perpetual peace' was chimerical. The verdict on right and wrong in the international sphere must be left to history: as Schiller had put it, 'world history is the world's court of justice'.   WHW

Reading

Avineri, S.: *Hegel's Theory of the Modern State*. Cambridge: Cambridge University Press, 1972.

Hegel, G.W.F.: *Philosophy of Right* (1821), trans. T.M. Knox. Oxford: Oxford University Press, 1942.

——: *Political Writings*, trans. T.M. Knox with intro. essay Z.A. Pelczynski. Oxford: Oxford University Press, 1964.

——: *Lectures on the Philosophy of World History* (1857) intro. and trans. H.B. Nisbet. Cambridge: Cambridge University Press, 1975.

Pelczynski, Z.A.: *State and Civil Society: studies in Hegel's political philosophy*. Cambridge: Cambridge University Press, 1984.

Hobbes, Thomas (1588–1679)   English philosopher, tutor, and royalist. Author of *Leviathan* (1651), one of the most influential works of political thought ever written. Though Hobbes did not, as he had hoped, supply models for concrete political systems, he introduced secular notions of government and authority through a powerful theory of the structure and mechanics of SOVEREIGNTY. Hobbes attempted to construct a scientific approach to politics based on true philosophical knowledge. From human nature he inferred the unlimited right to realize desires and hence the inevitability of conflict. Political order was therefore both artificial and essential to human survival, and was the necessary consequence of a transfer of individual rights to a sovereign who is not contractually bound to his subjects. Civil society was merely an arrangement to forestall harmful relations among individuals, and was held together by the sovereign. The body politic was reduced to one main attribute: sovereignty as absolute coercive power. By defining LAW as the will of the sovereign, Hobbes bequeathed two principles to political analysis: a political system establishes its own impartial rules by which right and wrong may be judged; effective power (see POLITICAL POWER) must underpin legally unchallengeable authority. Although that authority orginated in the people, REPRESENTATION meant the non-accountable and irreversible substitution of the sovereign's will for theirs. Political practitioners have understood Hobbes to argue that the successful test of a state – and one which obligates its subjects – is in its exercise of power and maintenance of their security, and that it is devoid of other communal ends. His theory has been described as authoritarian, but not totalitarian, since subjects are left to their own devices in areas that do not affect their preservation. MSF

Reading

Goldsmith, M.M.: *Hobbes's Science of Politics*. New York: Columbia University Press, 1966.

Hobbes, T.: *Leviathan* (1651).

Leyden, W. von: *Hobbes and Locke*. London: Macmillan, 1981.

Macpherson, C.B.: *The Political Theory of Possessive Individualism: Hobbes to Locke*. Oxford: Clarendon Press, 1962.

Strauss, L.: *The Political Philosophy of Hobbes*. Chicago, Ill.: University of Chicago Press, 1963.

Warrender, H.: *The Political Philosophy of Hobbes*. Oxford: Clarendon Press, 1957.

Watkins, J.W.N.: *Hobbes's System of Ideas*. London: Hutchinson, 1973.

Holy Roman Empire The supreme political authority in central Europe between its establishment by Charlemagne in 800, and 1806, when the last emperor Francis II resigned under pressure from Napoleon. It was conceived as the successor to the Roman Empire in the west, but the term Sacrum Romanum Imperium is not encountered before the thirteenth century and was always a misnomer (as Voltaire recognized in a famous quip). Increasingly limited in practice to the German-speaking lands, the Empire was often known from the fifteenth century as the 'Holy Roman Empire of the German nation'. Its chronic conflict with the papacy did much to unleash the Lutheran Reformation: no emperor was crowned by the pope after 1530. The decaying empire retarded the formation of modern states in the area but its unique institutions, however weak, represent an important example of CONFEDERAL structure, with an elective sovereign and elaborate constitutional checks and balances. The legacy of the Holy Roman Empire passed directly to the emperors of Austria (the style assumed by

Habsburg rulers in 1804), indirectly to the Second German Empire of 1871–1918.

RJWE

Reading

Barraclough, G.: *The Origins of Modern Germany*. Oxford: Blackwell, 1946.

Bryce, J.: *The Holy Roman Empire* (1864), rev. edn. London: Macmillan, 1904.

Zophy, J.W. ed.: *The Holy Roman Empire: a dictionary handbook*. Westport, Conn.: Greenwood, 1980.

home rule See DEVOLUTION.

House of Commons The elected chamber of Britain's bi-cameral legislature. All adult British nationals, with certain exceptions, can vote in a general election to return members of parliament. There are currently 650 members, each returned to represent a single constituency.

The House has its origins in the thirteenth century, when the king summoned two knights from each shire – and subsequently the leading freemen (burgesses) of the boroughs – to approve the raising of more money (supply) to meet the king's needs. In 1275 Edward I held his 'first general parliament', to which knights, burgesses and citizens were summoned in addition to the king's principal advisers – the earls, barons and leading churchmen of the kingdom. After 1325 the representatives of the communities, or *communes* (the Commons), were regularly summoned and under Edward III – who had to summon parliaments regularly to raise extra taxation – they began to make the grant of supply conditional upon the redress of grievances. At various times in the fourteenth century the Commons deliberated separately from the earls and barons, leading to the eventual separate development of the House of Commons and the HOUSE OF LORDS.

The House of Commons became a powerful political body under the Tudors as the monarch became increasingly dependent upon it for political as well as financial support. The attempt by Stuart kings to assert the divine right of monarchs to rule generated tension between crown and parliament resulting in the civil war, the beheading of Charles I, and, later, the flight of James II and his replacement under parliament's will by William of Orange. The new king owed his position to parliament, and the constitutional dominance of the latter was asserted in the Bill of Rights of 1689. The crown was denied the power to make or dispense with laws or to raise money without the consent of parliament.

During the eighteenth century the House of Commons was powerful but rarely assertive. Little public legislation was passed and members recognized a duty to maintain the king's government. Members of parliament were returned for constituencies which were notable for having few electors and in which open voting took place. Electors were often in the pay of leading aristocrats. The grip of the aristocracy was loosened by the 1832 Reform Act which enlarged the electorate by 49 per cent. The effect was to produce more independent members while encouraging the growth of embryonic political organizations. The 1867 Reform Act had an even more profound effect. It produced an electorate too large to be contacted other than through highly-organized political parties. The parties served as a conduit for the transfer of power from the Commons to a party-dominated executive (responsible for making public policy) and to the electorate (responsible for the choice of party government). Within parliament, recognition of the Commons as the democratically-elected chamber resulted in its being able to assert its position as the pre-eminent of the two chambers. For the House of Commons, the advent of a mass electorate was thus a double-edged weapon.

The relationship of the House of Commons to the government established by the end of the nineteenth century has remained largely unchanged in the twentieth. Constitutionally it remains a powerful body. It is the dominant element in the triumvirate of the Queen-in-Parliament, the body responsible for passing Acts of Parliament; under the doctrine of PARLIAMENTARY SOVEREIGNTY such Acts cannot lawfully be set aside by any other body. The government remains dependent upon the House for grants of supply. Politically, the House is less central. It is party-dominated, party cohesion being a marked feature of members' voting behaviour. The party with a majority of seats in the House usually forms the government and is assured normally of a majority when votes (divisions) are held. In the making of public policy, the role of the House is often characterized as being both marginal and predictable.

Once returned, the House fulfils three essential functions. Firstly, it provides the personnel of government. By convention, ministers are drawn from (and remain within) parliament and, again by convention, are drawn predominantly from the House of Commons. The House also provides a forum in which potential ministers can undergo a form of apprenticeship. Secondly, it provides the function which is common to national assemblies: that of legitimization. The House serves to legitimize the measures of government and also, through votes of confidence, the government itself. By virtue of being the elected chamber, the Commons constitutes the most powerful legitimizing agent within the formal body of the Queen-in-Parliament. Thirdly, the House fulfils a function most commonly subsumed under the heading of being a 'watchdog'. Under this head it debates public policy and, before giving its assent to government measures, subjects the government and its legislation to a process of scrutiny and influence. Subjecting government measures and actions to scrutiny occupies most of the time of the House.

Scrutiny of government actions takes place through debate, through question time (occupying up to fifty-five minutes on four days a week, before the start of public business) and through investigative SELECT COMMITTEES. In 1979 the House appointed fourteen such committees to examine 'the expenditure, administration and policy' of the principal government departments. Scrutiny (and legitimization) of legislation takes place through a long-established procedure: the formal first reading (when a measure is introduced); the second reading, when the principle of the measure is debated and approved; Committee stage, when a BILL is sent to Committee – usually a STANDING COMMITTEE but sometimes a COMMITTEE OF THE WHOLE HOUSE – for detailed consideration; Report stage, when changes made in Committee (and new amendments) can be considered; and third reading, when the measure receives its final approval. The House may also have subsequently to consider amendments made to the measure by the House of Lords.

The House has been variously criticized for failing to subject government to effective scrutiny, and for lacking the political will, the structures and the resources that would allow it to do so. Many critics would like the Commons to move away from a party-dominated, chamber-oriented and under-resourced body to a more independent, committee-based body, able to influence public policy at its formulative stages. Parliamentary reform has been variously canvassed. Some critics seek further change within the institution, such as a strengthening of select committees; others believe significant reform can only be achieved by wider constitutional and political change, for example a written constitution, a formal SEPARATION OF POWERS, or by proportional representation which would lead to coalition government. Nevertheless, the Commons has re-asserted its influence since the 1970s, and it remains the model for many Commonwealth parliamentary systems.   PN

Reading

Butt, R.: *The Power of Parliament*. London: Constable, 1967.

Judge, D. ed.: *The Politics of Parliamentary Reform*. London: Heinemann, 1983.

Norton, P.: *The Commons in Perspective*. Oxford: Martin Robertson, 1981.

——— ed.: *Parliament in the 1980s*. Oxford: Blackwell, 1985.

Walkland, S.A. ed.: *The House of Commons in the Twentieth Century*. Oxford: Oxford University Press, 1979.

——— and Ryle, M. eds: *The Commons Today*. London: Fontana, 1981.

House of Lords   The Upper House of the Parliament of the United Kingdom has been composed since its origins in the early middle ages of the Lords Spiritual and Temporal. In 1985 its composition was as follows: 26 archbishops and bishops; 726 peers by succession (18 of them women); 30 hereditary peers of first creation; 345 life peers (48 of them women); and 20 Lords of Appeal.

All lay members are for life, but archbishops and bishops retire at about age seventy. There is a leave of absence scheme for Lords who do not wish to attend. Members receive no salary but may recover expenses within specified limits. Party allegiance in 1985 was Conservative 413, Independent or Cross-Bench 230, Labour 127, Liberal 42 and Social Democrat 44. In 1968 a White Paper stated that 'the Conservatives have always in modern times been able to command a majority', but in recent years this has by no means always been so, and the present Conservative administration has often been defeated in the Lords.

Until 1911 the House possessed unrestricted powers except as limited by the Commons' financial privilege, but in that year the Parliament Act removed the Lords' power to reject 'money bills' and provided that an ordinary public bill could become law if passed by the Commons in three successive sessions and after two years: this was cut down to two sessions and one year by the Parliament Act 1949.

The House of Lords has eight principal functions.

(1) Supreme Court of Appeal, i.e. the ultimate court of appeal in the United Kingdom.
(2) A forum for debate on matters of public interest, on which the House spends about a fifth of its time, especially on Wednesdays.
(3) Revision of public bills brought from the Commons, which occupies over a third of the time of the House and more than any of its other functions.
(4) Initiation of public legislation, including government bills, especially technical bills of uncontroversial nature in party political terms, and bills on law reform, such as Consolidation and Law Commission Bills. Private members possess an unfettered right to introduce bills.
(5) Consideration of delegated legislation, on which the Lords have uncurtailed powers, but use them with restraint. Technical scrutiny is carried out by a joint committee.
(6) Scrutiny of activities of the executive, by oral questions, private notice questions on matters of urgency, questions for written

answer, and 'unstarred questions', or questions with debate.

(7) Scrutiny of private legislation, on which both the powers and the workload of the two Houses are equal.

(8) Select committees. These include the European Communities Committee, which reports on EEC proposals, working through sub-committees and making some twenty reports a year, which are debated; also the science and technology committee which has three sub-committees and produces two reports a year, also debated. A number of other *ad hoc* select committees have been set up in the last decade including those on the bill of rights (1978), unemployment (1982) and overseas trade (1985).

Until the nineteenth century the procedures of the two Houses were in many ways similar; latterly they have diverged as the Lords have not yet been forced by PARLIAMENTARY OBSTRUCTION radically to alter their procedure, which has evolved slowly to meet changing conditions. The Lords is the only legislative assembly whose Speaker has no power to maintain order. All Lords share equally the responsibility for maintaining order, though the Leader of the House has a duty to advise the House. The Lord Chancellor as ex officio Speaker has no power to maintain order. There are relatively few standing orders, and the practice of the House is laid down in the *Companion to Standing Orders*. There continues to be no selection of amendments, no guillotine, no fixed times for adjournment, no (with few exceptions) time rules, and no priority for the government.

MAJW-B

Reading

Bromhead, P.A.: *The House of Lords and Contemporary Politics 1911–1957*. London: Routledge & Kegan Paul, 1958.

Companion to the Standing Orders and Guide to the Proceedings of the House of Lords. London: HMSO, 1984.

House of Lords Reform. London: HMSO, Cmnd. 3799, 1968.

Morgan, J.P.: *The House of Lords and the Labour Government 1964–1970*. Oxford: Oxford University Press, 1975.

Pike, L.O.: *Constitutional History of the House of Lords*. London and New York: Macmillan, 1894.

Shell, D. *The House of Lords*. London: Philip Allen, 1988.

House of Representatives
See CONGRESS.

Hume, David (1711–1776) Scottish philosopher, historian and essayist. Hume's political theory, though developed with an eye to contemporary political conflicts, was firmly rooted in his general philosophical system. He was an empiricist with a radically sceptical view of the scope of reason in human affairs. Rejecting rationalist theories of government with their pretensions to demonstrative proof, Hume advocated an empirical science of politics, one that would be grounded in an empirical understanding of human nature, and a historically based knowledge of the causes operative in social and political life. His own study of politics led him to stress the importance of well contrived institutions. Good government, he argued, depends less on the qualities of rulers than on the laws and institutions through which they govern: the mark of a well designed constitution being the degree to which it constrains those in authority to act, despite themselves, in the public interest, and to act predictably, in accordance with known laws that protect private property and personal liberty. This virtue of 'regular' or 'civilized' government is compatible, Hume thought, with a variety of institutional forms, from absolute monarchies to pure republics – provided they are not too democratic. Particular forms of government were to be defended less on abstract principle than on their compatibility with existing customs. Despite this open-mindedness, in theory, towards alternative forms of government, Hume was deeply committed to the British constitution, not because he thought it the best possible but because it had, since 1688, taken root in the affections of the people. Without their loyalty, even the wisest of constitutions would, in his view, come to grief.

FEMcD

Reading

Forbes, D.: *Hume's Philosophical Politics*. Cambridge: Cambridge University Press, 1975.

Hume, D.: *Essays Moral Political and Literary* (1777), ed. E. Miller. Indianapolis: Liberty Classics, 1985.

————:*A Treatise of Human Nature* (1739–40), ed. L.A. Selby-Bigge. Oxford: Clarendon Press, 1978.

Miller, D.: *Philosophy and Ideology in Hume's Political Thought*. Oxford: Clarendon Press, 1981.

Stewart, J.B.: *The Moral and Political Philosophy of David Hume*. New York: Columbia University Press, 1963.

hung parliament   Colloquial term used to describe a situation in which no single party has a majority in the British House of Commons, so that there must be either a MINORITY GOVERNMENT or a COALITION. The term is derived from 'hung jury', a jury unable to agree and so deadlocked, with a retrial being necessary. The term was first used in Britain in the *Economist* (3 August 1974, p. 13): 'This Parliament has been called many names: the hung, the cynical, the shiftless, the cowed.' The implication of the term is that, given the plurality system of election, a hung parliament is a temporary aberration from the norm; in proportional representation systems, they are of course normal. In recent years, political scientists have devoted some attention to the constitutional and political problems likely to arise from a hung parliament in Britain.   VBB

Reading

Bogdanor, V.: *Multi-Party Politics and the Constitution*, part 2. Cambridge: Cambridge University Press, 1983.

Butler, D.: *Governing without a Majority*. 2nd edn. London: Macmillan, 1986.

I

ideology The term was first used in France by a minor *philosophe*, Destutt de Tracy (1754–1836), who coined it in 1796 to stand for a possible 'science of ideas'. This science has never developed. The word however was useful and writers in post-Napoleonic France and Romantic Germany took it up to represent two things at once. To them an ideology was a systematic outlook on the world, both a theory and a programme, showing a coherence of logic and/or feeling, but it could also be a distorted outlook, departing from positivistic objectivity to embody the passions, fears, desires, or mere errors of the ideologue. Ideology was therefore a presentation of the world in falsified terms and the falsification lay within the mind and expression of the falsifier. To MARX and Engels, therefore, it was 'false consciousness'.

Whence does 'false consciousness' come? How can its different forms be explained? What thinking is possible that is not 'ideological'? The Marxist answer to the first question is not interesting since it is so obvious: ideology is the distortion of thought by economic concern with the interest and the service of class domination. Feudal, romantic, positivist ideologies and so forth, therefore, all belong to the same family. The differences the Marxists detected in ideologies are historically specific in terms of the evolution of class politics and the various exigencies of economically dominant groups in search of the legitimation of their power or their aspirations. But if so much thinking is ideological why should the theory of ideology itself be other than a new form of ideology?

'Unmasking ideology', to use the Marxist phrase, might well itself be an ideological exercise. If all political regimes require a legitimation for their exercise of power, then all power enlists ideology. If all political aspirations claim legitimacy, then all must be ideological. So Marxism itself can be regarded as merely another ideology.

After Marx and Engels, the analysis of ideologies went on without necessarily using the word itself. PARETO's 'manifestations', MOSCA's 'political formula', SOREL's 'myths', WEBER's concerns with traditional legitimacy and so on, are all concerned with aspects of ideology. What is more, Freudianism could at once individualize and enormously expand ideology, for all individual psychology is to be understood in the unmasking of the ideology of individual formation, and yet this formation is claimed to be uniform for all cultures, places, and times. Ideology had become like a serpent with its tail in its mouth. There might seem to be no escape from its dilemmas.

The sociologist Karl Mannheim strove to distinguish between two main kinds of ideology and also suggested that there was an escape from the difficulty unconsciously raised by Marx. Mannheim demarcated two forms of ideology: the first which he termed ideology *tout court* expressed the distortion of thought inevitable in a RULING CLASS desiring to conserve its power; the second was the distortion of thought directed to an impossible and ideal future for an aspiring class, and this he defined as a Utopia entailing a Utopian ideology. The distinction was useful enough but it did not solve the relativistic problem. Mannheim suggested that there was a solution in that, in the history of society, an independent grouping of 'free-standing intellectuals' (or clerisy) had emerged for the purposes of science and scholarship and which therefore was the master of techniques of critical judgement and objectivity quite separate from ideology. As Mannheim's critics at once pointed out, was this position not itself ideological in the tradition of Cometeanism? Mannheim's reply was in the proper sense of the term pragmatic: if the free-standing and critical intellectuals are the prey of ideology they are at once a self-correcting group and also to be justified by the practical triumphs of science, reason and scholarship.

Mannheim's writings are at their best in the 1920s. The word ideology now became widely disseminated; the 1930s and 1940s largely defined this as being 'engaged in a war of ideologies'. FASCISM, NAZISM, DEMOCRACY and COMMUNISM, were defined as ideologies and particular forms of action were supposed to flow from adherence to them. It was suggested that all four were largely complete systems of thought and that each embodied a specific form of political will. In the 1950s, 'the end of ideology' thesis was argued, above all by Daniel Bell. There were three elements in the case for this position: representative democracy was held to be non-ideological but both rational and pragmatic; communism (fascism was largely forgotten) was regarded as indeed being an internally consistent thought-system but was 'unmasked' by the gap between its consequences and its claims, and also by its failures in human terms. Thirdly, ideology, it was argued, was no longer necessary, for an age of affluence had arrived in at least the western capitalist countries and could extend elsewhere so that class, passions, and desires would no longer move mankind.

As this case was being argued old ideologies of nationalism, religion, and international rivalry were re-establishing themselves throughout the third world and finding plenty of manifestations elsewhere. Political scientists have come to study ideologies empirically in the analysis of opinion formation and policy preferences. Ideologies remain among the most important objects of social and political studies and the best the student can hope for is that Mannheim was in part right.   DGM

Reading

Converse, P.E.: The nature of belief systems in mass politics. In *Ideology and Discontent*, ed. D. Apter. New York: Free Press, 1964.

Lichtheim, G.: *The Concept of Ideology and other Essays*. New York: Random House, 1967.

MacRae, D.G.: *Ideology and Society*. London: Heinemann, 1961.

Mannheim, K.: *Ideology and Utopia*. New York: Harcourt Brace; London: Routledge & Kegan Paul, 1936.

———: *Essays on Sociology and Social Psychology*. London: Routledge & Kegan Paul, 1953.

Marx, K. and Engels, F.: *German Ideology* (1845). London: Lawrence & Wishart, 1938.

Plamenatz, J.: *Ideology*. London: Macmillan, 1970.

Shils, E.: Ideology. *International Encyclopedia of Social Sciences*, Vol. VII. New York: Macmillan and the Free Press, 1968.

Stark, W.: *The Sociology of Knowledge*. London: Routledge & Kegan Paul, 1958.

Thompson, J.B.: *Studies in the Theory of Ideology*. Cambridge: Polity, 1984.

image, party   Voting behaviour is influenced by a number of factors – social background, issues, party identification, and the leaders and events associated with each election. A more general influence may be the voter's image of the party or candidate. One of the first uses of the term was by Graham WALLAS in his *Human Nature in Politics* (1908). Wallas held that voters required: 'something simple and more permanent, something that can be loved and trusted, and which can be recognized at successive elections as being the same thing that was loved and trusted before; and party is such a thing'. Images therefore enable voters to simplify and interpret a complex flow of messages and influences. People may vote for a party in spite of disagreements with it about specific issues or leaders because of the party image. Much of a party's campaigning is aimed at reinforcing positive features of its image.

To take specific examples, surveys in Britain have shown that many voters regard Labour as the party of 'fairness', 'the working class', and 'public ownership'. The Conservatives are widely seen as the party of 'free enterprise', 'the middle class', and often, 'the national interest'. In the United States the Democrats, until recently, were regarded as the party of prosperity and of war, while the Republicans were linked with the economic depression of the 1930s.

There is much evidence in western states of an increase in ELECTORAL VOLATILITY as voters have become weaker in their attachment to particular parties, and become more inclined to vote on the basis of issue and candidate factors. Attachment to a party image is a way of promoting electoral stability, and the decline of one is related to the decline of the other.   DK

Reading

Crewe, I. and Denver, D. eds: *Electoral Change in Western Democracies: patterns and forms of electoral volatility*. London: Croom Helm, 1985.

Wallas, G.: *Human Nature in Politics*. London: Constable, 1908.

impeachment is a legal process for removing undesirable persons from public office. It originated in medieval England and was revived in the seventeenth century during the struggle between king and parliament. In a bicameral legislature, such as the British Parliament or the United States Congress, the lower house will present articles of impeachment to the upper house. Vote of the upper house settles the question of the defendant's guilt or innocence. The process thus partakes of the nature both of a trial in which all the usual procedural niceties are observed, and of party politics. In the most famous impeachments, such as those of the earl of Strafford in 1641 and Warren Hastings in 1787, the element of party warfare was all too evident (and partly explains why in neither of these cases was conviction obtained). However, it is the development of the doctrine of ministerial RESPONSIBILITY and the exceedingly cumbrous nature of the process which explains why impeachment has fallen into complete disuse in Britain. It was last used in the case of Lord Melville in 1806. Defeat in a general election or loss of a vote of confidence in the House of Commons are much swifter methods of evicting ministers, while judges can be removed when necessary by address of Parliament. The situation is slightly different in the United States, where under the Constitution 'the president, vice president and all civil officers of the United States' (Art. II. § 4) – this is thought not to include members of Congress – as well as state governors, (except in Oregon), and state judicial officers may be impeached (the King, as head of state, cannot be impeached under British law). Under the US Constitution 'treason, bribery or other high crimes and misdemeanours' are the sole impeachable offences. President Andrew Johnson was impeached in 1868; President Richard Nixon was arraigned in 1974. Neither episode was a convincing advertisement of the merits of impeachment in a modern government. Johnson was the intended victim of something very like a COUP D'ÉTAT by the Republican party in Congress. Had he been driven from office the essential balance of the Constitution would have been destroyed. Impeachment was launched against Nixon, successfully, as the only way of forcing his resignation. The threat of removal from office thus showed its value in an emergency, but the difficulties of arriving at a satisfactory definition of 'high crimes and misdemeanours', and related legal problems, showed that the process could have been drawn out indefinitely, to the serious injury of government. Impeachment proceedings have occasionally been brought against federal judges and state officials, but have proved little more satisfactory than the presidential impeachments.   HB

Reading

Berger, R.: *Impeachment: the constitutional problems*. Cambridge, Mass.: Harvard University Press, 1973.

US House of Representatives: *Impeachment of Richard M. Nixon, President of the United States: the final report of the Committee on the Judiciary*. New York: Viking, 1975.

imperial federation With the concession of self government to many colonies and moves towards federal governments in Canada and Australia, a few enthusiasts dreamed of a wider federation of the British Empire, but even with the technological advances in communication a century later it would be a prodigious, even impossible, task to federate an EMPIRE scattered across the world. Within ten years the Imperial Federation League (founded in 1884) had suspended operations for lack of support. Colonists were reluctant to surrender any powers recently secured, while British governments refused to share with remote colonists authority in European diplomacy so crucial to Britain. There were many of course who saw the empire as a potential source of greater mutual protection. If in Britain, however, there might be general support for a *kriegsverein*, colonies for the most part preferred to develop their own forces which they could control rather than hand over to a British War Office or Admiralty. If colonists had some support for an imperial *zollverein*, a mutually inter-dependent and sufficient economy, the British were not yet prepared to surrender free trade for tariff reform and to buy dearer from the colonies, while colonists were not prepared only to produce raw materials for Britain and were anxious to develop their own industries to compete with the British. For a formal federation, a *staatsverein* which would establish in Britain a central government, remote from the colonies but giving them a voice in European affairs, there was nowhere much support. A looser, less demanding COMMONWEALTH was to emerge. AFM

implementation The process through which national, state or local governments translate policy into action, for example in areas such as education, energy, health or welfare. Implementation can be seen as the conversion of political intentions into action sometimes as a response to demands and pressures put on the governmental system and sometimes as a result of initiatives taken by governments themselves. However, such a neat model does not always correspond with reality; action does not always follow political rhetoric and when it does, results are often not as anticipated. This has led writers to talk of 'implementation failures' or 'implementation gaps' between policy and action. It has also drawn politicians, administrators and scholars

to look more closely at the process of implementation itself.

It is frequently claimed that political scientists took little notice of implementation issues until the 1970s. This claim is exaggerated as any examination of the literature of political development would indicate. Hence, as states have struggled to industrialize or to introduce agriculture or land reform, differences between stated intentions and what has actually materialized have often been sharply demonstrated. Such problems are features of both third world and industrial countries and of both federal and parliamentary systems. Implementation difficulties also characterize the operation of supra-national bodies such as the European Community, particularly in fields such as agriculture and energy.

Questions therefore arise as to why implementation is so difficult, whether it is more problematic in some policy areas than others or a specific feature of particular political systems. To address these questions it is first essential to realize that many discussions of implementation are based on simplistic models of how governments operate and how policy is made. These often assume that politics and ADMINISTRATION are sharply separate as are policy formulation and implementation. This perspective leads to a model of governmental behaviour which sees decisions made first at a political level then implemented without question by BUREAUCRACIES. It also assumes that policy goals are clearly specified, resources released to achieve them and that implementing agencies and organizations are subject to a system of hierarchical control. This perspective, often called the 'top-down' view of implementation, leads to a specific set of remedies for 'implementation failures': goals should be clearly specified, resources made available, control established and co-ordination between implementing agencies ensured. It is argued that while such action might not achieve 'perfect implementation' it would at least lead to substantial policy improvement. Such suggestions are not without value but they may also fail to appreciate that policy can itself evolve in the process of implementation.

The idea that politicians articulate clear goals which can then be speedily implemented makes particular assumptions not only about the nature of politics but also about the organization of government and the ability of the latter to change and control its environment. For politicians vague goals or symbolic utterances are often preferred to specific statements that carry high political costs if not realized. Moreover, in some areas (e.g. agriculture, education, health care) policy may evolve with the state of knowledge as a response to changing social and economic environments or as a result of interactions between those who implement the policy and the client groups they deal with.

To the above must be added the fact that control by political actors over policy implementation cannot be taken for granted. This is particularly the case where implementation involves interaction between levels of GOVERNMENT – central and local government in Britain; federal and state agencies in the United States. In these instances differences in values and goals in policy areas such as education and housing may lead to difficulties in implementation. Yet, even in areas where there are no ideological differences and the merits of initiatives may seem agreed, problems may still arise since national and sub-governments may have different policy priorities and compliance with central initiatives cannot be assumed. Policy implementation therefore often depends on the co-operation of organizations within and outside government who have their own values and interests and whose co-operation may be achieved only through processes of negotiation and bargaining in which the nature of policy may itself be shaped and altered (e.g. the influence of health professionals on health policy in the UK).

These arguments, often referred to as 'bottom-up' perspectives on implementation, stress the need to qualify the simple model of implementation outlined initially with the recognition that policy formulation and implementation are often inter-dependent activities and that implementation can be influenced both by the nature of the policy itself and by the political system in which implementation takes place. In particular any study of implementation needs to take account of the relation of a government with its bureaucracies and with groups in the wider political system. Implementation difficulties are therefore not aberrations subject to a quick technical or political fix but a reflection of the problems faced by governments of controlling the environments in which they function. There is no one model of implementation since the process varies both with policy and political context. Indeed the value of implementation studies is less to offer a panacea to improve poor policy as to open a window onto the real power struggles within and between levels of government in the context of policy development.　　　　WIJ

Reading

Bardach, E.: *The Implementation Game*. Cambridge, Mass.: MIT Press, 1977.

Barrett, S. and Fudge, C. eds: *Policy and Action*. London: Methuen, 1981.

Dunsire, A.: *Implementation in a Bureaucracy*, Vol. I. Oxford: Martin Robertson, 1978.

Ham, C. and Hill, M.: *The Policy Process in the Modern Capitalist State*, ch. 6. Brighton, Sussex: Wheatsheaf, 1984.

Hogwood, B.W. and Gunn, L.A.: *Policy Analysis for the Real World*, ch. 11. Oxford: Oxford University Press, 1984.

Lewis, D. and Wallace, H. eds: *Policies into Practice*. London: Heinemann, 1984.

Mazmanian, D.A. and Sabatier, P.A. eds: *Effective Policy Implementation*. Lexington, Mass.: Heath, 1981.

Pressman, J.L. and Wildavsky, A.: *Implementation*. Berkeley: University of California Press, 1973.

impoundment　Term used to signify a refusal by the president of the United States to spend funds appropriated by law. The term is also used loosely to describe a presidential decision to defer spending such funds until a later fiscal year. Although occasional impoundments have occurred since the early nineteenth century, the practice became highly controversial when President Nixon aggressively used it to curtail or eliminate programmes enacted and funded by law. Though several impoundment orders have been challenged in the lower federal courts, the constitutional conflict over the president's impoundment powers has not been definitively decided by the Supreme Court. The Congressional Budget and Impoundment Control Act of 1974, which was signed by President Nixon, mediated the confrontation by granting the president express statutory authority to impound or defer appropriated funds, subject to the right of Congress to review and disapprove any such action by a legislative veto. This disapproval procedure has since been held unconstitutional (see LEGISLATIVE VETO), leaving the president's statutory as well as his constitutional right to impound in doubt.

LNC

Reading

Abascal, R. and Kramer, J.: Presidential impoundment, Part I: historical genesis and constitutional framework. *Georgetown Law Journal* 62 (1974) 1549–618.

Fisher, L.: Note, impoundment of funds. *Harvard Law Review* 86 (1973) 1505–35.

————: Note, protecting the fisc: executive impoundment and congressional power. *Yale Law Journal* 82 (1973) 1636–58.

————: *Presidential Spending Power*, pp. 147–201. Princeton, NJ: Princeton University Press, 1975.

————: Note, addressing the resurgence of presidential budgetmaking initiative: a proposal to reform the Impoundment Control Act of 1974. *Texas Law Review* 63 (1984) 693–719.

incomes policy This euphemism became fashionable in the 1960s when governments sought to restrain wages for the purpose of reducing inflation. While it was presented as a policy for controlling the volume and distribution of all incomes, in practice it was largely confined to curbing the capacity of TRADE UNIONS to increase wages – what an incautious senior French official once called a wages *police*. This concentration upon wages was due to the fact that in advanced industrial societies wages were the largest source of income and were regarded as easier to control than profits; the trade unions were sometimes considered susceptible of being co-opted into the process so that the poachers could become gamekeepers. In return for accepting the invidious role of ceasing to extract the maximum increases in wages in a process of free collective bargaining, the trade unions were

usually offered a number of incentives. To ensure that the real value of wages was maintained, prices might be controlled or wage rates might be indexed to the cost of living. To give incomes policy a 'social justice' connotation, the lower paid might be accorded a higher percentage increase in wage rates and minimum wages. More generally, trade union leaders might be allowed an influence over macro-economic policy, notably in matters such as employment policy, aimed at achieving full employment.

Incomes policies quickly ran into difficulties when they were implemented. Where the government or public enterprises were the employers, it could be considered that they had, in a more or less co-ordinated way, always pursued a wages policy. A hierarchy of more or less accepted intra-public sector differentials had developed, but differentials were a much more controversial matter in the private sector (where market forces were relied upon) as were comparabilities between the public and private sectors generally. The capacity of trade union leaders to enter into binding wage restraint commitments depended upon their ability to control the behaviour of their members. Where trade unions were strong and centralized, as well as enjoying close ties with a Social Democratic Party that played an important or dominant role in the policy process – which was notably the case in Austria and Sweden – the individual and political prerequisites of incomes policy existed. Elsewhere the lack of both prerequisites (the cases of the USA or France) or their only partial presence (Britain and the Federal German Republic) meant that incomes policy either failed to get off the ground at all or only existed for brief periods.

The institutions set up to regulate incomes generally proved to be ephemeral, notably because trade unions were either unwilling or unable to accept formal incorporation into the decision making system. However, even in France, which did not establish such institutions in their 1960s heyday, an Incomes and Costs Study Centre was created to collect accurate information about the incomes of the non-wage and salary earners, it having been argued that it was unfair to control incomes without first obtaining such data. The fact that this body still survives when more ambitious attempts at institutional innovation (such as the Prices and Incomes Board in Britain) have disappeared, contains a lesson in the virtues of modesty. But factors in the economic and social environment were not the only reasons for the difficulties of incomes policies in Britain. Electoral and party factors were of importance also; indeed between 1961 and 1975 every British government resorted to an incomes policy without an electoral mandate. This, and the expected short life of incomes policies are also among the main reasons for their failure. In the 1970s, although there were still attempts at incomes policies, notably in the Labour Party–Trade Union Congress 'Social Contract' in Britain, governments increasingly turned to monetary policy in the fight against inflation while increasing unemployment reduced the capacity of trade unions to raise wages to an extent that the government regarded as excessive. By the 1980s, incomes policy had ceased to be a fashionable instrument of state intervention.   JESH

Reading

Blackaby, F. ed.: *An Incomes Policy for Britain.* London: Heinemann Educational, 1972.

Faxén, K.-O.: Incomes policy and centralized wage formation. In *The European Economy*, ed. A. Boltho. Oxford: Oxford University Press, 1982.

Flanagan, R.J., Soskice, D.W. and Ulman, L.: *Unionism, Economic Stabilization and Incomes Policies: the European Experience.* Washington, DC: Brookings Institution, 1983.

Goldthorpe, J.H. ed.: *Order and Conflict in Contemporary Capitalism.* Oxford: Clarendon Press, 1984.

Hayward, J.: Interest groups and incomes policy in France. *British Journal of Industrial Relations* 4 (1966) 137–53.

OECD: *Collective Bargaining and Government Policies in Ten OECD Countries.* Paris: OECD, 1979.

Panitch, L.: *Social Democracy and Industrial Militancy: the Labour party, the trade unions and incomes policy, 1945–1974.* Cambridge: Cambridge University Press, 1976.

independent agency A major administrative organization that has greater autonomy than that possessed by a ministry or department. (In the United States government the term also applies to any organization that is not in a cabinet department.)

The substantial autonomy accorded by independent status is advocated principally for quasi-judicial, business-type, and regulatory functions. Among organizations freed from full hierarchical administrative control and accountability are ADMINISTRATIVE COURTS, the PUBLIC CORPORATION, the QUANGO, and the INDEPENDENT REGULATORY COMMISSION. An independent agency is often headed by a board or COMMISSION whose members have long and overlapping terms, which reduces the appointing executive's opportunity to control the agency's decision making. Some independent agencies are meant to be financially self-sufficient and so escape normal budgetary and appropriation processes or report only net financial needs. Some are exempted from CIVIL SERVICE laws. Multiplication of independent agencies conflicts with the doctrine of accountability to politically reponsible executives, with government-wide policy consistency, and with budgetary comprehensiveness.   JWF

Reading

Dogan, M. ed.: *The Mandarins of Western Europe: the political role of top civil servants*, pp. 210–37. London: Halstead, 1975.

Kettl, D.F.: *Leadership at the Fed.* New Haven, Conn. and London: Yale University Press, 1986.

Sharkansky, I.: *Whither the State? Politics and Public Enterprise in Three Countries.* Chatham, NJ: Chatham House, 1979.

United States Government Organization Manual. Washington, DC: US Government Printing Office, annual.

Wade, E.C.S. and Bradley, A.W.: *Constitutional and Administrative Law.* London: Longman, 1985.

Walsh, A.H.: *The Public's Business: the Politics and Practices of Government Corporations.* Cambridge, Mass. and London: MIT Press, 1978.

independent regulatory commission A multi-member body that has broad regulatory power over one or many industries, and whose autonomy is formally greater than that of ministries or departments.

Independent regulatory commissions, whether in Britain, commonwealth countries, or the United States, differ in legal status, organization, funding, and actual enjoyment of autonomy. Normally they are intended to insulate public regulation of an industry from politics, certainly in day-to-day, quasi-judicial decision making, less clearly in broad policy making. In Britain, for example, ministers guide such bodies as the Monopolies and Merger Commission through powers of direction and approval of certain key decisions, and parliamentary oversight serves as a constraint. Ministers and members of parliament also intervene in practice in day-to-day decisions.

In the United States the formal independence of commissions rests on statutes typically requiring bipartisan membership, overlapping terms of five to fourteen years, and removability by the president only for cause, not for policy views. Their independence, though anomalous in a SEPARATION OF POWERS system, was upheld in 1935 by the US supreme court. In 1937 the President's committee on administrative management called the commissions 'a headless fourth branch of the government, a haphazard deposit of irresponsible agencies and unco-ordinated powers'.

A president nevertheless gains effective influence through the expiration of terms, the ambitions of sitting commissioners for re-appointment, mid-term resignations, and the availability of compatible candidates in the opposition party. The president designates commission chairmen, who play strong leadership roles. Commissions' proposed legislation, budgets, and litigation are reviewable in the executive branch.

The commissions were long attacked as captives of the regulated industries. Recent scholarship discounts this view. Commissions' support of deregulation in the 1970s and 1980s confirms the new interpretation, at least for this period.

See also QUANGO. JWF

Reading

Derthick, M. and Quirk, P.J.: *The Politics of Deregulation*. Washington, DC: Brookings Institution, 1985.

Kettl, D.F.: *Leadership at the Fed*. New Haven, Conn. and London: Yale University Press, 1986.

Steel, D.R.: Britain. In *Government and Administration in Western Europe*, ed. F.F. Ridley. New York: St Martin's, 1979.

US Senate Committee on Governmental Affairs: *Study on Federal Regulation*, vol. 5. *Regulatory Organization*. Washington, DC: US Government Printing Office, 1977.

Welborn, M.: *Governance of Federal Regulatory Agencies*. Knoxville: University of Tennessee Press, 1977.

Wilson, J.Q. ed.: *The Politics of Regulation*. New York: Basic Books, 1980.

indirect election Where an office holder or representative assembly is elected by a larger body of persons that has in turn been elected by a still larger electorate, that office holder or assembly is said to have been indirectly elected by the still larger electorate. Indirect election may be chosen as a principle and the intermediate body set up for that purpose (see ELECTORAL COLLEGE). It may also result from deciding that some representative bodies which already exist for other purposes (for example, regional councils or local branch committees) may themselves need representing at a higher level; in several liberal democracies SECOND CHAMBERS (for example, the German *Bundesrat*) represent regional or local authorities and are therefore, but only incidentally, indirectly elected. Indirect election was formerly more common than it is today: there is a tendency to move away from it in the name of democracy, which is presumed to mean direct election. Indirectly elected chambers have been either abolished (Sweden, 1969) or made directly elected (the United States Senate, 1913); recent Conservative government legislation in the United Kingdom requiring trade unions to change from indirect to direct election of their executive committees follows the same general development. MS

indirect rule A form of colonial administration particularly characteristic of British Colonial Africa in the inter-war years. All systems of colonial rule depended upon the assistance and co-operation of the subject populations, especially in the absence of substantial settler communities. Indirect rule elevated this pragmatic habit into a system and an ideology. Its roots as a policy lay in Northern Nigeria where the combination of extremely meagre British administrative manpower and the robust traditional authority of the emirs encouraged Lord Lugard to establish the essential principles of the system: viz. that interference with the traditional ruling elite should be kept to the minimum, and that local organs of traditional authority should be fully incorporated into the colonial administrative apparatus and strengthened appropriately. Two influences promoted the dissemination of indirect rule as a system after 1918: its cheapness in an age of depression, and the way that it chimed in with the new anthropological emphasis on the value of traditional cultures and the danger of disrupting them. Even before 1939 indirect rule was criticized for its indiscriminate application in societies where no strong traditional authorities existed, as well as for its implicit abdication of any modernizing role by the colonial power. Indeed it was the post-war emphasis on the mobilization of colonial resources and the co-operation of modern-minded social groups that led to its progressive abandonment after 1945.   JGD

Reading

Iliffe, J.: *A Modern History of Tanganyika*. Cambridge: Cambridge University Press, 1979.

Perham, M.: *Lugard: the years of authority 1898–1945*. London: Collins, 1960.

industrial democracy In industrial relations, as in political discourse, the notion of democracy is a battleground of conflicting definitions. There are few avowed anti-democrats to be found, but the arrangements under the elastic title of industrial democracy are diverse. This is evident from the array of concepts often presented as synonyms or constituents of the generic notion: joint regulation, employee participation, workers' control, self-management, autonomous group functioning, joint consultation, co-operative production, economic democracy, self-government in industry.

Many of the contemporary meanings of industrial democracy straddle the uncomfortable interface between socialist humanism and enlightened managerialism. Early theories and programmes were explicitly anti-capitalist, often stemming from an insistence that political democracy was contradicted and subverted by minority ownership and control of industry. While some schools of SOCIALISM envisaged little change in the nature of management within state-owned industry, others insisted that workers' citizenship rights should extend to the organization of production itself. During the second decade of the present century, SYNDICALIST challenges to statist socialism, and the rise of workers' councils and shop stewards' movements, gave rise to varied schemes of workers' control as both a means of attacking capitalism from within and a system of economic organization under socialism. Such programmes, at times diluted and transmuted, have exerted enduring influence in a number of LABOUR MOVEMENTS. Perhaps the most notable modern example of these ideas in practical application is the system of 'workers' self-management' introduced in Yugoslavia after the break with Stalin in 1948.

Yet paradoxically and by contrast, industrial democracy has also been presented as a strategy for stabilizing rather than displacing CAPITALISM. The past half-century has seen widespread management concern with 'human relations'. While some employers and management theorists insist that managers must manage, others emphasize that success depends on the initiative, resourcefulness and co-operation of subordinate employees. This, it is argued, requires the mobilization of their goodwill, and is undermined by authoritarian styles of management. In this view, industrial democracy represents the means of harnessing workers' consent to management's priorities and policies.

While both approaches identify industrial democracy with employee involvement in decision making at work, there are two key principles of differentiation: the level of decision making, and the degree of worker influence. The latter may range from various forms of subordinate or minority representation, through structures of 'dual power' or co-determination, to majority or exclusive worker direction. The former may involve merely peripheral questions such as the colour of canteen walls; operational decisions within the workplace; issues of general policy and long-term strategy for the employing organiz- ation as a whole; or even plans for the entire industry or economy. Such higher-level strategic policy necessarily constrains, often severely, the range of options available at lower levels.

In general, managerial conceptions of industrial democracy have concerned detailed, low-level issues; the higher the level of decision making, the less worker influence have employers been willing to contemplate. Socialist conceptions, by contrast, have usually emphazised the importance of strategic decision making while dismissing forms of minority representation as 'pseudo-democ- racy'. Yet there exists no clear dichotomy of approaches to the question: partly because of the many gradations which exist in both level of decision making and degree of influence; partly because both trade unions and govern- ments, as major participants in contemporary debate, articulate interests and perspectives which transcend any simple capitalist/socialist division. Union policies may reflect an amalgam of socialist ideas and managerial notions of efficiency; the same may be true of govern- ments of the left, while those of the right (particularly in Catholic societies) may em- brace philosophies of participation in industry. In all cases, the rhetoric and reality of policy can differ confusingly.

It is possible to identify a hierarchy of contemporary issues in the politics of industrial democracy. The first involves economic owner- ship: the creation of structures in some sense intermediate between conventional capitalism on the one hand, NATIONALIZATION on the other. One such system is employee share- ownership (sometimes under such labels as profit-sharing or co-partnership): popular with some liberals as a form of wealth- spreading, among some conservatives as a means of stabilizing private ownership through encouraging the growth of 'worker-capitalists'. Gaullist governments in France have required larger companies to implement worker share-

holding; recent British governments have offered tax advantages for voluntary schemes; employee stock ownership plans are wide- spread in the USA. A more radical variant of such schemes is the system of wage-earner funds enacted in Sweden in 1983: companies are required to make an annual allocation of shares, not to individual employees but to investment funds with majority worker (and, it is assumed, normally union) representation. The bitter opposition of Swedish employers to this legislation reflected a belief – shared by its supporters – that the outcome would be significant collective worker influence over strategic decision making. A third form of ownership is the workers' co-operative, in which capital is held exclusively or predomi- nantly by the employees. Familiar for more than a century, this structure has attracted considerable recent attention with the success of the interlinked system of co-operatives at Mondragon in the Basque country. A number of governments offer fiscal encouragement to such arrangements – seen by some on the left as a form of workers' management prefigurative of a post-capitalist economic order (hence the enthusiasm in Britain in the 1970s for the 'Benn co-operatives' supported by the then Industry Minister); by some on the right as a means of accommodating workers to the disciplines of market efficiency.

A second contemporary issue is board-level representation. In several European countries with two-tier systems of company boards there is a tradition of employee representation on supervisory boards. In the West German coal and steel industries equal worker and share- holder representation has existed since 1952; and after intense political controversy a modi- fied form of parity was extended to all major firms in 1976. For over a decade proposals for obligatory worker directors (the draft Fifth Directive) have been under discussion within the EEC. In Britain, a Committee of Inquiry (the Bullock Committee) was appointed in 1975 to propose machinery for 'a radical extension of industrial democracy in the control of companies by means of represen- tation on boards of directors'. Its proposals for parity representation, qualified by the appoint- ment of additional 'neutral' directors (the

287

2x + y formula), were vehemently opposed by employers' organizations (partly because they envisaged trade union appointees rather than, as in Germany, elected worker shareholders), received only lukewarm trade union support, and were abandoned by the then Labour government.

One argument of British employers was that board-level representation would be unsatisfactory in the absence of 'substructures' at establishment level. Works councils are a widespread institution in continental Europe. In a number of countries their existence and functions are legally prescribed; statutory powers are commonly weak (as in France), though in Germany and the Netherlands they extend to rights of co-determination – in effect, the power of veto – over aspects of employment policy. Elsewhere, such councils exist only on a voluntary basis – though in Sweden their operation has been specified since 1946 in a national union–employer agreement. In Britain the formation of joint production committees received enthusiastic government support during the 1939–45 war, and in the past decade there has been a marked revival of joint consultative committees. Since 1974 there have also been statutory provisions for safety representatives and committees at the workplace.

The fourth focus of recent discussion is the individual job or work group. As suggested above, the 'humanization' of work has long been advocated by some management theorists, both through enlarging individual employee discretion and through encouraging forms of teamwork and group decision making over immediate production issues. A notable example of this strategy is the Volvo company, which – troubled by problems of worker dissatisfaction and labour turnover – organized its Kalmar factory in 1974 on the basis of team production rather than conventional assembly lines. In Japan there is a widespread practice of 'quality circles', in which work teams regularly discuss production issues and take responsibility for quality control: a system which has attracted many recent imitators in Europe and America. Some trade unionists are suspicious of such managerial initiatives; but others, notably in Scandinavia, have long

been critical of fragmented, isolated and monotonous work tasks, and regard it as an important service to their members to win improvements in the quality of working life (QWL).

All four areas of 'democratization' involve new institutional arrangements. Many trade unionists, particularly in the USA and Britain, deny the need for such innovations. *Industrial Democracy* was the title of the Webbs' classic analysis of trade unionism; their view that workers can best influence industrial policy through independent union organization has been reiterated in recent times by Clegg. On both the left and the right of the trade union movement it is commonly argued that the most viable means to industrial democracy is to strengthen and extend collective bargaining – possibly through statutory support for union recognition, obligatory disclosure of information relevant to bargaining, and a requirement to negotiation before changes are implemented in working arrangements. The existence of consultative committees separate from collective bargaining machinery has always evoked suspicion.

Other trade unionists accept the utility of new institutions but demand a role in their operation. The Swedish policy on wage-earner funds has already been noted; Swedish legislation on worker directors requires that their appointment shall be through union channels, and only by the request of relevant unions. The Bullock recommendations were couched in similar terms, on union insistence. While German unions accept that works councils should formally possess almost complete autonomy, in practice they ensure a close working relationship. In many southern European countries, unions have obtained legislative provision for trade union sections in the workplace, and attempt to strengthen their position at the expense of works councils. Far more generally, QWL issues are commonly regarded as an additional item on the bargaining agenda, rather than a topic for special institutional arrangements; though in France there has been some union support for recent legislation establishing 'expression groups' through which employees are entitled to voice opinions on questions of work organization.

See also TRADE UNIONS   RH

Reading

Blumberg, P.: *Industrial Democracy: the sociology of participation*. London: Constable, 1968.

Clegg, H.A.: *A New Approach to Industrial Democracy*. Oxford: Blackwell, 1963.

Coates, K. and Topham, T. eds: *Workers' Control*. London: Panther, 1970.

Cole, G.D.H.: *Self-Government in Industry* London: Bell, 1917.

Committee of Inquiry on Industrial Democracy (Chairman Lord Bullock): *Report*. London: HMSO, Cmnd 6706, 1977.

Cressey, P., Eldridge, J. and MacInnes, J.: *Just Managing: authority and democracy in industry*. Milton Keynes: Open University Press, 1985.

Goodrich, C.L.: *The Frontier of Control*. London: Bell, 1920.

Schuller, T.: *Democracy at Work*. Oxford: Oxford University Press, 1985.

Vanek, J. ed.: *Self-management*. Harmondsworth: Penguin, 1975.

Webb, S. and Webb, B.: *Industrial Democracy*. London: Longman, 1897.

industrial society A form of society distinguished by a division of labour based on mechanized production and factory organization. This definition refers primarily to its economy and technology but its characteristics include certain political and social correlates, particularly urbanization, an elaborate law of contract, separation of household from enterprise, a demographic transition from high to low fertility and mortality, formal systems of education and research and a kinship system of isolated nuclear families. The category of industrial societies is accordingly heterogeneous economically, politically and culturally.

The term has not, on the whole, been used statically. Saint-Simon popularized it in the early nineteenth century, conceiving it in terms of the rise of new men of power – the entrepreneurs – to replace the previous domination by priests and warriors. Herbert Spencer also thought in terms of a transition from 'military' to 'industrial' society. But the main definitional focus of evolutionary or historical conceptions of industrial society remained economic. There had been an industrial 'revolution' out of agrarian society. Advances in agricultural productivity released labour and capital for industrial development. The most famous interpretation along these lines was MARX'S theory of the genesis of capitalist society, emphasizing the economic base, the political and social superstructure, and surplus value accruing to capital as a result of exploited labour. The most famous contrary thesis is Max WEBER'S, linking the origins of capitalist industrial society to the economic ethic of some protestant forms of Christianity. Later economic theorists (for example Colin Clark) distinguished between economies with their centre of gravity in the primary, the secondary or the tertiary sector of industry. The idea of the service society (see Gershuny) emerged from this line of work.

A larger and sharper debate about industrial society arises from the conflict and competition between its two opposed political forms – CAPITALISM and communism. The first is a type of industrial society evolving 'spontaneously' in Britain, western Europe and America, with private capital and relatively small governmental involvement – political economies in which polity and economy are relatively separate. The second is one in which the state plays a direct role in capital accumulation. Such states come into being through political revolution; the economy is administered politically.

During the twentieth century the further development of capitalist industrialism has not only produced intermediary forms of socialist or social democratic countries such as Sweden or Austria but also some greater or lesser development of the WELFARE STATE in the first (capitalist) and the second (communist) worlds while the third world is seen as evolving towards industrial society.

Interest in capitalist and communist forms of industrialism provoked prolonged debate in the 1960s and 1970s over the 'end of ideology' and the theory that industrial societies, whether capitalist or communist, would converge in their political, administrative and cultural character. Weber identified a fundamental element of convergence in the 'iron cage' of industrial development, namely BUREAUC-RACY. But the more general question of the degree of independence of political and economic structures remains in contention and more recently discussion has moved from the origin to the destiny of industrial society, variously termed post-industrial, super-industrial or post-modern. In this newer context industrial society has become an ever-changing historical phase in the development of economy and technology that has permitted and permits a wide range of political and cultural variation.   AHH

Reading

Aron, R.: *Eighteen Lectures on Industrial Society.* London: Weidenfeld & Nicolson, 1967.

Bell, D.: *The Coming of Post-Industrial Society.* New York: Basic Books, 1973.

Clark, C.: *The Conditions of Economic Progress.* London: Macmillan; New York: St Martin's, 1957.

Gershuny, J.L.: *After Industrial Society.* London: Macmillan, 1978.

————: *Social Innovation and the Division of Labour.* Oxford: Oxford University Press, 1983.

Pahl, R.E.: *Divisions of Labour.* Oxford: Blackwell, 1984.

informateur   The office of negotiator in the GOVERNMENT FORMATION PROCESS in some continental multi-party systems. The term was first used in Belgium in 1935, when M. Theunis was asked by King Leopold III to make a rapid inquiry concerning a programme for government, and in the Netherlands in 1951, although use of the informateur did not become formalized until 1956.

In Belgium and the Netherlands, the sovereign generally appoints an informateur when a new government has to be formed so as to protect the monarchy from direct political involvement. The informateur is usually someone without personal political ambitions and so acceptable as a negotiator; an elder statesman is a frequent choice, but occasionally an active politician is appointed.

In Belgium, but not the Netherlands, the informateur has always been a member of one of the two chambers of the legislature. In the Netherlands, the informateur can be, for example, a provincial governor; and it has been the custom in recent years for more than one informateur to be chosen. The informateur plays a highly active role in the government formation process, initiating the search for

290

agreement on the composition of a coalition government, the distribution of posts and the programme of the government; the informateur then reports back to the sovereign.

The informateur has also been used on occasion in Denmark and Norway, but there the role is more passive, confined simply to registering the view of the parties.   VBB

Reading

Andeweg, R.B., Van der Tak, Th. and Dittrich, K.: Government formation in the Netherlands. In *The Economy and Politics of the Netherlands since 1945*, ed. R.T. Griffiths. The Hague: Nijhoff, 1980.

Bogdanor, V.: The government formation process in the constitutional monarchies of North West Europe. In *Comparative Government and Politics*, ed. D. Kavanagh and G. Peele. London: Heinemann, 1984.

initiative   A device by which a specified number of electors may invoke a popular vote on a proposal of their choice. (See REFERENDUM AND INITIATIVE.)

institution   Central to social science use of the term is the sense of the Latin verb *instituere* (to set up or establish) from which it is derived. This is in line with the notion of an 'institution' as an established form of activity which long antedates the development of modern political science and sociology. The debates initiated by Burke and Rousseau raised *inter alia* first the issue of institutional continuity versus the 'spontaneous' creation (or re-creation) of institutions, and second the question of the effectiveness both political and other, and the constraints they impose.

Most sociological definitions – since Herbert Spencer's day – have in common the general idea of institution as the locus of a regularized or crystallized principle of conduct, action or behaviour that governs a crucial area of social life and that endures over time. There is general agreement too that the term does not denote the behaviour itself nor the organizations of which individuals or groups are members; an influential definition has been made by R. M. MacIver and C. H. Page which differentiates between institution and association – though social scientists have been known to blur this distinction. The focus has been on established procedures. Blondel has written: 'there is no real difference between institutions and procedures, as institutions are sets of procedures. A political party is an institution: it is also a set of procedures by which leaders are chosen, decisions are taken, election campaigns are organized . . .' It will be noted that on another level a party is an association in the MacIver and Page sense of something to which people belong, as compared with a set of procedures which regulate what they do.

Some important analytical questions have been raised concerning the relation between institution and norm and some writers in social science have tried to provide a checklist of institutions corresponding to functional problems. Issues then arise as to how far various institutions (including political) form a 'system'; what kind of system this is; what may be the relations between institutions that compose the system. To other writers this whole concern with the concept of system appears to be only a new set of questions. Certain of these cruces may be illuminated by the observation of S. E. Finer, rejecting the preoccupation with system, that 'government is institutionalized politics'. 'Politics', he writes, 'is an activity: it is a kind of behaviour and it is not a set of roles and institutions (or structures and associations) which regulate this activity. "Government" on the other hand, may be an activity but, in another sense, may also be an association (or structure) of some kind.' Though this appears to leave open the difference between structures and associations the vital point is the warning which is implied against confusing an *activity* with the *procedures* for regulating that activity: those regulatory concerns clearly require structures for their maintenance and application, but whether or not such structures form a system cannot be presupposed. Nor does the empirical and theoretical concern either with 'groups' or 'processes' entail the abandonment of the idea of institutions in politics.

Another aspect crucial to the debate has been the contrast between two kinds of analysis: that which, it is claimed, sticks to the level of formal institutions, and that which

gives priority to behaviour, activity and interaction. No doubt the primacy of institutions has at times been exaggerated – to the neglect of micropolitical behaviour, and of problems of power and decision making at the micro level – but it is hard to justify a fundamentalist 'either/or' position on such matters. Some early or classical approaches to politics may have overstated the formal nature of such regular procedures and given insufficient weight to the less formal processes which themselves become institutionalized through repetition or duration over time. It does not however follow that we can, or should, dispense with a concept that pinpoints regular processes or mechanisms for channelling certain activities, meeting certain recurrent challenges and contingencies and settling disagreement on and about the allocation of values – or indeed determining what the values are which will be allocated in a given territory in a specific era. Another area of discussion in political studies distinguishes between two kinds of inference that have come from sociology. One has been to suggest that political institutions are epiphenomena; that is they derive from social processes and especially those that crystallize in a society's pattern of stratification. This inference feeds broadly into a concern with group interests as the organizing principle of political involvement or participation. An alternative approach, equally grounded in sociology and now absorbed into the study of politics, comes from assumptions about the (relative and variable) 'primacy of politics'. Formal institutions, such as the party system and the practices of bureaucratic organizations (all of which are shaped by culture and history) play a causal rather than a dependent part in political life and are active determinants of political conflict and the social changes that either precede or follow from such conflicts. Having recognized that social forms and regularities are relevant to the behaviour of power holders and decision makers (or to their interactions with others), we need not concede further that 'power' and 'decision making' are reducible to data on social organization or to what may follow from inferences from that data. On the contrary the institutions that are more narrowly political have their own role in channelling what results from the complex and varied working through of influences that stem from social organization.

SJG

Reading

Blondel, J.: *Thinking Politically*. London: Wildwood, 1976.

Easton, D.: *The Political System: an inquiry into the state of political science*. 3rd edn. Chicago, Ill.: University of Chicago Press, 1981.

Emmet, D.: *Function, Purpose and Powers: some concepts in the study of individuals and society*. London: Macmillan, 1958.

Finer, S.E.: *Comparative Government*. London: Penguin, 1970.

————: Almond's concept of 'The Political System'. *Government and Opposition* 5 (1969–70) 3–21.

Parsons, T.: *The Social System*. London: Tavistock, 1952; New York: Free Press, 1961.

intelligence A term traditionally used to describe either news and information from any source (The London *Times* between the wars still headed its foreign news section 'Foreign Intelligence') or, more specifically, information from secret sources. The same ambiguity survives in a number of major languages (for example *renseignements* in French, *Nachrichten* in German). In contemporary English usage, however, intelligence refers principally to information collected by covert means. It is also used to describe the agencies which collect that information and the other activities in which they engage. In 1979 the American Consortium for the Study of Intelligence agreed on a fourfold classification of the 'major elements of intelligence' which has since been widely accepted:

Clandestine collection: Human intelligence (HUMINT) nowadays provides much less information than technical intelligence whose two most important varieties are signals intelligence (SIGINT) and imagery intelligence (IMINT). SIGINT includes both communications intelligence (COMINT), derived from the interception of radio transmissions in cipher or cleartext, and electronic intelligence (ELINT), derived from machine-generated signals such as those from rockets. IMINT

includes the interpretation of photographic, infra-red and radar imaging data. Other forms of technical intelligence, such as acoustics intelligence, are developing rapidly. The advocates of HUMINT argue that on such important questions as political intention it cannot be replaced by the more plentiful supply of technical intelligence.

Analysis and estimates: A distinction is commonly drawn between the 'raw intelligence' supplied by the various systems of collection and the 'finished intelligence' derived from it by the intelligence analyst. Most analysts are nowadays confronted by an information explosion and the problems of distinguishing the crucial intelligence signals from irrelevant or misleading background 'noise'. Analysts are sometimes divided between current intelligence specialists and the producers of long-term 'estimates' or forecasts of future trends.

Counter-intelligence: Attempts to identify, to neutralize, and sometimes to manipulate the activities of foreign intelligence services and 'subversive' groups. Passive counter-intelligence seeks to safeguard sensitive official information and to protect the government bureaucracy from penetration by hostile or subversive agencies. Active counter-intelligence aims to manipulate these agencies by techniques such as penetration and deception (as in the Double Cross System of the second world war). Counter-intelligence is usually more controversial than foreign intelligence because of the greater potential threat to domestic CIVIL LIBERTIES and differing views as to what constitutes subversion.

Covert action: Clandestine attempts to influence the affairs of other states by methods ranging from peaceful propaganda to paramilitary operations. Though covert action is employed to some extent by most intelligence services, it is believed to be most developed in the range of 'active measures' (*activinye meropriyatiya*) used by the KGB and Soviet Bloc intelligence services: among them disinformation, forged documents, front organizations and agents of influence. Peacetime covert action is commonly criticized in the West as both immoral and, at least in the long term, ineffective. Short term 'successes', such as the CIA/MI6 removal of the Mossadeq regime in Iran in 1953, may become counterproductive when the covert action behind them is eventually disclosed. Covert action is probably more effectively, as well as more extensively, employed by the KGB than by the CIA because secrecy is easier to enforce and maintain in the East than in the West.

See also SECRET SERVICE.   CMA

Reading

Andrew, C.: *Secret Service: the making of the British intelligence community*. London: Heinemann, 1985.

————— and Dilks, D. eds: *The Missing Dimension: governments and intelligence communities in the twentieth century*. London: Macmillan, 1984.

Godson, R. ed.: *Intelligence Requirements for the 1980s*. 7 vols. Lexington, Mass.: Lexington Books, 1975–85.

Hinsley, F.H. et al.: *British Intelligence in the Second World War*. 3 vols. London: HMSO, 1979–86.

Laqueur, W.: *World of Secrets: the uses and limits of intelligence*. London: Weidenfeld & Nicolson, 1985.

Leggett, G.: *The Cheka: Lenin's political police*. Oxford: Clarendon Press, 1982.

Ranelagh, J.: *The Agency: the rise and decline of the CIA*. London: Weidenfeld & Nicolson, 1986.

Richelson, J.T. and Ball, D.: *The Ties that Bind: intelligence co-operation between the UK, the USA, Canada, Australia and New Zealand*. London: Allen & Unwin, 1985.

US Congress, House Committee on Intelligence: *Soviet Active Measures*. Hearings, 97th Cong., 2nd sess. Washington, DC: Government Printing Office, 1982.

See also the journal *Intelligence and National Security* (1986–).

interest articulation and aggregation

The general acceptance of POLITICAL PARTIES and INTEREST GROUPS as legitimate institutions of democratic politics is a matter only of the last half century. The American and British party systems are exceptional from this point of view, having acquired their legitimacy in the nineteenth century. On the European continent, politics was dominated by conservative parties which tended to be 'restorationist' and anti-democratic, and by rising social democratic parties which accepted parliamen-

tary participation as a means towards the overthrow of capitalism and the establishment of a socialist society. The liberal view of parliamentarism was a relatively minor trend in nineteenth-century continental European politics, and it was flanked on the left and right by movements which only accorded instrumental legitimacy to parliamentary competition. It was not until the 1950s that the German Social Democrats dropped their Marxist class struggle doctrine and fully accepted parliamentarism. The adaptation of the left to parliamentarism in countries such as France, Italy, Spain, Portugal, and Greece is still taking place, and there remains some ambivalence and uneasiness about parliamentarism on the right in these countries.

Interest groups, pressure groups, the 'lobby', have become legitimate parts of democratic politics even more recently than parties. It was not until the late 1930s in the United States and Britain with the emergence of large labour movements that interest groups were acknowledged to be components of a democratic PLURALISM. On the European continent left-wing scholarship viewed trade unions as aspects of the working class, and trade associations as instruments of the bourgeoisie; while conservative scholarship tended to view all interest groups as well as parties as illegitimate threats to the sovereignty of the state, and the authority of the bureaucracy which represented the public interest.

The introduction of such concepts as interest articulation and interest aggregation may be understood in the context of this process of the emergence of the democratic infrastructure. Early efforts at legitimizing the activities of parties and interest groups took the form of somehow trying to squeeze these institutions into the constitutional framework of SEPARATION OF POWERS. The 'lobby' was viewed as a third legislative chamber, as performing part of the legislative function, and parties were treated as components of the electoral and legislative processes.

The rise of these specialized organizations drew attention to the complexity of the democratic policy making process. It was not simply a matter of making general rules, of legislating, of making policies. There were phases and sub-processes, and rigorous description and comparison required some conceptual innovation. A family of concepts came into use. Harold Lasswell proposed a scheme involving some seven steps from initiation to termination; May and Wildavsky more recently suggested a five phase division, beginning with AGENDA SETTING, and proceeding with issue analysis, decision taking, implementation, evaluation, and termination. The division of the policy-making process into interest articulation, interest aggregation, and policy making, simply was an effort at codifying the conclusions of research on political parties and pressure groups of the inter-war and the early post second world war periods.

The model of American politics which came out of this research was that of organized interest groups formulating and expressing the political demands of economic and other groups and transmitting these demands to political parties, legislatures, and administrative agencies. Political party leaders on the other hand were viewed as brokers attempting to convert these particularistic demands into policy alternatives, which would attract votes in electoral campaigns and structure debates in the legislative process. Though deriving from the American context it seemed reasonable to use these two broadly defined process categories, for general comparative purposes. Thus one could compare Italian interest groups and political parties with their American counterparts according to the way in which these organizations articulated and aggregated interests. Interest groups dominated by the church and the communist party, and a polarized and fragmented party system would articulate and aggregate interests in ways very different from those of a relatively autonomous interest group system, and a consensual two-party system. The introduction of these concepts led to useful ways of classifying interest groups and party systems, according to the way they structured the political process.

The theory coming out of this essentially American political party and interest group research, argued that a responsive and effective democratic process was associated on the one hand with a situation in which all the interests in a society are organized through associations, independent of political parties; and on the other hand with consensual party systems of the two- or multi-party variety. Such structural patterns would assure a relatively free flow of demands into the political process, which would be assimilable in an orderly and coherent policy making process. Essentially, this is a rational-bargaining-coalitional model of democratic politics.

Neo-CORPORATISM, a theory developed recently by Phillipe Schmitter, Gerhard Lehmbruch, Peter Katzenstein, and others, disputes this approach to democratic stability, citing a number of countries in Europe where organized interest groups, fostered and often established by the state, are involved in regular consultation with parliamentarians and bureaucrats in bargaining about wages, prices, welfare benefits, and investment policy. They argue that the corporatist mode of 'interest intermediation' may be more clearly associated with democratic stability than the competitive model. It tends to depoliticize economic issues that otherwise might produce sharply conflictual propensities.   GAA

Reading

Almond, G.A. and Coleman, J.: *The Politics of the Developing Areas*. Princeton, NJ: Princeton University Press, 1960.

Almond, G.A. and Powell, G.B.: *Comparative Politics: systems, process, policy*. Boston, Mass.: Little, Brown, 1978.

Ehrmann, H. ed.: *Interest Groups on Four Continents*. Pittsburgh, Penn.: University of Pittsburgh Press, 1958.

Finer, S.E.: *Anonymous Empire*. London: Pall Mall, 1958; 2nd edn 1966.

Herring, E.P.: *The Politics of Democracy*. New York: Norton, 1940.

Katzenstein, P.: *Small States and World Markets*. Ithaca, NY: Cornell University Press, 1985.

LaPalombara, J. and Weiner, M.: *Political Parties and Political Development*. Princeton, NJ: Princeton University Press, 1966.

Lipset, S.M. and Rokkan, S.: *Party Systems and Voter Alignments*. New York: Free Press, 1967.

Neumann, S.: *Modern Political Parties*. Chicago, Ill.: University of Chicago Press, 1956.

Ostrogorski, M.: *Democracy and the Organization of Political Parties*. London: Macmillan, 1902.

Schmitter, P. and Lehmbruch, G.: *Trends Towards Corporatist Intermediation*. Beverly Hills, Calif.: Sage, 1979.

Truman, D.B.: *The Governmental Process*. New York: Knopf, 1951.

interest groups The study of interest groups became a major preoccupation of students of politics in the 1950s and 1960s. This was in part a response to the burgeoning numbers and activities of these groups, and in part a reflection of a shift away from the study of the formal constitutional and institutional aspects of politics towards an emphasis on political process and the exercise of political power.

Interest groups are organizations which attempt to influence the direction of government policy without themselves seeking to form the government. At one time attacked as subversive of democratic processes, interest groups became widely regarded as the essence of the system of democratic PLURALISM where, it was argued, they stand as a buffer between the individual citizen and the overarching state. Political theorists such as BENTLEY and Truman argued that groups were the fundamental building blocks of the political process, and that political institutions could be seen as being driven by group pressures. Interest groups were not regarded as a threat to democratic processes because individuals were considered to be free to form groups, and as a group formed on one side of a political issue, another could arise which would redress the balance.

More recently, however, the inegalitarian elements of the universe of interest groups have received more attention, with the recognition that there are 'insider' groups, regularly consulted by governments and active in policy formation and implementation, and 'outsider' groups which are often regarded as illegitimate by governments, and which struggle to gain a foothold on the political agenda. Instead of being a mechanism whereby a wide range of differing views could be absorbed into the democratic process, the increased attention being paid to the 'filtering' mechanisms whereby certain groups achieved a 'public status' and others were excluded, showed that privileged interest groups were exercising quasi-public powers relatively immune from democratic scrutiny.

Writers on CORPORATISM have linked the incorporation of favoured groups to the extension of state intervention in the economy and welfare fields, where governments have sought directly to negotiate policies with interest groups representing economic producers and the professional providers of services. They have pointed to the extent to which relatively stable and interdependent relationships between governments and favoured groups have come to exercise a significant role in a number of policy fields.

There have been various attempts to classify interest groups, with the most common distinction drawn between groups which defend a particular sectional interest, such as that of farmers or employers, and those which seek to promote a cause, such as nuclear disarmament. The latter groups correspond most readily to the pluralist model, which is characterized by a large but fluid number of groups competing with each other for members and influence. Case studies of the successful exercise of influence over policy-making have stressed the importance of financial and organizational resources, and the capacity of such groups to mobilize popular support through the mass media. The relationship between favourable policy outcomes and the successful mobilization by interest groups of political resources in a competitive context seems to hold most strongly for moral and distributional issues rather than those which involve state intervention in production.

Many sectional groups, whose interests are peripheral to the policy concerns of governments, may also fall into this competitive sphere of the group world, but more important ones, which derive their identity from the function that their members perform in the social division of labour, do not. These latter groups derive their power and importance from the system of production and its corresponding interests, which is not readily amenable to challenge by conventional lobbying techniques. The most important of these groups, the trade unions, employer and trade associations, are based on interests which derive from the major class division in society between capital and labour. A long history of institutionalized consultation between government and these groups in Britain, especially intense during the two world wars, led to their becoming part of the governing institutions of the state, which moderated class conflict at least until the impact of economic recession in the 1970s polarized economic attitudes and led to the relative exclusion of the trade unions from discussions on the management of the economy.

The analysis of interest group activity has shifted considerably in the last twenty years from the characteristics of the groups themselves to the study of their environments, which shape the constraints facing them and the opportunities open to them. In this way the study of interest groups has become more integrated with the central concerns of politics, and is less of a distinctive sub-field of political science. AC

Reading

Beer, S.H.: *Modern British Politics*. 3rd edn. London: Faber & Faber, 1982.

Bentley, A.F.: *The Process of Government*. Harvard: Belknap, 1967.

Finer, S.E.: *Anonymous Empire*. 2nd edn. London: Pall Mall, 1966.

Middlemas, R.K.: *Politics in Industrial Society*. London: Deutsch, 1979.

Offe, C.: The attribution of public status to interest groups. In *Organizing Interests in Western Europe*, ed. S. Berger. Cambridge: Cambridge University Press, 1981.

Richardson, J.J. and Jordan, A.G.: *Governing Under Pressure*. Oxford: Martin Robertson, 1979.

Truman, D.: *The Governmental Process*. New York: Knopf, 1971.

intergovernmental relations The term originated in the United States of America in the 1930s. It was a conceptual innovation intended to describe new features and novel patterns of the interactions among public officials functioning within the US federal system which was then experiencing the stress and strain of the world-wide economic depression. Despite having originated in a political system that was formally and operationally

a federal structure, the term IGR has subsequently been applied to sets of relationships among officials in non-federal nations, such as Japan and the United Kingdom.

The apparent originator of the term, William Anderson, later defined IGR as:

An important body of activities or interactions occurring between [or among] governmental units of all types and levels within the US federal system. ... Underlying the concept ... is the fact that the nation as a whole, each one of the [fifty] states, and every county, town, city, school district, and other special district or local unit is a territorial and corporate or quasi-corporate entity that has a legal existence, rights, functions, powers, and duties within its territory [that are] distinct from those of every other such unit. (Anderson 1960, p. 3)

In the USA this definition includes all the combinations and permutations of exchanges (of information, ideas, resources) among more than 80,000 units of government in the political system, i.e. one national government, fifty state governments, counties (3,043), cities (19,083), townships (16,148), school districts (15,032), and special districts (28,733). As applied to Japan (Institute of Administrative Management (1982)) intergovernmental relations encompass the combinations and permutations of relationships among the central (national) government, the forty-seven prefectural governments, and the 3255 municipalities (*shi, cho, son*). For the United Kingdom intergovernmental relations are essentially the equivalent of what has recently been studied and practised under the title of CENTRAL/LOCAL RELATIONS (Jones 1980; Rhodes 1981).

In the United States IGR has been considered from various angles, especially its differences from FEDERALISM. One author implies that IGR has essentially displaced or replaced federalism: 'Federalism – old style – is dead. Yet federalism – new style – is alive and well and living in the United States. Its name is *intergovernmental relations*.' (Reagan 1972, p. 3.)

In contrast Wright (1982, p. 26) views IGR as a conceptual and descriptive supplement to the political and structural relationships described by federalism: 'IGR is not, I think, a substitute for federalism; IGR includes a range of activities and meanings that are neither explicit nor implicit in federalism.' Several writers have used IGR with reference to interjurisdictional relationships in nations where the concept of federalism is clearly inappropriate (for example, Japan and the United Kingdom). (See IIAS 1982; Jichi Sogo Center 1984; Jones 1980; Rhodes 1981; Rose 1982.)

Federalism has been distinguished by and has emphasized several features: predominant focus on national-state relationships; formal legal relationships; implied hierarchical relations based on the ultimate supremacy of the national government; and the modest or limited focus on *policy* questions or issues in federalism analyses (Macmahon 1954; Riker 1964). In contrast to this cluster of federalism features a focus on IGR has been marked by five distinctive characteristics:

(1) national-state-local, state-local, national-local, and inter-local relations;
(2) the attitudes and actions of public officials especially their perceptions of actors from other political jurisdictions;
(3) the regularity, consistency, and patterned nature of day-to-day working relationships that span political boundaries within a country;
(4) the importance of *all* public officials, both popularly elected and appointed administrative officials;
(5) the prominence of policy issues, with particular attention to fiscal relationships, for example grants-in-aid, revenue raising, taxing authority, and policy implementation.

The utility and visibility of IGR as a concept has been enhanced in the USA by the creation and continuation of the Advisory Commission on Intergovernmental Relations. This body, created in 1959, is composed of twenty-six presidentially-appointed members who are representative of local, state, and national interests and viewpoints. The Commission and its staff have engaged in extensive research, published numerous reports, and made hundreds of policy recommendations on intergovernmental issues. Despite the emergent and wider usage of IGR as an organizing concept, there is a noteworthy absence of systematic cross-national comparative studies on the subject.   DSW

Reading

Anderson, W.: *Intergovernmental Relations in Review*. Minneapolis: University of Minnesota Press, 1960.

IIAS Tokyo Round Table Organizing Committee, ed.: *Public Administration in Japan*. Tokyo: Institute of Administrative Management, 1982.

Jichi Sogo Center: *Local Public Administration in Japan*. Tokyo, 1984.

Jones, G.W. ed.: *New Approaches to the Study of Central–Local Government Relationships*. Farnborough: Gower/SSRC, 1980.

Macmahon, A.W. ed.: *Federalism: Mature and Emergent*. New York: Doubleday, 1955.

O'Toole, L.J. ed.: *American Intergovernmental Relations*. Washington, DC: Congressional Quarterly Press, 1985.

Reagan, M.: *The New Federalism*. New York: Oxford University Press, 1972.

Rhodes, R.A.W.: *Control and Power in Central–Local Government Relations*. Farnborough: Gower, 1981.

Riker, W.H.: *Federalism: origin, operation, significance*. Boston, Mass.: Little, Brown, 1964.

Rose, R.: *The Territorial Dimension in Government: understanding the United Kingdom*. Chatham, NJ: Chatham House, 1982.

Wright, D.S.: *Understanding Intergovernmental Relations*. 2nd edn. Monterey, Calif.: Brooks/Cole, 1982.

internal colonialism A relationship of exploitation between component geographical areas of a single state. According to this theory a state can be divided into two unequal areas: a 'core' or 'centre' which exploits the resources (such as cheap labour or raw materials) of a 'periphery'. Since the individuals and institutions which own or control the means of production are predominantly located in the core area the profits generated by economic activity in the periphery tend to flow to the centre. The dependent and subordinate role of the periphery may be buttressed by the centralization of transport, communications and markets in the core area, by the centre's dominance of cultural life as well as by coercive governmental measures, such as those outlawing symbols of peripheral identity.

Internal colonialism was originally associated

with Lenin's writing on the economic and political development of Russia. Although it has been used by non-Marxists it is strongly identified with Marxist scholarship of third world and especially of Latin American countries. In western Europe the theory has been explored as a means of explaining regional economic inequalities as well as the persistence of regional identities and nationalist movements in France (Brittany and Occitania), the United Kingdom (Scotland, Wales and Northern Ireland), Spain (Basque country and Catalonia) and Italy (the *Mezzogiorno*) among other countries. Most studies of internal colonialism in the West European context have concluded that on its own the theory cannot explain contemporary regional economic and political differences.

See also LENIN; MARX.   ECP

Reading

Frank, A.G.: *On Capitalist Underdevelopment*, pp. 72–80. Bombay: Oxford University Press, 1975.

Hechter, M.: *Internal Colonialism: the Celtic fringe in British national development 1536–1966*. London: Routledge & Kegan Paul, 1975.

Smith, A.D.: *The Ethnic Revival*, ch. 2. Cambridge: Cambridge University Press, 1981.

Tiryakian, E.A. and Rogowski, R. eds: *New Nationalisms of the Developed West*. London and Boston, Mass.: Allen & Unwin, 1985.

International Court of Justice   Principal judicial organ of the UNITED NATIONS. The Court was established in 1946 as the successor to the Permanent Court of International Justice. Its composition and powers are governed by its Statute. The Court consists of fifteen judges appointed by the General Assembly and the Security Council. Only states may bring contentious cases before the Court; its jurisdiction in these depends on the consent of the states parties. The Court's decisions are made under international law; it may also give Advisory Opinions at the request of the General Assembly, Security Council and specialized agencies of the United Nations.

CDG

Reading

Rosenne, S.: *The Law and Practice of the International Court*. Dordrecht: Nijhoff, 1985.

interpellation   Device designed to hold the executive to account in a number of parliamentary systems. It consists of a request by a member of the legislature to a member of the government to explain an action of a department or a matter of government policy. It generates a debate usually culminating in a vote of confidence. The *interpellation* was frequently used in France in the Third and Fourth Republics, and was indeed one of the causes of the instability of French government between 1871 and 1958.   VBB

Reading

Inter-Parliamentary Union: *Parliaments of the World*. 2 vols. Gower: Aldershot, 1986.

iron law of oligarchy   Formulated by Roberto MICHELS, this 'law' asserts that democratic organizations inevitably become subordinated to the interest of their leaders and that the leadership becomes an entrenched oligarchy: 'He who says organization, says oligarchy.' Michels based his general thesis on the organization of political parties and specifically on his study of the German Social Democratic Party (SPD) at the beginning of the century. He saw the SPD as a test case, since it was the most important MASS MEMBERSHIP PARTY of its time and undeniably dedicated to the cause of inner-party democracy.

Michels published his findings in his treatise *Zur Soziologie des Parteiwesens in der modernen Demokratie* (1911; translated as *Political Parties* (1962)). He advances a number of arguments which support the idea of a pervasive tendency towards oligarchy. It partly results from the nature of organization; it is also a question of political power; and partly too it can be ascribed to 'human nature' – the psychological disposition of leaders and the led. It is the mutual reinforcement of these three factors that lends such apparent inevitability to the 'iron law'. First, there is the technical problem of democratic organization. A large democratic party faces insuperable problems in the way of ensuring equal and direct participation, and requires some division of labour and specialization of function. Within the party a class of professional politicians emerges. They possess expertise and develop organizational skills that distinguish them from ordinary party members; as full-time party functionaries their interests also become different. Second, and related to this divergence, the question of the power relationship within the organization becomes significant: it is natural for the elite to try to perpetuate its position and to insist on its indispensability. Third, although in theory the leaders can be challenged and replaced by the normal democratic processes, in practice this is difficult to achieve because their followers accept their subordination and feel incompetent. Michels found the veneration accorded to the leadership to be particularly true in the case of working-class leaders who most rapidly move away from ordinary party members as they become adept in handling political matters.

Michels's pessimism about democratic socialist parties led him to conclude that they were unlikely to fulfil their ideals. The irony was that as they apparently became more successful in winning support, the need for stronger party organization would grow too and democratic goals would become displaced by an entrenched oligarchy.

The 'iron law' can be criticized from many points of view. On one level it can be dismissed as a trite observation: it is in the nature of organization that decisions will be made by minorities. The question of whether those minorities become immune to the will of the majority can only be settled by reference to particular cases, and there is sufficient evidence to show that leaders can be toppled and that the mass membership does on occasion simply withdraw its support. Michels also neglected the importance of FACTIONS within the party: even though the success of one faction over another did not guarantee democracy in the party, the continuing factional struggle ensures that no one group will wield permanent power – an argument transferred to the wider democratic stage in the theory of democratic elitism.

There is a sense in which the observations made by Michels are time-bound and over-specific. His work relates to an era in which parties were operating under regimes that were themselves often far from democratic; it was unrealistic to expect the parties to have entirely different standards. Working-class parties also faced handicaps, and it was natural for them to emphasize loyalty, discipline and obedience – qualities which unduly favoured an uncritical attitude towards party leaders. Loyalty to the leadership and a dedication to the party organization was often based on the premise of imminent revolutionary change, but with victory not forthcoming and a more realistic view of what could be achieved, the membership became less inclined to treat the existing leadership as indispensable.

Michels was undoubtedly correct in stressing the strong position of the professional politician and the independent role that a powerful party bureaucracy could play. In certain circumstances they are able to subvert the will of the democratic majority, but Michels tended to neglect the extent to which political parties are voluntaristic organizations which depend for their vitality on an unforced commitment: a party that becomes too professional and bureaucratic risks losing its following. Michels underestimated the part played by the amateur in politics and by party outsiders who are not products of the party MACHINE or dependent on it. The major weakness of Michels's analysis was to postulate an undifferentiated mass membership and a unified party elite. In practice neither assumption is valid. To the extent that Michels was primarily concerned with class-based mass parties and hence with a largely homogeneous social composition, oligarchical tendencies may be favoured, but the weakening of such parties in the modern era means that – at best – the 'iron law' is properly applicable only to certain types of party and then only in particular circumstances.

See also DEMOCRACY; ELITES; OLIGARCHY.

GSm

Reading

Beetham, D.: From socialism to fascism: the relation between theory and practice in the work of

Roberto Michels. *Political Studies* 25 (1977) 3–4, 161–81.

Cassinelli, C.: The law of oligarchy. *American Political Science Review* 47 (1953) 773–84.

Duverger, M.: *Political Parties: their organization and activity in the modern state*. London: Methuen, 1964.

May, J.: Democracy, organization, Michels. *American Political Science Review* 59 (1965) 417–29.

Michels, R.: *Political Parties*, ed. and intro. S.M. Lipset. New York: Crowell-Collier, 1962.

Minkin, L.: *The Labour Party Conference: a study in the politics of intra-party democracy*. London: Allen Lane, 1978.

Parry, G.: *Political Elites*. London: Allen & Unwin, 1969.

issue network   First used by Hugh Heclo in 1978 to describe a pattern of decision making, its significance lay in its conception of the political network in which policy was made as ad hoc: a changing pattern of participants for different issues and for the same issue over time. In using this image to characterize current American policy making Heclo was therefore deliberately challenging terms such as 'group subgovernment', 'iron triangle' and similar concepts which were often interpreted as presenting policy as being made by restricted, predictable, and specialized sets of participants. 'Looking for closed triangles of control' he argued (1978, p. 88), 'we tend to miss the fairly open networks ... that increasingly impinge upon government.'

Heclo was claiming that in the 1970s there had been an increased mobilization of competing INTEREST GROUPS, and a decay in the comparatively settled dominance of policy sectors by coalitions of established and legitimate pressure groups, government agencies and congressional committees. While the emergence of this new pattern perhaps satisfied complaints about lack of access to subgovernments, the very unpredictability was seen to make any political management difficult.

In Kelso's terms (1978) there has been a movement from corporate pluralism to laissez faire pluralism as the common decision process. Other observers have noted this proliferation of interests. Wilson (1981) argued that the increase in pressure group activity meant that PLURALISM as a theory better 'fitted' the US

in the 1970s than the 1950s in which the theory was so influential.

See also CORPORATISM.   AGJ

Reading

Chubb, J.E.: *Interest Groups and the Bureaucracy*. Stanford, Calif.: Stanford University Press, 1983.

Gais, T.L., Peterson, M. and Walker, J.L.: Interest groups, iron triangles and representative institutions in American national government. *British Journal of Political Science* 14.2 (1985) 161–185.

Heclo, H.: Issue networks and the executive establishment. In *The New American Political System*, ed. A. King. Washington, DC: American Enterprise Institute, 1978.

Jordan, A.G.: Iron triangles, woolly corporatism and elastic nets: images of the policy process. *Journal of Public Policy* 1.1 (1981) 95–123.

Kelso, W.: *American Democratic Theory*. Westport, Conn.: Greenwood, 1978.

Wilson, G.: *Interest Groups in the United States*. Oxford: Clarendon Press, 1981.

issues, issue perception and issue voting   Broadly speaking a political issue is any point of disagreement on political affairs. The disagreement may be actual or potential, real or supposed; it may be disagreement among elites (parties, candidates) or among masses; it may be about day-to-day policies, about values and goals, about personalities, about choices or about competence. The list is endless. So, such deceptively simple questions as 'do issues matter?' are too ill-defined to allow an equally simple answer.

The simplest RATIONAL CHOICE model assumes that the voter begins by adopting a position on a political issue, then checks the positions of the various parties or candidates on the issue, and finally votes for the party or candidate whose issue-position comes nearest to his or her own.

There are several faults with this simple model. First, issues are many and the voter must therefore select and/or weigh the issues by some criterion of importance. Second, there is no such thing as a party position on an issue – different observers have different perceptions of party positions. Third, voters are not born with built-in, ready-installed, positions on any and every political issue.

Their own issue positions derive from outside sources.

On the other hand, voters are born into families and into social milieux which already have commitments to parties and to some general political ideas, so when an issue emerges its influence is constrained by a web of existing political attitudes and commitments.

Before an emergent issue can have a large effect upon voting it must overcome four constraints which may be called the salience, persuasion, projection and damping effects. Voters may react to a new issue that would disturb their existing party commitments either by denying its importance (the *salience* effect), by accepting their own party's policy (the *persuasion* effect), by wantonly misperceiving their party's policy in such a way as to allow them to claim that their party has the same policy as themselves (the *projection* effect – since the voters project their own policies on to their image of their party), or simply by staying with their existing party despite open disagreement with it on an important issue (the *damping* effect – older, more socially integrated, and more consistent partisans may be better able to cope with issue disagreement while remaining loyal to their party).

There is evidence that all these constraints operate, and the impact of an issue is usually much less than the simple rational choice model of issue voting would imply. Some issues however can have substantial impact despite the constraints. More generally, there is a trend towards weaker political commitment and hence towards less constraint on issue voting. In consequence, Nie *et al.*'s *Changing American Voter* claimed to detect a huge 'rise of issue voting' during the mid-1960s which has been maintained ever since.

The question of a rise in issue voting involves difficult problems of trend analysis and two-way causation. First, it is now clear that the question-formats used to measure issue-attitudes in political surveys were radically improved during the mid-1960s. This purely technical change in itself produced an apparent quantum leap in the coherence of voters' issue attitudes and in their correlation with voting choice (Abramson 1983). Changes in measurement techniques therefore make long-term trend analyses almost impossible, and there is reason to doubt the scale and permanence of the 'rise in issue voting' in the 1960s. Second, while the static correlation between issue attitudes and voting choice is well established, the dynamics of the interplay between issue attitudes, partisan loyalty and voting are still obscure. We know that both issue attitudes and PARTY IDENTIFICATION can and do change, we know that each influences the other, but as yet there have been relatively few studies of their interaction. (Though for some pioneering attempts, see Markus and Converse 1979; Page and Jones 1979; or Miller 1983.)

See also DEALIGNMENT.   WLM

Reading

Abramson, P.R.: *Political Attitudes in America*. San Francisco: Freeman, 1983.

Kinder, D.R.: Diversity and complexity in American public opinion. In *Political Science: the state of the discipline*, ed. A.W. Finifter. Washington, DC: American Political Science Association, 1983.

Markus, G.B. and Converse, P.E.: A dynamic simultaneous equation model of electoral choice. *American Political Science Review* 73 (1979) 1055–70.

Miller, W.L.: The denationalisation of British politics. *West European Politics* 6 (1983) 103–29.

Nie, N.H., Verba, S. and Petrocik, J.R.: *The Changing American Voter*. 2nd edn. Cambridge, Mass.: Harvard University Press, 1979.

Page, B.I. and Jones, C.C.: Reciprocal effects of policy preferences, party loyalties and the vote. *American Political Science Review* 73 (1979) 1071–89.

J

Jackson/Jacksonian democracy

(1) *Andrew Jackson* (1767–1845) President of the United States from 1829–37. Jackson was neither a mere political figurehead nor a great creative statesman. His fame as the victor in the battle of New Orleans (1815) won him the presidency; his adroitness as a politician ensured his re-election in 1832 and his dominance of the political scene so long as he held office. His greatest achievement was the suppression of the nullification movement in South Carolina (1832–3) by which he averted civil war for nearly thirty years. A firm believer in the maxim, 'that government is best which governs least', he left the federal government appreciably weaker than he found it, but within that government he enormously increased the prestige and the power of the presidency. This achievement was somewhat offset by his part in building up the party system which was to keep the presidents, with one exception, in leading-strings until the twentieth century; the exception was Abraham Lincoln. Lincoln used Jacksonian precedents and, more important, the expectations which Jackson aroused, to justify dealing with the Southern rebellion of 1861 in a manner which showed how great was the power of the presidency when an emergency had to be surmounted.

(2) *Jacksonian democracy* A somewhat misleading label used by academic historians to characterize the United States political system between approximately 1815 and 1849. This was a period of rapid westward expansion and economic growth. It was also the era in which universal white manhood suffrage was achieved, something to which America's already vigorous electoral politics had to adjust. It saw the emergence of permanent two-party politics, tightly-disciplined party machines, and the presidential nominating convention. It was an age of religious enthusiasm and exuberant reformism, marked by campaigns for the abolition of slavery, the reform of the prison system, universal schooling, improved health and diet, and, by the end of the period, votes for women. But the central issues of party politics were economic. Followers of Jackson's, organized in the Democratic party, were intensely suspicious of banks, and especially of the Bank of the United States, which carried out some of the functions of a central bank. They also came to oppose any use of public funds, whether state or federal, for what were called 'internal improvements' (roads, canals, railways). Their opponents, who set up the Whig party, were strong supporters of the Bank. The central episode of the age was therefore Jackson's presidential veto of the re-charter of the Bank in 1832, which led to the so-called Bank War.

HB

Reading

McCormick, R.P.: *The Second American Party System*. Chapel Hill: University of North Carolina Press, 1966.

Meyers, M.: *The Jacksonian Persuasion*. Stanford, Calif.: Stanford University Press, 1957.

Schlesinger, A.M. Jr: *The Age of Jackson*. Boston, Mass.: Little, Brown, 1945.

Ward, J.W.: *Andrew Jackson: symbol of an age*. New York: Oxford University Press, 1955.

Jefferson/Jeffersonian democracy

(1) *Thomas Jefferson* (1743–1826) Author of the DECLARATION OF INDEPENDENCE and a leading American statesman during and after the AMERICAN REVOLUTION. Jefferson served as Secretary of State under the first President, George Washington, but he also inspired a party opposed to the centralizing and industrializing policies that Washington's administration was pursuing under the influence of Alexander HAMILTON. Jefferson's party, which elected him to the presidency in 1801 and dominated American national politics for a generation thereafter, called itself the Republican (not the 'democratic') party. It was however democratic in its idealistic faith in enlightened, moral peoples and its jealousy towards governments. Jefferson was also a strong believer in the separation of church and state.

(2) *Jeffersonian democracy* Originally built around the ideal of the independent farmer, the term later inspired diverse non-agrarian popular political movements in America and elsewhere. The term also implies an emphasis on the territorial decentralization of power characteristic of many Federal States (see FEDERALISM). The US DEMOCRATIC PARTY traces its origins to Jefferson; but perhaps the Jeffersonian ideal exerted its greatest influence upon the Populist and PROGRESSIVE movements at the turn of the century, movements animated in part by a nostalgia for the supposed simplicities of Jefferson's America.   JZ

Reading

Jefferson, T.: *The Papers of Thomas Jefferson*, ed. J.P. Boyd and C.T. Cullen. 21 vols. to date. Princeton, NJ: Princeton University Press, 1950– .

Malone, D.: *Jefferson and his Time*. 7 vols. Boston, Mass.: Little, Brown, 1948–83.

Peterson, M.D.: *The Jefferson Image in the American Mind*. New York: Oxford University Press, 1960.

———: *The Portable Thomas Jefferson*. New York: Viking, 1975.

judge In modern nations a governmental official appointed or elected to administer justice in a court of law. Scholars in comparative law often make a distinction between the Weberian ideal model of the judge as an objective professional and that of the judge as a partisan. The former emphasizes the development of an independent professional judicial elite, trained for judicial service and socialized for objective, rational interpretation and application of recognized principles of law; the latter suggests that judges are often active or discreet participants in ruling elites to whom they may render favourable decisions. Most common law countries place some reliance on lay judges as well as professionals, with England being exceptional in that lay judges outnumber professionals by around 60 to 1. In the US and the Soviet Union, lay judges are popularly elected, for fixed terms, rather than appointed. Professional judges are typically appointed or elected after they have had considerable experience as lawyers, but in civil law countries the judge is appointed by the minister of justice, upon passing examinations in his twenties, and has many of the characteristics of a civil servant.   JRS

judicial activism and self restraint

The debate over judicial activism and self-restraint is a latter-day out-growth of the constitutional institution of JUDICIAL REVIEW. It followed the successful challenge finally mounted by President Franklin Roosevelt to the conservative 'Old Court' majority on the US Supreme Court after his re-election in 1936, and the President's use thereafter of the executive appointing power to name judges to the Court, many of whom had enjoyed direct executive or legislative experience with the drafting and adoption of the NEW DEAL programme and who shared the President's own essentially liberal activist philosophy. While the main constitutional rationale for reversing the conservative 'Old Court' jurisprudence was the presumption of constitutionality in favour of Congressional legislation, the new wave of New Deal judges, led by Justices Hugo Black and William O. Douglas, began to apply an increasingly interventionist approach, involving a priority, 'preferred position' for the constitutional First Amendment (free speech) values over other constitutional guarantees, and an especially vigorous judicial assertion and protection of all the other political and civil rights contained in the constitutional BILL OF RIGHTS. The projection of this particular judicial philosophy was immensely assisted by Black's and Douglas's unusually long tenure – from the late 1930s to the 1970s – and by the fact that they were joined from 1953 to 1969 by an unusually powerful Chief Justice, Earl Warren, with the same essential values. The logical counterpoint was provided by Justice Felix Frankfurter – like Black and Douglas a Roosevelt appointee – who claimed, in stated reliance on the great Justice Oliver Wendell Holmes Jr, that the judicial role involved a general deference or self restraint in regard to the popularly-elected executive and legislative authorities; and that for the new Court majority now to inject liberal activist values into its adjudication would be to commit the same constitutional error as the 'Old Court' did before 1937 when it imposed its own conservative philosophy as constitutional dogma.

In a sense, activism/self restraint is a false judicial dichotomy, the two positions being better represented as different points on a continuum ranging from strict ('logical', 'legalistic') construction to more teleological, goal-oriented ('policy', 'legislative') judicial interpretations. As such it is to be found represented, in its different aspects, in the jurisprudence of all main constitutional courts. We could well number among the leading judicial activists not only Black, Douglas and Warren of the US Supreme Court, but Rand of the Canadian Supreme Court, Fazl Ali of the Indian Supreme Court, Leibholz of the West German Constitutional Court, and Jessup and Lachs of the International Court of Justice.   EMcW

Reading

Biddle, F.: *Justice Holmes, Natural Law and the Supreme Court*. New York: Macmillan, 1961.

Frankfurter, F.: *Mr Justice Holmes and the Supreme Court*. Cambridge, Mass.: Belknap, 1961.

————: *Of Law and Men, Papers and Addresses of Felix Frankfurter 1939–1956*, ed. P. Elman. New York: Harcourt, Brace, 1956.

McWhinney, E.: *Judicial Review in the English-Speaking World*. 4th edn. Toronto: University of Toronto Press, 1969.

————: *Supreme Courts and Judicial Law-Making: constitutional tribunals and constitutional review*. Dordrecht: Nijhoff, 1986.

Mendelson, W.: *Justices Black and Frankfurter: conflict in the Court*. Chicago, Ill.: University of Chicago Press, 1961.

judicial function and process The capacity to hear, evaluate, and determine the outcome of cases in controversies between competing litigants. Most governmental systems try to maintain a reputation of objectivity and impartiality by providing a variety of safeguards designed to insulate JUDICIARIES from external pressures such as executive or legislative authority and from private influences whether economic, social, or religious.

The judicial process varies from nation to nation in accordance with the broad historical influence (or lack of it) of families of law. Legal systems may be classified by their historical origins and lines of development; by their emphases in legal principles and philosophy; by their distinctive institutional structure and organization; by the kinds of legal authorities they accept and the manner in which they acknowledge them; by the ideological bases of their approaches to legal interpretation. Though there have been considerable differences of opinion among specialists in comparative law, a comprehensive rigorous evaluation of over eighty years of scholarly assessment of families of law by Zweigert and Kotz identified eight families. These are: Anglo-American common law, the Romanistic, Germanic, and Nordic civil law, the Socialist family, and the Far Eastern, Hindu and Islamic religiously based families. The historical development of each family has varied. Some variations followed military conquest, such as the establishment of law 'common to the realm' after the Norman conquest of Anglo-Saxon England. Differences in legal style – such as the traditional English common law emphasis on the judge whereby law is made on a case by case basis as against the practice in continental European systems of treating law systemically and abstractly – are the result of historical as well as attitudinal differences. English law has more often than not been influenced by judges, while continental law has more frequently reflected the analyses of legal scholars.

Fundamental historical differences in the objectives as well as in the procedures of dispute resolution are particularly noticeable in the comparison of western with Far Eastern systems, which traditionally emphasized the subordination of disputes and legal confrontations to arbitration in order to maintain the stability and harmony of society. In western families of law, both common law and continental, individual or group success in an adversarial judicial process was generally considered socially acceptable. These differences in social definitions of the proper role of law result in significant differences in legal institutions: in western families of law there is a considerably larger social and institutional role for lawyers and judges than in Far Eastern systems; in the East alternative modes of dispute resolution were developed, with correspondingly different solutions in regard to its institutions and personnel.

The major families of law enjoy fundamental conceptual similarities as well as differences. Virtually all families of law accept, in theory, the assumption that the judicial function and process were developed to institutionalize conflict resolution based on objective principles and procedures. All families have developed some system to distinguish the role of the legal professional and the judge from other private and public roles; when however the actual administration of justice is utilized as an instrument of power or to the advantage of an economic, military, religious or family elite, the exemplary theoretical principles of fair and objective law making are modified or abandoned. Absolute monarchs and contemporary dictators have from time to time found it useful or necessary to attempt to create the appearance of objectivity in their judicial systems. These departures from the ideal purpose of judicial objectivity were frequently based upon short term expediency. More fundamental departures arise because of basic differences of principle over the optimum goals of law: conflicts, for example, between religious and secular principles or capitalist and socialist ideals of justice. Such fundamental divisions have recurred throughout the

centuries-old development of conceptions of the judicial function and process. Nevertheless the goal of objectivity based upon fair procedures and professional judicial decision making, remains the central principle associated with the judicial function and process within all the major families of law. JRS

Reading

Abraham, H.J.: *The Judicial Process*. 4th edn. New York and Oxford: Oxford University Press, 1980.

Ehrmann, H.W.: *Comparative Legal Cultures*. Englewood Cliffs, NJ: Prentice Hall, 1976.

Li, V.H.: *Law without Lawyers: a comparative view of law in China and the United States*. Boulder, Col.: Westview, 1978.

Murphy, W.F. and Tanenhaus, J.: *Comparative Constitutional Law: cases and commentaries*. New York: St Martin's, 1977.

Tiger, M.E. and Levy, M.R.: *Law and the Rise of Capitalism*. New York: Monthly Review Press, 1977.

Trubeck, D.M.: Max Weber on law and the rise of capitalism. *University of Wisconsin Law Review* (1972) 720–53.

judicial review Emerging in the early nineteenth century as a distinctively American constitutional conception, it had, by the middle and late twentieth century, been 'received' in many other legal systems. Judicial review may perhaps be considered today as the master institution of western, and also western-influenced, CONSTITUTIONALISM, being present in key succession states to the old British Empire (for example in Canada, Australia, India); in Japan and West Germany after the second world war; diverse states such as Socialist Yugoslavia, post-Franco Spain; and even in the Fifth French Republic's somewhat unique CONSEIL CONSTITUTIONNEL.

Judicial review is not mentioned, as such, in the US Constitution, and it was not until some years after the adoption of that charter that it was advanced, by way of constitutional innovation, by the great early Chief Justice of the US SUPREME COURT, John Marshall, in his celebrated judgment in *Marbury* v. *Madison* in 1803. Chief Justice Marshall, using as his basis the US Constitution's status as 'superior paramount law, unchangeable by ordinary means' and its inner logic in the arrangement and distribution of governmental powers, postulated a constitutional power, inhering in the courts, to strike down 'unconstitutional' laws.

The term judicial review is a comprehensive one that necessarily implies judicial competence to go beyond SEPARATION OF POWERS questions, involving the interaction of executive, legislative, and judicial power – what West German constitutional law calls institutional conflicts. Today, the agenda of judicial review in the major systems in which it is in operation involves also regional (Federal–Provincial) conflicts, CIVIL LIBERTIES (citizen against the state or state authority), even the supervision of the fairness of the electoral system and electoral laws and the regulation of the internal self-government of the political parties. With innovations in legal procedures today facilitating access by citizens and private interest groups to the courts, constitutional complaints related to CIVIL RIGHTS (whether or not formally enshrined in a constitutional BILL OF RIGHTS) have come to supply the bulk of the business of court-based constitutional review.

Once successfully asserted by Chief Justice Marshall, the power of judicial review was not seriously disputed, on legal grounds, in the United States. The challenges that emerged over the years tended to be political ones, going to the concrete consequences of the court decisions when applied and to the general legal and political philosophy of the judges making up the Court at any particular time. In the so-called 'Gilded Age' of American society, from the late nineteenth century on to the world economic Depression of the end of the 1920s and the early 1930s, a politically conservative majority on the Supreme Court, in the name of a 'liberty of contract' stated to be inherent in the English Common Law-derived DUE PROCESS OF LAW clauses of the Fifth and Fourteenth Amendments to the Constitution, applied *laissez-faire* principles to strike down early social and economic planning legislation. The resulting political conflicts between court and executive–legislative authority came to a head in the 1930s with the Old Court majority's invalidation of President Roosevelt's New Deal reform legislation. After the President's 1936 re-election, the court beat a hasty and ill-disguised political retreat and, with the 'Court Revolution' of 1937, began to apply a general presumption of constitutionality to Congressional legislation. Thereafter, the politically conscious presidential utilization of the executive power to appoint judges has generally ensured judicial majorities consonant with dominant societal attitudes.

Outside the United States, although the constitutional–legal roots are often widely different, as with the historical role of the old British Imperial tribunal, the Privy Council, in the case of the Commonwealth countries, and the influence of civil law conceptions of the judicial process and court function in the case of West Germany and Japan, the impact of American constitutional thinking has been direct and marked after 1945. The institution of a specialized Constitutional Court, of which the West German *Bundesverfassungsgericht* (with its judges elected for a term of years) is the archetype, is a logical projection of all the American experience over the years.

See also JUDICIAL ACTIVISM AND SELF-RESTRAINT.

EMcW

Reading

Cardozo, B.N.: *The Nature of the Judicial Process.* New Haven, Conn.: Yale University Press, 1921.

Freund, P.A.: *On Understanding the Supreme Court.* Boston, Mass.: Little, Brown, 1951.

Hughes, C.E.: *The Supreme Court of the United States.* New York: Columbia University Press, 1928.

McWhinney, E.: *Judicial Review in the English-Speaking World.* 4th edn. Toronto: University of Toronto Press, 1969.

————: *Supreme Courts and Judicial Law-Making: constitutional tribunals and constitutional review.* Dordrecht: Nijhoff, 1986.

Mason, A.T.: *The Supreme Court from Taft to Warren.* Baton Rouge: Louisiana State University Press, 1958.

Pritchett, C.H.: *The Roosevelt Court: a study in judicial politics and values 1937–1947.*

Swisher, C.B.: *The Supreme Court in Modern Role.* New York: New York University Press, 1968.

judiciary A governmental institution empowered to decide legal conflicts. A judiciary or a court generally has in most nations been granted or has successfully asserted a distinctive, independent role. In ideal conceptual models judiciaries are often defined as specialized organizations designed to institutionalize conflict resolution in a manner ensuring fairness and justice to the adversarial parties in litigation. Such judicial objectivity is guaranteed by a variety of institutional safeguards of independence such as life tenure on good behaviour (United States) or historic statutory guarantees (Britain). In contrast with the Anglo-American tradition, the continental European tradition tries to ensure judicial independence, in part through development of specialized professional training and the career ladder advancement of judges which is differentiated from the training of ordinary lawyers. In both traditions objectivity in decision making is often associated with methods of internal judicial operation intended to provide such impartiality.

In reality judicial objectivity and independence vary a great deal between nations and within specific nations longitudinally. Consequently courts have been vehicles for what Otto Kirchheimer called 'political justice'. Modern examples of the use of judiciaries as instruments of power are the special Nazi courts and the Soviet judiciaries which were tribunals for the Stalin show trials of the 1930s. Several analysts of judiciaries have suggested that the basic tasks of courts make a completely objective resolution of disputes exceedingly hard to achieve. In regimes far less extreme than those of Hitler and Stalin judges, as agents of the regime, will occasionally take into consideration factors other than the adversarial positions of the opposing litigants. Social control, public reputation, regime stability, as well as elite preferences or prejudices may intrude. The Dreyfus case is a specific French example, but it is also symptomatic of a problem which may affect any national judiciary.

Criteria for proper judicial procedure and organization vary broadly between nations, but certain general patterns embody the characteristics of pervasive 'families of law'. These are the Anglo-American common law system, the continental codification system, the socialist system, and a variety of religiously based systems of which the Islamic is the most influential. While the standards for the attainment of justice and fairness vary according to system, these families embrace virtually all national judiciaries and so represent powerful cross-national legal cultural systems whose common characteristics generally overshadow parochial national judicial differences.

See also JUDICIAL FUNCTION AND PROCESS.

JRS

Reading

Becker, T.L. ed.: *Political Trials*. Indianapolis: Bobbs-Merrill, 1971.

David, R. and Brierly, J.E.C.: *Major Legal Systems in the World Today: an introduction to the comparative study of the law*. London: Stevens, 1978.

Kirchheimer, O.: *Political Justice: the use of legal procedure for political ends*. Princeton, NJ: Princeton University Press, 1961.

Shapiro, M.: *Courts: a comparative and political analysis*. Chicago, Ill.: University of Chicago Press, 1981.

junta An ad hoc body for political purposes, usually at local level and often self-appointed. In revolutionary periods in Spain, when the central power was weak, urban radicals set up local juntas. The central government recovered control by the creation of a *Junta Central* which subsumed local juntas. The collapse of the central government authority on the outbreak of the Civil War (July 1936) revived the junta tradition, e.g. the Junta de Defensa of Madrid and the Anti-Fascist Militia Committee of Barcelona. The Juntas de Defensa (1917) were an officers' trade union which brought severe pressure on governments.

RC

jury A number of lay persons summoned to participate in the disposition of a trial, normally by deciding on the facts. Trial by jury, used in England from the twelfth century, came to be regarded as an important safeguard against oppression and was enshrined in the United States Constitution. Elsewhere it has been little employed, although the people's assessors of courts in the Soviet Union and Eastern European countries perform a somewhat similar role. Jury trial remains widely available in the United States, but in England doubts about the institution have been reflected in its diminished use, particularly in civil law.

CRM

Reading

Cornish, W.R.: *The Jury*. Harmondsworth: Penguin, 1971.

Devlin, P.: *Trial by Jury*. London: Stevens, 1956.

Frank, J.: *Courts on Trial*. Princeton, NJ: Princeton University Press, 1949.

Kalven, H. and Zeisel, H.: *The American Jury*. Boston, Mass.: Little, Brown, 1966.

Justice of the Peace   In England, a lay person appointed by the Lord Chancellor in the name of the Queen to discharge (without remuneration) judicial functions in a particular area as a MAGISTRATE and also to exercise certain administrative powers, principally in the granting of licences for the sale of alcohol or for music, dancing etc.   JKBN

justiciability   The term is sometimes used to describe existing legal arrangements. If a particular issue lies within the jurisdiction of a court or tribunal it may be said to be justiciable there. Justiciability is frequently (and sometimes confusingly) used in a prescriptive or critical sense to assert or imply that an issue is *suitable* or *appropriate* for settlement in a judicial forum. So when legislation is under discussion it may be argued that some questions are 'non-justiciable' in the sense that their subject-matter makes them unsuitable for submission to the judicial process. Legislators have often felt it appropriate to exclude the courts from reviewing the exercise of powers conferred by them on ministers or administrative agencies. Such 'privative' clauses in legislation have often met with judicial criticism or resistance.

Where the law is unclear, courts and judges may develop doctrines about what are or are not suitable issues for judicial settlement or review. In the United States the SUPREME COURT accepted a category of 'political questions', mainly to do with the conduct of foreign relations and war, which may be held unsuitable for reference to the Court because of the inherent difficulty of weighing judicially evidence about the matters in dispute. The French doctrine of *acte de gouvernement* and the British law as to act of state reflect a similar judicial reluctance to interfere in the exercise of certain kinds of executive authority, mainly when exercised outside the boundaries of the state.

In recent years British courts have narrowed the area within which they are prepared to treat executive powers as non-justiciable. One area of contention that remains is the extent to which the exercise of prerogative powers by ministers or civil servants is justiciable or reviewable in the courts. Whether the courts will review the exercise of a prerogative power now seems to depend on its content. Matters still regarded as non-justiciable seem to be executive action under the prerogative that involves the armed forces, treaty making, the award of honours and the personal acts of the sovereign (see PREROGATIVE).

See also ADMINISTRATIVE TRIBUNALS; JUDICIAL FUNCTION AND PROCESS; JUDICIAL REVIEW; JUDICIARY.   GM

Reading

Fuller, L.L.: The forms and limits of adjudication. *Harvard Law Review* 92 (1978) 358.

Harlow, C. and Rawlings, R.: *Law and Administration*, ch. 2. London: Weidenfeld & Nicolson, 1984.

Marshall, G.: Justiciability. In *Oxford Essays in Jurisprudence*, ed. A.G. Guest, 1st ser. Oxford: Clarendon Press, 1961.

Summers, R.S.: Justiciability. *Modern Law Review* 26 (1963) 530.

K

Kant, Immanuel (1724–1804)

Kant, Immanuel (1724–1804) Celebrated German philosopher. Kant argued that political arrangements should wherever possible accord with the demands of morality. This meant that the state should have a 'republican' constitution, one which assured the RULE OF LAW, observed the SEPARATION OF POWERS and gave the last word in legislation to representatives of the people. Only 'active' citizens were to have the vote, an active citizen being defined as one who was 'his own master'. Passive citizens included apprentices, servants and 'women in general'. Kant recognized that actual states diverge markedly from the republican ideal, but was adamant that rebellion against the state could never be legitimate. Despite this he held that the 1789 French Revolution was an event of major significance in human history, though he said somewhat unplausibly that it was a phenomenon not of revolution, but of 'the evolution of a constitution governed by natural rights'.

Kant's other main interest in politics was in 'perpetual peace'. Sovereign states related to one another like individuals in a Hobbesian state of nature: they were always at war or preparing for war. To set up republican constitutions is one step towards removing this condition, since republics are 'incapable of bellicosity'. But it is necessary to institute the rule of law on the international plane too. Kant's proposals under this head were modest: he advocated that republican states form an alliance on the understanding that disputes between them be henceforth settled by peaceful means. No indication was given of the institutional machinery needed to produce this result.   WHW

Reading

Kant, I.: *Political Writings*, ed. H. Reiss and trans. H.B. Nisbet. Cambridge: Cambridge University Press, 1970.

Murphy, J.G.: *Kant: the Philosophy of Right*. London: Macmillan, 1970.

Riley, P.: *Kant's Political Philosophy*. Totowa, NJ: Rowman & Littlefield, 1983.

Williams, H.: *Kant's Political Philosophy*. Oxford: Blackwell, 1983.

Kelsen, Hans (1883–1973)

Kelsen, Hans (1883–1973) Austrian legal philosopher and public lawyer. Kelsen's chief fame is as the author of *Reine Rechtslehre* (1934) and the originator of the legal theory advanced in it, the 'pure theory of law'.

Kelsen's theory depicts legal systems as hierarchically ordered systems of norms, those higher in the hierarchy authorizing the creation of lower-order, more concrete norms. Of humanly created (positive) norms, the most abstract and general is the constitution. To treat a system as valid or binding is to presuppose a highest-order nonpositive norm which validates the 'historically first' constitution in a series. Revolutions occur when nonconstitutional changes are made and a new *Grundnorm* has to be presupposed. Such a legal order is constitutive of a STATE in the political sense. States exist as juristic persons both in municipal and in international law. LAW as such is neutral as between various moralities and ideologies, being nothing other than a normative order which provides at its most concrete level for coercive sanctions and which is largely efficacious in a given territory over some stretch of time.

In its insistence on the ideological and

ethical neutrality or purity of legal science Kelsen's theory is the most rigorous version of 'legal positivism' yet advanced. As well as contributing to legal theory in Europe and (since the Nazi period) in the USA, Kelsen was draftsman of the Austrian Constitution of 1919, and was for a time a judge of the constitutional court. His writings include contributions to international law and to the critique of Marxist legal theory as well as to general jurisprudence.   NMacC

Reading

Kelsen, H.: *The Pure Theory of Law*, trans. M. Knight. Berkeley: University of California Press, 1967.

Twining, W. and Tur, R.H.S. eds: *Essays on Kelsen*. Oxford: Oxford University Press, 1986.

Key, V. O. Jr. (1908–1963) One of the most prominent American political scientists of the post-war generation. Key was a leader of the effort to intensify behavioural approaches and quantitative techniques as research tools in American political science. His studies of American political parties, public opinion, pressure groups, electoral behaviour and Southern politics are all imbued with a deep faith in the vitality of American democracy. Much of Key's work constituted an effort to discover through empirical data the precise character of American democracy, thereby contributing to the construction of a new theory of how democracies actually function. A Texan, Key received his doctorate from the University of Chicago in 1934. He served as a faculty member at UCLA, Johns Hopkins, Yale and Harvard. He was a frequent consultant to various governmental agencies and commissions, and chaired some of the American Political Science Association's most important research committees, serving as president of that organization in 1958.

Key's writings tried to answer two fundamental questions. First, to what extent were American political leaders held accountable to the voting public through elections? Second, what role did American political elites and activists play in maintaining a consensus about democratic values and practices? His answer to the first seemed to cast doubt on the representativeness of American democracy, for he argued that elections effectively translated only the will of highly organized groups into public policy. Key discovered that voters maintained historical allegiances to political parties even though the voters' stated interests didn't seem to correspond to their preferred party's platform. But Key also found that if American elections were far from perfect, they still represented effective, if only occcasional, popular intervention into the direction of government. Key identified as 'critical elections' occasions when the depth and intensity of electoral participation led to a profound readjustment in power relations. Unlike other political scientists who employed psychological and sociological approaches to the study of voting behaviour, Key found elements of what he called a 'responsible electorate' – voters moved by rational concerns over central questions of governmental performance. In answer to the second question, Key argued that the successful maintenance of American democracy rested heavily not only on the presence of a 'responsible electorate', but perhaps more importantly on a 'political subculture' of elites and activists who respected democratic norms in their beliefs and activities. Public opinion, he held, was the result of interaction between an elite subculture on the one hand and the mass public on the other. It was therefore essential that the elite subculture appeal to the electorate as if it were responsible, at least if democracy was to be maintained. He argued that the corruption of democracy derived not from the cupidity of the masses but from the influence of leaders. He urged political leaders not to succumb to the temptations of public relations gimmickry, but to preserve democratic norms by placing meaningful public policies into the electoral realm.

Key's work has sometimes been criticized for its over-optimism. He died several years before his kind of faith in American democracy was seemingly undermined by the conflicts of the 1960s. Yet his legacy is one of enormous influence on electoral studies in the United States.   RMS

310

Reading

Key, V.O. Jr: *Public Opinion and American Democracy*. New York: Knopf, 1961.

———: *Parties, Politics and Pressure Groups*. New York: Crowell, 1964.

———: *The Responsible Electorate*. New York: Vintage Books, 1966.

Natchez, P.: *Images of Voting/Visions of Democracy*. New York: Basic Books, 1985.

Keynes/Keynesianism John Maynard Keynes (1883–1946) was an academic, economic statesman, financial operator and patron of the arts. He is primarily remembered as the author of the most important book on economics of the twentieth century, *The General Theory of Employment, Interest and Money*.

Keynes became a household name in 1919 when he published *The Economic Consequences of the Peace*, attacking the post-war settlement imposing heavy reparations on Germany. Though critical of Britain's return to the Gold Standard at the pre-war parity, his monetary theory was in the conventional mould. But in the next ten years he became increasingly sceptical of orthodox economics. After 'a long struggle of escape from habitual modes of thought and expression', the *General Theory* was published in 1936. The central message which Keynes now gave was that capitalist economies did not always and everywhere tend to full employment. The equilibrating mechanisms of orthodox economics, lower wages and interest rates, might not work in the manner prescribed, and the economy could become stuck with persistent unemployment. There was, however, no need to jettison the entire capitalist system in favour of some centrally planned economy. Free markets did quite well in determining *what* things should be produced: the failure lay in determining *how much*. Deficiency of aggregate demand could be made good by the appropriate monetary policy and, more importantly, by fiscal policy which increased public expenditure or lowered taxes. Keynes made the additional point that a 'somewhat comprehensive socialization of investment' would be needed to secure full employment, but he added that

beyond this there was no obvious case for a system of state socialism embracing most of the economy (see *Collected Writings* vol. VII, p. 378). Keynes's ideas were quickly absorbed into the main stream of economics and of policy making, undoubtedly helped by the experience of economic management and finance during the second world war. Active policies of 'demand management' to maintain full employment were adopted by most advanced countries after the war, though they were delayed in the United States and Germany until the 1960s.

Many countries set up councils of advisers and the like backed by strengthened statistical services to supply governments and the public with analyses of national income, production, employment and trade. Some governments went a stage further, creating institutions for ECONOMIC PLANNING or for the operation of INCOMES POLICIES. *Keynesian/Keynesianism* are expressions embracing both the theoretical ideas of the *General Theory* and, sometimes rather uncritically, the policy prescriptions which are believed to follow from them.

As economic adviser to the government, Keynes drafted the British proposals for the establishment of an International Clearing Union after the second world war. Members drawing on overdraft facilities would pay interest, but so also would creditors. This embodied Keynes's view, derived from experience of the Gold Standard, that when trade was unbalanced the whole burden of adjustment should not be placed on deficit countries, which might be forced into deflation and unemployment. The mechanisms of the International Monetary Fund created at Bretton Woods in 1944 followed more closely the United States proposals, which did not embody this symmetrical treatment of debtors and creditors. Even so, with true statesmanship, Keynes argued for the acceptance of this second best scheme, an important factor in its adoption. In the event, the new institutions facilitated the unparalleled growth of world production and trade which followed the war.

Until the late 1960s it was widely believed that Keynesianism had banished mass unemployment for ever. But inflation was growing, and the Bretton Woods system of fixed exchange rates crumbled, to be replaced by floating rates subject to violent and unpredictable swings. Mass unemployment reappeared. The simpler Keynesian prescriptions seemed no longer adequate. Whether, nevertheless, the solution of renewed unemployment might still be found among the ideas of Keynes remained to be seen.   GDNW

Reading

Buchanan, J.M. and Wagner, E.R.: *Democracy in Deficit: the political legacy of Lord Keynes*. New York: Academic Press, 1977.

Keynes, J.M.: *Collected Writings*. 29 vols. London: Macmillan, 1971–83.

Keynes, M. ed.: *Essays on John Maynard Keynes*. Cambridge: Cambridge University Press, 1975.

Lekachman, R.: *The Age of Keynes*. London: Allen Lane, 1967.

Thirlwall, A.P. ed.: *Keynes and Laissez-faire*. London: Macmillan, 1978.

Wattel, H. ed.: *The Policy Consequences of John Maynard Keynes*. London: Macmillan, 1986.

Worswick, G.D.N. and Trevithick, J. eds: *Keynes and the Modern World*. Cambridge: Cambridge University Press, 1983.

KGB   A body attached to the COUNCIL OF MINISTERS of the USSR which performs both intelligence and police functions. Founded in 1918 and known successively as the Cheka, GPU, OGPU, NKVD, NKGB, and MGB, the KGB (*Komitet gosudarstvennoi bezopasnosti* or Committee for State Security) exercised a variety of extraordinary powers during the STALIN era. Since the 1950s, however, its powers have been confined in principle to espionage, treason, terrorism, and other anti-state activities although it also controls the state borders and plays a prominent role in the regulation of domestic dissidence and in foreign intelligence operations.

See also SECRET POLICE.   SLW

Reading

Barron, J.: *The KGB Today*. London: Hodder & Stoughton, 1984.

Butler, W.E.: *Soviet Law*. London: Butterworth, 1983.

kibbutz   (Hebrew: commune; pl. *kibbutzim*) Communal villages in Israel, originating in the socialist Zionist ideology of settling the Land of Israel and creating a socio-economic collectivist infrastructure for a Jewish society in Palestine. The first kibbutz, Deganiah, was formed in 1909 in the Jordan Valley. Today there are about 300 kibbutzim in Israel, housing about 3 per cent of the overall population of the country. They are organized in a number of federations according to the nuances of their socialist-Zionist ideologies. Most kibbutzim are affiliated with the Israel Labour Party or the more left-wing Mapam (United Workers Party).

The General Assembly is the supreme authority of each kibbutz and meets at frequent intervals. It elects, on an annual basis, kibbutz officials such as secretary and treasurer, committees responsible for various aspects of kibbutz life (finance, education), and it also legislates the kibbutz by-laws. Jobs are allocated to individual members on the principle of rotation, though with increasing technological advance professionalization is becoming much more common. Each individual member or couple is allocated a housing unit; children are mostly raised in communal crèches and homes, spending only a few hours a day with their parents. Most meals are taken in communal dining halls. Kibbutz members do not receive wages but are allocated their provisions on an egalitarian basis from communal stores, with some extra cash for additional expenses. Kibbutz members sent to work outside the kibbutz receive a living allowance, and their salaries go directly to the kibbutz treasury. Kibbutz educational, cultural and recreational features are among the best in Israel. An average kibbutz has around 300–500 members. Originally mainly agricultural, most kibbutzim have recently branched out into industrial production as well, and some are involved with hi-tech industries. Kibbutz members are very prominent in the labour movement and trade unions, and their number in the Israeli Knesset and government has traditionally been above their proportion in the population. Kibbutz members are also prominent in elite formations of the Israeli army.

A modified form of co-operative village, the *moshav*, has evolved over the years alongside the kibbutz. In this the family unit is central, and each family owns its own house and plot of land; only marketing, credit institutions, and some of the machinery are jointly managed.

See also ZIONISM.   SA

Reading

Krausz, E. ed.: *The Sociology of the Kibbutz.* New Brunswick, NJ and London: Transaction Books, 1983.

Rosner, M.: *Democracy, Equality and Change: the kibbutz and social theory.* Darby, Penn.: Norwood, 1981.

Spiro, M.E.: *Kibbutz – Venture in Utopia.* New York: Schocken, 1963.

kremlinology   The name given to the art of deciphering Soviet politics from indirect and allusive sources. An understanding of what is happening in the USSR is widely believed to require the ability to read not only the lines themselves but often what lies between them as well. The conventions of Soviet politics inhibit the airing of political differences in public and prescribe the image of monolithic unity. Yet behind the conflictless facade there are at times severe and, on occasion, bloody power struggles. Sometimes the evidence breaks surface in a dramatic fashion as in the execution of police chief Beria and his associates in the early 1950s, the overthrow of Khrushchev in 1964 or the jockeying for position that accompanied the Brezhnev succession. More often the signs of conflict and political manoeuvrings are oblique. Changes in the manner of presentation and coverage of a particular leader's speeches in the party press or a sudden alteration in the protocol-governed seating arrangements on major public occasions have been shown to correlate with power shifts at the top. Policy disputes at all levels are habitually conducted in Aesopian terms or in an obscure, coded terminology whose purpose is to confine exchanges to the initiated. Soviet leaders often talk to their own people in similar terms. It has been remarked that when Pravda starts carrying articles on famine in Africa it is a sign to tighten one's belt for the coming Soviet grain harvest. The revelations of the scale of the Chernobyl nuclear power plant disaster in May 1986 were preceded by a sudden release of news of similar disasters in the West.

TPMcN

Reading

Conquest, R.: *Power and Policy in the USSR.* London: Macmillan, 1961.

Hoffmann, E.P.: Methodological problems of Kremlinology. In *Communist Studies and the Social Sciences,* ed. F.J. Fleron, Jr. Chicago, Ill.: Rand McNally, 1971.

Nove, A.: The uses and abuses of Kremlinology. In *Was Stalin Really Necessary?*, ed. A. Nove. London: Allen & Unwin, 1964.

Rush, M.: Esoteric communication in Soviet politics. *World Politics* (July 1959) 614–20.

Tatu, M.: *Power in the Kremlin: from Khrushchev to collective leadership.* London: Collins, 1969.

Tucker, R.C.: The conflict model. In *Problems of Communism* (November–December 1963) 59–61.

L

labour camp First established in 1918, supposedly for 're-education', the Soviet system of corrective labour camps, generally known as the 'gulag', was expanded in the 1930s under STALIN into a vast network of slave labour settlements in the remote and inhospitable areas of the USSR. It is believed that at their peak, after the second world war, the gulag may have held as many as twenty million forced labourers spread over more than two hundred camps. Ordinary criminals and 'enemies of the people' were herded together in abominable conditions that produced phenomenally high mortality rates. Works such as Solzhenitsyn's *Gulag Archipelago* and *One Day in the Life of Ivan Denisovich*, and Marchenko's *My Testimony* provide insight into the inhuman conditions inflicted upon inmates.

The slave labour system played an important role in the development of the early Soviet economy and was responsible for numerous major projects (the Amur railway, the White Sea Canal, Karaganda mining, the towns of Molotovsk and Magadan, countless airfields, roads and industrial plants). It is recorded that in 1941 the camps were responsible for as much as 14 per cent of the building work, 12.5 per cent of the timber, 40.5 per cent of gold chromium production and 75 per cent of gold production for the entire Soviet Union. After Stalin's death there was for the first time some public admission of the existence of the slave labour camps. Millions were amnestied in the years 1954–6. Though the numbers incarcerated nowadays are much smaller than in Stalin's time, testimony suggests that the treatment of inmates has little improved. In China, also, there is a system of forced labour known as Lao Jiao (education through labour) and Lao Dong Gai Zao (reform through manual labour). Official statistics are not published, but unofficial estimates claim that there are 16 million forced labourers, some 3 per cent of the population.

In Nazi Germany, the CONCENTRATION CAMPS became in effect labour camps in the second world war, and by September 1944, nearly 10 million prisoners of war and foreign civilians were engaged in forced labour.

TPMcN

Reading

Bunyan, J.: *The Origins of Forced Labour in the Soviet State: documents and materials*. Baltimore, Md.: Johns Hopkins University Press, 1967.

Conquest, R. : *Kolyma: the Artic Death Camps*. London: Macmillan, 1978.

Dallin, D. and Nicolaevsky, B.: *Forced Labour in the Soviet Union*. London: Hollis & Carter, 1948.

labour court An institution with the function of adjudicating upon issues relating to employment or issues arising in the application of the labour laws of a state. Labour courts are not confined to any particular type of political regime but they reflect their political regime more closely than do courts in general. Indeed it is the political nature of their function that is usually the reason for having a specialized labour court to discharge that function. Their jurisdiction will normally be concerned with some combination of the following matters: disputes between employers and individual workers, for example about discipline or dismissal; disputes arising out of collective

314

agreements between employers and trade unions; the conduct of, and limits placed upon, industrial conflict and industrial action; the conduct and government of trade unions. Different systems may have labour courts with different styles of adjudication, important variations being between: formal and informal procedure; tribunal composed entirely of independent judges, or partly of representatives of employers and workers (tripartite), or wholly thereof (bipartite); lay or professional advocacy. The powers of labour courts will also vary greatly and may include: the provision of conciliation, mediation or arbitration between the parties to labour disputes; adjudication upon claims for civil legal sanctions in labour disputes; the execution of state powers or the imposition of state sanctions in relation to labour disputes. They may be solely concerned with rights, or also with resolving disputes between competing interests. Their role is often controversial. MRF

Reading

Aaron, B.: *Labor Courts and Grievance Settlement in Western Europe*. Berkeley, Los Angeles and London: University of California Press, 1971.

labour movement An imprecise term which can be used both descriptively and normatively to characterize a variety of organizations of wage earners in industrializing and industrialized societies. It may be taken as synonymous with trade unionism, as in the United States in the twentieth century; or, as in Europe, it may be used as a collective reference to the variety of organizations of wage earners within a given society – co-operatives, mutualist societies, political parties claiming a special relationship with the working classes, and TRADE UNIONS. It is most frequently used to describe the relationship between political parties of the left and trade unions. The term movement is used to describe both collective actions by labour organizations to advance their own specific interests and the idea of a commitment to a broad range of issues of interest to all citizens. When used in this sense the labour movement can be regarded as a particular type of SOCIAL MOVEMENT.

The most frequently utilized theory of labour movements has been that based upon MARXISM which seeks to explain their growth in terms of changes in the technology of production and the system of property relations which create an irreconcilable antagonism between capital and labour. A necessary relationship is posited between the working class and SOCIALISM, and between labour movements, properly conscious of their real interests, and socialism. The more sophisticated versions of this theory emphasize the fact that the development of labour movements is marked by inherent contradictions. Capitalist wage labour is seen as generating grievances and conflicts to which workers respond by creating protective organizations which by their involvement in grievance regulation become institutions conducive to the stabilization of the capitalist system. But whatever the emphasis on such contradictory developments there remains a core assumption that the basic conflict in modern societies is derived from the capitalist mode of production and that a necessary relationship exists, in the last instance, between the working class and its organizations and socialism.

A priori assumptions also characterize the most influential non-Marxist general theory of labour movements. In *A Theory of the Labour Movement* (1928) Selig Perlman claimed to identify a universal scarcity consciousness among workers based upon a limited and defensive psychology which led them to try to create, through negotiations with employers, collective regulations governing the conditions and terms of work. Socialism was seen not as a necessary feature of labour movements but as a doctrine introduced by intellectuals for their own purposes. Much subsequent Anglo-American work on labour movements has adopted this frame of reference.

Both general theories are essentially ahistorical in their assumption that labour movements have a particular essence and 'normal' path of development. Additionally, both theories assume the centrality of workplace relations in shaping working-class consciousness and tend to treat as synonymous organized labour and the working class. No labour movement however has ever been able to mobilize all wage earners within its ranks, nor has the culture of labour movements ever been identical with that of the working classes. While the productive order has generated basic cleavages within industrial societies so also have the forces of ethnicity, gender, language, race and religion. Labour movements in Europe have been divided along confessional and political lines while ethnicity and race have divided the American labour movement.

Outside Europe the importance of particular configurations of cultural, economic, political and historical experiences in shaping the attitudes, behaviour and structure of labour movements is even more marked. In the new states of Africa labour movements emerged as much in response to colonial rule as in conflicts over working conditions, hence many observers have seen them primarily as political organizations. Since independence there has been a marked tendency for governments to attempt to subordinate labour movements and to assign to them a role in preserving industrial peace and explaining development programmes; this has certain similarities to the place of trade unions within the communist countries. Although organized labour accounts for only a small proportion of the total population, the strategic importance of the industries within which it is located has led the governments of new states to play an active role in shaping the structure and actions of its organizations. Similar patterns of government intervention have been a feature of the development of labour movements in the new states of Asia and in the countries of Latin America, though the efficacy of the intervention has varied.

While all labour movements exhibit certain structural similarities, historicist theories of their development have been unable to explain the differences in form, structure and behaviour which are apparent not only between different societies but within the same society at different periods. Such variations may be historical facts susceptible only to historical explanations.

See also SOCIALIST AND SOCIAL DEMOCRATIC PARTIES.   JSR

Reading

Bean, R.: *Comparative Industrial Relations: an introduction to cross-national perspectives*. London: Croom Helm, 1985.

Bergquist, C. ed.: *Labor in Latin America: comparative essays on Chile, Argentina, Venezuela and Colombia*. Stanford, Calif: Stanford University Press, 1987.

Coleman, J.C. and Rosberg, C.G. Jr: *Political Parties and National Integration in Tropical Africa*, ch. 9. Berkeley: University of California Press, 1964.

Currie, R.: *Industrial Politics*. Oxford: Oxford University Press, 1979.

Dunlop, J.T. and Galenson, W. eds: *Labour in the Twentieth Century*. New York: Academic Press, 1978.

Kassalow, E.M. and Damachi, U.G.: *The Role of Trade Unions in Developing Societies*. Geneva: International Institute for Labour Studies, 1978.

Kendall, W.: *The Labour Movement in Europe*. London: Allen Lane, 1975.

Kerr, C., Dunlop, J.T., Harbison, F.H., and Myers, C.A.: *Industrialism and Industrial Man*. London: Heinemann, 1962.

Perlman, M.: *Labour Union Theories in America: background and development*. Evanston, Ill.: Harper & Row, 1958.

Perlman, S.: *A Theory of the Labour Movement*. New York: Harper & Row, 1928.

Sandbrook, R. and Cohen, R.: *The Development of an African Working Class: studies in class formation and action*. London: Longman, 1975.

language and politics   Language is related to politics in several ways: in the formation of states and political boundaries, as a source of divisions in plurilingual or multilingual societies, or as a series of domains for policy choices. The occasional use of the phrase in connection with the linguistic analysis of political discourse will not be considered here.

In historical perspective the relation between language and political boundaries is complex and reciprocal. In Europe the frontier of the Romance languages reflects roughly the limits of Roman imperial power. On the other hand the late medieval national monarchies tended to develop the dialects spoken at their centres into national languages: there is some validity to the linguists' quip that a language is a dialect with an army behind it. Dynastic regimes and empires could live comfortably with linguistic pluralism, but in the early nineteenth century Romantic nationalism gave language an ideological dimension that contributed strongly to patterns of state formation in the nineteenth and twentieth centuries. Language may be either a help or an obstacle to state formation. After 1918 it provided the principal rationale for the constitution or reconstitution of several European polities (Poland, Hungary, Finland, Czechoslovakia, the Baltic states) though some of these retained significant linguistic minorities of their own. In the dismantling of colonialism and the proliferation of new states after 1945 language often proved a divisive factor, the selection of an official language or languages becoming in many cases a major political issue. Since about 1960, a sharpened ethnic consciousness in western societies has led to the revival or enhancement of linguistic claims among several Western European minorities (for example in the Celtic fringe) and among the supposedly assimilating immigrant communities of North America. Ethnic and ethno-regional movements however do not invariably emphasize *language*: in Scottish nationalism, for example, the linguistic component is marginal. In this sense linguistically divided societies may be seen as a sub-category of a larger group of PLURAL SOCIETIES characterized by divisions of language, race, religion, or other criteria of ethnic or cultural particularism.

Analytically, it is convenient to divide contemporary plurilingual states into three categories: first, those with a dominant language and one or more linguistic minorities; second, those with two or a few groups in relative balance; third, those with highly diversified language patterns. In the first type the predominant policy concern is usually with the fair treatment of minorities, and here fairness must be related to both dominant-group attitudes and minority aspirations (see MINORITIES, PROTECTION OF). In the second type it may be the preservation of intergroup equilibrium and political stability. In the third type a central problem is effective communication through some common language, whether this be a regional lingua franca, an

international language, or a modified version of an indigenous language. Some literature on third world development, influenced by unilingual western models, has seen linguistic pluralism as an obstacle that must be overcome before economic development can succeed.

Some modern writers have seen conflict as unavoidable in any racially or linguistically divided society, while others emphasize potential strategies of accommodation. The issue has earlier precedents. John Stuart Mill, in his essay on *Representative Government* (1861), considered that in multinational and multilingual states 'the united public opinion, necessary to the working of representative government, cannot exist'; whereas Lord Acton's essay on *Nationality* (1862) argued to the contrary that 'a State which is incompetent to satisfy different races condemns itself' and lacks the moral basis for self-government. In developed societies having parliamentary systems and free elections, linguistic divisions are likely to be one of the continuing major sources of societal cleavage, along with divisions of race, religion, or social class. Whether the potential for language conflict remains latent or becomes open appears to depend on a variety of factors, including most obviously: the relative economic status (both perceived and actual) of the groups in question, the social status of the linguistic groups and of their respective languages, the level of modernization and urbanization, relative numbers, geographic concentration or dispersion of languages, the degree of political accommodation (whether through power sharing at the centre or through decentralization), the situation of cultural kin groups in neighbouring states, any external support for irredentism, and the general international milieu (for its demonstration effect). In institutional terms linguistic divisions are more often mediated *within* political parties than *between* parties organized on linguistic lines, though the influence of fringe parties upon language-related issues should not be underestimated. In western parliamentary systems the party structure usually reflects social divisions that antedate linguistic conflict. Stable linguistic parties, such as the Swedish People's Party in Finland, are relatively scarce, and the formal splitting of all the traditional parties in Belgium after 1968 is a highly unusual example of the influence of languages on party structure.

In bilingual and multilingual political systems language usage and language rights become a subject for important policy choices. Such decisions may be highly structured through legislation or regulations, or else left largely to custom or judicial decision. They may be centralized or else decentralized through some form of federalism, devolution, or special status. Subordinate and superordinate groups often differ over the appropriate form and degree of regulation. The basis for regulation may vary according to the geographical distribution of language: the *territorial principle* prescribes language usage for a given territory or region, while the *personality principle* attaches language rights or obligations to legal and natural persons within a prescribed political unit. In practice many contemporary language regimes combine elements of both principles. Where the territorial principle prevails, questions of regional economic development tend to assume added salience.

In this century the domains of language usage subject to conflict and to political or constitutional regulation have been increasing. The language of education, crucially important for intergenerational language maintenance or language shift, became contentious with the spread of universal public education. In communications, the rise of electronic media has transferred important language decisions from the private to the public regulated sector. In the administration of justice, long a sensitive area, a heightened emphasis upon linguistic fairness in courts and tribunals has emerged as a matter of human rights. More generally the expansion of the public sector, and of the tertiary sector of the work force as a whole, has made language competence – and indirectly mother tongue – an important criterion for access to employment. In plurilingual systems the language of work in the public sector is often a major issue, and some jurisdictions (for example Ticino, Flanders, Quebec) have also regulated various aspects of language usage in the private sector. Even in nominally unilingual states or regions the requirements of language standardization, modernization, or alphabetization may require important or difficult policy decisions concerning language development (termed 'corpus planning'), followed by programmes of implementation. Such policies may also lead to international treaties or agreements on language standardization across political borders (Netherlands–Belgium, Indonesia–Malaysia).

See also ETHNIC NATIONALISM; ETHNIC PARTIES; ETHNICITY. KDMcR

Reading

Allardt, E.: *Implications of the Ethnic Revival in Modern Industrialized Society: a comparative study of the linguistic minorities in Western Europe*. Helsinki: Societas Scientiarum Fennica, 1979.

Beer, W.R. and Jacob, J.E. eds: *Language Policy and National Unity*. Totowa, NJ: Rowman & Littlefield 1985.

Esman, M.J. ed.: *Ethnic Conflict in the Western World*. Ithaca, NY: Cornell University Press, 1977.

Laponce, J.A.: *Langue et territoire*. Quebec: Les Presses de l'Université Laval, 1984.

LePage, R.B.: *The National Language Question: linguistic problems of newly independent states*. London and New York: Oxford University Press, 1964.

McRae, K.D.: *Conflict and Compromise in Multilingual Societies*, Vol. I: *Switzerland*, Vol. II: *Belgium*. Waterloo, Ont.: Wilfrid Laurier University Press, 1983, 1986.

O'Barr, W.M. and O'Barr, J.F. eds: *Language and Politics*. The Hague and Paris: Mouton, 1976.

Rabushka, A. and Shepsle, K.A.: *Politics in Plural Societies: a theory of democratic instability*. Columbus, Ohio: Merrill, 1972.

Savard, J.-G. et al.: *Linguistic Minorities and Interventions: towards a typology*. Quebec: Les Presses de l'Université Laval, 1978.

—— and Vigneault, R. eds: *Multilingual Political Systems: problems and solutions*. Quebec: Les Presses de l'Université Laval, 1975.

Stephens, M.: *Linguistic Minorities in Western Europe*. Llandysul, Dyfed: Gomer, 1976.

Laski, Harold Joseph (1893–1950)

One of the most prominent and prolific political thinkers in Britain in the inter-war years. Most of Laski's working life, during which he acquired a legendary reputation as a teacher, was spent at the London School of Economics where he became a lecturer in 1920 and Professor of Political Science in 1926, a post he held until his death. A life-long member of the Labour Party, he served on its National Executive Committee from 1937 to 1949. He was Chairman of the Labour Party in 1945 and became the central figure in the 'Red Scare' which was one of the features of the general election of that year.

There were two distinct phases in Laski's approach to politics. From the first world war until the early 1930s he was mainly concerned with using ideas derived from Liberalism to construct a programme of economic, social and political reform, designed to produce a just and 'pluralist' society with the state as its servant not its master. The main work which embodied Laski's ideas in this phase was *A Grammar of Politics* published in 1925 and for many years a widely used textbook in political theory.

With the Great Depression, the collapse of the second Labour government in Britain in 1931, and the triumph of Nazism in Germany, Laski's thought came to be deeply influenced by MARXISM. Books such as *Democracy in Crisis* (1933), *The State in Theory and Practice* (1935), and *Parliamentary Government in England* (1938), as well as many other of his books, pamphlets and articles have as their main themes the class nature of the state, the degree to which capitalism in crisis is incompatible with democratic forms, and the extreme difficulty this must present for a peaceful transition to socialism, of which Laski remained a fervent advocate. During this period he also used historical materialism in the interpretation of the evolution of political doctrines: a notable example of this endeavour was *The Rise of European Liberalism* (1936).

In the main, Laski's importance as a political thinker lies in the fact that he was a pioneer in the exploration of many crucial questions about the nature and limitations of capitalist democracy at a time when such questions were largely ignored by 'mainstream' political theorists.

See also PLURALISM.   RM

Reading

Deane, H.A.: *The Political Ideas of Harold J. Laski* New York: Columbia University Press, 1955.

Eastwood, G.: *Harold Laski*. London and Oxford: Mowbray, 1977.

Laski, H.J.: *A Grammar of Politics*. London: Allen & Unwin, 1925.

———: *The State in Theory and Practice*. London: Allen & Unwin, 1935.

———: *The Rise of European Liberalism*. London: Allen & Unwin, 1938.

Martin, K.: *Harold Laski: a biographical memoir*. London: Gollancz, 1953.

law A form of normative order, in the prescriptive rather than descriptive sense. Law is 'normative' in that it sets standards for human conduct and its critical judgement; these standards include customs and legislatively or judicially determined rules of conduct and general principles expressive of the overall sense or point of the other standards. It is an 'order' in the sense both that it has some overall ordered coherence in the standards it sets and that it actually succeeds to some extent in ordering the conduct and affairs of the members of a relevant community. To this needs to be added that such an order has to be conceived as having some objective existence and binding quality external to the momentary will of any particular subject of the system. This is sometimes taken to mean that the law or the legal system necessarily has to be supported by coercive measures in the way of sanctions and has to set up, or try to set up, a monopoly on the use of force in the relevant community.

The supposition that coercion or its monopolization is essential to the very nature of 'law' is evidently false when such phenomena as church law (canon law) or the laws of golf or cricket are brought into consideration, to say nothing of international law or the laws of primitive communities or of 'moral law'. Here we have a classic case of species/genus confusion. Coerciveness is not a mark of law as such, but rather of law as the law of the STATE. States are *inter alia* coercive associations, hence the laws that are constitutive of states are coercive, but that is because of the kind of laws they are, not because of what law is. In politics, it is important to keep this in mind, even though for the purposes of politics it is the law of states that is of primary concern (though the law between states cannot be ignored). This article is henceforth concerned primarily with state law.

Following H. L. A. Hart, we may differentiate a primary and a secondary level of law. The primary level is concerned with the regulation of what persons must and must not do; it comprises a set of requirements for acceptable interpersonal conduct. The secondary level establishes institutions in various ways concerned with regulation at the primary level. For example, it may authorize some persons acting as judges to adjudicate on accusations or disputes arising out of alleged breaches of primary requirements, and to give orders which the parties or other persons specially empowered must or may implement to conclude the dispute; or it may enable individuals or groups to add to or vary primary requirements or alter the rules which constitute and regulate adjudicative enforcement or even legislative agencies. A primary level is common to all forms of law, but what is specific to state law is the special form of the institutions it establishes at the secondary level for the enactment and enforcement of law, for judicial determination of its meaning and effect both in individual cases and in general terms, and increasingly for the implementation of policies and for the realization of goods (e.g. general health and welfare, education, national defence) as determined by superior governmental authorities.

The importance of such institutions and their internal articulation, regulation and mutual interconnection and interaction for such legal–political doctrines as those of 'SEPARATION OF POWERS' or 'the RULE OF LAW' is clear. In fact it is the form of the law, and in particular the structure of its secondary level, that is constitutive of the various organs of government possessed by modern societies, and these agencies, envisaged as a coherent and interlocking group with single corporate being and set of purposes, are constitutive of the state.

A distinction of considerable importance, between public and private law, can therefore be drawn in legal thought. Public law is that body of law at the secondary level that is concerned with the establishment and legal powers (also limits on powers) of governmental organs, and also with the duties of these organs both to individuals (above all in respect of their fundamental rights) and to the political community at large. One essential duty of the latter sort is that of acknowledging and giving effect to all valid laws of the community, validity being grounded on the satisfaction of some commonly acknowledged criterion or criteria. (Such criteria are the substance of what Hart calls a 'rule of recognition'.) So constitutional and administrative law belong classically to the field of public law, as also do taxation and welfare law, defining as these do duties towards and rights against the state. Criminal law is also frequently reckoned to be public: the parties to all criminal causes being the state and the alleged wrongdoer, and the victim (if any) of the offence being, at this stage, a witness or even a spectator rather than a party.

The private law, by contrast, is that to which private citizens are the direct parties, state agencies being no more than bystanders (not necessarily wholly disinterested ones) and upholders of pre-determined rights of persons. Private law concerns persons, their status in law and their family relationships, the law of property and of succession to or other transfer of or exercise of property rights, and obligations whether created by contracts or other voluntary acts or arising from some form of wrongdoing. The sphere of private law relationships may be envisaged as that of civil society to which the state stands in the relation of a guarantor and upholder of rights and enforcer of duties.

It is a highly contentious question whether the existence and essence of law can be captured simply by description of positively established and largely efficacious rules and institutions such as those mentioned above, or whether it is necessary, as proponents of 'natural law' propound, to add some ascription of moral considerations. Conversely, where evil is done in the name of law, it is a question whether that name is misused as it is certainly abused.

See also ADMINISTRATIVE LAW; CONSTITUTIONAL LAW.   NMacC

Reading

Finnis, J.M.: *Natural Law and Natural Rights*. Oxford: Oxford University Press, 1980.

Hart, H.L.A.: *The Concept of Law* Oxford: Oxford University Press, 1961.

MacCormick, N. and Weinberger, O.: *An Institutional Theory of Law*. Dordrecht: Reidel, 1986.

Paton, G.W. and Derham, D.P.: *A Textbook of Jurisprudence*. 4th edn. Oxford: Oxford University Press, 1972.

leadership The power of one or a few individuals to induce a group to adopt a particular line of policy. Leadership has always fascinated the general public as well as observers of political life because of the element of 'miracle' which seems embedded in the phenomenon. It appears to belong to the realm of the divine, of the sacred, as it creates a bond between rulers and ruled which defies ordinary explanations. Not surprisingly, therefore, leadership has proved difficult to measure and to assess; works on the subject have tended to be descriptions of the deeds of heroes rather than careful analyses of the subject.

Part of the difficulty comes from the fact that the qualities required of a leader are hard to define. Social psychologists and psychologists, who more than other academics have attempted to analyse the phenomenon and who have set up experiments designed to detect the components of leadership, have found it difficult to agree as to which personality characteristics are most important. Many 'traits' are felt to be essential, from energy to intelligence and from the ability to communicate to the capacity to take decisions rapidly and firmly. The results so far do not provide a clear outline of what is or is not required, any more than the biographies of 'illustrious' men have made it possible to determine what exactly were the qualities of Alexander or Caesar, Napoleon or Churchill.

One reason why the personal qualities required of a leader may be diverse is because

leadership cannot be divorced from the environment within which it occurs. The role of this environment is manifest in several ways. To begin with the personal qualities of leaders are personal only in the sense that these leaders happen to possess them: they may also be viewed as being in part the product of the environment, from the family in which the leaders grew up to the nation to which they belong. But there are two other essential ways in which leadership is related to and indeed depends on the environment. First, leadership is, usually at least, clearly connected to the holding of a particular position: a prime minister may exercise his or her leadership more or less successfully; in the first instance, however, the fact of being prime minister provides opportunities which others do not have. The holder of such a post is expected to be a leader; other politicians and the population as a whole look to the head of the government for guidance. What needs explanation is more why some prime ministers or presidents do not succeed in becoming 'real' leaders, rather than why they succeed in doing so. Indeed, more generally, the institutional framework truly fashions the characteristics of leadership in that it provides opportunities to exercise power: the British prime minister, for example, has an easier task in this respect than the Italian prime minister, who heads a coalition government whose many components are more likely to rebel than to follow.

There is, however, a second and even more fundamental way in which the environment appears to condition or even mould leadership: the circumstances are not equally advantageous to all those who hold top positions. Of course, a 'real' leader is the one who can seize the opportunities and exploit them to the full; but the opportunities may be rare. Some leaders may benefit from the disunion of their enemies at home and abroad; others may benefit from the fact that external circumstances are favourable. Indeed, it is in the context of foreign affairs that the characteristics of leadership have tended to emerge most strongly, in part because foreign affairs have always been more glamorous than internal policy-making and in part because, the stakes being much higher, up to and including the destruction of the country, the successes can be immense. MACHIAVELLI knew this well: most of his recommendations to the Prince were connected to the aim of establishing leadership through prestigious victories against foreign enemies. Closer to our own day, one wonders how Winston Churchill would have fared – indeed whether he would still play a significant part in the history books, despite having been minister several times – had he not 'met with destiny' in 1940; the same might be said of Charles de Gaulle, as a result of the brutal French defeat of the same year.

Not unnaturally, psychologists and others have come increasingly to note that the qualities required of leaders cannot be defined in the abstract; they must, on the contrary, be related to the circumstances in which the leader emerges. Leaders and their environment are so closely related that the question of the assessment of their role becomes extremely difficult to undertake. Here too, biographies have described the achievements of large numbers of great rulers but are of little help in answering the question: how have leaders changed the course of history? The question has become the subject of a major debate between those who emphasize 'heroes' and those who interpret the past on the basis of broad economic and social trends in which leaders are mere symbols.

So far there has been no definite answer to the question and none is likely to be given in the near future. Attempts to compare different situations and assess how much of the variation could be attributed to leaders have occasionally been made. Even if these efforts are not wholly convincing they make the case of those who suggest that leaders merely reflect their environment more difficult to sustain: it goes against common sense; it goes against the way people have always behaved, not least those who have professed that the environment was all powerful. It is the political regimes that are most closely built on this philosophy, the communist systems, that produce the politicians who place most emphasis on leadership as though the socio-economic forces needed LENIN, MAO, Tito, and others to materialize themselves in the reality of political life.

It seems reasonable to continue to assume that leaders play a major part in determining political actions though it is also reasonable to believe that this part is larger in some circumstances than in others and especially large at times of crisis or when a new country is created. This is probably why the strongest form of leadership, that which WEBER described as 'charismatic', often prevailed during the post second-world-war period, when dozens of states became independent and many others underwent revolutions.   JFPB

Reading

Blondel, J.: *World Leaders*. London and Los Angeles: Sage, 1980.

Burns, J. McG.: *Leadership*. New York: Harper & Row, 1978.

Hook, S.: *The Hero in History*. Boston, Mass.: Beacon, 1955.

Kellermann, B. ed.: *Leadership*. Englewood Cliffs, NJ: Prentice-Hall, 1984.

Machiavelli, N.: *The Prince*.

Neustadt, R.E.: *Presidential Power: the politics of leadership from FDR to Carter*. New York: Wiley, 1980.

Paige, G.D. ed.: *Political Leadership*. New York: Free Press, 1972.

Tucker, R.C.: *Politics as Leadership*. Columbia: University of Missouri Press, 1981.

Verba, S.: *Small Groups and Political Behaviour: a study of leadership*. Princeton, NJ: Princeton University Press, 1961.

Weber, M.: *On Charisma and Institution-Building*. Chicago, Ill.: University of Chicago Press, 1968.

leadership selection Some writers use 'leadership selection' as synonymous with 'elite recruitment' – the processes by which some people became members of a society's most honoured and powerful groups. Others use it more narrowly to mean the processes by which social and political organizations choose those who take the lead and guide other members. Others again use it still more narrowly to denote the processes by which a political party chooses a single officer (or, rarely, a committee) to exercise paramount but responsible authority over its national organizations inside and outside the government. That is the meaning discussed here.

In a few instances POLITICAL PARTIES have no formal procedures for choosing their leaders. The leaders of the hegemonic parties in many third world and communist countries, for example, are still chosen by analogous procedures. Until 1964 the leaders of the British Conservative party 'emerged' from a quasi-consensual process of revelation understood by few insiders and fewer outsiders. In 1964 the Conservatives adopted formal rules for the selection of their leader by secret votes of Conservative MPs. Some other democratic parties choose their leaders similarly, but the most common method is selection by a special committee, delegate convention, or ELECTORAL COLLEGE chosen for the purpose by the party's rank-and-file members and/or affiliated interest groups. In most instances the party leader can be deposed and replaced by the same procedures, but by far the most frequent occasion for changing the leader is when the incumbent dies, voluntarily resigns, or is forced to resign and a replacement is chosen.

The United States is unique in that for most of the time only one of the two major parties has a single national leader. The president is always the recognized leader of his party, but the other party has no single generally acknowledged leader from the day it loses the presidential election to the day, nearly four years later, when it selects its next presidential candidate.　　　　　　　　AR

Reading

King, A.: How not to select presidential candidates: a view from Europe. In *The American Elections of 1980*, ch. 9.2, ed. A. Ranney. Washington, DC: American Enterprise Institute, 1981.

McKenzie, R.T.: *British Political Parties*, chs 2 and 6. New York: Praeger, 1966; London: Heinemann, 1955.

Matthew, D.R. and Keech, W.R.: *The Party's Choice*. Washington, DC: The Brookings Institution, 1976.

league An imprecise term for a loose union such as that between sovereigns for a campaign. It was first used in connection with a military alliance made in 1167 between cities in Lombardy, and was later favoured by the papal states. In France the term was used for a sixteenth-century conspiracy of Catholic nobles. It was assimilated to Bund in German because of a false derivation from *ligare*, to glue or tie together. In French, the old Swiss Confederacy was called *les ligues suisses*, and Graubünden *les ligues grises*. In English the word retains chivalric, archaic overtones, and is used by campaigning lobbies, for example the Anti-Corn Law League. In French League of Nations is rendered *société*.

See also CONFEDERATION.　　　　　CJH

League of Nations International organization created after the first world war; the Covenant establishing it was part of the Treaty of Versailles. The aims of the League were 'to promote international co-operation and to achieve international peace and security'. The original members were allied states signatory to the Treaty of Versailles and neutral states invited to accede; it was open to others to apply for membership. However, the League never achieved universal membership. In particular, the refusal of the United States to join harmed the prestige and effectiveness of the League.

The main organs of the League were the Council, the Assembly and the Secretariat. Autonomous but closely connected to the League were the Permanent Court of International Justice and the International Labour Organization; the League also established subsidiary bodies to promote co-operation on economic and social matters. The central Articles of the Covenant provided for the pacific settlement of disputes, reduction of armaments, the guarantee of territorial integrity and political independence against external aggression, and the imposition of sanctions against states unlawfully resorting to war. The Covenant has been criticized for the vagueness of its provisions, the unanimity rule governing Council decisions, and the decentralized nature of decision making on the imposition of sanctions. But the failure of the League was the result not of these weaknesses but of the unwillingness of its member states to fulfil their obligations under the Covenant. The League proved unable to act effectively against the aggression of Japan, Italy and Germany in the 1930s. It was inactive during the second world war and was replaced in 1946 by the UNITED NATIONS.   CDG

Reading

Walters, F.P.: *A History of the League of Nations*. London, New York and Toronto: Oxford University Press, 1952.

left and right   Each of these terms denotes one or the other of two contradictory sets of political attitudes into which, it is claimed, all political viewpoints can be divided. The terms have often been emotionally loaded and neither is scientifically precise: nor, taken together, do they exhaust the range of political alternatives as expressed in the programmes of political parties or regimes.

The terms originally defined the stance taken for or against the political principles of the French Revolution of 1789. When Europe began to industrialize in the latter half of the nineteenth century they indicated the stance taken for or against the interests of labour or of private capital.

The terms originated in a meeting of the revolutionary National Assembly in Paris in 1789 in which the more revolutionary members sat on the left of the speaker's rostrum and the less revolutionary on the right. After the restoration of the French monarchy in 1815 'left' meant for the Revolution and 'right' against it: the Left believed that sovereignty resided in the people and favoured a republican and anti-clerical policy, while the Right believed in 'Throne and Altar', i.e. an authoritarian and monarchical regime buttressed by, and upholding the values of the church.

The industrial revolution added a new sense to the original one, identifying 'left' with a favourable attitude towards the interests of the working classes and 'right' with a favourable one towards proprietors and capitalists. In consequence there are not two sets of attitudes but four.

(1) *The political left.* This usually embraces a belief in the progressive perfectibility of men and women and the possibility of making the individual and society better by political agency; a favourable attitude towards change and innovation; a commitment to maximizing civil and moral liberty, to equality in political matters and hence to the insistence that sovereignty resides in the people; a commitment to fraternity, and hence, to internationalism. The political left is associated with an IDEOLOGY which affirms the superiority of reason and science over tradition and religious dogma; and, through this, a belief in the evolutionary betterment and progress of humanity as a whole.

(2) *The political right* tends to be sceptical as to whether human nature can be improved by political agency, is attached to the prevailing social, political and moral order, tends to the rejection of popular sovereignty, sees certain virtues in social and economic inequalities, and tends to be nationalistic in its approach. Its ideology often appeals to non-rational beliefs and sentiments, including religious ones, as well as to reason, and it affirms the traditional morality of the family.

(3) *The economic left* pursues the interests of the industrial worker and landless peasant and supports the intervention of the state in the market-mechanism, along with fiscal and social-security benefits to the disadvantaged.

(4) *The economic right* believes in freedom of choice in the economic sphere, and favours a free-market economy with the minimum of state intervention. It prefers voluntary self-help and personal insurance schemes to state organized social-security systems wherever that is possible.

Where (1) and (3) combine, *political left* and *economic left*, the outcome is a labour, socialist or communist party or regime. Where (1) and (4) combine, *political left* and *economic right*, the outcome is a party such as the French Radicals (of whom it has been said that their heart was on the left but their wallet on the right), the German Free Democratic party, or the Belgian, Dutch and Italian Liberal parties. These parties combine a strong attachment to civil liberties with policies favouring free enterprise. The combination of (2) and (4), *political right* and *economic right*, generates conservative parties ranging from constitutional ones such as the British Conservative Party to the highly authoritarian forms found in some military dictatorships. The (2) and (3) combination of *political right* and *economic left* yields a radicalism of the right which embraces reformist military regimes such as that of Juan Perón which ruled Argentina from 1946 to 1955 and, more markedly, the fascist or 'National Socialist' regimes of inter-war Italy and Germany.

Even this fourfold classification, however, is imperfect. The Soviet Union, for example, combines (1) and (3), but its trade unions are not independent nor are its elections free. The classification of political positions as left or right cuts across the more important distinction between liberal DEMOCRACIES and AUTHORITARIAN or TOTALITARIAN regimes. Democratic socialism has more in common with constitutional conservatism than either has with communism or fascism.

Even if the classification is restricted to liberal democratic regimes, however, it is still inadequate. Christian Democratic parties (see CHRISTIAN DEMOCRACY), for example, can and do adopt policies of the (2) + (3) type, but equally, those of the (2) + (4) type, and some, such as the Italian Christian Democratic Party, combine both tendencies in their ranks. LIBERAL PARTIES claim to find illiberal tendencies both on the left and on the right, and often resist classifications in left/right terms. In general, centrist parties as well as parties of the right are less willing to accept a position on a typological map of political allegiances than parties of the left. Moreover, some political scientists would argue that the left/right classification is of less use in an advanced industrial society when new issues come to supersede the conflict between capital and labour. Nevertheless, the classification remains a useful shorthand guide to alternative clusters of political attitudes.   SEF

Reading

Bell, D.: *The Radical Right*. New York: Doubleday, 1963.

Brittan, S.: *Left or Right: the bogus dilemma*. London: Secker & Warburg, 1968.

Caute, D.: *The Left in Europe*. London: Weidenfeld & Nicolson, 1966.

Laponce, J.A.: *Left and Right: the topography of political perceptions*. Toronto: University of Toronto Press, 1981.

Lipset, S.M.: *Political Man: the social basis of politics*. London: Heinemann, 1959; New York: Doubleday, 1960.

Rémond, R.: *The Right Wing in France from 1815 to de Gaulle*. Philadelphia: University of Pennsylvania Press, 1969.

Rogger, H. and Weber, E. eds: *The European Right*. London: Weidenfeld & Nicolson, 1965.

Smith, D.: *Left and Right in Twentieth Century Europe*. London: Longman, 1970.

legislative committees The functions and activities of LEGISLATURES include considering and making laws, scrutinizing administration, and representing and informing people. Committees exist in legislatures to help fulfil all these functions and can be defined as specialized, often permanent, organizations to which responsibilities are devolved. There are many types of committees in legislatures, with very different duties and special concerns and jurisdiction. The major ones are standing, select, special, joint, investigating and conference committees, all established by the legislature. In most instances they provide an intermediary level of decision making between the individual legislator and the legislature, allowing an opportunity for legislators to become more specialist in knowledge about, and more influential on specific areas of policy or proposed legislation.

Committees are often the organizations through which legislators consider the complex details of taxing and spending policies, reflecting the important role of the legislature with respect to the financing of governmental activities. Other specialist areas of policy where committees can be useful include foreign affairs or defence. The manner in which these committees make decisions, and their significance, depends upon the terms of reference set out by the parent legislature. It is difficult to generalize about legislative committee behaviour, because there are few common factors either within a particular legislature or between legislatures in different countries. Legislative committees differ in importance, in organization and in function.

In the United States CONGRESS, for example,

many important legislative decisions are made by permanent standing committees and sub-committees. In other legislatures, such as the British HOUSE OF COMMONS, STANDING COMMITTEE recommendations or the reports of SELECT COMMITTEE investigations carry much less weight. Legislative committees, however, normally consist of a group of elected politicians, some more senior or experienced than others, who for a variety of reasons are required or are prepared to spend time and energy in committee work. Many committees are primarily fact-finding bodies and use formal hearings or other devices to obtain information from witnesses of all kinds. Their activities are heavily influenced by the behaviour and attitudes of those who chair the committees.

The most numerous legislative committees are the standing committees. Their principal task is to consider the detail of proposed bills, including those on finance. Standing committees are permanent in the US Senate and House of Representatives. They consider bills before they are debated by the full legislature, and often have a crucial influence on the fate of a particular bill. However, in parliamentary systems such as those of the United Kingdom or India (though not Canada) most standing committees are less permanent in nature and composition, consider bills after floor debate, and have less influence. There are other differences and contrasts. Scrutiny of administration in the British House of Commons is conducted by specialist select committees, while such select committees in the Congress (with some exceptions, such as the House and Senate select committees on Intelligence) are more temporary in nature, with the standing committees combining the consideration of legislation relating to a particular department and scrutiny or oversight of the implementation of legislation by permanent sub-committees.

Another important contrast with respect to standing committee and sub-committee behaviour in legislatures relates to the influence of party on composition and decision making. While party is important in assigning legislators to committees through different kinds of committees of selection, standing committees differ markedly in the US Congress with respect to the degree of partisanship they exhibit, while standing committees and most select committees in the British House of Commons are partisan in their individual and collective behaviour. Committees of Congress also have large permanent professional staff, whereas there are few specialist staff beyond clerks of the House to assist the members of standing or even select committees at Westminster. A further contrast is demonstrated in the case of Congress, where the Senate is at least the co-equal to the House of Representatives and where a range of parallel standing committees with similar jurisdictions and powers has developed (for example the House and Senate Armed Services committees to deal with defence matters), also permanent joint committees composed of senators and representatives. The most distinctive development however is the use of special bipartisan conference committees composed of members of the relevant standing committees in charge of particular bills, when differences occur between the House and Senate versions of a bill. These legislative committees are especially significant because their decisions often become the final decisions of Congress as a whole. In some legislatures, party committees are important.

Committees are often used in legislatures for special investigations or to consider and recommend reforms in procedures and practices. Almost all committee and sub-committee meetings in the US Congress are open to the public, but in many legislatures much committee work is conducted in private.

Committees are used in most legislatures; their work is especially important to members of the US House of Representatives where constituency and personal attitudes may be more important than party, and where committee work has an important effect on individual careers and re-election prospects. This is much less the case in parliamentary systems where party loyalty and performance on the floor of the legislature are more important than committee work in advancing individual careers. In many parliamentary systems the use of legislative committees and their autonomy is influenced and controlled by the attitudes of the executive. However where the executive is unstable, as in Italy, some legislative committees have acquired the authority to decide on legislation and can make law. Where the legislative branch is formally separate from the executive, as with the American Congress, legislative committees serve the needs of the legislature and individual legislators, and are likely to be permanent organizations with important functions and considerable influence on all aspects of legislative behaviour.   JDL

Reading

Drewry, G. ed.: *The New Select Committees: a study of the 1979 reforms*. Oxford: Clarendon Press, 1985.

Eulau, H. and McCluggage, V.: Standing committees in legislatures: three decades of research. *Legislative Studies Quarterly* 9 (1984) 195–270.

Fenno, R.F. Jr: *Congressmen in Committees*. Boston, Mass.: Little, Brown, 1973.

Hill, D.M. ed.: *Parliamentary Select Committees in Action: a symposium*. Glasgow: Strathclyde Papers in Government and Politics 24, 1984.

Lees, J.D. and Shaw, M. eds: *Committees in Legislatures: a comparative analysis*. Durham, NC: Duke University Press; Oxford: Martin Robertson, 1979.

Loewenberg, F. and Patterson, S.C.: *Comparing Legislatures*, ch. 4. Boston, Mass.: Little, Brown, 1979.

Mezey, M.L.: *Comparative Legislatures*. Durham, NC: Duke University Press, 1979.

Smith, S.S. and Deering, C.J.: *Committees in Congress*. Washington, DC: Congressional Quarterly Press, 1984.

Unekis, J.K. and Rieselbach, L.N.: *Congressional Committee Politics: continuity and change*. New York: Praeger, 1984.

Walkland, S.A. ed.: *The House of Commons in the Twentieth Century*. Oxford: Oxford University Press, 1979.

legislative drafting   Contrary to popular belief, the drafting of legislation involves more than just putting legislative proposals into legal language and ensuring that there are no loopholes. Before starting to draft a law the legislative drafter needs to know in some detail what its promoters wish to achieve and what alterations of or additions to the existing law are considered necessary for the purpose.

Ideally, this information should take the form of written instructions prepared by a team of administrators and lawyers familiar with the subject-matter of the proposed law.

Having digested the instructions and, if need be, clarified them in discussion with those who prepared them, the drafter is in a position to start work. One of the first tasks is to devise a suitable set of concepts in which to embody the basic ideas of the draft law, and to design an appropriate structure for the law as a whole. This 'design' aspect of the drafting process is of fundamental importance and affects not only the overall organization of the draft but also the internal organization of each component provision. An experienced drafter will aim to produce a structure that will stand up even if the draft law is considerably amended during its passage through the legislature.

Most new laws deal with topics which are already the subject of legal rules – and, except where it is practicable to repeal the existing law and make a fresh start, each new law has to be meticulously woven into the existing fabric. This means that the drafter's room for manoeuvre is often severely limited both by the need to make the new law fit the structure and language of existing statute law and by constraints imposed by case-law, ADMINISTRATIVE LAW, international law or where relevant, European Community law.

The drafter's primary task is to produce a legally effective text. Complaints that statutory provisions are complicated and therefore difficult to understand overlook the fact that modern legislation must take account of the complexity of modern society, technology and business operations. It is reasonable to expect STATUTE LAW to be clearly intelligible to a reader who knows and understands the factual and legal context in which it operates and is willing to devote the necessary minimum of time to studying it. But to expect every statute to be easily understandable by all whom it affects is to demand the impossible.

Legislation is usually prepared under considerable pressure of time in order to meet parliamentary or party-political deadlines. The drafter is rarely allowed the luxury of a period of calm in which to consider how a draft law could be improved. Given time, the drafter can nearly always perceive ways in which the structure and wording of a draft could be bettered, but this is not something that can be done in a rush. And once a draft law has been presented to the legislature, the promoters are as a rule understandably reluctant to prolong the proceedings on it by moving amendments whose only purpose is to cure infelicities of structure and wording.

It is often supposed by those unfamiliar with modern statutes that laws are written in a special jargon peculiar to legislative drafters. This may be true in some parts of the world, but in countries where the technique of legislative drafting has been developed over a long period it will be found that laws are mostly expressed in ordinary language and contain an irreducible minimum of (not necessarily legal) technical terms. In particular, laws are (or ought to be) free of antiquated expressions such as 'whereby', 'hereinafter' and 'the said' – which continue to be used, for reasons best known to themselves, by the drafters of wills, leases and other legal documents of a private character.

In Britain, the present system under which the government's public bills are prepared by a body of professional drafters available to all government departments dates from the establishment of the Parliamentary Counsel Office by Treasury Minute in 1869. This system has been adopted in most Commonwealth countries though there is still a serious shortage of experienced legislative drafters in many of them. In France, by contrast, primary legislation is drafted by departmental officials under the supervision of the CONSEIL D'ÉTAT which scrutinizes and where necessary revises it before it is presented to the legislature – this scrutiny being required by the Constitution.

Attempts have been made to compare the drafting styles of different countries with a view to showing that, for example, the so-called 'continental' method of drafting alleged to be used in most European countries and by the institutions of the European Community, produces laws that are shorter and less detailed and so easier to understand. These comparisons tend to be deceptive, since the circumstances in which legislation is produced and enacted differ from country to country. Some countries are content with a fairly broad-brush approach. Others aim to set out the principles of the new law in primary legislation, leaving the details to be spelt out in regulations of a subordinate character. By contrast, most Commonwealth legislatures insist on a high degree of specificity in the laws they are prepared to pass, regarding this as an essential safeguard for the rule of law and the only way of ensuring the legislature's ultimate control over the law.   GE

Reading

Bibliography of Materials on Legislative and other Legal Drafting and the Interpretation of Statutes. 2nd edn. London: Commonwealth Secretariat, 1982.

Dale, W.: *Legislative Drafting: a new approach.* London: Butterworth, 1977.

Dickerson, R.: *Fundamentals of Legislative Drafting.* Boston, Mass.: Little, Brown, 1965.

Driedger, E.A.: *The Composition of Legislation* (1956). Ottawa: Department of Justice, 1976.

Ilbert, C.: *Legislative Methods and Forms.* Oxford: Clarendon Press, 1901.

Renton Committee: *Report of the Committee on the Preparation of Legislation.* London: HMSO Cmnd 6053, 1975.

Thornton, G.C.: *Legislative Drafting* (1970). 2nd edn. London: Butterworth, 1979.

Thring, Lord: *Practical Legislation: the composition and language of Acts of Parliament.* London: Murray, 1902.

legislative veto   In the United States, a procedural device, derived from and going beyond the British practice of 'laying on the table', which Congress inserted in numerous statutes delegating regulatory or other powers to the president or executive agencies. A typical provision delayed the effectiveness of action taken pursuant to the delegation for a specified period and set the action aside if, during that period, a majority of one House (or under some statutes, both Houses) voted to disapprove it. The device was declared unconstitutional by the United States Supreme Court in *Immigration and Naturalization Service* v. *Chadha*, 462 US 919 (1983). The Court ruled that under the Constitution (Article I, § 1 and § 7), the 'veto' device is 'legislative action' – that is, action that alters legal rights and duties of persons outside the Legislative Branch – and must be enacted by majority vote of both Houses of Congress and either approved by the president or, if vetoed, passed by a two-thirds overriding vote in both Houses.

LNC

Reading

Fisher, L.: *The Politics of Shared Power: Congress and the executive*, pp. 92–103. Washington, DC: Congressional Quarterly Press, 1981.

Martin, D.: The legislative veto and the responsible exercise of congressional power. *Virginia Law Review* 68 (1982) 253–302.

Watson, H.: Congress steps out: a look at Congressional control of the executive. *California Law Review* 63 (1975) 983–1094.

————: Note, 'laying on the table' – a device for legislative control over delegated powers. *Harvard Law Review* 65 (1952) 637–48.

legislatures Political institutions whose members are formally equal to one another, whose authority derives from a claim that the members are REPRESENTATIVES of the political community, and whose decisions are collectively made according to complex procedures. Typical aspects of the organization and composition of legislatures derive from these defining characteristics. Because of the equality of their status, members of legislatures are reluctant to apply sanctions against each other. Legislative procedure therefore depends to a remarkable degree on the implicit folkways of the group. These are to some extent registered as precedents and to some extent merely sanctioned by habit and custom comprising informal norms of behaviour. Only a small part of legislative procedure takes the form of explicit rules enforced by explicit sanctions. The equality of the status of members also determines that they work in groups, either as committees, as party caucuses, or in meetings of the whole membership. The claim to representativeness affects the composition of the legislature and the method for selecting its members. Modern legislatures are typically elected by a process that produce a membership which the community can recognize to be in some salient respects like itself.

Defined in this way, legislatures are clearly distinguished from bureaucratic institutions. Their members are not hierarchically related in positions of subordination and control. There is no formal division of labour among them, although an internal committee system often results in specialization. What distinguishes one member from another is the CONSTITUENCY he or she represents, and in that sense there is a territorial rather than a functional diferentiation among members. The mode of decision making in those legislatures containing a multiplicity of political parties is a bargaining mode rather than a system of command and obedience.

Contemporary legislatures are the result of a historical evolution which began in medieval Europe. Originally they were assemblies of aristocrats irregularly convened by monarchs in order to secure support for taxation or war. Gradually they became regularly convened bodies which provided essential communication between monarchs and the most powerful groups of their subjects. The term 'legislature' to denote such an assembly came into use in seventeenth-century revolutionary England out of the constitutional controversy over the proper location of the law-making power. While the older term 'parliament' prevailed in England, the term 'legislature', like other aspects of seventeenth-century English constitutional doctrine, took root in revolutionary America a century later. In the United States, it is the general term used to denote the representative assembly. Elsewhere the same institution may have one of a variety of names, denoting its meeting place (chamber), its time of meeting (Bundes*tag*), its structure as a gathering of members (Congress, Knesset), or its characteristically deliberative mode of operation (*parle*ment). Some features of the organization of legislatures can only be explained by their historical origins. Approximately half of the world's legislatures continue to consist of two houses, recalling the distinction between the house of the nobility and the house of commoners. Though this bicameral structure subsequently took many different forms, it was generally maintained to permit representation of two different kinds of constituencies, an advantage in federal systems and in large, territorially differentiated countries. Most legislators continue to represent territorially defined constituencies. Similarly most legislatures have borrowed heavily from the quaint but serviceable body of parliamentary procedure which developed in the British HOUSE OF COMMONS and was preserved by generations of its able parliamentarians.

Other aspects of legislatures are the result of the adaptability of the institution to a great variety of political settings. It is remarkable both that legislatures have such an ancient lineage and that they are nearly ubiquitous throughout the modern world and not just in the political systems influenced by Britain. The influences of the political environment affect the functions that legislatures perform in the political system, their relationship to the political executive, and their composition.

From its origins in medieval Europe, the legislature was transplanted first into colonial North America, where the assembly was the only political institution which the colonists could control. Their insistence that the law-making power reside in the assembly was therefore part of their effort to obtain political independence from England. For justification they drew on the political theory of seventeenth-century Puritan England. This combination of pragmatic and theoretical considerations transformed the representative assembly as a deliberative parliament into a genuine legislature 3,000 miles from its native environment. The colonial assemblies played a leading role in the American revolution, becoming thereafter models for the state and national legislatures which were established in the political system of the newly independent United States. This history, which created uniquely powerful law-making assemblies in the United States, has not been repeated elsewhere.

In the United States a distinctive relationship also developed between this powerful legislature and a presidential executive modelled after monarchy. It was a relationship expressing an eighteenth-century European theory of the desirability of locating distinct governmental powers in separate institutions. Inscribed in a written constitution which did not easily permit change, the separation of the legislature from the executive became a permanent feature of its condition in the United States. It was imitated eventually in most of Latin America and, in the twentieth century, in less developed countries looking for a constitution which assured strong executive powers; however, the American manifestation of a balance of powers between legislature and executive was not easily imitated.

A much closer relationship between the representative assembly and the executive evolved in nineteenth-century Europe, where the assembly became the principal symbol of national independence in new nation states such as Belgium, Switzerland, Italy, and Germany. Nearly everywhere it became the instrument of liberal democracy. Liberal political leaders tried to make monarchy responsive to an expanding electorate by imposing accountability to the assembly on the ministers of the crown or on republican executives. The institution, which continued to be called parliament, eventually became the centre of a political system in which the effective executives required the confidence of parliament to govern.

As political parties began to organize parliaments selected by a broad electorate, the ability of ministers to obtain the confidence of the assembly depended increasingly on their standing within their own political parties. Parliamentary systems in which relatively few strongly-led political parties existed, as in the United Kingdom, enabled the ministers to dominate the parliament. Systems in which numerous weakly-led political parties existed, as in pre-war France and Germany, made the executives highly dependent on parliament. The relationship between the assembly and the executive was therefore determined by the party system, and was changeable to the extent that the party system changed. The dominant position of the assembly in Third and Fourth Republic France was substantially altered because of a changed party system in the Fifth Republic. A similar transformation occurred between the pre-war and post-war German political systems. Because the relationship between the assembly and the executive in Europe has been subject to evolution, influenced principally by changing party systems, the institution in its European manifestation never became simply identified with the law-making function.

The differences among legislatures are most striking with respect to the functions they perform. The US CONGRESS is the principal example of a legislature that significantly participates in the drafting and enactment of legislation and of budgets. The legislatures of the American states perform the same functions in the more limited political systems over which they have jurisdiction. The British House of Commons is the leading example of a legislature that legitimates the enactments and the budgets formulated by political executives through the process of publicly debating these proposals and voting on them. It is also the principal example of a legislature whose members are the reservoir from which the political executives are chosen. It is the most widely imitated model in the democratic world.

In newly independent Asian and African states legislatures serve to integrate new nations, connecting the central government to the local communities, communicating between the civil servants in the national government and the villagers whom they must reach, and symbolizing the existence of the state. In these settings legislators add to the important network that comprises the elements of nation-building, reminiscent in some respects of the role they played in the creation of European states. In communist states legislatures function to legitimate the rule of the party and to demonstrate its popularity: both their composition and their decisions are controlled by a single party which uses the legislature to express and legitimate party decisions.

In both North America and Europe the composition of the legislature has been affected by social change. Assemblies were originally composed of the nobility and of landowners and leading citizens of the towns, usually identified by ascription. Gradually systems of electing members developed, and during the nineteenth century the franchise expanded rapidly in nearly all countries. The result of these electoral systems was to recruit the members of the legislature more broadly.

The occupational composition of legislatures varies with popular expectations of the relevant qualifications for membership, and with the social composition of the political parties which are the principal agencies of recruitment. In the United States lawyers were from the outset conspicuous by their numbers in most legislatures, but farmers were gradually displaced by business and professional men. After the middle of the twentieth century numbers of women and members of non-white ethnic minorities gradually increased. The occupational composition of European legislatures is more diverse than it is in the United States because European political parties, which include working class based parties, vary socially from each other more than do American political parties. The precursors of legislatures in states which became independent after the second world war were the territorial assemblies composed of colonial settlers. At the moment of independence these consultative bodies were transformed into national legislatures composed of representatives of the indigenous population. Political control over the composition of the legislature and of its decisions by a single political party replaced colonial domination, sometimes after an interval of party competition. India with its multi-party system is the most notable exception to this pattern. In communist states, the party explicitly plans the composition of the legislature to reflect the occupational, ethnic and regional diversity of the country at least as it is officially conceived. The composition of these assemblies is designed to project an image of representativeness which will help to legitimate the regime. But naturally, legislatures also reflect the partisan divisions of the electorate, although the precise extent will depend upon the ELECTORAL SYSTEM and the extent of the incumbency effect, at present very considerable in the United States.

Over time, every legislature develops a distinctive form of organization and a distinctive way of proceeding, independent of the particular individuals composing it at any moment. In the older legislatures of Europe and North America the level of institutionalization is high, which means that the boundary between the legislature and other political institutions is clear, the rules governing its members are impersonal, and its ways of working are complex. In the newer legislatures of the third world, and the assemblies of communist states, the legislature is permeated by other political institutions, typically by the dominant political party and by the political executives. In these settings the turnover of members of the legislature is high, meetings are infrequent, and procedures are relatively simple. Most legislatures are subject to re-election at least every four or five years. Where elections are non-competitive, the political parties which, in effect, choose the members of the legislature generally provide for rapid turnover of the membership. This increases both party patronage and control. In multi-party democracies, where elections are competitive, sitting members generally enjoy a re-election advantage with the result that there is considerable continuity of membership. This in turn promotes the institutionalization of the legislature.

Organization
Although the members of a legislature are formally equal to each other, they characteristically organize themselves into committees which afford them a measure of functional specialization and create a division of labour (see LEGISLATIVE COMMITTEES). In addition, legislatures have officers, notably a presiding officer known as a 'speaker' in the legislatures influenced by the British tradition, or elsewhere a president. Overlaid on this part of the legislature's organization is the party organization of its members. Legislators belonging to the same political party generally select their own leader and often their own committees. Finally, most modern legislatures are served by a staff of quasi-civil servants who record their actions, maintain their procedures, perform a wide variety of housekeeping functions, and provide expert advice on substantive questions of policy.

The US Congress has developed the most elaborate committee structure, having thirty-eight committees and 231 sub-committees. With this elaborate division of labour, the US Congress has established by far the largest legislative staff in the world, with over 3,000 individuals serving the committees alone; its total staff exceeds 15,000. A parallel development has occurred in Western Europe but on a much smaller scale, with staffs of between 1,000 and 2,000 members. Through committee specialization and legislative staffing, legislatures are responding to the pressure towards bureaucratization in the modern world. The incentive to this development is given by the need of legislatures to match the expertise of political executives. The danger is that the distinctive character of the legislative institution will be lost, that it will devolve into a collection of individual political entrepreneurs who have lost their capacity to make collective decisions.

Procedure
The ability of legislatures to transform a set of contentious political leaders into a collectivity able to make decisions depends on the effectiveness of parliamentary procedures and the success of the modes of legislative bargaining. The British House of Commons has exceptionally elaborate procedures, the product of a continuous 500-year evolution. Its accumulated experience, carefully maintained in journals and in compilations of precedents, has been transmitted to an extraordinary proportion of the world's legislatures, those established in colonial America, in the British Commonwealth, and on the continent of Europe. The diffusion of British parliamentary practice sometimes occurred through direct imitation, for example the *Manual* which Thomas Jefferson wrote for the US Senate, sometimes through the writing of political theorists, for example Bentham's *Essay on Political Tactics* which influenced Belgian, French and later German legislatures. In the twentieth century the spread of British procedure resulted explicitly from technical assistance to the parliaments of newly independent states provided by clerks of the House of Commons.

At home British parliamentary procedure was first used to establish the autonomy of the House from the monarchy, then further evolved to protect the rights of individual members and minorities, and finally established the ways in which majorities could control decisions. These are the objectives of procedure in all parliamentary bodies.

The study of legislatures has attracted the skills of political historians who have traced the history of the institution, and of lawyers who interpret its legal processes and products. It has become the special province of those political scientists who study the behaviour of its individual members, the patterns of influence among its principal internal components, and the relationship between them and the legislature's various external constituencies.

Knowledge of the world's legislatures is unevenly developed. The US Congress is by far the most studied example of the institution, followed at a great distance by Western European legislatures. Since 1960 the volume of research has grown enormously, and it has begun to include work on legislatures in less developed countries and in communist states. Most research is still country-specific. The comparative study of the institution continues to be rare.

See also RESPONSIBLE GOVERNMENT; SECOND CHAMBERS; SEPARATION OF POWERS.

GL

Reading

Aydelotte, W.O. ed.: *The History of Parliamentary Behavior*. Princeton, NJ: Princeton University Press, 1977.

Cherot, J.-Y.: *Le Comportement parlementaire*. Paris: Economica, 1984.

Eulau, H., Wahlke, J.C. et al.: *The Politics of Representation*. Beverly Hills, Calif.: Sage, 1978.

Griffith, J.A.G., Ryle, M. and Wheeler-Booth, M.: *Parliament*. London: Sweet and Maxwell, 1989.

Inter-Parliamentary Union, ed.: *Parliaments of the World*. 2 vols. Aldershot: Gower, 1986.

Jewell, M.E. and Patterson, S.C.: *The Legislative Process in the United States*. 4th edn. New York: Random House, 1986.

Jones, C.O.: *The United States Congress*. Homewood, Ill.: Dorsey Press, 1982.

Kim, C.L., Barkan, J.D., Turan, I. and Jewell, M.E.: *The Legislative Connection: the politics of representation in Kenya, Korea, and Turkey*. Durham, NC: Duke University Press, 1984.

Loewenberg, G.: *Parliament in the German Political System*. Ithaca, NY: Cornell University Press, 1967.

—— and Patterson, S.C.: *Comparing Legislatures*. Boston, Mass.: Little, Brown, 1979.

——, Patterson, S.C. and Jewell, M.E. eds: *Handbook of Legislative Research*. Cambridge, Mass.: Harvard University Press, 1985.

Vanneman, P.: *The Supreme Soviet: politics and the legislative process in the soviet political system*. Durham, NC: Duke University Press, 1977.

legitimacy This concept denotes one or more aspects of the lawfulness of a regime, its representatives and their 'commands'; it is a quality derived not from formal laws or decrees but from social acceptance (or acceptability) and 'appropriateness' as judged by reference to norms to which 'subordinates' accord (more or less) active assent. It has become central to debates first over how, and whether – in terms of an accepted pattern of values, or value-based norms, within a community or society – rulership, government or power is validly exercised, and second about the extent, grounds and sources of such validity. The debate over legitimacy extends and reformulates traditional discussion of political obligation. For the legitimacy of a rule rests upon a sense of obligation within a shared sense of what is appropriate or right. Such debates cannot be fully separated from two other areas of fundamental concern, neither of which is 'value-free': the precise nature and status of a society's 'systems' or 'range' of values and norms; and the moral and constitutional differences between democratic and tyrannical forms of rule. As with most key concepts in political science, legitimacy points to a real 'non-academic' problem – one that concerns practitioners of politics as well as students. This is because it highlights issues governing the grounds of power and authority and the justifications that are offered by, or on behalf of, those who hold power or authority – especially but not solely in modern societies. A purely coercive form of rule would not be preoccupied by elaborate claims to legitimacy: its legitimacy would, in a sense, be self-evident or self-justifying – at least in the eyes of its 'holders'. But such a form of rule would be a limiting case, rarely found in practice. Existing 'impure' coercive forms of rule may rest upon, or over time acquire, legitimacy depending upon the acceptance of their supporting ideologies or myths or upon their achievements (including that of killing, outlawing or intimidating actual or potential areas of opposition).

Sociological attention to legitimacy (especially since the seminal writings of Max WEBER) has been concerned both with the quality of the beliefs about their rule which satisfy rulers themselves and which they (or others) circulate in their support, and the quality of that support among ancillary or subordinate groups, classes, or strata within the population so any claim as to the validity or legitimacy of the exercise of power will be judged from more than one perspective; again, it will only be in a limiting case that such perspectives will be uniformly consistent or one-dimensional. The varieties of political legitimacy may be viewed not only from the trichotomy (traditional, charismatic and legal-rational) set out by Weber but also through brief reference to some more recent approaches. Lipset, for example, in his influential text *Political Man* was concerned with the roles of effectiveness and legitimacy in maintaining 'stable democracy'. 'While effectiveness is primarily instrumental, legitimacy is evaluative . . .' But he concedes that 'legitimacy, in and of itself, may be associated with many forms of political organization, including oppressive ones' (p. 77). It has been claimed that some leading sociologists (notably Talcott Parsons), through an a priori conceptual framework that stressed consensus, have conflated power with legitimate authority and so narrowed the empirical utility of both concepts. On the whole those who make this claim also tend to regard legitimacy (and its 'crises') as derivative from the use (or misuse) of POWER, and to view the use of the concept by others (though not by themselves) as an ideological (or idealist) obfuscation.   SJG

Reading

Friedrich, C.J.: *Man and his Government: an empirical theory of politics*. New York: McGraw-Hill, 1963.

Habermas, J.: *Legitimation Crisis*. Boston, Mass. Beacon, 1975.

Lipset, S.M.: *Political Man: the social bases of politics*. London: Heinemann, 1959; New York: Doubleday, 1960.

Parsons, T.: *Politics and Social Structure*. New York:

Free Press; London: Collier-Macmillan, 1969.

Weber, M.: *Selections in Translation*, ed. W.G. Runciman and trans. E. Matthews. Cambridge: Cambridge University Press, 1978.

Wrong, D.H.: *Power: its forms, bases and uses*. Oxford: Blackwell, 1979.

Lenin/Leninism

(1) *Lenin (Ulyanov), Vladimir Ilich* (1870–1924) Russian revolutionary leader and writer. Lenin was the founder of the BOLSHEVIK organization, the forerunner of the COMMUNIST PARTY of the Soviet Union. He was the principal architect of the Bolshevik revolution and the first head of the Soviet state. Although he proclaimed fidelity to the principles of MARX and Engels, he in fact reinterpreted certain of their doctrines and developed their analysis of CAPITALISM both in terms of Russia's own experience, and internationally in its imperialist aspects. Whereas Marx had assumed that revolutionary SOCIALISM would flourish first in advanced industrial societies and principally through the efforts of a highly politically conscious proletarian majority rejecting capitalism, Lenin showed that a socialist revolution could be made in an underdeveloped country by exploiting the grievances of peasant, ethnic and other disaffected social elements. In *What is to be done?* (1902), he put forward his theory of the Bolshevik party as the 'vanguard of the proletariat', and argued for a centralized, disciplined party led by professional revolutionaries. His enemies argued that such a conception could lead to a dictatorship over the working class. Lenin provided the classic example of how a small minority, organized in a highly disciplined political machine, could seize power, hold on to it and transform society by means of pressure from above. His success in seizing and retaining power elevated the USSR to the role of the leading centre of world communism and made the Soviet communist party the paradigm for communist parties generally.

(2) *Leninism* In *The state and revolution*, written in 1917 shortly before the Bolshevik revolution, Lenin argued that this would provide for direct rule by the workers and peasants, and that the STATE would eventually

'wither away' in a classless communist society. He therefore called in his *April theses* (1917) for 'All Power to the Soviets', since these institutions exemplified the principle of direct democracy. Leninism has become instead the foundation stone of a new kind of political order, sometimes referred to as a 'partocracy'. In this system government is essentially extra-constitutional and is exercised with some regard for the semblance of democracy but little for its substance. Real power resides in the hands of a self-selected party elite which uses a mixture of manipulation and coercion to perpetuate its rule. State and other public bodies such as trade unions and supposedly voluntary associations are reduced to the role of largely passive instruments in the hands of party bosses.

See also DICTATORSHIP OF THE PROLETARIAT. TPMcN

Reading

Aron, R.: *Democracy and Totalitarianism*. London: Weidenfeld & Nicolson, 1968.

Eissenstat, B.W. ed.: *Lenin and Leninism*. Lexington, Mass.: Heath, 1971.

Harding, N.: *Lenin's Political Thought*. 2 vols. London: Macmillan, 1977, 1981.

Lane, D.: *Leninism: a sociological interpretation*. Cambridge: Cambridge University Press, 1981.

Lenin, V.I.: *What is to be done?* In *Collected Works*, Vol. I. London: Lawrence & Wishart, 1965.

————: *State and revolution*. In *Collected Works*, Vol. XXV. London: Lawrence & Wishart, 1965.

Meyer, A.G.: *Leninism*. Cambridge, Mass.: Harvard University Press, 1957.

Liberal parties Originated as the organized expression of what may be termed the political left (see LEFT AND RIGHT) in nineteenth-century Europe. Their demands for constitutional, parliamentary government and for a secular state, and especially a secular national educational system brought them into conflict, respectively, with conservative forces espousing older monarchical or aristocratic principles of government and with clerical, usually Catholic, defenders of a religious view of the state. The subsequent development of Liberal parties varied considerably according to whether their principal opponent on the right was a CONSERVATIVE party (as in Britain

and Scandinavia), a CHRISTIAN DEMOCRATIC party (as in Belgium or the Netherlands) or both (as in France or Germany). All Liberal parties found themselves subsequently in opposition to Socialist parties on the economic left and, thereby deprived of their historic role as the major force of the left, were pushed towards a position in the political spectrum at the centre or towards the right. Generally Liberal parties historically opposed to Conservative parties tend towards a centrist position in modern politics (see CENTRE PARTY). Those in competition with Christian Democrats usually have more middle-clss electorates than their Christian Democratic opponents and at least on socio-economic issues are more right wing.

Having often been parties with enough popular support to form majority governments on their own in the late nineteenth century, they tend now to be small parties. Some historically strong Liberal parties such as the French Radicals, Greek Liberals or Norwegian *Venstre* have today all but disappeared; others such as the British, Belgian or Dutch Liberals have expanded their electoral support in recent decades. Whereas the other families of political parties are distinguished by their electoral appeals to particular sections (Communist and Social Democratic parties to the working class; Agrarian parties to farmers; Conservative parties to the middle class) or to religious or ethnic loyalties (Christian Democratic and Nationalist parties), Liberal parties are unique in lacking any such characteristic electoral base. This is probably the main reason for their decline in twentieth-century Europe. Certain Liberal parties however have acquired the support of such a group because of the history of alliances between groups and ideologies in particular countries: the Danish *Venstre* party has a substantial agrarian base and the British and Swedish Liberal parties have had strong support among dissenting churches. Consequently, Liberals tend to be more dependent than others on local or regional pockets of electoral support and tend also particularly to attract floating voters who respond to their tactical position in the party system.

Because of their pivotal position in West

LIBERAL PARTIES

European party systems Liberal parties are frequent coalition partners, acceptable to parties both to their right and to their left, and in many countries Liberal parties are therefore in power more often than not, but in coalition governments. Brief minority one-party Liberal governments in Denmark and Sweden during the 1970s and the exclusion of the British Liberals from power by the British electoral system are the main exceptions to this rule.

All Liberal parties are still characterized by an emphasis on political freedom, human rights, and constitutional questions. On economic issues some tend to be either social–liberal (the German/Scandinavian term) or radical (the British term), supporting public expenditure on welfare and favouring the mixed economy. Others maintain an emphasis on classical liberal market economics (as in Belgium or the Netherlands). The German Free Democratic Party combines both traditions, which makes it an important pivotal party within the transnational groupings of Liberal parties as well as in domestic politics. In certain countries (for example Denmark, Italy) both strands of liberalism are represented by separate parties.

Most modern Liberal parties are staunchly in favour of European integration, and where national opinion is divided on that issue, Liberal parties are usually the strongest proponents of European unity. Generally on issues of defence and foreign policy there is no common Liberal position, Liberal parties tending to reflect their countries' national history. Austrian Liberalism became entwined with Pan-Germanism in the last century and this led to pro-Nazi sympathies in the 1930s; the Austrian Freedom party today retains a particular attraction for former Nazi supporters. Within NATO, most Liberal parties are strong supporters of the Atlantic Alliance and supporters of expenditure on defence; but the British Liberal party and Danish *Radikale Venstre* reflect particular pacifist traditions.

Outside Europe, Liberal parties appear in both Spanish and English speaking countries but the label can be misleading; the Australian Liberal party, for instance, is clearly a Conservative party, and in Latin America the use of European ideological labels often means very little. In the nineteenth century in Latin America however there were several Liberal and Radical parties whose name had essentially the same significance as in nineteenth-century Europe. Today the Liberal party in Canada and the Radical party in Argentina are perhaps the two strongest Liberal parties in the modern world. The Canadian party has the greatest experience of governing, with an overall parliamentary majority, while the Argentinian Radicals, taking over power from the military dictatorship in 1982, face the classic Liberal tasks of installing democracy and protecting human rights. Their success may presage a generally favourable atmosphere for Liberal parties in Latin America, with their emphasis on constitutionalism and the liberal democratic agenda, in the wake of the waning of military dictatorships.

Liberal parties in the European Community are grouped in a Federation; the strength of the liberal heritage in Europe is indicated by its having a member-party in eleven out of twelve countries. The Liberal International covers the world, but with member-parties in only twenty-one countries (sixteen in Europe, three in Latin America plus one each in Canada and Israel). Characteristically these two transnational organizations do not have precisely the same parties as members in six out of the twelve countries in which they overlap; a certain degree of argument and confusion over just what a Liberal party is exists among these parties, as it does also among political scientists. In Portugal, no party formed after the collapse of the dictatorship claimed a liberal heritage and the Liberal International has no member-party – but the Federation of Liberal, Democratic and Reform Parties of the European Community has attracted the support of one of the country's strongest political parties even though that party's label is the Social Democratic Party. The biggest party in the Liberal, Democratic and Reform group in the European Parliament since 1962, the French Republican Party, is the modern expression of the French Conservative tradition, yet was not a member of the Liberal International until 1986. MS

Reading

Beyme, K. von: *Political Parties in Western Democracies*, pp. 31–46. Aldershot: Gower, 1985.

Bogdanor, V. ed.: *Liberal Party Politics*. Oxford: Clarendon Press, 1983.

Kaack, H.: *Die F.D.P.*. Meisenheim am Glan: Anton Hain, 1978.

Kirchner, E. ed.: *Liberal Parties in Western Europe*. Cambridge: Cambridge University Press, 1988.

Steed, M.: The liberal parties in Italy, France, Germany and the UK. In *Moderates and Conservatives in Western Europe*, ed. R. Morgan and S. Silvestri. London: Heinemann, 1982.

Tarr, F. de: *The French Radical Party from Herriot to Mendès–France*. Oxford: Oxford University Press, 1961.

limited vote An ELECTORAL SYSTEM with multi-member constituencies in which each elector has fewer votes than there are candidates to be elected. This system was used in a small number of constituencies in Britain between 1867 and 1885, and it is now used to elect the lower house in Japan, where the elector has one vote in a constituency returning up to five members of parliament, and in Spain to elect the upper house. The system is sometimes also known as the single non-transferable vote.

The purpose of the system is to allow for the representation of minorities but, although it often achieves this aim, it also offers considerable power to party leaders, and provides encouragement to factionalism and the growth of personal political machines. It yields a greater degree of proportionality in representation than plurality systems, but less than systems of proportional representation. For this reason, it has sometimes been described as a semi-proportional system.

VBB

Reading

Stockwin, J.A.A.: Japan. In *Democracy and Elections: electoral systems and their political consequences*, ed. V. Bogdanor and D. Butler. Cambridge: Cambridge University Press, 1983.

lobbying The term derives from American politics, and originally described attempts to influence elected representatives during the passage of legislation through Congress. It came into common usage in Britain during the mid-nineteenth century when it was applied exclusively to influences directed at Parliament. The contemporary meaning is broader, referring to the practices of INTEREST GROUPS, directed not only at seeking support from elected members, but also from political parties, public bureaucracies and other public bodies, and from the general public through the mass media. This broader meaning reflects a decline in the power of Parliament and a corresponding increase in the power of the executive branch of goverment.　　AC

local government A type of political institution whose authority or jurisdiction is confined to a territorial portion of the state. It is characterized by long historical development, constitutionally subordinate status, local participation, powers of taxation, and a wide range of responsibilities.

There is a long tradition, especially in Western Europe, of *towns* being permitted a measure of political autonomy. Some British cities for instance have an unbroken tradition of self-government dating back to the grant of CHARTERS by medieval monarchs. In many parts of the world, community involvement in *village* governments is even older. Nevertheless neither urban nor rural local government has ever been allowed unlimited discretion. Its constitutional status was and is subordinate.

Unlike states or provinces in a federal political system, local government units have no share in sovereignty. Local government is subordinate to the national or, in a federation, provincial government; it must operate within the legislative framework they prescribe. The sovereign higher levels of government may create or dissolve local government units and add to or subtract from their responsibilities. Despite this constitutionally subordinate status, local government generally enjoys wide discretion in democratic political systems and wields significant political influence. This is largely because local government provides for substantial local participation. The organs of local governments are invariably directly or indirectly elected by the local residents. This gives local government democratic legitimacy and political authority which appointed public bodies do not possess.

The authority of local government can be strengthened by the arrangements for LOCAL GOVERNMENT FINANCE. Most local government units raise at least part of their income locally; they also invariably receive some grants and loans from higher levels of government. Nevertheless even a degree of financial autonomy enhances discretion.

Local government is responsible for a range of public services. Depending on the law and traditions of particular countries, local government provides some or all of the following: roads, public housing, education, welfare, public transport, health, water, sewerage, electricity and other types of power, sports facilities, support for the arts, and a host of miscellaneous environmental, personal, and recreational services. Local government units are typically multi-purpose. A city government, say, may provide a whole range of these services. Nevertheless alongside the multi-purpose local government units in most countries exist varying numbers of special purpose bodies providing a single service or closely related group of services: for instance passenger transport authorities, water supply authorities, health authorities, harbour authorities, perhaps even school authorities, such as, for example, the Inner London Education Authority in Britain. Yet these too, if they are locally elected or appointed by the multi-purpose local government units, are properly considered part of the local government system, especially if they have local taxation powers. Where special purpose bodies are entirely appointed by higher levels of government however they are not strictly local governments.

Alderfer (1964) has suggested that local government has four basic patterns: the British, the French, the Soviet and the traditional, and that the first three prevail everywhere leaving only remnants of the last (indigenous forms of village government) persisting in some parts of Asia and Africa. For Alderfer the British local government system was relatively decentralized with central controls of a legislative type and little supervision of one local government unit

by another; the French system was characterized by heavy central supervision through administrative controls and an hierarchical chain of command; the main feature of the Soviet system was an even stricter hierarchy through both formal structure and the DEMOCRATIC CENTRALISM of communist party control and single candidate elections. It is doubtful whether the differences between the French and British systems are so profound as Alderfer suggests. There is indeed significant convergence. During the 1980s British local government has been subjected to ever more central control, often administrative; French local government has enjoyed some easing of hierarchical supervision. In any case CENTRAL/LOCAL RELATIONS are influenced as much by POLITICAL CULTURE and party politics as by formal structural considerations. French local government has always had as much bargaining power as its British counterpart, if not more.

The basic difference between patterns of local government is twofold not fourfold. On the one hand there are political systems in which local government has sufficient autonomy, status, and separate legitimacy to enable it to bargain with higher levels of government. This is the basic pattern in all the liberal democracies. On the other hand there are systems in which local government has no significant autonomy, status, or separate legitimacy and therefore no effective bargaining power – as in the Soviet Union and other authoritarian regimes. Indeed in such circumstances perhaps local government is nothing more than deconcentration of central administration.

That local government is so universal an institution suggests its value, perhaps indispensability, for the modern state. Marxists traditionally see local government in the West as an extension of the state, playing its part in maintaining the capitalist system. Some neo-Marxists have adapted this view; while they agree that local government has a role in 'capitalist reproduction' they see it as creating interests distinct from those of the state nationally and thus generating separate tensions and conflicts. Liberal democrats explain the importance of local government in the

West differently. In the first place it is justified on practical grounds as a *convenient* method of providing public services. Without local government these services would be the responsibility of national (or, in a federation, provincial) government or of new appointed institutions, any of which would be administratively more cumbersome and would moreover entail significant loss of innovation. Each local government unit with its measure of discretion can try new ways of providing the services for which it is responsible. More centralized arrangements would by definition reduce the scope for polycentric experimentation. In the second place local government is justified on the basis of less tangible values such as democratic participation, local community self-government, and political education. On the latter, for instance, John Stuart MILL argued that the opportunitites local government provided for participation and political behaviour outside the national government strengthened people's understanding of free political institutions. Naturally such arguments only carry weight in democratic political systems.

There is sometimes a tension between the justifications on practical and on democratic grounds. LOCAL GOVERNMENT REORGANIZATION tends in all countries to produce fewer and larger local government units on the grounds of administrative efficiency. Yet this reduces the scope for participation. Moreover, survey evidence indicates that people identify more easily with small local government units and with those which retain their traditional boundaries.

Despite this tension local government seems likely to remain a prominent feature of democratic political systems. In authoritarian or totalitarian political systems local government, in the sense of deconcentration of central administration, also seems to be a practical necessity.

See also ALDERMEN; AREAL DIVISION OF POWER; CENTRALIZATION AND DECENTRALIZATION; CITY GOVERNMENT; LOCAL POLITICS; MAYOR; PARISH.   DER

Reading

Alderfer, H.F.: *Local Government in Developing Countries*. New York: McGraw-Hill, 1964.

Anton, T.J.: *Governing Greater Stockholm*. Berkeley: University of California Press, 1975.

Dahl, R.A.: *Who Governs? Democracy and power in an American city*. New Haven, Conn.: Yale University Press, 1963.

Dunleavy, P.J.: *Urban Political Analysis: the politics of collective consumption*. London: Macmillan, 1980.

Dye, T.R.: *Politics in States and Communities*. 4th edn. Englewood Cliffs, NJ: Prentice-Hall, 1981.

Feldman, L.D. and Goldrick, M.D.: *Politics and Government of Urban Canada: selected readings*. 3rd edn. Toronto: Methuen, 1976.

Humes, J. and Martin, E.: *The Structure of Local Government: a comparative survey of eighty-one countries*. 2nd edn. The Hague: IULA, 1969.

Jacobs, E.M. ed.: *Soviet Local Politics and Government*. London: Allen & Unwin, 1983.

Mawhood, P. ed.: *Local Government in the Third World*. Chichester: Wiley, 1983.

Robson, W.A. and Regan, D.E. eds: *Great Cities of the World: their government, politics and planning*. 3rd edn. London: Allen & Unwin, 1972.

Rowat, D.C. ed.: *The Government of Federal Capitals*. Toronto: University of Toronto Press, 1973.

Smith, B.C.: *Decentralization: the territorial dimension of the state*. London: Allen & Unwin, 1985.

Stewart, J.D.: *Local Government: the conditions of local choice*. London: Allen & Unwin, 1983.

local government finance   The study of local government finance involves examining the processes by which revenue is raised and spent. This revenue can be raised by local taxation, by charging fees to users of services, by borrowing from public or private lenders, and by receiving grants from other levels of government. Though local finance has been primarily studied by economists (particularly in the United States and the United Kingdom), political scientists studying advanced industrial democracies have increasingly become interested in the topic both for its own sake and because of intergovernmental relations. Macro-economic policy debates (particularly in the UK) and economic development policies (especially in the USA) are tied to local finance. Local finance generally has not been of so much concern to students of the Third World where local governments are often not politically significant, do not exercise financial autonomy, and are almost completely dependent on the central government.

Most literature has focused on the system of local taxation and the system of grants prevailing in any one country. (Such funds finance the current, or operating, budget.) The basic distinction is between those systems (the USA and UK) in which local government taxes primarily property, those systems (Scandinavia) in which local government taxes income, and those systems (France and Italy) in which localities tax little and rely extremely heavily on central grants. While most systems rely on central grants to even out disparities in the wealth of local jurisdictions, Germany is notable for its complex system of tax-sharing among local governments. While British and American local governments share a reliance on property taxes, they differ in the extent of their reliance on central grants and on the central government generally. British localities are much more heavily dependent on the national government than are American localities. British localities receive a 'rate support grant' which is not earmarked for specific services. In many policy areas the centre sends out a stream of regulations and directives which, while not necessarily tied to any specific stream of money, nevertheless regulate local activity. In the United States, by contrast, local governments are more dependent in the aggregate on their state governments for aid than on the federal government. State aid is primarily directed towards elementary and secondary education, which is firmly controlled by local officials. Federal aid, however, while not so bountiful as state aid, is not insignificant, especially since it is directed towards a wider variety of policy sectors than is state aid and generally carries more restrictions.

In Britain parliament decides the type of taxes localities may levy and has supported the property tax exclusively. Until the early 1980s, however, British local authorities enjoyed, comparatively speaking, unusual freedom in that they could determine the level at which property would be taxed; property tax restrictions were imposed by the Conservative government, which also proposed a radical reform of the rating system, replacing the property tax by a community charge which is

in effect a poll tax. American localities have not had the freedom enjoyed by British local authorities in the pre-Thatcher era. Local taxes are controlled by state legislatures as to both their type and their level. For example, a city cannot usually levy taxes on commuters who work in the city but live in the suburbs unless specifically permitted to do so by the state legislature; furthermore property tax rates are controlled to a significant degree by state statutes. Local governments in the United States, United Kingdom, France, Italy and the Federal Republic of Germany have significant responsibilities in the area of capital investment for the building of schools, airports, roads, sewers, public housing and so forth. While the type of capital investment financed by local as opposed to central government varies cross-nationally, local governments usually pay for their portion of an investment by borrowing rather than by paying it out of their own revenue. In the United States public investment at the local level is regulated by state not national law and local governments are, for example, restricted in the level of debt they are allowed. Local officials have found it possible to circumvent these limits by establishing new, single-purpose governments (often referred to as public authorities) with borrowing power independent from that of a general-purpose government. The establishment of these authorities has dramatically restructured the landscape of American local government. Public investment carried out by local authorities is much more controlled by central government in Britain than in the United States: even the state governments in the USA do not control capital expenditure to the degree that it is controlled by London. British capital expenditure in any sector must be approved by a central government agency before it can proceed, and such expenditure is often controlled with reference to the needs of macro-economic policy rather than to the needs and desires of local authorities.

Of increasing interest to political scientists is the way in which the current and capital budgets are being used to pursue economic development. The United States has the longest history of local public monies being used to help develop the private sector; in the nineteenth century, for example, midwestern cities in particular were active financiers of private railroads. In the early 1980s British local authorities also became more active in the pursuit of private employers; in the mid-1980s, French, Italian, Danish and Japanese authorities joined the competition for private industry and began considering financial inducements to private sector firms.

See also BLOCK GRANT; LOCAL GOVERNMENT; RATE SUPPORT GRANT; RATES.

AMS

Reading

Bahl, R.W.: *Financing State and Local Government in the 1980s.* New York and Oxford: Oxford University Press, 1984.

Bennett, R.J.: The finance of cities in West Germany. *Progress in Planning* 21 (1983) 1–62.

Cathelineau, J.: Local government finance in France. In *Local Government in Britain and France,* ed. J. Lagroye and V. Wright. London: Allen & Unwin, 1979.

Foster, C.D., Jackman, R.A. and Perlman, M.: *Local Government Finance in a Unitary State.* London: Allen & Unwin, 1980.

Newton, K.: *Balancing the Books: financial problems of local government in Europe.* London: Sage, 1980.

———— ed.: *Urban Political Economy.* London: Pinter, 1981.

Rose, R. and Page, E. eds: *Fiscal Stress in Cities.* Cambridge: Cambridge University Press, 1982.

Sbragia, A. ed.: *The Municipal Money Chase: the politics of local government finance.* Boulder, Col.: Westview, 1983.

local government reorganization The process of revising the boundaries and functions of LOCAL GOVERNMENT. Until the nineteenth century local government reorganization was generally incremental and spasmodic. Since then, however, there have been radical reorganizations in a number of political systems stimulated by economic and social changes on the one hand and by political and philosophical ideas on the other.

Most countries have experienced rapid growth of urban populations over the last two centuries. Moreover technological improvements in transport, allowing people to live some distance from their place of work, have

permitted lower density development. Traditional local government boundaries have in consequence become increasingly anomalous as built-up areas have sprawled indifferently over them. The development of huge urban agglomerations has at the same time necessitated the wider provision of public services such as roads, housing, paving, sewerage and water supply. On top of these economic and social necessities local government reorganization has been shaped by intellectual fashions. The two most recurrent have been administrative rationality and democratic legitimacy.

Napoleonic rationality established a radically new structure of local government in France which persists substantially to this day. The British counterpart, Utilitarianism, profoundly influenced the development of local government in the first half of the nineteenth century with its stress on coherent administrative units, adequate finance and central inspection. Equally important to the thrust of rationality is the influence of democratic principles which in the nineteenth century were seen as particularly safeguarded by local government. In Britain and the USA this influence took the principal form of liberalism. It favoured the creation of powerful, elected units of local government both for the services they could provide to their citizens and for the rôle they could play in the political system generally.

Faced with such economic, social and political pressures local government reorganization has followed one or more of four strategies.

(1) Traditional multi-purpose local government units have had their boundaries extended; in most countries cities have since 1800 widened their areas of jurisdiction.

(2) New multi-purpose local government units have been created to embrace new populations, or whole conurbations, for instance as upper tiers in metropolitan areas. For example the Metropolitan Board of Works was established in 1854 covering the built-up area of London; this was replaced by the London County Council in 1888 and then by the even bigger Greater London Council in 1964. Similarly a Municipality of Metropolitan Toronto was established in 1954 and strengthened in 1967.

(3) Existing multi-purpose local governments have been given increased responsibilities. Cities, towns, counties, *communes, départements, Kreise* and the like have accumulated functions over the last 150 years.

(4) New special purpose units have been established – health boards, sanitary districts, poor law authorities, public transport authorities, and so on.

The first great wave of local government reorganization occurred in many countries during the nineteenth century and by contrast the first half of the twentieth century was a period of relative stability. There then followed a second period of reorganization which affected much of the western world. This time considerations of administrative rationality were even more dominant. Through mergers and restructurings units of local government were generally made fewer and larger. In many countries such reorganization was accompanied by centralist moves, transferring certain functions from local government to higher levels of government or to new national bodies (as with gas and electricity supply in Britain).

Opposition to local government reorganization has come principally from the forces of entrenched LOCALISM. These have generally not been strong enough to resist the reorganizing zeal of national or provincial governments. The USA is a major exception. Most American states provide for local referendums on reorganization schemes and they have often been defeated. The boundaries of New York City for instance have been unchanged since 1897. More principled opposition came in nineteenth-century Britain from the school of romantic constitutionalists led by Joshua Toulmin Smith and from the German Rudolf von Gneist with their stress on the participative value of small, traditional units of local government. More recent critics of local government reorganization have seen it as costly and ineffective. Where there was naive structural determinism which expected reorganization itself dramatically to improve the performance of local government, there was disappointment when this did not happen. There has even been some unscrambling of reorganization, as

with the abolition in 1986 of the Greater London Council in Britain.

See also CITY GOVERNMENT.   DER

Reading

Bourjol, M.: *La Réforme municipale: bilan et perspectives.* Paris: Berger-Levrault, 1975.

Davey, K.J.: *Financing Regional Government: international practices and their relevance to the third world.* Chichester: Wiley, 1983.

Dearlove, J.: *The Reorganization of British Local Government: old orthodoxies and a political perspective.* Cambridge: Cambridge University Press, 1979.

Gourevitch, P.A.: *Paris and the Provinces: the politics of local government reform in France.* London: Allen & Unwin, 1980.

Gunlicks, A.B. ed.: *Local Government Reform and Reorganization: an international perspective.* New York: Kennikat, 1981.

Loughlin, M., Gelfand, D.M. and Young, K. eds: *Half a Century of Municipal Decline 1935–85.* London: Allen & Unwin, 1985.

Redlich, J. and Hirst, F.W.: *A History of Local Government in England*, ed. B. Keith-Lucas. London: Macmillan, 1958.

Rowat, D.C. ed.: *International Handbook on Local Government Reorganization: contemporary developments.* London: Aldwych, 1980.

local politics   A phrase used to designate the way in which elections, political participation, party leadership and party competition at the lowest level of elected government relate to political behaviour and political outcomes. An analytical rather than a substantive phrase, it is used in at least three very different senses.

First, it is used to describe political behaviour within the lowest level of elected government, as in the study of local electoral behaviour or local party competition. The study of localized politics may be the nature of local elites and distribution of power within the local unit of government or the association of demographic, socio-economic features of local units of government to political activity within the local unit. The self-contained study of local politics was perhaps most highly developed by the American community power studies which tried to link local participation to local politics as part of a larger defence of pluralist politics. The main object of localized political studies has most often been to determine how, if at all, local political forces influence policy outcomes at the local level.

Second, the phrase is used to describe how local political organizations, parties or even bureaucracies intervene at higher political levels in order to achieve particular aims of the local unit. In these instances the local unit is treated as a political actor in a larger arena of regional, national and even international decision making where it attempts to maximize its political, social and economic self-interest. In this usage, local politics may have very different meanings across countries. From late Victorian Britain until the 1920s, local political intervention for particular local needs was organized by the Association of Municipal Councils (now the Association of Metropolitan Authorities) whose skill in organizing parliamentary support for private bills of local interest was remarkable. In the United States local politics of this kind more often occurs in Congressional bargaining over 'porkbarrel' laws which allocate huge amounts of money to the states and cities for land reclamation, highways, water provision, etc. Local politics in the sense of access and influence at higher levels of government for specific purposes varies with structural features of the political system and how political risks and rewards are distributed within the political system.

Third, the term local politics may refer to the ways in which the local government structure as a whole exercises influence on behalf of its collective interests at the national or higher levels of government. The long tradition of 'town vs. country' that remains embedded in the British system has made collective intervention in national policy making difficult, while the close association of French mayors, departmental and regional councillors with party organizations and elections (and until recently the ability to hold multiple elected office) made local politics an effective check on national level policy-making. Differences in local political capacities to intervene collectively at higher levels have often been attributed to structural features of political systems, for example federal or unitary systems of government. More recent work suggests that the systemic balance of power between national and local politics may have more to do with constitutional, historical and even cultural features of political systems. For example, the deeply ingrained custom of party discipline in the British House of Commons makes it extremely difficult for local politics collectively to affect national policy making.

In relation to political philosophy and political development, local politics has traditionally been associated with the vitality and strength of democratic governance, most clearly in TOCQUEVILLE's famous account of American local politics. On the whole liberal political philosophy associates self-sufficient, autonomous local politics with effective and rational self-government. In Britain, France and the United States early twentieth century socialists often considered municipal forms of ownership and co-operation a testing ground for socialist ideas. More recent socialist views of government, in particular neo-Marxist theories of politics, see local politics as an obstacle to achieving socialist reforms because local politics smothers class conflict and protects private interests. These philosophical positions are now confused because conservative governments in both the United States and Britain have tried to place severe fiscal restrictions on local government.

See also CENTRAL/LOCAL RELATIONS; CENTRALIZATION AND DECENTRALIZATION.

DEA

Reading

Ashford, D.E.: *British Dogmatism and French Pragmatism: central–local policymaking in the welfare state.* London, Boston, Mass. and Sydney: Allen & Unwin, 1982.

Bulpitt, J.G.: *Party Politics in English Local Government.* London: Longman, 1967.

Cockburn, C.: *The Local State: management of cities and people.* London: Pluto, 1977.

Dearlove, J.: *The Politics of Policy in Local Government.* Cambridge: Cambridge University Press, 1973.

Gyford, J.: *Local Politics in Britain.* London: Croom Helm, 1976.

———: *The Politics of Local Socialism.* London and Boston, Mass.: Allen & Unwin, 1985.

——— and James, M.: *National Parties and Local*

Politics. London and Boston, Mass.: Allen & Unwin, 1983.

Hain, P. ed.: *Community Politics*. London: John Calder, 1976.

Hampton, W.: *Democracy and Community Power*. London: Oxford University Press, 1970.

Hill, D.M.: *Democratic Theory and Local Government*. London and Boston, Mass.: Allen & Unwin, 1974.

Jones, G.W.: *Borough Politics: a study of the Wolver-hampton Borough Council*. London: Macmillan, 1969.

Keith-Lucas, B. and Richards, P.G.: *A History of Local Government in the Twentieth Century*. London and Boston, Mass.: Allen & Unwin, 1978.

Newton, K.: *Second City Politics: democratic processes and decision-making in Birmingham*. Oxford: Oxford University Press, 1976.

Sharpe, L.J. ed.: *Voting in Cities*. London: Macmillan, 1967.

localism A term often used to explain other political phenomena, but rarely examined as a subject in its own right. It has a number of meanings. First, it can be employed to describe a POLITICAL CULTURE favourably disposed to local citizens, local interests, LOCAL POLITICS, and LOCAL GOVERNMENT. In this sense it is just one of a number of themes associated with, and supportive of, local democracy. Second, it is sometimes used to denote national policies which are either given a local character to improve implementation, or are offloaded on to local governments and local politicians to insulate the central government from potentially embarrassing problems. This is localism 'from above' in the interests of administrative efficiency and/or political advantage. Third, the term localism is employed to describe a particular pattern of party politics in which local parties or local constituency representatives have a large displacement in a national party's power structure, the national inter-party battle, or the policy process in the capital city. As a concept, then, localism feeds into a number of other subjects: local democracy, national policy implementation, and party politics. The common theme is CENTRAL/LOCAL RELATIONS, broadly defined.

So though the concept is well known and well used it is employed in a number of different ways. All countries exhibit some degree of localism, but systematic measurement of the variations has proved difficult; neither the causes nor the effects of the phenomenon are well understood. Take, for example, the causes and effects of localism in party politics, probably the most interesting dimension of the subject. Some popular explanations of its causes are: a constitution formally committed to decentralization (for example FEDERALISM); the existence of territorially concentrated cleavages in society; elite or mass opinion antagonistic towards, or suspicious of, the central government; a high propensity of citizens to vote for local, rather than national, issues in countrywide elections. This particular list is only too easily undermined. Such explanations may not be mutually exclusive and it is often difficult to distinguish causes from effects. Again, empirical evidence suggests that localism can flourish in constitutionally centralized and decentralized systems (for example France and the USA) and in societies which are reasonably homogeneous (for example the Republic of Ireland). Moreover, all such explanations suggest that politicians respond passively to structurally-induced localism. But the evidence we have suggests that politicians can sustain or destroy localism for their own advantage. Both the demise of localism in British party politics after 1918 and its re-emergence after the mid-1970s reflect more deliberate political intent than is commonly supposed. Finally, there is little consensus among liberal commentators as to whether this particular form of localism is a good or bad thing. For some it is a logical derivative of PLURALISM, for others an affront to majority rule and policy rationality.

See also CENTRALIZATION AND DECENTRALIZATION. JB

Reading

Ashford, D.E.: *British Dogmatism and French Pragmatism: central-local policymaking in the welfare state*. London, Boston, Mass. and Sydney: Allen & Unwin, 1982.

Birch, A.H.: *Small Town Politics*. London: Oxford University Press, 1959.

Bulpitt, J.: *Territory and Power in the United Kingdom*. Manchester: Manchester University Press, 1983.

Grodzins, M.: *The American System: a new view of*

government in the United States. Chicago, Ill.: Rand McNally, 1966.

Gyford, J.: *The Politics of Local Socialism*. London: Allen & Unwin, 1985.

Thoenig, J.-C. and Dupuy, F.: *Sociologie de l'administration française*. Paris: Colin, 1983.

Locke, John (1632–1704) English philosopher and political thinker, adviser to the first Earl of Shaftesbury, and supporter of the Glorious Revolution of 1688. Author of *Two Treatises of Government* (1689) and *Essay Concerning Human Understanding* (1690). One of the most important influences on liberal democratic practice, Locke employed a theory of natural individual rights to form the basis of a consensual political association. The idea of a social contract that created a civil society encompassed a notion of responsible and restricted government. Civil society enabled the defence of individuality by means of the RULE OF LAW, as well as the regularization and centralization of executive power; political power, however, was neither paternal nor arbitrary but constituted a trust which limited its wielders. The moral justification of government lay in its protection of natural human rationality, with its concomitant of free and equal individuals, and of property rights. Hence government could also be regarded as a neutral umpire among its citizens. Here lay the foundations of liberal CONSTITUTIONAL-ISM, with its dual stress on general rules and on ultimate ethical ends. To protect against the abuse of power Locke advocated the separation of the legislature – the supreme power of the commonwealth – from the executive. Central to Locke's analysis was his location of SOVEREIGNTY in the political community, which exercised its constituent power through the popular right to resist tyranny, tacit consent to government being otherwise assumed. However an incipient, though undeveloped, majoritarian doctrine allowed the community to act through its representatives in the legislature. The possibility of a democratic suffrage was not entertained. Locke's theories supplied the framework, if not the details, for rights-oriented, accountable government, and have their most faithful echo in American constitutional and political practice. MSF

Reading

Dunn, J.: *The Political Thought of John Locke*. Cambridge: Cambridge University Press, 1969.

Gough, J.W.: *John Locke's Political Philosophy*. Oxford: Clarendon Press, 1973.

Leyden, W. von: *Hobbes and Locke*. London: Macmillan, 1981.

Locke, J.: *Two Treatises of Government*, ed. P. Laslett. Cambridge: Cambridge University Press, 1970.

Parry, G.: *John Locke*. London: Allen & Unwin, 1978.

Tully, J.: *A Discourse on Property: John Locke and his adversaries*. Cambridge: Cambridge University Press, 1982.

Yolton, J.W.: *John Locke: problems and perspectives*. Cambridge: Cambridge University Press, 1969.

M

Machiavelli/Machiavellianism

(1) *Niccolo Machiavelli* (1469–1527) was a Florentine politician, historian and political thinker. During the turbulent period witnessing the expulsion and then return of the Medici to Florence, the foreign wars and the Florentine Republic under Savonarola, Machiavelli held high offices of state in his native city, including that of secretary for the militia. He also suffered imprisonment, torture and involuntary retirement which gave him the opportunity to formulate his thoughts on politics. His chief works are *The Prince, The Discourses on the First Ten Books of Livy, The Art of War* and *The History of Florence*. Writing vividly and with great originality, drawing on his personal experience as well as his erudition in classical texts, Machiavelli's chief concern is with political POWER, specifically in respect to the foundation and maintenance of states. He broke with the medieval Christian tradition in defining the STATE as an autonomous association, with its own morality and mode of operation. The state, or the ruler, had its own 'reason' or overriding claim to maintain itself against internal and external oppposition. For Machiavelli it is power that creates stability and makes for orderly relations among individuals, not the other way around. Machiavelli regarded people as fickle and prone to evil; only under good laws made and enforced by strong-willed rulers are they kept well-behaved. He extolled the classical and martial virtues of courage, perseverance, foresight and patriotism, and called upon would-be rulers to unite the qualities of the lion and the fox in themselves: statesmen, as well as states, had constantly to fight against fortune. Since the qualities needed for statemanship are rarely to be found in one person, Machiavelli concluded that republics are preferable to principates because they will allow government to be conducted by a wider range of characters better able to adapt to changing circumstances. Although single rulers are generally needed to found and reform states, republican governments are better at maintaining them, once established. History alternated between citizenly virtue and corruption; Machiavelli saw country and city in his own age as corrupt: hence his call for the 'Prince' to conquer and create order out of chaos. Machiavelli's political science, centred on the notion of power, consists for the most part of historical generalization, sometimes of dubious value.

(2) *Machiavellianism* refers to a salient aspect of Machiavelli's political doctrines, often taken out of context. In common parlance it signifies lack of moral scruple in the pursuit of one's aims, or more succinctly: the end justifies the means. It is true that Machiavelli himself, especially in the notorious *Prince* (1513), quite unambiguously recommends the use of physical violence and fraud, in disregard of moral principles, in the service of the ruler. His detractors however, from the papacy through English Elizabethan writers and Frederick II of Prussia to modern political philosophers, pay inadequate attention to Machiavelli's principles as more fully set out in the *Discourses*. Machiavellianism in this generalized sense of ruthless power politics or an overriding REASON OF STATE has been more or less openly adopted and practised by nationalist politicians in the modern age. The Italian

communist Antonio Gramsci, in paying tribute to Machiavelli's insight into politics, likened his *Prince* to the role of COMMUNIST PARTIES. It might be said that in a minimal sense Machiavellianism is necessarily involved in the conduct of any state, government and political movement; its maximal and exclusive pursuit however clearly spells political immorality.

RNB

Reading

Butterfield, H.: *The Statecraft of Machiavelli*. London: Bell, 1940.

Chabod, F.: *Machiavelli and the Renaissance*. London: Harper Torchbacks, 1965.

Fleischer, M. ed.: *Machiavelli and the Nature of Political Thought*. New York: Atheneum, 1972.

Gilmore, M.P. ed.: *Studies on Machiavelli*. Florence: Sansoni, 1972.

Gramsci, A.: *The Modern Prince*. London: Lawrence & Wishart, 1958.

Hulling, N.: *Citizen Machiavelli*. Princeton, NJ: Princeton University Press, 1983.

Machiavelli, N.: *The Prince*, trans. G. Bull, Harmondsworth: Penguin, 1961.

———: *The Discourses*, trans. L.J. Walker, ed. B. Crick. Harmondsworth: Penguin, 1970.

Meinecke, F.: *Machiavellianism: the doctrine of raison d'état and its place in modern history*, ed. W. Stark, and trans. D. Scott. London: Routledge & Kegan Paul, 1957.

machine This term can be used in two senses. In the broader sense it can mean the professional staff, election agents and politicians, both central and local, who direct the activities of a political party. The term can thus be a synonym for PARTY ORGANIZATION.

In its narrower sense the term, more commonly used in the United States than elsewhere, refers in a derogatory manner, to a state or local party organization whose members are motivated and controlled by expectations of sharing in the 'spoils' of government (see SPOILS SYSTEM), favouritism based on political criteria in appointments, contracting, and administration of the laws. Machines are enduring, well organized (by American standards of party administration), and hierarchical. A machine need not, however, have all the power in its party and locality. One local machine might be opposed by another, each sustained by spoils from a different level of government. The presence of a machine need not signify centralized power within one local party or the other. For this reason, and because the incentive structure of machines is antithetical to doing so, machine politics is neither a source of policy coordination in municipal government nor a response to a need for such coordination.

Machines are concerned not with substantive issues but with those routine governmental operations that are not automatically decided and allocate benefits or penalties to specific individuals, not classes of persons. A variety of such decisions can be made according to political criteria. The beneficiaries are expected to help their party with financial contributions and/or work during election campaigns. It should not be assumed that influence is acquired from such contributions. 'Political participation' based on PATRONAGE is usually involuntary. Patronage employees are often assessed a percentage of their salaries. In places where machines flourish, government contractors assume that they must contribute.

At the lowest organizational level of the machine are precinct (neighbourhood) workers who are expected to know the people in their territory, ease their dealings with local government, and keep their party superiors informed of politically relevant developments. In return for favours, or to ingratiate themselves with the machine, some of these citizens can be counted on to attend nominating CAUCUSES and vote in the obscure primaries that maintain the machine in power.

In the US machines are most common in the Northeast and parts of the Middle West; they are almost wholly nonexistent in the West and other parts of the Middle West. Some areas with large immigrant populations have machines in one or both parties, others do not. By the same token some places with few immigrants have machines, others do not.

The decline of political machines has been announced for most of the twentieth century. One explanation is that the welfare state removed the need for the charity that machines doled out to the poor, at the same time that the flow of immigrants dwindled. In fact the welfare state provides many more opportunities for the exercise of petty favouritism. Moreover, many of the benefits of machine politics go not to poor people, but to middle-class business-men and professionals. American cities continue to receive waves of immigrants from rural areas and foreign countries. As govern-ment services increase, these unacculturated newcomers have, if anything, greater need for help with expanded bureaucracies.

Nevertheless, political machines, while flourishing in some places (one of the strongest is the Republican organization in the Long Island suburbs of New York City), have declined somewhat both in number and in-fluence. This modest trend has not been satisfactorily explained.   REW

Reading

Banfield, E.C. and Wilson, J.Q.: *City Politics*. New York: Vintage Books, 1963.

Key, V.O. Jr: *Politics, Parties and Pressure Groups*. New York: Crowell, 1964.

Mayhew, D.R.: *Placing Parties in American Politics*. Princeton, NJ: Princeton University Press, 1986.

Whyte, W.F.: *Street Corner Society*. Enlarged edn. Chicago, Ill.: University of Chicago Press, 1955.

Wilson, J.Q.: The economy of patronage. *Journal of Political Economy* 69 (1961) 369–80.

Wolfinger, R.E.: *The Politics of Progress*. Englewood Cliffs, NJ: Prentice-Hall, 1974.

Madison, James (1751–1836) No other individual in America's history has played a greater part in shaping his country's political institutions and political thought. Madison's standing in this respect eclipses his service as member of Congress, Secretary of State (1801–9) and President (1809–17).

A rising star in the politics of Virginia during the American Revolution, Madison early became convinced that the so-called Articles of Confederation, the first consti-tution of the United States, could not make the Union of American states permanent. He saw a danger that the Union would break up into three smaller CONFEDERATIONS, and exerted himself to find means of preventing this since he was convinced that the Union offered much the best prospects for the future

greatness and happiness of the states and people of America. Madison made a systematic study of political institutions, particularly those of earlier confederations, and by the time the Constitutional Convention met in 1787 to draft a new constitution he was better pre-pared than any other delegate with constructive proposals. Although many of his specific suggestions were not approved, his sobriquet, 'Father of the Constitution', was well-earned, for his influence on the other delegates was enormous. Furthermore, he kept by far the fullest record of the convention's proceedings. After the finished Constitution was sent to the states for ratification he collaborated with Alexander HAMILTON and John Jay in writing the FEDERALIST PAPERS, the most authorita-tive commentary on the Constitution ever compiled and America's one certain classic of political thought. It was largely because of his efforts that Virginia ratified the Constitution. During the first session of the new Congress, he led the successful campaign to pass the first ten amendments to the Constitution, known collectively as the BILL OF RIGHTS. Madison gradually moved into opposition to the admin-istration of President George Washington and became, with Thomas Jefferson, the co-founder of the Republican party, the fore-runner of the Democratic party. In his old age, partly in response to the growing controversy over STATES' RIGHTS, he made the preparation of his convention records for publication the occasion for extended reflection on his consti-tutional handiwork, and in these last writings showed himself to be, as always, a staunch republican and nationalist, in this way typify-ing American democracy.

Madison was a liberal: his great, charac-teristically American contribution to liberalism was his insistence at all times on the importance of practical politics. He could never have rested content with the lofty generalizations of some thinkers (such as those of Jefferson in the Declaration of Independence), nor would he accept detailed laws or constitutions based merely on deductions from first principles. Madison arrived at his first principles through political experience and activity. Experience of the confused and feeble Confederation govern-ment convinced him that each part – he accepted the conventional categories of executive, legislature and judiciary – had to be safe from encroachment by the others, and yet be prevented from exceeding its own powers. (In *The Federalist* no. 51, he identified the central problem of politics as the necessity first to 'enable the government to control the governed; and in the next place oblige it to control itself'.) In this way the famous doctrine of CHECKS AND BALANCES was evolved. Madison saw that the House of Representatives ought to be the democratic element in the Constitution, to act as a corrective to the privileges accorded to the states and to property; but he was also the first to raise the spectre of 'the tyranny of the majority'. In *The Federalist* no. 10 he argued that factions were inevitable, but that their malign effects could be mitigated in a large state within which a number of interests would jostle for recognition. Madison was therefore, with MONTESQUIEU, one of the first to recognize not only that popular government could be achieved in a large state, but that liberty might actually be better safeguarded in a larger than in a smaller unit. Madison's views did much to shape those of Alexis de Tocqueville, and through this and other channels, above all the Constitution itself, his ideas are still influential today.

See also SEPARATION OF POWERS.   HB

Reading

Brant, I.: *The Fourth President*. Indianapolis: Bobbs-Merrill, 1970.

Hamilton, A., Madison, J. and Jay, J.: *The Federalist* (1788), ed. J.E. Cooke. Middletown, Conn.: Wesleyan University Press, 1961.

Madison, J.: *Papers*, ed. W.T. Hutchinson and W.M. Rachel. 6 vols. Chicago, Ill.: University of Chicago Press, 1962–9.

————: *Writings*, ed. G. Hunt. New York: Putnam, 1900–10.

magistrate   In a broad sense anyone discharging judicial functions; in England the term is confined to those who do so in Magistrates' Courts. They may be either JUSTICES OF THE PEACE (JPs) or Stipendiary Magistrates. The latter, who are legally qualified, are appointed for large cities and usually sit alone, whereas between two and seven JPs normally sit together. All criminal proceedings begin in a Magistrates' Court. Depending on the gravity of offence, the court may either decide the whole matter or rule on whether there is sufficient evidence to justify committing the defendant to the Crown Court. The court has a limited civil jurisdiction, primarily in family matters.   JKBN

Reading

Walker, R.O and Walker, M.G.: *The English Legal System*. 6th edn. London: Butterworth, 1985.

majority government   A government supported by at least half the members of the national legislature in a parliamentary democracy. If the legislature has more than one chamber the government normally only needs the support of the lower house, and its support in this chamber determines its classification. The opposite of a majority government is a MINORITY GOVERNMENT. If a government is non-partisan it may be impossible to classify it as majority or minority. Majority governments may be composed of a single party, as is normally the case in two-party systems. Alternatively, majority governments may represent coalitions of two or more parties. Majority coalition governments are the most common form of government in many countries with multiparty systems, such as the German Federal Republic, Italy and the Netherlands.

Coalition theories distinguish between minimum winning and oversized majority governments. Minimum winning governments have no member parties that are unnecessary for majority status, whereas oversized coalitions do contain one or more such parties. Oversized majority governments are especially common in small democracies with deep social divisions, such as Belgium and Switzerland. This type of government often forms during wars and other national emergencies. Dodd (1976) has shown that oversized majority governments are generally less durable than minimum winning governments.   KS

Reading

Blondel, J.: Party systems and patterns of government in western democracies. *Canadian Journal of Political Science* 1 (1968) 180–203.

Dodd, L.C.: *Coalitions in Parliamentary Government.* Princeton, NJ: Princeton University Press, 1976.

Lijphart, A.: *Democracies: patterns of majoritarian and consensus government in twenty-one countries.* New Haven, Conn. and London: Yale University Press, 1984.

Powell, G.B. Jr.: *Contemporary Democracies: participation, stability and violence.* Cambridge, Mass.: Harvard University Press, 1982.

Strom, K.: Party goals and government performance in parliamentary democracies. *American Political Science Review* 79 (1985) 738–54.

See also under COALITION.

majority rule   This term can be used in two ways: one refers to the majority principle as a technique for making decisions in case of disagreement; the other refers to government by the majority of the people. The former is the primary sense; majority rule in the latter sense can be seen as derivative, as an application of majority rule in the former sense to decision making by the people and/or their representatives.

Majority rule (in the first sense above) comprises several techniques for decision making in case of disagreement. These differ with respect to the groups compared or to the size of the required majority. According to the *absolute* majority rule that course of action is chosen which is favoured by a majority of all the votes; according to the *relative* majority rule that course of action is chosen which is favoured by more votes than is any alternative. The simple majority rule selects the option that is favoured by more than half the votes; the qualified majority rule selects the option that is favoured by some specified proportion of votes above a simple majority (two-thirds, three-fourths, five-sixths, etc.). Majority rule presupposes the counting of votes but not necessarily the counting of individual participants in voting; it can be used whether individuals have one or several votes each.

Majority rule has been widely used for centuries but it has been accepted with misgivings and has been subject to restrictions.

In the formula 'maior et senior pars', which was used by certain bodies within the medieval Christian church, the quantitative majority rule was combined with a qualitative element: among the majority should be included those with superior judgement. John LOCKE favoured majority rule on the assumption that society would fall apart unless it followed the lead of its strongest section, i.e. the majority. Locke also maintained that individual rights must be safeguarded from violation by the majority. Jean-Jacques ROUSSEAU believed in legislation by the 'general will' in the form of directly expressed popular preferences. In order to qualify as a general will, however, such majority preferences must be aimed at promoting the public interest, not private interests. Jeremy BENTHAM's principle of 'the greatest happiness of the greatest number' involved a justification of majority rule. Fearing that majority rule might lead to unwise decisions and to violation of minority rights, John Stuart MILL argued in favour of proportional representation and plural votes to more highly qualified voters. John C. CALHOUN, writing in defence of slavery in the Southern United States, wanted to limit majority rule by the principle of 'concurrent majorities', which would enable a minority of the nation to veto measures endorsed by its majority.

Majority rule involves two main types of problems. The first is that it does not necessarily produce decisions favoured by a majority since, when there are more than two options, there may be no majority in favour of any particular outcome. This is illustrated by the 'paradox of voting' in which, for example, three voters – A, B, and C rank three options – x, y and z – in the following manner: A ranks x before y and y before z; B ranks y before z and z before x; C ranks z before x and x before y. A majority $(A+C)$ therefore ranks x before y, a majority $(A+B)$ ranks y before z, but a majority $(B+C)$ ranks z before x. Consequently there is no majority for any particular rank order. Only if the distribution of rankings has a certain shape (i.e. is 'single-peaked' as, for example, when the votes are distributed along a unidimensional political continuum from left to right) can this result be avoided. Moreover even when there is a majority in favour of a certain outcome, one majoritarian technique, the qualified majority rule, allows a minority – possibly quite small (say just over one-sixth) – to block action favoured by a majority. In addition voting rules (about the selection of options for each choice, the sequence of choices, etc.) may in fact, if not by intention, prevent the majority's preferences from being translated into decisions.

The second main problem with majority rule is the justification for it. Why should the majority decide? In its primary sense, majority rule seems to be incontrovertible. It is procedural and non-discriminatory: it is not affected by the content of the votes or the characteristics of the voters. In its derivative sense of government by the majority of the people, its justification is not self-evident. One problem is that the majority of the people, and even their representatives, cannot be assumed to possess the requisite knowledge about difficult issues in today's complex society. To compensate for this, a host of formal and informal expert advisers are brought into decision making processes on different levels of government. Another, and more controversial, difficulty is the extent to which majority rule is compatible with the rights of minority groups and individuals. Electoral methods, such as various forms of proportional representation, are often designed to deal with this problem by ensuring that minorities are represented in the legislative assembly. Constitutional protection of certain human rights – backed up by the courts and removable only by new elections or referenda and/or by the use of the qualified majority rule – is also used as a barrier against 'majority tyranny'; lists of such rights are included in the constitutions of many countries. Yet neither electoral methods nor constitutional protection of rights provide any guarantees against serious disagreement between majority and minority. Majority rule must co-exist with conflicts of interest in society.   EB

Reading

Arrow, K.J.: *Social Choice and Individual Values.* New York: Wiley, 1951.

Bentham, J.: Constitutional code. In *The Works of*

Jeremy Bentham, Vol. IX. ed. J. Bowring. Edinburgh: Tate, 1838–1843.

Berg, E.: *Democracy and the Majority Principle.* Stockholm: Scandinavian University Books, 1965.

Calhoun, J.C.: *A Disquisition on Government* (1854). New York: Political Science Classics, 1947.

Locke, J.: The second treatise of civil government. In *John Locke: The Second Treatise of Civil Government* and *A Letter on Toleration*, ed. J.W. Gough. Oxford: Blackwell, 1946.

Mill, J.S.: Considerations on representative government. In *J.S. Mill: On Liberty* and *Considerations on Representative Government*, ed. R.B. McCallum. Oxford: Blackwell, 1946.

Pennock, J.R.: *Democratic Political Theory.* Princeton, NJ: Princeton University Press, 1979.

Rousseau, J.-J.: The Social Contract. In *Jean-Jacques Rousseau: The Social Contract* and *Discourses*, ed. G.D.H. Cole. London: Dent, 1966.

Spitz, E.: *Majority Rule.* Chatham, NJ: Chatham House, 1984.

maladministration   Literally, bad administration. The term is used particularly of failures to observe the proper standards of good government by public authorities or officials. A paradigm is provided by the Crichel Down affair, which led to a British minister's resignation in 1954: the Ministry of Agriculture had refused to sell back to a landowner after the war part of his farmland which had been purchased by another ministry for government use and was no longer required for the purpose for which it had been requisitioned.

The term maladministration became an art form when used to delineate the British OMBUDSMAN's jurisdiction over complaints. The term itself was undefined in the legislation, but Richard Crossman explained in debate that it would cover such failings as 'bias, neglect, inattention, delay, incompetence, ineptitude, perversity, turpitude, arbitrariness and so on' and that 'it would be a long and interesting list'. This has become known as the Crossman catalogue. It is clearly not exhaustive, and does not exclude inquiry into the merits of decisions, although it more obviously comprises procedural errors.

The faults described by the term are not generally such as to amount to illegality, and so typically lie outside the purview of courts and tribunals. The creation of other institutions to consider or provide redress for them signifies that existing political controls and institutions were perceived to be deficient. That perception was widespread, for the ombudsman device or something similar, such as the French *médiateur*, has taken root in most of the world's mature democracies.   CRM

Reading

Gellhorn, W.: *Ombudsmen and Others: citizens' protectors in nine countries.* Cambridge, Mass.: Harvard University Press, 1967.

Schwartz, B. and Wade, H.W.R.: *Legal Control of Government.* Oxford: Oxford University Press, 1972.

Wheare, K.C.: *Maladministration and its Remedies.* London: Stevens, 1973.

mandate   A non self-governing territory over which sovereignty was technically suspended but lodged, in effect, in a supranational authority, the LEAGUE OF NATIONS (1919–46). Mandates were created to provide for the colonial territories conquered from Germany and Turkey in the first world war. Administrative control passed to the victor powers: Britain, France, Belgium, Japan, Australia, New Zealand and South Africa, though an annual report to the Permanent Mandates Commission of the League was required. Mandates were divided into three classes, *A*, *B*, and *C*, depending on the rapidity with which they were expected to attain independence; for *C* mandates this was infinitely remote. In principle mandates were to be governed in the interests of their indigenous populations, and internationalization was intended to lessen the colonial rivalries thought to have been partly responsible for the conflagration of 1914. In practice, since the League was dominated by colonial powers, international scrutiny was undemanding. (See TRUSTEE SYSTEM.)   JGD

Reading

Hall, H.D.: *Mandates, Dependencies and Trusteeship.* London: Stevens, 1948.

Louis, W.R.: *Germany's Lost Colonies.* Oxford: Clarendon Press, 1967.

mandate theory   The 'doctrine of the mandate' can imply either that a government is bound to follow instructions given by the electorate in a general election; or, negatively, that a government ought not, in a democracy, to adopt some new policy unless it has first been put before the electorate. The doctrine thus implies that a party elected to office on the basis of its programme is 'mandated' to carry it out; it has both the duty and the right to do so. The doctrine also implies that electors vote in the full knowledge that their behaviour will determine not only the composition of the next government, but also its policy on a dominant issue. This has sometimes occurred in Britain; the 1831 election was dominated by the issue of whether the system of representation should be reformed, that of 1868 by whether the Irish church should be disestablished, the 1906 and 1923 elections largely over the issues of protection versus free trade.

However it is difficult to maintain the doctrine when, as in modern British general elections, the programmes of the two major parties each contain well over 70 specific policy commitments, since the opinion surveys show that few if any voters prefer (even if aware of) every single item in one party's programme to every single item in another's. The doctrine is even more difficult to maintain in countries with multi-party systems, none securing an absolute majority in the legislature. Sometimes the notion of a specific mandate is weakened so that it becomes simply a 'mandate to govern', the implication being that a government, by virtue of being elected, has the right to take difficult and unpopular decisions, even if these were not put before the electorate at the last general election. In a number of political systems, it is argued that general elections cannot yield to any government a mandate to change the constitution of a country, and that, for constitutional change, a different 'weapon' is needed such as the REFERENDUM.   SEF

Reading

Birch, A.H.: *Representative and Responsible Government.* London: Allen & Unwin, 1964.

Bogdanor, V.: *The People and the Party System: the*

referendum and electoral reform in British politics. Cambridge: Cambridge University Press, 1981.

Emden, C.S.: *The People and the Constitution*, rev. edn. Oxford: Oxford University Press, 1956.

Jennings, I.: *Cabinet Government*, rev. edn. Cambridge: Cambridge University Press, 1959.

Marshall, G. and Moodie, G.: *Some Problems of the Constitution*. 5th edn. London: Hutchinson, 1971.

manifesto   See ELECTION PROGRAMME.

Mao Zedong and his thought 'Maoism', which the Chinese themselves prefer to call 'Mao Zedong Thought', may be defined as the end product of Mao Zedong's efforts, over a period of more than half a century, to adapt MARXISM, or Marxism–Leninism, to Chinese conditions.

Mao's administrative philosophy, which is the most important dimension of his thought from the standpoint of this volume, was shaped by three distinct influences: LENINIST organizational principles, the Chinese tradition, and his experience of armed struggle as the primary mode of revolutionary activity from the 1920s to 1949. To take the last point first, Mao put forward his famous aphorism, 'Political power grows out of the barrel of a gun', in 1927 *before* he had actually launched the guerrilla warfare from rural bases which was to lead to victory in 1949, having grasped already that, in a country with no effective centralized government, military force was the only solid foundation for political control. (See GUERRILLA WARFARE.)

Nevertheless, despite the emphasis on the gun during the period of armed struggle, Mao Zedong and the Chinese Communist Party underwent a long apprenticeship in the exercise of political power in the base areas, and in the process developed distinctive methods of leadership. One important element of these was the 'mass line'. This was not so much an alternative as a complement to Lenin's DEMOCRATIC CENTRALISM. Mao repeatedly stressed, both before and after 1949, that Party discipline and obedience to higher authority were indispensable, and that in the last analysis centralism was even more important than democracy. The mass line called for listening to people and taking

account of their views, but it was clearly stipulated that the 'scattered and unsystematic' ideas of the 'masses' must be synthesized by the 'processing plant' at the centre before they could be of any use. There is a clear parallel between this concept, and Lenin's view that class consciousness can only be injected into the working class from outside.

A second highly characteristic trait of Chinese Communist methods of leadership, the emphasis on thought reform, indoctrination, and psychological transformation, may be seen as flowing rather from traditional Chinese roots than from Leninism. The idea of the state as supreme educator, and of moral example and moral suasion as key instruments of political control, were central to Chinese political thought in earlier centuries, and such an approach is clearly echoed in the theory and practice of Mao Zedong.

During the so-called 'Great Proletarian Cultural Revolution' of 1966–1976, it appeared for a time that Mao had repudiated the emphasis on centralism and on discipline which had always marked his thought in the past, and was seeking to promote some kind of institutionalized chaos. It is possible that he may have toyed for a brief moment at the outset with some variant of the Paris Commune model which he explicitly evoked in summer 1966 as the solution for China, but by February 1967 he had already abandoned such notions. The proposal that 'heads' should be abolished was, he said, 'extreme anarchism' and therefore 'most reactionary'. In reality there would always have to be leaders, whatever one might call them.

Mao Zedong's views regarding the exercise of political power must be seen in the broader context of his overall goals: to combat bureaucracy, to transform human nature, and to build a new society and develop the economy through popular participation. Looking at Mao's life and thought as a whole, there is no doubt that he did genuinely seek to enhance the role of ordinary people in the life of society, but only in pursuit of the aims he had fixed and in the framework of the movements he promoted. If he often used the masses to challenge, shake up, or even to destroy others in the Party leadership, he was wholly unwilling, especially during the last twenty years of his life, to tolerate any lack of respect for his own authority.

In China, a decade after his death, Mao's great historical contributions are abundantly recognized but it is increasingly suggested that his economics, and even his conception of political power, owed more than a little to STALIN. Thus, while Mao Zedong Thought, defined as the totality of Mao's 'correct' works (mostly prior to 1957), plus writings by his contemporaries such as Liu Shaoqi, Zhou Enlai and Zhu De, is regarded as an important contribution to the theory China needs to guide her revolution, Marxism flexibly interpreted is becoming more and more the watchword.   SRS

Reading

Communist Party of China: *Resolution on CPC History (1949–1981)*. Beijing: Foreign Languages Press, 1981.

Friedman, E.: Three Leninist paths within a socialist conundrum. In *Three Visions of Chinese Socialism*, ch. 2, ed. D. Solinger. Boulder, Col.: Westview, 1984.

Meisner, M.: *Marxism, Maoism, and Utopianism*. Madison: University of Wisconsin Press, 1982.

Schram, S.R.: Decentralization in a unitary state: theory and practice 1940–1984. In *The Scope of State Power in China*, ch. 4, ed. S. Schram. London: SOAS; Hong Kong: Chinese University Press, 1985.

———: *The Thought of Mao Tse-tung*. Cambridge: Cambridge University Press, 1987.

Tang Tsou: *The Cultural Revolution and Post-Mao Reforms*. Chicago, Ill.: University of Chicago Press, 1985.

marginal seat   A legislative seat liable to change hands between parties. Their number determines the relationship between seats and votes in single member ELECTORAL SYSTEMS which have no formal allocative rule. Commonly there have been sufficient marginal seats for a change in votes between two parties to produce a disproportionate transfer of seats, ensuring an overall majority of all seats for the largest party. In contrast, small parties win few seats. But neither feature is invariant. For example, the number of Conservative/Labour

marginals in Britain halved between 1955 and 1983, significantly reducing the electoral system's exaggerative quality.

See also CUBE LAW.   JKC

Reading

Curtice, J. and Steed, M.: Electoral choice and the production of government: the changing operation of the electoral system in the United Kingdom since 1955. *British Journal of Political Science* 12 (1982) 249–98.

———: Proportionality and exaggeration in the British electoral system. *Electoral Studies* 5 (1986) 209–28.

Gudgin, G. and Taylor, P.: *Seats, Votes and the Spatial Organisation of Elections*. London: Pion, 1979.

martial law   The imposition of MILITARY RULE on the civil population. In one sense, which is recognized by international law, it may refer to the rule imposed by a military commander in occupation of a foreign territory. In some constitutional systems a country under its own law may be subjected in time of war or emergency to military rule and a suspension of ordinary law by the proclamation of a 'state of siege'.

In the United States the president's right to impose martial law in cases of extreme necessity has been held to be not allowable when the civil courts are open and functioning. In the United Kingdom no such authority exists either under statute or common law, though it could of course be imposed by Act of Parliament. During the two world wars emergency parliamentary legislation gave wide powers to the executive but no attempt was made to impose military rule or to suspend the operation of the ordinary courts and there has been no attempt by the crown to exercise martial rule in England since the seventeenth century. In so far as martial law can be said to be recognized by English law it would appear to be merely an aspect of the crown's right to maintain order in cases of necessity arising out of insurrection or invasion, by whatever degree of force may be necessary – the crown's acts and their necessity being subject to question in the ordinary courts after the emergency. It seems that no such necessity could arise in times of peace. What may be done in the United Kingdom by the army and by military tribunals in emergency depends therefore on the necessity of the case and does not rest upon any proclamation of martial law. The law cannot be stated with complete certainty however since it derives from cases arising from events now remote in time, in Ireland, Canada and South Africa, rather than in Britain.

See also EMERGENCY POWERS.   GM

Reading

Dicey, A.V.: *Introduction to the Study of the Law of the Constitution.* 10th edn (1959), ch. 8, ed. E.C.S. Wade. Repr. Basingstoke: Macmillan, 1985.

Heuston, R.F.V.: *Essays in Constitutional Law.* 2nd edn, ch. 6. London: Stevens, 1964.

Holdsworth, W.: Martial law historically considered. *Law Quarterly Review* 18 (1902) 117.

Keir, D.L. and Lawson, F.H.: *Cases in Constitutional Law.* 6th edn, ch. 3. Oxford: Clarendon Press, 1979.

Marxism   This radical critique of capitalist society, enunciating and advocating its overthrow by a proletarian revolution leading to SOCIALISM, was developed in the writings of Karl Marx (1818–83), a German thinker of Jewish descent who lived most of his life in exile in England.

Marx's thought initially developed as an internal critique of HEGEL's political philosophy. Marx especially challenged Hegel's contention that in modern society the STATE appears as a force independent of the economic forces of civil society. In numerous articles, books and unpublished treatises culminating in *The Communist Manifesto*, Marx propounded the idea that the modern state, far from representing common interests, is 'nothing else than the executive committee of the ruling classes'. All history to Marx is class history, as man is basically a producing animal (*homo faber*); according to this philosophical anthropology man is distinct from other animals in his active relationship to nature, which he transforms in the process of satisfying his needs. Man's needs are themselves historically conditioned, hence his productive capacities are central to historical development ('histori-cal materialism'). Out of this struggle over the control of production there arises human history as the history of class warfare. According to Marx modern society is divided into the bourgeoisie, which controls the capital, and the proletariat, which sells its labour for wages. In *Das Kapital* Marx argues that wages never rise above the subsistence minimum, the surplus thereby accruing to the capitalist forms the exploitative basis of bourgeois society. This attempt to keep wages at their minimal level is also however the basis for the internal contradictions of capitalism: it restricts the purchasing power of the workers; this in turn causes restraints on the level of production, accompanied by cyclical crises in the industrial system, constant threats of unemployment and bankruptcies, and the immanent inability of the capitalist system to produce abundance despite the technology available to it.

Marx advocated the organization of workers both as an economic force (TRADE UNIONS) and as a political one (a revolutionary movement). According to him capitalist societies are doomed because of their periodic crises of over-production and under-consumption: only an industry directed by overall social goals, rather than by the profit motive of individual capitalist owners, will be able to ensure abundance without crisis. The proletariat, which according to Marx comprises the majority of the population in most industrialized societies, will through organizing itself into a revolutionary force succeed in gaining power; the transition to socialism could, in some countries, such as Britain and the US, be peaceful, but the proletarian revolution would, more possibly, be a violent one especially in countries with strong authoritarian traditions, such as Germany and France. This DICTATORSHIP OF THE PROLETARIAT will concentrate all productive power in the hands of society: class differences will thus disappear, and this classless society will eventually lead to the WITHERING AWAY OF THE STATE.

Marx's theories were further developed after his death into the popular and simplified doctrine known as *Marxism*, which tended to emphasize the deterministic elements in Marx's thought at the expense of the dialectical heritage of the Hegelian tradition inherent in it. This became the main doctrine of most SOCIALIST PARTIES on the European continent until the first world war. During this period the revolutionary belief in a radical transformation of society was mitigated in western Europe by electoral reforms, which offered most working-class people access to political participation, as well as by social welfare reform. This tended to transform the erstwhile revolutionary movement, mainly in Germany and France, into 'reformist' parties working within the parliamentary system. In eastern Europe, and especially in Czarist Russia (where the proletariat was small and could not aspire to become a majority) such developments could not occur. Marx did not exclude the possibility of a revolution in Russia, but believed that it would be most likely to occur in more advanced industrial societies in which capitalism was fully developed. Under LENIN Russian Marxism became an elitist ideology, legitimizing a revolutionary dictatorship by a party led by professional revolutionaries imposing their radical policies on a recalcitrant population, mainly made up of peasants.

Between the two world wars this rift between the reformist and the revolutionary wings of Marxism became institutionalized in the split between the social democratic and COMMUNIST PARTIES. The emergence of TOTALITARIANISM under STALIN further exacerbated this split. After the second world war, the Leninist version of Marxism became the ruling ideology in most eastern European countries liberated from the Nazis by the Soviet army, while the process of decolonization in the third world introduced variants of Marxism into the non-European world. These variants included, especially, Maoism (see MAO ZEDONG AND HIS THOUGHT).

The discovery and propagation, after the second world war, of Marx's early philosophical writings did much to introduce a humanistic dimension into the understanding of Marxism in the West. This further divorced western interest in the theoretical aspects of Marxism from the bureaucratic regime prevalent in the Soviet Union.   SA

Reading

Althusser, L.: *For Marx*. New York: Vintage Books, 1970.

Avineri, S.: *The Social and Political Thought of Karl Marx*. Cambridge: Cambridge University Press, 1968.

Cohen, G.A.: *Karl Marx's Theory of History: a defence*. Princeton, NJ: Princeton University Press, 1978.

Colletti, L.: *Marxism and Hegel*. London: Verso, 1979.

Elster, J.: *Making Sense of Marx*. Cambridge: Cambridge University Press, 1985.

Kamenka, E.: *The Ethical Foundations of Marxism*. London: Routledge & Kegan Paul, 1972.

Kolakowski, L.: *Main Currents of Marxism: its origins, growth and dissolution*. 3 vols, trans. P.S. Falla. Oxford and New York: Oxford University Press, 1978.

Lichtheim, G.: *Marxism*. London: Routledge & Kegan Paul; New York: Praeger, 1961.

Marx, K.: *Selected Writings*, ed. D. McLellan. Oxford: Oxford University Press, 1977.

Tucker, R.C.: *The Marxist Revolutionary Idea*. London: Allen & Unwin, 1970.

mass communication and mass media

The term mass communication refers to the abundant, openly available and relatively standardized messages, intended for more or less simultaneous consumption by large numbers of individuals in diverse social or geographical locations, which are 'professionally' produced and distributed by specialized institutions termed *mass media*, using advanced technologies. The technical developments that have successively facilitated the growth of newspapers and magazines, the cinema, radio and records, and television have also: extended communication capabilities in space, time and audience reach; forged more links between previously less connected sectors of national and international society; enlarged vicarious experience; and created new forms of entertainment, information, rhetoric and culture.

Several sorts of 'media dependence' with implications for social and political order have resulted. At the individual level, much leisure time is devoted to media consumption, which in turn provides handy 'coins of exchange' for conversation with family and friends and often prompts reflection on self, social values and political issues. At the societal level, mass communication is now indispensable to: the acquisition of power; the legitimation of authority; the enforcement of social norms; and the organization (including the definition) of public opinion. At the sub-system level, many organizations, including political parties, rely heavily on mass media access to mobilize support for their objectives. Consequently the publicity process of modern democracies has increasingly become a competitive struggle to influence popular perceptions of key political events and issues through the mass media. Indeed one effect of 'media politics' is the sheer amount of planning, resources and activity that are invested by opinion makers in efforts to generate favourable publicity. Another may be the exposure of the political system to faster-flowing, though sometimes ephemeral, currents of change. Guided by essentially transitory news values – topicality, novelty and conflict – a media-dominated environment is liable to be a less stable one.

Six features of mass communication are specially significant. One is the heterogeneous composition of the audience, entailing shared experiences (though not necessarily common reactions) among individuals drawn from all classes, occupations, regions, life cycle phases, life styles and belief systems. This undergirds consensus building, social integration and the vaunted agenda-setting power of mass communication.

Second, the mass media typically disseminate general interest materials for consumption by people at leisure in free-time periods. Consequently political communications must compete with messages of many other kinds for mass media selection and audience attention. Political communicators also have to reckon on audiences that tend to associate media use less with work and duty and more with relaxation and diversion.

Third, mass communication is predominantly the one-way transmission of materials from organized sources to collective audiences. Stratification, unevenness of power relations, difficulties of targeting messages, potential mismatches of intention and reception may all result, especially in the case

of political communication, which has even been defined as 'the transmission of messages and pressures to and from the highly informed and abysmally ignorant; ... the highly powerful and the pitifully impotent; ... the highly involved and the blissfully indifferent'. Although mass media communicators may be motivated to attend to audience feedback, such as ratings, opinion surveys, organized research and informal soundings, the ensuing lessons are sometimes incorporated into rather generalized audience images which can be grossly stereotyped and self-serving.

Fourth, mass communications are mediated communications. They are therefore only a small subset of the vast array of events and messages that could have been chosen – greatly amplifying the significance of their selection. Moreover they are processed within large and complex organizations with their own purposes, survival needs and control structures, and they often reflect the organization's work routines, financial resources and linkages to other institutions. Thus media organizations are intermediary bodies, standing between and exposed to influences from both would-be message sources and opinion advocates on the one side and prospective audience members on the other. In political communication, media relations to sources can become highly complex and mutually absorbing, entailing much accommodation and exchange alongside adversarial attitudes and sporadic outbreaks of conflict.

Fifth, mass communication is associated with the rise of a new social role, that of the professional communicator. Its holders have been likened to symbol brokers or translators, relaying information, attitudes and concerns from one part of society in terms that can be understood by others. The role can be varyingly defined and performed, depending partly on how orientations to several possible points of reference are valued and mixed; for example, toward communication sources, the audience, peer standards, the organization itself or some form of service to society at large. Schemes for classifying journalistic models have distinguished: gatekeepers versus advocates; interpreters, information providers and adversarials; prudential, reactive, conventionally journalistic and analytical stances towards mass media agenda setting. Since, however, the message produced by the professional communicator is not *necessarily* related to his/her own ideas and value preferences, certain characteristic norms have often been associated with the role, such as objectivity, neutrality, impartiality and fairness.

Sixth, the mass media are exposed to contact with an extraordinary variety of external systems – political, economic and cultural. Media arrangements are partially dependent on the latter. Political systems, for example, not only provide the legal framework for media operations, they also include spokesperson roles (President, Prime Minister, Leader of the Opposition, etc.) that translate more or less automatically into 'rights' of mass media access. Regardless of the form of financial support, media systems also operate within the constraints imposed on their resources by the economic base. Yet knowing the economic and political systems of a society does not permit easy derivation or prediction of what its media system will be like. Media systems have *sui generis* qualities, among which may be a sense of the vulnerability of their independence from other systems and a special striving to preserve it.

None of this is intended to suggest that media arrangements are everywhere broadly alike. On the contrary, six different press system models have been distinguished according to their normative principles: authoritarian; totalitarian; liberal; socially responsible; development journalism; and democratic–participant. Linkages to external systems are also highly variable. Although comparative communication systems analysis is still in its infancy, research has already traced differences of mass media performance to differences of political structures, political cultures, funding arrangements, levels of source activity, professional cultures and the relative subordination of media institutions to (or autonomy from) political institutions.

Due to their complexity, the mass media are open to study at several levels and from diverse points of departure, making integrated scholarship difficult. They may be examined as organizations (from a sociological per-

spective), as industries and businesses (economics), for their relations to government, public opinion and pressure groups (political science), as suppliers of patterned 'texts' and discourses (cultural studies) and as builders of audiences, seeking certain gratifications and open to certain effects (social psychology). They are eminently ubiquitous forces, not only in audience reach but in the range of topics, issues and relationships covered, excluding no area of social reality. Yet mass communications are received by audience members under the influence of a host of other social commitments and loyalties; and their knowledge-producing function is shared with the institutions of education, politics, industry and religion. Such conflicting tendencies help to explain the divide in the academic literature between scholars who subscribe to modest 'limited effects' models of media impact and those who are prone to speak of 'powerful mass media' in society and politics.

Six other master divisions structure debate in the field. One concerns the discretionary power of the mass media and the degree of their dependence on or independence from society's other main centres of power gravity. Theories of the agenda-setting function of the press typically treat the news media as able to stamp their own priorities on political discourse. Scholars differ, secondly, over the uniformity or diversity of mass media coverage of major policy questions. According to Marxists and critical theorists, the media are constrained to project relatively homogeneous and conventional impressions of what is at stake in such issue areas as industrial relations, social welfare spending, race relations, law and order, terrorism and other forms of deviance. Pluralists, however, find more scope for rival standpoints to be aired in the mass media, depicting television, for example, as affording a 'cultural forum', inviting reflection on alternative approaches to social issues and moral dilemmas. Third, the typical audience member has been characterized by certain authorities as relatively passive (emphasizing media use as a low involvement, unconsidered, pastime activity with high vulnerability to effect) and others as relatively active (selective, bending content to the person's own purposes, mingling it with interpersonal communication flows, erecting barriers to effect). Fourth, the social function performed by mass communication through the provision of common points of reference across the heterogeneous audience has been assessed quite differently. Functionalists see it as integrative, relating the claims and demands of different sub-systems to society's core values and standards, while Marxists treat it as hegemonic, bolstering ideologies that sell the status quo, mask injustices and tame oppositions. Fifth, vigorous controversy has arisen over the part played by the mass media (particularly television) in the social construction of reality. Some researchers allege that media portrayals cultivate misleading and exaggerated impressions of a wide range of social institutions and relationships – the family, industrial conflict, provision of health care, violence in society, and images of women, the elderly and ethnic minorities. Others are sceptical, stressing instead audience awareness of media distortions and the differential incorporation of media information into people's views of the world. Finally, many of these points of conflict shape different perspectives on the role of the mass media in democracy. Whereas some scholars regard them as providing a sort of national debating chamber, framing alternatives between which citizens may choose, others claim that they are not only unsuited to such a task but are also corrosive of the party system and other political institutions, from which alone coherent choices can emerge.

Latterly, new technological developments – diffusing video cassette recorders, remote control switches, cable and satellite television, videotext, teletext and home computers – have raised questions about the future of the mass audience and blurred the distinctness of mass communication processes. Prospects beckon for segmented rather than heterogeneous audiences, plural rather than common cultures and agendas, interactive rather than one-way communication, and personalized rather than collective consumption. The ultimate shape of the communicatons future will turn partly on outcomes of intensified competition between established providers and newcomers to the field and partly on the still uncertain appeal to audience members of the new devices and facilities. Though prediction is hazardous, mass communication in the traditional sense may be sheltered from obsolescence by the significance for society and the individual of the many needs it serves. A degree of fragmentation (if not segmentation) of the mass audience appears inevitable, however, and this is likely to make the job of political communicators, aiming to aggregate exposure to their appeals, even more difficult than it has been in the recent past.

See also POLITICAL COMMUNICATION.

JGB

Reading

Alexander, J.C.: The mass media in systemic, historic and comparative perspective. In *Mass Media and Social Change*, ed. E. Katz and T. Szecsko. Beverly Hills, Calif. and London: Sage, 1981.

Arterton, F.C.: *Media Politics: the news strategies of presidential campaigns*. Lexington, Mass. and Toronto: Lexington Books, 1984.

Ball-Rokeach, S.J. and Defleur, M.L.: A dependency model of mass media effects. *Communication Research* 3.1 (1976) 3–21.

Blumler, J.G.: The political effects of television. In *The Effects of Television*, ed. J. Halloran. London: Panther, 1970.

—— and Gurevitch, M.: The political effects of mass communication. In Gurevitch et al. 1982.

—— and Gurevitch, M.: Politicians and the press: an essay in role relationships. In *Handbook of Political Communication*, ed. D.D. Nimmo and K.R. Sanders. Beverly Hills, Calif. and London: Sage, 1981.

Carey, J.: The communications revolution and the professional communicator. In *The Sociology of Mass Media Communicators*, ed. P. Halmos. Keele Sociological Review Monograph 13, University of Keele, 1969.

Gurevitch, M., Bennett, M., Curran, J. and Woollacott, J. eds: *Culture, Society and the Media*. London: Methuen, 1982.

Hall, S.: The re-discovery of ideology: return of the repressed in media studies. In Gurevitch et al 1982.

Janowitz, M.: The study of mass communication. *International Encyclopedia of the Social Sciences*, Vol. III. New York: Macmillan and the Free Press, 1968.

McQuail, D.: *Mass Communication Theory: an intro-*

duction. Beverly Hills, Calif. and London: Sage, 1983.

————— and Siune, K.: *New Media Politics: comparative perspectives in western Europe.* Beverly Hills, Calif. and London: Sage, 1986.

Newcomb, H.M. and Hirsch, P.M.: Television as a cultural forum: implications for research. In *Interpreting Television: current research perspectives,* ed. W.D. Rowland, Jr and B. Watkins. Beverly Hills, Calif., London and New Delhi: Sage, 1984.

Noelle-Neumann, E.: *The Spiral of Silence: our social skin.* Chicago, Ill.: University of Chicago Press, 1983.

Ranney, A.: *Channels of Power: the impact of television on American politics.* New York: Basic Books, 1983.

Siebert, F., Peterson, T. and Schramm, W.: *Four Theories of the Press.* Urbana: University of Illinois Press, 1956.

Wright, C.R.: *Mass Communication: a sociological perspective.* New York: Random House, 1975.

mass membership party A party relying on formal membership as an organizational feature, in contrast to those which have no strict requirements and no clear-cut distinction between members and supporters, such as a 'party of notables' or a CADRE PARTY. A corollary aspect of a mass membership party is the formal specification of the obligations and rights of members as well as the detailed attention in party statutes given to PARTY ORGANIZATION and the processes of decision making in which members participate, especially the election of party officials and the determination of the party's programme.

Mass membership parties developed in Europe during the late nineteenth century primarily as a response to the extension of the franchise. Forerunners of the mass party are to be found in nationalist movements and the political institutions of the Roman Catholic church, but the SOCIALIST PARTIES in Europe were the first to develop a mass base together with a distinctive and permanent organization. The socialist parties were successful in mobilizing working-class support, thereby becoming a significant electoral force, and the model of the mass membership party was later adopted by the 'bourgeois' parties. This process of 'contagion from the left' (Duverger) did not always apply: in the United States

socialist parties failed to develop. In Britain both the Conservatives and the Liberals acquired some features of the mass party before the advent of the Labour Party. In principle, mass membership parties are democratic organizations in the sense that party policies are ultimately decided by the members who should also be able to control the party leaders; in practice, initiative usually lies with party activists since most members participate very little. More fundamentally MICHELS with his IRON LAW OF OLIGARCHY held that a mass membership party would inevitably be controlled by the party elite whatever the extent of its democratic pretensions.

Mass membership parties are an efficient way of ensuring a high and stable level of electoral support and more generally of securing the political mobilization of particular social groups. Historically, and especially for socialist parties, a high degree of 'social encapsulation' was sought in integrating the members with the party, and for the members the party was important in expressing a collective identity over and above any tangible benefit. In this respect the mass party differs from other mass organizations which are chiefly instrumental in character.

Some mass parties have succeeded in achieving a high 'membership density' (proportion of members to voters), but this can conceal an actual weakness in appealing to a wider electorate. Emphasis on securing a large membership has declined, and the weakening of strong PARTY IDENTIFICATION is reflected in a general fall of membership density for mass parties. But it can be argued that contemporary parties no longer require a large and committed membership and that, for their part, voters do not depend greatly on parties either as expressions of social identity or as means of furthering their own ideals and interests. GSm

Reading

Daalder, H. and Mair, P. eds.: *Western European Party Systems.* London and New York: Sage, 1983.

Duverger, M.: *Political Parties: their organization and activity in the modern state.* London: Methuen, 1964.

Epstein, L.: *Political Parties in Western Democracies*. New Brunswick, NJ: Transaction Books, 1980.

Kirchheimer, O.: Party structure in mass democracy in Europe. In *Politics, Law and Social Change*, ed. F. Burin and K. Shell. New York: Columbia University Press, 1969.

LaPalombara, J. and Weiner, M. eds: *Political Parties and Political Development*. Princeton, NJ: Princeton University Press, 1966.

Neumann, S. ed.: *Modern Political Parties*. Chicago, Ill.: University of Chicago Press, 1956.

Sartori, G.: *Parties and Party Systems*. London and New York: Cambridge University Press, 1976.

mayor   The political head of a town or CITY GOVERNMENT. The office of mayor has a long history in Europe. The English title, like the French *maire*, derives from the Latin *major* (greater) meaning a superior official. However, the office has equivalents in other European languages drawn from different etymological roots: *sindaco* (Italian), *alcalde* (Spanish), *borgmester* (Danish), and so on. The office has now been adopted in LOCAL GOVERNMENT well beyond Europe.

Despite the ubiquity of the office, the role and status of mayors vary widely. There are three main dimensions of difference: central versus local appointment, direct versus INDIRECT ELECTION, and chief executive versus chairman responsibilities. In authoritarian political systems mayors are appointed by central authorities and may be dismissed by them – or at least such appointments are subject to their approval. In most liberal democracies on the other hand, mayors are appointed locally without central interference. There are some exceptions. For instance the Dutch *burgemeester* is a central government appointee, though with independent power once appointed. Even where mayors are usually appointed locally, capital cities may be subject to special arrangements. Mexico city, for example, in contrast to other Mexican cities, is headed by a *Jefe del Departamento del Distrito Federal* appointed by the national government.

Where mayors are local appointments the principal difference is between those directly elected by the local citizens, and those elected by the city or town council after it has been elected by the citizens. The former system,

direct election, is usual in American, Canadian, and New Zealand cities. British, Swedish, and French mayors are indirectly elected.

The third dimension of difference involves the mayor's powers and responsibilities. One major possibility is to make the mayor a political chief executive for the town or city with powers commensurate with this role over finance, appointments, and direction of policy. The other main possibility is to make the mayor merely a chairman and to allocate few special powers to the office. French, West German, Israeli, American, and Canadian mayors are expected to provide powerful executive leadership. British and Swedish mayors are only chairmen; executive leadership may however be provided instead by the leader of the majority party on a town or city council.

This leads to a consideration which can override in importance the powers attached to the office, namely the party political situation. Even where mayors have little formal authority, if backed by an effective party apparatus they may in practice wield enormous power. Richard Daley was a particularly dominant mayor of Chicago betwen 1955 and 1978 because of his control of the Cook County Democratic Party machine, even though technically the city has a WEAK MAYOR system.

Where mayors are powerful municipal executives then, they are important, not only in running towns or cities but in CENTRAL/LOCAL RELATIONS, representing their citizens in negotiations with higher levels of government.

Because mayors are such prominent political figures they are highly accountable to their electorates. There is indeed a danger that citizens may have unrealistic expectations of what a mayor can achieve in either a local or a central–local role.   DER

Reading

Becquart-Leclerc, J.: *Paradoxes du pouvoir local*. Paris: Fondation Nationale des Sciences Politiques, 1976.

CNRS: *Pouvoirs* no. 24. 'Le Maire'. Paris: Presses Universitaires de France, 1983.

Froger, P.J.: *Le Maire et son village*. Éditions le Cercle D'or, 1976.

Garrard, J.: *Leadership and Power in Victorian Industrial Towns*. Manchester: Manchester University Press, 1983.

Jones, G.W. and Norton, A.L. eds: *Political Leaders in Local Government*. Birmingham: Birmingham University Inst. of Local Government Studies, 1978.

Lagroye, J.: *Chaban-Delmas à Bordeaux*. Paris: Éditions Pedone, 1973.

Lee, J.M.: *Social Leaders and Public Persons*. Oxford: Oxford University Press, 1963.

Lowi, T.J.: *At the Pleasure of the Mayor: patronage and power in New York City 1895–1958*. Glencoe, Ill.: Free Press of Glencoe, 1964.

Rakove, M.L.: *Don't Make No Waves, Don't Back No Losers*. Bloomington: Indiana University Press, 1975.

Regan, D.E.: *A Headless State*. Nottingham: University of Nottingham Press, 1980.

Souchon, M.F.: *Le Maire: élu local dans une société en changement*. Paris: Édition Cujas, 1968.

mayor–administrator plan   An ADMINISTRATOR PLAN in which an administrator, by whatever title, is appointed (and may be dismissed) by the mayor, who is thereby freed from routine administration for work on policy development and leadership, ceremonial duties, and lobbying in the state and national capitals. (Usually the mayor and the administrator jointly prepare the budget.) The plan was first used in San Francisco in 1931 and spread to many large, and some small, cities after the second world war. It helped overcome the common problem of an elected executive lacking administrative capacity. The plan has been supported by reformers for cities where there is strong political opposition to the council-manager plan.   CRA

Reading

Adrian, C.R.: Recent concepts in large city administration. In *Urban Government*, ed. E.C. Banfield. New York: Free Press, 1961.

mayor–council   plan   Whenever the mayor is popularly elected, or is not dependent upon the council for reaching office, the form of city government is known as the mayor–council plan. The authority of the mayor may vary greatly from one city to another. Depending upon the extent of administrative authority, the system may be one of a STRONG MAYOR PLAN or a WEAK MAYOR PLAN. The council is almost always popularly elected, though candidates may first be screened and nominated by a political party or by some other method. Councils perform the traditional legislative functions of debate, criticism, investigation, and declaration of the law (or of the ordinances).   CRA

McCarthyism   The fear of communist subversion which pervaded American politics and government during the years 1946 to 1955. Wisconsin senator, Joseph R. McCarthy (1908–57), became the leading figure in the anti-communist agitation after a speech at Wheeling, West Virginia, on 9 February 1950 when he claimed to possess a list of 205 'communists' in the US State Department. A series of ever more dramatic allegations (not one of which was substantiated) regarding the pervasive influence of communists in government followed, and the senator achieved widespread publicity and public support. McCarthy became chairman of the Senate's Governmental Operations Committee in the Republican-controlled 83rd Congress (1953–4), but his inability to substantiate claims of communist influence in the US Army in televised hearings and attempts to secure special treatment from the army for a former aide, led to his censure by the Senate in November 1954 and the rapid disintegration of his political influence.

Anti-communist measures undertaken by the US government in the period 1946–55 were more important than McCarthy's activities. These included Truman's and Eisenhower's purges of the federal bureaucracy and the outlawing of the Communist party.

McCarthyism was a consequence of the Cold War between the US and the Soviet Union, and more specifically of frustrations experienced by the US in foreign policy – the end of America's nuclear monopoly, the 'loss of China' and the Korean war. McCarthy's disgrace and the lessening of international tensions by the mid 1950s drained much of the impetus from the anti-communist crusade. During the period 1956–58, the Supreme Court under chief Justice Earl Warren struck down much of the internal security legislation and circumscribed the power of congressional investigation (*Cole* v. *Young* 1956; *Pennsylvania* v. *Nelson* 1957; *Yates* v. *US* 1957; *Watkins* v. *US* 1959).

McCarthyism has been analysed by some political scientists as an example of a POPULIST political movement; but its social basis of support was not confined to the lower middle-class as was the case with POUJADISM for example. Some political scientists have analysed McCarthyism as a type of moral panic characteristic of certain periods of American history; while S. M. Lipset has characterized it like NAZISM as an extreme of the centre. Unlike Nazism, however, McCarthyism was never racist although it shared with populist movements a suspicion of political elites and of the institutions of representative democracy. NCR

Reading

Bell, D. ed.: *The Radical Right.* Garden City, NY: Anchor, 1964.

Caute, D.: *The Great Fear: the anti-communist purge under Truman and Eisenhower.* London: Secker & Warburg, 1978.

Fried, R.N.: *Men Against McCarthy.* New York: Columbia University Press, 1976.

Lipset, S.N.: *Political Man: the social bases of politics.* London: Heinemann, 1959; New York: Doubleday, 1960.

—— and Raab, E.: *The politics of unreason: right-wing extremism in America 1790–1970*, ch. 6. London: Heinemann, 1971.

Reeves, T.: *The Life and Times of Joe McCarthy.* London: Blond & Briggs, 1983.

Rogin, M.P.: *The Intellectuals and McCarthy: the radical specter.* Cambridge, Mass.: MIT Press, 1967.

McKenzie, R. T. (1917–1981)

McKenzie, R. T. (1917–1981) Professor of political sociology at the London School of Economics. McKenzie is best known for his *British Political Parties* (1955), the publication of which had more impact on the study of British political institutions than almost any other book in the post-war period.

He was also joint author (with Allan Silver) of *Angels in Marble* (1968), a study of working-class supporters of the Conservative Party.

The scope of *British Political Parties* is indicated by its sub-title, 'The Distribution of Power within the Conservative and Labour Parties'. McKenzie claimed that the power relationships within the two parties were broadly similar.

Whatever the role granted in theory to the extra-parliamentary wings of the parties, in practice final authority rests in both parties with the parliamentary party in its leadership. In this fundamental respect the distribution of power within the two major parties is the same (2nd edn, p. 365).

This claim challenged the established view (and in some degree the parties' caricatures of themselves and each other) of the Conservative Party as elitist and leader-dominated, and of the Labour leaders being controlled by the mass membership.

McKenzie was of course following the ideas of Roberto MICHELS who claimed that there was an IRON LAW OF OLIGARCHY in all organizations. His thesis created a stir in the Labour Party, particularly his claim that the party's belief in inner party democracy was incompatible with the British constitution. If the party conference could *instruct* Labour MPs, what was left of the independence of MPs and cabinet responsibility to the House of Commons? For McKenzie a Labour prime minister and cabinet had to be independent of dictation by any outside body. This view gained support when the party leader Hugh Gaitskell defied the 1960 conference vote over defence (eventually reversing it the next year), and the Wilson government ignored conference votes opposed to government policy in the late 1960s.

The thesis has been criticized on the grounds that it generalized from the immediate post-war period, and that power relationships were more variable than McKenzie had appreciated. The parliamentary leaders had managed to 'guide' the conference because of agreement on major issues with leaders of the main trade unions. In the late 1960s this alliance broke down and conference was less supportive of the parliamentary leadership.

Since 1979 there have been changes in the structure of the party – particularly the mandatory re-selection of MPs between elections and the system of electing the party leader by an electoral college, representing all sections of the movement (and no longer by MPs exclusively). These have increased the leverage of extra-parliamentary elements and lessened the autonomy of MPs. Further, McKenzie underestimated the importance of divisions within the leadership, each section seeking to appeal to the rank and file; neither the parliamentary leadership nor the extra-parliamentary movement are unitary actors, but are themselves factional bodies.

More generally, McKenzie never properly defined his main terms, and his lack of conceptual clarity detracts from the scientific status of his conclusions. He has also been criticized, especially by Beer, for ignoring the importance of IDEOLOGY in political life. Nevertheless *British Political Parties* remains one of the most important books on political science to be published in Britain since the war; it permanently altered conceptions of party democracy and greatly encouraged behavioural research into political parties.

DK

Reading

Beer, S.H.: *Modern British Politics*. 3rd edn. London: Faber, 1982.
Kavanagh, D.: Power in British political parties: iron law or special pleading? *West European Politics* 8 (July 1985).
McKenzie, R.T.: *British Political Parties* (1955). London: Heinemann, 1963; New York: Praeger, 1966.
–––––– and Silver, A.: *Angels in Marble*. London: Heinemann, 1968.
Minkin, L.: *The Labour Party Conference: a study in the politics of intra-party democracy*. London: Allen Lane, 1977.

Michels, Roberto (1876–1936) Belonging to the classical period of European political sociology at the start of the twentieth century, Michels came of Franco-German ancestry, and was educated in Germany, France and Italy. As a student he became a committed socialist and a member of the SPD (Sozialdemokratische Partei Deutschlands), though of a strongly syndicalist orientation.

His political views prevented him from obtaining an academic post in his native Germany and in 1907 he moved to take up a position at Turin. Here he came under the influence of Gaetano MOSCA and his doctrine of the 'political class', which crystallized his growing disenchantment with Social Democracy. It was from this perspective that in 1911 he published his classic work *Zur Soziologie des Parteiwesens in der modernen Demokratie* (translated as *Political Parties*), based upon his detailed personal knowledge of socialism in three countries. He took Italian citizenship in 1913 and, despite a long period as professor at Basle, regarded Italy as his home country. He joined the Fascist party after Mussolini's accession to power, and returned to a university post in Italy in 1928 to help develop a pro-fascist political science.

Although a prolific writer Michels is still only, and probably justly, known for this one work on political parties. Its purpose was to explain the reformism of European Social Democracy by demonstrating that movements and parties of the left must necessarily become deradicalized as they grow in size. In order to organize a mass movement effectively, so the argument goes, it is necessary to have a full-time leadership and a permanent apparatus of trained officials. Although recruited from the proletariat, these gradually become divorced from their origins in a variety of ways: they acquire specialist knowledge and expertise that is not available to the rank-and-file; their life is spent in the rarefied environment of industrial bargaining or parliamentary intrigue; above all, their position frees them from manual labour, and gives them a secure salaried employment with the accompanying life-style and outlook of the petty bourgeoisie. Having secured their own social revolution their radicalism is blunted, and they become opposed to any militant policy which might threaten the persistence of the organization and with it their own privileged existence. Furthermore, the position which divorces them from their following also guarantees them the means to determine the policy of the movement. Thay have the advantage over the rank-and-file of continuity of operation, superior knowledge and control over organizational resources, including the dissemination of information. Reformism thus comes to permeate the labour movement via its own structures of power.

Michels's work has made an important contribution to a number of overlapping areas of political science: to the theory of elites, to the study of movements and parties of the left, to the analysis of bureaucracy and the relation between democratic theory and practice. In the field of the theory of ELITES Michels's work offered a valuable test-case of PARETO's doctrine of elite circulation, according to which new elite forces repeatedly rise from the masses and become assimilated into established elite structures. In particular, the work provided plentiful evidence that it is not past social origins but present political roles which determine elite perceptions and behaviour. However, writing before the Bolshevik revolution, Michels seems to have overlooked the possibility, anticipated by Pareto, that established elites might be either too enclosed or too inept to accommodate a rising counter-elite, and that the latter's radicalism could be thereby sustained to the point of revolutionary overthrow. In other words, Michels's study accords with only one of two contrasting modes of elite circulation: that of assimilation rather than outright replacement.

Michels's explanation of the deradicalization process itself has not been accepted by all students of LABOUR MOVEMENTS. Some point to the wider economic and ideological forces that have moulded the working class, and see the antithesis between a potentially revolutionary mass and a reformist elite as unduly simplistic. Others argue that progressive deradicalization is the product of strategic choices which impose their own logic on subsequent activity; thus it was the decision of the SPD to embrace a purely parliamentary tactic that gave its organization the character it had, whereas the anti-parliamentary strategy of the Bolsheviks or the Communists after the first world war led in a very different direction. These examples call into question Michels's assertion that organization is necessarily conservative in its effects. However, to the extent that these examples are also exceptional, Michels's work highlighted a significant tendency for organization to become an end in itself and this has become a commonplace of subsequent studies of BUREAUCRACY. From a Michelsian perspective, administrative systems cannot be understood apart from the interests and values of those who work within them, since both personal and organizational imperatives can affect the goals to which the administration is supposedly subservient.

At the heart of Michels's work lay a deep scepticism about the democratic nature of mass organizations, and about the possibility of popular control over leadership, whatever its character. He documented in convincing detail the combination of personal prestige, organizational power and psychological manipulation that enables established leaders to maintain their position and outwit opposition from below. In so doing, however, he painted a bleaker prospect for democracy than is actually warranted – for example by playing down the changes that popular initiatives can bring in the content of policy, and the greater scope for this where elites are disunited or where pluralism is institutionalized within elite structures themselves.

Michels's pessimism about democracy can be partly traced to a faulty scientific method which assigned significance to historical uniformities rather than variations, and presented oligarchy as an IRON LAW rather than as a tendency that could with conscious effort be counteracted. In this respect a work such as *Industrial Democracy* by Michels's British contemporaries, the WEBBS, which explored the differing possibilities for democratic control offered by different types of trade union structure, was methodologically sounder than *Political Parties*. Yet the history of the two works suggests that a one-sided and provocative thesis can do more to stimulate subsequent research and debate than the most thorough and judicious compendium.   DB

Reading

Beetham, D.: Michels and his critics. *European Journal of Sociology* 22 (1981) 81–99.
Hands, G.: Roberto Michels and the study of political parties. *British Journal of Political Science* 1 (1971) 157–72.

Michels, R.: *Political Parties*. New York: Dover Publications, 1915; also ed. and intro. S.M. Lipset. New York: Crowell-Collier, 1962.

military regimes The expression relates to states where the top political decisions are made exclusively or predominantly by members of the armed forces. It therefore covers the cases where an alien army of occupation rules a conquered state (as in the Allied military governments in Germany and Italy during and after the second world war); more frequently it is used in reference to states whose military forces have supplanted a former civilian government and rule in their own name. The literature has mostly addressed the differences between military regimes but it is also necessary to ask whether common characteristics of such regimes entitle them to be regarded as a specific type of government *vis à vis* civilian regimes.

Broadly speaking, different military governments can be distinguished by the place the military hold in the decision making structure of the state and/or by what they do with the power they wield.

The place of the military in the decision-making structure

Sub-types of military governments shade into civilian ones, and it can be hard to know where the line should be drawn between them. It seems useful to confine the definition to the class of states where the current regime is the outcome of a previous illegal usurpation of power by the military, and where the head of state, or chief executive, is a member of the military. Within this broad category the roles played by the military in top decision making vary: three can be distinguished.

The military-junta type in which the supreme policy-making organ is a JUNTA or command council of officers representing the three services (army, navy, air force). It usually appoints a civilian cabinet to administer under its authority. Parties and the legislature are suppressed or else only a single official party is permitted. Often nominal and usually, at any rate, feeble, it is however a subservient artefact of the military executive. In this type the military, as 'represented' by its senior officers, plays the active and supreme role in policy making. These governments come nearest to the stereotype of a 'military government' and, to distinguish them from those where the military plays a lesser role are, properly speaking, *stratocracies*.

The presidential type in which the military play a supportive rather than a creative role, and the cabinet is formed largely or wholly from civilian rather than military personnel. In Zaire the army's role is supportive of the president, while the official party is largely nominal: hence a personalist-presidential regime. In Iraq and Syria, however, the local Ba'ath parties are true vanguard parties, in a 'symbiotic' relationship with the officer corps. The military play a more creative role than in the previous type, but the existence of the party enables the president to arbitrate, and so exert independent leadership over both civilian and military sectors.

There remain a few states where the entire cabinet personnel are civilian except possibly the head of state – and where, though founded by a coup, a (limited) competitive party system has developed, providing a legislature and a degree of press freedom. Egypt is such a state and should properly be regarded as an authoritarian civilian state and not a military government.

This classification is based on the military's control over the executive, the parties and the legislature; but in some countries they exercise great influence in the bureaucracy and/or the economy. In Ghana and Nigeria, for example, the military rulers have entrusted administration to the bureaucracy, whereas in Burma and Indonesia they have extensively taken over from it, both at central and local level. Similarly with the economy: the socialized Burmese economy is largely administered by the military and in Indonesia these administer the commanding state corporations and hundreds of individual firms.

The uses of power

Some military governments confine themselves to supervising or 'patrolling' the society. In Thailand the largely military cabinets permit the civil service a wide autonomy in running affairs, and preside over what is on the whole a free-wheeling economy. In Ghana and Nigeria however, the governments go further: they direct a national programme, but they leave the civil service to administer it. Finally, as in Burma, the military not only exert supreme authority on the direction via their hold on the socialized economy and the party, but play a large part in actual administration.

How distinctive are military governments?

Many studies of the political or the economic performance of military governments have been conducted on the assumption that these all exhibit a mix of attributes which makes them a separate category, clearly distinguishable from civilian regimes. They are certainly distinguishable in the trivial sense that they are the products of military coups, and that their presidents or heads of state are military or ex-military men.

Military governments also exhibit a common political style: by the indicators laid down by Freedom House all but two out of thirty-six military governments ranked as authoritarian and lacking basic civil freedoms, while among the seventy-three civilian regimes examined only 60 per cent ranked in this way. But absolute numbers convey a different impression: there were thirty-four military governments ranking as authoritarian as against forty-three civilian governments; there were thirty military governments lacking in civil rights as against thirty-eight civilian governments.

Military governments do not demonstrate any distinct economic style. Using the categories of Freedom House, nine were market economies, ten were statist-market, twelve were socialist-market, and four were out-and-out socialist economies. Nor do they follow a distinctive line in foreign affairs, some being pro-western, others pro-Soviet, and others being non-aligned. They are a mixed bag, where the only single differentiating characteristic is the use of military men in positions which would normally be held by civilians.   SEF

Reading

Finer, S.E.: *The Man on Horseback.* 2nd edn. Harmondsworth: Penguin, 1976.

———: The morphology of military regimes. In Kolkowicz and Korbonski, 1982.

Gastil, R.: *Freedom in the World: political rights and civil liberties.* New York: Freedom House, 1980.

Jackman, R.W.: Politicians in uniform. *American Political Science Review* 70.3 (1976) 1078–97.

Kelleher, C.M.: *Political–Military Systems.* New York: Sage, 1974.

Kolkowicz, R. and Korbonski, A. eds: *Soldiers, Peasants and Bureaucrats.* London: Allen & Unwin, 1982.

Nordlinger, E.A.: *Soldiers in Politics.* Englewood Cliffs, NJ: Prentice-Hall, 1977.

Perlmutter, A.: *The Military and Politics in Modern Times.* New Haven, Conn.: Yale University Press, 1977.

Mill, James (1773–1836) British philosopher. Mill was born in Scotland and moved to London in 1802 to earn a living as a writer; in 1817 he published *The History of British India* which earned him a post with the East India Company, where he later became Chief Examiner. After meeting Jeremy BENTHAM in 1808 he became the chief political propagandist for the school of philosophical radicals. A contributor to numerous journals, he applied the utilitarian philosophy to jurisprudence, education, political economy and, most famously, to government. Between 1816 and 1823 he wrote a series of essays for the Supplement to the fifth edition of the *Encyclopaedia Britannica* including one on 'Government' regarded by, among others, his son, John Stuart MILL, as the classic statement of utilitarian political theory. The essay marks a shift of emphasis away from the traditional question of who should rule to the question of how to control and restrain the rulers. Mill's central argument was that the very reasons which make government necessary for order and security point to REPRESENTATIVE GOVERNMENT as the sole security against oppression. Human nature is such that unless constantly checked rulers will look to their own interests at the expense of those of the community. To prevent this there must be an identification of interest between rulers and ruled, and representative democracy is the only means to this end. Along with freedom of expression – the ability to control our rulers depends on our knowledge of their actions – this is the main security for good government, logically deduced from the utilitarian view of man as driven by self-interest. Mill was an early advocate of democratic institutions, therefore, as a means of combating sinister interests. He also favoured the secret ballot. He was, however, criticized by Macaulay and by his son John Stuart Mill, for neglecting the problem of leadership in a representative system.

GLW

Reading

Halévy, E.: *The Growth of Philosophic Radicalism*. London: Faber & Faber, 1952.

Hamburger, J.: *James Mill and the Art of Revolution*. New Haven, Conn.: Yale University Press, 1963.

Lively, J. and Rees, J. eds: *Utilitarian Logic and Politics: James Mill's 'Essays on Government', Macaulay's critique and the ensuing debate*. Oxford: Clarendon Press, 1978.

Mill, J.: *An Essay on Government*. New York: Liberal Arts Press, 1955.

Mill, John Stuart (1806–73) British philosopher and economist. The eldest son of the radical reformer James Mill, who was himself a leading disciple and friend of the utilitarian philosopher Jeremy Bentham, the young Mill received a remarkable education from his father, beginning Greek at the age of three and Latin at eight. He was instructed in a wide range of subjects including economics, history, philosophy and natural science, and became convinced that Benthamite utilitarianism was the complete philosophy of life. In 1823 he entered the East India company where he worked until his retirement in 1858. His early commitment to the utilitarian cause was modified during a lengthy period of depression in 1826 after which he became open to new influences, especially those of poetry and art, which helped him towards a view of happiness as the development of character in a rich and diverse manner rather than the mere maximization of pleasurable consequences. Mass conformity posed a threat to such development; the power of public opinion in an age of increasing democratization therefore needed to be limited. In this way Mill began the movement away from his inherited opinions, a process influenced further by the French writer Alexis de TOCQUEVILLE, whose study of America pointed out the danger in a democracy of the 'despotism of the majority'. As a result a major problem that Mill faced in his political writings was how to combine popular participation with a high quality of political leadership, how to balance the virtues of democracy with the importance of freedom which he increasingly came to see as the essential climate for a progressive society as it was for the development of individual character.

After his retirement in 1858 and his wife's death in the same year Mill retired to Avignon in the south of France where he began to publish his mature judgements on matters political and moral. His fame brought an invitation to stand as parliamentary candidate for Westminster where he was elected in 1865; he was defeated three years later and retired once more to Avignon where he died in 1873.

In his mature works, most notably *On Liberty* (1859), *Considerations on Representative Government* (1861) and *Utilitarianism* (1863) much of the early utilitarian optimism regarding the beneficial consequences of political and social reform is replaced by an awareness that theoretical argument has to allow for historical change and cultural conditions. Democratic reform could no longer be seen simply as a rationally proven solution guaranteed to sweep away all injustice and corruption; it must be adapted to local conditions, and its weaknesses as well as its strengths must be recognized. Society had a high potential but equally powerful dangers; the crucial factor influencing future development would be the presence or absence of freedom and individuality. Mill's view of happiness, comprising nobleness of character, personal affection, social feeling, intellectual development, truth, and virtue led him to an awareness of the dangers of conformity and mediocrity which he saw as the results of unlimited popular power. Conformity whether to tradition and custom or to majority domination robbed the individual of his humanity, rendering him a servile creature and society a stagnant pool. Could the democratic system be so arranged that freedom and excellence might triumph over despotism and mediocrity?

The answer for Mill lay in giving representative government an educative as well as a utilitarian role. Popular power was not merely a security for good government, given the right conditions, but also an important training whereby people became citizens rather than mere subjects. Participation should improve standards as well as protecting interests. Of course this general approach carried with it detailed proposals to ensure the harmony between public involvement and informed judgement. The electoral system must be devised to allow the representation of all opinions, not just those of the majority, and this called for a form of proportional representation to ensure the representation of minorities (see ELECTORAL SYSTEMS). Again the better educated were entitled to more than one vote so that their voices would not be drowned in a sea of mediocrity. So the system was not seen simply as a register of individual self-interest but as an exercise in public spirit. (It was for this reason that Mill abandoned his defence of the secret ballot in favour of the view that a public duty should be publicly performed.) The resulting representative assembly was primarily intended to debate policy rather than actually govern. Its power lay in its control; the framing of legislation and the administration were tasks for experts. Parliament could inspect, scrutinize, criticize, censure, or expel but not itself govern. Laws were to be drafted by a specialized commission and the assembly could accept or reject or refer back its proposals. Similarly, administration needed to be in the hands of qualified experts not the mediocre amateurs so often found and tolerated in the civil service. This would give a balance between control by popular power and action by professional experts, leading both to the welfare and to the education of a people. Toward these ends Mill supported local representative bodies; they performed their tasks more efficiently and responsibly than could national government,

and they nourished a sense of public spirit and citizenship, essential for the kind of democratic state Mill envisaged. For the same reason, Mill favoured democratic participation in industry in the form of workers collectively owning the capital of the firm in which they were employed. His proposals always had at their heart his belief that institutions must be directed towards the improvement of man and the progress of society and so must preserve freedom and diversity and encourage participation and involvement. If the dangers of despotic majority rule could be avoided then popular representative government could help to make a people collectively greater and individually more enlightened, though at the same time it should be recognized that the key element of human happiness was individual improvement and in this area the role of government was necessarily limited.

Mill was one of the earliest students of comparative government, seeking to determine the conditions under which representative democracy was possible, and to analyse the educative effects of participation. His work has exerted a considerable influence upon modern political science, and especially upon democratic theory where Mill has been enlisted as an opponent of the elitist school of theorists whose intellectual ancestry can be traced to Joseph SCHUMPETER.

See also DEMOCRACY. GLW

Reading

Burns, J.H.: J.S. Mill and Democracy 1829–1861. *Political Studies* 5 (1957) 158–75, 281–94.

Duncan, G. and Lukes, S.: The new democracy. *Political Studies* 11 (1963) 156–77.

Halliday, R.J.: *John Stuart Mill*. London: Allen & Unwin, 1976.

Hamburger, J.: *Intellectuals in Politics: J.S. Mill and the Philosophical Radicals*. New Haven, Conn.: Yale University Press, 1965.

Kern, P.B.: Universal suffrage without democracy: Thomas Hare and J.S. Mill. *Review of Politics* 34 (1972) 306–22.

Mill, J.S.: *The Collected Works of John Stuart Mill*, ed. F.E.L. Priestley. Toronto: University of Toronto Press, 1963–1984.

Rees, J.C.: *John Stuart Mill's 'On Liberty'*. Oxford: Clarendon Press, 1985.

Robson, J.M.: *The Improvement of Mankind*. Toronto: University of Toronto Press; London: Routledge & Kegan Paul, 1968.

Ryan, A.: *J.S. Mill*. London and Boston, Mass.: Routledge & Kegan Paul, 1974.

Thompson, D.F.: *John Stuart Mill and Representative Government*. Princeton, NJ: Princeton University Press, 1976.

Williams, G.L. ed.: *John Stuart Mill on Politics and Society*. London: Fontana, 1976.

minister/ministry   In general a minister is the political head of a government DEPART-MENT. First among government ministers are heads of government. Others form the cabinets working around government leaders, though in some systems (such as in Britain) there is also an outer ring of non-cabinet ministers. Most ministers are placed in charge of defined sectors of government (portfolios) but some operate as 'ministers without portfolio', assisting heads of government in tasks they determine; others (usually at non-cabinet level) serve within large departments as assistants to ministers carrying primary administrative responsibility.

There has been a striking growth in the number of ministerial offices around the world since the second world war. The first systematic study of the ministerial profession, conducted by Jean Blondel in the early 1980s, estimated that the group then comprised about 3000 persons in all. The extent to which they can cope with the complexities of governing modern states has become a leading area of contemporary political research.

Ministerial office is mostly seen as representing the peak of a political career. In some countries however, civil servants or military officers are easily translated into these offices, so that the distinction between political and administrative careers characteristic of Westminster systems is not always so clear. The office of US departmental 'secretary' roughly combines the roles of minister and permanent/departmental secretary in true ministerial systems. The WESTMINSTER MODEL projects a very precise view of ministerial RESPONSIBILITY, which is less clear in some other systems.

The word ministry has two quite distinct political uses. The first refers simply to the body of ministers making up a government (the Thatcher ministry). The second refers to units of government under the direct supervision of particular ministers (the UK Ministry of Defence). In this sense ministry may be synonymous with department, but some difficulty arises in clarifying this relationship. Exercises in codification have pointed to the existence of several patterns. First: the terms ministry and department are totally interchangeable, as in the Australian Commonwealth government. Second: ministry is reserved for some or all larger, more important departments, as in Britain. Third: ministry is used to describe the field of a minister's total jurisdiction (or portfolio) when that field contains several departments in the public service sense, or one or more departments plus non-departmental agencies. There are subdivisions here. Sometimes there are co-ordinating secretariats to assist such ministers; at other times they stand face to face with a plurality of official heads at department and agency level without benefit of secretariat. Australian State governments provide a rich variety of such arrangements, the word ministry being sometimes used to denote the co-ordinating secretariat only. Where ministry is unambiguously the total portfolio organization, the permanent secretary is at that level and the constituent departments are headed by technical chiefs. Occasionally in this progression, the departments disappear altogether, being replaced by units at division level.   RLW

Reading

Blondel, J.: *Government Ministers in the Contemporary World*. London: Sage, 1985.

Headey, B.: *British Cabinet Ministers: the role of politicians in executive office*. London: Allen & Unwin, 1974.

Weller, P. and Grattan, M.: *Can Ministers Cope? Australian Federal Ministers at Work*. Melbourne: Hutchinson, 1981.

Wettenhall, R.L.: *Organising Government: the uses of ministries and departments*. Sydney: Croom Helm, 1986.

minorities, protection of Compared with dominant groups, minorities vary according to their relative size, their distinguishing characteristics – national, racial, religious or linguistic; their goals – acculturation, integration or separateness; and according to the obstacles, if any, that the dominant group puts in the way of achieving these goals. The techniques used for their protection will therefore vary according to types and circumstances.

Numerical and sociological minorities
The Swedish Finns are a numerical minority in Finland but sociologically they are, in greater proportion than the Finnish Finns, a part of the ruling elite. The blacks in South Africa are a numerical majority but a sociological minority. Certain scheduled castes of India are both a numerical and sociological minority.

DEMOCRACY, in some of its variations on the 'one-person one-vote' principle, will often be sufficient to protect a sociological minority that happens to be numerically large. In Belgium, as in the white South African polity, democracy helped the formerly dominated group – Flemish or Afrikaans – to become politically dominant. Even when the minority is numerically weak some common techniques of democratic rule may be so selected as to maximize its representation in the organs of government or give it the control of, or at least significant influence over, specific levels or branches of government. FEDERALISM may be used to protect territorially concentrated minorities; proportional representation may be favoured by minorities that are territorially dispersed. One may also resort to consociational techniques such as grand coalitions or mutual vetoes (see CONSOCIATIONAL DEMOCRACY).

Frequently however the common practices of equalitarian democracy will not be sufficient to protect minorities; their protection may require the institution of minority privileges that take the form of restrictions to the freedom of coalition formation. Examples of such deviations from strict equalitarianism and freedom of choice are: communal elec-torates of the kind used in pre-war India for the representation of religious and ethnic minorities in parliament; the Lebanese electoral system of the 1950s and 1960s requiring that candidates run as multi-ethnic teams; the Canadian custom (not formally binding, it is true) that francophones and anglophones alternate in the leadership of the Liberal party; the American and Indian practice of AFFIRMATIVE ACTION which consists in giving an advantage to the members of certain minority groups to compensate for past wrongs.

When a minority is geographically concentrated – concentration is more common for linguistic than for religious minorities – decentralization or deconcentration will often give the minority the possibility of administering its own locally made rules (constitutional federalism) or of administering locally the rules originating from the central authorities (administrative federalism). The two types of federalism may, as in Switzerland, reinforce each other. The advantages (from the ethnic if not from the economic point of view) inherent in federalism have led a unitary bi-ethnic state such as Belgium to adopt a territorial division of power not unlike that of states regulated by federal constitutions.

When the minority is not concentrated geographically, a system of so called 'personal federalism' may be used as a substitute for territorial federalism. The Ottoman Empire used the Millet system to give to some of its religious minorities, then to some of its linguistic groups, the possibility of administering their communal affairs in a more or less autonomous fashion. Similarly in Poland the Kahal was used to give the Jewish communities, locally and nationally, some powers of self-administration.

Among modern states the most systematic use of personal federalism was made by Estonia and Lithuania in the 1920s. Some of the minorities of these states – those that were territorially dispersed – availed themselves of the legal possibility of forming ethnic councils that had powers similar to those of a local government, in particular the powers to tax their members and administer their schools.

Administering the relations between minority and dominant groups

Proper protection of a minority requires that its group objective, rather than those of the dominant group, be taken as a test of the functionality of the measure intended to be protective.

Laponce (1960) distinguishes minorities that are prepared to accept their minority status for the sake of preserving their identity (minorities by will) from minorities that are prevented from assimilating to the dominant groups (minorities by force). Wirth (1945) distinguishes *assimilationist* (those who want to assimilate), *pluralist* (those who want to remain distinct), *secessionist* (those who want to separate), and *militant* minorities; the latter being those who want to turn the dominant group into a minority. Schermerhorn (1970) obtains four distinct types by comparing the attitudes of both the minority and the dominant group, which can be either centripetal or centrifugal. Laponce (1984) obtains sixteen types by relating the attitudes of both dominant and dominated groups according to whether each group wants to be assimilated, is indifferent to assimilation, rejects assimilation, or wants to assimilate the other group.

According to the type of relations between the dominant group and the minority, the protective techniques should be either universal or specific and should be given either to individuals or to groups. Furthermore, the administration of the protection may be left to the intra-state regulation or may require international intervention in the form of treaties or reciprocal agreements.

The guaranteeing of equality and individual rights is well adapted to protecting a minority that wishes to be assimilated (for example the blacks in the United States, at least before the 1960s); it is equally well adapted to a minority that wishes to remain distinctive but not at the cost of equal treatment – Catholics in Britain when they were allowed into the public service; or the Jews in France who welcomed the Clermont-Tonnerre revolutionary formula: 'As Jews nothing, as French citizens everything.' The sole granting of individual rights however can be – and often is – dysfunctional when equality reinforces an existing power differential. The Swiss Constitution proclaims the equality of all citizens but the Swiss courts have recognized that some individual rights must take second rank to collective rights, notably in matters of language. The Swiss Federal Tribunal has ruled that the right to speak the language of one's choice can be overruled by the right of a canton to impose the sole public use of a community's language in order to prevent penetration of the territory of one ethnic group by another.

Tajfel (1974) has argued that in the case of ethnic groups that refuse assimilation, a healthy minority is one thinking of itself as superior to the dominant group on at least one trait that distinguishes it from the latter. The best protective techniques of such a minority may well be those that allow its members, at least cost, to continue to value or even, and why not, overvalue themselves.

See also CIVIL LIBERTIES; CIVIL RIGHTS; ETHNIC NATIONALISM; ETHNICITY; LANGUAGE AND POLITICS.   JAL

Reading

Horowitz, D.L.: *Ethnic Groups in Conflict*. Berkeley: University of California Press, 1985.

Laponce, J.A.: *The Protection of Minorities*. Berkeley: University of California Press, 1960.

————: *Langue et territoire*. Quebec: Presses de l'Université Laval, 1984.

McRae, K.D.: The principle of territoriality and the principle of personality in a multilingual state. *Linguistics* (1975) 33–54.

Schermerhorn, R.A.: *Comparative Ethnic Relations: a framework for theory and research*. New York: Random House, 1970.

Tajfel, H.: Social identity and intergroup behaviour. *Social Science Information* (1974) 6–93.

Van Dyke, V.: *Human Rights, Ethnicity and Discrimination*. London: Greenwood, 1985.

Wirth, L.: The problem of minority groups. In *The Science of Man in the World Crisis*, ed. R. Lindon. New York: Columbia University Press, 1945.

minority government A government supported by fewer than half the members of the national legislature in a parliamentary democracy. If the legislature has more than one chamber the government normally only needs the support of the lower chamber, and its support in that chamber determines its classification. The opposite of a minority government is a MAJORITY GOVERNMENT. In some cases, particularly when a government is a non-partisan business administration, it may be impossible to calculate its legislative support and classify it as majority or minority. References to minority government therefore assume party government. Most minority governments are composed of only one party, but about one-third are coalitions of several parties. Many minority governments also have formal or informal agreements for legislative support with parties outside the government.

Minority governments were prevalent in Germany during the Weimar Republic (1919–1933) and in France during the Fourth Republic (1946–1958). In both cases, the large number of such governments may have contributed to political instability and ultimately to the collapse of these regimes. In recent years however minority governments have been most common in smaller and more stable European democracies, especially in Scandinavia. Since 1945 Denmark has seldom had majority governments, indeed there has been no Danish majority government since 1971. Italy, Canada, and the Republic of Ireland have also often had minority governments. Minority governments form under a variety of circumstances, and it is not easy to specify the conditions most conducive to their formation.

Minority governments are an anomaly because they contradict the basic notion that parliamentary democracy implies control of the executive branch by the legislative majority. They are liable to parliamentary defeat and resignation if confronted by a united and hostile opposition. Nor can minority governments safely count on legislative approval of their policy initiatives. These features of minority governments should render them unstable and ineffective. Empirical studies have shown that minority governments are in fact less durable than majority governments, but not necessarily much less effective.

KS

Reading

Herman, V. and Pope, J.: Minority governments in western democracies. *British Journal of Political Science* 3 (1973) 191–212.

Lijphart, A.: *Democracies: patterns of majoritarian and consensus government in twenty-one countries.* New Haven, Conn. and London: Yale University Press, 1984.

Luebbert, G.M.: A theory of government formation. *Comparative Political Studies* 17 (1984) 229–64.

Robertson, J.D.: Economic issues and the probability of forming minority coalition cabinets. *Social Science Quarterly* 66 (1985) 687–94.

Strom, K.: Minority governments in parliamentary democracies: the rationality of nonwinning cabinet solutions. *Comparative Political Studies* 17 (1984) 199–227.

See also under COALITION.

mixed government Political theorists have always looked for ways to set limits on the exercise of the power of government and to prevent that power being exercised by one section of the community to the detriment of other sections. The theory of mixed government has the longest pedigree of such theories. It was based upon two assumptions. First, that every section of the community was likely to abuse its position if the government was left solely in its hands. Second, that the only effective check on the exercise of power by one section was the exercise of a countervailing power by other sections. In applying these assumptions to the problem of the control of power, the theory of mixed government was an overtly class-based theory, unlike the later doctrine of the SEPARATION OF POWERS which looked for checks on the exercise of power through a *functional* distribution of authority.

In the *Laws* PLATO described the need for compromise in the state if 'the wantonness of excess' was to be avoided. A mixture of democracy and monarchy, with their conflicting interests, if properly harmonized in the constitution, would ensure that each section would be able adequately to defend its interests. ARISTOTLE developed this idea in the *Politics* where he argued that a *polity*, the form of state most likely to be generally beneficial, should be a mixture of democracy and oligarchy. POLYBIUS later adapted the ideas of Plato and Aristotle in analysing the history of the Roman Republic. CICERO echoed him in his treatment of the excellence of mixed government, and in medieval times the ancient concept was received, through Aquinas and other writers, as the *regime bene commixtum* of monarchy, aristocracy and democracy. It had however little practical importance until, with the development of parliamentary institutions in England, it became the theoretical basis for an attack upon Stuart absolutism, and then in turn, as the monarch was faced with ever more radical threats, the defence of constitutional monarchy, and of the aristocracy, against demands for a thorough-going democracy. After 1689, the theory of mixed government became the basis of the accepted ideology of the mixed and balanced constitution in which the differing powers of King, Lords and Commons each kept the others in check, and provided that happy blend which was eulogized by MONTESQUIEU and Blackstone as the envy of the world. As the eighteenth century progressed, the claim that the British constitution embodied the best elements of monarchy, aristocracy and democracy came increasingly under attack, drawing from Bentham the jibe that it could equally be described as a system which combined the worst elements of all three, making it 'all-weak, all-foolish and all-knavish'.

In the second half of the eighteenth century the attack by ROUSSEAU on the concept of mixed government, the objections of the American colonists to a system which seemed to them simply to mask a tyranny, and the opposition in Britain to the aristocratic exercise of power, through a corrupt and unrepresentative House of Commons, brought the theory to a low ebb. Nevertheless its central concept, the need to check power with power, found expression in the mid-nineteenth century theory of parliamentary government in Britain; above all, it formed the basis for that theory of CHECKS AND BALANCES embodied in the Constitution of the United States, and indeed lives on still in the form of PLURALIST theories of democracy.   MJCV

Reading

Fritz, K. von: *The Theory of the Mixed Constitution in Antiquity: a critical analysis of Polybius' political ideas.* New York: Columbia University Press, 1954.

Weston, C.C.: *English Constitutional Theory and the House of Lords.* London: Routledge & Kegan Paul, 1965.

modernization   See POLITICAL DEVELOPMENT.

monarchy Since Aristotle states have been classified on the basis of the proportion of the population holding power: one (monarchy), the few (aristocracy), all the people (democracy). For Plato a distinction could be made between the pure and the corrupt form of each type of regime. The essence could be judged by what was actually done and for whose benefit. In the corrupt form authority was exercised for selfish ends; in the pure form in the public interest. For Aristotle monarchy was the good government of one, tyranny the depraved form.

The notion of monarchy was based on a system of values that was essentially religious, paternalistic and conservative. Accompanying this was the idea of the divine right of kings and the idea that the king could do no wrong. The relationship of kingship and religion evolved in three stages. First the king was considered a living God. In Ancient Egypt, for instance, the Pharaohs married their sisters or daughters so that royal authority remained within the sacred family. Later the king was considered as a descendant of a God; the emperors of China and Japan were thus 'sons of the skies'. This concept evolved and the monarch became simply God's chosen man. The basis of legitimacy became the religious ceremony, the coronation during which the monarch became God's anointed. With the decline of the hold of religion on society and the rise of rationalism the foundations of traditional monarchy were eroded. Conservative ideologies developed to replace religion in the upholding of the monarchy. Monarchy was justified on the grounds of history and tradition, on the grounds of utility and the natural order of things.

Before the democratic revolutions of the eighteenth, nineteenth and twentieth centuries monarchy was the most widely known form of government. In some cases the kingship was elective (Poland, the Holy Empire, Russia, France up to Clovis and in the eighth and ninth centuries) but most monarchies were hereditary. The majority were based, in Europe, on an indisputable law of succession indicating from infancy the successor to the throne; in the Orient the principle of heredity was sometimes imputed to a family or group of families and not to one individual. Assassination of one's potential rivals thus became a necessary precaution.

The two major types of traditional European monarchies were the aristocratic monarchy and the absolute monarchy. The first came into being after the fall of the Roman Empire and the barbaric and Norman invasions, when Europe had broken up into feudal dukedoms. The relation between the king and the lord was similar to that between lord and vassal. The bond between them was the tenure of the land. As regions aggregated under him, the power of the monarch developed steadily. The feudal system gave the king a limited right to military service and to certain aids, both of which were inadequate to meet expenses especially in time of war. The king therefore had to get contributions from his people and he consulted them in their respective orders. The right of representation in its origin was a right to consent to taxation.

Absolute monarchies developed as monarchs progressively rid themselves of the checks put on them by the lords and began to exercise total political power themselves. There were many such monarchs (Babylonian, Inca, Aztec, Byzantine, Chinese in the Han and Ming periods) but the term is used more specifically to refer to western monarchies between the sixteenth and eighteenth centuries especially in France and Spain. These monarchies were founded on reference to God – a single God, a single Prince. It was in France that absolute monarchy lasted longest, but it also came later to Prussia (Frederic II), Austria (Joseph II) and Russia (Catherine II). Absolute monarchy was always highly centralized and of necessity developed an efficient administrative system. Even at its height absolute monarchy was never entirely absolute. Custom was a major limit to absolute power, especially in those countries where it was a source of law. Absence of means of action was also a major obstacle to royal absolutism. With the rise of absolute monarchies came the notion of the enlightened despot: the king, thanks to his power, could transform society in the interest of all. The state became not only centralized but highly interventionist.

In Britain the power of the crown increased greatly under the Tudors. Parliament met rarely and its meetings were short; legislation was for the most part drafted by the monarch and his advisers and Parliament's proceedings were closely directed by the crown. It was not rare for the monarch to withhold the Royal Assent to a bill. But neither Henry VIII nor Elizabeth I were absolute monarchs. They had great regard for parliamentary conventions. Advice, criticism and dissatisfaction were openly expressed by Parliament.

Under the Stuarts, the Commons began to free itself of royal control. It claimed that its privileges were of inheritance and right, it was 'the sovereign court of Parliament'. The doctrine of the separation of powers was assimilated to the 'mixed monarchy' with the king in the role of independent executive; a second balance, that of legislative against executive, was added to the conventional balance of King, Lords and Commons.

After the civil war Parliament emerged greatly strengthened. Its sovereignty with regard to legislation and taxation was undisputed. There was no longer any subject on which it could not act and it was supreme over the church. The king was obliged to accept both legal and political limitations of his authority. Constitutional monarchy, in which kingship was to be rendered subordinate to the principles or the text of a constitution, was in the making.

Steps in the movement towards constitutional monarchy include the right of the Commons to share the power of the King and Lords in legislation, the exclusive right of the Commons to impose taxes, the disappearance of the clergy as a separate order and the rise of the Cabinet. In Britain the settlement of 1688 put an end to all claims to authority based on Divine Right.

In democratic states, monarchy has had to become constitutional to survive. Where it has not, it has been abolished. In 1914, only France, Portugal and Switzerland, of the twenty-three states in Europe, were republics. By the 1980s, however, only eight of the seventeen democracies of Western Europe (excluding ministates such as Lichtenstein), were monarchies.

The essence of constitutional monarchy is that the sovereign acts on the advice of his ministers who are willing to assume responsibility for his actions. For the principle of ministerial responsibility has as its corollary that the acts of the sovereign are not his own acts, but those of his ministers. Thus the sovereign can remain politically neutral.

The sovereign however, retains various formal and ceremonial powers, and also what BAGEHOT termed 'the mystic reverence, the religious allegiance which are essential to a true monarchy'. In addition, most consti-tutional monarchs retain certain prerogative powers, essentially residual in nature, but which could be used *in extremis* as emergency powers to guard the constitution against abuse. The central purpose of these residual powers is generally to ensure the smooth functioning of parliamentary government; and the main powers retained by constitutional monarchs – the nomination of a prime minister, and the summoning and DISSOL-UTION OF PARLIAMENT – are designed to secure this end. These so-called prerogative powers cannot be used at the sovereign's discretion, but have generally come to be regulated by constitutional conventions. This is to ensure that the sovereign's use of his prerogative powers does not become the subject of partisan controversy.

But a constitutional monarch, while his acts cannot be personal or arbitrary, is none the less not a mere automaton. He can exert influence upon government, since he possesses Bagehot's trinity of rights – the right to be consulted, the right to encourage and the right to warn – and these rights can allow a sagacious monarch to exercise considerable influence which, however, by its very nature must remain a secret influence.

See also GOVERNMENT FORMATION PROCESS.   MCh

Reading

Bagehot, W.: *The English Constitution* (1865). In *Collected Works*, Vol. V, ed. N. St John-Stevas. London: The Economist, 1965–86.

Jennings, W.I.: *Cabinet Government*. 3rd edn. Cambridge: Cambridge University Press, 1959.

Loewenstein, K.: *Die Monarchie im modernen Staat*. Frankfurt: Metzner, 1952.

Molitor, A.: *La Fonction royale en Belgique*. Brussels: Crisp, 1979.

Nicolson, H.: *Kings, Courts and Monarchy*. New York: Simon & Schuster, 1962.

———: *King George V: his life and reign*. London: Constable, 1952.

Petrie, C.: *Monarchy in the Twentieth Century*. London: Dakers, 1952.

Monnet, Jean (1888–1979) Although the founder of both the French Planning Commissariat and the EUROPEAN COM-MUNITY, Monnet was neither an academic economist, an elected politician, nor a career civil servant. Born in Cognac in the Charente, he attended the local *collège*, and left at the age of sixteen to learn English in London. At eighteen he was sent by his father, a brandy merchant, to sell the family's wares in North America. In 1914 he returned to France, but was found unfit for military service. He persuaded the prime minister to employ him to co-ordinate Franco-British war supplies and at the end of the war was appointed deputy secretary-general of the LEAGUE OF NATIONS, which he later left for the family business and for banking, notably helping to reorganize the Chinese Railways. In 1939 he headed the Franco-British war-supply organiz-ation. In 1940, as France was falling, he persuaded Winston Churchill and Charles de Gaulle to accept his plan for Franco-British political union; it was overtaken, however, by the armistice and the installation of Marshal Pétain's Vichy regime. Monnet then served on the British Supply Council in Washington. In 1943 he was sent by President Roosevelt to Algiers where he helped to reconcile General de Gaulle and General Giraud, later serving on the former's National Liberation Committee. He devised and headed the French Plan (sometimes still known as 'the Monnet Plan'), established in 1946.

In 1950, Monnet put to Robert Schuman, then French foreign minister, what became known as the Schuman Plan for the European Coal and Steel Community, to reconcile France and Germany and begin the unification of Western Europe by pooling French and German coal and steel resources in a common market open to other countries of Europe. Belgium, Italy, Luxemburg, and the Netherlands also joined. Monnet headed the preparatory conference and was appointed first president of the Schuman Plan's High Authority, based in Luxemburg. Meanwhile, he had proposed to the French prime minister René Pleven the 'Pleven Plan' for a European Army or European Defence Community. The same six countries signed a treaty to this effect, but only Belgium, Germany, Luxemburg, and the Netherlands ratified it, and it collapsed after defeat on a procedural vote in the French National Assembly in 1954. Monnet subsequently resigned from the High Authority, and set up the Action Committee for the United States of Europe, consisting of virtually all the non-communist and non-Gaullist political parties and trade unions of the six Community countries. With their backing, he helped initiate the 'relaunching of Europe' following the Messina Conference of 1955, which led to the European Economic Community and Euratom. He also played a large part in assisting British membership of the European Community and promoting the objective of an equal partnership between it and the United States.

Contrary to some suggestions, Monnet was not a formal advocate of FEDERALISM. Experience had taught him, however, that the nations of western Europe faced common problems, which they could solve only by collective, not national, action. Since this was unnatural, it had to be fostered by common institutions whose task was to identify and represent the common interest. This was in sharp contrast to traditional intergovernmental co-operation, in which there was no delegation or merger of national SOVEREIGNTY but only low-level bargains between conflicting short-term national interests.

In 1950 Monnet believed that the Community institutions would involve, or evolve into, SUPRANATIONAL GOVERNMENT. He later regarded this belief as mistaken. The essence of the Community method, he concluded, was a permanent dialogue between the COUNCIL OF MINISTERS, representing national governments, and the COMMISSION, representing their collective longer-term interests.

Monnet also espoused lateral thinking. In an impasse he always preferred to change the context of the problem rather than attacking it head on. By tackling a practical side-issue he would try to reach limited agreement between antagonists, then build on the new situation thus created. Coal and steel were the key to political unification: he even proposed, in later years, joint desalination projects to change the context of conflicts in the Middle East. By uniting Western Europe, Monnet believed, it would also be possible to transform relations between Europe and America – and, ultimately, between East and West.   RJM

Reading

Mayne, R.: *Postwar: the dawn of today's Europe.* London: Thames & Hudson, 1983.

————: 'Gray Eminence'. *American Scholar.* Autumn (1984) 533–40.

Monnet, J.: *Les États-unis d'Europe ont commencé.* Paris: Laffont, 1955.

————: *Memoirs.* London: Collins; New York: Doubleday, 1978.

Montesquieu, Charles-Louis de Secondat, Baron de (1689–1755)

The outstanding exponent in the French Enlightenment of parliamentary liberalism inspired by English political experience and John LOCKE's political philosophy. A lifelong enemy of DESPOTISM, Montesquieu's earliest writings, such as his brilliantly satirical *Lettres persanes* (1721), betray a certain yearning for republican government and the civic virtues of the ancient world. When Montesquieu toured the republics of his own time, however, he was profoundly disillusioned. Venice, Genoa, Lucca, and above all Holland, seemed to him to offer only a mockery of civil freedom. In England, by contrast, he found a system of parliamentary monarchy which achieved an exemplary fusion of liberty and law.

A parliamentarian himself, having been chief magistrate of the *parlement* of Bordeaux before he resigned to devote his life to authorship, Montesquieu became a key figure in the struggle of the French *noblesse de robe* to recover a share in the sovereignty of France. But he was far from being a mere ideologue of his class. He did not argue legalistically, as did other champions of the *thèse nobiliaire*, for the ancient constitutional rights of the *parlements*; he wrote as a political sociologist.

Montesquieu diagnosed the key to the success of the English system in the division of power between the executive, legislative and judicial institutions, each of which served to counteract any tendency towards despotism on the part of the others. Freedom, he argued, was preserved – and could only be preserved – by a mechanism of CHECKS AND BALANCES. His long, rambling masterpiece *De l'esprit des lois* (1748) is packed with such empirical generalizations about government in general. Among other things he argued that the political arrangements which any society can expect to make for itself must depend on such factors as climate, geographical situation and history, so that there can be no ideal constitution for everyone. What suited the English, for example, would not suit the French. Nevertheless, Montesquieu could not conceal his desire to see France reformed on the basis of principles he had worked out in his studies of the government of England.

See also SEPARATION OF POWERS.   MWC

Reading

Baum, J.A.: *Montesquieu and Social Theory*. New York: Pergamon, 1979.

Montesquieu, C.-L. de Secondat: *The Persian Letters* (1721). Harmondsworth: Penguin, 1973.

———: *The Spirit of the Laws* (1748), ed. F. Neumann, trans T. Nugent. New York: Hafner, 1949.

———: *Considerations on the Causes of the Greatness of the Romans and Their Decline*, trans. and ed. D. Lowenthal. Ithaca, NY: Cornell University Press, 1968.

Pangle, T.L.: *Montesquieu's Philosophy of Liberalism:*

a commentary on 'The Spirit of the Laws'. Chicago, Ill.: University of Chicago Press, 1973.

Shackleton, R.: *Montesquieu: a critical biography*. London: Oxford University Press, 1961.

Mosca, Gaetano (1858–1941) Italian political theorist. Mosca was of Sicilian origins but spent his academic and public career in northern Italy. He was a professor at the University of Turin until 1923 and then at the University of Rome until 1933. He was a deputy and later a senator in pre-fascist Italy. His translation to Rome rewarded the publication of his most famous work *Elementi di scienza politica* (The Ruling Class). The *Fascisti* did not regard him, as they did PARETO, as one of the sources of their ideology; nevertheless his views, which tended in his latter years to a kind of democratic populism, were not inconsistent with the propaganda of fascism before 1935.

Mosca held that all political power would reside in an OLIGARCHY (or ruling class). Basically these oligarchies would be either democratic, and capable of innovation and renewal without altering the general system of power, or aristocratic (by which Mosca did not necessarily mean noble) and therefore conservative or hereditary. The alternation of these two modes of rule anticipated Pareto's theories of the circulation of ELITES. As a result of his parliamentary experience Mosca regarded representative parliamentary government as a degenerate form of democracy. Until his death he vacillated about his adherence to some form of populist plebiscitary regime. For his general theory of ruling class (and for the political formula) see RULING CLASS.   DGM

Reading

Albertoni, E.: *Mosca*. Oxford: Blackwell, 1987.

Bobbio, N.: *On Mosca and Pareto*. Geneva: Droz, 1972.

Meisel, G.H.: *The Myth of the Ruling Class: Gaetano Mosca and the elite*. Ann Arbor: University of Michigan Press, 1962.

Mosca, G.: *The Ruling Class* (1896), trans. and ed. H.D. Kahn and A. Livingston. New York: McGraw-Hill, 1939.

———: *Partiti e sindicata nella crisi del regime parlamentare*. Bari: Gius, Laterza & Figli, 1949.

N

nation building The sum of policies designed to promote national integration. Nation building is an architectural metaphor for the process induced within a state to integrate the country and tie the inhabitants together in a national fellowship. The most immediate and simple type of nation building produces shared national institutions, communications, and symbols of unity. Institutions such as schools, associations, administration and army may serve the goal of national integration; status projects, national celebrations, flags, heroes and public architecture may also be visible manifestations of nation building in progress. These policies are particularly crucial in recent states with artificial or accidental borders, and in states with different traditions, religions, and ethnic groups.

As a theme in political studies nation building became prominent after the dissolution of European colonialism. The borderlines drawn by the colonial powers became the frontiers of new states, largely irrespective of ethnic and cultural criteria. Nation building became a clue to the political aspects of modernization: the break-up of primordial loyalties was a prerequisite for modern citizenship and for a viable polity in a universe of nation-states. Nation building as a state policy dates back to the American and French revolutions of the late eighteenth century. In this context nation building meant the dual development of public authority and loyalty through citizenship. The FRENCH REVOLUTION also founded an original idea of nation building when the Third Estate proclaimed itself as a 'national assembly' and made

patriotism its specific ideology. The state was no longer dynastic. The nation became the new symbol of fellowship, the tie between citizens without a monarch, and the source of sovereignty. The nation was subsequently built by standardization and centralization.

In modern political studies nation building has been conceptualized in terms of progressive stages of political development: territorial penetration by state power; cultural standardization on the model of a nation-wide code (with standard education and assimilation of minorities); participation of wider sections of the population (by political citizenship mobilizing peripheries and lower classes); finally, by redistribution and welfare policies as mechanisms of national integration. Nation building is here a dual conception, with growing public authority and control on the one hand, and the extension of civil rights on the other. The ideal of nation building is nevertheless relative to the concept of a nation. When the nation is conventionally made synonymous with a modern state, or with the inhabitants of any established state, nation building is simply the policies for real state control and public obedience. When the nation is an expression of cultural fellowship or ethnic characteristics, nation building implies active assimilation and standardization towards an authorized national code – linguistic, religious or ethnic. Historical myths of identity and uniqueness often serve the same end. When the nation is seen as an emotional fellowship, nation building means the policies intended to stimulate national fellow feeling, irrespective of the more objective characteristics of various sub-national groups. The historical experience of nation building shows that the underlying ambiguities of nationality often lead to a rather opaque mix between these three conceptions.

Nation building also signifies a critical leap in the ways and means of politics: the appearance of a secularized political style where formally equal citizens compete in a national political arena. Politics no longer emanates from local communities, tribal affiliations or patron–client relationships. This is the sociological meaning of nation building as a leap in political culture. Still there are institutional policies that may promote nation building across sociological heterogeneity and group cleavages, ranging from expatriation to assimilation and from federalism to centralization. A pattern of cross-cutting cleavages may also reduce political tension and contribute to national integration in a more spontaneous way. It is, on the whole, difficult to distinguish clearly between nation building as an explicit policy and the more spontaneous processes involved. Nation building may even be regarded as the unintended consequence of policies with a more narrowly specific purpose. The architectural image might then be somewhat misleading.

See also CITIZENSHIP; NATIONALISM; ROKKAN.   ØØ

Reading

Bendix, R.: *Nation-Building and Citizenship*. Berkeley: University of California Press, 1977.

Deutsch, K.W. and Foltz, W.J. eds: *Nation-Building*. New York: Atherton, 1963.

Eisenstadt, S.N. and Rokkan, S. eds: *Building States and Nations*. 2 vols. Beverly Hills, Calif.: Sage, 1973–74.

Emerson, R.: *From Empire to Nation*. Cambridge, Mass.: Harvard University Press, 1960.

Seton-Watson, H.: *Nations and States*. London: Methuen, 1977.

Tilly, C. ed.: *The Formation of National States in Western Europe*. Princeton, NJ: Princeton University Press, 1975.

nation-state   A fusion of two dissimilar structures and principles, the one political and territorial, the other historical and cultural. The 'state' element here signifies the modern, rational STATE which came to fruition in the early modern West as a set of public institutions, autonomous of other institutions, differentiated, centralized and possessing the monopoly of coercion and extraction in a demarcated and recognized territory. The nation, defined as a named human community with a myth of common ancestry, historical memories and standardized mass culture, possessing a single territory, division of labour and legal rights for all members, includes elements of ethnic culture (ETHNIC NATIONALISM) and modern 'civic' features. The resulting dualism and ambiguities in the concept of the nation affects its subsequent fusion with the state. The more pronounced the civic, territorial elements of the nation the less difficult has been the process of fusion; conversely, the more prominent the ethnic elements the less likelihood of harmony or a close knit between state and nation. Even in the few cases where state and nation are more or less co-extensive in territory and congruent in social and cultural composition, this is more the result of an ethnic nationalism which strove to gain independent statehood for an ethnically defined nation, than a parallel development of state institutions and a civic nationality.

The great majority of so-called nation-states are polyethnic in composition and could more adequately be described as state-nations. This applies particularly in sub-Saharan Africa and parts of Asia. Here the decolonized new states must base their nationalist aspirations on the territory and institutions of the state and integrate ethnically heterogenous populations through a civic NATIONALISM. Often lacking an ethnic core on which to build a state, let alone a nation, these nations-to-be are furthest removed from the nation-state goal that has become the criterion of international legitimacy. Next come those new states that possess an ethnic core (Burma, Sri Lanka, Malaysia, Iran, Egypt, Zimbabwe) but also significant ethnic minority communities, many of which are politically active and unwilling to accept the culture and ascendancy of the dominant *ethnie*; here too the prospects of achieving the status of nation-state in the foreseeable future seem remote. The chances of the more advanced and older western states doing so are greater, but they also may suffer from deep internal ethnic cleavages, as in Spain, Belgium and Canada. Nevertheless, they possess the advantage of more solidly entrenched state institutions and widely diffused civic ideals; these are also features of polyethnic immigrant societies in the Americas and Australia. While it is common to term the western and even the immigrant societies nation-states, recent developments such as the 'ethnic revival' have revealed the error of this assumption. Only in a very loose and historical sense can they be called nation-states, since they enjoyed that status internationally before ethnic nationalism had spread to their own ETHNIC NATIONALISM had spread to their own Basques, Scots, Flemish, Quebecqois, etc.). But in reality only some 10 per cent of the world's states can be accorded the status of nation-state, in the strict sense – that is, where state territories and institutions are occupied by members of a single ethnically defined nation with a homogeneous culture. It was the historical error of according that status to certain western seaboard states, notably England and France at the height of their power, that endowed the ideal of the homogeneous nation-state with such prestige and allowed the internal political agenda to focus on less divisive issues than ethnicity. It remains to this day a powerful, but no longer universal, political ideal.

See also ETHNICITY.   ADS

Reading

Akzin, B.: *State and Nation*. London: Hutchinson, 1964.

Breuilly, J.: *Nationalism and the State*. Manchester: Manchester University Press, 1982.

Deutsch, K. and Foltz, W.J. eds: *Nation-Building*. New York: Atherton, 1963.

Mayall, J.B. ed.: *The Community of States*. London: Allen & Unwin, 1982.

Smith, A.D.: *State and Nation in the Third World*. Brighton, Sussex: Harvester, 1983.

Tilly, C. ed.: *The Formation of National States in Western Europe*. Princeton, NJ: Princeton University Press, 1975.

Tivey, L. ed.: *The Nation-State*. Oxford: Martin Robertson, 1980.

national liberation movements (NLM) Movements with the avowed aim of liberating the people of a specific nation from colonial or foreign rule or oppression. The term came into currency during the era of decolonization during the 1950s and 1960s, but it has been appropriated by a wide variety of movements rebelling against national governments in the post-colonial period. The label has often been adopted by groups trying to achieve liberation from an illegitimate, corrupt or oppressive government, or from a regime which is an instrument of foreign domination. Examples of particularly effective and influential NLMs are the Front de Libération Nationale (FLN) in Algeria, and the National Liberation Front (NLF) in Vietnam. National liberation movements vary widely in the degree of popular support and sympathy they enjoy and the extent to which they depend on foreign rather than purely indigenous support and assistance. Some self-proclaimed NLMs, such as the Palestine Liberation Organization (PLO) and the Armenian Secret Army for the Liberation of Armenia (ASALA) are forced into exile. This greatly reduces their prospects of overthrowing the regime in their native country. But once an NLM has a sizeable base of mass support and an organizational structure for rebellion within the target country, it does not necessarily need to have majority support among the national population. Determined and ruthless minorities succeed by using violence, subversion and other covert means, in intimidating and controlling the populations.

Most NLMs have fused nationalism with some variant of MARXISM in their ideologies, and have made no secret of their profound hostility to the western powers and the capitalist economic system. The Soviet Union has frequently supported what Lenin terms 'wars of national liberation' and has encouraged various local communist parties concerned to participate in these struggles with the aim of weakening the West European powers. Ironically, the Soviet Union has treated her own many national minorities with cynical indifference to the principle of self-determination. Only the trappings of cultural identity are allowed: any attempt at real political self-determination would be ruthlessly crushed.

On the other hand, the Soviet Union has taken the opportunity of aiding a wide variety of NLM rebellions against western powers in the 1950s and 1960s. Moscow encouraged the non-bloc communist parties to join NLM coalitions even though it usually meant temporary collaboration with what they term 'bourgeois-nationalist' forces in a united front. The communists would move rapidly to eliminate these 'bourgeois' elements once victory had been obtained. Soviet tactics of sponsoring NLMs have been fairly successful in parts of South East Asia and Africa, but they have met with strong rebuffs in Muslim countries.

In the longer term NLM 'wars of national liberation' present both superpowers with major dilemmas. The Soviets' decisions to subordinate party-to-party relations to state-to-state relations has meant that local revolutionary groups have often felt betrayed by Moscow, as was the case with the Chinese Communist Party (CCP) in the 1920s and 1930s. This has helped to cause friction and division among communist countries and movements. At the same time the Soviet leadership's frequent desire to improve diplomatic and economic relations with major western and third world states has tended to place some restraints on Soviet use of NLMs as instruments of communist expansion. The American dilemma is summed up by the popular political cry of 'no more Vietnams' voiced whenever there appears a possibility of US military intervention to counter an insurgent threat in a Third World state. One school of thought favours America mounting and aiding its own 'freedom fighter' movements against Marxist regimes. Others argue for a policy of strict non-interventionism, on the grounds that the peoples of foreign countries should be left to sort out their own political systems.

National liberation struggles also present the international community as a whole with grave dilemmas. The United Nations Charter emphatically guarantees sovereign states domestic jurisdiction over all internal matters. At the same time UN declarations on decolonization have made it a duty of member states to aid legitimate national liberation struggles. As there are no universally accepted criteria for defining a legitimate national liberation movement, each state in practice decides for itself which NLMs, if any, it will regard as legitimate, and what steps, if any, it will take to assist them.

See also REVOLUTION; SELF-DETERMINATION.

PW

Reading

Chaliand, G.: *The Palestinian Resistance*. Baltimore, Md.: Penguin, 1972.

Cobban, A.: *The Nation State and National Self-Determination*, rev. edn. New York: Crowell, 1970.

Emerson, R.: *Self-Determination Revisited in the Era of Decolonization*. Cambridge, Mass.: Harvard University Press, 1964.

Fanon, F.: *The Wretched of the Earth*. Harmondsworth: Penguin, 1967.

Hodges, D.C. and Abu-Shanab, R.E.: *National Liberation Fronts 1960–1970: essays, documents, interviews*. New York: Morrow, 1972.

Horne, A.: *A Savage War of Peace: Algeria 1954–62*. Harmondsworth: Penguin, 1979.

Johnson, H.S.: *Self-Determination within the Community of Nations*. Leiden: Sijthoff, 1967.

Kedourie, E. ed.: *Nationalism in Asia and Africa*. Cleveland, Ohio: World Publishing, 1970.

Miller, N. and Aya, R. eds: *National Liberation: revolution in the third world*. New York: Free Press, 1971.

nationalism A political doctrine and sentiment. The doctrine affirms basically that the legitimate political unit is co-extensive with the *national unit*. The assumption is that all human beings are characterized by something called nationality, that they live in politically centralized units, that this unit is the only legitimate agency of coercion, and that it constitutes the 'correct' unit only if it is felt to be the expression of that nationality. On this theory legitimacy and political propriety are violated if some members of a given nationality are incorporated in political units dominated by other nationalities or indeed if their own unit has an excessive number of members drawn from other nationalities.

As an unrestricted generalization about the human condition, each of the three assumptions of nationalist theory is false. Not all human beings live in politically centralized units: decentralized 'acephalous' communities are not uncommon. Though all human beings have some kind of culture and speak some kind of language, they are by no means always familiar with the notion of nationality and cannot always say to which nationality they belong. Many people, for instance, can specify the tribe to which they belong, but although the tribe may share a language and culture with other tribes, there may be simply no socially and politically effective notion linking them together as one 'nation'. Or again, in many parts of the Indian sub-continent men are acutely aware of their 'caste', but have no clear idea about their 'nationality'; when ethnic ideas and nationalism are imported from outside, they tend to make caste characterization do the work otherwise attributed to ethnicity.

Although blatantly false as an unrestricted generalization for all periods for all social positions, nationalism is nevertheless a very close approximation to the truth for a certain set of conditions in a certain historical period, namely our own. Modern societies are almost invariably centralized, except for periods of acute breakdown. The central political agency which governs a given territory is characteristically concerned not merely with the maintenance of order and the extraction of taxes, but also with the servicing, and initially with the establishment, of the cultural and educational infrastructure of modern society. Modern industrial society is occupationally mobile and technically complex, and requires literacy and a considerable degree of education and sophistication from its members. This cannot be achieved without universal standardized education.

All this means that modern society is one in which High Culture, in other words culture transmitted by formal education and written text, has become dominant and pervasive, rather than a minority accomplishment. This, in conjunction with occupational mobility, means that the most important qualification a person possesses, and which alone confers effective moral incorporation in society and genuine political citizenship on him, is the capacity to communicate and read and write in that culture, which in turn is associated with a given political unit and protected by it. It is this simple mechanism which is really responsible for the strength of nationalist sentiment in the modern world, and for the fact that the political arrangements which contradict the nationalist principle are widely felt to be offensive and indeed politically scandalous. In an exceptionally mobile and anonymous society pervaded by a formalized, literate, educationally transmitted culture, a person only feels comfortable, acceptable and 'at home' if his or her own culture and that employed by the central state bureaucracy are identical. If they are not, discontent, and 'irredentism' result, and are only quietened by assimilation, migration, re-drawing of frontiers or annihilation. Subjectively, the sentiment appears as an inherent and natural 'love of country'. Objectively, it is a by-product of the new relationship between culture and polity which prevails in industrial and industrializing societies. Consequently, political turbulence of a nationalistic kind is extremely characteristic of regions undergoing the transition from an agrarian to an industrial social order. The former seldom engenders the principle of *one culture, one state*. The latter seldom fails to do so.

Nationalism is not the only force operating under modern conditions, but it is an extremely powerful and dominant one. Conversely, during the pre-industrial past of humanity, nationalism was not wholly absent, but was an untypical and a minority phenomenon.

See also ETHNIC NATIONALISM.   EG

Reading

Deutsch, K.: *Nationalism and Social Communications.* 2nd edn. Cambridge, Mass. and London: MIT Press, 1966.

Gellner, E.: *Nations and Nationalism.* Oxford: Blackwell, 1983.

Kamenka, E. ed.: *Nationalism.* London: Hutchinson, 1976.

Kedourie, E.: *Nationalism.* London: Hutchinson University Library, 1966.

Kohn, H.: *The Age of Nationalism.* 2nd edn. New York and London: Greenwood, 1977.

Minogue, K.R.: *Nationalism.* London: Batsford, 1969.

Seton-Watson, H.: *Nations and States.* London: Methuen, 1977.

Smith, A.D.: *Theories of Nationalism*. 2nd edn. London: Duckworth, 1983.

nationalization The transfer from private to public ownership. Nationalization was the major feature in the programme of the British Labour government elected in 1945. Yet clause IV of the Labour Party's constitution does not use the term but calls for the 'common ownership of the means of production, distribution and exchange'. Herbert Morrison came to prefer 'socialization'. The term does however convey the meaning that the public ownership is on a national basis, e.g. the whole of the coal industry, and not municipal ownership which was an earlier objective of the Labour Party.

The arguments used in favour of nationalization range from the highly theoretical to the very practical. The Marxist argument based on the labour theory of value claims that the flow of unearned income – rent, interest and profits – in the capitalist system is a toll laid upon the workers by the owners of capital. It is therefore essential to remove such ownership from private hands. It is also claimed that a system of private ownership gives too much power to those individuals who own the capital and that competition to maximize profits leads to economic fluctuations and a disregard of socially desirable goods and services. In the case of several of the industries nationalized in the years 1946–50, for example gas and electricity, nationalization was claimed to be the most effective method of securing reorganization and greater efficiency. It was thought to be a particularly appropriate treatment for the commanding heights of the economy or the basic services such as fuel and transport. The nationalization programme of Mr Attlee's Labour government covered the Bank of England (1946), civil aviation (1946), coal (1947), transport (1948), gas (1949), and iron and steel (1951).

The process of nationalization involves decisions on two major issues. First, should compensation be paid for the enterprises taken over from their former owners and if so on what basis? A move at the Labour Party conference of 1934 to the effect that dispossessed owners should not have any right to capital repayment save in the case of working-class funds or of proven hardship was heavily defeated. The issue of principle having been decided it remained to determine the method of fair compensation in each case, e.g. valuation of shares at current market value or net maintainable revenue.

The second issue is how should the industries be organized and managed after nationalization? The earliest ideas favoured the normal ministerial department with the minister responsible to parliament. But the establishment of the London Transport Board in 1933 led to the acceptance of the PUBLIC CORPORATION. This form of organization was seen to have several advantages; it would enable trade union representatives to take part in the management and would provide the freedom from political control enjoyed by private management. All the industries and services nationalized between 1946 and 1951 were accordingly vested in public boards, appointed by the appropriate minister but independent of him so far as day to day running of the industry was concerned.

Since then nationalization has ceased to be the foremost element in the programme of the Labour Party. Instead emphasis is placed on forms of control and influence which fall short of public ownership. DNC

Reading

Barry, E.E.: *Nationalization in British Politics*. London: Cape, 1965.

Chester, N.: *The Nationalization of British Industry 1945–51*. London: HMSO, 1975.

Gaitskell, H.: *Socialism and Nationalisation*. Fabian Tract 300 (1956).

Hanson, A.H. ed.: *Nationalization: a book of readings*. London: Allen & Unwin, 1963.

Morrison, H.: *Socialism and Transport*. London: Constable, 1933.

Pryke, R.: *Public Enterprise in Practice*. London: MacGibbon, 1971.

Trades Union Congress: *Interim Report on Post-War Reconstruction*. London, 1944.

navette See SECOND CHAMBERS.

Nazism/Nazi Party An extreme nationalist, imperialist, and racist movement which developed in Germany after 1918 and which established a dictatorship under its leader, Adolf Hitler, from 1933–45. Nazism had something in common with FASCISM, and some historians and political scientists have seen it as the German variant of a European phenomenon. Both Nazism and fascism were anti-democratic, anti-liberal, anti-communist and anti-socialist. Both movements sought alliances with traditional conservative parties to assist with the conquest of power, but both fascism and Nazism are to be sharply distinguished from orthodox conservatism. For one thing, they did not hold to the doctrine of limited governmental interference in society and the economy; further, both movements glorified violence and terror.

Yet the differences between fascism and Nazism are as important as the similarities, for Nazism was essentially a racist movement with foreign policy aims which were far more ambitious than those of fascist leaders.

The German Workers Party, founded in Munich on 5 January 1919, was renamed the National Socialist German Workers Party (NSDAP: *Nationalsozialistische Deutsche Arbeiterpartei*) on 24 February 1920. In September 1919 it was joined by a thirty-year-old lance-corporal, Adolf Hitler, whose demagogic talent quickly won mass support for the party in Bavaria. He took over as leader on 29 July 1921. The NSDAP attracted a considerable following among ex-soldiers and middle class youth who were organized in a paramilitary force attached to the party, the SA (*Sturmabteilungen*: Storm Detachments). On 8–9 November 1923, Hitler attempted a *putsch* (coup) in Munich with the aim of leading a 'March on Berlin', similar to Mussolini's 'March on Rome' of October 1922. He failed, was imprisoned for nine months and his party banned.

Hitler's ideology derived from racist anti-Semitism, social Darwinism, and pan-German imperialism, ideas already current before 1914, which he now integrated into a coherent political programme in *Mein Kampf* (1925–6). He saw mankind as a hierarchy of races, all struggling to secure the available land and raw materials. The Aryans, of whom the Germans were the purest example, were the supreme

culture-bearing race, while the Jews represented the lowest race, which was bent on world conquest by parasitically infesting the Aryan race and undermining it. For Germany to win this racial struggle and secure world hegemony for the Aryan race, it must eliminate the Jews and conquer sufficient 'living space' in western Russia. This would require the full mobilization of the nation's mental and physical resources, in turn necessitating a complete transformation of the political and social order. Parliamentary democracy must be replaced by a Nazi dictatorship, and class conflict overcome in a socially harmonious 'people's community'; liberal and humane values were to be eliminated through the indoctrination of a ruthless will to power, involving adherence to the 'laws of nature' interpreted as the struggle for survival of the fittest, and an acceptance of the subordination of the individual to the community. Although in practice Nazism was to contain a variety of ideas and emphases from the archaic 'blood and soil' visions of the agrarians to the technocratic perspectives of the engineers and bureaucrats, the key elements were defined by Hitler's programme: racism, the cult of struggle and war, and the eradication of the belief in the intrinsic value of the individual human being and its replacement by an exclusive emphasis on his or her functional relationship to the nation and its goals.

When the party was re-formed on 26 February 1925, Hitler determined to pursue a legal path to power by winning elections. The NSDAP achieved a breakthrough between 1928 (with 2.8 per cent of the vote) and 1930 (with 18.3 per cent) by exploiting the effects of agricultural depression, and its rapid advance continued until July 1932 (achieving 37.3 per cent), when it became the largest party in the Reichstag. Its electoral support was strongest in the Protestant and rural districts of north and east Germany, weakest in large industrial cities and in Roman Catholic rural areas in the south and west. Like its voters, its membership covered a broad social spectrum, though weighted somewhat towards the middle class and the young. The NSDAP owed much of its success to a sophisticated propaganda machine which was financed mainly by membership

385

dues, entrance fees to its meetings, and donations from small rather than big business, whose contribution to Nazi success has been exaggerated. The party's nationalist and populist vision of a 'people's community' appealed to a nation humiliated by defeat and riven by sharp cleavages of class, religion and ideology, while its hostility to the left was welcomed by middle class groups who resented the increased power of Social Democrats and trade unions and feared communism. Hitler's image as a strong national leader appealed to a society in which democratic traditions were weak and whose political culture had been shaped by a semi-autocratic monarchy, and by military-style values. Untainted by the failures of the other political parties, the Nazis created the impression that they alone had the drive to restore Germany's fortunes. The Nazis did not come to power by winning a majority in the Reichstag. Indeed in the November 1932 election they lost over 4 per cent of their vote (33 per cent). The party was rescued from a grave crisis by the decision of conservative politicians to try and use Nazi mass support to replace parliamentary democracy by a right-wing authoritarian system.

On 30 January 1933 Hitler was appointed Chancellor in a coalition cabinet containing only two other Nazis. During the years 1933–4 however the Nazis secured total power through legal measures, terror against their opponents by the Nazi organizations, and a sustained propaganda campaign to create the impression of overwhelming public support for the new order, an impression somewhat marred by their vote in the last relatively free election of 5 March 1933 (43 per cent). The key legal measures were: first, the Decree for the Protection of People and State of 28 February 1933, of which § 1 suspended civil rights and provided the legal basis for the CONCEN-TRATION CAMPS, and § 2 permitted the Reich Government to take power in the federal states in the event of a breakdown of order. Between 5 and 10 March 1933, the SA ensured there was a breakdown in those states, for example Bavaria, where the Nazis were not yet in control. Second, the Enabling Law of 24 March 1933 permitted the government to issue laws without the participation of either the Reichstag or the Reich president. Third, on 14 July 1933, a law declared the NSDAP to be the sole legal party. Fourth, with the death of President von Hindenburg a law of 1 August 1934 abolished the office of president and appointed Hitler 'Leader [*Führer*] and Reich Chancellor'. The armed forces and civil services were then obliged to swear an oath of loyalty to him personally. From then on Hitler's rule was justified in charismatic rather than legal terms.

Having achieved their goal of total power, Hitler and the Nazis set about implementing their programme. Opposition was ruthlessly crushed through the GESTAPO. The population were indoctrinated with Nazi values through a new Ministry for Popular Enlightenment and Propaganda, which controlled the media and cultural activities, and also through the education system and the Hitler Youth organization, membership of which was eventually made compulsory. The economy was geared to rearmament and, through the acquisition of Austria (March 1938), the Sudetenland (October 1938) and the rest of Czechoslovakia (March 1939), Hitler prepared the ground for his main goal: a war for living space in the east.

With the outbreak of war in September 1939 Nazism came into its element. Its ruthless exploitation of the population and economies of the occupied territories through slave labour and plunder, particularly in Poland and Russia, showed a contempt for human life which was the product of racial arrogance and ideological fanaticism. The Nazis were responsible for the 'final solution' whose aim was the extermination of the entire Jewish population of Europe. German Jews had already been subjected to increasing persecution, losing their citizenship in 1935, and their property in 1938. During the war, they and the Jewish population of occupied Europe were deported to the EXTERMINATION CAMPS in Poland. The catastrophe unleashed upon Europe by Germany ended in its total defeat in May 1945. The scale of the destruction and loss of life reflected the nihilism and inhumanity at the core of Nazism.

See also ANTI-SEMITISM; GAULEITER; RACE IN POLITICS; TOTALITARIANISM.

JDN

Reading

Bracher, K.D.: *The German Dictatorship*. London: Penguin, 1973.

Broszat, M.: *The Hitler State: the foundations and development of the internal structure of the Third Reich*. London: Arnold, 1981.

Fest, J.: *Hitler*. London: Penguin, 1975.

Hildebrand, K.: *The Third Reich*. London: Allen & Unwin, 1984.

Kater, M.: *The Nazi Party: a social profile of members and leaders 1919–45*. Oxford: Blackwell, 1983.

Kershaw, I.: *The Nazi Dictatorship*. London: Arnold, 1984.

Mosse, G.: *The Crisis of German Ideology: intellectual origins of the Third Reich*. London: Weidenfeld & Nicolson, 1966.

Noakes, J. and Pridham, G.: *Nazism 1919–1945: a documentary reader*. 3 vols. Exeter: Exeter University Press, 1986.

Orlow, D.: *A History of the Nazi Party 1919–45*. 2 vols. Newton Abbot: David & Charles, 1969 and 1973.

New Deal The movement for social and economic change launched during the peacetime presidency of F. D. Roosevelt, 1933–9. It followed the collapse of the American economy with some fifteen million unemployed. The early emphasis, especially during the 'Hundred Days' (March–June 1933), was on economic recovery. Measures included the Banking Act, the National Recovery Act to raise industrial prices, the Agricultural Adjustment Act to restore farm prices through limits on production, work programmes for the unemployed, and the Tennessee Valley Authority as a model for regional planning. In 1935–6, a new social thrust appeared, with the Social Security Act, and the Wagner Labour Relations Act to protect trade unions, along with measures to protect securities and attack monopolies. Roosevelt's landslide re-election in 1936 confirmed the popularity of the New Deal.

Thereafter difficulties mounted. The SUPREME COURT had already obstructed several New Deal measures, but Roosevelt's attempt to reform it in 1937 was blocked in Congress. Nevertheless, the Court ceased to strike down federal legislation in economic and social matters, and has adopted a stance of self-restraint on such issues since the 1930s (see JUDICIAL ACTIVISM AND SELF-RESTRAINT). Recession in the economy and divisions within the Democratic Party also slowed down the New Deal, although major bills dealing with agriculture and housing were passed in 1938. However in 1939 Roosevelt announced that the New Deal was mainly over and that the main emphasis henceforth would be on the threat of world war.

The New Deal was far from wholly successful. Unemployment remained at a high level until 1941 and it was the war which finally restored the economy to full vigour. The New Deal was most effective for large combines, powerful farmers, and big labour unions; it had less to offer the blacks or the poor. Yet it had an extraordinary long-term effect. It committed the US government henceforth to support for the economy and for social welfare. It powerfully encouraged labour and ethnic minorities, and revived the south and farming areas. It notably reinforced the powers of the presidency, and of the federal government over the states. Its use of intellectual advisers ('the brains trust') was also a key feature. In party political terms it is associated with an electoral REALIGNMENT which made the Democrats the natural majority party and the voice of liberalism and urban reform from the 1930s to the 1970s. It ranks with the War of Independence and the Civil War as a pivotal phase in the making of the United States.

KOM

Reading

Blum, J.M.: *From the Morgenthau Diaries*. 3 vols. Boston, Mass.: Houghton Mifflin, 1959–65.

Burns, J.M.: *Roosevelt: the lion and the fox*. New York: Harcourt Brace, 1956.

———: *Roosevelt: soldier of freedom*. New York: Harcourt Brace, Jovanovich, 1970.

Friedel, F.B.: *Franklin D. Roosevelt: launching the New Deal*. Boston, Mass.: Little, Brown, 1974.

Leuchtenburg, W.E.: *Franklin D. Roosevelt and the New Deal, 1932–1940*. New York: Harper & Row, 1963.

Louchheim, K.: *The Making of the New Deal: the insiders speak*. Cambridge, Mass.: Harvard University Press, 1984.

Schlesinger, A.M. Jr: *The Coming of the New Deal.* London: Heinemann, 1960.

————: *The Politics of Upheaval.* London: Heinemann, 1961.

Zinn, H. ed.: *New Deal Thought.* New York: Bobbs-Merrill, 1966.

New Left A movement of neo-Marxism which came to prominence in the 1960s proclaiming a libertarian SOCIALISM as opposed to the scientific socialism of traditional MARXISM. Inspired by the humanistic writings of the younger Marx, by the Frankfurt school of dialectical sociology, by radical forms of phenomenology and existentialism, and by the dissident communist ideas of Antoni Gramsci, New Left theory was essentially eclectic. As a movement with little faith in the revolutionary potential of the industrial working class, it assigned historic roles both to intellectuals and to alienated protest groups in bourgeois society. It could claim to have shaken universities to their foundations in 1968 and to have mobilized American opinion against the Vietnam war but, through the lack of any organized structure, the New Left endured rather as a tendency than as a fixed political grouping.   MWC

Reading

Cranston, M.W.: *The New Left.* London: Bodley Head, 1970.

New Right A broad ideological movement associated with the conservative revival of the 1970s and 1980s. Although elements of the movement can be found in a number of western countries, its significance is greatest in the United States and the United Kingdom where two political leaders (Ronald Reagan and Margaret Thatcher) have been popularly associated with it. While the New Right is not monolithic, some common themes in its political beliefs and some common features of its political style can be identified.

First, the New Right draws ideological inspiration from the classical liberal theory of the nineteenth century and from the school of economics based upon it. Among twentieth-century theorists, it is especially indebted to the writings of F. A. von Hayek and the Austrian school of political economy, to the free market ideas of Milton Friedman and the Chicago school, and to the political ideas of the American philosopher, Robert Nozick. These intellectual foundations distinguish the New Right from both the collectivist ideologies of MARXISM and SOCIALISM on the one hand and from the pragmatic British approach – dubbed Butskellism after the moderate Tory R. A. Butler and the Labour leader Hugh Gaitskell – associated with the welfare consensus of the period between 1945 and 1970 on the other. The individualism of classical liberalism also distinguishes it from traditional British Toryism and paternalistic varieties of conservatism which emphasize the importance of hierarchy and order. In the United States the New Right has developed a strong libertarian strand, although other elements in the New Right coalition (such as the neo-conservatives who emphasize the importance of traditional national, religious and family values as integrating mechanisms and the religious right who assert the need for a return to biblical morality) oppose the libertarians' assertion of freedom of choice in matters of personal morality.

Second, the New Right has an aggressive and POPULIST style which distinguishes it from traditional conservatism. It has a Manichean view of political conflict and rejects attempts to compromise between freedom and the various forms of collectivism, both in domestic politics and in the international arena where the New Right's instincts are fiercely anti-communist. The New Right tends to be suspicious of institutions and, in the United States, has been skilful at using instruments of DIRECT DEMOCRACY such as the REFERENDUM. In the United States the political style of the New Right has enabled it to adapt to an increasingly competitive electoral environment by using such techniques as computerized direct mail. It has also been adept at putting together coalitions of like-minded pressure groups, such as those concerned with preserving the traditional family, with committees, such as the National Conservative Political Action Committee, which are altogether broader in scope.

Finally, although this is not entirely consonant with the New Right's economic liberalism, there has been a reassertion of the need for authority in society. In the United States, because of the religious contribution to the conservative revival, this has taken the form of a demand for the suppression of abortion, homosexuality, and pornography and for a return to a biblically-based pro-family morality. In the United Kingdom the moral and religious dimension of New Right politics has been much less evident but there has been a strong populist emphasis on law and order and patriotism. In both the United States and the United Kingdom the New Right has expressed a developing criticism of the ethical permissiveness and cultural nihilism associated with the 1960s and has celebrated the values of enterprise, responsibility, and conventional morality. In both countries it has also lost some of its distinctiveness as many of its ideas, particularly on the economy, have been absorbed into the mainstream of political life.

GRP

Reading

Bosanquet, N.: *After the New Right*. London: Heinemann Educational Books, 1983.

Levitas, R. ed.: *The Ideology of the New Right*. Oxford: Polity, 1986.

Peele, G.: *Revival and Reaction: the Right in contemporary America*. Oxford: Oxford University Press, 1984.

nomenklatura The name given to the lists of positions in the Soviet Union appointment to which is the prerogative of the CPSU, and also to the lists of persons who are candidates for them. The *nomenklatura* system operates at all levels of the party, from the all-Union CENTRAL COMMITTEE down to *rayon* (district) committees. The total number of positions in the *nomenklatura* is estimated at over two million, giving the party comprehensive control of recruitment into the political elite and of career advancement in general. The Central Committee's *nomenklatura* powers cover, as well as party positions at all-Union level and the most important at republic and *oblast* (regional) level, top officials in the military, the media, and mass and professional organizations, a total currently estimated at about fifty thousand posts.

Personal factors are likely to be involved in selection, but so are impersonal bureaucratic ones, since at each level the apparatus of the appointing committee plays a substantial role. The main qualifications include political reliability. The wielding of the power of appointment by higher bodies over lower means that patron–client relationships often bypass relations of authority within a given body.

There has been some debate among western and emigré scholars over the question of whether the category of people who occupy *nomenklatura* positions comprises a RULING CLASS (this category is also commonly referred to as the *nomenklatura*, but its members are more properly called *nomenklaturnye*). The penetration of the system to relatively low levels of society makes this identification implausible. However the *nomenklaturnye* of the all-Union Central Committee more plausibly merit such a description, the issue hingeing on the connotation given to ownership in the definition of ruling class. SW

Reading

Harasymiw, B.: *Nomenklatura*: the Soviet Communist Party's leadership recruitment system. *Canadian Journal of Political Science* 2 (1969) 493–512.

————: *Political Elite Recruitment in the Soviet Union*. London: Macmillan, 1984.

Hill, R.J. and Frank, P.: *The Soviet Communist Party*. 3rd edn. London: Allen & Unwin, 1986.

Nove, A.: Is there a ruling class in the USSR? *Soviet Studies* 27 (1975) 615–38.

Voslensky, M.: *Nomenklatura: anatomy of the Soviet ruling class*. London: Bodley Head, 1984.

non-violent action A technique of political action in the use of which practitioners exert pressure on opponents but themselves abstain from violent means that injure, or threaten to injure, the persons of opponents. Damage to property is not necessarily excluded; some advocates of the technique emphasize the moral distinction between violence to persons and violence to property. Defining non-violent action (NVA) in largely negative terms suggests that the contrast is with political action involving use of overtly violent means. But some argue that NVA is also distinguishable from conventional constitutional action since the latter assumes that any change of policy or law so obtained will be upheld, if necessary, by the state's use of 'legitimate violence'. From this perspective, NVA is seen as a 'third way' to achieve political objectives, involving, typically, DIRECT ACTION by those looking for change rather than indirect action through representatives.

In practice NVA overlaps with, and is often used to supplement, constitutional action, even when civil disobedience is involved. It is also commonly used by revolutionaries as a prelude, or adjunct, to violent action. Further, states may use certain non-violent methods in dealing with other states, for example diplomatic non-recognition and economic sanctions. Sharp has identified some 200 methods classified as follows. *Non-violent protest* comprises methods which are primarily symbolic in their effect and intended to indicate dissent to a particular policy or, on occasions, to a whole regime, for example mass petitions, picketing, marches and walkouts. *Non-violent non-cooperation* comprises methods characterized by a withdrawal of cooperation with the opponent, the effect being to make it difficult or impossible to maintain the normal efficiency and operation of the system, for example social boycotts, consumer boycotts, strikes – including GENERAL STRIKES, and acts of political boycott such as tax refusal and boycott of elections. *Non-violent intervention*: methods which, in contrast to those of the second type, involve heightened interaction with the opponent, challenge his power more directly, and, unless countered effectively, tend to alter abruptly the status quo, for example sit-ins, work-ins, non-violent invasions, and the setting up of alternative institutions and a system of parallel government.

When used successfully, NVA produces change in one of three ways. Opponents may be converted to the viewpoint of the practitioners; they may be non-violently coerced into doing what is demanded; or there may be some accommodation between the opposed viewpoints. Although associated with contemporary PACIFISM, NVA does not require a principled commitment to non-violence. In fact, historically, it has been used most frequently by people with a pragmatic attitude to non-violence. The technique rests on the theory of 'voluntary servitude' which maintains that structures of power depend, ultimately, not on the physical force wielded by power-holders but on the 'consent', willingly or reluctantly given, of those over whom power is exercised. Although NVA has a long history, its extensive use is associated with the rise of nationalist and labour and socialist movements. Its increased popularity in recent decades owes much to its successful use by Gandhi in the struggle for Indian independence and Martin Luther King in the campaign for CIVIL RIGHTS in the USA. It is currently used by a wide variety of movements, including campaigners for nuclear disarmament, some of whom suggest that it could provide an alternative to military defence.　　　　GNO

Reading

Alternative Defence Commission: *Defence Without the Bomb*, ch. 7. London: Taylor & Francis, 1983.

Carter, A.: *Direct Action and Liberal Democracy*. London: Routledge & Kegan Paul; New York: Harper & Row, 1973.

Sharp, G.: *The Politics of Nonviolent Action*. Boston, Mass.: Porter Sargent, 1973.

O

oligarchy Two distinct meanings and connotations of the term can be distinguished. In the original Greek sense the word means rule by the few, and is distinguished from MONARCHY and AUTOCRACY (rule by one person) on the one hand, and from DEMOCRACY (rule by the many, or the people) on the other. The oligarchs rule in their own interest and accumulate special powers and privileges denied to ordinary people. A prevailing tendency of oligarchy is towards plutocracy, in which power and privileges are based on wealth. Both PLATO (*Republic*, ch. 30) and ARISTOTLE (*Politics*, bk V, ch. 6) discuss this tendency together with other aspects of oligarchy.

During the nineteenth and twentieth centuries oligarchy has been discussed and analysed less as a form of government than as a management style seen to operate in organizations and institutions such as POLITICAL PARTIES and TRADE UNIONS. POWER rather than wealth is the key factor. Various scholars and commentators have noted a rooted propensity for those in power to show oligarchic tendencies. This happens for a number of reasons, including the oligarchs' superior knowledge of the organization, the extra power that comes with continuity in office, and the ability to manipulate information, even events, in their own interest. As the process develops their subordinates, or in the case of a political party the mass membership, have little alternative but to cede more power to the oligarchs whose grip on the organization is thereby further strengthened and so the process continues. 'Who says organization says oligarchy' was a famous phrase of Roberto MICHELS. The proclivity is seen in many organizations and institutions such as large-scale businesses, corporations, and the hierarchy of a church. Commentators on Michels's IRON LAW OF OLIGARCHY are divided between those who deplore the process, arguing that it is undemocratic in practice and anti-democratic in principle, and those who argue that it is unavoidable in any large enterprise where expertise, continuity and a degree of bureaucracy are necessary parts of the structure. (See also RULING CLASS.)

The term has also been discussed by writers such as C. Wright Mills, MOSCA and PARETO in connection with the study of ELITES and elite theory. These writers also divide between those who see a danger in elites, and those who regard them as inevitable. ESAI

Reading

McKenzie, R.T.: *British Political Parties*. London: Heinemann, 1955; New York: Praeger, 1966.

Michels, R.: *Political Parties*, ed. and intro. S.M. Lipset. New York: Crowell-Collier, 1962.

Mills, C.W.: *The Power Elite*. New York: Oxford University Press, 1956.

ombudsman There is no elegant English translation for this Scandinavian word with German origins. Literally it can mean agent, representative, guardian or perhaps grievance officer. Ombudsmen in the English-speaking world are formally styled commissioners, others ombudsmen, but all tend to use the title ombudsman in their everyday work, and the word may now be regarded as absorbed into English terminology. Non-English titles for similar officers include Médiateur in France and the flowery El Defensor del Pueblo in Spain. The world's first ombudsman institution was created in Sweden in 1809 and the second in Finland in 1919. Since the second world war many other countries – Denmark in 1954, New Zealand in 1962 and Britain in 1967 – have followed suit, and ombudsman institutions are to be found today in most countries other than those in Central and South America and those with communist regimes. There are many variations: some ombudsmen are single officers (such as the Parliamentary Commissioner for Administration in Britain and in Northern Ireland, and the Médiateur in France), others operate within the framework of a commission (for example the three Local Commissioners in the Commission for Local Administration in England), and yet others, especially in Africa, work as a type of collegiate body (for example the People's Assembly Committee in Sudan). Most ombudsmen are set up by statute (e.g. the Parliamentary Commissioner Act, 1967 in Britain; Loi 73–6 in France; the Ombudsman Act, 1976 in Australia). Others are created as a result of voluntary agreement by those in a profession, trade or area of business which is to be subject to investigation by the ombudsman (for example the Insurance Ombudsman Bureau set up in 1981, and the Banking Ombudsman set up in 1986, in the United Kingdom); some of these agreements are put into statutory form, for example, the British Lay Observer (Solicitors Act 1974) and the Police Complaints Authority (Police and Criminal Evidence Act 1984).

The task of the statutory ombudsman is to investigate complaints against administrative action by government authorities. Most countries with ombudsmen empower them to deal with complaints against central government. In federal countries there may be separate ombudsmen dealing with complaints against state (Australia) or provincial (Canada) governments; and in others there may be ombudsmen concerned with regional (Italy), cantonal (Switzerland) or local (United Kingdom, USA) government authorities. Canada has provincial ombudsmen, though there are three specialist federal ombudsmen dealing

respectively with matters concerning privacy, information and the official languages. In the USA there are many municipal ombudsmen but few state ombudsmen (Hawaii and Alaska), and no federal ombudsman. Ombudsmen for special areas of administration include those dealing with the armed forces (Federal Republic of Germany), the health service (United Kingdom), education, consumer affairs and small businesses (all USA). Caseloads vary greatly: extremes are represented by the Pakistan ombudsman who receives over 30,000 complaints each year, and the ombudsman for the Indian State of Uttar Pradesh with less than 200.

The ground upon which ombudsmen may investigate complaints is the supposition of some administrative fault, not necessarily illegal, causing injustice. This jurisdiction is often expressed widely in the governing statute: the New Zealand ombudsman may investigate complaints that decisions or actions were 'unreasonable, unjust, oppressive' or 'wrong', while in the United Kingdom the word used is 'MALADMINISTRATION' – a term which is undefined but which has been held by ombudsmen to cover error which is both intentional, such as malice, bias or perversity, and unintentional, such as incompetence, unjustified delay, failure to follow procedures already established, and failure to establish or revise procedures where a clear need to do so has been shown. Ombudsmen may not normally investigate complaints about issues which could be litigated in courts or other tribunals, but they often have specific discretion to do so if satisfied that it would be unreasonable in all the circumstances of the case to expect the complainant to take such other action. Most ombudsmen have little or no restrictions placed upon their area of jurisdiction but some, notably in the United Kingdom, are prevented by their statutes from considering certain matters (for example personnel complaints, and the internal conduct of schools and colleges). In many countries complaints may be lodged orally (Canada, Pakistan), while in others they must be in writing, and referred by a Member of Parliament (British Parliamentary Commissioner) or local councillor (United Kingdom Local

Ombudsmen). Some ombudsmen may investigate on their own initiative (Denmark, New Zealand, Pakistan).

Because ombudsmen are dealing with matters of wider administrative morality than simple illegality, their findings do not have the force of law and are put in the form of reports, often made directly to the legislature as in Sweden, Denmark, Spain, Britain (Parliamentary Commissioner), or to the local or other authority against whom the complaint was made (municipal ombudsmen). There is no direct method of enforcement, though the administrative authorities almost always comply with the findings and provide the remedies recommended. Exceptionally a complainant remaining dissatisfied by the response of the relevant authority to a report by the Northern Ireland Commissioner for Complaints (who investigates complaints against local authorities, hospitals, health authorities and some other province-wide bodies) may seek a court remedy for the fault found in the report. The ombudsman is therefore an office which, while discharging an almost judicial function in a citizen's dispute with a public authority, yet forms no part of the judiciary. In some countries, such as Britain, the office is seen as an extension of Parliament, in others as part of the administration.　　　　　　　　　DCMY

Reading

Caiden, G.E. ed.: *International Handbook of the Ombudsman.* 2 vols. Westport, Conn.: Greenwood, 1983.

Gellhorn, W.: *Ombudsmen and Others: citizens' protectors in nine countries.* Cambridge, Mass.: Harvard University Press, 1967.

Gregory, R. and Hutchesson, P.: *The Parliamentary Ombudsman: a study in the control of administrative action.* London: Allen & Unwin, 1978.

Rowat, D.E. ed.: *The Ombudsman: citizens' defender.* 2nd edn. London: Allen & Unwin, 1968.

Stacey, F.: *Ombudsmen Compared.* London: Allen & Unwin, 1978.

Wheare, K.C.: *Maladministration and its Remedies.* London: Stevens, 1973.

Williams, D.W.: *Maladministration: remedies for injustice.* London: Oyez, 1976.

one-party states　　Polities where only one political organization calling itself a party is permitted to operate legally or politically. One-party states are in many respects the political norm around the world: the number of genuine multi-party democracies, as opposed to those systems which claim to be multi-party but are really variants of the one-party system, is relatively small. One-party states have proved particularly popular outside Europe and the main areas of European settlement. The category 'one-party state' however embraces a variety of forms and some of these are substantially more flexible and more responsive to pressure from below than others.

The roots of the one-party state can be traced to the imperative of communal unity and enforced homogeneity, whether the community in question is a tribe, a clan, an empire or a republic. In pre-modern polities the unification of power and its legitimization in the hands of a single ruler were regarded as desirable and efficient. The alternative, especially in poorly administered polities with cross-cutting loyalties, was the threat of anarchy and vulnerability to invasion from outside.

In the modern period the one-party system has been legitimated either explicitly by reference to a transcending ideology (MARXISM–LENINISM, NAZISM, religion, NATIONALISM) or by a more implicit set of teleologies (modernization, stability, fear of neo-colonialism). These systems may or may not be totalitarian in their aspiration (see TOTALITARIANISM), although no modern system, however effective its administrative machinery, has achieved totalitarian control in practice; they should therefore be seen as occupying a position on a spectrum between AUTHORITARIANISM and degrees of informal pluralism.

Soviet-type systems are characterized by the rule of an organization, the Communist Party, which aims to be the sole agent of power and control. In these systems the political sphere tries to encompass others and to insist that political rationality, as defined by the party, must remain dominant over all others such as the economic, legal, social and aesthetic. In this respect the party claims a monopoly of rationality, efficiency in execution, organization, political thought and control in structuring the future; its legitimacy is claimed to derive from the revolution inspired by Marxism–Leninism.

The Soviet-type party therefore, as the self-styled possessor of historic truth through scientific socialism, cannot tolerate challengers in the political sphere because these can rapidly erode its power and legitimacy, given that it claims to rule in the name of a single, cohesive whole. It administers the political system by a variety of instruments: the most important of these are its power over the instruments of coercion; its monopoly over appointments through the NOMENKLATURA, a list of posts in all bureaucracies (i.e. in the party, the state, local government, the administration of justice, social institutions, trade unions, the press, armed forces, police etc.) which are filled by reference to political criteria; its control of economic and other material benefits by which individuals and groups can be co-opted or integrated. Currently, the use of coercion has become less important in the management of power than the threat of it. Mass terror, used to exact compliance, was associated with STALIN, but this was abandoned under Khrushchev, together with the demand for total compliance. Nowadays, the Soviet-type party plays a more complex role as goal-setter in politics, economics, society; as executor of the strategies it has chosen; as arbitrator among different socio-political interests. The practice of these three roles is frequently confused and the absence of open conflicts of interest results in the near impossibility of determining the 'best interests' of the polity. Hence partial interest groups can distort the political or economic rationality of the system for their own purposes (for example, by diverting investment through their control of central planning). In this sense the single party, especially if its ideological fervour has declined, can become a coalition of factions, which informally represent different interests. These divergent interests, however, will not be so far-reaching as to destroy the unity of the party *vis-à-vis* society.

The one-party state of the non-Soviet type tends to be less far-reaching in its claims and less cohesive in its organization. It will seek to control politics by reference to homogeneity and to regard conflict as undesirable. One-party systems of this kind may have a fairly overt teleology as their political legitimation, or they can be the *ex post facto* constructs of a dictator who has seized power and requires a political organization to support his political objectives. One-party systems of this kind can permit autonomous institutions to coexist with the single party, such as a less than fully controlled press. Some one-party systems are military in origin, arising in the aftermath of a military take-over.

One-party systems of all types tend to suffer from a process of decay, of a growing conservatism over time, and of corruption; often finding it difficult to renew their legitimacy they become resistant to innovation or renewal; isolation from the wider aspirations of society is not infrequent. This can create a cycle of take-overs, as one group in power is ousted by another claiming to be better fitted to lead the polity. In certain circumstances the absence or weakness of the legitimacy of the party when coupled with a major crisis, either external or domestic, can result in the rapid collapse of the system (for example Poland in 1980). The positive side of one-party systems is that, over short periods, they can stabilize a polity which has been torn apart by dissension; this stabilization demands that those who have taken supreme power should recognize the transitory quality of their rule (Turkey offers an example). Equally, these systems can be effective in mobilizing energies for a particular purpose, ususally that of modernization interpreted as creating a modern industrial base. Over the longer term, however, they become vulnerable to the cycle of degeneration.

See also MILITARY REGIMES.   GSch

Reading

Allardt, E. and Rokkan, S. eds: *Mass Politics: studies in political sociology*. New York: Free Press, 1970.

Finer, S.E.: *Comparative Government*. London: Penguin, 1970.

Harding, N.: *The State in Socialist Societies*. London: Macmillan, 1984.

Held, J. ed.: *The Cult of Power*. New York: East European Monographs, 1983.

Linz, J.: An authoritarian regime: Spain. In Allardt and Rokkan, 1970.

Sartori, G.: The typology of party systems. In Allardt and Rokkan, 1970.

Wiatr, J.: The hegemonic party system in Poland. In Allardt and Rokkan, 1970.

open government Though sometimes used as synonymous with FREEDOM OF INFORMATION in describing laws that provide a legally enforceable right of public access to government records, the term open government embraces activities which go beyond the limits of these laws. The law relating to government information (or to information of any kind) can prohibit communication, require it, or remain neutral. Freedom of information laws only require certain kinds of communication by establishing a legally enforceable right of public access to government records. The laws prohibiting communication of information, such as widely-drawn statutes defining 'espionage' may also have an effect on the openness of government. One particular issue is whether an unauthorized disclosure of classified government information may be permitted the defence that it has been made in the 'public interest'. A similar issue is whether there should be such a defence when a civil action is brought against a breach of confidentiality. The Civil Service Reform Act of 1978 in the USA established an Office of Special Counsel to prevent administrative retaliation against civil servants who 'blow the whistle' by disclosing information which reveals government wrongdoing.

Legal rules are not the only determinants of the relative openness of government (or of other institutions). The law may be neutral, or at least largely so, leaving disclosure of information to other factors. In the United Kingdom a policy of open government was adopted in 1978 by the senior civil servant in charge of the Civil Service Department (since abolished). Because he later became Lord Croham his circular establishing the policy became known as the 'Croham Directive'. The directive instructed civil servants to disclose as much information as possible, and to draft documents so that policy advice to ministers (which was not to be made public) could be easily segregated from other information. The policy was criticized and has been abandoned, at least so far as any system for monitoring compliance existed.

While freedom of information laws apply only to the executive functions of government, open government can embrace the publicizing of other governmental functions, particularly legislative ones.

It can also include other forms of openness, requiring for example that meetings of various governmental bodies should be open to the public. Examples are state and municipal laws in the USA, the federal 'Government in the Sunshine' Act of 1976, and the Public Bodies (Admission to Meetings) Act of 1960 in the UK (introduced as a Private Member's Bill by Margaret Thatcher).   JRM

Reading

Galnoor, I.: *Government Secrecy in Democracies*. New York: Harper & Row, 1977.

Michael, J.: *The Politics of Secrecy: confidential government and the right to know.* Harmondsworth: Penguin, 1982.

opinion polls Parties and candidates have long relied on intuition and impressions for interpreting the mood of voters and explaining election outcomes. Opinion polls, based on the questioning of a representative and systematically drawn sample of the electorate, date from the 1930s. A key date is 1936 when the Gallup and Elmo Roper polls correctly predicted the outcome of the Roosevelt-Landon presidential election in the United States. It was not until the 1960s that polls were widely used by the mass media and parties for election purposes. Since then the use of polls has grown almost exponentially, and competition between them has stiffened.

An easily overlooked condition for the activity of market and opinion research is the freedom, found mainly in Western European and Anglo-American societies, to interview people and publish the findings of polls on political views and voting intentions. A number of third-world states in Africa, the Middle East and South-east Asia have opinion polls, but these usually avoid questions on national politics. In France, West Germany, Brazil, and South Africa opinion polls freely report between election campaigns – but for the duration of the official campaign, or in its later stages, these countries ban reports of the polls' findings or, as in West Germany, their forecasts.

By interviewing a sample of 1000 or so voters drawn randomly from the electorate, the polls claim to be correct within a margin of plus or minus 3 per cent in 95 per cent of cases. In Britain the polls have a good record in predicting election winners, though they have been spectacularly wrong on two occasions. In 1970 four public polls out of five wrongly predicted a Labour win, while in February 1974, the polls unanimously but insistently predicted a Conservative victory: though the Conservatives gained more votes and fewer seats than Labour, each poll understated the Labour vote. In 1979 and 1983 the polls were remarkably close to the final result. The average error in the final forecasts of five major polls was 1 per cent in 1979, and it was only slightly larger in 1983.

Pollsters are now usually careful to poll to the last day in order to measure any late change in sentiment. They were disastrously wrong in the 1948 presidential election when they forecast an easy victory for Dewey over President Truman. The allocation of undecided votes and adjustments for differential turnout are matters for subjective not scientific judgement.

It is frequently alleged that by making forecasts the polls influence election results, for example by creating a 'bandwagon' of support for the leading party. Certainly more voters are now aware of what the polls are saying and are potentially more open to influence. But it is not clear that 'bandwagons' are created. In British general elections since 1945 the polls have underestimated the winning party's margin of victory six times and overestimated it four times. It is worth noting that surveys in the October 1974 and 1979 general elections found that people were less likely to vote for the front-running party if a landslide victory seemed probable. Futher, the polls by informing the electors of the tactical situation in the constituency can provide opportunities for tactical voting.

Opinion polls have probably led to more informed coverage and analysis of elections. Evidence takes the place of hearsay or other impressions. The polls can also inform politicians about what voters think. They can be used to evaluate an incumbent party's claim to have a MANDATE for its programme. They can also provide a check on the claims of parties, pressure groups and the mass media about PUBLIC OPINION. Above all, most political parties and party leaders use private polls to plan election strategies.

Polls may also be used by government leaders to time an election for when it is most favourable to their party; furthermore parties and, in presidential systems, candidates often commission private polls from commercial organizations. These polls are less important for predicting the election result than for enabling parties to make a more effective presentation of policies, monitor the impact of campaign themes and issues, and target on key voters.

Polls are regularly attacked and praised as surrogates for direct democracy. They may offer a check on the mediating or representative claims of parties, pressure groups, and mass media. Where they are centrally commissioned, local candidates often resent them as yet another instance of the centralization and nationalization of campaigning; they may therefore strengthen the position of leaders within the parliamentary parties, and the parliamentary parties against the mass members. Used with care, however, opinion polls remain an important feedback device for decision makers and citizens between and during elections.

See also ELECTIONS.   DK

Reading

Clemens, J.: *Polls, Politics and Populism*. London: Gower, 1983.

Kavanagh, D.: Public opinion polls. In *Democracy at the Polls*, ed. D. Butler, H. Penniman and A. Ranney. Washington, DC: American Enterprise Institute, 1981.

Mendelsohn, H. and Crespi, I.: *Polls: television and the new politics*. Scranton, Penn.: Chandler, 1970.

Penniman, H. ed.: *At the Polls: a series of election studies*. Washington, DC: American Enterprise Institute, 1975– .

Worcester, R. ed.: *Political Opinion Polling*. London: Macmillan, 1983.

opposition In the political process the term refers to the right of minorities to criticize the majority, to exercise control, and to seek popular/electoral support by advocating alternative positions. Opposition can be loyal and aim at political change within the given constitutional parameters; or it can be fundamentalist (opposition of principle) and defy the political consensus by advocating an abolition/transformation of the political system. Parliamentary opposition is directed against the government and consists of the party or parties who are not involved in a coalition or similar agreement. Extraparliamentary opposition emanates from political parties or movements either too weak or not inclined to gain parliamentary representation. Opposition can also occur within political parties or interest groups.

The role of opposition depends on the POLITICAL CULTURE in which it developed and the constraints imposed by the political system. Where the articulation of conflicting positions in parliaments through elected representatives and political parties is a cornerstone of the political process (as in democracies), opposition perpetrates innovation and change. Where politics is supposed to express a pre-existent common good (as in communist systems), opposition is deemed an obstruction or illegitimate. Where the state proclaims itself to be above-party, political parties and parliaments are despised as divisive while opposition tends to be criminalized as a danger to the stability of the political system itself. This has been an element in the German tradition. Where socio-economic groups or political parties have little confidence that their positions and interests could effect change, opposition of principle may proliferate (for example the French Fourth Republic, Italy, the Weimar Republic).

Based on British parliamentary practice, the classical model sees parliamentary opposition as a shadow government ready to take over the affairs of state at a moment's notice. Two equally legitimate political forces, government and opposition, compete in parliament and two political parties seek popular support. Political change rests on their alternation in government; i.e. both sides could command an electoral majority. Opposition is expected to control government policies through criticism and offering alternatives; it has no role in formulating government legislation. In 1937 the leader of the opposition in Britain became an official appointment by the Crown. This signifies the legitimacy of opposition in the political process and bestows rights of parliamentary reply upon the largest opposition party, although several parties have shared the opposition benches since the Labour Party gained parliamentary representation. Voting preferences and electoral DEALIGNMENT in recent years have strengthened tendencies towards party pluralism. The plurality electoral system has, however, served to maintain the two-party structure in parliament and shadow government as the dominant voice of parliamentary opposition.

In democratic PRESIDENTIAL SYSTEMS the party affiliation of the president can differ from party majorities in elected chambers. In the United States the government/opposition divide may go either way between Senate and Congress. Opposition is determined by issues with changing alliances according to the local/regional interests or political judgement of individual delegates since political parties themselves are regionally too diverse to prescribe common policies.

The measure of success for opposition must be its ability to form the government. In two-party systems, this is normally accomplished by winning a majority of parliamentary seats in national elections although all-party coalitions may temporarily suspend opposition. In multi-party systems (see PARTY SYSTEMS, TYPES OF), parliamentary majorities depend on coalitions. Opposition parties might switch to government roles if policies converge sufficiently for common approaches to be found between different parties. Coalition politics reduce the need to articulate distinct political alternatives in search of popular support. Opposition parties without prospects to form or join a government are inclined towards fundamentalist positions.

In federal systems, government and

opposition overlap since the governing party or parties at national level may be in opposition in several regions or vice versa; or the opposition parties in the national parliament may command a controlling majority and legislative veto in the SECOND CHAMBER. In West Germany, the Constitutional Court can censure government policies and initiate political change, i.e. function as political opposition.

Parliamentary procedure can incorporate opposition parties into the legislative process. In addition to the rights of opposition to confront the government in public, 'integrated' opposition can influence legislation in specialist non-public committees, and table its own legislative proposals. To imprint policy aims of the opposition on to legislation becomes a yardstick of success; in parliament, most legislation is passed unanimously. Opposition as co-government fosters centre-based politics, curtails political partisanship, and contributes to policy continuity between governments. It also restricts political diversity and the articulation of policy alternatives.

Extra-parliamentary opposition can range from fringe parties to protest movements, and has two major political functions. Extra-parliamentary opposition *challenges* the legitimacy of parliament and its ability to generate political change. It aims at a transformation of the parliamentary parameters or the political system itself. Elites, displaced in a transition towards democracy, or disaffected groups in advanced industrial societies, have tended towards extra-parliamentary opposition including violent confrontations or terrorism. Extra-parliamentary opposition *articulates* issues which have been ignored/omitted by parliamentary oppositions and catch-all parties. Salient issues in society (e.g. environmentalism) may generate extra-parliamentary movements which tend to act as catalysts of policy innovation at party and parliamentary level. EK

Reading

Beyme, K. von: *Political Parties in Western Democracies*. New York: St Martin's; Aldershot: Gower, 1985.

Dahl, R.A. ed.: *Political Oppositions in Western Democracies*. New Haven, Conn.: Yale University Press, 1966.

Ionescu, G. and Madariaga, I. de: *Opposition: past and present of a political institution*. London: Watts, 1968.

Kolinsky, E. ed.: *Opposition in Western Europe*. London: PSI & Croom Helm, 1987.

Oberreuter, H. ed.: *Parlamentarische Opposition: ein internationaler Vergleich*. Hamburg: Hoffman & Campe, 1975.

organization theory Takes as its frame of reference all artificial or consciously designed units of human organization. It is defined more by subject-matter than by discipline, and in that sense resembles political science and PUBLIC ADMINISTRATION. Unlike political science it is mainly concerned with organization below state level (enterprises, associations, plants, work units); unlike public administration it deals with all formal organizations in society, not just those providing public services. Organization theory aims: to define issues generic to all formal organization (for instance, issues as to how tasks and responsibilities are to be divided up, how the activities or decisions of different component units are integrated, what rules govern the conduct of business, how communication among component parts is structured, how subordinates are controlled and motivated by superordinates); to explore commonalities, differences and 'family groups' in the world of formal organizations; thereby, to produce theories consistent with observations drawn from only sub-classes of that population (for instance, in 'contingency theory', which tries to determine the extent to which structure and operating procedures relate to size, environment and type of work).

Organization theory developed with the growth of large-scale enterprise over the past century or so. Before that, large corporate entities were to be found mainly in military, government and ecclesiastical affairs, with separate 'sciences' for each of these fields of organization. Outside those spheres the legal fiction (followed by classical economics) that corporations can be understood as though they were individual persons, was convenient enough in a small-firm economy, but with the growth of trusts, giant corporations, mass political parties, large-scale trade unions, and massive expansion in the scale of public bureaucracy, the traditional function of the enterprise as a person was set aside and a new kind of theory developed to describe and understand its internal workings. The first phase was the development of 'how to do it' principles by practitioners, but professional academics began to take over the field at least fifty years ago, as an age of innocence gave way to one of 'sophisters, economists and calculators' (Burke, p. 170).

Some of the major strands of modern organization theory are as follows:

(1) Economics-based theories relating to the management of the large firm, and the exercise of discretion by managers in firms and public bureaucracies (classic works include Williamson 1975; Leibenstein 1976).
(2) Social psychology-based theories about the motivational effects of alternative organization designs, physical structuring, work routines and management styles.
(3) Sociology-based theories about the relation between informal group behaviour and formal rules, about the way the different tasks, technologies and other factors shape organization (see Miller 1976), and about the strengths and weaknesses of the classic Weber model of BUREAUCRACY.
(4) Cybernetics-based theories about the general principles underlying the operation of communication and control systems (see Beer 1966).

CCH

Reading

Beer, S.: *Decision and Control.* London: Wiley, 1966.

Child, J.: *Organization: a guide to problems and practice.* London: Harper & Row, 1977.

Burke, E.: *Reflections on the Revolution in France* (1790), ed. C.C. O'Brien. Harmondsworth: Penguin, 1969.

Crozier, M.: *The Bureaucratic Phenomenon.* Chicago, Ill.: University of Chicago Press, 1964.

Leibenstein, H.: *Beyond Economic Man: a new foundation for microeconomics.* Cambridge, Mass.: Harvard University Press, 1976.

Miller, E.J.: The open systems approach to organizational analysis. In *European Contributions to Organization Theory*, pp. 43–61, ed. A. Rice, M.S. Kassem and G. Hofstede. Assen: Van Gorcum, 1976.

Perrow, C.: *Complex Organizations: a critical essay.* 2nd edn. Glenview, Ill.: Scott, Foresman, 1979.

Williamson, O.E.: *Markets and Hierarchies.* London: Collier-Macmillan, 1975.

Ostrogorski, Moisei Yakovlevich (1854–1919)

Ostrogorski was born in Tsarist Russia and died in Soviet Russia. After a legal education and a career in the Ministry of Justice he moved, partly because of increasing unhappiness with the oppressiveness of the regime, to France. He studied at the École Libre des Sciences Politiques in Paris where he presented a thesis on the development of universal suffrage, a subject which was to be the germ of a lifelong concern. A book arising out of his work in Paris entitled *La Femme au point du droit public – étude d'histoire et de legislation comparée* was published in 1892, and subsequently translated and published in both English and German. In it Ostrogorski commented on the radical origins and conservative resistance to the suffrage demands of the women's movement that followed the egalitarianism of the French Revolution 'as a logical sequel. It comes and meets with a cold welcome.' This laconic recognition of the defeat of hope was characteristic, and the frustration of the expectations of democrats of all kinds – not just of feminists – was to be a recurring theme of his work. The extension of the vote, the reasons and arguments for it, its consequences and potential, all had become his overwhelming interest, and by 1892 he was already at work on his massive pioneering comparative study of political parties published in London in 1902 under the title *Democracy and the Organisation of Political Parties.* It is this work which made his reputation, and which led him to be seen as one of the founders of modern political science.

The theme of the book was the causes and effects of organization on political life in the two major examples of representative democracy, Britain and the United States, each of which was the subject of a separate volume. Although the book contains a massive amount of evidence gained from Ostrogorski's research into the practice of party politics, it is essentially a sustained qualitative appraisal of politics and an insistence on the fundamental importance of ideas and of human choice in forming institutions and events. It is this element which gives purpose to the whole enterprise, but though it is the central theme of the two volumes, it has, like Ostrogorski's work on sexual exclusion, frequently been unnoticed or ignored in later accounts of his work, and is largely missing from the bowdlerized edition prepared in the United States by S. M. Lipset. Ostrogorski described his intention as being to look below the surface of constitutional forms; what he saw underneath was not behavioural laws, but the power of culture and ideas, and 'the workings of the wills which set political society going'.

Ostrogorski's argument was that the social and political order which had been maintained by traditionally stratified society, and which had been eroded by individualism, was now provided not by the rational choices of informed and free citizens, but by the mechanical organization of political life by professional politicians, the managers of the caucus. 'Organization' was the key term, for it indicated the essential corruption of contemporary societies. Whereas for writers such as MICHELS organization was harmful because it led to oligarchy, for Ostrogorski it was incompatible with the desirable conduct of politics. It replaced considered individual action with the manipulated responses of masses, subverting the individualism whose consequences it had been developed to meet. Elections were organized so that the votes cast reflected not the informed thinking of responsible and intelligent citizens but the marshalling of consent; opinion was subverted by the liturgies of campaigning which cajoled voters through spectacle and emotion. The independent opinion of public representatives was subjected to controls which were exercised through the popular organizations of the party but which were under the control of the caucus; elected representatives were thus more and more mobilized and controlled in the interests of party leaders who masked their power by working through the seemingly democratic mass organizations of supporters. Not only had the promise of democracy been dishonoured but a sham democracy had been constructed in which the people traded their support in return for a mere semblance of popular power. While Ostrogorski's criticism of democracy was a liberal one, it expressed a whiggish liberalism which valued distinctions so long as they were based on acknowledged merit. What he wanted was not so much an egalitarian society as one where everyone had an equal opportunity to recognize and accept their betters. So Ostrogorski recommended changes which would restore both rational choice and rational deference, reinstate the leadership of statesmen and rescue the electorate from the clutches of those whose methods of thought and action debased public life and deprived it of its higher possibilities. He proposed the dissolution of the party system and the election of individual representatives on the basis of personal worth. Government likewise should become a coalition of statesmen rather than a reflection of party strength.

The stress on values was characteristic not only of Ostrogorski's prescription but of his analysis also. Organization had corrupted political life, but it had been able to do so because the ideas which formed the political culture had themselves become corrupt. For this reason he saw nothing inevitable in the growth of party or of machine politics. The intellectual culture of a society was the root of politics, and what people had chosen they could alter or abolish. So while Ostrogorski may rightly be seen as the founder of the exact and scholarly study of political parties, he is also the founder of the persistent commitment to reform which has so often characterized that study and made it interesting.   RB

Reading

Barker, R. and Howard-Johnston, X.: The politics and political ideas of Moisei Ostrogorski. *Political Studies* 23.4 (December 1975) 415–29.

Ionescu, G.: Moysei Ostrogorski (1854–1919) and the theory of the professional organization. In

Rediscoveries, pp. 139–60, ed. J.A. Hall. Oxford: Clarendon Press, 1986.

Ostrogorski, M.Y.: *Democracy and the Organisation of Political Parties*. London: Macmillan, 1902.

————: *The Rights of Women: a comparative study in history and legislation*. London: Swan Sonnenschein, 1893.

————: *Democracy and the Organisation of Political Parties*. 2 vols, ed. and abridged S.M. Lipset. Chicago, Ill.: Quadrangle Books, 1964.

overload A term popularized in the 1970s referring to the increasing difficulties which governments appeared to be having in effectively governing. It may be less significant in the 1980s, an era in which big government finds itself under serious challenge in many democracies. Overload was thought to be caused by two factors. First was the increasing number of demands being placed upon government by the public. Citizens had learned to turn to government for services and benefits during a period of rapid expansion of the public sector during the post-war era and had no reason to expect that government could not provide more benefits. Second, overload was produced by changes in the social, political and economic systems which rendered authoritative decision making and IMPLEMENTATION more difficult. To some degree the problems posed by overload were fiscal, with apparent resistance to increased levels of taxation but no budget constraint that would keep citizens and groups from demanding more benefits for themselves. Other problems included the ineffectiveness and incoherence of government policies and a growing disrespect for government arising from its perceived failures. Overload reflected a general crisis in confidence for governments.

Sources of demands
Although citizens were blamed for increased levels of demand for governmentally provided benefits other sources of pressure must also be considered. First, organized groups rather than individual citizens are the main source of pressures upon government. Interest groups have every reason to look for concentrated benefits for their members and it has been difficult to organize groups to block the expansion of the public sector. Some such groups have been formed, for example the 'taxpayers' revolt' in the USA which was manifested by popular movements to reduce taxes (Proposition 13 in California) as well as by greater readiness to evade or avoid taxes. These, though, have been the exception rather than the rule.

Those in government also serve as a source of demands for government actions. These demands may come from active politicians attempting to advance their own careers, or from career civil servants trying to expand their organization, but the demands may address a real policy problem; action by government can create a real need for further government action.

Finally, overload may result simply from the inertia of previous decisions. This is particularly true for the financial aspects of overload. A decision to initiate a policy, e.g. social security, or to make a seemingly minor change in a policy, e.g. indexing benefits, may have major financial consequences which were not anticipated at the time of adoption. Governments then face the difficult choice between continuing an increasingly expensive programme and risking public outrage when a programme has been cancelled.

Capacity to deliver
One factor commonly cited as a cause of the inability of government to govern effectively is that modern government involves increasing interdependence with the private sector and with organized groups within the public sector; many groups in society have a virtual veto over governmental action. Fewer and fewer public policies are purely governmental and government increasingly depends upon third parties to make and implement policy in its name. Even those groups which may be entirely within the public sector seem to be less reluctant to challenge the authority of government by striking and engaging other forms of non-compliance.

In addition, the policy space within which government functions is increasingly crowded. This implies first that any new initiatives which a government may undertake will have to be co-ordinated with other policies, with the possibility of incompatibility or duplication. At best the need to co-ordinate policies will require time and possibly other resources. In addition the crowding of the policy space means that there is little new that government can do other than try to live up to the commitments made by past governments. It may not have the money to do anything, and there may be similar policies already in existence. This is at once discouraging for politicians who come into office with ideas for new policies, and may make citizens believe that the current government is ineffective because it is not doing anything new and innovative. The one exception to this is the ability of conservative governments to implement their own agenda of reducing the size of the public sector.

Finally, government actions may be slowed or curtailed because of the increasing availability of procedural checks on action and an increasing use of the legal system as a means of challenging government action. This is especially true in the United States but appears to be somewhat the case in less litigious cultures as well. The increasing number of steps which have to be taken in order to make secondary legislation, the requirement of greater public participation in decisions, and required studies such as environmental impact statements, all slow down and may even prevent decisions being made.   BGP

Reading

Brittan, S.: The economic contradictions of democracy. *British Journal of Political Science* 5 (1975) 129–59.

Crozier, M., Huntington, S.P. and Watanuki, J.: *The Crisis of Democracy.* New York: New York University Press, 1976.

King, A.: Overload: problems of governing in the 1970s. *Political Studies* 23 (1975) 284–96.

Rose, R. ed.: *Challenge to Governance: studies in overloaded politics.* London: Sage, 1980.

—— and Peters, B.G.: *Can Government go Bankrupt?* New York: Basic Books, 1978; London: Macmillan, 1979.

P

pacifism The doctrine and movement which opposes on grounds of principle all wars, including 'internal wars', and advocates personal non-participation in them except, possibly, in a non-combatant role. When first used in 1901 the word referred to the broader movement (labelled pacif*ic*ism by some) which has the aim of abolishing war and which strives to create or maintain peace between nations by such means as disarmament, the use of arbitration, and the strengthening of international law and organizations. In current Anglo-American usage pacifism implies conscientious objection to military service, but such service may in particular wars also be opposed by 'anti-militarists' on political rather than religious or moral grounds. 'Nuclear pacifism' is selective opposition to nuclear, but not 'conventional', war.

Until the twentieth century, pacifism in the west was largely confined to Christian sects whose inspiration derived from the Sermon on the Mount, especially the precept 'resist not evil'. Two post-Reformation sects have been particularly important in developing the tradition: the Anabaptists who hold that true Christians must withdraw from the un-regenerate world, abstaining from all politics, and the more influential Quakers who aim, in contrast, to Christianize the world. Today pacifists are represented in many other churches.

Pacifism may also rest on secular ethical principles. Contemporary pacifism has been greatly influenced by Gandhi's philosophy of non-violence. Pacifists now tend to emphasize 'non-violent resistance', rather than 'non-resistance', and to argue that NON-VIOLENT ACTION provides the functional equivalent of war and could be used as an alternative to military defence and to armed liberation struggle. They also espouse Gandhi's concept of 'non-violent revolution' which implies the peaceful transformation of all social relations and individual life-styles as the way to developing a universal non-violent society.

GNO

Reading

Brock, P.: *Twentieth-Century Pacifism*. New York: Van Nostrand Reinhold, 1970.

Ceadel, M.: *Pacifism in Britain 1914–1945*. Oxford: Clarendon Press, 1980.

Dungen, P. van den, ed.: *West European Pacifism and the Strategy for Peace*, ch. 2. London: Macmillan, 1985.

Sharp, G.: *Gandhi as a Political Strategist*, ch. 10. Boston, Mass.: Porter Sargent, 1979.

panachage   See ELECTORAL SYSTEMS.

Pareto, Vilfredo (1848–1923) Italian sociologist and economist, Pareto was born in Paris. His family belonged to the minor north-Italian nobility and he could have used the title of Marquis had he wished. He died on the shores of Lac Leman as one of the first senators appointed by Mussolini. He was always cosmopolitan but the Suisse Romande was his ideal home where he could be a professor at the University of Lausanne, rich, and maliciously cynical. His reputation is deservedly high as an economist, sociologist, and political scientist.

The style of life which Pareto expected was one which the minor Italian nobility could not afford. He therefore trained as an engineer, and showed a most unusual ability in applied mathematics. (He is far from being the only major social scientist whose intellectual foundations were in engineering: Spencer and Whorf provide interesting parallels.) Civil engineering in the Italy of the Risorgimento and the problems of civil engineering, property rights, and democratic politics shaped his subsequent career. He became at once technical and cynical, probably exaggerating the degree of corruption in the new Italy which Cavour had created.

Unlike many north Italians of his generation, Pareto easily resisted the historicism of German economics to accept and develop the revolution in economic analysis which took place around 1870 and whose principal figures were Jevons, Menger and other Austrians and, above all, Walras. Marginalist economics dissatisfied those who found the felicific calculus of Bentham too subjective: more than anyone else Pareto provided the formally separate and objective code of analysis in terms of indifference curves. More important however is the still theoretically unjustified long *s*-shaped curve of income distribution which is still known by Pareto's name. Income distribution in almost all societies, formal socialist or capitalist, seems to follow this curve. It leads to speculation about its short but privileged top: whence does this income elite come?

By the 1890s Pareto wanted to go beyond economics into the social and political foundations of society. To him economics belonged to the rational logic of action paralleled only by the rational order of natural science, but society and politics belonged to what he called the realm of 'non-logical' action ruled by other forces. Similar ideas were to be found in the writings of such diverse contemporaries as Freud and Nietzsche, and in *fin de siècle* art. To recognize the irrational and even to over-estimate it was not unusual, but to do it with such enormous thoroughness was unique to Pareto.

What, he asked, is left over when one has analysed the logic of economics and science? Almost everything. Pareto identified six 'residues' as he called them, and in terms of these and the forms they take in social action we can understand the course of society.

Two of these derive from his analysis of what he believes are the six basic elements which lead to social action ('residues'). One is ELITES and 'their manifestations by means of external acts' are central to Pareto's politics. These acts are the impulse to retain, if only for the purposes of power, the existing relations of power, and on the other hand to establish new combinations of such relations. If in all human groupings there are to be found a small number of individuals (families, sodalities, etc.) these elites will be involved in a 'circulation' as he called it, or an alternation at the deep level of social chaos where logical action is of little importance, and disjunction will always arise between an essentially dominating conservative elite and the world in which it rules. By one mechanism or another – revolution, conquest, *coup d'état*, conspiracy, parliamentary democracy, etc. – such an elite will be replaced by an innovatory one: out of inertia, greed, friendship and age, all innovatory elites become conservative and are therefore in turn overthrown. The whole of society and politics is sorrowful return.

As senator in the new Italy of Mussolini, Pareto did not withdraw his analysis, first published in 1916, but foresaw a long future for European societies in a Byzantine rigidity. As he said, whoever loves that future will be happy, but there is no reason to hope that the reign of logical action, which is the essence of science, and the possibility of economic behaviour will ever triumph. Byzantine rigidity will end, but not in logic, only in innovation for its own sake. The great theorist who had carried the concept and the analysis of moving equilibria from engineering to economics found this equilibrium only in sociology.

See also IRON LAW OF OLIGARCHY; MOSCA; MICHELS; WEBER.   DGM

Reading

Bobbio, N.: *On Mosca and Pareto*. Geneva: Droz, 1972.

Borkenau, F.: *Pareto*. London: Chapman & Hall, 1936.

Bucolo, P. ed.: *The Other Pareto*. London: Scolar Press, 1980.

Pareto, V.: *Fatti e teorie*. Florence: Vallenchi, 1920.

——: *Introduction aux systémes socialistes*. 2 vols. Paris: Giard, 1902.

——: *Manuale di economica politica* (1906), trans. as *Manual of Political Economy*. New York: Kelly, 1971; London: Macmillan, 1972.

——: *Trattato di sociologia generale* (1916). 3 vols, trans. and ed. A. Livingston and A. Bongioro as *The Mind and Society*. 4 vols. London: Cape; New York: Harcourt Brace, 1935.

parish The smallest unit of local elective government. Traditionally, in Britain, the area served by one church and one priest. In the sixteenth century the parish became the unit for civil administration through the parish vestry and the parish officers, responsible for the relief of the poor, maintenance of the roads, and so on.

By the Local Government Act (1894) parish councils (now called community councils in Wales) were established as elected local authorities in the rural areas, responsible for civil administration, including that of footpaths, allotments, playing fields and public halls, and representing the view of the parish. As spokesmen for the interests of the countryside and the villages, closely in touch with their electors, parish councils have considerable influence – although they are not (with a few exceptions) elected on a party political basis.

Many other countries have rural local councils similar to the parish councils of England, for example townships in the USA, panchayats in India, village councils in Sri Lanka, rural communes in France, parishes in Ontario and Quebec, etc., with widely varying degrees of self-government.   BK-L

Reading

Arnold-Baker, C.: *Local Council Administration*. London: Longcross, 1981.

Report of the Royal Commission on Local Government. London: HMSO Cmnd 4040 XXXVIII, 1969.

Webb, S. and B.: *English Local Government: the parish and the county* (1906), repr. London: Cass, 1963.

parliamentary obstruction The term applied to attempts within the existing rules of procedure, by a minority of members of a legislature, to delay legislation or other parliamentary business.

Parliamentary obstruction can take various forms. The most common is that in which one or more legislators try to prolong proceedings by speaking at great length, a practice known as filibustering. Obstruction may also take the form of tabling and speaking to numerous amendments, speaking on early items of business to reduce the time available to consider the main business, forcing votes on all motions before the House, raising at length points of procedure, moving procedural motions, and being absent from the chamber when quorum votes are called.

Over the past century various LEGISLATURES have introduced rules of procedure designed to reduce the opportunities for obstruction. Greater restrictions have been applied in legislative chambers in which there are a large number of members, in which business is substantial and complex, and in which there is no general agreement on unwritten rules of the game. In the US House of Representatives, for example, the growth of legislation and the increase in the number of representatives in the late nineteenth and early twentieth centuries forced the introduction of procedural rules designed to facilitate the passage of measures which enjoyed majority support. In the British House of Commons, the growth of government business and sustained parliamentary obstruction by Irish Nationalists in the 1880s precipitated a similar imposition of limitations on the private member.

Various procedural measures which can now serve to limit the ability of members to delay business are: time limits on speeches (notably in the case of the US House of Representatives), closure motions (allowing the question to be voted upon forthwith), guillotines (imposing a specific timetable for deliberations on a measure), and powers vested in the presiding officer to select and group amendments (kangaroo), to refuse to accept dilatory motions and to employ sanctions against members who refuse to accept the rulings of the chair. Opportunities to move and debate certain procedural motions have also been removed. In the House of Commons, for example, it is no longer possible to call attention to the absence of a quorum.

These restrictions are less apparent in legislative chambers in which the membership (or, in the case of the British House of Lords, the active membership) is small, in which business is often less extensive than in other chambers, and in which there is a gentleman's agreement on methods of procedure. In such chambers the opportunity to engage in obstruction is formally extensive. In practice consistent use of obstruction often incites the majority to impose rules to limit it. In the US Senate, for example, the power to filibuster has been variously if somewhat reluctantly restricted after its effective and not infrequent employment by southern senators.

In most western legislatures opportunities to engage in parliamentary obstruction are more restricted than hitherto. None the less, opportunities still exist. Only in chambers in which party control is total (and votes usually non-existent) is the concept of obstruction an irrelevant one.   PN

Reading

Bradshaw, K. and Pring, D.: *Parliament and Congress*. London: Quartet, 1981.

Campion, Lord: *An Introduction to the Procedure of the House of Commons*, ch. 1. 3rd edn. London: Macmillan, 1958.

Wilding, N. and Laundy, P.: *An Encyclopaedia of Parliament*. 4th edn. London: Cassell, 1972.

parliamentary privilege The constitution or legislation of many countries confers on the members of the legislative body legal immunities which protect them from the potential legal consequences of acts carried out in their capacity as legislators, or protect them from legal scrutiny when engaged in activities internal to the legislative chamber. In Britain and Commonwealth countries such immunities stem from the privileges historically claimed by parliament.

In Britain, parliamentary privilege designates the sum of the special rights conferred by the law and custom of the parliament of the United Kingdom, and recognized by the common law, on each House of Parliament. It has been defined by Erskine May as consisting of 'the peculiar rights enjoyed by each House collectively as a constituent part of the High Court of Parliament and by members of each House individually without which they could not discharge their functions and which exceed those possessed by other bodies or individuals'.

There are a number of specific heads of privilege. The most important of the Commons' privileges are the freedom of speech and debate, freedom from arrest, and the right to punish contempts of the House. The last of these has probably been the most contentious, since it allows the House to summon and through its Committee of Privileges to cross-examine and punish, without any right of representation, individuals or groups who have disobeyed orders of the House or its committees or have committed contempts of the House by speech or writing. In the past at times of political excitement, Members of Parliament have been known to lose their sense of proportion in the exercise of this last – and arguably unprincipled – power, but reformers have failed to persuade them to give it up.

Criticism has also been made of the extent to which the House's right of free speech may be carried. Though sometimes exercised at the expense of private reputations it creates a forum in which any assertion, report or allegation may be made with absolute immunity and protection from any threat of an action for defamation, with extensive though not absolute privilege for newspaper and broadcast reports of parliamentary proceedings.

There is to some degree an unresolved tension between the claims of both Houses to exercise and control the application of their own privileges and the power of the courts. Where a privilege is exercised especially within the confines of either House the courts in general have declined to interfere or review what has been done. But Parliament cannot create new privileges and the courts retain the power to decide whether a particular claim falls under an acknowledged privilege, and also to determine what activities of a member come within the ambit of 'proceedings in Parliament'. GM

Reading

Inter-Parliamentary Union: *Parliaments of the World*. 2 vols. Aldershot: Gower, 1986.

Marshall, G.: The House of Commons and its privileges. In *The House of Commons in the Twentieth Century*, ed. S.A. Walkland. Oxford: Oxford University Press, 1979.

May, T.E.: *Parliamentary Practice*. 20th edn, ed. C. Gordon, ch. 10. London: Butterworth, 1983.

Report from the Select Committee on Parliamentary Privilege. London: HMSO H.C. 34, 1967–8.

parliamentary question Addressed by a member of the legislature to a member of the government, the parliamentary question is a process widely used in democratic states to secure information from the government as a means of helping to make government accountable and also to ventilate grievances. Questions may be oral or written. The practice of the parliamentary question originated in Britain and 'question time' became a distinct procedure in 1849, with written answers being introduced in 1902. The parliamentary question is to be distinguished from the INTERPELLATION since it is not followed by either a debate or a vote.

In the United States where the heads of executive departments are not members of the legislature, the procedure does not exist in either the House of Representatives or the Senate, but members of the executive can be questioned in standing committees of CONGRESS. PGR

Reading

Borthwick, R.: Questions and debates. In *The House of Commons in the Twentieth Century*, ed. S.A. Walkland. Oxford: Oxford University Press, 1979.

Chester, N.: Questions in the house. In *The Commons Today*, ed. S.A. Walkland and M. Ryle. Glasgow: Fontana, 1981.

——— and Bowring, N.: *Questions in Parliament*. Oxford: Oxford University Press, 1962.

May, T.E.: *Parliamentary Practice*. 20th edn, ed. C. Gordon. London: Butterworth, 1983.

Inter-Parliamentary Union: *Parliaments of the World*. 2 vols. Aldershot: Gower, 1986.

parliamentary sovereignty Where a parliament is sovereign (as is the parliament of the United Kingdom) it has an unlimited authority, recognized by the courts, to make any law or to amend any law already made. In consequence no other body or court has the right to overrule or set aside its legislation. Very few of the world's LEGISLATURES are free in this sense of all constitutional limitations. The British and New Zealand parliaments are, but those, for example, of Canada, Australia, the United States, India, Germany and Italy are not, since their legislative powers are limited by federal divisions of law-making authority, or by the provisions of constitutional enactments that deny to the legislature power to make laws that violate fundamental freedoms (typically set out in a BILL OF RIGHTS).

The sovereignty of parliament in England was slow to develop. In the early seventeenth century Chief Justice Coke asserted that the Common Law courts would control Acts of Parliament and adjudge them void if contrary to right reason. But the courts did not in practice claim such a role and Sir William Blackstone in his *Commentaries on the Laws of England* (1765–70) described the power and jurisdiction of parliament to be so transcendent and absolute that it could not be confined within any bounds.

The implications of this unlimited parliamentary authority are in theory far-reaching and astonishing. Parliament might in principle extend its laws to any part of the world (so, as Sir Ivor Jennings once pointed out, to prohibit Frenchmen from smoking on the streets of Paris), though such exercises would be treated as law only in the United Kingdom. With equal awkwardness the sovereignty of parliament places difficulties in the way of constitutional change. A federal system, a bill of rights, a treaty arrangement which is initiated by one parliament may be repealed and swept away by a subsequent Act of Parliament. Parliament might in theory extend its own life and abolish general elections. The one thing that it cannot do is bind the future or its own legislative freedom of action.

Parliamentary sovereignty in this sense was given its classical exposition in DICEY's *Law of the Constitution* written in 1885. In recent years these implications have been much debated and some of them questioned. A number of Scots lawyers have held that Acts of Parliament might be challenged if in breach of the Treaty of Union. In addition, a number of the implicit assumptions of the traditional doctrine have under closer examination been seen to yield far-reaching possibilities. How fundamental for example is the rule that an Act of Parliament must be constituted by the three-fold assent of the present two Houses and of the queen? Can that rule be changed by an Act passed in the existing manner and form? On this point there is no clear agreement and no decisive legal authority. If however an Act of Parliament can change the future manner and form of legislation for particular purposes it may be possible for a bill of rights or a treaty or a new federal arrangement to be protected or 'entrenched' against future repeal by making such repeal subject to special procedures or special majorities.

Two other developments have posed questions for parliamentary sovereignty in its traditional form. One is the development of independent commonwealth states and the formal assertion in British independence legislation (such as the Canada Act 1982) that, from the date of adoption of the new constitution, no future Act of Parliament shall have effect as part of the law of the commonwealth state. This suggests that, whatever the orthodox doctrine implies, the sovereign parliament of the United Kingdom may limit a portion of its authority geographically defined.

A further major development is the creation of the legal system of the European Economic Community of which the United Kingdom is a member. In the European Communities Act of 1972 the British Parliament has purported and attempted to subordinate its sovereign legislative authority to that of the legislative organs of the Community whose law British courts must now apply. The law of the European Community appears to treat the legislatures of the member-states as sub-ordinate bodies, subject to a new and superior legal order and therefore as being no longer sovereign. That theory has not as yet been accepted in the British courts' approach to Community law. Nevertheless it may be, in the

long run. The doctrine of parliamentary sovereignty was a creature of the judges and its future remains in their hands.

See also ENTRENCHMENT.   GM

Reading

Bradley, A.W.: The sovereignty of parliament – in perpetuity? In *The Changing Constitution*, ed. J. Jowell and D. Oliver. Oxford: Clarendon Press, 1985.

Dicey, A.V.: *Introduction to the Study of the Law of the Constitution*. 10th edn (1959), chs 1–3 and 8, ed. E.C.S. Wade. Repr. Basingstoke: Macmillan, 1985.

Hart, H.L.A.: *The Concept of Law*, chs 4 and 6. Oxford: Oxford University Press, 1961.

Marshall, G.: *Parliamentary Sovereignty and the Commonwealth*. Oxford: Clarendon Press, 1957.

Street, H. and Brazier, R. eds: *De Smith's Constitutional and Administrative Law*. 5th edn, chs 4–5. London: Penguin, 1985.

parliamentary system   The term is used in two main senses. Broadly, it denotes all political systems where there exists an assembly of elected representatives of the people which, in theory or in practice, has considerable responsibility for legislation, including finance. The legislative assemblies of both the United States and the Soviet Union have been members of the Inter-Parliamentary Union. More commonly, it means a system which is distinguished both from the PRESIDENTIAL SYSTEM of the USA (and elsewhere) and from the arrangements of the USSR (and other socialist countries where government is under the direction of a dominant communist party). The principle underlying parliamentary government is sometimes referred to as parliamentarianism or parliamentarism.

Unlike presidential government, which is based on the SEPARATION OF POWERS principle, the parliamentary system involves the fusion of the executive and legislative powers. This means that the legislative assembly is transformed into a parliament or an equivalent body. At the same time, the executive branch of government is divided into a largely formal head of state (for example a monarch or president) who remains physically separate from the parliament, and a head of government (for example a prime minister or chancellor) who exercises most of the executive powers together with members of the ministry (or CABINET). The ministers exercise individual responsibility (for a government department for example) and answer to parliament for their actions. The ministry as a body is also collectively responsible for government policy – hence the principle of cabinet secrecy and solidarity.

Parliamentary government is RESPONSIBLE GOVERNMENT. This means that individual ministers may have to resign if they are judged by parliament to have mishandled their departments (though they may retain their seats in parliament). The ministry or cabinet as a whole may be compelled to resign if parliament loses confidence in its ability to govern. Since a parliamentary system depends on the continued support of a majority of members of parliament, it usually relies on the loyalty of members of one or more parties. Parliamentary government is therefore also party government and tends to be more successful where there is party discipline. Because responsible government originated in eighteenth-century Britain, the English (after 1707, British) parliament has been called the mother of parliaments. There are however various types of parliamentary systems. The two-party adversarial Westminster type operates somewhat differently from the multi-party consensual form found in much of Western Europe, since in Britain responsible government preceded the extension of the FRANCHISE.

Parliamentary government in Britain moulded the development of the party system and the transformation of the constitution. This may be contrasted with the more common continental pattern where the franchise was extended, and parties developed, before responsible or parliamentary government. This was the pattern in, for example, the German Empire before the first world war. The British parliament is the mother of those parliaments of the Commonwealth which are based on the WESTMINSTER MODEL.

The balance of forces between the executive and legislative elements in parliament varies considerably. The Westminster model has favoured strong cabinet government based on a disciplined majority party elected by single-member constituencies. The consensual model in Western Europe has led to coalitions of several parties elected on the principle of proportional representation. In some Westminster-type systems there is a dominant party, with the opposition usually divided into many smaller parties which find it difficult to reach a consensus and form a coalition government (for example India, 1977–9). The British parliamentary system is unique because there is no single document referred to as the constitution: there is no agreed legal or formal interpretation of the system against which the practice may be judged. Explanations of the nature of British parliamentary government customarily investigate its historical evolution.

Parliamentary systems may be distinguished from other forms of government by the practice whereby ministers sit as members of parliament and play a double role in the fusion of executive and legislative powers. Parliamentary government is not to be confused with convention (or assembly) government in which supreme power, both executive and legislative, lies with the assembly of representatives. Convention government is often favoured by revolutionaries (for example France, 1793), but usually gives way to another form of government once the revolutionary phase is over. In the United States, the prototype of presidential government, Congress remains an assembly of representatives of the people. The president, the chief executive, is responsible to the people, not to the legislature.

Since parliamentary heads of government have to deal with the American president, there has been a tendency for them to find the presence of another person as formal head of state an inconvenience. In 1958, France replaced its parliamentary system with a SEMI-PRESIDENTIAL SYSTEM. A number of other countries have replaced the parliamentary system with something more 'presidential', not always successfully in regard to the principle of responsible government.

See also LEGISLATURES.   DVV

Reading

Birch, A.H.: *Representative and Responsible Govern-*

ment: an essay on the British constitution. London: Allen & Unwin, 1964.

Inter-Parliamentary Union: Parliaments: a comparative study on the structure and functioning of representative institutions in forty-one countries. London: Cassell, 1962.

Lijphart, A.: Democracies: patterns of majoritarian and consensus government in twenty-one countries. New Haven, Conn. and London: Yale University Press, 1984.

Verney, D.V.: The Analysis of Political Systems. London: Routledge & Kegan Paul, 1959.

Wilding, N. and Laundy, P.: An Encyclopaedia of Parliament. 4th edn. London: Cassell, 1972.

parties, political: development of

The emergence of political parties in the modern world is closely linked to the emergence of CONSTITUTIONALISM and REPRESENTATIVE GOVERNMENT. Parties today are found under almost all forms of government, and in socialist and third-world states as well as advanced liberal democracies, but their origins are essentially western. Almost all commentators have observed that a critical juncture in western political development was reached when national cohesion in particular societies began to be sufficient for the toleration of political divisions and their institutionalization into organized competition for power. By the late eighteenth century, Edmund BURKE was already arguing (before parties in the sense in which he conceived them actually existed) that organized competition for power constructed along lines of principle rather than factional self-interest, was acceptable and even desirable.

Thereafter, as Sartori has observed, if parties found little favour in the intellectual climate immediately emerging from either the French or the American revolutions, they found a firm base in the ideology of social and intellectual pluralism on which the practice of nineteenth-century liberalism was constructed. Moreover, the institutional expression of this liberalism – representative government – and the subsequent extension of the FRANCHISE, created powerful incentives to the formation of alliances in the legislature, and hence to potential party groupings. Initially unstable, these alliances were gradually firmed up, firstly by the need to counterbalance and control the executive, secondly by the incentive to establish a nation-wide electoral apparatus, and thirdly with the gradual nationalization of political competition, by the importance of fixing a clear-cut political identity for each group in the minds of the electorate.

However, as the restricted franchise of liberalism gradually yielded to mass democracy, those groups hitherto excluded from the legislature, but already assuming an organized identity outside it, were also given an incentive to establish a clear-cut party connotation. A second common feature of the literature on the origins of political parties is therefore the emphasis on a distinction between those parties generated initially inside the legislature, and those born as social movements or interest groups outside it – the latter frequently but not invariably moved into the legislature at a later stage. Notable examples of the former type are CONSERVATIVE and LIBERAL PARTIES in nineteenth-century Europe. Among the latter, SOCIALIST PARTIES and other parties representing the emerging working class, religious interests, and the defence of territorial or cultural identity against the national metropolitan centre, stand out as the three clearest types; examples are, respectively, the German Social Democrats, the Italian (Catholic) Peoples' Party, and the Irish Nationalists. The different origins of political parties are frequently characterized in terms of their organization; the former type being CADRE PARTIES and the latter type MASS MEMBERSHIP PARTIES; although over the course of time distinctions of both origin and organization have become blurred, as parties have operated for long periods under similar political conditions.

The distinction by origin also has some affinity with another distinction of importance: that between parties which accepted the notion of free competition for power under a liberal framework (party government in a party state), and those such as FASCIST and COMMUNIST parties which, during the crisis of democratic government that reached its peak between the two world wars, sought to impose a monolithic conception of society (AUTHORITARIAN or TOTALITARIAN government by state parties) denying the very notion of free party competition. However, the two sets of ideal types – parliamentary and extra-parliamentary parties on the one hand, and representative and regime parties on the other – are not congruent. While most modern totalitarian parties were born from extra-parliamentary origins, by no means all extra-parliamentary parties proved to be opposed to the liberal–democratic framework. Moreover, some ultra-conservative groups generated inside the legislature have proved less than whole-heartedly committed to that framework.

The distinction between parties of sectional defence operating under a regime of free competition, and regime-parties which deny other parties the right to exist, might be thought to be so great as to negate the utility of the word 'party' in covering both types of arrangement. Even where the origins of parties are similar (social–democratic and communist parties, for example) it could be argued that their subsequent role in the political system differs too greatly across regimes to give the single word a common connotation. Yet 'party' in this general sense has continued as a key element in the language of both political science and ordinary political discourse, and this is perhaps a consequence less of linguistic inertia than of the retention, in the nature of almost all political parties, of at least some common traits as political institutions.

The most important of these is their role in linking the formal structure of government with the various elements of 'civil society': individual citizens, and the many types of economic, cultural, religious and other groups which they constitute. This linkage role may clearly vary greatly in the direction in which lines of response and control run. However, in almost all cases there is likely to be a combination of, on the one hand, responsive-ness of the party *to* society, and on the other, controls exercised by the party *over* society. Most Soviet specialists, for example, now accept that the CPSU acts not just as a mechanism of social control, but also as a broker of a variety of more or less constrained interests, some well institutionalized, others less so. Equally, western parties frequently

lead public opinion, rather than follow it, and, given the restrictions on freedom of entry to the political market place even under liberal democracy, this agenda-setting function clearly entails elements of control.

Parties, then, operate on the boundary between the formal (i.e. legal/constitutional) and the informal (societal) parts of the political system. They differ from other social formations such as interest groups (or in Weber's famous definition, classes or status groups) in that they seek not just to influence *but to occupy positions within* the legally con-stituted structure of power. Yet they them-selves are not part of that structure, even if they are *regulated by it* (as in the case of state laws governing party organization in the United States) or *granted from it* a specially privileged status vis-à-vis other parties (for example by an outright ban on 'totalitarian' parties as in the Basic Law of the Federal German Republic). Indeed, even the limiting case of the Communist Party of the Soviet Union, granted a monopoly of power by the constitution of the USSR, illustrates this point. For despite the many levels at which party and government structures mesh together, it is still perfectly possible and useful to make a conceptual distinction between them when analysing the way in which the Soviet Union is governed.

The defining characteristic of parties as political institutions is that they serve (or are candidates to serve) as mechanisms which link the institutions of the state to those of civil society. When party representatives come to occupy positions of power within the state, they do so on the basis at least of contact with, if not some sort of mandate from, the society from which they spring. Similarly, when decisions are taken within the structure of government they can generally be justified, either implicitly or explicitly, in terms of the aims and values of one or more political parties. Such a linkage role, which applies independently of whether or not a party has been freely elected to office, can, in its turn, be broken down into a series of component functions: goal formation; interest articulation; socialization and mobilization; elite formation and recruitment (see PARTIES, POLITICAL:

411

FUNCTIONS OF). By no means all of these functions are performed all the time by all political parties, and in at least some societies several of them are performed by mechanisms other than parties. A minimal definition of party would in fact have to be that of a vehicle through which at least some public office-holders acquire office. But the reality is rarely restricted to this minimum, despite the much-heralded 'decline of parties' in contemporary societies. Indeed, although constitutional theory has rather little to say about the linkage role, it is difficult to imagine how complex modern societies could be governed efficiently for any length of time unless this role is performed satisfactorily by political parties.

DJH

Reading

Beyme, K. von: *Political Parties in Western Democracies*. Aldershot: Gower; New York: St Martin's, 1985.

Duverger, M.: *Political Parties: their organization and activity in the modern state*. London: Methuen, 1964.

Epstein, L.D.: *Political Parties in Western Democracies*. New Brunswick, NJ: Transaction Books, 1980.

Lawson, K. ed.: *Political Parties and Linkage: a comparative perspective*. New Haven, Conn. and London: Yale University Press, 1980.

Michels, R.: *Political Parties: a sociological study of the oligarchical tendencies of modern democracy*. New York: Collier, 1962.

Neumann, S.: *Modern Political Parties*. Chicago, Ill.: University of Chicago Press, 1955.

Pombeni, P.: *Introduzione alla storia dei partiti politici*. Bologna: Il Mulino, 1985.

Rokkan, S. and Lipset, S.M. eds.: *Party Systems and Voter Alignments: cross-national perspectives*. London: Collier-Macmillan; New York: Free Press, 1967.

Sartori, G.: *Parties and Party Systems: a framework for analysis*, Vol. I. Cambridge: Cambridge University Press, 1976.

Schattschneider, E.E.: *Party Government*. New York: Holt, Rinehart & Winston, 1942.

parties, political: functions of Political parties serve a number of functions within the political system. The main ones are goal formulation; interest articulation; socialization and mobilization; and elite formation and recruitment.

(1) Many observers believe that the function of *goal formulation* is no longer being satis-factorily fulfilled by de-ideologized CATCH ALL parties. In fact the attraction of IDEOLOGIES declined in the mid-twentieth century as parties lost part of their educational and socialization function to the media. Someone interested in politics no longer needed to join a party to find out what it was doing. However, the thesis of the 'end of ideology' has proved an over-simplification. Scarcely had it been established when a new wave of re-ideologization developed in parties in western democracies. The whole process led not to de-ideologization but to the ideologies becoming more competitive and more directly related to action.

The 'end of ideology' hypothesis developed into a self-destructive prophecy in the time of the re-ideologization of European parties. This theoretical orientation had some con-sequences for internal decision making within parties.

First, the party conventions and conferences became more important even in countries such as Britain which were traditionally said to favour a pragmatic and anti-ideological approach to politics. Even the Conservative Party no longer follows Balfour's famous 'bon mot' that on policy he would sooner consult his valet than a Conservative Party conference. Though the party conference has not de-veloped into a policy-making body the discussions are of some importance for the guidelines of politics. Since 1967 there have been formal resolutions after the debates and since 1965 the Conservative Party leader has tended to be present for the whole conference.

Second, the pragmatic everyday work of parliamentary groups is much closer to goal implementation than it was in the age of the radical alternatives offered by the old parties. In most parliamentary systems the parlia-mentary groups have become more responsible to the party outside parliament and this normally means a stronger influence of party ideology on the deputies.

Third, the concept of parliamentary rep-resentation changed. The radical democratic concept of an imperative MANDATE by the constituency was not realized in any system, but the new wave of mobilization created more responsible parties and deputies who were forced to attend more carefully to some resolutions of their decision-making party bodies in their constituencies.

Factionalism within the parties grew under the revival of ideology (see FACTIONS). This was not so much the traditional type of clientele factionalism prevailing in traditional party structures as in Italy, Japan or Israel, but a new type caused by ideological opposition within the parties. These changes were partly due to a revitalization of the goal-finding functions of the parties. Sometimes ideological conflicts, having been transformed into power quarrels between parliamentary groups, developed disruptive tendencies, as in the case of the British Labour Party, when the SDP (Social Democratic Party) split off in 1981.

(2) This change in party programmes would not have been possible without a change in the function of *interest articulation*. In many western democracies social and regional strongholds have been reduced or reshuffled. Capitals such as Paris and Berlin, whose 'red belts' were once the strongholds of the working-class parties, now have an increasing share of votes for the bourgeois parties, as they have become perforated in some areas by the suburbs of the new middle classes. The parties became less preoccupied with their main target groups and their respective organizational infrastructure. Indirect membership of unions in Labour parties also came under attack – no longer only from the Conservative side, but increasingly from groups to the left of the established Labour parties. The decline of party strongholds – unless protected by plurality ballot – made electoral campaigns more competitive on a national scale. As traditional ties with social groups were reduced the parties found that they had to devote attention to their voters. This, however, to some extent strengthened the professional elites of party campaigners more than the rank-and-file organization. But even the elites can no longer afford to ignore voters' wishes as OSTROGORSKI described in the case of the early party machines in Britain and in the USA. The party elites concern themselves

with their voters not only through individual effort but very much as a collective and they can now be compared to 'professional teams' in sports 'playing for votes in their own unique television league'.

(3) The function of mobilization and socialization. The crudest indicator of the legitimacy of a party system is the share of votes polled by anti- and a-system parties. The most important anti-system parties have been the Communists and the neo-Fascists. Neo-Fascist parties have been a problem only in Italy and in Germany, though the latent fascist potential in many countries is bigger than electoral output suggests. The share of communist votes is considerable only in four European countries: Italy, France, Finland, and Iceland, in all of which except Italy communists have been in power. Sartori, who strongly emphasized the type of POLARIZED PLURALISM, refused to see the voluntary relinquishing of power by Communists in Finland and Iceland as proof that they had grown into the position of integrated parties, because of the marginality and special situation of those two small countries. Only between 1981 and 1984 was there the possibility that France might grow into a major example for the integration of communists. Other a-system parties were the neo-populist parties such as the POUJADISTS in France and Glistrup's Progressive Party in Denmark, the ETHNIC PARTIES, especially the Volksunie in Belgium and some left-wing socialist parties. All of them contributed to make coalition building more complicated, but none of these movements endangered the system as a whole. In Belgium the ethnic split through the established three parties (Christian Democrats, Socialists and Liberals) had more serious consequences than the existence of explicitly regional parties. The ecological parties and their equivalents, such as the new radicals in Italy or the D'66 in the Netherlands, have recently challenged some of the rules of the established party systems. But in spite of many claims that majority rules should not apply to vital ecological questions, no danger for these systems is yet apparent. Unconventional behaviour proved to be by no means incompatible with conventional be-

413

haviour during elections. In the long run the participatory revolution may well create more parties that claim to be parties of a new type (almost every new movement in history started as a party of a new type) and end up in coalition building and power sharing, thereby helping to change the rules of the game as well as the contents of the political process. Indicators of crisis have been identified besides the rise of extremist anti-system parties, such as the growing fragmentation of party systems and increasing volatility of voters. There was growing volatility especially in Denmark, Norway, and the Netherlands, but there is no overall explanation for this. Ecological concern, anti-welfare state sentiment, conflicts over the issue of entering the EEC in Denmark and Norway in 1973 all contributed to growing volatility. Volatility is only one possible indicator of change. Most of it did not take place between right and left but within each camp. Fragmentation of party systems may be one of the consequences of volatility (see ELECTORAL VOLATILITY). The number of relevant parties was largest in the early 1970s. Some countries, for example Germany and possibly also France, experienced a lasting concentration of parties. Neither indicator, however, suggests a growing delegitimation of party systems.

The legitimacy crisis would also appear to be an exaggeration in terms of the capacity of party systems in western democracies to mobilize the voters to participate during elections. Participation declined slightly, but did not decline drastically even when a country, such as the Netherlands, gave up compulsory voting in 1970. The overload on the voters through continuous referenda in Switzerland and the special problems of American registration policies are deviant cases.

(4) Elite formation and the recruitment function are more exclusive prerogatives of the parties than at any other period of party history. The independent member and the independent citizens' movement have not succeeded in eroding party privilege. The socialization function with regard to the mass of party members has been reduced. But with

regard to the elite it has been intensified. In many parties future elites are exposed to a long and wearisome process of testing in party offices and on the backbenches before they are admitted to the highest executive offices. With the exception of the USA and the SEMI-PRESIDENTIAL SYSTEMS (for example, Finland and France) non-party ministers are of virtually no significance.

Researchers from Ostrogorski to MICHELS have developed an 'iron law' (see IRON LAW OF OLIGARCHY) for this phase of party development, according to which the parties are said to develop increasingly towards bureaucracy and an oligarchical structure. Although there is still room for very much more democracy in the internal structure of modern parties, no straight-line progression towards oligarchy can be established. The bureaucratization of the party machines observed by earlier party theoreticians was rather the helpless and hardly well-prepared attempt by the parties to channel and integrate the sudden access of voters brought about by the extension of the franchise. The progressive bureaucratization which had been forecast for the parties was halted by the lack of readiness on the part of the general public to join parties. The degree of organization which leapt up during the period when the parties were developing their great ideological philosophies dropped back again. Unlike many associations the parties did not have negative sanctions at their disposal and positive sanctions had no effect on the mass of members who were not aiming for a political career. They could only be applied to a small elite who wanted to make a profession of politics or hoped that party membership would further their career in administration. Hence the parties were largely dependent on their ideologies and programmes to attract new members.

On the level of government formation the term 'party state' is still appropriate in some countries. The process of democratization has meant that since the second world war elections have acquired a much more direct influence on the composition of the government than formerly. Only rarely are there 'party states' in the narrower sense, in which the party and parliamentary party leaders have almost sole power of decision on the composition of the government. Only Belgium, the Netherlands, and Italy at most can still be called party states in this sense. In many systems a form of party dominance has become established which the general public is least willing to accept: an increasing number of administrative posts which are treated as political offices.

In view of the increasing power of patronage in the parties and the funds they now receive from the state in many countries, analysts have felt that there is increasing danger to their internal democracy. On the whole, however, it cannot be argued that there is a clear tendency towards authoritarian oligarchy. On the contrary, parties are often accused of losing the ability which they once had, of controlling parliamentarians, activists, members and voters. Many of these complaints draw too heavily on American experience.

This summary of the main functions conceals the fact that the parties today exercise far more functions than formerly. This increases the tendency to overstrain their resources, especially since their organization has not grown noticeably more stable. Broad policy areas which used to be regarded as unpolitical have now been taken into the parties' agendas. Specialization – the result of former ideological stances – has been cut down. Modern parties have to be able to take a stand on every issue. Socialists can no longer grind their teeth and accept a partial deterioration in general living conditions in the hope that this will hasten the establishment of a socialist system. The Christian Democrats cannot specialize on family and education policy as in the period of the struggle against the laicist state; nor can the Liberals display their laicism, uphold the doctrine of free trade and cultivate a general humanist attitude without taking a stand on the details of social policy, once ideologically so far removed from them. What has been lost in unity of vision has been gained in orientation to competition. The more active members of the general public who take part in citizens' initiatives, protest movements or other forms of anomic behaviour keep raising further points for the parties' programmes. Where the cartel formation of the established parties has

threatened to mean that they would only split into 'caps' and 'hats' for the sake of appearance new forms of unconventional behaviour on the part of the general public ensured that there will be no political ossification.

The restriction of political participation to voting at elections has been held responsible for the external control of parties and their restriction to a policy which conforms with the requirements of stability and sales strategy calculations, bowing to the 'dictates of the floating voter'. However, breaking through this limited rationale with new unconventional forms of participation in extra-parliamentary opposition, citizens' initiatives and 'public interest groups' will bring new risks if majority decision rules are no longer accepted by militant groups. No modern democracy can survive without majority decisions and the individual group's assessment of the 'public interest' may well amount to no more than the strengthening of veto positions with very little attempt at participation in new compromises or solutions. This also conceals a risk to equality of participation, the development of which has been one of the most important contributions the parties have made to the evolution of the modern democracy. Participation in less conventional and looser forms of organization is more selective and fragmentary than in the parties. Efforts are made to speak in 'advocate planning' for groups which have so far hardly participated, but the 'concrete general interest' which is supposed to be the main focus of attention cannot be politically generalized in decisions which the majority really accepts. Hence the aggregation achievement of the parties will not be superfluous in future in a modern democracy either, even if parts of the interest articulation are now exercised less within the parties than with respect to them. It is therefore too early to proclaim the 'end of the parties'. The 'participation revolution' since the end of the 1960s has so far not brought a straight-line decline in participation in parties and elections in the Western democracies, as can be seen from the figures on election turnout and membership trends. There is not even a uniform trend in the individual countries. In a crisis-prone country such as Italy, the Christian Democrats and communists have proved astonishingly capable of easing their way out of old organizational encrustations, and they have developed new organizational forms, while a party such as the PSI (Partito Socialista Italiano) has proved less able to do this, even when its membership figures and voters were rising. Even if support for the parties seems to be declining, this need not necessarily entail delegitimization. Support of the parties – unlike support for the democratic system as a whole – has always been partial and many citizens have retained anti-party feelings. Delegitimization, moreover, is a function of the level of expectation among citizens. Since many people continue to prefer other forms of politically relevant activities (interest-group adhesion, citizens' action groups, un-conventional behaviour) expectations of the parties may be lowered without delegitimization of the whole system.   KvB

Reading

Beyme, K. von: *Political Parties in Western Democracies*. Aldershot: Gower; New York: St Martin's, 1985.

Duverger, M.: *Political Parties: their organisation and activity in the modern state*. London: Methuen, 1964.

Epstein, L.D.: *Political Parties in Western Democracies*. New Brunswick, NJ: Transaction Books, 1980.

Henig, S. ed.: *Political Parties in the European Community*. London: Allen & Unwin, 1979.

Lipset, S.M. and Rokkan, S. eds: *Party Systems and Voter Alignments: cross-national perspectives*. London: Collier-Macmillan; New York: Free Press, 1967.

Merkl, P.H. ed.: *Western European Party Systems: trends and prospects*. New York: Free Press; London: Collier-Macmillan, 1980.

Sartori, G.: *Parties and Party Systems: a framework for analysis*, Vol. I. New York and Cambridge: Cambridge University Press, 1976.

party convention The American national party convention is the central institution for the nomination of major party candidates for President of the United States. The United States Constitution, having made no provision for political parties, offered no structural arrangements for certifying party candidates for president. Yet by 1800 an incipient two-party system was already in existence. For a short period the problem of concentrating party support around one authorized nominee was solved by a caucus of party members in Congress. For an even shorter period the problem was met through nomination by party members in state legislatures. But from 1831 to the present, the national party convention was the institutional solution to this recurring political problem.

Early conventions set most of the precedents for convention organization. The convention was to be composed of delegates apportioned to (and chosen by) the individual states, and while the formula apportioning these delegates has varied over time the underlying arrangement has remained the same. From the first, balloting was to be by individual delegates, from among as many candidates as were presented, until a given majority was achieved. The Republican Party always interpreted this to mean individual votes and a simple majority, but the Democratic Party required a two-thirds majority until 1936 and permitted a 'unit rule' whereby a majority within each state could cast the total state vote, until 1968. Early in their existence conventions also developed internal sub-committees for dealing with their major operational problems – for judging the credentials of their delegates, for adopting rules to govern their deliberations, and for issuing a statement of party principles – and these, too, have continued down to the present, with varying names but consistent functions.

While convention organization remained remarkably stable, forces surrounding the convention have changed substantially in ways which substantially influence their operation. The selection of delegates to national party conventions has changed tremendously from the nineteenth century, when they were peopled entirely by delegates selected through the internal procedures of state political parties, usually in parallel state party conventions, occasionally by a meeting of a central state party committee. Since 1972, on the other hand, an overwhelming majority of national convention delegates have been selected through state presidential primary elections, where the voters either choose the delegates directly, or choose a presidential preference who in turn creates the delegates. The reporting of convention developments has changed as well, with first the appearance of the national wire services, then the addition of comprehensive radio coverage, and finally the coming of television broadcasting. As a result of the interaction of these changes (in delegate selection and in mass media coverage), conventions have become less central to resolving the nomination – the identity of the nominee usually being well known in advance – and more critical to launching the general election campaign.

See also CANDIDATE SELECTION.   BES

Reading

Congressional Quarterly, Inc.: *National Party Conventions, 1831–1980*. 3rd edn. Washington, DC: Congressional Quarterly Press, 1983.

David, P.T., Goldman, R.M. and Bain, R.C.: *The Politics of National Party Conventions*. Washington, DC: The Brookings Institution, 1960.

Davis, J.W.: *National Conventions in an Age of Party Reform*. Westport, Conn. and London: Greenwood, 1983.

party identification   The first two voting studies carried out in the United States used social characteristics and group memberships to explain individual voting behaviour (Lazarsfeld, Berelson and Gaudet 1944; Berelson, Lazarsfeld and McPhee 1954). Electors who belonged to a set of groups with the same partisan preference were almost bound to vote for the party indicated: only those with a mixed social background would experience cross-pressures and either not vote or change votes. This assumption of relative stability in voting habits and of the 'conserving' effects of the election campaign was associated with the re-election of Roosevelt in 1940 and the re-invigoration of the New Deal alliance by Truman in 1948.

National surveys of the Eisenhower elections of 1952 and 1956 revealed a contrasting pattern of great change as electors switched votes under the attraction of the candidate and to a lesser extent of issues, while in many cases continuing to profess loyalty to the Democrats. The notion of stable group memberships seemed unable to explain such changes so the

investigators switched their emphasis to psychological factors in the voting choice – the short-term attractions of candidates and issues which could (only temporarily however) overcome the effects of an underlying sense of party identification. In the long run this identification would pull the voter back to support his or her own party (Campbell, Gurin and Miller 1954; Campbell, Converse, Miller and Stokes 1960). Party identification replaced social group membership as the measure of long-term predispositions towards the support of a particular party. It was avowedly a social-psychological attachment, defined as 'a psychological identification, [a] sense of attachment with one party or the other' (Campbell et al. 1960, p. 121). Empirically, party identification was measured through a standard survey question: 'Generally speaking, do you think of yourself as a Republican, a Democrat, an Independent or what? [IF CLASSIFIES SELF AS RE-PUBLICAN or DEMOCRAT:] Would you call yourself a strong (REP,DEM) or a not very strong (REP,DEM)?' (Campbell et al. 1960, p. 122). This was adopted, but with considerable variants, in voting surveys of many other national electorates.

The great popularity and influence which the concept acquired in studies of political socialization, voting and attitudes was due: first, to its ease of conceptualization and measurement; second, to the complete assimilation of the general concept of long-term predispositions towards a party with this particular measure of predispositions; third to the very sophisticated development of the concept in a variety of contexts. Two of these were of particular importance: first, the characterization of elections as maintaining, deviating or realigning in terms of their effects on the partisan identification of the electorate (Campbell et al. 1966, pp. 63–77). Second, the concept of the 'normal vote' as a baseline from which to measure the effect of issues and candidates in an election. The normal vote was the aggregate vote produced when either short term effects were zero or balanced each other out: it was a vote which directly reflected the proportions of partisan identifiers in the relevant group. In the case of the United

PARTY IDENTIFICATION

States as a whole this would be between 54 per cent and 57 per cent Democrat and between 46 per cent and 43 per cent Republican – very much the national vote recorded by each party in the (low-stimulus) congressional elections, in contrast to the (high-stimulus) presidential elections where both parties on average get around 48 per cent of the vote.

Party identification was thought to influence American voters because of the clear guidance it provided for party choice in a confusing political environment, characterized by internally fragmented parties and elections at multiple levels (local, state, federal). It was however used without modification as a central organizing concept in voting studies of other democracies, particularly those of Western Europe which are characterized by united, ideological parties and single national elections. Findings that identification varied over successive elections almost as much as the vote in Western Europe raised some doubt about the independence of the two, and therefore about the status of party identification as an independent explanatory variable (Butler and Stokes 1971, p. 60; Budge, Crewe and Farlie 1976, Part I *passim*). In spite of this it has continued to be used as a central explanation of voting developments: most recently a decline in the aggregate level of party identification among the British electorate has been characterized as 'partisan dealignment' and credited with producing increased ELECTORAL VOLATILITY (Särlvik and Crewe 1983; Crewe and Denver 1985, p. 61). Evidence of increased issue-voting in the United States after 1968 was also used to criticize the notion of party identification – unfairly since the way it was used clearly allowed for issue and candidate effects (for a review of this debate see Margolis 1977).

In some ways party identification has become the prototype of the sociological explanation of political phenomena as opposed to the RATIONAL CHOICE approach. The contrasts are mainly rhetorical however. At an operational level both party identification and rational choice explanations, as well as those based on social groups and characteristics, single out two classes of factors as influencing

voting decisions: long-standing predispositions or attachments to a party, and short-term stimuli (chiefly candidates and issues) (Budge and Farlie 1977, ch. 3). The real problem lies in distinguishing these and measuring them independently of each other and of the vote. The mistake of most investigations basing themselves on party identification is to regard it as the only way in which predispositions can be measured; or indeed to dispense with the idea of predispositions entirely in favour of party identification. This then provokes irrelevant debate on what is the 'real' measure of predispositions, when in fact a variety of indicators, including social groups and party identification, can be used, and when it is quite rational given imperfect information to use any or all of these as a guide to voting behaviour.

See also DEALIGNMENT; REALIGNMENT; ISSUES, ISSUE PERCEPTION AND ISSUE VOTING.   IB

Reading

Berelson, B., Lazarsfeld, P.F. and McPhee, W.: *Voting*. Chicago, Ill.: Chicago University Press, 1954.

Budge, I., Crewe, I. and Farlie, D.J. eds: *Party Identification and Beyond: representations of voting and party competition*. London and New York: Wiley, 1976.

Budge, I. and Farlie, D.J.: *Voting and Party Competition: a theoretical critique and synthesis applied to surveys from ten democracies*. London and New York: Wiley, 1977.

Butler, D. and Stokes, D.: *Political Change in Britain*. London: Penguin, 1971; Macmillan, 1974.

Campbell, A., Converse, P.E., Miller, W.E. and Stokes, D.E.: *The American Voter*. New York and London: Wiley, 1960.

————: *Elections and the Public Order*. New York: Wiley, 1966.

Crewe, I. and Denver, D. eds: *Electoral Change in Western Democracies: patterns and sources of electoral volatility*. London: Croom-Helm, 1985.

Lazarsfeld, P.F., Berelson, B. and Gaudet, H.: *The People's Choice*. New York: Duell, Sloan & Pierce, 1944.

Margolis, M.: From confusion to confusion: issues and the American voter. *American Political Science Review* 71 (1977) 31–43.

Särlvik, B. and Crewe, I.: *Decade of Dealignment.* London and Cambridge: Cambridge University Press, 1983.

party list   See ELECTORAL SYSTEMS.

party organization   Refers generally to the internal structuring of political parties, but a wide range of organizational variables has to be taken into account: the composition and powers of party decision-making bodies and the relationships between them; the extent to which authority is centralized or decentralized; the structure and size of the party bureaucracy; the nature and functions of the basic or local units of party organization. Two features stand out as of overriding importance: the question of party membership and the nature of leadership within the party.

Significant differences in party organization are attributable to contextual and ideological influences. The 'context' affects all parties in a particular system – the terms of their historical development and the constitutional constraints under which they operate. Variations also arise because parties have different goals and priorities, so that distinctive forms of party organization can coexist in the same party system. For some of these reasons party organization in the United States differs markedly from the pattern established in Western Europe even though the framework of a competitive party system is common to both. The kind of party organization engendered by party competition differs fundamentally from party organization where competition is absent, as is the case in single-party regimes. All parties require some degree of organization in order to perform their basic functions, and parties are by definition a special form of organization – 'organized opinion' in Disraeli's description. In competitive systems at least a minimal level of organization is necessary in order to contest elections and to retain that capability from one election to another; without continuity, the party would risk falling apart. To a limited extent the party as a whole (its membership) can take decisions, but the impossibility of continuous participation makes it inevitable that responsibilities are delegated to rep-

resentative elected bodies and to full-time officials. Those tendencies led MICHELS to believe that inner-party democracy would always succumb to the power of party elites, and he employed various arguments in support of his IRON LAW OF OLIGARCHY. In a similar vein, OSTROGORSKI argued that the development of the party machine and the party caucus was inimical to the representation of individual interests.

The importance attached to party membership can be viewed as a decisive factor in determining the type of party organization. Parties that serve purely electoral purposes may make little or no provision for formal party membership, and their organization may depend on a small group of individuals, a few notable personalities giving rise to a so-called CADRE PARTY. Large-scale membership has never been a feature of the major parties in the United States; instead, they rely on relatively few core party workers, and in the hey-day of patronage politics, the patronage machine could be relied upon to deliver the vote. The decentralized character of the American political system also ensured that national party organization remained rudimentary and non-authoritative, so power was vested in state-level committees and city 'bosses'. The weak organizational structure has persisted, and the institution of the 'primary' (see PRIMARY, DIRECT) has further acted against any strengthening of party organization or the build-up of party membership since selection/nomination of candidates is opened up to a wider range of voters.

In contrast to the American experience, European parties developed their organization largely on the model of the MASS MEMBERSHIP PARTY which entails a relatively complex structure in order to balance the requirements of organizational efficiency with the aims of securing the participation of members and democratic decision making within the party. Ultimate responsibility of the organization to the membership is vested with the highest party organ, the (usually) annual party congress at which the membership is represented by delegates (typically but not exclusively on a territorial basis). The party congress, as the sovereign body, has the final say on the party's programme and constitution as well as deciding the composition of the party's leading organs, especially the party executive, which act on behalf of the party from one congress to another, and the same applies to the party leader. In practice however the party leader may enjoy a large measure of autonomy, and the difficulties of ensuring party control are greater if the leader has a strong base in the parliamentary wing of the party. In fact it is the parliamentary party which fits most uneasily into the scheme of party organization and control since parliamentary deputies also bear a responsibility to the electorate at large.

The organization of mass membership parties varies considerably according to the kind of membership and the role the party plays for its members. Some parties rely on a large indirect membership, for instance the affiliation of trade unions to the British Labour Party, allowing a part of its organization to be external to the party itself. Direct membership gives rise to a greater organizational density which may be reflected in a large variety of ancillary organizations serving diverse sectional interests and purposes. At the limit, the party may seek a kind of omnicompetence for its members.

Organization in an authoritarian or totalitarian party can bear a striking, if superficial, resemblance to that of the typical mass party. The cardinal difference lies in the direction of control: effectively all authority resides with the leader or with a small leadership group which itself can dictate recruitment to the group and perpetuate its own power. Party organization is subordinated to the will of the leadership and the party members serve the purposes of the leadership, a process which is rationalized in communist theory by the principle of DEMOCRATIC CENTRALISM.

GSm

Reading

Beyme, K. von: *Political Parties in Western Democracies*. Aldershot: Gower; New York: St Martin's, 1985.

Crotty, W. ed.: *Approaches to the Study of Party Organization*. Boston, Mass.: Allyn & Bacon, 1968.

Duverger, M.: *Political Parties: their organization and activity in the modern state*. London: Methuen, 1964.

Eldersveld, S.: *Political Parties: a behavioral analysis*. Chicago, Ill.: Rand McNally, 1964.

Epstein, L.D.: *Political Parties in Western Democracies*. New Brunswick, NJ: Transaction Books, 1980.

Kirchheimer, O.: Party structure and mass democracy in Europe. In *Politics, Law and Social Change: selected essays of Otto Kirchheimer*, ed. F.S. Burin and K.L. Shell. New York and London: Columbia University Press, 1969.

Raschke, J.: *Organisierter Konflikt in Westeuropäischen Parteien*. Opladen: Westdeutscher Verlag, 1977.

Sartori, G.: *Parties and Party Systems: a framework for analysis*, Vol. I. New York and Cambridge: Cambridge University Press, 1976.

party systems, types of A widely accepted approach to classifying party systems according to the number of parties which they contain. The most familiar distinction, and that used by Duverger, is between 'two-party' and 'multi-party' systems, although the non-competitive 'one-party' system, which will not be discussed here, is also an important variant. Two-party systems are those in which two parties of equivalent size compete for office, and where each has more or less equal chance of winning sufficient electoral support to gain an executive monopoly: Britain and the United States are the most frequently cited examples. Multi-party systems involve the competition of more than two parties, and government is usually formed by COALITIONS. In Italy, for example, the multi-party system has invariably produced multi-party or coalition governments. In some multi-party systems, however, one of the competing parties sometimes manages to win sufficient support to form a majority on its own, and office may alternate between single-party government and coalition government. Norway, Sweden and the Republic of Ireland have shown examples of this pattern during the post-war period.

Traditional analyses of party systems tended to emphasize the advantages of the two-party type. First, it was seen as a more accountable system in which voters were presented with a clear choice between alternative governments. Second, it was seen as a fair system, encouraging alternation in government and preventing any one party or group of parties from gaining an executive monopoly for an extended period. Third, it was seen to encourage a politics of moderation, with each of the two contenders competing to win the centre ground.

Multi-party systems were seen to enjoy none of these advantages. Voters did not have a direct voice in deciding who was to form the government; rather, the decision emerged from the often difficult rounds of post-election bargaining between the parties themselves. In the aftermath of the 1972 elections in the Netherlands, for example, it took 164 days for the parties to reach agreement on the formation of a coalition. Second, alternation in government was not necessarily encouraged, in that the support of certain pivotal parties was vital to the formation of every government, and further, such pivotal parties often enjoyed a degree of influence quite disproportionate to their electoral strength. In West Germany, for example, despite averaging less than 10 per cent of the vote, the Free Democrats have formed part of every coalition government since 1969. Third, the sheer multiplicity of parties was seen to encourage intense ideological competition and to discourage centre-seeking competition. In addition, since multi-party systems often involved coalition government, they were seen to lead to political instability: individual parties or groups of parties found it difficult to win majority support in the legislature, while such alliances as did form were vulnerable to inter-party squabbling and to subsequent collapse. Critics of multi-party systems frequently contrasted the evident stability produced by the two-party system in Britain with the unhappy governing experiences of Weimar Germany, Fourth Republic France and post-war Italy.

This simple association of two-partism with stability and multi-partism with instability was soon to be confounded, however, as other writers pointed to the experiences of such countries as Switzerland and the Scandinavian democracies, where despite a multiplicity of parties and the frequency of coalition governments, the political systems themselves proved to be both stable and conducive to a politics of moderation. In short, it was argued that multi-party systems were not alike, and that the crude distinction between two parties and more-than-two parties was itself an inadequate basis for classification.

The search for a more effective method of classifying party systems accordingly moved away from a simple numerical criterion and began to incorporate additional dimensions. Initially, writers such as Gabriel Almond subdivided the multi-party category into two groups – 'working' and 'non-working' or 'immobilist' party systems, the one representing the more stable and consensual Scandinavian democracies, the other representing the fragmented and ideologically divided French and Italian systems. The distinction was further refined by Arend Lijphart's elaboration of the CONSOCIATIONAL DEMOCRACY model, which applied to Austria, Belgium, the Netherlands and Switzerland, and which essentially described the sharing of political power in culturally divided or PLURAL SOCIETIES. More recently, Giovanni Sartori has emphasized the importance of the ideological distance which separates political parties and the number of poles around which they compete, employing these additional criteria to distinguish between moderate and POLARIZED PLURALISM (that is, multipartism). In this case, however, Sartori also returns to the more traditional numerical emphasis, arguing that where there are fewer than six parties there is a tendency for moderate pluralism to develop, and where there are six or more parties there is a tendency towards polarized pluralism.

Apart from the supposed merits of the different types of party system, there remains the essential problem of distinguishing these types in the first place. When does a two-party system cease to be a two-party system? When does one type of multi-party system become another type? The first problem here is the level at which the distinction is made. Given the disproportionality of certain types of ELECTORAL SYSTEMS, what may be a multi-party system at the level of electoral competition can turn out to be a two-party one when the parliamentary seats are distributed. This problem is most easily illustrated by the British case in 1983. At the parliamentary level, the Conservatives and Labour together won more than 93 per cent of the seats, creating what would seem to be a clear example of a two-party system. At the electoral level, on the other hand, the combined vote of the two parties was only 70 per cent, which would seem to place a question mark over the inclusion of the British case in the two-party category.

A second problem is to decide when, even at the parliamentary level, one can speak of a true two-party system. Again taking the British case, though the two main parties completely dominate the legislature, other parties nevertheless also manage to win representation. The .Liberals and Social Democrats are obvious examples, but the Welsh and Scottish Nationalists and at least four Ulster parties must also be included. Does this make for a multi-party system? In other words, when does a party count as being relevant to the classification of a party system into one type or another? Sartori has suggested some simple rules for this. In order for a party to be counted as relevant, first it must win parliamentary representation, and second it must have an effect on government formation, either by having coalition potential itself or because its presence encourages particular coalition alliances between its opponents. Following these criteria the British case would clearly be an effective two-party system, in that even the parliamentary presence of the minor parties rarely affects government formation.

Establishing cut-off points at the electoral level is more difficult, however, particularly when distinguishing between different types of multi-party system. In his analysis of the smaller European democracies, Stein ROKKAN suggested a three-fold classification based on the different sizes of the parties and their relative proximity to a majority point. In 'even multi-party systems' there are three or more parties of equivalent size (1 *vs.* 1 *vs.* 1 etc.); in the Scandinavian model, on the other hand, there is one big party competing against three or four smaller parties of more or less equal size (1 *vs.* 3 or 4); finally, in what Rokkan called the 'British-German' model, there are two large parties and one very small

party (1 *vs.* 1 + 1). Jean Blondel has explored a similar vein, defining as two-party systems those in which the leading two parties win an average of more than 90 per cent of the vote, and as multi-party systems those where the two leading parties win no more than two-thirds of the vote. In between Blondel suggests the intermediary category of two-and-a-half party systems, characterized by the presence of two major parties and one minor party, arguing that straight three-party systems, where three parties of equivalent size competed, were not likely to exist.

Either way, the general conclusion is that while the number of parties is important, a numerical criterion alone is an inadequate basis for classifying party systems. Rather, one must take account of the relative sizes of the different parties and their pattern of competition. Second, it is evident that the simple distinction between two and more-than-two parties tells us little, and that it is distinctions between types of multi-party systems that are often most relevant. Finally, any attempt at a classification of party systems must make clear the level which is being addressed, be it electoral or parliamentary.

See also COMPETITIVE PARTY SYSTEMS; POLITICAL PARTIES. PMM

Reading

Almond, G.A.: Comparative political systems. *Journal of Politics* 18.3 (1956) 391–409.

Blondel, J.: Party systems and patterns of government in western democracies. *Canadian Journal of Political Science* 1 (1968) 180–203.

Duverger, M.: *Political Parties: their organisation and activity in the modern state*, pp. 206–280. London: Methuen, 1964.

Lijphart, A.: Typologies of democratic systems. *Comparative Political Studies* 1.1 (1968) 3–44.

Rokkan, S.: *Citizens, Elections, Parties: approaches to the study of comparative development*, pp. 93–6. Oslo: Universitetsforlaget, 1970.

Sartori, G.: *Parties and Party Systems: a framework for analysis*, Vol. I, chs 5–6. New York and Cambridge: Cambridge University Press, 1976.

passive resistance See NON-VIOLENT ACTION.

patronage This term is increasingly used in political literature as synonymous with CLIENTELISM. However patronage is also a legitimate and formal procedure, the outcome of which is similar to that of clientelism only in degenerative situations. Patronage is indeed defined as the power and the acknowledged right of a political authority to appoint people to positions of responsibility following its own opinion, preference or interest. The authority's choice is discretionary and is based on trust, loyalty and political affinity rather than on competence and skill.

Some political systems provide for patronage to some degree. Heads of state or prime ministers, governors and mayors can appoint people from their own entourage or party to various positions at the diplomatic level as well as at the level of local organizations. In the USA a well-defined system of patronage exists; this is the so-called 'spoils system' which allows the leader of the ruling party ample appointive powers.

Following the ever growing influence of governments within society, particularly on the economy, patronage has become common practice in many areas such as the civil service, state industry and the banking system. Extended and uncontrolled patronage can lead to misuse of public resources and consequently to clientelism.

General literature on patronage as defined here does not exist; rather it is dealt with in specific studies on some political systems, typically in those of the USA. This fact contributes to the confusion between the two interpretations of the term.   MC

permanent revolution The theory of permanent revolution was an attempt to apply Marxist theory to Russian conditions following the 1905 revolution. It was developed by Parvus and by TROTSKY to explain how an industrially backward society such as Russia could, nevertheless, prove ripe for a socialist revolution. The theory declared that, precisely because of Russia's backwardness, its bourgeoisie was too weak to make a bourgeois revolution unaided, and would need the help of the proletariat. The duty of the proletariat, however, was to maintain the revolution 'in permanence'; this would ignite revolutions in the countries of western Europe and, thus aided, the proletariat would be able to establish a socialist order in Russia. Thus the two central ideas of the theory were that, instead of two revolutions, a bourgeois revolution and a proletarian revolution, there need be only one continuing revolution, and that the Russian Revolution would directly inspire revolutions in other capitalist countries.

Although the theory was attacked for underestimating the role of the peasantry, it nevertheless proved to be a reasonably accurate forecast of LENIN's methods in leading the October Revolution in 1917, and also the Chinese Revolution of 1949. Indeed, Marxist revolutions have occurred in developing societies marked by industrial backwardness, rather than in advanced industrial societies as Marx believed. But the real weakness of the theory was that it over-estimated the revolutionary potential of the societies of western Europe. After coming to power, the Russian Bolsheviks found that they were left to defend their revolution on their own. So it was that the idea of 'Socialism in One Country' associated with STALIN replaced earlier internationalist aspirations.   VBB

Reading

Deutscher, I.: *Trotsky*. 3 vols. London: Oxford University Press, 1954, 1959, 1963.

Knei-Paz, B.: *The Social and Political Thought of Leon Trotsky*. Oxford: Oxford University Press, 1978.

Trotsky, L.: *The Permanent Revolution: results and prospects*. London: New Park, 1962.

Zeman, Z.A.B. and Scharlau, W.B.: *The Merchant of Revolution*. (A Biography of Parvus.) London: Oxford University Press, 1965.

personal federalism See MINORITIES, PROTECTION OF.

pillarization The literal translation of the Dutch *verzuiling*. It has been used mainly to describe the religiously and ideologically divided societies of Belgium and the Netherlands, although many of its characteristics can also be observed elsewhere. The authoritative definition of the term pillar (*zuil*) by the Dutch sociologist J. P. Kruijt, the first scholar to study this phenomenon systematically, reads as follows: 'an integrated complex of social institutions organised on a religious and/or ideological basis'. Other scholars have found it more convenient to apply the term to a segment of the population united by means of a set of exclusive organizations instead of this organizational complex itself.

A pillarized society is a special case of a plural society, that is, a society deeply divided by religious, ideological, regional, cultural, ethnic, or racial cleavages into separate segments, which tend to have their own political parties, interest groups, media of communication, schools, and voluntary associations. A pillar differs from a segment in two ways. First, a pillar has an exclusively religious or ideological character. In Belgium and the Netherlands, for instance, the Roman Catholics, Protestants, Socialists, and Liberals can be regarded as pillars; while the Flemings and French-speakers in Belgium are not pillars although they are clearly segments in a culturally plural society. Second, the usual assumption is that pillars are *vertical* segments, cutting across the horizontal socio-economic cleavage, though this assumption makes it difficult to apply the term to the largely class-based Socialist and Liberal pillars.

See also CONSOCIATIONAL DEMOCRACY.

AL

Reading

Daalder, H.: *Politisering en Lijdelijkheid in de Nederlandse Politiek.* Assen: Van Gorcum, 1974.

Huyse, L.: *Passiviteit, Pacificatie en Verzuiling in de Belgische Politiek: Een Sociologische Studie.* Antwerp: Standaard, 1970.

Kruijt, J.P.: *Verzuiling.* Zaandijk: Heijnis, 1959.

Lijphart, A.: *The Politics of Accommodation: pluralism and democracy in the Netherlands.* 2nd edn. Berkeley: University of California Press, 1975.

Lorwin, V.R.: Segmented pluralism: ideological cleavages and political cohesion in the smaller European democracies. *Comparative Politics* 3.2 (January 1971) 141–75.

Schendelen, M.P.C.M. van, ed.: Consociationalism, pillarization and conflict-management in the Low Countries. Special issue of *Acta Politica* 19.1 (January, 1984).

Steininger, R.: *Polarisierung und Integration: eine Vergleichende Untersuchung der Strukturellen Versäulung der Gesellschaft in den Niederlanden und in Österreich.* Meisenheim am Glan: Hain, 1975.

platform A programme or set of proposals presented by a group, such as a political party, for more general approval is described in terms of an analogy with the platform or hustings from which a spokesman or candidate for office has traditionally made his appeal. The analogy can be developed to particularize the planks or components of the programme, their strengths or weaknesses.

Democratic bodies may develop procedures for constructing platforms, through representative conferences or conventions, but their significance varies widely. Australian parties have in the past avoided producing more than vague and curtly worded platforms for fear of misquotation during campaigns, and have left party leaders to formulate objectives. American party platforms appear to itemize inducements to diverse, even disparate interests to join an electoral coalition. Their importance lies in the fact that they signal the ability of party factions to combine in the essential task of backing a winning candidate. They paper over cracks and emerge out of intensive horse-trading between presidential front-runners. Substantial changes in their content over the years reflect a pragmatic sensitivity to shifting electoral possibilities. The British Conservative Party, while acknowledging the help of constituency parties, has always regarded platform construction as the prerogative of the party leadership. Conference procedures in the Labour Party, by contrast, reflect a view of the platform as the mandate (see MANDATE THEORY), the authoritative voice of the party membership.

See also MANIFESTO.

GS-K

Reading

McKenzie, R.T.: *British Political Parties.* London: Heinemann, 1964; New York: Praeger, 1966.

Porter, K.H. and Johnson, D.B.: *National Party Platforms, 1840–1956.* Urbana: University of Illinois Press, 1961.

Plato (*c.*427–347BC) Greek philosopher. Plato's contribution to the modern study of politics has been to pose in dramatic fashion the underlying tension between philosophical understanding and the exigencies of political practice. In attempting to answer fundamental questions such as 'what is the best way of life?' or 'what is the best constitution?', through the analysis of the basic concepts of ethics and politics, he reveals both a profound pessimism and a measure of optimism which at times seem almost at odds. The pessimism emerges in the frequent allusions in numerous dialogues to the trial and death of Socrates or to the tragic fate of the philosopher, as in the Cave Allegory in the *Republic*. So severe are his criticisms of the pretensions of the sophists and rhetoricians and the practices, not only of Athenian democracy but also of every political regime, that no political system seems worthy of approval and no way of life which is just and wise seems able to survive.

Plato does commit the philosopher, whatever the perils, to a life in politics and his prescriptions, however foreign and often unpleasant they seem to modern commentators, still point to problems and develop philosophical approaches which remain of great interest today. One of these is his study of both the political and psychological aspects of tyranny. In the *Gorgias* he explores the psychological disposition towards tyrannical power with great insight; in the *Republic* he develops this theme in the way in which he links the democratic soul and constitution with the tyrannical soul and constitution. A second theme may be found in the way in which he explores the relationship between understanding and politics on numerous levels: through the critique of the sophists; the distinction between knowledge (*epistemē*) and belief (*doxa*); the notion of the unity of virtue and its dependence on wisdom; the claims for the philosopher-king; and the theory of forms. Although modern problems are not posed in precisely the same language, many of the issues are similar: for example, in the distinction between theory and ideology; in the exploration of the concept of false consciousness in Marxist theory; in the problem of knowing one's interests in utilitarian thought;

and even in the question of voter rationality. In the *Statesman*, Plato, anticipating ARISTOTLE, advocated MIXED GOVERNMENT and argued that extreme forms of government would encourage instability.

Most of Plato's dialogues contain underlying political themes and allusions, although the works most commonly read are the *Republic*, *Statesman* and *Laws*. To this list should be added the dialogues concerned with the trial and death of Socrates (*Euthyphro*, *Apology* and *Crito*), the *Protagoras* where Plato examines at length the claims of the sophists, and the *Gorgias* where the memorable meeting between Socrates and Callicles raises the spectre of the superman which has continued to haunt the modern world to the present. Many of the terms and concepts which Aristotle has made familiar to modern political thought may be found originally in Plato, and often in a more subtle and profound, if less definite, form. FR

Reading

Annas, J.: *An Introduction to Plato's Republic*. Oxford: Clarendon Press, 1981.

Bambrough, R.E.: *Plato, Popper and Politics*. Cambridge: Heffer, 1967.

Barker, E.: *Greek Political Theory: Plato and his predecessors*. London: Methuen, 1960.

Klosko, G.: *The Development of Plato's Political Theory*. London: Methuen, 1986.

Morrow, G.: *Plato's Cretan City*. Princeton, NJ: Princeton University Press, 1960.

Plato: *Euthyphro, Apology of Socrates, Crito, Protagoras, Gorgias, Republic, Statesman, Laws* (various editions).

Strauss, L. : *The City and Man*. Chicago, Ill.: Rand McNally, 1964.

plebiscite See REFERENDUM AND INITIATIVE.

plural society Term coined by J. S. Furnivall and defined as 'a society comprising two or more elements or social orders which live side by side yet without mingling in one political unit'. In such societies, he argued, each sector was likely to develop its own form of nationalism, setting one against the other. POLITICAL CLEAVAGES in such societies, therefore, are likely to be reinforcing rather than cross-cutting leading to very great tensions.

Political scientists have devoted considerable attention to the problem of how stability is to be achieved in plural societies, and whether, in order to achieve stability, departures may be needed from the WESTMINSTER MODEL of government. There is some agreement that tensions are best contained by separating groups in the light of the saying that high fences make good neighbours, rather than requiring them to intermingle. Amongst the mechanisms devised to solve this problem are proportional representation, grand coalitions, FEDERALISM, DEVOLUTION, COMMUNAL REPRESENTATION and, more generally, CONSOCIATIONAL DEMOCRACY.

See also PILLARIZATION.   VBB

Reading

Furnivall, J.S.: *Netherlands India*. Cambridge: Cambridge University Press, 1939.

pluralism A condition in which political power is dispersed amongst a wide variety of social groups. Pluralist ideas of dispersed political power among autonomous groups and dispersed political decision centres are arguably the most influential of political concepts in western countries in the twentieth century, but pluralism is ill defined as a concept and its accuracy as a description of current western society is often challenged.

Historically the term pluralism was identified with a school of philosophy which argued against the concept of an absolute and sovereign state. In works such as LASKI's *Studies in the Problem of Sovereignty* (1917) and *The Foundations of Sovereignty* (1921) classical pluralists attacked the legal doctrine of the sovereign state, both on the grounds that it did not fit empirical reality and that as a normative goal it was undesirable.

The classical pluralists were thus reacting against a legalistic approach to political study which, it was claimed, accepted constitutional nostrums at face value. Garson (1978, p. 18) writes that Laski 'performed the pleasant task of rendering explicit an idea whose time had come', though he did go on to suggest that the

pluralists had themselves over-simplified the approach they sought to replace. Ehrlich (1982) in the older classical tradition but written from a context of Eastern Europe, is still interesting.

Contemporary pluralist thought developed in the 1950s and is associated with works such as Dahl's *A Preface to Democratic Theory* (1956) and *Who Governs* (1961), and Dahl and Lindblom's *Politics, Economics and Welfare* (1953). These works shared with classical pluralism an empirical/observational approach and a normative belief in limiting the power of the state (though the focus was now government rather than state). However the new pluralism was developed not in contra-distinction to state sovereignty but to the theory of ELITES. The central assumptions were that there was widespread distribution of political resources, and that different interests prevailed in different political disputes and at different times. Pluralism was also a reaction to classical democratic theory. It played down the importance of voting as a democratic check and provided an intellectual legitimation of pressure group activity – activity that once had a suspect place in democratic practice.

The most famous statement of this version of pluralism is Dahl's (1967, p. 386) remark, 'few groups in the United States who are determined to influence the government – certainly few who are organized, active and persistent, – lack the capacity and opportunity to influence some officials somewhere in the political system in order to obtain at least some of their goals'. Also noteworthy is Polsby's comment (1963, p. 113) that there is an unspoken notion in pluralist research that at bottom *nobody* dominates.

Pluralism exists in an ambiguous relationship with Dahl and Lindblom's term POLYARCHY. Reserving 'democracy' as an ideal type, Dahl used the concept of polyarchy as a label for the western political systems which approximated to democracy. At some points pluralism is only a component dimension of polyarchy but in *Who Governs* Dahl himself used pluralism as the natural contrast with oligarchy (e.g. 1961, p. vi, p. 11). Dahl's work does not to any great extent rest on the classical pluralists but his intellectual roots go back to MADISON and TOCQUEVILLE and their arguments that since a 'general will' consensus is unattainable in complex modern states, then organizational pluralism is desirable. Given that pluralism has been often presented as the ruling intellectual orthodoxy of political science, Dahl's own comments (1984, p. 240) on the definitional vacuum are significant. About *Who Governs* he wrote: '*Pace* some interpretations, the book was not written to advance a general "pluralist theory of politics"; in fact "pluralism" and "pluralist democracy" are not included in the index. In hindsight, it might have been better to set out a more explicit theory. But perhaps not.' To use Dahl's words again (1984, p. 232): '"Pluralist theory" came to designate a strange melange of ideas. In fact, a good deal of the "theory" consisted of interpretations by hostile critics . . . Frequently the result was a "theory" that probably no competent political theorist – pluralist or not – would find plausible.'

The major vein of criticism is probably that the empirical studies which pluralists made to discover (or at least confirm) their belief that different interests prevail in different contexts cannot be convincing because there is 'a second face of power' which is not uncovered by case studies. Bachrach and Baratz (1970, p. 7) argued that important power holders did not need to win on a particular issue but could, 'limit the scope of the political process to public consideration of only those issues which are comparatively innocuous . . . ' to them. As developed by Lukes (1974, p. 25) with his 'third-dimension of power', the criticism is that power holders can so manipulate the wants of others that their *real interests* (his emphasis) are suppressed.

The most significant of such attacks is probably Charles Lindblom's later work *Politics and Markets*. He finds that there is a privileged position of business in the market-dominated polyarchies of the west – that they are controlled undemocratically by business and property. He claims (1977, p. ix) that 'when political science turns to institutions like legislatures, civil service, parties and interest groups, it has been left with secondary questions'. Dahl too in his later work (1982) and in the introduction to the 1976 edition of

Politics, Economics and Welfare is a critical supporter of pluralism. These sorts of criticisms are more fundamental than the simple misinterpretation that pluralism is about open competition between reasonably equal political forces.

Other criticisms emerged as criticisms of GROUP THEORY, but the main theme of works such as Connolly (1969) was that the pluralist picture of Western democracy was too un-critical of the inequalities of resources and access that existed.

An amended version of pluralism is to retain the idea of a fragmented government, but to concede that access is far from open and find a pattern of sub-governments where government departments reach accom-modation with clientelist groups. Labels such as group sub-governments, iron triangles, policy communities, corporate pluralism, have been developed to describe these extra-constitutional structures in the political system. CORPORATISM has more similarities with this segmented pluralism than the simple *laissez-faire*, competitive, version (see Kelso 1978).

See also INTEREST GROUPS; POWER. AGJ

Reading

Bachrach, P. and Baratz, M.: *Power and Poverty*. New York and London: Oxford University Press, 1970.

Connolly, W.E. ed.: *The Bias of Pluralism*. New York: Atherton Press, 1969.

Dahl, R.A.: *A Preface to Democratic Theory*. Chicago, Ill.: University of Chicago Press, 1956.

————: *Who Governs? Democracy and Power in an American City*. New Haven, Conn.: Yale University Press, 1963.

————: *Pluralist Democracy in the U.S.* Chicago: McNally, 1967.

————: *Dilemmas of Pluralist Democracy*. New Haven, Conn.: Yale University Press, 1982.

————: Polyarchy, pluralism and scale. *Scandinavian Political Studies* 7.4 (1984) 225–40.

Dahl, R.A. and Lindblom, C.E.: *Politics, Economics and Welfare*. New York: Harper & Row, 1976.

Ehrlich, S.: *Pluralism on and off Course*. Oxford: Pergamon, 1982.

Garson, G.D.: *Group Theories of Politics*. Beverly Hills, Calif. and London: Sage, 1978.

Kelso, W.A.: *American Democratic Theory*. Westport and London: Greenwood, 1978.

Lindblom, C.: *Politics and Markets*. New York: Basic Books, 1977.

Lukes, S.: *Power: a radical view*. London: Macmillan, 1974.

Polsby, N.: *Community Power and Political Theory*. New Haven, Conn. and London: Yale University Press, 1963; repr. 1980.

Truman, D.: *The Governmental Process*. New York: Knopf, 1951.

plurality method See ELECTORAL SYSTEMS.

polarized pluralism In proposing a new analysis of party systems, Giovanni Sartori introduced the notion that a distinction should be made between two types of multi-party systems: moderate and polarized pluralist systems. A polarized pluralist party system may account for general political immobility and, in some cases, the collapse of democracies.

Sartori's theory of party systems derives from the spatial theory of electoral competition first elaborated by Anthony Downs. The spatial theory depicts parties as vote-maximizers, competing within a unidimensional spectrum of opinion (traditionally, but not necessarily, a left–right ideological dimension) along which voters are distributed. As a specific type of party system within this rational choice framework, polarized pluralism is distinguished from other multi-party systems by four characteristics.

First, the number of *relevant* parties usually exceeds five. The relevance of a party is determined not by its electoral strength but rather by its systemic import; to be relevant, a party must either have a coalition potential (i.e. be crucial to the formation of at least one feasible coalition) or have a blackmail potential (i.e. be capable of affecting the tactics and direction of party competition).

Second, a polarized pluralist system is characterized by a high degree of ideological (or other) *distance* between its outer relevant parties (as measured by a polarization index). That is to say the political spectrum encompasses a wide spread of opinions and

the level of consensus among both elites and masses is consequently low. Third, the system is multipolar; it contains more than two poles, including a centre pole. The polarized nature of extreme pluralism and the physical occupation of the centre results in a fourth characteristic, namely centrifugal drive. The rewarding direction of party competition is generally outward to the extremes, stimulating extremist politics.

The interrelation of these four characteristics is what distinguishes polarized pluralist polities from other multi-party systems. Polarization is stimulated by the competitive interaction of more than five relevant parties on one and the same dimension of competition, be this an ideological, ethnic, religious, or linguistic dimension. Conversely, while moderate pluralist systems may also be characterized by the presence of more than five parties, the domain of party identification in such politics is multidimensional and competition on any one dimension is limited to three or four parties.

Similarly interrelated are the competitive drives of the system and the degree of polarization. The latter can be viewed both as a static *condition* of a polity and as a dynamic *process* within it. As such, centrifugal competition produces a process of increasing polarization within a country and eventually maintains a condition of high polarization, or wide ideological distance.

It should be stressed that there is an inherent logic in the model's conceptual progression. The degree of polarization and the number of relevant parties are the determining features of the model. A high degree of polarization (itself partly the result of a large number of relevant parties) leads to the physical occupation of the centre by one or more parties. The centre's occupation, in turn, encourages centrifugal competition.

Any party system characterized by the interaction of these four factors is likely to witness a number of additional features, each of which contributes to the immobility of the polity. First, ANTI-SYSTEM PARTIES, i.e. parties which have a delegitimizing impact upon the regime, will tend to dominate the opposition at one or both sides of the political spectrum.

The centre, or pro-system parties, will therefore be confronted with an anti-systemic opposition; the greater the polarization the more likely it is to engender, in feedback manner, a bilateral opposition.

The prevalence of anti-system mentalities, as well as the more general ideological patterning of politics, when combined with the physical occupation of the centre results in the centre being placed outside electoral competition. Centrist voters are too far removed from the opposition to vote for it rather than the centre, leading to the opposition parties becoming uninterested in competing centripetally for votes at the centre of the spectrum. Hence, whereas the centre's occupation is itself a result of polarization its very occupation further encourages centrifugal competition thereby stimulating increased polarization.

Yet another feature, that of irresponsible opposition, can be traced to centre-based politics. Once the opposition knows that it will not be held accountable for its actions and promises made in opposition (given that the prospects of coming to power are small), it can behave irresponsibly while engaging in outbidding. In turn, the mechanics of government imply that there is only a 'peripheral turnover', one of coalition partners, rather than a complete alternation of governments.

Polarized pluralist party systems, then, are likely to witness centre-based politics, anti-system opposition, irresponsible and highly ideological politics, and an absence of alternative governments, resulting in only a peripheral turnover of coalitions. Such a form of party politics tends to stimulate immobility throughout the polity, and lead to the inherent fragility of the entire political system.

As a result, such systems are especially vulnerable to external shocks and internal turmoil, ultimately leading to their potential disintegration. Such was the case with Weimar, the French Fourth Republic, and Chile. At other times, the polity stabilizes in its polarized condition and comes to accept the large degree of immobility as 'natural'. Here, Italy and Finland appear to be examples of the continuing viability and acceptance of the polarized condition.

The introduction of the notion that different types of multi-party systems exist has been an especially useful one for the analysis of political institutions. In this sense Sartori's contribution has been truly important. Yet the model falls short in at least two important respects: namely, in its discussion of the centre and in its reliance on a unidimensional, left-right imagery of politics.

The notion that in polarized pluralist systems the centre is necessarily placed outside competition, even if logically deduced from the theory's premises, would seem to be inconsistent with the reality of politics. Parties, as vote-maximizers, are interested in gaining maximum support. To the extent that parties at the extremes (even if anti-system parties) share this principle, such parties will be encouraged to seek the support of the largest possible voting-bloc. If this voting-bloc is located at the centre, parties will be compelled to attract that support if they are to remain viable. Hence, centripetal electoral competition may co-exist with, or come to dominate, centrifugal processes, even in polarized polities.

A second drawback of the theory is its reliance on a left–right imagery of politics. While this imagery has obvious theoretical and conceptual attractions, the analyst interested in quantification will time and again run into the problems of definition and hence of measurement. When relying on a left-right continuum to measure degrees of polarization and centrifugation, the analyst must assume that there is an *a priori* agreed-upon definition of left, right and centre and that such definitions are readily quantifiable. Such is not the case however. There are many lefts and rights – political, economic, social, religious, and so forth. Even then, one person's extreme-left may be another's centre-left. Hence, while most people have an intuitive notion of what these categories entail, agreed definitions are notable only for their absence.

See also CENTRE PARTY; SPATIAL MODELS.

IHD

Reading

Daalder, H.: In search of the centre of European party systems. *American Political Science Review* 78 (1984) 92–109.

Daalder, I.H.: The Italian party system in transition: the end of polarized pluralism? *West European Politics* 6 (1983) 216–36.

Downs, A.: *An Economic Theory of Democracy*. New York: Harper & Row, 1957.

Sani, G. and Sartori, G.: Polarization, fragmentation, and competition in western democracies. In *West European Party Systems: continuity and change*, ed. H. Daalder and P. Mair. London and Beverly Hills, Calif.: Sage, 1983.

Sartori, G.: *Parties and Party Systems: a framework for analysis*. New York and Cambridge: Cambridge University Press, 1976.

——: *Teoria dei partiti e caso italiano*. Milano: SugarCo Edizioni, 1982.

police A body of persons employed to maintain civil order and investigate breaches of the law. Persons employed to maintain order and investigate offences on private property may also be referred to as police. Furthermore it is customary to describe any person engaged in the enforcement of the rules as being engaged in policing. Many organizations, including the professions, and religious bodies, have private arrangements for policing their members. Investigative officials (for example in the customs and excise), prosecutors, and sometimes magistrates, may be engaged in policing or its supervision without being regarded by the public as being police. In industrialized countries police officers are usually assisted by a variety of auxiliaries: finger-printing technicians, forensic scientists, mechanics, photographers, telephonists, traffic wardens, typists, etc. The public image of who counts, or does not count, as a police officer may therefore pose interesting questions to the political scientist but it does not provide any foundation for generalizing about the police as an institution.

As societies have become more complex the volume of criminal laws has grown and with it the volume, size and variety of law enforcement agencies. This in turn has created new problems of control. In some countries, such as Sweden, the national government employs a national police force with jurisdiction throughout the country. Several European countries (France, Belgium, Italy, Spain) have both a national police and a *gendarmerie* or civil guard. In France the minister of the interior has administrative control of the national police while the minister of defence has similar control of the gendarmerie (but the director-general of the gendarmerie is a civilian and not a military officer). The minister of justice oversees the judicial control of both the national police and gendarmerie in the investigation and proof of crime. In systems of this kind national police organizations may be complemented by municipal police responsible for local matters such as the enforcement of traffic regulations (for example the *Vigili Urbani* in Italy). The supervision of the police is achieved in a different way in the Netherlands where the local mayor can direct the police in respect to the maintenance of public order but not in respect to the investigation of offences.

In countries with legal institutions based upon common law, police administration is less centralized (though New Zealand has a central ministry of police). In the United Kingdom the police are accountable to the courts for their actions in investigating offences; their resources are controlled by a police authority whose duty is 'to secure the maintenance of an adequate and efficient police force for the area' but the Home Office is also influential. For the Metropolitan Police (London) the police authority is the Home Secretary. For the thirty-eight other police forces of England, the four of Wales, the eight of Scotland, and the one in Northern Ireland, the police authority is a local committee which draws its funds partly from central and partly from local sources. In addition there are specialist police forces for the transport system, defence and atomic energy establishments, and fourteen separate forces responsible for particular docks, airports and a tunnel.

In the United States there are six major types of police agency: federal, including the Federal Bureau of Investigation (FBI), and the Narcotics Bureau; state police forces and criminal investigation agencies established by each of the 50 states of the union, often concerned primarily with highway patrol; county sheriffs and deputy sheriffs in over 3000 counties; municipal police forces for about 1000 cities and 20,000 towns; the police of some 15,000 villages and boroughs; and semi-private police forces for bridges, tunnels, parks, university campuses, etc. Apart from their common accountability to the courts, these bodies are controlled in a great variety of ways and there is a remarkable overlap of jurisdictions. For example a suspected offence by an overseas visitor on a university campus involving a victim taken across a state boundary might be investigated simultaneously by the campus police, the city police, the county sheriff, the FBI, the immigration authorities, and, in some circumstances, the Narcotics Bureau.

Overlapping jurisdiction gives rise to inefficiency but it can be a safeguard against corruption. When police misbehave, officials in another agency may be able to take action where ordinary members of the public could not. This points to the problem of accountability which is often summarized in the Latin tag: *quis custodiet ipsos custodes*? (Who guards the guardians?) Efficiency is desirable, but not if it confers excessive or unregulated power. The bigger the organization the greater is this problem. It is convenient, following Geoffrey Marshall, to distinguish between two kinds of accountability. There is a 'subordinate and obedient' kind of accountability in which the supervisor's responsibility is accompanied by administrative control and a power to direct and veto. A police officer has, within the law, to be accountable in this mode to a senior officer or to a prosecutor. This is insufficient, since police resources are limited and much depends upon a senior officer's ability to direct the police officer, as to where he shall patrol and what kinds of offence he shall look out for. A police chief therefore needs to be held accountable in an 'explanatory and co-operative' mode to a body representative of the public who can question his general policies and whose advice he must respect.

Police officers are recruited from the general public (if not evenly from all sections of it). They, and their relatives, live among the public and share many of the same opinions. This can be both a strength and a weakness. It makes it easier for them to understand the people whose behaviour they want to influence.

They are less likely to offend public susceptibilities. At the same time they share the prejudices of the groups with which they identify. Reacting to the conflicting expectations of them manifested by different groups, police officers usually develop a very strong sense of occupational solidarity.   MPB

Reading

Bayley, D.H.: *Forces of Order: police behavior in Japan and the United States*. Berkeley: University of California Press, 1976.

Goldstein, H.: *Policing a Free Society*. Cambridge, Mass.: Ballinger, 1977.

Holdaway, S.: *Inside the British Police*. Oxford: Blackwell, 1983.

Marshall, G.: Police accountability revisited. In *Policy and Politics*, ed. D. Butler and A.H. Halsey. London: Macmillan, 1978.

Muir, W.K., Jr.: *Police: street corner politicians*. Chicago, Ill.: University of Chicago Press, 1977.

Punch, M.: *Conduct Unbecoming: the social construction of police deviance and control*. London: Tavistock, 1985.

Reiner, R.: *The Politics of the Police*. Brighton, Sussex: Wheatsheaf, 1985.

Skolnick, H.: *Justice Without Trial*. New York: Wiley, 1966.

police state   A translation of the German *polizeistaat* which entered common English usage in the 1930s to refer to the control features of NAZISM, and in particular to a political system in which the police *apparat* dominated government, wielding arbitrary power in a repressive state. The police state is generally regarded as an essential element of a TOTALITARIAN regime and the term is conventionally used to describe any political system regardless of its ideology, where the use of organized violence is not under social control, where the instruments of coercion are free to act arbitrarily, or where these serve the ends only of the ruling elite. This implies the absence of RULE OF LAW, or any autonomous legal framework operating independently of the police and the ruler and, therefore, the existence of an authoritarian or totalitarian system.

In such states the police has wide and unquestionable discretion in regard to law. It

431

will be able to make arrests, to detain at length those arrested, to use torture, to interpret existing legislation for its own ends and to overrule independent judicial inquiry. The police will also possess a good deal of autonomy over its own budget; it may even have the *de facto* power to extort money from the population or engage in criminal activity to finance itself. Its primary objective will be to suppress all activity regarded as undesirable by the ruler and by itself. In general, the police will be the judge of whether any distinction is to be made between political crime and political error.

It is rare for the activity of the police to be entirely free from the political control of the ruler: some political control over the police will usually persist, not least because the ruling elite itself will be reluctant to see its power jeopardized by excessive power falling to the police. The ruling elite's ideal, in this respect, is that the police should act as its private army. Over time, the functioning of the police can become bureaucratized and to some extent even made routine, though the ultimate freedom to act independently of the law will not be lost. With the loss of this freedom the state will cease to be a police state.

The chief goal of the police is generally the suppression of political opposition. This can include the repression of activity which is only marginally political (for example the attempt to organize independent trade unions in Soviet-type systems). Another key function of the police is the collection of information, surveillance of all activity and the creation of a climate in which individuals are atomized in order to prevent the emergence of any social solidarity which might threaten the power of the ruler. In some cases the use of the police remains restricted to the enforcement of compliance, and often the threat of intervention by the police is as effective as actual police intervention. In other circumstances, notably when the ruling elite is attempting to pursue a political strategy seriously at variance with popular aspirations, the activity of the police, rather than simply suppressing action, can have the aim of forcing the population to take part in certain types of behaviour. The mass rituals of the STALINIST period provide an

illustration of this. Finally, in the vocabulary of political abuse, any action by the police, even when taken in a legal framework, can be qualified by those affected as evidence of the existence of a 'police state'.   GSch

Reading

Adelman, J.R. ed.: *Terror and Communist Parties*. Boulder, Col.: Westview, 1984.

Chapman, B.: *Police State*. London: Pall Mall, 1981.

Conquest, R.: *The Soviet Police System*. London: Bodley Head, 1968.

Delarue, J.: *The History of the Gestapo*, trans. M. Savill. London: Corgi, 1966.

Payne, H.C.: *The Police State of Louis Napoleon Bonaparte 1851–1860*. Seattle: University of Washington Press, 1966.

policy analysis The 'science of social engineering', policy analysis is concerned with the content, development and outcomes of action programmes designed to deal with social problems (or at least what are perceived to be social problems). It is primarily concerned with public policy – i.e. action taken directly by government or involving the legal powers of the state in some way.

Within policy analysis, one can distinguish between a 'professional' approach and an 'academic' approach. The professional approach is concerned with analysis for policy or 'speaking truth to power' (Wildavsky 1980). Policy analysis received much of its initial impetus from an interest in improving public policy, in learning from mistakes and in solving (or at least redefining) problems. In that sense it may be seen as a branch of operational research, and as related to PUBLIC ADMINISTRATION, the study of what governments may properly and successfully do. The profession of policy analysis, argue Hogwood and Peters (1985, pp. 3–4), is to social science what medicine is to biology. It is applied, requires specific subject-matter and case knowledge, but also a degree of 'generalism' allied with the ability to communicate across fields of expertise and the mystic craft of a good 'bedside manner'.

The academic approach to policy analysis is less applied and more detached – analysis of policy rather than analysis for policy. Its interests include the cognitive and political processes involved in policy formulation, the evaluation of results, the understanding of IMPLEMENTATION processes, the exploration of cause-effect assumptions, and the identification of alternative instrumentalities or policy principles.

Among the characteristic features of academic policy analysis are the following:

(1) Analysis is usually focused on policy programmes: that is, the set of instruments and institutions which are directed to purposes such as defence, health care, income maintenance, education.

(2) Analysis tries to be interdisciplinary, including all the 'policy sciences' from qualitative political theory to microeconomics (Jenkins 1978, p. 32).

(3) Considerable interest has been devoted to identifying what Richardson (1982) terms 'national policy styles', as different characteristic mixes of policy-formulation processes (for instance, consultation versus unilateral decision, long-term planning versus day-to-day reaction to events). Others are sceptical about this approach: Rose (1984) argues for example that government growth is best understood not in terms of overall national policy styles but by disaggregating government into its major component programmes and exploring the characteristics and dynamics of each programme area.

Just as the practice of social engineering pre-dates the term itself, the study of policy was established long before the generic term 'policy analysis' was coined, going back at least to the eighteenth century. But in the 1960s and 1970s, three things happened. First, policy analysis gained a generic intellectual brand name and emerged as a self-conscious, 'go-anywhere' approach, with new journals and universities training students for careers in policy analysis. It went furthest in the USA, where university-trained 'generalist' policy analysts found a ready market, given the diffuseness of the government structure and the absence of a permanent corps of generalist senior civil servants. Second, there was a wave of quantitative analyses of statistical indicators of policy outputs, to supplement the traditional

qualitative case history method. Third, interest in policy formulation was supplemented by greater emphasis on policy implementation.

Like many academic trends these developments followed US federal dollars. The 'Great Society' programme of the 1960s – ambitious social engineering projects funded by the federal government – stimulated both professional and academic policy analysis. Professional policy analysis was stimulated by a demand for causal models and quantitative studies comparing actuality with promises. Academic policy analysis was stimulated by the perceived failure of many Great Society projects, leading to efforts towards a better understanding of policy implementation, to chart the various reefs on which policy intentions could founder, and the conditions in which learning could occur. Later, from the mid 1970s, a second phase of thought in policy analysis reacted to the first, attempting, for instance, to construct 'bottom up' models as better descriptions of how policy processes actually work than the 'top down' models of the earlier generation of policy analysts, which came under attack as centralist and *étatist* in focus. (Sabatier, 1986 has attempted a synthesis.)

CCH

Reading

Heclo, H.: Review article: policy analysis. *British Journal of Political Science* 2 (1972) 83–108.

Hogwood, B. and Peters, B.G.: *The Pathology of Public Policy*. Oxford: Clarendon Press, 1985.

Jenkins, W.I.: *Policy Analysis: a political and organisational perspective*. Oxford: Martin Robertson, 1978.

Richardson, J.J. ed.: *Policy Styles in Western Europe*. London: Allen & Unwin, 1982.

Rose, R.: *Understanding Big Government: the programme approach*. London: Sage, 1984.

Sabatier, P.A.: Top-down and bottom-up approaches to implementation research: a critical analysis and suggested synthesis. *Journal of Public Policy* 6 (1986) 21–48.

Wildavsky, A.: *The Art and Craft of Policy Analysis*. London: Macmillan, 1980. Published in the USA in 1979 as *Speaking Truth to Power*.

Wilson, W.: The study of public administration. *Political Science Quarterly* 2 (1887) 197–220.

policy output studies The outputs of a

government consist of the sum total of its decisions, activities, and products. These include, most notably, the laws and rules that it enacts and enforces, the public and private policy statements that it makes, the taxes it extracts, and the services and facilities it provides for public consumption. Policy output studies, therefore, concentrate on the question of what governments do and produce, and particularly on the question of how and why governments vary in the policies they pursue and the services they provide. These are among the fundamental and timeless questions of political science, going to the heart of Harold Lasswell's definition of the subject as the study of 'Who gets what, when and how'.

The term 'political outputs' was introduced into modern political science by the systems and structural-functional theorists of the 1960s, particularly David Easton and Gabriel Almond, who drew an important distinction between the inputs into the POLITICAL SYSTEM which then generates outputs. These outputs, in their turn, cause a feedback loop into the system by affecting the nature of the environment and its inputs. In fact, this early theoretical literature had little to say about outputs, mainly because the great bulk of political-science research at the time was concerned with inputs – ELECTIONS, PARTIES, pressure groups, PUBLIC OPINION, the media – and the way in which they were processed in the political system.

A few social scientists had been making output studies, without so describing them, before the 1960s, but the work was scattered and mainly carried out by economists who were primarily interested in the economic determinants of public expenditure levels. It was not until a series of empirical studies were carried out by American political scientists in the late 1960s and early 1970s that research on policy outputs gathered momentum. Initially a comparison was made of different nation-states in an attempt to discover how and why they varied over a range of policy outputs.

The research method employed was usually the collection of data relating to the inputs of the environment (population size, national wealth, population age structure, for example), to the political system (election turnout, federal-unitary features, party in government), that were then related by statistical means to a set of output variables. This work soon ran into a set of difficulties which forced it to limit its ambitious scope. First, it proved difficult to compare nation-states because they varied so much in their history and their social, economic, and political circumstances, as well as in the form and nature of their outputs. In addition the limited number of nation-states which may sensibly be compared presented statistical problems. Research therefore moved quickly into a comparison of sub-national units of government, states and local authorities, which are more plentiful and more comparable. Second, research quickly focused on public expenditure as an easily quantifiable and reliable indicator of policy outputs. Critics pointed out that spending may be a highly imperfect measure of service quantity and quality, but so far have failed to suggest anything better. Besides, public expenditure levels are important in their own right as an output, especially in an era of cuts.

In comparing the policy outputs of the sub-national units of government within a nation-state, political scientists were in effect trying to establish the causes of variation in public policy among a set of mini-political systems. Whereas much of political science examines one small part of the political system, policy output studies had total systems to examine, and could therefore ask some broad and high-level questions about how and why they vary in what they do. The first wave of studies of this kind reached a rather startling conclusion – they found that politics did not matter. That is, they found that political variables had little or no impact on output variation which was explained, statistically speaking, by social and economic variables. This was startling because it meant that most of the traditional concerns of political science – elections, mass participation, elite characteristics, party in government – had little impact on what governments do or how they perform. By and large it was found that level of economic development and population characteristics were the most important determinants of policy outputs. In short governments were the helpless prisoners of social and economic circumstances.

It became apparent however that these studies were deficient in some respects: most were carried out in the United States where parties are often weak and ideologically similar; they tended to be cross-sectional (i.e. they examined outputs at a given time); and they often defined politics in a narrow way. It was argued that research in Europe, where parties are stronger and cover a wider ideological spectrum, would find that politics play a larger role, particularly if research traced changes over time. By and large these predictions proved correct. A series of studies in the nations of Western Europe found that party politics in particular, and politics more generally, were often associated with some important variations in expenditure levels. Politics were re-established as a determinant (but certainly not the only determinant) of output variation at both the local and national levels of government.

By this time output studies had gone through a few other transformations as well. They had long ceased any special connection with systems or structural-functional theory, and had been carried out within a range of other theoretical approaches including PUBLIC CHOICE or RATIONAL CHOICE theories, and PLURALIST theory. These were later joined in terms of a theory of the STATE and its contradictory role in producing the conditions of profit-making on the one hand, and political stability on the other.

At the same time, interest in policy outputs grew with a broader development in policy studies, and the term took on a rather different and specialized meaning. Policy output studies have now come to cover that part of public policy analysis which is mainly concerned with the understanding and explanation of variations in national or sub-national government performance, especially with variations in the level of service expenditure and provision. As such it is also identified with (large) data sets relating to the social, economic, and political characteristics of political systems and their outputs, and with elaborate and complex statistical methods of analysing these data. Most recently attention has switched from

attempts to explain the rise of welfare policies and services, to a study of cuts and contraction. This is likely to consume the interests of policy output specialists for a few years to come and, although there are unlikely to be major breakthroughs in statistical method-ology, the field will quite probably have to develop new theory if it is to make much headway.   KN

Reading

Almond, G.A. and Powell, G.B.: *Comparative Politics: a developmental approach*. 3rd edn. Boston, Mass.: Little, Brown, 1982.

Dye, T.: *Understanding Public Policy*. Englewood Cliffs, NJ.: Prentice-Hall, 1972.

Easton, D.: *A Systems Analysis of Political Life*. New York: Wiley, 1965; 2nd edn, Chicago, Ill.: University of Chicago Press, 1979.

Fried, R.C.: Comparative urban policy and per-formance. In *The Handbook of Political Science*, Vol. VI, ed. F.I. Greenstein and N. Polsby. Reading, Mass: Addison-Wesley, 1975.

Heidenheimer, A.J., Heclo, H. and Adams, C.T.: *Comparative Public Policy: the politics of social choice in Europe and America*. 2nd edn. New York: St Martin's, 1983.

Sharpe, L.J. and Newton, K.: *Does Politics Matter? The Determinants of Public Policy*. Oxford: Oxford University Press, 1984.

Politburo (and Presidium)   The Politi-cal Bureau (Politburo) of the CENTRAL COM-MITTEE of the CPSU is the most authoritative organ of the party and hence of the entire Soviet political system; it is the functional equivalent of a cabinet. Similar bodies exist in the other Soviet-type states.

Members – currently, after March 1986, numbering twelve, with seven candidates – are elected by the Central Committee in plenary session, but membership is in fact determined by the Politburo itself, under the leadership of the GENERAL SECRETARY. Other office-holders who (nowadays) invariably sit on the Politburo are the Premier (Chairman of the COUNCIL OF MINISTERS) and the President (Chairman of the Presidium of the SUPREME SOVIET). The remaining members are drawn from the Central Committee Secretariat, from the ranks of regional party secretaries, and from the state apparatus. Only one woman has sat on the Politburo: Ye. A. Furtseva, from 1957 to 1961.

The role and power of the Politburo have not been constant since its creation – actually only formalizing an existing state of affairs – at the Eighth Party Congress in 1919. Until Lenin's death supreme political authority lay with the Council of People's Commissars (from 1946 Council of Ministers), of which Lenin was chairman. The transfer of power to the party body coincided with the arrogation by STALIN, the General Secretary, of increasing power to himself. However, the latter process culminated in the virtual ossification of the Politburo as a collective body; its members, terrorized after 1934 by Stalin's PURGES, were consulted as he saw fit and in ad hoc groups or subcommittees. At the Central Committee plenum following the Nineteenth Party Congress of 1952, the Politburo was, at Stalin's instigation, renamed Presidium and expanded to twenty-five members and eleven candidates, a development which presaged a further round of terror. Only the smaller Bureau of this body, whose existence was acknowledged later, ever met. Two days after Stalin's death in March 1953 the size of the Presidium was reduced to ten, with four candidates.

During the Khrushchev years the Presidium, though meeting more regularly, continued to be treated in a high-handed manner by the party leader, a fact which contributed to his ultimate downfall. In the Brezhnev period and thereafter the authority of the Politburo (as it was renamed in 1966) has become more firmly established, preventing the arbitrary exercise of power by the General Secretary.

The precise nature of the Politburo's deliberations is unclear, but in any case it is likely that matters such as the extent to which consensus is sought and the weight given to the views of the General Secretary vary with circumstances and with the personalities involved. Formal voting is known to have taken place under Khrushchev, while a familiar tactic under Brezhnev was the setting up of a temporary commission of Politburo members to deal with unresolved disputes. Meetings are usually held once a week, sometimes twice.

The agenda is probably drawn up by the General Department of the Central Committee under the General Secretary's supervision, and covers foreign affairs as well as domestic issues too important or controversial to be settled in the Presidium of the Council of Ministers or the Central Committee apparatus.

SW

Reading

Hough, J.F. and Fainsod, M.: *How the Soviet Union is Governed.* Cambridge, Mass. and London: Harvard University Press, 1979.

Khrushchev, N.: *Khrushchev Remembers.* London: Deutsch, 1970.

———: *Khrushchev Remembers: the last testament.* London: Deutsch, 1974.

Löwenhardt, J.: *The Soviet Politburo.* Edinburgh: Canongate, 1982.

Schapiro, L.: *The Communist Party of the Soviet Union.* 2nd edn. London: Methuen, 1970.

political action committee (United States) A non-party fund of a sponsoring labour union, business, trade organization, or independent political group used to contribute money to candidates for public office. While there have always been political action committees (PAC) in one form or another, the number and kinds of PACs have grown sharply since the passage of the Federal Election Campaign Act of 1971 and its 1974 amendments, which strictly limited the amounts and conduits of campaign contributions. Each PAC is permitted to give up to $5000 per election to each candidate for federal office, and many states have more generous limits (or no limits at all) on PAC gifts. From 608 in 1974 the number of PACs has grown rapidly, and there were over 4000 by 1985; contributions to congressional candidates have similarly multiplied, from $12.5 million in 1974 to $105.3 million in 1984. PACs now supply more than a third (34 per cent) of all funds raised by House candidates, and close to a fifth (17 per cent) of the war chests accumulated by Senate contenders. Incumbent members of Congress receive the vast majority of PAC gifts (up to 70 per cent in 1984), and this largesse has fuelled charges of influence-peddling and vote-buying, though the relationship between PAC money and members' floor votes is not strong in most cases. (The legislator's party affiliation, ideology, and the needs of his or her constituency explain far more of his voting choices than do PAC contributions.) Some of the largest and most active PACs include the National Conservative Political Action Committee (NCPAC), the National Congressional Club (affiliated with Republican Senator Jesse Helms of North Carolina), the Realtors' R–PAC, the American Medical Association's AMPAC, the AFL–CIO's Committee on Political Education (COPE), and the National Education Association's NEA–PAC.

See also POLITICAL FINANCE.   LJS

Reading

Alexander, H.E.: *The Case for PACs*. Washington, DC: Public Affairs Council, 1983.

Drew, E.: *Politics and Money: the new road to corruption*. New York: Macmillan, 1983.

Jacobson, G.C.: *Money in Congressional Elections*. New Haven, Conn.: Yale University Press, 1980.

Malbin, M.J.: *Money and Politics in the United States: financing elections in the 1980s*. Washington, DC: American Enterprise Institute/Chatham House, 1984.

Sabato, L.J.: *PAC Power: inside the world of political action committees*. New York: Norton, 1984.

Sorauf, F.J.: *What Price PACs?* New York: Twentieth Century Fund, 1984.

political attitudes An attitude is a mental predisposition that need not ever be translated into observable acts or specifically formulated thoughts or beliefs. An attitude is usually defined by psychologists as more specific than a value while vaguer than behaviour. Political scientists have often ignored the distinction between value and attitude, treating the two as interchangeable concepts.

A seminal experiment developed by LaPierre (1934) was to reveal the difference between attitude and behaviour as well as the risks one takes when one extrapolates from the one to the other. LaPierre toured the United States by car in the company of a Chinese couple and stayed with them at a variety of hotels and motels. In nearly all cases the reception had been courteous. A few months later LaPierre sent letters to each of the establishments where he and his friends had spent a night, asking whether the hotel or motel would accept as patrons a Chinese couple. In nearly all cases the answer was negative: it was not the practice of the establishment to accept Chinese guests. Although it may not have been the same individuals who answered the letters and who stood at the reception desk, the institutions concerned were the same. LaPierre concludes that one should not extrapolate from attitude to behaviour. Reinterpreting the experiment, Rokeach (1972) noted that in both cases LaPierre had, in fact, recorded attitudes – one might also say behaviour – that varied according to changes in the context of the answer. Writing in the isolation of one's office is markedly different from reacting verbally to the presence of a potential customer, possibly in the full view of other clients and under the potential threat of an unpleasant exchange of words.

Whether we label it 'verbal behaviour' or 'anticipated behaviour' or 'opinion' or call it by some other name, the set of mental constructs more commonly called political attitudes has been frequently studied by political scientists; especially since the early 1960s when the technique of survey research became widely used to gather information on such large populations as national electorates. Indeed, the importance given to attitudes measured by verbal responses to verbal stimuli led John Wahlke to criticize his own discipline for having failed to study actual behaviour while giving itself the illusion of having done so under the labels of political behaviour and political BEHAVIOURALISM. Survey research and the testing of attitudes, argued Wahlke, had put a regrettable distance between political scientists and political actors and led the former to downplay the importance of actual behaviour.

Specific and generalized attitudes
Very specific questions that narrow precisely the perceptual field may be used as stimuli in what one wishes to be a well controlled mental

437

experiment. A question such as 'do you think that the government should stop immigration from country X' tests the opinion of the respondent regarding immigration and may test the attitude of that same respondent vis-à-vis the country mentioned; it does not tell one whether the respondent who answers positively is more ethnocentric than a respondent who answered negatively. To get at generalized attitudes, one needs either less specific questions (for example a question that would not mention the name of a country) or a battery of questions that would vary the stimulus by which the attitude is triggered.

Such batteries of questions are often summed up into scale values, for example the ethnocentric and fascist scale values postulated by Adorno and his colleagues (1950) in their study of the authoritarian personality, the conservative scale values postulated by McClosky (1958) or Wilson (1973), the left–right scale values postulated by Laponce (1981), the soft minded–tough minded as well as liberal/conservative scale values postulated by Eysenck (1954). The resulting scales number over a hundred; see for example the classics reprinted by Robinson and Shaver (1969).

The scales of attitudes commonly used in political research are of two major kinds: the researcher-determined and the subject-determined scales. Those of the first kind (the Adorno scales for example) have values that are predetermined by the researcher. The latter decides what response measures what attitude and how much weight should be given to each of the answers resulting from the battery of questions. The scale values are determined exclusively by the researcher's judgement. The second type of scale – such as the Guttman or the Loevinger scale (Mokken 1971) – does not assume that all the questions in the battery measure the same attitude; scaling seeks, then, to determine whether the questions form a hierarchical mental structure. If such a hierarchy is found after going through a permutation of questions and respondents, one is able to say that if a respondent believes x he or she is also highly likely to believe y and z but not w. Unless the number of respondents and questions is very small, the search for hierarchical attitudinal structures by means of the Guttman or Loevinger's scaling techniques requires the use of computers.

The computer has also facilitated the application of other correlational techniques such as factor analysis, tree analysis and smallest space analysis to the study of attitudes in order to determine the existence of a general syndrome or to break it into its component parts. Factor analysis enables Wilson, for example, to differentiate his general syndrome of conservatism into religious, economic, political and social components whose relative overlap can then be measured.

But the hierarchical ordinal scale, though better than the merely additive scale, is not without limitations. It orders questions and responses but cannot measure the 'distance' between them; it cannot determine adequately the magnitude of the variation in intensity of the stimulus as one goes from one question to another down the scale.

The recommended strategy for the study of attitudes is thus to use both single questions and summary scales and report the findings in such a way that the reader is then able to disaggregate the averages or scale values into their components and reinterpret and eventually rename the attitudes under observation. The study of the composition and of the naming of attitudinal scales is indeed a revealing field of research, revealing of the attitudes and beliefs of those who do the naming (see for example the criticisms of the assumptions underlying the Adorno scales by Christie and Jahoda, 1954).   JAL

Reading

Adorno, T.W., Frenkel-Brunswick, E., Levinson, D.J. and Nevitt, S. eds: *The Authoritarian Personality*. New York: Wiley, 1964.

Christie, R. and Jahoda, M.: *Studies in the Scope and Method of the Authoritarian Personality*. Glencoe, Ill.: Free Press of Glencoe, 1954.

Eysenck, H.J.: *The Psychology of Politics*. London: Routledge & Kegan Paul, 1954.

LaPierre, R.T.: Attitudes vs. actions. *Social Forces* (1934) 230–7.

Laponce, J.A.: *Left and Right: the topography of*

political perceptions. Toronto: University of Toronto Press, 1981.

McClosky, H.: Conservatism and personality. *American Political Science Review* (1958) 27–45.

Middendorp, C.P.: *Progressivism and Conservatism*. The Hague: Mouton, 1978.

Mokken, R.J.: *A Theory and Procedure of Scale Analysis*. The Hague: Mouton, 1971.

Robinson, J.P. and Shaver, P.: *Measures of Social Psychological Attitudes: appendix to measures of political attitudes*. Ann Arbor: University of Michigan, Institute for Social Research, 1969.

Rokeach, M.: Attitude toward situations. *Journal of Personality and Social Psychology* (1972) 194.

Schubert, G.: *Political Attitudes and Ideologies*. Beverly Hills, Calif.: Sage, 1977.

Wahlke, J.: Pre-behavioralism in political science. *American Journal of Political Science* (1979) 9–31.

Wilson, G. ed.: *The Psychology of Conservatism*. London: Academic Press, 1963.

political behaviour   The branch of political science which studies people's attitudes to politics and the way they express those attitudes, in contrast to the study of political structures and constitutional frameworks. The 'behavioural approach' (not to be confused with the behaviourism of psychologists) developed in the early post-war years as a reaction to the weight put on institutions of government and formal rules. Political behaviour attempted to explain rather than to describe and to use quantitative evidence rather than qualitative testimony. A technical innovation, the advent of the political opinion survey, fostered the subject's growth. Students of political behaviour emphasized the opinions and behaviour of ordinary citizens which had hitherto been neglected by conventional political science but could now be established through sample surveys.

Political behaviour begins with the study of POLITICAL SOCIALIZATION. What accounts for the persistence (and the disruption) of regimes, and how are political attitudes perpetuated? How do children learn about the institutions of their society? How are a society's political values handed down from one generation to another? Political socialization consists of more than deliberate indoctrination. Much political learning is a by-product of other activities; so the spread of education has a political spin-off in that it promotes feelings of self-confidence which equip people to participate more in politics. Political socialization does not end with childhood, but through influences from the workplace, the trade unions and voluntary associations, continues throughout life. Indeed, present research lays more stress on adult experience. Differences in the extent and form of political participation by various social groups reflect differences in the pattern of socialization. Middle-class groups generally participate more, so enhancing their political leverage.

Research into political socialization highlights two basic themes of political behaviour: POLITICAL CULTURE and the nature of the party system. The study of political culture is that of popular attitudes towards government, and towards different social groups. A simple comparison between Britain and Northern Ireland shows at once that there are huge divergences in the character of politics in the two areas which owe little to differences in political institutions and which arise from radically contrasting popular attitudes. In some societies government is seen as essentially beneficial, in others as alien and malign; in some countries, citizens find it easy to live at peace with other groups, in others their relationships are marked by suspicion and violence. More broadly, the differences between the politics of stable western democracies and most countries of the third world reflect contrasts in popular orientations to government.

The inability of political parties to work together or at least to restrain their antagonism often mirrors the deep hostility between adherents of different churches or members of separate ethnic groups. Academic and commercial opinion surveys enable a much more precise assessment of the social bases of party choice, of the extent to which electors' policy preferences parallel the way they vote and the degree of commitment to their party. There has been renewed interest in the origins and evolution of political parties; Lipset and ROKKAN's model which attempts to account for both the similarity and diversity of the various European party systems is

439

the most exciting and stimulating of these exercises.

Regime stability has been another prominent issue. Almond and Verba's cross-national investigation, *The Civic Culture*, an appraisal of popular attitudes to governments in five western countries, is a classic example. Scholars reflecting on the collapse of democracy in inter-war Europe, and its failure in post-colonial territories elsewhere, sought to verify the conditions under which liberal-democracy could survive and flourish. Comparative work of this kind has been prompted by the wish to move away from narrow single-country studies and to formulate more general laws of political stability. Britain, with its special blend of participatory and deferential attitudes, was for long held up as the model of stable democracy.

Political behaviour has been criticized on three grounds for excessive concentration on election studies.

(1) The accessibility of data from opinion surveys has imparted to the subject, it is said, an implicit ideological bias favouring liberal-democracy, and has led scholars to assume that the character of a country's polity is the sum of the attributes of the individuals who compose it. In principle there is no reason why we should not undertake research into political behaviour in countries without free elections and indeed much work using data other than survey responses has been done on such societies. Moreover, for elections at least, the overall national decision *is* no more than the aggregate of individual preferences.

(2) Election studies are said to attach too much importance to the mass-public, too little to the political elites. Nevertheless, the methods developed by students of political behaviour have generated new advances in the study of elites.

(3) Work in political behaviour is said to be informed by crude determinism and by a misplaced ambition to make the study of politics 'scientific'. Critics often charge more than proponents claim; research in political behaviour cuts across the argument as to whether politics can be truly scientific. At a minimum, the methods and data used make possible a much more *systematic* study of political life than was hitherto feasible. Even the great masters of the past were implicitly behavioural and tacitly quantitative: Walter BAGEHOT foreshadowed the concept of status-discrepancy as an explanation of extreme political beliefs; and the relevance of 'the tyranny of the majority' notion which loomed so large in the nineteenth-century debate about universal suffrage can now be more accurately assessed. Every discussion of the working of political institutions rests on implicit or explicit empirical assumptions, whether valid or not. The purpose of the study of political behaviour is to test such assumptions, and to discard those found wanting.

See also SOCIAL STRUCTURE AND PARTY ALIGNMENTS.   HBB

Reading

Butler, D. and Stokes, D.: *Political Change in Britain*. 2nd edn. London: Macmillan, 1974.

Dawson, R.E., Prewitt, K. and Dawson, K.S.: *Political Socialisation*. 2nd edn. Boston, Mass.: Little, Brown, 1977.

Jaros, D. and Grant, L.V.: *Political Behaviour*. Oxford: Blackwell, 1974.

Kavanagh, D.: *Political Science and Political Behaviour*. London: Allen & Unwin, 1983.

Lipset, S.M.: *Political Man: the social bases of politics*. New York: Doubleday, 1960; London: Heinemann, 1983.

Lipset, S. and Rokkan, S. eds: *Party Systems and Voter Alignments: cross-national perspectives*. London: Collier-Macmillan; New York: Free Press, 1967.

Nie, N.H., Verba, S. and Petrocik, J.R.: *The Changing American Voter*. 2nd edn. Cambridge, Mass.: Harvard University Press, 1979.

Rose, R. ed.: *Electoral Behavior: a comparative handbook*. New York: Free Press, 1974.

political cleavages The criteria that divide society into politically-relevant groups and subgroups. The most fundamental bases of cleavage are usually assumed to include social class, religion, nationality, language, race and gender. Cleavages define the underlying social structure that forms the basis for political activity. In a stable political system they may well be represented in the established political process – the party system, the system of interest groups, the administrative structure and so on. In a deeply divided society particular cleavages may even define the battle lines in a civil war. The Lebanon provides a recent tragic example of an intractable civil conflict defined in terms of a complex religious cleavage. A number of properties are held to affect the political impact of a particular set of cleavages.

In the first place, cleavages may take one of four basic forms. There are 'socio-structural' cleavages such as socio-economic class. There are 'trait' cleavages, such as race or gender. There are 'attitude' cleavages, such as those between unionists and nationalists in Northern Ireland. These may in practice cut very deeply indeed, but are in principle amenable to change. There are behavioural cleavages, such as those between people working in the public sector and the private sector. Obviously, differences on one type of cleavage may generate differences on another. For example, blacks develop different political attitudes from whites, while particular political attitudes lead to particular forms of voting behaviour. One influential model based on cleavages is that of Lipset and ROKKAN. This attempts to account for the variations in western European party systems in terms of the historical development of the cleavage structure and in particular of the state/church cleavage, the centre/periphery cleavage, the urban/rural cleavage and the capital/labour cleavage. There has been much recent interest in the role of 'consumption' and 'production' cleavages in the explanation of political behaviour in general (see Castells) and voting behaviour in particular (see Dunleavy). These analyses highlight the increasing role of, for example, the cleavage between state and private sector employees, or between owner-occupiers and public authority tenants. They explain the apparent decline in 'class voting' in many western systems by arguing that the cleavages that determine voting have changed in nature and become much more specific. (For a counter argument see Franklin 1985, and Franklin and Page 1984.)

The second important property of a political cleavage is its salience. Some cleavages, such as social class, appear always to be salient.

Others, such as religion, vary dramatically in salience both from one time period to another in the same system, and between systems. What is clear is that fundamental social cleavages (a good example being gender) may for long periods be ignored by the mainstream political system. What is also clear is that the salience of cleavages can be manipulated for political ends. This has periodically been the case in Irish political history and is also, to an extent, an endemic feature of US electoral politics, which often put a premium on the mobilization of clearly-defined ethnic and demographic groups such as women, blacks, Jews and so on.

In the third place, different cleavages fragment society in different ways. Some break society into a cluster of small groups; others break it into a couple of large groups. Meanwhile two cleavages that each divide society into two groups can cut in many different ways. One may produce two equal fractions, the other may put an overwhelming majority against a small minority. In an influential discussion, Rae and Taylor proposed a definition of fragmentation that has since been widely adopted. The level of fragmentation, F, is the probability that two people, selected at random from the society, will be put into different groups by the cleavage in question. This gives a measure ranging from zero (absolute homogeneity) to unity (absolute heterogeneity). It can be easily computed for any cleavage when we know the size of the relevant subgroups; it also has considerable intuitive appeal. The very high level of religious fragmentation in the Lebanon, for example, is clearly one factor that makes the situation there so intractable.

Moving beyond a single cleavage considered in isolation, the most important property of a set of political cleavages is the manner in which they interact. In particular, cleavages may reinforce or cut across one another. If two cleavages each divide the society into two groups they may cut along the same lines, reinforcing one another and producing two groups between them; or they may cut across one another and produce four subgroups. The table shows two quite different societies of 100 people.

Society A

Religion

		Catholic	Protestant	
Class	Upper	25	25	50
	Lower	25	25	50
		50	50	100

Society B

Religion

		Catholic	Protestant	
Class	Upper	0	50	50
	Lower	50	0	50
		50	50	100

Looked at in isolation the two cleavages appear similar in each society: each cleavage breaks both societies into equal groups. The two societies, however, differ starkly. This difference is produced by the interaction of the class and the religious cleavage. In one society a person's religion can be predicted from his or her social class with absolute certainty, in the other society the one is impossible to predict from the other. It is typically argued that a lack of cross-cutting (as in Society B) may make for unstable politics. This is because certain groups may find themselves on the losing side of every issue, thereby becoming alienated and hostile. (Lipset is probably the best-known proponent of this argument.) This is one of the conventional arguments used by political scientists, for example, to explain the developing political alienation of Catholics in Northern Ireland. But Lijphart's model of CONSOCIATIONAL DEMOCRACY (1975), shows how, under certain circumstances, the *absence* of cross-cutting can

make for stability. Rae and Taylor also proposed a measure of cross-cutting (XC) that has since been widely used to capture the interaction between two cleavages. This is the probability that two people who are put in the same group by one cleavage are put in different groups by the other. This can be easily calculated from tables such as those above. (The level of cross-cutting in Society A is 0.5; that in Society B is zero.)

There is no such thing as 'cleavage theory'. Rather, political cleavages are associated with a vocabulary of concepts. These can be applied systematically in a range of theories that specify factors affecting the salience of cleavages, and consequences flowing from the fragmentation and cross-cutting caused by a particular cleavage structure.

See also GENDER AND POLITICS; RELIGION IN POLITICS; SOCIAL STRUCTURE AND PARTY ALIGNMENTS. MJL

Reading

Castells, M.: *City, Class and Power*. London: Macmillan, 1978.

Dunleavy, P.J.: The political implications of sectoral cleavages and the growth of state employment (two parts). *Political Studies* 28 (1980) 364–83, 527–48.

Franklin, M.: *The Decline of Class Voting in Britain*. Oxford: Oxford University Press, 1985.

——— and Page, E.: A critique of the consumption cleavage approach in British voting studies. *Political Studies* 32 (1984) 521–36.

Lane, J.-E. and Ersson, S.O.: *Politics and Society in Western Europe*. London: Sage, 1987.

Lijphart, A.: *The Politics of Accommodation: pluralism and democracy in the Netherlands*. 2nd edn. Berkeley: University of California Press, 1975.

Lipset, S.M.: *Political Man: the social bases of politics*. New York: Doubleday, 1960; London: Heinemann, 1983.

Rae, D. and Taylor, M.: *The Analysis of Political Cleavages*. New Haven, Conn.: Yale University Press, 1970.

Rokkan, S. and Lipset, S.M. eds: *Party Systems and Voter Alignments: cross-national perspectives*. London: Collier-Macmillan; New York: Free Press, 1967.

political communication The flow of messages and information that gives structure and meaning to the political process. Political communication involves not just the ELITES sending signals to their mass publics, but the whole gamut of informal processes of communication throughout a society which affect politics in any manner, whether in the shaping of public opinion, the political socializing of citizens, or the mobilizing of interests. Some theorists have seen government as one vast communications process, involving the collection, storage and dissemination of messages and information.

Political life in any mass society is impossible without established methods of political communication. No individual alone can discern directly all the activities that make up the political process; leaders and followers are equally dependent upon the communication function to learn what others are assuming to be the political news of the day. The dominant flow of political communication, whether its content is correct or not, becomes the crucial force in defining and explaining what is significant in politics at any time.

The mass media are the prime institutions for political communication in modern countries today. Professional communicators working in the various fields of journalism have become autonomous forces shaping political attitudes and the priority of issues. In pre-modern societies much of the communications process involved the word-of-mouth transmission of messages. In imperial bureaucratic societies, such as ancient Rome and China, government messengers ensured uniformity of rule by delivering orders that upheld the cohesion of the government. Throughout history the scope of governments has been limited by the technologies of communication.

The study of political communication covers a wide variety of activities. In the early years research attention was focused on questions concerning the influence of mass media on public opinion. These studies included analysis of the relationship of the media to informal channels of communication, the role of the media in influencing voters in election campaigns, the techniques of dictators in the use of propaganda, and issues about the economic and political control of the press and radio. During the 1950s and 1960s there was considerable interest in the role that political communication might play in facilitating the process of political development in the new states of Asia and Africa. Communications patterns were seen as being decisive in bringing about regional and international integration.

Theories have been developed about the potential of political communications for mobilizing people in the newly independent states and socializing them into becoming effective citizens in the national life of their countries. It was assumed that governments could rapidly disseminate new information and ideas, especially to total populations, and thereby speed the process of modernization. Political communication was also closely associated with the diffusion of innovations – governments could teach people through radio and television what they needed to know to be able to exploit the advances of science and technology.

The control and manipulation of political communications has been a key factor in the development of TOTALITARIANISM. State control of the mass media and of all other means of communication, including attempts to intimidate informal processes of communication, has been essential for the monopolizing of power that is necessary for building such systems. Precisely because centrally-controlled systems attach such importance to controlling political communications, outside observers have recognized the importance of engaging in detailed analyses of the content of the media in totalitarian states. The result has been the emergence of sophisticated techniques for interpreting the esoteric communications of such governments, as is done by students of 'KREMLINOLOGY'.

The study of political communication has also involved research into the changing patterns of political symbols and the emotional or affective dimensions of politics, such as the practices of charismatic leaders in mobilizing mass support. Since political communication normally has a high quotient of slogans and symbols, the measurement of the rise and decline of specific symbols can be used as an index of shifts of political sentiments in societies.

443

POLITICAL COMMUNICATION

In recent years political scientists have become more interested in the problems raised by the spread of new technologies of communication, especially electronic communications. The advances in such technologies have raised new issues of law and freedom, and posed questions as to whether norms developed for the protection of freedom of speech and of the press will be adequate or even appropriate when print is being rapidly displaced by cables, computers, video-disks, and satellites. The problems involve questions about privacy and the public's right to know.

A second major area of contemporary research on political communications concerns the effects of the media, and especially of the electronic ones, on how people learn about politics and how political events are perceived. What happens to public life when people rely mainly upon television for political news? Furthermore, questions arise about the power of the media, especially because they have enjoyed considerable autonomy in democratic societies and are therefore burdened with few restraints of responsibility.

In advanced industrial societies the power of the media is thought by some to be great enough to set, or at least distort, the agenda of national political issues. That is, television in particular is thought to be able to direct the public's attention by dramatizing some issues and ignoring others that are less readily popularized. The political agenda has hitherto been set by politicians, who are vulnerable to criticism, but this responsibility is now shared with the media, though the technology and the economics of mass communications set limits on the kinds of issues that can be popularized, and the media are seen as biasing the flow of politics. In particular, television's method of holding the public's attention produces a political environment in which single issues are dramatized so that the traditional ways of aggregating interests through political parties are weakened.

Advances in communications technology have had a profound effect on the electoral process in many democratic societies. Political advertising and the practice of candidates' debates has altered the format of politics, to say nothing of changing the image of the personal qualities essential for political success. The result has been a change in political rhetoric and the style of political competition.

The power of the media in advanced industrial societies has also affected international communications. In some third world countries the western press has been accused of being unfair to the developing countries, and there have been calls for a new order in international communication – an idea strongly resisted by western democracies that favour press freedom.

Although attention is generally concentrated on the ways and means of persuasive communication in politics, the structure and methods of mass communications can have profound unintended consequences for a society's public life. The media not only pass on the news of the day; they also set norms for evaluating events and standards for criticizing public figures. In this respect political communication can be thought of not only as influencing current events but also as influencing the thinking of coming generations of citizens. Debates will continue over the precise power of the media, but there is no questioning the central place that political communication plays in the politics of all countries.

See also MASS COMMUNICATION AND MASS MEDIA.   LWP

Reading

Chaffee, S.H. ed.: *Political Communication: issues and strategies for research*. Beverly Hills, Calif.: Sage, 1975.

Deutsch, K.W.: *The Nerves of Government*. New York: Free Press, 1963.

Hovland, C.I., Janis, I.L. and Kelley, H.H.: *Communication and Persuasion: psychological studies of opinion change*. New Haven, Conn.: Yale University Press, 1953.

Katz, E. and Lazarsfeld, P.L.: *Personal Influence: the part played by people in the flow of mass communication*. Glencoe, Ill.: Free Press of Glencoe, 1955; paperback 1964.

Lerner, D.: *The Passing of Traditional Society*. Glencoe, Ill.: Free Press of Glencoe, 1958.

MacBride, S.: *Many Voices, One World*. 'The MacBride report'. Paris: Unesco, 1980.

McQuail, D.: *Mass Communication Theory: an intro-*

duction. Beverly Hills, Calif.: Sage, 1983.

Nimmo, D. and Sanders, K.R.F.: *Handbook of Political Communication.* Beverly Hills, Calif.: Sage, 1981.

Pool, I. de S.: *Technologies of Freedom.* Cambridge, Mass.: Harvard University Press, 1983.

Pye, L.W. ed.: *Communications and Political Development.* Princeton, NJ: Princeton University Press, 1963.

Schramm, W.L.: *Mass Media and National Development: the role of information in the developing countries.* Stanford, Calif.: Stanford University Press, 1964.

Weaver, D. et al.: *Media Agenda-setting in a Presidential Election: issues, images and interests.* New York: Praeger, 1981.

political corruption   The use by political actors, politicians or officials of official decision-making processes, resources and facilities, to which they have access through their public position, for the advantage of another party, in return for some proposed or actual benefit to themselves contrary to the formal rules forbidding such behaviour. This definition is narrower and more legalistic than those which consider any misuse of office or all self-regarding behaviour by political actors as corrupt. It does, though, distinguish corruption from other types of illegal or unethical conduct by identifying the presence of the benefit to the actor, the bribe, and rules that preclude or forbid their offer or acceptance. The ingredients of corruption are that it is a transaction between at least two parties, that it is a means to achieve an outcome which one of them at least does not consider attainable through official means, and that those means specifically proscribe the use of bribes. These ingredients provide identifiable and generally-understood foci for analytical and comparative studies of corruption. Such studies concentrate on the three major issues raised by corruption: its causes, its significance, and its relevance to political activity.

Several theories attempt to explain the causes of corruption. None of them offers a universally-valid explanation but together they provide useful and often overlapping perspectives. Theories which focus upon rules consider corruption as just another law-breaking activity: a political actor should be seen as a criminal in a public position who is aware of both the opportunity and the personal incentive for breaking the law and who weighs these against the possibility of detection and the severity of the sanction that may be invoked if he is caught.

Theories focusing upon rules see the causes of corruption in a situational and functional context. The political actor may become involved in corruption because he has no commitment to or identity with his official position or duties. The political environment may not exert sufficient moral, professional or ideological pressure against such conduct or the office or institution may not have adequate procedures for accountability or place high value on standards of conduct, particularly in terms of performing its functions or satisfying the demands of political or client objectives. Theories which look at public office in a wider context fall into two general categories. Developmental theories deal with newly-established political systems. They argue that corruption is caused by the persistence of traditional gift-giving, and a sharp increase in government expenditure and in the number of spending agencies without the concomitant development of standards of conduct or procedures of accountability, so that there is a lack of loyalty to and trust in the political system and its decision-making processes. Cultural theories see corruption as the result of divergences between official and normative standards, between public and private sector values or between political goals and public service.

The significance of corruption can be assessed in terms of three categories: individual, systematic and systemic. Individual cases of corruption at whatever level are invariably treated as covert, sporadic, opportunist acts of criminality that happen to occur in a political or administrative context. Systematic or institutional corruption is of more concern because it points to corruption as a regular or standard activity where formal procedures and responsibilities are disregarded and actors, if they do not participate in the bribery, must collude with the behaviour of their colleagues. This type of corruption persists if the corruption or the collusion is hierarchical and can become institutionalized if the actors deliberately organize and market the powers and functions of their office in return for bribes. Systemic corruption occurs where public positions and official authority are openly used for personal enrichment throughout the political system. Its pervasive presence and, in particular, the involvement of senior actors encourages the institution-alization of a tariff or commission system within the decision-making processes that involves everyone, from individuals to multi-nationals and foreign governments.

Systemic corruption is normally associated with third world countries and is clearly highly relevant to the functioning of their political systems. While there are those who see certain beneficial functions of corruption – in, for example, providing a means of access or expediting the decision-making processes – the growth of corruption can help to create a downward spiral of exploitation, cynicism and misappropriation. Non-third world countries tend to see systemic corruption as an historical phenomenon; the circumstances that gave rise to it have either been legislated against, abolished or, occasionally, legitimized. Cor-ruption in these countries is invariably seen in the context of individual corruption and, without regular evidence of systematic cor-ruption, without any immediate victim or loss as in other crimes, it is not considered an important public issue. When examples of institutional corruption occur – and most major scandals or controversies over corrup-tion in non-third world countries concern this type of corruption – official inquiries tend to avoid looking for functional, cultural or other explanations. They try and play down the cases as aberrational or raise the threshold of tolerance of individual corruption so avoiding the question of whether major institutional reforms are necessary.

This conveniently forgets that corruption is a means to an end. The offer of bribes indicates, in part at least, that the donor does not accept the official decision-making processes and procedures. For a political actor to ask for or accept them is to indicate that

neither does he or she – and, for any political system, that is cause for concern.   ADo

Reading

Clarke, M. ed.: *Corruption: causes, consequences and control*. London: Pinter, 1983.
Heidenheimer, A.J. ed.: *Political Corruption: readings in comparative analysis*. New York: Holt, Rinehart & Winston, 1970.
Scott, J.C.: *Comparative Political Corruption*. Englewood Cliffs, NJ: Prentice-Hall, 1972.

political culture   A fairly new term for an old idea. The notion of a culture, spirit, mood or set of values which shapes the conduct of politics of a nation or groups is as old as the analysis of politics itself. Aristotle wrote about a 'state of mind' which encouraged political stability or revolution, Burke praised the 'cake of custom' which affected the working of political institutions. TOCQUEVILLE, DICEY and BAGEHOT gave an explicit place to political values and sentiments in their theories of political stability and change. Anthro-pologists and historians have, until very recently, written about the importance of a 'national character' or 'tradition' in shaping behaviour. The term itself was first explored by Herder.

Gabriel Almond (in Almond and Verba 1980) has suggested that the concept emerged from the confluence of three separate intellec-tual influences:

(1) Social psychology and psychoanthro-pology, especially the work of Freud and the insights of anthropologists such as Malinowski and Benedict.
(2) European sociology, represented in the work of WEBER, PARETO and Durkheim. Weber had challenged MARX on 'cultural' grounds, by claiming that religion and values were crucial influences upon economic activity and political structures. Many of these writers' ideas, particularly on the role of social norms and values, were developed in the United States by Talcott Parsons.
(3) Survey research, and the development of more sophisticated techniques of sampling, interviewing and analysing data. Public-opinion surveys enabled students to move

beyond what had been largely speculative and impressionistic statements about a culture to collect data about a group's or a nation's psycho-cultural orientations to politics.

Interest in political culture was part of the reaction against a legal institutional approach to political study, which involved, in the eyes of its critics, too great a concentration on the formal apparatus of politics – government, institutions, constitutions and states.

Events were also important in promoting awareness of political culture. Developments in continental Europe in the inter-war years, particularly the collapse of constitutional regimes in Germany, Italy and Spain, had been disillusioning for those who had anticipated the gradual spread of liberal democratic regimes and enlightenment values. In the 1950s and 1960s the collapse of constitutions in many newly independent 'third world' countries was again a forceful reminder of the complex relationships between political institutions, political behaviour and political culture. Explanations of stable democracy which rested heavily on institutional and socio-economic factors were clearly incomplete.

The most influential working definition of political culture was offered by two American political scientists, Almond and Verba, in *The Civic Culture*, a pioneering study of political culture in five countries. Political culture was defined as the 'pattern of orientations' to political objects, for example parties, courts, constitution, and history of a state. Orientations are predispositions to political action and are determined by such factors as tradition, historical memories, motives, norms, emotions and symbols; the culture therefore represents a set of propensities. These orientations may be broken down into: cognitive orientations (knowledge and awareness of the political objects), affective orientations (emotions and feelings about the objects), and evaluative orientations (judgements about them).

There have been many applications of the cultural approach to explaining political phenomena. Almond and Verba drew on their survey evidence about attitudes in Britain and the United States to propose a theory of the cultural bases of stable democracy. In his *Man on Horseback* (1962) S. E. Finer explained the propensity of the military to stage a *coup d'état* in terms of the level of political culture of a state – or popular support for the government. This in turn depends on two things. First, it depends upon whether there is a consensus about the procedures for assuming and transferring political power and general recognition of one sovereign power. This is the LEGITIMACY factor: where legitimacy is well-established the government does not depend on the military for its existence and a military takeover would be widely rejected as 'unconstitutional'. Second, it depends upon the extent to which the society is mobilized into various associations. Where both factors are high political culture is a more reliable prop for the civil government.

A number of conceptual and technical difficulties beset the relating of political culture to other political phenomena in a causal sense. If we do find a relationship between culture and structure or performance, how do we establish the link? The actual relationship may be one of mutual reinforcement over time, and this may make it well-nigh impossible to separate values from the performance of the political system as a whole.

There is also the macro-micro problem of analysing the survey material. While data collection is usually performed at the micro-level of the individual, culture is a collective phenomenon. The 'individualistic' fallacy involves a causal argument from the aggregated features of individuals to the global characteristics of a group of which the individuals are members. The proportion of respondents who express their support for, let us say, liberal democratic values does not tell us how 'democratic' the political system or political culture is. Where the political culture is seen as the aggregate of beliefs, emotions and values in society, the tendency is to overlook the problems of weighting the individual's values according to his or her political influence. Political values may be conditioned by history, social structure and the direct experience of people with the performance of the political system, yet the 'distal' historical and structural factors still have to be connected with the behaviour of groups and individuals. And it is here, even as an intervening variable, that values and attitudes have to be included in any strategy of explanation. Even if political values are shown to be derivative at one moment they may, once established, be important thereafter in affecting political behaviour.

A useful test case of the extent to which the culture can be 'engineered' from above is afforded by the communist regimes in Eastern Europe and China, where the party has enjoyed a monopoly control over education, mass media and socialization. These countries have also seen conscious and elaborate attempts to remake the political culture along socialist lines and to create a 'new' socialist man. Yet a recent study of political culture in these countries (Brown and Gray 1977) emphasizes the points of continuity and the tenacity of many old values regardless of change in the regime.

See also CIVIC CULTURE.   DK

Reading

Almond, G.A. and Verba, S. eds: *The Civic Culture: political attitudes and democracy in five nations.* Princeton, NJ: Princeton University Press, 1963.

———: *The Civic Culture Revisited: an analytical study.* Boston, Mass.: Little, Brown, 1980.

Brown, A. and Gray, J. eds: *Political Culture and Political Change in Communist States.* London: Macmillan, 1977.

Finer, S.E.: *The Man on Horseback* (1962). 2nd edn. Harmondsworth: Penguin, 1976.

Kavanagh, D.: *Political Culture.* London: Macmillan, 1972.

Pye, L. and Verba, S. eds: *Political Culture and Political Development.* Princeton, NJ: Princeton University Press, 1965.

political demography Defined by Weiner as 'the study of the size and distribution of population in relationship to government and politics', it is concerned with the political determinants and consequences of population change and includes governmental policies that relate to population numbers and their distribution. The political connotations of population exercised the minds of the early demographers. Thomas Malthus, for example, was concerned with the question of optimum population size, while William Petty gave the title 'Political Arithmetic' to his pioneering study on demography that first appeared in the seventeenth century. Nowadays however the term political demography is rarely used in demographic literature. For instance, there is no entry under this heading in the International Dictionary of Demography; nor does the authoritative abstract series on population, the Population Index, devote a specific section to the topic. Yet this does not mean that demographers ignore the political importance of population characteristics; rather it reflects the very diversity of these political aspects which impinge on most areas of population studies.

Compared with more formal demographic analysis, political demography lacks a coherent set of guiding principles. Rarely are the relationships between population and politics straightforward, because they are first filtered through the diverse social, economic and cultural systems that characterize different countries. Consequently, the political significance of a given set of demographic characteristics is not easy to predict; there is no simple connection between a country's size or growth rate and its political stability or the nature of its political institutions. Nor does a large population necessarily signify military and political strength as it did in previous centuries. Furthermore no firm link has been established between population density and the potential for social conflict despite analogies drawn with animal populations.

In regard to broad issues of population that concern governments there is a large array of diagnoses as well as prescriptions. For example, western countries view the population explosion in the third world almost exclusively as a problem of excessive population growth, whereas from the conventional Marxist perspective it is a reflection of basic inequalities in the world system of resource distribution. Attitudes vary, moreover, between third world countries. Governments with comparatively sparse populations believe that benefits may accrue from rapid population growth, whereas the high density industrializing countries of

East Asia regard excessive growth as hindering their development. Even when there is agreement about the desirability of curbing rapid growth it does not necessarily imply a consensus as to how this should be achieved: whereas western governments and agencies emphasize family planning programmes, third world countries appear to see these as a form of western neo-colonialism and urge economic development, which erodes the desire for large families, as the means of curbing population growth.

In Europe governments are again, as in the 1930s, occupied with the consequences of static or declining populations. Concern about low growth first emerged in Eastern Europe in the early 1960s, mainly for economic reasons but also for reasons of ideology and national pride, and strongly pro-natalist policies have since been pursued in countries such as Hungary and Czechoslovakia. In Western Europe the stance has been less interventionist. Because of modern technologies there is not the same concern about the size of the labour force, nor are there the ideological overtones as in Eastern Europe. However, one of the consequences of no-growth, ageing, is regarded as a potentially serious problem, with the connotation that populations are becoming less flexible, less innovative and more conservative in outlook. There is also the important political consideration of how the growing number of retired are to be supported financially. In addition a falling birth rate has meant that there are fewer children in the population and this has created problems for the rational planning of education at all levels.

When loyalties and aspirations conflict in populations that are heterogeneous by ethnic or religious group a dynamic towards new political arrangements and groupings may be set in train. The balance between competing groups may be disturbed if faster population growth confers a numerical advantage on minorities, with implications for electoral success as well as power-holding consequences. In the most extreme circumstances this may transform a former minority into the majority as has happened in the Lebanon where the conflict between Moslem and Christian partly hinges on attempts by the now Christian minority to preserve its political privileges. Equally destabilizing can be the fact that a minority is increasing its proportion in a population, as is happening in Northern Ireland where Catholic nationalist confidence is boosted in the belief that demography will eventually give them a voting majority that will lead to a united Ireland. Because Protestant fears of eventual incorporation into an all-Ireland state are intensified, demographic trends only serve to sharpen the Northern Ireland problem. Yugoslavia constitutes another example of national and religious differences creating acute political tensions, as between Serb and Albanian, Moslem and Christian, Serb and Croat. These too are partly linked to differential growth rates which have intensified traditional antagonisms and fuelled secessionist tendencies. Even the Soviet Union faces a potentially serious problem in Central Asia where a continuation of the very high rates of growth of the Moslem population could eventually upset the balance between Slav and non-Slav; this helps explain the sensitivity of Moscow to the rise of fundamentalist Islam in Afghanistan and Iran.

Patterns of migration across international boundaries are governed not only by economic factors but also by the entry and exit rules of countries, which are the result of political decisions. It may be noted that these movements can affect the ethnic and racial composition of populations and can therefore help shape both domestic and international relationships. Hence migrants may promote or actively work against the political interests of their country of origin, while expulsions may be a source of international conflict.

On a practical level accurate demographic data are necessary for the good administration of any state, and population censuses constitute an important method of collecting such information. The availability of accurate population head counts is crucial for the equitable allocation of funding and resources between local administrative areas. Similarly, the conduct of elections in a democracy where fair representation is the objective is dependent upon constituency boundaries being drawn so as not to favour any one particular group. Furthermore the size of the electorate in a constituency can be allowed to vary only within fairly narrow limits while still preserving representativeness.   PAC

Reading

Berelson, B. ed.: *Population Policy in Developed Countries*. New York: McGraw-Hill, 1974.

Besemeres, J.F.: *Socialist Population Politics*. White Plains, NY: Sharpe, 1980.

Clinton, R.I., Flash, W.S. and Godwin, R.K. eds: *Political Science in Population Studies*. Lexington, Mass.: Lexington Books, 1972.

Council of Europe: *Population Decline in Europe*. London: Arnold, 1978.

Pressat, R. and Wilson, C.: *The Dictionary of Demography*. Oxford and New York: Blackwell, 1985.

Ross, J.A. ed.: *International Encyclopedia of Population*. 2 vols. New York: Macmillan and Free Press, 1982.

Schubnell, H. ed.: *Population Policies in Asian Countries: contemporary targets, measures and effects*. Hong Kong: The Dräger Foundation and the Centre of Asian Studies, University of Hong Kong, 1985.

Weiner, M.: Political demography: an inquiry into the political consequences of population change. In *Rapid Population Growth*, ed. R. Revelle, et al. Baltimore, Md.: The Johns Hopkins University Press, 1971.

political development A concept in political science used to describe the processes of NATION BUILDING and state building, especially in the newly independent countries of Africa and Asia which emerged from colonial rule after the second world war. Political development is closely associated with the concepts of modernization and economic development, and it is now applied to processes of political change throughout the third world. The idea of political development implies that societies can consciously direct the course of their own nation building rather than submit to the blind forces of social and political evolution or revolution.

In the immediate post-colonial period there was hope that the leaders of the new states might successfully transform their nationalist and anti-colonial movements into effective governments and thereby advance the condition of life in their countries. Since it was believed that political development depended upon advances in economic and cultural progress, the richer countries of North America and Europe initiated programmes of economic and technical assistance. Concern over the prospects of political development was also heightened by cold-war competition and anxieties about the spread of communism.

By the 1950s political scientists were sceptical about the pace of political development, especially in the poorer countries. Although there was general agreement that the flow of history was in the direction of a transition from traditional society founded on agricultural and rural patterns of life toward more modern conditions based on urban and industrial life-styles, this did not ensure that all societies would move at the same pace. It was recognized that many countries had severe handicaps, some in the shape of objective conditions and others because of their traditional cultures.

Theories of political development were influenced at an early stage by the work of nineteenth-century social theorists who had tried to explain the industrial revolution and the transformation of western societies. Influential works included those of Max WEBER, Karl MARX, Emile Durkheim, Henry Maine, and others. Theorists of political development also looked to anthropology for an understanding of the processes of acculturation and social change, and research in political development was also identified with the study of POLITICAL CULTURE and POLITICAL PSYCHOLOGY.

In the 1970s thinking about political development was affected by the popularity of dependency theory, especially as advanced by Latin-American scholars. According to dependency theory under-developed countries had little hope of economic progress because of international capitalism. Multi-national corporations were said to inhibit progress and to force the governments of under-developed countries to become increasingly authoritarian. Although most dependency theorists claimed to be neo-Marxists they did not accept Marx's unilinear view of progress from FEUDALISM to CAPITALISM to SOCIALISM, but adhered to LENIN'S theory of imperialism and of 'semi-colonies'. By the 1980s however dependency theory had lost popularity among political scientists, in part because of the remarkable progress of those Asian countries that had relied heavily upon foreign investments and relations with multi-nationals, but even more because of the collapse of authoritarian regimes and the revival of democracy in Latin America – a development which contradicted dependency theory.

Empirical studies of political development have covered a wide range of phenomena. Work has involved both institutional analyses and survey studies of attitudes and cultural predispositions. In particular there have been many comparative studies of institutions such as bureaucracies, parties, religious organizations, educational systems and rural development projects. Policy analyses have covered not only the policy performance of different institutions of government but also their larger political roles, and especially the importance of armies because of the frequency of military coups. Attitudinal studies have focused on the rise of religious fundamentalism, especially after the Iranian revolution of 1979.

A central problem in political development has been that of national integration. This is because so many of the developing countries are deeply divided along ethnic, linguistic, tribal or religious lines. A challenge to leadership has been the need to create new ideologies that will bind a country together without stirring up traditional animosities. This manifest need for greater national cohesion has encouraged the emergence of charismatic leaders who try to embody the national will in their own personalities.

The first generation of leaders after independence included a large number of charismatic leaders, such as for example, Sukarno in Indonesia, Jawaharlal Nehru in India, Mao Zedong in China, Kwame Nkrumah in Ghana, and U Nu in Burma. The successors to the first generation tended to be either tyrants or technocrats. In some cases the resulting military regimes were little more than repressive, authoritarian governments, as in the succession of coups in Africa which brought rule first by generals, then by colonels and in some cases even by sergeantry. In other cases army rule was transformed into technocratic regimes, as with Suharto in Indonesia, and Park Chung Hee in South Korea. Civilian pragmatists have brought a high degree of technical and rational planning to national development in several countries, most notably in China after the rise of Deng Xiaoping in the post-Mao era.

Academic research into the processes of political development has led to a re-examination of European history with an eye to better understanding of the sequence of change that produced the western nation-state system. This has produced new insights into such matters as the role that war played in advancing the ability of European states to mobilize resources and the conditions that led to peasant rebellions and other forms of civil violence. Interest in such matters was heightened by the problems posed by the outbreak of insurgencies in several developing countries, and most particularly by the war in Vietnam.

The study of political development has enriched political science by forcing the discipline to look for knowledge in several other social science disciplines, including sociology, anthropology, economics, psychology and history.   LWP

Reading

Almond, G.A. and Powell, G.B.: *Comparative Politics: a developmental approach.* 3rd edn. Boston, Mass.: Little, Brown, 1982.

Binder, L. et al.: *Crises and Sequences in Political Development.* Princeton, NJ: Princeton University Press, 1974.

Cardoso, F.H. and Falleto, E.: *Dependency and Development in Latin America.* Berkeley: University of California Press, 1979.

Frank, G.: *Capitalism and Underdevelopment in Latin America.* New York: Monthly Review Press, 1967.

Geertz, C.: *Old Societies and New States.* New York: Free Press, 1967.

Huntington, S.P.: *Political Order in Changing Societies.* New Haven, Conn.: Yale University Press, 1968.

——— and Dominguez, I.: Political Development. In *Handbook of Political Science,* ed. N. Polsby and F. Greenstein. Reading, Mass.: Addison-Wesley, 1974.

Mahler, V.A.: *Dependency Approaches to International Political Economy*. New York: Columbia University Press, 1980.

Packenham, R.A.: *Liberal America and the Third World: political development ideas in foreign aid and the social sciences*. Princeton, NJ: Princeton University Press, 1973.

Pye, L. and Verba, S. eds: *Political Culture and Political Development*. Princeton, NJ: Princeton University Press, 1965.

political ecology A variety of approaches to the study of environments of POLITICAL BEHAVIOUR. The term is commonly applied in sociological and political methodology in relation to the well known inferential problem of the ecological fallacy. Moreover the term is used substantively in a wide sense to describe any environmental impact upon political behaviour; such as the organizational ecology of a group of individuals. In a more narrow sense the term covers the study of the spatial territorial environments and political behaviour with close links to POLITICAL GEOGRAPHY. Lately, a fallacious usage has been registered confusing political ecology with conservationist issues and 'the ecological movement'.

Political ecology is characterized by attempts to measure the influence of different surroundings upon individuals and groups which can be considered similar, in terms of one or more features, across surroundings. In Herbert Tingsten's classical *Political Behaviour* of 1937, he demonstrates a significant difference between groups of Swedish workers in their propensity to vote for the class-based Social Democratic party. Workers living in working class areas displayed a considerably higher tendency to left voting than workers living as 'minorities' in middle class areas. This Law of Social Gravity illustrates well the basic structure of an argument based on political ecology.

A unit of observation only characterized by variables describing its environment is commonly known as an ecological unit, for example a constituency described in terms of its election returns is an ecological unit. Analyses juxtaposing variable characteristics of ecological units is often referred to as ecological analysis, for example regressing the election returns for a given party on information about the social composition of the same constituencies.

Inferences may be drawn from ecological analysis concerning the ecological units entered into the analysis. Attempts to infer how individuals behave on the basis of a purely ecological analysis is often termed 'the ecological fallacy'. The percentage of the population of each constituency in Britain employed as domestic servants is probably a good predictor of Conservative voting strength. We may not, however, infer from this ecological analysis that domestic servants tend to vote Conservative. To do so would mean committing an ecological fallacy.

Cross level ecological analysis entails that both ecological and individual data exist, as in the above analysis by Tingsten. This enables the researcher to measure the impact of different environments upon individual behaviour and is certainly not a fallacy.   FA

Reading

Dogan, M. and Rokkan, S. eds: *Quantitative Ecological Analysis in the Social Sciences*. Cambridge, Mass.: MIT Press, 1969.

Goodman, L.: Some alternatives to ecological correlation. *ASA* 64 (1959) 610–25.

Robinson, W.S.: Ecological correlations and the behavior of individuals. *ASA* 15 (1950) 351–57.

Siegfried, A.: *Tableau politique de la France de l'Ouest sous la Troisième République*. Paris: Colin, 1913.

Tingsten, H.: *Political Behaviour*. London: King, 1937.

political economics A term covering the analysis of a set of problems which are of common interest both to political science and to economics. It is to be distinguished from the term political economy, although there is much overlap. The latter has come to be partly associated with a Marxist-type focus on problems in which major issues are seen in terms of their distributional implications – especially as between workers and capitalists.

Political economics concentrates upon trying to understand the interaction between political and economic forces in the determination of aggregate economic policy. The concern is largely with modern industrial countries, though developing countries are not excluded. The topics of interest, however, are not generally relevant in centrally planned economics. Two distinct strands form the core of political economics; they can best be identified in the form of two questions. First, in what way does the state of the economy influence the electoral popularity of elected governments? Second, to what extent does the fact that economic policy is made by politicians (rather than by neutral technocrats) influence the kinds of economic policies that emerge?

While both of these questions are the subject of considerable debate the first of them is certainly the less controversial, probably because it is the more specific. It would be widely agreed that success in terms of economic policy will increase the popularity of a government and increase its chances of re-election. However, it is a central part of the method of modern political economics that hypotheses should be explicitly formulated and tested against data. Accordingly a long literature has emerged which tries to explain the popularity of governments (or electoral performance) as being determined by major economic indicators such as inflation, un-employment, balance of payments, rate of growth of real income per head, and so forth.

The statistical relationship between popularity and the economy is known as a *popularity function*. Many attempts have been made to estimate popularity functions, but these relationships appear to be very unstable. For example, the impact upon popularity of a 1. per cent increase in unemployment in the 1960s appears to be very different from the impact of the same increase in the 1980s. Furthermore the significance of the balance of payments has changed since the advent of floating exchange rates, so while it is usually possible to explain popularity over a specific period by reference to economic data it has proved difficult to discover stable relationships which are robust enough to *forecast* the impact upon popularity of future economic changes. Theoretical debates associated with the search for popularity functions have considered issues such as whether popularity should depend upon the past performance of governments or

whether expectations of future performance are more important. Another central issue is the extent to which the state of the economy is seen to be a result of government policy as opposed to the outcome of uncontrollable forces such as the world economy or the price of oil.

The second major strand in political economics is the influence of political factors on the formation of economic policy. Political factors can influence economic policy in a potentially large number of ways. Political economics is concerned mainly with influences upon the aggregate economy or upon macro-economic policy. The best known hypothesis in this field is that of the political business cycle, according to which governments attempt to generate boom conditions in the run-up to an election in order to increase their popularity and improve their chances of re-election.

Though the presence of a political business cycle is widely believed, the evidence for it is remarkably weak. One reason for this may be that the tactics can only pay off if the electorate can be fooled in the short run: it is unlikely that it could be fooled repeatedly. In any event, if the popularity function is not stable there is no guarantee that the boom will influence re-election chances.

An alternative form of political business cycle is based upon the fulfilment of commit-ments in the early years of a government. A newly elected party may have to pay off its supporters in terms of manifesto pledges. Eventually economic realism may take over and the government indulges in a U-turn. This is especially true if it has promised major spending programmes without planning too carefully how it will pay for them. In any event changes of government will involve swings in economic policy that are unlikely to be generally beneficial.

Another major line of research involves the question of whether the ideological complexion of the party of government significantly influences the macro-policy goals which are adopted. This question has been the basis of many international comparative studies fol-lowing the pioneering work of Douglas Hibbs of Harvard University. Hibbs tested the hypothesis that left-of-centre parties are

453

concerned with unemployment and right-of-centre parties are concerned with inflation. The evidence appears to be broadly consistent with this view. This evidence should not be taken as in any sense predictive of what will happen in the future, but it does indicate that party changes in government are likely to lead to swings in economic policy goals.

Political economics can therefore be seen as a line of enquiry which uses modern statistical and econometric techniques to test hypotheses about the interaction of the economy and the polity. Given this imperative of confronting hypotheses with data it is almost wholly free of the ideological overtones which are associated with the more traditional term political economy.   KAC

Reading

Alt, J.E. and Chrystal, K.A.: *Political Economics*. Brighton, Sussex: Wheatsheaf and University of California Press, 1983.

Hibbs, D.A. Jr. and Fassbender, H. eds: *Contemporary Political Economy*. Amsterdam: North Holland, 1981.

Mosley, P.: *The Making of Economic Policy*. Brighton, Sussex: Wheatsheaf, 1984.

political education   This should be distinguished from political indoctrination. Indoctrination aims at promoting belief in doctrine or ideology irrespective of any critical discussion of the validity of evidence. Hence political education is attached to ideas of tolerance and free discussion. Walter Bagehot spoke of 'the political education given by Parliament to the whole nation'; however, the phrase is now used in a narrower but more precise sense – as an essential part of secondary or pre-adult education. In most countries of Western Europe and in the USA it is a compulsory part of school curricula; in Britain it was long resisted, being either speciously thought to be implicit in the whole character of a school or else nervously thought to be inevitably political in the sense of partisan.

In recent years a movement has got under way in Britain to remedy gross political ignorance among young people and to fit them for citizenship. A Politics Association of teachers of the subject was founded in 1970.

About forty per cent of schools now have some significant political education, and it is a medium size not a small, General Certificate of Education examination subject. There are no national or state guidelines as in the Federal Republic of Germany or in each of the United States, but in 1978 the Department of Education and Science published an advisory paper, 'Political Competence', and appointed an advisory inspector in the subject. In the same year the Hansard Society published a report that made 'political literacy' a widely shared objective: the values, knowledge and skills that people need to be effective in the adult world of citizenship. People can be politically literate with remarkably little formal knowledge while many learned people can be politically illiterate. Most school examination syllabuses now ask for an empathetic understanding of issues and ideas as well as for knowledge of institutional structures.

BRC

Reading

Brennan, T.: *Political Education and Democracy*. Cambridge: Cambridge University Press, 1981.

Crick, B. and Porter, A.: *Political Education and Political Literacy*. London: Longman, 1968.

———— and Heater, D.: *Essays in Political Education*. Brighton, Sussex: Falmer, 1977.

Stradling, R., Nocter, M., and Baines, B.: *Teaching Controversial Issues*. London: Arnold, 1984.

political finance   The funding of political parties, leaders and candidates contending for public office and/or control of the state. The term encompasses the raising and spending of money, its sources and means of collection together with the purposes, objects and pattern of expenditure. The study of political finance entails assessments of the differential need for and availability of funds, the influence of contributors and fund-raisers on the strategies, tactics, policies and selection of contenders, and the impact of financial regulations on intra- and inter-party competition. The broad connotation of the term subsumes the monetary aspects of non-electoral or clandestine and revolutionary forms of struggle in democratic as well as authoritarian and one-party states, and the transactions of POLITICAL ACTION COMMITTEES, parallel action groups, sponsor and conveyor organizations.

In Anglo-American and European liberal democracies money is needed for effective election campaigns, the support of inter-election organizations and party infrastructures, and services to leaders and elected representatives in various branches and levels of government. The highest priority is generally placed on the campaign fund whereas organizational maintenance tends to reflect the parliamentary or extra-parliamentary orientations of the parties. The Austrian Socialist Party (Sozialistische Partei Oesterreich) on the Central European mass party model maintains a complex web of educational, research, women's, youth, sports, recreational and quasi-commercial bodies resting on the dues paid by a membership of hundreds of thousands. This pattern has been widely emulated notably by the more totalistic parties of the extreme left and right, in contradistinction to both the skeletal inter-election structures of the classical European and Canadian liberal and conservative cadre parties, and the highly personalized candidate orientation of the American electoral process where campaign needs, including lengthy and burdensome primary contests for the nomination, pre-empt the satisfaction of other demands. By contrast British election law, which strictly limits local candidate spending, fosters expenditure on organization, intra-party communications and central office publicity during the run-up to the formal campaign period.

The dilution of ideological commitments and the communications revolution have altered the pattern of campaign expenditures and sharply escalated the need for funds in western democracies. The move from closed membership to open consensual voters' parties has lessened the stress on the mobilization of ideologically committed sectors of the electorate in favour of the projection of leader, party and candidate images through the mass media. Expenditures on rallies of the faithful and a party-subsidized press have given way to paid advertising by way of the print media, posters and billboards, personalized direct mail produced by computer, and radio and television announcements and spots where broadcasting time is available for sale as in the United States, Canada, Australia, Japan and the European *postes périphériques*. The political consultant, pollster and advertising agency purchasable at a price have displaced the full-time party official and backroom operative and eroded the role of the traditional volunteer militant and activist. The candidate orientation of American electoral politics has been most conducive to commercial marketing techniques but no western-type democracy has been spared its impact on costs.

In most democracies the bulk of the money required has come from interest groups and business corporations, notably the peak industrial trade associations, trade unions and special conveyor or sponsor groups; American political action committees (PACs) are the most recent and prominent of such conduits for election funds. Traditionally, European and Commonwealth social democratic and labour parties were supported from periodic dues systematically assessed on their membership; such resources however provide a diminishing share of the monetary requirements of the Canadian New Democratic Party, the British Labour Party and the German and Scandinavian Social Democrats who depend increasingly on direct assistance from trade unions. Likewise individual donations to liberal, centre, conservative and right-wing parties have declined in significance in contrast to financial assistance from organized business. The recent Flick Affair in West Germany and the American Congressional revelations of the transfers to Italian, Japanese and other parties and politicians by US-owned multi-national corporations and *sub rosa* payments by the Central Intelligence Agency to Italian and other parties bespeak the diminished role of individual gifts in party war chests as well as the influence of foreign donors on the internal affairs of states. Such activities have their parallel in the purported Soviet support of Communist parties abroad and the documented evidence of sums provided to fraternal political groups by the West German party foundations (Stiftungen) and the American AFL/CIO (American Federation of Labour and Congress of

Industrial Organisation) in southern Europe, Africa and Latin America. Financial anxieties, together with organizational concerns, have also led parties to found commercial subsidiaries, travel agencies, trading companies, retail outlets and banking operations, a share of whose profits is allocated to the political work of the parent parties. Such institutions have been established by social democratic and communist parties in Scandinavia, Italy, Israel and France; noteworthy examples are the Bank für Gemeinwirtschaft and the Sparkasse controlled by the West German and Austrian socialists respectively.

Continuing shortages and the growing threat of scandal have encouraged recourse to the public treasury and the acceptance by political competitors of a modicum of statutory control of their financial operations. Incumbents have usually been able to exploit the benefits of office in their electoral interests through the macing of government employees, toll-gating, and kickbacks from the beneficiaries of governmental contracts, concessions, and patronage. These very abuses prompted Puerto Rico in 1957 and Quebec in 1963 to pioneer in the adoption of public subsidies; similar measures followed in more than a score of democracies in the past quarter century. The initiative has not been confined to government parties of one particular stripe. Based on a fixed or variable amount per parliamentary seat held, or the number and proportion of votes gained at an election, subventions for parties or candidates were introduced in West Germany by the Adenauer Christian Democrats, in Sweden by the Social Democrats, in Italy by the Christian Democrats, in Canada and its provinces by a mix of Liberal, Conservative and New Democratic governments, and most recently in Australia by the Labour Party. In the United States subsidies are confined to the race for the presidency. Parallel efforts have been made to stimulate individual giving in small amounts through tax deductions, tax credits and the American tax check-off. Yet the main beneficiaries are the established institutionalized parties.

There is little evidence that the trend towards complex control systems involving disclosure, limits on contributions, and monetary and quantitative ceilings on the objects of expenditure has been effective in stemming the persistent rise in costs. More information is now available to the public and a measure of equity has been introduced, but it appears that the liberal dream of equal chances for all has yet to be achieved.

See also CADRE PARTY; MASS MEMBERSHIP PARTY. KZP

Reading

Alexander, H.E.: *Financing Politics: money, elections and political reform.* 2nd edn. Washington, DC: Congressional Quarterly Press, 1980.

———: ed.: *Political Finance.* Beverly Hills, Calif. and London: Sage, 1979.

Campana, A.: *L'Argent secret: le financement des partis politiques.* Paris: Arthaud, 1976.

Malbin, M.J. ed.: *Parties, Interest Groups and Campaign Finance Laws.* Washington, DC: American Enterprise Institute, 1980.

Paltiel, K.Z.: Campaign finance: contrasting practices and reforms. In *Democracy at the Polls: a comparative study of competitive national elections*, pp. 138–72. ed. D. Butler, H.R. Penniman and A. Ranney. Washington, DC and London: American Enterprise Institute for Public Policy Research, 1981.

———: The control of campaign finance in Canada. In *Party Politics in Canada.* 5th edn, pp. 115–27, ed. H.G. Thorburn. Scarborough, Ont.: Prentice-Hall, 1985.

———: *Political Party Financing in Canada.* Toronto: McGraw-Hill, 1970.

Pinto-Duschinsky, M.: *British Political Finance 1830–1980.* Washington, DC: American Enterprise Institute, 1981.

political generations Broadly, a political community based on common experiences during the formative years of those born at about the same time. Whether a political generation is created among those with common birth dates depends on their experiences during their politically formative years, from about seventeen years of age to about twenty-five years. These years include, at least in modern western society, such personal landmarks as entry into the work-force, higher education, military conscription, and first marriage, all symbols of movement from childhood to a larger social setting. Childhood may be crucial in personality formation, but lifelong political beliefs are more likely to be acquired by those becoming adults. After young adulthood ends, new experiences will be accepted or rejected on the basis of their congruence with previously formed political beliefs.

Some large-scale social events, such as wars, economic depressions or inflations, and political changes which may amount to revolutions, are so important as to mould the political beliefs of many, sometimes most, of those in their formative years during these events. Since such decisive events occur irregularly, the frequency with which political generations are created is irregular, without a predictable pattern. The number of political generations co-existing (not always peacefully) at any given moment fluctuates, essentially as a function of the rate of social change. The faster this rate, the more frequently will a new political generation be created. Therefore the common assumption that there are only two generations in politics at any given moment is mistaken. Also mistaken is the assumption that every younger political generation is more progressive than every older political generation. For any new political generation being created, beliefs of older political generations will be irrelevant rather than objects of agreement or disagreement.

Some large-scale social events (such as the American Civil War, the Dreyfus Affair in France, the 1923 German inflation) mould the political beliefs of young adults in only one nation; others (such as the first and second world wars) operate in a cross-national context. The first world war, for instance, created a European war generation, not confined to one nation, if essentially confined to Europe. Some survivors of 1914–18 reacted to their war experience by becoming apolitical because they saw politics as having caused and continued the war; others reacted with a militant embrace of their war experience (this group included almost the entire eventual leadership of the National Socialist Party in Germany; see NAZISM); still others determined to prevent another such war by collective security (in the

League of Nations or, later, the United Nations) or pacifism or even sometimes (illogically) both. These different responses (what Karl Mannheim, the pioneer student of political generations, called 'generation units') had in common the conviction that the first world war had been the central experience of their political lives, creating a community which only death could dissolve.　　MR

Reading

Heberle, R.: *Social Movements: an introduction to political sociology*, pp. 118–27. New York: Appleton-Century-Crofts, 1951.

Mannheim, K.: *Essays on the Sociology of Knowledge*, pp. 276–320. London: Routledge & Kegan Paul, 1952.

Neumann, S.: *Permanent Revolution: totalitarianism in the age of international civil war*, pp. 230–56. New York: Praeger, 1965.

Rintala, M.: *The Constitution of Silence: essays on generational themes*. London: Greenwood, 1979.

Treves, R.: Il fascismo e il problema delle generazioni. *Quaderni di sociologia* (April/June 1964) 119–147.

Wohl, R.: *The Generation of 1914*. London: Weidenfeld & Nicolson, 1980.

Zeitlin, M.: *Revolutionary Politics and the Cuban Working Class*, pp. 211–41. New York: Harper & Row, 1970.

political geography This has been a recognized subdivision of geographical study since about 1900. It embraces a diversity of political institutions endowed with basic spatial content such as boundaries (between and within nations), territory, capital cities, the national state, land power and sea power. What influence have geographical factors had on politics and political institutions? This question has been at the heart of political geography, and the popular saying that 'the limits of his constituency are the limits of a politician's wisdom' emphasizes the importance of boundaries and of location.

The oldest discussion in western culture of geographical factors in politics is to be found in PLATO (*Laws*, Bks 4 and 5) and ARISTOTLE (*Politics*, Bk. 7); the debate on the ideal *polis* stresses size and organization of territory and its relationship to the sea. These characteristics of the state, and the role of maritime interests, are still among the major concerns of the founders of modern political geography, namely, Friedrich Ratzel in Germany and Halford Mackinder in Britain. The latter originated the concept, influential to this day, of the *Heartland* to designate the large land area controlled by Russia in Eurasia – a natural fortress that seemed immune to the sea power and trade more developed by Great Britain and the western powers. After 1917 political ideologies added to the opposition between East and West; and after 1945 air power and rocketry appeared to have devalued the land-sea dichotomy without, however, eliminating the significance of Heartland in terms of mass and capability for self-sufficiency and isolation. The concept of super powers is certainly related to the possession of a large land mass with adequate population.

The debate about an open or closed national system, symbolized by the relationship to the sea in the past, remains very much alive in modern political geography, and has been closely related to national culture and policy. Started by Plato on the philosophical level, and recurring in Chinese political history, it was traditional among French writers such as J. Bodin, MONTESQUIEU and TOCQUEVILLE, and further developed in France during the first half of this century with the work of André SIEGFRIED and Albert Demangeon who emphasized the relative decline of Europe and the rise of American supremacy; their political analysis stressed economic resources.

The years 1920–38 saw rapid developments in political geography, especially in Europe and the United States. At that time nations that claimed to be 'Have-nots' in terms of land and resources opposed the 'Haves'. Germany saw the birth of the new *Geopolitik* school directed by Karl Haushofer, which expressed the need to commit geography to a political aim – in their case, Germany's expansion from its 'central' and 'too crowded' position in Europe. German *Geopolitik* was too obviously biased to obtain scholarly credit, and the reputation of political geography suffered as a result. The term 'GEOPOLITICS' was avoided for some time after 1945. Being convenient, it has recently reappeared notably in the writings of Henry Kissinger.

Boundaries and border regions have long been a prime concern of geographers, who have worked on these problems with multi-disciplinary teams comprising politicians, jurists and students of politics and strategy. Sovereignty and jurisdiction must be defined spatially, which calls for full knowledge of the physical and human geography of the areas involved. The proliferation of national states on the one hand, and the rise of regionalisms and the spread of federal structures on the other, have multiplied all sorts of boundary disputes at various scales. The space at stake is now three-dimensional, having extended to the depths of the oceans and the air space above land and territorial seas. New concepts and institutions are arising in the field of political geography. The State Department in Washington DC has established and expanded an Office of the Geographer, working mainly on boundary problems and the law of the sea. The International Political Science Association has since 1976 had a research committee on political geography. The delimitation and analysis of political spatial units within nations increasingly claim the attention of geographers. These relate to the jurisdiction of regional or local governments and to electoral re-districting. Physical features and human regional characteristics must be accounted for. In the contemporary world, rapid socio-economic change and widespread migrations cause a need for frequent revision. In its famous decision in *Reynolds* v. *Sims* (15 June 1974), the US Supreme Court stated that 'legislators represent people, not acres or trees'. In a related minority opinion Justice Potter Stewart observed that 'legislators do not represent faceless numbers. They represent people . . . with identifiable needs and interests . . . which can often be related to geographical districting'. The implied dilemma underscores an old conflict built into both politics and geography.

In a rapidly changing world the field of political geography evolves and expands constantly. New trends have appeared in the last twenty years, tying scholarship to political ideology: there is now a 'Marxist geography' and a 'radical geography', while Soviet geographers accuse the Americans of reviving the anti-Soviet Geopolitik of the 1930s. Political geography strives to avoid these pitfalls and to preserve independent scholarship in a field replete with political conflicts and debate.   JG

Reading

Blij, H.J. de: *Systematic Political Geography*. 2nd edn. New York and Chichester: Wiley, 1973.

Gottmann, J.: *The Significance of Territory*. Charlottesville: University Press of Virginia, 1973.

———— and Laponce, J.A. eds: Politics and geography. *International Political Science Review*, Vol. I. Beverly Hills, Calif.: Sage, 1980.

Jackson, W.A.D. ed.: *Politics and Geographic relationships: readings on the nature of political geography*. New York: Prentice-Hall, 1964.

Pounds, N.J.G.: *Political Geography*. 2nd edn. New York and London: McGraw-Hill, 1972.

Soja, E.W.: *The Political Organization of Space*. Washington, DC: Association of American Geographers, 1971.

political influence The general term 'influence' is defined by Banfield (1961, p. 3) as 'the ability to get others to act, think, or feel as one intends'. In political life such influence may be exercised either by individuals or by groups. The holders of power clearly have influence, whether they are absolute monarchs, dictators, constitutional governments, or revolutionary assemblies; so too may philosophers, social thinkers, demagogues, charismatic leaders, wealthy individuals and families, parties, social movements, pressure groups, trade unions, professional associations, and the mass media.

Political influence is difficult to study empirically in a systematic way, since part of it occurs 'behind the scenes', and even where it is more or less public its extent and intensity cannot easily be measured. Nevertheless, some general statements about its nature can be formulated. First, it is evident that the forms and channels of influence will vary from one type of political system to another. In modern democracies, for example, there is a considerable number and diversity of individuals and groups possessing some kind of influence, as well as competition between opposing currents of influence. Second, there are distinct types of influence, ranging from the fairly precise and mainly public activities of specific pressure groups to the quite diffuse influence that may result from the work of intellectuals (for example the *philosophes*, the Fabians, the Frankfurt School, and various modern 'think tanks'). Third, there are considerable differences, closely related to the distribution of economic resources, among individuals and groups in the extent of their effective influence in political life. Much of the research that bears upon political influence has been done in connection with studies of pressure groups or the mass media, but Banfield's (1961) study of Chicago provides a good account of a variety of influences at work in a particular community. (See also INTEREST GROUPS; POWER; PROPAGANDA.)   TBB

Reading

Banfield, E.D.: *Political Influence*. New York: Free Press of Glencoe, 1961.

political integration The combination of political parts into a whole. While the political parts need not in principle be geographically defined, the term is usually applied to the integration of independent states. Usage has been less clearcut with respect to the whole which integration produces: its tightest definition is as a state into which two or more states are integrated. Against an historical background of conquest and empire, a process of voluntary union has emerged, whether as a unitary state, such as the Union between England and Scotland (1707), or a federal state (see FEDERALISM), such as the United States of America (1789) or Switzerland (1848). Such unions tend to be preceded by a period of CONFEDERATION, so that even under the tightest definition of the whole, the establishment of a confederal system may be seen as part of a process of political integration. The term is less often applied to the development of closer international links, unless these are being considered in the perspective of the establishment of a confederal or federal union.

In contemporary literature the paradigm for political integration has been the EUROPEAN COMMUNITY. Robert Schuman, the French Foreign Minister, launching the European Coal and Steel Community in May 1950, called it 'the first concrete foundation of a European federation': that is, a stage in a process of political integration with a federal end. The founder of the neo-functionalist school saw political integration as a 'process whereby political actors in several distinct national settings are persuaded to shift their loyalties, expectations and political activities towards a new centre, whose institutions possess or demand jurisdiction over the pre-existing national states' (Haas, p. 16). The attention of neo-functionalists became focused on the behaviour of political actors rather than on the institutions which they were creating or within which they were acting. Neo-functionalists were more concerned about political institutions than were functionalists, or pluralists who related integration not to institutions but to 'dependable expectations of peaceful change' (Deutsch et al., p. 5). But the neo-functionalists' focus drew attention away from the conflict between the jurisdiction of the new institutions and the sovereignty of the member states. This conflict blocked any decisive transfer of powers to the EC institutions after the rise of GAULLIST policy in the 1960s; and the lack of movement towards union induced a hiatus in the literature on political integration. The term is, however, likely to remain useful if political integration is seen as a response to a secular growth of international interdependence; such a view has been reflected in a renewal of proposals for European Union and a continued interest in integration plans elsewhere in the world.

JP

Reading

Deutsch, K.W. et al.: *Political Community in the North Atlantic Area: international organisation in the light of historical experience*. Princeton, NJ: Princeton University Press, 1957.

Etzioni, A.: *Political Unification: a comparative study of leaders and forces*. New York: Holt, Rinehart & Winston, 1965.

Forsyth, M.: *Unions of States: the theory and practice of confederation*. Leicester: Leicester University Press, 1981.

Haas, E.: *The Uniting of Europe: political, social and economic forces 1950–1957*. London: Stevens, 1958.

Lindberg, L:N. and Scheingold, S.A.: *Europe's Would-be Polity: patterns of change in the European Community*. Englewood Cliffs, NJ: Prentice-Hall, 1970.

Pentland, C.: *International Theory and European Integration*. London: Faber & Faber, 1973.

political myth In common usage, this is simply an erroneous political belief subscribed to by someone else, but in its more precise (and less pejorative) sense, it is a story told for the purpose of supporting or expressing a political claim, principle or point of view.

Most political myths fall into one of two main groups: foundation myths and eschatological myths. A foundation myth tells the story of how a particular political order was founded, and it generally serves to give support and legitimacy to the status quo; the Spartan myth of the Heraclids and the Roman myths of Aeneas and Romulus are examples. Eschatological myths, by contrast, tell the story of how a new political order is to be established in the future, and their purpose is to stiffen the resolve of oppressed groups in their opposition to the status quo. Christian millennialist myths are cases in point, so are certain secular doctrines such as the Marxist doctrine of the proletarian revolution. (In his *Reflections on Violence*, SOREL used 'political myth' to mean myths of this kind only.)

A political myth (unlike a parable or a fable) must be presented, and accepted, as a true narrative of events. The impartial observer may at times find the narrative fanciful but if a political myth is to be effective it must be based, either wholly or in part, on what the myth-maker and his audience believe to be hard historical fact. And as often as not it is so based. The Norman Conquest, the American War of Independence, and the Great Trek of the Afrikaaners are undoubtedly historical events; yet they have all been made the subject of powerful political myths.

In addition to being accepted as true, the events described in a political myth must hang together as a story. They must follow one another so as to form a plot and they must lead to a dramatically satisfactory conclusion. Most political myths trade on the same dramatic theme, namely that of exile and return, loss and recovery, a theme which, with its implication of an injustice set right, lends itself particularly well to the expression of political claims.

Finally, a political myth always addresses the practical problems and aspirations of a specific group or community – if only because, as a story, it deals not in abstract principles and universal truths but in concrete events. The myth of the Norman Yoke is concerned not with civil rights in general, but only with the rights of Englishmen; the myth of the Heraclids vindicates not every claim to hegemony, but only the Spartan claim to hegemony in the Peloponnese. In short, political myths are allegedly true stories, the practical significance of which is limited to the communities to which they belong.   HT

Reading

Cohn, N.: *The Pursuit of the Millennium*. London: Paladin, 1970.

Galinsky, G.K.: *Aeneas, Sicily and Rome*. Princeton, NJ: Princeton University Press, 1969.

Sorel, G.E.: *Reflections on Violence*, trans. T.E. Hulme and J. Roth. New York and London: Macmillan, 1950.

Tudor, H.: *Political Myth*. London: Pall Mall, 1972.

political participation   The act of taking part in the formulation, passage or implementation of public policies. This broad definition applies to the activities of any person, whether an elected politician, a government official or an ordinary citizen, who is active in any way in the production of policy within any type of political system. It is not part of the definition that political participants must be successful or effective in affecting public policy although their actions might be expected to have more than a purely symbolic function. Some scholars would add that participation must be voluntary to be genuine.

Participation is a central concept in both the theoretical and empirical study of politics. It has played a particularly important part in analyses of DEMOCRACY. Theories of democracy may be divided into those which emphasize citizen participation and those which limit it. Participatory democrats, including ROUSSEAU, J. S. MILL or in recent years Pateman and Barber, advocate maximizing the opportunities for ordinary citizens to take part directly in the making of political decisions. In modern large-scale states this would involve decentralization of many decisions to local communities or extensive use of the REFERENDUM to determine policies. By contrast those who, like SCHUMPETER, favour a more limited citizen participation argue that there should be a division of political labour between the elected professional politician who has responsibility for taking policy decisions and the ordinary citizen whose role is to elect or reject the politicians and their parties at periodic elections. On this view modern democracy is government by the politician and the participation of the ordinary citizen is restricted and intermittent.

Citizen participation, when it is defended, is usually justified on instrumental, developmental or communitarian grounds. Instrumental participation is aimed at promoting or defending the interests of the participant. Whether persons participate will depend upon an assessment of the anticipated benefits and costs, and of their power to attain their objectives. Developmental or educative notions suppose that the process of participation may extend the participants' general moral, social and political awareness. A communitarian view justifies participation by its contribution to the common good.

Most empirical studies of political participation have assumed that is is basically instrumental in character. It was long assumed that voting behaviour constituted the core element in political participation since it was the one form of political action in which the mass of citizens engaged. Participants were placed in a hierarchy according to whether they did or did not vote and whether they took part in other forms of activity particularly associated with party campaigning. Citizens were divided into the 'apathetic' who were largely outside the political process, the 'spectators' who were only minimally involved, and the small group of 'gladiators' who were active in several ways. Subsequent survey-based research, led by Verba and Nie, has replaced this view with a multi-dimensional interpretation. Participation is shown to comprise a number of 'modes', notably voting, party campaigning, communal activity (involving working with others for some community objective) and contacting a representative or official about a particular personal matter. These modes were found to exist in a number of contrasting countries, but only a small group of people were active in all these different ways. Instead, apart from the totally inactive section of the population, people tend to concentrate on one manner of action. Those deeply involved in community work may not engage in party campaigning. Those who contact officials on personal matters may have little or no involvement in other forms of action.

There are rival explanations for these differing patterns of participation. Psychological approaches point to differences in personal orientation in terms of political interest, a sense of political effectiveness, a readiness to be involved in conflict, as opposed to a preference for co-operative activity, and a sense of civic-mindedness. Utilitarian theories explain differences by reference to a calculation of the expected benefits and costs of the different modes of participation. The common finding that a person with higher social status and education participates more in politics may therefore be explained either by their more positive orientation to politics and greater knowledge of its operations or by their calculation that their economic and social power can also be effectively employed to gain political advantages. Organizations such as political parties, TRADE UNIONS and INTEREST GROUPS can, however, draw into politics people who might otherwise not participate on an individual basis and have been shown by Verba, Nie, and Kim to modify significantly the association between social class and participation in different countries.

Protest activities, including petitioning, marches, boycotts, rent strikes and even political violence, can be regarded as forms of political participation. Although few people in the liberal democracies take part in or support political acts involving violence, research suggests that many regard milder types of direct action as supplementary to conventional political action rather than as alternatives.

The effectiveness of citizen participation is essential to understanding democratic politics in particular but has proved difficult to measure. It involves the study of the responsiveness of ELITES to the various modes of action. Elites may, for example, vary in their readiness to listen to pressure groups or to protest marches. Research in liberal democracies has suggested that participation can be effective in shaping elite attitudes even though the participants are not themselves a representative group of the population.

Studies of political participation have tended to concentrate on the liberal democracies, but have also been made of developing countries and of communist states. Researchers on developing countries have discussed how far a relatively rapid growth in political participation coupled with weak political organizations has resulted in political instability. In communist systems citizen participation is concerned not so much with shaping decision making, which is in the hands of a restricted group, as with communicating problems to the leadership, raising complaints about services and administering some services at the neighbourhood level. There are also opportunities to participate in organizations such as trade unions and youth organizations as well as in the Communist Party, although some critics would interpret these as instances of political mobilization involving control from above, rather than as genuine participation. GBP

Reading

Barber, B.: *Strong Democracy: participatory politics for a new age*. Berkeley, London and Los Angeles: University of California Press, 1984.

Barnes, S. and Kaase, M. et al.: *Political Action: mass participation in five western democracies*. Beverly Hills, Calif. and London: Sage, 1979.

Hough, J.F. and Fainsod, M.: *How the Soviet Union is Governed*, ch. 9. Cambridge, Mass. and London: Harvard University Press, 1979.

Huntington, S.P.: *Political Order in Changing Societies*. New Haven, Conn. and London: Yale University Press, 1968.

Milbrath, L.W.: *Political Participation*. Chicago: Rand McNally, 1965.

Parry, G. ed.: *Participation in Politics*. Manchester: Manchester University Press; Totowa, NJ: Rowman and Littlefield, 1972.

Pateman, C.: *Participation and Democratic Theory*. Cambridge: Cambridge University Press, 1970.

Verba, S. and Nie, N.H.: *Participation in America: political democracy and social equality*. New York: Harper & Row, 1972.

————, Nie, N.H. and Kim, J.O.: *Participation and Political Equality: a seven nation comparison*. Cambridge and New York: Cambridge University Press, 1978.

political power In the social science literature there are a number of definitions of the concept of power. It is possible to classify these into ten major groups (Lane and Stenlund 1984). The basis of the classification is the occurrence of different key words in the definitions: causality, intention, conflict, sanction, influence, prevention, utility, punishment, dependence, decisiveness or pivotal. It cannot be claimed that power is a special word to any of the social sciences, although it has been claimed that it is at the heart of political science. Today the qualification of political, economic or social power seems to be accepted. One may distinguish between two distinctive modes of defining power: the causal and decision approaches.

The causal approach
Power is interpreted as basically a causal relation, that is as social causality. It is argued that a measure of causation also measures power. In a general sense path analysis provides measures of causal effect. According to one interpretation coefficients from path analysis may be used to measure power (Nagel 1975). An actor's power is indicated by appropriate path measures of the causal effect of his action *i*. The standard path equation reads:

$$r_{jj} = \Sigma_i d_j^2 + 2 \Sigma_{ik} d_{ij} d_{jk} r_{ik} + d_{jj}^2 = 1$$
$$i = k$$

where *i* and *k* stand for the variables that affect the *j* variable. Since r_{jj} is equivalent to the variance of the explained *j* variable (s_j^2) we have

$$s_j^2 = 1 = \Sigma_i d_{ji}^2 + d_{jj}^2$$

for the case when exogenous variables explaining *j* are uncorrelated ($r_{ik}=0$); the squared path coefficient d_{ji}^2 measures the amount of explained variation in *j* by variable *i* and consequently it measures the power of action *i*. The causal approach may be developed by placing restrictions on the variables that are allowed to be included. It may be argued that only intended actions are to be permitted, or actions involving sanctions or persuasion. The causal approach therefore includes a wide number of interpretations of the concept of power where causality may only be a first step in identifying power. Additional properties such as the use or threat of sanctions or the employment of force distinguish power from other social relations that also include causality.

According to one interpretation (Dahl 1957) the concept of power covers the fundamentals of a number of quasi-synonyms: INFLUENCE, authority, and control. Against the causal interpretation it has been objected that it is impossible to estimate stable power measures because of the differential way that power may be activated and depleted (March 1966). It has also been argued that the causal interpretation is open to the Santa Claus argument and fails to recognize power by anticipation. Some claim that the concept of power is more of a structural concept than an action concept (Lukes 1974); others go further claiming that the concept is an essentially contested one or inapplicable (Riker 1964). The causal approach to power may cover so-called non-issues or the mobilization of bias (Bachrach and Baratz 1970; Gaventa 1980).

The decision approach
The power indices are based on the notion of a swing or the ability to change the outcome by changing the vote (Stenlund and Lane 1984). The power index assumes that the power of an entity *i* is a function of the number of times in which *i* is in the position of making a swing in formal voting contexts. It should be pointed out that the power index only has meaning in a formalized voting context in which it is clear which players are involved,

what the weights of the players are, and what the decision rule states.

Let $V = v_1, v_2, \ldots v_N$ be a set of voters where the number of voters is N. To each voter i there is assigned a natural number w_i or the number of votes of voter i and where $w_i \geq 1$. A voting procedure is futhermore characterized by a *decision rule* saying that if $\Sigma w_i \geq d$ then a proposal is passed, otherwise not. The choice of d specifies the decision rule; a majority decision rule implies that $d = \Sigma w_i/2 + 1$ if Σw_i is even or $d = \Sigma(w_i + 1)/2$ if Σw_i is odd. With N voters there are 2^N subsets of the set V in which there are two groups of which one is supporting a proposal and the other is opposing it, calling such a group supporting (or opposing) a proposal a coalition. W denotes the set of those coalitions that are winning – that is, such coalitions where $\Sigma w_i \geq d$; $\overline{W}$ is then the set of all losing coalitions (where $\Sigma w_i < d$). Let S be a coalition; by the *characteristic function* of S is meant a function δ such as

$$\delta(S) = \begin{array}{l} 1 \text{ if } S \, \varepsilon \, W \\ 0 \text{ if } S \, \varepsilon \, \overline{W} \end{array}$$

We are now ready to define an index of power of the voters in V.

Definition: The power of voter i in V is

$$POW_i = \mathop{\Sigma}\limits_{\substack{i\varepsilon S \\ S\varepsilon W}} R_1(S) [\delta(S) - \delta(S - i)]$$

$$+ \mathop{\Sigma}\limits_{\substack{i\varepsilon S \\ S\varepsilon\overline{W}}} R_2(S) [\delta(S + i) - \delta(S)]$$

where $R_1(.)$ and $R_2(.)$ are functions defined on the set of coalitions. The first part is based on the number of coalitions S in which i is a member and that are swinging from winning to losing when i is leaving the coalition. The second part counts the number of coalitions S that change from losing to winning when i is joining the coalition. By choosing $R_1(.)$ and $R_2(.)$ in specific ways we get the well-known power indices.

The power indices based on a decision interpretation of the concept of power, share one common property and they are different in terms of another property. These indices

(Shapley and Shubik 1954; Banzhaf 1966; Coleman 1971) start from the so-called characteristic function of a game, describing the outcome of each coalition S by means of a function δ having the values one and zero, corresponding to pass and fail. The basic formula in each index is $\delta(S) - \delta(S-i)$, where the power of the voting unit is his differential contribution to the coalition S. We then have

$$POW_i = \mathop{\Sigma}\limits_{\substack{ScN \\ i\varepsilon S}} P(S)(\delta(S) - \delta(S - i))$$

The differences between the indices concern the interpretation of $P(S)$. What is critical in the power indices is the assumption that each possible coalition is equally probable. If one wants to know what voting units are decisive in a set of issues it is necessary to study not simply the formal constitutional rules but also the actual coalitions in order to arrive at empirical estimates of $P(S)$. If certain coalitions are less probable due to ideological strife or political tactics, any index concerning decision power would have to reflect deviations from the equal probability assumption.

It is possible to define an infinite number of power indices, one index for each choice of a weight $P(S)$. The weights chosen in the power indices discussed above are in one way or the other based on considerations as to what should be regarded as equally probable. This means that the power measures are a priori in the sense that they disregard any information concerning the actual probability distribution for different conceivable coalitions. If the power indices discussed above are denoted as a set of theoretical power indices, then we should be able to calculate a set of empirical power indices based on a posteriori assumptions concerning which coalitions are probable and which are not.

J-EL

Reading

Bachrach, P. and Baratz, M.S.: *Power and Poverty: theory and practice*. New York: Oxford University Press, 1970.

Banzhaf, J. III: Multimember electoral districts: do they violate the 'one man, one vote' principle. *Yale Law Journal* 75 (1966) 1309–38.

Coleman, J.S.: Control of collectivities and the power of a collectivity to act. In *Social Choice*, ed. B. Lieberman. New York: Gordon & Breach, 1971.

Dahl, R.: The concept of power. *Behavioral Science* 2 (1957) 201–15.

Gaventa, J.: *Power and Powerlessness*. Chicago: University of Illinois Press, 1980.

Lane, J.E. and Stenlund, H.: Power. In *Social Science Concepts*, ed. G. Sartori. Beverly Hills, Calif.: Sage, 1984.

Lukes, S.: *Power: a radical view*. London: Macmillan, 1974.

March, J.G.: The power of power. In *Varieties of Political Theory*, ed. D. Easton. Englewood Cliffs, NJ: Prentice-Hall, 1966.

Nagel, J.: *The Descriptive Analysis of Power*. New Haven, Conn.: Yale University Press, 1975.

Shapley, L.S. and Shubik, M.: A method for evaluating the distribution of power in a committee system. *American Political Science Review* 48 (1954) 141–64.

Riker, W.: Some ambiguities in the notion of power. *American Political Science Review* 58 (1964) 341–9.

Stenlund, H. and Lane, J.E.: The structure of voting power indices. *Quality and Quantity* 18 (1984) 367–75.

political psychology The branch of study that explores the impact of individual personality, and of the relationships between people, on politics. Its area is potentially vast and it is not easy to determine where political psychology begins and POLITICAL BEHAVIOUR ends. For reasons of academic convenience alone it is expedient to limit the subject to the significance of psychology for political decision making, for the recruitment of political elites, and for the development of political values. Political psychology is eclectic, and different authors draw on disparate schools of psychology. The subject can accommodate work influenced by the doctrines of Freud and his disciples, and the research of behaviouralists such as H. J. Eysenck. The span of the subject is wide and its range diverse but the main focus of political psychology lies in the effects of human motivation, sometimes unconscious, and human perceptions on political consequences.

The usefulness of psychology in the study of politics is one of the most keenly disputed issues in political science. Structural factors, it is argued, such as the role constraints of the decision maker play a much larger part than psychological characteristics. Political actors who differ in temperament will respond in similar ways when faced by the same situation. This view is over-simple: it is not reality which governs people's behaviour but their perceptions of reality. Political situations are sometimes highly ambiguous; political leaders often have insufficient knowledge, or contradictory advice, and some features of a situation, such as the intentions of the counter-players, are inherently hard to assess. Faced with a complex and confusing picture of events political actors may impose their own, perhaps idiosyncratic mental pattern upon events.

POLITICAL RECRUITMENT is one of the chief themes of political psychologists. Whereas POLITICAL SOCIOLOGY is concerned with the social location of political actors – their social class, their occupation, their educational backgrounds – political psychology looks at their psychological attributes, especially their self-esteem. One tradition postulates that politics attracts, paradoxically, a disproportionate number of those low in self-esteem who suffered emotional deprivation, ridicule or other forms of ill-treatment in childhood, or failure or frustration in adult life. These individuals, it is said, are looking for compensation through the prestige and power that politics offers. Another school, in contrast, argues that politics draws to it those with high self-esteem, people who can cope with the anxieties, the setbacks and the risks of political life.

Political psychology, as the emphasis on recruitment implies, has a distinctive interest in political elites, seeking to classify political actors in ways which will make it possible to identify regularities of behaviour. Barber, for instance, categorized legislators and American presidents on two dimensions – the extent of their activity in office, and the enjoyment they derived from it. Payne, Woshinsky et al., exploring the motivation of politicians, distinguished seven 'incentive types' – such as the Status, the Adulation and the Mission.

Christie and Geis developed the notion of the 'Machiavellian Personality'. Some people seem to be natural politicians; these 'Hi-Machs' are adept at influencing and manipulating others. Single-case studies of political actors or psychobiographies explore in some depth a leader's psychological characteristics and trace the effect of these in his or her attainment and use of power. In *Woodrow Wilson and Colonel House* Alexander and Julienne George draw a fascinating picture of President Wilson, relating both his triumphs and his setbacks in the political arena to a personality shaped by bitter childhood struggles.

Some of the most well-known, if controversial, work has traced the evolution of political values to childhood conflicts. No book in the field has had such a wide and lasting influence as Adorno et al.'s seminal study *The Authoritarian Personality*, which examined the growth of ethnic prejudice and political authoritarianism. The book is notable for the way in which it sets out to validate psychodynamic hypotheses with quantitative evidence. It prompted a series of major studies (for example Rokeach's investigation of closed-mindedness) into questions which the authors had either not answered or had not adequately explored. *The Authoritarian Personality* was intended to account for the broad spread of authoritarian and ethnocentric attitudes in the American population, even though the main interest of political psychology has been with elites. The core of the subject lies nevertheless in the impact of individual personality on political outcomes. Would things have turned out differently if, say, Winston Churchill had not become prime minister in 1940? Would the second world war have occurred, or at any rate reached the scale it did, if Hitler had been killed in the first world war? In short, are political actors dispensable? Would another leader have acted differently?

Despite this emphasis, interest has grown in the collective properties of decision-making groups, attributes which have little reference to the personal strengths and weaknesses of their members. The social psychologist Irving Janis, in his innovative study *Victims of Groupthink*, explored the reasons why decision making or advisory committees composed of expert, well-informed and apparently stable individuals, sometimes made choices, culminating in disaster, without proper scrutiny of the costs and risks of the policy adopted. *Groupthink*, the tendency of committees to foster concurrence seeking at the expense of critical appraisal also throws light on the failure of intelligence services to predict and warn of enemy attacks. Research in dynamics of group decision making springs from a long tradition in experimental social psychology. Conformity to group pressures, attitude change and ways of coping with dissonant information are some of the politically relevant issues which have been investigated by social psychologists.

Political psychology stands at the intersection of politics and psychology. Its nature highlights the more general debt of political science to other disciplines.

See also POLITICAL ATTITUDES.   HBB

Reading

Adorno, T.W., Frenkel-Brunswick, E., Levinson, D.J. and Nevitt, S. eds: *The Authoritarian Personality*. New York: Wiley, 1964.

Barber, J.D.: *The Lawmakers*. New Haven, Conn.: Yale University Press, 1965.

———: *The Presidential Character*. 2nd edn. Englewood Cliffs, NJ: Prentice Hall, 1977.

Christie, R. and Geis, F.: *Studies in Machiavellianism*. New York and London: Academic Press, 1970.

Elms, A.C.: *Personality in Politics*. New York: Harcourt, Brace, Jovanovich, 1976.

Greenstein, F.I.: *Personality and Politics*. Chicago, Ill.: Markham, 1969.

Janis, I.: *Victims of Groupthink*. Boston, Mass.: Houghton-Mifflin, 1972.

Knutson, J.M. ed.: *Handbook of Political Psychology*. San Francisco: Jossey-Bass, 1973.

Lasswell, H.: *Power and Personality*. New York: Norton, 1976.

Payne, J.L., Woshinsky, O. et al.: *The Motivation of Politicians*. Chicago, Ill.: Nelson-Hall, 1984.

Sniderman, P.: *Personality and Democratic Politics*. Berkeley: University of California Press, 1975.

political recruitment The processes through which people are inducted into political roles or offices. Unless the number of places to be filled coincides exactly with the total population, an unlikely eventuality in even the smallest or most undeveloped society, political recruitment necessarily involves some method of selection. Techniques of selection are appointment, inheritance, lot or rote, more or less rigorous examination, more or less violent appropriation of office and, finally, election. Whatever the method or methods adopted in a society those selected act, or are supposed to act, on behalf of and in the interests of the larger community. It is the possibility of a disjuncture between acting on behalf of a fragment or the whole of society that underlies interest in the recruitment of political actors since, by definition, those recruited are less numerous than those represented. All extant methods of recruitment necessarily result in selecting a group of people who, along one or another dimension which is considered important, are unrepresentative of the wider population. In potential conflict with this fact is the consideration that recruitment techniques involve attempts to determine or control the behaviour of those recruited. Although rarely explicit, academic studies of political recruitment are predicated on the same interest: the relationship between recruitment – techniques and personnel – and the policies/behaviour of those selected.

Every study of the personnel outcome of political recruitment has demonstrated that in no serious sense are those recruited to political office or roles a microcosm or representative sample of the total population. However the political is defined, whether widely inclusive or narrowly exclusive, those recruited are better educated, older, usually male, wealthier, more urban than the population as a whole; they are drawn from the dominant strata of the society – and the higher up the ladder of political success, power or esteem the more this is true. Most academic studies of recruitment concentrate on how this state of affairs comes about and there is broad agreement that recruitment should be conceptualized as a continuous screening process by which some are rejected at every stage of a potential political career. Clearly, this way of examining political recruitment involves the following

considerations: (1) what is 'political', (2) what sort of people offer themselves for selection, (3) what are the structural locations of such people, and (4) does the process make any difference to policy outcome?

If the word political is narrowly defined as relating to membership of parties, legislatures, pressure groups and so on the task of data collection under headings (2) and (3) is obviously more limited than if the political is widely defined to include all those actually or potentially seeking to influence policies. The latter would include civil servants, officers in the armed forces, trade-union leaders, terrorists, rioters, and so on: this procedure, although massively swelling the data to be analysed, has the merit that the leading echelons of such groups have fairly similar SES (socio-economic status) and demographic profiles under headings (2) and (3) to those in the more narrowly defined categories. This advantage is however offset by a major analytical problem: why do people of similar background 'choose' different paths to political influence?

Those offering themselves for selection are usually categorized by their SES, gender, and demographic background, by their personal histories and/or by their psychological constitutions. Nothing under SES and demographic differentiates the politically involved from massive numbers with the same profile but uninvolved except that the former are more likely than the latter to have come from politically involved milieux. Psychologically, the politically involved may score higher than most on characteristics such as sociability, ego regression, need to achieve, sense of efficacy, etc. which could lead them to wish for a political career. On the other hand, first, the higher scores may be consequences of political involvement and, second, massive numbers of the uninvolved have the same psychological profile. Similarly, it is hard to believe that a political career is uniquely or even specially suited to those people who score high on various psychological or psychiatric scales. Studies combining structural and individual mental features are rare but the evidence, admittedly not very tight, is that they are additive. Even so, large numbers with similar

467

profiles do not consider political involvement or are unsuccessful if they do and it is this fact that underlies the theoretical importance attached to the psycho-history or analysis of successful politicians.

Since the politically recruited are not a cross section of the population the question arises, does it matter? Obviously, if significant political outcomes are the consequences of factors that no one individual or group controls, it does not matter; some are, but most are not. If policy preferences are related directly to a person's structural location then the recruiting bias is important, but research has not shown any close connection between these two factors. Similarly, most recent work on gender demonstrates that politically women and men do not differ significantly. Additionally, both Marxist and non-Marxist accounts of the origins of state policy emphasize the structural constraints that impinge on policy makers to the extent that their personal preferences may be relatively insignificant. So, although it is intuitively obvious that recruitment is important, both analysis and empirical investigation suggest that it is not as significant as is often believed – or as the massive literature on the topic suggests.

See also CANDIDATE SELECTION; GENDER AND POLITICS; REPRESENTATION.   RED

Reading

Birch, A.H.: *Representative and Responsible Government: an essay on the British constitution*. London: Allen and Unwin, 1964.

Coates, D.: *The Context of British Politics*. London: Hutchinson, 1984.

Dowse, R.E. and Hughes, J.A.: *Political Sociology*. Chichester: Wiley, 1985.

Eulau, H. and Czudnowski, M. eds: *Elite Recruitment in Democratic Politics: comparative studies across nations*. Beverly Hills, Calif.: Sage, 1976.

Iremonger, L.: *The Fiery Chariot: a study of British prime ministers and the search for love*. London: Secker & Warburg, 1970.

Prewitt, K.: *The Recruitment of Political Leaders: a study of citizen-politicians*. New York: Bobbs-Merrill, 1970.

Rush, M.: *The Selection of Parliamentary Candidates*. London: Nelson, 1969.

Stanworth, P. and Giddens, A. eds: *Elites and Power in British Society*. London: Cambridge University Press, 1974.

political science   An academic discipline which seeks to systematically describe, analyse and explain the operations of government institutions and overtly political organizations; plus all those social activities and interactions which help determine binding allocations or decisions by legitimate sources of authority; and in addition the values, views of human nature and prescriptive theories which inform debates about such institutions, decisions and allocations. This broad and eclectic scope of concerns has generally been seen as a weakness by writers attempting to define the subject's *raison d'être* or 'theoretical object' (for example, Poulantzas 1978; Akoun et al. 1979). Easton's (1968) thumbnail sketch of the discipline looked forward to the construction of a new consensus about its purposes, centring on the concept of a POLITICAL SYSTEM. This expectation has not been borne out, and in the two intervening decades political scientists have adopted more diversified approaches and defined more specialized fields of investigation than ever before. But the impression of incoherence is more apparent than real, for since the early twentieth century the major avenues of work in the discipline can consistently be grouped under three main headings: empirical analyses, political theory and the theory of the STATE.

Empirical analyses include the most basic activities of the discipline in monitoring and explaining mass POLITICAL BEHAVIOUR (for instance, electoral trends); the activities of specialized political organizations (such as political parties and interest groups); the arrangement of government institutions; the formulation of public policies; and the relations between states. In the early post-war period proponents and opponents of the 'behavioural revolution' in political science conducted a largely sterile controversy about the utility of highly quantitative versus more qualitative/descriptive methods. The crumbling of an 'institutionalist' position asserting the primacy of a legalistic or formal analysis of government machinery, was succeeded by a wave of quantitative studies which in most cases did not live up to the prospectus painted for them by enthusiastic behaviouralists. Although behavioural methods are now generally accepted as legitimate and useful, they are consequently no longer seen as defining a distinctive approach to political analysis, but rather simply one element in the discipline's toolkit. Most political scientists now accept that the only sensible approach to many explanatory problems is to use several methods of investigation to analyse different aspects of complex phenomena. Reliance on undiluted number crunching survives chiefly in isolated areas where quantitative methods were over-developed in the 1960s and 1970s (especially some types of psephology and budgetary analysis). Stylistic objections to quantification are equally confined to enclaves which the behavioural revolution never penetrated, such as the study of constitutions and public law. For the rest, modern empirical research typically involves both qualitative and quanti-tative modes of explanation, with historical investigation, institutional analysis, statistical testing, and empirical theory all deployed where they can make a contribution to under-standing.

Political theory is an ancient field of study, which has accumulated an impressive inherit-ance of major texts in the course of its evolution. In the modern period political philosophy has developed as a sub-field which explores the foundations of thinking about politics in a more systematic, analytic and logically rigorous way. All political thought is intrinsically normative, concerned with what ought to happen – with the clarification of values, the meaning of major political concepts (such as freedom, justice or equality), the composition of 'human nature', and the end-purposes of political life. But these preoccu-pations are closely and inextricably interwoven with a more properly theoretical concern, with the systematization of empirical observations of political phenomena into over-arching explanations, and with testing the logical consistency and explanatory adequacy of those theories already formulated. Again the aggress-ive empiricism characteristic of the behavioural revolution period sparked an overdrawn debate

between proponents of a 'positive' political science no longer linked to the normative concerns of earlier epochs, and those such as Wolin (1968) who saw in political theory's assigned role as documentor of 'pre-scientific' modes of thinking only the sterilization of its traditional mission.

The slow transcending of this debate has been accomplished partly by the decay of BEHAVIOURALISM as a distinctive school of thought, and partly because of the waning of post-war liberal/pluralist dominance in political science. The unexpected strength of Marxist and radical thought in the late 1960s and 1970s, and the growth of distinctive 'new right' thinking in the 1970s and 1980s, have both increased the recognition of irreconcilable value diversity underlying empirical political analysis. Many contemporary political scien-tists accept that their subject is an inherently multi-theoretical discipline – where a unified body of universally accepted laws or a single theoretical paradigm analogous to those per-taining in the natural sciences cannot emerge. This fundamental reorientation safeguards a continuing and central role for political thought and philosophy in maintaining a live debate over the values and ethics which should inform competing political theories. In addition differences in style and orientation between the study of historical political thought and empirical research have been considerably reduced by the growth of more sophisticated methodologies for textual analysis, expounding the logic of arguments, and charting the influence of ideologies and knowledge on political developments.

Theories of the state constitute the central link between empirical political science and politi-cal thought. In the early twentieth century in Germany and the USA the label *Staatstheorie* denoted a highly formalized account of the origins and purposes of government institu-tions derived from constitutional law, a sense of the term which has now lapsed. The modern conception of theories of the state is a much broader one, which includes all the most important accounts of how government insti-tutions as a whole interrelate with civil society. From the eighteenth century onwards liberal political thought tended to neglect the concept of the state, and the problem of state/society relations, focusing primary emphasis instead upon the interrelationship of individual citizens with government. The reintroduction of 'the state' into the mainstream of contemporary political science owes a great deal to the revival of Marxism as a tradition of political analysis in the late 1960s, and the more long term influence of WEBERIAN political sociology. The challenge posed by these traditions, and liberal responses to them, have brought into clearer focus some powerfully developed if partly implicit liberal theories of state, especially in PLURALIST and elite theory accounts (Alford and Friedland 1985; Dunleavy and O'Leary 1987). Much of the behavioural literature focusing on concepts such as power and decision making, or on the notion of a political system in comparative politics, in practice operates within one or other of these liberal theories of the state.

The overlap between theories of the state and political thought is constituted in the modern period chiefly by 'empirical political theory', which seeks to systematize the findings of empirical analyses and relate them to the fundamental value controversies over the purposes of government and the make-up of human nature. POLITICAL SOCIOLOGY, a subfield of political science focusing on the social context of political decision making, mass behaviour, and the composition of leadership elites, has also constituted a strong overlap between theories of the state and political thought – especially by using classic texts by Marx, Weber, Durkheim and others as starting points for analysing contemporary state/ society relations.

The overlap between theories of the state and empirical analyses is constituted by a substantial body of theory-guided research in fields as diverse as international relations, public policy studies, comparative politics and URBAN POLITICS. Of course, much empirical work in modern political science remains very descriptive. For example, some institutional analysis and much contemporary political history is justified primarily in terms of the intrinsic interest of its subject matter, rather than by its relevance for theoretical controversies. And the still thriving 'zoological' tradition in comparative politics simply collects strange stories about foreign species of political system. But in most countries the development of numerous specialized sub-fields (especially in research into national politics) has constituted a vanguard of theoretically informed empirical work, concerned to address issues of over-arching explanatory importance and closely linked to one or another of the available theories of the state.

The ageing of the conflicts between institutional and behavioural methods, and between the apostles of a 'positive' political science and defenders of normative political thought, has coincided with the strong revival of two political economy approaches closely linked with different theories of the state. The first is PUBLIC CHOICE THEORY, which essentially uses the deductive methods and some of the concepts of neo-classical economics to analyse political phenomena (Mueller 1979). Despite an initial preoccupation with first-principles reasoning similar to welfare economics and game theory, public choice theory in the last twenty years has progressively sketched an alternative view of standard political science topics – such as party competition, the interest group process, the behaviour of legislatures, the operations of bureaucracies, and the organization of sub-national governments. The second political economy approach is neo-Marxist. Especially in Western Europe the refurbishment of Marx' and Engels' thought has been considerable since the slow intellectual de-Stalinization of Western academic MARXISM began in earnest during the 1960s. Although most neo-Marxist work initially operated at the level of macro-level generalization, some more applied analysis has been produced in fields such as corporatism, the politics of industrial relations and socialist parties, and urban politics. Both public choice theory and radical political economy have strengthened the linkages between empirical analyses and normative political thought in several ways. They re-emphasize the inescapably value-laiden and theory-dependent qualities of political research. They try to make empirical findings address some of the fundamental issues about political choices raised in the classic texts of political thought.

Some public choice theory has also linked normative principles (such as advancing 'freedom') closely with politically successful 'new right' policy analysis. And while neo-Marxist work is generally more critical than prescriptive, it too has has had a modest theoretical influence upon the policies of socialist parties in Western Europe.

The emergence of theories of the state as the central linking element between political thought and empirical analyses in contemporary political science, together with the strong development of political economy approaches, have both tended to marginalize some perspectives important in earlier periods. For example, social psychological theories of politics no longer play the major role which seemed possible in the 1950s and 1960s. Some sociological approaches (such as functional theories of political development and modernization in comparative politics) have ceased to grow in influence. The distinctiveness of political sociology as a sub-field of analysis has faded dramatically, since many of its central themes are now generalized to apply to the whole terrain of political science in neo-Marxist and elite theory work. In international relations a vigorous academic momentum has been maintained, but the direction of development has been less integrated with trends in mainstream political science – although this change also reflects the strong institutional separation of the sub-discipline studying international relations in most Western countries. However, the growth of interest in international political economy is an offsetting trend. And much foreign policy analysis decodes the conduct of external relations less in terms of interactions between unitary states and more in terms of the exigencies of domestic politics and of complex decision-making games within the executive branch of government. Hence it is as relevant for 'decisional' political science as for international relations specialists (see, for example, Allison 1971).

Many other areas of political science have flourished with the new importance of the theory of the state. The neuroses of post-war political theorists about their marginalization within the discipline have been largely dis-pelled. Public policy studies have broadened out from pluralist decisional research in the 1960s to encompass systematic attention to policy outputs and budgetary analysis, a focus reinforced by the increased influence of economic methods. The influences of POLITICAL ECONOMICS have strengthened work on cross-national policy outputs (such as the post-war expansion of the welfare state in most liberal democracies, or the evidence for political-business cycles). Along with a growing literature on organizational studies, PUBLIC CHOICE THEORY and radical political economy have also contributed to the considerable reintegration of public administration into the mainstream of political science thinking. The first signs of a similar impact on other enclaves previously uninfluenced by the theory of the state are apparent in sub-fields as diverse as electoral analysis, public law, and political geography.

Discussions of the agenda for political science as a discipline have a generally poor record of spotting future trends (for examples see Akoun et al. 1979; Blondel 1976; Easton 1968; Heller 1934; Mackenzie 1967). But the recent emphasis upon the theory of the state does not look as if it will disappear quickly. Equally the current bifurcation of much intellectually vigorous political science between public choice approaches and radical political economy seems more deeply rooted in key branches of the discipline than previous trends. And the eclectic methodological approaches now accepted as valuable by most political scientists probably will not change dramatically in the near future. Even if unexpected directions of development open up, it seems unlikely that they will halt the general growth of the discipline towards a simultaneously more unified and yet intrinsically multi-theoretical field of research.   PJD

Reading

Allison, G.: *Essence of Decision: explaining the Cuban missile crisis*. Boston, Mass.: Little, Brown, 1971.

Alford, R. and Friedland, R.: *Powers of Theory: capitalism, the state and democracy*. Cambridge: Cambridge University Press, 1985.

Akoun, A. et al.: *Dictionnaire de politique: le présent en question*, pp. 245–7. Paris: Larousse, 1979.

Blondel, J.: *Thinking Politically*. Harmondsworth: Penguin, 1976.

Crick, B.: *The American Science of Politics*. London: Routledge & Kegan Paul, 1959.

Dunleavy, P.J. and O'Leary, D.B.: *Theories of the State: the politics of liberal democracy*. London: Macmillan, 1987.

Easton, D.: Political science. In *International Encyclopedia of the Social Sciences*, Vol. XII, pp. 282–98, ed. D. Sills. New York: Macmillan and Free Press, 1968.

Finifter, A.W. ed.: *Political Science: the state of the discipline*. Washington, DC: American Political Science Association, 1983.

Heller, H.: Political science. In *Encyclopedia of the Social Sciences*, Vol. III, pp. 207–24, ed. E.R. Seligman and A. Johnson. New York: Macmillan, 1934.

Mackenzie, W.J.M.: *Politics and Social Science*. Harmondsworth: Penguin, 1967.

Mueller, D.: *Public Choice*. Cambridge: Cambridge University Press, 1979.

Poulantzas, N.: *Political Power and Social Classes*, pp. 37–56. London: New Left Books/Verso, 1978.

Ricci, D.: *The Tragedy of Political Science*. New Haven, Conn.: Yale University Press, 1984.

Seidelman, R.: *Disenchanted Realists: American political science 1884–1984*. Albany, NY: State University of New York Press, 1985.

Somit, A. and Tanenhaus, J.: *The Development of American Political Science*. New York: Livingstone, 1982.

Waldo, D.: *Political Science: tradition, discipline, profession, science, enterprise. In The Handbook of Political Science*, Vol. I, ed. F.I. Greenstein and N. Polsby. Reading, Mass.: Addison-Wesley, 1975.

Wolin, S.: Political theory: trends and goals. In *International Encyclopedia of the Social Sciences*, Vol. XII, pp. 318–31, ed. D. Sills. New York: Macmillan and the Free Press, 1968.

political socialization People have no innate knowledge of political tradition or of political roles and their associated behaviours: political socialization is the process or processes by which these are acquired. The study of these processes gained considerable academic cachet in the two decades following the publication of Herbert Hyman's book *Political Socialization* (1959) when many books and articles on the subject were published. Broadly, the field was divided between adherents of systems theory and adherents of one or another of the MARXIST schools. Amongst systems theorists the successful induction of people into a national political culture was thought to be a major determinant of political stability, of democracy or authoritarianism, or whatever else was under consideration. Similarly, Marxists paid attention to the concept of ideology, false consciousness, alienation, following, usually, *The German Ideology* directly or indirectly through Antonio Gramsci's notions of hegemony.

Attention was initially focused upon the pre-adult origins – as they were asserted to be – of adult political notions and behaviour. Social scientists investigated family, school, peer and sex differences, structures and ideas, and related these to class, income, putative vote, political knowledge, sense of political efficacy and dozens of other matters thought to relate to adult behaviour. Inter-generational transmission and the more manifest and deliberate transmission (as opposed to the latent transmissions of less directed polities) of ideas and attitudes of authoritarian systems were studied. Slightly later political socialization was thought of as a life-long process with the result that more attention was paid to adults and the manner in which they respond to changing adult circumstances: adaptations such as divorce, bereavement, changes in significant aspects of social structure, migration and emigration, amongst many other factors, have been analysed.

By the mid-1970s a reaction had set in as a consequence of a number of crippling objections which have yet to be fully dealt with. A major difficulty is the nagging doubt whether inferences about future behaviour or ideas drawn from accounts taken either directly by face to face interviews or from children's answers to questionnaires have much to do with how they will act when they become adults. This is both because for many young people a political interview or questionnaire is almost meaningless and also because circumstances may change dramatically between childhood and adulthood making previous dispositions much less relevant. Recall by adults of their childhood political ideas are very likely to be inaccurate. The only solution to this difficulty is the longitudinal panel survey which is massively expensive and, necessarily, very protracted (see Himmelweit et al.). An associated difficulty is that what people think, or report themselves as thinking – either as children or as adults – does not account for political behaviour: people think Conservative and vote Labour, think racist and have to behave neutrally, are sexist and obey anti-discrimination laws. A great deal of politically relevant behaviour is not ideationally determined.

A second area of difficulty centres upon the usually unarticulated assumption that the POLITICAL CULTURE into which a person is inducted is neutral between classes. The implication of this is that – assuming ideas do shape action – people are inducted into a way of behaving that systematically supports the *status quo*. This, however, has still to be demonstrated. The Marxist notion that the 'ruling ideas of each age have ever been only the ideas of its ruling class' addressed this problem squarely and usually looked at the manner in which, historically, ruling classes disseminated their ideas among populations. However, another strand of Marxist thinking pays less attention to this, arguing that people's political behaviour is broadly conditioned by the logic of CAPITALISM or, more widely, by the constraints of a system that must needs reproduce itself.

The final difficulty concerning socialization is that it is nearly always studied by instruments – interviews, questionnaires, historical reconstructions – which are inadequate to capture the complex phenomena that constitute political life. An ethnographic approach of total immersion in a political meaning system may capture this but at the cost of being unreliable about the wider context within which the behaviour/idea is located.

RED

Reading

Dale, R. et al. eds: *Schooling and Capitalism*. London: Routledge & Kegan Paul, 1976.

Dowse, R.E.: Political socialization. In *New Trends in British Politics*, ed. D. Kavanagh and R. Rose. London: Sage, 1977.

—— and Hughes, J.A.: Pre-adult origins of adult political activity: a sour note. In *British Political Sociology Yearbook*, ed. C. Crouch. London: Croom Helm, 1977.

Easton, D. and Dennis, J.: *Children in the Political System: origins of political legitimacy*. New York: McGraw-Hill, 1969.

Gramsci, A.: *The Modern Prince and Other Writings*. London: Lawrence & Wishart, 1957.

Himmelweit, H. et al.: *How Voters Decide: a longitudinal study of political attitudes and voting extending over fifteen years*. London: Academic Press, 1981.

Hyman, H.: *Political Socialization: a study in the psychology of political behavior*. New York: Free Press, 1959.

Joyce, P.: *Work, Society and Politics*. Brighton, Sussex: Harvester, 1980.

Niemi, R., ed.: *The Politics of Future Citizens*. San Francisco: Jossey-Bass, 1974.

Volgyes, I.: *Political Socialization in Eastern Europe*. London: Praeger, 1975.

political sociology As a term political sociology has sometimes been misunderstood; it sounds like a mistake or at least a misnomer. It refers to the study of the interrelationship between social structures and political institutions, between society and politics. Political sociology lies on the boundary betweeen POLITICAL SCIENCE and sociology, and it encompasses the overlap between these two neighbouring disciplines. Although it is a young discipline it has become accepted as a genuine border field rather than a special branch of sociology or of political science. Its primary aim is to analyse the relationship between social structure and politics, not to set up a political programme of action. Political sociology is in no sense more political than other branches of sociology so why, it has been asked, not use the term sociology of politics – which moreover better corresponds to the general terminology for special branches of sociology. The answer is that there are reasons for maintaining a distinction between political sociology and the sociology of politics.

Many sociological studies are based on stratifications of one kind or another. Social phenomena of a wide variety including political behaviour are explained by social and economic factors which constitute the social structure; politics is regarded as one phenomenon among many that can be explained on the bases of social and economic groups but which does not itself offer or contain explanatory factors. It is for this approach that the term sociology of politics is usually reserved. Political science in its turn often emphasizes what can be called an institutional aspect. Social phenomena are described as results of political action or as effects of prevailing political institutions, and it is assumed that politics is the institutional area where most great decisions about society are shaped. Typical of political sociology, on the other hand, is the attempt to balance the stratification and the institutional aspects and to study the inter-relationship between social structure and political institutions.

Political sociology covers a vast area of research including the study of revolutions, bureaucracy, nation-building processes, electoral behaviour, the history and future of party systems, and so on. Certain general theoretical themes are recurrent. Among those may be mentioned the role of conflict and consensus in the development of society, the sources of power in society, the prerequisites of democracy, the position and rise of bureaucracy, liberty versus authority, and the role of rational calculations versus emotions in political action. These questions were all favourite themes of the forerunners and classical writers of today's sociology and political science such as Marx, Tocqueville, Weber, Durkheim, Pareto, Michels, Mosca and many others.

Political sociology has been strongly comparative as regards both theory-building and empirical research. The importance of international comparison is partly a consequence of the focus on the large scale effects of the industrialization and the democratization of society. Many new methodological devices such as comparative survey research and the retrieval of information in internationally accessible data archives have been developed by scholars working in the field of political sociology.

Despite its many distinguished forerunners political sociology can be regarded as a fairly young discipline. As a label for a group of scholars conscious of their mutual research interest it did not develop until after the second world war. It was institutionalized as a

distinct sub-field of sociology by the establishment of the Committee of Political Sociology at the Fourth World Congress of Sociology in Stresa in September 1959. The sponsors for the proposal to create the committee were Shmuel Eisenstadt, Morris Janowitz, Seymour Martin Lipset, and Stein ROKKAN. Lipset became the committee's first chairman and Rokkan its first secretary. Under the guidance and leadership of these two scholars political sociology became established as a sub-field both within sociology and political science. The committee has sponsored numerous conferences and publications, and since the Stresa meeting in 1959 has organized sessions at all world congresses of both the International Sociological Association (ISA) and the International Political Science Association (IPSA).

The end of the 1950s saw not only the institutionalization of the field but also the establishment of political sociology as a distinct sub-field. A landmark was the publication of S. M. Lipset's *Political Man* (1960). In comparison with later works this book highlights some of the crucial developments within the field of political sociology. For example in *Political Man* Lipset still uses the term sociology of politics, and the book's content also conforms to what can be considered as the topic of the sociology of politics. His subtitle is 'The Social Bases of Politics', and the book clearly reflects the stratification aspect. Lipset argues that in every democracy conflicts between social groups are expressed through the party system, which at the core represents a democratic transformation of the class struggle. True, he points out that the cleavage between social classes is not the only one that is expressed through the political parties, but nevertheless the main thread of the book deals with the question of how political behaviour can be explained on the basis of the class structure. In the wake of Lipset's book and under the auspices of the Committee of Political Sociology there was at the time an upsurge of studies dealing with the social bases of political movements, voting behaviour, political systems, the emergence of new parties, etc.

By the early 1960s new orientations were developing. Political sociology was adopted as the proper term. There was a new interest in how the party system itself forms and elicits political behaviour. These new developments were clearly expressed in the comprehensive volume *Party Systems and Voter Alignments: cross-national perspectives*, edited by Seymour Martin Lipset and Stein Rokkan (1967). Here the question was no longer simply whether the party system corresponds to the social structure but rather how, under what conditions and by what political processes cleavages and interest antagonisms in the social structure are transformed into the party system, and how the party system in turn influences integration and the allocation of resources in the society.

Simultaneously with the new interest in the institutional aspect there was a strengthening of the historical orientation. Processes of nation- and state-building came to be a central theme in modern political sociology. This is very clearly reflected in S. N. Eisenstadt's large and comprehensive reader *Political Sociology* (1971). The subtitles of the different parts of the reader such as 'Major types of premodern political systems and their social conditions', 'Patterns of centres in developed traditional societies', 'Major types of modern political systems: political modernization and the political sociology of the modern state', are revealing. Interest in the interplay between political institutions and social structure in the course of historical development has become one of the hallmarks of the field of political sociology. It has also meant an increasing involvement of both historians and political geographers in the field. An important work reflecting many traditional and new orientations in comparative political sociology was *The Breakdown of Democratic Regimes*, edited by Juan Linz and Alfred Stepan (1978). It is comparative and historical, it deals with the preconditions of democracy and the relationship between liberty and authority, and it combines both the stratification and institutional aspects.

During the course of its development after the second world war the impact of the stratification aspect seems to have weakened in comparison with the institutional approach. Nevertheless political sociology has not been isolated from the renewed interest in Marxist

sociology which is especially typical in the development of sociology during the early 1970s. The impact of Marxism on political sociology has however been very indirect. It has brought a new interest in the effects of the economy and in the constraints produced by the economy. There has also been a new interest in analysing the state as an expression of the economic system.

The focus on the interplay between society and polity meant that new societal tensions rapidly become incorporated with and reflected in the themes of political sociology. In the early 1970s at least three new themes, and with them also certain research policies became incorporated into the body of political sociology: neo-corporatist theory; the RATIONAL CHOICE THEORY and, studies of ETHNICITY. All three became particularly important during the 1970s and early 1980s.

The strengthening of the *neo-corporatist* approach is a reflection of the fact that decision making in developed societies has become increasingly centralized in terms of collective bargaining between representatives of the state, the trade unions, and the employers. Such a pattern seems to be especially typical for decision making in west-European societies. Combined with the neo-corporatist approach there is a strong interest in issues related to governability and to the future of the modern WELFARE STATE. Studies of the fate of the welfare state are important not least because they represent an interdisciplinary effort in line with the best traditions of political sociology. A large number of studies of the effects of social policies on both politics and the social structure have been conducted during the early 1980s.

Rational choice theory is based on the assumption that every individual acts to maximize his or her benefit, or at least to minimize his or her cost, given a certain amount of information. The theory has largely implied an application of economic theory to political phenomena, and particularly to voting. Its importance has lain in a renewed discussion of political motivation. Traditional explanations in a clearly macro-oriented political sociology were strongly functionalist in nature. Functionalist explanations have emphasized needs and values which are collective whereas the rational choice theory is individualistic and emphasizes the self-interest of the individuals as the moving force. Rational choice theory was mainly developed within American political science but during the 1980s it has also gained a following in Europe. It has clearly renewed the analysis of some methodological issues which in the heyday of the rapid development of political sociology tended to be forgotten.

In the 1970s ETHNICITY as a politically motivating force and a ground for political alignments became a major research interest within political sociology. The importance of ethnic factors was largely denied or forgotten during the 1950s and 1960s and the renewal of interest was a clear reflection of the recrudescence of ethnic mobilization at the turn of the 1960s and 1970s not only in the third world but especially in advanced, industrial states. Studies of ethnic mobilization have introduced new conceptual schemes and have also raised methodological issues which tended to be neglected. Studies of ethnicity have as a rule strongly emphasized the differences between centres and peripheries because many ethnic and linguistic minorities tend to be located in the peripheries. Ethnic studies have also raised issues with regard to the explanatory value of social class. There are no satisfactory generalizations concerning the interplay of economic, political, cultural, and geographic factors in the rise of ethnic activism. Yet research questions have become more precise than previously, and the study of ethnic mobilization has become established as an important sub-field within political sociology.

Because of its constant focus on the interplay between society and polity, societal change has been of particular interest in political sociology. Political sociologists are often tempted to anticipate future developments. During the 1980s the effects of the new information technology on the future of the political system has been a special interest.

See also CENTRE/PERIPHERY ANALYSIS; CORPORATISM.   EA

Reading

Allardt, E. and Rokkan, S. eds: *Mass Politics: studies in political sociology*. London: Collier-Macmillan, 1970.

Dowse, R.E. and Hughes, J.A.: *Political Sociology*. Chichester: Wiley, 1985.

Eisenstadt, S.N. ed.: *Political Sociology: a reader*. New York and London: Basic Books, 1971.

Linz, J. and Stepan, A. eds: *The Breakdown of Democratic Regimes*. Baltimore, Md. and London: The Johns Hopkins University Press, 1978.

Lipset, S.M.: *Political Man: the social bases of politics*. Garden City, NY: Doubleday, 1960.

——— and Rokkan, S. eds: *Party Systems and Voter Alignments: cross-national perspectives*. London: Collier-Macmillan; New York: Free Press, 1967.

Pizzorno, A. ed.: *Political Sociology*. Harmondsworth: Penguin, 1971.

Rokkan, S. and Urwin, D.W.: *Economy, Territory, Identity: politics of West European peripheries*. London: Sage, 1983.

Rose, R. et al. eds: *The Welfare State East and West*. New York: Oxford University Press, 1986.

Schmitter, C. and Lembruch, G. eds: *Trends Towards Corporatist Intermediation*. London: Sage, 1979.

political succession The process by which leadership changes hands in a country. This is the most sensitive moment in internal political life, being the clearest test of the institutions and procedures of regimes. What is at stake is whether the current office-holders and those who have ambitions to replace them are prepared to accept and abide by pre-arranged rules regulating the duration of leaders in office and the means by which they are appointed and dismissed. Rules about political succession have to exist if political life is to be other than 'nasty, brutish, and short'; without them, anyone who has ambitions and anyone who strongly objects to current leaders will try and overthrow these rulers by any means. Arrangements for political succession are therefore the first step towards an orderly political life. However the existence of arrangements is not sufficient: in order to be effective, these have to be accepted by the population as well as by current and by aspiring leaders.

This acceptance is obviously difficult to obtain, for reasons which range from the most personal to the most ideological. There is no point in imagining that politicians might be without ambition: only ambitious men and women can sustain the toughness – and indeed dangers – of political life. Many will want to hasten the moment at which current leaders are replaced, while the leaders themselves obviously have the converse aim. It is important to note in this context that the time-horizons of politicians are usually rather short and that, consequently, a leader who has been in office for some years and shows no signs of wanting to leave appears to those who wish to take over the post as an obstacle to be overcome. For even if there is a high turnover of rulers there is only one post of head of government at a time.

One must therefore start from the recognition that there is only one 'crown' and that this crown cannot frequently pass to another head. Many ambitions will therefore be frustrated and tension is likely to increase in the polity as a result. But there are also other reasons which militate for the maintenance of leaders in office or for their replacement. The success or failure of policies, the fear that candidates for leadership might bring about social or economic disaster, the sheer repressiveness of the current rulers or the worry that possible successors might be authoritarian are among the more 'elevated' reasons; one should also include such motivations as the desire to receive patronage or favours, regional, tribal, ethnic or party origins, as well as deeply-engrained likes or dislikes of an affective character. If to these reasons are added opportunities, such as the ability to control the armed forces and therefore to replace physically those who are in power, the temptation to intervene may become – indeed does often become – irresistible.

The rules organizing political succession must be strong enough to overcome these pressures. Yet the strength of these rules ultimately lies in the belief which population and politicians have in their validity. This means that they must appeal both to the more elevated sentiments and to the self-interest of the persons concerned. To appeal to more elevated sentiments, rules about succession must be viewed as fair, both in themselves and

in the way in which they are administered: for instance, arrangements which decide that leaders will be appointed by an electoral mechanism must be seen to be applied in such a way as to give reasonable chances to various candidates. The arrangements relating to succession must also appeal to the self-interest of those concerned: they must make current and aspiring leaders feel that it is too risky to set them aside, as the outcome of the battle for the succession may be very uncertain and personally dangerous; the population must also believe that the stability of the regime is preferable to the upheaval which an irregular maintenance or change of leadership might provoke.

Naturally enough, the conditions required for a regular succession are not often met; they tend in particular not to be met in new countries in which, by definition, there has been no time to test whether the institutions are fair and whther it is in the interest of everyone to maintain them. But the conditions may not be met in many older polities either, especially where internal tribal, ethnic, or religious divisions are such that it is almost impossible for a fair system of succession to be devised, at any rate rapidly, or where economic and consequential social conflict are such that much of the population is divorced from the political system and believes – or can easily be made to believe – that there is nothing to be lost in an abrupt upheaval, beginning with an irregular change of leadership.

It is therefore not surprising that, historically, political succession should frequently have been irregular and that, in the contemporary world, countries in which successions have been occasionally or frequently irregular should be the large majority. Only a small number of states, principally Western European, North American, and members of the British Commonwealth have experienced regular successions since the end of the second world war. Communist systems have had ostensibly regular successions after the regimes were set up, but in most cases the succession has been in fact plainly irregular or a result of intense blackmail. On the other hand, nearly all the Latin American states have had at least one irregular transfer of power, together with the large majority of Middle Eastern and African countries, as well as a substantial number of south and southeast Asian nations. Indeed, in some states, irregularity of succession has almost been the norm, in particular in parts of the Middle East and parts of Latin America; although there has been a tendency for changes of leadership to be more regular since the early 1980s in Latin America, past experience casts some doubt as to the permanence of this trend. Irregular succession is an endemic feature of political life in most parts of the world. It would be wrong to conclude, however, that the efforts of political theorists and of constitutional lawyers have all been in vain: the mechanisms which they proposed and which were designed to smooth the process of political succession have had some effect: the problem has been posed and solutions have been offered. But there is still a need to reflect further on the conditions which are likely to bring about less tension in the succession process and to strengthen beliefs in the value of the succession rules.   JFPB

Reading

Apter, D.E.: *The Politics of Modernisation*. Chicago, Ill.: University of Chicago Press, 1965.

Blondel, J.: *World Leaders*. London and Los Angeles: Sage, 1980.

Finer, S.E.: *The Man on Horseback*. 2nd edn. Harmondsworth: Penguin, 1976.

Huntington, S.P.: *Political Order in Changing Societies*. New Haven, Conn. and London: Yale University Press, 1968.

Rush, M.: *How Communist States Change their Rulers*. New York: Cornell University Press, 1974.

political system Those social interactions and institutions through which a society makes decisions considered binding by most members of society most of the time (Easton 1981). Some scholars have argued that private organizations make similar kinds of decisions for their own members: hence we ought to broaden the notion of political system to apply to such organizations as well. This would increase enormously the numbers and variety of political systems that might be studied and provide a broad statistical base for comparisons. However, such proposals have not been generally accepted, largely on the grounds that the political systems of society are *sui generis* and have traditionally been the focus of attention of students of politics.

We now take the term political system for granted as a way of referring to the political life of a society; this was not always so. As a term with specific analytic implications it has only recently emerged, arguably entering into popular use in political science in 1953, the year in which *The Political System* first appeared. The term gradually spread from academe to general use, so that by the 1980s it was regularly being used in both technical and lay terminology to refer to the specifically political aspects of social life. In American political science especially it quickly displaced the dominant idea of the STATE as the most comprehensive orienting concept for political research, even though the state concept remained very much alive in Europe and has even undergone a renaissance in the United States since the 1970s.

The notion of a political system represents more than just a new term: it reflects a transformation in the way in which students of politics are able to theorize about their subject matter and pursue empirical inquiries. It is not accidental that its emergence coincided with and reinforced the introduction, through the so-called behavioural revolution, of rigorous methods for empirical research about political phenomena. But the term also reflects and contributed to the occurrence of a far broader intellectual movement, the 'system revolution' (Emery 1969). Just as the ideas of mechanism and evolution dominated thought and perspectives in the seventeenth and nineteenth centuries, the idea of system has become pervasive in the twentieth century.

What would distinguish political from other types of systems? There has been much debate in the social sciences in the attempt to establish a consensual description of the scope and boundaries of political life – what contemporary philosophy of science might call the 'domain' of a discipline. It was once thought that such discussions were unnecessary; instead, political science ought only to be precisely what political scientists do.

This pragmatic approach to an understanding of the subject matter of political inquiry had a certain appeal to the practising political scientist. It seemed to have the virtue of side-stepping the whole theoretical issue and of offering maximal freedom to the empirical research worker to define the subject as he or she saw fit. Philosophers of science have since discovered however that underlying all organized efforts at understanding an aspect of nature, whether physical or social, are certain important assumptions about the domain of the particular field of inquiry (Suppe 1977). Although a discipline may never agree on a general description of the limits of its area of inquiry, differences in the description do lead to significantly different theoretical outcomes: they help to account for different kinds of assumptions, questions posed, procedures used and answers obtained.

In political science before the second world war the dominant way of describing its subject matter was to say that it dealt with the study of the state. One person however unearthed over 140 different uses of the word state. The doubt and confusion engendered by a term with such variety of meaning led to constant efforts to achieve a more acceptable description of the domain of political science. Since the second world war, political life has been identified in a number of ways: as the study of the will; of power; of decision making; of a monopoly of the legitimate use of power, after Max Weber; of the authoritative allocation of values – or the making and implementing of binding decisions – for a society (Easton 1981). No one of these alternatives appealed to all students of politics. It is probably fair to say however that the last formulation has attracted considerable support.

If the concept of the political system drew renewed attention to possible meanings for the idea of 'the political' it also for the first time raised the question as to how we might profitably conceptualize political life for purposes of empirical analysis. What justification might there be for interpreting politics as a 'system' of some sort, however we might choose to define the unique properties that made that system political?

Whether users of the term were aware of it or not, the very idea of a set of phenomena constituting a system carried with it certain intellectual suppositions. First, it assumed that society must consist of other kinds of systems that were not political. Second, it presumed that it would be possible to extricate or abstract the political system from these other systems so that it could be dealt with in its own terms. Finally, it implied that if there are systems other than the political all these systems might interact in such a way as to have important consequences for each other and for all the systems taken as a whole. In short, the very notion of system evoked an image of the whole society as an over-arching system of behaviour composed of a variety of less extensive sub-systems (such as the political, cultural and economic) and demanded a mode of analysis that would permit the analyst to identify and separate out the political system for special attention.

Here two points of view emerged. One has held that a set of behaviours, or social interactions, and institutions can form a system only if they have a certain natural coherence. Whatever the elements of the political system, whether they are units of power, decisions or authoritative allocations, the interactions and institutions connected with them must hang together such that changes in one area will probably have important effects on other areas. The choice of the elements forming a system cannot be arbitrary: one must search nature to find those elements which cohere sufficiently to have a common fate and thereby provide evidence that they do constitute a system. In practice there is little difficulty in doing this with respect to the political system: legislatures, courts, parties, interest groups, electorates and the like show the kind of close relationships required by this interpretation of the nature of a system.

There is another conception, however, that relieves the investigator of the need to search for a naturally cohering body of phenomena. In this alternative view any set of elements can be designated as a system. The only question that arises is whether it constitutes an interesting system; that is, one that does something. What distinguishes a political system from others, such as a cultural or an economic system, is that it is a dynamic one with a special output. It converts the desires, opinions, wishes and the like of the powerful members of the system into binding decisions. Typically these may have important consequences for the lives of all members of the system, for other parts of society, and for other societies as well. In this view we can include within any political system at the focus of attention all those aspects of society which are more or less directly related to making these kinds of decisions. The constituent elements of a political system may therefore vary depending on which interactions and institutions seem, in a given society, to be most closely related to the making and implementing of political decisions (Easton 1979). This apparently arbitrary, although by no means capricious or whimsical formulation of a system permits us to account for and address the vast variety of institutional arrangements found in political systems across space and time.

Regardless whether we see a political system as given in nature or as a conceptual artefact, the idea of system itself commits the investigator to a set of problems and theoretical commitments about which not all those who use the term have seemed to be aware. None the less, the idea of system suggests identifiable inputs and outputs which provide linkages with other systems of society, such as the culture and economy, through which each influences the other; that processes occur within the system to convert the inputs into relevant outputs; that there are feedback processes whereby what happens at one moment may influence action at the next. In addition, it draws attention to the fact that social systems as such have special properties: normally they are able to regulate themselves, set and change their own goals and structures and take action to achieve or avoid these goals.

DE

Reading

Buckley, W.: *Sociology and Modern Systems Theory*. Englewood Cliffs, NJ: Prentice-Hall, 1967.

Easton, D.: *The Political System* (1953). 3rd edn. Chicago, Ill.: University of Chicago Press, 1981.

————: *A Framework for Political Analysis* (1965). 2nd edn. Chicago, Ill.: University of Chicago Press, 1979.

————: *A Systems Analysis of Political Life* (1965). 2nd edn. Chicago, Ill.: University of Chicago Press, 1979.

————: The political system besieged by the state. *Political Theory* 9 (1981) 303–25.

Emery, F.E. ed.: *Systems Thinking*. Harmondsworth: Penguin, 1969.

Suppe, F. ed.: *The Structure of Scientific Theories*. Urbana, Ill.: University of Illinois Press, 1977.

Sutherland, J.W.: *A General Systems Philosophy for the Social and Behavioural Sciences*. New York: Brazilier, 1973.

political violence Nominally the term refers to any use of physical violence for political purposes. Since the 1960s it has been used as a catch-all phrase for a wide variety of episodes or manifestations of political opposition within states in which coercion is used or threatened. It encompasses such specific events as anti-government riots, assassinations, TERRORISM, COUPS D'ÉTAT, peasant wars, rebellions, CIVIL WARS, and revolutionary warfare. Terms such as protest, insurgency and internal war, on the other hand, are sometimes used to refer to broader categories of conflict episodes. In addition to denoting a general subject of inquiry, political violence is also an indicator or property of conflict which is the object of theoretical explanation. Thus, theories have been developed to explain variables such as 'magnitudes' of political violence and the 'extent' and 'intensity' of rebellion and collective protest.

While there are established traditions of research on revolutions, peasant wars and coups d'état, the study of political violence as a general phenomenon began in the early 1960s. Three contributing factors can be identified: the emergence of new theoretical arguments, the development of a cross-national approach to political analysis using aggregate data, and a coalescence of public and scholarly concern with the rise of insurgency in the third world and violent protest in western societies.

A seminal article by Eckstein in 1965

opened up a number of theoretical perspectives on internal war, as he called it. At the same time pioneering studies which compared quantitative measures of 'conflict behaviour' across nations began to appear. These studies examined the relations between internal and external conflict, between inequality and political violence, and between 'systemic frustration' and political instability. Other such studies examined the relations between economic development and violence, and the effects of government coercion on oppositional violence. These cross-national studies were made possible by the development of cross-national data banks containing information on the demographic, economic, social, and political characteristics of all independent countries. The World Data Analysis Program at Yale University led the way in this movement, publishing the first *World Handbook of Political and Social Indicators* in 1964. This and subsequent editions have included extensive data on numbers and events such as riots, armed attacks, deaths from political violence, and seizures of power.

Data on patterns of political violence from 1950 to 1980 show that it has been most intense and widespread by far in the less-developed countries of Africa, Asia, and the Middle East, especially those with weak but autocratic regimes. Violent conflict in the communist regimes of Eurasia is relatively uncommon but quite deadly when it does occur. Latin American countries tend to occupy an intermediate position between Afro-Asia and the western democracies, where episodes of protest have been very numerous but seldom violent, except in the United States. Much empirical research has focused on the correlates or 'causes' of such variations among countries, and across time within countries. For example there is convergent evidence that the extent and intensity of political violence tend to increase in the earliest stages of capitalist economic development and then to decline as societies move toward the stage of mass consumption. High levels of political violence are also associated with high degrees of economic inequality, with ethnic heterogeneity, and with persisting patterns of discrimination against minorities.

In the 1970s there were several general attempts to integrate theory and evidence about the causes of political violence. T.R. Gurr and Edward N. Muller among others emphasized the importance of socio-psychological factors such as relative deprivation, political culture, and political beliefs. Others such as Douglas A. Hibbs, Jr. demonstrated that characteristics of social and political structure were crucial. In sociology the 're-source mobilization' school, led by Charles Tilly, argued that the nature of collective organization and the interaction between challengers and regimes determined the extent of political violence. Many scholars now, including some of the protagonists in debates about these contending approaches, would agree that a comprehensive explanation of political violence – either in general or in specific cases – requires the analysis of social and economic structure, psychological and ideological factors, the process of mobilization, and interactions between oppostion and government.

These theories have stimulated criticism to the effect that the phenomena of political violence are too diverse for general explanation and that some of them, revolutions in particular, require very different kinds of explanation (see REVOLUTION AND COUNTER-REVOLUTION). Theda Skocpol has taken the most extreme position on this issue, proposing an exclusively structural approach to explaining social revolutions which takes account of class relationships, the role of the state, and the international environment. She argues that 'consensual and voluntaristic conceptions of social order and disruption or change . . . are quite naive'. She also challenges Tilly's resource mobilization approach on grounds that 'no successful social revolution has ever been made by a mass-mobilizing avowedly revolutionary movement'. Skocpol has demonstrated the plausibility of her structural theory in a comparative historical analysis of a handful of social revolutions. It is inadequate or irrelevant to the explanation of other and more numerous kinds of violent political conflicts, precisely because it ignores the importance of grievances, ideology, and mobilization for collective action which are

481

essential for explaining why political opposition and violence can take such diverse forms.

Three newer kinds of issues are emerging in the analysis of political violence. One is the question of the effects of violent conflict on public policy, political institutions, and society more generally. There is accumulating evidence that violent protest often leads to changes in policy which are of some benefit to the protesting group. This pattern is observed in both democracies and autocracies, though the conditions associated with success are different in the two types of political system.

Second, government violence (more commonly characterized as coercion or repression) is the subject of new theoretical and empirical research. Two kinds of question are being raised. One is the circumstances under which regimes choose to use violence against citizens, especially in its more extreme forms of state terrorism and genocide. The origins and characteristics of the state, the nature of its coercive apparatus, and elites' ideologies and class bases are crucial to explaining such excesses. The second question concerns the effects of government violence in suppressing opposition. Evidence suggests that regimes which increase coercion in an attempt to control opposition are likely to stimulate increasingly violent resistance. Once an escalating cycle of internal conflict has begun, only very high and consistent levels of government repression seem to inhibit protesters and rebels.

Finally there is renewed recognition that internal political violence must be understood in its international context. Internal and international conflict have complex interrelations: wars are particularly likely to lead to increased political violence and instability in countries on the losing side. Successful revolutions play a major part in stimulating international conflicts of expansion and containment, and also spark imitative political violence elsewhere. And there is accumulating evidence that countries which are constrained by their dependency on international investment and trade have distinctive kinds of class conflicts in which both state and opposition are likely to use political violence.   TRG/JIR

Reading

Eckstein, H.: On the etiology of internal wars. *History and Theory* (1965) 133–62.

Gurr, T.R.: *Why Men Rebel*. Princeton, NJ: Princetön University Press, 1970.

——— ed.: *Handbook of Political Conflict: theory and research*. New York: Free Press, 1980.

Hibbs, D.A. Jr: *Mass Political Violence: a cross-national causal analysis*. New York: Wiley, 1973.

Lopez, G.A. and Stohl, M. eds: *Government Violence and Repression: an agenda for research*. Westport, Conn.: Greenwood, 1986.

Muller, E.N.: *Aggressive Political Participation*. Princeton, NJ: Princeton University Press, 1979.

Skocpol, T.: *States and Social Revolutions: a comparative analysis of France, Russia and China*. Cambridge: Cambridge University Press, 1979.

Stohl, M. and Lopez, G.A. eds: *The State as Terrorist: the dynamics of government violence and repression*. Westport, Conn.: Greenwood, 1984.

Taylor, S.: *Social Science and Revolutions*. New York: St Martin's, 1984.

Tilly, C.: *From Mobilization to Revolution*. Reading, Mass.: Addison-Wesley, 1978.

Zimmermann, E.: *Political Violence, Crises and Revolutions: theory and research*. Cambridge, Mass.: Schenkman, 1983.

politics   The activity by which decisions are arrived at and implemented in and for a community. Three important consequences follow from this definition. First, politics is an activity: common sense suggests that this is the case but the point is sometimes forgotten. Because politics is an activity it has a dynamic character; it evolves over time in different ways and, indeed, in a very complex manner. Equally importantly, politics, being an activity, is essentially a process by which certain actions take place. This is why, as a moment's reflection shows, it is concerned with a large variety of questions. As a matter of fact the field of political activity cannot be defined, *a priori*, by reference to particular objects: what counts is that decisions have to be taken, or are deemed to be needed, in a given field.

This leads to the second essential element of politics: it is the activity by which decisions are arrived at and implemented. Politics is about the taking of decisions. We often think in terms of politics being concerned with

POWER or with IDEOLOGIES. Politics is closely associated with power and ideology, as well as with other concepts, such as AUTHORITY and LEGITIMACY; however this is because politics is an activity aimed at taking and implementing decisions. The decisions which have to be taken concern an infinite number of questions and it is therefore natural that there should be different views about what should be the substance of the decision, that is to say the direction that the policy should take. The need for direction in the decision-making process results in the need for an ideology: one cannot decide, for instance, to increase or decrease pensions, to expand or contract educational services without calling on an ideology. Ideologies are inextricably linked with politics, but they are linked because a decision has to be taken. Indeed, the form in which decisions will be arrived at and implemented also involves ideology: for instance, decisions may be taken more or less democratically, or in a more or less liberal manner.

The role of power in politics also results from the need to take decisions: because decisions have to be arrived at and implemented there has to be some 'force' which will result in members of the community 'resolving' the problem. Hence the inevitable use of various means of pressure ranging from gentle influence to outright coercion: power is the word most commonly used to cover these types of pressure, though there is considerable controversy as to what the concept covers. What is important is to recognize that power becomes an essential ingredient of political activity because decisions have to be taken and implemented. It is not so much that 'politics is about power' but that there could not be any decision – any resolution – without the use of a force such as that which power constitutes, and which allows for the imposition of an authoritative sanction.

Other forms of pressure also play a major part, for instance tradition: we are accustomed to do certain things in a certain way and this 'structures' our activities. There is, too, the crucial part played by INSTITUTIONS and procedures which help the decision process because they resolve in advance a large number of problems, such as who will be involved in decision making and when.

Institutions on the one hand, traditions on the other ensure that obedience occurs most of the time: decisions can be accepted and, to a large extent at least, implemented. Without this acceptance politics would be extraordinarily difficult to conduct as well as extremely dangerous. The process of decision making would be very slow since at every point specific agreements would have to be obtained; it would be dangerous because there would always be the temptation to obtain agreement by physical violence. Politics needs acceptance; to operate smoothly it also needs institutions which are recognized and which are legitimate. This is why it is sometimes said that politics is an authoritative process: this 'authority' is indeed required, but only as a consequence of the fact that decisions have to be taken and implemented.

The third characteristic of politics is that it is an activity which takes place in and for a *community*. The point has two aspects. On the one hand politics takes place in a collective setting. There are no politics unless at least two individuals have to take a decision together. Where there is no need for a joint decision there is no political activity, though there will have been a previous political decision that joint action is not needed on the particular point. For instance if prices are fixed by governmental decree each decision relating to each price is political, but if prices are fixed as a result of supply and demand the only political decision is that by which it is agreed at the outset that prices would result from the operation of the market mechanism (a decision which, of course, is always revocable).

Political activity is inherently collective. It takes place in the context of a community – any community: in the STATE, of course, but also in local authorities, in trade unions, in businesses, in churches, in the family and clearly also internationally. Politics is therefore not merely an activity within the state, as is often believed. It may be true that political activities within the state are more important than other political activities – it may also be true that the state may have the power to regulate the political activities which take place in other organizations: for instance, the state may specify that only certain types of associations are allowed or that associations may engage only in certain types of activities. This may result in political activity within the state being dominant; it does not result in the end of political activity in other bodies. Furthermore, we often exaggerate the extent to which political activity within the state prevails over political activities in other communities: the extent of state dominance varies markedly from country to country and over time. JFPB

Reading

Crick, B.: *In Defence of Politics*. Harmondsworth: Penguin, 1966.

Dahl, R.A.: *Modern Political Analysis*. Englewood Cliffs, NJ: Prentice-Hall, 1963.

Duverger, M.: *The Idea of Politics*. London: Methuen, 1966.

Easton, D.: *The Political System*. 3rd edn. Chicago, Ill.: University of Chicago Press, 1979.

Sabine, G.H. and Thorson, T.L.: *A History of Political Theory*. New York: Holt Saunders, 1973.

Weldon, T.D.: *The Vocabulary of Politics*. Harmondsworth: Penguin, 1953.

polity The term may be understood in three different ways. (1) Any politically organized society; (2) the form of government in a society, synonymous with *regime*; (3) the English translation of Aristotle's word, *politeia*, by which he meant a MIXED form of GOVERNMENT. SEF

polyarchy In contemporary political science the term is generally used to refer to the institutions or political processes of modern representative democracy. It draws directly on a much older use of the word in its etymological meaning 'many rulers' in which sense it can be found in English as early as the seventeenth century. The word was uncommon before 1953 when Dahl and Lindblom introduced it in *Politics, Economics, and Welfare* as one of four major sociopolitical processes: 'In some societies the democratic goal is still roughly and crudely approximated, in the sense that non-leaders exercise a relatively high degree of control over leaders. The constellation of social processes that make this possible we call polyarchy.' The word was intended to provide a straightforward way of distinguishing democracy as an ideal and as a generic type from the democratic or popular component employed (together with non-democratic processes such as hierarchy) in governing certain modern nation states that in common parlance would be considered 'democracies'.

Since then the term has acquired a life of its own, with some confusion resulting from different attempts to specify its meaning. The prevailing interpretation is perhaps closest to that intended by Dahl and Lindblom, however, though the emphasis is now more likely to be placed on the distinctiveness of polyarchy as a set of institutions than as a socio-political process.

(1) Polyarchy can be interpreted as a distinctive kind of regime for governing the modern state. Its distinctiveness arises from the combination of two general features: its relatively high tolerance of oppositions and the relatively widespread opportunities for participating in influencing the conduct of the government. These opportunities extend all the way to participating in processes for replacing incumbent governing officials by peaceful means. Taken together, the institutions of polyarchy distinguish it from all regimes before the nineteenth century, including centralized or feudal monarchies, the Roman Empire, the historical regimes of China and Japan, and even the regimes of the democratic states of classical Greece, the Roman Republic, or the Italian city state republics. The institutions of polyarchy also distinguish it rather sharply from most other regimes existing among the nation states of the world today.

(2) Polyarchy can be understood historically or developmentally as a set of institutions that evolved in large part, though not exclusively, as a product of movements to democratize and liberalize the political institutions of nation-states. In this perspective polyarchy is a unique historically conditioned set of modern institutions resulting primarily from attempts since the eighteenth century to adapt demo-

cratic ideas and practices to the large scale of the nation-state. (For a description of these institutions, see DEMOCRACY.) This historically unique complex of political institutions has tended to acquire the name democracy, although its institutions have largely superseded the distinctive political institutions of the earlier democratic or republican city states. In democratic Athens, for example, the citizen assembly was of primary importance whereas organized political parties were unknown, as were most of the other autonomous interest organizations common in polyarchies.

(3) Polyarchy can be understood as a set of political institutions necessary in order to provide a satisfactory approximation to the democratic process when the objective is to apply that process on a large scale, and specifically on the scale of the nation-state. This interpretation emphasizes the importance of the scale or size of the political system, not only territorially but in number of citizens, and on the need for the institutions of polyarchy to exist in order to maximize democracy in such large-scale systems. On the smaller scale of the city state, as in municipalities and associations of the present day, a high level of democracy (at least among those eligible to participate) could arguably be attained without the full range of polyarchal institutions. But when the locus of democracy was shifted to the large scale of the nation-state, a new complex of democratic institutions necessarily had to be created.

(4) Polyarchy can be understood as a system of political control in which, as a consequence of its special set of institutions, the highest officials of the state face the prospect of their own displacement by means of popular elections, and hence tend to have strong incentives to modify their conduct in such a way as to win elections in political competition with other candidates, parties, and groups. This perspective is very close to Joseph SCHUMPETER's interpretation of democracy in *Capitalism, Socialism, and Democracy* (1942). From this perspective the most distinctive feature of polyarchy is the open competition among political ELITES for office, which in turn helps to create a certain measure of mutual influence between elites and masses. Because of elite competition in elections, polyarchies manage to avoid, or at least greatly weaken, the unilateral dominance by elites described as inevitable by Roberto MICHELS in his famous IRON LAW OF OLIGARCHY (*Political Parties*, 1915).

(5) Finally, polyarchy can be interpreted as a system of rights in which certain rights are institutionally guaranteed and protected. Each of the institutions of polyarchy prescribes definite rights that are necessary to the existence and functioning of the institution itself. To institutionalize free speech, for example, citizens must possess a legally enforceable claim to speak freely on political matters, and it must be an obligation of officials of the state to uphold that claim, if need be by punishing violators. In order for the political institution to exist in a realistic sense the right cannot be merely abstract or theoretical: it must be actually enforceable in courts of law. As an extensive and highly institutionalized system of rights polyarchy is once again distinguishable not only from all non-democratic regimes, modern and historical, but also from earlier democracies and republics. The range of protected rights guaranteed in modern polyarchies is far greater than existed in any of the ancient democracies or republics, and far greater than the supporters of popular governments in ancient times would have thought desirable.

These five interpretations – and others might be suggested – are not inconsistent. They simply emphasize different aspects or consequences of the institutions that serve to distinguish polyarchy from non-polyarchical regimes. It is these institutions that, taken in their entirety, distinguish polyarchies not only from all non-democratic systems, present and past, but also from small-scale democratic systems, present and past, that lack the full range of polyarchical institutions. RAD

Reading

Dahl, R.A.: *Polyarchy: participation and opposition.* New Haven, Conn.: Yale University Press, 1971.
—— and Lindblom, C.E.: *Politics, Economics and Welfare*, rev. edn. New York: Harper & Row, 1976.

Lijphart, A.: *Democracies: patterns of majoritarian and consensus government in twenty-one countries*. New Haven, Conn.: Yale University Press, 1984.

Mansbridge, J.: *Beyond Adversarial Democracy*. New York: Basic Books, 1980.

Michels, R.: *Political Parties*. New York: Dover, 1915. Also ed. and intro. S.M. Lipset. New York: Crowell-Collier, 1962.

Schumpeter, J.: *Capitalism, Socialism and Democracy*. 5th edn. London: Allen & Unwin, 1976.

Polybius Hellenistic historian, whose *Histories* in forty books analysed the evolution of Roman domination of the Mediterranean between 220 and 146 BC. His work is notable, as regards constitutional theory, for his description of the history and confederal institutions of his native Achaean League (II, chs 37–44), and above all his account of the Roman constitution (Bk VI). Polybius explained Rome's political and military resilience on the basis that it represented an effective example of the mixed constitution, a blend of monarchy, aristocracy and democracy, a concept established by PLATO and ARISTOTLE; but he did not propound any theory of CHECKS AND BALANCES. Less clearly, he also applied to Rome the notion, again derived from Greek political theory, of the 'transformations' (*metabolai*) of constitutional forms. Modern opinions are divided as to the appropriateness of applying to Rome an analysis according to which Roman institutions are characterized as a mixture of the monarchic (the two consuls), the aristocratic (the senate) and democratic (the popular assemblies).

See also MIXED GOVERNMENT. FGBM

Reading

Fritz, K. von: *The Theory of the Mixed Constitution in Antiquity: a critical analysis of Polybius' political ideas*. New York: Columbia University Press, 1954.

Millar, F.: The political character of the classical Roman republic (200–151 BC). *Journal of Roman Studies* 74 (1984), 1–19.

Momigliano, A.D.: *Alien Wisdom: the limits of hellenization*, ch. 2. Cambridge: Cambridge University Press, 1975.

Polybius: *The Histories*.

Walbank, F.W.: *Polybius*. Berkeley, Los Angeles and London: University of California Press, 1972.

populism A political mentality rather than a philosophy or an ideology, which has failed almost everywhere to form political parties of its own. Since the nineteenth century it has emerged during periods of modernization in different political cultures, different historical periods and in different continents. The populist mentality has historical, psychological and socio-economic roots.

The beginning of modernization – usually linked with the two past industrial revolutions and with the ongoing tertiary one – in one's own country, or in related countries, has deep effects on the national psychology. The relations between national urban/rural sectors and labour/capital industrial factors or, on the international plane, between developed and underdeveloped countries, have all been profoundly affected, and this has in turn affected the mental outlook of the peoples. Hence the two different, albeit contemporary, forms of populism during the 1870s to the 1890s, the one occurring in the Russian empire, the other in the USA. Both were concerned with the peasant: but while the Russian populists, the *narodniki*, originated in the intelligentsia, which 'went to the people' (*narod*) and attempted to share its problems and prospects in a society in dissolution, in the United States, the mentality of populism originated directly among 'the cash conscious commercial farmers, concerned with exploitation through the monetary system, railways, and disposal of public lands' (Hofstadter 1964).

The populist mentality is an instinctive reaction against changes in the traditional way of life, imposed by unknown and all-powerful social and economic forces, which are located either in the national capitals or, worse still, in foreign capitals. Hence also the similar, original revolt against 'the conspirators' in such different movements, with such different motivations, as FASCISM and NAZISM on the right, and co-operativism or extreme forms of SOCIALISM and communism on the left, before the second world war; a revolt which has recurred after the war in such movements as *Qualunquismo* in Italy, *Peronismo* in Argentina,

POUJADISM in France and in the students' revolt in 1968 in USA and Europe. Hence the mentality of *dependencia* prevailing in the politics of all Latin-American countries, and under other names in those of most under-developed countries or continents.

Psychologically, the mentality of populism consists of a deep, individual and collective, inferiority complex and persecution mania sublimated into an absolute longing for a human brotherhood of justice, participation and purity. The 'little man' (typical hero of novels of G. K. Chesterton, Hans Fallada and George Orwell) who lives in 'the periphery' and who feels that his fate is conditioned, or indeed manipulated by obscure supreme powers located in 'centres' of decision and at the same time of corruption, is the individual who represents the populist mentality. The feeling that the Gomorrahs, where the power-ful live and decide, should be seized and cleansed by 'the people' projects upon that ill-defined concept a sense of revenge and redemption. The 'peasant' or the 'worker' acquire in the imagination of classical populism the mythical attributes of Parsifal. When the 'people', peasants, workers and 'little men', will have destroyed the conspiratorial citadels of capitalists, bankers, Jews, puppet-politicians and manipulating media, the people will administer itself directly, everyone will par-ticipate in all decisions. Populists are generally suspicious of the institutions of representative democracy and tend to favour the instruments of DIRECT DEMOCRACY such as the REFER-ENDUM. Indeed the influence of populism can be seen in the United States in the constitutional provisions in many states for the referendum, the INITIATIVE, the TOWN MEETING and the RECALL.

The socio-economic causes of this political mentality are to be found in the massive and abrupt changes brought about by the three industrial revolutions which have taken place until now, and the chain reactions they have set off everywhere in the modern world. Yet one of the characteristics of the mentality of populism is that it is not always anti-market and anti-capitalist. Neither American popu-lism, nor populist movements in pre-fascist Italy, pre-Nazi Germany, nor Peronist popu-lism in Argentina were anti-capitalist. Their hatred was directed against those who had taken possession, in a conspiratorial way, of the levers of financial and political power, and exerted that power to their advantage, without the participation of the people. This is why populism can be an additive, a political colourant, to most doctrines and political parties whether they are Thatcherist or Reaganist, socialist or liberal parties, ecologists or anarchists. It is significant that the pro-gressives' revolt in Czechoslovakia and the students' movement in Paris in 1968, both simultaneously proclaimed 'participation' as their principal slogan. The more remote, foreign, and elitist the centres of power of decision making seem to be, the more frequent the manifestations of populism in contem-porary history; the more abruptly socio-economic changes are brought about by modernization and technology, the greater the number of 'persecuted' in rural areas, or in declining industrial areas, who will succumb to the populist mentality. But in the majority of these cases, anti-capitalism is the *leitmotiv* of the populist movements. Given however the inability of populism to crystallize in an authentic ideology and political organization of its own, such anti-capitalist sentiments tend to be channelled into socialist and communist ideologies and parties, better organized and more constructive than the essentially negative, anti, populist mentality.

The association of populism with, or its transformation into, other ideologies or parties has taken two different forms, according to the role these latter give the state. The first form is the absorption of populist movements or groups into Socialist or COMMUNIST PARTIES. The view put forward is that the state must be taken over, or in the case of underdeveloped countries created, as the instrument of justice and of development. No objection is raised, or indeed suspicion harboured, against the monopolization of 'power' in the hands of an 'elitist' minority or of a leader almost func-tionally, but also voluntarily installed in the seat of absolute power, as a result of the inevitable trend towards monolithic power implicit in any statist–political regime. The second alternative is the absorption into democratic parties and regimes (etymologically almost pleonastic: *populus* into *demos*), in which contrary to socialism, let alone communism, the state and its bureaucracy and coercive forces are held in check by the institutions of popular control and decision making at all levels of the process of government. As noted above, the more decentralized the structure of the state, as in federal systems, and notably the Swiss system, the nearer the structure comes to the essentially de-centralizing, anti-statist, participationist ideals of populism.

Forms of populism vary according to their geographic and historical origins. Students of the populist movements have found as many similarities as differences between the Russian, American, Central and Eastern European, Western European, Canadian, Latin American and African kinds of populism. In each of these there are internal differences between nineteenth- and twentieth-century formulations, and further subdivisions into generational periods. Since the 1968 revolt of the students (inspired in part by Mao's Cultural Revolution) which combined opposition to the political as well as to the moral (or to them immoral) rules of bourgeois capitalist society, populism has gradually turned into *plebeianism*. The *populus* has been replaced by the *plebs* in the new model.

There are many diverse, but converging, reasons for the new situation. One is the displacement of attention from the peasant in the villages to the workers in the towns, to the unskilled or unemployed worker, as against increasingly skilled and well-paid worker-technicians required by the new technology. The nuclear industry was especially attacked in 1968, not only for technological but for pacifist and ecological reasons. In general the movement was anti-technological (computers were defenestrated from university buildings) and essentially escapist. The 'peasant' was also abandoned because of his religious traditions and values (which had on the contrary been idealized by the *narodniki*) and because of his practical, capitalist mentality (idealized by American populism). The plebeian populists, and notably the hippies, do go back to 'nature' but not to the boring traditional villages. They create their own 'communes' in which they can live according to their own rules of promiscuity, gregariousness and the pursuit of escapism.

A second reason is that, given their fundamental aversion to the industrial technological revolution, and the improvements, indeed luxuries, it has brought into every home in town and countryside, the new populists denounce the '*embourgeoisement* of the masses'. The external sign of the new populism is sartorial: jeans and T-shirts are their uniform, disfigurement, as in the punk hair-dos, is the object of their fashion.

Finally, they practise systematically a cult of Youth. The 'young' are pure and idealistic; this is why Youth must join forces with the proletariat. Populism at its vaguest links together these two marginal groups of the developing technological society. More than an exercise in working-class consciousness this is an exercise of 'déclassement' and in anti-elitism. And therein lies the contradiction that a part of the future generation is opposed to the future.   GI

Reading

Canovan, M.: *Populism*. London: Function Books, 1981.

Goodwyn, L.: *Democratic Promise: the populist movement in America*. New York: Oxford University Press, 1976.

Hofstadter, R.: *Anti-Intellectualism in American Life*. London: Cape, 1964.

Ionescu, G. and Gellner, E. eds: *Populism: its meaning and national characteristics*. London: Weidenfeld & Nicolson, 1969.

Kitching, G.: *Development and Underdevelopment in Historical Perspective: populism, nationalism and industrialization*. London: Methuen, 1982.

Venturi, F.: *Roots of Revolution*. London: Weidenfeld & Nicolson, 1950.

postmaterialism A set of values that gives such goals as self-expression and belonging higher priority than economic and physical security. Since the second world war postmaterialist values have become increasingly widespread in advanced industrial societies as a result of intergenerational cultural change.

The hypothesis of an intergenerational shift

from materialist toward postmaterialist values is based on two key concepts: people value most highly those things that are relatively scarce; though, to a large extent, a person's basic values reflect the conditions that prevailed during his or her pre-adult years.

Taken together these two hypotheses imply that, as a result of the unprecedented prosperity and the absence of war in western countries that have prevailed since 1945, the post-war generation in these countries might be expected to place less emphasis on economic and physical security than older age groups who had experienced the hunger and devastation of the second world war and possibly the Great Depression, and even the first world war. Conversely, the younger birth cohorts would give a higher priority to non-material needs such as a sense of community and the quality of the environment.

These hypotheses were first tested in cross-national surveys carried out in 1970. Those respondents whose top two choices emphasized economic and physical security were classified as 'materialists'; those whose top two choices emphasized non-material values such as self-expression were classified as 'mixed'. As hypothesized, tremendous differences were found between the values of old and young. Among the oldest group, materialists outnumbered postmaterialists by more than twelve to one. But among the post-war generation postmaterialists were about as numerous as materialists.

Subsequent surveys carried out in the United States and a score of other countries confirm this pattern: survey after survey reveals dramatic differences between the goals emphasized by old and young. Moreover, cohort analysis shows that there is no tendency for given birth cohorts to become more materialist as they age, as would be the case if these differences reflected life-cycle effects. In 1985 virtually all the cohorts were fully as postmaterialist as they had been fifteen years earlier in 1970. There were significant short-term fluctuations. But by 1985 inflation had subsided almost to the 1970 level. With period effects held constant there is no sign of the gradual conversion to materialism that would be present if a life-cycle interpretation were

applicable. The pattern reflects intergenerational value change.

This implies that, other things being equal, we should witness a long-term trend towards postmaterialist values as one generation replaces another. A good deal of intergenerational population replacement has already taken place. In 1970 the post-war generation comprised only 20 per cent of our sampling universe; in 1985 it constituted almost 50 per cent.

There was a corresponding shift in the distribution of value types. In 1970, materialists outnumbered postmaterialists in these six nations by a ratio of 3.4 to one. By 1985 this ratio had fallen to about 2 to 1. Despite the intervening economic crises the process of intergenerational change continued to function from 1970 to 1985 though its effect was sometimes masked by period effects. When short-term forces returned to normal the results were manifest: a substantial net shift toward postmaterialism had taken place – most of it due to intergenerational replacement.

Because the postmaterialists' values reflect the presence of economic and physical security during their formative years, they tend to be recruited from the more prosperous strata of society. As traditional patterns of POLITICAL CLEAVAGE continue to prevail, their social class background would tend to link them with the political parties of the right – but their personal values work in the opposite direction. They give top priority to values that are fundamentally different from the materialist emphasis on economic growth and domestic order that has long prevailed in industrial society. Instead they place greater emphasis on the quality of life, social solidarity, and opportunities for self-expression. In so far as these goals conflict with prevailing societal priorities the postmaterialists constitute a change-oriented constituency, and in so far as the parties of the left are relatively open to change – which is generally, though not inevitably the case – this constituency tends to gravitate towards the left.

One consequence has been a decline in traditional patterns of social class voting. One of the long-standing truisms of political sociology is the fact that throughout western society working-class voters tend to support the parties of the left and middle-class voters those of the right. This still tends to be true, but the tendency has been getting steadily weaker. In the late 1940s and early 1950s, in the United States, Great Britain and West Germany, working-class voters were more apt to support the left than middle-class voters, by margins ranging from thirty to forty-five percentage points. In the most recent national elections in those three countries (from 1980 to 1984), this spread had shrunk to the range from ten to twenty points. Though long-established political party loyalties tend to maintain the traditional pattern, this is being eroded by the fact that new support for the left increasingly comes from middle-class post-materialists, and by the fact that there are occasional working-class shifts to the right in defence of familiar materialist values.

The political impact of value change is by no means limited to voting behaviour. Perhaps its most striking consequence has been the impetus it has given to new political movements. For postmaterialists not only have fundamentally different priorities from those that have long prevailed in their societies, they are also more likely to engage in direct political action on behalf of these priorities.

The development of nuclear power has been virtually halted in certain countries by determined public opposition, coming quite disproportionately from postmaterialists. Similarly, the rise of environmentalist movements, and environmentalist political parties such as the West German Greens, reflects the political expression of postmaterialist values. Finally, the peace movement that has recently emerged in western Europe and to a lesser extent in the United States is in large part a postmaterialist phenomenon.

See also ECOLOGY/ENVIRONMENTAL PARTIES; SOCIAL STRUCTURE AND PARTY ALIGNMENTS.   RI

Reading

Abramson, P.R. and Inglehart, R.: Generational replacement and value change in six West European societies. *American Journal of Political Science* 30 (February 1986) 1–25.

Baker, K.R., Dalton, R.J. and Hildebrandt, K.: *Germany Transformed*. Cambridge, Mass.: Harvard University Press, 1981.

Dalton, R.J., Flanagan, S.C. and Beck, P.A. eds: *Electoral Change in Advanced Industrial Democracies: realignment or dealignment*. Princeton, NJ: Princeton University Press, 1984.

Deth, J. van: The persistence of materialist and postmaterialist value orientations. *European Journal of Political Research* 11 (1983) 63–79.

Inglehart, R.: The silent revolution in Europe: intergenerational change in post-industrial societies. *American Political Science Review* (1971) 991–1017.

————: *The Silent Revolution: changing values and political styles among western publics*. Princeton, NJ: Princeton University Press, 1977.

————: Postmaterialism in an environment of insecurity. *American Political Science Review* (1981) 880–900.

————: Aggregate stability and individual-level change in mass belief systems: the level of analysis paradox. *American Political Science Review* (1985) 97–116.

Lafferty, W.M. and Knutsen, O.: Postmaterialism in a social democratic state: an analysis of the distinctness and congruity of the Inglehart value syndrome in Norway. *Comparative Political Studies* (1985) 411–30.

Poujadism The Poujade Movement was formed in 1953–54 to defend the interests of independent workers. It became a political movement when it put forward candidates at the French general election of 2 January 1956. In the short term the transformation from pressure group into political party gave it an unexpected impetus, but the movement soon failed and disappeared. None the less Poujadism remains a political symbol in France.

The *Union de Défense des Commerçants et Artisans* (UDCA) was founded in November 1953 by a small bookseller Pierre Poujade, in Saint Céré in the Lot. Small commerce had developed after the war because of scarcity and inflation. The end of rationing and inflation in 1952 forced small shopkeepers to modernize if they did not want to be eliminated. From July 1953 Poujade organized violent demonstrations against the tax offices. This revolt of the small against the big, of independent workers against Parisian technocrats and State intervention, was the result of a crisis situation among small tradesmen.

When Poujadism entered politics in 1955–6 under the title *Union et Fraternité Françaises*, it added anti-capitalist and anti-state themes to its anti-parliamentarianism. It also put forward political ideas which linked it to the nationalistic extreme right: defence of French Algeria, anti-Semitism, xenophobia and racism. In the political context of the times, it appeared as the opposite of Mendesism which stood for decolonization and modernization. The demagogic oratory of Pierre Poujade and the unpopularity of the Fourth Republic brought the Poujadists their unforeseen success of 2 January 1956 (12 per cent of the vote, 51 MPs). However as the party had no programme and no unity the movement disappeared in a matter of months, not only from the political scene but also out of society; other movements and other leaders took over the defence of tradesmen and artisans.

In France Poujadism is still the political symbol of negative, demagogic revolt with no real political objective other than bringing together the dissatisfied and exploiting politically all sources of discontent. The Communist Party, which supported the Poujadist movement in its early stages, is itself sometimes accused of Poujadism. Elsewhere the term is used to describe a POPULIST, know-nothing movement such as the Scandinavian tax protest parties based on a rag-bag of grievances amongst the lower middle-class, and led by a demagogic exploiter of discontents.　　JC

Reading

Hoffmann, S.: *Le Mouvement Poujade*. Paris: Colin, 1956.

PPBS (Programming, Planning, Budgeting System)

This was initiated in the United States in the 1960s as a revolutionary departure from existing methods of governmental budget formulation, and was quickly adopted as an ideal for budget systems at all levels of government all over the world.

PPBS is also known as programme budgeting. Instead of classifying expenditures on the basis of objects purchased, such as salaries, equipment or travel, it organizes them into programmes. Budget decisions are made according to the comparative effectiveness of each programme, based upon quantitative analysis of results. The aim is to rationalize the budget process through explicit appraisal of objectives and alternatives, multi-year forecasting and planning, linking together programme and budget decisions, and re-aligning government organizations.

The introduction of PPBS into the United States federal government was the culmination of a reform movement dating back over fifty years. Budget systems had traditionally been classified according to a line item or object of expenditure format. This classification was criticized since it gave no information on the purposes for which monies were expended, nor any indication whether they were spent efficiently. During the New Deal and post-war years a performance approach to budgeting became the substance of budget reform proposals resulting in activity classifications, narrative descriptions of organizational functions and work-cost-measurement techniques in the federal budget.

PPBS failed for both practical and intrinsic reasons. Practically, across-the-board implementation of a radically new budget system proved beyond the capacity of personnel and existing institutions. Quantification of programme effectiveness was difficult and decision making across organizational lines was impractical. The new system generated immense amounts of paperwork which hindered rather than helped policy-making and administration. Centralization provoked hostility and misunderstanding. In addition, several assumptions of PPBS appear to be untenable. First, neutral analytical techniques are incapable of determining which measures will result in greater social utility: this function lies in the realm of the political process. Second, changes in formal budget procedures do not necessarily determine the substance of budgetary decision making. Third, there is no single best way of conducting public budgeting; rather, budget processes are adapted to purposes and to their environment.

It is not surprising that countries with far fewer resources have experienced difficulties in implementing PPBS and it is unlikely that it will be successful in transforming budgetary decision making. But it is possible that certain elements of the system may remain of use in improving budget information and methods.

See also BUDGET/BUDGETING.   NJC

Reading

Schick, A.: The road to PPB: the stages of budget reform. *Public Administration Review* 26 (December 1966) 243–58.

————: A death in the bureaucracy: the demise of federal PPB. *Public Administration Review* (March/ April 1973) 146–56.

Prefect   A senior government official who is the direct agent of central government in the localities. The prefectoral model is generally contrasted with other models of LOCAL GOVERNMENT which provide for greater local autonomy.

In 1800 Napoleon created the French Prefects to play a key role in the re-centraliz-ation of the local government system estab-lished during the Revolution. In each of the eighty-one (later raised to ninety-six) *départe-ments* (or counties) – the upper level of local government – a Prefect was appointed as the direct representative of the central govern-ment, the local overlord of all local councils and field services of ministries, and the head of police services. In Paris, alongside the Seine department Prefect, a special Prefect of Police was given responsibility for law and order. From their offices and official residences, the Prefects (in the administrative 'capitals' of the *départements*) not only wielded huge legal powers but also considerable social and political influence. In the nineteenth century, and especially during the Second Empire, they were often accused of using their influence – and the patronage power of appointments in local administration – to 'make' elections for pro-government candi-dates. At the same time, as local police chiefs, they were criticized for persecuting and repressing opponents of the government – usually on the left. In practice, the real power of the Prefects never matched up to the popular mythology. From the start the Prefects faced rivals who aspired to freedom from prefectoral *tutelle* (supervision). Some field services – the treasuries, the courts and the army – won autonomy in 1800. Others remained subordinate, although the 'control' was more theoretical than effective. The elected municipal and departmental councils only gained freedom from *tutelle* in 1982 by the Defferre law.

Similar offices have been created else-where. In Italy, after the *Risorgimento*, Prefects were appointed to head the *provinces*, but their responsibility did not cover the field services or state agencies (apart from a vague co-ordinating role) and their supervision of local councils was never very effective. They became local police chiefs and directors of Ministry of the Interior services. Algeria, too, has a local administrative overlord modelled on the French Prefect. Since 1964 France has also had Regional Prefects, one in each of 22 regions.

See also TUTELAGE.   HM

Reading

Gourevitch, P.A.: *Paris and the Provinces: the politics of local government reform in France*. London: Allen & Unwin, 1980.

Hough, J.F.: *The Soviet Prefects*. Cambridge, Mass.: Harvard University Press, 1969.

Lagroye, J. and Wright, V. eds: *Local Government in Britain and France: problems and prospects*. London: Allen & Unwin, 1979.

Machin, H.: *The Prefect in French Public Adminis-tration*. London: Croom Helm, 1977.

Mény, Y. and Wright, V. eds: *Centre Periphery Relations in Western Europe*. London: Allen & Unwin, 1985.

Tarrow, S.: *Between Center and Periphery: grassroots politicians in Italy and France*. New Haven, Conn.: Yale University Press, 1977.

preferential voting   See ELECTORAL SYSTEM.

prerogative   An exclusive right or privilege vested in a person or body of persons, especially a political ruler or sovereign. Historically the royal prerogative in England was, according to DICEY 'the residue of discretionary or arbitrary authority left in the hands of the Crown' (1959, p. 424). In practice today prerogative powers are the discretionary powers of the executive government for whose exercise they do not need the authority of an Act of Parliament or other legislative instrument, and which are not analogous to powers exercised by any private person.

In origin many of the CROWN'S powers were feudal prerogatives. The king dispensed justice, but could not be sued in his own courts; he could pardon offenders and create peers. He could take emergency action for the defence and well-being of the realm. In the seventeenth-century struggle between the crown and parliament the crown's arbitrary powers were controlled and the supremacy of statute law established. The courts continued to recognize various kinds of prerogative power but developed legal doctrines to curb extensions of the prerogative. Constitutionally it became accepted that the major personal prerogatives of the crown could only be exercised through responsible ministers. The crown now has no personal involvement in the exercise of the prerogative powers that relate to the conduct of foreign affairs, the making of war and peace, of civil and military appointments, and the summoning and dissolution of parliament. (Though in some circumstances elements of personal discretion may be acknowledged, notably in relation to governmental requests to dissolve parliament.)

Where prerogative powers are exercised by ministers and civil servants the courts have been reluctant to exercise powers of control or review, particularly where powers in question related to the control of the armed forces or to acts done outside the realm. The courts now however seem prepared to treat many prerogative powers in domestic matters as similar to executive powers derived from statute and to subject them (with some reservations) to judicial review on the same principles. (See JUSTICIABILITY.)

In other systems of government, the term prerogative refers to the autonomous executive power of the head of state.   GM

Reading

Dicey, A.V.: *Introduction to the Study of the Law of the Constitution*. 10th edn (1959), ed. E.C.S. Wade. Repr. Basingstoke: Macmillan, 1985.

Heuston, R.F.V.: *Essays in Constitutional Law*, ch. 3. 2nd edn. London: Stevens, 1964.

Phillips, O.H. and Jackson, P.: *Constitutional and Administrative Law*, ch. 14. 6th edn. London: Sweet & Maxwell, 1982.

Jennings, I.: *Cabinet Government*, ch. 13. 3rd edn. Cambridge: Cambridge University Press, 1959.

Keir, D.L. and Lawson, F.H.: *Cases in Constitutional Law*, ch. 2. 6th edn, ed. F.H. Lawson and D.J. Bentley. Oxford: Clarendon Press, 1979.

Wade, W.: Procedure and prerogative in public law. *Law Quarterly Review* 101 (1985) 180–99.

president/presidential system The United States of America, under the Constitution of 1789, defines the leading uses of such terms as presidency, presidential system, or presidential government (a coinage of Walter Bagehot in 1867). An elected official styled 'President of the United States' serves as chief of state with reference to the external world, and simultaneously serves as the system's nearest thing to chief of government. The latter role is limited on the one hand by federalism and on the other by the independence of the law courts. It is further limited by the extraordinary position of CONGRESS, the national legislature.

Since the second world war those limits have frequently been obscured by the presidential exercise of certain constitutional and customary powers, among them conduct of diplomacy, command of the armed forces, preservation of internal peace, presentation annually of legislative programmes, and – harking back to Lockean prerogative – extraordinary action in perceived emergencies. More recently, the limits have been obscured still more by the prominence accorded presidents in television, the primary news source for most Americans. Successive presidents however have had to face congressional competition in diplomacy, restrictions on the use of military force, rejection of proposed domestic programmes, criticism or reversal of extraordinary acts – and all the pains attendant on unfavourable television coverage or images.

The constitutional relations of the presidency and Congress give American government a special character, distinguished from nominal

493

counterparts throughout the modern world. These relations were established in the eighteenth century to secure the newly-independent British colonists from the vicissitudes of English government in the seventeenth century and since. Drawing on Blackstone's Commentaries, among other sources, the American constitution-makers undertook (without acknowledgement) to perfect and to assure perpetuation of the balance between crown and parliament achieved by the Glorious Revolution. To settle once and for all the question of royal taxation, the Constitution requires Acts of Congress. To guard against the spectre of royal armies, Congress has to authorize the military forces, funding them for no more than two years at a time. To limit royal prerogative, only Congress may declare war (a limit technologically outmoded in the missile age). To ensure against such things as secret subsidies from France, one House of Congress, the Senate (originally representing states, now popularly elected), must consent to every treaty. To curb appointive power, presidential nominations require the consent of the Senate. To curb corruption through royal patronage, Senators and members of the other congressional body, the House of Representatives, cannot hold executive offices. And while the president can VETO legislation, Congress may override his veto by a two-thirds vote of both houses.

The Americans call these CHECKS AND BALANCES. They amount to making president and Congress sharers in each other's constitutional authority. Even with respect to the executive establishment, which actually administers the laws, that sharing is maintained. The president appoints department heads (Senate concurring) and is charged constitutionally to 'take care that the laws be faithfully executed'. But Congress creates the departments, enacting their functions by statute, appropriates their money, and through subcommittees, 'oversees' them, vetting performance. The president is known as chief executive; traditionally he talks with 'his' department heads in 'cabinet' meetings, among other places (though the cabinet is a body of advisers not collectively responsible to anyone for anything). He, they, and their senior assistants – appointed usually from private life, not civil servants – are known colloquially as 'the Administration'. But Congress and its subcommittees are as much participants as those in actual administration.

What has sustained these arrangements for two centuries? The answer seems to be that president and Congress both can claim to represent the sovereign people (who in 1776 replaced George III by God's grace as legitimator of the government). Presidents are popularly elected by a majority of voters in enough states to produce a majority in the so-called ELECTORAL COLLEGE – pledged electors being chosen by each state's majority. Members of the House of Representatives are directly elected by majorities (or pluralities) in geographic districts within states. For most of the twentieth century Senators have been similarly elected, two from each state, both at large. Since the constituency of each of these officials is geographically distinct from all the others, while TICKET-SPLITTING has become endemic in most districts, the presidency and the congressional Houses are effectively separated from each other by distinct electorates. The distinctions are reinforced by fixed terms of differing length: four years for a president (renewable once), two years for Representatives and six for Senators (renewable indefinitely).

Each official has a political base different from that of the others. The differences grow sharpest at the stage of nomination. Regardless of party label, presidents and members of Congress have limited effect, or none, on choices for each other's posts by party officers and voters in those distinct constituencies.

The result is perpetuation of the scheme of overlapped authority, hence 'checks' or 'balances', between the president and Congress. The power-sharing persists because their independence of each other institutionally is supported by their separateness politically. Separate institutions sharing powers, checking one another, was a Whig ideal implanted in the American Constitution. This is the case not only from the White House to the Capitol, where Congress sits, but also between both of them and the departments they each supervise. Serving two masters, the executive departments are and have to be somewhat in business for themselves. Least of all are they in business for each other: their statutory duties usually are assigned them individually.

In other countries, notably Britain, the formal separation among institutions and their separate political bases have been bridged by political parties. In the United States, as voter coalitions and as organizations too, the parties are state and district centred, with the principal exception of the presidential contest, a quadrennial source of national focus. As links across national government, American parties can and do ameliorate, somewhat, relations among president and members of Congress with the same party label. Also, automatically, labels decide who gets the chairmanships and leaderships in House and Senate, as well as who competes for higher-level posts in the administration. Winner-takes-all is the rule on both scores. Otherwise, however, political parties are weak reeds in Washington, compared with their roles elsewhere.

Unlike virtually all other industrialized or industrializing nations, the United States has no stiffening element in its governmental system, neither parties in the British sense (or in the Japanese, the Indian, the Mexican, the Leninist), nor civil services akin to those of France, nor military juntas, nor religious mullahs, nor even traditional royalty; the president comes closest to that last. The separateness of Congress and departments – and the courts and of course states – makes him or her at most a sort of Tudor monarch, or a later Stuart, never claiming to be Charles I, and unable ever, even in dire straits, to play Napoleon – not even Napoleon III, distinguishing Americans from the French under Charles de Gaulle. Even Abraham Lincoln at the outset of the Civil War – the greatest test of the American system yet – looked for early sanction for what he had done, not directly from the people but from Congress.

See also SEMI-PRESIDENTIAL SYSTEMS; SEPARATION OF POWERS.   REN

Reading

Corwin, E.S.: *The Presidency: office and powers*. 3rd edn. New York: New York University Press, 1949.

Cronin, T.E.: *The State of the Presidency*. 2nd edn. Boston, Mass.: Little, Brown, 1980.

Greenstein, F.I.: *The Hidden Hand Presidency*. New York: Basic Books, 1982.

Heclo, H. and Salamon, L.M. eds: *The Illusion of Presidential Government*. Boulder, Col.: Westview, 1982.

Neustadt, R.E.: *Presidential Power: the politics of leadership from FDR to Carter*. New York: Wiley, 1980.

Rockman, B.A.: *The Leadership Question*. New York: Praeger, 1984.

Rose, R. and Suleiman, E.N. eds: *Presidents and Prime Ministers*. Washington, DC: American Enterprise Institute, 1980.

Presidium   See POLITBURO.

pressure groups   See INTEREST GROUPS.

pre-state political systems   The broad category of simpler political systems which existed prior to the development of centralized states and which in many instances have been absorbed or destroyed by them.

During the course of human history, as the population of the world has risen, the number of autonomous political units into which it is divided has declined. The last 150 years have seen the emergence of the NATION-STATE as the major form of political organization, incorporating earlier forms of state and prestate organization. These range from very simple systems such as those to be found in hunter-gatherer societies, to large complex states. Different typologies have been suggested to cope with this variation (for examples see Fortes and Evans-Pritchard; Mair; Cohen and Middleton; and Fried), but similar ideas underlie all of them. As societies have become more complex so they have developed increasing degrees of specialization and inequality in the distribution of power. In the more complex states this culminated in complex hierarchies of office holders and elaborate rules for the transfer of leadership and power over time. This development was linked to other factors: changes in productive technology, in population density and in settlement size.

For most of its history the human population made its living through hunting and gathering and it was only with the development of agriculture and the domestication of animals that this changed. Although groups of hunter-gatherers survived into the twentieth century including Australian aborigines, African pygmies and bushmen, and the Eskimo, very few people even in these societies still pursue their former way of life.

They were succeeded by what are usually called 'tribal' societies (Sahlins 1968), consisting of a number of small autonomous units. Pastoral societies survive in many parts of the world. They are mobile in their search for pasture, fiercely independent and notoriously difficult to bring under administrative control. Separate groups of herders may be linked by ties of lineage – descent from a common ancestor – or age divisions cutting across social groups, but feuding and raiding are still common and a high value is placed on being able to defend one's own interests and those of one's close kinsmen. These wider links make it easy for pastoralists to bring together large mobile forces during a conflict, and they have often been able to establish political control over surrounding agricultural populations, producing stratified societies and even large states.

Shifting cultivation allowed still higher population densities and permanent settlements to develop, and these in turn allowed the accumulation of wealth and political power. In the 'big man' systems of New Guinea, the big man builds up his political following through elaborate exchanges of pigs and other valuables with other big men. The goods for exchange are obtained using the labour of wives, kin and allies who support him in the expectation that they will also benefit. Big man status is fragile and requires constant effort in creating and maintaining alliances, unlike the authority of chiefs which is accepted by others as legitimate and can be transferred to one's heirs over time.

The development of chiefship thus involved the adaption of existing authority patterns or the development of new ones. Even in many small-scale societies without chiefs some hereditary offices such as leadership of lineages or priesthoods existed. Forms of ranking based on skill in warfare, wealth, or supposed supernatural powers were widespread and formed a basis for the later development of more centralized political institutions. The crucial step in the development of chiefship is for one of the existing leaders to be recognized as *primus inter pares* by the others and as having some responsibility for the group as a whole. However even when chiefship is established there is a considerable degree of variation in the extent to which decision making is centralized in the hands of the chief or a hierarchy of officials with specifically delimited powers.

Why pre-state systems evolved into states is a complex question. It happened independently in six different parts of the world: Central America, the Andes, Mesopotamia, Egypt, the Indus Valley and China. From these centres centralized political institutions spread to other areas through processes of conquest, colonization and imitation. Primary state formation was associated with factors such as agricultural intensification producing a larger surplus, higher population densities, increasing social inequality, the growth of trade, and urbanization. Processes of secondary state formation, radiating outwards from these original centres, gradually affected more and more of the globe. Finally, colonialism, coupled with the rise of the nation-state, has, in the present century, led to the progressive absorption or demise of the remaining pre-state political systems.   JSE

Reading

Claessen, H.J.M. and Skalnik, P. eds: *The Early State*. The Hague: Mouton, 1978.

Cohen, R. and Middleton, J. eds: *Comparative Political Systems*. Garden City, NY: The Natural History Press, 1967.

Cohen, R. and Service, E.R. eds: *Origins of the State*. Philadelphia: Institute for the Study of Human Issues, 1978.

Fortes, M. and Evans-Pritchard, E.E. eds: *African Political Systems*. London: Oxford University Press, 1940.

Fried, M.H.: *The Evolution of Political Society*. New York: Random House, 1967.

Krader, L.: *Formation of the State*. Englewood Cliffs, NJ: Prentice-Hall, 1968.

Mair, L.: *Primitive Government*. Harmondsworth: Penguin, 1962.

Sahlins, M.D.: *Tribesmen*. Englewood Cliffs, NJ: Prentice-Hall, 1968.

Service, E.R.: *Origins of the State and Civilization*. New York: Norton, 1975.

primary, direct As early as the mid-nineteenth century, some local American parties had their voters nominate candidates in a 'primary' election. But as developed in most of the United States during the early decades of the twentieth century, the direct primary is a state-conducted election in which voters choose candidates to compete against each other in a subsequent general election. The adjective 'direct' distinguishes the method of candidate selection, or nomination, from the older American practice of party voters meeting in caucuses (also called primaries) to elect delegates to a convention which actually names the candidates. Customarily, however, Americans use the word 'primary' alone, applying it not only to elections in which voters choose party candidates but also to non-partisan elections for many municipal and other offices, in which voters cast ballots merely to reduce the field to two individual contestants for each office. The method's political significance is more striking in partisan contests where numerous voters replace smaller and more active organized memberships in bestowing party labels for general election ballots and campaigns.

The American primary differs sharply from CANDIDATE SELECTION in other democratic nations. What may occasionally be called a primary elsewhere is no more than a party's own poll of its organized and ordinarily dues-paying members. Only in the United States are party candidates chosen in an election provided by the same governmental authority that manages the general election. The relevant authority is that of the American state and its statutes (even in the few states that authorize parties to conduct their own primaries).

Almost all American states have adopted the direct primary as the standard means for nominating major-party candidates for their executive and legislative offices, for numerous local offices, and for both houses of the US Congress. A few states allow nominations for these offices by other methods, and some require a primary only if convention choices are challenged. But in most states the primary is mandatory. Presidential nominations are the principal exceptions. In the absence of a national primary both Republicans and Democrats have continued to choose their presidential and vice-presidential nominees in national conventions. By the 1970s, however, most delegates to these conventions reflected the candidate-preferences of voters as recorded in 'presidential primaries' conducted by over half the states. These resemble direct primaries, and they have, unsystematically, much the same effect by way of voter-determination of party nominations.

For the more pervasively established primaries for non-presidential offices as well as for presidential primaries, American statutes vary greatly from state to state. About half the states require the voter, at some specified date before a primary election, to record a preference for a particular party in whose primary he or she wishes to participate. The party preference is listed along with the voter's official registration as an eligible elector. About fifteen other states require an oral declaration of party preference at the primary election itself. In contrast to these more or less 'closed' primaries, the remaining minority of states open their primaries to all eligible voters without requiring any public expression of preference for the party whose nominees they want to help select. Within each broad category of closed and open primaries other variations occur. For example, certain primaries requiring advance registration are more liberal than others in allowing changes between elections or in allowing unaffiliated voters to declare for a party on a given election day, and a few of the open-primary states do not even confine voters to a single party's primary but permit choices of candidates of different parties provided they are not candidates for the same office.

The anti-organizational thrust of the direct primary accords with the reform purposes of the PROGRESSIVE movement that inspired the selection of candidates by rank-and-file voters.

Although turnouts in primaries are considerably lower than those in general elections, the numbers casting primary ballots are well above those likely to participate in caucuses and conventions. Moreover, in one-party states or constituencies, the primary serves as the only meaningful election. It may thus deter the development of a second party even as it also seems to deter the emergence of a significant third party in a two-party situation. The primary provides an alternative route to office for protest candidates rejected by an established party leadership. In this respect the primary fits the American pattern of candidate-centred politics in which parties are permeable and their organizations limited in unusual ways. Although American party organizations can and often do endorse and campaign for particular candidates in primaries, they do not always win. Understandably, therefore, many party leaders would prefer other nominating methods. But, apart from the still disputed presidential selection process, the primary appears firmly established in most of the United States. LDE

Reading

Jewell, M.E. and Olson, D.M.: *American State Political Parties and Elections*, ch. 4. Homewood, Ill.: Dorsey, 1982.

Merriam, C.E. and Overacker, L.: *Primary Elections*. Chicago, Ill.: University of Chicago Press, 1928.

Polsby, N.W.: *Consequences of Party Reform*. New York: Oxford University Press, 1983.

Price, D.E.: *Bringing Back the Parties*, chs. 5–7. Washington, DC: Congressional Quarterly Press, 1984.

Ranney, A.: Candidate selection. In *Democracy at the Polls: a comparative study of competitive national elections*, pp. 75–106, ed. D. Butler, H.R. Penniman and A. Ranney. Washington, DC: American Enterprise Institute, 1981.

primary party organization Formerly known as cell, this is the basic membership unit of communist and other Marxist–Leninist parties. In the Communist Party of the Soviet Union, for instance, there were about 450,000 primary party organizations in 1986, each of them serving as a branch or basic unit of the party's nineteen million members. The rules of the CPSU specify that PPOs are the 'basis of the party' and that they are formed at places of work such as factories and collective farms wherever there are three or more party members. If necessary, PPOs may also be organized on a residential basis (rule 52). They hold meetings at least once a month; they also elect a bureau for a term of two or three years, and a secretary and deputy secretary to take care of current tasks (rules 54 and 55). PPOs are responsible for the admission of new members and for political leadership at the local level, including ideological work and the organization of production. PPOs within ministries and other state bodies also enjoy the right to supervise the work of leading personnel within these bodies (rules 58 and 59). Analogous provisions are made in the statutes of other ruling COMMUNIST PARTIES. PPOs are supposed to function in accordance with the principles of inner-party democracy, criticism and self-criticism, and broad publicity. Reports in the party press suggest that they are more frequently dominated by elected officials and that ordinary party members have very little opportunity to influence their decisions. SLW

Reading

Hill, R.J. and Frank, P.: *The Soviet Communist Party*. 3rd edn. London: Allen & Unwin, 1987.

Simons, W.B. and White, S. eds: *The Party Statutes of the Communist World*. The Hague: Nijhoff, 1984.

prime minister/prime ministerial government Prime ministers are the leaders of governments by virtue of their leadership of the majority party or coalition in parliament. A prime minister is normally the head of the government; where there is a separate elected president (as in France or Portugal) he or she is the second person in rank or, as the leader of the largest party, an alternative source of power (see also SEMI-PRESIDENTIAL SYSTEMS).

Prime ministers are generally referred to as the 'first among equals' because they work mainly through the collective will of cabinet. But they retain their authority only so long as they remain the elected leader of their party.

The constituency to which they owe their position is at its widest in Canada where a large convention representing all sections of the party is convened to choose the leader, and at its narrowest in a country such as Australia where only the parliamentary party has a vote. Prime ministerial security depends in part on the ease with which he or she can be removed. In Canada election by convention means that it is virtually impossible to displace a prime minister who wants to stay. In Australia prime ministers can be, and have been, removed at any time by a vote of the parliamentary party; they are always vulnerable.

There can be no job description to define what prime ministers are constitutionally required to do; they define the job in terms of what they want to achieve. Their success can then be judged against normative and implicit assumptions (what the observer thinks they should do) or operational criteria of effectiveness. Some roles they must play: chair cabinet, prevent fragmentation, arbitrate, meet the media, fight fires, and fulfil international duties. Others they may choose to pursue: control the details of policies, initiate policies. There are a few roles which observers think that they ought to fill – and think that they often have difficulty in filling well: acting as guardian of the government's strategy, focusing on priorities. Each category contains political, policy, and administrative problems. The pressures and range of duties are immense for the problems that come to the prime minister are those which cannot be solved elsewhere or those in which they are personally interested. The skill is in determining the balance.

Richard Crossman and others have argued that in Britain there has been a growth in prime ministerial power that can be attributed to six factors: the right to select and dismiss ministers; the right to control the structure and proceedings of the cabinet; the development of disciplined parties through which the prime minister can control parliament; increased direct influence on the media, particularly the development of election campaigns into personalized appeals for votes; an increase in the level of patronage; and the development of new processes of co-ordination so that prime ministers can control the vast bureaucratic machines of which they are head. Similar arguments – that CABINET GOVERNMENT has been displaced by prime ministerial power – can be found also in Canada, Australia, and New Zealand.

Prime ministers are undoubtedly the most powerful of ministers, but each of their powers has to be exercised within constraints. They need to choose a cabinet that is balanced to represent the party factions, regions, and coalitions; some items force themselves on to the cabinet agenda, particularly if a powerful minister wants them discussed; cabinets and parties do not blindly follow orders and need to be wooed to ensure the security of the leader's position; prime ministers cannot control all those that they appoint to important posts. Even the most dominant prime ministers must constantly compromise to maintain the cohesion of their support.

Prime ministers have immense potential power; however it needs to be used carefully. They cannot make every decision. Prime ministers are not presidents with personalized power. Even if they try to dominate, they must work with and through their cabinet and party whose support and consent they need in order to survive.   PMW

Reading

Crossman, R.H.S.: *Inside View: three lectures on prime ministerial government*. London: Cape, 1972.

Hockin, T.A. ed.: *Apex of Power: the prime minister and political leadership in Canada*. 2nd edn. Scarborough, Ont.: Prentice-Hall, 1977.

King, A. ed.: *The British Prime Minister*. 2nd edn. London: Macmillan, 1985.

Punnett, R.M.: *The Prime Minister in Canadian Government and Politics*. Toronto: Macmillan, 1977.

Rose, R. and Suleiman, E.N. eds: *Presidents and Prime Ministers*. Washington, DC: American Enterprise Institute, 1980.

Weller, P.: *First Among Equals: prime ministers in Westminster systems*. Sydney and Boston, Mass.: Allen & Unwin, 1985.

private bill This is a bill for conferring particular powers or benefits on any person or body in excess of or in conflict with the general law.

Private bills in the United Kingdom parliament are founded on petitions from their promoters. The stages through which they pass are essentially the same as for PUBLIC BILLS, but the details of their procedure are very different; in particular opportunity is provided for opponents of a bill to petition against it and to be heard, and evidence may be called in support of both the promoters and the petitioners.   MTR

Reading

May, T.E.: *Parliamentary Practice*. 20th edn, Part III. London: Butterworth, 1983.

private members bill   This is a PUBLIC BILL introduced by a Member other than a Minister. Some such bills propose minor amendments of the law; others express a party point of view; often they deal with controversial moral or social issues.

The procedure in the HOUSE OF COMMONS on these bills is essentially the same as for any public bill. Time for their consideration is however strictly limited and there is much competition to secure a favourable place for the second reading stage. Priority is decided by a ballot. Members unlucky in the ballot can still introduce a bill, but the chances of it making further progress are slight unless it is totally uncontroversial. Private members may also take up bills agreed by the Lords. In recent sessions between 10 and 20 private members bills have received Royal Assent.
MTR

Reading

Richards, P.: *Parliament and Conscience*. London: Allen & Unwin, 1970.

————: Private Members' Legislation. In *The Commons Today*, ed. S. Walkland and M. Ryle. London: Fontana, 1981.

privy council   A body in the United Kingdom appointed by the crown whose role, once important, has become formal. It emerged under the Norman kings as a policy-making group of officials and advisers, and reached the zenith of its influence during the Tudor period. In the seventeenth century the abolition of its judicial arm, the Court of Star Chamber, and parliament's curtailment of the prerogatives led to its decline. It may be regarded as a precursor of the CABINET, which came to perform similar functions. Though its practical importance has diminished, formally it still remains at the centre of the machinery of government. Its members, appointed by the crown and numbering upwards of 300, are styled 'the Right Honourable'. Cabinet ministers and senior judges are appointed to it by convention, complemented by others distinguished in public or political service. Membership is for life, subject to removal. The Council's principal function is its use for the enactment of some of the government's subordinate legislation (proclamations and orders in council), normally performed by a few members summoned to the monarch's presence, the quorum being three. The council meets in full only on ceremonial occasions. It has a few miscellaneous functions exercised through committees, including some responsibilities for the Channel Islands, universities, and advice on proposals for the conferring of honours. The Judicial Committee of the privy council is a court with specialized jurisdiction. Issues of national security or constitutional importance are sometimes referred to *ad hoc* committees.   CRM

Reading

Dicey, A.V.: *The Privy Council*. London: Whittaker, 1860.

Morrison, H.: The privy council today. *Parliamentary Affairs* 2 (1948) 10–17.

Progressive Movement   This term is conventionally applied to a broad movement of reform which transformed the course of American politics during the first two decades of the twentieth century. It was an impassioned reaction to the domination of the US social and political system by business interests and associated party corruption during the years following the end of the civil war in 1865. Progressivism emerged in full flood during the presidency of Theodore Roosevelt in 1901–9, and reached its climax, perhaps, in the 1912 presidential campaign. It petered out effectively with America's entry into the first world war in 1917.

The movement focused on three main areas. First, it was an attempt to impose governmental and legal control on big business, especially through the anti-trust movement and railroad regulation. Second, it stimulated the social justice movement, with crusades against poverty, slum housing, and the exploitation of child and female labour. Third, it aimed to restore direct democratic control and accountability through such methods as the PRIMARY system for electing senators and other public officials, the secret BALLOT, the RECALL, INITIATIVE, and REFERENDUM. The movement was most effective locally, at the city and state level. In cities such as Cleveland, Cincinnati or Toledo, effective urban reform movements outflanked the old machines. City managers were often appointed to run cities on non-partisan, honest lines, free from corrupt CAUCUS politics. At the state level spectacular achievements came in Wisconsin, where 'Fighting Bob' La Follette, first as governor, then as US senator, spearheaded such reforms as railroad regulation, tax changes, workers' compensation and unemployment insurance, together with the extension of DIRECT DEMOCRACY. The direct primary had spread to all but four states by 1918.

From around 1904, progressivism also began to make its impact upon federal politics, fanned by the powerful exposure journalism in the so-called 'muck-raking' press, from writers such as Lincoln Steffens and Ida Tarbell. There were federal measures, often aimed at protecting the consumer, such as the 1906 Pure Food and Drugs Act and major curbs on the railroad companies in 1906 and 1910. The department of justice gave new life to the anti-trust campaign in the courts; Standard Oil and other industrial monopolies were among the victims. In a remarkable presidential contest in 1912 both the victorious Democrat Woodrow Wilson, and Theodore Roosevelt the former Republican president who had now founded a 'Progressive Party' (or 'Bull-Moosers'), claimed to be champions of progressivism. Wilson passed several important social reforms as late as 1916. By then, however, the

tide of reform was ebbing and progressivism fragmenting. The nationalist hysteria of the first world war finally killed it, until temporarily revived by La Follette's candidacy in the 1924 presidential election as a protest movement against the conservative administrations of Harding and Coolidge.

The success of progressivism lay in its identification with contemporary, urban America, unlike the agrarian 'free silver' Populists of the 1890s. Progressivism also afforded scope for the reformist enthusiasms of professions such as lawyers, journalists, teachers, ministers of religion, and even enlightened businessmen. It was distinctly Anglo-Saxon, Protestant and, on balance, nationalist in tone, and its weakness stemmed from this ideological and ethnic limitation. It failed to appeal effectively to immigrants, farmers, or organized labour. Its roots in evangelical Protestantism led to its placing the emphasis unduly on reforming individuals through direct democracy rather than reshaping the political structure more fundamentally. The New Dealers of the 1930s were more sober and disenchanted, but also in the longer term more effective. In terms of political institutions, however, the Progressives have left a heritage which remains important in American politics today.   KOM

Reading

Davis, A.F.: *Spearheads for Reform: the social settlements and the progressive movement.* New York: Oxford University Press, 1967.

Goldman, E.F.: *Rendezvous with Destiny.* New York: Vintage Books, 1955.

Hofstadter, R.: *The Age of Reform.* New York: Vintage Books, 1955.

Link, A.S.: *Wilson: the new freedom.* London: Oxford University Press, 1956.

Morgan, K.O.: The future at work. In *Contrast and Connection: bicentennial essays in Anglo-American history,* ed. H.C. Allen and R. Thompson. London: Bell, 1976.

Mowry, G.: *The California Progressives.* Berkeley: University of California Press, 1951.

————: *The Era of Theodore Roosevelt and the Birth of Modern America 1900–1912.* New York: Harper & Row, 1958.

Thelen, D.P.: *Robert La Follette and the Insurgent*

Spirit. Boston, Mass.: Little, Brown, 1976.

Wiebe, R.H.: *Businessmen and Reform: a study of the progressive movement*. Cambridge, Mass.: Harvard University Press, 1962.

Witt, B.P. de: *The Progressive Movement*. Seattle: University of Washington Press, 1968.

promotional group See INTEREST GROUPS.

pronunciamento Overthrow of a government or political system by an officers' revolt. Examples of anti-system pronunciamentos from Spanish history are: Riego (1820) against absolutism; Primo de Rivera (1923) against parliamentary liberalism; Franco (1936) against democratic republic.

In most of the 'classic' mid-nineteenth-century pronunciamentos, party politicians, excluded from government, appealed to generals as 'swords' to install them in office. In the late nineteenth century the Spanish army developed a political theory to justify military intervention. If the political system ceased to represent the general will then that will, in their view, was expressed by the officers. This set limits on the pronunciamento when a government or a political system clearly embodied the general will. Hence Colonel Tejero's invasion of the Cortes (February 1981) was a *golpe* (a COUP) not a pronunciamento.   RC

propaganda The calculated manipulation of symbols (including words, slogans, signs, music and visual displays) so as to change an audience population's attitudes and behaviour in designed directions. The term now has pejorative connotations, and it is common to use concepts such as persuasion, advocacy, and political advertising as more neutral expressions for purposeful political communication. Lenin, who popularized the term, defined it as the reasoned use of argument to influence educated people, reserving the concept of 'agitation' for emotional appeals to the uneducated masses.

The systematic study of propaganda began after the first world war and it expanded greatly with the rise of NAZISM and FASCISM. During the second world war and in the early cold war years the western allies' counter-propaganda effort was known as 'psychological warfare'. Devious propaganda includes 'black propaganda', in which the source of the communication is falsely identified, 'grey propaganda', which leaves the source ambiguous, and 'disinformation', involving inaccurate stories being planted in legitimate news channels. International propaganda is at present carried out largely through 'cultural diplomacy', national 'information' services, and state-run radio programming, activities that re-affirm the adage that what is education for one is propaganda for another.

Early research on propaganda led to the development of methods for rigorous content analysis and to the art of deciphering Aesopian communications in totalitarian-controlled societies. More recent work has focused on the psychological dynamics of attitude change and the influence of the mass media in electoral campaigns and in setting the agenda for popular politics. As populations have become more sophisticated in responding to mass communications the art of propaganda has had to become increasingly subtle in order to avoid any suggestion of being 'propaganda'.

LWP

Reading

Doob, L.: *Public Opinion and Propaganda*. New York: Holt, 1948.

Ellul, J.: *Propaganda*. New York: Knopf, 1965.

George, A.L.: *Propaganda Analysis: a study of inferences made from Nazi propaganda in World War II*. Evanston, Ill.: Row Peterson, 1959.

Hale, H.: *Radio Power: propaganda and international broadcasting*. Philadelphia: Temple University Press, 1975.

Jervis, R.: *The Logic of Images in International Relations*. Princeton, NJ: Princeton University Press, 1970.

Lasswell, H.D.: *Propaganda Techniques in the World War*. New York: Smith, 1938.

Lerner, D.: *Propaganda in War and Crisis*. New York: Stewart, 1951.

Roetter, C.: *The Art of Psychological Warfare*. New York: Stein & Day, 1974.

proportional representation
See ELECTORAL SYSTEMS.

protectorate　A state which has, by agreement, handed the management of certain important functions, usually its defence and foreign relations, to another power. Although there were European cases the commonest kind of protectorate in the nineteenth and twentieth centuries was the colonial protectorate. As well as having their foreign relations and defence controlled by the protecting power these were colonies in all but name, the most significant distinction being that, since annexation had not taken place, the inhabitants did not become national subjects of the protecting power. The treaties with native rulers establishing such protectorates were considered to have no force in international law, and to be only morally binding.　JGD

Reading

Madden, A.F.: *Imperial Constitutional Documents: a supplement*. Oxford: Blackwell, 1966.
Wight, M.: *British Colonial Constitutions 1947*. Oxford: Clarendon Press, 1952.

Protestant parties　By contrast with CONFESSIONAL PARTIES and the parties of CHRISTIAN DEMOCRACY, Protestant parties arise only under special conditions. The Scandinavian countries being homogeneous Lutheran societies faced no competition from Catholicism, and so there was little need for mass-based Protestant parties to defend the position of the church. In recent years, however, these countries (except for Norway where the Christian Peoples Party goes back to the 1930s), have seen the formation of Christian Peoples Parties dedicated to combating what they see as excessive liberalism in sexual matters. Such parties rarely secure more than 5 per cent of the vote and generally act with the bourgeois bloc in parliament. In the Netherlands, where there was competition, both from the Catholic church and from secularism, there were two Protestant parties – the Anti-revolutionary Party and the Christian Historical Union – but these merged in 1977 with the Dutch Catholic party to form the Christian Democratic Appeal. In Northern Ireland, where political allegiance is based upon ethnic/religious communities rather than socio-economic factors, the Unionist parties are in effect parties for the Protestant majority, and generally obtain the vast majority of the votes cast by Protestants.　VBB

Reading

Madeley, J.T.S.: Scandinavian Christian Democracy: throwback or portent? *European Journal of Political Research* (1977) 267–86.

psephology　This term for the study of elections derives from the greek ψηφος, the pebble which Athenians dropped into an urn to vote. (The verb ψηφεζω is still used in modern Greek for voting.) Psephology was first coined in 1949 by Frank Hardie, an Oxford academic, and first used in print in 1952. In popular parlance it has become associated with the analysis of voting figures and with the forecasting of election outcomes, but it properly covers the whole subject-matter of electoral analysis, including legal frameworks, ELECTORAL SYSTEMS, individual behaviour, CANDIDATE SELECTION, campaigning by parties and by media, OPINION POLLING, statistical exploration of the results and ELECTORAL GEOGRAPHY.

Psephology should not be regarded as a distinct discipline. It can be seen as a branch of history, sociology, geography, statistics or political science. Among the main pioneers have been the French geographer André SIEGFRIED, who from 1913 onwards encouraged a cartographic approach linking the social characteristics of voters with their party allegiance; Paul Lazarsfeld, the Austro-American sociologist who explored with panel polls the way in which Ohio voters reacted to the 1940 presidential campaign; and R. B. McCallum, the Oxford historian who launched the Nuffield College series of election studies. Other approaches have included studies of electoral systems and electoral law. The main thrust of psephological studies, however, has developed from Lazarsfeld's survey approach. Much has emerged from ordinary newspaper polling but the leading force has undoubtedly come from the University of Michigan studies, most notably exemplified in *The American Voter* by Angus Campbell and others. This has led to comparable work in many countries, for example, Britain.

At the same time the more descriptive approach has been covered by Howard Penniman of the American Enterprise Institute who has sponsored a worldwide series of studies *At the Polls* covering all the major democracies of the world in turn.

The study of elections and referendums has the attraction of covering the most essential of democratic acts – the ordinary citizen's choice of representative, leader, government or policy. But elections are enormously complex phenomena involving all aspects of political and social life. The explanation of these 'locks on the river of history', as Sir Lewis Namier described them, has in the last generation challenged an increasing range of academic inquirers. Moreover, elections themselves have been fought with increasing sophistication as the contenders have called to their aid pollsters, public relations consultants, and advertising agents. But these experts, like the academic specialists, still remain mercifully uncertain about what decides the voter and how he or she may be manipulated.   DEB

Reading

Butler, D., Penniman, H.R. and Ranney, A.: *Democracy at the Polls: a comparative study of competitive national elections*. Washington, DC and London: American Enterprise Institute, 1981.

―――― and Stokes, D.: *Political Change in Britain*. 2nd edn. London: Macmillan, 1974.

Campbell, A., Converse, P.E., Miller, W.E. and Stokes, D.E.: *The American Voter*. New York and London: Wiley, 1960.

Heath, A., Jowell, R. and Curtice, J.: *How Britain Votes*. Oxford: Pergamon, 1985.

Lazarsfeld, P., Berelson, B. and Gaudet, H.: *The People's Choice*. New York: Duell, Sloan & Pierce, 1944.

McCallum, R.B.: *The British General Election of 1945*. London: Oxford University Press, 1947.

Rokkan, S.: *Citizens, Elections, Parties: approaches to the study of comparative development*. Oslo: Universitetsforlaget, 1970.

Särlvik, B. and Crewe, I.: *Decade of Dealignment*. Cambridge: Cambridge University Press, 1983.

Siegfried, A.: *Tableau politique de la France de l'ouest*. Paris: Colin, 1913.

public administration In lower case (p.a.), institutional arrangements for the provision of public services; in upper case (P.A.), the study of those arrangements. 'Institutional arrangements' is a general term to denote the complex of agencies, authorities and enterprises, the formal rule structures, mixes of instruments, and conventions of behaviour which describe the organizational means of delivering public services. To some extent the study of institutional arrangements can be distinguished from the study of the content of public policy, which is the central concern of POLICY ANALYSIS, but obviously the two things are closely related.

The meaning of 'public' in public services is more ambiguous. Some authorities take the terms public administration and government ADMINISTRATION to be synonymous. There are common-sense advantages in defining public administration in this way. But this apparently down-to-earth approach leads to real problems too. For instance some public services (for example lifeboat, telephone, rural fire services) are provided in some countries by specifically government enterprises and in others by ostensibly private or independent enterprises. Moreover, the boundaries of government are by no means self-evident. For instance, US state grand juries may make determinations about public service provision, but there might well be scope for argument as to whether such institutions should be counted as part of government administration.

An alternative way of treating public services is to define them either as services which involve the use of the 'public power' (the generic Roman law term for the power to compel, forbid, permit, punish) or as services which involve some or all of the three properties of a 'public good' in economic theory (i.e. jointness of consumption, benefits which are non-zero-sum, impracticability of excluding from benefit those who would choose not to pay). Most of the traditional concerns of government (arms, justice, foreign affairs and 'police' in the continental European sense of public health, public security and market regulation) are public services in both senses. But public power and public goods do not always go together: the most controversial areas of public administration in fact often occur in situations where the public power is used to provide services which have little or none of the character of public goods – as might occur, for instance, if government compelled citizens to buy boots and shoes from a government-operated boot and shoe factory.

Public administration has been described (by Waldo, in Charlesworth 1968, p. 2) as 'a subject-matter in search of a discipline', and there is no single dominant analytic paradigm in this field. Traditional mainstream public administration theory developed out of continental European public law and political science at the end of the last century, as epitomized in a famous essay on the study of administration by Woodrow WILSON (1887) and an equally famous essay on bureaucracy by the German scholar Max WEBER, originally written about 1911, and very influential in the USA after it had been translated into English in the 1940s (Gerth and Mills 1948, pp. 196–244.)

The tradition that developed from such work took as its main area of concern the study of public BUREAUCRACY – that is (in its classic form) monocratic hierarchies of salaried career officials under direct political oversight, with non-transferable ownership rights in the enterprise, characteristically financed by annual block allocations from a general-fund budget, and typically endowed with a legal monopoly of certain activities. Given this traditional 'core' of the subject, 'comparative public administration' in practice tended to mean comparison of public bureaucracies in different countries and likewise 'development administration' came to mean a focus on the development of public bureaucracies.

In the USA the academic study of public administration which built on the continental European theory of bureaucracy has two distinctive features. First, it was linked to vocational training within universities for those seeking careers in public bureaucracy, by the study of 'generic' aspects of administration – contrasting with the traditional European preparation for such careers by the study of law, humanities or engineering. Second, it was concerned to change the world as much as

(if not more than) to understand it, while European work in general has been less *engagé* and more concerned with realistic description. In the US public administration, 'administrative improvement' came to be associated with a set of generic prescriptive principles, notably: the professionalization of administrative work within orderly hierarchies: the appointment of administrators on non-political 'merit' principles (based on academic examinations or professional qualifications) for a lifetime career, rather than appointment on the basis of party loyalties and subject to instant dismissal when a different party or incumbent gained government office; the separation of the details of policy execution from the political task of policy formulation; the removal of all rivalry and conflict between public bureaucracies by rationalizing and broadening jurisdictions.

The classic European bureaucracies which were built upon such principles had operated in their imperial heyday in the context of ruling-class ideas of group honour and *noblesse oblige*, militaristic ideas about a disciplined society, ideals of Christian service (Freemasonry in Prussia) and ideas of racial supremacy in the colonies. The civil services of Napoleon's France and Frederick the Great's Prussia were modelled on military organization and followed the same principles of centralization, discipline, the solidarity of an 'officer class' (Dunsire 1973, p. 78). Scholars such as Wilson thought that the techniques of the Prussian civil service would work equally well in the very different social context of the USA, with its characteristic ideas of social egalitarianism, self-help individualism, opportunistic entrepreneurship. But no close account was given of what would motivate public bureaucrats in such a context, and it was this motivational Achilles heel of the Woodrow Wilson theory that the economics of bureaucracy school began to explore in the 1960s.

In addition to the American and continental European stream of thought, Thomas (1978) argues that there was also a distinct British school of public administration in the years 1900–39. This school, she claims, diverged considerably from mainstream American ideas

505

in that it stressed the unity of policy and administration, believed the study of administration to be a branch of moral philosophy rather than of natural science, and did not espouse the sharp distinction between 'human relations' approaches and 'classical' organizational design principles which emerged in US administrative thought. However, this British school of administrative thought was always fragmented, its ideas were not expressed in major academic treatises (in contrast to the USA), and it excluded Sidney and Beatrice WEBB, who were the foremost scholars of British public administration at that time. This perhaps explains why American ideas came to dominate even British administrative thought from the 1940s. In any case, this British school was just as 'bureaucracy-minded' as the dominant American school, equally preoccupied with the aggrandizement of professional management and broadly centralist in orientation.

The dominant paradigm of public administration – as the study of public bureaucracies, and the effort to bring such enterprises to perfection – is still strongly entrenched, for instance, in institutes of public service development all round the world. But it has come under a wave of intellectual attacks since the second world war. In the 1940s Appleby (1949) attacked the 'policy-administration dichotomy' and Simon (1947) attacked the traditional prescriptions of public administration theory as a set of mutually inconsistent 'proverbs'. In the politically turbulent 1960s there emerged a new public administration movement in the USA (see Marini 1971), as an administrative echo of the radical politics of that decade. The new public administration group was concerned with how public bureaucracies could be made more responsive to some kinds of 'clients' (especially the poor) and less responsive to others (particularly the corporate middle-class). The new public administration lacked conceptual coherence, was easily dismissed by its opponents as a mere gust of emotion with no clearly-defined constitutional underpinnings (something of which the British administrative radicals of the early 1900s could not have been accused) and failed to take root.

Strangely, perhaps, no strong Marxist school of public administration has emerged, in spite of the debate within Marxism about public bureaucracy as a force autonomous from other class interests, and of the interesting questions to be asked about the expropriation of the means of public administration in modern industrial societies, as represented by managerialism, the growth of independent public enterprises and more recently privatization of public enterprises in many countries. This may be no more than a matter of title: Marxists have pursued such questions in the realm of URBAN POLITICS, but there is no major treatise developing such ideas in the context of public services generally.

Perhaps the greatest intellectual challenge to the traditional public administration paradigm has come from the rediscovery of institutional theory in economics, particularly since the early 1960s. A quite different approach to public administration developed outside the orthodox schools and boundaries of the subject. Instead of taking public bureaucracy as its central focus of concern – the traditional point of departure – the economics-based public choice school typically began with the problem of public goods and related problems of human interdependence such as the tragedy of the commons and the Prisoners' Dilemma (see also PUBLIC CHOICE THEORY). As Ostrom (1974, pp. 19–20) put it 'When the central problem in public administration is viewed as the provision of public goods and services, alternative forms of organization may be available for the performance of those functions, apart from an extension and perfection of bureaucratic structures.'

Like the mainstream theory which it challenges, the economics-based approach to public administration is associated with a set of prescriptive principles, in particular the attempt to apply a competitive model to the operation of public services wherever possible. The normative implications for the organization of public services tend to include a bias towards small-scale rather than large-scale enterprise in public service provision; a bias towards performance contracting rather than direct labour through open-ended employment contracts; a bias towards multiple-provider structures of public service provision (preferably involving rivalry among competing providers and means for control of providers by users, as in the US system of elected school boards) rather than single all-purpose provider structures; a bias towards user charges (or at least earmarked taxes) rather than general tax funds as the basis of funding public services other than pure public goods; a bias towards private or independent enterprise rather than public bureaucracy as the instrument of service provision.

All these biases are subject to the conventional *ceteris paribus* assumption, and all rest on arguments concerning allocative and X-inefficiency – a subject which was hardly treated by traditional theorists of public administration. The economics-based approach offers a serious challenge to traditional mainstream theory of public administration because it involves a common language of analysis and a broadly consumer-oriented approach to public services. If the traditional mainstream approach to public administration echoed and lent academic respectability to US administrative trends of the early years of the twentieth century, it is perhaps the economics-based approach which now holds that position – for instance, in offering a rationale for the introduction of competition in US telecommunications, from the Federal Communications Commission's 'above 590 MHz' decision on microwave transmission in 1959 to the break-up of the Bell system in 1982. Ironically, such serious criticism of the economics-based approach as there has been is largely couched in the language and style of the public choice approach itself, and no strong defence of the old orthodoxy has yet been mounted.

The emergence of basic paradigm conflict, in what has traditionally been rather a torpid and under-developed field of study in theoretical terms, can do nothing but good if it spurs greater rigour in argument, the selection of case studies designed to test the assumptions of competing paradigms (rather than to describe what is held to be intrinsically interesting in an a-theoretical way), and a search for a new synthesis.   CCH

Reading

Appleby, P.H.: *Policy and Administration*. Montgomery: University of Alabama Press, 1949.

Charlesworth, J.C. ed.: *Theory and Practice of Public Administration: scope, objectives and methods*. Philadelphia: American Academy of Political and Social Science/American Society for Public Administration, 1968.

Dunsire, A.: *Administration: the word and the science*. London: Martin Robertson; New York: Wiley, 1973.

Gerth, H.H. and Mills, C.W.: *From Max Weber: essays in sociology*. London: Routledge & Kegan Paul, 1948.

Marini, F. ed.: *Toward a New Public Administration: the Minnowbrook perspective*. Scranton, Penn.: Chandler, 1971.

Ostrom, V.: *The Intellectual Crisis in American Public Administration*. 2nd edn. Alabama: Alabama University Press, 1974.

Savage, P.: Dismantling the administrative state: paradigm reformulation in public administration. *Political Studies* 22 (1974) 146–57.

Simon, H.A.: *Administrative Behavior: a study of decision-making processes in administrative organization*. New York: Macmillan, 1947.

Thomas, R.: *The British Philosophy of Administration: a comparison of British and American ideas 1900–39*. London: Longman, 1978.

Wilson, W.: The study of public administration. *Political Science Quarterly* 2 (1887) 197–220.

public bill   This is a legislative proposal relating to public policy. Such bills normally apply to all citizens or to all persons of a specified class or classes. When passed by the LEGISLATURE and assented to by the HEAD OF STATE, a bill becomes an ACT and thus part of the general law.

Bills may be introduced into either House of the United Kingdom parliament. Bills concerned with major policy or financial matters normally start in the HOUSE OF COMMONS. Government bills are introduced by a MINISTER; those introduced by other Members are called PRIVATE MEMBERS BILLS.

Bills are published after a formal first reading. The second reading permits a full debate on the principle and main purposes of the bill, and, if opposed, a vote. If carried in the Commons the bill is then examined in detail by either a STANDING COMMITTEE or a COMMITTEE OF THE WHOLE HOUSE.

The committee considers amendments and also each clause and schedule of the bill. After committee stage, bills may be further considered by the House itself and amendments are again debated and often accepted. There follows a brief third reading debate; the bill is then sent (or sent back) to the Lords.

Procedures in the Lords are similar. Any amendments made by the Lords to a Commons bill have to be considered by the Commons; and vice versa. Once agreement is reached between the two Houses, the bill is submitted to the Queen for Royal Assent.

Under the Parliament Acts 1911 and 1949, bills which have passed the Commons in essentially the same form in two successive sessions may, subject to certain conditions, be presented for Royal Assent without being agreed by the Lords.   MTR

Reading

Drewry, G.: Legislation. In *The Commons Today*, ed. S. Walkland and M. Ryle. London: Fontana, 1981.

Griffith, J.A.G.: *Parliamentary Scrutiny of Government Bills*. London: Allen & Unwin, 1974.

May, T.E.: *Parliamentary Practice*. 20th edn, ch. 22. London: Butterworth, 1983.

Miers, D.R. and Page, A.C.: *Legislation*. London: Sweet & Maxwell, 1982.

public choice theory Examines the provision of public goods. A public good is anything that is at least partly non-rival and/or non-excludable. Non-rival means that the addition of new beneficiaries does not reduce the value of the good to the original beneficiaries: a law excluding black students from white schools is non-rival – its value to any white racialist is not reduced by the arrival of more white racialists. Non-excludable is self-explanatory: clean air is normally non-excludable, so is national defence – if anybody gets them, everybody does. If there is no government public goods will be underprovided in relation to the true demand for them, or not provided at all, because each beneficiary is tempted to free-ride on the efforts of others by reasoning: 'Either the good will be provided without my contribution, or it will not be provided even with my contribution. If I free-ride, nobody can punish me by denying me access to the good. Therefore it is always in my interest to free-ride.' Public goods are therefore normally supplied only by governments, and public choice in practice becomes a study of voters, governments, parties and pressure groups: 'the subject matter . . . of political science [studied by] the methodology . . . of economics' (Mueller 1979, p. 1).

However, the provision of government is itself a public good. If anybody enjoys its benefits (whatever they are) everybody does. So public choice theory examines (and has not yet explained, but see for example Axelrod 1984) how any government ever comes into existence. Likewise, the first question it asks about any lobby is 'why does this lobby exist at all – why does not everybody free-ride?' (See especially Olson 1965, 1982.) Olson's work deeply affects the debate between ELITISTS and PLURALISTS, both of whom fallaciously argue from the existence of interests to the existence of interest groups. Lobbies and governments may be provided by political entrepreneurs, whose activities may be studied analogously to economic entrepreneurs (see for example Frohlich et al. 1971). Bureaucrats have economic ends of their own, studied by Niskanen (1971) and his followers, whose work is marred by ideological special pleading but is nevertheless important.

Most public choice theorists argue that free-riding dilemmas are 'prisoners' dilemmas' (see BARGAINING THEORY), though some of them are really 'chicken' games. Theoretical advance depends on careful labelling and modelling of these multi-person interactions. Empirical advance is most likely in the study of lobbies of all kinds, notably lobbies concerned with the environment. Clean air and water are classically non-excludable goods (see for example Hardin 1982). Olson (1982) makes an ambitious attempt to explain economic decline via public-choice theory: he argues that lobbies for excludable goods that are good for their beneficiaries but bad for society (tariffs and subsidies, for example) will emerge, whereas lobbies for non-excludable goods for everybody will not. Whether right or wrong, these ideas have set the terms for subsequent discussion. IMcL

Reading

Axelrod, R.: *The Evolution of Cooperation*. New York: Basic Books, 1984.

Frohlich, N. et al.: *Political Leadership and Collective Goods*. Princeton, NJ: Princeton University Press, 1971.

Hardin, R.: *Collective Action*. Baltimore, Md.: The Johns Hopkins University Press, 1982.

Mueller, D.C.: *Public Choice*. Cambridge: Cambridge University Press, 1979.

Niskanen, W.A.: *Bureaucracy and Representative Government*. Chicago, Ill.: Aldine, 1971.

Olson, M.: *The Logic of Collective Action: public goods and the theory of groups*. Cambridge, Mass.: Harvard University Press, 1965.

————: *The Rise and Decline of Nations*. New Haven, Conn.: Yale University Press, 1982.

public corporation The simplest definition is 'a body incorporated by Act of Parliament, Royal Charter or other instrument of government endowed with powers and duties to provide goods or services'. It differs from the two other main forms of public administration – in which executive power is vested in a MINISTER or in a local council elected by the voters for a limited area. The essence of the concept of the public corporation is that it is not accountable to a minister for its day to day operations and therefore not answerable to Parliament in detail for those operations, nor is it directly accountable to the electorate.

As a device for the management of public utilities the public corporation was pioneered in Victoria, Australia where it was claimed as 'the most significant contribution . . . to State Socialism'. It is a very variable constitutional form. When recommending the formation of the Tennessee Valley Authority to Congress in 1933 President Roosevelt referred to 'a corporation clothed with the powers of government but possessed of the flexibility of a private enterprise'. Herbert Morrison saw the public corporation as providing a combination of public ownership, public accountability, and business management for public ends.

As such it came to be regarded as being more effective than the ministry form for the management of a publicly owned industry or service. The traditional form of central government was thought to have features which rendered it unsuitable for efficient management of commercial enterprises, for ministries are subject to detailed treasury control and the minister is personally answerable, for example at parliamentary question time, for all the actions or failures to act by ministry staff. The employees are civil servants subject to the traditions and controls developed over a long period, sometimes categorized as red tape. The work of a ministry is subject to political pressures, even in respect of quite small actions. While these features are thought to be essential to securing the democratic administration of foreign policy, defence and the social services, Morrison and others keen to extend public ownership saw them as inimical to the best kind of management provided in the private sector. Hence the stress on independence and flexibility. Arguments of this kind were reinforced by two other general ideas.

It was claimed that it was not essential for the efficiency of the managers of an industrial concern for them to own its capital. Indeed the obligation on the management of a private company to maximize its profits did not always lead to the most advantageous distribution of goods and services nor to the best relations between managers and workers. Providing the board of the nationalized industry were not answerable to shareholders with an equity capital demanding a share of the profits the management would be free to run the industry efficiently and in the social interest. It was not necessary to vest the industry in a minister to secure the public interest.

The other general argument arose from the increasing demand for workers' control. The idea of direct worker management was very strong among the miners. But this was incompatible with the normal structure of the ministerial DEPARTMENT, for the minister could hardly share his accountability with a board, whose members could act only as advisers. In contrast the public corporation offered the opportunity for the minister to appoint people of different interests, including the interests of workers, to the board charged with the management of the industry.

Though there is general political support for this form of public management opinion differs on the degree of freedom which should be accorded to the board. In the absence of competition and the target of profitability there is no certainty that left alone the board will be progressive and efficient. Moreover those who support public ownership are not content to allow the industry to be run as though it were purely private enterprise. For these and other reasons the tendency is to favour more rather than less ministerial and political control.

The degree of political dependence can be varied in several ways. First, by the method of appointment and the tenure of members of the board. Normally, appointment is by the minister of the appropriate department but occasionally (for example the Bank of England) it is placed in the hands of the crown which means the prime minister or the cabinet. In the case of the London Passenger Transport Board, appointments were made by five appointing trustees, composed of such representatives as the President of the Law Society. Tenure may be for a fixed term, five or seven years, or for only the length of notice normally required for dismissal. The last clearly puts the minister in a commanding position. In some countries serving civil servants are appointed to a board, which can hardly make for its political independence.

Second, there are the specific powers of intervention given to the minister. In the nationalization legislation of 1945-51 these were kept in general terms, for example the approval of a board's capital programme. The main Acts gave the minister power to issue directions of a general character to a board, i.e. not in respect of specific operating decisions.

Third, the financial arrangements are obviously important. The earlier idea was that capital needed by these bodies should be raised by the issue of fixed interest securities on the market, but this apparent independence of government is reduced when the treasury guarantees the payment of the principal and interest. The general conception is that the corporation should cover its costs by its sales and so be financially independent. But where this proves impossible the exchequer may be asked to provide a subsidy and so require a say in the operations of the industry.   DNC

Reading

Ashley, C.A. and Smails, R.G.H.: *Canadian Crown Corporations*. Toronto: Macmillan, 1965.

Eggleston, F.W.: *State Socialism in Victoria*. London: King, 1932.

Friedman, W. ed.: *The Public Corporation: a comparative symposium of thirteen countries*. Toronto: Carswell, 1954.

public inquiry   The holding of a public inquiry is, in Britain, a means of adjudication on disputes arising mainly from government intervention in a wide range of civil affairs. The use of a public inquiry as an investigative procedure began in the mid-nineteenth century, seen first in recognizable form in the Education Act, 1870. The Act gave power to a Department to hold an inquiry into matters in dispute. The general procedure largely followed since appears first in the Public Health Act, 1875. Since then governments have made gradually increasing use of an inquiry as a means of settling administrative disputes between individuals and firms with public authorities, public authorities and private interests, and public authorities with each other.

The public inquiry is a statutory means by which governments try to resolve conflicts by striking a recognizable balance betwen public and private good when making administrative decisions. The system largely supersedes appeals and objections to the courts, petitions to parliament and private legislation. It passes the resolution of conflict to departmental determination.

The end of the second world war saw a vast increase in public intervention in civil affairs. With it came an increase in public inquiries. But little development in the system of inquiries has occurred since Edwardian days. From 1863 judicial decisions had offered some fundamental rules on the conduct of inquiries, largely to ensure the rules of natural justice were observed. Little light had been shed on the general principles to be followed. The Franks Committee (on Administrative Tribunals and Inquiries, Cmnd 218), which reported in 1957, provides those principles. Openness, fairness and impartiality were the characteristics that should inform the public inquiry system. The committee's proposals were largely enshrined in the Tribunals and Inquiries Act, 1958.

Public Inquiries have now become a substantial part of the government's administrative decision-making apparatus. The fields with which such inquiries deal are identified in over one hundred statutory provisions. In 1986 some 18,000 appeals were made in the UK. Their subject matter included industrial accidents, the outbreak of epidemics, the provision of highways, water supplies, harbours, airports, power stations, the compulsory acquisition of land, development plans, disputes over the grant of permission or consents for development, the enforcement of statutory controls and many other administrative disputes.   FL

Reading

Wraith, R.E. and Lamb, G.B.: *Public Inquiries as an Instrument of Government*. London: Allen & Unwin, 1971.

public opinion   A freely used but far from precise or unambiguous concept. The problems arise both from the status of public opinion at the core of the liberal democratic ideal, and from its role as the principal legitimizer of regimes, parties and causes. It is frequently defined in terms of the ideological stance it is intended to serve.

The word public is not precise in this context. Attempts to limit it to the informed or involved sections of the population straitjacket it into what liberal democratic ideology suggests it ought to be. It is more fruitful to define 'the public' as the total population, accepting the fact that many issues, even of grave public consequence, may not interest large numbers of the public, and that those with the strongest opinions may be the least adequately or the least accurately informed. There is always a public, but it does not have opinions on every question.

The concept of opinion involves two elements. The first is that opinions relate to contested or controversial matters: there is no opinion on matters of demonstrable truth or where there is consensus. This is not so clear-cut as it might be; as societies become more sophisticated, the range of things that are opinions widens, with matters once taken for granted being increasingly challenged. The second element is that opinions should be rationally defensible. This does not require each specific opinion to be rationally formulated by each individual. In the complicated processes of opinion formulation, logical deduction from objective premises is only sometimes a factor. Opinions may be accepted on the authority of others or be born out of a complex of habitual attitudes or psychological dispositions.

Opinions are only rarely unanimous. Much more usual is a spread of contrary opinions, held with varying degrees of intensity and salience. There are also likely to be those who have no opinion, either from ignorance or indifference or from an unwillingness to decide.

In sum public opinion may be defined as the range of views on some controversial issue held by some significant portion of the population.

As a political force it expresses itself as the majority, or perhaps some vociferously articulated minority component of that total opinion. The link between public opinion and the formulation of public policy is far more tenuous than traditional liberal democratic theory would seem to require. While public opinion does not govern, it may set limits on what governments do.   THQ

Reading

Best, J.: *Public Opinion: micro and macro* Homewood, Ill.: Dorsey, 1973.

Childs, H.L.: *Public Opinion: nature, formation, and role*. Princeton, NJ: Van Nostrand, 1965.

Crotty, W.J.: *Public Opinion and Politics*. New York: Holt, Rinehart & Winston, 1970.

Lippmann, W.: *Public Opinion*. London: Allen & Unwin, 1922.

Wilson, F.G.: *A Theory of Public Opinion*. Chicago: Regnery, 1962.

purge A term used by COMMUNIST PARTIES to describe the process of removing undesirables from their ranks, now normally associated with the issue of new party cards. First applied by the Bolshevik Party before the October Revolution but officially sanctioned for the first time in the Twenty-One Conditions for Admission to the Communist International – penned by Lenin in August 1920 – and then included in the Decree on Party Unity at the Tenth Congress of the Russian Communist Party (Bolsheviks) in March 1921. A two-thirds majority of the Central Committee was then necessary to expel a member.

Purges were a common occurrence after the October Revolution. About one fifth of the membership was removed in 1922, for example, for 'refusing to carry out party directives, passivity, careerism, drunkenness, bribe taking and extortion'. Purges reached their climax under STALIN's rule, culminating in the Great Purges which were carried out under Stalin's direction during 1936–8 and linked to the three Great Show Trials of the same period. Bolsheviks who had entered the party before 1917 were then a special target. Under Stalin those purged normally faced imprisonment and often death, and the Great Purge was in fact a period of terror for many party members. Purges were also carried out in East European communist states in the 1950s and 1960s.

The Russian word *chistka* (cleansing) was not originally so ominous as purge, but *Pravda* (13 February 1986) used the alternative word *ochishchenie* (cleansing) to describe the process of ridding the party of corrupt and incompetent elements, set in train by Gorbachev. It also stated that a *chistka* was not envisaged since that term denoted a mass expulsion of members; what was now needed was for each member's credentials to be examined and if found wanting for the member to be removed.

The term has now acquired an extension of its original meaning to indicate mass arrests, imprisonment or execution of those thought to be politically undesirable; and it has been held to be a particular feature of totalitarian regimes, with ideological goals. For example, the term is used to describe the shooting of Ernst Röhm and his supporters by the Nazis in the so-called 'blood purge' of June 1934. It remains a characteristic of the purge that it is applied not to elements outside the system, such as Kulaks or Jews, marked out for destruction, but to those within the system who, while apparently loyal, might constitute an alternative to the regime.

See also TOTALITARIANISM.   MMcC

Reading

Conquest, R.: *The Great Terror*, rev. edn. Harmondsworth: Penguin, 1971.

Schapiro, L.: *The Communist Party of the Soviet Union*. 2nd edn. London: Methuen, 1970.

putsch Conspiratorial attempt to overthrow the legitimate government of a state, usually though not always by a faction of the army and generally of a right-wing character. First applied to the abortive attempt by Wolfgang Kapp to overthrow the Weimar Republic in 1920.

See also COUP D'ÉTAT.   VBB

Q

quango Originally a shortened form of the term 'quasi-non-governmental organization' devised by Alan Pifer, President of the Carnegie Corporation, to cover a new genus of organization on the American scene. Quangos are bodies established by the normal process of incorporation in the private sector yet financed entirely or largely by the federal government, e.g. by contracts or by grants for research. Among British political scientists it was thought that such bodies should more properly be labelled 'semi-private' and that the term quango might more appropriately be used for bodies usually known as non-departmental, i.e. bodies which performed functions in the public sector but were not an integral part of a ministerial department: they were 'quasi-autonomous non-governmental bodies'. Such bodies had become increasingly popular, ranging from the PUBLIC CORPORATIONS to various advisory and regulatory boards and commissions. In a Report for the prime minister in 1980 Sir Leo Pliatsky listed 489 governmental bodies principally executive in nature and 1,561 advisory bodies. The report resulted from the political criticism of the growth of these bodies which were said to increase ministerial patronage and obscure public accountability.

The term is not particularly useful when applied to such a disparate group of administrative bodies. Its chief value is that it draws attention to the fact that the public sector is not confined to ministries and locally elected councils, the two traditional forms of administration, but contains a large number of bodies which perform a public function but are neither ministries nor local authorities. Most of these bodies have some connection with a minister, e.g. the minister may appoint all or some of its members, but is not answerable to the House of Commons for its activities.

There are four main reasons for this growth. First, the spread of state activity to roles previously regarded as appropriate only to the private sector is achieved not by the function being taken over by a minister but by devices, such as grants, which leave the body a large measure of political independence. Second, the measure of control exercised over ministers by the Treasury and the House of Commons is thought to be unnecessary, and indeed inimical to proper administration of certain services, and a buffer is said to be needed against the normal political pressures, i.e. the function should not be vested in a minister. Third, the boards of such bodies provide an opportunity to draw upon the experience and expertise of many who would not emerge from the political process. Finally, in Britain the employees of these bodies are not counted as civil servants. Their use, therefore, enables governments to extend the role of the state without incurring criticism focused on the size of the civil service.

The degree of independence of non-departmental bodies with executive or regulatory functions varies considerably. Some receive the whole of their finance from the Exchequer, others have their own resources. Bodies set up to advise the government must be independent of political control if their recommendations are to have special weight.

See also INDEPENDENT REGULATORY COMMISSION.   DNC

Reading

Barker, A. ed.: *Quangos in Britain*. London: Macmillan, 1982.

Carnegie Corporation of New York. Annual Report for 1967.

Chester, D.N.: Public corporations and the classification of administrative bodies. *Political studies* 1 (1953) 14–52.

Giddings, P.J.: *Marketing Boards and Ministers*. Lexington, Mass.: Saxon House, 1974.

Pliatsky, Sir Leo: *Report on Non-departmental Public Bodies*. London: HMSO Cmnd 7797, 1980.

Smith, B.L.R. and Hague, D.C. eds: *The Dilemma of Accountability in Modern Government: independence versus control*. New York and London: Macmillan, 1971.

quantitative methods in politics The conversion of empirical evidence into numerical form (data) so as to enable the evidence to be more easily presented in support of some theoretical proposition. Typically, quantitative methods implies that a particular body of data has been subjected to some sort of statistical analysis which shows that two or more 'variables' are empirically associated. For example, from the evidence of several mass surveys we know that in British general elections people belonging to trade unions are more likely to vote Labour than for other political parties: the two variables, 'being a trade-union member' and 'voting Labour' are empirically associated or 'correlated'. This should not be taken to imply that surveys of individuals are the only source of variables which might be correlated: quantitative methods are also applied to data which describe not individuals but social or political aggregates such as political organizations, geographical regions, nation-states or even groups of nation-states. In general, quantitative methods are used in politics as a means either of *providing empirical descriptions* or of *testing hypotheses* about causal relationships which are thought to underlie some aspect of political behaviour.

Descriptive statements are in most cases quite straightforward, since they usually entail simplification, which will also imply a 'loss of information'. For example, the observation that 'in the British general election 1983, 39 per cent of trade union members voted Labour' is a typical descriptive empirical statement. It tells us nothing, however, about the extent to which members of different unions might have varied in their propensities to vote Labour and, obviously, it does not provide us with the names of the particular trade-unionists who voted Labour. None the less, in spite of this clear 'loss of information', the statement is still valuable in the context either of arguments about the support base of the Labour Party or of speculations as to the possible political implications of trade union membership.

The use of quantitative methods for *hypothesis testing* is rather more complicated. While statistical analysis can never in itself establish causality, it is possible to hypothesize that a causal relationship exists between phenomena and then to examine the appropriate statistical evidence in order to establish how far it is consistent with that hypothesis. For example, assuming there were good theoretical reasons for doing so, we might hypothesize that 'in Britain, people participate in violent political action only because they are relatively deprived'. Suppose that a 'representative' 2000-person survey of the British public had been undertaken and that it had established whether or not each respondent had recently participated in 'violent political action' and been 'relatively deprived'. Suppose further that we then observed a pattern of survey responses similar to that identified in Table 1. According to the table, people who experienced relative deprivation (RD) were no more likely to take violent political action than people who did not experience RD. This pattern strongly falsifies the original hypothesis that political violence and relative deprivation are causally related.

Table 1 *No empirical association between two variables (Refutes hypothesis)*

	Not relatively deprived	Relatively deprived	
Did not participate in violent political action	500	500	1000
Did participate in violent political action	500	500	1000
	1000	1000	2000

If the initial hypothesis were true, however,

we would at least expect to find that there was an empirical relationship between violent action and RD: that all (or most) of the respondents who had participated in political violence had also been relatively deprived. This sort of pattern is indicated in Table 2 where only people who participated in political violence were those who experienced RD.

Table 2 *Very strong empirical association between two variables (Supports hypothesis)*

	Not relatively deprived	Relatively deprived	
Did not participate in violent political action	1000	0	1000
Did participate in violent political action	0	1000	1000
	1000	1000	2000

It should none the less be stressed that even if we observed this kind of strong statistical association with 'real' data (which is not very likely), we could not cite it as proof that it is relative deprivation which causes (British) people to take violent political action: we could merely affirm (subject to the spurious correlation qualification made below) that it supports the hypothesis that relative deprivation causes people to take such action. This represents an important limitation to the use of quantitative methods in politics but it is one that needs to be recognized from the outset.

There are three other major problems associated with the use of quantitative methods in politics. The first of these is *representativeness*. In the context of the hypothetical survey mentioned above, for example, if we wished to generalize the survey results to the British public as a whole, we would have to show that the 2000 respondents selected for the interview were in some sense representative of 'the British people'. Fortunately, using probability theory, it can be shown that if a sample of around 2000 people is randomly selected from a target population (in this case, the British public) then with a high level of probability this sample will be representative of the population from which it is drawn. Tests of statistical significance (such as the chi-square test) provide researchers with a means of assessing how far they are justified in generalizing their sample findings to some wider population.

A second problem concerns *operationalization*: how far a particular theoretical concept is really measured by a given operational indicator. Although there are certain quantitative techniques available for coping with such 'measurement error' problems, these techniques are not as important as the provision of a plausible theoretical argument which links *concept* to *indicator*. For example, the concept 'social class' could only be operationalized on the basis of the indicator 'type of occupation' (using, say, the Registrar-General's classification scheme) if a coherent and plausible theoretical argument were provided which explained why this was a better way of assessing social class than any of the alternatives, such as an individual's 'relationship with the means of production'.

Finally, there is the problem of *spurious correlation*. This refers to the danger of wrongly inferring from a given statistical association that the variables involved are causally related. Quantitative researchers always need to consider the possibility that any observed two-variable correlation could be the result of the effects of some third variable(s) which itself causes the first two. There are various *causal modelling* techniques which assist in the identification and elimination of such spurious correlations. These, however, can at best act only as supplements to careful theoretical reasoning which closely scrutinizes any potentially spurious correlations and ensures that all possible tests are undertaken to prevent spurious inferences being drawn.

See also POLITICAL ECOLOGY.   DJS

Reading

Blalock, H.M.: *Social Statistics*, rev. edn. New York: McGraw-Hill, 1981.

——: *Causal Inferences in Nonexperimental Research*. Chapel Hill: University of North Carolina Press, 1964.

Erikson, G. and Nosanchuk, T.A.: *Understanding Data*. Milton Keynes: Open University Press, 1979.

Gurr, T.R.: *Politimetrics: an introduction to quantitative macropolitics*. Englewood Cliffs, NJ: Prentice-Hall, 1972.

Lewis-Beck, M.S.: *Applied Regression: an introduction*. Beverly Hills, Calif.: Sage, 1980.

Williams, F.: *Reasoning with Statistics: how to read quantitative research*. 3rd edn. New York: Holt, Rinehart & Winston, 1979.

quasi-judicial   A term that has been used in differing senses in British, Commonwealth, and American administrative law. The report of the Committee on Ministers' Powers of 1932 defined a quasi-judicial decision as one that involved a hearing and a finding of facts in a dispute between parties where the dispute is resolved by the application (usually by a minister) of administrative policy to the dispute. This distinguished it from a judicial decision in which the dispute is resolved by applying the law of the land.

In the courts 'quasi-judicial' seems to have been used at various times to indicate the role of some person who is not himself a judge but who is said to have a duty to act judicially in the sense of respecting the rules of natural justice or fair decision making. The American usage of quasi-judicial seems to have related to this second sense and has been used to describe the decisions of administrative bodies that are not courts of law but may be charged with resolving factual or legal disputes.

In Britain the distinction between judicial, quasi-judicial, and administrative decisions had at one time some importance when the courts were inclined to hold that persons acting administratively were free from any duty to obey the rules of natural justice. More recently the duty to act fairly has been imposed by the courts on a much wider range of bodies and persons. So the distinction between quasi-judicial and administrative action is now of much less significance.

GM

Reading

Report of the Committee on Ministers' Powers. London: HMSO Cmd 4060, Section III, 1932.

Smith, S.A. de: *Judicial Review of Administrative Action*. 4th edn, ch. 2, ed. J.M. Evans. London: Stevens, 1980.

Wade, W.: *Administrative Law*, p. 5. Oxford: Clarendon Press, 1982.

R

race in politics For social scientists and for geneticists the definition of the word 'race' is not without controversy. Among political scientists the politics of 'race' have come to cover a varying range of situations where contests and competition between different ethnic groups, different cultural groups, or even different nationality groups, occur within the same political system.

Race and race-related politics have been a feature of many formally democratic systems during both the nineteenth and twentieth centuries. ANTI-SEMITISM, for example, was a feature of the politics of the German Empire and explicitly anti-Semitic parties were represented in the Reichstag from the late nineteenth century to the first world war. Anti-Semitism also featured strongly in the politics of the area that became Austria and was of course important in the inter-war politics of many countries. Since the end of the second world war, however, there has been a change in the predominant nature of the politics of race in formally democratic countries: two types of society, not being colonies, have exhibited an explicitly racial dimension in their politics. One type includes those with long-standing habitation by different racial groups: either by importation for slavery or indentured labour, as in the United States of America, or else due to patterns of evolution or settlement, as in the Republic of South Africa or Australia, or in formerly colonial countries with a significant minority of white settlers, such as Zimbabwe. The second type includes those that since the second world war have allowed substantial immigrations of non-indigenous workers to function as replacement labour in certain native industries: either from former colonies as in the cases of Britain, France or the Netherlands, or from countries such as Greece, Spain and Turkey on the southern European periphery in the cases of the various more affluent countries in northern Europe, or from third world countries in the cases of the United States and again in some countries in northern Europe.

The politics of race in formally democratic political systems take three major forms.

(1) Many countries have seen reactions taking a political form by indigenous (usually white) populations against the presence of non-indigenous/non-white groups.
(2) There have sometimes, though not always, been political mobilizations by anti-racists (non-white and indigenous white groups) against what they see as racist reactions among sections of the population of their country.
(3) There have usually been various types of mobilization by non-indigenous/non-white groups, although the form that these have taken and how militant or pacific they have been vary from one situation or period to another within the same country and from one country to another.

Reactions by the indigenous population in situations of total or near-total domination of one race by another tend to be incorporated into the political system by means of governing parties explicitly committed to programmes of racial domination. However, in those political systems, as in the countries of western Europe which formally subscribe to a non-racial democratic ideal, reactions among the indigenous population may take the form of explicitly racist political parties and they have led the mainstream parties (especially but far from exclusively those on the right) to make concessions on race matters in order to accommodate known or anticipated negative reactions to the presence of non-indigenous/non-white groups. In Britain, France, the Netherlands, and Switzerland there have at various times since the 1960s been significant explicitly racist or exclusionist parties, while in all these countries there have also been noticeable political concessions to racist reactions from the indigenous population, usually taking the form of greater restrictionism in immigration policy.

Political mobilization by anti-racists may involve publicity, marches, demonstrations, and similar activities intended to propagate opposition to what are seen as racist politics in the country in question. The best-known examples, such as the Anti-Nazi League against the National Front in the late 1970s in Britain or SOS Racisme against the Front National in the mid-1980s in France, tend to occur outside the forum of conventional party politics, partly because the mainstream parties of the left are sometimes nervous about loss of support from a too public identification with them. Instead, such movements comprise a number of more marginal left groups. They are usually relatively evanescent, unable to sustain longer-term mobilization from a large uncoordinated base of support. However, more formally bureaucratic pressure groups, such as those concerned with civil liberties, whose activities are in whole or part oriented to the furtherance of the interests of non-indigenous/non-white groups, are usually more permanent.

The forms taken by political mobilization among non-indigenous/non-white groups vary substantially and a significant factor is whether, and on what conditions, members of these groups are enfranchised. In the case of the United Kingdom, for example, the franchise was immediately available to incoming settlers from former colonies. In 1975 Sweden extended the franchise in local elections to migrant workers of three years' residence but, in the mid-1980s, the question of whether France should introduce a similar provision is a highly contentious issue in national politics. Whether or not a non-indigenous/non-white group has immediate access to the vote has important consequences upon how its members see their political and social role, and also how they are perceived by many of the indigenous population, particularly the extent to which their economic function as replacement labour is recognized. Where such groups do not have the franchise, seeking it has been one important activity among their residentially more permanent activists. However, even in political systems in which they do have the vote, the levels of their electoral registration and/or participation have tended to be perceptibly lower than those of otherwise equivalent members of the indigenous population. When they do vote, they have tended to opt strongly for the mainstream left political parties of the country concerned, far more so even than their social-class position would predict. Similarly, as in the cases of the British Labour Party and the American Democratic Party, their activists have tended to obtain entry into, and sometimes reform of, the bureaucratic structures of that same party. There is some dispute about the relevance of the concept of a 'black political agenda', i.e. a collection of issues that uniquely concern and motivate the non-indigenous/non-white population. Certainly in some political systems there are issues that may have this specific character; on the other hand voters from these groups typically share many of the issue-concerns of socially and economically comparable members of the indigenous population.

See also ETHNICITY.   CTH

Reading

Banton, M.: *The Idea of Race.* London: Tavistock, 1977.

Ebels-Dolanova, V. ed.: *The Extreme Right in Europe and the United States.* Amsterdam: Anne Frank Stichting, 1985.

Husbands, C.T.: Contemporary right-wing extremism in western European democracies: a review article. *European Journal of Political Research* 9 (1981) 75–99.

——: Race and gender. In *Developments in British Politics 2*, ed. H. Drucker, P. Dunleavy, A. Gamble and G. Peele. London: Macmillan, 1986.

Knoke, D.: *Change and Continuity in American Politics: the social bases of political parties*, pp. 38–51. Baltimore, Md. and London: The Johns Hopkins University Press, 1976.

Layton-Henry, Z.: *The Politics of Race in Britain*. London: Allen & Unwin, 1984.

Levy, M.R. and Kramer, M.S.: *The Ethnic Factor: how America's minorities decide elections*. New York: Simon & Schuster, 1972.

Miles, R.: *Racism and Migrant Labour*. London: Routledge & Kegan Paul, 1982.

Wistrich, R.: *Hitler's Apocalypse: Jews and the Nazi legacy*. London: Weidenfeld & Nicolson, 1985.

Radical parties A loose term applied most frequently to parties on the left of the family of LIBERAL PARTIES, as with the Danish Radikale Venstre, and the Swiss Radical (Freisinnig) Democratic party. The most significant Radical party was that in France whose origins lay in the Revolution of 1848, and which was a leading force in the Third and Fourth Republics. ANTICLERICALISM was a central plank in the Radical programme at the beginning of the century. The Italian Partito Radicale, founded in 1955, also lies on the left of the Liberal family, while possessing some affinities to ECOLOGY AND ENVIRONMENTAL PARTIES. There are or have also been radical parties in Argentina, Chile and Ecuador. In general such parties are committed to social liberalism, a concern to extend civil liberties while also improving social provision.

The term radical is also applied, however, to parties of the Right – both TAX REVOLT PARTIES and parties of the radical Right (see FASCISM). What all the various parties called radical have in common is probably little more than a professed commitment to popular participation in politics and a hostility to established interests. Radical parties generally favour the extension of democratic rights, but the parties of the radical Right are only dubiously committed to democratic procedures.   VBB

radical Right parties See FASCISM.

rate support grant A payment by central government in Britain to local authorities in order to supplement their local rate income to provide services. It was designed to equalize the position in local authorities and make available resources correspondent with their needs. The grant thus contained a 'needs' element based on relative assessments of local need, a 'resources' element which compensated for relative levels of local rateable capacity, and a domestic element which subsidized local ratepayers. There was no earmarking of how the grant should be spent and it was designed to encourage local autonomy and equality.

See also LOCAL GOVERNMENT FINANCE.

NTB

rates A local tax levied by local authorities in England and Wales on the occupiers of land or buildings, in proportion to the valuation of such property. Rates are collected by district councils on behalf of themselves, the county councils and the parish (or community) councils. The basis of this tax was established by the Poor Law Act (1601) which codified the law and has, with many amendments and judicial interpretations, been the foundation of the system ever since.

The estimated amount of rates to be raised in England in 1986–7 is £15,019,000,000. The total revenue expenditure is estimated at £25,328,500,000, the balance being made up of government grants. (See BLOCK GRANT; GRANT IN AID; RATE SUPPORT GRANT).

There is considerable dissatisfaction with the system, for three main reasons: the unevenness of the rate burden between different families, the fact that about half of those who have votes in local government elections do not also pay rates and so have little incentive to economy in local expenditure, and the fact that occupiers of shops, offices and factories pay rates but do not as such have votes and so cannot exercise electoral control over the expenditure of the local authorities. In 1985 the British government announced its intention to abandon rates as a source of local government revenue.

The use of some form of property tax as the basis of the revenue of local authorities is almost universal in western countries, though it is often combined with other taxes such as sales taxes or local income tax. In the USA and the Commonwealth countries whose local government is based on the English pattern, the rating system is generally more or less similar to that of the UK.

See also LOCAL GOVERNMENT FINANCE.

BK-L

Reading

Cannan, E.: *The History of Local Rates in England*. London: Longmans Green, 1896.

Hepworth, N.P.: *The Finance of Local Government*. 7th edn. London: Allen & Unwin, 1984.

Report of the Committee of Enquiry into Local Government Finance. London: HMSO Cmnd 6453, 1976.

rational choice   These methods in a sense date back to Hobbes and Hume, but were first systematically applied to political science by economists in the 1950s. They assume that political actors (voters, politicians, lobbyists, bureaucrats) consistently choose the most efficient means to their various ends. Rational choice deductive methods are modelled on neoclassical microeconomics. They start with meagre assumptions (whatever people desire, they prefer more of it to less; but rival goods display diminishing marginal substitutability). From these assumptions are derived non-obvious conclusions which can then be tested against observed behaviour. Rational choice theorists are often wrongly accused of arguing that all political actors are narrowly self-interested: some early formulations (for example Downs 1957, pp. 27–8) encouraged this misapprehension. The rational choice paradigm now holds the commanding heights of US political science. Its subdivisions include PUBLIC CHOICE THEORY, SPATIAL MODELS, and SOCIAL CHOICE THEORY. Although still often criticized as abstract and unreal, it does at least generate testable hypotheses, unlike most earlier paradigms, and applications are becoming more sophisticated.   IMcL

Reading

Barry, B. and Hardin, R. eds: *Rational Man and Irrational Society?* Beverly Hills, Calif.: Sage, 1982.

Downs, A.: *An Economic Theory of Democracy*. New York: Harper & Row, 1957.

realignment   An idea which is central to an understanding of the dynamics of electoral politics in democratic regimes. At most elections there is a 'natural' party balance within the legislature which can be expected to be reproduced at election after election to within a few dozen seats. Occasionally one party may win an exceptionally large majority, only for the natural balance to be restored at the following election. Even more occasionally, the natural balance itself is changed: a party that had previously played only a peripheral role moves into prominence, replacing the former majority party. If the changed situation proves durable then the new party balance comes to be regarded as natural; when such a change occurs it is often referred to as a 'realignment' of the party system.

Strictly speaking, a party system is said to be aligned with major cleavages in the social structure of a country (see SOCIAL STRUCTURE AND PARTY ALIGNMENTS), and realignment takes place when a new POLITICAL CLEAVAGE becomes dominant. The term 'realignment', however, is most customarily employed by American historians and political scientists (especially V. O. KEY, Walter Dean Burnham and James Sundquist) to describe the several occasions in American history when a new party balance was established; for example at the time of the 1860 Civil War, in 1896, and during the New Deal era of the 1930s. In this context the linkage between social structure and party alignment is not always explicit. The term has also been used by American political scientists (and by others writing within the same academic tradition) to refer to the establishment of new and lasting alignments in other countries (for example, Butler and Stokes (1974) use the word to describe the establishment of the Labour Party as a major contender for power in Britain in the 1920s, at the expense of the Liberals).

Some controversy surrounds the question of how realignments take place. Classical democratic theory would regard a realigning election as one in which substantial numbers of voters reassess their political allegiances and switch their votes from one party to another in response to events and issues; most commentators have made the assumption (implicitly or explicitly) that major changes in the electoral fortunes of political parties reflect voting decisions of this kind. This assumption fits poorly, however, with findings from survey research which show that most voters inherit a political allegiance which becomes ingrained and is unlikely to be abandoned. Voters who do abandon a previous allegiance are, moreover, particularly likely to return to it at a subsequent election. So it is hard to see how permanent realignments can result from the conversions of existing voters.

Campbell et al. (1960) in the United States, and Butler and Stokes (1974) in Britain, brought to bear survey data which support the contention of Samuel Lubell (1951), based on non-survey evidence, that realignments are primarily due to the influx into the electorate of large groups of previously non-voting individuals, as a consequence of changes in franchise laws or for other reasons. This suggestion has recently been confirmed (in respect to the New Deal realignment) through the painstaking re-analysis of historical survey data by Kristi Andersen (1979), and it seems likely that the rise of the British Labour Party can be ascribed to a similar process.

Considerable contemporary debate surrounds the question whether the United States is currently undergoing one of its periodic realignments of the party system. The fact that Republicans have controlled the presidency for all but four years out of the past eighteen makes it seem that the Democratic Coalition forged by Roosevelt in the 1930s no longer exists. On the other hand, Democrats have continued through all these years to control the House of Representatives, and more Americans still claim to identify with the Democratic Party than with the Republicans.

Many of the characteristics associated with previous realignments appear to be present in the contemporary American electorate, and to have been present since at least the early 1970s. Among these are low levels of political participation and involvement, and declining turnout at elections. The disaffection with the existing party system is particularly marked among new voters. This has led many commentators to predict the coming of a new partisan alignment, though there is little agreement as to what form this realignment might take. For example, Phillips (1968) and others have predicted a new Republican majority, Broder (1971) hypothesizes either a coalition of blacks and young professionals or a populist realignment, and more recently Phillips (1975) has predicted a realignment based on the POST-MATERIALIST cleavage popularized by Inglehart.

Given our new-found understanding of the mechanics of realignment, all of these alternative scenarios require the mobilization of young voters in support of a single political programme, and it is hard to see what programme could achieve the mobilization of a group united only by their age. Moreover, this group is smaller than the groups available for mobilization at previous periods of realignment. Andersen supports Burnham, and also Ladd and Hadley, in suggesting that it is at least as likely that disaffection with existing parties will continue without any new alignment arising, and with people casting their vote increasingly on the basis of issues rather than partisan identification. A similar process may well be under way in Britain, where Franklin has shown that the tendency to vote for the party of one's social class has fallen most extensively among younger voters, who are disproportionately likely to make their electoral choices on the basis of issues rather than group loyalties. (See also DEALIGNMENT.)

MNF

Reading

Andersen, K.: *The Creation of a Democratic Majority 1928–1936*. Chicago, Ill.: University of Chicago Press, 1979.

Broder, D.: *The Party's Over*. New York: Harper & Row, 1971.

Burnham, W.D.: *Critical Elections and the Mainsprings of American Politics*. New York: Norton, 1970.

Butler, D. and Stokes, D.: *Political Change in Britain*. 2nd edn. London: Macmillan, 1974.

Campbell, A., Converse, P.E., Miller, W.E. and Stokes, D.E.: *The American Voter*. New York and London: Wiley, 1960.

Franklin, M.: *The Decline of Class Voting in Britain*. Oxford: Oxford University Press, 1985.

Inglehart, R.: *The Silent Revolution: changing values and political styles among western publics*. Princeton, NJ: Princeton University Press, 1977.

Key, V.O.: A theory of critical elections. *Journal of Politics* 17 (1955).

Lubell, S.: *The Future of American Politics*. New York: Harper & Row, 1951.

Phillips, K.: *The Emerging Republican Majority*. New York: Arlington House, 1968.

——: *Mediacracy*. New York: Doubleday, 1975.

Sundquist, J.: *Dynamics of the Party System*. Washington, DC: Brookings Institution, 1973.

Williams, P.M.: Review article: party realignment in the United States. *British Journal of Political Science* 15.1 (1984) 97–115.

reason of state The principle that the defence of public order takes precedence over ordinary moral and legal rules. The term itself, derived from the Latin *ratio status*, was first employed in this modern sense by the Italian writer Guicciardini in the sixteenth century. The principle came to be widely adopted as an adjunct to the theory of modern state sovereignty and was elaborately justified in the writings of MACHIAVELLI and HEGEL in particular. Reason of state has more recently been discredited as it is deemed contradictory to international law and CONSTITUTIONAL GOVERNMENT. However in emergencies most states act on it – for example in the face of terrorism.   RNB

Reading

Friedrich, C.J.: *Constitutional Reason of State*. Providence, Rhode Island: Brown University Press, 1957.

Meinecke, F.: *Machiavellism: the doctrine of raison d'état and its place in modern history*, ed. W. Stark, trans. D. Scott. London: Routlege & Kegan Paul, 1957.

recall A procedure by which voters can remove a public official before the expiration of his or her elected term. Although advocated by Marx in his writings on the Paris Commune, it has been most extensively used in the United States. There, it constituted one of the reforms advocated by the early twentieth-century PROGRESSIVES, along with the initiative and referendum, to minimize the influence of political parties. Less accepted than these other reforms, it now is in effect in thirteen states and a number of cities. In essence, in a constitutional system of divided branches of government, it provides a substitute for a parliamentary vote of no-confidence. Recalls originate in petitions signed by the requisite proportion of voters, followed by a special election to decide whether the designated official shall be removed from office. If the recall is approved, a successor is chosen either at the same balloting or in a subsequent election. Sometimes the instrument of recall was a letter of resignation signed by the elected official before taking office. It could then be evoked by a quorum of officials. Recall movements are not usually successful, but constitute a possible check to official abuse of power. The only successful recall of a state governor was that of Lynn J. Frazier, an agrarian radical in North Dakota in 1921, who was subsequently elected to the US Senate. Recalls have also been employed to oust judges who have made unpopular decisions and mayors who have been accused of corruption.   GMP

Reading

Magleby, D.: *Direct Legislation*. Baltimore, Md.: The Johns Hopkins University Press, 1983.

Munro, W.B.: *The Initiative, Referendum and Recall*. New York: Appleton, 1912.

redistribution The adjustment of district boundaries to reduce inequalities caused by population changes. There are two components of redistribution: the apportionment of seats to different areas of the country, and the redrawing of lines in individual seats. The philosophical justification for redistribution is that if each vote is to count equally the numbers in every CONSTITUENCY should be as identical as possible. The specific interpretation of this goal has changed over time however and varies widely across political systems. In earlier periods rural areas were allowed to deviate substantially from the norm. The trend in all Anglo-American countries has been in the direction of greater equality, but the United States has unquestionably the strictest equality requirement: US Congressional seats, for instance, must have a variance of less than 1 per cent of the ideal population. Countries also differ in what they are equalizing. The United States insists on equality of population, whereas most Anglo-American democracies aim for equality of eligible voters or officially registered voters.

In addition to equality of numbers redistribution reflects a number of other values. Some believe that it is important for districts to be contiguous and as compact as possible. Properly shaped districts, proponents contend, ease the task of REPRESENTATION and make gerrymandering more difficult. Others maintain that there is no necessary connection between district shape and political balance. Another common redistribution criterion is respect for communities of interest. This is a broad and sometimes hard to define standard since it can mean rural interests, racial and ethnic communities, or areas demarcated by distinctive geographical features. Racial and ethnic groups have been specially protected by the United States courts but on the whole figure less significantly in the deliberations of Commonwealth commissions.

Population equality, district shapes and communities of interests are referred to collectively as 'formal' criteria, because they focus on the physical features of constituencies. A second type of criterion governs the political outcomes of redistribution. The most common example of an 'outcome' standard is the proportionality of seats to votes. A plan is said to be fair by this measure if it leads to outcomes that most nearly equalize the seats to votes ratio. Since single member districts do not readily yield proportionate outcomes a second and more sophisticated version of proportionality requires 'symmetry'. This means that if party A gets x per cent of the seats with y per cent of the vote, party B should also get x per cent of the seats with y per cent of the vote. Critics point out that natural population concentrations and the unpredictable effects of money, incumbency, or campaign strategy make this goal difficult to achieve.

Because people weigh the importance of these goals differently, because the criteria are not always consistent with each other, and because boundary lines affect political outcomes, the task of redistribution can be very controversial and this has led to much debate over the best method to use. There are two basic approaches to redistribution procedure.

In the American model redistribution is highly decentralized and political. In the year after the decennial census each state has the responsibility of drawing the boundary lines for the congressional seats apportioned to it as well as for state legislative seats. Most states leave the task of drawing constituency boundaries to their state legislatures. Only nine states use a commission for state legislature lines and only two for congressional lines. Even when a commission controls the process the legislature is often represented. Most of the commissions either include legislators themselves or désignés of the legislature. Since these commissions are delicately balanced between the two parties, the so-called 'tie-breaking member' is a controversial appointment.

The other model is the British or Commonwealth approach. Britain, for instance, has permanent Boundary Commissions for England, Scotland, Northern Ireland and Wales. These Commissions are charged with the responsibility of producing parliamentary constituency redistributions every ten to fifteen years. In contrast to the American exemplar the British Boundary Commissions are not controlled by elected officials or party representatives. The English Commission, for instance, consists of the Speaker of the House of Commons as Chairman, a High Court Judge as Vice-Chairman, the Surveyor-General, the Registrar-General and two additional members (usually lawyers). After allocating the appropriate number of seats to each shire and metropolitan county the Commission draws up a provisional map that is published for public scrutiny. Assistant Commissioners then hold local inquiries which allow private citizens and local parties to voice their objections. These criticisms are relayed back to the Commissioners in London who then decide whether or not to incorporate them in their final map. In contrast with America, neither the Commissioners nor the

Assistant Commissioners are supposed to consider party or political considerations. Similar approaches are also used in Canada, Australia, and New Zealand.

The Commonwealth Commissions have on the whole attracted less controversy than the American Commissions and redistribution committees. No one has seriously accused the Commissioners of political bias although some have suggested that the outcomes have favoured one party over another. The British Labour party, for instance, brought suit in 1982 against the Commission for giving too much weight to 'natural communities' and too little weight to 'equal numbers'. The practice of allowing the legislature to redistribute has been hotly debated in the United States. In a couple of instances where one party has simultaneously controlled the legislature and the governorship the majority party has drawn lines that disadvantage the minority party. This has caused American reformers to search for less political approaches to redistribution.

BEC

Reading

Butler, D.: *The Electoral System in Britain since 1918.* Oxford: Clarendon Press, 1963.

————— and Cain, B.E.: Reapportionment: a study in comparative government. *Electoral Studies* 4.3 (December 1985) 197–214.

Cain, B.E.: *The Reapportionment Puzzle.* Berkeley: University of California Press, 1984.

Dixon, R.G.: *Democratic Representation and Reapportionment in Law and Politics.* New York: Oxford University Press, 1968.

Grofman, G., Lijphart, A., McKay, R. and Scarrow, H. eds: *Representation and Redistricting Issues in the 1980s.* Lexington, Mass.: Lexington Books, 1981.

Symposium: gerrymandering and the courts. *UCLA Law Review* 33.1 (October 1985).

Waller, R.J.: The 1983 boundary commission: policies and effects. *Electoral Studies* 2.3 (December 1983) 195–206.

referendum and initiative The referendum is a device of DIRECT DEMOCRACY by which the electorate can pronounce upon some public measure put to it by a government, or, in the case of a transfer of sovereignty, by an international organization. Where changes of sovereignty are in question, the referendum is sometimes called a plebiscite, although there is no uniformity of usage. The modern origins of the referendum are to be found in sixteenth-century Switzerland when delegates to the Swiss Assembly were normally required to consult their constituents on important questions. This procedure was known as a commission *ad audiendum et referendum*. The referendum was first used for constitutional ratification in Massachusetts in 1778 when a proposed constitution was rejected by the electorate. The first constitutions ratified by the referendum were those of Massachusetts in 1780 and New Hampshire in 1783. The referendum was first used to ratify ordinary laws in the Swiss canton of St Gallen in 1831. It was also used in France following the FRENCH REVOLUTION in accordance with the notion of the sovereignty of the people, in 1800 to ratify a new constitution, in 1802 to appoint Napoleon Life Consul and in 1804 to appoint him Emperor of France. Its use by Napoleon and later by Hitler and other dictators in the 1930s led to the belief that the referendum, far from being a democratic device, was in reality a method of legitimizing dictatorship.

Yet almost every democracy uses the referendum. There are only five major democracies which have never had nation-wide referendums. They are India, Israel, Japan, the Netherlands and the United States. (The referendum has, however, been widely used at state level in the United States.) Yet although use of the referendum is almost ubiquitous in democracies, most countries use them infrequently. Only five democracies – Australia, Denmark, France, New Zealand and Switzerland – have held more than ten nation-wide referendums. Switzerland is truly exceptional in that between 1945 and 1980, the country held 169 referendums out of a total of 244 held in 21 democracies identified by Lijphart (1984). Switzerland, therefore, which is sometimes thought of as typical in its use of referendums, is in fact highly untypical, indeed unique.

A number of different kinds of referendum may be distinguished. The constitutional referendum requires the referral for ratification of any constitutional amendment to the electorate. This is required by the constitutions of Australia, Denmark, Ireland, Spain and Switzerland and also in every one of the states of the United States except Delaware. Referendums can also be required for certain ordinary legislative measures, or alternatively they may be called at the discretion of the government as, for example, in Britain and Sweden. Occasionally, qualified majorities are specified for proposed changes; and in the FEDERAL states of Australia and Switzerland, constitutional amendments must be ratified by a double majority comprising a majority of those voting and a majority of the constituent units in the federation.

Two other instruments of direct democracy are to be distinguished from the referendum; the popular veto (sometimes called the petition referendum) and the initiative. The popular veto allows a specified number of registered electors to demand a referendum on a particular law. This instrument is provided for in the constitutions of Italy and Switzerland, and also in the constitutions of twenty-four of the states of the United States.

The initiative, first adopted by the Swiss Canton of Vaud in 1845, is a device by which a certain percentage of registered electors can require that a proposal of their choice be put to the popular vote. The legislature is sometimes first given the opportunity to pass the proposal of its own accord; but if it fails to do so, the proposal is put directly to the electorate. Italy and Switzerland are the only democracies to provide for the use of the initiative at the nation-wide level; but twenty-three of the states in the United States, only five of which lie East of the Mississippi, provide for its use either for consitutional measures, for ordinary statutes or for both.

Use of the referendum and initiative is most prevalent in societies with experience of direct democracy in other forms. In both Switzerland and a number of the states of the United States, there was a tradition of taking decisions by means of the TOWN MEETING; while in many of the western states of the United States, political institutions and parties were less firmly rooted than in the north-east, and the development of the institutions of direct democracy in these states reflects the impact of the Populist and PROGRESSIVE movements at the beginning of the century.

The referendum divides legislative power allowing the elector to share it with the legislature. It is, as a matter of logic, a conservative instrument, offering to the electorate, conceived of as the ultimate source of political power, a check against government. The referendum does not allow the electorate to put a measure on the statute book unless it has already been endorsed by the legislature. It is a device intended to repair the legislature's sins of commission. The initiative, by contrast, is a device intended to repair the legislature's sins of omission. There is no reason in principle why the initiative should prove to be either a conservative or liberal weapon. In the late 1970s, it was advocated and used with varying success in the United States by the NEW RIGHT, but in both Switzerland and the United States, the majority of initiative proposals not endorsed by the legislature are rejected.

The referendum and initiative are used not to replace representative institutions but to supplement them when it is felt that they are not working effectively; they are also advocated so as to secure greater popular legitimacy and support for government policies. The general effect of the referendum is to weaken parties since it enables the voter to separate his or her opinion on issues from party allegiance. The referendum and initiative have also been held to have increased the influence of interest groups since organization is essential to the effective running of a referendum or initiative campaign. However, these instruments of direct democracy tend to arouse controversy only when their frequent use is advocated. Where, as in most democracies, they are employed only very infrequently, they tend to be taken for granted as a useful if limited adjunct to the normal machinery of the democratic state. VBB

Reading

Bogdanor, V.: *The People and the Party System: the referendum and electoral reform in British politics.* Cambridge: Cambridge University Press, 1983.

Butler, D. and Ranney, A. eds: *Referendums: a*

comparative study of practice and theory. Washington, DC: American Enterprise Institute, 1978.

Delley, J.D.: *L'Initiative populaire en Suisse: mythe et réalité de la démocratie directe*. Lausanne: Éditions L'Age d'Homme SA, 1978.

Lijphart, A.: *Democracies: patterns of majoritarian and consensus government in twenty-one countries*, ch. 12. New Haven, Conn.: Yale University Press, 1984.

Magleby, D.B.: *Direct Democracy: voting on ballot propositions in the United States*. Baltimore, Md.: The Johns Hopkins University Press, 1984.

Ranney, A. ed.: *The Referendum Device*. Washington, DC: American Enterprise Institute, 1981.

regionalism An ambiguous and much-debated concept often confused with 're-gionalization', though their meanings are entirely different. Regionalism refers to the practice of redistributing certain central government powers to give to territorial authorities an intermediate position between the central and local levels; regionalization refers to the process by which central political and administrative authorities have responded to regionalist demands. Regionalism is a matter of politics; regionalization a matter of policies: regionalism stems from the periphery; regionalization is the answer of the centre.

The term regionalism has in the past been linked with individuals and groups who criticized both the centralization and the organization of the nation-state without, however, questioning its existence. In nineteenth century France, regionalism was an expression of traditionalist currents of thought which accepted the nation's territorial integrity but attacked the excessive influence of Paris and the artificial character of *départements* which, according to Edmund Burke, had 'dismembered' France. They therefore advocated a return to territorial divisions with deeper historical roots. Later, the term changed its meaning as it came to be used by civil servants, economists and military strategists. They talked of administrative, economic or military 'regionalism' to refer to divisions of the state that were bigger than the basic structures they normally used (provinces in Spain, Italy or Belgium and *départements* in France). Very often and particularly in the 1950s and 1960s this type of 'regionalism' represented a watered-down technocratic response from government elites to demands emanating from the periphery. It resulted in various hybrid forms of DEVOLUTION policy in regimes as diverse as Franco's Spain, de Gaulle's France or Britain under the Labour Government.

The ambiguity of the term, with its numerous different applications, has given rise to much debate. For a long period it was seen as a subversive doctrine, particularly in nation-states built on the Jacobin model (France, Italy, Spain and Belgium). Here, the established authorities (the Republicans in France under the Third Republic, Franco and his supporters in Spain, the central elites in Belgium) saw regionalism as a threat to the regime to be vigorously fought. Eventually, though, regionalism acquired respectability in all four countries. In France it seemed possible to integrate its activists into the political mainstream without threatening the unity of the State; in Spain and Italy it was defined as a constitutional guarantee (*garantismo*) against dictatorship; in Belgium it appeared as a lesser evil in comparison with the threatened breaking up of the State. But as regionalism lost its subversive character, it was rejected by the most radical groups in favour of a greater degree of autonomy. Today the Welsh and Scottish nationalist movements and the Spanish autonomists are not prepared to support regionalism, which they see as a mere technical adjustment of the existing state. The finest hour of regionalism may therefore have passed. As one Italian observer noted in relation to his own country, we have reached a period of 'regionalization without regionalism'.

YM

Reading

Bogdanor, V.: *Devolution*. Oxford: Oxford University Press, 1979.

Cameron, D.M.: *Regionalism and Supranationalism*. London: Policy Studies Institute, 1981.

Cornford, J.P. ed.: *The Failure of the State*. London: Croom Helm, 1975.

Gras, C. and Livet, G. eds: *Régions et régionalisme en France du XVIIIe siècle à nos jours*. Paris: Les Presses Universitaires de France, 1977.

Mény, Y. and Wright, V. eds: *Centre–Periphery*

Relations in Western Europe. London: Allen & Unwin, 1985.

Morgan, R. ed.: *Regionalism in European Politics*. London: Policy Studies Institute, 1986.

Rokkan, S. and Urwin, D. eds: *Economy, Territory, Identity: politics of West European peripheries*. London and Beverly Hills, Calif.: Sage, 1983.

—— eds: *The Politics of Regional Identity*. London: Sage, 1982.

Tarrow, S., Katzenstein, P.J. and Graziano, L. eds: *Territorial Politics in Industrial Nations*. New York: Praeger, 1978.

registration of electors An orderly election demands an exact definition of who is entitled to vote. Since the early nineteenth century the compilation of an authoritative record of those in each locality who satisfy the legal qualification for the franchise has been a key element in electoral administration. In most countries the electoral register consists of a listing of those citizens of full age who were normally resident on a given date. It is usually compiled by the local authority, although in some countries, such as Australia and Canada, it is prepared by a separate force of election officials. In some countries (notably the United States) registration is a voluntary act and the numbers registered are only 50 to 70 per cent of those who satisfy the franchise conditions. In other countries the quality of the register varies widely: studies in Britain in the 1950s and 1960s suggested an error rate of about 3.5 per cent (with 'dead' names almost exactly equalling omissions); in 1981 the figure had risen to 7 per cent and was much higher in decaying city centres, and among ethnic minorities, than in rural and middle class areas. In countries where democratic norms are not well-established, manipulation of the register is one of the commonest forms of electoral malpractice.

See also TURNOUT.

DEB

religion and politics Two ubiquitous complexes with no agreed definitions, and no generally accepted view as to their precise interaction or relationship. Even in early and small tribal societies with relatively little social differentiation both regal and priestly functions are ascertainable, although usually combined in one person: at times the fusion was such that the king was viewed as god as well and this same configuration is also found frequently in later periods and in more complex societies. Even where a heteronomic situation prevailed in which different persons or groups of persons held the two roles, and even where at times there might have been struggles between them over resources, the priestly side as a rule accepted the primacy of the king and together they strove to exalt the supremacy of their god over others. At all times religion was called upon to provide both a legitimizing support for the ruler and a measure of communal solidarity with him; as often as not the exchange deal provided for some enforcement measure for the religious side.

With the growth and complexity of societies the relationship between politics and religion became of major concern, particularly in the great civilizations and wherever universal churches prevailed. In some of these a deep cleavage between the worldly and the transcendental orders emerged, accompanied by a growing tension between them. Even in basically this-worldly religions the temporal and the non-temporal can be analytically distinguished; for example in Hinduism, a religion in which it is difficult to determine where the temporal ends and the non-temporal begins, the king was regarded as representative of the deity on earth by the *brāhmans* who themselves claimed to be gods on earth. And at least in some of its historical forms in Buddhism, a church-like establishment emerged with a clearly structured institutional distinction between the laity and the monastic orders. In Islam things were different again; here, within the framework of monotheism, no proper church emerged and hence no CHURCH AND STATE distinction could arise. The integrated governing institutions included religious dignitaries and functions. Moreover, the status of various sectors of the population was determined according to religious affiliation, and many Islamic regimes were galvanized by religious fervour.

This shows that church–state relations, although the central element of the wider religion–politics dualism, by no means exhausts it. The mainstream history of the

Islamic world shows throughout a pronounced politicization of religion, and, though to a much lesser extent, a thorough permeation of politics with religious elements and considerations. The history of medieval christendom has been presented as the history of the conflict between two opposing theories of government and law. On the one hand there was what has been termed the ascending theory, whose main feature was that original authority was located in the people or in the community, that is to say in an earthly source. Opposed to this was the descending theory of government, in which the original source of authority came to be seen as located in divinity itself with the earthly ruler designated from above. The latter is basically a theory of theocracy, in which the temporal elements of the polity became totally subservient to clericalism. In reality, however, it seems that other notions, and certainly forces of anticlericalism, were of greater prevalence than official historiography, either contemporaneous or later, cared to admit. Still, it is a measure of the success of the clerical side that even the regal side adopted for itself the claim of rule by divine right, whether accepting the intermediary of the clerus or not. With the protestant schisms, and even earlier in eastern christendom, the subservient role of the state churches to the temporal powers, even their functioning as branches of the state apparatus became a widespread feature, whereas in most Catholic countries the state–church equilibrium prevailed.

One of the main factors which has determined the religion–politics nexus in the modern era is the process of secularization. Indeed, these two phenomena, namely modernity and secularization are usually seen as intrinsically and causally interconnected. The common experience has been that with the decline of religious belief and observance the official status of the church(es) has been abrogated or abolished altogether, but this is by no means always the case. There are, for instance, established churches in some of the most secular states, such as in Scandinavia, while in countries which have formally separated church and state, religion plays an important role in society and in politics.

Developments in the US during the 1970s and 1980s are a good example of the widening and, more questionably, the deepening of religious experiences with religion exerting a more forceful impact on politics. In Italy the Catholic Church in 1983 relinquished by concordat its cherished status as the only church of state, thereby not only bowing to the inevitable change in the religious beliefs and behaviour of Italians, but also symbolizing a reversal of the church's estimation of itself.

The entire gamut of formal church–state relationships, namely the constitutional status, the powers and resources accorded to the church and the legal positions of individuals and groups vis-à-vis the church – running from the establishment of one state church through state support for churches and religious activities to disestablishment and the separation of church from state, on to state-directed anti-church and anti-religious activities – constitutes the focus for related conflict areas of religion and politics. One of the major conflicts in the contemporary world affects the role of the church in the educational system and the provision of social services. The taking of stands by the churches and church-related organizations and individuals on public issues of the day, the propagating of these stands and attempts by the churches to influence public opinion in accordance with them, their support of some political parties and their condemnation of others, are all part of what, from a secular point of view, are seen as improper intrusions of religion into politics. Other elements of this syndrome are such variegated matters as the religious persuasion of voters in elections (recent research seems to have established a greater influence of religious factors than would have been thought likely, given the secularizing tendencies in society, thereby proving religion to be still a cause of societal cleavages), the emergence and persistence of so-called religious or CONFESSIONAL PARTIES, including the phenomena of Social Christianity and CHRISTIAN DEMOCRACY, and of religiously inspired trade unions and the whole plethora of religious and church-related associations. In most societies mainstream religions have, for different and often contradictory reasons, been among the conservative, status-quo maintaining forces in society and politics. Given exceptions, this has generally been true of established churches, but not much less so of sects and schismatic denominations. One of the novel features of recent times has been the growing tendencies of religions and church groups if not of whole churches, to adopt radical, reformist and even revolutionary orientations.

Another crucial and comparatively recent component of religion in politics is the role of theology, church activities and the use of religious labels in connection with the rise and pursuit of movements of NATIONALISM. Indeed, some observers view modern nationalism as a religion or surrogate religion. The emergence and existence of so-called civil religions, i.e. a set of myths, symbols, rituals and ceremonies, and perhaps of beliefs, which may or may not be derived from prevailing religious traditions though not necessarily church-connected, and which serve the public authorities as instruments for public legitimation and solidarity, is a fairly newly observed phenomenon. This seems essential in order to overcome those cleavages in modern society which originate in religious heterogeneity of adherents of different religions and denominations and of devout and secular people.

All the foregoing can be subsumed under the heading of religion and politics. Politics in religion views the churches and other religious institutions as arenas for their own internal politics.

See also ANTI-CLERICALISM; CLERICALISM; CHURCH AND STATE.   EGu

Reading

Baron, S.W.: *Modern Nationalism and Religion*. New York: Harper, 1974.

Berger, S. ed.: *Religion in West European Politics.* London: Cass, 1983.

Hammond, P.E. ed.: *The Sacred in a Secular Age.* Berkeley: University of California Press, 1985.

Irving, R.E.M.: *The Christian Democratic Parties of Western Europe*. London: Allen & Unwin, 1979.

Lenski, G.E.: *The Religious Factor: a sociological study of religion's impact on politics, economics and family life.* Garden City, NY: Doubleday, 1963.

Lewy, G.: *Religion and Revolution*. New York: Oxford University Press, 1974.

Martin, D.: *A General Theory of Secularization.* Oxford: Blackwell, 1978.

Merkl, P.H. and Smart, N. eds: *Religion and Politics in the Modern World*. New York: New York University Press, 1983.

Smith, D.E.: *Religion and Political Development.* Boston, Mass.: Little, Brown, 1970.

Turner, B.S.: *Religion and Social Theory*. London: Heinemann, 1983.

Whyte, J.H.: *Catholics in Western Democracies*. New York: St Martin's, 1981.

Yinger, J.M.: *The Scientific Study of Religion*. New York: Macmillan, 1970.

representation   A concept which may be defined as the making present again, in some non-literal sense, of some entity, whether personal or abstract. Behind this lie complexities and ambiguities: in what sense, and under what circumstances, does one entity 'stand for' another, and on what grounds can one say that representation is or is not taking place? Such questions are of fundamental importance to political representation, since what is at issue is the outcome of processes of decision making in which small numbers of people are taken to be acting, in some sense, on behalf of much larger groups, even on behalf of society as a whole. Since all political systems are alike in this respect, the idea is both older and more general than that of REPRESENTATIVE GOVERNMENT, and the issue of representation includes but is by no means confined to questions relating to ELECTORAL SYSTEMS.

Representation has been given very different inflections in the context of conflicting assumptions about society and politics, and historical and empirical studies reveal its complex, shifting and ambiguous nature. The medieval belief that law was something to be discovered rather than created by men reflected a conviction that society was underwritten by supernatural sanctions, in the light of which monarch and assembly should sustain and symbolically represent a coherent hierarchy of 'estates' or 'orders': the pursuit of individual rights or group interests through representation was firmly subordinated to this. The idea that the religious principles of order bonding an entire society should be represented in the structure of the state has taken other forms. Only the church faithful could be chosen to represent the early theocratic state in Massachusetts, and Edmund Burke consolidated widely shared ideas about the natural and providential combination of 'interests' whose legislative representation constituted in miniature the integral Christian commonwealth. Modern commentators tend to cite Burke for another, less metaphysical aspect of his argument: that, given good sense, independence and time for deliberation, a representative assembly will arrive at judgements in the best interests of society as a whole. But the implications are not necessarily democratic, since the REPRESENTATIVE has the obligation to consider his judgements on the welfare of the whole of society, over the long term, rather than the preference even of majorities. There is a distinction to be made here between representation and representativeness. The qualities required for informed and far-sighted judgements are rare in any society. The interests of some groups may indeed be better represented through VIRTUAL REPRESENTATION, by people with economic and social characteristics very different from their own. There has been much argument about the statistical representativeness of legislative assemblies. Legislators chosen from large populations by random sampling would be statistically representative, but would they be capable of acting collectively as effective representatives?

Authoritative representation by elites has been accepted where there has been an affirmative sense of membership in society, overriding the fact of exclusion from the franchise. But the question of what constitutes the social whole requiring representation and how it should be represented is always open. As economic change has created new bases for political power and undermined consensus, the emergence of an indefinite range of assertive interests has overrun the too simple categories that had seemed self-evident to Burke. The logic of this development, in the expanding populations of America and Europe, pointed towards an unrestricted franchise and the principle of political individualism, so that all interests could find expression in relation to their strengths.

The radical principle of one person one equal vote emerged slowly against the weight of existing assumptions, though more rapidly in America than in Europe, and in France earlier than in Britain. The idea of representation had been deeply permeated by a concept of property, as a social entity, the substance of society, that required representation through its owners. In Virginia, a landholder owned additional votes for every county in which he met a property qualification, and Burke too conceived of 'land' in this general sense. The new property interests had no radical commitment to widening the franchise, but paradoxically they accelerated the growth of political individualism. The Massachusetts Constitution of 1780, which allocated seats in the legislature on the basis of population, resulted from an expedient alliance between emerging mercantile, city property and urban numbers, against the weight of 'land'. The modest advance towards individualism in England in 1832 was the product of a similar alliance, rather than of radical demands for the franchise. But political individualism, once established, gives a different emphasis to the idea of representation: Burkean trusteeship recedes, and the delegate, directly responsive to and disciplined by his constituency, emerges.

Contemporary argument struggles with this ambiguous legacy. Pluralist theorists have argued that open competition among organized interests, refereed by the state, arrives at an outcome roughly in line with the public interest. But leaving aside a contentious conception of the state, pluralists have underrated the inherently oligarchical nature of organizations, their advantage over the disorganized and their capacity for thwarting collective decisions costly to themselves. Such structural biases must be set beside the uncertain performance of electoral representation, however equitable, as a means of transmitting popular demands and controlling representatives. The refinements of alternative electoral systems are less important here than the variable and selective response of political parties to interests and constituencies. Increasingly, attention turns to the prospects for a responsive and participatory respresentation of individuals in more local and meaningful contexts, such as the workplace.

See also POLITICAL RECRUITMENT.

GS-K

Reading

Birch, A.H.: *Representation*. London: Pall Mall, 1972.

Bogdanor, V. ed.: *Representatives of the People? Parliamentarians and Constituents in Western Democracies*. Aldershot: Gower, 1985.

Cawson, A.: Functional representation and democratic politics: towards a corporatist democracy. In *Democratic Theory and Practice*, ed. G. Duncan. Cambridge: Cambridge University Press, 1983.

Cnudde, C.F. and Neubauer, D.E. eds: *Empirical Democratic Theory*. Chicago, Ill.: Markham, 1969.

Doel, H. van den: *Democracy and Welfare Economics*. Cambridge: Cambridge University Press, 1979.

Lowi, T.: *The End of Liberalism*. New York: Norton, 1969.

Pitkin, H.F.: *The Concept of Representation*. Berkeley: University of California Press, 1967.

Pole, J.R.: *Political Representation in England and the Origins of the American Republic*. London: Macmillan, 1966.

Redenius, C.M.: Representation, reapportionment and the Supreme Court. *Political Studies* 30 (Dec 1982) 515–32.

representative Someone who stands for or acts on behalf of another person or persons and who, normally, has been chosen by them for that purpose. The main type of political representative is the member of an elected legisative assembly (such assemblies being frequently referred to as 'houses of representatives'). Elected representatives are found at all levels of government, however, local as well as central, and also in other forms of non-political organization, such as trade unions and other private associations.

The functions of political representatives vary according to the different senses and aspects of REPRESENTATION. In one sense the representative may be seen simply as an agent chosen to act on behalf of the electors and their interests. In another sense, the 'typical' or 'micro-cosmic' sense of representation, a representative may be expected to share the characteristics of those represented. Thus a representative from, for example, a farming or a mining district may be said not to be 'representative' of the electors of the district unless he or she is a farmer or miner; assemblies are unrepresentative of the community as a whole if they do not provide an accurate cross-section in terms of such characteristics as social class, gender, age or ethnicity.

Typical representatives may be valued simply because they reflect and appropriately symbolize the community. They are also sometimes, mistakenly, considered to be necessary and sufficient for the effective agency representation of interests. But an effective representative as agent need not share the characteristics of those represented. It is true that representatives may tend to favour their own interests, especially where they are not sufficiently accountable to the electors. If the representatives have different characteristics and different interests from their electors they may therefore act against their electors' interests. However, the connection between the two aspects of representation is an empirical one, to be established by evidence, and does not follow as a matter of logic.

The proper role of the representative in relation to the voter has long been the subject of debate. The classic statement is that of Edmund BURKE in his speech to the electors of Bristol (1774) in which he claimed that Parliament was not a 'congress of ambassadors from different local interests ... but ... a deliberative assembly of one nation, with one interest, that of the whole'. Two related distinctions are made: one concerns the nature of the interest which the representative should pursue, the local interest of the electors or the common interest of the whole community; the other is between the representative as a delegate, acting under instructions of the electors and following their views wherever possible, and the representative as independent advocate of the electors' interests, acting on their behalf without necessarily following their views on how their interests should be furthered. In terms of these distinctions, the role of representatives differs in different political cultures (see REPRESENTATIVE

531

GOVERNMENT). In practice, however, neither model can predominate to the exclusion of the other. In all parliaments, representatives must give some attention to both local and national interests. All representatives are called on to exercise their own independent judgement to a certain extent while none can afford to ignore public opinion completely. Moreover, Burke was writing before the growth of organized political parties. Today the representative in most democracies is expected to speak for his or her party's viewpoint.

See also LEGISLATURES.   RGM

Reading

Birch, A.H.: *Representation*. London: Pall Mall, 1971.

Bogdanor, V. ed.: *Representatives of the People? Parliamentarians and Constituents in Western Democracies*. Aldershot: Gower, 1985.

Mackintosh, J.P.: Member of Parliament as representative or as delegate. *The Parliamentarian* 52 (1971) 14–21.

Pennock, J.R. ed.: *Representation*. New York: Atherton, 1968.

Pitkin, H.F.: *The Concept of Representation*. Berkeley: University of California Press, 1967.

representative government May be briefly defined as government in which legislative and political authority is located wholly or mainly in an assembly of representatives chosen in regular free ELECTIONS. It has become the dominant form of government in the modern western political tradition. Though distinct in its origins, representative government is now commonly identified with DEMOCRACY or, more specifically, with indirect or representative democracy as distinct from direct democracy.

Representative assemblies may vary in function and structure. In systems of parliamentary government, the government or executive is formed by members of the representative assembly who have the support of a majority of the representatives. In systems of presidential government, such as the United States, where there is constitutional separation of powers, the assembly may be confined to largely legislative rather than executive func-

tions but the system overall can still be described as representative government.

Representative assemblies may be elected according to different electoral systems with either one or a number of representatives for each district or constituency. There may also be a second chamber, an upper as well as a lower house. In federal systems, the upper house is normally representative of the states or provinces which make up the federation and may provide equal representation for each state or province regardless of differences in respective populations, while representatives in lower houses are representative of individual electors. Members of upper houses may be appointed in a number of ways, by direct election, by indirect election, by nomination from the government or, as in the British House of Lords, by hereditary title.

The role of the representative in relation to the voter varies in different political traditions and cultures. In terms of Burke's distinction between instructed ambassadors or delegates and independent members of a deliberative assembly (see REPRESENTATIVE) both liberal and conservative politicians in Europe have tended to give more weight to the independence of the individual parliamentary representative. Thus, J. S. Mill, in his *Consideration on Representative Government* (1861), claimed that the representatives should be more educated and experienced than the electors and that while they owed their electors the benefit of their wisdom they should not be bound to follow their constituents' judgement. Radicals, however, adopted the delegate model which also took root in the United States and the British dominions with their less aristocratic and more egalitarian political cultures.

The Burkean models of representation predate the rise of mass political parties. In twentieth-century representative government almost all representatives are members of a political party and owe their election to that membership. As party members they are committed to support their party's principles and platform and cannot act as completely independent individuals. All parties now accept, to some extent, the doctrine of the electoral MANDATE, whereby each party submits a political programme to the electorate which it is committed to follow if it achieves power. This practice allows the voters a choice not just between alternative governments but also between alternative government policies and is an accepted part of modern representative government.

Nevertheless, there is still considerable variation between different countries and different political traditions in the extent of such commitment. Party rules and conventions differ over the degree to which individual party members may be allowed to dissent from official party policy. Moreover, some parties come to power with a very detailed and precise set of policies which determine much of their decision making in government. Other parties have programmes which are limited to vaguely worded generalities and which allow a government a considerable degree of initiative and discretion. These variations often reflect the balance of power between the party members in parliament, particularly the parliamentary leadership, and the extra-parliamentary party organization. Left-wing parties with radical origins, such as socialist parties, tend to favour tight party discipline and detailed manifestos, thus continuing the radical support for the delegate model of representation. Conservative and liberal parties still tend to emphasize the independence of the individual representative and to give more weight to the parliamentary members of the party. (Because of its presidential system, the United States is an exception. In spite of its egalitarian background and the strength of the delegate model of representation, the separation of powers has enabled political parties to remain loose coalitions generally uncommitted to particular policies. Detailed electoral commitments are still common but are made by the individual congressmen to the electors of their individual districts rather than to a nationwide party programme.)

Because of its connection with democracy and the democratic principles of equality, representative government is now expected to ensure that each citizen is equally represented. The ELECTORAL SYSTEM, the method by which individual votes are converted into seats won in the representative assembly, should allow each vote to count equally; electoral boundaries should be drawn in such a way that each representative represents an equal number of citizens. In the United States, for example, a series of Supreme Court decisions, beginning with the pivotal case of *Baker* v. *Carr* (1962) have held that electoral districts of unequal size are unconstitutional. Though some degree of variation is usually allowed to cater for such factors as community of interest or topography, almost all systems of representative government now espouse equality as the norm and provide some mechanism for periodic review of boundaries or, in multi-member systems, of the number of members (see REDISTRIBUTION).

As representative assemblies are now chosen on party lines and elections have become primarily contests between competing political parties, equality requires not only that each individual representative should represent an equal number of citizens but also that each party should have an equal chance of winning seats in the assembly. Under the single-member plurality system, as used, for example, for electing the British House of Commons and the United States House of Representatives, one party may have an advantage over another because of the way in which its supporters are distributed among the various constituencies, even if the constituencies are of equal size. Boundary setting may therefore become a matter of considerable partisan contention. Such problems are largely avoided under systems of proportional representation, but not always (see CONSTITUENCY). Those European countries which did not adopt the institutions of representative government until the late nineteenth or twentieth century, when mass political parties had become accepted as a necessary and legitimate part of modern democratic government, mostly opted for electoral systems incorporating party lists. These systems are designed to ensure parliamentary representation more or less in proportion to nationwide party support. However, those countries with a longer political tradition of representative government, particularly the English-speaking democracies, have not been willing to accord that degree of formal recognition to political parties. In so far as they have favoured proportional representation (which still remains, for them, the exception rather than the norm) it has been that form of proportional representation which does not rely directly on party lists, the single transferable vote (STV).

In sum a representative government would normally be held to require that there were no restrictions upon the right to vote of all sane adults (see ELECTIONS); that the apportionment of constituencies was reasonably fair; and that the method of nomination of candidates for office was reasonably open (see CANDIDATE SELECTION).

See also LEGISLATURES.   RGM

Reading

Birch, A.H.: *Representative and Responsible Government*. London: Allen & Unwin, 1964.

Birch, A.H.: *Representation*. London: Pall Mall, 1971.

Fishkin, J. et al.: Special issue on representation. *Ethics* 91 (1981) 353–490.

Mill, J.S.: Considerations on representative government. In *J.S. Mill: On Liberty* and *Considerations on Representative Government*, ed. R.B. McCallum. Oxford: Blackwell, 1946.

Pennock, J.R. ed.: *Representation*. New York: Atherton, 1968.

Pitkin, H.F.: *The Concept of Representation*. Berkeley: University of California Press, 1967.

republic/republicanism

(1) *Republic* The term originally derives from the Greek *politeia* which Roman jurists, notably CICERO, rendered in Latin as *res publica*, meaning public affairs, and best translates into English as common weal or Commonwealth. Hence the root meaning of republic is simply the STATE. In modern times however two further meanings came to be attached to the word. The first and best known is the sense of republic as a form of state and government, sharply distinguished from MONARCHY: a republic has a constitutionally and periodically appointed, as opposed to an hereditary, HEAD OF STATE, and the functions of a republican government are legally defined and limited. The vast majority of present day states are republican in this formal sense and so the term has lost some of its previous

informative value: republics may vary from personal dictatorships through one-party states to liberal-democracies. The second modern meaning of republic refers to a style of politics, emphasizing equality, political DEMOCRACY, POLITICAL PARTICIPATION and public spiritedness; here the intended contrast is both to liberalism, with its private orientation, and to SOCIALISM, involving authoritarian state policies.

(2) *Republicanism* as the term is now used, signifies adherence to and advocacy of republic as a form of state and style of politics; it also has a more restricted sense in some countries for example the USA and France, as support for political parties of the same name.

RNB

Reading

Arendt, H.: *On Revolution*. New York: Viking; London: Faber, 1963; Harmondsworth: Penguin, 1973.

Geise, J.P.: Republican ideals and contemporary realities. *Review of Politics* 46 (January 1984) 23–44.

Hamilton, A., Madison, J. and Jay, J.: *The Federalist Papers* No. 17, ed. C. Rossiter. New York: Mentor, 1964.

Pocock, J.G.: *The Machiavellian Movement: Florentine political thought and the Atlantic republican tradition*. Princeton, NJ: Princeton University Press, 1975.

Republican Party

Created in 1854 in the anti-slavery mood preceding the Civil War. The circumstance of this major conflict contributed to the party's immediate electoral success. In 1856 the Republican candidate for president, John C. Fremont, narrowly lost the election. In 1860, Republican presidential candidate Abraham Lincoln was elected, ushering in a seventy-two-year era in which only two Democrats (Grover Cleveland and Woodrow Wilson) were elected to the White House. The word republican was commonly used to refer to those supporting social reform and a popular government, for example Thomas Jefferson. Those forming the new party liked the name for the ideas it represented.

The Great Depression resulted in a dramatic turnabout in Republican Party success.

Democrats became the majority party in voter registration and dominated presidential and congressional elections for 20 years. In 1952 the voters elected a military hero, Dwight D. Eisenhower, the Republican candidate, to the White House. Republicans also won narrow majorities in the House of Representatives and the Senate. The Democrats regained their majorities in both houses of Congress in 1954, beginning a period of split-party control – Republicans frequently winning the White House; Democrats maintaining majorities in one or both houses of Congress.

The Republican Party has traditionally been supported by voters with high income, education, and social status. It has been associated with big business more than labour and has espoused a philosophy of a limited central government and protection of states rights. This conservative dogma found considerable support in the 1980s under the leadership of President Ronald Reagan. The national Republican Party under the leadership of Reagan developed impressive organizational strength, due primarily to successful fund raising. Republican presidential candidates have been elected by landslide Electoral College margins despite the minority status of the party among the voters.   COJ

Reading

Hess, S. and Broder, D.: *The Republican Establishment: the present and future of the GOP.* New York: Harper & Row, 1967.

Huckshorn, R.J.: *Political Parties in America.* 2nd edn. Monterey, Calif.: Books/Cole, 1984.

Jones, C.O.: *The Republican Party in American Politics.* New York: Macmillan, 1965.

Moos, M.: *The Republicans: a history of their party.* New York: Random House, 1956.

Price, D.E.: *Bringing Back the Parties.* Washington, DC: Congressional Quarterly Press, 1984.

reselection   Elections in a representative political system generally involve a two-stage procedure: first, the selection of party nominees by party supporters, members, or activists and, second, the election of such party nominees by the wider electorate. Reselection is a procedure for enabling the party selectors to

pass judgement on the performance of the party's elected representatives. The term has been most frequently used in recent years in the specific context of the Labour Party in Britain. Until 1979 Labour MPs went through a restricted reselection procedure in which the procedural constraints on Party activists were considerable. In only a very limited number of cases was an incumbent Labour MP rejected by such procedures. In 1981 new reselection procedures were introduced which require an incumbent MP to face formal renomination (with the possibility of rival nominations), followed by a selection conference culminating in a vote to choose the Party nominee.

Between 1981 and July 1986, thirteen Labour MPs were 'deselected' (although a number of others resigned knowing that they would not win a reselection contest). The new reselection procedures have become acceptable to all factions within the Labour Party and the major point of difference is now who should do the reselecting. Some wish the powers to remain with the Party activists (i.e. General Committee delegates) but others would prefer to extend the power to all individual Party members.

See also CANDIDATE SELECTION.   PS

Reading

Kogan, D. and Kogan, M.: *The Battle for the Labour Party.* London: Kogan Page, 1983.

Seyd, P.: *The Rise and Fall of the Labour Left.* London: Macmillan, 1987.

Young, A.: *The Reselection of MPs.* London: Heinemann, 1983.

responsibility   The terms 'responsibility' and 'responsible' are used in a number of different, though not entirely unconnected, senses. The sense used most frequently in moral and legal contexts is liability for one's own actions; one is responsible if one could have acted otherwise and is therefore open to praise or blame or liable to punishment (*liability responsibility*). In politics and public administration, the most common and straightforward sense refers to the duties associated with a particular office or institution, as, for example, the responsibilities of a postmaster or of a commission of inquiry (*role responsibility*). Responsibility implies that there are certain tasks or functions which people, in virtue of the position they hold, are obliged to perform. It also usually implies that there is some other person or body to whom the office-holders are responsible or answerable for performance of these duties and who may call them to account. These people in turn may themselves be responsible to some further person or persons. In organizations such as government departments or corporations which are organized hierarchically, there is usually a vertical chain of responsibility whereby each person is responsible to a superior for the performance of his or her own duties, which duties may include the supervision of those lower down the chain and themselves responsible to that official. Because those responsible can be called to account and may be subject to blame and even punishment for non-performance of their duties, role responsibility is closely linked to liability responsibility.

The most important political use of the term is in the Westminster system of parliamentary government, which is itself sometimes known as RESPONSIBLE GOVERNMENT and in which ministers, both collectively and individually, are responsible to Parliament. There has been much discussion of the sense in which ministers are responsible and of how this type of responsibility is related to the other, more everyday senses of the term. The main requirement of responsibility on ministers is that they should be answerable to parliament; they are obliged to provide parliament with accurate information about any action taken by them or the various departments and agencies of government under their control. Ministers are thus clearly answerable for many actions of their subordinates of which they themselves cannot have had knowledge and for which they cannot personally be praised or blamed. Though, in theory, ministers take responsibility for everything done by their departmental officers, in practice they do not admit fault or resign when acts of MALADMINISTRATION in their departments are brought to light. Ministers are thus answerable without being morally responsible or liable. There might

therefore appear to be a clear distinction between ministerial responsibility, i.e. answerability, and liability responsibility.

However, considerations of moral liability and praise or blame are not entirely absent from ministerial responsibility. Though ministers may not be blamed for every act of maladministration in their departments, they are culpable if, once a fault has been revealed, they do not take steps to remedy it and prevent its future occurrence. That is, ministers are held personally liable for those actions which they could reasonably be expected to take themselves. Ministerial responsibility is not restricted simply to the duty to answer in parliament but also implies action appropriate to someone in overall charge of an organization. Such responsibility is similar to other instances of role-responsibility in administrative hierarchies where someone may be responsible for work performed by others. Though not personally responsible for every action taken by subordinates, the person in charge is expected to take all reasonable steps to ensure that the subordinates act sensibly in terms of the objectives set for them.

Moreover, though individual ministers are not necessarily forced to resign when they or their departments are found to be incompetent or negligent, the ministry or government as a whole is still liable to defeat in parliament. Indeed, it is this aspect of responsibility, the fact that the government continues in office only so long as it has the support of a majority in parliament, which is the major connotation of the phrase 'responsible government'. There is thus no reason to suggest that ministerial responsibility is a peculiar, or particularly attenuated, form of responsibility. It is merely a species of role responsibility.

There are other senses of responsibility which are of less importance politically but need to be distinguished. One is found in such phrases as 'acting responsibly' or 'irresponsibly' and refers to the manner in which those holding positions of role responsibility perform their particular functions and duties. In this sense, the ascription of responsibility implies a judgement about the behaviour appropriate to a particular role, a judgement which owes much to the observer's individual and often partisan point of view; what appears to be responsible behaviour to one observer may be thought of as grossly irresponsible by another. This sense is sometimes, confusingly, associated with the notion of acting responsively, that is responding to the demands of those to whom one is accountable. Responsiveness is an important and generally desirable feature of democratic governments but it is conceptually quite distinct from responsibility.

A final sense, sometimes known as causal responsibility, refers to the relationship of cause and effect, as in, for example, 'the change of government was responsible for a fall in the exchange rate' or 'the minister's speech was responsible for a backbencher's revolt'. Though this type of responsibility is clearly linked to, and often overlaps with, liability-responsibility, it is not identical; people can cause effects without being liable to praise or blame for them.   RGM

Reading

Birch, A.H.: *Representative and Responsible Government*, chs 1 and 17. London: Allen & Unwin, 1964.

Marshall, G. ed.: *Ministerial Responsibility*. Oxford: Oxford University Press, 1989.

Marshall, G. and Moodie, G.C.: *Some Problems of the Constitution*. 5th edn, chs 4 and 5. London: Hutchinson, 1971.

Thynne, I. and Goldring, J.: Government 'responsibility' and responsible government. *Politics* 16 (1981) 197–207.

responsible government An executive that is required to explain and justify its decisions to an electorate, through the legislature on which it depends, satisfies the requirements of a formal definition of responsible government. But this confident formal interpretation derives from a liberal constitutionalism which lived comfortably with a restricted conception of politics and a state apparatus of modest proportions. The concept is increasingly used to identify contemporary problems associated with the responsiveness of government.

In its formal sense, responsible government is central to the conception of liberal democracy. It brought into focus, for instance, the issues raised by the scheme for constitutional advance in British India under the Government of India Act of 1919. Complete and immediate transition to REPRESENTATIVE GOVERNMENT was at the time inconceivable. A redistribution of powers however with that as the ultimate goal, but without any acceptance of formal responsibility to a new Indian electorate, would have been meaningless. So the Act defined a transitional transfer of responsibilities that delegated certain policy areas to the provinces, where Indian ministers would be responsible to elected legislatures. More sensitive areas were retained by the central government in India, which was responsible for them as before, through the Secretary of State to the House of Commons, and through the House to the British electorate. How far such re-programming of formal political responsibility reflects significant shifts in the balance of political forces is another and more complex question.

Ministerial RESPONSIBILITY maintains the useful fiction that ministers themselves make all decisions taken in their name. The extent to which formal constitutional conventions can be used as a vehicle for effective accountability depends on the accidents of history that have produced one kind of parliamentary system and civil service rather than another. State structures in Britain have evolved in a direction that has roughly approximated to the ideal Weberian hierarchy, to the supervision of lower offices by higher ones, and to a distinction between politics and administration. Parliamentary critics have been able to bring the buck to rest before specific ministers. Formal responsibility in other political and institutional contexts can have very different implications.

It has been observed that nothing that went wrong under the French Fourth Republic, not even the war in Indo-China, was ever imputed to anyone, or even to any political group. A traditional hostility to governments found expression in the individualism of legislators and in fragile coalitions which provided volatile bases for successive governments. A powerful legislature kept governments in their place under the constant threat of dissolution, but not in any coherent sense through the formal constraint of responsibility. At ministerial level the buck was adroitly passed around. At the same time, long range policies, including some with strong public support, such as economic expansion and European co-operation, were the work of officials in powerful and independent bureaucracies who were not formally accountable.

The crisis that produced the French Fifth Republic gave fresh form and some fresh substance to the principle of responsibility, by maintaining accountability to the legislature of a party government that was no longer, however, to be representative of that legislature or even necessarily selected from it. Various devices were introduced to protect governments, under a president elected in 1962 on popular vote, from the continuous threat of destruction by irresponsible guerrilla tactics in the legislature, while still exposing them to the parliamentary criticism that is an essential component of any form of responsible government. Responsible government in any meaningful sense depends, such illustrations suggest, on institutional provisions, but also on the structure of party politics. Increasingly it is seen to depend on the nature and organization of the civil service bureaucracies, and on the nature of their relationships with the government and the public.

The difficulty of attaching blame for specific unsatisfactory decisions is not the primary consideration, though clearly important. Legislatures can at least be precise about what powers are delegated to civil servants, expose them to questioning, make some provision for the investigation of complaints and monitor the performance of officials through a select committee or similar body. More problematic is the relationship between public preferences and the myriad unreviewed administrative decisions through which they are supposedly aggregated and adjusted. Modern bureaucracies have outgrown constitutional constraints, inevitably acquiring extensive discretion, in the initiation, promotion and assessment of legislative programmes, in addition to their notional role as implementers of policy.

One response would re-emphasize the importance of formal responsibility and accountability, by stiffening the hierarchical relationship between policy and administration. But who is to put the scrutinizing procedures into effect? Would the procedural criteria natural to legislative committee staff, for instance, realistically meet the case? It is also argued that bureaucracies can act effectively on behalf of the disadvantaged interests, if they are trained to do so. Exclusive reliance on an abstract principle of professional impartiality however, even over apparently technical issues, is naive. Appropriate forms of participation could tilt the balance but, while special bodies, such as the so-called QUANGOS, can increase informed participation and administrative responsibility in specific areas, they also raise the same problems in another form. Open pluralist access to the policy process by organized interests may in principle transform the civil servant into a subordinate administrator of regulations congenial to the interests themselves, but which interest will be accorded legitimacy and who, if not the bureaucrats, will adjudicate between their conflicting claims? The balance is not inevitably tilted against the less organized; state bureaucracies have experimented with subsidizing and encouraging participation in local bureaucracies, but such projects are difficult to sustain and the risk remains of creating captive groups to endorse essentially bureaucratic decisions.   GS-K

Reading

Bates, E.: Can the public voice influence bureaucracy. *Public Administration Review* 60 (1982) 92–8.

Birch, A.H.: *Representative and Responsible Government*. London: Allen & Unwin, 1964.

Finer, S.E.: The individual responsibility of ministers. *Public Administration* (1954) 377.

Marshall, G. and Moodie, G.C.: *Some Problems of the Constitution*. 5th edn. London: Hutchinson, 1971.

Self, P.: *Econocrats and the Policy Process*. London: Macmillan, 1975.

Suleiman, E.N.: *Politics, Power and Bureaucracy in France*. Princeton, NJ: Princeton University Press, 1972.

Thompson, D.F.: Bureaucracy and democracy. In *Democratic Theory and Practice*, ed. G. Duncan. Cambridge: Cambridge University Press, 1983.

Thynne, I. and Golding, J.: Government 'responsibility' and responsible government. *Politics* 16
(1981) 197–207.

Williams, P.M.: *Crisis and Compromise: politics in the
Fourth Republic.* London: Longman, 1964.

responsible party government A
model for the organization of democratic
government; also a doctrine that the model
should be followed by all governments aspiring to democracy. Both the model and the
doctrine have been developed and advocated
mainly by American writers, notably Woodrow
WILSON, Frank J. Goodnow, A. Lawrence
Lowell, E. E. Schattschneider, and James
MacGregor Burns, all of whom have based
their briefs in part upon their understanding
of how the British party system works.

The model has the following principal
features: the nation has at least two (preferably
only two) major political parties, each of which
makes the case for its programme, leaders, and
candidates. Voters decide which party they
prefer and vote in constituency elections
for that party's candidate because of the
party ticket and regardless of the candidate's
personal qualities. The party that wins the
most votes elects a majority of the public
office-holders and thereby acquires control of
the government's entire power. Moreover, its
office-holders exercise that power cohesively
as a party and not as autonomous individuals.
As a result, the governing party collectively
controls, and assumes collective responsibility
for, all that the government does or fails to do
during its term in office. Between general
elections the opposing party has no power over
government decisions, but constantly criticizes
the governing party's policies, advocates
different policies, and presents itself as the
alternative government.

At the following general election the voters
ask themselves whether, on balance, the
governing party has governed and is likely to
govern better than the opposition party. If a
majority say yes they return the governing
party to power for another term. If a majority
say no they accordingly give a majority of the
offices to the opposition party; that party
assumes full power over and responsibility for
government policies for the next term of office

and in turn is held accountable at the succeeding general election.

The *model* of responsible party government
therefore has four basic features: the voters
vote for parties, not individual candidates;
each party's officeholders act cohesively, not
independently; the governing party holds the
entire power of government and is collectively
and solely responsible for all public policies
and their results; popular control of government is achieved by the voters' ability at
regular intervals to renew the governing party's
mandate to rule or transfer it to the opposition
party.

The *doctrine* of responsible party government
begins with the proposition that democratic
government in a modern nation with a large
population should be both efficient and
accountable. The great complexity and difficulty of modern governments' problems
coupled with the rapidly growing number and
heterogeneity of government agencies have
made efficiency not merely desirable but a
condition of survival. Now more than ever
efficiency requires that a government's policies
be made and carried out by a team of office-
holders working together, not by an agglomer-
ation of autonomous representatives each
working only for his own constituents. The
same complexity of problems and heterogeneity of agencies has also made it much
more difficult for ordinary citizens to know
just which public officials are responsible for
government successes and failures.

Full power is a necessary, though not
sufficient, condition for full responsibility. If a
public official has only limited power shared
with many others, it makes no sense for his
constituents to hold him personally responsible
for the government's performance. A political
party is the only kind of organization that is
both large enough to provide the teamwork
necessary for developing consistent and effective policies and visible enough for ordinary
people to know it is in charge and hold it
accountable for government performance.
Pressure groups operate largely out of public
sight, work only for special interests and
narrow goals, and form only temporary, shifting, and dimly-seen coalitions. Accordingly,
only a political party that collectively holds the

entire power of government and wields it cohesively is capable of providing both the efficiency and the accountability that modern democratic governments require.

The doctrine of responsible party government has been used mainly by American writers to criticize the organization and performance of American parties. The most detailed attack was made by the members of the American Political Science Association's Committee on Political Parties in its 1950 report, 'Toward a More Responsible Two-party System'. In their present state, the report declared, American parties could not provide the coherent policy direction and accountability the governmental system so desperately needed. They were fragmented into hundreds of national, state, and local organizations, none of which had any effective authority over the others. Even at the national level party power was dispersed between the president, the congressional floor leaders and CAUCUSES, and the national committees and conventions. Moreover, the parties had no control over who can participate in their affairs, for state election laws stipulate that any voter may vote in the PRIMARY elections of any party he or she chooses. The committee listed a number of measures it believed would make the party system more like the model of responsible party government: for example, biennial national conventions, stronger national committees, party councils to make policy between the quadrennial national conventions, regular and frequent meetings of national, state, and local party leaders, and tighter control by the congressional party leaders over the membership and behaviour of congressional committees.

The model and the doctrine have received little attention from political analysts outside the United States, and even in the US it has had at least as many critics as advocates. Even so, it continues to frame a considerable part of the perennial discussion among American political writers about the proper organization and role of political parties.   AR

Reading

American Political Science Association, Committee on Political Parties: Toward a more responsible two-party system. *American Political Science Review* 44 (1950) supplement.

Burns, J.M.: *The Deadlock of Democracy*. Englewood Cliffs, NJ: Prentice-Hall, 1963.

Epstein, L.D.: What happened to the British party model? *American Political Science Review* 74 (1980) 9–22.

Kirkpatrick, E.M.: Toward a more responsible two-party system: political science, policy science, or pseudo science? *American Political Science Review* 65 (1971) 965–90.

Pomper, G.M.: Toward a more responsible two-party system: what, again? *Journal of Politics* 33 (1971) 916–40.

Ranney, A.: *The Doctrine of Responsible Party Government*. Urbana: University of Illinois Press, 1954.

Schattschneider, E.E.: *Party Government*. New York: Holt, Rinehart & Winston, 1942.

revenue sharing   In its narrowest sense this refers to the systematic apportioning of the revenues from a particular tax among different units of government within a political system according to a formula established by the constitution or a statute. Examples may be found in the Federal Republic of Germany, Switzerland and India. In a broader sense the term may refer to the whole system of intergovernmental transfers intended to balance the revenues of each government with its exependiture responsibilities. In this sense various forms of revenue sharing are found in all federations as well as in other political systems with local units of government. The particular arrangements in a given country may involve a blend of some or most of the following: assignment of different taxes to different governments (e.g. most federations); concurrent taxing powers assigned to different governments (e.g. USA); supplements levied by provincial governments as a percentage of national taxes (e.g. Canada); systematic apportioning of particular tax proceeds (e.g. Federal Republic of Germany, Switzerland and India); intergovernmental transfers of general purpose and specific purpose grants (e.g. most federations).

The term revenue sharing has developed a particular connotation in the United States where it refers to arrangements adopted by Congress in 1972 for sharing on a formula basis over $30 billion of federal revenues with state and local governments in the form of general purpose grants. See also FEDERALISM; INTERGOVERNMENTAL RELATIONS. RLWa

Reading

Glendenning, P.N. and Reeves, M.M.: *Pragmatic Federalism: an intergovernmental view of American government*. 2nd edn, ch. 6. Pacific Palisades, Calif.: Palisades, 1984.

Hunter, J.S.H.: *Federalism and Fiscal Balance: a comparative study*, chs 4–10. Canberra: Australian National University Press and Centre for Research on Federal Financial Relations, 1977.

Mathews, R.: Revenue sharing in federal systems. *Australian National University Research Monograph* 31. Canberra: Centre for Research on Federal Financial Relations, 1980.

revolution and counter-revolution

Modern social scientists tend to reserve the term revolution for historical periods involving change of regime follwed by major reconstitution of the political, social and economic order. Such 'great revolutions' (a term we owe to the American writer Lyford P. Edwards) are extremely rare and are associated with major social change and innovation, examples being the English Civil War (1642–9), the AMERICAN REVOLUTION (1775–89), the FRENCH REVOLUTION (1789–1815), the RUSSIAN REVOLUTION of 1917, and the Chinese Revolution of 1949. Counter-revolution is the attempt or desire to reverse or anticipate the forces that make such major social changes possible.

The term revolution (*rivoluzione*) came into use in Italy in the late fifteenth century to designate what would now generally be called a COUP D'ÉTAT, the sudden overthrow of a ruler by force, and derives from the notion of the sudden reversal of fate to be expected by astrologers at certain conjunctures of the revolving planets. Its first use in English was by Edward Hyde, 1st Earl of Clarendon, in 1662, referring to the restoration of King Charles II; its later use, describing the fall of James II, originated the idea that by such changes an ideal order could be attained – an idea integral to Jacobinism. Karl MARX (1818–83) gave the word its present more

technical meaning, though in popular usage it is still often employed to designate political revolutions – the overthrow of governments or regimes) through the use or convincing threat of force.

Marx believed that in the evolution of society the bourgeoisie, the dominant class in capitalist society, had attained power through the violence of the French Revolution. In *The Communist Manifesto* (1848) he and Friedrich Engels predicted that in due course the bourgeoisie would be overthrown in the same way, by a social revolution that would usher in the DICTATORSHIP OF THE PROLETARIAT. In Marx's historical writings, however, he also used the word revolution to designate political revolutions – as did most of his contemporaries. V. I. LENIN claimed that the October Revolution of 1917 in Russia was the first true socialist revolution, and this remains the official view of the Soviet Union today. But it was made not by the proletariat but by the Social Democratic (later Communist) Party on behalf of the proletariat, and recent Marxist revisionists have argued that this was a fundamental breach with Marx himself, and that STALINISM was not the product of the personal idiosyncrasies of an individual but of the failure to engage the masses in the revolutionary process. Ironically later pro-communist revolutions have taken place in the less developed parts of their respective continents, and generally only with substantial Soviet help. The two major autonomous revolutions do not follow the Soviet pattern. The Chinese Revolution led by MAO ZEDONG was the product not of the proletariat, but of the peasantry, while in Cuba (1959–61) revolutionary change was carried out in great haste before a party apparatus had been formed to guide it.

Some non-Marxists regarded the similarities between the Russian Revolution and the French Revolution as evidence that the former was not, as its proponents argued, an entirely new phenomenon. Two US sociologists Lyford P. Edwards and George Sawyer Pettee, however, helped consolidate the view that revolution was a social rather than a political phenomenon. This view was strengthened by the historian Crane Brinton, whose influential

Anatomy of Revolution (1938) drew parallels between revolutions in England, the United States, France and Russia, and predicted that the Russian Revolution too would some day reach the stage at which counter-revolution would set in, a stage which he termed 'the Thermidorean reaction'. For some, the emergence of a 'new class' in eastern Europe has confirmed this prediction. Theda Skocpol has also argued that the French, Russian and Chinese Revolutions are fundamentally similar instances of social revolutionary transformation. Barrington Moore, on the other hand, used a Marxist comparative historiography to try to explain why some states had social revolutions, others, such as Britain, evolved participatory democracy without significant levels of violence, and Germany and Japan followed a very different course of development, controlled by violence and guided by an essentially counter-revolutionary ideology.

Analysis of revolution as a political phenomenon has been handicapped by the absence of agreed definitions and the extreme rarity ascribed by most writers to the phenomenon of social revolution; few writers could agree on as many as twenty genuine social revolutions. The term revolution is variously applied to the *process* of disenchantment with an incumbent regime, the *event* of its overthrow, the *programme* of the new regime, or the *myth* with which they legitimize their seizure of power. Some writers have therefore eschewed the use of the term altogether. Others approach the problem of violent political change and the transformation of society in a variety of ways: Ted Gurr by finding the psychological causes of POLITICAL VIOLENCE in frustration/aggression theory, Chalmers Johnson by thinking in terms of a contest of ideologies and value systems, and Charles Tilly by seeing violence as a special form of political contest for control. This last view appears most directly relevant to the central concerns of the political scientist. If social revolutions are rare, political revolutions are quite common, and can be incorporated with social revolutions in common typologies. The analytical method therefore offers the most promise for the future study of revolution by political scientists. PARC

Reading

Brinton, C.: *The Anatomy of Revolution*, rev. edn. New York: Vintage Books, 1965.

Calvert, P.: *Revolution*. London: Pall Mall; Macmillan, 1970.

Friederich, C.J. ed.: *Nomos VII: Revolution*. New York: Atherton, 1966.

Johnson, C.A.: *Revolution and the Social System*. Stanford, Calif.: The Hoover Institute; Stanford University Press, 1964.

Meisel, J.H.: *Counterrevolution: how revolutions die*. New York: Atherton, 1966.

Moore, B. Jr: *Social Origins of Dictatorship and Democracy*. Boston, Mass.: Beacon, 1966; London: Allen Lane; Penguin, 1967.

Skocpol, T.: *States and Social Revolutions: a comparative analysis of France, Russia and China*. Cambridge: Cambridge University Press, 1979.

Tilly, C. *From Mobilization to Revolution*. Reading, Mass.: Addison-Wesley, 1978.

Rokkan, Stein (1921–1979)

Born in Vagan (Lofoten) in the periphery of Norway, Rokkan grew up in Narvik. He studied philology and political theory at the University of Oslo in 1939. He later joined the philosopher Arne Naess in a UNESCO study of the meaning of democracy and spent some years in the USA and England before he became, in 1951, the first research associate and then Director of Research of the privately financed Institute of Social Research in Oslo until 1960. He was fellow of the Christian Michelsen Institute in Bergen from 1958 to 1966, and Professor of comparative sociology and comparative politics at the University of Bergen from 1966 until his death in 1979.

From his earliest days in Oslo Rokkan took an active part in international collaborative research. He was engaged in the 1950s in an international study of social mobility and a seven-nation study on the political attitudes of teachers. At the same time, he became involved in the analysis of elections in Norway, which resulted in a long-term partnership with Henry Valen in the Norwegian Programme of Electoral Research. American electoral studies exercised a powerful influence on electoral analysis in Norway as in other European countries. Rokkan and his associates consciously sought to involve scholars, notably from the University of Michigan (for example, Angus Campbell and Daniel Katz), in work on Norway. At the same time, the analysis of surveys administered to Norwegian voters made Norwegian scholars profoundly aware of the rather different party alternatives which faced voters in Norway compared to American voters. In trying to account for such differences, Rokkan and his colleagues became highly conscious of historical and regional factors, which also left a strong mark on contemporary attitudes. From an early period, the Norwegian programme of Electoral Research therefore emphasized the need for supplementing survey research with ecological analysis, and longitudinal analysis on the manner political attitudes were initially formed and retained. This concern led Rokkan to emphasize the lasting importance, nationally and comparatively, of early mass mobilization processes, which in turn were strongly affected by institutional factors, notably the timing and manner of FRANCHISE extension in relation to the coming about of responsible parliamentary government. He began to draw up varying analytical schemes, trying to account for the manner in which different cleavages had historically been politicized, or not. One basic feature of such schemes was a strong emphasis on CENTRE/PERIPHERY tensions, which opposed modernizing centres in countries to peripheries along dimensions of force, law, economics and culture. A strong awareness of the lasting importance of cleavage structures also led him to formulate his famous 'freezing proposition', according to which 'the [European] party systems of the 1960s reflect, with few but significant exceptions the cleavage structures of the 1920s'.

If his earlier concern was mainly to account for differences in European party systems, his later work focused more strongly on processes of state formation, his chief ambition being to develop what he termed a 'topological–typological macro-model of Europe'. In elaborating various versions of such a 'conceptual map of Europe', he revealed an astounding knowledge of geographical, historical, political, economic and social factors in the development of European countries, as well as an unrivalled mastery in

his attempt to account for different developments within and across countries through parsimonious explanatory schemes. Much of his work remained tentative and in his own view subject to further elaboration, criticism and amendment. Rokkan took considerable pain – and pleasure – in comparing and contrasting his own schemata of political development with those of other authors, for example the scholars in the Committee on Political Development of the American Social Science Research Council, Karl W. Deutsch, Alfred Hirschmann, Barrington Moore and more Marxist-oriented scholars such as Perry Anderson and Immanuel Wallerstein. Although much of his work remained on a conceptual level, he strongly emphasized the need to validate explanations by empirical analysis with the aid of comparative time-series data.

Apart from being a scholar of great originality and erudition, Rokkan also was one of the great organizers of modern social science. He planned and participated in many international conferences, which brought together scholars from many countries and disciplines, and he was a tireless editor of volumes which resulted from such encounters. He set great store on making data accessible, through publication of guides to data resources and the establishment of an International Data Information Service. He retained a special link with UNESCO and was President of the International Social Science Council from 1973–77. He was vice-president of the International Sociological Association (1966–70), president of the International Political Science Association 1971–73, founding member and first chairman of the European Consortium for Political Research, and an active proponent of Nordic cooperation in a variety of roles. Some of his best work was done in a typically informal group of scholars brought together as the Committee on Political Sociology which functioned under ISA and IPSA jointly, and of which he was for many years the secretary. Rokkan had a strong pioneering spirit. He was fascinated by the potential contribution of data archives for cumulative comparative and developmental research. He promoted the publication of guides to data resources and founded the ECPR data information service and newsletter.

In his later years Rokkan developed a strong interest in political geography. His last research project concerned an ECPR research project on economics, territory, identity, of which two volumes were published posthumously by his fellow editor in that project, Derek W. Urwin.

See also FREEZING OF PARTY ALTERNATIVES; SOCIAL STRUCTURE AND PARTY ALIGNMENTS. HD

Reading

Allardt, E. and Valen, H.: *Stein Rokkan: an intellectual profile*. In Torsvik, 1981; pp. 11–38.

Daalder, H.: Stein Rokkan 1921–1979: a memoir. *European journal of political research* 7 (1979) 337–56.

Rokkan, S.: *Citizens, Elections, Parties: approaches to the study of comparative development*. Oslo: Universitetsforlaget, 1970. [A volume of essays collected by the author].

—— and McKeon, R. eds: *Democracy in a World of Tensions*. Chicago, Ill.: University of Chicago Press, 1951.

—— and Urwin, D.W.: *Economy, Territory, Identity: politics of West European peripheries*. London: Sage, 1983.

—— and Urwin, D.W. eds: *The Politics of Territorial Identity: studies in European regionalism*. London: Sage, 1982.

Saelen, K.: A full bibliography of Rokkan's writings. In Torsvik, 1981; pp. 525–53.

Torsvik, P. ed: *Mobilization, Center-periphery Structures and Nation-building: a volume in commemoration of Stein Rokkan*. Bergen and Oslo: Universitetsforlaget, 1981.

roll-call analysis The investigation of recorded votes in LEGISLATURES. The term roll-call comes from the American CONGRESS. In the Senate votes are recorded by calling out the name of each member in turn and requiring those on the floor to say 'yea' or 'nay' or 'present' (i.e. abstention) to the proposed measure. Since 1973 the House of Representatives has achieved the same end by electronic voting. In Britain votes on the floor of the HOUSE OF COMMONS are recorded by the MPs walking through the division-lobbies – Ayes or Noes, as appropriate – with the vote of each member being noted and published.

Students of the American Congress were the first to analyse roll-call votes; these often provide a rich storehouse of material which can be exploited by scholars in a systematic way. Students of other legislatures followed suit, and in Britain both historians and political scientists are increasingly using such data. One of the earliest studies (1901) by the American scholar A. L. Lowell examined the relationship of party affiliation to voting behaviour for selected sessions in Congress, some state legislatures and the British House of Commons. Lowell concluded that party influence had increased steadily in the British parliament during the second half of the nineteenth century, but had fluctuated sharply in the United States.

American scholars have exploited roll-call votes much more vigorously than students elsewhere, partly becaue party cohesion in the legislature is generally weaker in the United States than in Europe. The techniques used have become increasingly sophisticated. Cluster analysis or cumulative scales can be used to identify ideological or sectional blocs within, and across, parties. In the United Nations General Assembly votes cast by states have been analysed to identify voting blocs, and similar methods can be used for the same purpose in ostensibly non-partisan assemblies. In domestic legislatures votes have been related to social background variables and to the demographic characteristics of members' constituencies. Roll-call analysis is being increasingly used in the study of nineteenth century parliaments in Britain. Aydelotte constructed scales from parliamentary divisions in the 1840s to show within each party the relationship between the political opinions of members and the nature and size of constituencies.

In modern Britain the strictness of party discipline made roll-call analysis unrewarding until the 1960s. Surrogate measures have been used in Britain and elsewhere: lists of signatures to Early Day motions in the House of Commons have been analysed in a way not dissimilar to the roll-call votes of the US Congress.

Roll-call analysis is best seen as complementary to more traditional methods of observation. Although there are dangers in the uninformed use of such techniques they afford an important check on impressionistic accounts and furnish a way, sometimes the only way, in which accurate generalizations about certain kinds of legislative behaviour can be made.   HBB

Reading

Anderson, L.F. et al.: *Legislative Roll-Call Analysis.* Evanston, Ill.: Northwestern University Press, 1966.

Aydelotte, W.O. ed.: *The History of Parliamentary Behavior.* Princeton, NJ: Princeton University Press, 1977.

Finer, S.E. et al.: *Backbench Opinion in the House of Commons 1955–59.* Oxford: Pergamon, 1961.

MacRae, D. Jr: *Issues and Parties in Legislative Voting.* New York: Harper & Row, 1970.

Lowell, A.L.: *The Influence of Party upon Legislation in England and America.* Washington, DC: American Historical Association, 1901.

Norton, P.: *Dissension in the House of Commons 1974–79.* Oxford: Clarendon Press, 1980.

rotten borough This term became popular in Britain during the later eighteenth century to designate parliamentary constituencies in places so small or shrunken that they supplied few or no resident electors. Old Sarum (Wiltshire) and Dunwich (Suffolk) each returned two members to Parliament, though the former contained no houses and most of the latter had fallen into the sea by coastal erosion. These boroughs, most of which lay in southern England, were usually treated as property, the MPs being nominated by the owner. For long the chief target of the parliamentary reformers, they were swept away by the 1832 Reform Act.   MGB

Reading

Brock, M.: *The Great Reform Act.* London: Hutchinson, 1973.

Cannon, J.: *Parliamentary Reform, 1640–1832.* Cambridge: Cambridge University Press, 1973.

Porritt, E. and A.: *The Unreformed House of Commons.* Cambridge: Cambridge University Press, 1903.

Rousseau, Jean-Jacques (1712–1778)

Born in Geneva, the son of a watchmaker, Rousseau was apprenticed to an engraver at the age of thirteen. In 1728 he moved to Savoy where he lived for most of the next ten years. At the age of twenty-six he went first to Paris, then to Venice as secretary to the French Ambassador, eventually returning to Paris where he began to compose opera and ballet and became a contributor to Diderot's *Encyclopédie*. His first real fame came in 1749 with his prize essay on the question 'Has the revival of the arts and sciences done more to corrupt or purify morals?' This marked his break with those Enlightenment philosophers who believed in progress based on the development of science; on the contrary, argued Rousseau, modern civilization and the increase of scientific knowledge were bringing ruin, corruption, and vice. A virtuous society was a simple and unsophisticated one, like ancient Sparta or some contemporary Swiss cantons.

Rousseau's next major essay in 1745, on the question of the origin of inequality among men, reinforced this attack on contemporary society: how had men created a system which constrained all and kept most in subjection to the few? For Rousseau the life of man is a record of the suffering that he undergoes in the course of becoming civilized. Any inequalities to be found in nature have no importance or repercussions: the natural life is simple, uniform, and solitary. Man's innocence is shattered by the institution of private property which destroys equality and fills people with avarice, ambition, and vice. The solution to the chaos that ensues is found by the rich, powerful, and corrupt who persuade the poor that political institutions offer peace and justice while in fact they herald permanent subjection and an institutionalization and increase of inequality. Rousseau makes no plea for a return to the original innocence of nature; his purpose is to show how intolerable is its alternative – existing, degenerate society – and so to show that the cure lies where the fault is, in the nature of society; it must be rescued from group interests and made to serve the whole.

How this might be done is the subject of Rousseau's most famous political work, *Du contrat social* (1755), in which he constructs a society in which innocence is transformed into virtue rather than replaced by vice, where freedom and authority can coexist. The general will, expressing the equal participation of all, is to be sovereign; all law will emanate from this source and will be directed at the general good. The people will obey only laws made by themselves; supreme authority and freedom are both incorporated in this one idea. In contrast to this legislative concept which directs us towards freedom and morality, Rousseau sees government as a constant threat to such sovereign power. Once it attempts legislative activity or acts beyond its powers then the state is corrupted and man's obligation ceases; the result is the unjust and servile world which Rousseau saw around him.

With regard to political institutions, Rousseau's importance lies in his being a protagonist of DIRECT DEMOCRACY. He believed that individuals could not delegate their sovereignty to legislative institutions – will could not be represented. Representative democracy, therefore, was an illusion. Rousseau's ideas were exemplified in a draft constitution which he prepared for Corsica, and in his advice on the reform of the government of Poland, *Considérations sur le gouvernment de Pologne* (written 1771, published 1782). In recent years, Rousseau's ideas have again become fashionable amongst advocates of participation.   GLW

Reading

Barber, B.: *Strong Democracy: participatory politics for a new age.* Berkeley: University of California Press, 1984.

Cobban, A.: *Rousseau and the Modern State.* London: Allen & Unwin, 1964.

Rousseau, J.-J.: *Oeuvres complètes.* Paris: Gallimard, 1959–69.

————: *First and Second Discourses*, ed. R.D. Masters. New York: St Martin's, 1964.

————: *The Social Contract and Discourses.* London and New York: Dent, 1963.

————: *The Social Contract.* Harmondsworth: Penguin, 1968; with *Geneva Manuscript and Poltical Economy*, ed. R.D. Masters. New York: St Martin's, 1978.

————: *A Discourse on Inequality.* Harmondsworth: Penguin, 1984.

royal commission A body appointed by the Crown on the advice of ministers to investigate and report on a specified aspect of government. This form of inquiry has been used in Britain since the twelfth century, the Inquest of Sheriffs of 1176 being one of the most famous and significant of early commissions. The system has been adopted in other Commonwealth countries, particularly in Canada and Australia.

In Britain royal commissions were most extensively used in the sixteenth and the nineteenth centuries. In the nineteenth century 399 were appointed; among them commissions to inquire into the Poor Laws, municipal corporations, employment of children in factories, housing of the working classes, and colonial problems in a number of territories.

146 royal commissions have been appointed in the twentieth century. Among the more recent commissions have been those reporting on the constitution (devolution to Scotland and Wales), justices of the peace, local government, the press, common land, and the police. No new royal commissions have been appointed since 1979 when the Thatcher government came into office. Some existing royal commissions are of a different sort – more or less permanent bodies of experts appointed to monitor a specified subject, for example, Environmental Pollution (appointed in 1970), Historical Monuments (1908), Historical Manuscripts (1869), and one for the Great Exhibition of 1851.

Royal commissions collect information by examining witnesses and by written evidence. It is usual to appoint an independent chairman, commonly a judge or a senior academic. Other members may be either independent or chosen to represent a particular interest or point of view. The report is formally presented to the Crown, and the government of the day is not obliged to accept its proposals. In the past the members of commissions have not been paid. There is little difference between royal commissions and the more numerous departmental committees, except that royal commissions normally deal with more important topics, and are appointed by royal warrant.

Similar inquiries may be conducted by SELECT COMMITTEES of the House of Commons, but they have neither the political impartiality nor the expert membership of royal commissions. They may be quicker, but probably less thorough in their inquiries than royal commissions, which sometimes take several years to complete their work. The conclusions of select committees may sometimes be more acceptable to the government than those of independent royal commissions. In other countries the inquiries undertaken by royal commissions are more frequently carried out by LEGISLATIVE COMMITTEES.

It is sometimes argued that since the government may ignore the recommendations of royal commissions, their time and expertise may be wasted. It has been suggested that governments have on occasion appointed royal commissions more as a means of delaying or avoiding a decision on a difficult problem than as a means of getting informed guidance.

BK-L

Reading

Cartwright, T.J.: *Royal Commissions and Departmental Committees in Britain*. London: Hodder & Stoughton, 1975.

Chapman, R.A.: *The Role of Commissions in Policy Making*. London: Allen & Unwin, 1973.

Report of the Departmental Committee on the Procedure of Royal Commissions. London, HMSO Cd 5235, 1910.

Wheare, K.C.: *Government by Committee*. Oxford: Oxford University Press, 1955.

rule of law A political ideal to which, it is proposed, a state's constitutional arrangements should give effect. The concept has been used with such a variety of meanings, however, that it is not easily defined.

At its most basic the concept merely implies a preference for law and order as opposed to anarchy and strife. In this narrow sense it is compatible with any form of government, given some effectiveness of enforcement. Generally the concept implies also what is sometimes called the principle of legality: that government must be conducted according to law. That in turn may be taken to require that a person affected by government action is able to challenge its legality before a court, where an independent judge adjudicates. But if all that the rule of law means is that official acts must be clothed with legality, then arguably the German state during the Third Reich conformed to it, and the concept offers no guarantee that more fundamental values are not infringed. For that reason most formulations of the concept go further and include a moral or political content, but these interpretations are so varied as to make the concept one of open texture.

The belief that law is necessary to society, although not shared by anarchist thinkers, has been widely held throughout civilization. The notion that law might assist in the problem of subjecting governmental power to control is also of ancient origin. Aristotle argued that government by laws was superior to government by men. Under classical and Christian doctrines of natural law there were considered to be universal and fundamental laws, to which actual human laws and governments were in a relation of inferiority. In these doctrines lie the derivation of the idea of government under law which manifested itself in different countries. Bracton, who in the thirteenth century wrote the first systematic treatise on English law, affirmed that the King was under God and under the law. Doctrines of royal absolutism, although occasionally propounded, never prevailed in England, and the events of the seventeenth century finally confirmed the subjection of the British monarchy to the law (see SOVEREIGNTY). The curtailment of royal power and especially the part played in the process by the courts were to the fore in DICEY's thinking, when he presented the rule of law as an important and distinctive feature of the British constitution. According to Dicey the rule of law embodied three distinct but related conceptions:

It means, in the first place, the absolute supremacy or predominance of regular law as opposed to the influence of arbitrary power, and excludes the existence of arbitrariness, of prerogative, or even of wide discretionary authority on the part of the government . . . It means, again, equality before the law, or the equal subjection of all classes to the ordinary law of the land administered by the ordinary law courts . . . [It] lastly may be used as a formula for expressing the fact that with us the law of the constitution, the rules which in foreign countries naturally form part of a constitutional code, are not the source but the consequence of the rights of individuals, as defined and enforced by the courts . . . thus the constitution is the result of the ordinary law of the land.

A number of reservations and qualifications would have to be made before Dicey's account could be accepted as accurately describing either the nineteenth-century or the contemporary British constitution. For example the crown or central government enjoyed substantial immunities from the application of law until 1948, when they were reduced. Again, as the functions of government have expanded in the nineteenth and twentieth centuries, wide discretionary powers have frequently been conferred for effecting them. Dicey's glorification of 'ordinary law' and 'ordinary courts' was founded upon misunderstandings of the nature of *droit administratif* and the CONSEIL D'ÉTAT in France, and his comments inhibited the development of an ADMINISTRATIVE LAW in England.

Significantly, Dicey had trouble in reconciling the rule of law with the sovereignty of parliament in the United Kingdom. An unlimited sovereign parliament might pass laws of any form or content, so governments might be given wide or arbitrary powers or laws might be substantively unjust. The principle of legality as such offered little protection. Dicey's concept went beyond that, for he considered that the influence of the rule of law would act as a practical restraint on legislation. But the domination of parliament by the executive and burgeoning of executive power were not fully appreciated or foreseen by him, and from a contemporary perspective, they threaten to undermine his confident generalizations.

Others have employed the concept of the rule of law to express particular conceptions of justice. Sometimes it is linked to procedural desiderata in law making or law enforcement. For example it may be held to require that laws should be well promulgated, clear and prospective, or that their administration should be fair and impartial. Here it is related to the concept of DUE PROCESS. Sometimes it is linked to human rights, as in the United Nations Universal Declaration of Human Rights (1948), and formulations by the International Commission of Jurists. Often the concept implies a form of CONSTITUTIONALISM, to which it is closely related. Government by laws and not by men is facilitated when government is limited by a higher law such as the United States Constitution; it is typical of the slipperiness of the concept that Dicey could regard such special laws as a denial rather than an expression of it.

In its wider formulations the concept essentially favours limited government, and so its acceptance, and perceptions of it, will vary according to the form of government in different states. Unger argues that it has been used in liberal societies as a medium for preserving social order, in so far as the apparent generality of laws and autonomy of legal processes help to render tolerable the imbalances which exist. Certainly the concept loses much of its force if the courts are not seen to represent an impartial balance.

CRM

Reading

Dicey, A.V.: *Introduction to the Study of the Law of the Constitution* (1885). 10th edn (1959) ed. E.C.S. Wade. Repr. Basingstoke: Macmillan, 1985.

Lawson, F.H.: Dicey revisited. *Political Studies* 7 (1959) 109–126, 207–221.

Lyons, D.: *Ethics and the Rule of Law*. Cambridge: Cambridge University Press, 1984.

Marsh, N.S.: The rule of law as a supra-national concept. In *Oxford Essays in Jurisprudence*, ed. A.G. Guest. London: Oxford University Press, 1961.

McIlwain, C.H.: *Constitutionalism: ancient and modern*. Ithaca, NY: Cornell University Press, 1940.

Raz, J.: The rule of law and its virtue. *Law Quarterly Review* 93 (1977) 195–211.

———: *The Authority of Law*. Oxford: Clarendon Press, 1979.

Sutherland, A.E. ed.: *Government Under Law*. Cambridge, Mass.: Harvard University Press, 1956.

Unger, R.M.: *Law in Modern Society*. New York: Free Press, 1976.

The Rule of Law in a Free Society. International Commission of Jurists: Geneva, 1960.

rule-making power See DELEGATED LEGISLATION.

ruling class That rulers constitute a class and not just a category is a concept that evolves from the time of the Directory in revolutionary France and that became central to political analysis in monarchical Italy and the French Third Republic. The ruling class is not the economically dominant class, although very often the two will overlap. It consists of people interconnected (very often) by kinship, economic interest, ideological prejudices, but above all by the concern to obtain, hold, and exercise power. If it suggests any idea of exploitation it is of exploitation through power, not through economic position. Theories of the ruling class see politics not economics as primary in the political order.

A ruling class must have what SOREL called a myth and what MOSCA (*Elementi di scienza politica* (The Ruling Class), called a political formula. This myth or formula is a declaration in emotive terms of the justification of the rulers in their authority and of their intentions about action to maintain, and sometimes to innovate in, the political order. The phenomenon of the ruling class is essentially one of advanced societies wherein the possibility if not the fact of REPRESENTATIVE GOVERNMENT is always present. PARETO's ruling class is an ELITE, but the analysis of ruling classes does not necessarily involve any theory as to the sources of elites or their 'circulation'.

In journalistic hands the idea of 'ruling class' as a kind of conspiracy of political exploitation permeated the Third Republic, the Italian kingdom, and extended into the Catholic populism of Belloc in England and the propaganda of American populism in, for example, the writing of Ignatius Donnell.

DGM

Reading

Aron, R.: Classe sociale, classe politique, classe dirigeante. *European Journal of Sociology* I (1960) 1–2, 260–81.

Burnham, J.: *The Machiavellians*. London: Putnam, 1943.

Finer, S.E.: *The Man on Horseback*. 2nd edn. Harmondsworth: Penguin, 1976.

—— ed.: *Pareto: Sociological Writings*. London: Pall Mall, 1966.

Guttsman, W.: *The British Political Elite*. London: MacGibbon & Kee, 1963.

MacRae, D.G.: Foundations for the sociology of politics. *Political Quarterly* 37 (1966) 324–32.

Mosca, G.: *The Ruling Class* (1896), trans. and ed. H.D. Kahn and A. Livingston. New York: McGraw-Hill, 1939.

Russian Revolution The upheaval in Russia, culminating in October 1917 with the Bolsheviks in control of the whole of central Russia, was all things to all men and women. It was declared a SOVIET revolution, a workers' revolution, a peasants' revolution, a national revolution and a democratic revolution. It was 'soviet' since on 25 October 1917 the second All-Russian Congress of Soviets of Workers' and Soldiers' Deputies opened and declared that power had passed to it. 'All power to the soviets' seemed to have become a reality. The revolution was a workers' revolution since the Bolsheviks claimed that the DICTATORSHIP OF THE PROLETARIAT had been inaugurated. It was a peasant revolution since the peasants would be able to achieve their age-old dream, the seizure of the landlord estates, royal family and church lands. It was a national revolution since LENIN proclaimed that those nations which wished to could secede from the new Soviet state. It was democratic since it was alleged that the majority of the population supported it. The general expectation was that a broad socialist coalition composed of Bolsheviks, Mensheviks and Social Revolutionaries would take over until the Constituent Assembly was convened, drew up a constitution, and elected a new government. (It did meet, but for only one day in January 1918 before being dispersed by the Bolsheviks. Lenin's primary goal was the hegemony of the Bolshevik Party.)

The Soviet Congress set up two institutions: the All-Russian Central Executive Committee (CEC) which was to act in the name of the soviets between congresses, and the Council of the People's Commissars (Sovnarkom), the government, headed by Lenin. The Bolsheviks were in the majority in the CEC and they held all ministerial portfolios. A coalition government was formed in December 1917 and ended in March 1918; it included a few Social Revolutionaries, but in insignificant posts. Sovnarkom was subordinate to the CEC. All decrees having 'general political significance' were to be submitted for approval to the CEC which possessed the authority to request Sovnarkom representatives to appear before it and to remove and re-elect any of its members. This was not very precise and the Bolsheviks argued that the defence of the revolution took precedence over all formal arrangements. The CEC met five times during the first ten days of the revolution and then convened less and less frequently. Sovnarkom, in contrast, met almost daily and sometimes twice a day. Gradually more and more legislation bypassed the CEC. One estimate is that of the 480 decrees promulgated during the first year of Soviet power only sixty-eight had been forwarded to the CEC.

A third institution, the Bolshevik Party, was of key importance. Its Central Committee (the POLITBURO was set up in 1919) contained all the key political actors. Government ministers had the right to appeal to the Politburo, over Lenin's head, if they had lost a vote in Sovnarkom. In October 1917 the CEC had been the key institution, followed by Sovnarkom and the Central Committee of the Party. By 1921 the Politburo was supreme, followed by Sovnarkom and then by the CEC.

The main reason for this reversal was the civil war. Lenin had hoped that the middle and poor peasantry would support the urban proletariat giving the Communist Party majority support in the country. This never happened. The civil war (June 1918–December 1920) forced the Bolsheviks to seize peasant grain surpluses to feed the Red Army and the cities. The need to produce war *matériel* made Bolshevik industrial policy severe. Bolshevik support in the soviets dwindled. As their support base shrank the Bolsheviks became more and more coercive and the instruments of coercion, the Cheka (KGB) and the military, assumed greater and greater significance. Opposition to the Bolsheviks was classified as opposition to the revolution. All other political parties were banned. The country fragmented and the

Soviet state had to be welded together again militarily. In the summer of 1918, eighteen separate governments vied for power with the Bolsheviks, five others on territory occupied by the Germans, not to mention Finland and Georgia which had declared independence. By 1921 the Bolsheviks had triumphed and had gathered in almost all the lands of the old Russian Empire, but at the expense of democracy. The state until the civil war had been weak (influenced by the Paris Commune) but afterwards everyone became subjected to it in an effort to make it strong. The Bolshevik Party claimed to act in the best interests of the proletariat even though a majority of the proletariat opposed it as did the country at large. The new economic policy, launched in March 1921, was an admission that war communism (June 1918–March 1921) had failed. The Soviet Union was not yet ripe for socialism. One reason for the coercion was the failure of world revolution to materialize. Lenin believed that without it the Soviet Union could not survive. He believed in its imminence – hence the need to hang on to power at any cost until it occurred. But the outcome was a hitherto novel party DICTATORSHIP based upon IDEOLOGY. Historians and political scientists still dispute whether the roots of STALINISM lie in the dictatorship of the Bolshevik party or are a product of Stalin's own political personality.

See also BOLSHEVISM.

MMcC

Reading

Bunyan, J. and Fisher, H.H.: *The Bolshevik Revolution, 1917–1918: documents and materials*. Stanford, Calif.: The Hoover Institute, 1965.

Carr, E.H.: *The Bolshevik Revolution 1917–1923*. 2 vols. Harmondsworth: Penguin, 1966.

Fitzpatrick, S.: *The Russian Revolution*. Oxford: Oxford University Press, 1982.

Keep, J.L.H.: *The Debate on Soviet Power: minutes of the all-Russian Central Executive Committee of Soviets Second Convocation, October 1917–January 1918*. Oxford: Oxford University Press, 1979.

McCauley, M.: *The Russian Revolution and the Soviet State 1917–1921: Documents*. London: Macmillan, 1975.

Schapiro, L.: *The Origin of the Communist Autocracy:*

political opposition in the Soviet state, first phase, 1917–1922. London: Bell, 1955.

———: *The Communist Party of the Soviet Union.* 2nd edn. London: Methuen, 1970.

———: *The Russian Revolutions and the Origins of Present-day Communism*. London: Smith, 1984.

S

Sainte-Laguë method See D'HONDT
METHOD.

Schmitt, Carl (1888–1985) Best-known
for his concept of the political as the relationship of 'friend or enemy' and his interpretation
of the EMERGENCY POWERS of the president
under Article 48 of the Weimar constitution.
The most important of Schmitt's works in the
development of German *Staatsrecht* into a
political science, *Der Begriff des Politischen*
(1927 and 1932) and *Verfassungslehre* (1928),
appeared late in the Weimar Republic. The
first asserted that 'the concept of the state
presupposes the concept of the political' which
Schmitt went on to specify as the relationship
of friend or enemy. Careful to point out that
this was a criterion, 'not an exhaustive definition or an indication of substantial content',
Schmitt's argument was nevertheless usually
interpreted as reducing the sphere of politics
to violent struggle and war. To a generation
that experienced the rise of National Socialism, it seemed a theoretical statement of the
FASCIST notion of politics. Others, such as
Julien Freund and Bertrand de Jouvenel, saw
Schmitt's argument as a major contribution to
a science of politics in the twentieth century.

Schmitt's political jurisprudence continues
to be a powerful influence on public and
constitutional law in Germany, largely through
his *Verfassungslehre* which argued that there are
certain inviolable provisions of a constitution
which cannot be changed without the whole
constitution being abrogated. In the case
of Weimar, these were the organizational
provisions of the first part which divided
power among the executive, legislative and
judicial branches and specified their duties
and powers. Combined with the democratic
electoral provisions of the constitution and
certain provisions in its bill of rights (the
guarantees of individual liberties and property
rights), these institutional features of the
Weimar constitution formed a specific instance
of the modern constitutional state, or *bürgerliche
Rechtsstaat*. He further distinguished between
laws and executive acts that temporarily violate
the constitution and those which alter it
permanently. On the basis of such distinctions,
Schmitt reinforced his earlier interpretation of
the emergency powers of the president in
Article 48 as forming a 'commissarial dictatorship' to defend the constitution (*Die Diktatur*,
1921).

Originally formulated in the context of
Friedrich Ebert's presidency, Schmitt's
argument for the emergency powers of the
president justified their extensive use by the
conservative nationalist Paul von Hindenburg
during the period of parliamentary incapacity
from 1930 onward. Under Adolf Hitler,
however, the provisions of Article 48 were a
first step toward the destruction of constitutional government, a constitutional change
which the Nazis' Enabling Act of March 1933
completed.

Schmitt sought to place the 'core' of the
Weimar constitution beyond change by either
a two-thirds majority in the parliament or by
popular initiative. This essentially conservative
element in his constitutional theory was recognized by the framers of the Bonn constitution
in 1949. In the light of the Nazis' 'legal
revolution' the *Grundgesetz*, or Basic Law,
of the Federal Republic places certain con-

stitutional provisions (democracy and the rule of law) under permanent guarantee. Closely associated with the Catholic Centre Party during the Republic Schmitt argued against giving the Nazis and Communists an 'equal chance' to compete in elections (*Legalität und Legitimität*, 1932) another feature of his political thought which was incorporated into the West German constitution.

In a dramatic about-face, however, Schmitt joined the Nazi party in May 1933 and played the role briefly of 'crown jurist of the Third Reich' until factions within the party and SS put an end to his influence in 1935. By then Schmitt's reputation as a fascist political thinker was made by writings which justified, among other things, the brutal purge of the SA in June 1934 ('Der Führer schützt das Recht', 1934). After 1945 Schmitt became something of a negative cult figure in the Federal Republic, a man about whom intellectuals are still deeply divided. Carl Schmitt, like Martin Heidegger, lost his chair in 1945 and lived in the provinces of the Sauerland, his birthplace, until he died at the age of 96 in 1985.   ELK

Reading

Bendersky, J.: *Carl Schmitt: theorist for the Reich*. Princeton, NJ: Princeton University Press, 1983.

————: The expendable *Kronjurist*: Carl Schmitt and National Socialism, 1933–1936. *Journal of Contemporary History* 14 (1979) 309–328.

Habermas, J.: Sovereignty and the *Führerdemokratie*. *Times Literary Supplement* (September 26, 1986) 1053–54.

Kennedy, E.: Carl Schmitt in West German perspective. *West European Politics* 7 (1984) 120–7.

————: Carl Schmitt and the Frankfurt School. *Telos*, 1987.

Schmitt, C.: *Die Diktatur. Von den Anfängen des modernen Souveränitätsgedanken bis zum proletarischen Klassenkampf*. Munich: Duncker & Humblot, 1921.

————: *Legalität und Legitimität*. Munich: Duncker & Humblot, 1932.

————: Der Führer schützt das Recht. *Deutsche Juristen-Zeitung*. 39.15 (1934) 945–50.

————: *The Concept of the Political* (1928, 1932). New Brunswick, NJ: Rutgers University Press, 1976.

————: *The Crisis of Parliamentary Democracy* (1923, 1926). Cambridge, Mass.: MIT Press, 1985.

————: *Political Theology* (1922). Cambridge, Mass.: MIT Press, 1985.

Schwab, G.: *The Challenge of the Exception: an introduction to the political ideas of Carl Schmitt, 1921–1936*. Berlin: Duncker & Humblot, 1970.

Strauss, L.: Comments on Carl Schmitt's *The Concept of the Political*. In C. Schmitt *The Concept of the Political*. New Brunswick, NJ: Rutgers University Press, 1976.

Schumpeter, Joseph Alois (1883–1950)

Austrian economist. Born into a middle-class family Schumpeter was introduced, following his mother's second marriage, into the aristocratic society of Vienna and from 1893 to 1901 attended an exclusive school for the sons of the aristocracy, the Theresianum. Subsequently, during the years 1901–6, he studied law and economics at the University of Vienna, where he attended the seminars of Wieser and Böhm-Bawerk and engaged in vigorous debates with two Austro-Marxist contemporaries, Otto Bauer and Rudolf Hilferding. After graduating he spent some months in England, living as a young man of fashion, and in 1907 married an Englishwoman, but the marriage soon proved a failure, though it was not dissolved until 1920. In 1907 he went to Egypt where he practised law, managed the financial affairs of an Egyptian princess (with considerable success), and the following year published his first book, on economic theory. He returned to Vienna in 1909 and accepted a professorship at the University of Czernowitz, moving two years later to the University of Graz, where he published a book which made him famous, *The Theory of Economic Development* (1911). After the first world war he acted briefly as a consultant to the Socialization Commission in Berlin, and was then for a few months finance minister, under socialist sponsorship, in the coalition government of the first Austrian Republic. From 1920 to 1924 he was the president of a private bank in Vienna, and in 1925 he accepted a professorship at the University of Bonn. Finally, in 1932 he moved to Harvard University where he remained until his death.

Schumpeter was primarily an economist, but he had very broad interests in social science and made important contributions to sociology and political science, as well as to the history of economic thought. The distinctive element in his *Theory of Economic Development* is the significance that he attributes to the role of the entrepreneur, as a new social type, in the development of modern captitalism. Two important monographs, on imperialism (1919) and on social classes (1927), show the extent of his interest in, and his ability to make an original contribution to, political and sociological studies. Scattered through the whole of Schumpeter's work can be found illuminating analyses of political institutions and processes. But the work which is undoubtedly of the greatest and most enduring interest to political scientists is *Capitalism, Socialism and Democracy* (1942). In this book Schumpeter first provided an admirably lucid assessment of various aspects of Marx's work, before examining the 'decline of CAPITALISM', which he explained (to some extent in accord with Marx, and especially with the Austro-Marxists) by the decline of the entrepreneur as a result of the growth of large corporations, and also by the crumbling of capitalism's political defences, in which, according to his view, the activities of radical intellectuals played a considerable role. In the third part of the book he turned to the question 'can socialism work?' and in opposition to those critics of socialism who had argued that it would be impossible for a centrally planned economy to allocate resources efficiently, he gave a very positive answer. In the following part he considered the relation between socialism and democracy, advancing a theory of democracy as 'competition for political leadership' which has a close affinity with the ideas of Max WEBER. He was one of the originators of the elitist theories of democracy, and criticized such conceptions as those of ROUSSEAU and the utilitarians whose work he found ignored the social realities of the modern world.   TBB

Reading

Plamenatz, J.: *Democracy and Illusion*. London: Longman, 1973.

Schumpeter, J.A.: *The Theory of Economic Development*. Cambridge, Mass.: Harvard University Press, 1934.

———: *Imperialism and Social Classes*. Oxford: Blackwell, 1951.

———: *Capitalism, Socialism and Democracy*. 5th edn. London: Allen & Unwin, 1976.

secession/accession Leaving/joining a (con)federation. When a loose union (confederation) is formed or when additional members join each member must assent individually. Members retain sovereignty and a military capacity, so in this sense it is easy to leave. The remaining states have a *jus ad bellum*, a right to wage limited war with the seceders – but there is no right to win a war. A CONFEDERATION is usually a unity for diplomatic affairs, so such a war should be confinable within its land boundaries. The closer union FEDERALISM however is a status not a contract, so accession may be by simple statute, and easy – but secession is insurrection, and provincial military capacity is weak.

Secession is the daily bread of a confederation (such as the EEC), as well as the ultimate medicine: each disobedience is momentary secession. The threat is ever present. To prevent dissolution, secession is institutionalized by the requirement of unanimity and procedures for arbitration.

However, the distinction between a confederacy and a federal state is blurred – all federations use the language of confederation and pretend to an origin in contract. All wars today are limited wars and belligerent rights are lightly conceded by superpowers, especially in insurrections within precise geographical areas. In any case, nearly all nations claim their origin and legitimacy from victory in a struggle to secede.

In the American war of secession the ten 'rebel' states acquired international belligerent rights from Lincoln's Declaration of Blockade in April 1861, but the federal power only reluctantly applied the laws of war regarding the conflict as insurgency. So when the southern states surrendered at Appomattox in April 1865 it was unclear whether there had ever, in federal law, been an effective secession. But two million citizens could not be executed for 'rebellion'. Successive presidents, Supreme Courts, and Congresses came to incompatible decisions. Eventually and illogically, the southern states were made to sue for readmission and accept the XIV Amendment. Full legality was not restored until the 1960s.

At around the same time Prussia seceded from the Germanic Union – but in this case it was the federal power, represented by Austria, that was defeated in battle and Austria that was expelled. Earlier, in 1847, seven (Catholic) Swiss cantons had tried to secede from the Swiss confederacy but were defeated in battle. Puppet governments were successfully installed in the principal defeated cantons and leading rebels punished. Catholics did not fully re-enter national life until 1919.

Accession of a new state to the USA requires only a Joint Resolution of the two Houses of Congress (US Constitution, Article 4 §.3). Special conditions and reservations have in the past been made for and by states, but all states are now regarded as equals (*Coyle v. Smith*, 1911). Application for admission to the European Community is under Article 237 of the Treaty of Rome. The practice is to require unanimity in the COUNCIL OF MINISTERS. In Switzerland, accession of the new canton Jura in 1980 was by constitutional amendment, a majority of voters and cantons.

CJH

Reading

Buchheit, L.C.: *The Legitimacy of Self-Determination*. New Haven, Conn. and London: Yale University Press, 1978.

Carpenter, J.T.C.: *The South as Conscious Minority, 1789–1861*. Gloucester, Mass.: Smith, 1963.

Huber, E.R.: *Deutsche Verfassungsgeschichte Seit 1789*, Vol. III. Stuttgart: Kohlhammer, 1960.

McNair, Lord and Watts, A.D.: *The Legal Effects of War*. Cambridge: Cambridge University Press, 1966.

O'Brien, W.: *The Conduct of Just and Limited War*. New York: Praeger, 1981.

US Supreme Court. 7 Wall. 700 (1869) *Texas versus White* (The leading Supreme Court case, with a dissenting Judgment).

second ballot An ELECTORAL SYSTEM used in France for the election of the president and for the National Assembly (except in 1986), as well as in presidential elections in the SEMI-PRESIDENTIAL SYSTEMS of Austria, Finland and Portugal. Under this system provision is made for a second ballot if no candidate wins an absolute majority of votes cast at the first. There is usually a restriction on the number of candidates allowed to participate in the second ballot. In French presidential elections, only the top two candidates in the first ballot can compete; in elections to the National Assembly there is a threshold – at present 12.5 per cent of the registered electorate (equivalent to roughly 15 per cent of the vote), and only parties which can surmount this threshold are allowed to compete in the second ballot.

The purpose of the second ballot, like the ALTERNATIVE VOTE whose mechanics it resembles, is to prevent a candidate winning an election on less than a majority of the vote. The second ballot does not, however, secure proportional representation and can, indeed, under certain circumstances, yield a more disproportional result than the plurality system. It differs from the alternative vote in that it allows, and indeed encourages, bargaining between parties and groups between the two ballots.

VBB

second chambers Historically second chambers are rooted in the medieval idea of representation of orders or ESTATES. The various social orders were considered to require representation in different chambers based upon different methods of selection. For example, the HOUSE OF LORDS, the oldest second chamber still in existence, originated at the end of the thirteenth century as a house for the Lords Spiritual and Temporal. With the development of democracy, the justification of second chambers as a means of securing aristocratic representation ceased to carry weight. Nevertheless the majority of democracies retain second chambers, justifying their existence in different ways.

The classical description of the functions of a second chamber is that of Lord Bryce in his Report on the Conference of the Reform of the Second Chamber (Cd 9038). Bryce declared that a second chamber had four functions: revision of legislation; initiation of non-controversial bills; delaying legislation of fundamental constitutional importance so as 'to enable the opinion of the nation to be adequately expressed upon it'; and public debate. In addition, there is a separate justification for the existence of second chambers in FEDERAL states, namely to protect the interests of the constituent parts of the federation. It is for this reason that every modern federal state is bicameral. The functions of delaying legislation of fundamental constitutional importance, and of protecting the interests of the constituent parts of a federation, may be regarded as democratic justifications of second chambers. In practice, however, in many democracies, second chambers are dominated by disciplined parties and this affects their performance of these functions.

Of thirty-nine democracies with populations of over 200,000 identified by Leonard and Natkiel, only ten are unicameral. Unicameralism is generally confined to small democracies. The largest unicameral state is currently Portugal with a population of around 10 million. In addition, communist countries are generally unicameral.

In most democracies the method or date of election or the composition of the electorate varies between the two chambers, thereby ensuring that the second chamber is complementary to the first rather than a mere duplication of it. Britain is the only democracy in which the majority of members of the second chamber sit by right of hereditary succession, together with a minority of members – around 25 per cent – who sit as life peers in virtue of appointment by the sovereign on the advice of the prime minister; and Canada is the only democracy to have a wholly nominated second chamber. The membership of all other second chambers is chosen mainly if not wholly through election, either direct or indirect, and in a number of countries (for example Australia, France, India, the Netherlands and the United States) the electoral cycle for second chamber elections is staggered to give greater continuity of membership.

In federal states, representation in the second chamber is generally on the basis of the constituent units and not proportionately to the size of population. The constituent units may enjoy either equal representation in the second chamber as in Australia, Switzerland and the United States, or representation which over-represents the smaller units as in Austria and the Federal Republic of Germany. Representatives of the constituent units may be chosen, by direct election, as in Switzerland (with the exception of the canton of Berne) and the United States, by INDIRECT ELECTION by the legislature of the constituent unit as in Austria and Spain, or they may be representatives of the executive of the constituent units as in Germany.

Even in non-federal states, however, provision can be made for the representation of local or regional interests. In France and the Netherlands, for example, there is indirect election through an electoral college composed – mainly in France and wholly in the Netherlands – of the elected representatives of local government. In Norway and Iceland a percentage of the elected members of the legislature, equivalent to a quarter in the case of Norway, and a third in the case of Iceland, constitute the second chamber; some would regard these two countries as not strictly bicameral. Finally, although the principle of FUNCTIONAL REPRESENTATION has sometimes been suggested as an appropriate basis for the composition of a second chamber, the Irish Republic is the only country whose second chamber exemplifies the principle.

It is rare for the two chambers of a legislature to enjoy absolutely equal powers. In general, governments in parliamentary systems are responsible to the first, popular chamber, and not the second. But in Australia in 1975, the Senate, by withholding Supply, made it impossible for the government to continue, so precipitating a constitutional crisis. In some countries (Fiji, the Netherlands, Norway) all bills must be introduced in the lower house, while in Britain, Canada, India and Ireland, all money bills must originate in the lower house, and the second chamber cannot amend or defeat these bills; in Britain, most government bills originate, by custom, in the House of Commons. In the United States, all tax legislation must be introduced in the House of Representatives. These restrictions reflect the principle that the people's consent is required, via their elected representatives, to measures authorizing expenditure or imposing taxation.

Where the two chambers enjoy equal or near-equal powers, a device is needed to resolve differences between them. The most common method is a joint committee of the two chambers called in some countries a mediation, conciliation or conference committee and composed of an equal number of members from each chamber. This method is used in Canada, France, the Federal Republic of Germany, Ireland, Japan, Switzerland and the United States. In France, Ireland and Germany (except for issues affecting the Länder) if the two chambers cannot agree the issue is decided by the vote of the first chamber; in Canada the Senate in practice gives way, while in Japan the opposition of the second chamber can be overcome by a two-thirds vote in the popular chamber.

A second method, which can be used in conjunction with the joint committee, is known as the *navette*. This provides for the two chambers to examine alternately the bill in question, each sending messages to the other until they can agree upon a common text. If agreement cannot be reached, the bill usually cannot become law. This procedure is used in Australia, Belgium, Canada (although in practice the Canadian Senate normally gives way), France, Italy, Malaysia, and Switzerland. In Australia and India, joint sittings of the two chambers can be held, while in Australia both houses can be dissolved if agreement cannot be reached within two months.

If agreement still cannot be reached, then if the powers of the two chambers are equal as in Belgium and Italy, the legislative process cannot be completed. In most democracies, however, the second chamber has no more than a delaying power and the popular chamber can therefore overcome its opposition.

The supremacy of the popular chamber does not necessarily mean that second chambers do not fulfil important legislative and constitutional functions as described by Bryce. It is true that some smaller democracies (Denmark, New Zealand, Sweden) decided to dispense with their second chamber in the post-war era, while there are some in Britain who would like to abolish the Lords and others who would like to reform it. But perhaps the best

justification for a second chamber was that given by Walter Bagehot in *The English Constitution* (1867) 'With a perfect Lower House it is certain that an Upper House would be scarcely of any value. If we had an ideal House of Commons ... it is certain we should not need a higher chamber.' It is because this ideal is so rarely fulfilled that most democracies retain a second chamber.

See also LEGISLATURES. VBB

Reading

Bryce, Viscount (Chairman): *Conference on the Reform of the Second Chamber*. London: HMSO, Cd 9038, 1918.

Inter-Parliamentary Union: *Parliaments of the World*. 2 vols. Aldershot: Gower, 1986.

Leonard, D. and Natkiel, R.: *World Atlas of Elections: voting patterns in thirty-nine democracies*. London: Hodder & Stoughton, 1987.

Marriott, J.A.R.: *Second Chambers*. London: Oxford University Press, 1927.

Mill, J.S.: *Considerations on Representative Government*, ch. 13.

The Role of Second Chambers. *Parliamentarian* 63.4 (October, 1982).

Wheare, K.C.: *Legislatures*, pp. 197–218. Oxford: Oxford University Press, 1963.

secret police Authoritarian systems generally use clandestine information gathering, surveillance and the threat of omniscience over their subjects as a way of maintaining their power: the agency for effecting these is known as the secret police. Their degree of secrecy varies and their functions usually merge with espionage and counter-intelligence activities. Every political system will attempt to keep hidden some of its activities, while trying to uncover those of its enemies.

The vital elements of a secret police organization are: far-reaching powers of arrest, interrogation, surveillance, information-gathering, and even of execution; an independent budget; relative freedom from political control; access to the highest levels of political power. Among early examples was the medieval Inquisition set up by the Roman Catholic church to eradicate heresy. The Tsarist *Okhrana* and the police surveillance of

Austria-Hungary and Prussia, both aimed at real or imagined enemies of the system, are more recent instances. The GESTAPO (GEheime STAatsPOlizei) in Nazi Germany and the KGB (Komitet Gosudarstvennoi Bezopasnosti) in the USSR are widely regarded as paradigmatic instances, but even an organization which is little more than a gang of armed ruffians, such as the Tonton Macoute of Duvalier's Haiti, can fall into this category. The remit of the secret police is likely to be virtually unlimited. The political leadership, which tries to maintain maximum supervision over it, will use it as an alternative instrument of control over the overlapping and interlocking bureaucracies which tend to proliferate in authoritarian systems. During the 1980s the KGB in the USSR has become a political actor of some weight, with a degree of informal autonomy in the system.

The purpose of secret police activity falls into several broad categories. Information-gathering aims to be as far-reaching as possible, with the intention of creating a climate of insecurity and preventing the emergence of organized opposition. There is reason to believe that information-gathering can become an end in itself and that its machinery can suffer from information overload. The discovery, pursuit and liquidation of clandestine activity aiming to destabilize the system is another key function of the secret police. The preparation of the Stalinist show trials in the USSR and Eastern Europe illustrates this. The show trials also provide an insight into another aspect of secret police activity: its propensity to 'discover' ever wider networks of hostile conspiracies, due partly to a genuine conviction on the part of its operatives; partly to the attitude that all unsanctioned activity is actually or potentially hostile and partly to the need to prove the organization's indispensability to its political masters.

Secret police organizations operate not merely through sizeable establishments, but also by the creation of networks of informants, some of them professional (i.e. paid) and others not. In contemporary Soviet-type systems, the network of such informants is thought to be very wide and to include members of diverse professions.　　　GSch

Reading

Adelman, J.R. ed.: *Terror and Communist Politics.* Boulder, Col.: Westview, 1984.

Barron, J.: *The KGB: the secret work of Soviet secret agents.* London: Hodder & Stoughton, 1974.

Emerson, D.E.: *Metternich and the Political Police: security and subversion in the Habsburg Monarchy (1815–1830).* The Hague: Nijhoff, 1968.

Mosse, G.L. ed.: *Police Forces in History.* London: Sage, 1975.

Nonas, S.: *The Third Section: police and society in Russia under Nicholas I.* Cambridge, Mass.: Harvard University Press, 1961.

secret service　A term traditionally used in Brtain to denote either clandestine operations ranging from intelligence collection to covert action (see INTELLIGENCE) or the secret agency which runs these operations. The second meaning has come to predominate. Secret Service is nowadays used to describe either the intelligence community as a whole or the Secret Intelligence Service (SIS or MI6) in particular. Since 1923 the chief of SIS ('C') has had the official title Head of the Secret Service. Secrecy has been and is an even greater priority in twentieth-century Britain than in previous centuries or in other countries. The foreign secretary Austen Chamberlain told the House of Commons in 1924: 'It is of the essence of a Secret Service that it must be secret, and if you begin disclosure it is perfectly obvious . . . that there is no longer any Secret Service and that you must do without it.' SIS, unlike the CIA and the KGB, remains officially unavowable. In the USA 'Secret Service' has a more restricted meaning and is usually used to denote the police force which guards the president.

　　　　　　　　　　　　　　　　　　　CMA

select committee　A body of members of a legislature appointed by it for consideration of or inquiry into matters referred by the plenary body. In general, select committees are an attempt to prepare complex matters for decision and to reconcile the conflicting demands of time available and business to be considered. Their development has varied. In the tradition of the British HOUSE OF COMMONS and certain Commonwealth parliaments political authority rests clearly with the executive, though in some of them reforms enhancing the role of select committees have recently been introduced. In other instances (particularly the United States CONGRESS) committees have a more influential and politically significant position.

Looked at another way, *ad hoc* select committees may be distinguished from permanent or standing bodies. The investigative mandate of the former normally comes to an end when their specific tasks are completed. The competence of the latter will usually cover the policy and actions of the executive and its agencies, and also (except in most of the countries influenced by the Westminster tradition) legislation. Most such committees (though the European Parliament and the Italian Parliament are exceptions) are constituted for an electoral term. A further variety of permanent committee is responsible for internal matters such as rules of procedure or privileges, notably the Rules Committee in the US House of Representatives.

The term committee is used here both for *ad hoc* and for permanent bodies. The latter are however often termed STANDING COMMITTEES a phrase which has a particular connotation in the UK House of Commons.

Permanent committees may be prescribed in the national constitution (France and Sweden) in statute (USA) or in parliamentary rules (UK, USA and the Netherlands). Disposition of parties normally mirrors that in the plenary assembly. The details will depend on legal requirements, as in Japan, on specific agreement (European Parliament) or the rules of procedure and custom. The chairman is usually elected by the committee itself, except in India (Rajya Sabha) and certain committees in the US Congress where the appointment is made by the SPEAKER. Whatever the method of appointment, the chairmanship may in practice depend on the political decision of the executive or committee seniority. A proportion of chairmanships is sometimes allocated to members of minority parties (Belgium and the European Parliament) and a number of committees with financial control functions are chaired by opposition members, as in Austria, Spain, the UK and the Irish Republic.

Where, as in Britain, the preponderant political initiative rests with the executive, much preparatory work on draft legislation will be complete before it reaches parliament. Where the principle of SEPARATION OF POWERS allows more initiative to the legislature, as in the USA, committees play a more decisive part in shaping legislation. The independent budgetary competence of US congressional committees is in striking contrast to the limited role of committees in Britain where the crown's (government's) recommendation must precede consideration of expenditure, creating a charge on the public revenue.

See also LEGISLATIVE COMMITTEES.

KB

Reading

Bradshaw, K. and Pring, D.: *Parliament and Congress*. London: Quartet, 1981.

Inter-Parliamentary Union: *The System of Parliamentary Committees*. In Constitutional and Parliamentary Information, 1st series, pp. 139–40 n.p., 1984.

self-determination A radical doctrine justifying the autonomy and independence of an individual or group conceived as possessing a distinctive identity and free will. As an ethical doctrine, it originated with Kant's postulate of the good will as free and autonomous; Kant applied this to the self-determining individual, who could only be deemed to be acting morally if he or she were free of external constraint. Kant's German Romantic followers, notably Fichte, applied the idea of individual free will to collectivities, especially cultural communities or 'nations'. In this form, the doctrine of national self-determination achieved great popularity in the wake of the French Revolution in the nineteenth century, especially in Eastern Europe, where neglected or oppressed ethnic communitites were persuaded by their romantic-nationalist intellectuals that the only way to exercise autonomy and determine their communal destiny was to claim political independence and the right to self-rule. The doctrine later spread to the Middle East, south Asia and finally Africa, where it became an important justification for anti-colonialism and later for a variety of secessionist and irredentist ETHNIC NATIONALISMS. In the post-war period, the doctrine was used by all kinds of anti-establishment movements to whom a radical subjectivism seemed to offer that combination of authenticity with revolutionary activism (*praxis*) which could replace the old social order with new modes of sentiment and structure. Classes, sects, despised minorities, women, even communes and nature itself, could be endowed with the right to self-determination and untrammelled self-expression in the face of bureaucratic and capitalist pressures.

This oscillation between a wider general ideal of self-determination and a more specific national right of self-determination highlights the ambiguities of the doctrine. Philosophically it assumes that human beings are capable of directing their lives in perfect freedom, and so fails to address the sources of inner compulsion as well as the structural constraints stemming from tradition, social institutions and collective history. Even more damaging is its failure to elucidate the 'self' that can exercise the right of self-determination which, as historical experience has shown, is so often the object of doubt, vagueness and conflict. As far as national self-determination is concerned other criteria have had to be adduced to delimit the determining 'self', notably language and later 'colour'. The problems caused by the doctrine are well illustrated, in different ways, by the strategies adopted by Lenin and Woodrow Wilson in the aftermath of the first world war; both acknowledged the right of self-determination on an ethnic-linguistic basis while seeking to limit its uninhibited exercise. A similar ambivalence to the principle accompanied the DEVOLUTION debate in Britain in the 1970s, and continues to haunt the practical politics of ethnic inclusion and SECESSION from Sri Lanka and the Punjab to Cyprus and the Falklands. Inscribed in the Charter of the United Nations, the principle is systematically flouted but universally acknowledged as the basis of national legitimacy and the main expression of political liberty. Its numerous critics, mainly situated in the West, decry the excesses committed in the name of national self-determination and ascribe to the attempts to implement the principle many of the conflicts and brutalities that disfigure international relations; however not only do they place too great a causal weight on the idea, they also fail to locate it within its social and political context as an attempt to escape conflicting modern structural and cultural realities.   ADS

Reading

Buchheit, L.C.: *Secession*. New Haven, Conn.: Yale University Press, 1978.

Cobban, A.: *National States and National Self-Determination*. Oxford: Oxford University Press, 1945.

Deutsch, K.: *Nationalism and Social Communications*. 2nd edn. Boston, Mass. and London: MIT Press, 1966.

Kedourie, E.: *Nationalism*. London: Hutchinson University Library, 1960.

Ronen, D.: *The Quest for Self-Determination*. New Haven, Conn.: Yale University Press, 1978.

Smith, A.D.: *Theories of Nationalism*. 2nd edn. London: Duckworth, 1983.

self-government A condition in which an individual or collectivity manages his/its own affairs and is solely responsible for his/its actions and destiny. More narrowly, a doctrine commending the virtues of autonomy or living according to one's distinctive 'inner rhythms', which require freedom from external constraint; hence self-government presupposes the right of SELF-DETERMINATION, and in its national form, the Whig doctrine of nationality, i.e. that nations are best ruled by their own representatives. The liberal doctrine, stated by J. S. MILL, is to be distinguished from 'organic' justifications of nationalism, according to which only national states are genuine ones and national self-rule is the only justifiable type of government. The latter doctrine stems from romantic preoccupations with the 'natural' units of society and politics, and from the cults of autonomy and authenticity put forward by cultural populists from ROUSSEAU and Herder to Gokälp and Aurobindo.

Traceable ultimately to the Greek love of political liberty or *autonomia*, the ideal of self-rule admits of various gradations in practice. At the lowest level attention is confined to cultural autonomy, the right to unfettered self-expression in literature, the arts, worship and education; a free press and theatre have often sparked off wider movements for self-rule. Second comes legal autonomy and rights, notably native judges and an unrestricted judicial process, and equality before the law; ethnic discrimination and social prejudice are regarded as arbitrary limitations of individual and collective dignity and self-expression. Third comes internal political autonomy or home rule, the control by representatives of the community of its economic, social and political affairs within the boundaries of that community; while this excludes defence, law and order and foreign affairs, home rule delivers a large measure of control over the community's resources and social policies to ethnic members. Finally, self-rule is equated with permanent independence in the form of a state exclusively for the community, and thus a NATION-STATE; but in practice not all NATIONALISMS aspire to full independence and statehood, and few states belong exclusively to a particular ethnic community. Hence self-rule is qualified in several ways. There is usually more than one community within the territory of the state; the community may well have to be content with legal autonomy or home rule; and in any case even nominally independent communal states (nation-states) may be forced to become clients of larger states or superpowers or have their sovereignty limited, in practice, by alliances or regional treaties, such as the Treaty of Rome for EEC members.

The right to self-rule is however valued both as a bulwark against external interference and influence and, in its frequent conjunction with the ideal of popular sovereignty since at least the French Revolution and its cult of republican Rome, against the tyranny of both individuals (monarchs or DICTATORS) and FACTIONS (oligarchies or classes). In fact, the myth of self-government may be used as a cloak for demagogues and totalitarian leaders; the movement or party and its leader are felt to mirror and express the self-determination and autonomy of the people, whose 'national soul' and 'mission' they personify.   ADS

Reading

Beitz, C.: *Political Theory and International Relations*. Princeton, NJ: Princeton University Press, 1979.

Hinsley, F.: *Sovereignty*. London: Watts, 1966.

Hodgkin, T.: *Nationalism in Colonial Africa*. 2nd edn. London: Muller, 1978.

Kautsky, J. ed.: *Political Change in Underdeveloped Countries*. Chichester: Wiley, 1962.

Plamenatz, J.: *On Alien Rule and Self-government*. London: Longman, 1960.

Smith, A.D.: *Nationalism in the Twentieth Century*. Oxford: Robertson, 1979.

semi-presidential systems A term first employed by the French political scientist Maurice Duverger in *Institutions politiques et droit constitutionnel* (11th edn, 1970) to designate a political system, such as that of the French Fifth Republic since 1962 in which a president elected by universal suffrage co-exists with a Prime Minister and Cabinet responsible to the legislature. Duverger identified seven examples of this system – the Weimar Republic in Germany 1919–33, and among contemporary states Austria, France, Finland, Iceland, Ireland and Portugal. An eighth, Sri Lanka, has since been added.

Such a system would at first sight seem to be a synthesis of the presidential and parliamentary models of government, but it is hardly possible to fuse two such different modes of government. Instead, the semi-presidential system can, under certain circumstances, operate according to the mechanics of a PRESIDENTIAL SYSTEM – as, for example, in France under de Gaulle (1958–69), Pompidou (1969–74), Giscard d'Estaing (1974–81), and Mitterrand (1981–86); or it can operate according to the mechanics of a PARLIAMENTARY SYSTEM as in Austria, Iceland and Ireland; or, finally, there can be a division of powers within the executive so that president and prime minister enjoy extensive powers within particular spheres. This method of operation has been characteristic of Finnish experience since the end of the second world war. The president is broadly responsible for foreign policy and enjoys various administrative and rule-making powers, while the prime minister and cabinet are generally responsible for domestic policy.

The precise mode of operation depends less upon constitutional rules than upon political factors, and most of all, upon the party system, the presence or absence of a parliamentary regime, and the relationship between the president and the majority party or bloc, if any, in the legislature. If the president is leader of the majority as were for example, de Gaulle, Pompidou and (until 1986) Mitterrand, he is likely to have a powerful political role. If he is a member of the majority without being its leader as in Austria between 1970 and 1986, the president is likely to exercise a merely symbolic role; while if he is in opposition to the majority in the legislature, as with Mitterrand from 1986 to 1988, or President Jonas in Austria between 1966 and 1970, he may enjoy some regulatory or supervisory powers but will not have a central political role. Where the political system does not create a stable parliamentary majority, the position of the president is likely to correspond closely to his constitutional powers.

In the main the countries which have adopted the semi-presidential system are those in which there were thought to be threats to the stable working of parliamentary institutions; and the semi-presidential system seems most appropriate for democracies characterized by multi-party systems and political fragmentation; for the institution of the presidency can encourage bipolarity in what might otherwise prove a fragmented political system.

See also COHABITATION.   VBB

Reading

Duverger, M.: A new political system model: semi-presidential government. *European Journal of Political Research* (1980) 168–83.

———— ed.: *Les Régimes semi-présidentiels*. Paris: Presses Universitaires de France, 1986.

senate   See CONGRESS.

seniority   The practice of awarding political offices on the basis of length of service in the institution. Its origins can be traced to hereditary monarchy and to tribal practices in many areas of the world. In the United States, it has been most important in designating the chairs of the substantive legislative committees in CONGRESS. The usual rule has been that the chair is the member from the majority party who has served the longest continual term on the specific committee.

The justifications for the use of seniority are that it insures that committee leadership will be held by experienced persons and that this automatic rule avoids disruptive conflict over the selection. On the other hand, the practice favours persons who have accumulated seniority because they come from constituencies with relatively limited electoral competition, and who may therefore be out of touch with the general electorate or uncooperative with their own party's legislative goals and leadership. This criticism was particularly strong when conservative Democrats from the South, an erstwhile one-party area, would use their committee chairmanships to thwart liberal Democratic programmes.

Congressional seniority was signficantly altered by Democrats in the House of Representatives in 1975 when they gave party leaders the power to nominate chairmen and provided for secret election by all members of the legislative party. Similar, but less stringent, changes have also been made by Republicans and in the Senate. In a few significant cases, these changes have brought a measure of party discipline to Congress. In most cases, however, seniority still governs the choice of chairmen.

See also LEGISLATIVE COMMITTEES.

GMP

Reading

Goodwin, G. Jr: The seniority system in Congress. *American Political Science Review* 53 (1959) 412–436.

Peabody, R.L.: *Leadership in Congress*. Boston: Little, Brown, 1976.

separation of powers   This doctrine is an amalgam of concepts and ideas drawn from centuries of political thought and practice, from the time of ancient Greece to the present day. It is a set of ideas, expressed as a theory of politics, which asserts that liberty can be safeguarded only in a political system which adheres to the principles of the doctrine. It has however no generally accepted form, and it is easy to read back into the writings of an earlier age ideas which were not in fact held by political theorists or practical men of the time. Nevertheless, there are a number of elements which go to make up the doctrine of the separation of powers.

(1) The first of these is the concept of law itself. The distinction between an arbitrary command and a *law*, whether made by God or man, is essential to the doctrine. The modern view of law as a man-made set of rules to govern social behaviour is of relatively recent origin, and until it emerged fully in the seventeenth century a coherent doctrine of the separation of powers was not feasible. An important aspect of the concept of law is its generality, that is to say that laws should be formulated in general terms and not directed at particular individuals. This was a vital step in the development of the next element of the doctrine, the functions of government.

(2) Initially theorists saw only two functions of government – those of making the law and of applying it. Aristotle divided political science into two parts, legislative science and politics or action, although for him law-making was not the continuous instrumental process it is today. The idea of the two functions of making law and of putting it into effect, were first clearly expressed by Marsilius of Padua at the begining of the fourteenth century, and in the writings of those who developed and defended the institutions of the Venetian Republic. Although, however, Marsilius and other medieval writers referred to the *legislative* and *executive* functions, the latter was conceived very differently from the executive power of modern times. Medieval writers meant by the executive power the application of the law by the courts, by judges, and in England by the highest judge in the land, the king in his high court of parliament. At the end of the seventeenth century John Locke still maintained this essentially twofold division of the functions of government, although he also recognized the *federative* power, the role of the executive in relation to foreign affairs. The modern view of the executive function, applying the law through an administrative rather than a judicial procedure, did not emerge fully until the eighteenth century when MONTESQUIEU and

Blackstone established a threefold division of the functions of government – legislative, executive and judicial.

(3) The concept of three branches of government – the legislature, the executive and the judiciary – also took time to emerge. It is possible to conceive of the functions of government being performed by the same person, an absolute ruler, or by the same group of people, an aristocracy or an assembly, however chosen. For over two thousand years or more, political institutions have been divided into a number of structures, constituted in different ways, and employing differing procedures. This was partly a result of the requirements of the division of labour, but mainly a response to the elaboration of different sets of values: the demand for representation leading to an elective assembly; the relative speed and efficiency of an administrative–bureaucratic procedure; the demand for fairness and impartiality in the settlement of disputes through an independent judicial system. As with the concept of the functions of government, it is not easy in practice to maintain these nice distinctions. Cabinets are created deliberately to link legislature and executive, and the emergence in recent times of hybrid animals such as ADMINISTRATIVE TRIBUNALS, or quasi-administrative, quasi-judicial bodies such as the INDEPENDENT REGULATORY COMMISSIONS in the United States, makes a simple tripartite classification of government virtually impossible.

(4) The more radical or extreme versions of the doctrine of the separation of powers introduce another concept – the idea that the different branches of government should be constituted by quite separate groups of people, no one person being allowed to be a member of more than one branch at one time. This idea was implemented rigorously in the Constitution of the United States (except for the role of the vice-president as the presiding officer of the Senate), but attempts have also been made to apply this idea in France during revolutionary periods; even in Britain the attacks upon 'placemen' led to a prohibition in the Act of Settlement of 1701 upon office-

holders being members of the House of Commons, a provision that was soon repealed. Unlike the United States with its presidential–congressional system, most western democracies are parliamentary–cabinet systems in which the personnel of the government link the legislative and executive branches at the top, although none go as far as Britain in having an official, the Lord Chancellor, who is a member of all three branches of government. However, there are a number of parliamentary democracies in which the personnel of government have to relinquish their parliamentary seats; for example, the Fifth Republic in France, the Netherlands and Norway. Nevertheless, a vitally important residue of this aspect of the doctrine of the separation of powers remains in the rules which prevent civil servants and serving military officers from being elected to the lower house of the legislature, and the rules providing for the independence of the judges.

(5) Finally the doctrine of the separation of powers links all these strands together into a theory of government which, in Montesquieu's words, states that 'When the legislative and executive powers are united in the same person, or in the same body of magistrates, there can be no liberty . . . Again, there is no liberty if the judicial power be not separated from the legislative and executive . . .' Initially developed as a theory during the English Civil War, elaborated by Locke, Montesquieu and Blackstone, the doctrine was embraced by the American colonists in their revolt against the British crown and parliament. It was given full expression in the Constitution of Virginia of 1776 which provided that: 'The legislative, executive and judiciary departments shall be separate and distinct, so that neither exercises the powers properly belonging to the other: nor shall any person exercise the powers of more than one of them at the same time . . .' Few modern theorists would accept this extreme view of the need for the strict separation of powers, conflicting as it does with the perceived need for a co-ordinated and effective system of government to deal with the complex social and economic problems of today; nor indeed was this extreme view accepted by the Founding Fathers in the

United States, and the American system of government has been characterized as one based on a separation of institutions sharing powers, rather than a separation of powers *tout court*. In France, however, the separation of powers has been interpreted to mean that one branch of government should not interfere with the work of another; it is for this reason that litigation involving administration is heard before separative administrative courts (see CONSEIL D'ÉTAT); for to confer on the judiciary the power to judge litigation involving administration would be to allow it to encroach upon the field of the executive.

Some have argued that the concept of the separation of powers is too porous to be of much use to the political scientist, but nevertheless there remains a kernel of truth in the doctrine without which western constitutional government could not persist.

See also CHECKS AND BALANCES; MIXED GOVERNMENT; PRESIDENT/PRESIDENTIAL SYSTEM; SEMI-PRESIDENTIAL SYSTEMS.

MJCV

Reading

Hamilton, A., Madison, J. and Jay, J.: *The Federalist Papers*, ed. C. Rossiter. New York: Mentor, 1964.

Gwyn, W.B.: *The Meaning of the Separation of Powers*. New Orleans: Tulane University Press, 1965.

Marshall, G.: *Constitutional Theory*. Oxford: Oxford University Press, 1971.

Montesquieu, C.-L.: *The Spirit of the Laws* (1748).

Vile, M.J.C.: *Constitutionalism and the Separation of Powers*. Oxford: Oxford University Press, 1967.

serfdom Found normally in societies where the majority of the basic producers are peasants who possess the holdings from which they derive their subsistence but who are subordinated to the class which owns the land. The institution has existed world-wide and many centuries before our era. Serfs differ from slaves, who are their owner's chattels, for serfs not only have their own means of subsistence but live in family units. Nevertheless they are unfree. This lack of freedom is necessary because the lords (or in some cases the state) need to guarantee the transfer of the surplus production from the peasant holding in the form of rents and services. Hence the serfs are bound to the soil or their lord; their offspring may only marry with the lord's permission; their movable goods are their lord's property which he can confiscate, for example as a death duty; there is no security of tenure; the lord may determine whether rent will be paid in labour services, in kind or in money; in addition to rent he may demand other taxes. Lords normally exercise private jurisdiction over their serfs, though its extent varies according to the strength of the state. Serfdom is usually judicially defined, though often imprecisely. The strictest forms of serfdom are based on the unfree, hereditary status of the serf, who would be excluded from law-courts and legal processes open to the free, especially processes which would permit legal action against the lord. The nature of the servile condition can vary from place to place and from time to time. Even peasants of supposed free status could in practice be subjected to conditions little different from those of serfs. This happens where the lords not only wield social and economic power over their tenants, but exercise public jurisdiction in their own private courts, as well as using their power to influence the public courts.

See also FEUDALISM; SLAVERY.   RHH

Reading

Bloch, M.: *Slavery and Serfdom in the Middle Ages.* Berkeley: University of California Press, 1975.

Hilton, R.H.: *The Decline of Serfdom in Medieval England.* 2nd end. London: Macmillan; New York: St Martin's, 1982.

Smith, R.E.F.: *The Enserfment of the Russian Peasantry.* Cambridge and New York: Cambridge University Press, 1968.

Société Jean Bodin: *Le Servage.* 2nd edn. Brussels: Editions de la Libraire Encyclopédique, 1959.

shadow cabinet The parliamentary executive committee of the main opposition party at Westminster and in some other WESTMINSTER MODEL parliaments. In the eighteenth-century British parliament it became the practice for leading figures of out-of-office factions to meet to organize OPPO-SITION to ministers of the day, and also for a list of potential ministers to be produced in anticipation of the fall of a government. Then former cabinet ministers would constitute a group to direct the policy of the opposition. These practices are reflected in the modern shadow cabinet's twin functions of managing the opposition party's parliamentary business and posing as an alternative team of ministers. At its weekly meetings the shadow cabinet deals with day-to-day party matters and decides the party's parliamentary tactics, short-term policy attitudes and longer-term policy commitments.

A Labour shadow cabinet (or 'parliamentary committee') has twenty-two members. Fifteen are elected annually by Labour members of parliament, and one by the Labour peers, while six are *ex-officio* members (the party leader and deputy leader, chief whip, chairman of the parliamentary party and leader and deputy leader of the Labour peers). After the annual election the party leader allocates members of the shadow cabinet to responsibilities as party spokesmen, 'shadowing' particular ministers.

The size and membership of a Conservative shadow cabinet (or 'consultative committee'), and the tasks of its members, are determined exclusively by the party leader. Since the 1950s MPs and peers who are not members of the shadow cabinet have also been allocated positions as spokesmen and assistant spokesmen, and the shadow cabinet is now the core of a shadow government of fifty or more members.   RMP

Reading

Punnett, R.M.: *Front-Bench Opposition.* London: Heinemann, 1973.

Turner, D.R.: *The Shadow Cabinet in British Politics.* London: Routledge & Kegan Paul, 1969.

Siegfried, André (1875–1959) French political scientist and geographer. Born at Le Havre into one of the leading Protestant families of France, André Siegfried was the son of an influential politician. While young he stood several times, unsuccessfully, for election to the National Assembly, then decided to study politics in order to 'discover its laws'. He was the author of three books which laid the foundations for the analysis of ELECTORAL

GEOGRAPHY and established a school and tradition which have greatly influenced many scholars around the world. He may, indeed, be regarded as one of the founders of modern political science.

The first of these books, the monumental *Tableau politique de la France de l'ouest* (1913) dissected local POLITICAL BEHAVIOUR and its variations in the constituencies of a large section of France which Siegfried knew well at first hand. The study takes into account all the available data on elections since the 1880s: voting statistics, campaigning, speeches and local media attitudes, issues debated, subsequent behaviour of the elected politicians, regional social-economic characteristics, religious and cultural traditions, etc. The human geography and sociology of each district were shown to be influencing the voters' choice, and their shifts or constancy. Siegfried later extended his study to other parts of France. He summarized his observations of the national arena in the *Tableau des partis politiques en France* (1930). This book remains one of the best available studies of national character. In the 1930s and 1940s Siegfried focused on south-eastern France. His small volume *Géographie électorale de l'Ardèche* (1949) is another much quoted classic. Siegfried's central conclusion was that patterns of political alignment were essentially stable, deriving as they did from deep-seated factors of temperament which could reasonably be analysed in geographical terms.

An indefatigable worker and traveller, Siegfried did not limit himself to the study of French politics. His Calvinistic background made him especially interested in the national character, the political institutions, and the modern evolution of the English-speaking nations. Much of his work shows the influence of Alexis de TOCQUEVILLE. Siegfried's books on democracy in New Zealand (1906), the race question in Canada (1907), followed by another on Canada as a rising power (1937), two books on the British economy (especially *La Crise britannique au XX siècle*, 1931) and two on the United States (especially *America Comes of Age*, 1927) form an impressive tableau to which were added long essays on the British Empire, Australia, India, and southern Africa.

While describing the individuality of each country, Siegfried stressed the common political traditions of the British and North American democracies; he emphasized the continuity of institutions achieved by their adapting to gradual change and constant evolution, and he foresaw the acceptance of a pluralistic society and institutional system, particularly in North America.

Altogether Siegfried published over twenty volumes and many essays, often drawing on his teaching at the École des Sciences Politiques and at the Collège de France in Paris. His influence was considerable and widespread, and his works remain a basic introduction to the analysis of politics in this century. His methods of electoral analysis, which were time-consuming and required hard work, have been simplified through the use of public opinion polls and computers. His conclusions about the importance of national and regional character and tradition are likely to endure.   JG

Reading

Bonnefous, E. ed.: *L'oeuvre scientifique d'André Siegfried*. Paris: Presses de la Fondation Nationale des Sciences Politiques, 1977.

Siegfried, A.: *Tableau politique de la France de l'ouest sous la troisième République*. Paris: Colin, 1913.

———: *America Comes of Age*. New York and London: Cape, 1927.

———: *Tableau des partis politiques en France* (1930). Trans. as *France: a study in nationality*. New Haven, Conn.: Yale University Press, 1930.

———: *What the British Empire Means to Western Civilization*. Toronto: Oxford Pamphlets on World Affairs, C4 (1940).

———: *Géographie électorale de L'Ardèche sous la IIIe République*. Paris: Colin, 1949.

single transferable vote (STV) See ELECTORAL SYSTEMS.

slavery The institution under which one person is the property of another. Slavery has existed in many societies, but often in modified forms such as SERFDOM. Societies in which slavery proper is a dominant form of labour are rare: only ancient Greece and Rome, and European colonies in America, have fallen into this category.

Typically a slave society arises as a result of the unwillingness or unavailability for labour of the native population, making it necessary to import a workforce from outside. Once introduced, the slaves are subject not merely to the will of their masters, but to various legal and social restrictions designed to reinforce their inferior status: thus in the ancient world a slave, unlike a citizen, was liable to corporal punishment, could not give evidence in court save under torture and, as in the USA, could not officially marry.

Despite the essential harshness of the institution, slave societies often reveal circumstances that mitigate or even undermine its inhumanity. In the ancient world a large proportion of slaves were freed, and slaves were often highly skilled. The slave of a powerful master could even wield great power himself. In America, the racial theories which sought to justify the enslavement of blacks prevented this, just as they prevented the freed slave from integrating into society. Few ancients, however, questioned the rightness of slavery as a whole. In modern times, by contrast, the growth of theories of human rights has led to the institution's being progressively outlawed.   DSL

Reading

Davis, D.B.: *Slavery and Human Progress*. New York & Oxford: Oxford University Press, 1984.

Finley, M.I.: *Ancient Slavery and Modern Ideology*. London: Chatto & Windus, 1980.

Stampp, K.M.: *The Peculiar Institution: slavery in the ante-bellum South*. New York: Knopf, 1956.

small group politics The validity of this concept can be challenged on two grounds: first, it could be argued that there are no features of politics in small groups that cannot be found in large groups; second, it could be argued that there are so many varieties of small groups that no useful generalization can be made about them anyway. It is true that 'small group politics' can be interpreted in different ways, and several can be distinguished. The politics of the primary group would refer to the family, the production team and the office, people in face-to-face relationships. Their position might be simulated in laboratory situations. The politics of the small town or neighbourhood refers to a rather large number of people, though still few in total compared with mass electorates. These may be, on occasions, micro-political units with a few powers; for example, the power to erect bus shelters or even to levy a modest tax. A complicating factor is the small group that is part of a large organization such as a political party. The two former types of small groups will usually produce the politics of the un-political, while the 'grass roots' ward party will be the arena of the consciously political. All however are likely to exhibit some common characteristics.

All politics are concerned with issues of power, authority, leadership, control, conflict and decision making. The likelihood is however that small groups will deal with these problems by different methods from large groups. For example, in primary groups it is likely that rules will not be formally promulgated, leaders will emerge by consensual processes rather than be elected and control will be exerted by pressures of conformity. The predisposition of such small groups will be to avoid conflict because in face-to-face situations personal disagreement will be painful and persistently damaging to the group. Conflict avoidance becomes an overriding necessity and is promoted in various ways. One is by maintaining an ideology of harmony. This involves emphasizing those norms, values and opinions with which most people are in agreement and suppressing those which cause dissent, argument and the emergence of oppositional sub-groups. Another is through the choice of decision-making methods which do not encourage criticism and organized opposition. Hence the more powerful members of small groups, who are likely anyway to be conformists holding group-norms, will try to prevent the institution of formal agendas and decision-making modes. They will be in favour of what Steiner and Dorff (1966) call 'decisions by interpretation' and against majority decision making which stimulates participation and innovative demands. When there is dissent in small groups, however, it may be expressed in personality clashes and with an intensity that seldom characterizes large groups.

Where, as in neighbourhood or parish councils, some representative framework exists, the community leadership is likely to stifle divisive tendencies. This implies preventing the development of cleavages existing in national politics. Bealey and Sewel (1981) explain how in Scottish small burghs the councils were elected at-large, because wards encouraged mobilization on the lines of class parties. A similar feature can be found in American LOCAL POLITICS. Such non-partisanship is a reflection of the ideology of consensus which frequently grips small groups and small communities. The assertion that national parties should not obtrude upon a small community's politics because they are not wanted has a populist ring.

With a small group such as a ward party, however, the position will be more complex. Here there will be highly political argument, though the smallness of the activist group may well lead to personality clashes. There will be many formal rules governing behaviour; but though they will often be quoted in disputes they will probably be subverted in practice by a set of entirely informal conventions. The politics of small political groups is a compound of political and unpolitical modes of behaviour.

In their simplified contrast of small-scale with large-scale politics, Dahl and Tufte (1974) mention as distinctive features of small group politics, the accessibility of leaders to followers and the reciprocal nature of the relationship, as well as the relative lack of functional specialization among leaders of small groups. (The leadership of large groups is generally in the hands of professional politicians.) FWB

Reading

Banfield, E.C.: *The Moral Basis of a Backward Society*. New York: Free Press, 1967.

Bealey, F. and Sewel, J.: *The Politics of Independence: a study of a small Scottish town*. Aberdeen: Aberdeen University Press, 1981.

Black, G.S.: Conflict in the community: a theory of the effects of community size. *American Political Science Review* (1974).

Dahl, R.A. and Tufte, E.: *Size and Democracy*. Oxford: Oxford University Press, 1974.

Homans, G.C.: *The Human Group*. London: Routledge & Kegan Paul, 1951.

Lee, E.C.: *The Politics of Non-Partisanship*. Berkeley: University of California Press, 1960.

Sprott, W.J.H.: *Human Groups*. London: Penguin, 1958.

Steiner, J. and Dorff, R.H.: *A Theory of Political Decision Modes*. Chapel Hill: University of North Carolina Press, 1960.

Vidich, A.J. and Bensman, J.: *Small Town in Mass Society*. Princeton, NJ: Princeton University Press, 1958.

social choice theory Examines the relationship between individuals' preferences and social choices. In 1785 the Marquis de Condorcet first noticed that for three individuals and three options, *a*, *b*, and *c*, it was possible that majorities would prefer *a* to *b*, *b* to *c*, and *c* to *a*. This is called a 'cycle' and its existence is called the 'paradox of voting' or 'Condorcet's paradox'. Arrow (1951) generalized this to show that no conceivable way of deriving a social choice from individual preferences could jointly satisfy four very undemanding conditions of fairness and rationality. Black (1958) showed that Arrow's result did not hold if there were only one ideological dimension and if nobody rated the options in the middle of the range worst ('single-peakedness') (see also SPATIAL MODELS). Social choice theory has now grown explosively and is mathematically intimidating. Its other main results are: that the 'weak Pareto rule' ('if everybody prefers *a* to *b*, choose *a*') is inconsistent with libertarianism (see Sen 1970, ch. 6); that no voting procedure is proof against manipulation; and that cycles are almost inescapable when there are many voters and several dimensions. These results are clearly interpreted for non-mathematicians by Riker (1982) and Dummett (1984). They have profound implications for electoral reform and democratic theory which have not yet been absorbed into mainstream political science. IMcL

Reading

Arrow, K.J.: *Social Choice and Individual Values*. New York: Wiley, 1951.

Black, D.: *The Theory of Committees and Elections*.

Cambridge: Cambridge University Press, 1958.

Dummett, M.: *Voting Procedures*. Oxford: Clarendon Press, 1984.

Riker, W.H.: *Liberalism against Populism*. San Francisco: Freeman, 1982.

social movements The word movement as applied to social phenomena first entered English usage in the late eighteenth and early nineteenth centuries. It denotes a series of actions or endeavours of a body of persons for a special object. For example, William Cobbett, commenting on disorders among the poor in 1812, observed: 'This is the circumstance that will most puzzle the Ministry. They can find no agitators. It is a movement of the people's own.' A different, now obsolete, use of the term was to describe certain 'innovatory' or 'progressive' parties as in the French term *parti du mouvement*, movement party, in early nineteenth-century Britain.

Social scientists and historians have found the concept of social movement indispensable in the study of collective behaviour. It implies a degree of self-generated and independent action, leadership, and a minimal degree of organization and participation on the part of the members of a group. It should not be confused with the unintended and unplanned social changes that come about as a result of general historical tendencies or trends. This is not to deny that such trends do often give rise to and promote organized social movements; as an obvious example, severe economic depression has frequently provoked radical protest movements among the poor, the unemployed, and the dispossessed. By no means all social movements however can be explained by changes in social and political conditions, though an influential American school of collective behaviour theorists argues that movements, like other forms of collective behaviour, arise out of behaviour in situations not clearly defined or problematic: it is a form of activity governed by new or emergent norms rather than by existing customs and rules. But other scholars have concentrated on the motivation of the individuals who establish and join movements and stress psychological mechanisms, such as the simultaneous expression of latent predispositions among many individuals, the 'contagion effect' brought about by the effects of mass communications, and imitation.

Historically social movements have been extremely important, both in the history of specific cultures and countries and internationally. One only has to reflect on such movements as those of communism, national liberation, peace and disarmament, and women's rights in the twentieth century, to appreciate their significance, not only for their effects on specific nation-states, but also in their world-wide influence as agents of political and social change. It is a considerable advantage that intellectuals have found the study of movements romantic and fascinating. There is an impressive scholarly literature on the history and theory of specific cases. The concept of social movement has also the enormous advantage that it is culturally interchangeable, ideologically neutral, and, like 'ideology' can be projected back into earlier periods of history.

Much of the general and comparative literature on social movements has been concerned with 'natural histories' and 'models' of movement development. In an influential pioneering work Rudolf Heberle (1951) set himself the ambitious task of 'the development of a comparative, systematic theory of social movements within a more comprehensive system of sociology' (p. 2). He emphasizes three key characteristics of social movements: group consciousness, a sense of group identity, and solidarity. They are invariably integrated by a specific pattern of normative commitments, 'constitutive ideas', or ideology. All social movements help society in the formation of the common will, and in the processes of socialization, training and recruitment of political elites.

Various attempts have been made to provide a typology of social movements. Some writers employ Max Weber's threefold categorization of forms of normative commitment: the value-rational fellowship of believers; the emotional–affectual following of the charismatic leader; the purposive–rational association for pursuing individual interests. Herbert Blumer (1951) distinguishes between 'general' and 'specific' movements. True social movements are of the 'specific' type, because they have some elements of organization and collectively defined values and norms. 'General' movements are uncoordinated trends in behaviour. Neil Smelser (1963) uses a twofold classification: value-oriented movements, deriving from a generalized belief that changes should be made in one or more of the basic values of the society, and norm-oriented movements which, while not challenging basic values, attempt to alter the processes for achieving the values of the society. Paul Wilkinson (1971) proposed a more complex typology, based on the predominant characteristics of the movement; hence all movements should be categorized in terms of the nature of their commitment to change, by their organizational mode and strategy, and also by the 'constituency' of the population which accords the movement normative commitment and participation.

The concept of social movement obviously encompasses a very wide range of phenomena. Inevitably it overlaps to some extent with the concepts of 'political party', 'pressure group' and 'voluntary association'. Most modern political parties, as Jean Blondel (1969) points out, have a movement dimension: they tend to be mass parties with well-defined policies and programmes. But some political parties, such as the US Democrats and the British Labour Party, contain more than one movement. Some movements use political parties as the spearhead of their campaigns for political power. But for many movements, political party activity is considered either irrelevant or profitless. There is a similar situation of overlap between voluntary associations and pressure groups and certain social movements. While some movements are willing to conform to the rules of party and pressure group participation in the political system, others contemptuously reject such constraints and function purely as extra-parliamentary campaigns or, in many cases, resort to violence and subversion to overthrow the political system. Other movements, such as many religious and cultural organizations, simply have no desire for direct political participation. Thus many social movements are *sui generis*. The concept of social movement is invaluable because it can embrace all major types of movement – including even conspiratorial societies, terrorist groups, millenarian sects and cults and prophetic movements – and not simply the more secular and conventional political parties, pressure groups, and voluntary associations with movement dimensions.

It would be a serious mistake to overlook or underestimate the positive political contribution that can still be made by certain social movements even in the most technologically sophisticated and bureaucratically organized political systems. It is unbalanced to dwell exclusively on movements which have become involved in civil violence and conflict, or which have become the vehicles or victims of dangerous illusions. Many great social movements have combined powerful moral concern for social betterment with non-violent, but highly effective techniques of rational reform and attempts to resolve or significantly alleviate major social and political problems. The Suffragettes and the Civil Rights Movement in America are notable examples. But recent history shows how social movements can also be exploited for destructive purposes, such as the inculcation of hatred and mistrust, terror, and aggressive war, with horrifying consequences for humanity.   PW

Reading

Blondel, J.: Mass parties and industrialised societies. In *Comparative Government: a reader*, ed. J. Blondel. London: Macmillan, 1969.

Blumer, H.: Collective behaviour. In *Principles of Sociology*. 2nd edn, ed. A.M. Lee, 1951.

Cohn, N.: *The Pursuit of the Millennium*. London: Paladin, 1970.

Etzioni, A.: *A Comparative Analysis of Complex Organisations*. Glencoe, Ill.: Free Press of Glencoe, 1961.

Heberle, R.: *Social Movements: an introduction to political sociology*. New York: Appleton-Century-Crofts, 1951.

Hobsbawm, E.: *Primitive Rebels*. Manchester: Manchester University Press, 1959.

Smelser, N.: *Theory of Collective Behaviour*. London: Routledge & Kegan Paul, 1962.

Tönnies, F.: *Community and Association*. London: Routledge & Kegan Paul, 1955.

Weber, M.: *The Theory of Social and Economic*

Organization, ed. T. Parsons. Glencoe, Ill.: Free Press of Glencoe, 1964.

Wilkinson, P.: *Social Movements: key concepts in political science*. London: Pall Mall, 1971.

social partnership A concept linking democratic ideals with corporatist structures (see CORPORATISM). It has been discussed and possibly realized in Austria, to a lesser extent in Scandinavian countries (especially Sweden), in the Federal Republic of Germany, in Switzerland, and in the Netherlands where, however, it has been in decline since the 1970s. From corporatism, social partnership takes the institutionalized co-operation between employers, employees and government. As a democratic ideal, this tripartite co-operation is considered to be the hard core of a general social system of economic (or industrial) democracy.

Social partnership has to be seen on different levels: as participation at the workplace; as co-determination on the plant level; as a free bargaining process between trade unions and employers; as a national institution to determine (or at least influence) social and economic policies. Trade unions usually emphasize more the higher, employers the lower levels of social partnership.

Historically, social partnership as corporatist co-operation has been especially stressed by the social doctrine of the Roman Catholic Church and – yet without freely organized labour – by Mediterranean fascism. As an important step towards economic democracy, social partnership is especially favoured by Central and Northern European Socialist (or Social Democratic) parties. In those parts of Europe, social partnership has been (and still is) an important component of a basic general consensus.　　　　　　　　　　　　　　　AP

Reading

Barkin, S. ed.: *Worker Militancy and its Consequences: the changing climate of western industrial nations*. New York: Praeger, 1983.

Industrial Democracy in Europe (IDE), International Research Group: *Industrial Democracy in Europe*. Oxford: Clarendon Press, 1981.

Roberts, B.C. ed.: *Towards Industrial Democracy: Europe, Japan and the United States*. Montclair, NJ: Allanheld, Osmun, 1979.

social structure and party alignments in western countries The 'alignment' of a party system is the way in which party support is predicated upon fundamental cleavages in social structure. For example, the British party system in the post-war era was said to be aligned with the class cleavage, so that working class voters generally supported the Labour Party and middle class voters generally supported the Conservatives. In France, differences between practising Roman Catholics and the rest of the population form the basis for the support of left and right wing parties. In these and other countries, political alignments have at one time or another been based on one or more of class, rurality, language, religion, REGIONALISM, ETHNICITY and other POLITICAL CLEAVAGES.

That not all potential bases for political cleavage are actually found within observable political conflicts underlies Schattschneider's discussion of the 'mobilization of bias', as a means of determining which social divisions are actually given political expression. Scholars such as Sartori, Kirchheimer and ROKKAN stress the variety of factors which mediate the expression of social divisions in political conflicts, ranging from the conditions prevailing at certain periods in a nation's history when the social cleavage emerged, to the behaviour of political elites who try to build support by either exploiting or playing down some particular division within an existing social structure. Once established, such a cleavage may endure long after the objective conditions that led to its establishment have passed, as new generations are subjected to POLITICAL SOCIALIZATION into the values associated with the cleavage concerned. (See also FREEZING OF PARTY ALTERNATIVES.)

Over time, new cleavages become established that cut across the frozen cleavages of previous eras. Given recent developments in our understanding of the process of political REALIGNMENT, it seems clear that new cleavages must generally involve differences between one POLITICAL GENERATION and the next (as, for example, in the case of the British Labour Party's success in establishing class as the dominant social cleavage in Britain between the wars, at the expense of religion);

Social cleavages and party support in western countries 1975–86*

	Working Class	Middle Class	Religious	Anti-Clerical	Rural	Linguis-tic/ethnic	Regional	Catch-All
Australia	Labour	Lib(1)			National			Lib(2)
Austria	SPO(1)	OVP(1) FPO(1)	OVP(2)	SPO(2) FPO(2)	OVP(3)			
Belgium	PS(1) SP(1)	PRL(1) PVV(1)	CVP(1) PSC(1)	PS(2) SP(2) PRL(2) PVV(2)		PS(3) SP(3) PRL(3) PVV(3) CVP(3) PSC(3) FDF(1) RW(1) Volks-unie(1)	PS(4) SP(4) PRL(4) PVV(4) CVP(4) PSC(4) FDF(2) RW(2) Volks-unie(2)	
Canada	NDP							Lib Con
Denmark	SocDem SPP	Con Radical			Venstre			Prog-ress
Finland	SocDem SKDL	NatCoal			Centre Rural	SPP		
France	PS(1) PCF(1)		RPR(1) UDF(1)	PS(2) PCF(2)				RPR(2) UDF(2) FN PS(2)
Greece	KKE		ND(1)	Pasok(1)				ND(2) Pasok(2)
Iceland	PA SocDem				Prog			Independence
Ireland	Labour							FF FG
Italy	PCI(1) PSI(1)	PLI(1) PR(1)	DC(1)	PCI(2) PSI(2) PLI(2) PSDI PR(2)				DC(2) PSI(2)
Luxemburg	POSL(1) PCL(1)	PD(1)	PSC	PCL(2) PD(2) POSL(2)				PSC
Netherlands	PvdA(1)	VVD(1)	CDA	PvdA(2) VVD(2) D'66				
New Zealand	Lab(1)	Nat(1)					Lab(2)	Nat(2) SC
Norway	Labour SV	Con	KF(1)		Centre(1)	Centre(2) KF(2)		

continued

* For party names see Mackie and Rose, *International Almanac of Electoral History*. Parties defined by more than one cleavage appear with numerical suffixes. Only parties gaining more than 5 per cent of the vote are included.

Social cleavages and party support in western countries 1975–86 cont'd

	Working Class	Middle Class	Religious	Anti-Clerical	Rural	Linguistic/ethnic	Regional	Catch-All
Portugal	PS(1) PCP(1)		CDS	PS(2) PCP(2)				PSD PS(3)
Spain	PSOE(1) PCE(1)		UCD(1) AP PNV(1)	PSOE(2) PCE(2)		CiU(1) PNV(2) EE(2) HB(1)	CiU(2) PNV(3) EE(3) HB(2)	UCD(2) PSOE(3)
Sweden	Comm SocDem	MS Lib Centre						
Switzerland	SocDem(1)		ChrDem	SocDem(2) Radical	Centre			
United Kingdom	Labour	Con(1)	SDLP(1) UUP(1) DUP(1) SF(1)			PC(1)	PC(2) SNP SDLP(2) UUP(2) DUP(2) SF(2)	Con(2) Lib SDP
United States						Dem(1)		Dem(2) Rep
West Germany	SPD(1)	FDP(1) Grs(1)	CDU(1) CSU(1)	SPD(2) Grs(2)			CSU(2)	CDU(2) SPD(2)

but, as soon as cleavages cross-cut one another, the potential arises for parties to establish themselves on the basis of sectional interests defined (as Duverger has pointed out) by the intersection of multiple cleavages. Where this happens, we commonly see a style of multi-party system politics quite different from the traditional Anglo-Saxon model of party competition.

The table identifies the major cleavages which define party support in twenty-two western countries. For each country, parties receiving more than 5 per cent of the vote (national or regional) are listed once for each cleavage that defines a major basis for their electoral support in the past decade. Parties with no numerical suffix are defined by only a single social cleavage, but for parties defined by more than one cleavage the suffix differentiates between successive bases of electoral support.

In one respect, the class cleavage is present in nearly every country. Only in the United States do none of the major parties owe any allegiance to a socialist political tradition. And even there the New Deal realignment resulted in majority working class support for the Democratic Party. In most countries, however, working class support has also gone to parties normally thought of as middle class; and in countries where the religious cleavage is important, many workers have also voted for confessional parties. In Scandinavia, middle class parties have tended to limit their appeal to middle class voters. This constitutes an exception to the normal pattern in which middle class parties deny the importance of social class as a basis for electoral choice.

Other cleavages are more country-specific. The religious cleavage does not exist in countries where religious conflict has been avoided in recent history (for instance in England or much of Scandinavia) or in Roman Catholic countries without an anti-clerical tradition (of which the Republic of Ireland is probably the only example). In Europe, the urban/rural cleavage (which is often also a centre/periphery cleavage) has been important only in Protestant countries because elsewhere the Roman Catholic church provided a link between rural and urban centres of political power. In Finland, Spain and Britain (Wales) parties have developed to defend the interests of linguistic minorities which are in general also regionally based (although the exceptions shown in the table are important). In multilingual Switzerland all the major parties cut across linguistic divisions, but in Belgium all the major parties are now divided by language. The ethnic particularities of New Zealand and the United States are well known.

The table represents only the latest stage in the long development of western party systems. Social structure is constantly changing, and with it the basis for party choice. Nevertheless, despite the dramatic social and economic changes of the first half of the present century, the basic characteristics of the party systems in most western countries remained unchanged until the mid-1960s. Only in those countries which saw changes of regime were there radical changes in the party system before that date. Elsewhere, the frozen manifestations of past cleavages continued to dominate electoral choice. But from about 1968 onwards change in party systems was rapid and widespread.

The most newsworthy of these changes involved the rise of nationalist parties in Scotland, Wales, the Basque Country, Catalina, Flanders, Wallonia and Quebec; but even within the countries concerned these movements involved relatively few voters. Far more important from a systemic viewpoint were changes involving religion (in continental Europe) and social class (in Scandinavia and Anglo-American countries). In continental Europe, while church-attenders have continued to give their overwhelming support to religious parties, nominal church members have ceased to give priority to the religious cleavage. Moreover, the number of church-attenders has itself declined, further reducing the base of support for religious parties. By contrast, in Scandinavia and Anglo-American countries, the decline of class voting has taken first place. In these countries the size of the manual working class community has declined, but more important has been the fact that all voters have come to show less loyalty to the

parties of their own class. In some countries this decline has been associated with the rise of new parties, but in all countries it has been associated with a change in the basis of support for existing parties.

Rather than a new cleavage in social structure arising to supersede the divisions that pre-existed within these societies, what seems to have happened is that issues have arisen which are not mediated through social structural loyalties. This development is generally referred to as the rise of issue voting (see ISSUES, ISSUE PERCEPTION AND ISSUE VOTING), and can be seen to be a counterpart to the general decline in the power of social structure to condition partisanship. To the extent that voters react to the issues of the day as individuals rather than as representatives of a sectional interest, then the distribution of party support will cut across traditional social cleavages without any new cleavage establishing itself. Some political scientists have argued that the emergence of certain issues does reflect the creation of new social cleavages based upon for example Inglehart's POST-MATERIALISM, or Dunleavy's consumption patterns; but while it can readily be shown that conflicts of interest exist in these spheres, no author has yet demonstrated that the cleavages concerned have any basis in social structure. Issues such as ecology, feminism, immigration and nuclear power create SOCIAL MOVE-MENTS that are quite different from the sectional interests of old. Whether the rise of issue voting caused the decline in the importance of social structure, or whether the ageing of the cleavage structure made room for issue voting is a subject of scholarly debate. (These developments are further discussed in Franklin (1985) chs 2, 6 and 7.)

See also LANGUAGE AND POLITICS.

TTM/MNF

Reading

Barnes, S. and Kaase, M. et al.: *Political Action: mass participation in five western democracies*. Beverly Hills, Calif. and London: Sage, 1979.

Daalder, H. and Mair, P. eds: *Western European Party Systems: continuity and change*. Beverly Hills, Calif. and London: Sage, 1983.

Dalton, R.J., Flanagan, S.C. and Beck, P.A. eds:

Electoral Change in Advanced Industrial Societies: realignment or dealignment? Princeton, NJ: Princeton University Press, 1984.

Dunleavy, P.J. and Husbands, C.: *British Democracy at the Crossroads: voting and party competition.* London: Allen & Unwin, 1985.

Franklin, M.: *The Decline of Class Voting in Britain.* Oxford: Oxford University Press, 1985.

Gunther, R. et al.: *Spain after Franco: the making of a competitive party system.* Berkeley: University of California Press, 1986.

Haerpfer, C. and Gehmacher, E.: Social structure and voting in the Austrian party system. *Electoral Studies* 3 (1984).

Inglehart, R.: *The Silent Revolution: changing values and political styles among western publics.* Princeton, NJ: Princeton University Press, 1977.

Kirchheimer, O.: The transformation of the Western European party systems. In *Political Parties and Political Development*, ed. J. LaPalombara and M. Weiner. Princeton, NJ: Princeton University Press, 1966.

Lipset, S. and Rokkan, S.: *Party Systems and Voter Alignments.* New York: Free Press, 1967.

Mackie, T. and Rose, R.: *The International Almanac of Electoral History.* London: Macmillan, 1982.

Nie, N.H., Verba, S. and Petrocik, J.R.: *The Changing American Voter.* 2nd edn. Cambridge, Mass.: Harvard University Press, 1979.

Rae, D. and Taylor, M.: *The Analysis of Political Cleavages.* New Haven, Conn.: Yale University Press, 1970.

Rose, R. ed.: *Electoral Behavior: a comparative handbook.* New York: Free Press, 1974.

————: *Electoral Participation.* Beverly Hills, Calif. and London: Sage, 1982.

Worre, T.: Class parties and class voting in the Scandinavian countries. *Scandinavian Political Studies* 3 (1980).

social structure and party alignments, theories of

The division of society by such dimensions as class, religion, race, age, gender, constitutes its social structure; the divisions of the electorate into groups that more or less consistently support a particular party constitutes the party alignment of a society. Theories of the relationship between social structure and party alignment usually start from the assumption that, to a substantial extent, social structure is the cause or chief determinant of party alignments. Theories differ in the particular dimensions of social structure said to be the cause of party alignments, and whether they recognize multiple causes (for example class *and* religion) or, as is the case with Marxist theories, reduce party alignments to a single cause.

The way in which social structure affects party alignments can be hypothesized as follows: first, by causing the organization of a party to represent a given group in the social structure; second, by causing parties to compete for votes by emphasizing appeals to different, and often conflicting social interests; third, by influencing electors to vote for particular parties; fourth, by making parties differ in the policies they pursue when in office. Nationalist theories of political action are deviant: they postulate that only one party should exist in a society in which the great majority of the people have a common identity (for example a country with a small imperial presence).

The multi-dimensional character of social structure creates the first problem: which dimension or dimensions of social structure are deemed relevant for the determination of party alignments? A theory provides an a priori answer to this question; by contrast, empirical studies (see SOCIAL STRUCTURE AND PARTY ALIGNMENTS IN WESTERN COUNTRIES) usually search inductively for those influences that determine the largest amount of voting behaviour.

The simplest theories reduce social structure to a single dimension of class. The interests of different classes are assumed to be in conflict; from this it is hypothesized that electors will vote for parties that represent different class interests. The approach is particularly common among sociologists, whether or not they are Marxist, because of the pervasive importance that class is assumed to have in most sociological theories. In Britain, for example, sociologists have conventionally described a two-party system as being determined by the social division between the middle class and working class. Analyses of class structure can be expanded to incorporate more classes and more parties. For example, farmers and peasant-proprietors can be differentiated from urban classes in order to explain the existence of agrarian parties. Within urban societies, intermediate classes of 'marginal' persons can be identified, and offered as explanations for the existence of a third party, whether centrist or extremist. Class theories may recognize the existence of other dimensions of social structure, but explain away any influence that they appear to have by asserting that such divisions have class differences as their underlying cause. Empirical evidence showing the importance of social divisions not defined by occupational class are then said to be really a reflection of the underlying class structure. If the concept of class is stretched indefinitely to embrace all economic and non-economic divisions in society it goes beyond empirical refutation. Logically, another dimension of social structure could be the cause of partisan alignments. In Northern Ireland, religion can explain fundamental alignments far better than class, and studies of pre-1914 England often give pre-eminence to religious divisions in explaining Conservative vs. Liberal alignments. Racial differences can explain alignments affecting parties and political movements in South Africa.

The comparative analysis of electoral behaviour requires a multi-dimensional concept of social structure. Historically and today many European societies show a great variety of non-class as well as class divisions, and a much greater number and heterogeneity of parties than exist within the conventional two-party systems of Britain and America. The most ambitious and comprehensive theory relating social structure to the creation and maintenance of party alignments is that propounded by S. M. Lipset and Stein ROKKAN. Unlike class theorists, they start with the social structure of pre-industrial society, and examine the way in which a variety of different social divisions can become politically salient. The divisions selected are loosely related to categories of social action developed by Talcott Parsons. The Lipset–Rokkan theory gives pre-eminence to cultural dimensions of social structure: religion, language, and ethnic identity. In order to create a state, central authorities must come to terms with such divisions. One way to do this

is by homogenizing the population so that everyone has the same religion, language and ethnic identity; this would make state and nation identical. The attempt to ignore, override or eradicate social differences can however produce a negative reaction, generating political cleavages along religious, linguistic and ethnic lines. The outcome of the process is that parties created in the initial phases of nation-building are likely to differ along cultural dimensions. A two-party system may be based on conflicts between practising Roman Catholics and anti-clericals, or Protestants and Catholics or, as in the Netherlands, on differences between Catholics, Protestants and anti-clericals. Linguistic parties may arise, claiming a distinctive national identity, or ethnic identity may be asserted independent of linguistic issues.

The Lipset–Rokkan theory identifies problems that societies must deal with in the course of creating conditions of party competition, but it does not posit a deterministic outcome. The long-term resolution of these conflicts is recognized as being contingent upon specific historical circumstances. Conflicts about national identity may lead to the creation of separate countries, each with their own party system (for example the withdrawal after 1918 of Irish Nationalists from the British party system at Westminster to create an independent Ireland). In most Scandinavian societies, religious, linguistic and ethnic homogeneity was achieved. In most continental European countries, religious cleavage was the outcome. In Switzerland and for generations in Belgium, religious cleavages were strong enough to override linguistic differences.

The industrial revolution is the second great influence upon parties. Lipset and Rokkan distinguish between the first stage, the confrontation between landed interests (whether aristocrat or peasant proprietors) and urban interests (factory workers as well as industrialists and financial groups), and a second stage, divisions between an industrial working class and a middle class. The theory incorporates contemporary class divisions emphasized in a one-dimensional model, while also giving independent recognition to a variety of historically important sources of political difference.

If each of the divisions identified by Lipset and Rokkan were to persist and remain significant electorally, then every party system would be divided into at least thirty-two different groups, each with a distinctive combination of religious, linguistic, ethnic, urban–rural and industrial class characteristics. In fact, such a high degree of differentiation is abnormal in social structure. The United States, Canada, Belgium and Switzerland are atypical in having politically salient differences along three or more dimensions of religion, class, race, language and/or national identity. After generations of social change resulting from wartime invasion, the diffusion of mass education and the mass media, and economic developments, most European countries today are linguistically homogeneous, and politically issues identified with other cultural differences have lost their historic salience. The typical European political system today reflects both cultural and economic cleavages; it has at least one party whose voters are aligned along religious, linguistic or ethnic lines, and at least one party alignment on class lines. It can also have parties whose voters have at least two social-structure characteristics in common; for example, they may be manual workers and anti-clericals.

Concentrating exclusively upon social structure as a determinant of electoral support ignores two sets of critical intervening influences. First of all, political elites and the organizations they head play a critical role in determining what kind and how many parties are organized to solicit votes within a given society. Moreover, the leaders of a party at any given moment have discretion to determine whether or not to devote their electoral appeal to a single social group within the electorate, or make a 'catch-all' appeal that ignores social differences within the electorate (see CATCH-ALL PARTY). In proportional representation with multi-party coalition governments, the secure support of a single group constituting a fifth or a tenth of the electorate (for example farmers, or a linguistic minority) could be sufficient to give a party a place in government. But in a British or American style first-past-the-post electoral system a more inclusive electoral appeal is required to win an election. Secondly, social structure is only one among many influences upon voting behaviour. As alternative to theories of determinism by social structure, it can be hypothesized that voting is primarily motivated by PARTY IDENTIFICATION, issues, political personalities or other factors independent of a voter's location in the social structure. Some theories maintain that the electoral influence of social structure is gradually declining with social change, and new types of differences, based upon issue or value conflicts, are gaining salience. Theories of the social determination of voting were developed long before modern empirical methods of examining the behaviour of voters. Decades of empirical testing of these theories, and particularly, tests that include European as well as Anglo-American societies, have revealed their limitations, both conceptual and empirical.

A two-class two-party model will not fit many competitive party systems in the world today, for there is usually a multiplicity of parties. Nor can all parties be reduced to different types of class party. Some parties do not fit because they make appeals that cut across class lines and other social differences too. Other parties do not fit because their supporters are aligned on the basis of religious, linguistic or other divisions. Attempts to classify people into classes reveal ambiguities and uncertainties about how many classes society is divided into, where the dividing lines fall and, therefore, how many parties should result. Even when material economic influences are found to influence voting, for example, trade-union membership, this does not conform to stereotype patterns of class divisions, for there are many middle class trade-union members, and many manual workers are outside trade unions. Only a minority of the electorate has all the ideal-type characteristics of the working class or the middle class. Most voters today have a mixture of attributes, combining characteristics of two or more classes. Proponents of particular social structure theories may attempt to defend their position by citing examples of a good fit between social groups and voting. But since there are more than two dozen countries having competitive party systems involving hundreds of parties in total, one example and one counter-example can be found for almost any theory. Another common defence is to argue that any non-random relationship between social structure and party is proof of causation. But to show a one per cent or a ten per cent correlation between class and party leaves 90 to 99 per cent of the relationship to be explained by other factors.

The literature on social structure and party alignments provides a framework for examining and testing whether and under what circumstances political parties appeal to particular social groups for support, and to what extent they succeed in winning such support. Moreover, changes in society and in party systems logically imply the need to adapt or expand early theories of the social determination of party alignments. The most significant modifications to the initially hypothesized relationships include, first, the voluntaristic choices of party leaders in merging, splitting and otherwise changing parties within the system; second, alternative appeals (for example, regarding personality, competence to govern, or new values) that can be used by parties seeking votes; third, the influence of economic conditions and the performance of the party in office; fourth, elite bargains between parties, and between parties and interest groups, to accommodate social interests independently of partisan alignments.　　　　　　　　　RR

Reading

Inglehart, R.: The changing structure of political cleavages in western society. In *Electoral Change in Advanced Industrial Democracies*, ed. R.J. Dalton, S.C. Flanagan and P.A. Beck. Princeton, NJ: Princeton University Press, 1984.

Kirchheimer, O.: The transformation of the Western European party systems. In *Political Parties and Political Development*, ed. J. LaPalombara and M. Weiner. Princeton, NJ: Princeton University Press, 1966.

Lijphart, A.: *Democracies: patterns of majoritarian and consensus government in twenty-one countries.* New Haven, Conn. and London: Yale University Press, 1984.

Lipset, S.M. and Rokkan, S.: Cleavage structures, party systems and voter alignments. In *Party Systems and Voter Alignments: cross-national perspectives*, ed. S.M. Lipset and S. Rokkan. New York: Free Press, 1967.

Przeworski, A.: *Capitalism and Social Democracy.* New York: Cambridge University Press, 1985.

Rose, R. and McAllister, I.: *Voters Begin to Choose: from closed class to open elections.* London: Sage, 1986.

—— and Mackie, T.T.: Do parties persist or disappear? The big tradeoff facing organizations. In *When Parties Fail*, ed. K. Lawson and P. Merkl. Princeton, NJ: Princeton University Press, 1987.

—— and Urwin, D.W.: Social cohesion, political parties and strains in regimes. *Comparative political studies* 2 (1969) 7–67.

socialism　A political doctrine that emerged during the industrialization of Europe. The term was applied independently to the followers of Robert Owen (1771–1858) in 1827 and those of Saint-Simon (1760–1825) in 1832 and came into general use during the 1840s. From the outset it covered a multitude of beliefs and practices rather than a single doctrine. There was no single classic socialism or golden age against which to compare later varieties. True socialism is as impossible to pinpoint as true liberalism or true conservatism.

The term now signifies one of the major ideologies of the last hundred years but it is also used to refer to the various political regimes, institutions, and policies of states that proclaim themselves socialist, as well as the various political parties and movements which are trying to establish socialism in different parts of the world. It is also used more narrowly to mean a new type of economic system, founded on principles different from those of CAPITALISM, representing a higher or transitional stage of economic development. Almost all socialists would argue that social relationships, especially those bound up with the industrial process, play a vital role in determining human possibilities. In particular, the unequal ownership of property in capitalist societies and the consequent need of the majority to sell their labour places crucial constraints upon individual freedom and upon the creation of a fraternal and co-operative society which will also be classless. This view was given its most sophisticated theoretical formulation in the work of Marx, who attacked earlier socialists as 'Utopian' and claimed to have discovered the basic laws of social development so rendering socialism 'scientific'.

As an ideology socialism has always had a complex relationship to liberalism. The experience from which socialism arose was hostility to an economy and society founded on the principles and practices of extreme individualism. Socialism as an ideology began as a critique of liberalism, but from the outset two major strands in socialist responses to liberalism were apparent. The first saw socialism as fulfilling liberalism, the second thought of socialism as the rejection of liberalism. These two responses were often voiced by the same individuals; only later did they form the basis for organizational division.

Socialists criticized liberals in the name of their own ideology. Liberals made universal demands for the recognition of fundamental human rights such as freedom and equality but their attachment to private property prevented them from proposing the kind of institutional change which could make such objectives realizable. Socialists argued that civil and political rights only created formal equality. They needed to be extended to include social and economic rights (substantive equality). Equality before the law needed to be accompanied by a wider equality of opportunity and of outcome. The restrictions placed on the realization of the ideals of the American and French Revolution by private property rights needed to be swept aside in a quest for social justice.

The demands such socialists made were often radical but once civil and political rights had been conceded, they proved ready in practice to pursue a strategy of patient reform of the existing institutions and policies of the liberal state. The second strand of socialist thought and experience was more uncompromising. These socialists sought not reform of the existing order by obliging it to live up to its own ideals, but its replacement by a new social and moral order. They wanted to overthrow capitalism not merely because the way in which it organized production and distributed

wealth denied social justice, but also because of its dominant ethos of materialism, selfishness, and competitiveness. They reasserted the importance of community, and the values of altruism, solidarity, and co-operation as the bases for organizing society. All socialists were united in condemning the concentration of power and of wealth that was associated with capitalism, but they were divided from the outset as to how this inequality should be remedied; and in particular upon whether it can be remedied within the existing framework of liberal democratic institutions. This division is a crucial one in the history of socialism.

This is what makes socialism such a contradictory ideology. R. N. Berki distinguishes four main strands; egalitarianism, moralism, rationalism, and libertarianism. Socialism draws on modern liberalism in its doctrines of equal rights and its faith in rationalist analysis and prescription but it also derives many of its ideas from pre-modern doctrines and attitudes. This is why some socialists can be proponents of efficiency, planning, and centralization while others are advocates of decentralization and non-materialistic values. In many socialists (MARX is perhaps the clearest example) there is a simultaneous embrace of modern industrial society, its techniques, its modes of organization, and its vast potential, and a deep moral rejection of it, because of its destructive impact on human relationships and its constant undermining of the basis of community which denies the conditions for individual and social emancipation.

The complexity of socialism as an ideology is not always understood by its critics who frequently identify it with one part of socialist doctrine, the centralized regulation of production. Public ownership of the means of production, distribution, and exchange did emerge as a key doctrine of revolutionary and reformist socialism alike during the early decades of the twentieth century, but there always remained great differences over how publicly-owned industries should be organized, and over whether the priority was to increase economic efficiency through planning, or to lay the foundations for a quite different kind of social order by reorganizing industries as public services or as self-governing communities.

The experience of the first socialist state after the 1917 BOLSHEVIK revolution in Russia polarized opinion among socialists and ultimately led to a strengthening of the commitment of socialist parties in the West to democracy and to a discrediting of the idea of central planning. Many of these parties no longer put forward an extensive programme of public ownership and emphasize instead the objective of social justice. In many third world states, however, socialism has become an ideology of national economic development, and is valued not for its libertarian critique of capitalism but for its guide to modernization through planning and organization. Socialism is here equated with state ownership or control of the main industrial sectors, some basic efforts at providing social services and in some cases land reform.

In the 1950s it became fashionable to proclaim the death of socialism because the claim that it offered a superior means of organizing industrial society had been discredited. Such a notion could only be sustained by arbitrarily identifying one strand of ideology as the essence of socialism. A cursory survey of political ideas and political movements in the contemporary world reveals that socialism has lost little of its vitality and capacity for new development.

See also FABIANS; GUILD SOCIALISM; LABOUR MOVEMENT; SOCIALIST AND SOCIAL DEMOCRATIC PARTIES; SYNDICALISM.

AMG

Reading

Bell, D.: Socialism. In *International Encyclopedia of the Social Sciences*, Vol. 14, pp. 506–34. New York: Free Press, 1968.

Berki, R.N.: *Socialism*. London: Dent, 1975.

Cole, G.D.H.: *A History of Socialist Thought*. 5 vols. London: Allen & Unwin, 1953–60.

Crosland, A.: *The Future of Socialism*. London: Cape, 1956.

Dunn, J.: *The Politics of Socialism*. Cambridge: Cambridge University Press, 1984.

Laidler, H.W.: *History of Socialism*. London: Routledge & Kegan Paul, 1968.

Landauer, C.: *European Socialism: a history of ideas and movements*. 2 vols. Berkeley and Los Angeles: University of California Press, 1959.

Lichtheim, G.: *A Short History of Socialism*. London: Weidenfeld & Nicolson, 1970.

socialist and social democratic parties

Communist and social democratic parties have a common origin in the socialist parties of nineteenth-century Europe, of which the most important in size and influence was the German Social Democratic Party (SPD). These parties hoped to replace capitalism with politico-economic systems in which the state would own and control the basic means of production. They were also committed to the construction of egalitarian societies, peace and international workers' solidarity.

The triumph of Bolshevism in Russia in 1917 led to a split in the socialist movement between those who were prepared to accept LENINIST principles and those who insisted on the parliamentary road to socialism. During the nineteenth century the terms socialist and social democrat were interchangeable; the label of social democrat distinguished essentially between the minority of democrats who were also socialists and the majority of democrats who were not. After 1917 social democratic parties were perceived as those socialist parties which gave primacy to the maintenance of liberal representative democracy as against those who gave primacy to the achievement of socialism.

The split among the socialist parties was most apparent internationally. The success of the Bolshevik revolution led to the formation of the Communist International (the Comintern or Third International) in 1919. This organization insisted on very stringent conditions of membership designed to bring about commitment to revolutionary transformation. Of the non-communist parties, only the Norwegian Labour Party, for a time during the 1920s, found itself able to accept these conditions. Reformist socialist parties founded the Labour and Socialist International which collapsed in 1940 but was refounded as the Socialist International at Frankfurt in 1951.

Socialist and social democratic parties have also been distinguished from COMMUNIST

PARTIES by contrasting principles of PARTY ORGANIZATION. Duverger has placed the social democratic party in an intermediate position along a continuum between the loose electoral aggregation typical of the bourgeois party and the DEMOCRATIC CENTRALISM of the Leninist party. Bourgeois parties normally have weak organizations and loose membership criteria while communist parties have strong organizations and an exclusive membership which gives the parties a 'ghetto character'.

These distinctions have become more blurred in recent years. Social democratic and socialist parties have much less of a class-specific character and throughout much of Western Europe they have become 'people's parties' with a broad membership and have made a successful electoral appeal across class lines. In recent years several Western European communist parties in pursuit of a Euro-communist strategy have largely shed their 'democratic centralist' vanguard characteristics.

Northern European democratic socialist parties have often been happy to call themselves social democratic parties while southern European parties have been uneasy with the term and have normally preferred to be called socialist parties. Attempts are sometimes made to define social democratic parties in contradistinction to labour parties as those which are friendly to labour but which do not have direct trade union affiliation. This distinction is not very helpful. In Holland, for example, the social democrats changed their name to the Dutch Labour Party just when they abandoned formal union affiliation. Most social democratic parties have had trade unions affiliated to them at some time but at present this relationship obtains amongst western European parties only in Britain, Norway and Sweden. In Britain unions are affiliated at the national level whereas in Norway and Sweden affiliated unions enjoy collective membership only in the local party branches.

Socialist and social democratic parties are committed to the electoral road to power. They have all been affected by the numerical decline of the manual working class in industrial societies. Different parties have responded differently in the struggle for electoral advantage. Some, like the German SPD, are now looking for new class allies, 'the technical intelligentsia'. Others, of which the southern European parties are the most obvious examples, though also seeking new class allies, have concentrated on projecting charismatic leaders. The early 1980s have seen an interesting reversal of electoral geography. Socialist and social democratic parties appear to be going through an electoral trough in their traditional heartlands of northern Europe, and have been electorally more successful in their traditional areas of weakness in southern Europe.

Geographically socialist and social democratic parties have been concentrated in Western Europe with the notable exception of Australia and New Zealand where the absence of an indigenous capitalist class has been an important contributory factor to the success of the Australian and New Zealand Labour Parties. North America has, in general, proved remarkably unfruitful territory but the New Democratic Party in Canada has had some limited success. In the third world the most successful parties have been the Chilean Socialist Party, the People's National Party in Jamaica and Accion Democratica in Venezuela.

Ideologically, socialist and social democratic parties exhibit wide variations although there have been some common developments. For a very long period ideological debate and prescriptions centred on the ownership question. A commitment to nationalization of the basic means of production was, until the 1950s, a central feature of party programmes in parties such as the British Labour Party as well as those such as the German Social Democratic Party which had been much more influenced by Marxist ideas.

The impact of the Cold War, allied to the pervasive character of post-war prosperity, moved most socialist and social democratic parties to weaken their commitment to nationalization. This change was most dramatically exemplified by the Bad Godesberg Programme of the German Social Democratic Party (1959) which dropped most of the party's ideological baggage including the commitment to nationalization. The Bad

Godesberg Programme had been anticipated by Anthony Crosland's *The Future of Socialism* (1956). Crosland distinguished five criteria which, have constituted the core values of most socialist and social democratic parties from the late 1950s onwards; political liberalism, the mixed economy, the WELFARE STATE, KEYNESIAN economics and a belief in equality. This was sometimes translated into formal programmatic change as in the case of the German and Austrian parties; sometimes it was more a matter of practice and convention as in the case of the British Labour Party.

This set of ideas has proved increasingly difficult to translate into practical terms and to defend at a theoretical level in recent years. After the oil price rise in 1973, when growth started to falter, the tax burdens imposed on the core clienteles of socialist and social democratic parties proved to be electorally disadvantageous. Moreover Keynesian economics often appeared to display an apparently inherent impetus towards an increase in government expenditure and inflation. At a more theoretical level, the statist nature of these policies came under increasing attack from the 1968 generation which was participation oriented. The assumptions made about the unquestioned desirability of growth have also come under increasing attack. During the last two decades Marxist critiques have been increasingly influential.

Ideologically the parties are now in a state of disarray; parties of the right are exploring the implications of market socialism and are attempting to weaken bureaucratic and centralizing elements; in the centre, there is a concentration on the workplace, on industrial democracy; in Scandinavia there has been a sustained attempt to change the conditions of capitalism, to tackle the ownership question indirectly by pension fund schemes; on the left there are continued attempts to incorporate ecological perceptions. Social democratic and socialist parties have traditionally been more subject to fission than their conservative and liberal rivals. The collapse of the ideological consensus in the 1970s led to renewed fission of which the most notable examples are the formation of the Greens in West Germany in 1980 and the SDP in Britain in 1981.

See also LABOUR MOVEMENT; SOCIALISM.

WEP

Reading

Beyme, K. von: *Political Parties in Western Democracies.* Aldershot: Gower; New York: St Martin's, 1985.

Crosland, A.: *The Future of Socialism.* London: Cape, 1956.

Duverger, M.: *Political Parties: their organisation and activity in the modern state.* London: Methuen, 1964.

Esping-Andersen, G: *Politics against Markets: the social democratic road to power.* Princeton, NJ: Princeton University Press, 1985.

Paterson, W. and Thomas, A. eds: *Social Democratic Parties in Western Europe.* London: Croom Helm, 1977.

————: *The Future of Social Democracy: problems and prospects of social democratic parties in Western Europe.* Oxford: Oxford University Press, 1986.

Sorel, Georges (1847–1922) French theorist of SYNDICALISM. Sorel was trained as an engineer at the *École Polytechnique.* After retiring from the department of highways in 1892 he wrote extensively on politics, ethics, science and religion and adhered to a variety of political opinions. The central element of continuity in his thought was based on his search for 'a historical genesis of morals'. This sociology of virtue he came to see as being based on a strong family and a combined warrior-work ethic based on struggle against foes or (by workers) against nature; such an outlook is sustained by an 'epic state of mind' that resists the corrupting attraction of consumption and leisure justified by a hierarchy of rationalist intellectuals schooled in philosophical rationalism.

In 1893 Sorel was attracted to Marx's ideas of the link between knowledge and production, but he became increasingly sceptical of economic determinism, historical teleology and the labour theory of value. He attacked evolutionary conceptions of socialism as represented, for example, by Karl Kautsky, the German socialist leader, and argued that to expect an inevitable socialist revolution would only demoralize the proletariat and strengthen bourgeois ideology. Sorel therefore abandoned political Marxism in about 1902, and, influenced by Proudhon, argued in *Social Foundations of Contemporary Economics* and in *Reflections on Violence* (1906) that SOCIALISM should be centred in autonomous workers' organizations acting through the GENERAL STRIKE and DIRECT ACTION. Here praxis consists in attention to immediate practical tasks, and socialism already exists in the hearts of the workers. Sorel refused to reject violence, claiming that it could strengthen the socialist cause. After a brief flirtation with royalism, Sorel was quoted as praising Mussolini, but he condemned fascist 'brutality'. Ultimately, he supported LENIN, thinking that the Russian SOVIETS were genuine workers' councils.

JLS

Reading

Jennings, J.R.: *Georges Sorel: the character and development of his thought*. London: Macmillan, 1985.

Sorel, G.: *Reflections on Violence*, trans. T.E. Hulme and J. Roth. New York and London: Macmillan, 1950.

————: *Social Foundations of Contemporary Economics*, trans. J.L. Stanley. New Brunswick, NJ: Transaction Books, 1984.

Stanley, J.L.: *The Sociology of Virtue: the political and social theories of Georges Sorel*. Berkeley: University of California Press, 1981.

sovereignty The condition of being sovereign or of being a sovereign. Despite constitutional courtesies a limited monarch such as the British monarch is not a 'sovereign' as conceived classically in legal and political theory. A sovereign in that sense is that organ in a state which holds and exercises supreme authority, and may be either an individual person or a collective entity. In the UK at present it is parliament (the monarch in parliament) which is constitutionally sovereign. Such a sovereign is sometimes considered to be necessarily above the law and in no way subject to any of its restrictions or limitations. On this view, parliament has a supremacy in law making which neither is nor logically could be subject to any form of legal regulation. (See PARLIAMENTARY SOVEREIGNTY.)

This view has ancient roots in the concept of the *princeps legibus solutus*, but modern ones in the work of Jeremy Bentham and John Austin, in which law is defined as the command of a sovereign, and the sovereign defined as the person or group habitually obeyed by a populace but habitually obeying no other. Hence a sovereign cannot be subject to legal limitations, though no doubt there may be moral constraints on what can rightly be done and practical ones on what can prudently be done without courting revolt by the subjects. Subsequent thinkers such as James Bryce and A. V. DICEY criticize this view for confusing legal and political sovereigns: the former being that to which the law ascribes supreme legislative authority; the latter being whoever or whatever has the ultimate practical influence over the exercise of legal authority – the electorate in parliamentary or democratic polities, as they, perhaps over-optimistically, supposed.

If sovereigns are defined by law, they can also be restricted by law since only those exercises of power which fall within the law's definition will count. The theory of legal sovereignty may take one back to pre-Austinian conceptions of sovereign power as, for example, conferred by some legally foundational instrument or compact: a 'social contract', indeed. But legally conferred legislative powers need not be absolute, and some constitutions, notably that of the United States of America, have manifestly failed to establish any organ under the constitution which is endowed with sovereign power. If this implies that the people remain sovereign, as constitutional rhetoric has it, this curiously vindicates Austin's theory in part, for he concluded that sovereignty lay behind the constitution in such a polity – but here a 'habit of obedience' seems hardly constitutive of a 'sovereign people'.

Even where no single governmental organ is superior to all others in a state, no external authority need have any legal or political power over that state. International law prohibits intervention by external powers; the concept of 'state sovereignty' can therefore be defined as either legal or political freedom from external control, whether or not an internal sovereign is a condition of statehood. A strict separation of powers under a constitution may therefore be envisaged as an (internal) division of (external) sovereignty. That the undertaking by a state of treaty obligations is an exercise of, not a limitation on, sovereignty may be taken as axiomatic. But the existence under treaties of standing supra- or trans-national entities (see SUPRANATIONAL GOVERNMENT) such as the European Communities seems plainly to entail derogation from the sovereignty of the member states without ascription of sovereignty to the con-federation as a whole. Here, a process of conceptual as well as political evolution is in progress.   NMacC

Reading

Austin, J.: *The Province of Jurisprudence Determined*, ed. H.L.A. Hart. London: Weidenfeld & Nicolson, 1954.

Bryce, J.: *Studies in History and Jurisprudence*, Vol. II, ch. 10. Oxford: Clarendon Press, 1901.

Marshall, G.: *Constitutional Theory*, ch. 3. Oxford: Oxford University Press, 1971.

soviet   The Russian word for council. In the Soviet Union today, the soviets are the popularly elected councils at all levels of government. The word soviet is also used nowadays to distinguish the present regime from that of the Tsars which was destroyed in the Bolshevik revolution of October 1917. Hence the official name for the USSR spells out The Union of Soviet Socialist Republics which is also referred to as the Soviet Union, or even as the Soviets, as shorthand for USSR. Similarly one speaks of Soviet influence or Soviet military power. The first soviets were councils of workers' deputies which formed spontaneously throughout the Tsarist Empire in 1905 in reaction to the hardships of the (unsuccessful) Russo-Japanese war. They served as vehicles for revolutionary and strike action. After the February Revolution of 1917, which limited and finally abolished the mon-archy of the Tsars, workers' and soldiers' soviets formed in the towns and countryside and took over authority as the central govern-ment collapsed. V. I. LENIN saw them as more revolutionary than the Provisional Government which had been established in Leningrad in February 1917, and in his quest for power for his BOLSHEVIK faction of the Russian Social Democratic party he launched the slogan of 'all power to the soviets'. In this way he hoped to destroy the Provisional Government which he regarded as bourgeois by replacing it with the soviets which were a prey to extremism. When his Bolshevik fraction seized power in a coup d'état in October 1917, they did it in the name of the soviets. The first (1918) Constitu-tion of the Great Russian Republic, and its successor in 1924, regularized local soviets which in turn elected deputies to higher soviets and so on all the way to the All-Russian Congress of Soviets, which was the highest organ of state power. This All-Russian Con-gress elected a Central Executive Committee as the country's supreme legislative, adminis-trative and supervisory body, to act in the (long) intervals between the meetings of the Congress. In 1936 however the new 'Stalin' constitution was introduced. This abandoned the above-mentioned indirect election of the supreme legislative body of Soviets for direct universal suffrage, so that nowadays the supreme legislature, which is still called the SUPREME SOVIET is directly elected by the voters as a whole. Every level of the Soviet Union is nowadays governed by a directly elected council called a soviet. In ascending order from the bases these are: Area Soviets of Working People's Deputies, regional Soviets, Supreme Soviets of the Autonomous Repub-lics, Supreme Soviets of the fifteen Union Republics, and at the apex, the Supreme Soviet of The USSR.

See also RUSSIAN REVOLUTION.   SEF

Reading

Hough, J.F. and Fainsod, M.: *How the Soviet Union is Governed*. Cambridge, Mass. and London: Harvard University Press, 1979.

spatial models   A subset of RATIONAL CHOICE models of political behaviour. They presuppose a 'policy space' in which all candidates and most voters can locate one another. It is assumed that voters are able to measure the distance between themselves and the candidates and that each voter will vote for the nearest candidate (or vote tactically for a remoter candidate with a better chance of winning). The dimensions of policy space are ideological ones such as left/right and religious/ secular and each voter is assumed to be able to measure leftness, religiosity, etc., cardinally (to award Neil Kinnock 80 points for leftness, oneself 60, David Owen 50 and Margaret Thatcher 5, for example). Given these assumptions the 'Euclidean distance' between any two points can always be measured, however many dimensions there are.

Hotelling (1929) was the first to suggest an analogy between traders competing in a High Street for business and politicians competing for votes. In both cases, locational theory predicted that the most successful candidate would set up shop in the median position. This theory was elaborated and disseminated by Downs who predicted that in two-party one-dimensional politics, parties starting off-median 'will converge on the same location until practically all voters are indifferent between them'. (1957, p. 117).

The Hotelling/Downs model attracted little interest at first; most political scientists joined Stokes (1966) in dismissing it because of the unrealism of suggesting that most voters used the concepts 'left' and 'right' at all, let alone measured their distance from politicians in those terms. However, in the 1970s intellectual fashion moved (with the evidence) towards regarding voters as better-informed and more ideological than Stokes and his colleagues had done. Multidimensional spatial theory was elaborated by Enelow and Hinich (1984), and applied by Page (1978) and Heath et al. (1985). Robertson (1976) and McLean (1982) contrasted the centripetal force of median-voter wooing with the centrifugal force exerted by party activists.

Spatial theory has been more damaged from within than from without. The prediction of convergence can be valid only if there is a median to converge on. If there are at least three voters and at least three options there may be a 'cycle' where each option can be beaten by another (see SOCIAL CHOICE THEORY). If there is a cycle, there is no median. Recent work non-technically summarized by Riker (1982) suggests that cycles are all but universal in multidimensional policy space with many voters. Spatial models are therefore of limited value except in analysing

small-group (e.g. committee) voting where small numbers make cycling less likely; and where one ideological dimension is of overwhelming importance *and* at least one candidate/party departs conspicuously from the median (as in the US presidential elections of 1964 and 1972 and the UK general election of 1983). Within those limits they provide the most parsimonious explanation of politicians' and voters' behaviour. IMcL

Reading

Downs, A.: *An Economic Theory of Democracy*. New York: Harper & Row, 1957.

Enelow, J and Hinich, M.: *The Spatial Theory of Voting: an introduction*. Cambridge: Cambridge University Press, 1984.

Heath, A. et al.: *How Britain Votes*. Oxford: Pergamon, 1985.

Hotelling, H.: Stability in competition. *Economic Journal* 39 (1929) 41–57.

McLean, I.: *Dealing in Votes*. Oxford: Martin Robertson, 1982.

Page, B.I.: *Choices and Echoes in Presidential Elections*. Chicago, Ill.: Chicago University Press, 1978.

Riker, W.H.: *Liberalism against Populism*. San Francisco: Freeman, 1982.

Robertson, D.B.: *A Theory of Party Competition*. London: Wiley, 1976.

Stokes, D.: Spatial models of party competition. In *Elections and the Political Order*, ed. A. Campbell et al. New York: Wiley, 1966.

Speaker The term is frequently used to designate the officer who presides over a legislative chamber. The office of Speaker originated in England where it can be traced back to the fourteenth century. The custom arose whereby the Commons selected one of their number to represent their grievances to the king and he became known as the Speaker because he spoke on their collective behalf.

The office of Speaker of the British HOUSE OF COMMONS is one of great prestige and authority. The Speaker presides over the House, maintains order, and interprets its rules and practice. He does not vote except to exercise a casting vote in the event of a tie. He is the traditional guardian of the privileges of the Commons and is its representative on all official occasions. He is elected for a constituency like every other member and elected to the chair by his fellow-members. The first business of a new parliament is always the election of a Speaker and should the office fall vacant a new Speaker must be elected before any further business can be transacted. Once elected to the chair the Speaker immediately severs his party connections and becomes totally impartial. A Speaker who seeks re-election at a general election does not conduct a political campaign and he is normally continued in office even if there is a change of government. In Britain no Speaker has been ejected from office since 1835, nor has any British Speaker ever been defeated in his constituency.

The office of Speaker exists in most Commonwealth countries and in certain others, but in few of them is its detachment from political influence so complete as in Britain. In countries where the British parliamentary system has been adopted the Speaker is likely to be a party member although not a political leader. The Speakership in Canada has a tradition of political impartiality although only one Speaker has succeeded in detaching himself completely from his party affiliation. Similarly in India Speakers normally remain members of their political parties while taking pains to minimize the influence that party membership inevitably exerts. In Australia on the other hand Speakers are openly partisan, remaining active members of their parties and conducting political campaigns at general elections. One result of the political nature of the office in Australia is that the rules of the House of Representatives allow very little discretion to the Chair. By contrast, the Indian Speaker enjoys wider powers than any other Speaker in the Commonwealth.

In some legislatures the Speaker is not required to be an elected member but may be chosen from outside the House. This is the case in Malaysia, Malta, Singapore, Trinidad and Tobago, Guyana and certain African parliaments of the Commonwealth. In Zimbabwe, Zambia, the Gambia and Kiribati, it is specifically provided that the Speaker may not be a member of the parliament. In Malawi the Speaker is not elected by the House but appointed by the president. In Tonga he is appointed by the King.

In the United States the Speaker of the House of Representatives wields considerable power and is one of the leaders of the majority party. He is expected to assist the passage of his party's legislative programme and he does not hesitate to declare his position on controversial political issues. His powers in the House are considerable and are legitimately exercised in his party's interests.

In European legislatures the position of the presiding officer has little in common with the British concept of the Speakership. The nature of the office varies with each parliament so it is difficult to generalize, but most European presiding officers are active party members with the right to vote in the House. Unlike the British Speaker they usually have direct involvement in the organization of parliamentary business. In France, the President of the National Assembly presides over a bureau consisting of deputies drawn from the various parties represented in the assembly. It guides and directs the procedure of the assembly and the authority of the Chair is vested in the bureau as a whole. It also manages the internal economy of the assembly. The parliamentary agenda is determined by a body consisting of the President and Vice-Presidents of the assembly, the chairmen of standing committees and the leaders of the parties represented in the Assembly. In West Germany the Bundestag elects a 'Council of Elders' similar to the French bureau, its main function being the arrangement of parliamentary business and the allocation of debating time to the various agenda items. In Sweden, the Speaker since 1974 has been responsible for initiating the GOVERNMENT FORMATION PROCESS in place of the monarch.

In bicameral parliaments the presiding officers of upper Houses often have somewhat different functions from their counterparts in the lower House. For example the Lord Chancellor is the Speaker of the HOUSE OF LORDS although he does not have the procedural and disciplinary powers of the Speaker of the House of Commons. In France the President of the Senate replaces the President of the Republic in the event of the latter's incapacity, and there are other countries where a similar constitutional provision is to be found. The President of the US Senate is the vice-president of the Republic, thereby providing a link between the executive and the legislature. The President of the Upper House of the Indian Parliament is likewise the vice-president of the Republic. Not all presiding officers of upper Houses hold office ex-officio. Some are elected by their fellow-members, as in Australia and various other Commonwealth countries. Some are appointed, usually by the head of state, as in Canada and Holland.

PACL

Reading

Britain, House of Commons: *Report of the Select Committee on Parliamentary Elections (Mr Speaker's Seat), 1938–9.* HC 98.

————: *First Report from the Select Committee on Procedure: Election of a Speaker, 1971–2.* HC 111.

Conference of Commonwealth Speakers and Presiding Officers: Reports – Canada 1969; India 1970–1; Zambia 1973; UK 1976; Australia 1978; Canada 1981; New Zealand 1984; India 1986.

Laundy, P.A.C.: *Office of Speaker.* London: Cassell, 1964.

————: *The Office of Speaker in the Parliaments of the Commonwealth.* London: Quiller Press, 1984.

May, T.E.: *Parliamentary Practice.* 20th edn. London: Butterworth, 1983.

Speaker's Conference An all-party committee of MPs in Britain, meeting under the chairmanship of the SPEAKER to consider matters of electoral change. It is distinguished from a SELECT COMMITTEE in that it is set up by the government under the chairmanship of the Speaker. There have been five such Conferences, in 1916–17, 1943–4, 1965–8, 1972–4 and 1977–8. In addition a Speaker's Conference was established in 1919–20 to deal with the issue of devolution.

The Conferences meet in private, take little evidence and the proposals which they make are in no way binding upon governments; indeed they have been frequently ignored. For these reasons, while it used to be held that a Speaker's Conference was an essential pre-condition of electoral change, the device seems now to have fallen into desuetude.

VBB

Reading

Butler, D.E.: Modifying electoral arrangements. In *Policy and Politics*, pp. 13–22, ed. D.E. Butler and A.H. Halsey. London: Macmillan, 1978.

specialist   See BUREAUCRACY.

spoils system   Spoils are the tangible benefits that can be given to individuals as a result of political favouritism. Often called PATRONAGE, spoils are bestowed on individuals, not categories of people. They typically result from the routine operations of government and their amount is not greatly affected by alternative policy choices. Among the most important examples are public jobs, contracts, franchises, exceptions to zoning laws and housing regulations, and guardianships of the estates of minors.

The desideratum of spoils is aid to the party organization in the form of electioneering and campaign contributions. Patronage can most usefully be understood as an incentive to political participation. Party organizations based on this incentive are called machines. Machine politics is the customary term for distributing these benefits according to political criteria. The beneficiaries of the spoils system are loyal to their sponsoring party organization, not to their nominal bureaucratic superior. Thus patronage fragments governmental administration rather than facilitating its co-ordination.

Machine politics is unimportant in the American federal government and in many states and cities as well. Public employees work under a civil service merit system unresponsive to election outcomes, contracts are a result of competitive bidding, and the laws are enforced impartially. In some places, however, party politicians make claims that are observed by government officials, and routine public administration provides resources that motivate political activity.

See MACHINE.

REW

587

Reading

Tolchin, M. and Tolchin, S.: *To the Victor....* New York: Random House, 1972.

Wolfinger, R.E.: *The Politics of Progress*. Englewood Cliffs, NJ: Prentice-Hall, 1974.

sponsored candidate Uniquely among major democratic political parties, the British Labour Party requires the election expenses of all its parliamentary candidates to be guaranteed by one of the organizations affiliated to the Party (Labour Party Constitution, Clause X, ¶ 4). But only an individual supported by a trade union or the Co-operative Party is termed a sponsored candidate. Contemporary sponsored candidates are successors to the first union nominees who began contesting elections to the House of Commons in the 1860s. Increased numbers of Constituency Labour Party (CLP) supported candidates in the 1920s and inter-union competition for seats after the 1931 election led the 1933 Party Conference at Hastings to adopt rules limiting the financial support a union might give its candidates. This Hastings Agreement, as modified, is the basis for sponsorship today. A union or the Co-operative Party may pay no more than 80 per cent of a candidate's allowable election expenses and no more than 60 per cent of an agent's salary (if there is one) or an annual constituency maintenance grant of £650–£750. Union choices are placed on the Party's list A of available nominees; CLPs select prospective candidates from that list or from list B which includes individuals not being sponsored.

Sponsored candidates normally stand in safe seats, and the proportion of sponsored MPs in the Parliamentary Labour Party is inversely related to the Party's electoral success. Sponsorship provided a route into the political elite for the working class but recent years have seen a decline in the number of sponsored candidates with a blue-collar background because traditional manual workers are less likely to secure adoption by CLPs and because some unions have begun sponsoring sitting MPs who are frequently not even members of the union.

Sponsored candidates elected to the House provide the unions and the Co-operative Party with a parliamentary voice and access to ministers, but they are not DELEGATES. Custom, tradition and PARLIAMENTARY PRIVILEGE ensure that the demands of Party and of the MP's geographic constituency come first even though some unions have ceased to sponsor MPs they disagree with, or have threatened to do so.   WDM

Reading

Ellis, J. and Johnson, R.W.: *Members from the Unions*. London: Fabian Society, 1974.

Harrison, M.: *Trade Unions and the Labour Party Since 1945*. London: Allen & Unwin, 1960.

Labour Party. *Rule Book, 1984/85*. London: Labour Party, 1985.

Muller, W.D.: *The 'Kept Men'? The First Century of Trade Union Representation in the House of Commons, 1874–1975*. Hassocks: Harvester, 1977.

Ranney, A.: *Pathways to Parliament*. London: Macmillan, 1965.

Taylor, A.J.: *The Politics of the Yorkshire Miners*. London: Croom Helm, 1985.

SS See GESTAPO.

Stalin/Stalinism

(1) *Stalin, Joseph V.* (1879–1953) Born at Gori, Georgia, the son of a cobbler, Iosif Vissarionovich Dzhugashvili, known as Stalin, was supreme ruler of the Soviet Union for over two decades. He studied at an Orthodox seminary in Tbilisi but was expelled in 1899 and thereafter became a professional revolutionary. He was first apprehended in 1902; this began a cycle of arrest, exile and escape until 1917. On Lenin's nomination, Stalin was co-opted to the Central Committee (CC) of the Russian Social Democratic Labour Party in 1912; he helped LENIN during the planning of the October Revolution but was less significant than TROTSKY. Commissar of Nationalities in the first Bolshevik government, Stalin was a founding member of the Politburo and Orgburo of the CC in 1919, and also a Commissar of the Workers' and Peasants' Inspectorate (Rabkrin). Appointed Secretary General in April 1922 he was master of the Party machine on Lenin's death in 1924. Striking astute tactical alliances he out-

manoeuvred Trotsky, Zinoviev, Kamenev and Bukharin so that by 1929 he was the undisputed leader. The cult of his personality then began, amid forced collectivization, industrialization and the subsequent famine, PURGES and oppression. Some have argued that, with the aid of the SECRET POLICE, he created the world's first totalitarian state (see TOTALITARIANISM). Show trials of his leading opponents in the party were held to eliminate rivals; while many in the population at large were persecuted and murdered under the pretext that they were opposed to the regime. He became Prime Minister, Defence Minister, Commander-in-Chief of Soviet Armed Forces, Marshal and Generalissimo during the war. He remained master of the USSR until his death. Stalin was a brilliant tactician, an incisive and ruthless politician whose abilities served two goals: his own power and the transformation of the Soviet Union into an industrial state.

(2) *Stalinism* Used essentially pejoratively, the term refers to the nature of the Soviet regime between 1929 and 1953. Not officially used in the USSR Stalinism is associated with the DICTATORSHIP OF THE PROLETARIAT exercised in the name of the vanguard of the Communist Party by Stalin; a monolithic, strictly disciplined, highly hierarchical party which claimed a monopoly of political and economic power, reducing all other social institutions to instruments of its will; the ruthless elimination of all perceived or actual opponents of Stalin's leadership; the cult of Stalin's personality; the idea that all culture is subservient to political goals and serves purposes of social engineering; a powerful ruling bureaucracy with a high turnover of office holders aiding social mobility; a strengthening of the state, involving the intensification of class struggle in order to eliminate classes, before the state would be able to 'wither away'. The ideology, Marxism–Leninism, was codified and simplified by Stalin as he became sole, legitimate interpreter. Stalin argued that socialism in one country was possible – in sharp contrast to Trotsky's allegedly adventurist internationalism. He established a centrally planned economy whose chief aim was to build up heavy industry and military power. Central to Stalinism was the idea of the inevitable intensification of the class struggle with the approach of socialism. This provided the justification for mass terror. The process of de-Stalinization began at the twentieth Party Congress in 1956 with Khrushchev's attack on the post-1934 record, but some aspects of Stalinism re-appeared after 1964. Political scientists continue to argue over whether Stalinism was the natural fulfilment of BOLSHEVISM, or whether, by contrast, a betrayal of it. The latter thesis is strongly defended by Cohen and by Tucker.

See also LABOUR CAMP. MMcC

Reading

Carr, E.H.: *The Russian Revolution from Lenin to Stalin*. London: Macmillan, 1979.

Cohen, S.F.: *Bukharin and the Bolshevik Revolution*. Oxford: Oxford University Press, 1974.

Deutscher, I.: *Stalin*. 2nd edn. Oxford: Oxford University Press, 1966.

McCauley, M: *Stalin and Stalinism*. Harlow, Essex: Longman, 1983.

Medvedev, R.: *Let History Judge*. London: Macmillan, 1971.

Rigby, T.H. ed.: *Stalin*. Englewood Cliffs, NJ: Prentice-Hall, 1966.

Stalin, J.V.: *The Essential Stalin: major theoretical writings 1905–52*. London: Croom Helm, 1973.

Tucker, R.C.: *The Soviet Political Mind: Stalinism and post-Stalin change*. 2nd rev. edn. London: Allen & Unwin, 1972.

———: *Stalin as Revolutionary, 1897–1929*. London: Chatto & Windus, 1973.

———: *Stalinism: essays in historical interpretation*. New York: Norton, 1977.

standing committee The term has a distinct meaning in the UK HOUSE OF COMMONS: despite the impression of permanence which it conveys, standing committees are principally appointed merely to debate the detailed provisions of particular BILLS. Their work finishes when their consideration of a bill ends. They have no continuing mandate, orders of reference, or membership. Continuing committees of other legislatures (such as the Australian House of Representatives or the French National Assembly) are not infrequently referred to as standing or permanent committees, while in the United Kingdom committees appointed by standing order are known as SELECT COMMITTEES.

Modern standing committees began at Westminster in the late nineteenth century when a few committees were set up to consider the details of particular classes of bills. Now however, they have lost that degree of specialization, are merely distinguished by letters, and have different members for each bill. Only the Scottish Grand Committee (a standing committee consisting of all members representing Scottish constituencies, which may consider the principle of Scottish bills, and debate estimates and matters) remains unchanged in its membership. Its Welsh counterpart, with similar but fewer responsibilities, may have up to five other members added to it. Members of standing committees are chosen by the Committee of Selection (itself a select committee), which is obliged to have regard to the qualifications of the members nominated and to the composition of the House. This requirement ensures that there is a considerable degree of expertise and similarity of membership on committees on similar bills. Typically they have between sixteen and twenty-five members.

Standing committees provide the normal mechanism for debating the details of bills following approval in principle by the House at second reading. They are microcosms of the House as a whole. Members are ranged on either side of the committee room, and they stand when called by the chair to speak – as in the House, but unlike the less formal, sedentary style of select committees in which members sit round a horseshoe table. Standing committees are basically committees of debate, not committees of inquiry. They invariably meet in public. Ministers are included in the membership. The chair is impartial and moderatorial, rather than innovative as in investigative select committees. Most bills are considered by standing committees, except those touching on the constitution, those urgently needed, and some minor bills; all these are considered in COMMITTEE OF THE WHOLE HOUSE.

The combination of evidence-taking and debate, the norm for committees in many LEGISLATURES, is extremely rare in the House of Commons, although in the 1980s a few 'special standing committees' have been empowered to hear some evidence. Unlike committees of, for instance, the United States Congress, standing committees do not exercise any legislative initiative. Nor do they combine a legislative role with political and administrative scrutiny as do committees in the USA and the Federal Republic of Germany. Pressure of business has, however, led the House of Commons to appoint *ad hoc* standing committees to deal with the second readings of minor bills, delegated legislation and other matters. See also LEGISLATIVE COMMITTEES.

KB

Reading

Bradshaw, K. and Pring, D.: *Parliament and Congress*. London: Quartet, 1981.

Lees, J.D. and Shaw, M. eds: *Committees in Legislatures: a comparative analysis*. Durham, NC: Duke University Press; Oxford: Martin Robertson, 1979.

May, T.E.: *Parliamentary Practice*. 20th edn. London: Butterworth, 1983.

Olson, D.M.: *The Legislative Process: a comparative approach*. New York: Harper & Row, 1980.

Pettifer, J.A.: *House of Representatives Practice*. Australian Government Publishing Service, 1981.

state A form of political association that began to emerge slowly and incoherently from the fifteenth century onwards and was recognized to differ from its predecessors – Greek, Roman and medieval. The idea and the practice of the modern state was forged out of conflict involving medieval parliaments, which centralizing rulers sought to extinguish or make subservient (as in France); the church, as rulers attempted to acquire its authority and thereby extend their moral function in relation to their subjects (as in Reformation Germany); and the nobility, who were either drawn into the service of the prince as members of the royal administration (as in Italy and Sweden) or ceded influence to a bourgeoisie rising as powerful officers (as in France). The term state came slowly into use but with little precision or consistency, reflecting in part the complexity of the new experience and in part the very different senses of the Latin word *status*. Medieval usage of *status* in a proprietary sense – *status regalis* – with the emphasis on the authority and prestige of the prince contrasted with its frequent use after Dutch Independence to distinguish a republic from a kingdom.

In achievement of clarity about the character of the new political association two contributions are noteworthy: MACHIAVELLI, who viewed the state as an autonomous, secular realm pursuing an exceptional morality – 'reason of state'; Jean BODIN, who emphasized its attribute of SOVEREIGNTY, an absolute and unique authority involving the ability to make as well as apply and guarantee law. The problem of the relationship between the state as an apparatus of power, concerned with its effective exercise, and the state as a legal institution has subsequently bedevilled the theory and practice of the modern state. In practice, 'state-building' was accompanied by immense conflict, uncertainty and failure, and disagreements remain about when the modern state reached maturity. There are advocates for seventeenth-century France under Cardinal Richelieu and then Louis XIV (*L'état, c'est moi*); for France after the radical elimination of the patrimonial and feudal legacy with the 1789 revolution; for Prussia after the accession of Frederick William in 1740 and his idea of himself as 'the first servant of the state' and its chief bureaucrat; or for the end of the Holy Roman Empire in 1806 and the response of the Prussian reformers to this crisis. In sum, these experiences contributed to the gradual emergence of the idea of the abstract, impersonal state, which controls a consolidated territory and possesses a system of offices that is differentiated from that of other organizations operating in the same territory. Max WEBER reflected this phenomenon when he referred to rational legal authority as the dominant type of authority in the modern world, displacing traditional and charismatic authority, and BUREAUCRACY as its structural expression. In the eighteenth century the German Cameralists and the French physiocrats and *philosophes* contributed to the spread of the idea of public office as a professional relationship to an abstract impersonal state dedicated to social improvement and public welfare. During the nineteenth century French and German lawyers, strongly influenced by Roman law and its distinction between public and private affairs (*res publica* and *res privata*), elaborated a powerful body of public law pertaining to the abstract impersonal state. Public law provided principles to guide legislation and administration and was applied in a distinct system of administrative courts. In this way the intimate relationship between law and state (*Rechtsstaat*) in modern continental Europe was established.

Despite this early lack of clarity and slow, uneven growth it was possible during the nineteenth century to agree on the basic features of the state as a form of political association. The state had a distinct territorial character as an entity in a system of sovereign states; its authority had a special quality (its sovereignty); it had extraordinary and growing resources of physical power at its disposal; it was distinguished by the peculiar power of the bonds among its members and by its distinctive purpose. Political and legal theorists were left with many open questions: were there certain principles, for example of natural law binding on the exercise of state authority and essential to its legitimacy; what were the implications for public and international law of the immense physical power of the modern state; was the state as a society to be understood as a necessary legal artefact to ensure the rule of pure reason (KANT) or as an alternative to the 'brutish' world of men exercising their individual free wills (HOBBES), as the expression of national identity (NATIONALISM) or as a historical phenomenon expressing the emergence of man's growing self-consciousness (HEGEL); was the purpose of the state to be understood in terms of sustaining certain moral rules of conduct (Kant), providing security and tranquillity (Bodin), pursuing the welfare of subjects (Leibniz) or having a cultural mission (Herder and the later Fichte)?

Some order has been brought into the subsequent complexity of theories of the state by making an analytical distinction between three conceptions of the state.

591

The state as might: This approach involves political 'realism' and a concern with problems of political survival and effectiveness of rule. The pedigree of these theories can be traced from Machiavelli's concern with 'reason of state' to nineteenth- and early twentieth-century German ideas of the *Machtstaat* (the later Clausewitz, Treitschke and Carl SCHMITT), to elite theorists (MOSCA and PARETO) and to Marxist analyses of the state as a coercive instrument used by one class to subjugate another.

The state as law: This approach was concerned with the state's legal powers and the means of their application by officials and judges. The state was seen as a set of offices whose rights and duties were laid down very precisely in law; the nature of the will of the state was not relevant to the work of officials, judges or even legal scholars. A formal conception of the *Rechtsstaat* (state based on law) can be found in the work of Hans KELSEN and Max WEBER; *Staatsrecht* was one of the most notable achievements of this German legal science. Legal scholars gained a position of prestige, helping to codify law that was seen as the articulation of the state and training entrants for state service. In this process of codification legal scholars borrowed heavily from Roman law concepts.

The state as legitimacy: This approach asked basic philosophical questions about the principles on which state action rested and by reference to which its actions achieved LEGITIMACY. Examples are provided by theories of the 'police state' (for example, the German Cameralists) with the emphasis on welfare, social improvement, and efficiency; by 'material' theories of the *Rechtsstaat* that were concerned with the basic values from which the quality of the will of the state derived and that rejected legal positivism (for example, Gierke, Mohl, and Stein in nineteenth-century Germany and the dominant French legal tradition including Esmein, Duguit, and Hauriou); by HEGEL'S and neo-Hegelian accounts of the state as an ethical community through participation in which groups, classes, and individuals could transcend their particularity and achieve

freedom in community; by the NATION-STATE in the sense that the nation could provide a unity of culture and solidarity based typically on common language or literature; and by the technocratic state, based on a disinterested scientific management of society in the name of progress towards the 'good society' (Saint-Simon).

Theories of the state can also be analysed historically by reference to the different social and economic experiences that they reflect.

The state as reflection of a hierarchical social order: The idea of society as a hierarchical order composed of different and unequal ranks that are bound together by reciprocal interest and mutual obligation found expression in *Ständestaat* theories, reflecting a feudal social order and advocating neo-corporatist ideas of state organization, and in theories of the patrimonial state of bureaucratic absolutism. The former theories maintained popularity in nineteenth- and twentieth-century Germany; the latter were characteristic of the French *ancien régime* and later theorists of Restoration monarchy in France.

The state as reflection of an individualistic social order: Liberal theories of the state were associated with the industrial revolution, the market economy, and an ascendant middle class. The rewards that accrued to individuals for their achievements in the economic sphere should be complemented in the political sphere by a competition of opinions and competition for office. At the same time the activities of the state would be closely delimited and constrained by law. In one variant the liberal state was an association of will, respecting above all the rights of the individual who was the sole arbiter of right and wrong and the source of all law (Esmein, Laband): in another variant, the public institutions of the state had the function of 'socializing' the individual into an objective, universal legal order that was accessible to reason (Hauriou). In the former case the state was to be neutral in the struggle of opinions; in the latter it had a didactic role.

The state as the embodiment of community in society: These theories of the state sprang from a concern about the enervating effects on the person of social fragmentation and utilitarianism, which were rooted in the market economy, and of the radical individualism associated with the FRENCH REVOLUTION. They stressed solidarity, the capability of individuals to co-operate in collective action, and the significant role of the state as an ethical community. For Hegel and neo-Hegelians the institutions of the state offered individuals the possibility of finding rational and universal values. Theorists of the social state were above all preoccupied with the 'social question' and with providing a social-scientific perspective on the functions of the state. Durkheim, Duguit, and Tönnies emphasized the importance of intimate working relations between the state and the major occupational associations.

A further distinction can be made between those societies (typically continental European) where the idea of the state as the institution of political rule and the embodiment of public power has taken deep root and other societies (typically English-speaking) where the state has not been central in political and legal discourse.

The latter societies are characterized by a remarkable continuity of medieval political ideas and institutions, the lack of the self-conscious 'state-building' that comes from protracted external challenge, and the absence of the reception of Roman law. As an intellectual tradition state theory is less strongly represented in these societies; political ideas are rooted more closely in experience and the analysis of practice. By contrast 'state societies' rest on a rationalistic search for political order.

Clear definition of the word state remains difficult because it is a contested concept with a complex of conservative, liberal, social democratic and Marxist variants. In particular, Marxists have had a critical perspective on the state, directing their attack on a key assumption of state theory – the idea of a distinction between state and civil society. This idea forms the precondition of the state's ability to take a disinterested view of the public interest and its claim to embody a unique authority. Marxist theory has varied from those who have denied the autonomy of the state altogether seeing it as 'mere super-structure' for class rule, to others who accord a 'relative autonomy'

to the state. In the twentieth century Antonio Gramsci, the Frankfurt School (for example Habermas) and the French structuralists (for example Althusser and Poulantzas) offered influential Marxist analyses of the state: Gramsci stressed the 'hegemonic' role of the state as an ideological actor (and not just a coercive force); Habermas accepted that the state, though fragile, could play off particular capitalist interests against each other; and Poulantzas saw the state as a 'unifying social formation' organizing and reconciling different social forces. Neo-Marxist theories of this type have been important in providing a more dynamic analysis of the functioning of the modern state.   KD

Reading

Bornstein, S. et al. eds: *The State in Capitalist Europe*. London: Allen & Unwin, 1983.

Dyson, K.: *The State Tradition in Western Europe*. Oxford: Martin Robertson, 1980.

d'Entrèves, A.P.: *The Notion of the State*. Oxford: Clarendon Press, 1967.

Held, D. et al. eds: *States and Societies*. Oxford: Martin Robertson, 1983.

Poggi, G.: *The Development of the Modern State*. London: Hutchinson, 1978.

Shennan, J.H.: *The Origins of the Modern European State 1450–1725*. London: Hutchinson, 1974.

Skocpol, T.: *States and Social Revolutions: a comparative analysis of France, Russia and China*. Cambridge: Cambridge University Press, 1979.

Tilly, C. ed.: *The Formation of National States in Western Europe*. Princeton, NJ: Princeton University Press, 1975.

states rights   Since the essence of FEDERALISM is the division of powers between the central authority and the units some element of tension is bound to be present, and to be increased where political parties play a prominent role. The likelihood will be that the party in power at the centre will stress central authority and that the parties in power in the states or provinces will adopt a States Rights position. Experience suggests that parties in power at the centre tend to lose support in the units; crises in the federal relationship have therefore been frequent both in the 'classical' federal systems and the newer ones.

The states or provinces expressing a states rights point of view may be always the same ones because of some distinctive character or set of interests marking them off from the rest – Quebec is the obvious example. Elsewhere states rights doctrines have emerged from a variety of different situations. Their first American exponents were the Virginians who raised objections to the legislation brought in by the federal government to combat sympathy for the French Revolution. The cause was later taken up by the New England states who objected to the war of 1812 and their commercial losses resulting from it. Then it was the turn of South Carolina in its hostility to protectionism and subsequently that of the entire South as part of its defence of slavery. Even after the abolition of slavery the South's distinctiveness in respect of race relations and of its economic priorities made the cry of states rights a powerful one there until our own day.

In Canada the position of the provinces was enhanced by the interpretation placed upon the British North America Act, its constitution, by the Privy Council in London, and proved an obstacle to Canada's achieving full responsibility for amending its own constitution until 1982. The feeling that agrarian interests were being sacrificed to those of the more highly industrialized and urbanized states led to Western Australia's unsuccessful attempt to be allowed to secede from the Commonwealth of Australia in 1934–5.

While divergences in economic interests, social philosophy or religious and cultural allegiance are the underlying reasons for taking up a states rights position, the case is usually argued in constitutional terms. In the pre-Civil War period in the United States, the upholders of the Union cause stressed that an American nation had existed before a federal constitution was adopted; the states rights partisans stressed their belief that the original states had been sovereign entities, delegating some powers to the federal institutions but entitled to recall them, if they felt they were being abused. SECESSION from the Union was thus a constitutional right not an act of revolutionary defiance. In Canada, where the provinces had had no previous status as independent sovereignties, the French Canadians produced a theory according to which the Confederation was the product of a bargain between the two founding nations, British and French, from which Quebec derived its specific rights.

See also CALHOUN.   B

Reading *See* under FEDERALISM.

statute law Laws which are enacted by a properly constituted LEGISLATURE in accordance with prescribed procedures. Statutes can be drafted either in the fullest detail, which assumes that the statute deals only with those cases which fall within its actual wording (this is the COMMON LAW approach), or in a very general and abstract way, leaving the courts to fill in the details by making reference to a presumed legislative intention (this is the continental European theory). In England there are three CONVENTIONS known as 'rules' which order the interpretation of laws: the mischief rule, which attempts to establish the purpose of the statute (it dates from the sixteenth century); the literal rule, which emerged with the growth of PARLIAMENTARY SOVEREIGNTY and the articulation of a SEPARATION OF POWERS doctrine, as well as with theories of law advocating that the words of the statute be taken at face value in the nineteenth century; the golden rule, which developed almost contemporaneously with the literal rule to allow flexibility in instances where literalism would lead to absurdity.

MDAF

Reading

Lloyd, Lord and Freeman, M.D.A.: *Introduction to Jurisprudence*. London: Stevens, 1985.

Miers, D. and Page, A.: *Legislation*. London: Sweet & Maxwell, 1983.

Statute of Westminster Enacted by the United Kingdom parliament in 1931, this statute gave practical expression to the principle of equality in the relationships between the United Kingdom and the self-governing DOMINIONS which was formulated by the

Imperial Conference of 1926. The statute recited important conventions in its preamble and this was followed by the legislative provisions.

At this time common allegiance to the Crown was seen as essential to the COMMONWEALTH relationship, and the equality of the United Kingdom and the dominions was recognized by the formulation of a convention requiring the assent of all dominions to changes in the succession and in the Royal Style and Titles. This was recited in the preamble, and was given early and unexpected application in the abdication crisis of 1936.

So, too, in the preamble it was declared that in accordance with the established position, no law made by the parliament of the United Kingdom should extend to a dominion, save at its request and consent. Then, in its body, the statute provided that dominion legislation should not be void and inoperative on the ground of repugnancy to United Kingdom legislation or to the law of England. It affirmed the power of dominion parliaments to legislate with extra-territorial effect, and it asserted in legislative form what was set down as convention in the preamble – that United Kingdom statutes would operate as law in the dominions only with their request and consent. The statute made specific provision safeguarding the operation of certain United Kingdom statutes: those which provided the statutes of Canada, Australia and New Zealand.

The dominions to which the statute had immediate application were Canada, the Irish Free State and South Africa; in the cases of Australia, Newfoundland and New Zealand it was provided that it should apply only when adopted; one Australian leader saw the legislation as a 'misguided attempt' to reduce to written terms something which 'was a matter of spirit and not of the letter'. Australia adopted the statute with retrospective effect in 1942, and New Zealand adopted it in 1947. Newfoundland ceased to be a dominion in the 1930s, and later became a province of Canada.

Neither South Africa nor the Irish Free State much liked the notion of a United Kingdom Act as the basis for their freedom. So South Africa adopted the substance of the statute in an Act of its own parliament, the Status of the Union Act 1934, and the Irish Free State moved towards the concept of a constitution whose authority purported to come directly from its own people. A new constitution, adopted in 1937 after a referendum, declared Ireland to be a 'sovereign, independent, democratic state', and the last remaining link with the Commonwealth was removed by the Republic of Ireland Act, 1948.

ZC

Reading

Marshall, G.: *Parliamentary Sovereignty and the Commonwealth*. Oxford: Oxford University Press, 1957.

Wheare, K.C.: *The Statute of Westminster and Dominion Status*. 5th edn. Oxford: Oxford University Press, 1953.

statutory instrument A form of DELEGATED LEGISLATION. An order issued under the authority of an Act. In the United Kingdom the rules governing such instruments are laid down by the Statutory Instruments Act 1946. This provides that an instrument either has the force of law once it is issued or that it acquires such force once it has been approved by Parliament. Only a minority of instruments, those which are most important and which are not urgent, are placed in the latter category (affirmative procedure). Other instruments may be annulled by Parliament within forty days from when the instrument was issued (negative procedure); for this purpose, only days when Parliament is sitting are counted. An instrument dealing with finance is subject to control only by the Commons. To annul an instrument either House has to agree to submit a humble address to the Crown asking the monarch to revoke the instrument. This procedure is commonly known as a 'prayer'.

Lack of parliamentary time causes severe restrictions to be placed on debate on statutory instruments in the Commons. Instruments cannot be amended: they must be accepted or rejected as a whole. Instruments may not be debated in the House after 11.30 p.m. They may be discussed in a STANDING COMMITTEE but such a committee has no right to express a formal opinion on the merits of an instrument. A Joint Committee of Lords and Commons reviews all instruments to ensure that correct procedures have been followed: this committee is concerned with constitutional decency, not with merits. PGR

Reading

Englefield, D.: *Whitehall and Westminster*. London and New York: Longman, 1985.

May, T.E.: *Parliamentary Practice*. 20th edn. London: Butterworth, 1983.

Select Committee on Procedure, First Report, 1977–8. HC588 British Parliamentary Papers XVIII.

strong mayor plan From the 1880s reformers of US urban government began to call for changes to the traditional WEAK MAYOR PLAN that would give strong administrative powers to the mayor and allow him or her to co-ordinate and control the various agencies and activities of city government. Boston and Brooklyn (then a separate city from New York) were the first to receive strong mayor charters. Others, especially large cities, soon followed. From early in the twentieth century, the COMMISSION PLAN became popular, but the strong mayor remained the form preferred in large cities, though it was often diluted by practices carried over from the weak mayor plan.

In its model form the plan allows the mayor to appoint or dismiss department heads, prepare the annual budget and control its execution, serve as a policy leader and, in more recent years, represent the city's interests in the state and national capitals. The mayor typically retains a veto but does not preside over council meetings. The council is usually small, with five to nine members, except in the largest cities (though Boston and Detroit have councils of nine). Reformers brought about a wholesale abandonment of both bicameralism and large councils from about 1910, leaving little concern for representativeness. The mayor dominates the city government and journalists focus on that office to the neglect of the council. The major weakness in the plan is the mayor's frequent lack of management skills, a problem the MAYOR-ADMINISTRATOR PLAN attempts to correct.

See also ELECTORAL SYSTEMS. CRA

Reading

Griffith, E.S.: *A History of American City Government: the progressive years and their aftermath*. New York: Praeger, 1974.

See also under WEAK MAYOR PLAN.

student politics Students have traditionally played a radical role in politics, for example, in the 1848 revolutions. But, more recently, the impact of young people in political affairs has been powerfully augmented by the expansion of student numbers since 1945, though economic recession began to depress their numbers in the late 1970s. Ever larger groupings of young people have been collected together in colleges and universities, and segregated from the influence of family, local community, and other societal controls. They constitute a powerful pressure group.

Given their privileged access to free time compared with employees of similar age, increased financial support from the state, their articulacy, and the natural tendency of young people towards rebellious idealism, student politics tends to be activistic and radical (see YOUTH MOVEMENTS). Local, national, and international student organizations have played a key role in periods of political strain, for example in the rise of National Socialism in Germany, the Hungarian revolution of 1956, the anti-nuclear movement, and in resistance to apartheid. Student activities are co-ordinated by organized national unions. In democratic societies they are politically divided, with competing factions associated with established parties and groupings. Commonly student politics tends to extremes, either of left or right, leading to recurrent conflict with these 'parent' bodies. In totalitarian societies student activity is closely controlled, as a source of positive support for the regime, and as a primary arena of potential rebellion. In some third world nations (where young people constitute a large portion of the population) a similar pattern has developed, with student political movements incorporated as an arm of national development. In others the student movement provides a primary source of challenge to authoritarian regimes. The International Union of Students was established after the second world war as a communist front organization. Although it did not achieve its objectives and students remained divided along conventional political lines, student politics everywhere still tend to become involved in problems beyond those which concern 'students as such'. DM

Reading

Flacks, R.: *Youth and Social Change*. Chicago, Ill.: Markham, 1971.

Forstenzer, T.R. and Ferrarotti, F.: *Youth in the 1980s*. UNESCO Press, 1982.

Keniston, K.: *Young Radicals*. Cambridge: Cambridge University Press, 1971.

Maanen, G. van: *The International Student Movement*. The Hague: International Documentation and Information Centre, 1966.

successive voting In certain elections it is useful or necessary to count the votes in order to place elected candidates in a certain order – for example the leading, or first elected candidate to chair a committee; the next two elected to be joint vice-chairmen and the remainder ordinary members of the committee. With voting by party lists this may be determined in advance by the order of names on the list, and the position of head of the list (often meaning prime minister designate or the party's candidate for the position of mayor) is a well known feature of campaigning in list elections. Successive voting is a means whereby voters may themselves determine this order using the single transferable vote system. The votes cast to elect a multiple number of places (N) are first counted as for a single place and one candidate declared elected; they are then re-counted for two places and two candidates declared elected, one of whom will already have been elected first and the other is therefore elected second; then successively for three places and so on until the final count is for N places and the additional candidate elected at this stage takes the Nth place. The method may of course be abbreviated: thus, in the committee example suggested above, the count would be first for one place, then for three places and then for all places. MS

supranational government The expression supranationality, like its congener supranational government, does not yet have one precise legal or political meaning. It gained currency in Europe with the Schuman Plan (1950) for the delegation of certain sovereign powers concerning the coal and steel industries to a new international organization. The plan resulted in the establishment of the six-nation European Coal and Steel Community (ECSC) in 1951.

Supranational government is literally the exercise of governmental functions at a level above the states over whom it is constituted. The entity exercising such functions is a supranational organization. Political concern with supranationality has focused on the extent to which supranational organizations impinge upon the sovereign powers of state governments. Drawing upon the work of lawyers such as Schermers and Capotorti, seven conditions for full supranationality may be posited:

(1) Decisions of the organization bind the member governments.
(2) The organization is at least partly independent of the member governments, either because it is composed of individuals or bodies acting independently of member governments, or because decisions taken by the majority of member states bind all member states.
(3) The organization is empowered to make rules directly binding on individuals.
(4) The organization has power to enforce its decisions even without the co-operation of the governments concerned, perhaps by using other organs of the member states, for example national courts.
(5) The organization has sufficient financial autonomy to be independent in practice.
(6) Withdrawal, or dissolution of the organization, by member states is not possible without the collaboration of the supranational organs.
(7) The supranational organs are part of a new legal system to which member states and individuals are also subject. Such a legal system will have its own rule-making bodies and a separate judiciary.

No existing supranational organization

meets all these conditions in full. On the other hand, most institutional international organizations satisfy some of the conditions. Thus supranationality and supranational government are relative terms, used primarily to indicate degrees above a threshold. The EUROPEAN COMMUNITY is generally characterized as supranational. It meets all the seven conditions to some degree; in particular, it clearly possesses the three essential elements stressed by Capotorti: decision making structures partially independent of member governments, legal systems with power to bind individuals and governments, and the capacity for direct relations with individual legal persons.

A small number of sub-regional organizations established in other parts of the world appear to have the constitutional potential to eventually become supranational, although the necessary political consensus may not develop easily. Examples are the Andean Common Market established under the Cartagena Agreement 1969, with its Court of Justice inaugurated in 1984, and the Economic Community of West African States created by the Treaty of Lagos in 1975. Such universal international organizations as the UNITED NATIONS and the World Bank lack the independence from member governments necessary for supranationality, and are more akin to organizations of intergovernmental co-operation.

Supranational government is sometimes compared to FEDERAL government, and in certain circumstances it might also be compared to international CONFEDERATIONS such as Senegambia. As it presently exists, however, supranational government is *sui generis*. It involves an independence from member States not found in international confederation, but it has not yet attained the degree of integration or permanence found in strong federations.

BWK

Reading

Bernhardt, R. ed.: *Encyclopedia of Public International Law*, Instalments 5 and 6. Amsterdam: Elsevier, 1983.

Capotorti, F.: Supranational Organizations. In *Encyclopedia of Public International Law*, Instalment 5, pp. 262–268, ed. R. Bernhardt. Amsterdam: Elsevier, 1983.

Claude, I.L. Jr: *Swords into Ploughshares: the problems and progress of international organisation*. 3rd edn. New York: Random House, 1964.

Hay, P.H.: *Federalism and Supranational Organisations: patterns for new legal structures*. Urbana: University of Illinois Press, 1966.

Peaslee, A.J.: *International Governmental Organisations: constitutional documents*. 3rd edn, ed. D.P. Xydis. The Hague: Nijhoff, 1974–79.

Schermers, H.G.: *International Institutional Law*. Alphen aan den Rijn: Sijthoff & Noordhoff, 1980.

Seidl-Hohenveldern, I.: *Das Recht der Internationalen Organisationen, einschliesslich der supranationalen Gemeinschaften*. 3rd edn. Cologne: Heymanns, 1979.

Taylor, P.: Elements of Supranationalism. In *International Organisation: a conceptual approach*, pp. 216–235, ed. P. Taylor and A.J.R. Groom. London: Pinter, 1978.

Supreme Court One of the three branches of the federal government of the United States, established under the constitution. Article 3 of the constitution – which defines the judicial power – gives the Supreme Court original jurisdiction in all cases affecting ambassadors, other public ministers and consuls, and those in which a state is a party. In all other cases, which in fact constitute the largest part of its workload, the supreme court has appellate jurisdiction under regulations to be determined by Congress which also has the power to set up inferior courts. Article 3 of the constitution provides that judges shall hold office during good behaviour but the appointment of judges under Article 2 is vested in the president subject to the ADVICE AND CONSENT of the senate. The original number of supreme court justices was five but Congress has changed the size of the court from time to time. Since 1869 the number of justices has been nine.

Although it is not explicit in the constitution, the Supreme Court has made itself the arbiter of the constitution and has asserted the right to review the acts of the state legislatures, of Congress, and of the federal executive. The supreme court first exercised the power of JUDICIAL REVIEW of an Act of Congress in

1803 when in *Marbury* v. *Madison* it struck down legislation purporting to alter the original jurisdiction of the supreme court. Under the first Chief Justice, John Marshall, the court handed down a number of decisions which were crucial for the future constitutional development of the United States. Of particular importance were *McCulloch* v. *Maryland* (1819) in which the court asserted the implied powers of Congress, the supremacy of the constitution, and the doctrine that the federal government possessed its powers directly from the people rather than indirectly from the states, and *Gibbons* v. *Ogden* (1824) which asserted broad federal authority over interstate commerce.

The power of the Supreme Court to strike down federal as well as state legislation has frequently brought it into conflict with the elected branches of government. The presidency of Franklin Roosevelt witnessed a major confrontation between the executive and the judiciary as a result of the court's holding unconstitutional a number of laws which gave the president new powers to intervene in the management of the American economy. Ultimately the court accepted the NEW DEAL legislation and implicitly deferred to the right of president and Congress to frame social and economic policy.

In the period after the second world war the court again encountered hostility as it articulated its interpretation of the individual rights and protections provided by the constitution. Under Chief Justice Earl Warren (1953–69) the court was especially active in developing the EQUAL PROTECTION and DUE PROCESS clauses of the constitution to strengthen the position of minorities in American society. Especially significant were the decisions declaring segregation unconstitutional (*Brown* v. *Board of Education of Topeka* 1954), affirming a constitutional requirement of equal electoral districts (*Baker* v. *Carr* 1962), and a range of decisions improving the procedural protections available to accused persons and poor prisoners (*Miranda* v. *Arizona*) and (*Gideon* v. *Wainwright*).

Many of the supreme court's decisions in the Warren years were controversial because they saw the court asserting new standards of constitutional morality rather than striking down Acts of Congress on the basis of incompatibility with some specific provision of the constitution. The broad reading of the equal protection clause of the Fourteenth Amendment and of the due process clause led critics to claim that the Supreme Court was making law rather than interpreting it. Richard Nixon's 1968 presidential campaign made the court's role a political issue and it seemed that his election and the retirement of Warren would produce a more conservative court. In fact, the Court under Chief Justice Warren Burger (1969–1986) has sustained much of the Warren court's jurisprudence and in 1973 it made itself as unpopular as its predecessor had been by declaring that women had a constitutional right to an abortion in the first trimester of pregnancy (*Roe* v. *Wade*).

Although the court enjoys a formidable constitutional power, its power is not unlimited. The formal control of impeachment is less important than the informal restraint imposed by the court's awareness of the need to keep in general harmony with public opinion and of the extent to which it is dependent on the other branches of government for the enforcement of its decision. The presidential power to appoint new justices ensures that in the long term the court will not become remote from the wider political system – although not all presidents have the opportunity to fill supreme court vacancies and supreme court judges, once appointed, may prove more responsive to the norms of the bench than to the aspirations of the president who occasioned the nomination.

See also CIVIL LIBERTIES; CIVIL RIGHTS; CONSTITUTIONAL COURT; CONSTITUTIONS/ CONSTITUTIONALISM; JUDICIAL ACTIVISM AND SELF-RESTRAINT; JUDICIAL FUNCTION AND PROCESS.   GRP

Reading

Abraham, H.J.: *The Judiciary: the Supreme Court in the governmental process.* 2nd edn. Boston, Mass.: Allyn & Bacon, 1972.

Freund, P.A.: *The Supreme Court of the United States.* Cleveland, Ohio: Meridian, 1962.

———: *The Oliver Wendell Holmes History of the*

Supreme Court. London: Collier-Macmillan, 1971– .

McCloskey, R.G.: *The Modern Supreme Court*. Cambridge, Mass.: Harvard University Press, 1972.

Schwartz, B.: *The Reins of Power: a constitutional history of the United States*. New York: Hill & Wang, 1963.

Warren, C.: *The Supreme Court in United States History*. 3 vols. Boston, Mass.: Little, Brown, 1922.

Supreme Soviet   In the USSR this is the legislative body, elected in union and autonomous republics as well as the national level, through which popular sovereignty is notionally expressed. As the national legislature it is described in the constitution as the 'highest body of state authority of the USSR' and enjoys the exclusive right to approve legislative acts of the USSR (Article 108). It is elected every five years by all citizens aged over eighteen and consists of two chambers, the Council of the Union (whose 750 deputies are elected from constituencies of equal population numbers) and the Council of Nationalities (whose 750 deputies are elected by the various national-territorial units of the USSR). Of the 1500 deputies elected in 1984 (the Eleventh Convocation), 71.4 per cent are members of the Communist Party of the Soviet Union, 51.3 per cent are workers or collective farmers, and 32.8 per cent are women. Sessions of the USSR Supreme Soviet take place twice a year. One of these meetings, usually in November or December, considers the annual plan and budget; the other, usually in the early summer, considers a variety of other matters. Each chamber of the supreme soviet elects seventeen standing commissions to deal with planning and budget, foreign affairs, industrial and other matters, with a total membership of 80.7 per cent of all deputies. The supreme soviet also elects the COUNCIL OF MINISTERS of the USSR (the Soviet government) and the Presidium (a kind of collective presidency). The USSR Supreme Soviet is conventionally dismissed as a 'rubber stamp' legislature. Particularly through its commissions, however, it has recently been showing signs of greater assertiveness, and even its formal sessions provide some opportunity for the advocacy of local interests as well as for the unanimous approval of government proposals.   SLW

Reading

Constitution (Fundamental Law) of the USSR. Moscow: Novosti, 1977.

White, S.: The USSR supreme soviet. In *Communist Legislatures in Comparative Perspective*, ed. D. Nelson and S. White. London: Macmillan, 1982.

survey research   See OPINION POLLS.

swing   A measure of the change in the relative strength of two parties between two elections. The term is of greatest utility in summarizing the results of an election held using a majority or plurality electoral system and where only two political parties or groupings have a realistic prospect of office. In consequence, it is most widely used in Britain, Australia and New Zealand, though surprisingly not in the United States.

The actual formula used to calculate swing varies. Three principal measures can be identified:

(1) *Total vote swing* between party A and party B is defined as:

$$\frac{\text{Change in party } A\text{s} \ \% \text{ share of vote} - \text{Change in party } B\text{s} \ \% \text{ share of vote}}{2}$$

(2) *Two party swing* between A and B is the change in A's share of the vote for A and B combined.

(3) *Electorate swing* is the same as total vote swing except that the calculation is based upon the change in A's and B's share of the electorate.

Total vote swing is the most apparently straightforward measure, but it has been criticized for its inconsistent and inadequate treatment of movement to and from third parties (Steed 1965). Two party swing has consequently been widely adopted in Australia (where the ALTERNATIVE VOTE system permits the redistribution of minor party first preferences between the two main parties) and New Zealand, and by some academics in Britain. Electorate swing has failed to achieve any widespread credibility; it can be shown to give misleading results when the level of turnout changes dramatically.

Following increased levels of support for third parties in Britain in the 1970s, some attempt has been made to develop methods of summarizing the movement of support in three-party contests. Most popular has been the use of the equilateral triangle which can be used to display graphically both the extent and the direction of the movement of votes in such contests, and from which summary measures can be derived. The technique is primarily a method of presentation and does not have any particular analytic utility.

The popularity of swing has been based upon its potential as a simple predictive tool. Plurality and majority electoral systems lack any rule linking seats won to votes cast across the country as a whole. But knowledge of the swing in the early results of a general election can enable one to state how many seats are likely to change hands between the two main parties, and therefore who is likely to form the next government. The seats expected to change hands are simply all those where the percentage majority of the party losing support is less than twice the swing. The calculation is based on the assumption that there is little variation in the swing from one constituency to another.

The assumption of 'uniform' swing is based upon a fundamental paradox. It assumes that a party will lose the same absolute percentage share of the vote in each constituency and not, as one might intuitively anticipate, the same proportionate amount. If the latter were true, the fall in a party's share of the vote would be greater where it had previously been strong and less where it had been weak. But the assumption of proportionate loss has been shown to involve logical absurdities and has in practice not occurred. Although one important attempt was made by Butler and Stokes (1975) to discover why swing was largely invariant with previous party strength, the phenomenon is still not fully understood.   JKC

Reading

Berrington, H.: The General Election of 1964.

Journal of the Royal Statistical Society 128 (Series A) (1965) 17–66.

Butler, D.: *The Electoral System in Britain since 1918.* Oxford: Clarendon Press, 1963.

——— and Stokes, D.: *Political Change in Britain,* pp. 140–51. London: Macmillan, 1975.

McLean, I.: The problem of proportionate swing. *Political Studies* 21 (1973) 57–63.

Miller, W.: Symmetric representation of political trends in three-party systems with some properties, extensions and examples. *Quality and Quantity* 11 (1977) 27–41.

Steed, M.: An analysis of the results. *The British General Election of 1964,* pp. 337–8, ed. D. Butler and A. King. London: Macmillan, 1965.

syndicalism   Known in France as 'revolutionary syndicalism' it also thrived in Italy, Spain and Latin America in the generation leading up to 1914. The word itself simply means trade-unionism, and stood for the particular form of unionism which predominated in those countries. The ideas of syndicalism shared with contemporary SOCIALISM a rejection of capitalist relations of production and a belief in a worker-led revolution; they differed in their espousal of DIRECT ACTION and in rejecting parliamentary activity and any compromise with the state, which was seen as an inherently oppressive institution. Influenced by Proudhon and Blanqui, syndicalism has some affinities with anarchism and militant syndicalism has sometimes been called 'anarcho-syndicalism'.

In the place of state or municipal control, syndicalists favoured a society based on worker-controlled production units, with no central authority. Such a system was to be brought about by class warfare culminating in a GENERAL STRIKE. The organization and leadership of the revolutionary workers should come from within the working class, rather than being provided from the outside by political parties (including the socialists).

Although variants of syndicalism existed in Britain (GUILD SOCIALISM) and the USA (the International Workers of the World), the guiding spirit of the movement was French, and with the coming of the first world war and the wartime collaboration of the French unions, it was weakened and became divided.

Some syndicalists became communists (see COMMUNIST PARTIES) for a time, others took their hostility to the liberal state into the nascent Fascist parties (see FASCISM); a significant number in Spain were active in the anarchist organizations during the Civil War. But the increased involvement of unions with the state resulting from the experiences of war, and the absorption of revolutionary energies into LENINISM effectively ended the appeal of syndicalism and its aspirations to all but a handful of industrial workers.

See also LABOUR MOVEMENT; SOCIALIST AND SOCIAL DEMOCRATIC PARTIES; SOREL; TRADE UNIONS.   TRJ

Reading

Geary, R.J.: *European Labour Protest 1848–1939*. London: Croom Helm, 1981.

Julliard, J.: *Fernand Pelloutier et les origines du syndicalisme d'action directe*. Paris: Éditions du Seuil, 1971.

Ridley, F.F.: *Revolutionary Syndicalism in France: the direct action of its time*. Cambridge: Cambridge University Press, 1970.

Roberts, D.L.: *The Syndicalist Tradition in Italian Fascism*. Chapel Hill: University of North Carolina Press, 1979.

Sorel, G.: *Reflections on Violence*, trans. T.E. Hulme and J. Roth. London: Macmillan, 1950.

Stearns, P.N.: *Revolutionary Syndicalism and French Labor*. New Brunswick, NJ: Rutgers University Press, 1971.

systems analysis   A specific concept in political science which came into general usage in the late 1950s (Easton 1957) and identifies a specific mode of analysis for the empirical understanding of the way in which POLITICAL SYSTEMS operate. As a conceptual framework it aims to provide a possible starting point for the development of a general theory of politics; that is, a theory which would be equally applicable to any and all political systems, whether contemporary or ancient, public or private, modern or developing, democratic, totalitarian or dictatorial. It differs from traditional political theory in that, while stressing the importance of moral issues, it focuses on an empirically based explanation of political life.

Systems analysis was developed as a specific way of analysing political life. It needs to be clearly differentiated from general systems theory which seeks to formulate a body of knowledge that applies to systems at all levels, from the subatomic, through the molecular to the cellular, organismic, social and galactic. It looks for isomorphic laws or generalizations applicable across the board. Systems analysis neither assumes that such isomorphisms need exist nor, if they do, that they would be sufficiently specific to be useful in analysing important social phenomena.

Systems analysis also needs to be distinguished from operations research. This is a form of analysis, sometimes called linear programming, which does encourage the spread of systems thinking as a way of solving problems. However, it is more concerned with the design of systems in which goals are externally specified than in the understanding and explanation of the way in which self-regulating and self-determining systems – characteristic of most social systems including political systems – operate.

Every theory distinguishes itself by the kind of central problem it addresses. Systems analysis poses the following question: how does it happen that political systems come into being, survive, take certain forms, change and disappear? In pursuit of answers to these questions systems analysis begins with the notion that politics, however we may define it, is embedded in all of social life. If we are to be able to understand it we must find some way of cutting through the complexities of the relationships within political life itself and with the rest of society.

Systems analysis seeks to achieve this by analytically separating politics from all other aspects of society. Even though it is obvious that we cannot do so empirically, this operation does enable us to simplify complex social processes and structures for the purposes of analysis. We are then in a position to identify specifically political issues and to trace out the way in which they are influenced by and in turn influence those other aspects of society of which they may be an integral part.

This objective informs the whole mode of analysis. To this end it introduces a simplified imagery of a political system viewing it as a 'box' into which inputs from the social environment flow. These inputs are then converted through various political structures and processes, within the 'box' or system, into outputs or policies; the latter in turn may influence the social environment – economy, culture, social structure, ecology and the like – or the political system itself. These effects then flow back (feedback) through various complex social processes into the political system. In that way they influence another round of inputs.

To further simplify the analysis, the significant inputs are reduced to two: demands and support; and outputs are reduced to one: binding decisions. Demands may arise from any source – the people, politicians, administrators, opinion leaders and so on – depending on the nature of the regime. Support is particularly relevant because its variability affects the destinies of the political authorities (often called governments), the regime (democratic, authoritarian, and the like), and the political community. Outputs are created in all political systems through special processes that lead to their acceptance as binding by most members of the society most of the time.

In this view the inputs and outputs are major ways in which, analytically as well as empirically, the effects of all kinds of social behaviour and institutions are communicated to political life and through which each thereby influences the other. Through the way in which a system copes with its inputs the stability of one or another major aspect of the system (its political authorities, regime or political community) is assured or changed.

Two other general theoretical approaches have stood as competitors to systems analysis. One, functional analysis (Almond 1970), ended by absorbing a systems analytic point of view with many of its major terms and sought to fuse it with traditional functional analysis borrowed from anthropology and sociology. The other has been MARXISM, particularly in its structuralist version as formulated by Althusser and Poulantzas. Systems analysis has always claimed that its scope was broader than that of Marxist theory and, without necessarily passing judgement on the latter, interpreted it as a subset or variant of systems thinking. The dependence of such Marxists as Miliband as well as Poulantzas himself, in his later work, on the notion of system can be said to give some credibility to this claim.

Many of the major concepts and orientations of systems analysis have now been absorbed into normal political research, such as the terms political system, policy outputs, demands, support, political feedback and the like. We can find them particularly evident in such varied areas as comparative politics, policy analysis, legitimacy, violence, alienation, political support, political socialization and opinion formation.

See also FUNCTIONALISM; POLICY OUTPUT STUDIES.

DE

Reading

Almond, G.A.: *Political Development*. Boston, Mass.: Little, Brown, 1970.

Easton, D.: An approach to the analysis of political systems. In *World Politics* 9 (1957) 383–400.

————: *A Systems Analysis of Political Life*. New York: Wiley, 1965; Chicago, Ill.: University of Chicago Press, 1979.

————: *A Framework for Political Analysis* (1965). 2nd edn. Chicago, Ill.: University of Chicago Press, 1979.

Miliband, R.: *The State in Capitalist Society*. London: Weidenfeld & Nicolson, 1969.

T

tax revolt parties Protest parties, generally although not exclusively appealing mainly to the lower middle class, the prototype of which was POUJADISM which gained 12.3 per cent of the vote in the French general election of 1956. Tax revolt parties in other countries are largely a phenomenon of the 1970s, especially in Scandinavia, where they are known misleadingly by the term Progressive or Progress Party. The leading such party was Mogens Glistrup's Progress Party which succeeded in winning nearly 16 per cent of the vote in Denmark in its first parliamentary electoral contest in 1973. Since then, however, its vote has steadily declined.

Tax revolt parties should not be assimilated to CONSERVATIVE or to FASCIST PARTIES. Although they might on occasion be xenophobic, they are rarely racist or authoritarian; and they often favour drastic reductions in defence budgets. Tax revolt parties symbolize a growing and specifically contemporary disenchantment with the WELFARE STATE and its concomitant BUREAUCRACY.

See also POPULISM.   VBB

Reading

Nielsen, H.-J.: The uncivic culture: attitudes towards the political system in Denmark and the vote for the Progressive Party in 1973–1975. *Scandinavian Political Studies* (1976) 147–55.

technocracy Rule or tendency to rule by technical experts. In *The Rise of the Technocrats* (1965), W. H. G. Armytage describes the St Simonians, followers of Count Henri de Saint-Simon (1760–1825), as 'the first technocrats: apostles of the religion of industry'. The term itself was coined by Californian engineer William H. Smyth in 1919 for an organization, Technocracy Inc. This arose from a group, the 'technical alliance', for whom Thorstein Veblen's book *The Engineers and the Price System* (1921) and especially its final chapter, 'A memorandum on a practical soviet of technicians', became a central text. In the early 1930s, thanks largely to Howard Scott, the concept achieved some popular resonance, only to be overtaken by the New Deal. Jean Meynaud in *Technocracy* (1968, p. 212) found the term 'common' in France but 'comparatively unknown' elsewhere in Europe. Several authors have coined similar neologisms. For example: President Eisenhower in his Farewell Address, 17 January 1961 warned that public policy could become the 'captive of a scientific-technological elite'; J. K. Galbraith defined the Technostructure as 'all who participate in group decision-making or the organisation which they form'; Nigel Calder (*Technopolis*, pp. 22–3) states that 'we inhabit Technopolis, a society not only shaped but continuously modified in drastic ways by scientific and technical novelty'; Zbigniew Brzezinski argues that 'the post-industrial society is becoming a technocratic society: a society shaped by the impact of technology and electronics'.

ECONOMIC PLANNING, operations research, SYSTEMS ANALYSIS and technology assessment, etc. are evidently all technocratic activities, and the technocratic tendency is seemingly inevitable in advanced industrial societies. However, political disagreements arise over ends as much as means and here technocrats have no special advantage. They can also disagree among themselves. Alvin M. Weinberg defines 'trans-scientific' questions as questions 'which can be asked by science and yet *which cannot be answered by science*'. It follows that although some societies (for example France under the Fourth Republic) and institutions (such as the Pentagon when Robert McNamara was Defence Secretary) seem to be more technocratic than most, true government by technocracy is an unrealized, and unlikely, extreme. RW

Reading

Armytage, W.H.G.: *The Rise of the Technocrats*. London: Routledge & Kegan Paul, 1965.

Brzezinski, Z.: *Between Two Ages*. New York: Viking, 1970; London: Greenwood, 1982.

Calder, N.: *Technopolis*. London: MacGibbon & Kee, 1969.

Galbraith, J.K.: *The New Industrial State*, chs 2 and 6. New York and Harmondsworth: Pelican, 1967, 1969.

Meynaud, J.: *Technocracy*, trans. P. Barnes. New York: Free Press, 1968.

Public Papers of the Presidents: Dwight D. Eisenhower, pp. 1035–40. Washington, DC: US Government Printing Office, 1961.

Veblen, T.: *The Engineers and the Price System*. New York: Viking, 1921.

Weinberg, A.M.: Science and trans-science. *Minerva* 10.2 (1972) 204–22.

territorial politics A subject that can be defined as 'that arena of political activity concerned with the relations between the central political institutions in the capital city and those interests, communities, political organizations and governmental bodies outside the central institutional complex, but within the accepted boundaries of the state, which possess, or are commonly perceived to possess, a significant geographical or local/regional character' (Bulpitt 1983). It is concerned with a new perspective on and a series of messages about a very old subject, namely CENTRAL/LOCAL RELATIONS. It should be stressed, however, that no coherent inter-

national school of territorial politics analysis exists. The label territorial politics, and some of the ideas associated with it, are increasingly used, but the subject is still at an early stage of development.

This perspective developed in the 1970s as a result of the perceived inadequacies of the traditional, and some of the emerging, analytical frameworks then employed to study central/local relations, inadequacies highlighted by their inability to effectively explain the politicization of those relations which occurred in many western countries during that decade. Academic memories however are notoriously short: it is rare for any new approach to develop from a *tabula rasa*. Carpenter (1963), Maass (1959) and Grodzins (1966) pay tribute to some earlier and excellent attempts to improve the study of central/local relations, attempts which should still influence territorial politics analysis today.

Traditionally central/local relations were examined within the confines of one or other of two related paradigms, namely the FEDERAL/unitary and the decentralization/centralization dichotomies. In the 1970s two further approaches surfaced, both linked with Marxism: the INTERNAL COLONIALISM thesis and the production/collective consumption theory of dual state functions. All these differed in well-known and important ways. The important point, however, is that they shared so many analytical weaknesses. For example, the scope of central/local relations analysis was largely confined (with the exception of the internal colonialism thesis) to INTERGOVERNMENTAL RELATIONS, particularly relations between the central government and elected local or regional governments. Again, running through all such approaches was a series of assumptions unfavourable to central controls, though curiously this was associated with a marked reluctance to examine seriously the resources or intentions of central authorities. Above all, these approaches exhibited a high propensity to explain central/local relations without recourse to politics. Explanations tended to be 'read off' from a variety of other determining factors – constitutional, organizational, cultural, economic – central/local relations analysis was depoliticized. Or, if politics did impinge it was as an activity separate from politics in the rest of the system.

The territorial politics perspective represents an attempt to avoid these weaknesses. 'Territory' is emphasized because it is the generic label which seems to encompass most appropriately the actors and interest in this arena. Its employment means that the analytical scenario is extended in a number of ways. First, as well as governments at the local level, consideration must be given to local party and pressure group organizations and, more generally, the interests of, and those within, local communities. And attention must be paid to the whole range of governments at the local level, nominated as well as elected. All this makes it possible to construct a broad picture of the local political system or systems. Secondly, it is accepted that territorial interests are often articulated by a variety of local organizations within the central institutional complex in the capital city. In other words, the paradox of territorial politics is that the defence and promotion of territorial interests may be a game played for the most part in the capital. This poses considerable problems for traditional definitions of centralization. Equally important, it suggests that variations in territorial politics between countries may be less the consequence of formal rules regulating intergovernmental relations and more a function of the differing displacements of territorial interests in the capital city institutions. Comparisons between supposedly centralized France and Italy, and Britain, the home of local self-government, may have to be revised if this dimension of territorial politics is stressed. Third, the resources, assumptions, or intentions of the central authorities require special attention within this framework. It cannot be casually assumed that all 'centres' desire more control over territorial interests, or that if they do, they have the resources to easily pursue that goal. The effective management of territory (in all its dimensions) is one of the most difficult tasks facing politicians at the centre in pluralist systems, but it is just one of many problems in the twentieth century. It follows that territorial managements and politics cannot be divorced from the management of, and politics in, other policy arenas. Fourth, in these circumstances, the analysis should be particularly concerned to identify the broad strategies, or management codes, or statecraft, pursued by governments at the centre in relation to territorial politics over time. In other words, the approach should be developmental or historical, paying particular attention to the rise and fall of territorial statecraft regimes. In the UK, for example, this sort of analysis has drawn attention to the existence of a highly idiosyncratic territorial regime which existed and persisted from the early 1920s to the early 1960s. Throughout this period the centre (in this instance the cabinet and the civil service) managed territorial politics via a docile parliament, insulated from territorial pressures, and what amounted to a complicated system of indirect rule in which both the centre and its local collaborators gained a degree of relative operational autonomy from one another. This sort of regime does not correspond to any of the models associated with the other approaches to central/local relations.

Both the methodology and the messages of territorial politics analysis are contested. It is easy to see why. Territory is a difficult currency in which to deal. And the stress on political strategies from the centre leads to criticisms that the approach is elitist and conservative in character. American political science, however, might regard the concerns of this approach as a statement of the obvious. If so, it gives some idea of the poverty of central/local relations analysis in Britain and Europe before this approach emerged.

See also CENTRALIZATION AND DECENTRALIZATION; URBAN POLITICS.   JB

Reading

Bulpitt, J.: *Territory and Power in the United Kingdom*. Manchester: Manchester University Press, 1983.

Carpenter, J.T.C.: *The South as a Conscious Minority, 1789–1861*. Gloucester, Mass.: Smith, 1963.

Duchacek, I.D.: *Comparative Federalism: the territorial dimension of politics*. New York: Holt, Rinehart & Winston, 1970.

Grodzins, M.: *The American System: a new view of government in the United States*. Chicago, Ill.: Rand McNally, 1966.

Maass, A. ed.: *Area and Power: a theory of local government*. Glencoe, Ill.: Free Press of Glencoe, 1959.

Madgwick, P. and Rose, R. eds: *The Territorial Dimension in United Kingdom Politics*. London: Macmillan, 1983.

Rokkan, S. and Urwin, D.W. eds: *The Politics of Territorial Identity: studies in European regionalism*. London: Sage, 1982.

Rose, R.: *Understanding the United Kingdom: the territorial dimension in government*. London: Longman, 1982.

Tarrow, S., Katzenstein, P.J. and Graziano, L. eds: *Territorial Politics in Industrial Nations*. New York and London: Praeger, 1978.

terror A technique used regularly through history to maintain power and enforce policies by arousing fear in the ruled. The objective is usually to assure compliance and preclude opposition, but it can go beyond this to become an instrument of socialization, by which the ruler seeks to internalize a set of values in the rule. In this sense, terror should be distinguished from arbitrary violence which may be little more than banditry and has no major objective other than itself. In the modern period terror has generally referred to revolutionary terror, when the newly established revolutionary rulers deliberately use high levels of force to destroy real or assumed enemies and to reshape society according to their vision. In these circumstances terror is usually mass terror, involving the exercise of violence on large numbers of people. Terror will often be practised highly visibly, conceivably in a ritualistic or liturgical fashion. The show trials in Eastern Europe in the 1950s could be regarded as symbolic acting out of the revolutionary party's claim to omniscience backed up by control of total force.

The Jacobins during the FRENCH REVOLUTION used terror in this way, with the aim of physically liquidating the former elite. Even more ambitious were the totalitarian systems of the twentieth century, such as Hitler's Germany and post-revolutionary Soviet Union, where terror was the expressly chosen instrument of the ruler wielded to effect a 'revolutionary transformation'. STALIN deployed what has been called 'prophylactic terror', with the aim of destroying the possibility of dissent even before it was conceived of by its agent. The most extreme instance has unquestionably been Cambodia, where Pol Pot's Khmer Rouge engaged in auto-genocide with the goal of liquidating all vestiges of the previous order in order to create the potential for a totally new system. The idea underlying this process is that only the elimination of all representatives of the *ancien régime* can ensure the lasting revolutionary purity of the revolutionary order.

The time-scale of terror is generally relatively short, lasting a few years at most. After this it tends to decline and give way to a more routinely ordered administration. In these circumstances however, without a change in the continuity of regime, the threat of terror alone can keep a population submissive for a long period. After experiencing terror, societies will look for a period of tranquillity. During this period even mild concessions offered by the ruler will be accepted by the population as a major step. The effectiveness of terror is considerable if the goal is the maintenance of regime power and all else is subordinated to this (as has been the case in Soviet-type systems). The population subjected to terror, however, becomes passive, resentful and unwilling to accord the system any more than external compliance. Terror undermines initiative and innovativeness, resulting in poor economic performance and technological impoverishment; it socializes the population more into external obedience than into the conscious acceptance of post-revolutionary norms. (See also POLITICAL VIOLENCE; REVOLUTION; TOTALITARIANISM.) GSsh

Reading

Adelman, J.R. ed.: *Terror and Communist Politics*. Boulder, Col.: Westview, 1984.

Conquest, R.: *The Great Terror*, rev. edn. Harmondsworth: Penguin, 1971.

Kuper, L.: *Genocide*. New Haven, Conn.: Yale University Press, 1981.

Mackenzie, W.J.M.: *Power, Violence, Decision*. London: Penguin, 1975.

Walker, E.: *Terror and Resistance*. London: Oxford University Press, 1969.

terrorism A term which is not a synonym for violence and insurgency in general, but describes a special kind of violence, a weapons system that can be used on its own or as part of a whole repertoire of unconventional warfare. In Central America, for example, terrorism is typically used in conjunction with rural GUERRILLA WARFARE and with economic and political warfare in all-out bids to topple government; in Western Europe, which experiences a great many international terrorist incidents annually, terrorism is not usually accompanied by any wider insurgency. It is extreme, often indiscriminate violence directed at innocent people, but it is at the pre-insurgency phase.

Terrorism can be briefly defined as coercive intimidation, or more fully as the systematic use of murder, injury, and destruction, or threat of same, to create a climate of terror, to publicize a cause, and to coerce a wider target into submitting to its aims. International terrorism is terrorism exported across international frontiers or used against foreign targets in the terrorists' country of origin. There is no case of purely domestic terrorism, but there are, of course, many campaigns in which the political violence is concentrated in a single national territory or region (for example, the Irish Republican Army (IRA), and the Basque and Corsican terrorists).

A major characteristic of political terror is its indiscriminate nature. This is not to deny that terrorists generally have a specific human 'target', whether individual or collective, which they intend shall be the victim of the most direct physical harm. Quite apart from the physical danger of persons who are not pre-selected targets being hurt, there is the unavoidable side effect of widespread fear that others might be harmed. As Raymond Aron remarks in one of his most percipient observations on terror:

An action of violence is labelled 'terrorist' when its psychological effects are out of proportion to its purely physical result. In this sense, the so-called indiscriminate acts of revolutionaries are terrorist, as were the Anglo-American zone bombings. The lack of discrimination helps to spread fear, for if no one in particular is a target, no one can be safe.

Terrorists are frequently prepared to engage in the indiscriminate murder of civilians. Men, women, and children alike, regardless of their role or position in society, may be regarded as potential victims for the sake of the 'cause'. As a policy the waging of terror necessarily involves disregarding the rules and conventions of war: non-combatants, hostages, prisoners-of-war and neutrals have no inviolable rights in their eyes.

It is also characteristic of acts of terror that they appear entirely unpredictable and arbitrary to the society which suffers them. One writer has expressed this point very clearly: '. . . no observance of commands, no matter how punctilious, on the part of the prospective victims can ensure their safety'. There are of course many instances of individual victims of terroristic assassination or mass murder being given preliminary warning that they are to die. The point is that such warnings are only 'selective' and 'predictable' according to the rationalizations of the terrorists. As Malraux writes 'le terroriste décidât seul, exécutât seul', and it is in this sense true to describe terrorism as a peculiar kind of tyranny in which the potential victim is unable to do anything to avoid his destruction because the terrorist is operating and judging on the basis of his own idiosyncratic code of rules and values. These characteristics of unpredictability and arbitrariness also apply in the case of the repressive terror of the STATE for two major reasons. First, leaders and agencies of force in the state, who have acquired the preponderance of coercive power, may disregard the underlying values and norms of the existing law with impunity within their domain. Second, tyrannical DICTATORS or totalitarian governments (see TOTALITARIANISM) tend in the process of consolidating their power to subvert and manipulate the legal structure in order to forge it into a weapon for the oppression of their internal opponents.

Political TERROR can be differentiated from other forms of violence, agitation, intimidation and coercion by virtue of its extreme and ruthlessly destructive methods. These may range from genocide, massacre, political murder and torture at one end of the scale of violence, to physical beatings, harassment and defamation campaigns at the other. For any large-scale campaign of repressive or of revolutionary terror, the terrorists find it necessary to arm themselves adequately to check any possible resistance. Whereas spears and machetes were once adequate weapons in African tribal regimes of terror, and the famous sect of the Assassins in the eleventh and twelfth centuries used the dagger, modern terrorists must depend upon a minimal supply of guns and explosives. The factor of dependence upon weaponry, combined with the reliance of many terrorist movements and agencies upon a military organizational structure and style, underlines the close relationship between terrorism and warfare. Indeed, many American and French scholars have been so impressed by this affinity that they have tended to study terror exclusively in the context of 'internal war' and problems of 'counter-insurgency'.

It is in practice extremely difficult to draw clear boundaries between war and terror. Walter (1969), in his pioneering sociological analysis of the regime of terror, argues that, unlike civil terror which has the aim of controlling the enemy population, military terror aims ultimately at its extermination. 'When violence is employed in the service of power, the limit of force is the destruction of the thing that is forced' (p. 13). But there are two serious confusions in Walter's argument. First, we cannot assume that all wars are wars of extermination: even in modern wars distinctions are sometimes made between the civilian population and the armed forces of protagonists, and one of the normal strategic objectives is still the acquisition and control of enemy territories and their inhabitants. Second, and more important, internal revolutionary and state terror can both be directed at the deliberate destruction of whole social groups who have been designated as enemies. Terrorists may believe such a policy of liquidation to be necessary in order to capture or sustain their political control, or it may be dictated by ideological reasons, or it may derive from motives of hatred, vengeance or even sadism or mass hysteria, or a combination of these factors. The point to be made is that, historically, acts of civil terror have not,

unfortunately, always stopped short at the subjugation of certain real or imagined opponents. Totalitarian regimes of terror have committed crimes against humanity on a vast scale. We have no right to assume that the perpetrators of civil terror will arrive by some rational calculation at a notional limit to violence, and that they will always rule out extermination. As for the implications for political control, mass murders will intensify rather than extinguish the general terror: everyone in the population will be terrified lest they be caught in the next wave of terror. Thus, although this entry does not attempt a detailed analysis of war terror (i.e. terroristic usages in military conflict), any discussion of terrorism must include consideration of the many kinds of destruction against the civil population which can be understood as what Hobbes called 'hostile acts', or acts of war against the population.

What fundamentally distinguishes terrorism from other forms of organized violence is not simply its severity, but its features of amorality and antinomianism. Terrorists either profess indifference to existing moral codes or else claim exemption from all such obligations. Political terror, if it is waged consciously and deliberately, is implicitly prepared to sacrifice all moral and humanitarian consideration for the sake of some political end. Ideologies of terrorism assume that the death and suffering of those who are innocent of any crime are means entirely justified by their political ends. In their most explicit and candidly amoral form such terrorist rationalizations amount to a Nietzschean doctrine of the Will to Power. Might is right; terror can always be justified as the expediency of the strong; and such Judaeo–Christian notions as mercy, compassion and conscience must go with the weak to the wall of history. Political terror is not always justified in such explicit terms. Some utopian or messianic sects and movements that have resorted to terror have attempted a teleological justification, generally involving the rejection of all existing ethical principles and codes on the grounds that morality is manipulated in the interests of the rulers. In some cases it is argued that the acts of terror are necessary sacrifices to be made on the

609

journey towards introducing a new revolutionary order which will introduce a New Man and a New Order and a Revolutionary Morality. But the first task is that the existing order and morality are destroyed.

Having identified some of the key characteristics common to all forms of political terror: indiscriminateness, unpredictability, arbitrariness, ruthless destructiveness and the implicitly amoral and antinomian nature of a terrorist's challenge, there remains the important distinction between political terror and political terrorism. Political terror may occur in isolated acts and also in the form of extreme, indiscriminate and arbitrary mass violence, such as the insurrectionary outburst that characterized the lynchings and sackings at the height of the popular Terror in parts of revolutionary France. Such terror is not systematic, it is unorganized and is often impossible to control. Therefore neither one isolated act, nor a series of random acts is terrorism. Political terrorism, properly speaking, is a sustained policy involving the waging of organized terror either on the part of the state, a movement or faction, or by a small group of individuals. Systematic terrorism invariably entails some organizational structure, however rudimentary, and some kind of theory or ideology of terror.

See also POLITICAL VIOLENCE   PW

Reading

Evans, A.E. and Murphy, J. eds: *Legal Aspects of International Terrorism*. Lexington, Mass.: Heath, 1978.

Friedlander, R.: *Terrorism: documents of international and local control*. 3 vols. New York: Oceana, Dobbs Ferry, 1979–81.

Fromm, E.: *The Anatomy of Human Destructiveness*. London: Cape, 1974.

Gross, F.: *The Seizure of Political Power*. New York: Philosophical Library, 1958.

Kuper, L.: *Genocide*. New Haven, Conn. and London: Yale University Press, 1981.

Laqueur, W.: *Terrorism*. London: Weidenfeld & Nicolson, 1977.

Norton, A.R. and Greenberg, M.H.: *International Terrorism: an annotated bibliography*. Boulder, Col.: Westview, 1979.

Walter, E.: *Terror and Resistance*. London: Oxford University Press, 1969.

Wilkinson, P.: *Political Terrorism*. London: Macmillan, 1974.

———: *Terrorism and the Liberal State*, rev. edn. London: Macmillan, 1986.

theocracy   A term derived from the Greek *Theos* (god) and *Kratia* (rule). Coined by Josephus (Contra Apion: Whiston edn, II.17) to describe the Jewish polity: '[Moses] ordained our government to be what, by a strained expression, may be termed a theocracy.' The term has sometimes been applied to polities where the head of the secular system is also the head of the religious hierarchy (see MacIver) but this is commonly rejected, (for example by Weber who defines this instead as '*Caesaropapism*' as, notably, in the Byzantine Empire. The two forms, commonly recognized as being theocracy are:

(1) Where God is recognized as the immediate ruler and His laws are taken as the legal code of the community and are expounded and administered by holy men as His agents. Such was the situation in ancient Israel under the Judges (Shofetim) up to the advent of the monarchy under Saul; writers, divines and lexicographers have generally taken this as the paradigm case (see Jellinek; MacIver). Parallels can be found in Geneva under Calvin and the Consistory after 1555. A variant was at times found in Tibet where the Dalai Lama, recognized as the incarnation of the Buddha, governed with the assistance of a monkly consistory as both religious and secular ruler. (2) Where the temporal ruler is subjected to the final direction of the theological head. Such a claim was made by the papacy at various times, notably by Gregory VII (1073–85) and stated most explicitly by Boniface VIII in Unam Sanctam (1302): the spiritual power is higher than the temporal and is to be judged by it. The temporal 'sword' is to be wielded by the kings, but only at the command and with the permission of the spiritual power.   SEF

Reading

Gierke, O.: *Political Theories in the Middle Ages*. Cambridge: Cambridge University Press, 1900.

Jellinek, G.: *Allgemeine staatslehre*. 3rd edn. Berlin: Altenburg, 1920.

MacIver, R.M.: *The Web of Government*. New York: Collier-Macmillan, 1965.

Vaux, R. de: *Ancient Israel*. London: Darlin, Longman & Todd, 1961.

Weber, M.: *Economy and Society: an outline of interpretive sociology*. 3 vols. ed. G. Roth and C. Wittich. New York: Bedminster, 1968.

think tank An imprecise term current since the early 1960s, used loosely of a wide range of different types of institutions engaged in public policy analysis and/or research. It was originally applied to scientific and other research institutes in the USA. Although such bodies undertook contract work for government they were usually not wholly dependent on government, being funded also by foundations and by private firms. The earliest of these was the Brookings Institution, founded in 1916. The Rand Corporation was set up in 1946 at the Douglas Aircraft Company by the US Air Force, but was turned into an independent non-profit enterprise in 1948. Other well-known think tanks include the Hudson Institute, and the Stanford Research Institute. 'Think Tanks' of this kind are multidisciplinary; they carry out research, publish, organize private and public discussion, and advise the executive and the legislature. They are permanent bodies but can provide half-way houses among their staffs for academics wishing to move closer to public affairs or for public servants wishing to think. Numbers of staff range from one to two hundred to several thousand.

During the 1970s these think tanks of a broadly liberal/Keynesian cast of character were joined by new bodies with a more openly free enterprise, right wing orientation, such as the American Enterprise Institute or the Heritage Foundation. These newer bodies seem to see their main function as providing intellectual support for politicians, moderate and radical, in government and in opposition. Professor Yehezkel Dror excludes some of these on the grounds that a true think tank should not be affiliated to a political party. (By his definition it should also contain at least twenty-five full-time professional staff.)

Both types of think tank are found in Britain where they are smaller in scale and usually less influential. The Policy Studies Institute (incorporating the former Political and Economic Planning), the National Institute for Economic and Social Research, or the Royal Institute of International Affairs are examples of the former kind. A more free-market philosophy is expressed by the Institute of Economic Affairs, the Adam Smith Institute, or the more recent Centre for Policy Studies. Staff members may be as few as eight or ten, and rarely exceed fifty. In Britain the term think tank was also commonly applied to a very different body, the Central Policy Review Staff. This was a policy analysis unit within government and was based in the Cabinet Office for the whole of its existence (1971–83). It was wholly funded by the government and worked exclusively for the prime minister and cabinet.

The term is not often used elsewhere in Europe though it could be applied to several institutions, such as the Netherlands Scientific Council for Government Policy (government-funded but independent). This reports to the cabinet and to parliament (all its reports are published). There are some multi-national think tanks in Europe, such as the International Institute for Applied Systems Analysis in Austria and the European Centre for Policy Studies in Brussels. WP

Reading

Dickson, P.: *Think Tanks*. New York: Atheneum, 1971.

Dror, Y.: Required break-throughs in think tanks. *Policy Sciences* 16 (1984).

Marsh, I.: *An Australian Think Tank*. Melbourne: New South Wales University Press, 1981.

Plowden, W.: The British Central Policy Review Staff. In *Policy Analysis and Policy Innovation: patterns, problems and potentials*, ed. P.R. Baehr and B. Wittrock. London: Sage, 1981.

—— ed.: *Advising Governments*. Oxford: Blackwell, 1987.

threshold See ELECTORAL SYSTEMS.

ticket-splitting The practice of splitting one's vote between candidates of different parties in American elections. It is the opposite

611

of straight-ticket voting, i.e. voting for all a party's candidates regardless of the office. In nineteenth-century American elections ballots in most states were issued by the parties themselves, thus making ticket-splitting both difficult and hazardous. Ticket-splitting was greatly expedited during the Progressive Era (1900–1917) by the universal replacement of the party ballot by the government-printed or 'Australian' ballot. The gradually diminishing number of states (nineteen in 1984) using the 'party-column' rather than the 'office-block' ballot has also made ticket-splitting much easier in recent decades. From the Progressive Era onwards levels of ticket-splitting have risen continuously reflecting the decline of party loyalties in the US and the decreasing relevance of parties in American government. America's liberal political creed further encourages ticket-splitting by stressing the virtues of political independence and voting for 'the person rather than the party'. Of course this also implies control of political institutions in the United States being divided between the parties. The frequency of divided partisan control of the federal government since the early 1950s has led many distinguished commentators to condemn ticket-splitting as highly detrimental to effective government. Some have proposed reforms, such as a presidential–congressional 'team ticket' or giving the party which wins the presidency 'bonus' seats in Congress, which would either make ticket-splitting more difficult or mitigate its effects. Anti-partisanship is so deeply ingrained in modern American political culture however that such proposals have little prospect of being implemented.

See also DEALIGNMENT. NCR

Reading

Burnham, W.D.: *Critical Elections and the Mainsprings of American Politics*. New York: Norton, 1970.

DeVries, W. and Tarrance, V.L.: *The Ticket-Splitter: a new force in American politics*. Grand Rapids, Mich.: Eerdmans, 1972.

Ladd, E.C. Jr. with Hadley, C.D.: *Transformations of the American Party System*. 2nd edn, pp. 320–33. New York: Norton, 1978.

Nie, N.H., Verba, S. and Petrocik, J.R.: *The Changing American Voter*. 2nd edn, ch. 4. Cambridge, Mass.: Harvard University Press, 1979.

Sundquist, J.L.: *Constitutional Reform and Effective Government*, pp. 75–84. Washington, DC: The Brookings Institution, 1986.

Wattenberg, M.P.: *The Decline of American Political Parties 1952–1980*. Cambridge, Mass.: Harvard University Press, 1984.

Tocqueville, Alexis de (1805–1959) The son of an ancient and distinguished noble family in France, Tocqueville's contribution to modern democratic political and historical thinking has been immense. His nine-month visit to the United States in 1831–2 resulted in the two volumes of *Democracy in America* (*De la démocratie en Amérique*, published 1835, 1840) which made him famous. He was elected to the French National Assembly and to the Académie Française. His political influence was limited; however, attention came to Tocqueville in 1848 when, in a speech in the Chamber, he alone predicted the coming of the revolution which soon overthrew the regime of Louis Philippe. During the short-lived Second Republic Tocqueville served as chairman of the committee drafting a new constitution; in 1849 he was, for a few months, Minister of Foreign Affairs. He opposed the imperial regime of Louis Napoleon. In 1850, suffering from his recurrent pulmonary illnesses, he retired to Sorrento where he wrote his *Recollections* (*Souvenirs*). This incomparable account of men and crises was meant only for himself; it was discovered and published by his nephew more than thirty years after Tocqueville's death.

In 1853 Tocqueville began to write a history of the origins and development of the French Revolution. The first volume, *The Old Regime and the French Revolution*, was published in 1856. He was at work on the succeeding volume, carrying his unique interpretation of events beyond 1789, when he fell ill again. He died in 1859. He had married Marie Mottley, a middle-class Englishwoman, and left no heirs.

Besides the above-mentioned three principal works and a number of shorter historical and political studies the corpus of Tocqueville's writing includes his astonishingly extensive and important correspondence. Letter-writing served him as a diary would another thinker. In some of his letters we find the germ of ideas he would later develop in a book; we may also find in his letters ideas about a variety of important themes that we cannot find elsewhere. The range of topics is enormous, including such matters as religion, race, India, China, America, and shortcomings in the thinking of Plato, Aristotle and Newton.

During the nineteenth century Tocqueville's influence on political thinking was limited. He was respected for his analysis of American DEMOCRACY, but mostly outside his own country, among certain American and English liberal thinkers. The very reception of *Democracy in America* reflected this. The first volume was received with universal acclaim, but the second was criticized and evoked less interest at the time. Yet we can now see that the second volume is even more important and enduring than the first. In the first volume Tocqueville dealt principally with a description of the United States and its then political and judicial institutions, whereas in the second he directed his interest to the tendencies of democratic society itself. He could not easily be categorized either as a liberal or as a conservative; and although an exceptional thinker he could, with equal justice, be classified as a historian or as a pioneer sociologist. After world war two interest in Tocqueville revived, mostly because of his analytical description of certain dangers inherent in modern democracy, including that of the tyranny of the majority.

This, however, was but one of his great contributions to the understanding of modern political institutions. Tocqueville's political thinking is inseparable from the main theme of his historical vision, according to which democracy is gradually replacing the age of aristocracy everywhere in the world: a development that is so immense and profound that all the previous and still existing political categories are losing their significance. This development, while revolutionary in its long-range implications, affecting as it does every sphere of public and private life, is not always and necessarily dramatic in its appearance,

because a certain kind of continuity prevails. One element in this continuity – and in this Tocqueville's view is the opposite of that of other conservative nineteenth-century thinkers who also feared 'the tyranny of the majority' – is that in the age of democracy great revolutions may become rare: the movement of ideas, instead of being rapid and feverish, is actually slowing down; the incessant churning of publicity and the commercialization of intellectual activities tend toward long periods of intellectual stagnation. Another element of continuity is the unbroken growth of the powers of the centralized state. This very development of centralization had been responsible for most of the abuses of the old monarchy before the French revolution; yet it turned out to be the only feature of the old regime that the radical revolutionaries adopted and furthered without thinking. In describing the effects of centralization Tocqueville saw the coming of the provider, or welfare, state (which would eventually 'spare' many people from 'the trouble of thinking'.) It would create, and perhaps even perpetuate, a reign of mediocrity – and include a novel kind of tyranny over individual lives of which most subjects would be unaware. In this respect Tocqueville foresaw the degeneration of democracies into the reign of enormous bureaucracies, even though the term 'bureaucracy' did not figure in his prose.

Tocqueville was not however a systematizer or a categorical pessimist of the Spenglerian kind. He took some of his hopes from the unpredictability of history, from the prevalence of free will, from the appetite for freedom, especially among peoples who had known it before, and from the existence of religion. The most frequently remembered and cited passage of his writings is the passage at the end of volume I of *Democracy in America* where he foretold the rise of Russia and of the United States, the former incarnating absolutism and the latter, freedom; yet at the time of that forecast of the rise of these two great extra-European powers Tocqueville was not alone. On the other hand, none of the political and historical thinkers of the nineteenth century shared his unique vision of the prospects and dangers of mass democracy. On every level (including his description of the 1848 revolutions in France) Tocqueville's analyses and foresight have proved more correct than those of Marx. One of the reasons for this was Tocqueville's existential and phenomenological view of developments, wholly different from a systematic or mechanistic analysis – including his description that revolutions occur not when a tyranny is at its most drastic but when it has, appreciably and evidently, begun to lessen. There is even now considerable argument among political thinkers as to whether Tocqueville was a 'conservative' or a 'liberal' – a possibly useless intellectual exercise, especially in view of Tocqueville's own observation about the necessity of a 'new science of politics which is necessary for a new world', suggesting implicitly the outdated character of political categories still extant. The development of Tocqueville's religious convictions, too, and the history of his personal Catholicism evident mostly in his letters to his intimate friends, have not yet received their proper interpretation.

JL

Reading

Jardin, A.: *Alexis de Tocqueville*. Paris: Hachette, 1984.

Lukacs, J.: Alexis de Tocqueville. In *European Writers*, Vol. VI, pp. 893–912, ed. J. Barzun. New York: Scribner, 1985.

Nantet, J.: *Tocqueville*. Paris: Seghers, 1971.

Redier, A.: *Comme disait M. de Tocqueville*. Paris: Perrin, 1925.

Tocqueville, Alexis de: *Oeuvres complètes*, ed. J.P. Mayer et al. Paris: Gallimard, 1951– .

———: *Democracy in America*, trans. G. Lawrence, ed. J.P. Mayer and M. Lerner. New York: Harper, 1966; London: Fontana, 1968.

———: *Recollections*, trans. G. Lawrence, ed. J.P. Mayer and A.P. Kerr. New York: Doubleday, 1970.

———: *The Old Regime and the Revolution*, trans. S. Gilbert. New York: Doubleday, 1955.

———: *The European Revolution and Correspondence with Gobineau*, intro. and trans. J. Lukacs. New York: Doubleday, 1959.

———: *Journeys to England and Ireland*, trans. G. Lawrence and J.P. Mayer. New York: Doubleday, 1968.

totalitarianism A political term first used against and by Mussolini in 1923–5, and a theoretical concept since the first world war. Although the revolutionary intensification of political domination or the conduct of war had occasionally been characterized earlier as 'total' or 'totalitarian' the term was applied above all to the three radical dictatorial systems of the inter-war period: Italian FASCISM, German National Socialism, and STALINISM in the Soviet Union. Originally characterizing a most extreme form of DICTATORSHIP during the 1920s and 1930s the term underwent a certain modification after the end of the Fascist and National Socialist regimes in 1945. It was the changes within the communist system after Stalin's death, however, that brought the concept increasingly into question. Was it permissible or helpful to compare past, fascist regimes with communist systems still in the process of development?

The intensified controversies over the question of the comparability, or even equation, of regimes so pronounced in their contrasts was caused in great part by the use of totalitarianism as a polemical concept. The problems were complicated further by the linking since the second world war of theories describing totalitarianism with the confrontations of the cold war. Indeed, much of the most important literature on totalitarianism appeared under the impact of the global conflict between East and West. No wonder many contemporary critics saw the concept of totalitarianism as a polemically employed anti-ideology rather than a usable tool of political analysis.

Profound differences do indeed exist between fascism, national socialism, and communism, but for this very reason modern dictatorship, in its most pointed and consequent manifestations, is an important subject for comparative analysis. The search for characteristics common to these regimes and for a general theory of their structure and operation has yielded rich data and a variety of interpretations. What follows will differentiate types or versions of totalitarianism, without rejecting the general concept. Characteristically this is done most emphatically by communists – who in turn make efforts to use a most extensive concept of fascism, applicable to non-communist states and 'capitalist' societies of the most divergent character.

Academic debate begins with the question of the essential points in which the structure and function of totalitarian regimes differ from the classical dictatorships in the form of DESPOTISM and TYRANNY which have been described time and again since PLATO and ARISTOTLE. Most definitions of totalitarianism depict modern dictatorship in terms of a model governed by complete centralization and uniform regimentation of all aspects of political, social, and intellectual life and in these respects transcending by far earlier manifestations of absolute or autocratic rule and their capacity to control the mass of their subjects. In this sense totalitarianism is truly a phenomenon of the twentieth century. The expansion and mobilization of modern industrialism and technology constitutes the inherent basis and legitimization of total rule and are its essential precondition. Organization, communication, and propaganda provide the instruments for and facilitate the all-encompassing controls, the total mobilization and co-ordination of the citizen's life and thought based on the coercion of terror or seductive persuasion.

Regimes tending towards totalitarianism also differ from earlier forms of dictatorships and absolutist government in their ambivalent relationship to modern democracy, yet simultaneously present themselves as a higher manifestation of popular sovereignty. The totalitarian claim to legitimacy by means of plebiscitary acclamation is central although no more than the manipulation of assent to the exercise of power by a leader or monopolistic party which in turn claim to represent the general will of state and society. Nevertheless, different though the historical conditions, the social and national framework, and the ideological positions and ends sought by totalitarian movements may be, they undoubtedly possess significant common features as far as the use of power and the techniques of government, manipulation, and oppression are concerned. Though not uncontroversial, efforts to determine the common denominator for totalitarian systems have helped to elucidate the character and functioning of these systems.

Fundamental to all totalitarian regimes is the claim to exclusive leadership on the part of one party and IDEOLOGY. Rival political parties or groups are precluded, and fundamental claims to individual liberty and civil rights are denied. In that sense, its pseudo-democratic legitimization notwithstanding, totalitarianism is a fundamental contradiction of the democratic creed of human rights – whether it denies them explicitly (fascism and national socialism), or undermines them by manipulation (LENINIST and especially Stalinist communism).

It can be counter-argued that totalitarian principles of order, in the form of one-man dictatorship or the DICTATORSHIP OF THE PROLETARIAT, are justified by their ideological ends, aiming at a higher and ultimate mode of 'freedom' for all (or consoling all with that hope). Such justification of the means of dictatorship by reference to their higher ends is part of the classical repertory of totalitarian apologetics; for the concretely affected individual however, oppression is not rendered less burdensome by the mere representation, in the garb of popular democracy, of a grandiosely and radically styled people's dictatorship. The claim is that individuals, as well as groups, are meant to be integrated into a tightly knit, all-encompassing system, incorporating or preparing the future order of state and society. In this process individuals are to be made into 'new men' whose assent, enthusiasm and revolutionary dynamic is founded on and fed by a sense of ideological mission. It is manipulated, obligatory faith in the superiority of nation, class, and race whose claims to power are to be realized by any means, domestically (dictatorship of the party and the leader) as well as abroad (expansion, imperialism, world domination).

The total monopoly of the party, the leading elite and the leader, of power and control over state and society, is sanctioned and elevated not only pseudo-democratically but also pseudo-religiously, with ideology becoming political religion. Equipped with the attitude of infallibility these highest echelons of totalitarian systems demand glorifying veneration on the part of the masses which are being organized, indoctrinated and mobilized to this end and led, in gigantic parades and public spectacles minutely ritualized and theatrically staged, to deafening orgies of mass adulation. The aim is total consensus, manipulated in terms of social psychology to the point of exalted submission. This dogma of total consensus, formulated in the motto 'the leader, the party is always right', aspires to solve definitively the perennial and basic problem of all government by insisting on the full identity of leadership and people.

The classical systems of totalitarianism appear to be part of the past, and history may not repeat itself. But in this age of crisis-prone mass democracies, mass movements, and profound social change, some fundamental premises and components of totalitarianism remain of contemporary concern. They constitute a potential which may be mobilized by future leaders whenever social crisis, the emotional need for security and order, the idealistic longing for a political creed capable of solving all problems, and the craving for power and the resulting world-wide tensions become too strong. These stimuli, then, may be tied to the conviction that only the concentration of all energies in one power centre and the complete subordination of individual liberty – sublimated as a 'moral sacrifice' – to the chiliastic visions (the 'Thousand-year Reich', the WITHERING AWAY OF THE STATE) of a total movement and its quasi-deified leader will solve the problems of modern society.

In this sense the precepts and claims of the totalitarian organization of state and society are not a phenomenon only of the past and due exclusively to the unique constellation of historical circumstances during the inter-war period. Rather, totalitarianism was dominant in communist systems over one-third of the world population, and will remain for the foreseeable future a possible consequence of and peril attendant upon the modernization process. It is still a threat to nations and societies in the second half of the twentieth century, in the era of mass democracies, super-bureaucracies, and pseudo-religious ideologies. The totalitarian vision, conjured up as a warning almost four decades ago by George Orwell's *1984* has not yet vanished.

KDB

Reading

Arendt, H.: *The Origins of Totalitarianism* (1951). Repr. Cleveland, Ohio.: Meridian, 1966.

Bracher, K.D.: *The German Dictatorship*. London: Penguin, 1973.

———: *The Age of Ideologies*. London: Methuen, 1985.

Friedrich, C.J. and Brzezinski, Z.: *Totalitarian Dictatorship and Autocracy*. New York: Praeger, 1967.

Friedrich, C.J., Curtis, M. and Barber, B.R.: *Totalitarianism in Perspective: three views*. New York: Praeger, 1969.

Groth, A.: The 'isms' in totalitarianism. *American Political Science Review* 58 (1964) 888–901.

Menze, E.A. ed.: *Totalitarianism Reconsidered*. Port Washington, NY: Kennikat, 1981.

Revel, J.-F.: *La Tentation totalitaire*. Paris: Laffont, 1976; *The Totalitarian Temptation*. London: Secker & Warburg, 1976.

Schapiro, L.: *Totalitarianism*. London: Pall Mall, 1976.

Talmon, J.L.: *The Origins of Totalitarian Democracy*. New York: Praeger, 1961.

———: *The Myth of the Nation and the Vision of Revolution*. London: Secker & Warburg, 1980.

Unger, A.L.: *The Totalitarian Party*. London: Cambridge University Press, 1974.

———: *Totalitarian Democracy and After*. Jerusalem: The Israel Academy of Sciences and Humanities, 1984.

town meeting The earliest form of self-government in Britain's American colonies, and still sometimes regarded as the purest form of DEMOCRACY. Derived from the practice of classic Greek democracy, it was most extensively used in New England and now survives in thirteen north-eastern states, although only in Vermont, Massachusetts and Connecticut does the town meeting play any significant part in local affairs. This form of self-government is also used in five Swiss cantons where the legislative authority is in principle subordinate to the *Landsgemeinde*, an open meeting of all citizens of voting age.

In New England the town meeting is held annually and is open to all members of the community. Topics for discussion and decision are presented in a 'warrant' drawn up by the 'selectmen', representatives chosen at the previous town meeting. The agenda will include specific policy decisions, such as the paving of roads, as well as the annual budget and tax rate.

In its original form the town meeting did provide an effective means of DIRECT DEMOCRACY for small rural communities with relatively simple problems. With the growth of population however the opportunity for extended discussion among all citizens diminished, and meetings came to be dominated by persons with special interests. At the same time modern government became too complex to be handled by non-experts in a single annual meeting. In New England one solution was to create 'representative town meetings' to which citizens are elected. Elsewhere, even without formal legislative power, town meetings are still held as forums for the exchange of views between representatives and their constituents. The heritage of the town meeting is also evident in requirements for public hearings on legislation and in 'sunshine laws' mandating open meetings of governmental bodies. The same form of self-government is used in very small PARISHES in Britain. In recent years urban areas in the United States have developed surrogate forms of participation by means of decentralization and neighbourhood control. Some have argued that modern telecommunications technology offers new opportunities for television town meetings.

GMP

Reading

Barber, B.: *Strong Democracy: participatory politics for a New Age.* Berkeley: University of California Press, 1984.

Becker, T.: Hawaii televote: measuring public opinon on complex issues. *Political Science* 33.1 (July 1981).

Malbin, M.: Teledemocracy and its discontents. *Public Opinion* (June/July 1982).

Mansbridge, J.J.: *Beyond Adversary Democracy.* New York: Basic Books, 1980.

Sly, J.F.: *Town Government in Massachusetts 1620–1930.* Cambridge, Mass.: Harvard University Press, 1930.

Yates, D.: *Neighbourhood Democracy: the politics and impacts of decentralization.* Lexington, Mass.: Heath, 1973.

trade unions Collective organizations of workers, established at least in part 'for the purpose of maintaining or improving the conditions of their working lives' (see Webb and Webb, p. 1). This classic definition allows ample scope for conflicting conceptions of the nature of unionism. Four key issues may be identified: objectives, constituency, internal organization and external relations.

Unions may be concerned predominantly with a narrow agenda of terms and conditions of employment; or their interest in members' 'working lives' may extend far more broadly to include such matters as education and health, social welfare and political rights. Where objectives are broadly defined, unions are likely to adopt as much a 'political' as an 'economic' role. Those preoccupied with immediate employment issues commonly assign priority to collective bargaining and assume a lower political profile. However, even job-oriented unions may be forced to behave politically if they lack the legal freedom to perform bargaining activities (including the right to strike); if they are too weak to negotiate effectively; or if the state itself is a major employer, or attempts to regulate the process and outcome of union–employer bargaining.

Union constituencies reflect criteria of inclusion and exclusion which often influence (and are influenced by) choices of objectives. Modern unions normally organize at the level of the nation-state. Local or regional unionism is however common in some countries; while international confederations (usually rather weak and politically divided) exist to co-ordinate relations with transnational enterprises and supra-national political institutions. At the national level, organization may display divisions by occupation, industry/employer, or ideological attachment. The main traditional form of occupational organization was the craft society of skilled workers; such bodies often concentrated on sectional job-related issues. More recently, occupational differentiation has commonly been expressed in the separate organization of white-collar from manual employees. The model of industrial unionism was initially advocated as a broader, solidaristic alternative to craft sectionalism; its application has normally required centralized, and at times external, imposition. The narrower pattern of company-based unions is particularly familiar in the Japanese context. Ideological lines of division commonly arose in countries where socialist and religious organizations competed for workers' collective allegiance; fragmentation was increased by conflict between communists and social democrats. The repairs effected in some national movements in the 1940s rarely survived the cold war.

Internal constitutional arrangements reflect conflicting models of character and purpose: as service agencies, fighting organizations or miniature democracies. Unlike most other 'private' interest organizations, trade unions commonly proclaim their democratic credentials, and in many countries their internal relations are closely regulated by law. But the meaning of democracy in unions, as more generally, is strongly contested: participative versus representative models of decision making; centralized authority versus local or sectional autonomy; membership activism and initiative versus control by professional officials. In Britain, the 1984 Trade Union Act brought such controversies forcefully into the public arena, requiring secret ballots of members to elect executive committees, to create and maintain political funds, and before official strikes.

Patterns of external relations are the outcome both of dominant conceptions of union objectives, and of the policies and priorities of those institutions with which trade unions deal (primarily, employers and the state). The possibilities range from permanent conflict, through regulated bargaining, to co-operative and integrative relationships. Unions espousing explicit anti-capitalist philosophies might be expected to show greatest readiness to fight employers; but the constraints of organizational survival have often induced them to seek (at least tacitly) a more accommodative relationship. Conversely, narrowly job-conscious unions may prove militant when conflict suits their interests. Collaborative relations with employers are perhaps most likely where unions organize on an industry or employer basis and recognize a common

interest in the prosperity of 'their' firm or sector; where a centralized leadership is able to discipline membership assertiveness; and where employers themselves pursue co-operative industrial relations.

Although conceptions of purpose will influence union dispositions in the political arena, increasingly governments themselves have set the pattern of relationships with unions. In some societies independent unionism is perceived as a threat to the stability of the state, and unions are either suppressed or co-opted. Even where the legitimacy of independent unions is accepted, the limits to such independence are increasingly apparent. 'Free collective bargaining' – where unions and employers conduct their relations without governmental interference – is not obviously compatible with contemporary government concerns as macroeconomic managers. Such concerns were widely reflected – particularly in the 1960s and 1970s – in attempts to draw unions into the formulation and administration of government policy, in exchange for their moderation in wage bargaining. Such 'corporatist' relationships have proved unstable in the 1980s: economic crisis has reduced government willingness or ability to offer concessions in such trade-offs; unions' economic strength, and disruptive potential, have declined; many regimes espouse vehemently anti-union ideologies.

The array of influences on trade union character, organization and policy has generated a confusing diversity of national patterns. British unionism is perhaps more complex than most. Collective bargaining is normally the overriding concern; but socialist philosophies have long been influential, and most leading unions are affiliated to the Labour Party (an attachment confirmed in a series of ballots in 1985–6). Developing originally on a craft basis, the movement now displays a variety of structural forms, including the giant 'general' unions. Almost uniquely among western nations, the central confederation – the Trades Union Congress – embraces virtually every union of significance; but its authority over member unions, jealous of their individual autonomy, is very limited. There is a strong tradition of 'lay' participation and involvement: though levels of membership are relatively high by international standards (approximately half the labour force), numbers of full-time officials are low; voluntary branch officers and shop stewards perform an essential function in sustaining union activities. Partly because of the relative weakness of central officialdom, 'corporatist' relations with employers and governments have remained comparatively underdeveloped.

In the USA, 'business unionism' has long been the dominant ideology, with unions (despite a largely Democrat orientation) lacking the will or ability to maintain a strong and co-ordinated political role. Central officials in many unions wield considerable powers, and have often been accused of corrupt or authoritarian practices. Anti-union employers and unfavourable legislation (particularly in the southern States) have contributed to a low and declining level of membership. Several important unions are outside the central federation, the AFL-CIO (itself the union of two erstwhile rivals, espousing respectively craft and industrial unionist principles).

Simplifying drastically, four other major patterns may be identified. The first, common in northern Europe, involves industry-based unions with social-democratic orientations and traditions of centralized authority; high membership levels; relatively cordial relations with employers and governments; and in particular a willingness to adopt wage restraint in return for favourable social and economic policies. The southern European pattern (with parallels in many third world countries) involves strong political identities, with divisions on the basis of party or confessional attachment; weak development of collective bargaining (often in part a consequence of employer opposition); low levels of formal membership; and a tradition of militancy, commonly expressed in brief and demonstrative mass mobilization. Eastern Europe provides a third pattern, with unions defined as 'transmission belts' of state and party policy, and often claiming virtually complete employee membership. In practice such unions may perform an uneasy combination of functions as social clubs, cheer-leaders in production drives, and partial protectors against managerial excesses.

That the latter function is not wholly cosmetic is perhaps indicated by the limited apparent support for intermittent attempts to establish 'free' trade unions – with the dramatic exception of the *Solidarity* union in Poland. Finally, the third world displays a variety of combinations of the second and third patterns: little tradition of 'free collective bargaining'; a predominant role as social welfare organizations, political mobilizers, or both; low levels of membership, except where state sponsored and regulated; a base among the relatively advantaged workforce of the industrial and service sectors (often state employees); and dependence upon professional leadership, often with political ambitions or even established status in government.

See also COMMUNIST PARTIES; LABOUR MOVEMENT; SOCIALISM; SOCIALIST AND SOCIAL DEMOCRATIC PARTIES. RH

Reading

Banks, J.A.: *Trade Unionism*. London: Collier-Macmillan, 1974.

Clegg, H.: *Trade Unionism Under Collective Bargaining*. Oxford: Blackwell, 1976.

Coates, K. and Topham, T.: *Trade Unions and Politics*. Oxford: Blackwell, 1986.

Crouch, C.: *Trade Unions: the logic of collective action*. London: Fontana, 1982.

Flanders, A.: *Trade Unions*. London: Hutchinson, 1952.

Hyman, R.: *Industrial Relations: a Marxist introduction*. London: Macmillan, 1975.

McCarthy, W.E.J. ed.: *Trade Unions*. 2nd edn. Harmondsworth: Penguin, 1985.

Sturmthal, A.: *Comparative Labor Movements*. Belmont, Calif.: Wadsworth, 1972.

Webb, S. and Webb, B.: *The History of Trade Unionism 1666–1920*. 2nd edn. London: Longman, 1920.

traditionalism in politics Tradition is distinguished from traditionalism by self-consciousness. Every society transmits from one generation to the next a set of skills and values which constitute its special character – language itself, most importantly. But when a traditional society finds many of its practices challenged and devalued by some outside model (for example, modern highly developed and technologically advanced societies) its members must begin to decide which among its practices must be retained, however disadvantageous, because they constitute its very identity. In the encounter between East and West, most eastern societies have been content to abandon most of their technology, but to retain customs, culture, art, religion, and often such elements of family life as a sheltered role for women. This response has commonly been articulated by intellectuals belonging to nationalist movements. The resurgence of Islam, and of many features of Hinduism which were beginning to die out in the last century, illustrates the way in which elements of a tradition become the materials for a self-conscious adherence to traditionalism. In India, the sacredness of cows was revived, but the practice of suttee was abandoned.

The first societies to face this problem were those of Europe, from the eighteenth century onwards when the modernizing pressures of thought and commerce began to make themselves felt. The French revolution was the apotheosis of modernization, and provoked a traditionalist response from writers such as Edmund BURKE in Britain and Joseph de Maistre in France. The great philosophical account of the place of tradition in constituting a modern society is HEGEL's *Philosophy of Right* (1821). But neither Burke nor Hegel were traditionalist in the strict sense because each rejected a fixed world as valuable, and recognized that a tradition can only be sustained by a process of constant reform and adaptation. In European politics, traditionalists tend towards nostalgia for absolute monarchy, aristocracy, visible signs of social gradation and a customary morality.

Religious traditionalism is marked by an addiction to long-established liturgical practices such as the Latin mass. All these materials have at times been used by nationalist movements seeking power both in European and third-world countries, but such movements tend to concentrate upon elements of the cultural tradition, since they are usually bent on sweeping away the *ancien régime* and installing a new elite whose legitimacy will be defended in populist terms. From this point of view, the politics of non-European countries

in the twentieth century has been one of conflict between traditionalists and modernizers, between Slavophils and Westernizers, and the spectrum of possible policies ranges from Kemal Atatürk's forcible modernization of Turkey in the 1920s to the violent traditionalism of the Ayatollah Khomeini in the Iran of the 1980s. KRM

Reading

Friedrich, C.J.: *Tradition and Authority*. London: Pall Mall, 1972.

Levenson, J.: *Confucian China and its Modern Fate*. 3 vols. London: Routledge & Kegan Paul, 1958–65.

Minogue, K.R.: *Nationalism*. London: Batsford, 1967.

Oakeshott, M.: *Rationalism in Politics*. London: Methuen, 1962.

tribal government/tribalism See PRE-STATE POLITICAL SYSTEMS.

Trotsky/Trotskyism

(1) *Trotsky, Leon* (1879–1940) Born on 7 November 1879 at Yanovka, Ukraine, the son of a Jewish farmer, Lev Davidovich Bronstein, known as Trotsky, was, after LENIN, the most brilliant orator and writer of the Russian Revolution. He was murdered, almost certainly on STALIN's orders, on 20 August 1940. A revolutionary from the age of eighteen, Trotsky spent most of the years 1902 to 1917 abroad. He encountered Lenin first in 1902 but sided with the Mensheviks when the Russian Social Democratic Labour Party split in London in 1903. He played an important role in the Russian Revolution of 1905–7 as chairman of the St Petersburg (Leningrad) Soviet of Workers' Deputies. He joined Lenin in July 1917 and claimed that this was because Lenin had adopted his concept of PERMANENT REVOLUTION. Trotsky became a leading member of the Petrograd SOVIET and its Military Revolutionary Committee, the General Staff of the October Revolution. He was Commissar for Foreign Affairs (1917–18), and as Commissar for War (1918–25) he masterminded the build up of the Red Army and played a key role during the Civil War (1918–20). The natural successor to Lenin, he refused to seize

the leadership, preferring to wait until it was offered to him. Stalin ensured that this did not happen. Leader of the Left Opposition (1923–7) Trotsky was outmanoeuvred by Stalin. Expelled from the Party in 1927, and exiled to Alma Ata in 1928, he was expelled from the USSR in 1929 but was permitted to take his personal archive with him. He spent the rest of his life in Turkey, France, Norway and Mexico.

(2) *Trotskyism* A major contribution to MARXIST thought, Trotskyism is synonymous with the theory of permanent revolution, itself part of the wider theory of uneven and combined development. According to this theory all countries do not have to follow an identical social evolution, from feudalism through CAPITALISM to SOCIALISM. It is possible for underdeveloped states to 'catch up' by telescoping stages so that some may exhibit features of advanced capitalist states alongside the underdevelopment of others. This occurs in some states outside western Europe, North America and Japan. A native working class can develop which is stronger than the bourgeoisie so that the latter is in no position to acquire political power. It is left to the proletariat to carry out the bourgeois revolution, but the revolution goes further and develops certain elements of a socialist society. Once in power the victorious proletariat must give priority to aiding the struggle for revolution abroad – by force if necessary. Trotskyism opposed coexistence and underlines conflict as a way of gradually wearing down capitalist institutions and values. Socialist internationalism takes precedence over nationalism and patriotism. For this reason Trotsky opposed Stalin's conception of 'socialism in one country' and sought to analyse the nature of the Stalinist dictatorship which resulted. The party and state bureaucracies can spawn a privileged elite, cut off from the masses, which can be used to promote personal power by leaders. Objective economic laws cease to exist under socialism as workers, through central economic planning, becoming masters of their own fate. Vilified by the Soviets as counter-revolutionary Trotskyism has split into many factions. It has more support in developed capitalist states and in the third world than in the socialist bloc.　　　　　　　　　　MMcC

Reading

Day, R.B.: *Leon Trotsky and the Politics of Economic Isolation*. Cambridge: Cambridge University Press, 1973.

Deutscher, I.: *The Prophet Armed: Trotsky, 1879–1921*. Oxford: Oxford University Press, 1954.

————: *The Prophet Unarmed: Trotsky, 1921–1929*. Oxford: Oxford University Press, 1959.

————: *The Prophet Outcast: Trotsky, 1929–1940*. Oxford: Oxford University Press, 1963.

Knei-Paz, B.: *The Social and Political Thought of Leon Trotsky*. Oxford: Oxford University Press, 1978.

Trotsky, L.: *History of the Russian Revolution* (1932–3), trans. M. Eastman. London: Gollancz, 1965; Ann Arbor: University of Michigan Press, 1967.

————: *The Revolution Betrayed*, trans. M. Eastman. London: Faber & Faber, 1937; New York: Pathfinder, 1972.

————: *My Life*. New York: Grosset & Dunlap, 1963; Harmondsworth: Penguin, 1975.

————: *The Permanent Revolution and Results and Prospects*, trans. J.G. Wright, rev. B. Pearce. London: New Park; New York: Pioneer, 1962.

————: *The Transitional Programme for Socialist Revolution*. New York: Pathfinder, 1974.

Wistrich, R.: *Trotsky*. London: Robson, 1979.

trustee system/trusteeship　　After 1945 any LEAGUE OF NATIONS mandates that did not quickly become independent were transferred with the agreement of the administering powers (with the notable exception of South Africa) to the United Nations Organization as trust territories. Like MANDATES, trust territories were meant to be governed in the interests of their inhabitants, subjected to international scrutiny (by the United Nations Trusteeship Council) and advanced towards self-government. But unlike mandates they were to undergo regular inspection on the spot and, generally, their progress to independence was rapid. In part this was symptomatic of the general dismantling of colonial empires after 1945, but it also reflected the much greater influence of the anti-colonial powers in the League's successor.　　　　　　　　　JGD

621

Reading

Hall, H.D.: *Mandates, Dependencies and Trusteeship.* London: Stevens, 1948.

Louis, W.R.: *Imperialism at Bay.* Oxford: Clarendon Press, 1977.

turnout The proportion of a given population who vote in an election, the most common form of POLITICAL PARTICIPATION in western countries. Nevertheless many citizens do not vote. Turnout in national elections since 1945 has averaged about 80 per cent. In Australia (with compulsory voting) a figure of 96 per cent has been recorded. Two countries, Switzerland and the United States, are exceptional in their low turnout rates. In local elections and referendums involvement has been even lower. In Britain only 32 per cent took part in the European Parliament elections in 1979 and 1984 and only about 40 per cent vote in local elections. In Switzerland, where referendums are held every three months, turnout has often fallen below 30 per cent. In the socialist countries of eastern Europe official turnout rates of virtually 100 per cent are habitually recorded. Estimates of the actual number of voters range from 75 to 95 per cent. The difference between the official figures and these estimates is due to the widespread misuse of absentee voting certificates, which are used as a device to avoid voting, the practice of third parties voting on an elector's behalf and omissions of illegal immigrants in the larger cities from the electoral register.

Although no major group, with the important exception of aliens, is nowadays excluded from the franchise, institutional barriers to voting still exist in western countries. The most important of these is REGISTRATION. In most countries where registration is compulsory and where the public authorities make considerable efforts to keep the register up to date some 95 per cent of the eligible population will be on the register. In countries where registration is either *de facto* (France) or legally (the USA) a voluntary act, voting becomes a two stage process and many otherwise qualified citizens fail to complete the first step. In France some 10 per cent and in the United States one third of the potential electorate is not registered (registration barriers are one major explanation for the abnormally low turnout rate in the United States).

Turnout rates are also affected by the social characteristics of the individual elector. Recent studies of electoral participation rates have all confirmed the findings of Lipset's early compilation of survey data. Men are more likely to vote than women, though the gender gap has declined over the last thirty years. The young and the mobile are less likely to vote than the middle-aged, the old and the immobile. Class differences are much more important, with higher turnout rates amongst the better educated, the better paid and white collar workers. In most countries the impact of these social factors is attenuated by other institutional or contextual variables. Again the United States is an exception and education especially has an important effect upon voter turnout.

In four western countries, Australia, Belgium, Greece and Luxemburg, voting is compulsory. Voting was compulsory in the Netherlands until 1970. In four of these cases turnout has averaged over 90 per cent with only trivial differences between social groups. But in some other countries, Austria and New Zealand for example, where voting is voluntary, turnout is as high. High turnout is associated not only with compulsion, but also with party systems where parties have close links with social groups, and organizations such as churches, trade unions and farmers' organizations. Once again the United States is a deviant case because of the very broad appeals of the Democrats and the Republicans.

Limited evidence from the United Kingdom, Canada and state-level elections in the United States suggests that constituency level turnout is positively related to the marginality of the seat. In MARGINAL SEATS the party organization has a stronger incentive to mobilize potential support. Low turnout rates in the United States may be associated with a high proportion of very safe seats in the House of Representatives. Powell has suggested that the Swiss anomaly may be similarly explained. Since there has been a permanent coalition government amongst the four major parties since 1943, the results of a particular election are of little importance and the incentive to vote much reduced. (See also ELECTION.)

Average turnout in national elections in twenty-four western countries since 1945

	%		%
Australia	94.3	Japan	72.5
Austria	93.9	*Luxemburg*	90.3
Belgium	92.7	*Netherlands (before 1971)*	94.7
Canada	75.4	Netherlands (from 1971)	83.7
Denmark	85.7	New Zealand	90.0
Finland	78.4	Norway	81.2
France	78.7	Portugal	83.2
Germany	87.3	Spain	75.5
Greece	79.3	Sweden	85.9
Iceland	90.1	Switzerland	61.3
Ireland	74.7	United Kingdom	76.7
Israel	80.9	United States	
Italy	92.0	Presidential	59.3
		House of Representatives	47.3

Countries where voting is compulsory are italicized. Voting was compulsory in the Netherlands until 1970. Turnout is reported as a percentage of the registered electorate, except for the United States where the percentage of the resident population of voting age is given. *Source*: Mackie and Rose 1982.

TTM

Reading

Crewe, I.: Electoral participation. In *Democracy at the Polls*, ed. D. Butler, H.R. Penniman and A. Ranney. Washington, DC and London: American Enterprise Institute for Public Policy Research, 1981.

Karklins, R.: Soviet elections revisited: voter abstention in non-competitive balloting. *American Political Science Review* 80 (1986) 449–469.

Lipset, S.M.: *Political Man*. London: Mercury, 1964.

Mackie, T.T. and Rose, R.: *The International Almanac of Electoral History*. New York: Facts on File; London: Macmillan, 1982. [Annual updates published in the *European Journal of Political Research*.]

Powell, G.B.: *Contemporary Democracies: participation, stability and violence*. Cambridge, Mass.: Harvard University Press, 1982.

——: American voter turnout in comparative perspective. *American Political Science Review* 80 (1986) 17–43.

Verba, S., Nie, N. and Kim, J.: *Participation and Political Equality: a seven-nation comparison*. Cambridge: Cambridge University Press, 1982.

Wolfinger, R. and Rosenstone, S.: *Who Votes?*. New Haven, Conn.: Yale University Press, 1980.

tutelage The system of legal control or supervision exercised by the central power over other public authorities in certain West European countries.

The roots of tutelage may be found in Roman civil law and it was defined by Cicero Servius Sulpicius as a power or authority destined to protect a person who, for reasons of sex or age, was unable to defend himself or herself. By way of extension tutelage gradually came to cover relationships between public authorities: the state has the right, indeed the duty, to supervise the activities of other public authorities which are viewed not only as subordinate but in some fundamental sense as minors. Tutelage is generally seen to regulate relations between central and local authorities, and rests on two pillars: a mistrust of intermediary bodies and a belief in the strong and beneficent state.

Under Napoleon, France developed a highly constraining system of *tutelle* – a system which was exported to territories occupied by France or, in some cases, voluntarily adopted. An elaborate system of judicial constraints was constructed, expressed in the development of administrative law and implemented by state officials such as prefects or governors.

Evidence tends to suggest that tutelage was often ineffective: local ingenuity and central tolerance or connivance often ensured a degree of local autonomy far greater than that permitted by the law. However, it provided a framework of inhibition and could, on occasion, be invoked by state officials. It was under constant attack by both local authorities and political decentralizers.

The system of tutelage has gradually been dismantled in Western Europe – in post-Franco Spain, in regionalized Italy and in Belgium since the reforms of the 1960s and 1970s. Even in France, as a result of the decentralization reforms of the Socialist government elected in 1981, it has now been largely abandoned. However, local authorities now complain that their dependence on the financial and technical resources of the centre enables the latter to continue effectively to control their activities. (See also CENTRAL/LOCAL RELATIONS; PREFECT.)

VW

Reading

Ridley, F.R. ed.: *Government and Administration in Western Europe.* Oxford: Robertson, 1979.

Scase, R. ed.: *The State in Western Europe.* London: Croom Helm, 1980.

tyranny   The rule of a tyrant; or a state which is ruled by a tyrant; or the action of a tyrannical ruler and so, generally, oppressive or unjustly severe government. In ancient Greece, from the seventh century BC the tyrant was a man who had seized the sole power in a state and held it in defiance of any previously existing constitution. He might do this by force in order to exercise personal power but tyrants could also do this by popular consent following provision of more efficient government than previously. Thus in the original historical sense the tyrant was not necessarily a wicked ruler. From quite early times the term came to be used in an unfavourable sense; PLATO and ARISTOTLE both defined tyranny as a corrupted, degraded form of one-man rule. This usage is the standard one today. Thus, although the Greek tyrant was the absolute master of his subjects and in this respect is the same as the DESPOT we can nowadays talk of a benevolent or an enlightened despot, whereas to speak of a benevolent or enlightened tyrant would seem to be a contradiction in terms.   SEF

U

unicameral Term used to signify that a legislature has only one chamber, like the parliaments of Israel, New Zealand and Denmark. A bicameral legislature is one with two chambers or houses, for example the British Parliament (the House of Commons and the House of Lords), the American Congress (the House of Representatives and the Senate) the French Parliament (the National Assembly and the Senate).

See SECOND CHAMBER. SEF

United Nations Formally established on 24 October 1945 when its basic constitutive instrument, the UN Charter, entered into force for the 51 founder states. The first blueprints for the UN were drafted by the USA, the UK, the USSR and their allies during the second world war, reflecting their conceptions of the post-war international order. The Charter was finally adopted by 50 states meeting at San Francisco in June 1945. Although membership had expanded to 159 states by July 1986, and the nature and work of the UN has evolved considerably, the Charter has remained virtually unchanged.

Six 'principal organs' of the UN were established by the Charter: the General Assembly, the Security Council, the Secretariat, the INTERNATIONAL COURT OF JUSTICE (ICJ), the Trusteeship Council, and the Economic and Social Council (ECOSOC).

The General Assembly as the plenary body controls much of the work of the UN. It approves the budget, adopts priorities, calls international conferences, superintends the operations of the Secretariat and of numerous committees and subsidiary organs, and debates and adopts resolutions on major issues on the international political agenda. The numerous subsidiary bodies created by the General Assembly include the United Nations Development Programme, the United Nations Children's Fund and the Office of the United Nations High Commissioner for Refugees.

The fifteen-member Security Council is dominated by its five permanent members (China, France, the UK, the USSR and the USA), each of which has power to veto any draft resolution on substantive matters. The remaining ten members are elected for two-year periods by the General Assembly. The Security Council has primary responsibility for the maintenance of international peace and security, and unlike the General Assembly is able to take decisions binding on all members of the UN. It meets frequently throughout the year, mainly to consider military conflicts and other situations or disputes where international peace and security are threatened. It is empowered to order mandatory sanctions, call for ceasefires, establish peacekeeping forces, and even to take military action on behalf of the UN. The veto power was intended to ensure that the UN could not act against the strong opposition of any of the most powerful states. Thus the Security Council could contribute little to the amelioration of conflicts over Suez (1956), Vietnam (1954–75), the Sino-Vietnamese dispute (1979), and Afghanistan (1979–). The Security Council has never ordered military 'enforcement' action (the closest approximation, the force in Korea, was merely an authorized force), and the agreements envisaged in the Charter placing national military units at the disposal of the

625

UN have not been concluded. Significant binding sanctions were applied only to Rhodesia and to arms sales to South Africa. The Security Council has nevertheless played an important role in easing or containing numerous crises, and provides a high-level forum for discreet diplomatic contact and negotiation. Peacekeeping forces ranging from small observer units to large interposition or policing forces have been established by the Security Council in the Middle East, the Balkans, Kashmir, the Congo, Cyprus, and other areas. The General Assembly did create the United Nations Emergency Force in the aftermath of the Suez crisis in 1956 when the Security Council was prevented by veto from acting, and issued recommendations concerning UN forces in Korea and the Congo in similar circumstances, but control of peacekeeping has now returned firmly to the Security Council. The Security Council also has a role, with the General Assembly, in the admission of new members to the UN, the appointment of the Secretary-General, and the election of judges to the ICJ.

The Secretary-General is head of the UN Secretariat, which employs some 16,000 people at UN Headquarters in New York and at other offices. The Secretariat is part of the 50,000 strong international civil service employed by agencies within the UN system at some 620 posts throughout the world. The UN Charter requires that Secretariat staff be answerable only to the UN and stipulates that merit is to be the paramount consideration in their employment, but the UN has not always been able to adhere unswervingly to these principles. While the nature and quality of the UN's work depend greatly on the comparatively 'faceless' Secretariat, the Secretary-General is also a significant figure in international diplomacy. The Secretary-General frequently assists with crisis negotiations, as in the Falklands/Malvinas war, and may take independent initiatives in fact-finding, diplomacy, and the raising of matters in the Security Council. The Secretaries-General have been Trygve Lie of Norway (1946–53), Dag Hammarskjöld of Sweden (1953–61), U Thant of Burma (1961–71), Kurt Waldheim of Austria (1972–81) and Javier Pérez de Cuéllar of Peru (1982–).

The Trusteeship Council superintended the transition of Trust territories to self-government, but the main pressure for decolonization has come from other UN quarters – the Special Committee on Decolonization, dominated by third world states, and the General Assembly's Fourth Committee.

The Economic and Social Council comprises 54 states elected by the General Assembly, although many non-governmental organizations also participate. It supervises the work of numerous commissions, committees and expert bodies in the economic and social fields, and endeavours to co-ordinate the efforts of the UN specialized agencies in this area.

The UN system extends beyond the UN organs created by the Charter to include a host of agencies with their own separate constitutions, memberships and budgets. The largest of the 16 specialized agencies are the Food and Agriculture Organization, the International Labour Organization, the World Bank, the International Monetary Fund and the United Nations Educational, Scientific and Cultural Organization. Other organizations closely associated with the UN include the International Atomic Energy Agency and the General Agreement on Tariffs and Trade.

Expenditure by the UN system is some $4 billion per annum in the 1986–87 biennium. More than half of this is financed by voluntary contributions, with most of the remainder contributed by member states in accordance with binding assessments based mainly on gross and per capita national incomes. The UN has been in financial difficulties arising from non-payment of assessed contributions since the early 1960s, and the deficit has increased sharply in the 1980s.

Although the UN has developed a strong institutional existence, at core it remains, as former US Secretary of State Dean Rusk once remarked, 159 member states pursuing their national interests as they see them.   BWK

Reading

Bailey, S.: *The General Assembly of the United Nations*, rev. edn. London: Pall Mall, 1964.

Cot, J.-P. and Pellet, A.: *La Charte des Nations Unies*. Paris: Economica, 1985.

Franck, T.M.: *Nation against Nation: what happened to the UN dream and what the US can do about it.* New York and Oxford: Oxford University Press, 1985.

Goodrich, L.M., Hambro, E. and Simons, A.P.: *Charter of the United Nations: commentaries and documents.* 3rd edn. New York: Columbia University Press, 1969.

Higgins, R.: *UN Peacekeeping.* 4 vols. Oxford: Oxford University Press, 1969–81.

Luard, E.: *The United Nations: how it works and what it does.* London: Macmillan, 1979.

Meron, T.: *The UN Secretariat: the rules and the practice.* Lexington, Mass.: Lexington Books, 1977.

Peterson, M.J.: *The General Assembly in World Politics.* Boston: Allen & Unwin, 1986.

Urquhart, B.: *Hammarskjöld.* New York: Knopf, 1972.

Wiseman, H. ed.: *Peacekeeping: appraisals and prospects.* New York: Pergamon Press, 1983.

Yearbook of the United Nations. New York: United Nations, annually.

urban politics The field of political analysis most concerned with LOCAL GOVERNMENT institutions, the politics of spatially delimited communities, and (most recently) the politics involved in the production of publicly subsidized consumption services. Urban politics as a sub-field originated in the USA, partly during the period of the PROGRESSIVE MOVEMENT when liberal reformers were attempting to eradicate CLIENTELIST politics in American city governments and promote the professionalization of their administration.

Many of the reformers' ideas derived from academic studies of 'good practice' in local public administration, orginally rather prescriptive in character, but with an increasing volume of descriptive studies during the 1920s and 1930s. What distinguished these American developments from similar writings in other countries was the later merging of institutional studies with developments in urban sociology. During the 1920s sociologists began to use community studies of small towns as microcosms of American society. Early community studies concentrated on giving an all round picture of social life in an area, but during the 1930s and 1940s they evolved under the influence of the Chicago school of urban sociology to focus more on single themes in larger communities. R. and H. Lynd (1937) concentrated attention on inequalities of power in the depressed mid-western community they termed 'Middletown', and W. Lloyd Warner in the late 1940s made an ambitious attempt to map the broader community politics of a larger 'Yankee City'.

The author who did most to pull together institutional studies of local government (and to a lesser extent state) politics with urban sociology's focus on community was Floyd Hunter in his study of Atlanta, Georgia (1953). Hunter claimed to have distinguished a pyramidal structure of 'community power', centred in business and social elites, which collectively dominated Atlanta politics. The implication from this elite theory study was that if American democracy was so basically flawed and inadequate at this most accessible level for citizens, it was scarcely likely to be in better shape elsewhere. Hunter's study triggered a major reworking of pluralist ideas about urban politics, culminating in the work of Robert Dahl (1963) and N. Polsby (1963) whose studies of New Haven used survey techniques as well as decisional case studies to argue contrary conclusions (see DEMOCRACY). They found that power over community decisions was widely dispersed amongst voters and a wide range of interest groups, and that control over public policy was focused in the hands of elected politicians rather than community elites (see POLYARCHY).

The Atlanta and New Haven studies inaugurated over a decade of feverish scholarly research into community power structures in which pluralist political scientists tended to uncover dispersed power structures, while elite theory sociologists (see ELITES, DOCTRINE OF) studying other cities claimed evidence of the domination of weak local political institutions by economic and social elites, especially business. The most important later developments were 'neo-elitist' studies by Bachrach and Baratz (1970) and Crenson (1971), who argued in opposition to pluralist decision-making studies that control over the political agenda was as important as the ability to win overt conflicts of interest. In their view elite influence was exerted mainly via 'non-decision making'. The community power debate petered out in the mid 1970s, both in the USA and elsewhere, as the non-cumulative character of individual case studies became apparent. Comparative community studies enjoyed a brief vogue, using expenditure and survey data from large numbers of localities to try to pinpoint causal patterns in urban politics.

Since the mid 1970s the key developments in urban political analysis have taken place in Western Europe. The most immediate stimulus was the growth of French Marxist research, which rejected traditional concerns with urban institutions (such as local government), or the distinctive spatial patterning of social life in major towns (the community politics focus). Instead their work, influenced primarily by Castells (1977) in political analysis, concentrated on the production of cities in a capitalist society, using a radical political economy approach. Castells rejected as ideological the notion that the physical environment of the city would somehow exert its own influence on social life, arguing that in particular need of study were those kinds of consumption processes in which the government intervened to provide public services or goods. These 'collective consumption' processes – such as public housing, schooling, health care, transport, etc. – now played a central role in the economic development and social stability of advanced industrial states. They were in turn the sites of new and important forms of social struggle, essentially class-based (as in all other areas of capitalist society), but with some important distinctive features. For example Castells saw a potential for urban social movements organized around collective consumption issues to forge new cross-class alliances, which could be of central importance in creating a left majority going beyond the (shrinking) industrial proletariat.

Neo-Marxist work stimulated by the French literature and by other political economy writings produced a rebirth of radical studies of urban politics in many countries during the late 1970s. For a time the new wave's reliance on structuralist methods, its focus on a more coherent set of social processes, and its willingness to tackle central issues of modern socio-economic development, carried all before it. But in the 1980s, especially in Britain, political economy approaches have diversified into a more liberal Weberian mould, tackling similar issues but with more attention to the specificity of consumption processes, and with greater emphasis upon the role of spatial differences in shaping local politics. The emergence of an invigorated political geography tradition of urban analysis is one consequence.

The main area of recent influence from American studies has come from the application of PUBLIC CHOICE THEORY to explain and defend the highly fragmented US local government system, and to outline the logic of CENTRAL/LOCAL RELATIONS which allocate functions to different tiers of government. Tiebout's paper on local public expenditures (1956) has been belatedly influential in defending fragmentation as a means by which citizens can 'vote with their feet', moving between municipalities in search of the best available tax/service mix.

Urban politics continues to have severe problems in defining a coherent focus of study. In an advanced industrial society almost all political processes take place in towns and cities: the question is how to define a sub-set of this unmanageable total that is somehow specifically related to urban themes and issues (see Dunleavy 1982). The available options seem to be: to focus on one category of urban institutions, which converts urban politics into the study of municipal government; to focus on those political processes which are most confined to particular localities, the 'community' politics focus; or to designate certain substantive social processes as most specifically related to urban themes or issues, such as collective consumption or the production of the built environment.

See also ELITES/ELITISM; PLURALISM.

PJD

Reading

Bachrach, P. and Baratz, M.: *Power and Poverty: theory and practice*. New York: Oxford University Press, 1970.

Castells, M.: *The Urban Question*. London: Arnold, 1977.

Crenson, M.: *The Unpolitics of Air Pollution*. Baltimore, Md.: The Johns Hopkins University Press, 1971.

Dahl, R.A.: *Who Governs? Democracy and Power in an American City*. New Haven, Conn.: Yale University Press, 1963.

Dunleavy, P.J.: *The Scope of Urban Studies in Social Science*. Milton Keynes: Open University Press, 1982.

Hunter, F.: *Community Power Structure*. Chapel Hill: University of North Carolina Press, 1952.

Lynd, R. and Lynd, H.: *Middletown in Transition* (1937). London: Constable, 1964.

Polsby, N.: *Community Power and Political Theory*. New Haven, Conn.: Yale University Press, 1963.

Tiebout, C.: A pure theory of local public expenditure. *Journal of Political Economy* 64 (1956).

Warner, W.L. ed.: *Yankee City*. New Haven, Conn.: Yale University Press, 1963.

V

veto   In the United States this is the power of a chief executive to refuse to assent to proposed laws (bills) passed by the legislature and to return them to the legislature with his objections. Unless the legislature succeeds in passing the bill again, usually by an extraordinary majority, the proposal does not become law. If the legislature passes a bill after a veto, this is called a *veto override*.

British royal governors exercised veto power to check American colonial assemblies before the American Revolution. The Constitutional Convention gave veto power to the President of the United States. The Convention discussed granting an absolute veto, but instead agreed to permit the Congress to pass laws over the president's objections by a two-thirds vote in both houses. If the president receives a bill passed by congress, and neither signs nor vetoes it within ten days (Sundays excepted), the proposal becomes law anyway. If, however, congress adjourns before the ten days elapses – thus removing the opportunity for the president to return it with a veto – the bill only becomes law with the president's signature. This situation makes it possible for the president to kill a proposal at the end of a congressional session without formally vetoing it. Such an action is called a *pocket veto*.

The framers of the constitution saw the veto primarily as a shield against congressional intrusion into the powers of the executive branch, and secondarily as a check by the executive on the passage of unwise laws. Early presidents used the power rarely, only twice in the first twenty years, but later executives relied on it more. Since the second world war presidents have vetoed an average of about eight bills per year. The veto is needed when the president fails to persuade congress to shape legislation in accordance with his wishes; it therefore tends to be used more frequently when the president's party is numerically weak in congress or when the president's popularity with the public declines.

All the American states save one (North Carolina) have given veto powers to their governors, although there are differences in specific practices. For example, six states permit a veto override by just a majority of elected legislators in both houses. Forty-three states permit a special form of veto called the *item veto*. This permits the governor to delete a part of an appropriations bill while approving the remainder of it. Some people argue that the item veto works to restrain the aggregate amount of government spending, but since research shows that per capita state spending in states with such a provision is higher than in states without it, this remains an unproven assertion. Still, advocates of fiscal restraint have proposed granting an item veto to the president for over a hundred years, and most recent chief executives have supported the idea. Congress, however, views this as an attempt to diminish its authority and continues to resist the proposal.

See also PRESIDENT/PRESIDENTIAL SYSTEM.   DWR

Reading

Abney, G. and Lanth, T.: The line-item veto in the states: an instrument for fiscal restraint or an instrument for partisanship? *Public Administration Review* (1985).

Copeland, G.W.: When Congress and the president

collide: why presidents veto legislation. *Journal of Politics* 45 (1983) 696–710.

Cronin, E. and Weill, J.: An item veto for the president? *Congress and the Presidency* 12 (1985) 127–52.

Lee, J.R.: Presidential vetoes from Washington to Nixon. *Journal of Politics* 37 (1975) 522–46.

Rohde, D.W. and Simon, D.M.: Presidential vetoes and congressional response: a study of institutional conflict. *American Journal of Political Science* 29 (1985) 397–427.

virtual representation The doctrine that one can be properly represented even if one lacks the vote, provided that the legislature contains a representative broadly in sympathy with one's own opinions. In 1765, during the controversy over the rights of the American colonists, a British pamphleteer cited 'many ... great names ... to prove that every Englishman, whether he has a right to vote for a representative or not, is still represented in the British Parliament'. This doctrine, known by 1790 as 'virtual representation', was a mainstay of opponents of parliamentary reform until 1832.   MGB

Reading

Brock, M.: *The Great Reform Act*. London: Hutchinson, 1973.

Cannon, J.: *Parliamentary Reform, 1640–1832*. Cambridge: Cambridge University Press, 1973.

Porritt, E. and A.: *The Unreformed House of Commons*. Cambridge: Cambridge University Press, 1903.

voting The act of indicating one's preference among competing policies or candidates. Voting may be performed by voice, show of hands, written communication such as a ballot paper, by electronic signal, or even by standing in one place rather than another as in the House of Commons where members vote by going into either the Aye lobby or the No lobby of the Chamber. The ancient Greeks voted by casting a pebble in an urn, hence the term *psephology* (from Greek *psephos*, pebble) for the study of voting behaviour. Voting goes back to ancient times: in the west, to the Greek city states from the fifth century BC onwards. Nowadays it is inseparably connected with the doctrine that ultimate authority, SOVEREIGNTY, resides in the people, who may express this directly via the REFERENDUM or plebisicite, or indirectly by electing representatives to the legislature. Voting for representatives had survived through the seventeenth century in Britain, and spread from there to the thirteen American Colonies, whereas most assemblies had died out or been suppressed in Europe. Assemblies revived from the French Revolution, 1789, especially after the fall of Napoleon in 1815; while they did so, so the importance of the popular vote increased. The right to vote, sometimes called the FRANCHISE sometimes the suffrage, was confined from the outset of the nineteenth century to males possessing a specified amount of wealth. By the end of the century most states had extended the franchise to all males irrespective of wealth. Voting rights were generally not extended to women until after the end of the first world war.

For reading, see ELECTIONS.   SEF

voting behaviour See SOCIAL STRUCTURE AND PARTY ALIGNMENTS.

W

Wallas, Graham (1858–1932) English political thinker. Wallas's historical reputation is strangely paradoxical. He is chiefly remembered as one of the founders of FABIAN socialism and contributor to the *Fabian Essays in Socialism*, and for his imaginative concepts of a 'behavioural' political science, yet neither of these is central to the thrust of his own life-work. (See BEHAVIOURALISM.)

Most writings on the historical development of modern political science make reference to Wallas's pioneering *Human Nature in Politics* (1908) with its warnings about the dangers of exaggerating the intellectuality of mankind. However, as Wallas later made clear, he was appalled more by the anti-intellectualism of the twentieth century than by the naive understanding of the nineteenth. Whether manifested in fascist appeals to irrationalism or in overly rigid deterministic psychologies, excessive anti-intellectualism – by denying even the possibility of a rational free will – made nonsense of any dream of a Good Society recreated in the setting of the urban-industrial Great Society.

Wallas had attacked earlier assumptions about the connections between reason and behaviour, principally to teach people to think more clearly and to apply their reason to the improvement of the human condition: he had no wish to deny them the capacity to think at all. Wallas was not a behavioural political scientist but a moral reformer who looked to a new science of politics and government as a means to a more democratic political order, challenging the self-confident assurances of the old ruling classes. Although his enthusiasm for scientific methods gradually faded he remained convinced of the value of more quantitative data in the social sciences while refusing to ignore those elements of political life that are not readily quantifiable. This left him out of sympathy with the new generation of scholars in search of a 'value-free' social science.

Wallas's socialism and collectivism are also misleading. He had joined the Fabian Society in 1886 but feeling that it had 'lost the soul of its socialism' he gradually drifted away, formally resigning in 1904. His socialism is unintelligible out of the context of his evangelical upbringing. Owing little to any systematic economic theory, it was really an outburst of moral outrage at the effects of the materialistic, competitive values of capitalism which demoralized and degraded its peoples. The ultimate object of his political thinking was still the liberal goal of maximum individual liberty and dignity to be accomplished through collective social action rather than through the competitive machinery of the market-place which so inequitably distributed its rewards. As Wallas grew older, and as the individual good took ever greater prominence in his mind, he increasingly came to distrust institutionalized socialism.

These are the major components of Wallas's thought. He attacked older assumptions about the basis of human social behaviour, and the established political and economic institutions for dealing with selfish individualism, but his vision of the purpose of political activity was always the recreation of the *polis*, the communal good life. In time the scientific criticisms faded as the moral passions which inspired them came to the fore. THQ

Reading

Qualter, T.H.: *Graham Wallas and the Great Society*. London: Macmillan, 1985.

Wallas, G.: *Human Nature in Politics*. London: Constable, 1908.

Wiener, J.: *Between Two Worlds: the political thought of Graham Wallas*. Oxford: Clarendon Press, 1971.

weak mayor plan A mayor with weak administrative powers, but with a voice in policy making because of independence from the council, became the dominant pattern of urban government in the United States in the nineteenth century. The nation inherited its local government system from England, but cities soon began to develop distinctive forms. Towards the end of the eighteenth century Baltimore led the way in applying the concept of separation of powers, borrowed from the new national constitution, for city charters. In 1822 Boston and St Louis voters elected the first mayors; populists also called successfully for the direct election of various other administrative officers, and in the 1850s the newly developed commissions (to head police, fire, water, etc.) became widely elective. Large bicameral councils (twenty to eighty or more members), elected for short terms (one or two years), were popular. They controlled the budgets and appointed some administrators.

This plan, in countless variations, became virtually universal for cities in the United States and remained so until the 1880s when reformers began to press for changes. The mayor was weak as an administrator, had few appointive powers, and was unable to co-ordinate the growing number of functions or the expanding budget as the nation urbanized. The mayor had a veto, often presided over council meetings, and in some cities was a full member. Cities with political bosses, a growing number after the civil war, made do with the plan while co-ordinating activities through political party.

The STRONG MAYOR PLAN has gradually, though not totally, replaced this one. The bicameral council has gone, ever fewer administrators are elected, but many small cities and some large ones retain important aspects of the plan. CRA

Reading

Adrian, C.R.: *Governing Urban America*. 4th edn. New York: McGraw-Hill, 1972.

Kotter, J.P. and Lawrence, P.R.: *Mayors in Action: five approaches to urban governance*. New York: Wiley, 1974.

Webb, Beatrice and Sidney English historians and politicians. A formidable intellectual partnership was formed when on 23 June 1892 Beatrice (1858–1943), daughter of the Victorian 'railway-king' Richard Potter, having already served her 'apprenticeship' in social research, married the civil servant and leader of the London FABIANS, Sidney Webb (1859–1947).

A lifetime of dedicated research into the history and functioning of British institutions resulted in their production of masterly studies of trade unionism (1894 and 1897), local government (10 volumes 1898–1929), and co-operatives (1921), with a strong emphasis on the evolutionary development of these institutions. These have provided the foundation of all later work, and entitle the Webbs to be ranked among the greatest Victorian and Edwardian historians. Their techniques of research (now labelled 'positivistic') were made explicit in their *Methods of Social Study* (1932).

In politics, Sidney Webb's main contribution was made as member of the London County Council from 1892 to 1910. He systematized the policy of the Progressive Party, the Liberal–Labour alliance which dominated the LCC for most of that period, in *The London Programme* (1891), and he played a leading part in administering and reorganizing the whole education system of the metropolis.

Beatrice Webb's political activities had begun as hostess of a Fabian 'salon', through which talented young Fabians were introduced to persons of influence and power. In 1905 she was appointed by Balfour a member of the Royal Commission on the Poor Laws. She played a vigorous and critical role in the Commission, and (with the assistance of her husband) produced its Minority Report (1909) recommending the break-up of the Poor Law and its replacement by a system of state welfare services. When these recommendations were rejected by the Liberal government the Webbs mounted a large-scale public campaign which engaged the enthusiasm of left-wing intellectuals, but was a political failure and marked the end of Fabian hopes of 'permeating' the Liberal Party.

During the first world war the Webbs were drawn into active membership of the Labour Party; this resulted in Sidney Webb's important contribution to the drafting of the 1918 constitution of the party and of its post-war programme *Labour and the New Social Order*.

Beatrice Webb remained sceptical of the ability of the Labour party and its leaders. The collapse of the second Labour government in 1931 confirmed Beatrice's pessimism, and disillusioned Sidney Webb. In old age the Webbs renounced the hostility they had expressed previously to Russian communism, and made their 'pilgrimage to Moscow', hoping to discover Fabian virtues in Stalin's 'socialism in one country'. This resulted in their last big work *Soviet Communism: a new civilization?* (1935). It had considerable impact in the fervid politics of the 1930s, but it showed (as the Webbs had revealed in earlier journeys outside Western Europe in 1898 and 1911–12) that they were too English in outlook and expertise to reach a deep understanding of foreign peoples or the working of foreign institutions.   AMMcB

Reading

Adam, R. and Muggeridge, K.: *Beatrice Webb: a life*. London: Secker & Warburg, 1967.

Cole, M. ed.: *Beatrice Webb's Diaries*. 2 vols, 1914–24; 1924–32. London: Longmans Green, 1952, 1956.

———: *The Webbs and their Work*. London: Muller, 1949.

Hamilton, M.A.: *Sidney and Beatrice Webb: a study in contemporary biography*. London: Low, Marston, 1933.

MacKenzie, N. ed.: *The Letters of Sidney and Beatrice Webb*. 3 vols, 1873–92; 1892–1912; 1912–47. Cambridge: Cambridge University Press, 1978.

——— and MacKenzie, J. eds: *The Diary of Beatrice Webb*. 4 vols, 1873–92; 1892–1905; 1905–1924; 1924–43. London: Virago, 1982, 1983, 1984, 1985.

Nord, D.E.: *The Apprenticeship of Beatrice Webb*. Amherst: University of Massachusetts Press, 1985.

Webb, B.: *My Apprenticeship*. London: Longmans Green, 1926.

———: *Our Partnership*, ed. B. Drake and M. Cole. London: Longmans Green, 1948.

Weber, Max (1864–1920)   German social scientist. Weber was born in Thuringia and died in Munich. On his mother's side he traced his descent from a long line of pastors and school teachers; on his father's side, from a background of small businesses. His mother was a very devout woman, his father a robust and bustling nationalist of few intellectual pretensions. The Webers belonged to a rising and multiplying new German professional world of academics, direct servants of the state, and nationalist politics.

Max Weber's extended years of study encompassed classics, particularly classical history and Roman law, jurisprudence and economics. They were unusual more in depth and devotion than in content. He attracted the attention of some of the greatest scholars of his time, particularly the dean of German historians, the great Mommsen, who predicted that Weber would carry forward his own work of learning and scholarship. Weber travelled in Europe and in North America extensively in the years 1899 to 1904. He suffered a nervous breakdown and was appointed to a chair at the University of Heidelberg which involved no teaching duties. Until 1918 he spent most of his life in Heidelberg, working in the university and for most of the war, as a military hospital administrator. In 1918 he went to teach in Vienna but returned a year later to the University of Munich. Despite the breakdown and his war service Weber worked titanically on the philosophy of the social sciences, jurisprudence, the economic history of the ancient world and of the Middle Ages. He also worked actively both for the Evangelical Christian Union, and in his collaboration with Sombart and Jaffé in the League for Social Politics and the editing of the *Archive for social science and social politics*. When he died in 1920 his written legacy consisted of contributions to all these fields, each densely written and each distinguished. He also left a great deal of unfinished work which appeared during the

1920s in variously edited forms and which is now being re-edited.

Yet it is not for these labours that Weber is most famous, but for his work as a sociologist, a title that he increasingly adopted to describe himself from his mid-forties. This involved a famous series of studies and articles on the sociology of religion in China, India, ancient Israel, and modern Europe. In these he devoted himself to a problem which can essentially be summarized as why industrial CAPITALISM as a dominant, highly rationalistic mode of life emerged in modern Europe and the United States and was not paralleled in any of the other world-historical civilizations. His answer is intellectual, cultural, and above all in terms of religion, though as a student and critic of Marx he did not neglect the importance of material forces. Law guided by reason and strict rules; science as a vocation of open, critical, rational investigation of nature and society; and economics as the science of the most rationally conducted area of human life all owe their being to the ascetic use of time and resources taught by the churches and sects of post-Reformation Protestantism, in particular Calvinism and the more rigorous kinds of Methodism. German and English Evangelicism within the Lutheran and Anglican Church were ancillary to these revolutions of the mind and of economic behaviour. At the heart of this is a general theory of the tendency of the 'rational' components of social behaviour to gain in strength and to displace emotive and traditional modes of choice and action.

In consequence the world is more and more enclosed in an 'iron cage' of reason and BUREAUCRACY. This can, by reaction, be one of the major causes of emotively directed mass religious and political movements, possibly to be led by some 'parliamentary *condottiere*' to whom could be ascribed a non-natural gift or grace, i.e. charisma. In this can perhaps be found not just the fruits of analysis, social and political, but also a reflection of his barren marriage, although the last years of his life were marked by greater happiness.

Weber also made fundamental contributions to the development of POLITICAL SOCIOLOGY in his analysis of different types of AUTHORITY,

each of which constituted its own legitimating principle. He distinguished forms of social organization in terms of particular imperatives, arguing that early capitalism was characterized by the dominance of property relationships, while SOCIALISM, in his view, would entail bureaucratic dominance even greater than was already apparent in an advanced capitalist society. Much of his political sociology was concerned with the meaning of modern electoral politics and the plebiscitary type of democracy to which they were giving rise. His work can most fruitfully be compared with that of MARX in terms of contrasting perceptions of capitalist development and of the machinery of liberal democracy.

Weber's own politics combined German nationalism with a strong criticism of *Junkertum*. He was fascinated by political parties and their tendency towards oligarchic organizations even when they had a mass basis as with the German Social Democrats. His attitudes to socialism were ambiguous, and he proposed to spend time lecturing on the subject before his untimely death overtook his hopes. On the whole, society for Weber was a bleak place but, as he grew older, an increasingly exciting one in which the interplay of class and party with power and bureaucracy provided not merely an endless cycle but also entertainment for the student and responsibility for the citizen.

See also IRON LAW OF OLIGARCHY.

DGM

Reading

Bendix, R.: *Max Weber: an intellectual portrait*, rev. edn. New York: Doubleday Anchor, 1962.

MacRae, D.G.: *Weber*. 2nd edn. London: Fontana, 1986.

Mommsen, W.J.: *Max Weber and German Politics 1890–1920*. Berkeley: University of California Press, 1985.

Weber, M.: *Wirtschaft und Gesellschaft, Grundriss der Verstehenden Soziologie*. 4th edn. 2 vols, ed. J. Winckelmann. Tübingen: Mohr, 1956. Trans. as *Economy and Society: an outline of interpretive sociology*. 3 vols, ed. G. Roth and C. Wittich. New York: Bedminster, 1968.

——: *Gesammelte Politische Schriften*, rev. edn. 3 vols, ed. J. Winckelmann. Tübingen: Mohr, 1971.

———: *Rechtssoziologie*, ed. J. Winckelmann. Neuwied: Luchterhand, 1960.

———: *Gesammelt Aufsätze zur Religionssoziologie*. New edn. 3 vols. Tübingen: Mohr, 1963. Pt. 1 trans. as *The Protestant Ethic and the Spirit of Capitalism*. London: Allen & Unwin; New York: Scribner, 1930.

welfare state A form of government in which the state through legislation takes on the responsibility of protecting and promoting the basic well-being of all its members. Essential elements include legislation which guarantees income maintenance and other kinds of support for individuals and families in cases of occupational accidents and diseases, sickness, old age, and unemployment.

The first person to use the term in English is generally assumed to have been William Temple, Archbishop of York, in a book published in 1941 in which he contrasted democratic welfare-oriented systems of the time with the totalitarian 'power states' of Hitler and Stalin. The term appeared in the *Oxford English Dictionary* in its 1955 edition. The German *Wohlfahrtsstaat* was used in a derogatory sense as early as 1932 to denounce the Weimar Republic. This is believed to have been the first time the term was used. The Norwegian version of the term, *velferdsstaten*, was used in public reports early in 1939, primarily to denote a vision of the good society to come – welfare for everybody. In fact, the first part of the term, 'welfare', can trace its etymological roots to the Old Norse *velferð*. It was not until the 1960s and 1970s that the term became widely used in many languages, in the political arena, mass media, and social science research reports.

The ideology of the welfare state grew out of the experiences of the second world war. Sir William Beveridge's plan (1942) for a 'social service state' and the Philadelphia resolutions of the International Labour Organization (1944) became basic reference documents for both the legitimation of and the practical build-up of welfare state institutions and programmes on a large scale after the war.

Britain in the 1940s and 1950s has been perceived as exceptional in the history of European welfare state development in that academic social scientists made an important impact on the development of social policy. In addition to Beveridge, the influence of T. H. Marshall and Richard Titmuss was significant. All three were affiliated to the London School of Economics and Political Science. Many of their concepts and conceptions have played a major role in social policy debates in West European countries since 1950.

The idea and practice of universal social security schemes, i.e. schemes that cover the entire population, are typical post-war constructs in European welfare states. The principle of universality has been carried farthest in Britain and the Scandinavian countries.

The welfare state did not rise spontaneously after the war. The origins of modern social insurance and security are generally traced to Bismarck's comprehensive social legislation of the 1880s, though modest attempts at worker insurance (for miners, railway workers, and seamen) had been tried in several countries even earlier, and Bismarck's legislation was motivated as much, or more, by political as by social or humanitarian reasons. As a result of the German example social insurance programmes and policies were gradually instituted throughout Europe and even beyond. National programmes varied in terms of extent of population coverage and characteristics of organization, financing and benefit structures.

The extent of a welfare state is normally measured either in terms of the scope and character of social legislation or in terms of the extent of government spending on health and social services, sometimes including spending on education.

The growth of the welfare state has been understood in a number of ways. Except for some special political factors pertaining to Germany under Bismarck it can broadly speaking be seen as a response to two fundamental developments: that of the formation of national states and their transformation into mass democracies, and that of the growth of capitalism after the Industrial Revolution. The welfare state can be interpreted as a response to the demand both for socio-economic equality and for socio-economic security. The growth of the welfare state has been interpreted both as a response to the functional needs of developing capitalist societies and as a result of the active mobilization of the labour movement, whether or not socialist or social democratic parties have exercised control of the policy-making structures of the state. The smooth development of the welfare state in many countries has also been interpreted as the result of growing political consensus between major political parties on crucial goals of social policy. Relatively constant massive voter approval of steadily expanding social rights has certainly helped to consolidate such consensus at elite level. Whatever the sets of factors explaining the emergence and growth of specific policies and institutions in various countries, the welfare state has grown in advanced industrial societies with or without a strong social democratic labour movement.

In developed welfare states the welfare sector demands a major share of government budgets. The welfare state has substantially widened the arena of public policies. It affects political institutions in several ways, for example by creating a need for better coordination of public policies, and by inspiring the organization of new interest groups which tend to become permanent participants in one way or another in policy-making processes.

The welfare state implies a transformation of the state itself, of its structure, functions and legitimacy. It has alleviated social cleavages and may have created new ones. In Western Europe its growth has coincided with processes of democratization, the development of mixed economies, and an unprecedented growth in mass material welfare. Cause and effect in this development can hardly be distinguished. It is commonly assumed that the welfare state has contributed to social security, social harmony and political stability; that it has weakened the appeal of orthodox socialism; that it has stabilized the economy; that it has contributed to the equalization of living conditions between social classes and groups. Probably the welfare state can safely be assumed to have reduced political polarization. The high proportion (c. 40 per cent in the Scandinavian countries) of the population directly dependent upon the welfare state in one way or another in the 1980s – patients, clients, pensioners,

professional personnel – makes it highly unlikely that the welfare state can, or will, be easily dismantled.   SK

Reading

Alber, J.: *Vom Armenhaus zum Wohlfahrtsstaat.* Frankfurt: Campus, 1982.

Flora, P. and Heidenheimer, A.J. eds: *The Development of Welfare States in Europe and America.* New Brunswick, NJ and London: Transaction Books, 1981.

Gough, I.: *The Political Economy of the Welfare State.* London: Macmillan, 1979.

Heclo, H.: *Modern Social Politics in Britain and Sweden: from relief to income maintenance.* New Haven, Conn.: Yale University Press, 1974.

Rimlinger, G.V.: *Welfare Policy and Industrialization in Europe, America and Russia.* New York: Wiley, 1971.

Spiro, S.E. and Yuchtman-Yaar, E. eds: *Evaluating the Welfare State.* New York: Academic Press, 1983.

Temple, W.: *Citizen and Churchman.* London: Eyre & Spottiswoode, 1941.

Titmuss, R.H.: *Essays on the Welfare State.* London: Allen & Unwin, 1958.

Tomasson, R.F. ed.: The Welfare State, 1883–1983. *Comparative Social Research*, VI. Greenwich, Conn. and London: JAI Press, 1983.

Westminster model

The English (since 1707, British) parliament is located in Westminster in London, as are the offices of government which are associated with the part called Whitehall. The nineteenth century colonies, which sought autonomy from the Colonial Office in Whitehall, looked to Westminster as the model of parliamentary government. Characteristics of the Westminster model which distinguish it from the continental European type include: strong CABINET GOVERNMENT based on majority rule; the importance attached to constitutional CONVENTIONS; a two-party system based on single-member constituencies; the assumption that minorities can find expression in one of the major parties; the concept of Her Majesty's loyal opposition; and the doctrine of parliamentary supremacy, which takes precedence over popular sovereignty except during elections.

The Westminster parliamentary system continues to evolve. The eighteenth-century notion of the balanced constitution comprised the monarch, House of Lords and House of Commons. Today power lies with the prime minister, the cabinet and the commons. Two unique features of the Westminster model are the absence of an enacted constitution and its flexibility in the absence of any special amending procedure. No parliament can legally bind its successor. It is important to distinguish between an idealized (and often outdated) Westminster model and the evolving practice of parliamentary government. Among recent deviations from the model in the United Kingdom are: minority government; the refusal of cabinets to resign except after explicit votes of no confidence; the occasional assertiveness of the House of Lords; the emergence of a potential multi-party system; and direct democracy in the form of referendums over such issues as membership of the European Community and devolution. Arend Lijphart has suggested that the New Zealand parliamentary system is closer to the Westminster model than the British. Commonwealth countries have modified the Westminster model through written constitutions. Canada, Australia and India have tried to adapt it to the requirements of large federal states, with emphasis shifting from parliamentary to constitutional supremacy and judicial review. The Canadian Constitution Act of 1982 contains a Charter of Rights and Freedoms which challenges the parliamentary supremacy of the Westminster tradition. The Indian constitution not only includes a set of fundamental rights but retains extensive pre-parliamentary powers for state governors and adds a list of directive principles. In general Commonwealth countries in Asia and Africa which did not gain their independence until after the second world war have made even greater modifications to the Westminster model than countries such as Australia, Canada and New Zealand which had gained independence earlier. Moreover the Westminster model itself is not a static entity, but was evolved to meet changing conditions. The phrase 'the Westminster model' is thus a form of shorthand which can easily mislead if one is not aware of the particular era under discussion. The Westminster model of the constitutional

theorists must be distinguished from government as this has evolved at Westminster, and still more from the practice of government in Commonwealth countries.   DVV

Reading

Bagehot, W.: The English Constitution. In *Collected Works*. Vol. V, ed. N. St John-Stevas. London: The Economist, 1965–86.

Lijphart, A.: *Democracies: patterns of majoritarian and consensus government in twenty-one countries*. New Haven, Conn. and London: Yale University Press, 1984.

Rose, R.: *Politics in England*. 4th edn. Boston, Mass. and Toronto: Little, Brown, 1986.

Smith, S.A. de: *The New Commonwealth and its Constitutions*. London: Stevens, 1964.

Wheare, K.C.: *The Constitutional Structure of the Commonwealth*. Oxford: Clarendon Press, 1960.

Whigs and Tories Colloquial labels for the two main parliamentary parties from the mid-seventeenth to the early nineteenth centuries. In the mid-seventeenth century the English authorities pejoratively referred to the Scottish Presbyterian subversives as whigs and Irish popish bandits as tories. During the great political crisis of Charles II's reign (1679–82) the 'Court' Party called opposition parliamentarians whigs and the 'Country' Party returned the insult by calling the conservatives tories. The whigs, with whom Locke associated, asserted a right to resist tyranny by all necessary means; the tories, the party of church and king, countered with the doctrine of the divine right of consecrated kings and the duty of subjects to obey. Experience of the arbitrary rule of the popish James II, however, induced tory notables to join with whigs in the summons to William of Orange and his wife Mary who received the throne from parliament whereby, as the triumphant whigs put it, were secured 'our lives, our liberties and properties and the Church of England, with a due liberty to Protestant Dissenters'. There followed until the eve of the 1832 Reform bill, four periods of parliamentary party history:

(1) 1689 to 1714 *A two-party system*: William and Mary and after them Queen Anne were

able to avoid subjection to either whigs or tories.

(2) 1714 to 1760 *A one-party system*: The first two Hanoverian monarchs acquiesced in the supremacy of the whig oligarchs and this was secured by a purge of tories from state offices, control of local government and two generations of proscription, which extended to the ecclesiastical hierarchy. Nevertheless an organized tory party, with deep roots in the counties and large boroughs, remained as a permanent minority in parliament.

(3) 1760 to 1807 *A no-party system*: No leading public figure considered himself as a tory. Among multifarious whigs and independents one whig connexion, of which Burke was the spokesman and Charles James Fox the virtual leader, arrogated to itself the title deeds of whiggery. Fox claimed that its existence as a set of vigilantes opposing the chosen ministers of George III (namely Lord North (1770–82) and the Younger Pitt (1783–1801)), saved the state from the 'euthanasia of absolute monarchy'.

(4) 1807 to 1828 *The rule of the Pittites*: By about 1820 ministers gave up objecting to the label tories and recognized as the whig party that rump of new whigs which Fox had bequeathed to Grey in 1806. But when in 1827 the ultra-tories refused to support the liberal tory Canning, most whigs bolted to Canning.

By the end of 1827 the whigs seemed to be extinct as a separate party. Only a strange concatenation of events between 1828 and 1830 so changed the face of politics that the deserted chieftain won fame as 'Lord Grey of the Reform Bill'. Whiggery, temporarily rehabilitated, could claim to be a 'body of men connected with high rank and property, bound together by hereditary feelings, party ties, who when the people are roused, stand between the Constitution and revolution, and go with the people, but *not to extremities*'. But they were old-fashioned and soon became anachronistic. The civil and religious liberty which they, but not they alone, had advocated was broadly achieved. A privileged caste, they had no interest in opening careers to talents, let alone equality of opportunity. Fraternity they

practised only among themselves, the members of Brooks' Club, and 'all cousins', viewing less well-connected liberals *de haut en bas*. By 1859 at the latest there was a Liberal rather than a whig party. Whigs were indigenous to what Earl Russell called 'the temperate zone of our ancient constitution in which the evils of despotism and democracy are alike unknown'.

The tory party had, at the time of Grey's Reform Bill, become officially the Conservative Party, to which most whigs fled, as apprehensive conservatives in the guise of Unionists, in 1886. The change of name suited Peel, of Pittite stock, as he thought the image of toryism illiberal and a handicap to winning the middle ground of politics.

Ever since the birth of the Conservative Party, many, friend and foe, have used 'conservative' and 'tory' as interchangeable words. But many have not. Serious historians, as well as romantics, carry the tory tradition back to Charles I, the 'royal martyr' and the cavaliers of the generation before the term was applied to parliamentary polticians. And the term is still used, with pride (as whig is not) by many who feel it has a ring to it which 'conservative' lacks. Critical of Conservative Party leadership and policy drift, right-wingers may call themselves high tories, or use other adjectives such as stout or staunch, unrepentant or even dyed-in-the-wool, while progressives are apt to form Tory Reform Committees (as in 1942 and in the 1980s).   DGS

Reading

Ayling, S.: *George III*. London: Collins, 1982.

Blake, R.: *The Conservative Party from Peel to Thatcher*. London: Fontana, 1985.

Brooke, J.: *King George III*. London: Constable, 1972.

Bulmer-Thomas, I.: *The Growth of the British Party System*, Vol. I: *1640–1923*. London, 1965.

Colley, L.: *In Defiance of Oligarchy – the Tory Party, 1714–60*. Cambridge: Cambridge University Press, 1982.

Derry, J.: *Charles James Fox*. London: Batsford, 1972.

Feiling, K.: *History of the Tory Party 1640–1714*. Milford, 1924.

Gash, N.: *Lord Liverpool*. London: Weidenfeld & Nicolson, 1984.

Jones, J.R.: *The First Whigs*. London: Greenwood, 1961.

Kenyon, J.P.: *Revolution Principles: the politics of party, 1689–1720*. Cambridge: Cambridge University Press, 1977.

Southgate, D.G.: *The Passing of the Whigs 1832–86*. London: Macmillan, 1963.

Thomas, J.A.: *The House of Commons in the Eighteenth Century*. Oxford: Clarendon Press, 1971.

Whig: US One of the two major political parties in the United States during the period of the second party system, from the election of Andrew Jackson as President in 1828 to the Civil War. The Whigs derived their name from English history, presenting themselves as opposed to Jackson's allegedly tyrannical policies. They closely contested national elections during this period, one of the most competitive in American history. The Whigs' most prominent leader, Henry Clay, was thrice defeated for the presidency, but the party succeeded in electing William H. Harrison in 1840 and Zachary Taylor in 1848.

The Whigs were a national party, gaining votes from all sections, but particularly strong in New England, the Middle Atlantic region, and the border states. Their most important programmes implied national government aid to economic development through internal improvements to the canal and railroad transportation infrastructure, a national bank, and high tariffs. These policies brought support from the developing capitalist groups in the nation, such as manufacturers in the North, as well as from larger plantation owners in the South, and the more established ethnic groups, such as the English and Dutch. As a self-professed national party, the Whigs were particularly eager to avoid conflict over slavery and their leaders, Clay and Daniel Webster, were prominent in efforts at regional compromise. Ultimately, the tensions derived from slavery could not be resolved within the party or the nation. By 1860 the Whigs were replaced by the anti-slavery Republican party.

GMP

Reading

Benson, L.: *The Concept of Jacksonian Democracy*. Princeton, NJ: Princeton University Press, 1961.

McCormick, R.P.: *The Second American Party System*. Chapel Hill, NC: University of North Carolina Press, 1966.

whip The title applied in LEGISLATURES to a party official responsible for maximizing the attendance and voting cohesiveness of party supporters. The term has its origins in the hunting field (where a 'whipper in' is employed) and was first used in a parliamentary context in Britain in the eighteenth century. The functions of the whips developed and today encompass those of management, communication and persuasion. Government whips, with the government's business managers, are responsible for the management of the parliamentary timetable. The whips of the main OPPOSITION party (and, less regularly, of smaller parties) are consulted, such contact constituting 'the usual channels'. The whips act also as channels of communication between front benchers and their supporters and are responsible for persuading hesitant members to support the party line.

The term applies also to a written document issued each week by the whips, detailing the parliamentary business for the forthcoming week. The importance attached to each issue is indicated by underlining, the most important issues – necessitating the presence and support of all party members – being underlined three times (a 'three-line whip').

The value of whips is such that they are appointed by all parliamentary parties in Britain and are commonly appointed in many other legislatures and public assemblies. They are sometimes powerful figures and 'voting against the whip' (in effect, against the party) is often, as in India, a serious disciplinary offence. Elsewhere, when party control and cohesion is weaker, the power of the whips is considerably limited. In the US House of Representatives, for example, they perform solely monitoring and communicative functions.

There is generally a correlation between cohesive parties and the effectiveness of whips. The causal relationship, though, is often misunderstood: the effectiveness of whips is the product of cohesive parties rather than *vice versa*. Whips facilitate cohesiveness; they cannot force it. PN

Reading

King, A. and Sloman, A.: *Westminster and Beyond*, ch. 8. London: Macmillan, 1973.

Norton, P.: The organisation of parliamentary parties. In *The House of Commons in the Twentieth Century*, ed. S.A. Walkland. Oxford: Oxford University Press. 1979.

Ripley, R.B.: The party whip organisation in the United States House of Representatives. In *Congressional Behavior*, ed. N.W. Polsby. New York: Random House, 1971.

Searing, D. and Game, C.: Horses for courses: the recruitment of whips in the House of Commons. *British Journal of Political Science* 7.3 (1977) 361–85.

Wilson, Woodrow (1856–1924) President of the United States, 1913–21, but before that a leading American political scientist. In contrast to most American political scientists of the turn of the century, Wilson insisted that modern self-government should be understood not as a set of formal constitutional restraints but as a set of habits and moral restraints acquired and acted upon by the citizen.

In his first book *Congressional Government* (1885), inspired in part by BAGEHOT, Wilson argued that CABINET GOVERNMENT presented a unified governmental structure needed to overcome the fragmentation of government inherent in the system of largely independent congressional committees and subcommittees. He went beyong Bagehot in proposing that government be reformed not only according to the expansion of tasks that followed from industrialism, but according to the need to instruct and educate the citizenry.

Wilson's second book, *The State* (1889), was a textbook of comparative government largely inspired by German legal and administrative scholarship to which he had been introduced during his years at The Johns Hopkins University. His most influential essay 'The Study of Administration' (1886) outlined the prospects for a science of administration in a republic rife with popular suspicion against bureaucracy. Wilson argued that administrative ideas and practices were best legitimized with reference to the spirit of science and rational business procedures, which allowed administration to be presented as a service to society rather than as an imposition by the state.

In 1890 Wilson returned to Princeton. He served as president of the university from 1902–1910. Inspired in part by the surge of patriotism in the wake of the war against Spain in 1898 and in part by the vigour of Theodore Roosevelt's presidency, Wilson turned his attention from congressional, legislative leadership to the practice of executive, presidential leadership. In his last book, *Constitutional Government* (1908), Wilson argued that American constitutionalism was to be seen in the growth of national power, not in strictly legal interpretations of the Constitution. Constitutional flexibility was demonstrated in the judicial system which had been able to serve as a sounding board for the growth of business forces towards a national scope. Wilson predicted that the presidency, the primary symbol of national power and unity, would increasingly become the repository of popular political aspirations. NT

Reading

Mulder, J.M.: *Woodrow Wilson: the years of preparation*. Princeton, NJ: Princeton University Press, 1978.

Rabin, J. and Bowman, S. eds: *Politics and Administration: Woodrow Wilson and American public administration*. New York: Dekker, 1984.

Wilson, W.: *Congressional Government: a study in American politics* (1885). New York: Meridian, 1961.

———: The study of administration. *Political Science Quarterly*, 2 (July 1887) 197–222.

———: *The State: elements of historical and practical politics* (1889). Boston, Mass.: Heath, 1918.

———: *Constitutional Government in the United States* (1908). New York: Columbia University Press, 1917.

———: *The Papers of Woodrow Wilson*, ed. A.S. Link et al. 53 vols to date. Princeton, NJ: Princeton University Press, 1966– .

withering away of the state In the Marxist tradition, this is to be the ultimate stage of the transformation of society when the STATE – the instrument of class domination – will cease to exist as a separate institution. The state, according to MARX, will lose its 'political character' when through the 'DICTATORSHIP OF THE PROLETARIAT' class distinctions are abolished and a classless society emerges. When all have equal access to socially-controlled production the need for a special political organization controlling the distribution of power will disappear.

Historically, Marx saw the Paris Commune of 1871 as a possible model for such a development: DIRECT DEMOCRACY, the dismantling of the hierarchic state bureaucracy, officials directly elected by the populace, open to immediate recall and paid salaries equal to workers' wages – all this appeared to Marx as an alternative to the existing state machinery. LENIN initially viewed the SOVIETS as becoming such an alternative to state institutions. Developments in the Soviet Union however, with the emergence of a monopoly of power in the hands of a highly centralized party, went in a different direction.

While obviously having some features in common with ANARCHISM, Marx's idea is basically related to HEGEL's political philosophy and to the Hegelian notion of *aufhebung*, meaning both abolition, overcoming and realization. When the state is *aufgehoben*, i.e. both abolished and transcended, its functions are absorbed into the structures supplanting it. The nature of the state in the Hegelian tradition – representing universality as against the particularity of civil society and its economic interests – is thus, dialectically, preserved in the Marxian idea of the *aufhebung* of the state. SA

Reading

Lenin, V.I.: State and revolution. In *Collected Works*, Vol. XXV. London: Lawrence & Wishart, 1965.

Marx, K.: *Critique of Hegel's Philosophy of Right*. Cambridge: Cambridge University Press, 1970.

————: The civil war in France and critique of the Gotha Program. In *The Portable Marx*. Harmondsworth: Penguin, 1983.

women's suffrage The nineteenth century saw the beginning of the sustained campaign for female suffrage in Europe and America as an aspect of the growing women's movement (see FEMINIST MOVEMENTS). In all

the major states, however, 'the Cause' was not finally successful until the twentieth century, in the wake of the world wars. Before this however, women had been granted the vote in the Isle of Man in 1881, in New Zealand in 1893 (the first country to give women the vote) and in the states of Australia between 1893 and 1909. When invidious comparisons were made in the House of Commons between the position of women in the colonies and that in the mother country, the argument was neatly turned against British women by the claim that it was precisely because the British had an empire to rule that they could not allow women the vote, which would give them a part in this great male responsibility.

In America individual states had granted women the vote, beginning with Wyoming in 1869, but it was not until 1918 that this was passed in the House of Representatives and even then the senate delayed it for a year. American women were finally enfranchised by the Nineteenth Amendment in 1919, by which time Russian women had already had the vote for two years, having gained it first from the Provisional Government and retained it under the Bolsheviks, who also introduced equal pay, maternity leave, and extensive protective legislation in an effort to win female support.

In Britain and Germany the first world war was the catalyst for the granting of votes for women. Nineteenth-century Prussian law had forbidden them, along with children and the mentally ill, to join political parties, but with the establishment of the Weimar Republic all women (and men) over twenty received the vote. In Britain the suffragettes had fought a long and sometimes violent battle, but they gave up their campaign of civil disobedience when war was declared in 1914 and many believed that it was their patriotic performance during the war that made it impossible for politicians to refuse the vote afterwards. In 1918 women over thirty who were householders (or over thirty-five and the wives of householders) gained the vote, and in 1928 women over twenty-one did so too. Around the same time, Danish women (1915) and Swedish women (1919, unmarried; 1921, all) were granted the vote, the Finnish and Norwegians having been enfranchised in 1906 and 1907 respectively. In Italy and France, women had to wait until the end of the second world war for voting rights. Although the French chamber of deputies passed female suffrage in 1919, the senate voted it down and it was left to de Gaulle to introduce political equality in 1945. Mussolini promised Italian women the vote but the fascists progressively excluded them from economic and political life and it was not until 1945 that they acquired the franchise. Later still, and last of all the European democracies, Switzerland gave women federal voting rights in 1971.

Although the form and emphases of their cases differed slightly from country to country the opponents of women's suffrage reiterated much the same argument everywhere throughout the campaigns: women were naturally men's dependents and had no experience of the world on which to base political judgements; they were primarily wives and mothers and as such the moral guardians of society, a role which would be put in jeopardy by their involvement in politics. In some cases women themselves feared the loss of their femininity and the end of the protection men had given them in return for their dependence. Governments too, particularly after the loss of men in wartime, were loath to create an electorate in which women would be in the majority and, in some Catholic countries, the influence on politics of women's traditional allegiance to the church was feared. In the end however these arguments lost to women's claim for justice, and perhaps finally to the growing appreciation that the female role had changed to such an extent that there was neither logic nor fairness in their continued exclusion from the franchise.

See also GENDER AND POLITICS.   EMV

Reading

Harrison, B.: *Separate Spheres: the opposition to women's suffrage in Britain*. London: Croom Helm, 1978.

Lovenduski, J. and Hills, J. eds: *The Politics of the Second Electorate*. London: Routledge & Kegan Paul, 1981.

Morgan, D.: *Suffragists and Liberals*. Oxford: Blackwell, 1975.

Pankhurst, S.: *The Suffragette Movement*. London: Virago, 1977.

world government Schemes for the management of world affairs by a centralized power have a long intellectual pedigree but a scant history of implementation. One form of world government is universal empire, and Dante's projected restoration of the Roman Empire in *Monarchia* (c. 1310) is one of several important advocacies of *imperium* in European political thought. After the emergence of the European system of sovereign states in the seventeenth century proposals for world government rested more frequently on the organization of leagues of sovereign states to maintain peace and settle disputes through concerted action. Early theorists of international organization included Crucé, Penn, Saint-Pierre, Rousseau and Kant, but they had little practical influence until the League of Nations Covenant (1919) and the United Nations Charter (1945). Proponents of world government since 1945 have emphasized the necessity of international control of force, including nuclear weapons, and the subordinating of state sovereignty in international affairs. Functionalists argued that co-operation through international organizations would gradually supplant the international role of the state, while others urged reform of the United Nations and modification of international law to achieve this. A third group – well-represented in such periodicals as *The World Federalist* and *Common Cause* – argued for the rapid establishment of a world federal government, with power over and responsibility to individual citizens in some versions, but this movement lost momentum by the 1970s as the stimulating imperative of the second world war became more distant. Arguments against world government often focus on its alleged impracticality, the threat it may pose to cherished political and social values, and the advantages of decentralization and diversity.

BWK

Reading

Clark, G. and Sohn, L.B.: *World Peace through World Law: two alternative plans*. 3rd edn. Cambridge, Mass.: Harvard University Press, 1966.

Hinsley, F.H.: *Power and the Pursuit of Peace*. Cambridge: Cambridge University Press, 1963.

Mitrany, D.: *A Working Peace System*. London and New York: Royal Institute of International Affairs, 1946.

Peace Classics. London: Peace Book Co., 1939.

Ter Meulen, J.: *Der Gedanke der Internationalen Organisation in seiner Entwicklung*. 2 vols. The Hague: Nijhoff, 1917 and 1929.

Y

youth movements Though it is now commonly recognized that youth and youth movements play a crucial part in political change the significance of young people in politics has been underestimated until comparatively recently. In consequence the relevant concepts are inadequately developed and the facts poorly researched, though Feuer's *The Conflict of Generations* provided a valuable corrective to these weaknesses. Youth movements are of various types: they may be autonomous or controlled by adults; legitimate and officially recognized or illegitimate and unofficial; left, right, or single issue; organized or, as with the hippie movement, diffuse. In all cases they arise from the characteristics of youth, best analysed by Eisenstadt in *From Generation to Generation*. Primary among them are young people's natural tendency towards rebellious opposition, and the idealism which their structural position protects from the influence of pragmatic expediency.

Two particularly important general features of youth movements are the role of students (see STUDENT POLITICS), and the key significance of youth sections in political parties of all sorts. Their impact has been felt in democratic, authoritarian, and totalitarian societies alike, and is currently especially powerful in third world developing societies. Instances are provided by: the intellectual and social ferment preceding the Russian Revolution; the rise of National Socialism in Germany; the influence of the Campaign for Nuclear Disarmament in Britain; the downfall of the Shah of Iran in 1979 and the subsequent upsurge of radical Islamic activity; and current developments in South Africa, where young people are in the forefront of the challenge to apartheid.   DM

Reading

Eisenstadt, S.N.: *From Generation to Generation.* New York: Free Press, 1956.

Feuer, L.S.: *The Conflict of Generations.* London: Heinemann, 1969.

Marsland, D.: *Sociological Explorations in the Service of Youth.* National Youth Bureau, 1978.

Rosenmeyer, R. and Allerbeck, K.: Youth and society: a trend report. *Current Sociology* 27.2/3 (1979).

Z

Zionism The movement calling for Jewish national self-determination and eventual independence in Palestine – the historical Land of Israel. Deriving its name from Zion, the ancient citadel of Jerusalem, Zionism was founded by Theodore Herzl in 1897 as a political movement aiming at creating, through massive immigration, a social, economic and cultural Jewish infra-structure able to sustain the emergence of a polity becoming a new focus for Jewish life in the modern era. It is distinctive amongst national movements in the diversity of the diaspora which it sought to unite, and because of the long period of time between the destruction of the Jewish state and its re-creation in the twentieth century, on a former national territory.

While drawing on Jewish traditional religious beliefs, Zionism is basically a modern phenomenon. It developed in the nineteenth and twentieth centuries mainly in central and eastern Europe, where conditions of modernization radically transformed the position of the Jews.

Secularism and liberalism each opened the door to Jewish emancipation and equal rights, but NATIONALISM raised new questions of identity for secularized Jews in the emerging new nation-states. Out of this tension arose a new cultural and national self-awareness among the Jewish intelligentsia, and the advent of modern, racist ANTI-SEMITISM posed new challenges to the meaning of Jewish identity in the age of nationalism and self-determination. This was greatly exacerbated by the Holocaust, and after 1948 by the exodus of Jews from Arab countries.

Herzl's activity was preceded by earlier sporadic attempts at immigration (*Hovevei Zion* – Lovers of Zion), mainly from Russia, as well as by tracts such as Moses Hess's *Rome and Jerusalem* (1862) and Leo Pinsker's *Auto-Emancipation* (1882). Successive waves of Jewish immigration, before and after the first world war, slowly created a significant Jewish community in Palestine, trying new modes of social experimentation such as the KIBBUTZ. While supported by the League of Nations MANDATE to Britain over Palestine, Zionism slowly gave rise to Arab resistance. The creation of the state of Israel in 1948 in a part of Palestine, in accordance with United Nations recommendations on the partition of the country, led to the intervention of neighbouring Arab states and a series of wars between Israel and its Arab neighbours.

While 17 per cent of Israel's citizens are Arabs, the country's Zionist credo is epitomized in the Law of Return: this grants to every Jewish person the right of immigration to Israel and immediate citizenship on arrival.

Zionism contains various political streams: Labour or Socialist Zionism; liberal 'bourgeois' Zionism; religious Zionism; and right-wing ('Revisionist') Zionism. The political life of Israel is largely determined by these divisions. SA

Reading

Avineri, S.: *The Making of Modern Zionism*. London: Weidenfeld & Nicolson, 1982.

Halpern, B.: *The Idea of the Jewish State*. 2nd edn. Cambridge, Mass. and London: Harvard University Press, 1969.

Hertzberg, A.: *The Zionist Idea*. New York: Schocken, 1969.

Laqueur, W.: *A History of Zionism*. London: Weidenfeld & Nicolson, 1977.

Index

The Editors and Publishers are grateful to Mary Norris who compiled the index.
Page references to major entries on a subject are in bold type.